THE PFA
FOOTBALLERS'
WHO'S WHO
2008-09

Edited by Barry J. Hugman

in association with
www.allfootballers.com

Assistant Editors
Gerald Mortimer (text)
Michael Joyce (statistics)

Photographs © PA Photos

MAINSTREAM
PUBLISHING

EDINBURGH AND LONDON

First published in Great Britain in 2008 by
MAINSTREAM PUBLISHING COMPANY (EDINBURGH) LTD
7 Albany Street
Edinburgh
EH1 3UG

ISBN 9781845963248

A catalogue record for this book is
available from the British Library

Typeset and designed by Typecast (Artwork & Design)

Printed and bound in Great Britain by
Clays Ltd, St Ives plc

Foreword

Welcome once again to the Footballers' Who's Who – a definitive guide to every one of the PFA members playing first-team football throughout the Premier League and the Football League in England and Wales in 2007-2008.

As ever, I am extremely pleased to give the PFA's full endorsement and recommendation to this unique publication which is now in its 14th year. Since the inception of the Who's Who, interest in the modern game – at all levels – has continued to grow at a remarkable rate, and this book once again reflects that growth.

Packed full of statistics and profiles on all PFA members, the Footballers' Who's Who provides the background to what the game is all about – the players. Having to deal with 4,000 PFA members, the book gives me a valuable source of information in an easily accessible, attractive and enjoyable format – as it does anybody involved in the game, whether it be an administrator, player, manager, spectator or commentator. It is especially invaluable for any football 'Brain of Britain' or football quiz aspirant!

The publication is compiled by Barry Hugman, whose record in this field is unsurpassed, and he is aided by a team of close on 100 people who provide him with the invaluable aspects of local information, which gives this book such credibility. It's a fascinating read and an unequalled source of reference. We hope you enjoy it.

Gordon Taylor, OBE
PFA Chief Executive

The Professional Footballers' Association
working for the players, working for the game

Acknowledgements

Formerly known as the *Factfile* and now in its 14th edition, we believe that the *PFA Footballers' Who's Who* has become an invaluable part-work which, in due course, will cover the season-by-season career record of all professional footballers operating at that time in the Premier and Football Leagues. To this end, I would once again like to express my thanks to **Gordon Taylor**, the chief executive, and all those at the PFA who have genuinely supported and helped to establish the *Who's Who*. Their continuing support is very much welcomed and appreciated.

The task of dealing with the text this year was carried out by **Gerald Mortimer**, whilst the stats were handled in conjunction with myself and **Michael Joyce**, the author of *Football League Players' Records, 1888 to 1939*. This title, which is still available from SoccerData, 4 Adrian Close, Beeston, Nottingham NG9 6FL, slots in perfectly with my post-war *Premier and Football League Players' Records*. Michael, who despite now living in Norfolk has supported Arsenal for as long he can remember, has accumulated data for a complete Football League database over many years and used it to produce the player indexes for the Definitive series of club histories and several other publications. He provides statistical information for the website: www.since1888.co.uk, including career details of every English League player since 1888.

The editorial team were also lucky to be able to call upon **David Barber** (English FA), **Marco McIntyre** (Scottish FA), **Niall Dicksee** (FA Premier League), **Ceri Stennett** (FA of Wales), and **Marshall Gillespie** (editor of the Northern Ireland Football Yearbook). I am also indebted to **Alan Platt**, who supplied the international honours and produced the Where Did They Go? section. My thanks also go to **Jenny Hugman**, who did the proof reading, and to many Premier and Football League members up and down the country.

For details provided on players, I have listed below, in alphabetical order, the names of the team without whose help this book would not have been possible to produce. Once again, I thank every one of them for all the hard work they put in.

Audrey Adams (Watford): Has supported Watford since primary school days and currently provides the results and statistics for the BBC's *Sports Report* on Radio 5 Live. Audrey was also the club statistician for *The Ultimate Football Guide*. Regardless of how the club performed last season her devotion to the Hornets remains undimmed.

Geoff Allman (Walsall): A retired university lecturer, having worked for more than 50 years without taking a day off, he saw his first ever game in February 1944, Walsall versus Wolves. Has written for Walsall's programme for over 30 seasons and, at one time or another, has provided articles for more than half of the clubs currently in the Premiership and Football League.

Stuart Basson (Chesterfield): Has contributed to the *Factfile/Who's Who* since its inception and is the author of three books on The Spireites. Stuart maintains the history section for the club's official website at www.chesterfield-fc.co.uk and writes for the match-day magazine. He is happy to receive enquiries about any aspect of the club's past via email at historian@chesterfield-fc.co.uk.

Harry Berry (Blackburn Rovers): As a season ticket holder ever since starting work, Harry has followed Blackburn Rovers for over 50 years, having been born only three miles from Ewood Park and living within 15 miles all his life. Coinciding with Rovers' good form, 2006 saw Harry's book, *The Men Who Made Blackburn Rovers Since 1945*, published. Has been a road-runner for many years and has completed a few marathons. By profession a financial director, prior to retirement he worked for the largest manufacturer in Blackburn.

Tony Bluff (Doncaster Rovers): First watched the Rovers in 1953. The club historian and statistician for over 20 years, Tony has contributed to the programme for many of those years but now contributes to the website and club newspaper with historical data and match reports for the first team and reserves. Is co-author of the official history of the club. Tony also wrote the text for *The Book of Belle Vue* (The ground is now an affectionate but distant memory) and is currently endeavouring to update the official history of the club to cover the escape from near extinction to some of the most successful times in their history.

Eddie Brennan (Sunderland): Eddie has followed the fortunes of Sunderland for over 30 years and is hoping that the Black Cats latest return to the Premiership is the dawn of a bright new era for the club. He is also a former contributor to the Football League Directory and is delighted to see that Roy Keane is well on the way to establishing Sunderland in the Premier League once again.

Rob Briggs (Grimsby Town): A former office employee of the Mariners, Rob, who lives a hefty goal-kick away from Blundell Park, has been a contributor to Grimsby's match-day magazine for almost 20 years and has also written for the club fanzine and various soccer magazines.

Jim Brown (Coventry City): The club's official statistician and historian and contributor to the programme, he also pens a weekly column in the *Coventry Evening Telegraph* on City's history and answers readers' queries. He is the author of *Coventry City-the Elite Era* (1998 and 2001) and *The Illustrated History* (2000), in addition to being the co-author of the *Breedon Complete Record* (1991). Jim has been a Coventry fan since 1962 and has almost a complete collection of Coventry programmes since the war, as well as having a large library of football writings. He also carries out research for a number of commercial bodies. Apart from just covering Coventry, Jim has written critically acclaimed books on *Huddersfield Town's Glory Years* (1923-26) and *The Busby Era at Old Trafford* (1946-71), while his latest book *Ghosts of a Vanished Stadium: The history of Highfield Road* was published in 2006. In 2007 he founded the club's Former Players Association.

Mark Brown (Plymouth Argyle): Mark has been supporting the Pilgrims for 33 years, having been introduced to them at the tender age of five by his Argyle-mad family. Being a season ticket holder with his son Ben, he attends all of Plymouth's home games and as many away games as he can. His wife and young daughter Libby will no doubt in time become converts to the Green Army. Mark has been contributing to the *PFA Footballers Who's Who* for the past ten years, in which it has been one of the most successful periods in Plymouth's history.

Gavin Buckland (Everton): A life-long Everton supporter

of over 30 years and co-author of *Everton: The Ultimate Book of Stats and Facts* and two other football quiz books, Gavin has also worked as a researcher and question-setter on several TV quiz programmes. As the club statistician, he has a trivia and facts column in every Everton home programme and provides factual data for Radio Merseyside. Gavin is also the author of *Everton Strange But Blue* published in 2007, a collection of the 50 Strangest Everton matches and is the joint-author of *2008 Reasons Why Merseyside is the Capital of Football*, also published in 2007.

Trevor Bugg (Hull City): A supporter of the Tigers for nearly 40 years, Trevor contributes to Hull City's official website, match-day programme and club magazine. He also continues to pursue a career in football statistics.

Bob Cain (Fulham): Bob has supported Fulham for 37 years, during which time he has not missed a single home match in any first-team competition. In all he has clocked up almost 1,750 first-team games while watching his club play in all four divisions. A strong advocate of all-seater stadiums he has been a contributor to the club programme for almost 20 years and has also produced work on occasion for the club website.

John Campbell (Blackpool): Is the editor of www. blackpool.vitalfootball.co.uk, the website hosted on the Vital Football network which has been running for nearly three years. The site is considered to be the second largest Blackpool fans' website, a great achievement in such a short time. As well as the website, John also helps out on match days at Bloomfield Road in playing match day music.

Tim Carder (Brighton & Hove Albion): Tim is chairman of both the Supporters' Club and the Albion's Collectors' and Historians' Society. Along with Roger Harris, he co-authored *Seagulls: The Story of Brighton and Hove Albion FC* and *Albion A to Z: A Who's Who of Brighton and Hove Albion FC*. He is also a respected local historian on matters ranging far beyond the Albion.

Wallace Chadwick (Burnley): Wallace has been a Burnley supporter since the late 1950s and was a contributor to the club programme for many years. More recently he was one of the co-authors of the club history *Clarets Chronicles 1882-2007*.

Paul Clayton (Charlton Athletic): Author of *The Essential History of Charlton Athletic*, Paul wrote a regular feature in the club programme between 1993 and 1998, having previously written other articles for the now defunct Charlton Athletic magazine and *Valiant's Viewpoint* (Supporters Club newsletter/fanzine). He has also provided the Charlton statistics for a number of publications, including the *Ultimate Football Guide* from 1987 to its final publication in 1999, along with the Charlton player information for the *Factfile/Who's Who* since its inception in 1995. Paul is a long-standing season ticket holder at The Valley and rarely misses a game, home or away, despite living in Wiltshire.

David Copping (Barnsley): A life-long Barnsley fan who was a regular columnist in the club match-day programme for many seasons, he also served on the committee that is currently involved in setting up a museum at Oakwell. For many seasons he commentated on both hospital radio and the club videos.

Frank Coumbe (Brentford): Frank, who has been the Brentford statistician for the *Who's Who* since it started and enjoys providing the club biographies each year, hasn't missed a competitive Brentford home game since 1977, a run of consecutive games that now totals well over 800. On the field, Brentford's fortunes improved when Andy Scott took over as Manager in 2007, turning a relegation-threatened side into one that finished comfortably mid-table. As usual, Frank's 12-year-old daughter Sally helped him look up the stats for his contribution.

Mick Cunningham (AFC Bournemouth): Mick has been programme editor at AFC Bournemouth since the 1995-96 season, having previously edited the clubs fanzine, as well as writing the programme. He also is the club photographer and has covered every game home and away for 15 years, working for the club and local and national media.

John Curtis (Scunthorpe United): A life-long Scunthorpe fan, John is a former editor of the award-winning club match-day programme. He also covered the club's affairs for the *Scunthorpe Telegraph*, where he now works as the chief sub editor.

Carol Dalziel (Tranmere Rovers): Carol, who has been watching Tranmere Rovers since 1968, is a shareholder with aspirations to buy the club should she win the Lottery. She has been the operator of the electronic scoreboard for the last 18 seasons and is a former contributor to, and assistant editor of, the match-day programme. Carol's 'proper' job is in the logistics department of a local chemical manufacturing and distribution company, where she has worked for 25 years.

Iain Dalziel (Barnet): Nineteen-year-old Iain is long-time Barnet fan and a student at Nottingham Trent University. This season has seen him have to commute from the East Midlands whenever possible to attend games. With a typical student budget, this has not been easy and he and a friend even hitch-hiked to an away game at Bury (which Barnet lost 3-0). Iain intends to continue travelling the country watching the Bees next season, one in which he hopes will see them make a push for the play-offs.

Denise Dann (Aston Villa): In her own words, Denise is a mad, crazy Villa supporter, who follows them up and down the country without fail. With the *PFA Footballers' Factfile/Who's Who* since its inception, her only previous football work was to help with the club's profiles required for the *Premier League: The Players* publication.

Gareth Davies (Wrexham): Gareth is the co-author of the *Who's Who on Welsh International Footballers* (1991) with Ian Garland; editor/compiler of *Coast of Soccer Memories*, the centenary publication of the North Wales Coast FA (1994); co-author of *The Racecourse Robins* with Peter Jones; author of *Who's Who of Wrexham FC, 1921-99* (1999); co-author of Tempus' *Images of Sport: Wrexham FC, 1872-1950* (2000) with Peter Jones and *Wrexham FC, 1950-2001* (2001) with Peter Jones. He is also a contributor to the Wrexham official programme, *The Holyhead Hotspur* (Cymru Alliance), as the club's press officer, and the Welsh Football magazine, while producing various articles and info for other magazines and books.

David Downs (Reading): David is about to begin his 25th year working for Reading Football Club. He is currently employed as the club's children's safety officer, supervising all under-18 activities that take place at Reading. On match days, and when other duties allow, he acts as a summariser for Hospital Radio Reading, which covers home games at the Madejski Stadium. He also contributes a 'Flashback' article to the award-winning Reading match-day programme. Away from football David has recently joined the Purley Players amateur dramatic group, and celebrated his debut by playing the

back legs of the horse in their Christmas Pantomime 'Dick Whittington' to rapturous applause!

Ray Driscoll (Chelsea): A life-long Chelsea fan born and bred two miles away from Stamford Bridge, whose 50 years spectating encompasses the era from Roy Bentley to John Terry, including the 'wilderness years' of the early 1980s – far removed from the present Abramovich days! Like all Chelsea fans, he is in 'Dreamland' following back-to-back Premierships and, now, Cup successes. An all-round sports 'nut', he has contributed to many football books as well as other sports such as cricket, golf, rugby and tennis. He has also contributed to more 'cerebral' literature such as reference books. He will appear in the 2008 series of BBC's prestigious *Mastermind* quiz but couldn't put his knowledge of Chelsea to good use as his specialist subject because the subject had been covered shortly beforehand!

Brian Ellis (Luton Town): A supporter for 41 years and one of the co-authors of *The Definitive Luton Town* that was published in 1997, Brian is a contributor to the Luton Town Supporters' Club Newsletter regarding historical articles on the club and recently he wrote an article for *The Non-League Retrospective* on the evolution of football in Luton. Brian still hopes to finish and see published his long-standing project *The Definitive Luton Town 'Who's Who.*

Dean Enderby and **Eddie Collins** (Nottingham Forest): Dean has been a season ticket holder for the last 17 years and this is the first book he has contributed to. However, having now helped with a number of other publications he would like to assist with more in the future. Eddie has been watching Forest since 1956 and derives much pleasure from being involved in this publication. He is also a member of the AFS.

Harold Finch (Crewe Alexandra): Season 2008-09 will be his 75th of supporting Crewe Alexandra, which started on 10th March 1934 when defeating Accrington Stanley 4-2. Some 50 years as club historian, Harold is still providing regular articles for the Official Programme and producing all the relevant statistical information. Book number three, an ongoing project, on the complete A to Z of all players to have represented Crewe Alexandra in league football is a real challenge but one he intends to complete. His two previous books on the club have been well received in football circles.

Mick Ford and **Richard Lindsay** (Millwall): After 56 years of following Millwall faithfully, to get to the FA Cup Final and into Europe was a dream come true for Mick, something he never thought he would see in his lifetime. For Mick, the past few years at The New Den have been great, apart from relegation in 2005-06. Having now moved to Spain (with selected memorabilia), he still manages to go to all weekend home fixtures and run the programme shop. Being a Millwall supporter means it is not just supporting them – it's a way of life and, in Sue, he is proud to acknowledge her as such an understanding and supportive wife who endures his passion. Meanwhile, his Who's Who partner, Richard, the author of *Millwall: A Complete Record*, continues to help establish the Millwall FC Museum at The New Den.

Harry Glasper (Middlesbrough): Harry has been the official historian/statistician of Middlesbrough FC since he first started contributing to the match-day programme for the 1975-76 season and has been with the *Who's Who* since 2002.

Paul Godfrey (Cheltenham Town): Paul watched his first Cheltenham Town game at the age of ten – the Robins losing 2-1 to Yeovil Town in an FA Cup Fourth Qualifying Round match. He followed similar near misses and disappointments religiously before events took a dramatic turn in the late 1990s. Having become the club's programme editor in 1990, he was able to witness at first hand the transformation at Whaddon Road brought about by Steve Cotterill and the Board, headed by the chairman, Paul Baker. Having joined the club on a full-time basis in 2001, he is now the club secretary and retains a keen interest in the history of Cheltenham Town.

Frank Grande (Northampton Town): A supporter for 50 years and club historian, statistician and programme contributor for the past 25, Frank has written five books on the club and players. Over the years he has been instrumental in re-unions and events involving ex players, plus fund-raising events for the club.

Michael Green (Bolton Wanderers): Michael is a follower of two clubs – Newcastle United (home town team) and Bolton Wanderers (local club) and has watched the latter for the past 28 years. He enjoys writing and is looking to carve out further opportunities, preferably in the fields of football or popular entertainment (music, film, television etc) and also plays guitar in Slipstream, an Indie Rock band who play in the North West of England.

Alan Harding (Swindon Town): Alan, who has been supporting Swindon Town since 1968, is a season ticket holder, travels home and away, and has been researching match stats and line-up details, plus details of players since 1981. Is also a member of the AFS.

Des Hinks (Stockport County): Des, who is now County's media manager, has been following his beloved Hatters for more than 40 years. His son, Des junior, who works with his father updating the club's website and producing *True Blue*, their award-winning match programme, has been following County since the tender age of four and rarely misses a game, either home or away.

Adrian Hopper (Yeovil Town): Joined Yeovil Town as media manager in 2002 after a long association through a local newspaper he owned. Also known as 'Fat Harry', Adrian is now a devoted Yeovil Town supporter attending every game, but has been known to have a slight leaning towards a certain team that plays in red at a Theatre!

Gary James and **Chris Nield** (Manchester City): A Mancunian, Gary has provided support and assistance to Chris with the Manchester City profiles. In 2003 Gary set up the Manchester City Experience (award winning museum & tour) and continues to be involved in that enterprise. Last year he researched and wrote a series for Channel M on the history of football in Manchester – and *Manchester: A Football History* is due to be published this year. Coming from a family of City supporters who have followed the club since it's formation, Chris attended his first game in 1993, aged ten and was lucky enough to enjoy standing on Maine Road's famous Kippax Stand during its final season. Since then, you can count on one hand how many home games he has missed as well as attending as many away matches as possible. Chris is now the club's curator working at City's ground-breaking museum and stadium tour centre, as well as studying for a Masters Degree in Art Gallery & Museum Studies at Manchester University and playing in a popular local rock band, Air Cav. In 2007 Chris was responsible for staging a combined music and football exhibition at the club's museum.

Martin Jarred (Leeds United): Martin saw his first Leeds United game in 1966, a 2-1 midweek home win against West Brom and was hooked. A member of the AFS for

many years, he collaborated with Malcom MacDonald on several Leeds' books published by Breedon Books, which include four editions of the *Complete Record*, two *Leeds Story Books*, a *Leeds United Cup Book* and *Leeds United, The Complete European Record*. He is also the co-author, with Dave Windross, of *Citizens and Minstermen, a Who's Who of York City*. A previous sports editor of the *Scarborough Evening News* and *The Press, York*, Martin is now a freelance journalist.

Mike Jay (Bristol Rovers): Mike, a long-standing supporter of nearly 40 years and a regular programme contributor since 1977, is also the official club historian. Having had four books published on Rovers, the latest being a joint collaboration with Stephen Byrne, titled *Bristol Rovers: The Definitive History 1883-2003*. A keen collector of Rovers' memorabilia, he is always adding to his extensive collection of programmes, photos, autographs etc.

Colin Jones (Swansea City): A fan since the early 1960s and a long-standing contributor to the club's match day programme, Colin was programme editor at the Vetch Field for four years up to January 2003. Played non-league football before being involved with the training, coaching and administrative side after retiring as a player. In November 2005 he published the *First Comprehensive Player A-Z of Swansea Town/City players from 1912 to 2005*, and in November 2007 published a supplement to Professor David Farmer's book, *The Swans, Town and City*.

Dave Juson and **Gary Chalk** are, with David Bull and Duncan Holley, members of the Hagiology Publishing collective and official historians of Southampton Football Club. Dave and Gary have had a regular page in the Southampton programme since 2003 and details on the books they have contributed to can be seen at http://www.hagiologists.com. Both have been chronic Saints sufferers from childhood.

Andrew Kirkham (Sheffield United): A United supporter since 1953, and a regular contributor to the club programme and handbook since 1984, Andrew is a member of the AFS and 92 Club. He was also a contributor to *Sheffield United: The First 100 Years*, and co-author of *A Complete Record of Sheffield United Football Club, 1889-1999*.

Geoff Knights (Macclesfield): Geoff is a retired bank manager who has supported Macclesfield Town since the late 1980s. Describing himself as an ordinary supporter from the terraces, and one who enjoys the friendly atmosphere of a small club, he keeps detailed statistics and records on the club, which have been used over the years in response to media, club and other enquiries. Geoff also contributes to the match-day programme and although there are no official appointments as such he is acknowledged as the club's statistician and modern-day historian.

Geoff Lea (Wigan Athletic): A life-long supporter for over 30 years who first started watching the club during the non-league days, Geoff is a former editor of the match-day programme and now plays a key role in the production of the official match-day magazine. A press officer for Athletic on match days, he is also the club's statistician and has missed only a handful of games since the club's election into the Football League. Has also worked for a number of radio stations and newspapers following the club's progress.

Gareth Lloyd-Johnson (Bury): Although still only 16, Gareth has been a regular at Gigg Lane almost since he could walk and recalls with pride Bury's rise from Division Two to the Championship in the mid-1990s. Unfortunately, he has also been suffering with the rest of the Bury fans on the downward slide ever since!

John Maguire (Manchester United): A first-team regular since the *Who's Who'* began, John continues to indulge his passion in the beautiful game. He dedicates this season's efforts to the memory of the 'Busby Babes' (the deceased and survivors) who 50 years ago were setting the foundations for what the present day team achieved in Moscow on 26th May 2008, namely winning the European Cup, the greatest club team prize of them all!

Carl Marsden (Oldham Athletic): A life-long supporter, Carl has been involved with his beloved Latics on several levels. Formerly the chairman of SAFE (Secure Athletic's Future Existence), a website editor and fanzine contributor, he is now news editor of the local paper, *The Oldham Advertiser*. Carl also does commentary and fans' phone-ins for the official Latics Live Service and hosts *SportTalk* on Oldham Community Radio. In addition, he contributes analysis on visiting teams for the club's match-day programme and can be reached by email on carl@oafc.co.uk.

Carl Marston (Colchester United): Carl has been reporting on the fortunes of Colchester United since they regained their Football League status in 1992, both for the *East Anglian Daily Times* and the *Green 'Un* newspapers. He has only missed a handful of games during those last 16 years, usually when away trekking up mountains or running marathons. Carl was relieved when the U's won automatic promotion on the final day of the 2005-06 season, not least because the League One play-off final clashed with his wedding day! His wife Helen was also mightily relieved! Carl relished covering the U's during their subsequent two years in the Championship, and will now be looking forward to sitting in a new press box at the club's new Community Stadium.

Tony Matthews (West Bromwich Albion): The historian, statistician and curator of The Hawthorns Museum, his 80 + books on football include *Complete Records/Histories of Aston Villa, Birmingham City, Leicester City, Stoke City, Walsall, West Bromwich Albion and Wolves; A-Z Encyclopaedias of Aston Villa, Birmingham City, Huddersfield Town, Manchester United, Sheffield United, Stoke City, Tottenham Hotspur, West Bromwich Albion and Wolves; Who's Who's of Arsenal (published 2007), Aston Villa, Birmingham City, Chelsea, England World Cup players (from 1950), Everton, Liverpool, Manchester United, Nottingham Forest, Sheffield Wednesday (published 2007), Stoke City, West Bromwich Albion and Wolves; 100 Greats/Legends of Aston Villa (published 2007), Birmingham City and Wolves; 100 Years at The Hawthorns 1900-2000; West Midlands Football (1874-2004); Images of Sport Series: Aston Villa, Birmingham City, Stoke City and West Bromwich Albion; The Unique Double (1930-31), League Champions: 1953-54; Midlands Soccer at War (1939-45); Albion Through The War (1939-46); 'Smokin Joe' (The Cyrille Regis Story: 25 years in football); The Complete Footballer (The Ronnie Allen Story as Player and Manager, 1944-84); 2,000 Football Oddities; Football Firsts (1863 to 2006)* and two photographic books. There are more to come, including *The Legends of Stoke City* and *The Complete Record of Wolverhampton Wanderers (1877-2008)* in September 2008.

Peter Miles and **Dave Goody** (Southend United): Peter and Dave's first venture into publishing, *A Century United – The Centenary History of Southend United,*

was launched last year to much critical acclaim, and has already gone to a reprint. Having got the 'bug', they intend to publish further books on both Southend and football in general, with their next book planned for this Christmas; further details can be found at www.shrimperpublishing.co.uk. Peter and Dave are both staunch fans of the Shrimpers, and Dave is now taking his two young sons, Matthew and Sam, with him to Roots Hall.

Ian Mills (Arsenal): Ian has been an Arsenal fan since he was five years old and after several seasons following the team at Highbury as well as away games he can now be found in the Upper Tier at Ashburton Grove. He has been a regular contributor to *The Gooner* fanzine since 1997 and has written and published a fanzine *Sunday Bloody Sunday* for his own Sunday side since 1996.

Paul Morant (Leyton Orient): Working for an insurance company in London, Paul is an out-and-out Orient fan who rarely misses a game, home or away, and takes great pride in being this publication's Orient contributor. Paul married Miranda in 2005 and their baby son, Nathan, was born June 2006. Has now been joined by stepson Tyler as an O's fan.

Gerald Mortimer (Derby County): Gerald saw his first game at the Baseball Ground in 1946 and from 1970 spent 32 years covering them for the *Derby Evening Telegraph*. His spell included two League Championships as well as four relegations and three promotions. The author of several statistical books on the club, he was delighted to be at Wembley in May 2007 to see Billy Davies and his team clinch a return to the Premiership. This year Gerald did a great job editing the Who's Who.

Ron Norris (Queens Park Rangers): A QPR fan for over 20 years, Ron runs and edits the successful unofficial website: www.qpr.net.com/ and has interviewed countless Rangers' stars, past and present, for the site. He also co-wrote and published the successful book *Loftus Road Legends* in 2002.

John Northcutt (West Ham United): Has supported the Hammers since 1959 and is the co-author of *West Ham: A Complete Record* and *West Ham United: An Illustrated History*. A regular contributor to the club programme, John was the club adviser to *The Ultimate Football Guide*. He also answers all the questions put to the Vintage Claret section on the club's web site. In 2003 he compiled the *West Ham United Definitive*, which can be purchased at SoccerData Publications. John has been a season ticket holder at Upton Park for many years and likes to spend his time adding to his array of West Ham memorabilia. His latest book, *On This Day* will be available in August 2008.

Simon Parker (Bradford City): Has covered Bradford City's fortunes for the *Bradford Telegraph & Argus* since 2000 – a period that has unfortunately coincided with a spectacular fall from grace. Simon, who previously worked for *The News, Portsmouth*, has now seen the Bantams play 83 different sides in league action and he would rather it had been considerably less! He still insists he is not a jinx and is desperately hoping that the decline will be ended before too long.

Steve Peart and **Dave Finch** (Wycombe Wanderers): A former programme editor of the club and a supporter for over 30 years, Steve put together the player profiles, while the club statistics were supplied by Dave, the official Wycombe statistician. Both were authors of *Wycombe Wanderers, 1887-1996: The Official History*, published in 1996. Dave has supported Wycombe regularly since 1964, although he saw his first game at the old Loakes

Park ground in 1958. He has just retired from Wycombe's programme team after contributing articles and stats since 1990.

Steve Phillipps (Rochdale): A Rochdale supporter for over 40 years, and the club's official historian, Steve is the author of T*he Survivors: The Story of Rochdale AFC* (1990), *The Definitive Rochdale* (1995) and, more recently, *The Official History of Rochdale AFC*. A founder member of the AFS, away from football he is a university professor.

Terry Phillips (Cardiff City): Now aged 55, Terry is still covering Cardiff City FC as the MediaWales chief sports writer for the *South Wales Echo*, *Western Mail* and *Wales on Sunday*. Having been a sports journalist for over 30 years – *Kent Evening Post* (1970-1977), *Derby Evening Telegraph* (1977-1986), *Gloucester Citizen* (1986-1994) – he has previously covered clubs at all levels, including Brian Clough's Nottingham Forest, Derby County, Gillingham, and Gloucester City. His specialist subjects are Cardiff City FC and Cardiff Devils (Ice Hockey).

Alan Platt (Liverpool): A dedicated football statistician and follower of Liverpool FC since 1960, whilst resident in London he was a member and official of the London branch of the LFC Supporters Club. Has assisted Barry Hugman in an editorial capacity on all his football publications since 1980, namely five updates of the post-war *Football* (now titled *Premier & Football*) *League Players' Records*, the two editions of *Premier League: The Players* and, for the last seven years, the *PFA Footballers' Who's Who* (formerly *The Factfile*). Now resident in Manchester, his main interest today is in non-league football and he keeps detailed records on all the senior semi-professional leagues, having compiled a database of over 6,000 players participating in that level of football.

Kevan Platt (Norwich City): Kevan has worked at Carrow Road in a variety of roles since 1980 and has been club secretary since December 1998, a role which takes him to the heart of all football matters relating to Norwich City. A keen amateur statistician, he has been able to expand his interest and knowledge in this area whilst acting as programme editor for the club for nine years, culminating in his co-authorship, with Mike Davage, of *Canary Citizens - Centenary Edition*, published in 2002. A founder member of the Norwich City Football Club Historical Trust, a registered charity with aims to preserve Norwich City's heritage for future generations to enjoy, Kevan will clock up 40 years of watching Norwich play in September 2008 and seldom misses a match. His enthusiasm for all matters Norwich City is shared by his wife Ann and two children, Lawrie and Alice, both of whom have match-day jobs at Carrow Road.

Richard Prime (Hereford United): Richard, the sports editor of *The Hereford Times*, has followed in the footsteps of distinguished journalists such as Ted Woodriffe and Laurie Teague as the paper's Hereford United correspondent. After a modern languages degree at the University of Bristol and careers in the insurance and travel industries, he now has the opportunity to travel the country to feed his addiction to the Bulls.

Mike Purkiss (Crystal Palace): Having supported Palace since 1950 and producing stats on them since 1960, Mike is the author of *Crystal Palace: A Complete History, 1905-1989*. Was the club statistician for T*he Ultimate Football Guide* and also contributed to *Premier League: The Players*.

Derek Quinn (Morecambe): Derek, the club press officer and local journalist, has been supporting Morecambe for almost 30 years. After watching Trevor Brooking star

for FA Cup winners West Ham in a friendly at Christie Park in the 1970s he went on to sell programmes before promotion to a turnstile operator. Missed a few seasons while at University but the lure of the award winning Christie Park pies proved too much and he got his dream job as sports editor of the local paper and getting paid to watch his heroes. Now a BBC match commentator and freelance contributor he spends his spare time following the Shrimps up and down the country, still living the dream after the club's promotion to the Football League for the first time.

Mick Renshaw (Sheffield Wednesday): Has followed Wednesday for over 40 years, despite all the ups and downs of a club that won the First Division title four times in past years, and will continue to do so regardless. Mick, who is a great supporter of European soccer, also produced the club section for *The Ultimate Football Guide*.

Mick Robinson (Peterborough United): Another life-long fan, for a number of years Mick has contributed to the club programme and was the joint editor of *The Posh*, the official Peterborough history. Was also club statistician for *The Ultimate Football Guide*.

Phil Sherwin (Port Vale): Phil is the Port Vale club statistician and has contributed to the club programme for many years as well as various books about the club. He has also written articles for the local newspaper and has featured on local radio.

David Simpson (Dagenham & Redbridge): The club's official statistician and programme editor, David has supported them since the days of Walthamstow Avenue though the mergers with Leytonstone/Ilford and Dagenham to its current guise. Since the club's formation in 1992 he has missed only five games, home or away, in all first-team competitions. When he gets the time he is continuing to research the complete record of Walthamstow Avenue FC from 1900 to their last game in 1988. David has edited all the Football Conference promotion final programmes since the first one in 2003, including the North and South play-off finals.

Mike Slater (Wolverhampton Wanderers): The Wolves' contributor to this publication since its inception, Mike produced a book on the club's history called Molineux Memories, which he published in 1988. He has also written two booklets about Wolves, and compiled several quizzes on them. Would like to write another book or booklet on the club, with an emphasis on his experiences as a supporter, and continues to help out with other Wolves' publications from time to time.

Gordon Small (Hartlepool United): Gordon has supported Pools since October 1965 and for over 40 years now has collected and compiled statistics on his adopted club. Has contributed to all 14 editions of the PFA Footballers' Who's Who, and in 1998 he produced The Definitive Hartlepool United FC. Has a wide range of football interests, and in 2007 was the author of *The Lancashire Cup - A Complete Record 1879-80 to 2006-07*.

Dave Smith (Leicester City): Dave has been the official Leicester City statistician and historian for many years and is a regular contributor to both the club programme and the club's extensive media guide. He is also the co-author of both Of Fossils and Foxes and The Foxes Alphabet and was editor of both Farewell to Filbert Street and Keeping the Faith, which together charted the final season at Filbert Street and the first campaign at the Walkers Stadium.

Paul Smith (Tottenham Hotspur): Paul is the webmaster of Spurs Odyssey (http://www.spursodyssey.com) and has been supporting Tottenham at home and away, including across Europe, for over 40 years. Married with two adult sons, one of whom accompanies him to matches, as he also supports Spurs! Paul has been a board member of the Tottenham Hotspur Supporters' Trust for seven years, and is often consulted and interviewed by various press and media companies. Is the author of *Spurs Odyssey: Season Review 2006-07*.

Phil Smith (Milton Keynes Dons): One of a number of former Wimbledon supporters who now follow the Dons in their new surroundings, Phil is a regular contributor to the club's programme and website.

Gerry Somerton (Rotherham United): Has contributed the details on Rotherham United every year since this publication's introduction. Retired from his former full-time position of media manager with the club in October 2006, he still keeps in touch by doing match reports for the new independent radio station *Rother FM*. Gerry has written several books on the club and is still regarded as the club's historian with his vast amount of records.

Don Starr (Portsmouth): From a naval family, Don has supported his home-town team for over 50 years, experiencing many highs and lows along the way. In the distant past he was an occasional contributor to the official programme but now confines his support to merely watching and keeping his own stats!

Paul A. Stead (Huddersfield Town): A passionate life-long supporter of his beloved home-town football club who has followed the fortunes of the Terriers for the last 28 years. Such is the sense of anticipation for the clubs ambitions during the Centenary season 2008-09 that Paul has purchased a season ticket for himself and his eight-year-old daughter Gracie, even though she thinks football is boring. Paul is in his 11th year with the Who's Who.

David Steele (Carlisle United): David has been associated with the Who's Who since its inception. He was a regular contributor to the Carlisle United programme for many years and two years ago wrote Carlisle United 1974/75 - A Season in the Sun which covers the club's solitary campaign in the First Division. He continues to research the history of the club and is a regular contributor to the local newspaper on such matters.

Richard Stocken (Shrewsbury Town): Having followed Town through thick and mainly thin for almost 50 years, Richard is a collector of all things Shrewsbury and has contributed to a number of books and programmes over the years. In his spare time he is a senior manager with one of the big four banks.

Chas Sumner (Chester City): Chas has been a supporter of Chester City for 40 years having seen his first game in 1967. The club's official historian and statistician, he is a long-time programme contributor and the author of three books on the Blues including On the Borderline: The Official History of Chester City Football Club published in 1997 and Images of Sport: Chester City Football Club published in 2002.

Bill Swann (Newcastle United): A supporter since the Jackie Milburn days of the early 1950s, and a long-term share-holder in the club along with his wife and three children, all season ticket holders, he is a keen collector of memorabilia connected with the club. Bill has consolidated his information on club matches, teams, scorers, and players into a data base for easy access and analysis, has assisted in the production of the club's volume in the Complete Record series, and is a co-author of The Essential History of Newcastle United. This is his

13th year as a contributor to this publication.

Colin Tattum (Birmingham City): Colin is the chief sports writer on the *Birmingham Evening Mail* newspaper, with more than 16 years experience in his field, and has special responsibility to cover the day-to-day fortunes of Birmingham City.

Paul Taylor (Mansfield Town): The historian for Mansfield Town, Paul has just completed his 39th season as a Town fan and has contributed to many publications over the years. He co-authored the club's centenary history in 1997 and a new pictorial history, co-written with Martin Shaw, in the autumn of 2007. Paul is always happy to help fellow historians and statisticians with any query on the Stags.

Richard and **Sarah Taylor** and **Ian Mills** (Notts County): Richard is a life-long Notts County fan from a Notts County family, travelling the length and breadth of the land in following the Magpies, and has seen them on all but a few current league grounds and many non-current grounds too. In the summer, he umpires cricket matches to while away the close season. Sarah, like her father and two brothers, became a dedicated fan at an early age and has made regular excursions home from university to support the Magpies. Having seen his first game at Gay Meadow in 1959-60, Ian, who once ran the match-day programme sales, has been hooked ever since and has completed over 1000 consecutive games for County, being presented with a memento by Chris Hull of Nationwide on the pitch in 2002-03. He now sits in the press box at County doing the press officer's job, after 23 seasons of programme involvement and wanting a change.

Philip Terry (Accrington Stanley): The club's official historian and statistician. Prior to Stanley's promotion to the Football League, his involvement with the game was at non-league level, first at Colne Dynamoes where he was the secretary for many years and then with Accrington Stanley. He became the Stanley club secretary in 1992 and also became involved with the match-day programme. He retired from the secretary's position in May 2006 but continued to have a considerable input with the programme and he also acts as match secretary, attending all the games, both home and away. Has produced two books, *The History of Colne Dynamoes Football Club* and *The Stanley Centenary*.

Roger Triggs (Gillingham): Roger has been a Gillingham supporter for over 40 years and has been collecting statistics and records on the club since he was a schoolboy. Co-author of the highly acclaimed centenary book, Home of the Shouting Men, published in 1993, Roger has since produced his images collection in conjunction with Tempus Publishing Company and, in August 2001, brought out *The Complete Who's Who of Gillingham's Football League Players, 1920-1938 & 1950-2001*.

Frank Tweddle (Darlington): The club's official historian and statistician, Frank has regularly contributed articles to the Darlington programme for the last 33 seasons. He has avidly supported the Quakers, home and away, for over 50 years and has seen them play on well over a 100 grounds. As well as being a member of the 92 Club and the AFS he is the author of *Darlington's Centenary History* published in 1983 and *The Definitive Darlington 1883 - 2000*, as well as producing work for various other football publications. Now early-retired, Frank can devote even more time to delving into Darlington's fascinating if mainly undistinguished past 125 years!

John Vickers (Lincoln City): A life-long Lincoln City supporter, John was appointed as the Imps' media manager in August 2001. He has been in charge of the club's official website since 1998, whilst he has edited their award-winning match-day programme since the 2002-03 season. Coached as a youngster in his back garden by future England international Mick Harford, who lodged with his family during his playing days at Sincil Bank, John edited his first book in 2007, which charted the City's first 100 seasons in the Football League.

Paul Voller (Ipswich Town): A life-long Ipswich fan who started attending matches at Portman Road in 1963, Paul is a member of the executive committee of the Supporters' Club and is responsible for the Supporters' Club page in the match-day magazine. He was the Ipswich statistician for the *Rothmans Football Yearbook* and the *Football Club Directory* during the 1990s and is the joint author of *The Essential History of Ipswich Town*, which was published in 2001. Paul also provided the questions for the official *Ipswich Town Quiz DVD*, which was launched last December.

Tony Woodburn and **Martin Atherton** (Preston North End): Both North End fans for well over 30 years, Tony and Martin provide statistical and historical information on the club for various outlets and maintain the National Football Museum's permanent Preston North End collection, as well as writing for the club programme and of course the *Who's Who*. Martin is a member of the International Football Institute and his book on *The Theft of the Jules Rimet Trophy in 1966* was published in 2008.

David Woods (Bristol City): An Ashton Gate regular since March 1958, though the first game David can actually recall seeing was the 2-2 draw at Swindon during the 1954-55 Third Division (South) Championship campaign. David has been involved with many books on Bristol City, as well as a history on Bristol Bulldogs Speedway. *Bristol City – The Early Years 1894-1915* was published by Desert Island in 2004, whilst *Bristol City - The Modern Era*, which was first published in 2000, was updated last year. Later this year *Bristol City 1915-1946* is due for publication. David is now leisurely engaged in visiting as many Scottish grounds as possible, but with only 14 notched up so far it is unlikely that his feat of visiting all the Football League grounds will be matched across the border. The Bristol City official club historian and a graduate of the Open University, David's other interests include geology, history, cricket (Gloucestershire), rugby (Bristol), speedway (Somerset Rebels) as well as tennis, which has seen him as a visitor to the Wimbledon Championships every year since 1973.

Peter Wyatt (Stoke City): Now in his mid-50s, having supported the Potters since he was about six years old, Peter is over the moon with Stoke's return to the top flight of English football. Alan Hudson and Eddie Clamp (very underrated as a ball player but remembered more for being Stan Matthews' minder) are his all-time Stoke heroes and his favourite player of more recent times is Peter Hoekstra. Although his days of going all over the country to watch the Potters are now sadly over, he remains a season ticket holder at the Britannia.

Finally, on the production side of the book, my thanks go to **Jean Bastin**, of Typecast (Artwork & Design) for her patience and diligent work on the typesetting and design, which again went far beyond the call of normal duty and was much appreciated.

11

Editorial Introduction

Following on from last year's edition, the Who's Who portrays the statistical career record of every FA Barclays Premiership and Coca-Cola Football League player who made an appearance in 2007-2008, whether it be in league football, the Football League Cup (Carling Cup), FA Cup, Community Shield (formerly the Charity Shield), UEFA Champions League, UEFA Cup, Inter-Toto Cup, Johnstone's Paint Trophy, or in the Play-Offs. Not included are Welsh Cup matches. It goes beyond mere statistics, however, with a write up on all of the 2,300 plus players involved, and also records faithfully last season's playing records separately by club.

The work falls into three main sections, all inter-relating. Firstly, the main core, PFA Footballers' Who's Who: A-Z (pages 13 to 452); secondly, the FA Barclays Premiership and Coca-Cola League Clubs: Summary of Appearances and Goals for 2007-2008 (pages 453 to 472); and thirdly, Where Did They Go? (pages 475 to 479); lists all players shown in the previous edition who either moved on or did not play in 2007-2008. Below is an explanation on how to follow the PFA Footballers' Who's Who. Transfers from 1 July 2008 until going to press in mid-July that involve players in the book are also recorded separately on pages 474/475.

As the title suggests, all players are listed in alphabetical order and are shown by Surnames first, followed by full Christian names, with the name the player is commonly known by shown in bold. Any abbreviation or pseudonyms bracketed.

Birthplace/date: You will note that several players who would be predominately classified as British, were born in places like Germany and India, for example. My book, Premier and Football League Players' Records, which covers every man who has played league football since the war, has, in the past, used the family domicile as a more realistic 'birthplace'. But, for our purposes here, I have reverted to that which has been officially recorded.

Height and Weight: Listed in feet and inches, and stones and pounds, respectively. It must be remembered that a player's weight can frequently change and, on that basis, the recorded data should be used as a guide only, especially as players are weighed several times during the season.

Club Honours: Those shown, cover careers from the Conference and FA Trophy upwards. For abbreviations, read:- European Honours: UEFACL (UEFA Champions League, formerly known as the European Cup), ESC (European Super Cup), ECWC (European Cup Winners' Cup, not contested since 1999) and UEFAC (UEFA Cup, formerly Fairs Cup). English Honours: FAC (FA Cup), FLC (Football League Cup), CS (Community Shield), FMC (Full Members Cup, which took in the Simod and Zenith Data sponsorships), AMC (Associated Members Cup, now known as the FL Trophy, which is currently sponsored by Johnstone's Paint and has previously involved Freight Rover, Sherpa Van, Leyland DAF, Autoglass, Auto Windscreens and LDV Vans), AIC (Anglo-Italian Cup), GMVC (GM Vauxhall Conference), NC (Nationwide Conference), FC (Football Conference), FAT (FA Trophy), FAYC (FA Youth Cup). Scottish Honours: SPD (Scottish Premier Division), S Div 1/2 (Scottish Leagues), SC (Scottish Cup), SLC (Scottish League Cup), SLCC (Scottish League Challenge Cup). Please note that medals awarded to P/FL, FLC, and AMC winners relate to players who have appeared in 25%, or over, of matches, while FAC, UEFACL,

ESC, ECWC and UEFAC winners' medals are for all-named finalists, including unused subs. For our purposes, however, Community Shield winners' medals refer to men who either played or came on as a sub. Honours applicable to players coming in from abroad are not shown at present, but the position continues to be reviewed.

International Honours: For abbreviations, read:- E (England), NI (Northern Ireland), S (Scotland), W (Wales) and RoI (Republic of Ireland). Under 21 through to full internationals give total appearances (inclusive of subs), while schoolboy (U16s and U18s) and youth representatives are just listed. The cut-off date used for appearances was up to and including 30 June 2008.

Player Descriptions: Gives position and playing strengths and, in keeping the work topical and positive, a few words on how their season went in 2007-2008. This takes into account key performances, along with value to the team, injuries, honours, and other points of interest, etc. Since 1999-2000, trainees were gradually superseded by scholars under the new scholarship scheme, but for our purposes the young players who come through the club are still denoted as trainees.

Career Records: Full appearances, plus substitutes and goals, are given for all FA Barclays Premiership and Coca-Cola Football League games. If a player who is in the book has played in any of the senior Scottish Leagues, his appearances with the club in question will also be recorded at the point of signing. Other information given, includes the players' source (clubs in the non-leagues, junior football, or from abroad), registered signing dates (if a player signs permanently following a loan spell, for our purposes, we have shown the initial date as being the point of transfer). Also, loan transfers are only recorded if an appearance is made, while transfer fees are the figures that have been reported in newspapers and magazines and should only be used as a guide to a player's valuation. Appearances, substitutions and goals are recorded by P/FL (Premiership and Football League), PL (Premier League), FL (Football League), FLC (Football League Cup), FAC (FA Cup), and Others. Other matches take in the Play-Offs, FL Trophy, Community Shield, and European competitions, such as the European Champions League, UEFA Cup, European Super Cup and Inter-Toto Cup. All of these matches are lumped together for reasons of saving space. Scottish appearances for players on loan to P/FL clubs in 2007-2008 are shown at the point of transfer and do not include games following their return to Scotland. That also applies to players transferred from England to Scotland. FA Cup appearances, subs and goals are only recorded when they are made playing for a P/FL club and do not cover appearances made by Conference sides prior to joining or after relegation from the Football League.

Career statistics are depicted as
Appearances + Substitutes/Goals

Whether you wish to analyse someone for your fantasy football team selection or would like to know more about a little-known player appearing in the lower reaches of the game, the PFA Footballers' Who's Who should provide you with the answer.

Barry J. Hugman, Editor,
PFA Footballers' Who's Who

A

ABBEY George Peterson

Born: Port Harcourt, Nigeria, 20 October 1978
Height: 5'10" **Weight:** 11.13
International Honours: Nigeria: 16
Released by Port Vale in the summer, George signed for Crewe as an experienced defender with eight years in the English game after arriving from Nigeria. He relishes the chance to link up with the attack but was on the bench in the early part of the season. From the end of December, he earned a regular place in defence, operating in both full-back positions. Is neat and tidy in his work.
Macclesfield T (Signed from Sharks FC, Port Harcourt, Nigeria on 20/8/1999) FL 79+21/1 FLC 5+1 FAC 5+4 Others 2 (Freed during 2004 close season)
Port Vale (Free, following various trials, on 17/12/2004) FL 53+9/1 FLC 4 FAC 3 Others 2
Crewe Alex (Free on 31/7/2007) FL 20+3

ABBEY Nathanael (Nathan)

Born: Islington, 11 July 1978
Height: 6'1" **Weight:** 12.0
Freed by Brentford in summer, the experienced goalkeeper remained on the MK Dons bench for the entire League Two season, thanks to the consistency of Willy Gueret. He was given three Cup starts and in the first endeared himself to the home crowd with a crucial save in the Carling Cup penalty shoot-out win over Ipswich Town. Though he had few opportunities, he always showed a good attitude and was popular with supporters.
Luton T (From trainee on 2/5/1996) FL 54+1 FLC 3 FAC 8 Others 2
Chesterfield (Free on 10/8/2001) FL 46 FLC 1 FAC 3 Others 3
Northampton T (Free on 6/8/2002) FL 4+1 FLC 1 Others 2 (Free to Stevenage Borough during 2003 close season)
Boston U (Free, via St Albans C, trials at Luton T, Macclesfield T, Ipswich T, Burnley, on 6/8/2004) FL 61 FLC 3 FAC 6 Others 3
Bristol C (Free on 17/2/2006) FL 0+1
Torquay U (Free on 4/8/2006) FL 24 FLC 1 FAC 3 Others 1
Brentford (Free on 29/12/2006) FL 16
MK Dons (Free on 10/8/2007) FLC 2 FAC 1

ABBOTT Pawel Tadeusz Howard

Born: York, 2 December 1981
Height: 6'1" **Weight:** 11.12
International Honours: Poland: U21
Darlington equalled the club transfer record when they signed Pawel from Swansea in the summer and he made his debut against Wrexham on the opening day, alongside the club's other record buy Julian Joachim. He showed his undoubted class in holding up the ball and, with his deft flick-ons, scored four goals in his first seven games. Unfortunately a series of niggling injuries limited his appearances to 17 starts and his clever play was sorely missed in the run in towards a play-off place. He ended as second top scorer with nine goals and surely would have weighed in with a fair few more had his outings not been limited.
Preston NE (£125,000 + from LKS Lodz, Poland on 16/2/2001) FL 8+17/6 FLC 0+1 FAC 1+3
Bury (Loaned on 9/8/2002) FL 13/5 FLC 2 Others 1
Bury (Loaned on 18/3/2003) FL 4/1
Huddersfield T (Signed on 16/2/2004) FL 83+28/48 FLC 4/2 FAC 2+2/1 Others 3+4
Swansea C (£150,000 on 22/1/2007) FL 9+9/1 FAC 0+1
Darlington (£100,000 on 12/7/2007) FL 16+8/9 FLC 1 FAC 0+2

ABDOU Nadjim

Born: Martigues, France, 13 July 1984
Height: 5'11" **Weight:** 11.3
After leaving French club Sedan in the summer, Nadjim impressed Plymouth manager Ian Holloway enough during the pre-season to be offered a one-year deal. As a strong-tackling central midfielder with good stamina and no shortage of ability on the ball, he began his Plymouth career on the bench but became more of a first-team regular towards the end of the season. He scored twice, against Scunthorpe in December and the first in Argyle's FA Cup win against Hull in January. At the end of the season, he was considering the offer of a further contract.
Plymouth Arg (Free from Martigues, France, ex Sedan, on 24/8/2007) FL 22+9/1 FLC 1 FAC 1/1

ACHTERBERG John

Born: Utrecht, Holland, 8 July 1971
Height: 6'1" **Weight:** 13.8
Following an uncertain close season, when it was rumoured that he would not be re-signing for Tranmere, John agreed a new two-year player-coach contract on the understanding that his main emphasis was to be on coaching and he would start the season as the second-choice goalkeeper. Due to the excellent form of Danny Coyne, John spent most of the campaign on the bench, making only a handful of early-season starts, but maintained a professional outlook throughout, concentrating largely on his coaching and commercial duties. When he does play, this self-confessed workaholic is calm, reliable, commanding in the area and handles crosses well. John has been granted a testimonial by Rovers in 2008-09.
Tranmere Rov (Free from FC Eindhoven, Holland, ex NAC Breda, on 22/9/1998) FL 246+4 FLC 17+1 FAC 23 Others 13

ADAM Jamil Buba

Born: Bolton, 5 June 1991
Height: 5'10" **Weight:** 10.0
A product of the Barnsley Academy, Jamil made his debut as a late substitute at Cardiff on the final day of the season. The striker made a positive impression in the reserves and much is expected of him.
Barnsley (Trainee) FL 0+1

ADAMS Daniel (Danny) Benjamin

Born: Manchester, 3 January 1976
Height: 5'8" **Weight:** 13.9
The experienced left-back was one of Morecambe's most consistent performers. Danny linked up again with former boss Sammy McIlroy when he signed a two-year contract at the start of the season after an impressive loan spell and Huddersfield's decision to release him. He arrived with a reputation as a hard man but showed he had far more to his game, with a neat touch and ability to work his way out of tight spots. What he lacked in pace, he more than made up for through experience and intelligence. He was the supporters' and players' 'Player of the Year'.

Danny Adams

Macclesfield T (£25,000 from Altrincham on 31/8/2000) FL 146+2/1 FLC 5+1 FAC 12 Others 3/1
Stockport Co (Signed on 5/3/2004) FL 39/1 FLC 1 FAC 2 Others 1
Huddersfield T (Free on 24/3/2005) FL 68 FLC 3 FAC 3 Others 3
Morecambe (Free on 21/2/2007) FL 42 FLC 3 FAC 1 Others 4

Nicky Adams

ADAMS Nicholas (Nicky)
William
Born: Bolton, 16 October 1986
Height: 5'10" **Weight:** 11.0
International Honours: W: U21-2
Nicky exploded on the scene at Bury and proved the hype about him to be justified. The young winger showed maturity and adaptability when appearing on either wing and as a forward for the Shakers. Consistently good performances in the first half of the season earned a call up to the Welsh under-21 squad in November. His best performance was against Barnet, when he scored twice in Bury's 3-0 victory. Nicky was rewarded for his efforts when named 'Young Player of the Season'.
Bury (From trainee on 1/7/2006) FL 61+16/14 FLC 3 FAC 8+1/1 Others 4+1

ADAMS Stephen (Steve) Marc
Born: Plymouth, 25 September 1980
Height: 6'0" **Weight:** 11.10
Club Honours: Div 3 '02; Div 2 '04
The experienced defensive midfielder joined Swindon on a six-month contract in the summer with a view to proving his fitness, having been released by Sheffield Wednesday after an injury-hit 2006-07. Steve made two League starts and had a couple of outings in the Johnstone's Paint Trophy. His last appearance was as a late substitute in the FA Cup at Wycombe in November. He was offered a contract extension but sought the security of a longer deal at Torquay in the Blue Square Premier.
Plymouth Arg (From trainee on 6/7/1999) FL 131+26/7 FLC 4 FAC 7+3 Others 4+2
Sheffield Wed (Free on 9/3/2005) FL 18+2 Others 0+1
Swindon T (Free on 10/8/2007) FL 2 FLC 1 FAC 0+1 Others 2

ADAMSON Christopher (Chris)
Born: Ashington, 4 November 1978
Height: 6'1" **Weight:** 11.12
Signed from Sheffield Wednesday in the summer, although given Stockport's goalkeeping jersey Chris seemed to lack confidence during pre-season friendlies and failed to make a League appearance as a string of loan 'keepers were preferred. When Conrad Logan, on loan from Leicester, was refused permission to play in the FA Cup against Staines, Chris stepped in. Unfortunate to concede from what should have been a routine stop that gave Staines a late equaliser at Edgeley Park, he saved the first spot-kick before County eventually lost the replay on penalties to the non-Leaguers. Was released in the summer.
West Bromwich A (From trainee on 2/7/1997) FL 12 FAC 2 (Freed on 7/4/2003)
Mansfield T (Loaned on 30/4/1999) FL 2
Halifax T (Loaned on 1/7/1999) FL 7
Plymouth Arg (Loaned on 10/11/2002) FL 1
Sheffield Wed (Free from St Patricks on 28/11/2005) FL 9+2 FLC 1
Stockport Co (Free on 9/8/2007) FAC 2

ADDISON Miles Vivien Esifi
Born: Newham, 7 January 1989
Height: 6'2" **Weight:** 13.3
Two years after his two previous appearances for Derby, Miles made his Premiership bow at Blackburn when relegation was already a certainty. The central defender spent the season in Derby's reserves, who were as unsuccessful as the seniors, but coped reasonably well with Blackburn's strong forward pair.
Derby Co (From trainee on 6/7/2007) P/FL 3

ADEBAYOR Sheyi Emmanuel
Born: Lome, Togo, 26 February 1984
Height: 6'2" **Weight:** 11.11
International Honours: Togo :37
Emmanuel was thrust into the season as Arsenal's main striker, as Thierry Henry's summer departure along with injuries to both Robin van Persie and Eduardo left the Gunners short of forward options. The Togo international certainly accepted the responsibility with great vigour. He scored 24 goals in his 36 Premier League games, including a brace at Tottenham and hat-tricks at home and away against Derby. Emmanuel improved his finishing enormously but it is his aerial strength that really lends a different dimension to Arsenal's playing style. He was on target in the San Siro to complete a magnificent Champions' League win against Milan and scored in both legs of the quarter-final against Liverpool as he featured nine times in the competition. He managed two more goals in his two FA Cup ties and one in his solitary Carling Cup appearance. Deservedly, as Arsenal fans

took him to their hearts, he also received recognition from his peers when he was voted into the PFA 'Premier League Team of the Season'.

Arsenal (£5,000,000 from AS Monaco, France on 31/1/2006) PL 65+13/36 FLC 3+2/3 FAC 3+2/4 Others 13+4/3

ADEBOLA Bamberdele (Dele)

Born: Lagos, Nigeria, 23 June 1975
Height: 6'3" **Weight:** 12.8
Although not Coventry's first choice at the start, a Carling Cup goal against Notts County put him in the frame and from then until his move to Bristol City in January, he was involved in every game bar one. He sets problems for defenders and scored some excellent goals, his best effort coming at Blackburn in the 4-1 FA Cup victory, when he muscled past three defenders and unleashed a sweet left-footed shot. He next scored against Bristol City on New Year's Day. Needing to redress the lack of presence in the penalty area that was threatening to derail the Robins' good half-season's work, it was with some relief that their fans heard of the transfer window signing of Dele from Coventry. While not a prolific scorer, he added the physique that was necessary and in so doing created opportunities for others as City kept in the promotion pack and eventually reached the play-off final. At Wembley Dele found himself frequently penalised by referee Alan Wiley, rather clipping his wings.

Crewe Alex (From trainee on 21/6/1993) FL 98+27/39 FLC 4+3/2 FAC 8+2/3 Others 10+1/2
Birmingham C (£1,000,000 on 6/2/1998) FL 86+43/31 FLC 13+4/8 FAC 2+1/2 Others 1+2/1
Oldham Ath (Loaned on 20/3/2002) FL 5
Crystal Palace (Free on 15/8/2002) FL 32+7/5 FLC 5/2 FAC 4
Coventry C (Free on 2/7/2003) FL 115+48/31 FLC 5+3/3 FAC 8+3/2
Burnley (Loaned on 25/3/2004) FL 0+3/1
Bradford C (Loaned on 13/8/2004) FL 14+1/3 Others 1/1
Bristol C (£250,000 on 31/1/2008) FL 16+1/6 Others 3

ADOMAH Albert Danquah

Born: Lambeth, 13 December 1987
Height: 6'1" **Weight:** 11.8
The 20-year-old right-winger, who signed from Ryman League side Harrow Borough in January, became an instant hit with the Barnet faithful when he scored on his debut in the 2-1 win at Hereford. Despite only being involved in the second half of the season, Albert has already attracted several enquiries from higher division

Gabby Agbonlahor

clubs and looks set for a bright future in the game.

Barnet (Signed from Harrow Borough on 14/1/2008) FL 22/5

AGBONLAHOR Gabriel (Gabby)

Born: Birmingham, 13 October 1986
Height: 5'11" **Weight:** 12.5
International Honours: E: U21-10; Yth
Gabby's speed, tricks and accurate finishing were an instant feature of Aston Villa's season. He was the Barclays Premier League 'Player of the Month' for

November and continued to impress for England under-21, named 'Man of the Match' against Romania. With Gabby on the right and Ashley Young on the other side, Villa used the flanks to devastating effect and their attacking pace and power provided a test for any defence. A local boy, Gabby is a huge hero with the fans and while he has been as quick and as lethal as ever, he now holds the ball more effectively. He is also useful in the air and scored some fine headed goals. Gabby only missed one game, because of a hamstring injury.

*Aston Villa (From trainee on 4/3/2005) PL
77+7/21 FLC 5/1 FAC 2
Watford (Loaned on 22/9/2005) FL 1+1
Sheffield Wed (Loaned on 28/10/2005)
FL 4+4*

AGGER Daniel
Born: Hvidovre, Denmark, 12 December
1984
Height: 6'2" **Weight:** 11.11
Club Honours: CS '06
International Honours: Denmark: 18;
U21-10; Yth
In 2006-07 the young Danish
international established himself as
an automatic choice in manager Rafa
Benitez's Liverpool team and became
a Kop hero with his vital goal in the
European Champions' League semi-final
against Chelsea. He had everything
to look forward to but after only six
games of the new season he damaged a
metatarsal in a foot at Portsmouth and
was out of contention for four months.
On returning to training in January he
suffered a recurrence of the problem and
it was decided that surgery was required,
thus sidelining him for the remainder of
the campaign. With little cover in central
defence, Benitez played the veteran
Sami Hyypia more often than he wished
and one can only speculate how much
Daniel's absence contributed to some
uncertain defensive displays in the first
half of the campaign. In the January
transfer window, Benitez solved the lack
of cover by signing Martin Skrtel and so
well did the Slovak international slot in
that the unfortunate Dane now faces a
fight to regain his place when he returns
to full fitness.
*Liverpool (£5,800,000 from Brondby,
Denmark, ex Rosenhoj BK, on 13/1/2006) PL
31+5/2 FLC 2/1 FAC 1 Others 14/1*

AGHAHOWA Julius
Born: Benin City, Nigeria, 12 February
1982
Height: 5'10" **Weight:** 11.7
International Honours: Nigeria: 32
As a striker with pace to burn and one
who uses space intelligently, Julius'
second season in the Premier League with
Wigan was frustrating as he became a
peripheral figure. Tricky on the ball, he
played a full game against Liverpool in
September but his only other start was
in the draw at Fulham in December. As
Wigan battled to climb away from the
relegation zone, Julius went on in the
home game against Blackburn and set up
the fifth goal for Marcus Bent. While his
awareness and finishing still need work,
his pace and movement sometimes added
zest to the attack. Like many of the fringe

players Julius made his biggest impact in
the FA Cup, enjoying his best game in the
victory at Sunderland as Wigan fans saw
for the first time his trademark back-flip
goal celebrations when his was deflected
into his own net by Paul McShane.
Following the signing of Marlon King
in the January transfer window, Julius
struggled to make the bench and, along
with team-mate Saloman Olembe, joined
Turkish side Kayserispor at the end of the
season.
*Wigan Ath (£2,000,000 from Shaktar
Donetsk, Ukraine, ex Bendel Insurance -
Nigeria, Herning Fremad, Esperance - Tunisia,
on 31/1/2007) PL 5+15 FLC 0+1 FAC 0+2*

AGOGO Manuel (Junior)
Born: Accra, Ghana, 1 August 1979
Height: 5'10" **Weight:** 11.7
International Honours: Ghana: 19. E:
SP-3
The Ghana international came to
worldwide prominence during an
impressive African Cup of Nations
tournament in which Junior's two goals
helped his country to the semi-finals.
He began the season in fine form for
Nottingham Forest, a powerful forward
who can operate either on his own or
together with a partner to great effect.
After returning from the tournament, he
never seemed to have the same spark but
13 goals made him Forest's top scorer.
*Sheffield Wed (Free from Willesden
Constantine on 8/10/1996) PL 0+2 FAC 0+1
(Free to Colorado Rapids, USA on 2/2/2000)
Oldham Ath (Loaned on 18/7/1999) FL 10/6
Chester C (Loaned on 3/9/1999) FL 10/6
Chesterfield (Loaned on 11/11/1999) FL 3+1
Lincoln C (Loaned on 17/12/1999) FL 3/1
Queens Park Rgrs (Free from San Jose
Earthquakes, USA on 28/3/2002) FL 0+2 (Free
to Barnet on 4/7/2002)
Bristol Rov (£110,000 + from Barnet on
1/7/2003) FL 109+17/41 FLC 3+1 FAC 5/2
Others 3+2/2
Nottingham F (Signed on 29/8/2006) FL
47+17/20 FLC 1+1 FAC 5+2/3 Others 2*

AGYEMANG Patrick (Paddy)
Born: Walthamstow, 29 September 1980
Height: 6'1" **Weight:** 12.0
International Honours: Ghana: 3
After scoring Preston's first League goal
of the season at Coventry and getting
two more as a late substitute in the home
demolition of Southampton, along with a
further three, Paddy joined Queens Park
Rangers in January and soon went on one
of the most incredible scoring runs ever
seen at Loftus Road. After a promising,
albeit fruitless, debut at Stamford
Bridge in the FA Cup third round defeat
by Chelsea, he scored his first goal at

Sheffield United the following week. He
then continued the run, scoring at least
once in the next five games to take his
streak to six consecutive matches. The
last person to do that for Rangers was
the great Rodney Marsh in 1967. Injuries
took hold in the later stages of the
season and he sat out the last few weeks,
but his great scoring blitz will be long
remembered.
*Wimbledon (From trainee on 11/5/1999) FL
68+53/20 FLC 3+2/1 FAC 8+3/1
Brentford (Loaned on 18/10/1999) FL 3+9
FAC 1
Gillingham (£200,000 on 13/1/2004) FL
29+4/8 FLC 1
Preston NE (£350,000 on 17/11/2004) FL
55+67/21 FLC 1+1 FAC 5+1 Others 0+5
Queens Park Rgrs (£350,000 on 3/1/2008)
FL 17/8 FAC 0+1*

AHMED Adnan Farooq
Born: Burnley, 7 June 1984
Height: 5'10" **Weight:** 11.12
International Honours: Pakistan: 8
Having been released by Huddersfield,
Adnan signed a two-year contract
with Tranmere in early summer. An
enthusiastic and talented midfielder
who can play either in the centre or on
the right, Adnan has the ability to both
win the ball and deliver a telling pass. A
strong and determined tackler, Adnan
received his first formal call up to the
Pakistani national squad for the World
Cup preliminary against Iraq in October
and made his debut in their 7-0 loss. He
scored his first international goal when
playing against Sri Lanka in the AFC
Challenge Cup qualifier.
*Huddersfield T (From trainee on 22/8/2003)
FL 24+17/1 FAC 1 Others 1+2/1
Tranmere Rov (Free on 5/7/2007) FL 3+3
Others 1*

AINGE Simon
Born: Shipley, 18 February 1988
Height: 6'1" **Weight:** 12.2
Centre-half Simon found opportunities
difficult to come by at Bradford because
of the consistent form of David Wetherall,
Mark Bower and Matt Clarke. He
started in the Johnstone's Paint Trophy
at Doncaster and made two substitute
appearances before being loaned out to
Farsley Celtic.
*Bradford C (From trainee on 18/7/2006) FL
5+8 FAC 2 Others 1+1*

AINSWORTH Gareth
Born: Blackburn, 10 May 1973
Height: 5'9" **Weight:** 12.5
One of only three players surviving from
Queens Park Rangers' promotion winning
side of 2004, Gareth continued to display
the battling qualities that have seen

him become something of a cult hero in Shepherds Bush. Despite age creeping up, he is still a key member of the squad and despite being kept out of the side for much of 2008, showed that he can still do a job when required. On top of his playing duties, Gareth took on some coaching responsibilities under Luigi De Canio and if he is not on the pitch, can be found encouraging the team from the sidelines. He was named as Rangers' club captain after the departure of Adam Bolder.
Preston NE (Signed from Northwich Vic, ex Blackburn Rov YTS, on 21/1/1992) FL 2+3 Others 1/1
Cambridge U (Free on 17/8/1992) FL 1+3/1 FLC 0+1
Preston NE (Free on 23/12/1992) FL 76+6/14 FLC 3+2 FAC 3+1 Others 8+1/1
Lincoln C (£25,000 on 31/10/1995) FL 83/37 FLC 8/3 FAC 2 Others 4/1
Port Vale (£500,000 on 12/9/1997) FL 53+2/10 FLC 2/1 FAC 2
Wimbledon (£2,000,000 on 3/11/1998) P/FL 21+15/6 FLC 1+1 FAC 5+2/1
Preston NE (Loaned on 28/3/2002) FL 3+2/1
Walsall (Loaned on 5/12/2002) FL 2+3/1
Cardiff C (£50,000 on 17/3/2003) FL 9
Queens Park Rgrs (Free on 17/7/2003) FL 102+38/21 FLC 2+1/1 FAC 3+2 Others 2

AINSWORTH Lionel Glenn Robert
Born: Nottingham, 1 October 1987
Height: 5'5" **Weight:** 10.5
International Honours: E: Yth
Lionel certainly made his mark at Hereford after being freed by Derby in the summer, scoring a Carling Cup hat-trick against Yeovil and thrilling Bulls' fans with his extraordinary pace and control that turned games in their favour. Terrifying League Two defences, he concluded his short spell at Edgar Street with another hat-trick, against Stockport, and signed off with the only goal of an FA Cup first-round replay at Leeds before joining Watford on loan in November, the deal being made permanent in January. A busy, skilful winger with a smart turn of pace and good crossing ability, he made his debut against Barnsley. Although happy to fit into any position, his opportunities were limited for the rest of the season but he promised well for the future.
Derby Co (From trainee on 10/9/2005) FL 0+2
Bournemouth (Loaned on 4/8/2006) FL 2+5 FAC 0+1 Others 1
Wycombe W (Loaned on 23/2/2007) FL 3+4
Hereford U (Free on 7/8/2007) FL 13+2/4 FLC 2/3 FAC 2/1
Watford (Signed on 22/11/2007) FL 3+5 Others 1+1

AISTON Samuel (Sam) James
Born: Newcastle, 21 November 1976
Height: 6'1" **Weight:** 12.10
Club Honours: Div 1 '96
International Honours: E: Sch
Sam never had a look-in at Northampton in 2007-08 and after a handful of substitute appearances he joined Burton on loan before moving to Wrexham in November. Arriving at the Racecourse, the striker became new manager Brian Little's first signing after taking over from Brian Carey and the initial loan deal became permanent when the January transfer window opened. A strong, forceful midfielder who likes to take on defenders, he was a regular when on loan but injuries later sidelined him. He was on the bench until mid-March, out of favour again in final run-in and offered a free transfer.
Sunderland (From juniors at Newcastle U on 14/7/1995) P/FL 5+15 FLC 0+2 FAC 0+2
Chester C (Loaned on 21/2/1997) FL 14 Others 2
Chester C (Loaned on 27/11/1998) FL 11 Others 1
Stoke C (Loaned on 6/8/1999) FL 2+4 FLC 1
Shrewsbury T (Loaned on 24/12/1999) FL 10
Shrewsbury T (Free on 21/7/2000) FL 99+34/7 FLC 3 FAC 2+2 Others 1+3
Tranmere Rov (Free on 5/7/2005) FL 23+13/3 FLC 1 FAC 0+1 Others 2
Northampton T (Free on 4/8/2006) FL 14+8 FLC 1+1 FAC 0+1
Wrexham (Free on 22/11/2007) FL 13+6

AKINBIYI Adeola (Ade) Oluwatoyin
Born: Hackney, 10 October 1974
Height: 6'1" **Weight:** 12.9
International Honours: Nigeria: 1
Still very much a crowd favourite at Burnley, Ade was seen mainly as an impact substitute and was effective in that role, his pace and sheer nuisance value to defenders often adding freshness to the Clarets' attack. He also maintained a healthy goals-to-games ratio and his never-say-die approach was an inspiration. Featuring more often in the starting line-up after the January departure of Andy Gray he had particular rave notices for his performance alongside Andrew Cole in Burnley's 4-2 win at Queens Park Rangers.
Norwich C (From trainee on 5/2/1993) P/FL 22+27/3 FLC 2+4/2 FAC 0+2 Others 0+1
Hereford U (Loaned on 21/1/1994) FL 3+1/2
Brighton & Hove A (Loaned on 24/11/1994) FL 7/4
Gillingham (£250,000 on 13/11/1997) FL 63/28 FLC 2 FAC 2/1 Others 0+1
Bristol C (£1,200,000 on 28/5/1998) FL 47/21 FLC 5/4 FAC 1
Wolverhampton W (£3,500,000 on 7/9/1999) FL 36+1/16 FAC 3

Leicester C (£5,000,000 on 28/7/2000) PL 49+9/11 FLC 1/1 FAC 5+1/1 Others 2
Crystal Palace (£2,200,000 + on 6/2/2002) FL 11+13/3 FAC 0+4
Stoke C (Loaned on 27/3/2003) FL 4/2
Stoke C (Free on 15/9/2003) FL 52+7/17 FLC 0+1 FAC 2
Burnley (£600,000 on 24/2/2005) FL 38+1/16 FLC 3/2 FAC 1
Sheffield U (£1,750,000 on 27/11/2006) P/FL 12+6/3 FLC 2/1
Burnley (£750,000 on 3/1/2007) FL 29+30/10 FLC 2+1/1 FAC 1+1/1

AKINFENWA Saheed Adebayo
Born: Islington, 10 May 1982
Height: 5'11" **Weight:** 13.0
Club Honours: AMC '06
Out of favour at Swansea, Adebayo moved to Millwall last November. Regarded as a short-term signing, he made a handful of appearances for the Lions, usually as a substitute, in midfield or attack and was always hard to shift off the ball. After suffering a nasty injury and having a long lay-off, he worked hard and his fitness was greatly improved by the time he left the New Den. It was a case of 'zero to hero' for striker Adebayo when he joined Northampton after being given a chance to prove his worth by manager Stuart Gray. He did so with six goals in his first six games. His strong running, ability to shield the ball and power in the air made him a great favourite with the home crowd and it is felt that the best of him will be seen when he regains peak fitness.
Boston U (Free from Barry T, ex FK Atlantas, on 15/10/2003) FL 2+1 Others 1/1
Leyton Orient (Free on 31/10/2003) FL 0+1 FAC 0+1
Rushden & Diamonds (Free on 11/12/2003)
Doncaster Rov (Free on 28/2/2004) FL 4+5/4
Torquay U (Free on 1/7/2004) FL 28+9/14 FLC 0+1 FAC 1 Others 1+1/2
Swansea C (£35,000 + on 13/7/2005) FL 41+18/14 FLC 1+1/1 FAC 2+3/1 Others 6+3/5
Millwall (Free on 15/11/2007) FL 1+6 FAC 1+1
Northampton T (Free on 18/1/2008) FL 13+2/7

AKINS Lucas Jordan
Born: Huddersfield, 25 February 1989
Height: 5'10" **Weight:** 11.7
Yet another to emerge from Huddersfield's Academy, Lucas made his only appearance of the season as a late substitute in the home victory over Yeovil in the opening game. The tall striker was loaned to Northwich in November to gain experience but was among several released at the end of the season.
Huddersfield T (From trainee on 5/7/2007) FL 0+5 Others 0+1

Martin Albrechtsen

AKURANG Cliff
Born: Ghana, 27 February 1981
Height: 6'2" **Weight:** 12.3
Club Honours: FC '07
Cliff arrived at Barnet on New Year's Day
from Blue Square Premier club Histon.
Although he took 11 games to break his
scoring duck for the Bees, he soon found
his form and finished the season with
seven League goals. Having now adjusted
to League Two and established himself
as a main-line striker in the Bees' attack,
Cliff will hope to continue his improving
scoring record.
*Barnet (£20,000 from Histon, ex trainee
at Luton T, Chesham U, Hitchin T, Purfleet,
Heybridge Swifts, Dagenham & Redbridge,
on 1/1/2008) FL 17+4/7 FAC 3*

ALBRECHTSEN Martin
Born: Copenhagen, Denmark, 31 March
1980
Height: 6'1" **Weight:** 12.13
Club Honours: Ch '08
International Honours: Denmark: 4;
U21-14; Yth
Out of action for 11 weeks after
suffering an injury in the home League
draw with Sheffield Wednesday in early
November, Martin returned to the West
Bromwich team as a central defender
in January. Despite having a variety of
partners, he produced some outstanding
performances before injury struck again,
this time a groin strain, with six crucial
games remaining. He scored two League
goals: his first helped Albion to a 3-0 win

at Watford and his second came in the 3-
3 draw with Cardiff at the Hawthorns.
*West Bromwich A (£2,700,000 from FC
Copenhagen, Denmark on 30/6/2004) P/FL
100+18/4 FLC 7+1 FAC 11+1*

ALCOCK Craig
Born: Truro, 8 December 1987
Height: 5'8" **Weight:** 11.0
Having risen through the youth system
at Yeovil, Craig broke into the first
team at the start of the season and put
in some excellent performances. The
youngster was the only Glovers' player
who remained fully fit throughout the
campaign and despite his age and
inexperience at League One level, the full-
back slotted in comfortably. Is a defender
who can play anywhere across the back
four.
*Yeovil T (From juniors on 7/7/2006) FL 5+4
FLC 0+1 FAC 1 Others 2+1*

ALESSANDRA Lewis Peter
Born: Bury, 8 February 1989
Height: 5'9" **Weight:** 11.7
Lewis, an Oldham youth product, was
a regular scorer for the reserves before
his senior debut as a substitute at
Huddersfield in October. He was given
his first start at Swansea in February and
within a month, had his first League goal.
A quick and energetic striker blessed
with trickery, Lewis went on to make 16
appearances and has been set the target
of adding more goals to his otherwise
excellent contribution. His promising
performances were rewarded with a new
three-year contract and he scooped the
club's 'Young Player of the Season' award.
*Oldham Ath (From trainee on 3/7/2007) FL
12+3/2 FAC 0+1*

[ALEX] DIAS DA COSTA Alex
Rodrigo
Born: Niteroi, Brazil, 17 June 1982
Height: 6'2" **Weight:** 14.0
International Honours: Brazil: 12
Chelsea's latest central defensive
acquisition arrived in a circuitous and
unusual manner having been 'parked'
at PSV Eindhoven for three seasons
while Chelsea held his registration.
The Blues paid the Dutch club one
euro for his permanent signature in
August and Alex came to England with
a scoring reputation, having netted to
eliminate Arsenal from the previous
season's Champions' League. He wasted
no time confirming this and his two
Premier League goals came directly
from a Brazilian coaching manual but
were poles apart in execution. His first,
against Middlesbrough at the Riverside in
October, was a 35-yard cannonball that

gave the 'keeper no chance. The second, against Aston Villa on Boxing Day, was a piece of pure class from the backstreets of Rio as he shimmied through the defence and slammed in a low drive. His other Chelsea goal was a long-range effort against Rosenberg in the frozen wastes of Norway in a Champions' League tie. The strapping, no-nonsense defender was nicknamed 'The Tank' at PSV and has certainly endeared himself to Chelsea fans since superseding Tal Ben Haim as central defensive cover.

Chelsea (Signed from Santos, Brazil, via PSV Eindhoven, on 14/8/2007) PL 22+6/2 FLC 3 FAC 2 Others 5+1/1

ALEXANDER Gary George
Born: Lambeth, 15 August 1979
Height: 5'11" **Weight:** 13.0
International Honours: S: 30; B-1
Signed from Leyton Orient in the summer, the bustling centre-forward went more than 20 games before scoring for Millwall but cracked it in style with a hat-trick against Brighton. The fans never got on Gary's back because his constant hard work suggested all he lacked was a bit of confidence. After that, he regained some of his scoring prowess. Strong in the air and hard to knock off the ball, he is an admired target-man.

West Ham U (From trainee on 6/7/1998)
Exeter C (Loaned on 19/8/1999) FL 37/16 FLC 1 FAC 3/1 Others 4/2
Swindon T (£300,000 on 11/8/2000) FL 30+7/7 FLC 3 FAC 2+1 Others 2+1/2
Hull C (£160,000 on 21/6/2001) FL 64+4/23 FLC 3/2 FAC 3/2 Others 4/3
Leyton Orient (Signed on 27/11/2003) FL 165+14/52 FLC 2+2 FAC 10/1 Others 2+4/2
Millwall (Free on 5/7/2007) FL 32+4/7 FLC 1 FAC 3/1 Others 0+1

ALEXANDER Graham
Born: Coventry, 10 October 1971
Height: 5'10" **Weight:** 12.7
Club Honours: Div 2 '00
International Honours: S: 33
Graham was a surprising arrival at Burnley when he moved from neighbours Preston in August. It was certainly a shock to Preston supporters, especially as the transfer came so soon after he joined a select group of players to make 400 appearances for the Lilywhites. Very familiar to Clarets fans from encounters with North End, he was initially deployed in midfield, with mixed results, but moved to his more familiar right-back slot following injury to Michael Duff. A composed and highly experienced defender who also proved a natural leader, he captained the side in the

extended absence of club skipper Steve Caldwell. Seemingly unflappable, he rarely put a foot wrong at the back and was not averse to helping out further upfield, although he failed to add to his impressive career goal tally until the penultimate game, when he netted in the 3-3 draw against Cardiff.

Scunthorpe U (From trainee on 20/3/1990) FL 149+10/18 FLC 11+1/2 FAC 12/1 Others 13+4/3
Luton T (£100,000 on 8/7/1995) FL 146+4/15 FLC 17/2 FAC 7+1 Others 6+2
Preston NE (£50,000 on 25/3/1999) FL 350+2/52 FLC 19+1/6 FAC 19/5 Others 8+1
Burnley (£200,000 on 31/8/2007) FL 43/1 FLC 0+1 FAC 1

ALEXANDER James **Neil**
Born: Edinburgh, 10 March 1978
Height: 6'1" **Weight:** 11.0
Club Honours: S Div 2 '99; S Div 1 '01
International Honours: S: 3; B-1; U21-10
Neil joined Ipswich on a free transfer from Cardiff during the summer and established himself as the club's number one goalkeeper, playing in every game until his surprise move to Glasgow Rangers at the end of the January transfer window. Best remembered at Portman Road for three penalty saves that proved vital in the promotion push. Against Colchester and Wolverhampton, the saves proved to be the spur for the team to go on to win the games, while his save against Plymouth preserved a point.

Stenhousemuir (Free from Edina Hibs on 8/8/1996) SL 48 SLC 1 SC 1 Others 1
Livingston (Signed on 22/8/1998) SL 60 SLC 2 SC 8 Others 5
Cardiff C (£200,000 on 6/8/2001) FL 212+1 FLC 5 FAC 11 Others 5
Ipswich T (Free on 20/7/2007) FL 29 FLC 1 FAC 1

ALGAR Benjamin (Ben) Christopher
Born: Dronfield, 3 December 1989
Height: 5'7" **Weight:** 9.11
The left-sided midfielder and full-back emerged from Chesterfield's youth team to make a creditable debut in September, showing neat control from a pleasingly light first touch and a decent cross. Although slight of frame, Ben has the confidence to take on and beat the most physical opponents. Injury delayed his progress but manager Lee Richardson saw enough to offer Ben a professional contract.

Chesterfield (Trainee) FL 1+1 Others 0+1

AL-HABSI Ali Abdullah Harib
Born: Muscat, Oman, 30 December 1981
Height: 6'5" **Weight:** 13.12
International Honours: Oman: 66
An Oman international, Ali made his first appearance since joining the club some 21 months earlier in the Carling Cup tie at Fulham. After an injury to first-choice goalkeeper Jussi Jaaskelainen, Ali made his Premiership debut in the 1-0 defeat by Wigan in March and went on to appear in every subsequent League game. He impressed many with a number of confident and competent performances, his outstanding display in the 1-0 victory at Middlesbrough being a particular highlight. Imposing physically, Ali an agile shot-stopper with very quick reactions. Outstanding in the UEFA Cup draw at Bayern Munich, he further enhanced his reputation with a fine run, including three clean sheets in the last five games, in the closing stages of the season.

Bolton W (Signed from Lyn Oslo, Norway, ex Al-Midhaibi, Al-Nasr Sports Club, on 10/1/2006) PL 10 FLC 1 FAC 1 Others 4

ALIADIERE Jeremie
Born: Rambouillet, France, 30 March 1983
Height: 6'0" **Weight:** 11.8
Club Honours: FAYC '01; PL '04; CS '04
International Honours: France: U21; Yth
During his Arsenal career, Jeremie was loaned out to Celtic, West Ham and Wolverhampton, who he joined at 16, until 2009, a lack of first-team opportunities frustrated the young Frenchman so much so that he accepted a guarantee of regular football by signing for Middlesbrough in June. He scored five Premiership goals in his first season at the Riverside. His first was against Manchester United at Old Trafford and he also had the personal satisfaction of scoring against his former employers at the Emirates Stadium in March. Jeremie was involved in controversy at Anfield in March when he was sent off for an incident involving Javier Mascherano, who escaped without punishment. Middlesbrough lodged an appeal that was turned down as 'frivolous' and the ban was extended to four games. The reverberations of this caused great debate in football circles.

Arsenal (From trainee on 4/4/2000) PL 7+22/1 FLC 9+2/8 FAC 3+4 Others 0+4
Glasgow Celtic (Loaned on 1/7/2005) Others 0+2
West Ham U (Loaned on 25/8/2005) PL 1+6 FLC 0+1
Wolverhampton W (Loaned on 14/2/2006) FL 12+2/2
Middlesbrough (£2,000,000 on 10/7/2007) PL 26+3/5 FAC 2

ALJOFREE Hasney
Born: Manchester, 11 July 1978
Height: 6'0" **Weight:** 12.1
Club Honours: Div 2 '04
International Honours: E: Yth
Signed from Bolton in the summer,
Hasney was given the captain's armband
by Paul Sturrock on his arrival at Swindon.
He led by example, giving a number of
fearless performances at the heart of the
Town defence. He also pressed forward
on a number of occasions, netting a
late equaliser against Leyton Orient in
November and ripping a ferocious drive
just over at Huddersfield during an
audacious late charge into the box.
*Bolton W (From trainee on 2/7/1996) P/FL
6+8 FLC 4+2 FAC 0+2*
*Dundee U (Signed on 9/6/2000) SL 52+2/4
SLC 5+1 SC 5+1/3*
*Plymouth Arg (Signed on 30/8/2002) FL
109+8/3 FLC 3 FAC 5/2 Others 2*
*Sheffield Wed (Loaned on 23/9/2004) FL
2 Others 1*
Oldham Ath (Loaned on 21/3/2007) FL 5
*Swindon T (Signed on 10/8/2007) FL 38+1/2
FLC 1 FAC 4/1*

ALLEN Christopher (Chris)
Martin
Born: Devizes, 3 January 1989
Height: 5'11" **Weight:** 11.10
A graduate of the Swindon youth side
in his first year as a professional, Chris
made his debut in the Johnstone's Paint
Trophy against Brentford. He was given a
full League debut at Southend and turned
in a classy performance. A busy central
midfielder who likes to pass the ball, he
is regarded as one of the best technical
players at Swindon and will hope to
maintain his progress.
*Swindon T (From trainee on 10/7/2007) FL
7+1 FAC 0+1 Others 1+1*

ALLEN Damien Samuel
Born: Cheadle, 1 August 1986
Height: 5'11" **Weight:** 11.4
Neat and compact in midfield, Damien
made a big impression when he first
arrived at Morecambe in September from
Royal Antwerp. The former Stockport
man gave a number of 'Man of the
Match' performances and showed some

great touches. But after a good start he
picked up a niggling injury and never
really regained his touch as the pitches
became heavier. As the season came to
an end he was struggling for selection
and was released.
*Stockport Co (From trainee on 12/7/2004)
FL 28+22/1 FLC 1 FAC 2+1 Others 3*
*Morecambe (Free on 24/8/2007) FL 16+4
FLC 2 Others 2*

ALLEN Joseph (Joe) Michael
Born: Carmarthen, 14 March 1990
Height: 5'6" **Weight:** 9.10
International Honours: W: U21-7; Yth
Joe is a diminutive central midfielder with
excellent close skills and was given his
opportunity in the early season Carling
Cup ties against Walsall and Reading,
going on to become a regular member
of Swansea's squad during the first half
of the season. His abilities were also
recognised by Brian Flynn, manager of
the Wales under-21 side, with regular
appearances at that level.
*Swansea C (From trainee on 23/8/2007) FL
2+6 FLC 2 FAC 2+1 Others 2+1*

Manuel Almunia

ALLISON Wayne Anthony
Born: Huddersfield, 16 October 1968
Height: 6'1" **Weight:** 12.6
Club Honours: Div 2 '96
Wayne (the Chief) made his 750th League appearance at Wrexham in October. The veteran Chesterfield forward was used from the bench, having become the club's third-oldest player ever. Wayne gave up his role as player and reserve coach in February and left in search of regular first-team football. He has since done media work for Sky and local radio.
Halifax T (From trainee on 6/7/1987) FL 74+10/22 FLC 3/2 FAC 4+1/2 Others 8+1/3
Watford (£250,000 on 26/7/1989) FL 6+1
Bristol C (£300,000 on 9/8/1990) FL 149+46/48 FLC 4+5/2 FAC 12+1/5 Others 5+2/3
Swindon T (£475,000 on 22/7/1995) FL 98+3/31 FLC 9/3 FAC 7/2 Others 3
Huddersfield T (£800,000 on 11/11/1997) FL 71+3/15 FLC 3+1/2 FAC 6/2
Tranmere Rov (£300,000 on 3/9/1999) FL 35+18/26 FLC 4+3/1 FAC 6+1/5 Others 1
Sheffield U (Free on 30/7/2002) FL 29+44/7 FLC 7+1/1 FAC 4+4/2 Others 0+2
Chesterfield (Free on 30/7/2004) FL 56+49/21 FLC 2+4/1 FAC 3 Others 5/1

ALLOTT Mark Stephen
Born: Manchester, 3 October 1977
Height: 5'11" **Weight:** 12.6
Mark arrived for a second stint with Oldham last summer on a two-year deal after six years with Chesterfield. Having originally left Boundary Park in 2001 as a former youth product and striker with almost 200 appearances under his belt, he returned as a central midfielder. With his energy, tireless work and eye for a defence-splitting pass, he quickly won over the fans again as a model of consistency, ever-present when fit. His efforts, including four goals, were justly rewarded when he made a clean sweep with five awards, including 'Player of the Season' and 'Players' Player of the Season'.
Oldham Ath (From trainee on 14/10/1995) FL 105+49/31 FLC 7+3/2 FAC 8+7 Others 2+3
Chesterfield (Free on 19/12/2001) FL 205+16/11 FLC 8+1/2 FAC 5 Others 5+3/1
Oldham Ath (Signed on 12/7/2007) FL 34+8/4 FLC 1 FAC 5 Others 2

ALMEIDA Mauro Alexandro
de Silva
Born: Viseu, Portugal, 29 January 1982
Height: 6'0" **Weight:** 11.5
A Portuguese defender who spent part of 2006-07 with Accrington, he was a surprise inclusion for Swindon against Brentford in the Johnstone's Paint

Trophy in September. He gave a solid, if unspectacular performance in the centre of defence. It emerged later that Mauro was brought in as part of a proposed takeover by Best Holdings. The collapse of the deal left him unwanted and he later joined Sligo Rovers.
Accrington Stanley (Free from Vihren Sandanski, Bulgaria, ex Porto, CD Estrela Amadora, FC Zwolle, on 31/1/2007) FL 5
Swindon T (Free on 20/8/2007) Others 1

ALMUNIA Manuel
Born: Pamplona, Spain, 19 May 1977
Height: 6'4" **Weight:** 11.8
Club Honours: FAC '05
The Spaniard was given his chance for Arsenal after two high-profile mistakes from Jens Lehmann in August and retained the goalkeeping jersey for the rest of the season. Manuel enjoyed by some distance his finest season at the club so far as he displayed his ability to protect his goal as well as quickly start attacking moves from the back. The goalie also showed an impressive knack of acting as sweeper when necessary. He really came to the fore in the North London derby when he saved a penalty from Tottenham's Robbie Keane at 1-1 and moments later Arsenal scored the winner. Manuel appeared in 29 Premier League games, keeping 11 clean sheets, and nine times in the Champions' League, registering six clean sheets, including five in succession. International honours remain elusive for Manuel but his place as Arsenal's last line of defence seems assured.
Arsenal (£500,000 from Celta Vigo, Spain on 19/7/2004) PL 40 FLC 14 FAC 9 Others 17+1

ALNWICK Benjamin (Ben)
Robert
Born: Prudhoe, 1 January 1987
Height: 6'2" **Weight:** 13.12
International Honours: E: U21-1 Yth
Having failed to extend David Forde's loan last September, the Luton manager Kevin Blackwell called in Tottenham's third-choice goalkeeper to bring stability to his defence. Given his debut at Huddersfield, Ben's lack of match fitness and understanding with his back four saw him beaten twice but three days later his two fine saves at Yeovil enabled the Hatters to keep their first clean sheet in the League. He followed this with a capable display at home to Doncaster before sustaining an injury soon afterwards, letting Dean Brill back into the side. A recurrence of the injury cut his loan short and Ben returned to White Hart Lane. After spending time in Spurs' reserves Ben then joined Leicester on loan in the January window

after their efforts to sign Marton Fulop fell through. His Foxes' career was book-ended by home and away fixtures against Coventry, as he then picked up a thigh injury in training that effectively brought his campaign to a premature end.
Sunderland (From trainee on 13/3/2004) P/FL 19 FLC 3
Tottenham H (£900,000 on 1/1/2007)
Luton T (Loaned on 28/9/2007) FL 4
Leicester C (Loaned on 7/1/2008) FL 8

ALONSO Mikel
Born: Tolosa, Spain, 16 May 1980
Height: 5'10" **Weight:** 12.0
The brother of Liverpool's Xabi, Mikel signed on a season-long loan from Real Sociedad and made his Bolton debut as a substitute in the opening defeat by Newcastle. Mikel's first start was in the away defeat by Portsmouth in August and he started the next three games. Despite glimpses of quality, especially with the ball at his feet, Mikel's only subsequent first-team action was in the Carling Cup and UEFA Cup and it became apparent that he did not figure in new manager Gary Megson's plans
Bolton W (Loaned from Real Sociedad, Spain on 6/7/2007) PL 4+3 FLC 2 Others 2+1

ALONSO Xabi
Born: Tolosa, Spain, 25 November 1981
Height: 6'0" **Weight:** 11.2
Club Honours: UEFACL '05; ESC '05; FAC '06; CS '06
International Honours: Spain: 47
Xabi, the Liverpool and Spanish international midfield playmaker, endured a frustrating season for the Reds due to a metatarsal injury suffered in September, coincidentally in the same week that Daniel Agger encountered the same problem. Brought back in late October for the vital Premiership clash with Arsenal at Anfield, he suffered a recurrence of the injury and was out for another two months. On his return to fitness in December he found it difficult to regain his place with Steven Gerrard and Javier Mascherano dominating central midfield. However, in March manager Rafa Benitez re-jigged his tactical formation to allow Xabi to partner Mascherano in midfield with Gerrard pushed further forward, a system that worked well, at least until the Reds' defeat by Chelsea in the Champions' League semi-final. Xabi scored only two goals in the campaign, both coming in the early season 6-0 rout of Derby and one a blistering 35-yard free kick. He also twice attempted to replicate his trademark 60-yard special of previous seasons but failed narrowly each time. Incredibly, after signing a new five-year

contract in 2007, he finds his future at Anfield placed in doubt by Benitez's attempts to sign Gareth Barry from Aston Villa. His departure would be mourned by Liverpool supporters, not only for his technical ability but also his sheer love of the club, expressed on many occasions. Xabi signed off his season as a member of the Spanish side that won the European Championship final when beating Germany 1-0 in June.

Liverpool (Signed from Real Sociedad, Spain on 27/8/2004) PL 94+16/11 FLC 1+2 FAC 9/2 Others 37+4/1

ALUKO Sone
Born: Birmingham, 19 February 1989
Height: 5'8" **Weight:** 10.0
International Honours: E: Yth
Made his professional debut as a 74th-minute substitute for Birmingham in the home Carling Cup tie against Hereford last August and was then loaned to Aberdeen for the season. A left-sided attacker who is comfortable on the ball, he can beat a man for pace or by trickery and has an eye for goal.
Birmingham C (From trainee on 29/8/2006) FLC 0+1
Aberdeen (Loaned on 31/8/2007) SL 10+10/3 SLC 1+1 SC 1+3 Others 4+1/1

ALVES Afonso
Born: Belo Horizonte, Brazil, 30 January 1981
Height: 6'1" **Weight:** 11.8
International Honours: Brazil: 8
In October, Afonso, making only his second appearance of the season for Dutch side Heerenveen, scored seven goals in the 9-0 demolition of Heracles Almelo. This piece of football magic thrust the Brazilian international into the spotlight of world football. Following complicated and protracted negotiations, he finally signed a four-and-a-half year contract with Middlesbrough, who shelled out a club record fee. The signing just managed to sneak through the closing transfer window at 23:32 GMT. He was gently eased into Premiership football at the Riverside Stadium as a second-half substitute for Dong-Gook Lee in a 1-0 win over Fulham in February. His first two goals for his new club came in the Riverside in April against Manchester United in a 2-2 draw that was played in a blinding snow-storm. Afonso ended the season in wonderful style with a hat-trick when Manchester City were humiliated 8-1 but the transfer rumblings from late January resurfaced when AZ Alkmaar demanded a payment of £5.9million from Afonso, claiming he broke a pre-contract agreement to join them from Heerenveen.

Middlesbrough (£12,000,000 from from SC Heerenveen, Holland, ex Atletico Mineiro, Orgryte, FF Malmo, on 31/1/2008) PL 7+4/6 FAC 2+1

AMANKWAAH Kevin Osei-Kuffour
Born: Harrow, 19 May 1982
Height: 6'1" **Weight:** 12.0
Club Honours: Div 2 '05
International Honours: E: Yth
An early toe injury saw Swansea's attacking right-back unable to stake his claim for a place and he was later sidelined by a hamstring injury. When fit, his only appearances came in the Carling Cup, FA Cup and FA of Wales Premier Cup ties.
Bristol C (From trainee on 16/6/2000) FL 35+19/1 FLC 2+1/1 FAC 1+1/2 Others 7+2/1
Torquay U (Loaned on 25/11/2003) FL 6
Cheltenham T (Loaned on 16/8/2003) FL 11+1
Yeovil T (Signed on 3/2/2005) FL 48+5/1 FLC 2 FAC 3 Others 1
Swansea C (£200,000 on 4/8/2006) FL 23+6 FLC 1 FAC 3+1 Others 4+1

AMBROSE Darren Paul
Born: Harlow, 29 February 1984
Height: 5'11" **Weight:** 10.5
International Honours: E: U21-10; Yth
Darren had probably his best season for Charlton, finishing as joint-second top scorer with nine goals, all from midfield. Darren was mainly used wide, either right or left, but played more centrally a few times. He has a powerful shot, is an accurate passer and reads the game well. Darren scored some excellent goals, including a sweet volley into the bottom corner for his second against Ipswich at the Valley and his blaster against Bristol City, also at home. He was sometimes inconsistent but when on form, Darren is one of the most accomplished players in the side. He had a groin operation at the end of the season but hopes to be fit for the new campaign.
Ipswich T (From trainee on 3/7/2001) P/FL 20+10/8 FLC 2/1 FAC 1+1/1 Others 3+1/1
Newcastle U (£1,000,000 on 25/3/2003) PL 18+19/5 FLC 1+1 FAC 0+2 Others 8+7/1
Charlton Ath (£700,000 + on 11/7/2005) P/FL 69+22/13 FLC 5+3/2 FAC 4+2/1

AMEOBI Foluwashola (Shola)
Born: Zaria, Nigeria, 12 October 1981
Height: 6'2" **Weight:** 12.0
International Honours: E: U21-21
Shola began last season on the bench and even when he started at Arsenal in the Carling Cup in September he had a groin problem. His only other start was

in January, after which he joined Stoke on loan in March, with the possibility of a permanent move in the summer. A surprise signing, Shola joined Stoke to increase their attacking options on the run-in to promotion. Unfortunately, he suffered a hamstring strain, and with most of his appearances coming from the bench he failed to score. Shola is the older brother of Leeds striker Tomi and Newcastle youth squad player Sammy.
Newcastle U (From trainee on 19/10/1998) PL 95+73/28 FLC 6+2/3 FAC 8+5/3 Others 26+15/12
Stoke C (Loaned on 27/3/2008) FL 3+3

AMEOBI Oluwatomiwo (Tomi)
Born: Newcastle, 16 August 1988
Height: 6'3" **Weight:** 12.10
The younger brother of Newcastle's Shola, Tomi made his senior debut for Leeds in their 3-0 Carling Cup defeat at Portsmouth. Three months later, the young striker joined Scunthorpe on loan, the deal being extended until the end of the season to gain more experience. Tomi showed a big physical presence for the Championship strugglers in ten substitute appearances for the Iron but failed to break into the starting line-up and did not figure at all after early January.
Leeds U (From trainee on 10/8/2007) FLC 1 Others 0+1
Scunthorpe U (Loaned on 15/11/2007) FL 0+9 FAC 0+1

AMOO Ryan Lee
Born: Leicester, 11 October 1983
Height: 5'10" **Weight:** 9.12
Club Honours: FAYC '02
Ryan, a right-sided attacking midfielder, found his appearances at Lincoln in 2007-08 mainly limited to the first half of the season, with a number of injuries, most notably a medial knee-ligament strain that he sustained in a reserve game, curtailing his second campaign at Sincil Bank. Ryan left the club by mutual consent shortly after the season came to a close.
Aston Villa (From trainee on 26/7/2001)
Northampton T (Free on 23/3/2004) FL 2+4 (Freed on 23/3/2004)
Lincoln C (Free from Barrow Town on 26/7/2006) FL 45+11/3 FLC 2 FAC 1+1 Others 3

ANANE Richard (Ricky) Amookohome
Born: Manchester, 18 February 1989
Height: 5'8" **Weight:** 10.3
A young full-back, Ricky made one senior start in Bury's Johnstone's Paint Trophy second-round win over Rochdale. He also featured from the bench in the FA

Cup third round defeat of Norwich. Ricky can also play on the right-wing and is regarded as a pacy player with good technique. He is also noted for his strong tackling and mature positional sense.
Bury *(Trainee) FAC 0+1 Others 1*

[ANDERSON] ABREAU OLIVEIRA
Anderson Luis
Born: Porto Alegre, Brazil, 13 April 1988
Height: 5'10" **Weight:** 10.12
Club Honours: PL '08, UEFACL '08
International Honours: Brazil: 4
A superb attacking Manchester United midfield player who had long been a target of Chelsea and Milan before the Reds signed him from FC Porto in May, Anderson made his long-awaited Premiership debut against Sunderland in September. Drafted into a Carling Cup side that consisted almost entirely of youth and reserve team players, Sir Alex Ferguson praised his new signing, describing him as 'one of the best of a very poor bunch' after the 2-0 defeat by Coventry. Seen as a long-term replacement for Paul Scholes, he really showed his mettle when he came on as a substitute for the concussed Nemanja Vidic in United's 4-0 home drubbing of Wigan in October. Putting in arguably his best performance of the season, his precise through ball set up Carlos Tévez to score the opener in an emphatic win. His impressive form continued after the international break as he helped United to a 4-1 away win over Aston Villa in October and he made his first Champions' League start in the same month as he put in a 'Man of the Match' performance to ease United to a 4-2 win over Dynamo Kiev. Yet to register a goal for the Reds, he has settled well into the side, and his pace and vision will bring an extra layer of creativity to United. Though the big question is how he deals with the physical element of the English game, there are no worries so far.
Manchester U *(Signed from Porto, Portugal, ex Gremio, on 3/7/2007) PL 16+8 FLC 1 FAC 2+2 Others 6+3*

[ANDERSON] SILVA Anderson
de Franca
Born: Sao Paulo, Brazil, 28 August 1982
Height: 6'2" **Weight:** 12.11
Anderson was signed in August on a month's loan from Everton, later extended, and made an immediate Barnsley debut against Plymouth. He returned to Oakwell in November and made an impact as the midfield anchor in Barnsley's unbeaten run of seven matches. Anderson is tall, mobile and has excellent distribution. Nor does he

shirk tackles, although referees did not always approve. After another return to Goodison Park, Anderson finally signed a two-and-a-half year contract for Barnsley in January but his season ended a month later with a knee injury at Norwich.
Everton *(Signed from Nacional, Brazil, ex Montevideo, Racing de Santander, Malaga - all loans from Nacional, on 22/1/2007) PL 0+1*
Barnsley *(Signed on 23/8/2007) FL 20 FAC 1*

ANDERSON Paul
Born: Leicester, 23 July 1988
Height: 5'9" **Weight:** 10.6
Club Honours: FAYC '06; Div 1 '08
International Honours: E: Yth
The right-winger joined Swansea on a season-long loan transfer from Liverpool, showing both electric pace and deadly finishing. A torn thigh muscle in the warm-up at Nottingham Forest in January and then a hamstring problem saw him sidelined until early April when he made a welcome return to first-team action.
Liverpool *(From trainee at Hull C on 6/1/2006)*
Swansea C *(Loaned on 7/8/2007) FL 22+9/7 FLC 2/1 FAC 3 Others 5/2*

ANDERSON Russell
Born: Aberdeen, 25 October 1978
Height: 5'11" **Weight:** 11.10
International Honours: S: 11; U21-15
A centre-half signed by Sunderland from Aberdeen, Russell made only two appearances before requiring reconstructive surgery on an ankle injury sustained in September. A full Scottish international, he was allowed to join Plymouth on loan in January, initially for one month. Within hours of meeting his new team-mates for the first time, Russell starred in a 2-0 Championship win at Southampton. Forming a formidable central defensive partnership with Krisztian Timar, Russell impressed manager Paul Sturrock and agreed terms for the loan to continue until the end of the season. Strong in the air and a player who can read the game well, Russell was rewarded for his performances by regaining his place in Scotland's squad towards the end of the campaign.
Aberdeen *(From Dyce Juniors on 1/8/1996) SL 263+17/18 SLC 20 SC 23+1/1 Others 4*
Sunderland *(£1,000,000 on 19/7/2007) PL 0+1 FLC 1*
Plymouth Arg *(Loaned on 19/2/2008) FL 14*

ANDERTON Darren Robert
Born: Southampton, 3 March 1972
Height: 6'1" **Weight:** 12.5
Club Honours: FLC '99
International Honours: E: 30; B-1; U21-

12; Yth
There was plenty of frustration for the gifted Bournemouth midfielder as, after sustaining an injury against Leeds in November, he missed all games until the tail-end of the campaign. Even without match-practice, Darren still showed the immense class that once made him an England international. He is undoubtedly one of the most talented players in the lower divisions and he also scored some vital goals.
Portsmouth *(From trainee on 5/2/1990) FL 53+9/7 FLC 3+2/1 FAC 7+1/5 Others 2*
Tottenham H *(£1,750,000 on 3/6/1992) PL 273+26/34 FLC 30+1/8 FAC 26+2/6*
Birmingham C *(Free on 11/8/2004) PL 9+11/3 FLC 2 FAC 2*
Wolverhampton W *(Free on 22/8/2005) FL 20+4/1 FLC 1/1 FAC 1*
Bournemouth *(Free on 11/9/2006) FL 48/9 FLC 1 FAC 2 Others 3*

Leon Andreasen

ANDREASEN Leon Hougaard
Born: Aarhus, Denmark, 23 April 1983
Height: 6'2" **Weight:** 12.10
International Honours: Denmark: 10; U21: Yth
Joining Fulham in January from Werder Bremen on a long contract, the Danish international midfielder went straight into the side for the next game at Bolton. Leon started eight of the next nine games, aptly demonstrating his commitment in a central midfield role. A firm tackler, he harries opponents and breaks up attacks. Leon is not afraid to have a pop at goal from distance and was unlucky not to score on debut with a long shot.
Fulham *(£2,000,000 from Werder Bremen, Germany, ex Hammel, Aarhus AF, on 29/1/2008) PL 9+4*

ANDREW Calvin Hyden
Born: Luton, 19 December 1986
Height: 6'2"   **Weight:** 12.11
The signing of two experienced forwards reduced Calvin's early opportunities at Luton last season but he was wise enough to learn from Paul Furlong, becoming better at holding up the ball and laying it off. These attributes, coupled with his speed and strength, made him a useful cover player. He spent the first few weeks on the bench; finally earning his chance when paired with Furlong. Calvin is not a prolific scorer but three of his four goals turned out to be winners. After Mick Harford became manager, he was back among the substitutes.
Luton T (From trainee on 25/9/2004) FL 26+29/4 FLC 0+2 FAC 4+3/2 Others 3
Grimsby T (Loaned on 4/8/2005) FL 3+5/1 FLC 1
Bristol C (Loaned on 30/1/2006) FL 1+2

ANDREWS Keith Joseph
Born: Dublin, 13 September 1980
Height: 5'11"   **Weight:** 11.5
Club Honours: AMC '08; Div 2 '08
International Honours: RoI: Yth
If ever a player led a team to a title by example, then Keith is that man. An inspirational figure in the heart of the MK Dons' midfield, he particularly shone when playing behind the main striker and after six goals from the first six games, continued to find the net throughout the campaign, ending with 14 goals. His ability to control the game was often too much for opponents to handle and after being voted the League Two 'Player of the Season' was one of four MK Dons to be chosen into the PFA League Two select team.
Wolverhampton W (From trainee on 26/9/1997) P/FL 41+24 FLC 3/1 FAC 4
Oxford U (Loaned on 10/11/2000) FL 4/1 Others 1
Stoke C (Loaned on 9/8/2003) FL 16
Walsall (Loaned on 13/3/2004) FL 10/2
Hull C (Free on 25/5/2005) FL 24+5 FAC 1
MK Dons (Free on 31/8/2006) FL 74+1/18 FLC 1 FAC 3 Others 6/3

ANDREWS Wayne Michael Hill
Born: Paddington, 25 November 1977
Height: 5'10"   **Weight:** 11.12
Very much a fringe player at Coventry, where he has yet to start a game, the burly striker was used as a substitute seven times, the last in early March soon after Chris Coleman took over as manager. With first-choice strikers Jermaine Beckford and Tresor Kandol suspended, Leeds brought in Wayne and Mark De Vries as loan replacements.

Wayne played twice, in the victory at Oldham and the Johnstone's Paint Trophy win at Darlington, before returning to Coventry. He then went to Bristol Rovers on loan in March but suffered a serious knee injury after 17 minutes of his debut against Yeovil. Was released at the end of the campaign.
Watford (From trainee on 5/7/1996) FL 16+12/4 FLC 3+2/1 FAC 0+2 Others 2/1 (Free to St Albans C during 1999 close season)
Cambridge U (Loaned on 2/10/1998) FL 1+1
Peterborough U (Loaned on 5/2/1999) FL 8+2/5
Oldham Ath (Free from Chesham U on 30/5/2002) FL 28+9/11 FLC 1+2 FAC 2+1 Others 3/1
Colchester U (Free on 9/8/2003) FL 36+10/14 FLC 1 FAC 4+1 Others 3+1/2
Crystal Palace (Signed on 9/9/2004) P/FL 5+28/1 FLC 3+1 FAC 2+1
Coventry C (Free on 17/7/2006) FL 0+10/1 FAC 0+1
Sheffield Wed (Loaned on 23/11/2006) FL 7+2/1
Bristol C (Loaned on 19/1/2007) FL 3+4/2 Others 2+1/1
Leeds U (Loaned on 1/10/2007) FL 1 Others 1
Bristol Rov (Loaned on 27/3/2008) FL 1

ANELKA Nicolas
Born: Versailles, France, 14 March 1979
Height: 6'0"   **Weight:** 12.3
Club Honours: PL '98; FAC '98; CS '98
International Honours: France: 51; U21; Yth
Nicolas began last season in fine form for Bolton, firmly establishing himself as one of the best forwards in the Premiership. A perfectly executed free kick against Aston Villa was a highlight, although the goal that etched him into Bolton folklore was the winner in the 1-0 victory over Manchester United in November. A clinical two-goal haul in the vital 3-0 victory over Birmingham was, in hindsight, perhaps his most important contribution. With such a fine run of form, it was no surprise when Nicolas was continually linked to some of Europe's top clubs and an inevitable transfer, to Chelsea, was confirmed during the January window. With Chelsea challenging for honours on four fronts but desperately short of fire-power, they made much-travelled Nicolas the most valuable player of all time with combined transfer fees of £86.8-million. Nicolas settled quickly at Chelsea as he reunited with former club-mates Ashley Cole, Shaun Wright-Phillips and Tal Ben Haim, plus France team-mates Claude Makelele and Florent Malouda. He played well in the Carling

Cup semi-final second leg victory over Everton and made a Wembley final appearance in his tenth Chelsea match. The decision to play Nicolas wide on the right mirrored the whole side as Chelsea limped to a disappointing defeat. Although not an automatic choice, with goals at a premium Nicolas made telling contributions against two of his former clubs. Against Arsenal, he created the winner for Didier Drogba, enabling the Blues to leapfrog their London rivals into the second place they held for the rest of the season. Against Liverpool in the epic Champions' League semi-final, his dribble and perfectly weighted pass to Drogba sealed the tie and put Chelsea into their first European Cup final. The season ended on a sour note when Nicolas' shoot-out penalty was saved in the Moscow final and Chelsea finished as runners-up in three competitions.
Arsenal (£500,000 + from Paris St Germain, France on 6/3/1997) PL 50+15/23 FLC 3 FAC 13+1/3 Others 7+1/2 (£22,900,000 to Real Madrid, Spain on 20/8/1999)
Liverpool (Loaned from Paris St Germain, France on 24/12/2001) PL 13+7/4 FAC 2/1
Manchester C (£13,000,000 from Paris St Germain, France on 16/7/2002) PL 87+2/37 FLC 4 FAC 5/4 Others 5/4 (£7,000,000 to Fenerbahce, Turkey on 31/1/2005)
Bolton W (£8,000,000 from Fenerbahce, Turkey on 31/8/2006) PL 53/21 FLC 1/1 FAC 2+1 Others 2+2/1
Chelsea (£15,000,000 on 12/1/2008) PL 10+4/1 FLC 2 FAC 2+1/1 Others 0+5

ANGUS Stevland (Stev) Dennis
Born: Westminster, 16 September 1980
Height: 6'0"   **Weight:** 12.0
Able to play anywhere in defence, Stev made only one appearance for Barnet, in the 2-1 defeat at Brentford in August after arriving from Torquay in the summer. This was his second spell at the club, following a stint in 2006 in which he failed to register a first-team appearance. He was sent off in his single Barnet run-out and released from his non-contract agreement a few days later, moving to Fisher Athletic.
West Ham U (From trainee on 2/7/1999)
Bournemouth (Loaned on 11/8/2000) FL 7+2
Cambridge U (Free on 19/7/2001) FL 134+1/1 FLC 5 FAC 10 Others 10+1 (Freed during 2005 close season)
Hull C (Loaned on 15/12/2004) FL 1+1 FAC 1
Scunthorpe U (Loaned on 31/1/2005) FL 9
Torquay U (Free from Grays Ath on 19/7/2006) FL 33+3/1 FLC 1 FAC 2
Barnet (Free on 23/8/2007) FL 1

ANICHEBE Victor Chinedu
Born: Lagos, Nigeria, 23 April 1988
Height: 6'1" **Weight:** 12.8
International Honours: Nigeria: 4
Continuing to develop, the big Everton striker was called up at international level by his native Nigeria, for whom he scored on his under-23 debut. Although predominately used from the bench, the youngster influenced several matches, especially in the UEFA Cup, when he scored four times as a substitute. At domestic level the striker was not so prolific but his powerful frame and brute strength, especially with his back to goal, enabled him to unsettle even the most experienced defenders. With greater experience this Everton Academy product has a fine future.
Everton (From trainee on 5/4/2006) PL 15+33/5 FLC 2+5/1 FAC 1+2 Others 1+8/4

ANKERGREN Casper
Born: Koge, Denmark, 9 November 1979
Height: 6'3" **Weight:** 14.11
International Honours: Denmark: U21-3; Yth
The big Danish goalkeeper was extremely consistent during Leeds' charge up the League One table, missing only three League games through injury. Once Leeds were finally given the go-ahead to start the campaign, he was back at Elland Road within hours of the transfer embargo being lifted to make his move from Brondby permanent. Casper impressed in the latter half of the previous season while on loan and benefiting from a more settled defence in front of him, distinguished himself with several key saves. He had a fine game in the League One play-off final defeat by Doncaster at Wembley. Casper became extremely popular with fans for his work within the local community.
Leeds U (Signed from Brondby, Denmark, ex Koge BK, on 31/1/2007) FL 57 FLC 2 FAC 2 Others 3

ANNERSON Jamie Paul
Born: Sheffield, 21 June 1988
Height: 6'2" **Weight:** 13.2
International Honours: E: Yth
A promising young goalkeeper, Jamie joined Rotherham on loan from Sheffield United as back-up for Andy Warrington and made one appearance in the Johnstone's Paint Trophy, saving a penalty in the shoot-out against Grimsby. Was later loaned to Chesterfield but failed to make an appearance before returning to Bramall Lane.
Sheffield U (From trainee on 5/3/2007)
Rotherham U (Loaned on 14/9/2007) Others 1

ANTHONY Byron Joseph
Born: Newport, 20 September 1984
Height: 6'1" **Weight:** 11.0
International Honours: W: U21-8; Yth
Byron was very unfortunate to suffer a metatarsal injury in Bristol Rovers' Johnstone's Paint trophy tie against Bournemouth in October. The former Welsh under-21 central defender was sorely missed and it was to be five months before he regained his place in the first team.
Cardiff C (From trainee on 7/7/2003) FLC 1+1/1
Bristol Rov (Free on 3/8/2006) FL 39+4/1 FLC 3 FAC 3/1 Others 7/1

ANTWI Agyei William (Will) Kwabena
Born: Epsom, 19 October 1982
Height: 6'2" **Weight:** 12.8
International Honours: Ghana: 1
Normally a first-choice central defender at Wycombe, Will was still recovering from the previous season's groin strain in August. He made his first start in October, in the 2-0 Johnstone's Paint Trophy defeat at Swansea, and became a regular again in November with five starts. His dominant and assured performances won him the PFA League Two 'Player of the Month'

award for November, before a knee injury at Hereford halted his season in December. He appeared once more, in the penultimate League game, and will hope for an injury-free season next time around.
Crystal Palace (From trainee on 12/7/2002) FL 0+4 FLC 1+2 (Free to Ljungskile SK, Sweden during 2003 close season)
Wycombe W (Free from Aldershot T on 6/7/2005) FL 36/1 FLC 5 FAC 2/1 Others 5

ANTWI-BIRAGO Godwin
Born: Tafu, Ghana, 7 June 1988
Height: 6'1" **Weight:** 13.1
Club Honours: FAYC '06
Having impressed in a short loan with Accrington in 2006-07, the young Liverpool defender joined Hartlepool in July on a season-long loan. Godwin began well and in the first half of the season was an automatic choice, usually playing as a central defender. However, the rigours of regular League One football seemed to take their toll and he was used only sparingly in the later stages.
Liverpool (Signed from Real Zaragoza, Spain on 8/8/2005)
Accrington Stanley (Loaned on 13/3/2007) FL 9
Hartlepool U (Loaned on 1/7/2007) FL 27/1 FLC 2 FAC 1+1 Others 3

Godwin Antwi-Birago

AN-AR   PFA FOOTBALLERS' WHO'S WHO

ANYINSAH Joseph (Joe)
Greene
Born: Bristol, 8 October 1984
Height: 5'8" **Weight:** 11.0
Unable to secure a first-team place at
Preston, Joe created a good impression
when he spent much of the autumn with
Carlisle on loan. His skill and commitment
endeared him to the League One
promotion chasers and he netted a fine
goal in the victory at Bournemouth on
his full debut for the club before being
recalled to Deepdale. The pacy winger
then joined Crewe on loan in March and
stayed for the remainder of the season,
having settled quickly and endearing
himself to the fans.
*Bristol C (From trainee on 24/10/2001) FL
2+5 Others 0+2*
*Preston NE (Signed on 13/7/2005) FL 0+6
FAC 0+2*
Bury (Loaned on 9/2/2006) FL 3
*Carlisle U (Loaned on 20/9/2007) FL 10+2/3
Others 2*
Crewe Alex (Loaned on 7/3/2008) FL 6+2

ANYON Joseph (Joe)
Born: Poulton-le-Fylde, 29 December 1986
Height: 6'2" **Weight:** 12.3
International Honours: E: Yth

Port Vale's goalkeeper had a fine season,
although involved in a constant and
unsuccessful struggle against relegation.
An excellent shot-stopper, Joe was widely
tipped for a move in the January transfer
window but nothing materialised so he
continued his education at Vale Park,
it being his first full season of League
football. He saved a penalty at Tranmere
and followed with another in the next
game at home to Gillingham, probably
his best performance. Joe was heading
for an ever-present campaign until a knee
injury forced him to sit out two of the last
three games.
*Port Vale (From trainee on 13/8/2005) FL
65+1 FLC 1 FAC 3 Others 2*

ARANALDE Zigor
Born: Guipuzcoa, Spain, 28 February
1973
Height: 6'1" **Weight:** 13.5
Club Honours: Div 2 '06
It was very much a season of two halves
for the popular and stylish Carlisle
defender. He was ever-present until
losing his place at the end of January
following defeat at Oldham. Thereafter,
he never appeared again and was
released at the end of the campaign.

Joe Anyon

Age is not on his side but he will be
remembered with affection at Brunton
Park for his positive performances, skill
and obvious love of the game.
*Walsall (Free from CD Logrones, Spain, ex
Albacete, Marbella, Sevilla, on 11/8/2000) FL
183+12/5 FLC 12/1 FAC 12 Others 5*
Sheffield Wed (Free on 24/3/2005) FL 1+1
*Carlisle U (Free on 1/8/2005) FL 108+1/6 FLC
5 FAC 3/1 Others 9*

ARBELOA Alvaro
Born: Salamanca, Spain, 17 January 1983
Height: 6'0" **Weight:** 12.0
International Honours: Spain: 3; U21
Purchased by Liverpool manager Rafa
Benitez in the January transfer window
to provide competition at right-back,
the young Spaniard started the season
at left-back in preference to John
Arne Riise. However, by November
he loosened Steve Finnan's firm hold
on the right-back position although
the Irishman came back strongly the
following month. In the closing weeks of
the campaign the two players alternated
and it was unclear which one Benitez
considered first choice, especially as
Jamie Carragher was selected as right-
back six times. Although he can be well
satisfied with his 38 starts for the Reds,
it is still uncertain if Benitez considers
Alvaro the long-term candidate for
right-back even if, as seems likely, Finnan
departs in the summer. His versatility
across the back line should make him a
valued squad player for years to come.
He made his international debut for
Spain in March.
*Liverpool (£2,600,000 from Deportivo La
Coruna, Spain, ex Real Madrid, on 31/1/2007)
PL 34+3/1 FLC 3 FAC 1 Others 12+2*

ARBER Mark Andrew
Born: Johannesburg, South Africa, 9
October 1977
Height: 6'1" **Weight:** 12.11
Mark failed to agree terms with
Dagenham at the start of the season
after being with them on loan for the
last two months of the promotion
campaign. Instead, he joined Stevenage
from Peterborough. A dispute with the
Borough manager led to Mark arriving at
Dagenham on loan in February and the
central defender's introduction coincided
with a five-match winning run for his new
side. He scored his first goal at Bradford
and, at the end of the campaign, agreed
a one-year deal with Dagenham.
Tottenham H (From trainee on 27/3/1996)
*Barnet (£75,000 on 18/9/1998) FL 123+2/15
FLC 4 FAC 3 Others 8/1*
*Peterborough U (Free on 9/12/2002) FL
67+2/5 FLC 1 FAC 3 Others 2*

26

Oldham Ath *(Free on 27/7/2004) FL 13+1/1 FLC 2 Others 1*
Peterborough U *(Free on 21/12/2004) FL 98+3/3 FLC 3 FAC 8/1 Others 5 (Freed during 2007 close season)*
Dagenham & Redbridge *(Loaned from Stevenage Borough on 12/2/2008) FL 16/1*

ARCA Julio Andres
Born: Quilmes Bernal, Argentina, 31 January 1981
Height: 5'10" **Weight:** 11.6
Club Honours: Ch '05
International Honours: Argentina: U21; Yth (World Yth '01)
With the emergence of Andrew Taylor at left-back, Middlesbrough manager Gareth Southgate transformed Julio into an attacking central midfielder. His performances there earned him many rave reviews, with many suggesting an international call could be on the cards. Julio scored two Premiership goals, one against Newcastle in August and the other against his former club Sunderland in September. Unfortunately, he damaged his knee ligaments against the Black Cats and was cheered and applauded off the pitch by the visiting supporters when he was substituted. The injury kept him out until early December. In January he was named the new captain in place of George Boateng but suffered a real slump in form, culminating in a poor display against Cardiff in the FA Cup defeat at the Riverside. Julio and Fabio Rochemback were left out of the side for the following game against Aston Villa. Strangely, Julio signed a new two-and-a-half-year contract on the day he was dropped.
Sunderland *(£3,500,000 from Argentinos Juniors, Argentina on 31/8/2000) P/FL 145+12/17 FLC 5/2 FAC 15/4*
Middlesbrough *(£1,750,000 on 9/8/2006) PL 41+4/4 FAC 12/1*

ARDLEY Neal Christopher
Born: Epsom, 1 September 1972
Height: 5'11" **Weight:** 11.9
International Honours: E: U21-10
An experienced holding midfield player, Neal served Millwall well in his brief stay. Vision and creativity were his main attributes but after only one appearance as a substitute early in the season, Neal decided to retire to the disappointment of players and supporters.
Wimbledon *(From trainee on 29/7/1991) P/FL 212+33/18 FLC 22+3/5 FAC 27+4/3*
Watford *(Free on 9/8/2002) FL 105+6/7 FLC 7+1 FAC 8+1*
Cardiff C *(Free on 23/3/2005) FL 30+8/1 FLC 1+1 FAC 1*
Millwall *(Free on 2/8/2006) FL 15+6 FLC 1 FAC 1*

ARMSTRONG Christopher (Chris)
Born: Newcastle, 5 August 1982
Height: 5'10" **Weight:** 11.0
International Honours: E. Yth. S: B-1
Chris was a regular in the Sheffield United side until March when a groin injury, requiring an operation, ended his season early. Playing mainly on the left side of midfield, sometimes in an attacking role, sometimes more defensively, he showed good anticipation to break up play and defend when needed, and produced searching crosses when coming forward. He made a few appearances at left wing-back when Gary Naysmith was unavailable and gained a Scotland 'B' cap in November.
Bury *(From trainee on 2/3/2001) FL 33/1 FLC 1 Others 3*
Oldham Ath *(£200,000 on 22/10/2001) FL 64+1/11 FLC 2 FAC 6 Others 6*
Sheffield U *(£100,000 on 1/8/2003) P/FL 76+19/6 FLC 4+1 FAC 3+1*
Blackpool *(Loaned on 13/10/2005) FL 5 Others 1*

ARMSTRONG Steven Craig
Born: South Shields, 23 May 1975
Height: 5'11" **Weight:** 12.10
Having joined Gillingham from Cheltenham before the start of last season, Craig immediately gained a regular place in the Gills' side. Comfortable on the ball, he tried to press forward and deliver crosses with his sweet left foot but was released in January. He then returned to Cheltenham as a free agent and after a handful of appearances for the reserves he was selected in midfield at Brighton in February, remaining in the side until the final game. Operating in the centre of both four and five-man midfield formations, Craig's enthusiasm and experience proved valuable in a tension-filled end to the season and earned him the offer of a new contract.
Nottingham F *(From trainee on 2/6/1992) P/FL 24+16 FLC 6+2/2 FAC 1*
Burnley *(Loaned on 29/12/1994) FL 4*
Bristol Rov *(Loaned on 8/11/1996) FL 4+1*
Bristol Rov *(Loaned on 28/3/1996) FL 9*
Gillingham *(Loaned on 18/10/1996) FL 10 FLC 2 Others 1*
Watford *(Loaned on 24/1/1997) FL 3*
Watford *(Loaned on 14/3/1997) FL 12*
Huddersfield T *(£750,000 on 26/2/1999) FL 101+6/5 FLC 7+1 FAC 2 Others 1+1*
Sheffield U *(£100,000 on 15/2/2002) FL 29+6/1 FLC 3 Others 2*
Grimsby T *(Loaned on 24/2/2004) FL 9/1*
Bradford C *(Free on 20/1/2005) FL 4+3*
Cheltenham T *(Free on 4/8/2005) FL 70+6/2 FLC 3 FAC 7+1 Others 8+1/1*

Gillingham *(Free on 10/7/2007) FL 12+1 FLC 1 Others 2/1*
Cheltenham T *(Free on 4/2/2008) FL 13+1*

ARNISON Paul Simon
Born: Hartlepool, 18 September 1977
Height: 5'10" **Weight:** 11.2
Club Honours: Div 2 '06
For Paul it was another season of restricted first-team duties for Carlisle and he was not retained at the end of the term. Nevertheless, his innate professionalism ensured that he always gave of his best in occasional appearances in his favourite right-back berth.
Newcastle U *(From trainee on 1/3/1996)*
Hartlepool U *(Free on 10/3/2000) FL 53+24/3 FLC 2 FAC 2+1 Others 8/2*
Carlisle U *(Free on 31/10/2003) FL 72+23/1 FLC 4 FAC 1 Others 10*

ARNOLD Nathan
Born: Mansfield, 26 July 1987
Height: 5'7" **Weight:** 10.4
Started last season on the Mansfield bench and struggled to gain a regular place in the side until late on, coming to the fore during March and playing well, scoring a cleverly-taken first goal in 2-1 win at Bradford. Played his best football when appearing centrally alongside Micky Boulding and also served the side well when used wide on the left.
Mansfield T *(From juniors on 27/8/2005) FL 32+30/8 FLC 1 FAC 2+2 Others 3*

ARRIETA Ibon Perez
Born: San Sebastian, Spain, 9 June 1977
Height: 5'10" **Weight:** 11.3
A journeyman Spanish striker, Ibon joined Swindon as part of the prospective takeover of the club by Best Holdings. He was used from the bench in the first five games, with his solitary goal coming on his only first-team start in the Johnstone's Paint Trophy against Brentford. He scored it with a spectacular overhead kick and showed himself to possess a clever touch. The subsequent collapse of the takeover deal left him in a difficult position and it was no real surprise when he left for Romanian club Pandurii Targu Jiu in mid-season.
Swindon T *(Free from UD Melilla, Colombia, ex Pollenca, Real Union, SD Huesca, Tallavera CF, Chaves, Sporting Braga, Chavez, Estoril-Praia, Racing Ferrol, CD Logrones, Maccabi Herzliya, PAS Giannina, on 6/8/2007) FL 0+4 FLC 0+1 Others 1/1*

ARTELL David (Dave) John
Born: Rotherham, 22 November 1980
Height: 6'2" **Weight:** 13.9
Dave joined Morecambe in pre-season after being surprisingly released by

Mikel Arteta

Chester. With more than 200 senior games behind him, his experience was seen as vital to the Shrimps in their first League campaign. He played for most of the season and linked well with skipper Jim Bentley at the heart of Morecambe's defence. Dave will be the first to admit his distribution is not the best at the club but he compensates for that with his never-say-die attitude. Like Bentley, he chipped in with some important goals, most notably in the Carling Cup tie at Preston.
Rotherham U (From trainee on 1/7/1999) FL 35+2/4 FAC 3 Others 1
Shrewsbury T (Loaned on 26/9/2002) FL 27+1/1 FAC 3 Others 5
Mansfield T (Free on 7/8/2003) FL 43+2/5 FLC 2 FAC 5+1 Others 1+1
Chester C (Signed on 29/7/2005) FL 76+4/3 FLC 1 FAC 9 Others 1
Morecambe (Free on 24/7/2007) FL 34+2/3 FLC 3/1 Others 5

ARTER Harry Nicholas
Born: Sidcup, 28 December 1989
Height: 5'10" **Weight:** 12.8
International Honours: RoI: U19
An exciting young midfielder, Harry made his Charlton debut as a second-half substitute in the Carling Cup tie at Luton last September. Tenacious in the tackle and comfortable on the ball, Harry has two good feet, an array of tricks and is very confident. He played for the Republic of Ireland under-19 side during the season. An ankle injury in March ruled him out for the rest of the campaign but he is expected to break into the first-team reckoning on a regular basis next season.
Charlton Ath (From trainee on 4/7/2007) FLC 0+1

ARTETA Mikel
Born: San Sebastian, Spain, 26 March 1982
Height: 5'9" **Weight:** 10.12
Club Honours: SPD '03; SLC '03
International Honours: Spain: U21; Yth
The gifted Spaniard – surprisingly still ignored by his country at international level – had a mixed campaign at Everton. Before Christmas the midfielder continued his imperious form of the two previous campaigns, starring as the Toffees enjoyed success at both home and abroad, as well as being voted North-West 'Player of the Year'. But a long-standing abdominal injury limited his effectiveness in the second half of the campaign and he missed most of the run-in. A beautifully balanced and strong midfielder who has real flair, Mikel is particularly adept from dead-ball situations and Evertonians hope that a good pre-season will restore him to peak form.

Glasgow Rgrs (£5,800,000 from Paris St Germain, France, ex Barcelona, on 1/7/2002) SL 49+1/12 SLC 5 SC 6/1 Others 7/1 (Transferred to Real Sociedad, Spain on 9/7/2004)
Everton (£2,000,000 from Real Sociedad, Spain on 31/1/2005) PL 99+5/12 FLC 5+1 FAC 6/1 Others 9+1/4

ARTHUR Kenneth (Kenny) James
Born: Bellshill, 7 December 1978
Height: 6'3" **Weight:** 13.8
Club Honours: S Div 1 '01
After joining Accrington from Partick Thistle in the summer, Kenny started as first-choice goalkeeper, soon becoming a favourite of the crowd as he demonstrated reliability and competence. Unfortunately, after playing in the first nine League games, he suffered a broken leg at Bradford. After proving his fitness in a couple of reserve games, he immediately reclaimed the number one spot in mid-February and stayed for the rest of the season. Stanley's far from healthy 'goals against' column would have been worse but for Kenny, one of the successes of the season. That was reflected by his winning the Website 'Player of the Year'.
Partick T (From Possil YMCA 0n 01/06/1997) SL 242+1 SLC 14 SC 24 Others 9
Accrington Stanley (Free on 1/6/2007) FL 24 FLC 1

ASAFU-ADJAYE Edward (Ed) Yaw
Born: Southwark, 22 December 1988
Height: 5'11" **Weight:** 12.4
At the start of last season, Ed sustained a serious leg injury that appeared to put his Luton career in jeopardy. He battled to regain fitness and made his way back through the reserves and a loan to Salisbury in the Blue Square Premier League before earning a recall as a right-back, despite usually playing as a centre-back. He made his debut at home to Crewe and showed he could cope with an unfamiliar position, keeping out the more experienced Richard Jackson. As a central defender for the final game, he was named 'Man of the Match'. Although making only seven starts, it was rumoured that he had attracted interest from other clubs.
Luton T (From trainee on 5/7/2007) FL 7

ASHBEE Ian
Born: Birmingham, 6 September 1976
Height: 6'1" **Weight:** 13.7
International Honours: E: Yth
With Hull's promotion to the top flight

for the first time in their 104-year history, the ultimate unsung hero completed the unique feat of captaining a team from what is now League Two to the Premier League in his six years with the club. As well as his leadership qualities and familiar role as a midfield enforcer, Ian scored spectacular goals in televised games at Blackpool and Barnsley before netting the crucial late winner with a towering header against Crystal Palace at the KC Stadium to secure a play-off position. He was third in the 'Player of the Year' voting and his efforts on and off the pitch were recognised with the inaugural 'Chairman's Award' for outstanding contributions. All this came two years after he was told that a knee injury meant he may never walk again, never mind play football. Amazingly, Ian still has his detractors. They should hang their heads.
Derby Co (From trainee on 9/11/1994) FL 1
Cambridge U (Free on 13/12/1996) FL 192+11/11 FLC 7 FAC 15 Others 9+1
Hull C (Free on 3/7/2002) FL 193/8 FLC 5+2/1 FAC 6 Others 4

ASHDOWN Jamie Lawrence
Born: Wokingham, 30 November 1980
Height: 6'3" **Weight:** 14.10
Club Honours: FAC '08
Before last season started, Jamie accepted it was mission impossible to displace the superbly in-form David James as Portsmouth's number-one goalkeeper. And so it proved. In the early part of the season Jamie was restricted to two Carling Cup appearances, in both of which he kept clean sheets. Making matters worse, a shoulder injury sustained in training sidelined him for most of December and January and a back injury caused him to miss three games in early April. His Premier League chance came, over two years since his last League appearance, with three games of the season left after James tore a calf muscle. He did not let Pompey down. To his huge credit he regards it as a challenge to attempt to take the place of the best goalkeeper in England.
Reading (From trainee on 26/11/1999) FL 12+1 FAC 1 Others 2
Bournemouth (Loaned on 22/8/2002) FL 2
Rushden & Diamonds (Loaned on 14/11/2003) FL 19
Portsmouth (Signed on 2/7/2004) PL 36 FLC 7 FAC 1
Norwich C (Loaned on 20/10/2006) FL 2

ASHIKODI Moses
Born: Lagos, Nigeria, 27 June 1987
Height: 6'0" **Weight:** 11.9
International Honours: E: Yth
A big, strong-running forward who joined

Dean Ashton

Swindon on loan to the end of the season
from Watford in January, Moses failed to
display the best of his ability, although
scoring frequently for the reserves. His
loan was curtailed in April when it was
found that he required surgery for a loose
screw on a plate in his leg.
Millwall *(Trainee) FL 0+5*
West Ham U *(Signed on 31/8/2004)*
Gillingham *(Loaned on 15/8/2005) FL 0+4*
Glasgow Rgrs *(Free on 1/1/2006) SL 0+1*
Watford *(Signed on 2/1/2007) PL 0+2 FAC 1/1*
Bradford C *(Loaned on 6/3/2007) FL 8/2*
Swindon T *(Loaned on 18/1/2008) FL 4+6*

ASHMORE James Charles
Born: Sheffield, 2 March 1986
Height: 5'8" **Weight:** 11.2
Having become a regular in the Sheffield
United reserve side, James moved
to Macclesfield on loan, making his
League debut at Peterborough in the
middle of January. He played alongside
Terry Dunfield in the centre of midfield
for some two months but a change
of formation on the appointment of
Keith Alexander saw James surplus to
requirements and he returned to Bramall
Lane in the middle of March. Was
released at the end of the campaign.
Sheffield U *(From trainee on 7/7/2004)*
Macclesfield T *(Loaned on 4/1/2008) FL
7+1*

ASHTON Dean
Born: Crewe, 24 November 1983
Height: 6'1" **Weight:** 13.11
International Honours: E: 1; U21-8; Yth
After a whole season out of the game,
the big striker returned to the West Ham
forward line to the delight of his fans.
In September he was beginning to look
more like his old self as he scored in
three consecutive matches and his fine
form earned him a call up to the England
squad. There was a major setback when
he sprained a knee against Aston Villa
in October, keeping him out for three
months. After returning he struggled for
full fitness for a time but by the end of
March was back to his best, a constant
menace to defenders. Dean, who has
fantastic hold-up play, good movement
and an eye for a goal, ended the season
as top scorer after a brilliant goal against
Manchester United with an overhead kick
and another superb effort in the final
home game with Aston Villa, when he
swivelled and crashed the ball into the
top corner for a stunning finish.
Crewe Alex *(From trainee on 6/2/2001) FL
131+28/60 FLC 6+1/3 FAC 6+3/5 Others 3/5*
Norwich C *(£3,000,000 + on 11/1/2005)
P/FL 44/17 FLC 1+1/1*
West Ham U *(£7,000,000 on 26/1/2006) PL
29+13/13 FLC 2/1 FAC 7/3*

ASHTON Nathan Wesley
Born: Beckton, 30 January 1987
Height: 5'9" **Weight:** 11.8
International Honours: E: Yth
Fulham snapped up the impressive young left-back following his release by Charlton in August and he went straight into the reserves as a left-sided defender, later tried out in a wide midfield role. Confident in possession, he moves forward to join the attack but is rarely drawn out of position. His form prompted then Fulham manager Laurie Sanchez to promote him and after sitting on the bench at Sunderland, he started the home game against Reading. He was later loaned to Crystal Palace for the final two months of the season and made his debut against Blackpool, playing in the first half only.
Charlton Ath (From trainee on 26/5/2005) FLC 1
Fulham (Free on 23/8/2007) PL 1
Crystal Palace (Loaned on 27/3/2008) FL 1

ASHTON Neil John
Born: Liverpool, 15 January 1985
Height: 5'10" **Weight:** 11.12
Strong, solid performances are consistently part of Neil's game at left-back or in midfield. A fractured arm bone, sustained in pre-season, meant that he missed much of the early season for Shrewsbury, making his first appearance in the Johnstone's Paint Trophy at Yeovil in September. With Marc Tierney settled at left-back, Neil was restricted to midfield. He made six League starts and nine appearances from the bench before moving on loan in January to Macclesfield, where he replaced Kevin McIntyre, who had gone in the opposite direction. Neil was almost ever-present at left-back or wing-back when Macclesfield used a line of five. He played with energy and commitment, his one goal coming in the home win against Barnet from a free-kick that sneaked through a crowd of defenders.
Tranmere Rov (From trainee on 10/4/2003) FL 0+1
Shrewsbury T (Free on 9/12/2004) FL 109+17/3 FLC 1+1 FAC 4 Others 9
Macclesfield T (Loaned on 10/1/2008) FL 19/1

ASSOU-EKOTTO Benoit Pierre David
Born: Arras, France, 24 March 1984
Height: 5'10" **Weight:** 10.12
International Honours: Cameroon
The Tottenham left-back was beset by ill-fortune early last season when sustaining a serious knee injury in training, having played a part in one UEFA Cup and one

Premier League game. Benoit was forced to sit out the rest of the season and it remains to be seen whether he can regain fitness to force his way back into the reckoning, with Gareth Bale being the logical first choice in that position. Strong in the tackle, he links well with team-mates down the left.
Tottenham H (Signed from Lens, France on 14/7/2006) PL 17 FLC 3 FAC 1 Others 6

ATKINSON Robert (Rob) Guy
Born: North Ferriby, 29 April 1987
Height: 6'1" **Weight:** 12.0
Rob played all his League football away from Barnsley last season. He went on loan to Rochdale in October and had a longer spell with Grimsby. The centre-half joined Rochdale for a month to bolster the squad when they had five defenders out injured and made a couple of useful substitute appearances. Signed by Grimsby in November at the same time as another loan player Sam Hird, Rob proved a key man in Town's rise up the League Two table to safety. The central defender's debut in a 3-0 win at Barnet coincided with the Mariners' first clean sheet of the campaign. Rob played with confidence and developed a good understanding within the team. On target in a 2-0 win at Chester, his loan was extended to the end of the season, allowing him to play in the Johnstone's Paint Trophy final at Wembley.
Barnsley (From trainee on 5/7/2006) FL 6+2 FAC 2
Rochdale (Loaned on 19/10/2007) FL 0+2
Grimsby T (Loaned on 22/11/2007) FL 24/1 FAC 1 Others 4

ATKINSON William (Will) Henry
Born: Driffield, 14 October 1988
Height: 5'10" **Weight:** 10.7
After being loaned out by Hull in October, the slightly built left-winger made the first senior appearance of his career as a substitute in Port Vale's home defeat by Brighton and did well enough to start the next three games. Back at the KC Stadium after a change of manager, Will made his Hull debut as an attacking substitute in the closing stages of the third round FA Cup tie at Plymouth, with the Tigers vainly trying to salvage a replay. To further his experience he went out on loan to Mansfield just before the January deadline and made quite an impression playing wide on the left and stayed for a second month before Hull refused a further extension.
Hull C (From trainee on 14/12/2006) FAC 0+1
Port Vale (Loaned on 12/10/2007) FL 3+1
Mansfield T (Loaned on 29/1/2008) FL 10+2

AUBEY Lucien Yann Sherril
Born: Brazzaville, Congo, 24 May 1984
Height: 5'11" **Weight:** 11.10
International Honours: France: U21
Lucien, a French under-21 international, joined Portsmouth on loan in the middle of January from Lens, having previously made 152 appearances in six seasons at Toulouse. A tall and pacy left-back or central defender who likes to go forward as much as he can, he made his full Premier League debut against Tottenham in March having previously come on as a 27th-minute substitute in the 1-0 win at Bolton. He made one other substitute appearance, in the 3-1 defeat at Manchester City.
Portsmouth (Loaned from RC Lens, France, ex Toulouse, on 18/1/2008) PL 1+2

AURELIO Fabio
Born: Sao Carlos, Brazil, 24 September 1979
Height: 5'10" **Weight:** 11.11
Club Honours: CS '06
International Honours: Brazil: U21
Liverpool's first Brazilian import, albeit from manager Rafa Benitez's former Spanish club Valencia, started last season with an Achilles problem and was not available until late September. A left-back or midfielder, he made only intermittent appearances under Benitez's rotation system up to Christmas and only in the closing stages of the campaign did he usurp John Arne Riise's place, scoring his first goal for the Reds in a rare 3-1 victory at Bolton in March. With Riise's immediate future at Anfield in doubt, Fabio is the only logical successor at left-back but, at 28, may not be a long-term solution and there are still reservations about his crossing and delivery of free kicks. However, two of his three goal assists during the season came in vital away matches in the Champions' League, first at Marseille and then in the San Siro against Inter Milan when his interception and pass set up Fernando Torres to score the only goal in an historic away victory.
Liverpool (Signed from Valencia, Spain, ex Sao Paulo, on 20/7/2006) PL 23+10/1 FLC 4 FAC 0+2 Others 10+5

AUSTIN Kevin Levi
Born: Hackney, 12 February 1973
Height: 6'0" **Weight:** 14.0
Club Honours: AMC '06; Div 1 '08
International Honours: Trinidad & Tobago: 1
An experienced defender, Kevin confounded his age by regular inclusion in the Swansea first-team squad, either at centre-back, left-back or as one of the substitutes. His consistency and

Neil Austin

experience allowed few opportunities for opposing players to get the better of him.

Leyton Orient *(Free from Saffron Walden on 19/8/1993) FL 101+8/3 FLC 4/1 FAC 6 Others 7*
Lincoln C *(£30,000 on 31/7/1996) FL 128+1/2 FLC 9 FAC 6 Others 4*
Barnsley *(Free on 5/7/1999) FL 3 FLC 2+1*
Brentford *(Loaned on 27/10/2000) FL 3*
Cambridge U *(Free on 21/11/2001) FL 4+2 Others 1*
Bristol Rov *(Free on 12/7/2002) FL 52+4 FAC 4+1*
Swansea C *(Free on 2/7/2004) FL 107+10 FLC 5 FAC 13 Others 14+1*

AUSTIN Neil Jeffrey
Born: Barnsley, 26 April 1983
Height: 5'10" **Weight:** 11.11
International Honours: E: Yth
A strong-tackling right-back who arrived at Darlington from Barnsley during the summer, Neil suffered an injury on the opening day of the season and did not establish himself in the side until after Christmas. He appeared more regularly during the second half of the season and, enjoying getting forward down the flanks, scored the first of his two goals at Morecambe in January.
Barnsley *(From trainee on 27/4/2000) FL 132+16 FLC 2+1 FAC 11+1 Others 1+1*

Darlington *(Free on 1/7/2007) FL 23+6/2 FAC 1*

AVINEL Cedric Mickael
Born: Paris, France, 11 September 1986
Height: 6'2" **Weight:** 13.3
The young French centre-half was limited to two appearances in the Carling Cup in 2007-08. In September he went on a month's loan to Stafford Rangers to widen his experience but otherwise was confined to being a regular in Watford's reserve side, giving confident displays.
Watford *(Signed from Creteil, France on 16/2/2007) P/FL 1 FLC 2*

B

BA Georges
Born: Abidjan, Ivory Coast, 24 January 1979
Height: 6'1" **Weight:** 13.7
A tall, sturdy and powerful centre-forward, Georges joined Gillingham at the end of March following trials at Preston and Leeds. Seen as an impact player in a season when the Gills were desperate to avoid relegation to League Two, Georges made just one start, along with three substitute appearances, and failed to score before being placed on a month-by-month contract at the end of the season.
Gillingham (Free from Maccabi Netanya, Israel, following a trial at Leeds U, ex Tours, Sannois St Gratien, Besancon, OGC Nice, Montpellier, Le Mans, Troyes, on 27/3/2008) FL 1+3

Ryan Babel

BABEL Ryan Guno
Born: Amsterdam, Holland, 19 December 1986
Height: 6'1" **Weight:** 12.6
International Honours: Holland: 23
The mercurial Dutch international winger or striker was signed by Liverpool from Ajax for a massive fee in the summer. Accordingly, expectations were high but although he was involved in 49 of Liverpool's 59 games, he was a substitute on 20 occasions and, when he started, was often withdrawn so that only eight times did he complete 90 minutes. In fairness many of Benitez's substitutions were tactical rather than a reflection on his form. Although normally deployed on the left, he can also play on the right and Benitez often switches his position during games. Of his ten goals, seven were scored late in games when he came on as substitute and the match was already won, such as the one in the 8-0 rout of Besiktas in the Champions' League and his last-minute solo against a tiring Arsenal defence in the quarter-final second leg at Anfield. Undoubtedly his finest goal was in the Champions' League semi-final second leg at Chelsea when, out of nowhere, he struck a stunning swerving volley from 25 yards that so surprised the normally faultless Chelsea 'keeper Petr Cech that in attempting to catch, he merely palmed the ball high into the net. Sadly, with Chelsea leading 3-1, it was a mere consolation, coming three minutes from the end of extra-time. Had he scored ten minutes earlier it could have been the away goal to take Liverpool to their third Champions' League final in four years. Dutch manager Marco van Basten has suggested that Ryan has the potential to be another Thierry Henry and while this may seem exaggerated after an inconsistent first season in the Premier League, he is only 21 and, barring injury, can only improve. It will be disappointing if, in two years time, he is not an automatic choice for Liverpool and a star for Holland.
Liverpool (£11,500,000 from Ajax, Holland on 25/7/2007) PL 15+15/4 FLC 2 FAC 4/1 Others 8+5/5

BAIDOO Shabazz Kwame Kussie
Born: Hackney, 13 April 1988
Height: 5'8" **Weight:** 10.7
International Honours: E: Yth
Shabazz joined Dagenham from Queens Park Rangers on the last day of the January transfer window on a four-month deal but missed the first few games as the result of a rib injury the day before he signed. He made his first start at Hereford, but the speedy forward's opportunities became limited following a well-publicised personal incident. Was out of contract in the summer and looking for a new club.
Queens Park Rgrs (From trainee on 8/6/2006) FL 10+18/3 FLC 1+2 FAC 1+1/1
Dagenham & Redbridge (Free on 17/11/2008) FL 1+2

BAILEY James Joseph
Born: Bollington, 18 September 1988
Height: 6'0" **Weight:** 12.5
Another young player who has come through the youth system at Crewe, James was on the bench on several occasions last season but was used only once, against Doncaster. A midfielder who can also perform well at right-back, he hopes to break into the League side in the coming season and Crewe's optimism was demonstrated by a further year on his contract.
Crewe Alex (From trainee on 4/5/2007) FL 0+1

BAILEY Matthew (Matt) John
Born: Crewe, 12 March 1986
Height: 6'5" **Weight:** 11.6
Having arrived at Crewe from Northwich two years earlier as a forward, Matt was converted into a defender in 2007-08. He has only ever been a substitute in the League but had his first full outing in the FA Cup second round against Oldham in November. Matt spent time on loan at Weymouth and was released at the end of the season.
Stockport Co (From trainee on 8/7/2003) FL 0+1 Others 0+1
Scunthorpe U (Loaned on 6/8/2004) FL 2+2 FLC 1
Crewe Alex (Free on 11/5/2005) FL 0+2 FAC 1

BAILEY Nicholas (Nicky) Francis
Born: Putney, 10 June 1984
Height: 5'10" **Weight:** 12.8
Club Honours: FC '05
Nicky joined Southend in the 2007 close season after three seasons with Barnet. Having been rejected by Fulham as a youngster he found a way back into the full-time game via Sutton United. Nicky started on the bench but Steve Tilson liked his energy and attacking mentality, so accommodated him in central midfield with Kevin Maher and Alan McCormack. Nicky enjoyed a superb season, blending seamlessly with McCormack, their offensive play and willingness to track back complemented each other. Nicky outdid his midfield partner by scoring 12 goals that, with so many different strikers employed, made him leading scorer for the Shrimpers. It was no surprise when the Roots Hall faithful voted him 'Player of the Year'.
Barnet (Signed from Sutton U on 2/7/2004) FL 88+1/12 FLC 5/1 FAC 5 Others 4/1
Southend U (£175,000 on 1/8/2007) FL 42+2/9 FLC 3 FAC 5/2 Others 3/1

BAILEY Stefan Kyon Lloyd
Born: Brent, 10 November 1987
Height: 5'11" **Weight:** 12.8
A young midfielder who came through the Queens Park Rangers' youth ranks, Stefan had a short spell on loan at Oxford United in the latter part of 2007 but only made two appearances for Rangers before leaving in July. He is a strong-tackling midfield player, always looking to win the ball.
Queens Park Rgrs (From trainee on 8/3/2006) FL 14+4 FLC 3 FAC 1

BAINES Leighton John
Born: Liverpool, 11 December 1984
Height: 5'8" **Weight:** 11.10
International Honours: E: U21-16
The England under-21 international had a frustrating first season at Everton after signing from Wigan in the summer. Injuries and the good form of fellow defenders prevented him from making the left-back berth his own. After establishing himself in the team in September, ankle and hamstring injuries restricted his chances from November onwards and with Joleon Lescott firmly established on the left-hand side of the defence, he began only four League matches after Christmas. A fast, mobile full-back who is particularly strong going forward, Leighton hopes for better luck ahead.
Wigan Ath (From trainee on 4/1/2003) P/FL 140+5/4 FLC 7+2 FAC 6 Others 1+1
Everton (£6,000,000 on 7/8/2007) PL 13+9 FLC 0+1 FAC 1 Others 3+2

BAIRD Christopher (Chris) Patrick
Born: Ballymoney, 25 February 1982
Height: 5'10" **Weight:** 11.11
International Honours: NI: 32; U21-6; Yth
Signed from Watford, Chris was one of several with Northern Ireland international links introduced by Laurie Sanchez in the summer. He went straight into the Fulham team for the opening game at Arsenal and was a regular through most of the first six months. Although mainly used at right-back, he can cover in central defence if required. He is a strong tackler, who reads the game well and adjusts his position accordingly, and had an outstanding game in the early season derby at Stamford Bridge. Chris had the honour of captaining Northern Ireland against Lichtenstein, although they narrowly missed qualification for Euro 2008.
Southampton (From trainee on 15/1/2001) P/FL 62+6/3 FLC 4 FAC 5 Others 2
Walsall (Loaned on 26/9/2003) FL 10
Watford (Loaned on 16/3/2004) FL 8
Fulham (£3,000,000 on 17/7/2007) PL 17+1 FLC 1 FAC 1+1

BAKAYOGO Zoumana
Born: Paris, France, 11 August 1986
Height: 5'9" **Weight:** 10.8
International Honours: Ivory Coast: U23
Nicknamed 'Zoom' by Millwall team-mates because of his lightning pace, Zoumana can play in midfield and defence. From the back, he likes to get forward, usually on the flanks, but made only fleeting appearances last season. Was released at the end of the campaign.
Millwall (Free from Paris St Germain, France on 4/8/2006) FL 8+7 FLC 2 FAC 2+2 Others 2

BAKER Carl Paul
Born: Prescot, 26 December 1982
Height: 6'2" **Weight:** 12.8
International Honours: E: SP-2
Carl is a player full of talent who attracted the attention of a host of scouts as he burst on the League scene with Morecambe after being signed from Southport in the summer. The attacking right-sided midfielder's performances in the first half of the season were instrumental in Morecambe's superb start and his habit of scoring injury-time winners ensured they were among the early front runners. His highlight was two pairs of goals as Morecambe drew with Stockport and beat promoted Peterborough despite being down to ten men. Great tight skills saw him bemuse many a defender and despite a dip in form in the New Year, Carl ended back at his best.
Morecambe (£30,000 from Southport, ex Prescot Cables, on 30/7/2007) FL 40+2/10 FLC 3/1 FAC 1 Others 2

BAKER Richard (Richie) Peter
Born: Burnley, 29 December 1987
Height: 5'7" **Weight:** 11.6
After being substituted at half-time during Bury's opening game at MK Dons, Richie struggled to secure a place in the first team. When Alan Knill took over as manager, he had faith in Richie, regularly including him in the centre of midfield. Although lack of experience can cause his aggression to boil over, he often shows maturity in his play. When combined with his obvious desire, this produces a creative midfielder, best illustrated when grabbing his only goal of the season in Bury's 2-0 win over Peterborough in November.
Bury (From trainee at Preston NE on 1/7/2006) FL 55+16/6 FLC 2+1 FAC 7+1/1 Others 1+1

BALANTA Angelo Jasiel
Born: Bogota, Colombia, 1 July 1990
Height: 5'10" **Weight:** 11.11
A prolific Queens Park Rangers' youth-team starlet who made his first team bow at Crystal Palace when coming off the bench to replace Ben Sahar, Angelo's full debut followed a couple of weeks later at Watford. He started the final three games of the season as strike partner to Dexter Blackstock. Angelo signed his first professional contract this season and hopes are high that the Colombian-born striker will go on to enjoy a productive career at Loftus Road.
Queens Park Rgrs (From trainee on 22/1/2008) FL 6+5/1 FAC 0+1

BALDOCK Samuel (Sam)
Born: Buckingham, 15 March 1989
Height: 5'7" **Weight:** 10.7
Club Honours: AMC '08
As the first player produced locally by MK Dons to appear in League football, Sam is a speedy and energetic young striker who had few opportunities to shine as Paul Ince's team strode to the League Two title. He made his only senior start in a Johnstone's Paint Trophy win at Gillingham and is a prolific scorer at youth level.
MK Dons (From trainee on 20/4/2006) FL 0+6 FAC 0+1 Others 1+4

BALDWIN Patrick (Pat) Michael
Born: City of London, 12 November 1982
Height: 6'2" **Weight:** 10.12
Like several at Colchester, Pat endured a difficult second season in the Championship. He was in the heart of defence for the first 18 games but the team struggled at the back-end of the campaign, ending with the worst defensive record. Pat was perhaps the pick of the many centre-halves used but injury blighted him from the turn of the year. Pat spent three months on the sidelines and dislocated a shoulder when he returned at West Bromwich at the end of March. He needed an operation and is a big doubt for the start of the new season.
Colchester U (From trainee at Chelsea on 16/8/2002) FL 127+23/1 FLC 7 FAC 11 Others 5+3

BALE Gareth Frank
Born: Cardiff, 16 July 1989
Height: 6'0" **Weight:** 11.10
International Honours: W: 11; U21-4; Yth
The Tottenham left-back was signed from Southampton in the summer for what will potentially be a massive fee. Gareth made an immediate impact and was used both at left-back and as an attacking left-side midfielder in his 12 games for Tottenham, which brought him three goals. One of these was a free-kick special against Arsenal but the other two were in open play where he

demonstrates great pace, coupled with all the skill desirable in a wide player. Gareth is a Welsh international and played in four matches for his country before his season ended in December with a serious ankle injury. If Gareth can recover fitness and form, there should be a memorable season ahead.

Southampton *(From trainee on 19/7/2006)*
FL 40/5 FLC 3 FAC 1 Others 1
Tottenham H *(£5,000,000 on 29/5/2007) PL*
8/2 FLC 1/1 Others 1+2

BALL Michael John

Born: Crosby, 2 October 1979
Height: 5'10" **Weight:** 11.7
Club Honours: SPD '04; SLC '02, '05
International Honours: E: 1; U21-7;
Yth; Sch

After originally joining Manchester City on a short-term contract from Dutch side PSV Eindhoven in January 2007, the former England international has settled at Eastlands. Michael started last season on the sidelines, seeing out the remainder of a three-match ban at the end of the previous campaign, and on his return he found Javier Garrido in his left-back position. However, after waiting patiently to get back into the starting line-up he was restored to his defensive duties in December and played in most of the games until the end of the season.

Everton *(From trainee on 17/10/1996) PL*
102+19/8 FLC 7+3 FAC 7+1
Glasgow Rgrs *(£6,500,000 on 17/8/2001)*
SL 49+6/1 SLC 5 SC 2 Others 12+2/1
(Transferred to PSV Eindhoven, Holland on
31/8/2005)
Manchester C *(Signed from PSV Eindhoven,*
Holland on 31/1/2007) PL 31+9 FLC 3+1
FAC 5/1

BALLACK Michael

Born: Gorlitz, Germany, 26 September 1976
Height: 6'2" **Weight:** 12.8
Club Honours: FLC '07
International Honours: Germany: 87; U21

The German midfield maestro made a welcome return after eight months on the sidelines and immediately dug Chelsea out of a hole. Overcoming an ankle injury, Michael left the bench in the Boxing Day fixture at home to Aston Villa to score with a brilliant free-kick around the wall, maintaining the Premier League's longest unbeaten home record after they had trailed. The player he replaced, Frank Lampard, was then forced to miss ten matches with a groin strain. Along with the forced absence of Chelsea midfield stars at the African Cup of Nations,

Michael Ballack

they seemed to be heading for a crisis but Michael responded magnificently, occasionally skippering the side, scoring vital goals and being an integral figure in the march to a second successive Carling Cup final and a club record-equalling nine consecutive victories. Surprisingly, Michael was left on the bench for the final and an insipid Chelsea flopped to a defeat, surely no coincidence. He was then paired with Frank Lampard (another combination said to be incompatible) and Chelsea's performances moved to another level as they remained unbeaten until the Champions' League final penalty shoot-out drama. Michael was arguably the most influential player in the country in the second half of the season, controlling matches from midfield and regularly scoring opportunist goals. His haul included beautiful efforts against West Ham and Newcastle and crucial goals against Olympiakos and Fenerbahce that turned tight matches Chelsea's way en route to the Moscow final. But his most memorable match was the Premier League showdown with Manchester United when his two goals decided the match and kept the door ajar for the Blues if United faltered. Each was special in its way, a peerless header after ghosting behind the defence to despatch Didier Drogba's cross and a coolly-taken penalty to clinch the match after heated protests delayed the kick. Always trust a German with a penalty. Following two near-misses with Bayer Leverkusen and Bayern Munich, Michael was set on a winners' medal in the Champions' League but despite his penalty United won the shoot-out. His bad luck continued when, having captained Germany to the European Championship final against Spain in June, he had to be satisfied with yet another runners-up medal as the Spaniards won their first major title since 1964.
Chelsea (Free from Bayern Munich, Germany, ex Chemnitz, Kaiserslautern, Bayer Leverkusen, on 17/7/2006) PL 39+5/12 FLC 6+3 FAC 4+1/1 Others 18/4

BALOGH Bela
Born: Hungary, 30 December 1984
Height: 5'10" **Weight:** 13.4
International Honours: Hungary: 9
A Hungarian international, Bela was signed on loan from MTK Hungaria for the season. He continued to make international appearances throughout the campaign but found it hard to settle at Colchester. More used to operating as a centre-half, he also played at right-back. Communication was a problem – his English was very limited – and he was often outpaced at the back, but he is an

unruffled defender who would probably flourish in a successful team. His loan deal was not extended so he returned to Hungary.
Colchester U (Loaned from MTK Hungaria on 16/8/2007) FL 10+7

BANGURA Alhassan (Al)
Born: Freetown, Sierra Leone, 24 January 1988
Height: 5'8" **Weight:** 10.7
Al attracted national headlines when he was threatened with deportation to his native Sierra Leone as an illegal immigrant. Thanks to a determined campaign spearheaded by Watford FC, the 19-year-old youngster was eventually granted a work permit and allowed to stay. A talented and tigerish midfielder, Al missed the first half of last season after breaking his arm during the Carling Cup tie at Southend in August. Now a firm favourite with the crowd, even before his residency problems, Al further secured his future by signing an improved contract.
Watford (From trainee on 2/6/2005) P/FL 27+33/1 FLC 6+1 FAC 3 Others 1+2

BARACLOUGH Ian Robert
Born: Leicester, 4 December 1970
Height: 6'1" **Weight:** 12.2
Club Honours: Div 3 '98; Div 1 '07
International Honours: E: Yth
Scunthorpe assistant manager Ian continued to roll back the years with 17 appearances in the Championship. He played six of the opening seven League games in his customary central midfield role, where his experience helped the side make a good start. A good passer with an excellent left foot, he deputised well for four matches at centre-half in December and then had a run of games at left-back in March.
Leicester C (From trainee on 15/12/1988) FAC 1 Others 0+1
Wigan Ath (Loaned on 22/3/1990) FL 8+1/2
Grimsby T (Loaned on 21/12/1990) FL 1+3
Grimsby T (Free on 13/8/1991) FL 1
Lincoln C (Free on 21/8/1992) FL 68+5/10 FLC 7/1 FAC 4 Others 7
Mansfield T (Free on 6/6/1994) FL 47/5 FAC 7 FAC 4 Others 4
Notts Co (Signed on 13/10/1995) FL 107+4/10 FLC 5+1/1 FAC 8 Others 5
Queens Park Rgrs (£50,000 on 19/3/1998) FL 120+5/1 FLC 7 FAC 6
Notts Co (Free on 5/7/2001) FL 93+8/5 FLC 6 FAC 6+1 Others 3+1
Scunthorpe U (Free on 2/8/2004) FL 124+9/7 FLC 2+1/1 FAC 10/3 Others 2+1

BARAZITE Nacer
Born: Arnhem, Holland, 27 May 1990
Height: 6'5" **Weight:** 15.3
International Honours: Holland: Yth

Signed from NEC Nijmegen in the summer, Nacer is a skilful Dutch midfielder who certainly provided his fair share of goals to Arsenal's reserve and youth sides. He appeared as a substitute in two Carling Cup ties, suffering a serious shoulder injury in the second of these, at Blackburn. Scored six goals in 15 reserve appearances and an impressive 13 in 17 FA Academy under-18 games.
Arsenal (From trainee on 2/7/2007) FLC 0+2

BARCHAM Andrew (Andy)
Born: Basildon, 16 December 1986
Height: 5'9" **Weight:** 11.11
Andy, who is a prolific scorer for Tottenham's youth team and reserves, joined Leyton Orient on loan last November to provide cover for the forwards. Before returning to White Hart Lane, he had scored a top-notch goal after breaking from the half-way line against Luton and had endeared himself to the fans. Fast and tricky, he can play on either wing if required.
Tottenham H (From trainee on 7/7/2005) FLC 1
Leyton Orient (Loaned on 22/11/2007) FL 15+10/1

BARDSLEY Philip (Phil) Anthony
Born: Salford, 28 June 1985
Height: 5'11" **Weight:** 11.8
Club Honours: FAYC '03
The right-back played once for Manchester United, in the Carling Cup defeat by Coventry before joining Sheffield United on loan in October for three months, following an injury to Derek Geary. He fitted in quickly with the Blades and was unlucky not to score with any of his powerful shots. Although they were keen to sign him permanently Phil chose to join Sunderland in the January transfer window and solved what had become a problem position for Roy Keane with a series of consistent performances. Comfortable in possession and always keen to get forward, Phil's wholehearted attitude endears him to Black Cats' fans. Unfortunately, an injury the day before Sunderland's derby against rivals Newcastle in April ruled him out of the last three games.
Manchester U (From trainee on 2/7/2003) PL 3+5 FLC 3+1 FAC 2+1 Others 2+1
Burnley (Loaned on 16/3/2006) FL 6
Glasgow Rgrs (Loaned on 16/8/2006) SL 5/1 Others 2
Aston Villa (Loaned on 8/1/2007) PL 13
Sheffield U (Loaned on 19/10/2007) FL 16
Sunderland (£2,000,000 on 24/1/2008) PL 11

BARKER Christopher (Chris) Andrew
Born: Sheffield, 2 March 1980
Height: 6'0" **Weight:** 11.8
Chris was one of John Gregory's summer signings for Queens Park Rangers when he moved from Cardiff. Suspension pushed back his debut to September but he soon became a regular in the side. Unfortunately for Chris, the arrival of a new manager and, as a result more competition for defensive positions, restricted his opportunities and he featured only three times after the turn of the year.
Barnsley (Signed from Alfreton T on 24/8/1998) FL 110+3/3 FLC 11+1 FAC 4 Others 0+1
Cardiff C (£600,000 on 12/7/2002) FL 144+15 FLC 9 FAC 8 Others 4
Stoke C (Loaned on 6/8/2004) FL 4
Colchester U (Loaned on 18/8/2006) FL 38 FAC 1
Queens Park Rgrs (Signed on 7/8/2007) FL 25 FAC 1

BARKER Richard (Richie) Ian
Born: Sheffield, 30 May 1975
Height: 6'0" **Weight:** 13.5
International Honours: E: Yth; Sch
Richie is a hard worker who played an important role for Hartlepool as target man. A powerful, old-fashioned centre-forward, he took plenty of punishment from opposing defenders and this eventually took its toll as he missed the final weeks of the season with knee and hamstring injuries. He is a reliable penalty taker and was Hartlepool's top scorer with 16 League and Cup goals.
Sheffield Wed (From trainee on 27/7/1993) Others 1+1 (Free to Linfield on 22/8/1996)
Doncaster Rov (Loaned on 29/9/1995) FL 5+1 Others 0+1
Brighton & Hove A (Free from Linfield on 19/12/1997) FL 48+12/12 FLC 1+1/1 FAC 1/1 Others 1
Macclesfield T (Free on 5/7/1999) FL 58/23 FLC 6/2 FAC 3 Others 1/1
Rotherham U (£60,000 on 3/1/2001) FL 69+71/12 FLC 8+2/3 FAC 5/2
Mansfield T (Free on 26/11/2004) FL 93+2/40 FLC 5/2 FAC 6/6
Hartlepool U (£80,000 on 5/1/2007) FL 49+5/22 FLC 2 FAC 2/2 Others 3/1

BARKER Shaun
Born: Nottingham, 19 September 1982
Height: 6'2" **Weight:** 12.8
Shaun's second term at Blackpool was again a success as he easily made the step up from League One to Championship. The majority of his season was spent at right-back, with the occasional game covering at centre-back. He is a great

asset to Blackpool with his aerial ability and attacking nature from the back. An ever-present in the League, along with goalkeeper Paul Rachubka, Shaun scored two goals, both at Bloomfield Road, against Colchester in a 2-2 draw and in a 3-2 defeat by Stoke.
Rotherham U (From trainee on 10/7/2002) FL 119+4/7 FLC 6 FAC 3 Others 1
Blackpool (Signed on 4/8/2006) FL 91/5 FLC 5 FAC 5/1 Others 4/2

BARMBY Nicholas (Nick) Jonathan
Born: Hull, 11 February 1974
Height: 5'7" **Weight:** 11.3
Club Honours: FLC '01; UEFAC '01; CS '01
International Honours: E: 23; B-2; U21-4; Yth; Sch
Ably assisted by a fellow veteran Hullensian in Dean Windass, one of Hull's most famous sporting sons wrote a glorious chapter in the autumn of his career as he guided the Tigers to the top flight for the first time in their history. Most notably, Nick scored crucial goals in each leg of the Championship play-off semi-final against Watford to take Hull to Wembley. Often used on the left of midfield as opposed to a more advanced role, he extended his contract in August to the end of next season but until the fairy-tale conclusion, suffered a frustrating campaign. An ankle injury in September and a torn groin in February curtailed the experienced and enthusiast contribution, if not the influence of the man Tigers' manager Phil Brown calls 'the little maestro'.
Tottenham H (From trainee on 9/4/1991) PL 81+6/20 FLC 7+1/2 FAC 12+1/5
Middlesbrough (£5,250,000 on 8/8/1995) PL 42/8 FLC 4/1 FAC 3/1
Everton (£5,750,000 on 2/11/1996) PL 105+11/18 FLC 2+3/3 FAC 12/3
Liverpool (£6,000,000 on 19/7/2000) PL 23+9/2 FLC 3+4/1 FAC 2+3/1 Others 10+4/4
Leeds U (£2,750,000 on 8/8/2002) PL 17+8/4 FLC 1 FAC 0+2 Others 3/1
Nottingham F (Loaned on 27/2/2004) FL 6/1
Hull C (Free on 6/7/2004) FL 71+29/19 FLC 1+1/1 FAC 3 Others 3/2

BARNARD Lee James
Born: Romford, 18 July 1984
Height: 5'10" **Weight:** 10.10
International Honours: E: Yth
Unable to break into the Tottenham side, Lee went out on a long-term loan to Crewe at the end of August, scoring on his debut against Huddersfield at Gresty Road in September. Unfortunate to be injured against Luton in October, he was out of action for two months

before signing for Southend in the January transfer window and scoring the winner against Leeds on his debut. The goals came thick and fast for the blond front-runner as he struck up a good understanding with fellow newcomer James Walker. Apart from his eye for goal, Lee shields the ball well and channels it to attacking colleagues. His quick feet and turn of pace meant he came in for some hard tackles and suffered knee and ankle injuries during the final matches of the campaign. Undoubtedly, with nine League goals in only 11 starts, it was a very shrewd acquisition by manager Steve Tilson.
Tottenham H (From trainee on 3/7/2002) PL 0+3
Exeter C (Loaned on 1/11/2002) FL 3 Others 1
Leyton Orient (Loaned on 5/11/2004) FL 3+5 FAC 1 Others 1
Northampton T (Loaned on 4/3/2005) FL 3+2
Crewe Alex (Loaned on 31/8/2007) FL 9+1/3
Southend U (Signed on 25/1/2008) FL 11+4/9 FAC 0+1 Others 2

BARNES Ashley Luke
Born: Bath, 31 October 1989
Height: 6'0" **Weight:** 11.3
Ashley is a striker who joined Plymouth from non-League Paulton. He impressed enough during an extended trial, in which he scored several goals for the reserves, to earn an 18-month contract. Struggling for first-team opportunities he made only one substitute appearance, against Wycombe in the Carling Cup in August before going on loan to Oxford United in November and to Salisbury in March. Ashley helped Plymouth to reach the quarter-finals of the FA Youth Cup.
Plymouth Arg (Signed from Paulton Rov on 22/3/2007) FLC 0+1

BARNES Giles Gordon
Born: Barking, 5 August 1988
Height: 6'1" **Weight:** 12.13
International Honours: E: Yth
A knee injury from the previous season, aggravated in the play-off final, meant Giles was a late starter for Derby in 2007-08. His Premiership debut, as one of the substitutes in a 5-0 defeat by Arsenal, was a chastening experience and he had to develop match-fitness as he went along. Ideally, he likes to play in the centre of midfield, where his strong running can upset defenders, and it did not help that his position varied, sometimes wide and occasionally an auxiliary striker. Giles remains a player of potential and was often the subject of transfer speculation, with Derby rejecting

Phil Barnes

voted 'Player of the Year'. The goalkeeper showed excellent reflexes and handling on many occasions, particularly in the Johnstone's Paint Trophy, in which his penalty shoot-out stops against Rotherham and Doncaster were key factors in Grimsby reaching the final. Town's best performer in the Wembley defeat by MK Dons, Phil received rare ten out of ten marks from the local press for a faultless display that ensured victory in the area final at Morecambe.
Rotherham U *(From trainee on 25/6/1997) FL 2*
Blackpool *(£100,000 on 22/7/1997) FL 141 FLC 7 FAC 7 Others 14*
Sheffield U *(Free on 2/7/2004) FL 1 FLC 3 FAC 1*
Torquay U *(Loaned on 3/2/2005) FL 5*
Queens Park Rgrs *(Loaned on 4/2/2006) FL 1*
Grimsby T *(Free on 27/7/2006) FL 88 FLC 2 FAC 3 Others 9*

BARNETT Leon Peter
Born: Stevenage, 30 November 1985
Height: 6'1" **Weight:** 11.3
Club Honours: Ch '08
Signed to replace his former Luton team-mate Curtis Davies, Leon had an excellent first season at the Hawthorns. Although forced out through injury from time to time, when fit and in the side he was outstanding, despite having several different partners at the heart of West Bromwich's defence. Leon's three goals helped Albion to a 3-2 victory at Scunthorpe and salvaged points from 1-1 home draws with promotion-chasing Stoke and Watford. Unfortunately Leon missed the FA Cup semi-final clash with Portsmouth through injury.
Luton T *(From trainee on 28/9/2004) FL 51+8/3 FLC 4 FAC 2+1 Others 3+1*
West Bromwich A *(£2,500,000 + on 1/8/2007) FL 30+2/3 FAC 4*

BAROS Milan
Born: Ostrava, Czech Republic, 28 October 1981
Height: 6'0" **Weight:** 11.12
Club Honours: FLC '03; UEFACL '05; FAC '08
International Honours: Czech Republic: 60; U21-19; Yth
As Portsmouth searched for more attacking options, Milan joined on loan from French club Lyon for the rest of the season in January. He made his Premier League debut for the club three days later in the 2-0 defeat at Manchester United. Although his shooting boots may have been left behind, he had a dramatic impact on Pompey's season as his workrate and darting runs unsettled defences. This was emphatically

an inquiry from Newcastle because it was well short of their valuation. He is confident but development was halted by a further knee injury in training at the end of February, necessitating an operation by Dr Richard Steadman in Colorado.
Derby Co *(From trainee on 10/9/2005) P/FL 60+19/10 FLC 2+1 FAC 3+3/1 Others 0+2*

BARNES Michael Thomas
Born: Chorley, 24 June 1988
Height: 6'3" **Weight:** 13.8
When Michael was signed on loan from Manchester United in January, Chesterfield hoped that the winger would bring the same pace, close control and crossing ability to Saltergate that he showed as an Old Trafford reserve. It became clear that he was not yet ready to step up to the League and he was

allowed to return after an unproductive month. He had trials with Inverness before another loan, to Shrewsbury in March with a view to a permanent deal. He looked useful in his debut in a 1-0 home defeat by Bury but was restricted to one further appearance. Was released in the summer.
Manchester U *(From trainee on 6/7/2006) FLC 0+1*
Chesterfield *(Loaned on 2/1/2008) FL 1+2*
Shrewsbury T *(Loaned on 27/3/2008) FL 2*

BARNES Philip (Phil) Kenneth
Born: Sheffield, 2 March 1979
Height: 6'1" **Weight:** 11.1
Club Honours: AMC '02
After a mixed first term as a Mariner in 2006-07, Phil was Grimsby's most improved player last season and was

demonstrated in the FA Cup quarter-final at Old Trafford when, as a 54th-minute substitute, he changed the course of the game and earned the penalty from which Pompey, against the odds, booked their semi-final place. In the semi-final it was his parried shot, turned in by Nwankwo Kanu, that ensured Pompey's first Cup final appearance since 1939. He played in the Czech Republic's Euro 2008 qualifying games and was in their squad for the finals in Austria and Switzerland.
Liverpool (£3,400,000 from Banik Ostrava, Czech Republic on 24/12/2001) PL 45+23/19 FLC 3+5/4 FAC 0+3 Others 18+11/4
Aston Villa (£6,500,000 on 23/8/2005) PL 34+8/9 FLC 3+2/1 FAC 3+1/4
Portsmouth (Loaned from Lyon, France on 29/1/2008) PL 8+4 FAC 1+3

BARRAU Xavier
Born: Lyon, France, 26 August 1982
Height: 5'10" **Weight:** 11.0
Having signed from Bradford during the summer, Xavier made an explosive impact on his only League appearance for Darlington when he was sent off for two rash tackles just 22 minutes after entering for his debut as a second-half substitute against Peterborough in September. A left-winger and a good crosser of the ball, he made one start, against Leeds in the Johnstone's Paint Trophy, but after another substitute outing against Northampton in the FA Cup, was released and returned to Scotland with Hamilton Academical.
Raith Rov (Signed from Meyrin, Switzerland, ex-Lyon, Viry-Chatillon, on 25/8/2006) SL 0+2
Airdrie U (Signed on 29/9/2006) SL 12+1 SC 1
Gretna (Signed on 27/1/2007) SL 0+1
Bradford C (Signed on 6/3/2007) FL 1+2/2
Darlington (Free on 28/8/2007) FL 0+1 FAC 0+1 Others 1

BARRETT Adam Nicholas
Born: Dagenham, 29 November 1979
Height: 5'10" **Weight:** 12.0
Club Honours: Div 1 '06
Only three yellow cards all season was an amazing and creditable statistic for Adam, whose 100 per-cent attitude at the heart of Southend's defence was fully appreciated by team-mates and supporters alike. As well as being a dominant header of the ball, Adam is equally at home on the ground, and his rampaging runs from defence set Southend on the way to victory more than once during an eventful campaign. He even managed to chip in with seven valuable goals during an ultimately disappointing time for the Shrimpers.
Plymouth Arg (From USA football scholarship, ex trainee at Leyton Orient, on 13/1/1999) FL 47+5/3 FLC 4 FAC 6+1 Others 1

Mansfield T (£10,000 on 1/12/2000) FL 34+3/1 FAC 3 Others 2
Bristol Rov (Free on 2/7/2002) FL 90/5 FLC 2 FAC 5/1 Others 2
Southend U (Free on 5/7/2004) FL 158+3/22 FLC 8/1 FAC 10 Others 14

BARRON Scott
Born: Preston, 2 September 1985
Height: 5'10" **Weight:** 11.0
The young left-sided player was signed in the summer from Ipswich but while having some excellent games in the reserves, Scott had to wait patiently for first-team opportunities at Millwall. When Andy Frampton and Marcus Bignot were injured, Scott had a run at left-back and acquitted himself well. With good pace and an excellent left foot, he loves to get forward, starting many attacks, and the next aim is a regular place.
Ipswich T (From trainee on 18/3/2004) FL 14+1 FLC 1 FAC 1
Wrexham (Loaned on 8/2/2007) FL 3
Millwall (Free on 9/8/2007) FL 7+5 FLC 0+1 FAC 2+1 Others 1

BARRY Anthony Jonathan
Born: Liverpool, 29 May 1986
Height: 5'7" **Weight:** 10.0
Club Honours: FC '06
Anthony's second full season saw him take responsibility in the centre of the Yeovil midfield in 2007-08. He has the ability to pick out a pass and after some spectacular performances in the previous season's play-offs, many expected him to shine, but some niggling injuries and inconsistent performances saw Russell Slade release the former Accrington player at the end of the season.
Yeovil T (Signed from Accrington Stanley on 31/1/2006) FL 42+22 FLC 1 FAC 2 Others 7/1

BARRY Gareth
Born: Hastings, 23 February 1981
Height: 6'0" **Weight:** 12.6
International Honours: E: 20; B-1; U21-27; Yth
In an outstanding season, Gareth starred for Aston Villa and England. Naturally left-footed, Gareth's versatility makes him invaluable to Villa because he performs to a high level at left-back, in central defence or midfield. And he is dangerous with the goal in his sights. Gareth continued as captain and is Villa's regular penalty-taker. The hub of the team and the most consistent performer, he completed a decade with Villa, missing only one game after suffering a pelvic injury in training. In October, he became the youngest player to feature in 300 Premier League matches and received the BBC Midlands 'Footballer of the Year' award in December. Villa have

known his worth for years and he amply confirmed it for England with his ability to keep possession, pass accurately and play the position on the left of midfield. Gareth was much coveted in the summer, Liverpool being open in their admiration.
Aston Villa (From trainee on 27/2/1998) PL 315+12/36 FLC 27/4 FAC 18+2/3 Others 17+1/1

BARRY-MURPHY Brian
Born: Cork, 27 July 1978
Height: 6'0" **Weight:** 12.4
International Honours: RoI: U21-6; Yth
Brian started by featuring in seven of Bury's first ten games before losing his place to loan signing Lee Bullock. Even after Bullock left, the good form of Richie Baker and David Buchanan kept him out of the three-man midfield favoured by Chris Casper. Alan Knill saw something he liked in the Irishman when he took over in February and Brian was a fixture in Knill's four-man midfield. Receiving praise for bringing another dimension to his game in terms of winning tackles and renowned for his strong left foot, Brian remains a threat from dead-ball situations.
Preston NE (Free from Cork C on 3/8/1999) FL 6+15 FLC 1+3 FAC 1+1 Others 1
Southend U (Loaned on 11/2/2002) FL 8/1
Hartlepool U (Loaned on 30/10/2002) FL 7 FAC 2
Sheffield Wed (Free on 31/1/2003) FL 55+3 FLC 1 FAC 2 Others 6
Bury (Free on 3/8/2004) FL 113+17/10 FLC 3+1 FAC 5+2 Others 5

BARTLEY Marvin Clement
Born: Reading, 4 July 1986
Height: 5'11" **Weight:** 12.6
It was a frustrating season for the young midfielder who stepped up from non-League Hampton to play for Bournemouth. An injury before the campaign was under way meant he had to wait until December for his debut. Once in the side, he quickly made himself a crowd favourite with his all-action style before he was again struck by injury and spent the end of the season on the bench.
Bournemouth (Free from Hampton & Richmond Borough, ex Burnham, Hayes, Didcot T, on 24/7/2007) FL 14+6/1 FAC 0+1

BARTON Joseph (Joey) Anthony
Born: Huyton, 2 September 1982
Height: 5'9" **Weight:** 11.2
International Honours: E: 1; U21-2
Last season was difficult for Joey, an aggressive, tough-tackling, midfield player who joined Newcastle from Manchester City in the summer to reinvigorate his

career, but while captaining the side in a pre-season friendly at Carlisle he suffered a partial fracture of the fifth metatarsal in his left foot. He finally made his debut in late October but well-publicised problems off the field interrupted his season again at the end of the year and it was February before he reappeared in the starting line up. His form improved, particularly after the arrival of his former boss Kevin Keegan as manager, and his surging box-to-box runs in support of the attack became a feature. He scored his only goal in December, a stoppage-time penalty to secure victory at Fulham.
Manchester C *(From trainee on 5/7/2001) PL 123+7/15 FLC 4/1 FAC 13+1/1 Others 2+3*
Newcastle U *(£5,800,000 on 3/7/2007) PL 20+3/1*

BASEY Grant William
Born: Bromley, 30 November 1988
Height: 6'0" **Weight:** 11.11
International Honours: W: Yth
A powerfully-built young Charlton left-sided defender, Grant began the campaign on loan to Brentford for two months and impressed by his solid defending. On returning to his parent club in October, he was thrust into the first team as left-backs Ben Thatcher and Chris Powell were injured and made an immediate impact with a 'Man of the Match' performance on his debut against Queens Park Rangers at the Valley. He kept his place for the next five games before a groin injury at Sheffield United set him back for several weeks. Grant scored his first senior goal for Charlton in the final game against Coventry at the Valley, when he looked comfortable on the left of midfield. A good passer, who has a tremendous shot and likes to get forward, perhaps that could be his best position. He was named in the Wales under-21 squad but has yet to make his debut at that level.
Charlton Ath *(From trainee on 17/7/2007) FL 8/1 FAC 0+1*
Brentford *(Loaned on 17/7/2007) FL 8 FLC 1 Others 1*

BASEYA Cedric
Born: Bretigny, France, 19 December 1987
Height: 6'4" **Weight:** 14.7
Cedric, a lithe and elegant striker brought in from Bretigny, has been turning the heads of spectators at Southampton reserve games in the past season. He had a brief loan spell at Crewe, starting against Northampton in November and then making three substitute appearances, before graduating to the Saints' first-team bench in March. His one excursion on to the pitch, against Ipswich,

came in injury-time and was over before he touched the ball.
Southampton *(From trainee on 4/4/2007) FL 0+1*
Crewe Alex *(Loaned on 16/11/2007) FL 1+2 FAC 0+1*

BASHAM Christopher (Chris) Paul
Born: Hebburn, 20 July 1988
Height: 5'11" **Weight:** 12.8
A versatile defender or midfielder for Bolton's youth and reserve sides, Chris joined Rochdale on loan last February after a spell with Stafford. He made his League debut as a substitute against Hereford and was used mainly on the right of midfield, although he stood in for David Perkins in the centre a couple of times. Chris was a regular in the Dale squad over the course of his three-month loan but unfortunately this ran out after the first leg of the play-off semi-final.
Bolton W *(From trainee on 20/10/2007)*
Rochdale *(Loaned on 8/2/2008) FL 5+8*

BASSO Adriano
Born: Jundiai, Brazil, 18 April 1975
Height: 6'1" **Weight:** 11.7
To Bristol City fans, it was one of the mysteries of the season that this brilliant Brazilian goalkeeper didn't feature in the PFA 'Championship Select' team. Undoubtedly a major reason behind City's Premiership bid, he rivals Mike Gibson as the best Ashton Gate 'keeper of the past 50 years. His brilliant reflexes brought several penalty saves but it is his amazing ability to be up off the floor in a flash that marks him out as a special talent. Indeed, there are none better. Signed from Woking in 2005, the question is how much longer City will be able to keep him. Adriano fully deserved the City supporters' club award as 'Player of the Season', although he had little opportunity to demonstrate his skills in the play-off final at Wembley where he was scarcely troubled apart from Hull's winner, which he had little chance of saving.
Bristol C *(Free from Woking, ex Atletico Paraense, on 14/10/2005) FL 118 FLC 1 FAC 6 Others 8*

BASTIANS Felix
Born: Bochum, Germany, 9 May 1988
Height: 6'2" **Weight:** 12.0
International Honours: Germany: Yth
The young German left-winger, son of noted sprinter Werner Bastians, failed to make much of an impression at Nottingham Forest in his three appearances early in the season and went on loan to Chesterfield in October. Playing on the left of midfield, he added

a productive threat to their attacking without neglecting defensive duties and the Spireites felt they lost a useful player when regulations forced him to return to Forest after three one-month loans. Again on loan, he played five times for Notts County and appeared to be settling when he left to try his luck with MK Dons. Then, having failed to make an appearance for the Buckinghamshire side, he was back at the City Ground to help the reserves to the title. Was released at the end of the summer.
Nottingham F *(From trainee on 4/8/2005) FL 2+12 FLC 1 FAC 0+1 Others 2*
Gillingham *(Loaned on 22/3/2007) FL 5/1*
Chesterfield *(Loaned on 2/10/2007) FL 12/1 FAC 1*
Notts Co *(Loaned on 4/1/2008) FL 5*

BATES Matthew (Matty) David
Born: Stockton, 10 December 1986
Height: 5'10" **Weight:** 12.3
Club Honours: FAYC '04
International Honours: E: Yth
Signed by Norwich on loan from Middlesbrough in January, Matty sustained a knee injury against Hull the following month and returned to the North-East ahead of schedule. In his brief three-match stay with the Canaries, he displayed some of the attributes that earned him England under-21 recognition. He is decisive in the tackle and progressive when in possession.

Julien Baudet

All at Carrow Road wish him a full and speedy recovery.
Middlesbrough *(From trainee on 25/1/2005)
PL 12+7 FLC 2+2 FAC 2+2 Others 5*
Darlington *(Loaned on 24/3/2005) FL 4*
Ipswich T *(Loaned on 17/11/2006) FL 2*
Norwich C *(Loaned on 31/1/2008) FL 2+1*

BAUDET Julien
Born: Grenoble, France, 13 January 1979
Height: 6'3" **Weight:** 14.2
An experienced, well-built central defender who had previous experience with Oldham, Rotherham and Notts County, Julien continued to be a major influence in his second season with Crewe in 2007-08. He is a consistent performer and deputised as captain on a number of occasions, being respected by fans and players alike. It was no surprise when he was chosen as 'Player of the Season'.
Oldham Ath *(Free from Toulouse, France on 9/10/2001) FL 34+10/3 FLC 2 FAC 2+2 Others 2*
Rotherham U *(Free on 6/8/2003) FL 8+3 FLC 0+1*
Notts Co *(Free on 7/7/2004) FL 80+1/11 FLC 2 FAC 4/2 Others 2*
Crewe Alex *(Free on 3/6/2006) FL 77/2 FLC 4 FAC 1 Others 4+1*

BAUZA Guillem
Born: Palma de Mallorca, Spain, 25 October 1984
Height: 5'11" **Weight:** 12.6
Club Honours: Div 1 '08
A summer signing from Spanish La Liga side Espanyol, Guillem's early senior opportunities were limited to Cup ties and he scored his first goal for Swansea in the Johnstone's Paint Trophy against Wycombe. A groin strain in February ruled him out but when he regained fitness, Guillem scored some valuable goals, none more so than the brace at Gillingham when Swansea clinched promotion to the Championship. He followed this triumphantly with a hat-trick in the last home game against Leyton Orient.
Swansea C *(Signed from Espanyol, Spain, ex Mallorca B, on 26/6/2007) FL 12+16/7 FLC 2 FAC 3+2/4 Others 5/2*

BAYLY Robert (Rob) Sean
Born: Dublin, 22 February 1988
Height: 5'8" **Weight:** 11.1
Rob, a Republic of Ireland youth international, penned a new extended Leeds' deal but injury restricted him to one appearance, in the 3-0 Carling Cup defeat at Portsmouth as a replacement for David Prutton. Leeds have high hopes for this central midfielder who enjoys a tackle and can make a pass.
Leeds U *(From trainee on 3/3/2006) FL 1 FLC 0+2*

James Beattie

BAYNES Wesley (Wes)

Born: Chester, 12 October 1988
Height: 5'11" **Weight:** 11.10
Wes was a shining light in Wrexham's darkest days. After progressing through the youth system, he was a regular in the reserves until the arrival of Brian Little, who made him a surprise inclusion against local rivals Chester at the end of November. The midfield player showed 'an old head on young shoulders', impressing enough to be kept in the struggling side for a further eight games before returning to the Pontins League. Little restored him for the last two games and Wrexham scored four in their final League game at Lincoln, some going considering the season's previous best was two. Wes scored with two stunning free kicks to highlight his promise. A direct, pacy player who makes things happen, he delivers quality crosses into dangerous areas.
Wrexham (From trainee on 30/7/2007) FL 10+2/2

BEAN Marcus Tristam

Born: Hammersmith, 2 November 1984
Height: 5'11" **Weight:** 11.6
Marcus is a promising Blackpool defender who gave valuable service to Rotherham during his loan spell in the early part of the season. Extremely versatile, he featured in midfield during his time at Millmoor, scoring a good goal in a victory over Mansfield. He would probably have stayed with the Millers but an injury crisis at Bloomfield Road forced his recall. Was out of contract in the summer and looking for a new club.
Queens Park Rgrs (From trainee on 29/7/2004) FL 44+23/2 FLC 2+1 FAC 2 Others 3+1
Swansea C (Loaned on 17/2/2005) FL 6+2
Swansea C (Loaned on 8/9/2005) FL 9/1
Blackpool (Free on 20/1/2006) FL 19+4/1 FLC 0+1 FAC 0+2 Others 1
Rotherham U (Loaned on 10/8/2007) FL 11+1/1 Others 2

BEARDSLEY Jason Clive

Born: Uttoxeter, 12 July 1989
Height: 6'0" **Weight:** 11.3
A product of the Derby Academy, Jason made a respectable debut at right-back in the Carling Cup against Blackpool. There was no chance of further experience in the competition as County lost on penalties. Jason went back to the reserves, who also struggled, and did not make the 16 again until he was an unused substitute against Fulham at the end of March. He awaits a League debut.
Derby Co (From trainee on 7/7/2007) FLC 1

BEATTIE Craig

Born: Glasgow, 16 January 1984
Height: 6'0" **Weight:** 11.7
Club Honours: SPD '04, '06, '07; SC '06, '07; Ch '08
International Honours: S: 7; U21-7
Signed from Celtic in the summer, Craig battled against injury throughout the campaign and even when fit he had the likes of Kevin Phillips, Ishmael Miller and Roman Bednar to contend with for a place in the West Bromwich attack. Netting only four goals, the best being a late winner against Leicester, he also struck the winner that knocked Bournemouth out of the Carling Cup. Because of his injury problems, Craig was left out of the Scotland squad by George Burley. He seemed to have set an unwanted record when he suffered a double hamstring tear after only 38 minutes of his Preston debut at Leicester, having joined them on loan in March. It represented the shortest post-war career for a Preston player starting a match, but he recovered more quickly than expected and returned to Deepdale, playing the last half-hour of the season.
Glasgow Celtic (From juniors at Glasgow Rgrs on 1/7/2003) SL 18+32/13 SLC 3+2/2 SC 0+4 Others 1+5/1
West Bromwich A (£1,250,000 + on 26/7/2007) FL 6+15/3 FLC 3/1 FAC 1+1
Preston NE (Loaned on 4/3/2008) FL 1+1

BEATTIE James Scott

Born: Lancaster, 27 February 1978
Height: 6'1" **Weight:** 12.0
International Honours: E: 5; U21-5
Brought to the club by new manager Bryan Robson on a four-year deal, James was Sheffield United's record signing and he had an excellent season. He scored the Blades' first goal of the season and went on to hit 21 more, six from the penalty spot, making him the club's highest League scorer since Tony Agana in 1988-89. James worked hard for the team, generally as a target-man. He played alongside Billy Sharp for much of the season, particularly after Kevin Blackwell's arrival, and was dangerous both with his feet and in the air. He was voted the supporters' 'Player of the Year' but missed the final two games through injury.
Blackburn Rov (From trainee on 7/3/1995) PL 1+3 FLC 2 FAC 0+1
Southampton (£1,000,000 on 17/7/1998) PL 161+43/68 FLC 11+3/6 FAC 14+1/2 Others 2
Everton (£6,000,000 on 5/1/2005) PL 51+25/13 FLC 2+1 FAC 4+1/1 Others 1+1/1
Sheffield U (£4,000,000 + on 9/8/2007) FL 36+3/22 FAC 2

BEAVAN George David

Born: Bexley, 12 January 1990
Height: 5'9" **Weight:** 12.2
The sale of Chris Coyne and the end of Jaroslaw Fojut's loan left Luton with a lack of height in the centre of defence. To remedy the situation, manager Mick Harford called on George, who was still a scholar. He made his debut as a substitute at Bournemouth, replacing Keith Keane, and on his first start, at home to Orient, kept former Hatter Adam Boyd at bay. George's season was ended by injury, although he returned in an end-of-season Legends game. His size and presence suggest a good future.
Luton T (Trainee) FL 1+1

BECKETT Luke John

Born: Sheffield, 25 November 1976
Height: 5'11" **Weight:** 11.6
Huddersfield's goal poacher enjoyed another fruitful season in the scoring stakes, always involved in the first-team plans. The experienced predator has a tremendous appetite to find the back of the net. He forages hard, is good in the air and shows a great touch, often punishing defenders before they realise there is danger. Luke enjoys playing up front with a partner he can feed off when chasing scoring opportunities. He was the regular penalty taker and scored in each of the first four rounds of the FA Cup, one against his former club Oldham, on his way to a respectable tally of 12 for the season.
Barnsley (From trainee on 20/6/1995)
Chester C (Free on 11/6/1998) FL 70+4/25 FLC 5/5 FAC 4/2 Others 1
Chesterfield (£75,000 on 19/7/2000) FL 58+4/22 FLC 4/2 FAC 3/2 Others 5
Stockport Co (£100,000 on 14/12/2001) FL 79+5/45 FLC 4/1 FAC 2/1 Others 1
Sheffield U (£50,000 on 15/11/2004) FL 1+4
Huddersfield T (Loaned on 14/1/2005) FL 7/6
Oldham Ath (Loaned on 18/3/2005) FL 9/6
Oldham Ath (Loaned on 14/7/2005) FL 27+7/18 FAC 1+2 Others 1
Huddersfield T (Signed on 6/7/2006) FL 57+20/23 FLC 2 FAC 3+3/4 Others 1

BECKFORD Jermaine Paul

Born: Ealing, 9 December 1983
Height: 6'2" **Weight:** 13.2
Club Honours: Div 1 '07
Hot-shot Jermaine enjoyed a superb first full season in Leeds' colours. He notched 20 League goals to become United's 'Player of the Season' and also earned a place in the PFA 'League One Select' team of the season. For good measure, his magnificent lob that sealed a 2-0 victory over Hartlepool was voted 'Goal of the Season' by Leeds' fans. An ankle injury

ruled him out of the last four League games, dashing his hopes of catching Swansea's Jason Scotland as the division's top scorer. He returned for the first play-off semi-final against Carlisle but the injury flared up again and he went off within an hour. However, he bounced back to feature in the second leg and in the final against Doncaster at Wembley. Fast and skilful, it was inevitable that his goals record should attract attention, with Crystal Palace and Derby believed to be among his admirers.

Leeds U (Signed from Wealdstone on 15/3/2006) FL 41+9/20 FLC 1+2 FAC 2 Others 3
Carlisle U (Loaned on 6/10/2006) FL 4/1 Others 1
Scunthorpe U (Loaned on 19/1/2007) FL 17+1/8

BECKWITH Dean Stuart
Born: Southwark, 18 September 1983
Height: 6'3" **Weight:** 13.4
Dean's commanding performances at centre-back in Hereford's promotion-winning side enhanced his reputation and made him vital to the Bulls in 2007-08. His calm reading of the game and ability to bring the ball out of defence before producing a telling pass were backed by a threat in opposing penalty areas that brought two goals at vital times. Dean was able to call up quickly with a number of defensive partners and only a fractured jaw, sustained at Chester, kept him out for any length of time. His importance to Hereford was acknowledged when he was declared runner-up in the 'Player of the Year' poll.

Gillingham (From trainee on 7/8/2003) FL 0+1 FAC 0+1
Hereford U (Free on 14/7/2005) FL 70/2 FLC 4 FAC 8 Others 2

BECKWITH Robert (Rob)
Born: Hackney, 12 September 1984
Height: 6'2" **Weight:** 13.5
After being freed by Luton in the 2006 close season and having a spell out of the game to recover from injuries, Rob returned to the League with Barnet after a successful pre-season trial. Before that, the goalkeeper spent time at non-League Hitchin. Rob had to wait until New Year's Day to make his Barnet debut but, following a number of impressive performances during Lee Harrison's absence through injury, he played a big part in the second half of the Bees' campaign.

Luton T (From trainee on 1/7/2004) FL 17 FLC 2 (Freed during 2006 close season)
Chesterfield (Loaned on 17/3/2006) FL 2
Barnet (Free from Hitchin T on 9/8/2007) FL 9 FAC 2

BEDNAR Roman
Born: Prague, Czech Republic, 26 March 1983
Height: 6'4" **Weight:** 13.2
Club Honours: Ch '08
International Honours: Czech Republic: 1; U21
Signed on loan from Heart of Midlothian, Roman had a superb season for West Bromwich, scoring 17 goals. A strong, powerful, striker, he partnered both Kevin Phillips and Ishmael Miller in the Baggies' attack and always looked the part, an honest battler who scored important goals. Indeed, he netted seven times in seven games in November and December, his efforts throughout the campaign acknowledged by the appreciative Hawthorns crowd and his manager, who could not praise Roman highly enough for his tremendous workrate.

Heart of Midlothian (Signed from FB Kaunas, Lithuania, ex Bohemians Prague, Mlada Boleslav, on 27/7/2005) SL 33+7/11 SLC 1 SC 1+3/1 Others 4+1/1
West Bromwich A (Loaned on 31/8/2007) FL 18+11/13 FAC 5/4

BEEVERS Lee Jonathan
Born: Doncaster, 4 December 1983
Height: 6'1" **Weight:** 12.10
International Honours: W: U21-7; Yth
With the exception of a dislocated shoulder that forced him to miss two months of the season, the versatile defender was a regular in the Lincoln back line and although scoring only one goal, he continued to be a threat at set pieces. Always one to give of his best, the former Welsh under-21 international produced a number of consistent and disciplined performances as the Imps recovered from a poor start to finish in mid-table under Peter Jackson.

Ipswich T (From trainee on 19/3/2001)
Boston U (Free on 27/3/2003) FL 71+1/3 FLC 2/1 FAC 5 Others 3/1
Lincoln C (Signed on 21/2/2005) FL 111+11/7 FLC 3/2 FAC 3 Others 7+2

BEEVERS Mark Geoffrey
Born: Barnsley, 21 November 1989
Height: 6'4" **Weight:** 12.9
International Honours: E: Yth
This fine young central defender stepped up from the Owls' Academy last season to become an established first-team player. Tall and commanding, Mark is resolute and has an unflappable presence in the heart of the defence. He scored his first Sheffield Wednesday goal in the FA Cup at Derby and has a bright future. Mark was tied up on a four-year contract to try and ward off Premiership

interest and won the National Football League Award for 'Best Apprentice of the Year'.

Sheffield Wed (From trainee on 1/12/2006) FL 28+2 FAC 2/1

BEGOVIC Asmir
Born: Trebinje, Herzegovina, 20 June 1987
Height: 6'5" **Weight:** 15.0
As Portsmouth's third-choice goalkeeper behind David James and Jamie Ashdown last season, Asmir made no appearances but played on loan for Bournemouth and Yeovil. The giant 'keeper played in Bournemouth's first nine games and showed what an excellent shot-stopper he is but lost his place after a series of errors and returned early to Pompey. Going on loan to Yeovil towards the end of March, Asmir kept a clean sheet on his debut but after one more game, Harry Redknapp took him back to Fratton Park when Ashdown was injured. While standing by for Ashdown or the injured James, Asmir was an unused substitute in 14 Premier League games and two FA Cup ties. The Canadian of Bosnian descent is considered to be an exceptional talent with a bright future and, already an under-20 cap, he was given further international recognition when called into the Canadian squad for the friendly against Iceland in August.

Portsmouth (From juniors on 19/10/2006)
Macclesfield T (Loaned on 23/11/2006) 2+1 FAC 1
Bournemouth (Loaned on 10/8/2007) FL 8 Others 1
Yeovil T (Loaned on 27/3/2008) FL 2

BELFORD Cameron Dale
Born: Nuneaton, 16 October 1988
Height: 5'11" **Weight:** 12.10
Having been freed by Coventry, the young goalkeeper was snapped up by former Bury boss Chris Casper at the start of the season as a free agent. Cameron did not feature for the Shakers until the final game of the season, when he came off the bench to make a 30-minute appearance, including a good save low to his left.

Bury (From trainee at Coventry C on 18/8/2007) FL 0+1

BELL David Anthony
Born: Wellingborough, 21 April 1984
Height: 5'10" **Weight:** 11.6
Club Honours: Div 3 '03
International Honours: RoI: U21-2; Yth
The influx of new players meant there was no immediate start at Luton in 2007-08 for David, a consistent performer in the previous season. Recalled for the home game against Gillingham,

he responded by scoring after only 16 minutes and playing a major part in setting up the other two goals. Back to his best form in the centre or on the right of midfield, David continued to find goals, including the winner against Nottingham Forest. He formed a useful partnership with David Edwards that almost caused an upset in the third round of the FA Cup at home to Liverpool but the sale of Edwards and Luton's problems after going into administration seemed to affect his performances, especially when a proposed move to West Bromwich fell through. Instead, David was a last-gasp deadline day loan signing for Leicester in March, with an agreement to make the deal permanent during the summer. He was thrust into a debut in the crucial clash against Scunthorpe without even having met his new team-mates but soon settled into his wide midfield role and looked capable of delivering the sort of crosses that the strikers had been crying out for most of the season.

Rushden & Diamonds (From juniors on 24/7/2001) FL 109+13/10 FLC 4 FAC 5+3 Others 3+2

Luton T (£100,000 on 12/1/2006) FL 62+13/7 FLC 6/1 FAC 7 Others 1

Leicester C (Loaned on 27/3/2008) FL 6

BELL James (Jay)

Born: Liverpool, 24 November 1989
Height: 6'0" **Weight:** 12.0
Jay is a young Accrington defender, in his second year as a scholar and the son of the club's assistant manager. He made his first-team debut at right-back in April at Wrexham, after being an unused substitute several times. In the last two seasons he played regularly for the youth and reserve sides and went to Prescot Cables on work experience. His progress was rewarded by an offer of professional terms for next season.

Accrington Stanley (Trainee) FL 2

BELL Lee

Born: Alsager, 26 January 1983
Height: 5'10" **Weight:** 11.10
A summer signing from Crewe, Lee staked his claim for a place in Mansfield's midfield during the pre-season games. He was sent off against Stockport and was subsequently suspended for three matches. After this he improved all the time and by mid-season was an invaluable asset to the side until suffering a knee injury at the beginning of December and being ruled out for six weeks. He injured his other knee at Darlington in February and was sidelined until the last game of the season when he returned, although obviously not fully fit and lacking

match practice. Out of contract in the summer, Lee was reported to be joining Macclesfield.

Crewe Alex (From trainee on 6/2/2001) FL 34+20/3 FLC 0+1 FAC 1+3 Others 1+3 (Signed for Burton A on 31/1/2007)

Mansfield T (Free on 7/8/2007) FL 23/1 FLC 1 FAC 3+1

BELLAMY Craig Douglas

Born: Cardiff, 13 July 1979
Height: 5'9" **Weight:** 10.12
Club Honours: CS '06
International Honours: W: 51; U21-8; Yth; Sch
West Ham paid Liverpool a club record fee for the services of the Welsh international who has searing pace and can score goals. He made an impressive start to his Hammers' career when scoring twice in the Carling Cup against Bristol Rovers and hit another at Reading a few days later. After he limped off against Middlesbrough in September, his season went from bad to worse. There were a series of operations for abdominal problems and, after a complete rest, he was able to go on as a substitute at Wigan in February. Following that brief appearance, he again faced an abdominal strengthening operation, followed by minor knee surgery, and did not take part in any further games. He added to his total of Welsh caps before injury struck.

Norwich C (From trainee on 20/1/1997) FL 71+13/32 FLC 6/2 FAC 1

Coventry C (£6,500,000 on 17/8/2000) PL 33+1/6 FLC 3/1 FAC 2/1

Newcastle U (£6,000,000 on 11/7/2001) PL 87+6/27 FLC 3+2/4 FAC 5 Others 24+1/11

Glasgow Celtic (Loaned on 31/1/2005) SL 12/7 SC 3/2

Blackburn Rov (£5,000,000 on 16/6/2005) PL 22+5/13 FLC 3+1/2 FAC 1/2

Liverpool (£6,000,000 on 7/7/2006) PL 23+4/7 FLC 2 Others 8+5/2

West Ham U (£7,500,000 on 10/7/2007) PL 7+1/2 FLC 1/2

BELLETTI Juliano Haus

Born: Cascavel, Brazil, 20 June 1976
Height: 5'9" **Weight:** 10.12
International Honours: Brazil: 23
In yet another attempt to solve the problem right-back position, Chelsea swooped for the Brazilian international from Barcelona in August. He describes himself as a typical Brazilian full-back who loves to get forward and he came to England with a reputation as a goalscorer after his winner for Barcelona against Arsenal in the 2006 Champions' League final. It did not take him long to show this quality in the Premier League. In his eighth match, at Wigan, he slammed

home a long-range rocket shot that gave the 'keeper no chance and later he repeated the dose with a carbon copy against Tottenham. He seemed to have made the position his own, until Paulo Ferreira reclaimed it, and subsequently signed a new five-year deal. Shortly before the Champions' League final, Chelsea made a hefty investment in yet another right-back, Jose Bosingwa from Porto. Undaunted, Juliano came off the bench shortly before the end of the Champions' League final and calmly rolled home his kick in the penalty shoot-out.

Chelsea (£3,700,000 from Barcelona, Spain, ex Cruizeiro, Sao Paulo, Atletico Mineiro - loan, Villareal, on 24/8/2007) PL 20+3/2 FLC 6 FAC 2 Others 4+3

BENAYOUN Yossi Shai

Born: Beersheba, Israel, 5 May 1980
Height: 5'10" **Weight:** 11.0
International Honours: Israel: 64
The Israeli international midfielder was a summer signing by Liverpool manager Rafa Benitez from West Ham United and a surprise because it was unclear where Yossi would fit in. At West Ham he was deployed as an attacking central midfielder or a playmaker behind a lone striker, but with other contenders for those roles at Liverpool he had to bide his time. Eventually Benitez decided to play him on the right flank in competition with Jermaine Pennant but later in the campaign he also played on the left. Although involved in 47 games, 21 were as substitute as Benitez alternated him with Ryan Babel, Jermaine Pennant and, later in the season, Dirk Kuyt in his perpetual rotation system. His first Liverpool goal was a wonderful solo effort in the Carling Cup at Reading in September followed, a few days later, by one in the Premiership at Wigan, another stunning shot that proved to be the winner. His total of 11 goals included two hat tricks, one in the 8-0 rout of Besiktas in the Champions' League and the other in the FA Cup fourth round against Havant & Waterlooville that saved the Reds from the biggest humiliation in their history, coming back from a 2-1 deficit against a mid-table non-League team playing five levels below them. A surprise selection for the second leg of the Champions' League semi-final at Chelsea, he had a quiet game until, midway through the second half, he set up Liverpool's equaliser, a precious away goal, with a darting run from the right into the heart of the Chelsea defence before a short pass released Fernando Torres to score. Yossi is a very useful squad player with the ability to carry the ball and create opportunities from

Yossi Benayoun

innocuous positions but perhaps lacks the consistency to be an automatic selection.
West Ham U *(£2,500,000 from Racing Santander, Spain on 27/7/2005) PL 55+8/8 FAC 7 Others 1+1*
Liverpool *(£5,000,000 on 20/7/2007) PL 15+15/4 FLC 1+2/1 FAC 3/3 Others 7+4/3*

BENCHERIF Hamza
Born: France, 2 February 1988
Height: 5'9" **Weight:** 12.3
International Honours: Algeria: U20
Still at the learning stage, the young Nottingham Forest central defender went out on loan to Lincoln in October,

spending three months with the Imps prior to the New Year and a return to the City Ground. Described by John Deehan as a player he had been tracking for over a year, City's Director of Football went on to say that Hamza would provide solid competition for an under-performing back line. Big and strong with plenty of potential, the Algerian under-20 international will be looking for further opportunities in 2008-09.
Nottingham F *(Signed from Guingamp, France on 16/11/2006)*
Lincoln C *(Loaned on 2/10/2007) FL 11+1/1 Others 1*

BENDTNER Nicklas
Born: Copenhagen, Denmark, 16 January 1988
Height: 6'2" **Weight:** 13.0
International Honours: Denmark:18; U21-4; Yth
The Danish international returned to Arsenal after enhancing a growing reputation in his year-long loan at Birmingham during the previous season. He could not be accused of lacking confidence and his ability, while still needing to be honed, promises goals both in the air and on the ground. His first Premier League goal was memorable,

headed in with his first touch after arriving as a substitute to win the North London derby 2-1. Nicklas scored in all four competitions, including five in his 27 Premier League appearances, two in the Champions' League and one each in the FA Cup and Carling Cup.
Arsenal *(From trainee on 1/12/2005)* PL 7+20/5 FLC 5+3/1 FAC 2/1 Others 3+3/2
Birmingham C *(Loaned on 4/8/2006)* FL 38+4/11 FLC 0+4/2 FAC 1+1

BEN HAIM Tal

Born: Rishon Le Zion, Israel, 31 March 1982
Height: 5'11" **Weight:** 11.9
International Honours: Israel: 40; U21: Yth
Five months after their initial approach, Chelsea finally got their man when the Israeli centre-back joined them in July as a free agent after his Bolton contract expired. Jose Mourinho saw Tal as the perfect utility central defender who could do a job as he sought to avoid the previous season's situation when Chelsea took the field without a recognised centre-back. Tal figured prominently in the season's first quarter as he filled-in for either Ricardo Carvalho or John Terry and showed the qualities that make him such a well-respected player. Two circumstances conspired against the classy Israeli and seemed to send his Chelsea career into a cul-de-sac. First, the impressive Brazilian Alex arrived at Stamford Bridge to supersede Tal as first replacement and then Mourinho was replaced as boss by Tal's compatriot Avram Grant, who did not seem impressed by the ex-Bolton man. His last appearance was against Everton in January and he became one of several forgotten men with question marks hanging over his Chelsea future.
Bolton W *(Signed from Maccabi Tel Aviv, Israel on 30/7/2004)* PL 81+7/1 FLC 6 FAC 9 Others 7
Chelsea *(Free on 1/7/2007)* PL 10+3 FLC 3+2 FAC 2 Others 2+1

BENJAMIN Trevor Junior

Born: Kettering, 8 February 1979
Height: 6'2" **Weight:** 13.2
International Honours: Jamaica: 2; E: U21-1
The powerful striker made a big contribution to Hereford's excellent start in 2007-08 with a crop of early goals after arriving from Peterborough in the summer. Trevor's massive physical presence provided an excellent contrast to the pacy, young players around him and they benefited from his ability to hold the ball and bring others into play.

A minor knee injury early in the New Year cost Trevor his place. He was then used mainly as a substitute before a prolonged eye infection meant another spell on the sidelines, followed by later appearances in Edgar Davids-style goggles. Was released in the summer.
Cambridge U *(From trainee on 21/2/1997)* FL 96+27/35 FLC 7+3/4 FAC 9+1/5 Others 3/2
Leicester C *(£1,000,000 + on 14/7/2000)* P/FL 33+48/11 FLC 2+3/1 FAC 2+3
Crystal Palace *(Loaned on 20/12/2001)* FL 5+1/1
Norwich C *(Loaned on 8/2/2002)* FL 3+3
West Bromwich A *(Loaned on 27/3/2002)* FL 0+3/1
Gillingham *(Loaned on 20/9/2003)* FL 1+3/1
Rushden & Diamonds *(Loaned on 14/11/2003)* FL 5+1/1
Brighton & Hove A *(Loaned on 16/1/2004)* FL 10/5
Northampton T *(Free on 31/12/2004)* FL 5/2 FAC 1
Coventry C *(Signed on 16/2/2005)* FL 6+6/1
Peterborough U *(Free on 8/7/2005)* FL 20+27/8 FLC 2+1/2 FAC 1+4 Others 3/1
Watford *(Loaned on 21/9/2005)* FL 2
Swindon T *(Loaned on 30/1/2006)* FL 5+3/2
Boston U *(Loaned on 9/2/2007)* FL 2+1
Walsall *(Loaned on 22/3/2007)* FL 8/2
Hereford U *(Free on 7/8/2007)* FL 15+19/10 FLC 2 FAC 6/1 Others 1

[BENJANI] MWARUWARI Benjani

Born: Bulawayo, Zimbabwe, 13 August 1978
Height: 6'2" **Weight:** 12.3
International Honours: Zimbabwe: 33
Benjani continued to show all his usual strengths and qualities for Portsmouth in 2007-08. His high workrate and jinking runs that unsettled defences endeared him to the fans, particularly with his hugely sunny disposition, while his performances earned him numerous 'Man of the Match' awards and 12 goals kept him as Pompey's leading scorer. He scored two hat-tricks, one in the 7-4 defeat of Reading that was a record aggregate for the Premier League. It was also the first hat-trick by a Pompey player for three years in a team performance rated by many as their finest ever. To the disappointment of his many fans and his own evident dismay, he was transferred to Manchester City in the January transfer window in a deal necessary to fund another acquisition. Benjani wasted no time in earning hero status among City supporters. On his first start following his move from Portsmouth, he glanced in a goal in the famous 2-1 victory over Manchester United, further silencing the Old Trafford crowd, and when Portsmouth visited the City of Manchester Stadium he ran their defenders ragged

and scored an excellent goal. Everybody wanted to cheer.
Portsmouth *(£4,100,000 from Auxerre, France on 13/1/2006)* PL 62+8/19 FLC 3+1 FAC 2+1
Manchester C *(£8,000,000 on 31/1/2008)* PL 13/3

BENNETT Alan John

Born: Cork, 4 October 1981
Height: 6'2" **Weight:** 12.8
International Honours: RoI: 2; B-1
With no first-team experience in English League football, the Republic of Ireland international was whipped into Southampton from Reading on loan for the start of last season when George Burley found himself without a fit centre-back. Alan was given a disproportionate amount of flack from some fans following the ensuing debacle, in which Saints lost 4–1 at home to Crystal Palace, and not until October did he have another start at St Mary's. Playing alongside a bona fide centre-back, he proved to be a hardy and accomplished defender, quickly winning over his detractors. His return to the Madejski Stadium was widely regarded as regrettable. The solid centre-half joined Brentford on another loan for the last two months of the season. Good in the air, with impressive positional sense, he scored a cracking goal against Bradford in April.
Reading *(Signed from Cork C, ex Richmond, on 30/1/2007)*
Southampton *(Loaned on 1/8/2007)* FL 10 FLC 1
Brentford *(Loaned on 7/3/2008)* FL 11/1

BENNETT Elliott

Born: Telford, 18 December 1988
Height: 5'9" **Weight:** 10.12
The promising right-sided midfielder was given two opportunities in the Carling Cup by Wolverhampton last season and, despite spending time away from Molineux, was their 'Young Player of the Season'. In his first loan spell, Elliott spent three months at Crewe and occupied several positions in the front line, scoring the winner against Port Vale in November. On becoming Chris Brass' only signing in his short spell as Bury's caretaker manager, Elliott had much to do if he was to turn their fortunes around. He succeeded in the challenge and, showing pace and skill on the right, could change a game in seconds. Bury were glad to have a player whose effectiveness is matched by style and delighted when his loan was extended to the penultimate game. That gave him time to grab a goal against Macclesfield in April.
Wolverhampton W *(From trainee on*

2/3/2007) FLC 2
***Crewe Alex** (Loaned on 26/10/2007) FL
4+5/1 FAC 0+2*
***Bury** (Loaned on 31/1/2008) FL 18+1/1*

BENNETT Ian Michael
Born: Worksop, 10 October 1971
Height: 6'0" **Weight:** 12.10
Club Honours: Div 2 '95; AMC '95
Ian was second-choice Sheffield United
'keeper behind Paddy Kenny but had
his chance in October when Kenny
was injured. He produced very good
performances, being a fine shot-stopper
as well as commanding his area, and
kept his place even when Kenny was fit.
Unfortunately an injury in training meant
he had to step down again and Ian made
only one further appearance, in April,
before being released in the summer.
***Newcastle U** (From trainee at Queens Park R
on 20/3/1989)*
***Peterborough U** (Free on 22/3/1991) FL 72
FLC 10 FAC 3 Others 4*
***Birmingham C** (£325,000 on 17/12/1993)
P/FL 285+2 FLC 38 FAC 16 Others 13*
***Sheffield U** (Loaned on 9/12/2004) FL 5*
***Coventry C** (Loaned on 17/2/2005) FL 6*
***Leeds U** (Free on 4/7/2005) FL 4*
***Sheffield U** (£100,000 on 27/7/2006) P/FL
8+1 FLC 3*

BENNETT Julian Llewellyn
Born: Nottingham, 17 December 1984
Height: 6'0" **Weight:** 12.7
Julian can look back on the season with
particular relish, especially as the left-
back was overlooked towards the end of
the previous campaign. His Nottingham
Forest prospects seemed even bleaker
after the arrival of Matt Lockwood in the
summer but Julian regained his place
after Matt's opening-day injury and never
looked back. The tough, uncompromising
defender also likes to press forward in his
rampaging style. Julian's season ended
with him being named in the PFA's League
One select team as well as being voted
Forest's 'Player of the Year'.
***Walsall** (From trainee on 2/7/2004) FL
47+4/3 FLC 1 FAC 4 Others 5/1*
***Nottingham F** (Signed on 10/1/2006) FL
75+7/8 FLC 2 FAC 5 Others 4+1*

BENNETT Ryan
Born: Grays, 6 March 1990
Height: 6'2" **Weight:** 11.0
International Honours: E: Yth
An excellent season for Ryan began on
the opening day with his first senior goal
for Grimsby in a 1-1 draw against Notts
County. The teenager proved a valuable
squad member for the Mariners, showing
confidence and good distribution from
either right-back or central defence, also
adding a dangerous long throw to his

game. Still eligible for Town's FA Youth
Cup defeat by Tranmere, Ryan made his
England under-18 debut against Austria
after earlier being on standby for the
Ghana game. Disappointment at being
an unused substitute in the Johnstone's
Paint Trophy final was tempered by being
voted the Nivea for Men 'League Two
Apprentice of the Year' at the Football
League awards.
***Grimsby T** (From trainee on 18/4/2007) FL
31+14/1 FLC 1 FAC 3 Others 4*

BENSON Paul Andrew
Born: Southend-on-Sea, 12 October
1979
Height: 6'2" **Weight:** 12.7
Club Honours: FC '07
International Honours: E: SP-1
Having won the Conference 'Golden
Boot' award the previous season, the
Dagenham striker missed the first few
games with a knee injury. He marked his
first appearance in the League with the
winner against Lincoln but was troubled
by injury throughout the campaign and
lost two teeth in the Boxing Day game
at Barnet, prior to cracking a leg bone in
training the week after. Paul finished on a
high, scoring the goal at Darlington that
secured Daggers' League status.
***Dagenham & Redbridge** (Free from White
Ensign on 26/5/2005) FL 19+3/6 FAC 2/3
Others 2*

BENT Darren Ashley
Born: Wandsworth, 6 February 1984
Height: 5'11" **Weight:** 11.7
International Honours: E: 3; U21-14;
Yth
Tottenham paid a massive fee for Darren
from Charlton last summer and the tag
was always likely to be a heavy burden,
through no fault of the player. He had
to compete for the right to play, with
three top-class strikers at White Hart Lane
in Dimitar Berbatov, Robbie Keane and
Jermain Defoe. Darren was in fact the
first striker to score, against Derby in the
third game of the campaign, and he went
on to hit eight in 15 starts and 21 games
as a substitute. An unused substitute
for the Carling Cup final, his most vital
goal was at home against Aalborg in the
UEFA Cup, the winner as Spurs recovered
from 2-0 down. Darren likes the ball to
be delivered over the top of the defence,
so that he can use his pace. Despite the
difficult times at club level, Darren won
England recognition when coming off the
bench against Croatia.
***Ipswich T** (From trainee on 2/7/2001) P/FL
103+19/49 FLC 6+1/3 FAC 2+2/3 Others
5+4/2*
***Charlton Ath** (£2,500,000 on 3/6/2005) PL

68/31 FLC 4+2/4 FAC 5/2
***Tottenham H** (£16,500,000 on 29/6/2007)
PL 11+16/6 FLC 0+1 Others 4+4/2*

BENT Marcus Nathan
Born: Hammersmith, 19 May 1978
Height: 6'2" **Weight:** 12.4
International Honours: E: U21-2
Marcus began the season as Charlton's
main target-man, scoring on the opening
day, but after starting the first four games
was surprisingly loaned to Wigan for the
remainder of the season in an attempt to
cut the wage bill after relegation from the
Premiership. Big and strong, he is good
in the air, his workrate is excellent and
he can play in midfield when required.
Marcus made his Wigan debut as a
substitute at Newcastle and scored in
his first start at Reading, heading in a
Jason Koumas corner. He uses his pace
to run on to passes played round or over
the defence and finished the season as
Wigan's top scorer with seven Premiership
goals, including two at Birmingham.
Forming an effective partnership with
Emile Heskey, Marcus became only the
second Wigan player to score a hat-
trick in the Premier League, his first
three-goal return, in the home win over
Blackburn, one of his previous clubs. He
was expected to leave Charlton in the
summer.

Marcus Bent

Brentford *(From trainee on 21/7/1995) FL 56+14/8 FLC 7/1 FAC 8/3 Others 5+1/1*
Crystal Palace *(£150,000 + on 8/1/1998) P/FL 13+15/5 FLC 0+2 FAC 0+1*
Port Vale *(£375,000 on 15/1/1999) FL 17+6/1 FLC 1*
Sheffield U *(£300,000 on 28/10/1999) FL 48/20 FLC 5/3 FAC 3/1*
Blackburn Rov *(£1,300,000 + on 24/11/2000) P/FL 22+15/8 FLC 0+1 FAC 5+1/3*
Ipswich T *(£3,000,000 on 23/11/2001) P/FL 51+10/21 FLC 0+2 FAC 4/1 Others 2+1/1*
Leicester C *(Loaned on 1/9/2003) PL 28+5/9 FAC 2/1*
Everton *(£450,000 on 8/7/2004) PL 38+17/7 FLC 1+2/1 FAC 3+1 Others 2+2*
Charlton Ath *(£2,000,000 on 17/11/2006) P/FL 32+14/4 FLC 5/1 FAC 1*
Wigan Ath *(Loaned on 31/8/2007) PL 25+6/7 FAC 1*

BENTHAM Craig Martin
Born: Bingley, 7 March 1985
Height: 5'9" **Weight:** 11.6
Craig is happy to play the holding midfield role in front of the back four. Used sparingly by Bradford he enjoyed a three-month loan spell in the Blue Square Premier with Farsley Celtic before returning in April when he made a surprise reappearance in City's draw at Brentford. Was released in the summer.
Bradford C *(From trainee on 4/8/2004) FL 18+12 FAC 0+2 Others 1*

BENTLEY David Michael
Born: Peterborough, 27 August 1984
Height: 5'10" **Weight:** 11.0
International Honours: E: 6; B-1; U21-8; Yth
David's status in the game increased as he became an England international and a much coveted transfer target. His skills are often sublime. He is perhaps the best crosser from the right since David Beckham and his natural mastery of the ball enables him to retain possession. David is also developing the skill to thread telling passes through defences. Often moved around according to circumstances, he is best out wide on the right but his ability to dictate the tempo of the game frequently saw him switched inside. Perhaps the most surprising moment of the season was when he headed a goal for Blackburn against Bolton. Few could have predicted that.
Arsenal *(From trainee on 8/9/2001) PL 1 FLC 4 FAC 0+3/1 Others 0+1*
Norwich C *(Loaned on 28/6/2004) PL 22+4/2 FLC 0+1 FAC 1*
Blackburn Rov *(Signed on 31/8/2005) PL 96+6/13 FLC 9/2 FAC 8/2 Others 14/4*

BENTLEY James (Jim) Graham
Born: Liverpool, 11 June 1976
Height: 6'1" **Weight:** 13.0
As the club captain and proverbial rock at the heart of Morecambe's defence, Jim had been one of the best players in the non-League game. Finally given the chance to play at a higher level, he showed why he should have been grabbed by a League club years ago. An inspirational leader who always gives 100 per cent, Jim formed a good partnership with Dave Artell and scored some vital goals, seven in all, including one in the Carling Cup victory over Preston at the start of the season. Rarely beaten in the air, his strength served him well and he missed only a couple of games.
Morecambe *(Free from Telford U on 31/5/2002) FL 43/6 FLC 3/1 FAC 1 Others 2*

BENTLEY Mark James
Born: Hertford, 7 January 1978
Height: 6'2" **Weight:** 13.0
Club Honours: Div 1 '06
Although Mark did not have the same impact as in the previous season, he was still an important member of the Gillingham midfield and when he was absent, through injuries or suspensions, his unselfish attitude and good work in the air were missed. At his best, he holds up the ball well and is always a threat at set pieces.
Southend U *(Signed from Dagenham & Redbridge on 15/11/2004) FL 70+23/12 FLC 1+1 FAC 0+1 Others 10+1/1*
Gillingham *(Free on 1/8/2006) FL 73+1/6 FLC 2 FAC 3/2 Others 2+1/1*

BERBATOV Dimitar Ivan
Born: Blagoevgrad, Bulgaria, 30 January 1981
Height: 6'2" **Weight:** 12.6
Club Honours: FLC '08
International Honours: Bulgaria: 65
The Bulgarian international striker had another great season at Tottenham. Dimitar was equal top-scorer with Robbie Keane, hitting 15 Premier League goals and 23 in total. He continues to win the acclaim of pundits and fans and is inevitably a constant subject of transfer speculation. Despite his ability in front of goal, one of his best performances was in a game in which he did not score. Tottenham had a player sent off at Manchester City in the Carling Cup and sacrificed his fellow striker. That meant that Dimitar had to play alone up front and he had everything to do with Tottenham's 2-0 win that put them through to the semi-final of the competition they went on to win. In the final, Dimitar was ultra-cool when he

scored from the penalty spot to put Spurs level. He scored four times in the 6-4 League win over Reading and continued to demonstrate class in ball-winning, holding and passing. Dimitar played seven times for Bulgaria last season, scoring three times.
Tottenham H *(£10,900,000 from Bayer Leverkusen, Germany, ex CSKA Sofia, on 12/7/2006) PL 63+6/27 FLC 7+2/2 FAC 6+1/5 Others 15+1/12*

BERESFORD Marlon
Born: Lincoln, 2 September 1969
Height: 6'1" **Weight:** 13.6
Club Honours: Div 1 '05
This veteran goalkeeper found his opportunities increasingly restricted at Luton after the appointment of Kevin Blackwell. Following an injury to Mark Crossley, Marlon joined Oldham – the 12th club of his professional career – on loan in October and enjoyed an excellent debut in the 1-1 draw at Huddersfield. He stayed at Boundary Park for a month, demonstrating his vast experience and trademark composure between the sticks.
Sheffield Wed *(From trainee on 23/9/1987)*
Bury *(Loaned on 25/8/1989) FL 1*
Northampton T *(Loaned on 27/9/1990) FL 13 Others 2*
Crewe Alex *(Loaned on 28/2/1991) FL 3*
Northampton T *(Loaned on 15/8/1991) FL 15*
Burnley *(£95,000 on 28/8/1992) FL 240 FLC 18 FAC 20 Others 16*
Middlesbrough *(£500,000 on 10/3/1998) P/FL 8+2 FLC 3*
Sheffield Wed *(Loaned on 12/11/2000) FL 4*
Burnley *(Free on 31/11/2002) FL 13*
York C *(Free on 5/8/2002) FL 6*
Burnley *(Free on 10/10/2002) FL 33+1 FLC 4 FAC 5*
Bradford C *(Free on 15/9/2003) FL 5*
Luton T *(Free on 24/10/2003) FL 11 FAC 5 Others 1*
Barnsley *(Free on 26/1/2004) FL 14*
Luton T *(Signed on 5/7/2004) FL 105 FLC 5 FAC 5*
Oldham Ath *(Loaned on 18/10/2007) FL 5 Others 1*

BERGER Patrik
Born: Prague, Czech Republic, 10 November 1973
Height: 6'1" **Weight:** 12.6
Club Honours: FAC '01; UEFAC '01; CS '01
International Honours: Czech Republic: 44; Czechoslovakia: 2; Yth
Even with a new 12-month contract, Patrik's opportunities were limited at Aston Villa and he made only nine appearances as a substitute. He is a talented and strong competitor with

David Bentley

a tremendous shot, a real threat from dead-ball situations. He has scored his fair share of goals since he arrived in England in 1996 but did not endear himself to Martin O'Neill by stating it would be in Gareth Barry's best interest to move. The manager clamped down on that and he was released during the summer.

Liverpool *(£3,250,000 from Borussia Dortmund, Germany, ex Slavia Prague, on 15/8/1996) PL 106+42/28 FLC 9+2/3 FAC 4+4 Others 17+12/4*
Portsmouth *(Free on 12/7/2003) PL 50+2/8 FLC 3+2 FAC 3*
Aston Villa *(Free on 6/7/2005) PL 8+21/2 FLC 1+2*
Stoke C *(Loaned on 23/11/2006) FL 1+6*

BERNER Bruno George
Born: Zurich, Switzerland, 21 November 1977
Height: 6'1" **Weight:** 12.11
International Honours: Switzerland: 16; U21; Yth
The Blackburn left-back broke a metatarsal in pre-season but made a good recovery to be back for the Carling Cup-tie at Portsmouth at the end of October. Used only sparingly he had a hard time coping at Premiership level and appears to have fallen behind young Martin Olsson. Able to play at wing-back or in midfield, Bruno is a natural athlete with a great left foot. Was out of contract in the summer and looking for a new club.
Blackburn Rov *(Signed from FC Basle, Switzerland, ex Grasshoppers Zurich, Real Oviedo, SC Freiburg, on 31/1/2007) PL 3 FLC 1 FAC 2*

BERRETT James Trevor
Born: Halifax, 13 January 1989
Height: 5'10" **Weight:** 11.13
International Honours: RoI: Yth
A first-year professional, James made his full debut for Huddersfield in the FA Cup victory over Premiership Birmingham with a strong and solid display from the centre of midfield. He shows great awareness both as a playmaker and an industrious holding midfielder and was rewarded with further experience, notably against Chelsea in the FA Cup and the derby win over Leeds. James collected further Republic of Ireland under-19 caps and scored his first League goal in the victory over Bristol Rovers. Only a training-ground injury kept him from first-team duties in the latter part of the season but he was recalled to the starting line-up and selected in the Irish under-21 squad for the Inter-Continental Cup in Malaysia.
Huddersfield T *(From trainee on 5/7/2007) FL 10+7/1 FAC 2*

BERTRAND Ryan Dominic
Born: Southwark, 5 August 1989
Height: 5'10" **Weight:** 11.0
International Honours: E: Yth
Ryan joined Oldham on loan from Chelsea last August and quickly showed all the attributes that mark him out as a highly-rated prospect. Quick, assured in the tackle and a quality distributor of the ball, the young left-back made 24 starts for the club before returning to Stamford Bridge in January. Just two days later, the England under-19 international was loaned out to Championship side Norwich, where he spent the second half of the season. Ryan's stylish displays won him a new army of admirers, while his pace and a real desire to go forward at every opportunity prompted Glenn Roeder to deploy him on the left of midfield on occasions.
Chelsea *(From trainee on 10/8/2006)*
Bournemouth *(Loaned on 3/11/2006) FL 5 FAC 2*
Oldham Ath *(Loaned on 21/8/2007) FL 21 FLC 1 Others 2*
Norwich C *(Loaned on 4/1/2008) FL 18 FAC 1+1*

BEST Leon Julian Brendan
Born: Nottingham, 19 September 1986
Height: 6'1" **Weight:** 13.3
International Honours: RoI: U21-1; Yth
Leon was signed by Coventry for a large fee, decided by tribunal, from Southampton in the summer but the first half of the season was frustrating for the tall striker because of a persistent groin injury. He scored on his first start, against Notts County, and hit his first League goal as a substitute at Crystal Palace in a 1-1 draw, Iain Dowie's first return to his old club. He was superb in the Carling Cup victory at Old Trafford and City fans saw his potential when he terrorised the West Bromwich defence and snatched two goals. Leon looked better alongside Michael Mifsud than Dele Adebola but his goal tally was disappointing. Strong rumours linked him to Nottingham Forest in January and City were reported to have turned down a £1-million bid. He was booed when he went on as a substitute against Millwall but all was forgotten a week later as he scored twice in his best performance of the season in the 4-0 win over Barnsley. Improved form won over fans and the new management and he worked hard as a sole striker in the last quarter of the season, winning the 'Young Player of the Season' award.
Southampton *(From trainee on 21/9/2004) P/FL 8+7/4 FLC 1+1 Others 1+1*
Queens Park Rgrs *(Loaned on 17/12/2004) FL 2+3*
Sheffield Wed *(Loaned on 4/8/2005) FL 2/1*

Sheffield Wed *(Loaned on 31/1/2006) FL 3+8/1*
Bournemouth *(Loaned on 4/8/2006) FL 12+3/3 FLC 1 Others 1*
Yeovil T *(Loaned on 23/11/2006) FL 14+1/10*
Coventry C *(Signed on 12/7/2007) FL 29+5/8 FLC 3/1 FAC 2+1*

BETSY Kevin Eddie Lewis
Born: Seychelles, 20 March 1978
Height: 6'1" **Weight:** 11.12
International Honours: E: SP-1
Kevin's only full appearance for Bristol City came early in the season, in a 3-0 success at Brentford in the Carling Cup before the wide midfield player or striker was seen to better advantage on loans to Yeovil and Walsall. Yeovil signed Kevin in October and, on the strength of his excellent performances, were keen to extend the loan man's stay. However, the former Wycombe man's wages meant that the Glovers could not afford to keep him and he scored against them in February when he made his home debut for Walsall after arriving in January. Kevin played regularly as a striker for Walsall in the last three months of the season and, at times, his thrusting forward play was just what Tommy Mooney needed in support up front but his final tally of two goals in 16 games was disappointing.
Fulham *(£80,000 + from Woking on 16/9/1998) P/FL 3+12/1 FLC 2+1 FAC 0+1 Others 1*
Bournemouth *(Loaned on 3/9/1999) FL 1+4*
Hull C *(Loaned on 26/11/1999) FL 1+1 Others 1*
Barnsley *(£200,000 on 28/2/2002) FL 84+10/15 FLC 2 FAC 6/1 Others 3*
Hartlepool U *(Loaned on 6/8/2004) FL 3+3/1 FLC 1*
Oldham Ath *(Free on 10/9/2004) FL 34+2/5 FAC 3 Others 5*
Wycombe W *(Free on 27/7/2005) FL 70+1/13 FLC 8 FAC 3 Others 7*
Bristol C *(£150,000 + on 29/1/2007) FL 16+2/1 FLC 1*
Yeovil T *(Loaned on 5/10/2007) FL 5/1 Others 1*
Walsall *(Loaned on 31/1/2008) FL 16/2*

BEVAN Scott Anthony
Born: Southampton, 16 September 1979
Height: 6'6" **Weight:** 15.10
Scott was signed by Shrewsbury in January from Kidderminster, where he was regarded as one of the best goalkeepers in the Blue Square Premier. He had to wait until Paul Simpson took over as manager for an April debut at Morecambe, where he played a significant part in securing a vital point. He subsequently made some important saves, especially in the 3-0 victory over Wrexham. Scott is confident, uses his

height to command the box and his kicking is quite a weapon.
Southampton (From trainee on 16/1/1998)
Huddersfield T (Loaned on 27/7/2002) FL 30 FLC 2 FAC 1 Others 1
Wycombe W (Loaned on 16/1/2004) FL 5
Wimbledon/MK Dons (Free on 12/3/2004) FL 17 FLC 1 Others 1 (Freed on 6/1/2006)
Shrewsbury T (Free from Kidderminster Hrs on 31/1/2008) FL 5

BEYE Habib
Born: Paris, France, 19 October 1977
Height: 5'11" **Weight:** 12.6
International Honours: Senegal: 35
Captain of Marseille before his summer transfer, Habib was a welcome addition to Newcastle's defence, primarily at right-back but with occasional outings at centre-back. He reads the game well, and his pace is a valuable asset, not only when defending but also in his frequent forays down the wing in support of his attack. Habib immediately made the first-team spot his own but his season was interrupted by a hamstring injury in January, followed by an enforced absence when playing for Senegal in the African Cup of Nations, after which he retired from international football to concentrate on his club career. Reinstated in the side on his return, Habib's continued fine form made him the club's 'Player of the Year'. His only goal was a near-post header to secure a win in the home game against Birmingham in December.
Newcastle U (£2,000,000 from Olympique Marseille, France, ex Paris St Germain, RS Strasbourg, on 31/8/2007) PL 27+2/1 FLC 1

BIALKOWSKI Bartosz
Born: Braniewo, Poland, 6 July 1987
Height: 6'4" **Weight:** 13.0
International Honours: Poland: U21
An outstanding prospect, who must sometimes wonder which deity he has offended as his progress at Southampton has been hindered by injuries ever since he arrived, Bartosz began last season as the first-choice goalkeeper. Unfortunate to have a couple of bad days behind a makeshift defence, he was then sidelined by a thumb injury that required surgery in late January which stopped him from reclaiming his place when Kelvin Davis was injured in March.
Southampton (Signed from Gornik Zabrze, Poland on 4/1/2006) FL 14 FLC 1 FAC 2 Others 1

BIANCHI Rolando
Born: Albano Sant'Alessandro, Italy, 15 February 1983
Height: 6'3" **Weight:** 11.12
International Honours: Italy: U21-13

Habib Beye

Signed from Reggina in the summer, Rolando made the perfect start to his Manchester City career when his delicate finish put City into an early lead in the opening day win over West Ham at Upton Park. He followed this with an excellent performance against Bristol City in the Carling Cup, including a cracking long-range goal that gave the Blues victory. Despite being a fans' favourite, speculation about a return to Italy was never far away and Lazio took the striker back to Serie A in the January transfer window. His debut as a substitute against Torino lasted only five minutes, enough time for him to collect two yellow cards.
Manchester C (£8,800,000 from Reggina, Italy, ex Atalanta, Cagliari - loan, on 19/7/2007) PL 7+12/4 FLC 3/1 FAC 0+2

BIGNOT Marcus
Born: Birmingham, 22 August 1974
Height: 5'10" **Weight:** 11.2
Club Honours: Div 3 '03
International Honours: E: SP-1

Marcus found his opportunities limited with Queens Park Rangers last season, making a solitary start and one substitute appearance before his loan to Millwall, which became permanent in the January window after he was released by Rangers. He will be remembered with affection at Loftus Road. An experienced defender, he can operate in both full-back positions and made an immediate impact at the New Den by his eagerness to get forward. Marcus has an excellent delivery when hitting crosses into the area and an engine that sees him strutting from box to box regularly, belying his 33 years.
Crewe Alex (£150,000 + from Kidderminster Hrs on 1/9/1997) FL 93+2 FLC 8 FAC 3
Bristol Rov (Free on 7/8/2000) FL 26/1 FLC 5/2 FAC 1 Others 3
Queens Park Rgrs (Signed on 16/3/2001) FL 49+5/1 FLC 1 FAC 1 Others 1
Rushden & Diamonds (Free on 8/8/2002) FL 68/2 FLC 1+1 FAC 4 Others 3
Queens Park Rgrs (Free on 25/3/2004) FL 123+5 FLC 5+1 FAC 2
Millwall (Free on 9/11/2007) FL 17+5 FAC 3

BIKEY Andre Stephane
Born: Douala, Cameroon, 8 January 1985
Height: 6'0" **Weight:** 12.8
International Honours: Cameroon: 10
Appearing in just over half Reading's games, Andre usually played at centre-back, deputising for the injured Michael Duberry and then later for Ibrahim Sonko, also sidelined through injury. But he also filled in as an effective midfielder, where he showed a surprisingly delicate touch on the ball and consummate passing ability. Of his three goals, one in the 2-1 home defeat by Chelsea set a new club record. It came just 20 seconds after he replaced Duberry and is the quickest ever scored by a Reading substitute. Andre scored with two headers, again from centre-back, in the 2-1 victory over Birmingham, a win that gave Reading hope of avoiding relegation. While remaining a member of the Cameroon international squad, once travelling 19,170 miles for a meaningless midweek friendly in Japan, he represented his country in the African Cup of Nations but missed the final through suspension.
Reading (Loaned from Lokomotiv Moscow, Russia, ex Espanyol, Shannik Yaroslav, on 1/8/2006) PL 21+16/3 FLC 3/1 FAC 5

BIRCHALL Adam Stephen
Born: Maidstone, 2 December 1984
Height: 5'7" **Weight:** 11.8
International Honours: W: U21-12
Adam had a fine first full season at Barnet, scoring 15 goals. His most memorable strike was the late equaliser at Swindon in the FA Cup third round, a magnificent effort from the edge of the box. The front man attracted the attention of the media when he suggested that only the captain of the team should be allowed to question refereeing decisions during games, to help improve discipline. It was a policy that led to a much-improved disciplinary record for the Bees.
Arsenal (From trainee on 2/7/2002)
Wycombe W (Loaned on 20/8/2004) FL 11+1/4 FLC 1 Others 2/1
Mansfield T (Free on 5/8/2005) FL 16+20/2 FLC 1+1 FAC 1+2/1 Others 1
Barnet (Signed on 22/11/2006) FL 58+7/17 FLC 1/1 FAC 7+2/3 Others 1/1

BIRCHALL Christopher (Chris)
Born: Stafford, 5 May 1984
Height: 5'9" **Weight:** 12.12
International Honours: Trinidad & Tobago: 26
The Trinidad and Tobago international midfield player spent the first half of the season on loan to St Mirren, making nine

appearances before suffering an injury. On his return to Coventry he started one League game in place of the suspended Michael Doyle at Leicester and also made a substitute appearance in the FA Cup defeat by West Bromwich.
Port Vale (From trainee on 1/5/2004) FL 53+25/7 FLC 0+3 FAC 4+4/1 Others 1+1/1
Coventry C (£300,000 on 5/8/2006) FL 18+11/2 FLC 1+1 FAC 0+2
St Mirren (Loaned on 31/8/2007) SL 5+4

BIRCHAM Marc Stephen John
Born: Wembley, 11 May 1978
Height: 5'10" **Weight:** 12.4
Club Honours: Div 2 '01
International Honours: Canada: 17; U23-1
Marc, a Canadian midfielder, suffered a second injury-plagued season in a row after signing from Queens Park Rangers in July and managed to reach full fitness for only 11 Yeovil games. The tenacious tackler showed his commitment to put his body on the line for the Glovers and, if he remains fit, should prove an asset to the club.
Millwall (From trainee on 22/5/1996) FL 86+18/3 FLC 3+1 FAC 6+1/1 Others 5+1
Queens Park Rgrs (Free on 10/7/2002) FL 138+14/7 FLC 6+1 FAC 2+1 Others 5
Yeovil T (Free on 17/7/2007) FL 9+4

BIRD David Alan
Born: Gloucester, 26 December 1984
Height: 5'8" **Weight:** 12.2
David's performances in the heart of Cheltenham's midfield constituted one of the real success stories of their season. A locally-born player, who came up through the youth and reserve teams at Whaddon Road, he started all 51 League and Cup matches and was voted supporters' 'Player of the Year'. Originally a defensive midfielder or full-back, whose hard running enabled him to break up opposition attacks and supply possession for others, David has added other aspects to his game. He spent most of the season in the centre of either a four or five-man midfield, apart from two matches on the right, and took on some of the set-piece duties. David scored three important goals, including a last-minute header in the relegation crunch match against Bournemouth and the opener in the 2-1 victory at Leeds in March.
Cheltenham T (Signed from Cinderford T on 1/2/2001) FL 146+39/7 FLC 5 FAC 10+2 Others 9+3

BIRD Louis Matthew
Born: Grimsby, 31 October 1990
Height: 6'0" **Weight:** 11.7
A product of Grimsby's youth ranks,

Matthew signed a two-year professional contract with the Mariners after a trial with Manchester United was cut short by injury. The promising central defender subsequently made his senior debut as a substitute in the 1-0 home defeat by Rotherham, performing competently for the final 12 minutes.
Grimsby T (From trainee on 28/3/2008) FL 0+2

BISHOP Andrew (Andy) Jamie
Born: Cannock, 19 October 1982
Height: 6'0" **Weight:** 11.2
International Honours: E: SP-4
Although a persistent knee injury threatened to disrupt the start of Andy's season, it did not stop him making a huge impact on the opening day. As a half-time substitute in Bury's game at MK Dons, he scored twice to secure victory. He further showcased his talent with a hat-trick in the last ten minutes of Bury's FA Cup first round win over Workington. It was his winner against Leeds in the Johnstone's Paint Trophy that sticks in fans' minds. Andy reached 20 goals for the season when he scored two against Morecambe in February and continued to impress as transfer speculation grew. Management and fans were keen to keep the tall striker and he carried on his prolific scoring to the final game against Accrington, his two goals taking the Shakers to victory.
Walsall (From trainee on 9/8/2002. Freed during 2004 close season)
Kidderminster Hrs (Loaned on 18/11/2002) FL 22+7/5 Others 0+1
Kidderminster Hrs (Loaned on 5/8/2003) FL 8+3/2
Rochdale (Loaned on 20/11/2003) FL 8+2/1 FAC 1
Yeovil T (Loaned on 5/2/2004) FL 4+1/2
Bury (Free from York C on 1/7/2006) FL 80+7/34 FLC 2+1/1 FAC 9/10 Others 2/1

BISHOP Neal Robert
Born: Stockton, 7 August 1981
Height: 6'0" **Weight:** 12.10
International Honours: E: SP-2
Neal signed for Barnet from York on a free transfer in July and a solid first season in League football ended with him as runner-up in the club's 'Player of the Year' award. With two goals along the way, Neal's no-nonsense approach in the centre of the midfield and good passing ability earned him rave reviews. In the final week of the season, he handed in a transfer request and could well be playing elsewhere in the coming season.
Barnet (Free from York C, ex Billingham T, Spennymoor U, Gateshead, Whitby T, Scarborough, on 9/7/2007) FL 39/2 FLC 1 FAC 6 Others 1

Neal Bishop

BLACK Paul Michael
Born: Middleton, 18 January 1990
Height: 6'0" Weight: 12.10
The future looks bright for Paul, a young left-back who penned his first-ever professional deal for Oldham – a two-and-a-half year contract – in January, many months ahead of schedule. He was an unused substitute for several games before being called into action for his senior bow in the closing stages against Huddersfield in March. Paul played for the full second half in a home win over Cheltenham and capped his rapid progress with the club's 'Apprentice of the Season' award.
Oldham Ath (From trainee on 16/1/2008) FL 0+2

BLACK Thomas (Tommy) Robert
Born: Chigwell, 26 November 1979
Height: 5'7" Weight: 11.4
Signed from Crystal Palace in the summer, Tommy had a great first season at Southend, making the wide-right berth his own after Jamal Campbell-Ryce's sale to Barnsley. His skill on the ball and quick feet often opened up the play and created chances for others. Tommy's attacking link with full-back Simon Francis was a notable success, especially given the quality of his crosses. During an injury crisis, he played two matches as a stop-gap centre-forward and scored in both before being freed in the summer.
Arsenal (From trainee on 3/7/1998) PL 0+1 FLC 1
Carlisle U (Loaned on 25/8/1999) FL 5/1
Bristol C (Loaned on 17/12/1999) FL 4
Crystal Palace (£250,000 + on 21/7/2000) FL 67+60/10 FLC 15+6/5 FAC 3+2/2
Sheffield U (Loaned on 17/9/2004) FL 3+1/1 FLC 1
Gillingham (Loaned on 27/1/2006) FL 17/5
Bradford C (Loaned on 17/11/2006) FL 4 FAC 1+1
Southend U (Free on 10/8/2007) FL 29+9/2 FLC 2+1 FAC 1+1 Others 2

BLACKBURN Christopher (Chris) Raymond
Born: Crewe, 2 August 1982
Height: 5'7" Weight: 10.6
Club Honours: NC '07
Chris returned to League football after a long absence but rarely had the chance to shine, making only four starts for Swindon and a further three appearances from the bench after arriving from Morecambe in the summer. He scored twice on his debut in the Johnstone's Paint Trophy victory over Brentford but went on loan to Weymouth in March. A well-built central defender, also able to play at right-back, he has a good touch and looks comfortable on the ball. Chris was released on 14 May.
Chester C (Trainee) FL 0+1
Swindon T (Free from Morecambe, ex Northwich Vic, on 10/7/2007) FL 4+3 Others 2/2

BLACKETT Shane Jerome
Born: Luton, 26 June 1981
Height: 6'0" Weight: 12.11
Club Honours: FC '07
International Honours: E: SP-2
Shane started the season as first-choice central defender at Peterborough but an injury put him on the sidelines for much of the time. If Shane manages to steer clear of injuries in the campaign ahead, he could make the position his own because he is quick off the mark, a good reader of the game and has two good feet.
Peterborough U (Signed from Dagenham & Redbridge, ex Arlesey T, on 29/1/2007) FL 21+3 FLC 2 Others 1

BLACKMAN Nicholas (Nick) Alexander
Born: Whitefield, 11 November 1989
Height: 6'2" **Weight:** 11.8
A young Macclesfield striker who missed the start of last season following knee surgery, he returned to training in October, after which his appearances were split between the youth and senior teams. Nick was used as back-up for the senior strike force, with most of his appearances coming as a late substitute, although for several matches he was not used. He scored in his first senior appearance of the season with a last-minute equalizer in the home match against Dagenham and Redbridge.
Macclesfield T (From trainee on 7/3/2007) FL 1+11/1

BLACKSTOCK Dexter Anthony Titus
Born: Oxford, 20 May 1986
Height: 6'1" **Weight:** 12.0
International Honours: E: U-21-2; Yth
After a fine debut season for Queens Park Rangers, Dexter struggled in the early stages this time, in common with most of the side. Although he was always in and around the team, he found goals elusive and perhaps too much was demanded of the young man during a torrid time on the pitch for Rangers. However, Dexter found a new lease of life under Luigi De Canio and really began to sparkle towards the end of the season when a run of four goals in five games showed his capabilities. He began to form a productive partnership with Patrick Agyemang towards the end of the campaign and there is little doubt more is to come from him.
Southampton (From trainee on 24/5/2004) P/FL 15+13/4 FLC 2+2/5 FAC 2+1
Plymouth Arg (Loaned on 13/2/2005) FL 10+4/4
Derby Co (Loaned on 27/10/2005) FL 8+1/3
Queens Park Rgrs (Signed on 11/8/2006) FL 63+11/19 FLC 1 FAC 3/1

BLAKE Darcy James
Born: New Tredegar, 13 December 1988
Height: 5'10" **Weight:** 12.5
International Honours: W: U21-5; Yth
Darcy, who landed a new contract this summer, is a strong, aggressive and athletic player who has not settled into one position as yet, being able to operate in central defence, at full-back, or in midfield. Darcy is a product of the Cardiff Academy and a member of the Welsh under-21 team that defeated France 4-2 at home as they went top of their Uefa qualifying group.
Cardiff C (From trainee on 26/10/2006) FL 7+12 FLC 0+2 FAC 0+3

BLAKE Robert (Robbie) James
Born: Middlesbrough, 4 March 1976
Height: 5'9" **Weight:** 12.6
Returning to the club where he had enjoyed the best time of his career, Robbie was a hugely popular signing by Steve Cotterill from Leeds in the close season. At the time he left Burnley previously, the team largely revolved around him; he returned to a stronger squad and was less of a focal point but showed no loss of the skills that had endeared him to the Turf Moor faithful. Usually deployed just behind either one or two main strikers, Robbie's trickery was instrumental in setting up many of the Clarets' goals and he scored plenty of his own, some of them spectacular. Still capable of controlling a game when really on song, he should remain a key man as Burnley renew their efforts to reach the Premiership.
Darlington (From trainee on 1/7/1994) FL 54+14/21 FLC 4+2/1 FAC 3+1 Others 3+1/1
Bradford C (£300,000 on 27/3/1997) P/FL 109+44/40 FLC 8+3/4 FAC 7/1 Others 3+1/2
Nottingham F (Loaned on 22/8/2000) FL 9+2/1 FLC 1
Burnley (£1,000,000 + on 25/11/2002) FL 103+17/42 FLC 11/5 FAC 6+1/4
Birmingham C (£1,250,000 on 5/1/2005) PL 2+9/2 FAC 1+1
Leeds U (£800,000 on 26/7/2005) FL 58+19/19 FLC 3+2/1 FAC 2+1 Others 0+2
Burnley (£250,000 on 13/7/2007) FL 41+4/9 FLC 1+2/1 FAC 1

BLANCHETT Daniel (Danny) William
Born: Wembley, 6 May 1987
Height: 5'11" **Weight:** 11.12
The young defender started only two games for Peterborough and could not manage the step up to League football before being released at the end of the season. Danny is predominantly left sided and likes to get forward whenever possible.
Peterborough U (Signed from Cambridge C, ex Hendon, Northwood, Harrow Borough, on 20/3/2007) FL 1+3/1 Others 1

BLINKHORN Matthew (Matty) David
Born: Blackpool, 2 March 1985
Height: 5'11" **Weight:** 10.10
Club Honours: AMC '04
After impressing on loan from Blackpool during 2006-07, Matty returned to Morecambe with a new deal in the summer. Having created a big impression in the previous season, the striker struggled to make an impact in the League and was not off the mark until December, in a 3-0 victory at Hereford.

Confidence restored, he went on to score six goals in the next seven games and ended with ten in the League. He often played as a lone striker and his effort never flagged.
Blackpool (From trainee on 28/6/2003) FL 13+31/5 FLC 0+1 FAC 2+1 Others 5+5/5
Luton T (Loaned on 31/7/2004) FL 0+2 FLC 0+1
Bury (Loaned on 22/11/2006) FL 1+9
Morecambe (Signed on 24/7/2007) FL 36+5/10 FLC 1+1 FAC 0+1 Others 5/1

BLIZZARD Dominic John
Born: High Wycombe, 2 September 1983
Height: 6'2" **Weight:** 13.5
Dominic arrived at Stockport from MK Dons on the eve of the new season but it was not until the second half of the campaign that he began to show his real form. Dominic, along with Gary Dicker, provided the midfield dominance that helped County pick up an incredible 55 points from their final 24 games. Unfortunately, a hamstring strain in the penultimate game at Chester kept him out of the Hatters' successful play-off campaign.
Watford (From trainee on 19/4/2002) P/FL 22+7/2 FLC 4+2/1 FAC 1
Stockport Co (Loaned on 8/2/2007) FL 7
MK Dons (Loaned on 22/3/2007) FL 8 Others 2
Stockport Co (Free on 10/8/2007) FL 22+5/1 FLC 1+1/1 Others 1

BLOOMFIELD Matthew (Matt) James
Born: Felixstowe, 8 February 1984
Height: 5'9" **Weight:** 11.3
International Honours: E: Yth
Wycombe's dynamic midfielder was first choice last season, apart from two brief spells on the bench when the manager juggled his wealth of midfield talent. Matt is always looking to put opponents on the back foot with his drive and pace. He can play wide or in a central role, providing a main link with the strikers. His finishing was noticeably improved and his five goals included four in the space of eight games, characterized by late runs into the box on through balls. Matt's season came to an early end in March with a cruciate knee ligament injury depriving the team of his attacking flair. He is not expected to be fit for the start of the coming season.
Ipswich T (From trainee on 3/7/2001) FLC 0+1
Wycombe W (Free on 24/12/2003) FL 130+23/16 FLC 8 FAC 3+3/1 Others 8+2

BLUNDELL Gregg Steven
Born: Liverpool, 3 October 1977
Height: 5'10" **Weight:** 12.2
Club Honours: Div 3 '04

2+3/1 Others 2+4/1
Southampton *(£500,000 + on 27/8/1999)*
PL 6+8/1 FLC 0+2 FAC 1
Fulham *(£1,700,000 on 31/7/2000) P/FL*
169+36/44 FLC 11+4/6 FAC 16+1/2 Others
10+2/2
West Ham U *(£4,500,000 on 5/1/2007) PL*
26+15/1 FLC 4 FAC 3

BOARDMAN Jonathan (Jon)
George
Born: Reading, 27 January 1981
Height: 6'2" **Weight:** 13.11
Jon took it in turns with Dagenham's three
other centre-halves to form the defence.
The no-nonsense defender played in
the club's first League game before an
ankle injury kept him out of the squad in
September but he was back after a month.
Jon has power in the air, both when
defending and going up for set pieces, but
was unable to find a first League goal.
Rochdale *(Free from Woking on 17/5/2005)*
FL 20+5/1 FLC 2 FAC 0+1 Others 3
Dagenham & Redbridge *(Free on*
25/1/2007) FL 22+5 FLC 1 FAC 3 Others 2

BOATENG George
Born: Nkawkaw, Ghana, 5 September
1975
Height: 5'9" **Weight:** 11.7
Club Honours: FLC '04
International Honours: Holland: 4;
U21-18
Despite some excellent 'Man of the
Match' performances, George was in and
out of the Middlesbrough side in his sixth
season at the Riverside. There were also
conflicting Press rumours that the player
and his manager had a training ground
dispute in January. George scored his only
goal of the season at the Riverside in a
1-1 draw against Liverpool shortly before
the incident and, following the problem,
Gareth Southgate relieved him of his
captaincy. With a year left on his contract,
George was philosophical enough to
admit that he could be set to leave during
the summer and insisted that he did not
want a repeat performance.
Coventry C *(£250,000 from Feyenoord,*
Holland, ex Excelsior, on 19/12/1997) PL
43+4/5 FLC 3/1 FAC 8/1
Aston Villa *(£4,500,000 on 22/7/1999) PL*
96+7/4 FLC 8+1/1 FAC 9 Others 13
Middlesbrough *(£5,000,000 on 8/8/2002)*
PL 177+5/7 FLC 9+1 FAC 13+2/1 Others 16/1

BOATENG Kevin-Prince (Kevin)
Born: Berlin, Germany, 6 March 1987
Height: 6'0" **Weight:** 11.9
Club Honours: FLC '08
International Honours: Germany: U21
The 21-year-old German midfielder was
signed in the summer from Hertha Berlin,

Matt Bloomfield

Gregg continued to impress with his
unselfish running and determination to
retrieve seemingly lost causes in order to
create chances for others. He was used
almost as many times from the bench
as he had starts, to bring fresh legs and
enthusiasm to a tiring Darlington attack.
Although he scored only half-a-dozen
goals, his contribution to forward play
was immense with his holding of the
ball and tricky footwork. He was sorely
missed when out injured for the final few
matches of the campaign.
Tranmere Rov *(From trainee on 9/7/1996.*
Free to Knowsley U on 30/11/1996)
Doncaster Rov *(Free from Northwich Vic on*
27/3/2003) FL 74+11/27 FLC 4/2 FAC 3/2
Chester C *(£100,000 on 15/7/2005) FL*
44+13/13 FLC 1+1 FAC 5+1/1 Others 2/2
Darlington *(Free on 31/1/2007) FL 31+20/9*
FLC 0+1 FAC 2/1 Others 1

BOA MORTE Luis
Born: Lisbon, Portugal, 4 August 1977
Height: 5'10" **Weight:** 11.5
Club Honours: PL '98; Div 1 '01; CS
'98, '99
International Honours: Portugal: 26;
U21-28; Yth
A left-sided midfielder at West Ham, the
Portuguese international was all action
with forceful running. He was 'Man of the
Match' against Sunderland in October,
creating two of the goals, and was often
brought on as a substitute to spice up
the play with some keen tackling. In
what was his best game of the season,
he excelled against Aston Villa in May,
tracking back, producing plenty of hard
running and generally being in the thick
of the action.
Arsenal *(£1,750,000 + from Sporting Lisbon,*
Portugal on 25/6/1997) PL 6+19 FLC 3/2 FAC

Ferrie Bodde

but only made one start for Tottenham under the leadership of Martin Jol. That was in an academic UEFA Cup game in Cyprus, when Spurs were already 6-1 up. Kevin was reputedly also chased by Juande Ramos when he was Sevilla coach, and under the latter's management Kevin made a further nine starts and 12 substitute appearances. He has yet to make a real impact but is a combative and powerful central midfielder.

Tottenham H (£6,000,000 from Hertha Berlin, Germany on 9/8/2007) PL 7+6 FLC 1+2 FAC 1+1 Others 1+2

BOCANEGRA Carlos

Born: Alta Loma, California, USA, 25 May 1979
Height: 6'0" **Weight:** 12.4
International Honours: USA: 56; U21
The United States international remained a firm favourite with Fulham fans in a difficult season, although he did not start another game after the FA Cup replay at Bristol Rovers in January. Usually a left-back, he can also play in the centre of defence and was used there for a four-game spell around the turn of the year. Dominant in the air, he is an effective tackler who rarely allows opponents space. His heading ability makes him a threat at set pieces and he was on target at Birmingham in December. Carlos continued to represent the United States,

having captained them in the 2007 Gold Cup. He led Fulham for the first time in the home game against Tottenham in September and inspired them to recover from a 3-1 deficit and draw. Carlos scored for United States in a friendly against Brazil, his eighth goal for his country. Was released in the summer.

Fulham (Free from Chicago Fire, USA on 14/1/2004) PL 105+11/8 FLC 6+1 FAC 13

BOCO Romauld

Born: Bernay, France, 8 July 1985
Height: 5'10" **Weight:** 11.3
Club Honours: FC '06
International Honours: Benin: 17; U21
Romauld played in his usual midfield position at Accrington in the first six League and Cup games before being injured. Even before that, he did not look the player he was and, in fact, did not score a goal after September 2006. It is fair to say that from early September until his departure in January, he was clearly unhappy and started only two more games. On his return from the African Nations Cup, in which he captained Benin in all three games, it was decided a parting of the ways would be beneficial for both club and player. It was a sad finale to what had started as such a strong relationship.

Accrington Stanley (Free from Niort, France on 3/8/2006) FL 34+9/3 FLC 2+1 Others 2

BODDE Ferrie

Born: Delft, Holland, 5 May 1982
Height: 5'10" **Weight:** 12.8
Club Honours: Div 1 '08
International Honours: Holland: U23
Cultured Swansea central midfielder signed from Dutch side Den Haag in the close season, Ferrie has excellent passing ability coupled with strong shooting from outside the penalty area. A tough challenger, his over-zealous tackling saw him suffer two red cards during the season. A hamstring injury in late March at Hartlepool ruled him out of the final dash for promotion but he was still one of the Swansea five nominated in the PFA League One select team.

Swansea C (£50,000 from ADO Den Haag, Holland on 8/8/2007) FL 33/6 FAC 1/1 Others 1+1

BODEN Luke

Born: Sheffield, 26 November 1988
Height: 6'1" **Weight:** 13.1
This versatile youngster already had a League debut as a substitute and a Carling Cup appearance to his credit from 2006-07. Luke may have expected to make more of an impact but was held back for his long-term benefit because Sheffield Wednesday spent the season struggling in the Championship. He can play in midfield or as a second striker, with the ability to hold the ball and bring others into play. Luke hopes the new season will bring him more appearances for the Owls and confirm his potential.

Sheffield Wed (From trainee on 5/7/2007) FL 0+3 FLC 1+1

BOERTIEN Paul

Born: Haltwhistle, 21 January 1979
Height: 5'10" **Weight:** 11.2
Signed from Derby in the summer, the left-sided defender showed up well for Walsall at the start of the season and, after sustaining an injury in September, came back strongly in January following Danny Fox's move to Coventry. Paul was injured again near the end of the season but had shown enough quality to be offered a further contract.

Carlisle U (From trainee on 13/5/1997) FL 16+1/1 FLC 0+2 FAC 1 Others 1
Derby Co (£250,000 on 25/3/1999) P/FL 92+22/2 FLC 4+1 FAC 5+2
Crewe Alex (Loaned on 11/2/2000) FL 2
Notts Co (Loaned on 23/1/2004) FL 5
Chesterfield (Loaned on 22/3/2007) FL 4
Walsall (Free on 27/7/2007) FL 20 FLC 1 FAC 0+1 Others 1

BOJINOV Valeri Emilov

Born: Gorna Oryahovitsa, Bulgaria, 15 February 1986
Height: 5'11" **Weight:** 12.4
International Honours: Bulgaria: 21

The powerful 21-year-old striker joined Manchester City last summer from Fiorentina, having earlier been the youngest overseas player ever to make his debut in Serie A, at 15 years and 11 months. Sven-Goran Eriksson moved quickly to add the striker to his squad and Valeri certainly looked the part in a substitute appearance against West Ham at Upton Park on the opening day. He started against Manchester United a week later but suffered a severe cruciate knee ligament injury after six minutes, landing awkwardly when challenging for a header, and was ruled out for up to five months. Valeri is making good progress in his battle to return to full fitness.
Manchester C (£5,800,000 from Fiorentina, Italy, ex Lecce, Juventus - loan, on 10/8/2007) PL 1+2

BOLAND William (Willie) John
Born: Ennis, 6 August 1975
Height: 5'9" **Weight:** 11.2
International Honours: RoI: B-1; U21-11; Yth; Sch
An industrious playmaker in the centre of midfield for Hartlepool Willie is a player who rarely hits the headlines, but with his tough, no-nonsense approach United invariably play better when he is on form. For much of the season, he had short runs in the first team, having to miss games through minor injuries and suspension, but he was able to finish strongly with more consistent appearances.
Coventry C (From juniors on 4/11/1992) PL 43+20 FLC 6+1 FAC 0+1
Cardiff C (Free on 24/6/1999) FL 187+22/3 FLC 12+1 FAC 11+4/1 Others 6
Hartlepool U (Free on 18/8/2006) FL 57+4 FLC 2 FAC 4 Others 1

BOLDER Adam Peter
Born: Hull, 25 October 1980
Height: 5'8" **Weight:** 11.0
As Queens Park Rangers' captain under John Gregory, Adam became one of many players moved on when the new regime changed things around to their liking. A highlight was the only goal in a 1-0 win at Charlton, a result that was highly unlikely in prospect and gave Rangers their first away win of the season. Adam joined Sheffield Wednesday in January to cover for injuries in midfield and made himself a regular and important player in midfield, missing a few games through injury but coming straight back as soon as he was fit. A hard worker who always seeks opportunities to support the forwards, he scored both goals at Bramall Lane when the Owls drew 2-2 with Sheffield United.

Hull C (From trainee on 9/7/1999) FL 18+2 Others 2+1
Derby Co (Signed on 3/4/2000) P/FL 109+57/11 FLC 6 FAC 5+2 Others 1+1
Queens Park Rgrs (Free on 29/1/2007) FL 36+4/2 FLC 1
Sheffield Wed (Loaned on 8/2/2008) FL 11+2/2

BOLLAND Paul Graham
Born: Bradford, 23 December 1979
Height: 5'11" **Weight:** 11.0
Paul was in good form at the start of the season, claiming three goals in five League games, including one against Stockport to mark his 100th appearance for the Mariners. Grimsby's most mobile midfielder, with his constant running and pressure on defenders, his subsequent form was hindered by an ankle ligament injury. However, he was back to his best to help them reach Wembley, his strike goal of the two-legged Johnstone's Paint Trophy Area final.
Bradford C (From trainee on 20/3/1998) FL 4+8 FLC 2
Notts Co (£75,000 on 14/1/1999) FL 153+19/6 FLC 3+6 FAC 7+1 Others 2+3/1
Grimsby T (Free on 1/8/2005) FL 114+4/13 FLC 5 FAC 5+1/1 Others 9/1

BOLLAND Philip (Phil) Christopher
Born: Liverpool, 26 August 1976
Height: 6'2" **Weight:** 13.8
Club Honours: FC '04
With the Chester manager Bobby Williamson favouring a central defensive partnership of Paul Butler and Paul Linwood, the former City captain had a chance only after Linwood's red card against Morecambe. Clear that he had no future, in January the central defender made the short journey to Wrexham along with goalkeeper Gavin Ward. Phil did a reasonable job at the Racecourse and was arguably one of Brian Little's better signings as several others arrived in an attempt to revive their season. Despite working well with full-back Simon Spender, he was left out of the final four games as relegation from the Football League became inevitable and was not retained.
Oxford U (Free from Southport, ex Altrincham, Salford C, Trafford, Knowsley U, Altrincham, on 9/7/2001) FL 20/1 FLC 1 FAC 1 Others 1
Chester C (Free on 4/3/2002) FL 54+4/2 FLC 2 FAC 2+1 Others 4
Peterborough U (Free on 19/1/2006) FL 17
Chester C (Free on 5/7/2006) FL 25+3/1 FAC 4 Others 3/1
Wrexham (Free on 8/1/2008) FL 18

BOOTH Andrew (Andy) David
Born: Huddersfield, 6 December 1973
Height: 6'0" **Weight:** 13.0
International Honours: E: U21-3
Huddersfield's modern-day saviour passed 350 appearances and 140 goals for the club in the course of the season, an occasion marked by his wearing the captain's armband for the match against Crewe. Andy was a tower of strength as he led the front line and a constant threat as he continued to dominate in the air. With his close control and intelligent distribution, he made his presence felt all over the pitch. Often used to help the defence at set pieces, Andy reads the game well and, as ever, found the net with some great headers among his season's tally of nine.
Huddersfield T (From trainee on 1/7/1992) FL 109+14/54 FLC 10+1/3 FAC 8/3 Others 12+1/4
Sheffield Wed (£2,700,000 on 8/7/1996) P/FL 124+9/28 FLC 10+1/1 FAC 9+1/5
Tottenham H (Loaned on 30/1/2001) PL 3+1
Huddersfield T (£200,000 on 22/3/2001) FL 220+31/72 FLC 5+2/1 FAC 8+1/2 Others 15/4

BOPP Eugen
Born: Kiev, Ukraine, 5 September 1983
Height: 5'10" **Weight:** 12.4
Freed by Rotherham in the 2007 close season, the experienced midfield player moved to Crewe but was unable to gain a regular place in the side. He scored his only goal in the home game against Huddersfield and at his best is a creative player who can open up opposing defences with precision passes.
Nottingham F (From trainee on 11/9/2000) FL 39+38/8 FLC 3+4/2 FAC 4 Others 1/1
Rotherham U (Free on 4/8/2006) FL 24+5/5 FLC 1 FAC 1
Crewe Alex (Free on 1/7/2007) FL 5+5/1 FLC 0+1 Others 1

BORE Peter Charles
Born: Grimsby, 4 November 1987
Height: 6'0" **Weight:** 12.2
After a good start to his Grimsby career in 2006-07, Peter was by contrast used only occasionally last season. Following brief substitute outings the forward earned a first-team recall in February. His initial start of the campaign was in a 4-0 win at Morecambe and Peter excelled with two goals in a 'Man of the Match' display. Such form then led to selection as substitute for Town's Johnstone's Paint Trophy final trip to Wembley, where he was in action for the entire second half.
Grimsby T (From trainee on 22/8/2006) FL 25+24/10 FLC 1+1 FAC 0+2 Others 2+4

BORI Gabor
Born: Szombathely, Hungary, 16 January 1984
Height: 5'10" **Weight:** 11.0
International Honours: Hungary: 1
Arrived at Leicester for a trial in December, having recently played for MTK Hungaria, and impressed sufficiently to earn a loan deal to the end of the season. He had a particularly good debut in the home win over Coventry but thereafter found integration difficult due to his lack of English. He had less impact as the team struggled during the latter stages of the campaign and soon faded from the picture.
Leicester C (Loaned from MTK Hungaria, Hungary, ex Bodajk - loan, on 11/1/2008) FL 4+2

BORROWDALE Gary Ian
Born: Sutton, 16 July 1985
Height: 6'0" **Weight:** 12.1
International Honours: E: Yth
A left-back signed for Coventry in the close season by Iain Dowie from Crystal Palace at a fee set by a tribunal. Gary was first choice left-back for two months but, other than the first few games, rarely excelled in a shaky defence. An injury in October kept him out for over a month and when Coventry signed Danny Fox in the transfer window, Gary lost his place. He appeared at centre-half in the Millwall FA Cup match but after that did not even have a place on the bench.
Crystal Palace (From trainee on 6/12/2002) P/FL 74+24 FLC 7+4 FAC 3+1 Others 1
Coventry C (Signed on 5/7/2007) FL 20+1 FLC 3 FAC 2

BOSHELL Daniel (Danny) Kevin
Born: Bradford, 30 May 1981
Height: 5'11" **Weight:** 11.10
Grimsby's midfield playmaker was to push team-mate Tom Newey close in the race to claim most goal assists, while also scoring on several occasions himself. Danny was usually seen aiding the attack with late runs into the opposing area and after Christmas assumed responsibility for Town's penalties, hitting two in a 4-2 home win over Chesterfield. He did, however, miss one in the Mariners' Johnstone's Paint Trophy final defeat by MK Dons at Wembley.
Oldham Ath (From trainee on 10/7/1998) FL 45+25/2 FLC 6/1 FAC 3+3 Others 3/1
Bury (Loaned on 24/3/2005) FL 2+4
Stockport Co (Free on 1/8/2005) FL 28+5/1 FLC 1/1 FAC 3 Others 1
Grimsby T (Free on 24/8/2006) FL 61+8/8 FLC 1 FAC 3 Others 8/1

BOSTOCK John Joseph
Born: Camberwell, 15 January 1992
Height: 5'10" **Weight:** 11.11
International Honours: E: Yth
Young John entered the pages of Crystal Palace history when he appeared as a 72nd-minute substitute for Ben Watson in the home game against Watford on 29 October to become the club's youngest player at 15 years 287 days, thus beating Phil Hoadley's record. A midfielder with a whole host of clubs tracking his every move, John, who is an English youth international, is likely to become a big player sooner rather than later.
Crystal Palace (Associated Schoolboy) FL 1+3 FAC 1

BOTHROYD Jay
Born: Islington, 7 May 1982
Height: 6'3" **Weight:** 13.6
Club Honours: FAYC '00
International Honours: E: U21-1; Yth; Sch
Despite scoring a cracker in a pre-season friendly against Aston Villa, Jay made his first start for Wolverhampton in 2007-08 against Charlton in October and celebrated by scoring one and making the other. He also netted with a low shot against Bristol City and had a run in the team around Christmas. Despite having mixed fortunes, Jay continued to show great ability without always making the required impact, and his last appearance for Wolves was in February, at Cardiff in the FA Cup. In March, Jay was one of several players taken on loan by Stoke as cover during their successful charge for promotion, but started only once, with another three substitute appearances.
Arsenal (From trainee on 8/7/1999)
Coventry C (£1,000,000 on 13/7/2000) P/FL 51+21/14 FLC 1+5/2 FAC 5/1 (Transferred to Perugia, Italy on 14/7/2003)
Blackburn Rov (Loaned on 9/9/2004) PL 6+5/1 FLC 1 FAC 0+1
Charlton Ath (Free from Perugia, Italy on 31/8/2005) PL 3+15/2 FLC 0+3/1 FAC 1+3/3
Wolverhampton W (Free on 31/7/2006) FL 32+23/12 FAC 3/1 Others 2
Stoke C (Loaned on 14/3/2008) FL 1+3

BOUAZZA Hameur
Born: Evry, France, 22 February 1985
Height: 5'10" **Weight:** 12.0
International Honours: Algeria: 5

Gary Borrowdale

Hameur joined Fulham from Watford in August and went straight into the team for the opening game at Arsenal. His early attempts to establish himself were dogged by a shoulder injury that forced him to leave the field early more than once. A winger with pace, he was usually employed wide on the left but occasionally switched flanks. His only goal came in the 3-3 home draw against Manchester City when he unleashed an unstoppable free kick from around 20 yards. Another of the early-season signings to feature less following the arrival of Roy Hodgson as manager, he was recalled for game at Derby and thereafter appeared occasionally among the substitutes. Although born in France, Hameur represents Algeria at international level and scored his first goal in a 3-2 win over Mali in November.
Watford *(From trainee on 2/7/2004) P/FL 46+37/9 FLC 8+2/3 FAC 5+1/2*
Swindon T *(Loaned on 7/10/2005) FL 11+2/2 Others 2/1*
Fulham *(£4,000,000 on 8/8/2007) PL 15+5/1 FLC 1 FAC 1*

BOUCAUD Andre Christopher
Born: Enfield, 9 October 1984
Height: 5'10" **Weight:** 11.4
International Honours: Trinidad & Tobago: 6
Andre is a midfield playmaker who joined Wycombe last summer after impressing in trial matches. He spent the previous season at Conference North side Kettering, where he played 43 games. Comfortable on the ball, Andre was used mainly as a squad player, with three starts and eight substitute appearances. He was released at the end of the season.
Reading *(From trainee on 25/3/2002)*
Peterborough U *(Loaned on 27/3/2003) FL 5+1*
Peterborough U *(Loaned on 25/7/2003) 7+1/1 FLC 1*
Peterborough U *(Free on 1/7/2004) FL 15+10/1 FAC 1 Others 1 (Freed during 2006 close season)*
Wycombe W *(Free from Kettering T on 9/8/2007) FL 2+8 Others 1*

BOUGHERRA Madjid
Born: Dijon, France, 7 October 1982
Height: 6'2" **Weight:** 14.0
International Honours: Algeria: 21
Big, strong and skilful, Madjid was a regular in Charlton's central defence for most of last season. Good in the air and extremely comfortable on the ball, Madjid likes to get forward and scored twice. He deflected in a Jerome Thomas free kick to collect his first for the club and earn a point off Hull at the Valley, adding

Micky Boulding

a close-range header against Blackpool also at home. A foot injury caused him to miss several games in the second half of the season and, when fit, found his place taken by Sam Sodje. An injury to Sodje meant a return for the last four games and Madjid finished strongly.
Crewe Alex *(Free from Gueugnon, France on 31/1/2006) FL 11/1*
Sheffield Wed *(Free on 3/8/2006) FL 28/2 FLC 1*
Charlton Ath *(£2,500,000 on 29/1/2007) P/FL 26+8/2 FLC 2 FAC 2*

BOULDING Michael (Micky) Thomas
Born: Sheffield, 8 February 1976
Height: 5'10" **Weight:** 11.4
After coming out of a year's retirement in the summer of 2006, he looked to have regained his sharpness and fitness last term. Started the season as Mansfield's main striker and opened his account with a cracking 30-yarder at Brentford. He led the scoring charts at Field Mill from the start after netting in each of Town's first four League games. By New Year, he had bagged 15 goals in all competitions before a hamstring injury at MK Dons

on New Year's Day forced him to miss a couple of matches. He claimed a hat-trick in the 3-1 win over Shrewsbury in April.
Mansfield T *(Signed from Hallam FC on 2/8/1999) FL 28+38/12 FLC 2+2 FAC 2+1 Others 1+1*
Grimsby T *(Free on 24/8/2001) FL 24+11/11 FLC 0+2 FAC 0+2*
Aston Villa *(Free on 9/7/2002) Others 2/1*
Sheffield U *(Loaned on 29/9/2002) FL 3+3 FLC 1/1*
Grimsby T *(Free on 10/1/2003) FL 37+2/16 FLC 1 FAC 1/1 Others 0+1*
Barnsley *(£50,000 on 12/2/2004) FL 27+8/10 FLC 1+1 Others 0+1 (Freed during 2005 close season)*
Cardiff C *(Loaned on 23/3/2005) FL 0+4*
Mansfield T *(Free, having been out of the game for a year and following a short spell at Rotherham U, on 3/8/2006) FL 68+14/27 FLC 2+1/1 FAC 5+1/3 Others 2*

BOULDING Rory Joseph
Born: Sheffield, 21 July 1988
Height: 6'1" **Weight:** 12.8
Missed Mansfield's opening games with an injury picked up during the close season, but then featured as a substitute until mid-September when, badly in need

of match practice, he was sent on a one-month loan to Hucknall. He returned and, through injury to Simon Brown, made his first start for the club in the FA Cup tie with Lewes. He set up the first goal for his brother Micky and scored the second himself. Not a regular but he is still young and his time will come.
Mansfield T (From juniors at Rotherham U on 8/8/2006) FL 4+16 FLC 0+1 FAC 2+1/1 Others 0+3

BOUMA Wilfred
Born: Helmond, Holland, 15 June 1978
Height: 5'11" **Weight:** 12.13
International Honours: Holland: 34
Wilfred is primarily a left-back but can also play in central defence, for Holland as well as Aston Villa, and has an abundance of power and pace. In his third season with Villa, Wilfred came on in leaps and bounds under Martin O'Neill's management and was an ever-present in the Premier League. He scored his first goal for Villa against Newcastle in February and was consistently reliable throughout the season.
Aston Villa (£3,500,000 from PSV Eindhoven, Holland on 31/8/2005) PL 81+2/1 FLC 1+1 FAC 3

BOWDITCH Dean Peter
Born: Bishops Stortford, 15 June 1986
Height: 5'11" **Weight:** 11.7
International Honours: E: Yth
Dean did not make a first-team appearance for Ipswich in 2007-8, spending much of the season on loan. In his short stay at Northampton, he showed some neat touches and scored a couple of excellent goals, both at home. Supporters hoped for a deal to keep him at Sixfields but he went back to Ipswich before a second loan to Brighton. In February, after recovering from surgery for a double hernia, Dean returned to Brighton where he had enjoyed a successful loan in 2006-07, albeit curtailed by injury. Played as a right-winger, he was unable to resurrect the sparkling form of that earlier spell and was substituted in four of his five games before returning to Portman Road.
Ipswich T (From trainee on 28/7/2003) FL 30+42/8 FLC 5+1/1 FAC 0+1 Others 0+2
Burnley (Loaned on 11/3/2005) FL 8+2/1
Wycombe W (Loaned on 27/1/2006) FL 9+2/1
Brighton & Hove A (Loaned on 1/11/2006) FL 1+2/1 Others 0+1
Northampton T (Loaned on 22/11/2007) FL 7+3/2
Brighton & Hove A (Loaned on 11/2/2008) FL 5

Lee Bowyer

BOWER Mark James
Born: Bradford, 23 January 1980
Height: 5'10" **Weight:** 11.0
A regular at the heart of Bradford's defence until last season, Mark suffered a bad knee injury while warming up before a game on New Year's Day. He recovered in time to win back his place at Easter and renew his long-standing partnership with David Wetherall. Mark is always a threat going forward at set pieces.
Bradford C (From trainee on 28/3/1998) P/FL 219+9/12 FLC 8 FAC 9+1/1 Others 4
York C (Loaned on 16/2/2000) FL 15/1
York C (Loaned on 30/11/2000) FL 21/1 FAC 3 Others 0+1

BOWES Gary Tyron
Born: Ilford, 18 October 1989
Height: 5'11" **Weight:** 12.0
Another player from the Millwall Academy, Gary earned a first-team chance as a substitute against Port Vale. As a striker, Gary shows strength and a desire to improve, backed by pace and a stinging shot.
Millwall (From trainee on 25/4/2008) FL 0+1

BOWLER Michael James
Born: Glossop, 8 September 1987
Height: 5'11" **Weight:** 12.0
Michael was given a short-term contract by Stockport at the start of last season to help him fully recover from injury. But while he started four games in November, all at right-back, the midfielder failed to earn a new contract in January and signed for Blue Square Premier side Northwich.
Stockport Co (From trainee on 31/7/2006) FL 9+4 FLC 2 FAC 1 Others 2

BOWYER George
Born: Stockport, 11 November 1990
Height: 6'0" **Weight:** 10.2
After making good progress as a scholar with Rochdale, becoming a regular in the youth team and reserve sides, George was given his senior bow as a substitute for Marcus Holness in the final League game of the season, when Dale rested most of their regulars ahead of the play-offs. Highly thought of at the club, George can play anywhere across the back four and puts hard work at the top of his requirements for a way into professional football.
Rochdale (Trainee) FL 0+1

BOWYER Lee David
Born: Canning Town, 3 January 1977
Height: 5'9" **Weight:** 10.6
International Honours: E: 1; U21-13; Yth
The experienced West Ham midfielder scored his first-ever goal for the club against Wigan last August and this started a run of consistent performances. Playing wide on the right, he was always looking to be in the action and to score more goals. At Derby in November he was the 'Man of the Match', combining a stunning performance with two finely taken goals. After that game, he had a hernia operation which forced him out until January. Unfortunately, he developed a groin injury after playing against Birmingham in February and missed the remainder of the campaign.
Charlton Ath (From trainee on 13/4/1994) FL 46/8 FLC 6+1/5 FAC 3/1 Others 2
Leeds U (£2,600,000 on 5/7/1996) PL 196+7/38 FLC 7+1/1 FAC 16/3 Others 38/13
West Ham U (£100,000 on 8/1/2003) PL 10 FAC 1
Newcastle U (Free on 7/7/2003) PL 61+18/6 FLC 1+1 FAC 3+1/1 Others 11+2/4
West Ham U (£250,000 on 12/6/2006) PL 30+5/4 FLC 2+1 FAC 1+1 Others 2

BOYCE Emmerson Orlando
Born: Aylesbury, 24 September 1979
Height: 5'11" **Weight:** 11.10
International Honours: Barbados: 2
A composed and impressive defender, Emmerson is a model professional who played his part in Wigan's third Premier League season. Used initially as a substitute, he made his first start at the heart of the defence in the home match against Liverpool in September. Solid and reliable, he showed his versatility by playing at right-back following an injury to Mario Melchiot in December. Tall and speedy, he is always anxious to advance down the wing to send in crosses. In February, he returned to the starting line-up as Paul Scharner's partner at the centre of defence, producing a series of impressive performances. Emmerson reads the game well, tackles under pressure and does the job with the minimum of fuss. He celebrated his 50th Premier League appearance in the home win over Bolton in March and became Wigan's newest international when he played for Barbados against Dominica in the same month.
Luton T (From trainee on 2/4/1998) FL 171+15/8 FLC 11 FAC 9+3/1 Others 3
Crystal Palace (Free on 9/7/2004) P/FL 68+1/2 FLC 3 FAC 3 Others 2
Wigan Ath (£1,000,000 on 15/8/2006) PL 58+1 FLC 1 FAC 2

BOYD Adam Mark
Born: Hartlepool, 25 May 1982
Height: 5'9" **Weight:** 10.12
Adam joined Leyton Orient during the summer on a free transfer from Luton and is a proven striker at this level. He showed during pre-season just what fans had to look forward to when scoring against England goalkeepers in friendlies with Tottenham and West Ham. Once the season started, he delighted O's fans with his goals and assumed responsibility for penalties following Matt Lockwood's departure.
Hartlepool U (From trainee on 20/9/1999) FL 89+55/53 FLC 4/1 FAC 6+2/3 Others 9+4/3
Boston U (Loaned on 14/11/2003) FL 14/4
Luton T (£500,000 on 1/8/2006) FL 5+14/1 FLC 2+1/1 FAC 2
Leyton Orient (Free on 8/8/2007) FL 40+4/14 FLC 1+1/1 FAC 2/2 Others 1

BOYD George Jan
Born: Chatham, 2 October 1985
Height: 5'10" **Weight:** 11.7
International Honours: E: SP-6
In his first full League season with Peterborough, George did not disappoint and a number of League Two defenders were glad to see the back of him, which was the only view many of them had when playing against him. Fantastic ball control coupled with a mazy dribble had many opponents going the wrong way and George scored 15 times in all competitions, many 'goal of the season' candidates. Although lacking lightning pace, his skill makes up for that and he will hope for more time and space in League One to weave his magic.
Peterborough U (£265,000 from Stevenage Borough on 8/1/2007) FL 60+6/18 FLC 1/1 FAC 4/1 Others 2/1

BOYLE Patrick (Pat) Joseph Gerard
Born: Livingston, 20 March 1987
Height: 5'10" **Weight:** 11.9
Pat joined Crewe on loan from Everton last January after recovering from a back injury. With several senior left-backs at Goodison Park, the Glaswegian, a regular in the reserves, gained valuable experience in League One. The young left-back played 17 times in four months and proved a capable defender before returning to Everton, where he has yet to make an appearance. Was released in the summer.
Everton (From trainee on 11/7/2005)
Norwich C (Loaned on 14/9/2006) FL 3
Crewe Alex (Loaned on 22/1/2008) FL 17

BRAATEN Daniel Omoya
Born: Oslo, Norway, 25 May 1982
Height: 6'1" **Weight:** 13.5
International Honours: Norway: 16
Much was expected of the Norwegian international striker when he joined Bolton from Rosenborg in the summer and introduced himself in style by scoring, as a substitute, in his third match, the 3-0 defeat of Reading. His first start for Bolton was in the Carling Cup victory at Fulham and, despite sporadic starts in Cup competitions, he failed to have one in the Premier League. Daniel did not make enough of a mark when he played and had few opportunities under Gary Megson in the latter part of the season.
Bolton W (£800,000 from Rosenborg, Norway, ex Tonsen U, Skeid, on 9/8/2007) PL 0+6/1 FLC 1+1 FAC 1 Others 3+2

BRACKSTONE John
Born: Hartlepool, 9 February 1985
Height: 5'11" **Weight:** 10.8
The young left-back was very much an understudy to the regular performers after being signed from local rivals Hartlepool in the summer. John made his Darlington debut in the Carling Cup tie at Barnsley in the second match of the season but went on to make only three League and two further Cup starts during the campaign. Out of contract in the summer, he was an able deputy with his quick tackling and strong runs down the flanks.
Hartlepool U (From trainee on 16/3/2004) FL 21+4 FLC 2 FAC 3/1 Others 5
Darlington (Free on 24/5/2007) FL 3 FLC 1 FAC 2

BRADBURY Lee Michael
Born: Cowes, 3 July 1975
Height: 6'2" **Weight:** 13.10
Club Honours: Div 1 '06
International Honours: E: U21-3
This highly-experienced forward started the season with Southend among a glut of front men, but still managed a memorable hat-trick against Cheltenham in the Carling Cup. Lee's home is on the south coast and when the chance to join Bournemouth was offered, he left Roots Hall on an August loan transfer, a deal that was made permanent within days of his arrival. Although finding the net on a number of occasions early in the season, because of injuries in the squad he was moved to right-back. Excelling in the position, Lee played a big part in the Cherries' fantastic run-in as they made a valiant effort to overcome the ten-point deduction for going into administration.
Portsmouth (Free from Cowes on 14/8/1995) FL 41+13/15 FLC 1+2 FAC 4/2

Exeter C *(Loaned on 1/12/1995) FL 14/5*
Manchester C *(£3,000,000 + on 1/8/1997) FL 34+6/10 FLC 6/1*
Crystal Palace *(£1,500,000 on 29/10/1998) FL 28+4/6 FLC 3+1/1 FAC 1/1*
Birmingham C *(Loaned on 25/3/1999) FL 6+1 Others 1+1*
Portsmouth *(£380,000 on 14/10/1999) FL 90+9/28 FLC 3+2 FAC 2/1*
Sheffield Wed *(Loaned on 24/12/2002) FL 2+1*
Sheffield Wed *(Loaned on 1/3/2003) FL 8/3*
Derby Co *(Loaned on 14/8/2003) FL 1*
Derby Co *(Loaned on 20/11/2003) FL 6*
Walsall *(Free on 25/3/2004) FL 7+1/1*
Oxford U *(Free on 12/7/2004) FL 57+6/9 FLC 2 FAC 4+1/1 Others 2+1*
Southend U *(Free on 31/1/2006) FL 40+7/5 FLC 2/3 FAC 3/1*
Bournemouth *(Signed on 24/8/2007) FL 33+2/3 FAC 2 Others 2/2*

BRADLEY Mark Simon
Born: Dudley, 14 January 1988
Height: 6'0" **Weight:** 11.5
International Honours: W: U21-5; Yth
A home-grown Walsall midfielder, Mark had made only one first-team substitute appearance before the start of last season but came into his own in October with goals in successive games against Doncaster and Huddersfield. Mark not only held a regular place for most of the rest of the season but was capped by Wales at under-21 level and voted Walsall's 'Young Player of the Season'.
Walsall *(From trainee on 3/7/2006) FL 30+10/3 FAC 5 Others 0+1*

BRAIN Jonathan (Jonny) Robert
Born: Carlisle, 11 February 1983
Height: 6'2" **Weight:** 12.4
At the start of last season Jonny was Macclesfield's second-string goalkeeper, making appearances only in the Johnstone's Paint Trophy until Tommy Lee incurred a hand injury at the end of November, after which he took over to become the first choice for the rest of the season. Although clean sheets were the exception rather than the rule, this was due to the indifferent form of the team as a whole rather than Jonny's personal performance and he often kept his side in contention with some excellent saves.
Port Vale *(Free from trainee at Newcastle U, via trials at Carlisle U, on 21/8/2003) FL 58+1 FLC 1 FAC 5 Others 4*
Macclesfield T *(Free on 7/7/2006) FL 38 FLC 1 FAC 2 Others 3*

BRAMBLE Titus Malachi
Born: Ipswich, 31 July 1981
Height: 6'2" **Weight:** 13.10
International Honours: E: U21-10

Recruited in the summer, Titus had an excellent season for Wigan after he was signed from Newcastle. Big and strong, with an ability to make long and accurate passes out of defence, he has all the attributes required of a top-class centre-back. He showed them during a series of fine performances at the start of the season, his best game being at the JJB Stadium against his former club. He made his debut in the opening match at Everton, netted his first goal in December against Aston Villa and followed it with a late equaliser in the next game at Liverpool as Wigan gained their first-ever point against one of the 'big four'. Unfortunately, at times he continues to let himself down by lapses in concentration and lost his place in February. He is popular with supporters because of his honest approach and returned to the team for the final match of the season, at Aston Villa, producing an excellent display as Wigan confirmed their Premier League status.
Ipswich T *(From trainee on 24/8/1998) P/FL 41+7/1 FLC 4+1/2 FAC 4+1 Others 4/1*
Colchester U *(Loaned on 29/12/1999) FL 2*
Newcastle U *(£5,000,000 on 19/7/2002) PL 96+9/3 FLC 5 FAC 8 Others 38+1/4*
Wigan Ath *(Free on 17/7/2007) PL 26/2 FAC 1*

BRAMMER David (Dave)
Born: Bromborough, 28 February 1975
Height: 5'10" **Weight:** 12.0
Club Honours: AMC '01
Dave, an experienced Millwall midfield player, was again was dogged by injury. An excellent passer of the ball, with a stinging shot, Dave missed around half of the season. It was a blow to stability of Millwall's midfield, because he is an essential player. Dave's movement and sound decisions were much missed.
Wrexham *(From trainee on 2/7/1993) FL 118+19/12 FLC 6+2 FAC 8+2/1 Others 12+1/1*
Port Vale *(£350,000 + on 24/3/1999) FL 71+2/3 FLC 2 FAC 2/1 Others 7*
Crewe Alex *(£500,000 on 10/8/2001) FL 86+1/4 FLC 6/1 FAC 8/1 Others 2*
Stoke C *(Free on 13/7/2004) FL 91+14/2 FLC 1+1/1 FAC 4+1*
Millwall *(Signed on 29/1/2007) FL 40/1 FAC 1+1*

BRANCH Graham
Born: Liverpool, 12 February 1972
Height: 6'2" **Weight:** 12.2
Signed from Burnley in the summer, Graham started as Accrington's first-choice left-back, playing most of the early games there despite being sent off in his third match against Peterborough. After

that his appearances were spasmodic, but when called upon he was able to demonstrate his versatility by filling various roles, something he has done throughout his career. When he played, his experience proved a steadying influence on the players around him. Was out of contract in the summer and looking for a new club.
Tranmere Rov *(Free from Heswall on 2/7/1991) FL 55+47/10 FLC 4+8/1 FAC 1+2 Others 2+1*
Bury *(Loaned on 20/11/1992) FL 3+1/1 Others 1*
Wigan Ath *(Loaned on 24/12/1997) FL 2+1*
Stockport Co *(Free on 31/7/1998) FL 10+4/3 FLC 1*
Burnley *(Free on 31/12/1998) FL 208+56/17 FLC 14+3/1 FAC 9+8 Others 1*
Accrington Stanley *(Free on 17/7/2007) FL 19+3*

BRANDON Christopher (Chris) William
Born: Bradford, 7 April 1976
Height: 5'7" **Weight:** 10.3
The lively Huddersfield winger showed greater determination and workrate as his trickery and clever wing play provided a valuable outlet. His turn of pace and a willingness to run at defenders often led to telling crosses into the danger area. Chris controls his centres well and supports his defence with strong covering tackles. A back injury midway through the season kept him on the sidelines, as did a stoppage-time sending off at Brighton in January. He scored three times, twice in the League and the winner in the memorable FA Cup home victory over Birmingham. A hamstring injury kept him out of the last three games, with further disappointment when he was released at the end of the season.
Torquay U *(Free from Bradford PA on 5/8/1999) FL 64+7/8 FLC 4/1 FAC 5/1 Others 3*
Chesterfield *(Free on 9/7/2002) FL 74+5/11 FLC 2+1/1 FAC 2 Others 4/4*
Huddersfield T *(Free on 5/7/2004) FL 120+15/12 FLC 3+1 FAC 6/2 Others 2+1*
Blackpool *(Loaned on 21/3/2007) FL 4+1/2*

BRANDY Febian Earlston
Born: Manchester, 4 February 1989
Height: 5'5" **Weight:** 10.2
Club Honours: Div 1 '08
International Honours: E: Yth
An exciting loan signing from Manchester United in mid-February, Febian was mainly used from the Swansea substitutes' bench to good effect late in games, releasing his close skills and pace to make an impact. He scored his first League goal in the 4-0

win at Doncaster and followed with the winner in a close game against Oldham at the Liberty Stadium.
Manchester U (From trainee on 6/7/2006)
Swansea C (Loaned on 18/1/2008) FL 2+17/3 Others 2

BRANSTON Guy Peter Bromley
Born: Leicester, 9 January 1979
Height: 6'0" **Weight:** 13.12
Guy started only one game for Peterborough but the central defender was involved with three other clubs in 2007-08. With Rochdale suffering early season injuries to several defenders, Guy was brought in to add his physique and experience to their back four. His arrival coincided with Dale picking up their first points and they were unbeaten in Guy's four games before he too was injured. Northampton turned to Guy in November when skipper Chris Doig was injured and, in a debut to remember, Guy ended the game covered in blood from a head wound, giving some idea of his commitment. He stayed a month and, after being allowed to leave by Peterborough in mid-December, was signed by Notts County, who were short of defenders through injuries and the end of Krystian Pearce's loan. Unfortunately, Guy could not plug the gap in the middle of defence. He was still recovering from injury when he arrived at Meadow Lane, short of match practice, was unable to do himself justice in the short time allowed and was quickly released.
Leicester C (From trainee on 3/7/1997)
Colchester U (Loaned on 9/2/1998) FL 12/1 Others 1
Colchester U (Loaned on 7/8/1998) FL 0+1
Plymouth Arg (Loaned on 20/11/1998) FL 7/1 Others 1
Lincoln C (Loaned on 10/8/1999) FL 4 FLC 2
Rotherham U (£50,000 on 15/10/1999) FL 101+3/13 FLC 5+1 FAC 4 Others 2
Wycombe W (Loaned on 19/9/2003) FL 9 Others 2/1
Peterborough U (Loaned on 25/2/2004) FL 14
Sheffield Wed (Signed on 2/7/2004) FL 10+1 FLC 1 FAC 1
Peterborough U (Loaned on 31/12/2004) FL 4/1
Oldham Ath (Free on 18/2/2005) FL 44+1/2 FLC 1 FAC 2 Others 2
Peterborough U (Free on 24/7/2006) FL 24+2 FLC 1+1/1 FAC 2+1 Others 1
Rochdale (Loaned on 24/8/2007) FL 4 FLC 1 Others 1
Northampton T (Loaned on 15/11/2007) FL 3 FAC 0+1
Notts Co (Free on 1/1/2008) FL 1

BRECKIN Ian
Born: Rotherham, 24 February 1975
Height: 6'0" **Weight:** 12.9
Club Honours: AMC '96
Ian's ever-present League record with Nottingham Forest, spread over two years, came to an end on the first day of the new season because of a calf injury. On his return to fitness he found it hard to regain his place due to the form of Kelvin Wilson alongside Wes Morgan but was always ready to answer the call. Despite his frustration, he remained a useful member of the squad. Ian returned to the side in February, in an attempt to address Forest's poor away record. The formation was changed and Ian was a regular in away games for the remainder of the season. He was rewarded with a new contract.
Rotherham U (From trainee on 1/11/1993) FL 130+2/6 FLC 6 FAC 5 Others 11
Chesterfield (£100,000 on 25/7/1997) FL 208+4/8 FLC 16/1 FAC 9/1 Others 12/1
Wigan Ath (£150,000 on 25/6/2002) FL 92+4 FLC 4 FAC 3+1 Others 1
Nottingham F (£350,000 on 8/7/2005) FL 114+6/12 FLC 2/2 FAC 8 Others 4

BREEN Gary Patrick
Born: Hendon, 12 December 1973
Height: 6'2" **Weight:** 12.0
Club Honours: Ch '05
International Honours: RoI: 63; U21-9
The experienced central defender was appointed captain of Wolverhampton and was not afraid to point players in the right direction. After doing well alongside Jody Craddock, one goal conceded in four games, Gary was injured in October. He was out for a long spell but returned in February for six games, bringing more composure to Wanderers' defence. He was soon out again until coming back with a commanding display in April. Gary has excellent timing and is not afraid to bring the ball out of defence but was released at the end of the season.
Maidstone U (From juniors at Charlton Ath on 6/3/1991) FL 19
Gillingham (Free on 2/7/1992) FL 45+6 FLC 4 FAC 5 Others 1
Peterborough U (£70,000 on 5/8/1994) FL 68+1/1 FLC 6 FAC 6 Others 6/1
Birmingham C (£400,000 on 9/2/1996) FL 37+3/2 FLC 4 FAC 1
Coventry C (£2,400,000 on 1/2/1997) P/FL 138+8/2 FLC 10+3 FAC 12
West Ham U (Free on 30/7/2002) PL 9+5 FLC 2 FAC 2
Sunderland (Free on 7/8/2003) P/FL 105+2/7 FLC 1 FAC 5 Others 2
Wolverhampton W (Free on 20/7/2006) FL 58+1/1 FAC 4 Others 2

BRELLIER Julien
Born: Grenoble, France, 10 January 1982
Height: 6'1" **Weight:** 12.8
Signed on a Bosman-free from Heart of Midlothian in the summer, the French midfielder struggled to adapt to both the English game and a change of management at Norwich. Defensively minded but with an eye for a pass, he was taken to Carrow Road by Peter Grant to play the holding role. However, an early-season injury set him back and he was unable to make a place in the team his own. His contract was terminated in January and he later signed for FC Sion in Switzerland.
Heart of Midlothian (Free from Venezia, Italy, ex Montpellier, Inter Milan, Lecco - loan, Legnano - loan, Salternitana - loan, on 3/8/2005) SL 44+8 SC 3+1 Others 3+1
Norwich C (Signed on 11/7/2007) FL 8+2 FLC 1

BREZOVAN Petr
Born: Bratislava, Slovakia, 9 December 1979
Height: 6'6" **Weight:** 14.13
International Honours: Slovakia: U21
After recovering from a broken arm sustained in 2006-07, the goalkeeper's early-season appearances for Swindon were limited to the Carling Cup and Johnstone's Paint Trophy. Initially, he gave some understandably nervous performances before his confidence was fully restored. Petr spent a period on trial with Everton and rumours persist of higher division clubs continuing their interest. Tall and imposing, Petr can be an exceptional shot-stopper but his kicking ability, previously so impressive, seemed to desert him.
Swindon T (Free from FC Brno, Czech Republic, ex PS Bratislava, Vinorhady Bratislava, SKP Devin, Slovan Breclav, HFK Olomouc, on 1/8/2006) FL 45 FLC 1 FAC 4 Others 2

BRIDCUTT Liam Robert
Born: Reading, 8 May 1989
Height: 5'9" **Weight:** 11.7
A young midfielder who came through the Chelsea youth set-up and was shipped out on loan by Avram Grant to Yeovil for the final three months of the campaign. After Liam arrived at the club, manager Russell Slade described him as a Michael Essien type of player who had two good feet and a great attitude. Used on the left-wing and in the centre of midfield the versatile youngster showed glimpses of ability in his short stay with Yeovil.
Chelsea (From trainee on 4/7/2007)
Yeovil T (Loaned on 8/2/2008) FL 6+3

Wayne Bridge

BRIDGE Wayne Michael
Born: Southampton, 5 August 1980
Height: 5'10" **Weight:** 11.11
Club Honours: FLC '05, '07; PL '05
International Honours: E: 30; U21-8; Yth
One of the first arrivals of the Roman Abramovich era, England left-back Wayne had a very satisfactory, and injury-free, season. But, yet again, he didn't play enough first-team football. The excellent form shown by fellow England international Ashley Cole restricted Wayne to 19 starts in all competitions, a situation that alerted covetous Premier League rivals, all of whom could offer this top-class player an automatic first-team place. He is, after all, good enough to keep adding to his England caps.
Southampton (From trainee on 16/1/1998)
PL 140+12/2 FLC 10+1 FAC 11
Chelsea (£7,000,000 + on 21/7/2003) PL
71+10/1 FLC 13+1/1 FAC 11 Others 21+3/2
Fulham (Loaned on 20/1/2006) PL 12

BRIDGES Michael
Born: North Shields, 5 August 1978
Height: 6'1" **Weight:** 10.11
Club Honours: Div 1 '96, '99; Ch '05;
Div 2 '06
International Honours: E: U21-3; Yth;
Sch
Despite an impressive pre-season and good form in the early games, including the opener in the Carling Cup win at Crewe, Michael remained out of favour at Hull and slipped further down the pecking order as they increased their attacking arsenal. With first-team opportunities becoming more limited, the experienced forward was made available for loan and chose an exciting challenge offered by Sydney FC in Australia's Hyundai A-League on a three-month deal. On his spring return to the KC Stadium, Michael's only further involvement was as a substitute in a 5-0 win against Southampton.

Sunderland (From trainee on 9/11/1995)
P/FL 31+48/16 FLC 8+3/5 FAC 2
Leeds U (£4,500,000 + on 29/7/1999) PL
40+16/19 FLC 3+2 FAC 1+1 Others 17+2/2
Newcastle U (Loaned on 2/2/2004) PL 0+6
Others 1+2
Bolton W (Free on 1/7/2004)
Sunderland (Free on 23/9/2004) FL 5+14/1
FAC 0+2
Bristol C (Free on 6/8/2005) FL 4+7 FLC
0+1/1 Others 0+1
Carlisle U (Signed on 15/11/2005) FL
28+2/15 FLC 0+1
Hull C (£350,000 on 31/8/2006) FL 9+13/2
FLC 2/1

BRIDGE-WILKINSON Marc
Born: Nuneaton, 16 March 1979
Height: 5'6" **Weight:** 11.8
Club Honours: AMC '01
The Carlisle side that Marc signed for last summer, on arriving from Bradford, was very different to the one he experienced

on loan in the spring of 1999, when the club was desperately battling to stay in the League. A fine striker of the ball with the ability to deliver a telling pass, he took over as the principal dead-ball kicker. These skills were perhaps seen to best effect in the victory over Millwall. In the first half, he set up two goals and then scored another with a superb 25-yard free-kick.

Derby Co *(From trainee on 26/3/1997)* PL 0+1
Carlisle U *(Loaned on 5/3/1999)* FL 4+3
Port Vale *(Free on 4/7/2000)* FL 111+13/31 FLC 3/1 FAC 2+2/1 Others 9/3
Stockport Co *(Free on 2/8/2004)* FL 19+3/2 FLC 1 FAC 2
Bradford C *(Free on 25/2/2005)* FL 87/12 FLC 2/1 FAC 5/1 Others 1
Carlisle U *(Free on 24/7/2007)* FL 44+1/6 FLC 1 FAC 2 Others 4/2

BRIGGS Keith
Born: Glossop, 11 December 1981
Height: 5'10" **Weight:** 11.6
While something of a cult hero at Edgeley Park, Keith had only a six-month contract at Stockport in 2007-08 as he recovered from injury. Although making regular appearances before Christmas, the Boxing Day game at Shrewsbury was his last, as he was not offered a new contract. Instead, the midfielder who can also play in defence signed for Shrewsbury on non-contract terms in January and made his mark with a spectacular goal on his debut in a 3-1 defeat at Hereford. After one further substitute appearance, Keith was released and joined Mansfield to help their fight against relegation. His debut for the Stags was at right-back in a surprise 2-1 win at Darlington. Keith showed his versatility by turning out in midfield on a couple of occasions and at left- back in a win over Shrewsbury in April that could have been vital.

Stockport Co *(From trainee on 27/8/1999)* FL 47+11/2 FLC 4/1 FAC 3+1 Others 2/1
Norwich C *(£65,000 on 16/1/2003)* FL 2+3
Crewe Alex *(Loaned on 5/8/2004)* FL 3
Stockport Co *(Free on 14/1/2005)* FL 74+16/8 FLC 0+2 FAC 3/2 Others 3
Shrewsbury T *(Free on 11/11/2008)* FL 1+1/1
Mansfield T *(Free on 14/2/2008)* FL 10+3

BRILL Dean Michael
Born: Luton, 2 December 1985
Height: 6'2" **Weight:** 12.5
Having become Luton's regular goalkeeper at the end of 2006-07, Dean appeared to confirm his position when he played in the first three games of last season. He did not convince manager Kevin Blackwell, who brought in David Forde and Ben Alnwick. When Alnwick was injured, Dean returned in the

Carling Cup against Everton, did well and maintained his form for the rest of the season, earning several 'Man of the Match' awards. Good in the air and agile, he organises the defence and his confidence grew. He was splendid in the 1-1 draw with Bristol Rovers, after three players had been sent off.

Luton T *(From trainee on 15/3/2005)* FL 55+3 FLC 4 FAC 6 Others 4
Gillingham *(Loaned on 8/12/2006)* FL 8

BRISLEY Shaun Richard
Born: Macclesfield, 6 May 1990
Height: 6'3" **Weight:** 12.7
Central defender and local boy, Shaun first started playing for Macclesfield in their under-13s and progressed to the youth team, where he impressed last season. He was called into the senior side for Keith Alexander's first match in charge at the beginning of March to make his League debut against Notts

Dean Brill

County. Shaun slotted in easily, showing skill and versatility at left-back, centre-back and right wing-back, and scored twice in the home win against Accrington at the end of March. Shaun was voted 'Young Player of the Year'.

Macclesfield T (Trainee) FL 9+1/2

BRITTAIN Martin

Born: Cramlington, 29 December 1984
Height: 5'8" **Weight:** 10.7

On being freed by Ipswich in the summer, Martin agreed a short-term deal with Carlisle, where as a right-sided midfielder he made one brief substitute appearance before being released. He then moved on to Walsall and made three substitute appearances in midfield for them in January, on each occasion replacing a striker. Is a player who likes to take the full back on, combining dribbling skills with pace, to get his crosses in.

Newcastle U (From trainee on 20/9/2003) PL 0+1 FLC 0+2 FAC 1 Others 0+4
Ipswich T (Free on 21/8/2006) FLC 0+1
Yeovil T (Loaned on 31/10/2006) FL 12+3 Others 0+1
Carlisle U (Free on 10/8/2007) FL 0+1 FLC 1
Walsall (Free on 3/1/2008) FL 0+1 FAC 0+2

BRITTON Leon James

Born: Merton, 16 September 1982
Height: 5'5" **Weight:** 9.10
Club Honours: AMC '06; Div 1 '08
International Honours: E: Yth

Leon is extremely brave, with a high level of skill on the ball. The diminutive Swansea central midfield player suffered a hamstring injury at Cheltenham during the first half of the season but once recovered, turned in top-class performances in a central midfield trio with Darren Pratley and Ferrie Bodde. The only criticism that could be levelled was a shortage of goals, just one in the FA Cup replay against Horsham, but Leon is one of the fittest players in the City team.

West Ham U (From juniors on 21/9/1999)
Swansea C (Free on 13/12/2002) FL 193+23/10 FLC 5+1 FAC 16+2/4 Others 7+3/1

BRKOVIC Ahmet

Born: Dubrovnik, Croatia, 23 September 1974
Height: 5'7" **Weight:** 10.8
Club Honours: Div 1 '05

The arrival of new players at Luton in the summer relegated Ahmet to the reserves and he was unable to earn selection in midfield ahead of Darren Currie, his only League game coming as a substitute at Tranmere. Ahmet's final appearance for Town, again as a substitute, came in the Johnstone's Paint Trophy and in October

Leon Britton

the experienced midfielder joined Millwall, originally on a two-month emergency loan because of the crippling injury crisis at the Den. Able to play anywhere across the middle with tremendous vision in picking out a pass when nothing seems available, his experience was invaluable and led to a permanent deal.

Leyton Orient *(Free from HNK Dubrovnik, Croatia on 14/10/1999)* FL 59+10/8 FLC 3/2 FAC 4+2 Others 2+2
Luton T *(Free on 4/10/2001)* FL 162+32/31 FLC 6+2 FAC 14/4 Others 6+1/3
Millwall *(Free on 25/10/2007)* FL 15+10/2 FAC 2/1

BROADBENT Daniel (Danny) James
Born: Leeds, 2 March 1990
Height: 5'10" **Weight:** 12.0
International Honours: E: Yth
In the final year of his Huddersfield Academy scholarship, Danny was drafted in as a substitute for the away defeat by Tranmere. This was followed up late in the season by further substitute appearances. Danny is quick and strong on the ball with a keen eye for goal that makes him a regular scorer at junior levels.
Huddersfield T *(From trainee on 3/3/2007)* FL 0+5

BROADHURST Karl Matthew
Born: Portsmouth, 18 March 1980
Height: 6'1" **Weight:** 11.7
Karl, a former Bournemouth skipper who moved to Edgar Street in the summer, slotted easily into the role at Hereford in 2007-08, showing himself a leader on and off the pitch with his commanding performances at centre-back. Karl immediately built a strong central defensive partnership with Dean Beckwith that was crucial to Hereford's good start but an ankle injury in a televised FA Cup tie against Leeds cost him his place. The good form of others kept him out until the closing stages, when Graham Turner decided his experience was vital to the promotion campaign. Four clean sheets and three wins from his first five games back proved the manager correct.
Bournemouth *(From trainee on 3/7/1998)* FL 176+16/3 FLC 9+1/1 FAC 18/1 Others 7+1
Hereford U *(Free on 25/7/2007)* FL 22+1 FLC 2 FAC 1

BROGAN Stephen (Steve) Patrick
Born: Rotherham, 12 April 1988
Height: 5'7" **Weight:** 10.4
Having emerged through the junior ranks at Rotherham, Steve earned a regular

place thanks to the versatility that saw him play with equal prowess at full-back and in midfield. His enthusiasm was contagious and he was an expert from the penalty spot until, in early February, he suffered a broken leg that is likely to keep him out of action until next December. He was sadly missed and there is widespread hope that the youngster will make a full recovery to return for his home-town team.
Rotherham U *(From trainee on 3/8/2006)* FL 47+8/3 FLC 1 FAC 2/1 Others 1+4

BROMBY Leigh
Born: Dewsbury, 2 June 1980
Height: 6'0" **Weight:** 11.8
International Honours: E: Sch
Leigh began the 2007-08 campaign at right wing-back for Sheffield United but lost his place to Derek Geary and then to Phil Bardsley. Around the New Year, he played a few games at centre-back, as ever performing competently, but with no guarantee of a place and his contract running out in summer it was decided to sell him to Watford in the January transfer window. An elegant and accomplished centre-half who reads the game well, he slotted in successfully alongside Danny Shittu, impressing with a prodigious long throw that paid an immediate dividend when producing a goal for Steve Kabba in the first minute of his debut against Wolverhampton. He scored his first goal for the Hornets at West Bromwich.
Sheffield Wed *(Free from Liversedge on 9/7/1998)* FL 98+2/2 FLC 8 FAC 6+1 Others 5
Mansfield T *(Loaned on 10/12/1999)* FL 10/1 Others 1
Norwich C *(Loaned on 24/2/2003)* FL 5
Sheffield U *(Free on 5/7/2004)* P/FL 104+5/6 FLC 7+1 FAC 8
Watford *(£600,000 on 31/1/2008)* FL 16/1 Others 2

BROOKER Paul
Born: Hammersmith, 25 November 1976
Height: 5'8" **Weight:** 10.0
Club Honours: Div 3 '01; Div 2 '02
The experienced Brentford outside-right took part in the first two games of last season but following a dispute with the management, his contract was cancelled. Later in the campaign he played for Chertsey. At his best, Paul was an excellent crosser of the ball who posed problems for defenders.
Fulham *(From trainee on 1/7/1995)* FL 13+43/4 FLC 1+2/1 FAC 1+3/1 Others 3+3
Brighton & Hove A *(£25,000 on 18/2/2000)* FL 102+32/15 FLC 5+1 FAC 3+3 Others 3/1
Leicester C *(Free on 5/7/2003)* PL 0+3 FLC

2 FAC 0+1
Reading *(Loaned on 27/2/2004)* FL 5+6
Reading *(Free on 5/7/2004)* FL 22+9 FLC 2 FAC 0+1
Brentford *(Free on 3/8/2005)* FL 56+15/4 FLC 4 FAC 5+2 Others 1+3

BROOKER Stephen (Steve) Michael Lord
Born: Newport Pagnell, 21 May 1981
Height: 5'10" **Weight:** 12.4
Club Honours: AMC '01
Injuries continued to frustrate this wholehearted Bristol City forward's efforts and it was not until after the turn of the year that he was fit enough to go on loan to Cheltenham, an arrangement designed to help him recover full fitness after a knee operation and to fire the Robins' attack into action in the fight to retain League One status. After taking a few matches to regain his sharpness, the plan worked perfectly and Steve's physical presence, hold-up play and scoring ability provided a vital injection of quality into Cheltenham's season. He scored five goals in his last six games, the final one, a late winner against Bristol Rovers, prompted City boss Gary Johnson to recall him. Returning to Ashton Gate, he scored a last-minute winner against Norwich towards the end of the season but any hope that he would reinvigorate City's promotion push were again thwarted by niggling injuries.
Watford *(From trainee on 9/7/1999)* PL 0+1 FAC 0+1
Port Vale *(£15,000 on 5/1/2001)* FL 120+11/35 FLC 5 FAC 4/1 Others 9+2/3
Bristol C *(£150,000 on 30/9/2004)* FL 87+10/35 FLC 1 FAC 4/1 Others 2
Cheltenham T *(Loaned on 11/1/2008)* FL 14/5

BROUGHTON Drewe Oliver
Born: Hitchin, 25 October 1978
Height: 6'3" **Weight:** 12.10
Club Honours: AMC '08, Div 2 '08
Drewe joined MK Dons after being released by Chester and impressing in a pre-season trial, soon showing himself to be a big and strong target player who never shirked a challenge. A mid-season change to a more fluid 4-3-3 system did not really suit him and he went on loan to Wrexham in January. He stayed for a month, returning to Dons in time to score the winning penalty in the Johnstone's Paint Trophy Southern Area final shoot-out against Swansea, before going back to the Dragons on a further loan the next day. Wrexham became Drewe's 12th Football League club when he joined them, giving the new manager Brian Little more options up front, but he did not solve the scoring problems as Wrexham

tried to escape from a precarious position. Despite being the captain on occasions and working tirelessly, Drewe did not enjoy much success in the scoring stakes and was back with the Dons by mid-April, prior to being released at the end of the campaign.
Norwich C *(From trainee on 6/5/1997) FL 3+6/1*
Wigan Ath *(Loaned on 15/8/1997) FL 1+3*
Brentford *(£100,000 on 30/10/1998) FL 1*
Peterborough U *(£100,000 on 17/11/1998) FL 19+16/8 FLC 2 Others 1+1/1*
Kidderminster Hrs *(£50,000 on 22/1/2001) FL 70+24/19 FLC 2 FAC 2/2 Others 5/2*
Southend U *(Free on 13/6/2003) FL 31+13/2 FLC 2/1 FAC 0+2 Others 4+4/5*
Rushden & Diamonds *(Loaned on 14/10/2004) FL 9/4 FAC 1/1*
Wycombe W *(Loaned on 17/12/2004) FL 2+1*
Rushden & Diamonds *(Free on 11/2/2005) FL 43+6/12 FAC 1 Others 1*
Chester C *(Free on 1/7/2006) FL 9+5/2 FLC 1*
Boston U *(Loaned on 26/10/2006) FL 25/8 FAC 1*
MK Dons *(Free on 27/7/2007) FL 2+11 FLC 1/1 FAC 1 Others 2+2*
Wrexham *(Loaned on 25/1/2008) FL 5*
Wrexham *(Loaned on 26/2/2008) FL 11/2*

BROWN Aaron Wesley
Born: Bristol, 14 March 1980
Height: 5'10" **Weight:** 11.12
Club Honours: AMC '03
International Honours: E: Sch
Freed by Swindon during the summer, Aaron joined Gillingham and proved to be a lively right-sided midfielder, who has good ball skills and likes to get forward at every opportunity. Extremely versatile, he can also be used up front or in a wide-right position.
Bristol C *(From trainee on 7/11/1997) FL 135+25/12 FLC 3+2 FAC 10+1 Others 12+4*
Exeter C *(Loaned on 6/11/2000) FL 4+1/1*
Queens Park Rgrs *(Free on 5/1/2005) FL 1+2 FLC 1*
Torquay U *(Loaned on 22/3/2005) FL 5*
Cheltenham T *(Loaned on 23/9/2005) FL 3*
Swindon T *(Free on 24/11/2005) FL 36+21/4 FLC 1 FAC 2+1 Others 1*
Gillingham *(Free on 23/7/2007) FL 10+1/1 FLC 1 FAC 1 Others 2/1*

BROWN Christopher (Chris) Alan
Born: Doncaster, 11 December 1984
Height: 6'1" **Weight:** 13.4
Club Honours: Div 3 '04; Ch '05, '07
International Honours: E: Yth
Chris never made the expected impact at Norwich last season, but not for want of trying. His willingness to run and work hard was always appreciated, but he could not find the net, scoring just one

goal in 24 appearances for the Canaries. Transferred to Preston in January he made an immediate impression with his ability to hold up the ball and bring team-mates into the game. The young forward's close control and vision brought some much-needed class to North End's play and he also used his height to great effect. Chris also contributed five important goals, including two in the victory at Charlton, and the partnership he formed enabled Neil Mellor to blossom, offering real potential for the coming season.
Sunderland *(From trainee on 9/8/2002) P/FL 33+33/9 FLC 1/2 FAC 0+2*
Doncaster Rov *(Loaned on 3/10/2003) FL 17+5/10*
Hull C *(Loaned on 9/9/2005) FL 13/1*
Norwich C *(£275,000 on 11/1/2007) FL 11+7/1 FLC 2+1 FAC 3*
Preston NE *(£400,000 on 10/1/2008) FL 17/5 FAC 2*

BROWN David Alistair
Born: Bolton, 2 October 1978
Height: 5'10" **Weight:** 12.6
Club Honours: FC '06
Once again David was unable to win a regular place in the Accrington side, so it was obviously a disappointing season for him, without even the satisfaction of scoring a goal. However, he played regularly on his two loans. He went first to Rushden and then, on transfer-deadline day, to Northwich, helping them to maintain their Blue Square Premier status. Was freed during the summer.
Manchester U *(From trainee on 27/10/1995)*
Hull C *(Free on 26/3/1998) FL 108+23/23 FLC 9+1/5 FAC 10/3 Others 3+1*
Torquay U *(Free on 9/11/2001) FL 2 FAC 1 (Freed to Chester C on 21/12/2001)*
Accrington Stanley *(Signed from Hereford U, ex Telford U, on 9/3/2005) FL 16+16/5 FAC 1 Others 1+2*

BROWN David Patrick
Born: Tadcaster, 29 May 1989
Height: 5'11" **Weight:** 11.9
As a small but very quick striker, former Leeds' trainee David returned to Yorkshire when he left Nottingham Forest bound for Bradford in January. He made a storybook start to his senior career when he came off the bench at Macclesfield and capitalised on a goalkeeping error to score the winner with his first touch. Was freed during the summer.
Nottingham F *(From trainee at Leeds U on 5/7/2007)*
Bradford C *(Free on 30/1/2008) FL 0+5/1*

BROWN James Peter
Born: Cramlington, 3 January 1987
Height: 5'11" **Weight:** 11.0
Hartlepool supporters have been

expecting much of this exciting young player and he more than lived up to expectations at the start of the season. He showed impressive form as an attacking right-sided midfielder and there was inevitable talk of a possible transfer to a bigger club. James answered by pledging his immediate future to Hartlepool but soon afterwards was sidelined by a knee injury. A player with a good scoring instinct, he bagged 13 League and Cup goals and was rewarded by being named the Hartlepool 'Players' Player of the Year'.
Hartlepool U *(Signed from Chester-le-Street T on 20/9/2004) FL 60+15/17 FLC 2+2 FAC 4/2 Others 3+1/2*

BROWN Jonathan (Jon) David
Born: Bridgend, 17 April 1990
Height: 5'10" **Weight:** 11.4
International Honours: W: U21-2; Yth
A highly-rated young midfield player or striker, Jon is the only second-year trainee in Cardiff's Academy who was offered a senior contract. Pushed forward into more of an attacking role last season, he scored the winner in an FAW Premier Cup tie at Welshpool. Was a former schools sprint champion who was also a highly proficient rugby union player before opting for football. Jon made his first-team debut when getting a two-minute run-out at Coventry before coming off the bench at home to Blackpool for the last 22 minutes of the match.
Cardiff C *(Trainee) FL 0+2*

BROWN Junior
Born: Crewe, 7 May 1989
Height: 5'9" **Weight:** 10.12
Having come through Crewe's youth system, Junior made his debut as a substitute against Brighton in 2007-08. A skilful midfielder who can spray the ball around, it was felt that he would benefit from wider experience and was sent out on loan to Kidsgrove and Witton before being released at the end of the season. Junior may be looking to further his education with a non-League side.
Crewe Alex *(From trainee on 8/5/2007) FL 0+1*

BROWN Michael Robert
Born: Hartlepool, 25 January 1977
Height: 5'9" **Weight:** 11.8
International Honours: E: U21-4
A combative, tireless worker with a biting tackle, Michael enjoyed a fine first season with Wigan following his summer move from Fulham. Always involved in the thick of the action, he displayed his best form after the arrival of Steve Bruce in December. He missed the opening two matches because of a suspension held over from the previous

Michael Brown

season before making his debut at home against Sunderland. Michael played in the 350th League game of his career against Manchester United in October. Solid and dependable in the central midfield-holding role, he was a model of consistency throughout the campaign, missing games only because of two suspensions for his ten yellow cards. The only disappointment for Michael was his failure to score, despite several long-range efforts.
Manchester C *(From trainee on 13/9/1994)*
P/FL 67+22/2 FLC 2+4 FAC 10+1/2 Others 4
Hartlepool U *(Loaned on 27/3/1997) FL 6/1*
Portsmouth *(Loaned on 19/11/1999) FL 4*
Sheffield U *(Signed on 17/12/1999) FL*
146+5/27 FLC 13+1/3 FAC 6/3 Others 3/2
Tottenham H *(£500,000 on 31/12/2003) PL*
39+11/2 FLC 4+1/1 FAC 9
Fulham *(£1,500,000 on 31/1/2006) PL 40+1*
FAC 3
Wigan Ath *(Signed on 31/7/2007) PL 27+4*
FLC 1 FAC 1+1

BROWN Nathaniel (Nat) Levi
Born: Sheffield, 15 June 1981
Height: 6'2" **Weight:** 12.6
The 2007-08 season was pretty much a stop-start affair for the Lincoln central defender, with a number of injuries, most notably a grade two medial ligament injury that kept him on the sidelines for two months. In and out of the squad for the second half of the campaign, Nat failed to find the back of the net, having scored ten times in his first season at Sincil Bank.
Huddersfield T *(From trainee on 8/7/1999)*
FL 56+20 FLC 1+2 FAC 1+1 Others 2+1
Lincoln C *(Free on 5/8/2005) FL 86+8/8 FLC*
3 FAC 3 Others 5+1/1

BROWN Scott
Born: Runcorn, 8 May 1985
Height: 5'7" **Weight:** 10.3
International Honours: E: Yth
Bubbly midfielder Scott returned to action for Cheltenham in November following an eight-month absence with a broken leg. After easing back in the reserves, he went on as a substitute at Tranmere in late December. Scott made his first start of the season in a 2-0 defeat at Bristol Rovers and made several more appearances, either in central midfield or on the left. Renowned as one of the jokers in the squad, Liverpudlian Scott's presence provided a lift to players and supporters with his energetic running and inventive passing. With a full pre-season, Scott aims to return to the form that won him a regular place at Bristol City before his transfer to Cheltenham.
Everton *(From trainee on 16/5/2002)*
Bristol C *(Free on 10/8/2004) FL 48+15/5 FLC*
0+1 FAC 0+3 Others 1+3
Cheltenham T *(Free on 12/1/2007) FL 13+11*

BROWN Simon Alexander
Born: West Bromwich, 18 September 1983
Height: 5'10"   **Weight:** 11.0
Simon missed Mansfield's pre-season and opening games through injury, making his return in September at Accrington. He soon scored at Barnet and then later in October he rattled in a first-half hat-trick in the 5-0 demolition of Macclesfield. He was out of the side again after a further injury and struggled to retain a regular place after that, prior to being released in the summer.
West Bromwich A (From trainee on 9/7/2003)
Kidderminster Hrs (Loaned on 25/3/2004) FL 8/2
Kidderminster Hrs (Loaned on 19/7/2004) FL 11+2 FLC 1/1 Others 1
Mansfield T (£50,000 on 6/12/2004) FL 76+37/21 FLC 3+1/1 FAC 5+2/1 Others 1+1

BROWN Simon James
Born: Chelmsford, 3 December 1976
Height: 6'2"   **Weight:** 15.0
An experienced goalkeeper who joined Brentford from Hibernian in the close season, he missed the start through injury and then found it difficult to displace loanee Ben Hamer. Established himself from October but was again injured at the end of December. With Hamer in good form, Simon sat on the bench until selected again in early March. A nine-game run was halted when he was dropped following the Lincoln game and he was transfer-listed at the end of the season.
Tottenham H (From trainee on 1/7/1995)
Lincoln C (Loaned on 19/12/1997) FL 1 Others 0+1
Colchester U (Free on 20/7/1999) FL 141+1 FLC 7 FAC 9 Others 8+1
Hibernian (Signed on 24/6/2004) SL 49 SLC 3 SC 8+1 Others 4
Brentford (Signed on 3/7/2007) FL 26 FAC 1 Others 1

BROWN Wayne Jonathan
Born: Kingston, 6 August 1988
Height: 5'9"   **Weight:** 12.5
The young professional was given his Fulham debut in the FA Cup third round replay at Bristol Rovers, where his solid performance won praise from manager Roy Hodgson. A combative midfielder with an eye for goal, who had been top scorer for the reserves in the previous two seasons, Wayne was then loaned to Brentford in February to get added experience. Playing on the right side of midfield for Brentford in the final three months of the season, Wayne was in the squad for every game. He initially found

it tough to impose himself in League Two but began to show flashes of skill on the ball to create chances.
Fulham (From trainee on 7/2/2007) FAC 1
Brentford (Loaned on 25/2/2008) FL 7+4/1

BROWN Wayne Larry
Born: Southampton, 14 January 1977
Height: 6'1"   **Weight:** 11.12
Club Honours: FC '04
After missing the first game of last season through injury, Wayne was quickly back in the Hereford side and enhanced his reputation as the most highly-regarded Edgar Street goalkeeper in a generation. Tremendous reaction saves, command of his penalty area and quick, decisive distribution of the ball were major factors in Hereford's promotion. Perhaps Wayne's finest moment was in stoppage-time at Mansfield in early March when his brilliant penalty save, on a night of many other top-class stops, preserved three points and set the Bulls up for their successful finale. His popularity and talent between the posts were recognised when he was voted 'Player of the Year'.
Bristol C (From trainee on 3/7/1995) FL 1 (Freed during 1996 close season)
Chester C (Free from Weston-super-Mare on 30/9/1996) FL 107 FLC 8 FAC 7 Others 3
Hereford U (Free on 5/7/2006) FL 83 FLC 3 FAC 10

BROWN Wayne Lawrence
Born: Barking, 20 August 1977
Height: 6'0"   **Weight:** 12.6
Signed from Colchester at a Hull record fee for a defender, Wayne proved to be worth every penny as his partnership with Michael Turner was the bedrock of the successful team that, on the way to reaching the Premier League via the play-offs, equalled the Tigers' previous best by finishing third in the Championship. A no-nonsense, left-sided centre-back with superb organisational skills, he became the 900th player to make a City debut in League and Cup matches. A personal highlight was his goal in the 3-1 win against his former club Ipswich in September and he was sorely missed when he suffered calf and hamstring injuries in March and April.
Ipswich T (From trainee on 16/5/1996) P/FL 28+12 FLC 3 FAC 2 Others 4+1/1
Colchester U (Loaned on 16/10/1997) FL 0+2
Queens Park Rgrs (Loaned on 22/3/2001) FL 2
Wimbledon (Loaned on 14/9/2001) FL 17/1
Watford (Loaned on 30/1/2002) FL 10+1/3
Watford (Free on 18/12/2002) FL 24+1/1 FAC 1
Gillingham (Loaned on 19/9/2003) FL 4/1
Colchester U (Signed on 17/2/2004) FL

138+2/4 FLC 5 FAC 7+1/1 Others 3+1
Hull C (£450,000 on 18/7/2007) FL 41/1 FLC 3 Others 3

BROWN Wesley (Wes) Michael
Born: Manchester, 13 October 1979
Height: 6'1"   **Weight:** 12.4
Club Honours: UEFACL '99, '08; PL '99, '01, '03, '07, '08; FLC '06; FAC '04; CS '07
International Honours: E: 17; U21-8; Yth; Sch
A solid Manchester United and England central defender or right-back who is commanding in the air, with pace and confidence to match, Wes continued as a beacon of hope for home-grown talent at Old Trafford among so many imports. Always present through another successful Premiership and European campaign, Wes appeared in all competitions. Though widely considered a one-goal-a-season player, he certainly picked his moment to score his first, a rare header to set up United for a fabulous 3-0 win over arch-rivals Liverpool in the Premiership at Old Trafford. With absence through niggling injuries seemingly a thing of the past, he has certainly done enough to convince Sir Alex Ferguson to keep his cheque book in the drawer. In April, he signed a new five-year contract, along with Rio Ferdinand and Michael Carrick, which will keep him at Old Trafford until 2013. On the international front, Fabio Capello named him as a starter in his first games in charge of England, against Switzerland and France.
Manchester U (From trainee on 13/11/1996) PL 175+23/2 FLC 16+2 FAC 29+2 Others 51+7/1

BRUCE Alexander (Alex) Stephen
Born: Norwich, 28 September 1984
Height: 6'0"   **Weight:** 11.6
International Honours: RoI: 1; B-1; U21-5
Alex consolidated his position at the heart of Ipswich's defence, alongside Jason De Vos, where his aerial ability and timing of tackles were to the fore in his performances. He is still striving for the first senior goal of his career but defensive duties take priority.
Blackburn Rov (From trainee on 4/7/2002)
Oldham Ath (Loaned on 23/12/2004) FL 3+3 FAC 1 Others 1
Birmingham C (Signed on 26/1/2005) PL 3+3 FAC 4+2
Oldham Ath (Loaned on 28/1/2005) FL 5+1 FAC 1 Others 1
Sheffield Wed (Loaned on 10/3/2005) FL 5+1 Others 3

Wes Brown

Tranmere Rov (Loaned on 17/8/2005) FL 10+1 FLC 0+1
Ipswich T (Signed on 3/8/2006) FL 75+2 FLC 2 FAC 4

BRUNT Christopher (Chris)

Born: Belfast, 14 December 1984
Height: 6'1" **Weight:** 11.8
Club Honours: Ch '08
International Honours: NI:17; U23-1; U21-2

With a wonderful left foot, Chris played his part in West Bromwich's successful season after he was signed from Sheffield Wednesday in August. His sale after the first match of 2007-08 was a blow to Wednesday's hopes as his attacking thrusts and some thunderous goals from his trusty left foot made him a valuable player and had already established him in the Northern Ireland side. At Albion he created plenty of chances with his teasing, swinging crosses and although he certainly expected to score more goals, his four were significant. His first was in a 3-2 League win at Scunthorpe and his second in the emphatic 5-0 FA Cup victory at Coventry. The third was a vital equalizer against Southampton at the Hawthorns in the penultimate game that effectively confirmed Albion's promotion back to the Premiership. A superb fourth, a 20-yard free-kick to celebrate the birth of his first child, in the 2-0 win at Queens Park Rangers on the last day, clinched the Championship title, Albion's first at any level for 88 years. Occasionally sidelined with a knee injury, Chris played at Wembley in the FA Cup semi-final against Portsmouth.
Middlesbrough (From trainee on 6/7/2002)
Sheffield Wed (Free on 2/3/2004) FL 113+27/24 FLC 4+1 FAC 4 Others 2+2/1
West Bromwich A (£3,000,000 on 15/8/2007) FL 22+12/4 FLC 1 FAC 3+3/1

BUCHANAN David Thomas Hugh

Born: Rochdale, 6 May 1986
Height: 5'8" **Weight:** 10.8
International Honours: NI: U21-15; Yth

David was in and out of the Bury side and rarely settled, although he put in good performances in several positions. Having featured as a left wing-back, left-sided midfielder and central midfielder, his form saw him collect two more Northern Ireland under-21 caps. He scored in both of his last two international matches, but has yet to break his duck for the Shakers. On arriving at Gigg Lane, Alan Knill moved David to left-back, where he flourished.
Bury (From trainee on 5/7/2005) FL 82+20 FLC 3 FAC 9+2 Others 5

BUCKLEY William (Will) Edward

Born: Oldham, 21 November 1989
Height: 6'0" **Weight:** 13.0

Will joined Rochdale from Curzon Ashton for a trial in July and scored twice in a pre-season friendly. Previously a student at Hopwood Hall College, for whom he also played, he signed a professional contract and despite a spell out injured, made his mark as a striker in the reserves. He was rewarded with a call to the first-team squad in February, making his League debut as a substitute against Hereford and his first start a couple of weeks later against Wycombe. A remarkable first season in the professional game for Will ended with a substitute appearance at Wembley in the play-off final.
Rochdale (Free from Curzon Ashton on 18/8/2007) FL 1+6 Others 0+1

BUDTZ Jan

Born: Hillerod, Denmark, 20 April 1979
Height: 6'5" **Weight:** 13.5

A big Danish-born goalkeeper, he was signed by Hartlepool from Doncaster last summer to replace the similarly powerful Dimi Konstantopoulos. In pre-season, it was apparent that Jan would have to battle with Arran Lee-Barrett for the jersey but he made the position his own early in the season and turned in some impressive displays as his confidence grew. However, after a number of defensive problems, the roles were reversed, with Lee-Barrett taking over the position for the final weeks.
Doncaster Rov (Free from FC Nordsjaelland, Denmark on 5/7/2005) FL 26+1 FLC 3+1 FAC 2 Others 0+1
Wolverhampton W (Loaned on 26/1/2007) FL 2+2
Hartlepool U (Free on 12/7/2007) FL 28 FLC 2 FAC 2 Others 2

BULLARD James (Jimmy) Richard

Born: Newham, 23 October 1978
Height: 5'10" **Weight:** 11.10
Club Honours: Div 2 '03

After taking over a year to battle back from the horrific knee injury sustained early last season at Newcastle, Jimmy finally displayed his talents for Fulham on a regular basis after returning as a late substitute at West Ham in January. Restored to the starting line-up, he quickly underlined his fitness with a wholehearted display over 120 minutes on a heavy pitch at Bristol Rovers. He has the ability to dominate the midfield area, always in the thick of the action, and dovetailed well with Danny Murphy and Leon Andreasen in a central role, picking

out key passes and prompting attacking moves as Fulham battled successfully to avoid relegation. His free kicks were dangerous as amply demonstrated when Fulham came from behind to beat Aston Villa. There was another late effort at Blackburn and it was Jimmy's well-placed free kick that led directly to the vital final-day goal at Portsmouth.
West Ham U (£30,000 from Gravesend & Northfleet on 10/2/1999)
Peterborough U (Free on 6/7/2001) FL 62+4/11 FLC 2 FAC 6/1 Others 3/2
Wigan Ath (£275,000 on 31/1/2003) P/FL 144+1/10 FLC 8/1 FAC 1+3
Fulham (Signed on 18/5/2006) PL 19+2/4 FAC 1

BULLEN Lee

Born: Edinburgh, 29 March 1971
Height: 6'1" **Weight:** 12.8

Sheffield Wednesday's captain is a versatile defender who gives his all for the team. His last season with the Owls was a mixed one. He is very likeable and his enthusiasm has helped on several occasions to compensate for errors. Lee was always guaranteed to give of his best and covered at full back in Frank Simek's absence. He will be missed at Hillsborough for his wholehearted displays and great professionalism.
Meadowbank (Signed from Penicuik Ath on 10/1/1990) SL 5+7 Others 0+1
Stenhousemuir (Signed on 13/11/1990) SL 15+7/4 SC 1 (Free to Whitburn Juniors on 10/10/1991)
Dunfermline Ath (Signed from PAE Kalamata, Greece on 3/2/2000) SL 104+26/22 SLC 5+2/1 SC 10+4/1
Sheffield Wed (Free on 6/7/2004) FL 108+26/8 FLC 4+1 FAC 4+1/1 Others 4

BULLOCK Lee

Born: Stockton, 22 May 1981
Height: 5'9" **Weight:** 11.7

Unable to achieve a starting place at Hartlepool last season, Lee went out on a one-month loan to Mansfield at the end of August in order to stiffen the Stags' midfield. This he did but refused a second month at Field Mill, saying he wanted to compete for a Hartlepool place. In early October, Bury were also seeking to strengthen midfield when they added Lee on loan and he made an instant impact in his debut against local rivals Rochdale when his superb through ball put in Andy Mangan to score. Against Shrewsbury, he played on after suffering an early leg injury until substituted against his will. Bury were keen to keep Lee but an agreement could not be reached. Back at Victoria Park Lee made his only appearance for Hartlepool in 2007-08, as a substitute

against Leyton Orient in December before going out on loan to Bradford, a deal that was made permanent immediately prior to the January window closing. Lee gave Bradford important height and presence in midfield, proving to be a strong, robust player and, after several near misses, scored his first goal against Rotherham. Unfortunately, he missed matches towards the end of the season after undergoing a hernia operation.

York C *(From trainee on 29/6/1999) FL 156+15/24 FLC 5+1/1 FAC 10+2/2*
Cardiff C *(£75,000 + on 11/3/2004) FL 12+20/6 FLC 3+1/2 FAC 0+1*
Hartlepool U *(Free on 20/7/2005) FL 30+27/5 FLC 1+2 FAC 2+1 Others 3/1*
Mansfield T *(Loaned on 30/8/2007) FL 5*
Bury *(Loaned on 5/10/2007) FL 8*
Bradford C *(Signed on 1/1/2008) FL 12/1*

BULLOCK Martin John
Born: Derby, 5 March 1975
Height: 5'5" **Weight:** 10.7
Club Honours: AMC '02, '04
International Honours: E: U21-1
Having quickly opened his account with Walsall, scoring against Swansea in the opening match of the season, Martin was reunited with his former manager Alan Buckley six games later when joining up with Grimsby on loan in October, a deal that became permanent in the January window. At Grimsby, manager Buckley likened him to past star Garry Birtles as Martin overcame a long-term injury to show fine form in the season's run-in. The experienced forward's back problem was frustratingly aggravated by regular travelling from his Midlands' home but on returning to fitness, he soon commanded a place, at one stage hitting four goals in four games. Unlucky to be Cup-tied for Town's Johnstone's Paint Trophy final visit to Wembley, he continued to show good alertness and presence in attack.

Barnsley *(£15,000 from Eastwood T on 4/9/1993) P/FL 108+77/4 FLC 14+4 FAC 4+11/3 Others 1*
Port Vale *(Loaned on 14/1/2000) FL 6/1*
Blackpool *(Free on 10/8/2001) FL 128+25/4 FLC 4+3 FAC 10+1 Others 13+1/3*
Macclesfield T *(Free on 4/7/2005) FL 76+7/11 FLC 1/1 FAC 6 Others 5*
Wycombe W *(Free on 3/7/2007) FL 17+8 FLC 1 FAC 1*

BUNN Mark John
Born: Southgate, 16 November 1984
Height: 6'1" **Weight:** 12.2
Northampton manager Stuart Gray calls Mark the best goalkeeper in League One and he had an exceptional season. He pulled off a number of outstanding saves, often making supporters wonder how he

reached the ball when he really had little chance of getting there. Since taking the position a regular basis in August 2006, he has been a model of consistency and could have joined the elite band of Northampton players to make 100 consecutive appearances had he not been injured in a training session at Manchester City.

Northampton T *(From trainee on 8/7/2004) FL 87 FLC 5 FAC 7 Others 2*

BURCH Robert (Rob) Keith
Born: Yeovil, 8 October 1983
Height: 6'2" **Weight:** 12.13
International Honours: E: Yth
Signed from Tottenham in the summer, Rob had to fight Lee Grant for Sheffield Wednesday's vacant goalkeeping slot. The more experienced Grant earned the first nod and his form limited Rob to a handful of appearances. Rob gave signs that he has what it takes to forge a good career as a goalkeeper, especially when he becomes dominant and takes command of his area. Was released at the end of the campaign.

Tottenham H *(From trainee on 3/7/2002)*
Barnet *(Loaned on 30/1/2007) FL 6*
Sheffield Wed *(Free on 11/7/2007) FL 2 FLC 1*

BURGESS Benjamin (Ben) Keiron
Born: Buxton, 9 November 1981
Height: 6'3" **Weight:** 14.4
International Honours: RoI: U21-2; Yth
Ben ended last season as Blackpool's top scorer with nine League goals and one in the Carling Cup. His place as striker was called into question by some occasionally lacklustre performances but his height continued to cause problems for a number of Championship defences. Out of his nine League goals, his strike against Charlton stands out. Blackpool lost 4-1 at the Valley but Ben lobbed Nicky Weaver in the Charlton goal from all of 30 yards. Ben's contract was extended at the end of the season a further year.

Blackburn Rov *(From trainee on 25/11/1998) FL 1+1 FLC 1*
Brentford *(Loaned on 16/8/2001) FL 43/17 FLC 2 FAC 2/1 Others 4*
Stockport Co *(£450,000 on 5/8/2002) FL 17+2/4 FLC 4 FAC 1+1/2 Others 2*
Oldham Ath *(Loaned on 10/1/2003) FL 6+1*
Hull C *(£100,000 on 27/3/2003) FL 54+16/24 FLC 3/1 FAC 1*
Blackpool *(£25,000 on 31/8/2006) FL 38+24/11 FLC 0+1/1 FAC 1+3/1 Others 0+2/2*

BURGESS Kevin Matthew
Born: Middlesbrough, 8 January 1988
Height: 6'0" **Weight:** 12.0
This young reserve defender made just one 20-minute substitute appearance in the centre of Darlington's defence in the

first round FA Cup replay at Northampton when regular central defender Alan White went off injured. After making his debut on the last day of the previous season as a substitute against Stockport, he was unlucky not to add more games to that total, but following the signing of Ian Miller from Ipswich he made only spasmodic appearances on the bench and was released in the summer.

Darlington *(From trainee at Middlesbrough on 9/1/2007) FL 0+1 FAC 0+1*

BURNELL Joseph (Joe) Michael
Born: Bristol, 10 October 1980
Height: 5'10" **Weight:** 11.1
Club Honours: AMC '03
It is fair to say that Northampton's central midfielder enjoyed the better of his two seasons at Sixfields, although he was released at the end of it. He controlled the centre of the midfield with some neat passing and encouraging runs and despite being still in his 20s, Joe is closing on 300 senior appearances for his three clubs.

Bristol C *(From trainee on 24/7/1999) FL 117+14/1 FLC 3+2 FAC 4+3 Others 17+1/2*
Wycombe W *(Free on 7/7/2004) FL 50+7 FLC 2 FAC 1/1 Others 1+1*
Northampton T *(Free on 4/8/2006) FL 50+7/1 FLC 2 FAC 5+2/1 Others 1*

BURNS Jamie Daniel
Born: Blackpool, 6 March 1984
Height: 5'9" **Weight:** 10.11
Club Honours: AMC '04
A former Blackpool wide player who firmed up the previous season's loan deal, Jamie never really established himself in the Morecambe side. The highlight of his season was undoubtedly the goal that gave the Shrimps an excellent 1-0 win at Tranmere in the Johnstone's Paint Trophy. He made only made a handful of starts, three of them at left-back when Danny Adams was suspended late in the season. Jamie did well in defence but was released at the end of the season.

Blackpool *(From trainee on 1/7/2003) FL 30+17/1 FLC 1 FAC 2+2/1 Others 5+3/2*
Bury *(Loaned on 23/3/2006) FL 1*
Morecambe *(Signed on 23/11/2006) FL 4+3 FLC 0+1 Others 2+1/1*

BURRELL Warren Matthew
Born: Sheffield, 3 June 1990
Height: 5'10" **Weight:** 10.6
Warren can play up front or in midfield and is captain of the Mansfield youth team. He came to Field Mill after being released by Sheffield United and progressed enough to be given his first outing from the bench on the final day of the season.

Mansfield T *(Trainee) FL 0+1*

BURTON Deon John
Born: Reading, 25 October 1976
Height: 5'9" **Weight:** 11.9
Club Honours: Div 1 '03
International Honours: Jamaica: 51
Deon had a good season for Sheffield
Wednesday in his own hard-working
style. Strong but not especially quick,
his role in a front two is as the hold-up
man. Never a prolific scorer, he had
a disappointing goals tally, perhaps
reflecting the struggles of the whole side.
Deon reclaimed his place in the Jamaican
national side after a two-year absence
and hopes to be involved in their World
Cup qualifying ties.
*Portsmouth (From trainee on 15/2/1994) FL
42+20/10 FLC 3+2/2 FAC 0+2/1*
*Cardiff C (Loaned on 24/12/1996) FL 5/2
Others 1*
*Derby Co (£1,000,000 + on 9/8/1997) P/FL
78+47/25 FLC 6+2/3 FAC 9+1/3*
Barnsley (Loaned on 14/12/1998) FL 3
*Stoke C (Loaned on 21/2/2002) FL 11+1/2
Others 2+1/2*
Portsmouth (Loaned on 9/8/2002) FL 6/3
*Portsmouth (£75,000 + on 12/12/2002) P/FL
5+5/1 FAC 1+1*
Walsall (Loaned on 12/9/2003) FL 2+1 FLC 1
Swindon T (Loaned on 17/10/2003) FL 4/1
*Brentford (Free on 4/8/2004) FL 38+2/10
FLC 1 FAC 7 Others 2*
*Rotherham U (Free on 1/8/2005) FL 24/12
FLC 2/1 FAC 1/1*
*Sheffield Wed (£100,000 on 2/1/2006) FL
73+26/22 FLC 2+1/2 FAC 2+2*

BURTON-GODWIN Osagyefo (Sagi) Lenin Ernesto
Born: Birmingham, 25 November 1977
Height: 6'2" **Weight:** 13.6
Club Honours: AMC '01
International Honours: St Kitts: 3
Sagi joined Barnet in pre-season after
he was released by Shrewsbury. An
experienced head at the back, he quickly
formed a solid partnership with Ismail
Yakubu. An injury at Burton in the FA Cup
second round put him out of contention
for a considerable period and in the
second half of the season he did not
feature as regularly prior to leaving in the
summer.
*Crystal Palace (From trainee on 26/1/1996)
P/FL 19+6/1 FLC 1 FAC 0+1 Others 0+1*
*Colchester U (Free on 26/5/1999) FL 9 FLC 2
(Freed in November 1999)*
*Port Vale (Free, via trial at Sheffield U, on
14/11/2000) FL 76+10/2 FLC 3/1 FAC 3 Others
6+1/1*
Crewe Alex (Free on 8/8/2002) FL 1
*Peterborough U (Free on 29/8/2002) FL
88+8/4 FLC 3 FAC 6 Others 4+1/1*
*Shrewsbury T (Free on 19/1/2006) FL
41+3/5 FLC 1 FAC 1 Others 1+2*
*Barnet (Free on 4/8/2007) FL 29+1/1 FLC 1
FAC 2 Others 1*

BUTCHER Richard Tony
Born: Peterborough, 22 January 1981
Height: 6'0" **Weight:** 12.12
Freed by Peterborough in the summer,
Richard is a central midfielder with an
eye for goal, as he proved by hitting 12
to finish as top scorer for Notts County.
Unusually, only the last of his goals
proved to be a winner as County drew or
lost all other games in which he scored.
Although preferring a central role, he
was employed in all areas of midfield as a
formula was sought to accommodate his
scoring ability. Some of his strikes were
memorable but none more so than the
winner against Wycombe that secured
County's League status.
*Rushden & Diamonds (From trainee at
Northampton T on 26/11/1999. Freed on
1/10/2001)*
*Lincoln C (Free from Kettering T on
19/11/2002) FL 95+9/11 FLC 3 FAC 3 Others
12/1*
*Oldham Ath (Free on 4/7/2005) FL 32+4/4
FAC 3*
Lincoln C (Loaned on 6/10/2005) FL 4/1
*Peterborough U (Signed on 28/6/2006) FL
35+8/4 FLC 2 FAC 4/1 Others 2*
*Notts Co (Signed on 23/7/2007) FL 46/12
FLC 1 FAC 1+1*

BUTLER Andrew (Andy) Peter
Born: Doncaster, 4 November 1983
Height: 6'0" **Weight:** 13.6
After a frustrating two years in League
One, Andy thrived on Scunthorpe's
step up to the Championship, having
an excellent season at the heart of the
defence. A strong, commanding left-
footed centre-half, he won his place in
the starting line-up for the third match
of the campaign and stayed first choice
for the rest, apart from missing six weeks
after fracturing a bone in his foot in the
defeat at Ipswich in December. Was in
talks with the club over a new three-year
contract at the end of the season.
*Scunthorpe U (From trainee on 2/7/2003) FL
123+12/16 FLC 3+1 FAC 10 Others 5*
*Grimsby T (Loaned on 6/10/2006) FL 4
Others 1*

BUTLER Martin Neil
Born: Wordsley, 15 September 1974
Height: 5'11" **Weight:** 11.9
Club Honours: Div 2 '07
When Martin arrived at Grimsby from
Walsall, manager Alan Buckley likened
him to past star Garry Birtles and he
overcame a long-term injury to show
fine form in the season's run-in. The
experienced forward's back problem
was frustratingly aggravated by regular
travelling from his Midlands' home but on
returning to fitness he soon commanded
a place, at one stage hitting four goals in

four games. Unlucky to be Cup-tied for
Town's Johnstone's Paint Trophy final visit
to Wembley, he continued to show good
alertness and presence in attack. Earlier,
Martin had quickly opened his account in
his second season back with his original
League club, scoring against Swansea at
home, but was reunited with Buckley at
Grimsby after seven games.
*Walsall (From trainee on 24/5/1993) FL
43+31/8 FLC 2+1 FAC 2+5/2 Others 2+2/2*
*Cambridge U (£22,500 on 8/8/1997) FL
100+3/41 FLC 9/6 FAC 9+2/5 Others 3+1/1*
*Reading (£750,000 + on 1/2/2000) FL
85+18/32 FLC 4+1 FAC 5/2 Others 4+1/2*
*Rotherham U (£150,000 on 2/9/2003) FL
90+7/28 FLC 3 FAC 2+1 Others 1/1*
*Walsall (Free on 13/7/2006) FL 49/12 FLC 1/1
FAC 2 Others 1*
*Grimsby T (Signed on 16/10/2007) FL
15+6/6 FAC 1*

BUTLER Paul John
Born: Manchester, 2 November 1972
Height: 6'2" **Weight:** 13.0
Club Honours: Div 2 '97; Div 1 '99
International Honours: Rol: 1; B-1
Arriving at Chester from MK Dons in the
summer, the vastly experienced centre-half
was handed the captaincy and became
a steady presence at the heart of City's
defence in the first half of the season, when
he linked effectively with Paul Linwood. His
positional play and reading of the game
proved a great benefit as City pressed for
a play-off place before Christmas. In the
second half of the season, Paul was in and
out of the side with a series of niggling
injuries and his form dipped as the Blues
slipped down the table with a string of
defeats that almost resulted in relegation.
Powerful in the air, Paul contributed goals
against Bury and Accrington when he came
up for set pieces.
*Rochdale (From trainee on 5/7/1991) FL
151+7/10 FLC 8+1 FAC 6+2 Others 12+1*
*Bury (£100,000 on 22/7/1996) FL 83+1/4
FLC 8 FAC 2 Others 3/1*
*Sunderland (£600,000 + on 15/7/1998) P/FL
78+1/3 FLC 11+1/1 FAC 4*
*Wolverhampton W (Loaned on 17/11/2000)
FL 5*
*Wolverhampton W (£1,000,000 on
31/1/2001) P/FL 118+1/3 FLC 5 FAC 7 Others 5*
*Leeds U (Free on 2/7/2004) FL 99/4 FLC 4
FAC 2 Others 1*
MK Dons (Free on 22/11/2006) FL 17 FAC 1
*Chester C (Free on 30/7/2007) FL 35/2 FLC 1
FAC 1 Others 1*

BUTLER Thomas (Tommy) Anthony
Born: Dublin, 25 April 1981
Height: 5'8" **Weight:** 10.8
Club Honours: Div 1 '08
International Honours: Roi: 2; U21-14; Yth

Overcoming an early season hamstring injury, the former Sunderland wide midfielder displayed consistency on Swansea's left flank. He also scored dramatic goals, with nothing better than the opener at Leyton Orient, pointing the Swans towards a 5-0 win. Even when switched to the right, he continued to show the skill to beat his opponent with ease.

Sunderland *(From trainee on 25/6/1998) P/FL 16+15 FLC 1+3 FAC 0+1*
Darlington *(Loaned on 13/10/2000) FL 8 FAC 2*
Dunfermline Ath *(Free on 10/9/2004) SL 6+6 SLC 2*
Hartlepool U *(Free on 24/3/2005) FL 31+6/2 FLC 2 FAC 2/1 Others 2+1*
Swansea C *(£50,000 on 4/8/2006) FL 46+26/7 FLC 0+1 FAC 5+2/2 Others 4+3*

BUTT Nicholas (Nicky)
Born: Manchester, 21 January 1975
Height: 5'10" **Weight:** 11.3
Club Honours: FAYC '92; CS '96, '97, '03; PL '96, '97, '99, '00, 01, '03; FAC '96, '04; EC '99
International Honours: E: 39; U21-7; Yth; Sch
At a time when player-rotation is in vogue, Nicky's appearance record of being almost ever-present last season demonstrates what a key member of Newcastle's midfield he has become. Calm and assured under pressure but with a competitive edge, his covering of the back four is an important feature of his play, while his intelligent use of the ball often provides the springboard for attacks. His wealth of experience was tapped when he was asked to captain the side on occasions and he contributed a delightful chipped goal against Everton in October to mark his 350th Premier League appearance. He also scored against Chelsea, and his strike at Tottenham in March sparked a revival that turned a 1-0 deficit into a 4-1 win.
Manchester U *(From trainee on 29/1/1993) PL 210+60/21 FLC 7+1 FAC 23+6/1 Others 67+13/4*
Newcastle U *(£2,500,000 on 30/7/2004) PL 78+6/5 FLC 3+2 FAC 6 Others 15+4*
Birmingham C *(Loaned on 4/8/2005) PL 22+2/3 FLC 3 FAC 2*

BUTTERFIELD Daniel (Danny) Paul
Born: Boston, 21 November 1979
Height: 5'10" **Weight:** 11.10
Club Honours: AMC '98
International Honours: E: Yth
An experienced Crystal Palace right-back, who is now one of the club's longest-serving players, Danny had a good season in 2007-08, free from major injuries. His

good form resulted in him signing a two-year extension to his contract in February. Danny is a popular player, inside the club as well as with supporters, and augments his defensive responsibilities by pressing forward effectively to supply consistently good crosses.
Grimsby T *(From trainee on 7/8/1997) FL 100+24/3 FLC 13+1 FAC 5+2 Others 1+1/1*
Crystal Palace *(Free on 7/8/2002) P/FL 157+12/5 FLC 13+1 FAC 7+1 Others 5+1/1*

BUTTERFIELD Jacob Luke
Born: Bradford, 10 June 1990
Height: 5'11" **Weight:** 12.3
Jacob, developed by the Barnsley Academy, made his debut as a late substitute in the Carling Cup defeat at Newcastle and was rewarded in September with a three-year contract. Jacob was a regular in the heart of midfield for Barnsley's reserves. He was a late substitute at Wembley in the FA Cup semi-final and made his first start on the

Nicky Butt

final day of the season at Cardiff.
Barnsley *(From trainee on 2/10/2007) FL 1+2 FLC 0+1 FAC 0+1*

BUTTERS Guy
Born: Hillingdon, 30 October 1969
Height: 6'3" **Weight:** 14.2
International Honours: E: U21-3
After signing for Brighton in 2002 at the age of 32, Guy could hardly have dared hope for another six years of League football but his intelligent positional play and peerless heading counterbalanced ageing legs and established him as the rock at the heart of Albion's defence for much of that time. Last season, though, he found it difficult to maintain consistency and finally gave way to the younger players he had nurtured alongside him. It was, therefore, no great surprise when he was not offered a new contract but he leaves the Withdean Stadium with the best wishes of the supporters.
Tottenham H *(From trainee on 5/8/1988) FL 34+1/1 FLC 2+1 FAC 1*
Southend U *(Loaned on 13/1/1990) FL 16/3 Others 2*
Portsmouth *(£375,000 on 28/9/1990) FL 148+6/6 FLC 16+1/1 FAC 7 Others 7+2*
Oxford U *(Loaned on 4/11/1994) FL 3/1 Others 1*
Gillingham *(£225,000 on 18/10/1996) FL 155+4/16 FLC 9 FAC 14/1 Others 11*
Brighton & Hove A *(Free on 29/8/2002) FL 183+4/8 FLC 5+1/1 FAC 7+1 Others 11*

BUXTON Jake Fred
Born: Sutton-in-Ashfield, 4 March 1985
Height: 5'11" **Weight:** 13.0
Jake is a local lad who has progressed through the ranks at Mansfield and is now club captain. He started last season as centre-half, pairing up well with new partner Martin McIntosh, but was suspended after he was ordered off for a second yellow card in September and missed the Boxing Day win over Peterborough through illness. Having led the side well, he suffered two more red cards towards the end of the season after giving away penalties when adjudged to have been the last man. Jake is a confident player who can operate anywhere across the back four and gives everything for the team.
Mansfield T *(From juniors on 21/10/2002) FL 144+7/5 FLC 5 FAC 11+1 Others 5+1*

BUXTON Lewis Edward
Born: Newport, Isle of Wight, 10 December 1983
Height: 6'1" **Weight:** 13.10
For the second successive season at Stoke, Lewis was blighted by injuries. The centre-half or full-back, having once

featured reasonably regularly, made only four appearances in the promotion season, all from the bench. Happily, he was able to take part in the last match of the season as Stoke took the point they needed off Leicester.

Portsmouth *(From trainee on 9/4/2001)* FL 27+3
Exeter C *(Loaned on 21/10/2002) FL 4 Others 2*
Bournemouth *(Loaned on 10/1/2003) FL 15+2 FAC 1*
Bournemouth *(Loaned on 30/10/2003) FL 24+2 FAC 1+1*
Stoke C *(Free on 24/12/2004) FL 40+13/1 FLC 0+1 FAC 4*

BUZSAKY Akos
Born: Budapest, Hungary, 7 May 1982
Height: 5'11" **Weight:** 11.9
International Honours: Hungary: 11; U21
Akos started the season well in Plymouth's midfield, with manager Ian Holloway saying he would pay to see him play, but in October the Hungarian informed Argyle that he would not be signing a new contract when his existing one ran out at the end of the campaign. With that in mind, he went on loan to Queens Park Rangers in October and the move was made permanent in January. He stepped into the then vacant, but still revered, Rs' number-ten shirt and immediately did it justice. One of the classiest players seen at Loftus Road for many years, Akos not only settled into midfield, he dominated it. His all-round play was excellent but it was his fantastic scoring record that really shone. Akos scored only nine times in three years at Plymouth but bagged ten League goals in seven months at Loftus Road, including the Rs' 'Goal of the Season' for his effort against Blackpool in March. Equally comfortable in midfield, on the wing, or playing off a lone front man, Akos looks likely to be a key man for Rangers next season.
Plymouth Arg *(£25,000 from FC Porto, Portugal, ex MTK Hungaria, on 21/11/2005) FL 65+31/8 FLC 4+1/1 FAC 4*
Queens Park Rgrs *(£500,000 on 30/10/2007) FL 24+3/10 FAC 1*

BYFIELD Darren
Born: Sutton Coldfield, 29 September 1976
Height: 5'11" **Weight:** 11.11
International Honours: Jamaica: 7
Having joined Bristol City from Millwall just after the start of last season, the experienced striker impressed early on at Ashton Gate and finished as top scorer, even though he found the net

only eight times. Surprisingly, all but two of his successful strikes were when he was used as a substitute, which explains why he was regarded as an impact player. Unfortunately there was to be no fairy-tale ending when he replaced Nick Carle for the last 14 minutes of the Championship play-off final at Wembley. To make it even worse for Darren was the fact that he was released by City just two days later.

Aston Villa *(From trainee on 14/2/1994) PL 1+6 FLC 1 FAC 0+1 Others 1*
Preston NE *(Loaned on 6/11/1998) FL 3+2/1 Others 1*
Northampton T *(Loaned on 13/8/1999) FL 6/1 FLC 1/1*
Cambridge U *(Loaned on 17/9/1999) FL 3+1*
Blackpool *(Loaned on 6/3/2000) FL 3*
Walsall *(Free on 21/6/2000) FL 45+32/13 FLC 2+3/2 FAC 4+2/1 Others 2+2/1*
Rotherham U *(£50,000 on 27/3/2002) FL 53+15/22 FLC 3+1/1 FAC 2*
Sunderland *(Signed on 6/2/2004) FL 8+9/5*
Gillingham *(Free on 23/7/2004) FL 54+13/19 FLC 2/1 FAC 1 Others 1*
Millwall *(Free on 7/7/2006) FL 28+3/16 FAC 3+1 Others 1*
Bristol C *(£100,000 on 30/8/2007) FL 17+16/8 FAC 1 Others 0+1*

BYGRAVE Adam Michael
Born: Walthamstow, 24 February 1989
Height: 5'9" **Weight:** 12.2
A stocky youngster who can play anywhere in defence, where he makes up for a lack of height by his reading of the game, Adam is highly rated by Reading as a player to watch. In order to gain added experience, he was loaned out to Gillingham in November and soon impressed with his defensive displays. He fitted well into the Gills' back line but following a 3-0 defeat at home to Crewe, was unable to find a way past Danny Cullip, Simon King and Garry Richards before returning to the Madejski Stadium at the end of April. Was out of contract in the summer and looking for a new club.
Reading *(From trainee on 6/7/2007)*
Gillingham *(Loaned on 20/11/2007) FL 13+2 Others 1*

BYRNE Clifford (Cliff)
Born: Dublin, 27 April 1982
Height: 6'0" **Weight:** 12.12
Club Honours: Div 1 '07
International Honours: RoI: U21-10; Yth
Popular full-back Cliff firmed up his position as Scunthorpe's first choice on the right with a battling season in the Championship. A strong-tackling player, his 100 per-cent effort and workrate saw him stick to his task well against difficult

opponents. His season was hampered by a couple of red cards and in November he suffered a hairline fracture of a leg during the home match against Stoke. Although he was playing again inside two months, it wasn't until April that he fully shook off the effects of the injury.
Sunderland *(From trainee on 27/5/1999)*
Scunthorpe U *(Loaned on 21/11/2002) FL 13 FAC 3*
Scunthorpe U *(Free on 2/7/2003) FL 131+18/3 FLC 5 FAC 15+2 Others 10*

BYRNE Mark
Born: Dublin, 9 November 1988
Height: 5'9" **Weight:** 11.0
After being rejected by a host of clubs, the young Irishman joined Nottingham Forest in the summer and impressed the City Ground management with his all-action displays in the centre of midfield. Mark was a regular in the reserves and his performances earned promotion to the senior squad. His debut came as a substitute against Cheltenham in April and he will be hoping for more opportunities during the new campaign.
Nottingham F *(Signed from Crumlin U on 12/1/2007) FL 0+1*

BYWATER Stephen (Steve) Michael
Born: Manchester, 7 June 1981
Height: 6'3" **Weight:** 13.2
Club Honours: FAYC '99
International Honours: E: U21-6; Yth
Steve was ever-present in Derby's goal until Christmas, with plenty of chances to shine behind an uncertain defence, prior to suffering a shoulder injury at Newcastle and then realising during the warm-up for the Boxing Day game against Liverpool that he was not fit. By the time he recovered, Derby were on the brink of signing Roy Carroll from Glasgow Rangers, a transfer triggered by Ipswich goalkeeper Neil Alexander's arrival at Ibrox as cover. Following that, Steve joined Ipswich on loan in January to fill the vacancy and played in every game from then onwards. After a jittery start, he grew in confidence as the season drew to an anti-climax, making some outstanding saves, particularly in away games. The loan was with a view to a permanent transfer, but Ipswich extended their search in the summer.
Rochdale *(Trainee) Others 1*
West Ham U *(£300,000 + on 7/8/1998) P/FL 57+2 FAC 5 Others 3+1*
Wycombe W *(Loaned on 23/9/1999) FL 2*
Hull C *(Loaned on 23/11/1999) FL 4*
Coventry C *(Loaned on 3/8/2005) FL 14*
Derby Co *(Signed on 12/8/2006) P/FL 55 FLC 1 FAC 3 Others 3*
Ipswich T *(Loaned on 31/1/2008) FL 17*

C

[CACAPA] DA SILVA Claudio Roberto
Born: Lavras, Brazil, 29 May 1976
Height: 6'0" **Weight:** 12.5
International Honours: Brazil: 4
An accomplished defender who is comfortable on the ball, as befits a Brazilian international, Cacapa joined Newcastle in the summer when his contract with Lyon expired, having led that club to a succession of French titles. His debut was as a substitute against Aston Villa in the first home game, making him the 1,000th player to represent the club in a competitive match, and he quickly became a fixture at the centre of the defence until November's home game with Portsmouth, when he was replaced after 22 minutes with Newcastle 3-0 down. He returned in December for the game at Fulham with a 'Man of the Match' performance but a groin injury in March sidelined him until the final day at Everton when he made a substitute appearance. His first Newcastle goal was in the October victory over Tottenham.
Newcastle U (Free from Lyon, France, ex Atletico Mineiro, on 7/8/2007) PL 16+3/1 FLC 1 FAC 2/1

CADAMARTERI Daniel (Danny) Leon
Born: Cleckheaton, 12 October 1979
Height: 5'7" **Weight:** 11.12
Club Honours: FAYC '98
International Honours: E: U21-3; Yth
Arriving at Huddersfield on a free from Leicester in the summer, Danny missed the opening games with a troublesome hamstring injury. Once fully fit, he showed the Galpharm faithful his array of pace, strength and trickery on the ball. Often used as a winger, he was also deployed as a striker to probe opposing defences with his strong and purposeful running. It was not long before goals flowed, notably his first two in successive home games against Luton and Nottingham Forest, the latter incurring a second yellow card for over-celebrating. Unfortunately, just as things were taking off his season was prematurely ended with a right knee-tendon injury shortly before Christmas.
Everton (From trainee on 15/10/1996) PL 38+55/13 FLC 6+3/2 FAC 6+3
Fulham (Loaned on 4/11/1999) FL 3+2/1
Bradford C (Free on 22/2/2002) FL 42+10/5 FLC 1/1
Leeds U (Free on 12/7/2004) FLC 0+1
Sheffield U (£50,000 on 30/9/2004) FL 14+7/1 FAC 0+1
Bradford C (Free on 4/8/2005) FL 25+14/2 FLC 1/1 FAC 2+1 Others 1 (Freed on 1/7/2006)
Leicester C (Free from Grays Ath on 29/12/2006) FL 0+9 FAC 0+2/1
Doncaster Rov (Loaned on 16/3/2007) FL 6/1
Huddersfield T (Free on 5/6/2007) FL 10+2/3 FAC 1+1

CAHILL Gary James
Born: Dronfield, 19 December 1985
Height: 6'2" **Weight:** 12.6
International Honours: E: U21-3; Yth
The central defender signed a three-and-a-half-year contract with Bolton in the January transfer window. Although highly regarded at Aston Villa, some questioned the lofty fee Gary Megson paid. The player quickly dispelled such

Cacapa

concerns with a series of assured and talismanic displays, in particular when making a very impressive debut in the 2-0 win over Reading. Pivotal in keeping a clean sheet in his UEFA Cup debut in a 0-0 draw with Atletico Madrid, Gary quickly forged a great understanding with Andy O'Brien at the heart of the Bolton defence. A series of resolute defensive displays during the latter stages played a huge part in Bolton retaining their Premiership place and Gary established himself as a first-team regular during this time, showing the sort of form that led to rumours of an England call-up. Earlier in the season, Bryan Robson strengthened the centre of Sheffield United's defence by signing Gary on a three-month loan from Aston Villa. He impressed throughout his stay, showing good awareness, strength in the air and tidy distribution and there were hopes of a permanent move before Gary found his way to Bolton.

Aston Villa *(From trainee on 23/12/2003) PL 25+3/1 FLC 2 FAC 1*
Burnley *(Loaned on 9/11/2004) FL 27/1 FLC 1 FAC 4*
Sheffield U *(Loaned on 20/9/2007) FL 16/2*
Bolton W *(£4,500,000 on 30/1/2008) PL 13 Others 4*

CAHILL Thomas (Tom)
Christopher
Born: Leyland, 21 November 1986
Height: 5'10" **Weight:** 12.8
Rotherham became Tom's first League club when he joined them from Matlock soon after passing his degree examinations. He struggled to make an impact and did not make his full debut until early April, although he scored regularly for the reserves. He could be a player for the future.
Rotherham U *(Signed from Matlock, ex Sheffield University, Euxton Villa, on 23/7/2007) FL 5+2 Others 0+1*

CAHILL Timothy (Tim) Joel
Born: Sydney, Australia, 6 December 1979
Height: 5'10" **Weight:** 10.11
Club Honours: Div 2 '01
International Honours: Australia: 28; W Samoa: Yth
It was another injury-plagued season for Everton's Australian international, but when fit the midfielder proved once again that he is amongst the best of his type in the top flight. Tim injured a foot in a pre-season friendly and only returned to the team in October but immediately set off on a sparkling run of form, netting eight times before the turn of the year. After some consistent displays

in the second-half of the campaign a broken foot, sustained against West Ham in March, ended his involvement. A measure of his importance to Everton is that the Toffees lost only two of the 18 League games Tim played, and he scored in both those defeats. A typically competitive Australian, Tim specialises in late runs into the box, matched with wonderful heading ability.
Millwall *(Signed from Sydney U, Australia on 31/7/1997) FL 212+5/52 FLC 9+1/1 FAC 10+2/3 Others 10+1/1*
Everton *(£2,000,000 on 29/7/2004) PL 100+1/29 FLC 7+3/3 FAC 4+1/2 Others 10/3*

CAICEDO Felipe Salvador
Born: Guayaquil, Ecuador, 5 September 1988
Height: 6'1" **Weight:** 12.4
International Honours: Ecuador: 15
An Ecuadorian international striker, Felipe signed for Manchester City from FC Basle during the January transfer window. The powerfully-built front man arrived at the age of 19, with 15 international caps and two goals under his belt, having previously played at under-20 and under-17 level for Ecuador. He was thrown straight into the action with a debut as a substitute in the 2-1 Manchester derby victory at Old Trafford in February. Happy to play through the middle or on the left he continued to improve in a succession of substitute appearances as the season progressed.
Manchester C *(£5,200,000 from FC Basle, Switzerland, ex Rocafuerte, on 31/1/2008) PL 0+10*

CAINES Gavin Liam
Born: Birmingham, 20 September 1983
Height: 6'1" **Weight:** 12.0
Central defender Gavin missed the start of the season with a knee injury but returned to make three appearances in September, scoring Cheltenham's goal in a 1-1 draw with Tranmere. After sitting out October, Gavin returned to partner first Shane Duff and then youngster Andy Gallinagh in the centre of defence. The latter was a makeshift arrangement, brought about by injuries, but the pair helped the Robins to five clean sheets in six games during January. A strong, robust defender with a fearsome shot who takes the occasional free-kick, Gavin missed the final two months of the season with a new knee injury that required an operation but had done enough to earn the offer of a new contract from manager Keith Downing.
Walsall *(From trainee on 25/7/2003)*
Cheltenham T *(Free on 26/7/2004) FL 110+25/6 FLC 4/1 FAC 11 Others 10+1*

CAIRO Ellery Francois
Born: Rotterdam, Holland, 3 August 1978
Height: 5'7" **Weight:** 11.0
The Dutch right-sided wide player, signed from Hertha Berlin in the close season, had few chances to display his promised speed and crossing ability, starting only four League and two Carling Cup games for Coventry. His last appearance was in early December in a home defeat by Sheffield United when most observers thought he had a good game. In April he was told he was not being retained and was looking for a new club.
Coventry C *(Signed from Hertha Berlin, Germany, ex Feyenoord, Excelsior, Twente Enschede, SC Freiburg, on 6/7/2007) FL 4+3 FLC 2*

CALDWELL Stephen (Steve)
Born: Stirling, 12 September 1980
Height: 6'0" **Weight:** 11.5
Club Honours: Ch '05
International Honours: S: 9; B-3; U21-4; Yth
It was a disappointing season for the Burnley club captain, as he missed almost half the games through injury, his longest absence being a two-month lay-off up to Christmas with a torn tendon. The second half of the season was a stop-start affair for him and with the side having more defensive options, he was not always a guaranteed starter when fit. However, he remains a commanding presence at the back and a threat up front, opening his Clarets' scoring account with goals at home to Coventry and at Southampton.
Newcastle U *(From trainee on 30/10/1997) PL 20+8/1 FLC 3/1 Others 1+5*
Blackpool *(Loaned on 12/10/2001) FL 6 Others 1/1*
Bradford C *(Loaned on 7/12/2001) FL 9*
Leeds U *(Loaned on 2/2/2004) PL 13/1*
Sunderland *(Free on 19/7/2004) P/FL 75+1/4 FLC 4/1 FAC 1*
Burnley *(£400,000 on 31/1/2007) FL 42+4/2 FLC 2 FAC 1*

CAMARA Henri
Born: Dakar, Senegal, 10 May 1977
Height: 5'9" **Weight:** 10.8
International Honours: Senegal: 52
Recognised as a speedy striker with an eye for goal, Henri was allowed to join West Ham on a season-long loan from Wigan. A goal-poacher, whose trickery round the box makes him a threat, his only Wigan game had come against Hull in the Carling Cup. Playing as a striker, he was never able to command a regular place at West Ham and started in only three League games. He was used as a substitute on seven occasions but usually too late to make an impression. Henri's

last match was against Birmingham in February.

Wolverhampton W *(Free from Sedan, France, ex Neuchatel Xamax, Strasbourg, Grasshoper Zurich, on 6/8/2003) PL 29+1/7 FLC 2*
Glasgow Celtic *(Loaned on 2/8/2004) SL 12+6/8 SLC 0+1 SC 0+1 Others 4+2*
Southampton *(Loaned on 31/1/2005) PL 10+3/4 FAC 2+1/2*
Wigan Ath *(£3,000,000 on 10/8/2005) PL 43+9/18 FLC 3+1*
West Ham U *(Loaned on 31/8/2007) PL 3+7*

CAMARA Mohamed (Mo)

Born: Conakry, Guinea, 25 June 1975
Height: 5'11" **Weight:** 11.9
Club Honours: SPD '06; SLC '06
International Honours: Guinea: 79

Mo was on the outside at Derby after the 2007 January transfer window and although he scored with a speculative shot against Blackpool in the Carling Cup, it was a surprise when he was picked to play at Liverpool. It proved to be the left-back's only Premiership appearance and he went on loan to Norwich in November to help fill the gap caused by injury to Adam Drury. The agreement was subsequently extended as Mo, strong in the tackle and with excellent positional sense, added maturity to the Canaries' back-line. Always keen to overlap and get forward, he also found himself on direct free-kick duties for a while.

Wolverhampton W *(Signed from Le Havre, France, ex AS Beauvais, Troyes, OSC Lille, on 11/8/2000) FL 27+18 FLC 2+1 FAC 1+1 Others 2*
Burnley *(Free on 18/7/2003) FL 90 FLC 7/1 FAC 6+1*
Glasgow Celtic *(Free on 22/6/2005) SL 19 SLC 3 Others 2*
Derby Co *(Free on 16/8/2006) P/FL 20 FLC 3/1 FAC 3*
Norwich C *(Loaned on 20/11/2007) FL 20+1 FAC 1+1*

CAMERON Colin

Born: Kirkcaldy, 23 October 1972
Height: 5'6" **Weight:** 10.6
Club Honours: S Div 1 '93, '95; SLC '94; SC '98; AMC '08; Div 2 '08
International Honours: S: 28; B

A former team-mate of manager Paul Ince at Wolverhampton, Colin fitted well into the style of play adopted at the MK Dons after arriving from Coventry last summer. Comfortable on the ball, he worked hard in midfield and was always a potential scorer. Although he missed the final few games after suffering a knee injury, he used his experience to good effect in helping the Dons to the double of the Johnstone's Paint Trophy and the

League Two title.
Raith Rov *(Signed from Lochore Welfare on 13/7/1990) SL 106+16/23 SLC 8+1/5 SC 6/3 Others 9/2*
Heart of Midlothian *(£400,000 on 31/3/1996) SL 152+3/47 SLC 13/6 SC 17+1/6 Others 6+3/1*
Wolverhampton W *(£1,750,000 on 24/8/2001) P/FL 136+32/22 FLC 4/2 FAC 8+3 Others 5*
Millwall *(Loaned on 3/3/2006) FL 5*
Coventry C *(Free on 5/7/2006) FL 16+8/2*

FLC 1 FAC 1/1
MK Dons *(Free on 1/8/2007) FL 21+8/3 FAC 0+1 Others 4+1/1*

CAMP Lee Michael John

Born: Derby, 22 August 1984
Height: 5'11" **Weight:** 11.11
International Honours: E: U21-5; Yth

After impressing during his second loan spell at Queens Park Rangers towards the tail end of the previous season, Lee returned from Derby on a permanent

Lee Camp

basis in summer. He instantly made the goalkeeping spot his own, producing a string of fantastic performances and countless vital saves. Whilst the exact number of points he earned or saved for Rangers can be debated, his contribution to the season was immense, particularly early on, when the side struggled for form. He went on to become Rangers' only ever-present, playing every minute of every League and Cup game.

Derby Co *(From trainee on 16/7/2002)* FL 88+1 FLC 2 FAC 4 Others 2
Queens Park Rgrs *(Loaned on 12/3/2004)* FL 12
Norwich C *(Loaned on 8/9/2006)* FL 3
Queens Park Rgrs *(Loaned on 19/2/2007)* FL 11
Queens Park Rgrs *(£300,000 on 7/8/2007)* FL 46 FLC 1 FAC 1

CAMPANA Alessandro (Alex)

Born: Harrow, 11 October 1988
Height: 5'11" **Weight:** 12.1
Recognised as a talented wide-midfield player, Alex is a product of the Watford Academy who made his first-team debut at the age of 16. Having been awarded a full contract, Alex scored the first senior goal of his career in the Carling Cup against Gillingham before going on loan to Wealdstone for a spell. There were no League appearances for him at Watford in 2007-08 and he was released in the summer.

Watford *(From trainee on 20/4/2007)* FLC 1+2/1

CAMPBELL Dudley (DJ) Junior

Born: Hammersmith, 12 November 1981
Height: 5'10" **Weight:** 11.0
A nimble striker signed by Martin Allen from Birmingham for a fee that, reportedly, could rise to over £1-million. However, any promotion-related clauses will have to be put on hold as DJ never really established himself as the first-choice front man at Leicester, with only one goal after early November as confidence slipped away. Pacy, but never prolific, seemed to be the majority verdict.

Brentford *(Signed from Yeading, ex Stevenage Borough, on 7/6/2005)* FL 13+10/9 FLC 1 FAC 4/3
Birmingham C *(£500,000 on 31/1/2006)* P/FL 19+24/9 FLC 2+2/1 FAC 3/2
Leicester C *(£2,100,000 on 7/8/2007)* FL 17+11/4 FLC 2+2/1

CAMPBELL Fraizer Lee

Born: Huddersfield, 13 September 1987
Height: 5'11" **Weight:** 12.4
International Honours: E: U21-1; Yth

Fraizer made one Carling Cup appearance for Manchester United in the defeat by Coventry City before moving on loan to Hull in October and turning into arguably the discovery of the season. The young striker was a vital factor in transforming Hull into a potent force as they reached the top flight of English football for the first time in their history. In addition to the invaluable contribution of 15 goals and despite his slender frame, Fraizer worked relentlessly to halt opposition attacks before they started. A clinical finisher, his remarkable campaign reached a perfect climax when he provided an exquisite cross for Dean Windass to volley the winner in the play-off final against Bristol City at Wembley. At either end of the experience scale, he was often referred to as 'my lad' by his 39-year-old fellow forward. A regular winner of 'Man of the Match' awards, he was runner-up in the club's and supporters' 'Player of the Year' awards. Fraizer had earlier Tigers' pedigree, having scored over 30 goals playing under former City manager Warren Joyce at Royal Antwerp in 2006-07. He made his England under-21 debut against Poland at Wolverhampton in March.

Manchester U *(From trainee on 29/3/2006)* PL 0+1 FLC 0+1
Hull C *(Loaned on 18/10/2007)* FL 32+2/15 Others 3

CAMPBELL Stuart Pearson

Born: Corby, 9 December 1977
Height: 5'10" **Weight:** 10.8
Club Honours: FLC '97, '00
International Honours: S: U21-14
Stuart enjoyed another good campaign, captaining Bristol Rovers from central midfield and being selected as the supporters' 'Player of the Season'. His contribution from set plays and his range of accurate passes were significant and he was one of only two players who were ever-present in all League and Cup matches, the other being goalkeeper Steve Phillips.

Leicester C *(From trainee on 4/7/1996)* PL 12+25 FLC 2+5 FAC 3+3
Birmingham C *(Loaned on 23/3/2000)* FL 0+2
Grimsby T *(£200,000 on 15/9/2000)* FL 154+1/12 FLC 6/1 FAC 7 Others 0+1
Bristol Rov *(Free on 5/7/2004)* FL 133+17/2 FLC 6 FAC 16+1 Others 16+1/1

CAMPBELL Sulzeer (Sol) Jeremiah

Born: Plaistow, 18 September 1974
Height: 6'2" **Weight:** 14.1
Club Honours: FLC '99; PL '02, '04; FAC '02, '05, '08; CS '02

International Honours: E: 73; B-2; U21-11; Yth (UEFA-U18 '93)
Sol enjoyed another excellent season at the centre of Portsmouth's defence, his partnership with Sylvain Distin proving to be particularly effective. Pompey kept 23 clean sheets in all competitions and the pair partnered one another in 19 of them. His performances were rewarded with a recall to the England side for the Euro 2008 qualifers against Estonia and Russia in October, the friendly international against Austria and the final Euro 2008 qualifier against Croatia in November, taking him to 73 caps. Despite his season being slightly disrupted by niggling injuries, he still made 31 Premier League appearances and retains all his old qualities, particularly his strength and his ability to time crucial tackles to perfection. Along with David James and four others, Sol has appeared in all 16 seasons of the Premier League, amassing 453 appearances along the way. That puts him fourth in the all-time Premier League list behind Gary Speed, David James and Ryan Giggs. He capped his season by lifting the FA Cup after Pompey's 1-0 victory against Cardiff.

Tottenham H *(From trainee on 23/9/1992)* PL 246+9/10 FLC 28/4 FAC 28+2/1 Others 2
Arsenal *(Free on 10/7/2001)* PL 133+2/8 FLC 2 FAC 19/2 Others 41/1
Portsmouth *(Free on 11/8/2006)* PL 63/2 FLC 1 FAC 7

CAMPBELL-RYCE Jamal Julian

Born: Lambeth, 6 April 1983
Height: 5'7" **Weight:** 11.10
Club Honours: Div 1 '06
International Honours: Jamaica: 7; Yth
Arriving at Oakwell last August on a two-year contract from Southend, Jamal made his Barnsley debut against Scunthorpe a couple of weeks later. Playing wide on either side of midfield, he was a constant threat to defenders, always willing to take them on at speed and deliver crosses. He can cut inside and has a vicious shot, as Southend were reminded in the FA Cup when he hit the winner. Jamal, who continued to be selected by Jamaica, had started the first three games for Southend before Barnsley revived their interest from the previous season and the player opted for a return to Yorkshire.

Charlton Ath *(From trainee on 9/7/2002)* PL 0+3 FLC 0+2
Leyton Orient *(Loaned on 10/8/2002)* FL 16+1/2 FLC 2/1
Wimbledon *(Loaned on 6/2/2004)* FL 3+1
Chesterfield *(Loaned on 20/8/2004)* FL 14 FLC 1 Others 1/1
Rotherham U *(Signed on 30/11/2004)* 27+4 FAC 1
Southend U *(Loaned on 27/9/2005)* FL 7+6

Jamal Campbell-Ryce

FAC 2 Others 1
Colchester U *(Loaned on 23/3/2006)*
FL 1+3
Southend U *(Free on 30/5/2006) FL 40+5/2*
FLC 5 FAC 3
Barnsley *(Signed on 31/8/2007) FL 34+3/3*
FAC 4+1/1

CAMPION Darren
Born: Birmingham, 17 October 1988
Height: 5'11"　**Weight:** 11.0
Signed initially on a short-term deal last
September, having been a trainee at
Birmingham, Darren made his full debut
for Carlisle in the last League match of
the campaign. Playing in central defence,
he gave an assured performance that
promises well for the future.
*Carlisle U (From trainee at Birmingham C on
11/9/2007) FL 1+1*

CAMPO Ramos Ivan
Born: San Sebastian, Spain, 21 February
1974
Height: 6'1"　**Weight:** 12.11
International Honours: Spain: 4
Seemingly frozen out of Sammy Lee's
designs for Bolton at the beginning of last
season, Ivan did not figure in any of the
first six League games. Indeed, such was
the belief that Ivan would leave the club
before the August transfer window closed
that he was not even registered as a UEFA
Cup squad member for the initial stages
of the competition. A change of heart
restored Ivan to the starting line-up for
the home game against Tottenham and
he duly responded with a 'Man of the
Match' display as well as netting Bolton's
goal in a 1-1 draw. In addition, Ivan
played in some UEFA Cup games, joining
the competition for the home victory over
Atletico Madrid in the knock-out stages.
A great cult favourite among the Bolton
fans, Ivan continued to bring much-
needed warmth and humour to the game
before being out of contract at the end of
the campaign.
*Bolton W (Free from Real Madrid, Spain, ex
CD Logrones, Alaves, Vallencia, Valladolid,
Real Mallorca, on 31/8/2002) PL 149+23/13
FLC 8+3/1 FAC 6+1 Others 3+1*

CANOVILLE Lee
Born: Ealing, 14 March 1981
Height: 6'1"　**Weight:** 11.3
International Honours: E: Yth; Sch
Lee joined Notts County as a late arrival
at the start of the campaign, having
been earlier released by Shrewsbury. An
experienced right-sided defender, who
can also play as centre-back, he loves to
join the attack with bursts of pace down
the flank. Was out of contract in the
summer and looking for a new club.

Arsenal *(From trainee, having earlier been transferred from Millwall juniors for an undisclosed fee, on 3/7/1998) FLC 0+1* **Northampton T** *(Loaned on 26/1/2001) FL 2* **Torquay U** *(Free on 14/9/2001) FL 107+5/2 FLC 2 FAC 3 Others 4* **Boston U** *(Free on 4/8/2005) FL 57+2/1 FLC 2 FAC 2 Others 2* **Shrewsbury T** *(Free on 30/1/2007) FL 6+1* **Notts Co** *(Free on 27/7/2007) FL 32+3 FLC 1 FAC 2*

CANSDELL-SHERIFF Shane Lewis

Born: Sydney, Australia, 10 November 1982
Height: 6'0" **Weight:** 11.12
International Honours: Australia: U23; Yth

Shane's preferred position is at centre-back, where he turned in the solid, unflappable performances that made him a virtual ever-present in the Tranmere side during the last campaign. Strong, reliable and tenacious, he is also sufficiently versatile to fit into any line-up but plays particularly well alongside Ian Goodison. Remaining more or less free of injury all season, Shane relished any chance to go up front and grabbed four League goals in the process. Out of contract in the summer, he was offered new terms by the Birkenhead side.

Leeds U *(Free from NSW Soccer Academy, Australia on 1/2/2000. Freed during 2003 close season)* **Rochdale** *(Loaned on 8/11/2002) FL 3 FAC 1* **Tranmere Rov** *(Signed from Aarhus GF, Denmark on 24/7/2006) FL 83+4/6 FLC 2/1 FAC 6/1 Others 2*

CAPALDI Anthony (Tony) Charles

Born: Porsgrunn, Norway, 12 August 1981
Height: 6'0" **Weight:** 11.8
Club Honours: Div 2 '04
International Honours: NI: 22; U21-14

Was out of contract at Plymouth during the summer of 2007 and opted for a move to Cardiff. Took time to settle at left-back, but finished the season strongly. Tony played a key role in a City back four, alongside Roger Johnson, Glenn Loovens and Kevin McNaughton, who were a major factor in the FA Cup run that took Cardiff to the final. Can also operate in the right-back position with confidence and possesses good passing ability.

Birmingham C *(From trainee on 9/7/1999)* **Plymouth Arg** *(Free on 3/5/2003) FL 122+19/12 FLC 4 FAC 5+1 Others 0+2* **Cardiff C** *(Free on 1/7/2007) FL 43+1 FLC 4 FAC 6*

CARAYOL Mustapha Soon

Born: Gambia, 10 June 1989
Height: 5'11" **Weight:** 12.0

Mustapha impressed MK Dons while on trial pre-season and after being given a two-year contract made a couple of substitute appearances in Cup competitions before being loaned out to Blue Square Premier side Crawley for the last two-thirds of the season. He is a pacy left-winger who will sharpen his shooting and crossing with further experience.

MK Dons *(From trainee at Swindon T on 10/8/2007) FLC 1 Others 0+1*

CARBON Matthew (Matt) Philip

Born: Nottingham, 8 June 1975
Height: 6'2" **Weight:** 13.6
International Honours: E: U21-4

An experienced and powerful central defender, Matt had trials with the MK Dons before the season but picked up an injury that meant that he was not signed until just before Christmas. He made his debut as a substitute in the Boxing Day win at Notts County, played three further games off the bench, but then picked up another injury that kept him out of the final two months of the campaign prior to being released in the summer.

Lincoln C *(From trainee on 13/4/1993) FL 66+3/10 FLC 4/1 FAC 3 Others 4+3* **Derby Co** *(£385,000 on 8/3/1996) P/FL 11+9 FLC 1 FAC 0+1* **West Bromwich A** *(£800,000 on 26/11/1998) FL 106+7/5 FLC 7+2 FAC 4* **Walsall** *(Free on 23/7/2001) FL 49+6/2 FLC 1 FAC 5* **Lincoln C** *(Loaned on 24/10/2003) FL 1* **Barnsley** *(Free on 5/7/2004) FL 37+13/1 FLC 2 FAC 3+1 (Freed during 2006 close season)* **MK Dons** *(Free from New Zealand Knights on 4/12/2007) FL 0+3 Others 0+1*

CARDEN Paul Andrew

Born: Liverpool, 29 March 1979
Height: 5'8" **Weight:** 11.10
Club Honours: FC '04

Arriving at Accrington from Burton in the summer after he had captained the England non-League side, his signing was regarded as a coup, with Stanley expecting a quality midfield player being added to their squad. Unfortunately, Paul's career at Stanley never really took off. He did not appear until late September because of injury and then played only four games before being sidelined with another injury. In November he went to Cambridge United on loan and on his return was selected only twice as an unused substitute. He returned to Cambridge in January, on loan for the rest of the season, and helped them to the

Blue Square Premier play-off final.

Blackpool *(From trainee on 7/7/1997) FL 0+1 FAC 0+1 Others 1* **Rochdale** *(Free on 3/3/1998) FL 30+15 FLC 0+2 FAC 3+1 Others 3+1* **Chester C** *(Free on 10/3/2000) FL 45+6 FLC 0+1 FAC 3 Others 3* **Peterborough U** *(Free on 4/7/2005) FL 43+1 FLC 1+1 FAC 2 Others 3 (Free to Burscough on 20/10/2006)* **Accrington Stanley** *(Free from Burton A on 5/7/2007) FL 4*

CARDLE Joseph (Joe)

Born: Blackpool, 7 February 1987
Height: 5'8" **Weight:** 9.5

Joe spent the first half of the season on loan to Clyde from Port Vale. The tricky left-winger was sent off on his debut against Dundee but the nine appearances he made helped his football education. He was recalled on New Year's Day by new manager Lee Sinnott and used as a substitute at Cheltenham the following day. Joe can cause problems for any defence on his day but struggled to make an impact until the last few games when he was given his first consistent run. He played well in a 3-2 victory at Brighton and despite suffering with the rest in a 6-0 drubbing at Swindon, was the only one who showed some fight. Was released at the end of the season.

Port Vale *(From trainee on 30/6/2006) FL 6+16 FLC 0+1 FAC 0+1 Others 1+1* **Clyde** *(Loaned on 30/8/2007) SL 7 SC 1 Others 1*

CAREW Ashley Wayne

Born: Lambeth, 17 December 1985
Height: 6'0" **Weight:** 11.0

Right-winger Ashley signed for Barnet after a successful trial in the close season, having been released as a youngster by Gillingham. Given a second chance of making it in professional football by Paul Fairclough, he took his opportunity eagerly, featuring regularly in the Bees' side and notching his first League goal in the 4-2 win at Stockport in October, when he completed the scoring.

Barnet *(Free from Fisher Ath, ex trainee at Gillingham, Beckenham T, on 19/5/2007) FL 18+15/1 FLC 1 FAC 5 Others 1*

CAREW John Alieu

Born: Strommen, Norway, 5 September 1979
Height: 6'5" **Weight:** 14.0
International Honours: Norway: 71; U21; Yth

Exceedingly tall, John provides the height in Aston Villa's attack but there is more to his game than that because

he is an all-round forward. Strong and physical, opponents find it extremely hard to knock him off the ball, especially as he has a deft touch to bring it under control. The target-man likes to have the ball played to his feet so that he can turn past defenders and create opportunities for himself or others. The season was especially productive from a goalscoring perspective and opponents know they have been in a contest. John was out for six matches early in the

season after suffering knee ligament damage but apart from that was always there, scoring a hat-trick in the home game against Newcastle. John received an international accolade in November when he was named Norway's 'Player of the Year' and scored for them against Argentina and Greece.
Aston Villa (Signed from Olympique Lyonnais, France, ex Lorenskog IF, Valerenga, Rosenborg, Valencia, AS Roma - loan, Besiktas, on 24/1/2007) PL 43/16 FAC 1

Clarke Carlisle

CAREY Louis Anthony
Born: Bristol, 20 January 1977
Height: 5'10" **Weight:** 11.10
Club Honours: AMC '03
International Honours: S: U21-1
Yet another magnificent season for the Bristol City captain, despite a mid-season injury disruption. He joined rarefied ranks, becoming only the fifth player to make more than 500 appearances for the club, unfortunately reaching this milestone when Plymouth knocked City off top spot by winning at Ashton Gate for the first time since 1931. As in the previous season, he combined well with Jamie McCombe as City almost stormed into the Premiership and in the Championship play-off final at the new Wembley, Louis was rated as City's star man.
Bristol C (From trainee on 3/7/1995) FL 301+11/5 FLC 15+1 FAC 18+1 Others 21+2/1
Coventry C (Free on 16/7/2004) FL 23 FLC 3 FAC 1
Bristol C (Free on 1/2/2005) FL 121+2/5 FLC 3 FAC 4 Others 8+1/1

CARLE Nicholas (Nick) Alberto
Born: Sydney, Australia, 23 November 1981
Height: 5'11" **Weight:** 12.2
International Honours: Australia: 7; U21; Yth
Bristol City paid £500,000 during the transfer window to sign the skilful Australian international from Turkish side Genclerbirligi. Unfortunately, despite being a fairly regular scorer with his previous clubs, goals just would not come for the attacking midfielder. Perhaps it would have been different if he had put away an easy chance in his first home game against Blackpool but he impressed for all that with his quick feet and high energy. Rated by his Socceroo team-mate Tim Cahill, of Everton, as an exceptional talent, all at Ashton Gate are hoping that Nick will blossom, especially after he put a relatively easy chance wide having skilfully setting up the opportunity for himself in the Championship play-off final at Wembley.
Bristol C (£500,000 from Genclerbirligi, Turkey, ex Sydney Olympic, Troyes, Marconi Stallions, Newcastle United Jets, on 18/1/2008) FL 14+3 Others 3

CARLISLE Clarke James
Born: Preston, 14 October 1979
Height: 6'1" **Weight:** 12.10
International Honours: E: U21-3
Released by Watford, Clarke joined Burnley in August as a straight replacement for the departed Wayne Thomas. A tall and imposing defender, his experience

at this level was clear as he often kept the opposition at bay. The latter half of his season was disrupted by injury and then suspension following an injury-time dismissal at Preston; he picked up another red card in the final game at Crystal Palace. If the occasional temerity can be eliminated, Clarke could easily become one of the best defenders in the Championship and he seems likely to remain a key player at the back for the Clarets.

Blackpool (From trainee on 13/8/1997) FL 85+8/7 FLC 4+1 FAC 3/1 Others 5
Queens Park Rgrs (£250,000 on 25/5/2000) FL 93+3/6 FLC 5 FAC 6 Others 5
Leeds U (Free on 12/7/2004) FL 29+6/4 FLC 3
Watford (£100,000 on 6/8/2005) P/FL 34+2/3 FLC 2/2 FAC 2
Luton T (Loaned on 1/3/2007) FL 4+1
Burnley (£200,000 on 17/8/2007) FL 32+1/2 FLC 2

CARLTON Daniel (Danny)

Born: Leeds, 22 December 1983
Height: 5'11" **Weight:** 12.4
The hero of Morecambe's victory over Exeter in the previous season's Conference play-off final, Danny found the going rather tougher in League One after signing for Carlisle in the summer. Undoubtedly a hard worker, he made only a handful of starts, although he was often brought on as a substitute. Despite his best efforts, the elusive first goal never came although he did assist in goals scored by fellow strikers. It is to be hoped that the summer break will help to restore his confidence.

Carlisle U (Signed from Morecambe on 20/7/2007) FL 5+26 FLC 1+1 FAC 0+2 Others 1+1

CARNEIRO Carlos Paulo Martins

Born: Pacos de Ferreira, Portugal, 27 December 1974
Height: 6'1" **Weight:** 12.4
Carlos arrived at Walsall from Panionios in the summer and hopes were high that the Portuguese striker would emulate the feats of his fellow-countryman Jorge Leitao in the Saddlers' front line. Although he looked useful in pre-season games, Carlos made only four starts, was substituted in three of them and booked in the other. He left Walsall with hopes unfulfilled.

Walsall (Free from Panionios, Greece, ex Vitoria Guimaraes, Gil Vicente, on 19/7/2007) FL 2+1 FLC 1 Others 1

CARNEY David (Dave) Raymond

Born: Sydney, Australia, 30 November 1983
Height: 5'11" **Weight:** 12.4
International Honours: Australia:11; Yth

Signed by Sheffield United on a three-year deal from Sydney FC, the Australian international took time to adjust the pace of the Championship. Playing as a wide attacking midfielder, usually on the left but occasionally on the right, he worked hard, showing the ability to beat an opponent and produce a searching cross. He had a good run in the side in November and December and scored a well-taken goal at Colchester but after a brief run under Kevin Blackwell lost his place. Dave continued his international career and was named by the Aussie 4-4-2 magazine as the Socceroos 'Player of the Season'.

Everton (From trainee on 15/1/2000)
Oldham Ath (Free on 8/8/2003) FLC 0+1 (Freed in February 2004)
Hamilton Academical (Free from Sydney U, Australia, ex Halifax T on 13/11/2004) SL 6+2 SC 1 (Free to Sydney U on 1/7/2005)
Sheffield U (Free from Sydney FC, Australia on 10/8/2007) FL 18+3/2 FLC 3 FAC 1+1/1

CAROLE Sebastien (Seb)

Born: Pontoise, France, 8 September 1982
Height: 5'6" **Weight:** 11.4
A French winger, Seb was a regular starter for Leeds in the early part of last season, scoring in the 1-1 draw at Gillingham, lashing in a superb equaliser in the home draw against Leyton Orient and netting in the 3-1 triumph at Bournemouth in November. But he was used sparingly from December onwards and did not start a Leeds' game after Gary McAllister replaced Dennis Wise as manager in January. Seb reminded everyone what he is capable of by going on in the final League One game, against Gillingham, and smartly fashioning a goal for Bradley Johnson.

West Ham U (Loaned from Monaco, France on 31/1/2004) FL 0+1
Brighton & Hove A (Signed from Monaco, France on 12/8/2005) FL 34+6/2 FLC 1 FAC 1
Leeds U (Free on 3/8/2006) FL 24+21/3 FLC 3 FAC 2 Others 1+1

CARR Stephen

Born: Dublin, 29 August 1976
Height: 5'9" **Weight:** 12.2
Club Honours: FLC '99
International Honours: RoI: 44; U21-12; Yth; Sch
Once again, Stephen's season was interrupted by injuries, a problem that has plagued him throughout his time at Newcastle. He is a strong-tackling right-back who takes any opportunity to support the attack, but after starting the first three games he tore a hamstring at Middlesbrough and was out until late

November. On the second substitute appearance of his return, he broke down with a recurrence of the injury and was not recalled for first-team action until January, when Habib Beye was away at the African Cup of Nations. Stephen lost his place when Beye returned and was released by the club at the end of the season. He added a further Republic of Ireland cap before retiring from international football in November.

Tottenham H (From trainee on 1/9/1993) PL 222+4/7 FLC 23/1 FAC 16+1 Others 6
Newcastle U (£2,000,000 on 12/8/2004) PL 76+2/1 FLC 1 FAC 8 Others 20

CARRAGHER James (Jamie) Lee Duncan

Born: Bootle, 28 January 1978
Height: 6'1" **Weight:** 13.0
Club Honours: FAYC '96; FLC '01, '03; FAC '01, '06; UEFAC '01; ESC '01, '05; CS '01, '06; UEFACL '05
International Honours: E: 34; B-3; U21-27; Yth
Jamie enjoyed another excellent season in the heart of Liverpool's defence, playing in all but four of the 59-match programme. He had a variety of partners in central defence, Daniel Agger at the start of the season, Sami Hyypia for most of the remainder and Martin Skrtel for the closing stages. He is the ultimate stopper who reacts to dangerous situations quickly and is nearly always in the right place to make a well-timed, last-ditch clearance. His tackling is hard but fair and, remarkably for a defender, he picks up few cautions. His composure and self-discipline probably allow him to get away with offences that would lead to sanctions if committed by other players, perhaps most notably in the October derby with Everton when every single refereeing decision seemed to go in Liverpool's favour. Strangely, in the latter part of the campaign, Rafa Benitez deployed him six times at right-back, a position Jamie dislikes, having spent his early career there, because, due to his lack of pace, he is reluctant to make forward runs. But in his first outing there, against Sunderland in February, he provided an inch-perfect cross for Peter Crouch to break the deadlock and a few weeks later, against Bolton, a similar run and cross provided a chance that Dirk Kuyt was unable to convert. Such incidents were rarely, if ever, seen when Jamie was a regular full-back six or more years earlier. Indeed, that was the reason Jamie called time on his England career in summer 2007. Disappointed at being passed over for selection in his natural position and given only occasional outings

at full-back, where he felt he could not do himself justice, he decided at the age of 29 that it was too late to become an automatic choice and that there were plenty of younger defenders available to make up the England squad. It was a logical decision and one to which Jamie has adhered despite various requests to reconsider.
Liverpool (From trainee on 9/10/1996)
PL 346+14/3 FLC 22+4 FAC 28+1 Others 107+1/1

CARRICK Michael
Born: Wallsend, 28 July 1981
Height: 6'0" **Weight:** 11.10
Club Honours: FAYC '99; PL '07, '08; CS '07; UEFACL '08
International Honours: E: 14; B-1; U21-14; Yth
As a highly-rated, classy and composed Manchester United and England midfield player, Michael was quick to acknowledge that a first-team place was no longer assured following the big money arrival of Owen Hargreaves from Bayern Munich in the summer. Competing with the likes of Hargreaves, Paul Scholes and Anderson, he was a regular until October, when he suffered a fractured elbow playing against AS Roma in the Champions' League. Michael returned in November as a substitute for Anderson against Arsenal at the Emirates Stadium and from then until the end of the season, he figured strongly in United's successful quest for domestic and European honours. His only goal of the season was in the Manchester derby defeat at home to City in February but he was crucial to the Reds' title and Champions' League ambitions. He signed a new five-year contract in April, along with defenders Rio Ferdinand and Wes Brown, that will keep him at Old Trafford until 2013.
West Ham U (From trainee on 25/8/1998)
P/FL 128+8/6 FLC 8 FAC 11 Others 3+1
Swindon T (Loaned on 12/11/1999) FL 6/2
Birmingham C (Loaned on 23/2/2000) FL 1+1
Tottenham H (£3,000,000 on 24/8/2004) PL 61+3/2 FLC 3+1 FAC 6+1
Manchester U (£14,000,000 + on 1/8/2006) PL 53+11/5 FLC 0+1 FAC 10+1/1 Others 24+1/2

CARRINGTON Mark Richard
Born: Warrington, 4 May 1987
Height: 6'0" **Weight:** 11.0
After making three appearances from the Crewe bench in 2006-07, Mark gained further valuable League experience last season. He made his full debut at home to Walsall in December and aims to make an impact in the season ahead. Is a player who can perform on either side

of midfield, in an attacking role or as the holding player.
Crewe Alex (From trainee on 3/7/2006) FL 3+9 FLC 0+1 Others 0+1

CARROLL Andrew (Andy) Thomas
Born: Gateshead, 6 January 1989
Height: 6'3" **Weight:** 11.0
International Honours: E: Yth
Andy is a tall, strong, young Newcastle striker, still raw but capable of development, with good ball control for a big man. His scoring potential was demonstrated with a hat-trick against Middlesbrough reserves for the second successive season and he netted in a pre-season friendly against Juventus, earning praise from opposing goalkeeper Gianluigi Buffon. He went on loan to Preston for three months to broaden his experience, making seven starts and five substitute appearances in his time at Deepdale. After scoring once and picking up a red card at Scunthorpe he returned to Newcastle, where he became a regular on the bench. Andy made his first Premiership start in the final game at Everton and scored on his England under-19 debut against Belarus in September.
Newcastle U (From trainee on 4/7/2006) PL 1+7 FAC 0+3 Others 0+2
Preston NE (Loaned on 14/8/2007) FL 7+4/1 FLC 0+1

CARROLL Neil Adam
Born: Cheltenham, 21 September 1988
Height: 5'11" **Weight:** 11.8
A graduate of the Chester Academy, Neil was one of a number of players given an opportunity by manager Bobby Williamson. The left-sided midfielder made his debut in the 2-1 victory at Macclesfield in September in what proved to be his only first-team appearance. In November, Neil went on loan to Leigh RMI of the Blue Square North in order to gain experience and remained there until the end of the season.
Chester C (From juniors on 24/1/2007) FL 1

CARROLL Roy Eric
Born: Enniskillen, 30 September 1977
Height: 6'2" **Weight:** 12.9
Club Honours: AMC '99; PL '03; FAC '04
International Honours: NI: 19; U21-11; Yth
Despite Derby's struggles, Roy made a good impression after arriving as last January's transfer window was closing. The transfer had been agreed for several weeks but Glasgow Rangers would not let him go until they signed a replacement. That merely added to Roy's frustration, as the summer move to Ibrox did not bring

him any League football. The goalkeeper simply wanted to be playing and the position at Derby was open to him when Steve Bywater joined Ipswich on loan. Roy has a strong presence, always letting defenders know what is required, and is probably coming into his best years as a goalkeeper. He had plenty of work as the Rams drifted towards relegation but handled safely until he had a bad day when Aston Villa put six past him. After that, he never recovered his certainty.
Hull C (From trainee on 7/9/1995) FL 46 FLC 2 FAC 1 Others 1
Wigan Ath (£350,000 on 16/4/1997) FL 135 FLC 11 FAC 8 Others 15
Manchester U (£2,500,000 on 27/7/2001) PL 46+3 FLC 5 FAC 7+1 Others 10
West Ham U (Free on 15/6/2005) PL 31 FAC 2 Others 2
Glasgow Rgrs (Free on 7/7/2007) SLC 1
Derby Co (Signed on 31/1/2008) PL 14

CARRUTHERS Christopher (Chris) Paul
Born: Kettering, 19 August 1983
Height: 5'10" **Weight:** 12.3
International Honours: E: Yth
Chris, a left-sided Bristol Rovers' midfielder, spent the first two months of the season at left-back but failed to hold down a regular place because of the form of Joe Jacobson. Due to be released in summer, it looks as if his future will be away from the Memorial Stadium.
Northampton T (From trainee on 9/4/2002) FL 52+22/1 FLC 2+1 FAC 7 Others 3+2
Bristol Rov (Free on 24/3/2005) FL 87+13/1 FLC 3+1 FAC 11+1 Others 11+1

CARSLEY Lee Kevin
Born: Birmingham, 28 February 1974
Height: 5'10" **Weight:** 11.11
International Honours: RoI: 39; U21-1
Once again the veteran midfielder proved an invaluable presence in the heart of the Everton midfield, missing only a handful of matches. Deployed in the key holding role, the Republic of Ireland international enjoyed a consistent campaign and played an important part as the Toffees finished fifth. The Birmingham-born player gives 100 per cent every match and uses his vast experience to break up play and distribute the ball quickly. A credit to his profession on and off the pitch, Lee is strongly involved in several charitable organisations.
Derby Co (From trainee on 6/7/1992) P/FL 122+16/5 FLC 10+3 FAC 12 Others 3
Blackburn Rov (£3,375,000 on 23/3/1999) P/FL 40+6/10 FLC 4/1 FAC 4/1
Coventry C (£2,500,000 on 1/12/2000) P/FL 46+1/4 FLC 2/1 FAC 3
Everton (£1,950,000 on 8/2/2002) PL 153+13/12 FLC 14/1 FAC 8+1 Others 9

CARSON Scott Paul
Born: Whitehaven, 3 September 1985
Height: 6'3" **Weight:** 13.7
Club Honours: ESC '05
International Honours: E: 2; B-2; U21-29; Yth

A pre-season injury to goalkeeper Thomas Sorensen prompted Aston Villa to sign Scott on a season-long loan from Liverpool in a deal costing £2-million. Apart from missing the two games against Liverpool, in which he was not allowed to play, Scott was absent on only one other occasion, through suspension after receiving a red card in the home game against Manchester United. Scott settled in well at Villa and became a consistent performer. He made his England debut in a friendly in Austria, was included in the squad for the friendly against Germany and made his first competitive start in the vital Euro 2008 qualifier against Croatia. Unfortunately, a high-profile error helped to scupper England and it was generally felt he had not been given enough chance to acclimatise to international football.

Leeds U *(From trainee on 5/9/2002) PL 2+1*
Liverpool *(£750,000 + on 21/1/2005) PL 4 FLC 1 FAC 1 Others 3*
Sheffield Wed *(Loaned on 10/3/2006) FL 9*
Charlton Ath *(Loaned on 14/8/2006) PL 36 FLC 2*
Aston Villa *(Loaned on 10/8/2007) PL 35 FAC 1*

CARTER Darren Anthony
Born: Solihull, 18 December 1983
Height: 6'2" **Weight:** 12.5
International Honours: E: Yth

As a left-footed midfielder, able to play wide or down the middle, Darren joined Preston from West Bromwich two years before the start of the season and was a fixture in the squad. Despite an impressive debut, Darren took time to win over the Deepdale fans. He does not have a ball-winning style but tackles firmly when necessary. Darren has a powerful shot and earned a priceless three points with a stoppage-time winner at Leicester.

Birmingham C *(From trainee on 13/11/2001) P/FL 28+17/3 FLC 1 FAC 2+3/2 Others 1+1*
Sunderland *(Loaned on 17/9/2004) FL 8+2/1*
West Bromwich A *(£1,500,000 on 5/7/2005) P/FL 30+23/4 FLC 6/1 FAC 3+2/1 Others 0+2*
Preston NE *(£1,250,000 on 10/8/2007) FL 30+9/4 FLC 1 FAC 3*

CARVALHO Alberto Ricardo
Born: Amarante, Portugal, 18 May 1978
Height: 6'0" **Weight:** 12.6
Club Honours: FLC '05, '07; PL '05, '06
International Honours: Portugal: 46

Chelsea's unsung hero, Ricardo has not been on the losing side in a Premier League match for over 18 months, since November 2006. Unsurprisingly, he was voted 'Players' Player of the Year' and forms, with John Terry, the most formidable central defensive partnership in the Premier League. They complement each other perfectly, with Terry steaming into tackles and Ricardo using his pace and awareness to nullify last-ditch chances and showing his confidence on the ball to step up into midfield and initiate attacks with probing passes to feet. His only goal of the season was a header that decided the match against Middlesbrough. Ricardo sustained a niggling back injury following an awkward fall against Everton in November and missed six matches. Unfortunately the scenario was repeated in the penultimate Premier League match at Newcastle, five days after a towering performance in the Champions' League semi-final had guided Chelsea into their first final. He recovered in time to put in a typically faultless performance in atrocious conditions in Moscow as the Blues blunted the free-scoring Manchester United attack. Obviously, the Portuguese influence at the Bridge has been immense since Jose Mourinho's arrival in 2004 and, although less flamboyant, Ricardo has made a similar impact to his famous mentor.

Chelsea *(£16,500,000 + from FC Porto, Portugal, ex Leca, on 30/7/2004) PL 96+5/6 FLC 11 FAC 11/1 Others 40/2*

CARVILL Michael Desmond
Born: Belfast, 3 April 1988
Height: 6'2" **Weight:** 12.11
International Honours: NI: U21-7; Yth

After his loan from Charlton in 2006-07, Michael joined Wrexham on a 12-month contract in the summer. Despite four successive outings in late September and early October and a return at the end of the campaign, the midfielder was released in May.

Charlton Ath *(From trainee on 11/5/2006)*
Wrexham *(Free on 14/2/2007) FL 6+8 Others 1*

CASEMENT Christopher (Chris)
Born: Belfast, 12 January 1988
Height: 6'0" **Weight:** 12.2
Club Honours: FAYC '05
International Honours: NI: U21-9; Yth

Chris is a valued member of the Ipswich squad but his first-team opportunities were again limited by the good form of the other defenders at Portman Road and he made just three appearances. A commanding centre-back who likes to bring the ball out of defence to make

constructive passes, he continued to add to his Northern Ireland under-21 caps throughout the campaign.

Ipswich T *(From trainee on 20/4/2006) FL 4+4 FLC 0+1 FAC 1+2*

CASTILLO Nery Alberto
Born: San Luis Potosi, Mexico, 13 June 1984
Height: 5'8" **Weight:** 9.8
International Honours: Mexico: 13

The pacy Mexican international who joined Manchester City in January on an extended loan from Shakhtar Donetsk, arrived at the City of Manchester Stadium aiming to show the fans that he would be an asset wide on the right or as a striker. Nery made his City debut at Upton Park in the goalless FA Cup third round tie against West Ham in January but made only one other appearance before breaking a small bone in his shoulder in the Cup replay, resulting in six weeks out. After that, he made only one more start and five appearances from the bench.

Manchester C *(Loaned from Shakhtar Donetsk, Ukraine, ex Danubio, Olympiakos, on 4/1/2008) PL 2+5 FAC 2*

CATTERMOLE Lee Barry
Born: Stockton, 21 March 1988
Height: 5'10" **Weight:** 12.0
International Honours: E: U21-3; Yth

This England under-21 international is a confident, dominant, ball-winning midfielder who, if he can steer clear of serious injury, will be a future star for Middlesbrough, despite enduring a frustrating season. He made 14 of his 24 Premiership appearances from the substitutes' bench and some were for only a few minutes of play. Lee has a wise head on his young shoulders and is sensible and patient enough to realise that by the time the 2010 World Cup starts in South Africa, he will be only 22. By then he envisages himself playing regularly in the Premiership and pushing for the full England squad.

Middlesbrough *(From trainee on 2/7/2005) PL 42+27/3 FLC 3 FAC 13+1/1 Others 3+2*

CAVANAGH Peter Joseph
Born: Bootle, 14 October 1981
Height: 5'9" **Weight:** 11.9
Club Honours: FC '06

For the third successive season, Accrington's long-serving captain and full-back missed a large chunk of the action through injury and, as always, the lack of his defensive and leadership qualities was keenly felt. After playing in 14 of the first 16 League games, he needed a hernia operation. Unfortunately, when well on his way to recovery, his return was

knocked back when it was discovered that he required an Achilles operation. He showed the fans what they had been missing with a superb performance in his first game back against Dagenham, as he did in all the remaining games. At Wrexham, in one of his rare appearances in midfield, he scored a fine goal.
Accrington Stanley (From trainee at Liverpool on 27/9/2001) FL 45/5 FLC 3 FAC 1/1 Others 1

CECH Petr
Born: Plzen, Czech Republic, 20 May 1982
Height: 6'5" **Weight:** 14.3
Club Honours: FLC '05, '07; PL '05, '06; CS '05
International Honours: Czech Republic: 62

Chelsea's brilliant goalkeeper collected another raft of awards, being voted UEFA 'Goalkeeper of the Year' for 2006-07 and Czech Republic 'Footballer of the Year' for the third consecutive season, the only player to achieve this feat. In his now-familiar black skull protector, a legacy from the previous season's horrific head injury, Petr endured another injury-stricken season that included calf and hip strains but the worst injury came on the training ground in April when a collision with a team-mate left him with a horrendous facial injury requiring 50 stitches. He defied medical opinion that demanded a long lay-off, bravely returning for the season's climax with a string of inspirational performances. Although he showed signs of human frailty with uncharacteristic errors that cost goals, he maintained his exceptionally high standards as the Blues strove desperately to clinch a Premier League and Champions' League double. He played exceptionally in the Champions' League semi-final against Liverpool and in the Moscow final pulled off an astonishing double save to take the match into extra-time. Although he saved Ronaldo's spot-kick brilliantly in the shoot-out it was to no avail as the Blues missed two at the other end. Chelsea boasted the second-best defensive record in the Premier League and Petr's total of just 17 goals conceded in 26 matches was a major factor in that impressive statistic.
Chelsea (£9,000,000 from Stade Rennais, France, ex Chmel Blsany, on 19/7/2004) PL 115 FLC 7 FAC 7 Others 37

CERNY Radek
Born: Prague, Czech Republic, 18 February 1974
Height: 6'3" **Weight:** 13.5
Club Honours: FLC '08
International Honours: Czech Republic: 3

Radek has been a great servant to Tottenham during his three-year loan spell from Slavia Prague. Last season the goalkeeper made more first-team appearances than in any other. Radek won a place ahead of Paul Robinson but lost out to him before the Carling Cup final, when he had to be satisfied with a place on the bench. He made 13 Premier League appearances and seven in other competitions. In a season where Tottenham conceded 79 goals in 57 games, Radek was not involved in the five when they let in four. His highlights include playing in both legs of the Carling Cup semi-final against Arsenal, including the 5-1 win for Tottenham, and he also relished the game against his home team in Prague. At the end of the season, Radek signed for Championship side Queens Park Rangers.
Tottenham H (Loaned from SK Slavia Prague, Czech Republic, ex Ceske Budejovice, Union Cheb, on 28/1/2005) PL 15+1 FLC 4 FAC 4 Others 4

CESAR Bostjan
Born: Ljubljana, Slovenia, 9 July 1982
Height: 6'4" **Weight:** 13.6
Club Honours: Ch '08
International Honours: Slovenia: 26

A big, strong centre-half, good in the air and competitive on the ground, the season-long loanee from Marseille to West Bromwich had five different partners in his first season in English football and

Bostjan Cesar

generally performed well. Bostjan had his off days, as did several other Albion players, his worst coming in a 2-1 League defeat at Barnsley when he was shown his eighth yellow card of the campaign. He scored a crucial goal in the 2-1 home League win over Burnley.

West Bromwich A *(Loaned from Oympique Marseille, France, ex Dinamo Zagreb, Croatia Sesvete - loan, Olimpia Ljubjana - loan, on 8/8/2007) FL 19+1/1 FLC 2 FAC 2*

CHADWICK Luke Harry
Born: Cambridge, 18 November 1980
Height: 5'11" **Weight:** 11.0
Club Honours: PL '01
International Honours: E: U21-13; Yth
Unfortunately, a recurring shoulder injury badly interrupted Luke's second season at Norwich and he was out of contention from November until late April. Although predominantly a wide player, he is not a traditional winger who likes to go past defenders on the outside, as he is equally likely to cut inside and link with his front men. He takes on defenders, finds scoring positions and is a good passer with the ability to make incisive breaks. Norwich fans have yet to see the best of Luke and hope, as he will, for better things ahead.

Manchester U *(From trainee on 8/2/1999) PL 11+14/2 FLC 5 FAC 1+2 Others 1+5*
Reading *(Loaned on 7/2/2003) FL 15/1 Others 1+1*
Burnley *(Loaned on 15/7/2003) FL 23+13/5 FLC 2/1 FAC 1+1*
West Ham U *(Free on 5/8/2004) FL 22+10/1 FLC 1 FAC 3*
Stoke C *(£100,000 on 4/8/2005) FL 46+5/5 FAC 4/1*
Norwich C *(£200,000 on 14/11/2006) FL 10+7/2 FLC 0+1*

CHADWICK Nicholas (Nick) Gerald
Born: Market Drayton, 26 October 1982
Height: 6'0" **Weight:** 12.8
Once again, Nick's season was severely hampered by injuries and he started only five games all season for Plymouth. When he is fit, Nick is a hard-working centre-forward who is strong on the ball, a willing runner and capable of taking chances. This was evidenced in the first month of the season when he scored his only goals against Barnsley and Wolverhampton. In April it was announced that Nick would not be offered a new contract.

Everton *(From trainee on 29/10/1999) PL 3+11/3 FLC 1+3/2 FAC 0+3/1*
Derby Co *(Loaned on 28/2/2003) FL 4+2*
Millwall *(Loaned on 26/11/2003) FL 6/2*
Millwall *(Loaned on 18/3/2004) FL 5+4/2*
Plymouth Arg *(Signed on 9/2/2005) FL 49+28/10 FLC 4+1 FAC 0+1*

CHALLINOR David (Dave) Paul
Born: Chester, 2 October 1975
Height: 6'1" **Weight:** 12.6
International Honours: E: Yth; Sch
Dave began the season as Bury's captain before losing the armband briefly after a knee injury in the opening minutes of a 2-0 win over Peterborough in November. His organisational ability was missed and his return against Dagenham was well received. He lost the captaincy and his starting position when Alan Knill became manager and installed Efe Sodje at centre-half. When in the team, Dave's famous long throws continued to provide an attacking option and his aerial threat from set pieces was always evident. Was out of contract at the end of the campaign.

Tranmere Rov *(Signed from Brombrough Pool on 18/7/1994) FL 124+16/6 FLC 17+1 FAC 9+2 Others 1*
Stockport Co *(£120,000 on 11/1/2002) FL 78+3/1 FLC 3 FAC 2 Others 4+1*
Bury *(Loaned on 9/11/2004) FL 15*
Bury *(Signed on 30/7/2004) FL 158/2 FLC 4/1 FAC 9/1 Others 5*

CHALMERS Aaron Anthony
Born: Manchester, 2 February 1991
Height: 5'10" **Weight:** 12.8
Aaron signed a two-year apprenticeship with Oldham in May 2007 after impressing in the youth team. Although predominantly a midfielder, he can also play in defence. A late-season spate of injuries at Boundary Park gave him an unexpected first taste of senior football. Aaron made his debut as a 74th-minute substitute in the 2-0 home League win over Leyton Orient in April and followed with another cameo a week later at Northampton.

Oldham Ath *(Trainee) FL 0+2*

CHAMBERS Adam Craig
Born: West Bromwich, 20 November 1980
Height: 5'10" **Weight:** 11.8
International Honours: E: Yth
Adam again proved to be a major asset in midfield for Leyton Orient. He is an excellent box-to-box player who is equally good at breaking up attacks as well as launching counters. Adam managed to develop a good understanding with Sean Thornton from the start of the season.

West Bromwich A *(From trainee on 8/1/1999) P/FL 38+18/1 FLC 4+2 FAC 5+1 Others 0+1*
Sheffield Wed *(Loaned on 19/2/2004) FL 8+3 Others 1*
Kidderminster Hrs *(Free on 24/3/2005) FL 2 Others 3*
Leyton Orient *(Free, via trial at Swansea C, on 29/8/2006) FL 81+2/7 FLC 1+1 FAC 4 Others 3*

CHAMBERS Ashley Renaldo
Born: Leicester, 1 March 1990
Height: 5'10" **Weight:** 11.6
International Honours: E: Yth
Highly promising young Leicester striker, Ashley was once the club's youngest-ever debutant. Still only a teenager and due to fill out a little, he gained invaluable experience in the first-team squad late in 2007 and started once. Ashley added to his international honours at youth level and rounded off the campaign as an added-time substitute in the denouement at Stoke.

Leicester C *(From trainee on 7/9/2007) FL 1+4 FLC 0+1*

CHAMBERS James Ashley
Born: West Bromwich, 20 November 1980
Height: 5'10" **Weight:** 11.8
International Honours: E: Yth
Utility right-sided Leicester player, comfortable at full-back or in midfield, was a Martin Allen signing from Watford during the close season but gradually faded out of the picture as managerial changes took effect. His versatility looked to be an asset when he first joined but he eventually struggled to oust the regular occupants from his favoured positions.

West Bromwich A *(From trainee on 8/1/1999) P/FL 54+19 FLC 5+1 FAC 1*
Watford *(£75,000 on 9/8/2004) P/FL 74+16 FLC 8+1/2 FAC 3+1 Others 3*
Cardiff C *(Loaned on 12/10/2006) FL 7*
Leicester C *(Free on 3/8/2007) FL 15+9 FLC 2+1*

CHAMBERS Luke
Born: Kettering, 29 August 1985
Height: 5'11" **Weight:** 11.0
Luke was converted into a right-back at the start of the last campaign with great success. He was always willing to overlap, his runs often ending with a telling cross, and is dangerous at set pieces. His total of eight goals materially helped Nottingham Forest's promotion challenge and his leadership qualities were recognised when he captained the team on a number of occasions.

Northampton T *(From trainee on 3/11/2003) FL 109+15/1 FLC 6+1 FAC 8+3 Others 6+1*
Nottingham F *(Signed on 30/1/2007) FL 50+6/6 FLC 2 FAC 3 Others 3/2*

CHAPLOW Richard David
Born: Accrington, 2 February 1985
Height: 5'9" **Weight:** 9.3
International Honours: E: U21-1; Yth
Although Richard played in seven of Albion's first ten games last season, three of them as a substitute, he was injured in the Carling Cup defeat by

Cardiff and took some time to recover. With the January transfer window open and with so many other midfielders at the Hawthorns, he was allowed to join Preston. Richard suffered a staccato start to his Preston career as a series of niggles meant almost half his appearances were as a substitute. Despite this, Preston fans saw enough of the energetic box-to-box midfield player to believe he will be a good addition to the midfield options. His three goals included both in the 2-0 win over Stoke and an injury-time equaliser at Plymouth, all vital in the successful battle against relegation.
Burnley (From trainee on 13/9/2003) FL 48+17/7 FLC 3+1 FAC 5
West Bromwich A (£1,500,000 on 31/1/2005) P/FL 25+19/1 FLC 6+2 FAC 5/2 Others 1
Southampton (Loaned on 8/2/2006) FL 11/1
Preston NE (£800,000 on 10/1/2008) FL 7+5/3 FAC 0+1

CHAPMAN Luke Richard
Born: Cannock, 10 March 1991
Height: 6'1" **Weight:** 11.10
A left-sided Port Vale midfield player who is still on a youth-team contract, Luke was called up for the final game at Southend. He made his debut as a substitute in the final minute and almost scored with his first touch as a cross-shot was heading his way until the goalkeeper deflected it wide. Luke has a decent turn of pace and starred in Vale's run to the FA Youth Cup quarter-finals, when they were beaten by Chelsea.
Port Vale (Trainee) FL 0+1

CHARLES Wesley Darius Donald
Born: Ealing, 10 December 1987
Height: 5'11" **Weight:** 11.10
The composed Brentford left-back, who started 2007-08 on loan at Sutton, returned to the Bees at the end of September and was a regular in the squad until the turn of the year. He was then rarely used and joined Blue Square Premier side Ebbsfleet on loan in March. During his time at Griffin Park, he was always reliable.
Brentford (From trainee on 27/6/2006) FL 18+19/1 FLC 1+1 FAC 1+1 Others 1

CHARLES Ryan Andrew
Born: Enfield, 30 September 1989
Height: 6'0" **Weight:** 12.0
Having gained a fine scoring reputation as a Luton youth player, Ryan graduated to the reserves and the lack of goals in League One earned him a debut, as a substitute for Steve Robinson, at Southend. Playing with confidence, the striker was not afraid to take on

experienced defenders, using his pace and strength. His first touch is neat, he is quick and has an effective body swerve. Ryan was given a first start at Carlisle alongside Paul Furlong and scored his first goal on his home debut against Oldham, when he gathered the ball and went past two defenders to earn the 'Goal of the Season' award. He was eventually preferred to Calvin Andrew and formed a successful partnership with Sam Parkin. After his seventh game, a cartilage problem kept him out after the end of March.
Luton T (Trainee) FL 6+1/1

CHARNOCK Kieran James
Born: Preston, 3 August 1984
Height: 6'1" **Weight:** 14.7
International Honours: E: SP-11
Central defender Kieran, signed from non-League Northwich in the summer, broke into the Peterborough side early on in 2007-08 and was not out of place in a team playing good football. An injury after eight games cut short his campaign and another only six games into his comeback curtailed it further. He showed good form in his time on the pitch and needs an injury-free season.
Wigan Ath (From trainee on 2/7/2002. Free to Southport on 14/3/2003)
Peterborough U (Signed from Northwich Victoria on 12/7/2007) FL 10 FAC 2 Others 2

CHILVERS Liam Christopher
Born: Chelmsford, 6 November 1981
Height: 6'1" **Weight:** 13.5
Club Honours: FAYC '00
Although Liam was the unlucky member of Preston's central defensive trio early in the season, losing out because of Youl Mawene's return from injury, he made himself indispensable once he returned to form and full fitness from December onwards. Strong in the air and a decisive tackler, Liam shows little emotion on the field and his Arsenal apprenticeship becomes ever more apparent. His ability to defend strongly but fairly was reflected by only one caution in 31 appearances. It was a major blow to Preston's relegation battle when Liam ruptured an Achilles tendon in a freak accident while warming up at Charlton. He is not expected to be back in contention until November at the earliest.
Arsenal (From trainee on 18/7/2000)
Northampton T (Loaned on 22/12/2000) FL 7
Notts Co (Loaned on 1/11/2001) FL 9/1 FAC 2
Colchester U (Loaned on 24/1/2003) FL 6
Colchester U (Loaned on 26/8/2003) FL 29+3 FLC 1 FAC 7 Others 5

Colchester U (Free on 6/8/2004) FL 73+2/3 FLC 3 FAC 6+2 Others 2
Preston NE (Free on 13/7/2006) FL 72+1/2 FLC 1 FAC 6

CHIMBONDA Pascal
Born: Les Abymes, Guadeloupe, 21 February 1979
Height: 5'11" **Weight:** 11.11
Club Honours: FLC '08
International Honours: France: 1
At the start of last season, it appeared that Tottenham's right-back was unsettled as he was being strongly linked with a move to Chelsea. He stayed and played 49 games in all, including the Carling Cup final, in which he did not endear himself to fans or management by disappearing down the Wembley tunnel when substituted. Pascal appears to have lost his automatic selection as right-back to Alan Hutton, who was signed from Glasgow Rangers in January, and was asked to play in all positions across the back four, proving capable of well-timed tackles as well as headed clearances. He likes to get forward and had a hand in a number of goals with his crosses and headed assists, also scoring three himself.
Wigan Ath (Signed from Bastia, France on 26/7/2005) PL 37+1/2 FLC 3+1 FAC 2
Tottenham H (Signed on 31/8/2006) PL 64+1/3 FLC 8/1 FAC 6 Others 19

CHOPRA Rocky Michael
Born: Newcastle, 23 December 1983
Height: 5'8" **Weight:** 9.6
International Honours: E: U21-1; Yth
Michael was in some way a controversial signing by Roy Keane last summer when he arrived from Cardiff, having started his career with Sunderland's arch-rivals Newcastle. However, the nippy striker soon won over the Black Cats' fans with a winning goal on the opening day against Tottenham, especially when he followed this with a brilliant volley at Birmingham four days later. Often asked to fill an unfamiliar role wide on the right as Keane opted for a lone striker in some games, particularly away from home, Michael was never less than a willing and committed worker. He served a one-match ban in January after five yellow cards and had what should have been a winning goal at Derby in February controversially ruled out. But he was the match winner at Aston Villa in March and followed up with goals at Fulham and at home to Middlesbrough in April as Sunderland cemented their place in the Premier League.
Newcastle U (From trainee on 4/1/2001) PL 7+14/1 FLC 1+2 FAC 1+1/1 Others 1+4/1

89

Watford (Loaned on 25/3/2003) FL 4+1/5 FAC 1
Nottingham F (Loaned on 6/2/2004) FL 3+2
Barnsley (Loaned on 27/8/2004) FL 38+1/17 FLC 1 FAC 1 Others 1
Cardiff C (£500,000 on 19/7/2006) FL 42/22 FAC 2
Sunderland (£5,000,000 on 13/7/2007) PL 21+12/6 FLC 1

CHORLEY Benjamin (Ben) Francis
Born: Sidcup, 30 September 1982
Height: 6'3" **Weight:** 13.2
Club Honours: FAYC '01
Ben joined Tranmere from MK Dons in July, signing a two-year contract with the Prenton Park club. A commanding centre-back, he was a regular until November when injury and competition for his position from Antony Kay restricted him to the substitutes' bench. Ben came back strongly towards the end of the season to regain his place, forming a good understanding with Ian Goodison. He is a brave player who can head the ball accurately and relishes any opportunity to go forward. Vocal in the extreme, he demands and draws out the best from his team-mates.
Arsenal (From trainee on 2/7/2001)
Brentford (Loaned on 14/8/2002) FL 2 FLC 1
Wimbledon/MK Dons (Free on 3/3/2003) FL 119+6/5 FLC 6 FAC 5+1 Others 2
Gillingham (Loaned on 26/10/2006) FL 24+3/1
Tranmere Rov (Free on 25/7/2007) FL 30+1/1 FLC 1 FAC 2+1 Others 1

CHRISTANVAL Philippe
Born: Paris, France, 31 August 1978
Height: 6'2" **Weight:** 12.10
International Honours: France: 6; U21
Philippe endured his most frustrating season at Fulham as a succession of knee and foot injuries kept him out for the first four months. Normally a central defender, his only 16 minutes of Premiership action came as a substitute at Bolton where he occupied a defensive midfield role. He duly completed this with his usual assured composure, only to suffer a slight recurrence of a previous toe injury. Was out of contract in the summer.
Fulham (Free from Olympique Marseille, France on 31/8/2005) PL 26+10/1 FLC 1 FAC 3

CHRISTENSEN Kim
Born: Fredriksvaerk, Denmark, 8 May 1980
Height: 6'2" **Weight:** 12.8
International Honours: Denmark: U21-9
Signed from OB Odense, Denmark on a

two-year contract, Kim soon made his Barnsley debut as a substitute against Colchester. The big, powerful forward was regularly on the bench in the first half of the season and scored his only goal to date, a last-minute equaliser at Charlton, but found himself out of the squad after the turn of the year.
Barnsley (£300,000 from OB Odense, Denmark, ex Lyngby, SV Hamburg, Twente-Enschede, Brondby, on 17/8/2007) FL 0+12/1 FLC 0+1

CHRISTON Lewis John
Born: Milton Keynes, 24 January 1989
Height: 6'0" **Weight:** 12.2
After some promising performances the previous season, the young central defender hoped to secure a first-team spot at Wycombe. The arrival of experienced defenders David McCracken and Leon Johnson pushed him down the pecking order. After two League appearances, he spent a month on loan at Blue Square Premier side Woking, making two appearances, and then joined AFC Wimbledon in March. His five appearances helped the Ryman Premier League side to promotion. Lewis was offered a one-year contract at the end of the season.
Wycombe W (From trainee on 27/3/2006) FL 7+1 Others 0+1

CHRISTOPHE Jean-Francois
Born: Creil, France, 13 June 1987
Height: 6'1" **Weight:** 13.2
A strong and versatile midfield player, Jean-Francois joined Bournemouth on a six-month loan from Portsmouth at the start of last season and although a broken hand kept him out for some time he signed off with his first goal in England, against Brighton. The Frenchman, aggressive in the challenge, next went on loan in March to Yeovil to assist their battle against relegation. He provided good cover for the injury-hit squad and impressed in his short stay. Has yet to play for Pompey.
Portsmouth (Signed from RC Lens, France on 3/8/2007)
Bournemouth (Loaned on 10/8/2007) FL 5+5/1 FLC 1
Yeovil T (Loaned on 10/3/2008) FL 4+1

CHURCH Simon Richard
Born: Amersham, 10 December 1988
Height: 6'0" **Weight:** 13.4
International Honours: W: U21-6
Simon, a Welsh under-21 international, joined Crewe from Reading on loan in October and stayed until January. While at Gresty Road he impressed with his willingness to work at his game but his

only goal was at Cheltenham in October. After returning to Reading, Simon had another loan at Yeovil, who signed him as a covering player for the forwards in January. For much of the time, he was an unused substitute but featured in a Wales under-21 European Championship qualifier.
Reading (From trainee on 4/7/2007)
Crewe Alex (Loaned on 19/10/2007) FL 11+1/1 FAC 2
Yeovil T (Loaned on 30/1/2008) FL 2+4

CID Gerald
Born: Talence, France, 17 February 1983
Height: 6'2" **Weight:** 12.6
Having been signed from Istres in the summer, Gerald made his Premiership debut in the opening-day defeat by Newcastle and gave the impression that he would be a Bolton regular under Sammy Lee, with six starts during the opening weeks. Despite showing his versatility by playing at left-back as well as centre-half, Gerald did not feature regularly under Gary Megson and returned to France to join Nice in January.
Bolton W (Free from Bordeaux, France, ex Istres - loan, on 5/7/2007) PL 6+1 FLC 1 FAC 1 Others 5

CISSE Kalifa
Born: Dreux, France, 9 January 1984
Height: 6'1" **Weight:** 12.8
International Honours: Mali: 1
Signed from the Portuguese club Boavista during the close season, Kalifa impressed during Reading's participation in the Peace Cup tournament in Korea. He might have made a firm bid for a regular midfield berth but a second yellow card in the first home Premiership game led to his sending off against Chelsea. Thereafter he was usually in the first-team squad without establishing a regular starting place. He looked more comfortable in several games at centre-back, where his height and strong tackling made him an effective if not cultured defender. His goal was at Tottenham, where he played only because Brynjar Gunnarsson was suspended. Kalifa scored from the edge of the area to level the score at 1-1 and Reading led three times before losing an extraordinary encounter 6-4.
Reading (£1,000,000 from Boavista, Portugal, ex Toulouse, GD Estoril, on 18/5/2007) PL 11+11/1 FLC 1 FAC 2

CLAPHAM James (Jamie) Richard
Born: Lincoln, 7 December 1975
Height: 5'9" **Weight:** 10.11
Jamie was signed by Leicester from Wolverhampton in January because Ian

Holloway hoped his vast experience at left-back would add stability to the back line, as well as providing cover for the developing Joe Mattock. Jamie continued to perform in the steady, if unspectacular, fashion that has served him so well in more than a decade in the game but Leicester struggled to find any consistency and ultimately fell below Championship level for the first time in their history. He was released at the end of the season and it was a sad contrast to his earlier loan at Leeds. Dennis Wise signed him in August, after one Wolverhampton appearance as a substitute in the Carling Cup against Bradford, to fill a problem position and Jamie made a significant contribution as United got off to a flying start, rapidly wiping out their 15-point deduction.

Tottenham H (From trainee on 1/7/1994) PL 0+1 Others 4
Leyton Orient (Loaned on 29/1/1997) FL 6
Bristol Rov (Loaned on 27/3/1997) FL 4+1
Ipswich T (£300,000 on 9/1/1998) P/FL 187+20/10 FLC 19+1/4 FAC 4+3/1 Others 16+2/1
Birmingham C (£1,000,000 + on 10/1/2003) PL 69+15/1 FLC 5+2 FAC 3+3
Wolverhampton W (Free on 3/8/2006) FL 21+5 FLC 1+1 FAC 1
Leeds U (Loaned on 20/8/2007) FL 12+1 FAC 0+1 Others 0+1
Leicester C (Free on 31/1/2008) FL 11

CLARK Benjamin (Ben)

Born: Consett, 24 January 1983
Height: 6'2" **Weight:** 13.0
International Honours: E: Yth; Sch
The reliable Hartlepool utility player's season was badly disrupted by injury. After starting out of the side, he was just establishing himself when he was sidelined by a hamstring injury. Soon after returning, he suffered a thigh injury and it was only in the final weeks that he was to have a clear run with games in central defence and latterly in midfield. Recognised as a great asset, he signed a new contract in December.

Sunderland (From trainee on 5/7/2000) P/FL 3+5 FLC 4
Hartlepool U (Signed on 22/10/2004) FL 103+13/4 FLC 1 FAC 9+2 Others 5+1

CLARK Christopher (Chris)

Born: Aberdeen, 15 September 1980
Height: 5'11" **Weight:** 10.8
International Honours: S: B-3
After spending his entire career with his hometown club Aberdeen, where he made over 230 appearances, the Scotland 'B' international joined Plymouth on a three-and-a-half-year contract in the January transfer window. Chris is a versatile midfielder blessed with a neat

and tidy touch that allows him to operate with great effect on either wing or in the centre. He made an immediate impact for Argyle by scoring five minutes into his debut against Portsmouth at Fratton Park in the FA Cup fourth round. It was the only goal Portsmouth conceded on their way to lifting the Cup at Wembley.

Aberdeen (Signed from Hermes on 16/8/1997) SL 167+32/8 SLC 7+3 SC 16+2/1 Others 5+2
Plymouth Arg (£200,000 on 17/1/2008) FL 8+4 FAC 1/1

CLARKE Clive Richard

Born: Dublin, 14 January 1980
Height: 6'1" **Weight:** 12.3
Club Honours: AMC '00
International Honours: RoI: 2; U21-11; Yth
The most dramatic incident of Leicester's season undoubtedly came at Nottingham Forest's City Ground when Clive, on loan from Sunderland, suffered a heart attack in the dressing room at half-time during the Carling Cup tie and required resuscitation before being rushed to hospital. He had previously impressed at left-back in a couple of undefeated League outings before his medical condition brought his playing career to an abrupt and sadly premature end. A host of subsequent tests have so far failed to establish the exact cause of his problem and Clive has taken the sensible decision to hang up his boots rather than risk further drama.

Stoke C (From trainee on 25/11/1997) FL 205+18/9 FLC 12+3 FAC 8+1 Others 17/1
West Ham U (£275,000 on 1/8/2005) PL 2 FLC 1
Sunderland (Signed on 8/8/2006) FL 2+2
Coventry C (Loaned on 23/10/2006) FL 12
Leicester C (Loaned on 16/8/2007) FL 2

CLARKE James (Jamie)
William
Born: Sunderland, 18 September 1982
Height: 6'2" **Weight:** 12.9
Having been freed by Boston, it was thought Jamie would have the tough task of replacing Grimsby legend John McDermott at right-back, but most of his outings last term were in midfield. After waiting patiently for his senior bow, the tough tackler also showed versatility as a wing-back in a 3-5-2 formation, being ever-present in the Mariners' run to the Johnstone's Paint Trophy final. Jamie gained a reputation for important goals, his strikes against Bury, the only goal of the game, and Stockport (JPT) both being from distance.

Mansfield T (From trainee on 5/7/2002) FL 29+5/1 FLC 2 FAC 3+1 Others 2

Rochdale (Free on 5/7/2004) FL 53+10/1 FLC 2 FAC 4 Others 2+2
Boston U (Free on 20/1/2006) FL 42+10/3 FLC 0+1 FAC 1
Grimsby T (Free on 5/7/2007) FL 27+2/2 FAC 2 Others 6+1/1

CLARKE Leon Marvin

Born: Birmingham, 10 February 1985
Height: 6'2" **Weight:** 14.2
Leon started the season as a Sheffield Wednesday substitute, not seeming to have a future at Hillsborough and was allowed out on loan to Southend in September, making a dramatic impact. The tall, strong centre-forward scored in his first five outings, something not achieved at Southend since Micky Beesley did it in 1962. There was talk of a fee being agreed with Wednesday, although Leon incurred a three-match ban after being sent off at Nottingham Forest. His demeanour changed, the goals dried up, almost as if he was resting on his laurels, and his performance in his final game at Doncaster led to the contract offer being withdrawn. Back at Hillsborough, he made little impression until a late appearance as substitute in the victory over Sheffield United and suffered a cartilage problem. In the crucial, penultimate match at Leicester, he went on to clinch victory with a delicate lob over the goalkeeper. Leon has all the ingredients to be a top striker but needs to work on it.

Wolverhampton W (From trainee on 5/3/2004) P/FL 32+42/13 FLC 2+4/1 FAC 1+2/1
Kidderminster Hrs (Loaned on 25/3/2004) FL 3+1
Queens Park Rgrs (Loaned on 31/1/2006) FL 1
Plymouth Arg (Loaned on 23/3/2006) FL 5
Sheffield Wed (£300,000 on 16/1/2007) FL 5+13/4 FLC 0+1 FAC 0+1
Oldham Ath (Loaned on 1/3/2007) FL 5/3
Southend U (Loaned on 31/8/2007) FL 16/8

CLARKE Matthew (Matt)
Paul
Born: Leeds, 18 December 1980
Height: 6'3" **Weight:** 12.7
Matt put the previous season's injury troubles behind him to turn in a run of consistent displays in the centre of Bradford's back four. Quick and strong, the left-footed centre-half also notched his first goal for the club at Accrington on New Year's Day.

Halifax T (From trainee at Wolverhampton W on 5/7/1999) FL 42+27/2 FAC 5+1 Others 2+2
Darlington (Free on 9/7/2002) FL 163+6/13 FLC 5 FAC 6 Others 4
Bradford C (Free on 24/6/2006) FL 20+5/1 FAC 2+1 Others 2
Darlington (Loaned on 27/10/2006) FL 2

CLARKE Nathan
Born: Halifax, 30 July 1983
Height: 6'2" **Weight:** 11.5
The young Huddersfield central defender was a regular throughout, as he cemented his place with some solid performances, helped by finally having an injury-free season. Nathan tackles strongly and distributes accurately to the front players. The calm and collected defender benefited from playing alongside a more senior partner. His attacking long throws were a feature of his game as he drove the team forward and he scored two goals.
Huddersfield T (From trainee on 6/9/2001)
FL 206+2/4 FLC 6 FAC 11 Others 9+1

CLARKE Peter Michael
Born: Southport, 3 January 1982
Height: 6'0" **Weight:** 12.0
International Honours: E: U21-8; Yth; Sch
Having missed only one League match all season, Peter was deservedly voted runner-up in the Southend 'Player of the Year' awards. His solid defensive partnership with Adam Barrett was the rock on which Southend's play-off charge was built and it is testimony to Peter's class that such a combative centre-back should suffer only a one-match suspension during the season. Well liked by the Southend faithful, who will look forward to more of the same in the coming season.
Everton (From juniors on 19/1/1999) PL 6+3 FLC 0+1 FAC 4
Blackpool (Loaned on 8/8/2002) FL 16/3
Port Vale (Loaned on 20/2/2003) FL 13/1
Coventry C (Loaned on 13/2/2004) FL 5
Blackpool (Signed on 18/9/2004) FL 84/11 FLC 2/1 FAC 5/2 Others 1+1
Southend U (£250,000 on 4/8/2006) FL 79+4/6 FLC 5+1 FAC 8 Others 3

CLARKE Shane Robin
Born: Lincoln, 7 November 1987
Height: 6'1" **Weight:** 13.3
One of ten products of Lincoln's Academy set-up to play first-team football in 2007-08, Shane's career did not get off to the best of starts with the tall midfielder being sent off in his second match, against Rotherham at Sincil Bank. His response was first class, however, and on his return from suspension he became a regular feature during the final couple of months. His good form was rewarded with the offer of a new one-year contract.
Lincoln C (From trainee on 6/7/2006) FL 11+5

CLARKE Thomas (Tom)
Born: Halifax, 21 December 1987
Height: 5'11" **Weight:** 12.2
International Honours: E: Yth

Yet another season of heartache for the tough-tackling young Huddersfield defender as a knee ligament injury plagued him. Tom spent time on loan to Halifax to aid his rehabilitation programme. Much to everyone's surprise, he was called up to the first team in an April victory over Tranmere and hailed for an astute display of strong tackling and forward forays from right-back. He also played at the back in the final game of the season.
Huddersfield T (From trainee on 18/1/2005)
FL 36+5/1 FLC 0+1 FAC 0+1 Others 1+1

CLARKE William (Billy) Charles
Born: Cork, 13 December 1987
Height: 5'8" **Weight:** 10.1
International Honours: RoI: U21-7
Billy featured in the majority of Ipswich's games in the first four months of the season, either from the bench or as a left-sided attacking midfield player, in which position he was able to cut in from the flanks for strikes on goal or to deliver telling crosses. Unfortunately his lack of goals told against him and he went to Falkirk on loan in January.
Ipswich T (From trainee on 26/1/2005) FL 20+29/3 FLC 0+2/1 FAC 3+2
Colchester U (Loaned on 23/3/2006) FL 2+4
Falkirk (Loaned on 31/1/2008) SL 1+7/1

CLEMENCE Stephen Neal
Born: Liverpool, 31 March 1978
Height: 5'11" **Weight:** 11.7
Club Honours: FLC '99
International Honours: E: U21-1; Yth; Sch
An experienced midfielder, signed by Martin Allen from Birmingham in the summer and handed the club captaincy, Stephen ultimately had a disappointing campaign at Leicester, where he never quite produced the form and level of consistency shown with previous clubs. He looked at his best in tandem with Matt Oakley, with two wingers providing width, but that was a formation used only sparingly by Ian Holloway. Not recognised as a goalscorer, Stephen did at least net the last-gasp winner to oust local rivals Forest from the Carling Cup.
Tottenham H (From trainee on 3/4/1995) PL 68+22/2 FLC 7+1 FAC 7+1/1 Others 2+1
Birmingham C (£250,000 + on 10/1/2003) P/FL 104+17/8 FLC 6 FAC 7+1/1
Leicester C (£750,000 + on 7/8/2007) FL 30+1/2 FLC 3/1

CLEMENT Neil
Born: Reading, 3 October 1978
Height: 6'0" **Weight:** 12.3
International Honours: E: Yth; Sch

West Bromwich's longest-serving player reached 300 senior appearances on the last day of the season against his father's former club, Queens Park Rangers. Neil hardly had a look-in until late in the season following a severe knee injury that threatened his career. After regaining full fitness, he found his accustomed left-back position filled by Paul Robinson, while Leon Barnett, Bostjan Cesar and then Martin Albrechtsen were ahead of him for a place at the heart of the Baggies' defence. Neil went on loan to Hull but returned to duty at the Hawthorns in March as a substitute against Colchester and after a 'Man of the Match' display against Cardiff in the next game, played in Albion's FA Cup semi-final defeat by Portsmouth at Wembley. He kept his place and became the first Albion player ever to gain three promotions with the club. Not only that, he was promoted with two clubs. Having gone to promotion rivals Hull to regain match fitness and provided superb cover for injured defender Wayne Brown it was agreed the loan would be extended to the end of the season. But, because of Albion's own injury concerns, Neil was recalled to the Hawthorns – at a time when Hull had overtaken Albion in the promotion race.
Chelsea (From trainee on 8/10/1995) PL 1 FLC 0+2 FAC 0+1
Reading (Loaned on 19/11/1998) FL 11/1 Others 1
Preston NE (Loaned on 25/3/1999) FL 4
Brentford (Loaned on 23/11/1999) FL 7+1
West Bromwich A (£100,000 + on 23/3/2000) P/FL 242+22/21 FLC 15+2/3 FAC 16/2 Others 2+1
Hull C (Loaned on 29/2/2008) FL 4+1

CLICHY Gael
Born: Paris, France, 26 February 1985
Height: 5'9" **Weight:** 10.0
Club Honours: PL '04; CS '04
International Honours: France: B: U21
The French left-back enjoyed his most impressive season to date at Arsenal and was the only member of the squad to feature in every Premier League game. Gael was outstanding as he quickly forged a tremendous defensive understanding with fellow countryman Bacary Sagna at right-back and, having previously suffered several injury-plagued seasons, this was without doubt his breakthrough. Defensively, he has few equals and links that to an ability to drive forward with pace and skill. Gael was ever-present in the Champions' League and made one FA Cup appearance. His marvellous season was rewarded by his inclusion in the PFA 'Premier League Team of the Season'. Amazingly, he has yet to receive full international recognition and was left out

of the provisional French Euro 2008 squad.
Arsenal (£250,000 from Cannes, France on 6/8/2003) PL 82+17 FLC 7+1 FAC 10+5 Others 19+5

CLINGAN Samuel (Sammy) Gary

Born: Belfast, 13 January 1984
Height: 5'11" **Weight:** 11.6
International Honours: NI: 15; U21-11; Yth; Sch
Sammy made a welcome return to the Nottingham Forest midfield in September after recovering from a broken leg. Operating just in front of the back four, his play is uncomplicated. He always looks for the easy ball and rarely loses possession. Sammy has a good shot but, surprisingly, had to wait 54 League games before his first goal for the club, against Crewe in November. He remained a regular member of the Northern Ireland squad during the campaign.
Wolverhampton W (From trainee on 18/7/2001)
Chesterfield (Loaned on 8/10/2004) FL 15/2
Chesterfield (Loaned on 31/8/2005) FL 14+7/1 Others 1
Nottingham F (Signed on 24/1/2006) FL 79+6/1 FLC 3 FAC 4+1 Others 3

CLOHESSY Sean David

Born: Croydon, 12 December 1986
Height: 5'11" **Weight:** 12.7
Another Gillingham player who had a difficult season, Sean was called upon only when first-choice Nicky Southall was missing. Although he struggled to gain a regular place at right-back, despite his adventurous play and good positional sense, he never let the team down and could be relied upon to step up when required.
Gillingham (From trainee on 31/7/2006) FL 37+6/1 Others 3

CLOUGH Charles (Charlie) David

Born: Taunton, 4 September 1990
Height: 6'2" **Weight:** 12.7
After some impressive youth and reserve team appearances for Bristol Rovers in central midfield, the 17-year-old Charlie made his League debut against Brighton at the Memorial Stadium as a substitute. He quickly made an impression, almost scoring with two long-range shots, and is one for the future.
Bristol Rov (From juniors on 4/9/2007) FL 0+1

COCHRANE Justin Vincent

Born: Hackney, 26 January 1982
Height: 6'0" **Weight:** 11.8
Following his release by relegated Rotherham in the previous season, Justin

signed a short-term deal with Yeovil last August. He scored two goals, the winner at Port Vale and the opener in a 2-1 win at Northampton, but was not offered an extension to his contract at the beginning of February. After taking time out, the skilful midfielder made the briefest of appearances for Millwall in March, as a substitute against Oldham, before being allowed to move on.
Queens Park Rgrs (From trainee on 16/7/1999) FL 0+1 (Free to Hayes on 12/8/2002)
Crewe Alex (£50,000 on 19/7/2003) FL 60+12 FLC 4+1
Gillingham (Loaned on 10/2/2006) FL 5/1
Rotherham U (Free on 3/8/2006) FL 29+2/1 FLC 1 FAC 0+1
Yeovil T (Free on 10/8/2007) FL 6+6/2 FLC 0+1
Millwall (Free on 20/3/2008) FL 0+1

COGAN Barry

Born: Sligo, 4 November 1984
Height: 5'9" **Weight:** 9.0
International Honours: RoI: U21-1
Arriving from Barnet during the summer, the skilful right-sided player failed to gain a regular spot in the Gillingham line-up under new manager Mark Stimson and joined Grays on loan in March. Finding his feet with the Blue Square Premier side, Barry had a good spell, scoring five goals in his first eight games. Was out of contract in the summer and looking for a new club.
Millwall (From trainee on 28/11/2001) FL 8+16 FLC 0+1 FAC 1+2 Others 0+2
Barnet (Signed on 11/8/2006) FL 33+6/3 FLC 1 FAC 4 Others 1
Gillingham (Free on 1/8/2007) FL 9+7/1 FLC 0+1 FAC 1 Others 3

COHEN Christopher (Chris) David

Born: Norwich, 5 March 1987
Height: 5'11" **Weight:** 10.11
International Honours: E: Yth
A summer transfer from Yeovil, Chris suffered an injury in pre-season that delayed the start of his Nottingham Forest career but after his debut against Port Vale in September, he became one of the key members of the side, operating either as a central midfielder or in the hole behind a central striker. Not blessed with lightning pace, Chris has a shrewd football brain and can slide a pass through to create a scoring chance for forwards. Surprisingly, he managed only two League goals.
West Ham U (From trainee on 1/4/2004) P/FL 2+16 FLC 2+1 FAC 0+1
Yeovil T (Signed on 10/11/2005) FL 73+1/7 FLC 1 FAC 2/1 Others 3+1
Nottingham F (Signed on 10/7/2007) FL 40+1/2 FLC 1 FAC 3

COHEN Tamir

Born: Tel Aviv, Israel, 4 March 1984
Height: 6'1" **Weight:** 11.9
International Honours: Israel: 6; U21-12; Yth
An Israeli international midfielder and the son of former Liverpool player Avi Cohen, Tamir signed on a free transfer from Maccabi Netanya in January. He was thrust straight into action in the FA Cup defeat by Sheffield United and was one of the few positives to emerge from a poor Bolton performance. His first League start came in the next game, against Blackburn, and despite another defeat Tamir again impressed. He scored his first Bolton goal in the 3-1 home defeat by Liverpool, leaving the bench to head in. Most of Tamir's appearances were as a substitute and he proved a reliable squad member. Energetic, committed and skilful, Tamir is a box-to-box midfielder and will be looking to break in with more regular starts.
Bolton W (£650,000 from Maccabi Netanya, Israel, ex Maccabi Tel Aviv, on 4/1/2008) PL 3+7/1 FAC 1

COID Daniel (Danny) John

Born: Liverpool, 3 October 1981
Height: 5'11" **Weight:** 11.7
Club Honours: AMC '02, '04
Danny's opportunities were limited last season by injuries and the good form of Stephen Crainey and Shaun Barker in the full-back positions. Having notched

Chris Cohen

up ten years at Blackpool, he started nine League games, often at left-back in place of Crainey, who also had his share of injuries. Danny is obviously eager for regular first-team football and, given his versatility in either full-back position or across midfield, remains an attractive proposition. It was no surprise when his contract was extended for a further season.
Blackpool (From trainee on 24/7/2000) FL 213+32/9 FLC 10+3 FAC 17/1 Others 20+1/3

COKE Giles Christopher
Born: Westminster, 3 June 1986
Height: 5'11" **Weight:** 11.10
After being signed from Mansfield during the summer, Giles was missing from the Northampton midfield for most of the season with an injury. However, once able to play in the first team, he made his presence felt with neat touches, flicks and some well-taken goals. A fully fit Giles should be a powerhouse in the centre of the park.
Mansfield T (Signed from Kingstonian on 17/3/2005) FL 55+15/5 FLC 4/1 FAC 6/1 Others 1+1
Northampton T (£70,000 on 2/7/2007) FL 11+9/5

COLBECK Philip Joseph (Joe)
Born: Bradford, 29 November 1986
Height: 5'10" **Weight:** 10.12
There was no doubt that a loan spell at Darlington revived the Bradford winger's fortunes and he came back to make a real impact in the second half of the season. Joe's pace and enthusiasm for tracking back could never be questioned and he also chipped in regularly with goals from midfield, all away from home. The speedy, direct right-winger started four games, with two outings from the bench at Darlington, being popular with the fans for his darting runs on either side of the full-back and scoring two goals in his short spell at the Arena.
Bradford C (From trainee on 18/7/2006) FL 46+30/6 FLC 1+1 FAC 0+1 Others 2
Darlington (Loaned on 25/10/2007) FL 4+2/2

COLE Andrew Alexander
Born: Nottingham, 15 October 1971
Height: 5'11" **Weight:** 11.12
Club Honours: Div 1 '93; PL '96, '97, '99, '00, '01; FAC '96, '99; CS '97; EC '99; FLC '02
International Honours: E: 15; B-1; U21-8; Yth, Sch
A much-travelled former England striker, Andrew left Portsmouth to sign for Sunderland in August on a season-long contract but a calf injury delayed his

debut. He managed only a handful of appearances, without adding to his impressive career goals tally, before joining Burnley on loan at the end of January for the remainder of the season. The striker, formerly known as Andy, brought all of his vast top-level experience to Turf Moor and it often showed, his coolness on the ball and excellent distribution adding an extra element to the Clarets' attack. He was off to a flying start with a hat-trick at Queens Park Rangers in only his second full game, and his goal ratio was every bit as high as expected from a player to whom scoring has always come naturally. Out of contract in the summer, whether this was his swansong in League football remains to be seen.
Arsenal (From trainee on 18/10/1989) FL 0+1 Others 0+1
Fulham (Loaned on 5/9/1991) FL 13/3 Others 2/1
Bristol C (£500,000 on 12/3/1992) FL 41/20 FLC 3/4 FAC 1 Others 4/1
Newcastle U (£1,750,000 on 12/3/1993) P/FL 69+1/55 FLC 7/8 FAC 4/1 Others 3/4
Manchester U (£6,000,000 on 12/1/1995) PL 161+34/94 FLC 2 FAC 19+2/9 Others 49+8/19
Blackburn Rov (£7,500,000 on 29/12/2001) PL 74+9/27 FLC 8/7 FAC 5/3 Others 2+2
Fulham (Free on 21/7/2004) PL 29+2/12 FLC 3/1 FAC 5
Manchester C (Free on 21/7/2005) PL 20+2/9 FAC 1/1
Portsmouth (Signed on 31/8/2006) PL 5+13/3 FLC 2 FAC 2/1
Birmingham C (Loaned on 22/3/2007) FL 5/1
Sunderland (Free on 24/8/2007) PL 3+4 FAC 0+1
Burnley (Loaned on 29/1/2008) FL 8+5/6

COLE Ashley
Born: Stepney, 20 December 1980
Height: 5'8" **Weight:** 10.8
Club Honours: FAC '02, '03, '05; PL '02, '04; CS '02; '04; FLC '07
International Honours: E: 64; B-1; U21-4; Yth
It takes an exceptional player to deny Wayne Bridge an automatic place at left-back in any side but Ashley demonstrated that he is the finest left-back in Europe if not the world. Like John Terry, he was unavailable for England's catastrophic European qualifying defeats against Russia and Croatia, a situation that was surely reflected in the results. Ashley appeared in more Premier League matches for Chelsea than any other defender and his strength and positional sense contributed hugely to their impressive goals-against column. He has carved a niche as an attacking left-back who loves to get forward at every

opportunity and scored his first Chelsea goal with a sweetly-struck drive at West Ham in the Premier League. His duels with Ronaldo are always fascinating and the Portuguese winger was forced to switch wings in the Champions' League final to get some joy. Ashley stepped up confidently in the shoot-out to convert his penalty with aplomb but suffered defeat for a second time in the final, having been in the Arsenal side beaten by Barcelona in 2006.
Arsenal (From trainee on 23/11/1998) PL 151+5/8 FLC 2+1 FAC 19+1 Others 46+3/1
Crystal Palace (Loaned on 25/2/2000) FL 14/1
Chelsea (Signed on 31/8/2006) PL 48+2/1 FLC 4+1 FAC 5+1 Others 20

COLE Carlton Michael
Born: Croydon, 12 November 1983
Height: 6'3" **Weight:** 13.4
International Honours: E: U21-19; Yth
Last season was an excellent one for the West Ham striker, whose confidence grew as he was given a regular run in the side. Often used as a lone striker, he holds up the ball superbly and brings others into play. At Manchester City in January, Carlton scored an incredible goal after controlling a pass on his chest, holding off a defender and swivelling to beat the goalkeeper with an overhead kick. His pace and height make him a constant threat to defenders.
Chelsea (From trainee on 23/10/2000) PL 4+21/4 FLC 1/2 FAC 1+3/2 Others 0+2
Wolverhampton W (Loaned on 28/11/2002) FL 15+2/1
Charlton Ath (Loaned on 20/8/2003) PL 8+13/4 FAC 1/1
Aston Villa (Loaned on 12/7/2004) PL 18+9/3 FLC 1+1 FAC 1
West Ham U (£2,000,000 on 6/7/2006) PL 26+22/6 FLC 3+1/2 FAC 3+1/1 Others 1+1

COLE Joseph (Joe) John
Born: Romford, 8 November 1981
Height: 5'9" **Weight:** 11.0
Club Honours: FAYC '99; FLC '05; PL '05, '06; CS '05, '07
International Honours: E: 50; B-1; U21-8; Yth; Sch
If the new regime at Chelsea was expected to play a more expansive game, the ideal player in Joe was already in-situ. The quicksilver wide man had an outstanding season and spent more time on the pitch than any other Chelsea player, a situation unthinkable a year or so before. He scored a string of smartly-taken goals, none better than the gem against Everton at Goodison Park that clinched the Blues' third Carling Cup final appearance in four years. He mastered

the most difficult skill of all, controlling a ball dropping over his shoulder and buried a rasping drive into the opposite corner of the goal. Almost perversely, Joe was omitted from the starting line-up at Wembley and how the Blues missed his trickery and intuitive flair. It was an error that the management did not repeat as Joe is now regarded as a big occasion player, able to take a match by the scruff of the neck and make the unexpected happen. In addition to his brilliant dribbling Joe scored consistently, with ten goals in all competitions. A cult hero to Chelsea fans, it was an easy decision to select their 'Player of the Year', an award that Joe richly deserved.
West Ham U (From trainee on 11/12/1998) PL 108+18/10 FLC 6+1/1 FAC 10+1/2 Others 2+3
Chelsea (£6,600,000 on 6/8/2003) PL 94+49/23 FLC 9+8/4 FAC 12+5/2 Others 32+14/4

COLES Daniel (Danny) Richard
Born: Bristol, 31 October 1981
Height: 6'1" **Weight:** 11.5
Club Honours: AMC '03
Having played at centre-back for Hull on the opening day of the season, a home defeat by Plymouth was his final appearance for the Tigers. Hartlepool manager Danny Wilson knew the defender from their time together at Bristol City and took him to Victoria Park on loan where he played three times at right-back before returning to Hull. Danny, a former Bristol City central defender, next joined Bristol Rovers, initially on loan in November, following the long-term injury to Byron Anthony. His experience was used to good effect alongside Steve Elliott but he was briefly out of the side with a cheekbone injury and suspension. He scored his first goal in an FA Cup tie at Premiership Fulham and signed a permanent two-and-a-half-year deal.
Bristol C (From trainee on 7/6/2000) FL 141+7/5 FLC 4/1 FAC 8+1 Others 19/1
Hull C (£200,000 on 26/7/2005) FL 26+5 FAC 1
Hartlepool U (Loaned on 1/10/2007) FL 3
Bristol Rov (Signed on 2/11/2007) FL 24/1 FAC 6/2

COLGAN Nicholas (Nick) Vincent
Born: Drogheda, 19 September 1973
Height: 6'1" **Weight:** 13.6
International Honours: RoI: 9; B-1; U21-9; Yth; Sch
Nick kept goal in Barnsley's first game of the season, a 4-1 defeat by Coventry, before losing his place to Heinz Muller.

After that he had few chances to show his fine shot-stopping and organising. Nick continued to figure in the Republic of Ireland squad but had a transfer request accepted in October and joined Ipswich on a short-term contract in January.
Chelsea (From trainee on 1/10/1992) PL 1
Brentford (Loaned on 16/10/1997) FL 5
Reading (Loaned on 27/2/1998) FL 5
Bournemouth (Free on 9/7/1998)
Hibernian (Free on 29/7/1999) SL 121 SLC 8 SC 16 Others 2
Stockport Co (Loaned on 8/8/2003) FL 14+1 FLC 2
Barnsley (Free on 20/7/2004) FL 99+2 FLC 2+1 FAC 5 Others 4
Dundee U (Loaned on 28/1/2005) SL 1 SLC 1
Ipswich T (Free on 31/1/2008)

COLLINS Daniel (Danny) Lewis
Born: Buckley, 6 August 1980
Height: 6'2" **Weight:** 12.1
Club Honours: FC '04; Ch '05, '07
International Honours: W: 5; E: SP-2
Often an unsung hero, Danny came to the fore last season and was deservedly voted the Sunderland supporters' 'Player of the Year'. Primarily a centre-half, where his aerial power is especially evident, Danny operated for most of the campaign at left- back and his consistency was crucial to the Black Cats' Premier League survival. Always dangerous at set pieces Danny had an injury-time header controversially ruled out against Aston

Danny Collins

Villa in December but was to be rewarded with the opening goal in the vital win at relegation rivals Fulham in April. Danny continued to represent Wales and made his 100th appearance for Sunderland in the December game against Manchester United.
Chester C *(Signed from Buckley T on 27/12/2001) FL 12/1 FLC 1*
Sunderland *(£140,000 on 13/10/2004) P/FL 96+15/2 FLC 2+1 FAC 4+1*

COLLINS James Michael
Born: Newport, 23 August 1983
Height: 6'2" **Weight:** 13.0
International Honours: W: 19; U21-8; Yth
The Welsh international centre-back endured a season to forget at West Ham. In the two League games he played, he gave his usual no-nonsense displays by battling for every ball and winning headers. Then, in a reserve fixture against Portsmouth in January, he suffered a bad knee ligament injury that put him out of action for the remainder of the campaign. He added to his Welsh caps during 2007-08.
Cardiff C *(From trainee on 5/4/2001) FL 49+17/3 FLC 5 FAC 4+5/3 Others 4+2*
West Ham U *(£3,200,000 on 5/7/2005) PL 31+2/2 FLC 3+1 FAC 3 Others 1*

COLLINS Lee Harvey
Born: Telford, 28 September 1988
Height: 6'1" **Weight:** 11.10
International Honours: E: Yth
Lee showed during his extended loan from Wolverhampton that he is one for the future. After first appearing for Hereford at right-back, Lee slotted in confidently at left-back for a stint before moving to central defence, where he also showed his promise. A defensive shake-up cost him his regular place at the end of January but he remained an important part of Hereford's squad for the rest of the season.
Wolverhampton W *(From trainee on 2/3/2007)*
Hereford U *(Loaned on 15/11/2007) FL 14+2 FAC 4*

COLLINS Matthew (Matty) Jeffrey
Born: Merthyr Tydfil, 31 March 1986
Height: 5'9" **Weight:** 11.9
International Honours: W: U21-2; Yth
Brought in on loan from Swansea at the beginning of November by manager Brian Carey, Matty showed competitive spirit in Wrexham's midfield and added much-needed thrust. After three starts, he returned to the Swans when his month's loan expired. Industrious

and a willing worker, his priority is to win the ball.
Fulham *(From trainee on 4/4/2003)*
Swansea C *(Free on 18/7/2007)*
Wrexham *(Loaned on 2/11/2007) FL 2 FAC 1*

COLLINS Michael Anthony
Born: Halifax, 30 April 1986
Height: 6'0" **Weight:** 10.12
International Honours: RoI: U21-2; Yth
What a difference a year makes. The influential Huddersfield midfielder was a regular either in the centre or a wide midfield position and showed his versatility when operating at right-back. He made his international bow with two substitute appearances for the Republic of Ireland under-21 team in their European Championship campaign. Michael has a great appetite for the game and holds his own with his physical presence as he grows in maturity. He can act as the team's creator with quality passes into the danger area and scored four goals, the highlight being an FA Cup equaliser against Chelsea. Michael received a further call up to the Irish under-21 squad for the Inter-Continental Cup in Malaysia.
Huddersfield T *(From trainee on 11/5/2005) FL 90+19/7 FLC 3 FAC 4+4/1 Others 2+1/1*

COLLINS Neill William
Born: Troon, 2 September 1983
Height: 6'3" **Weight:** 13.0
Club Honours: Ch '05
International Honours: S: B-1; U21-7
Neill twice conceded penalties as he helped out in an unfamiliar left-back role at Wolverhampton last season. His effort never waned and it was some reward when he headed a late winner at home to Coventry. He had some games at centre-half, his preferred position, without looking comfortable and also pitched in at right-back. From mid-October Neill made 21 consecutive appearances and also went on as a substitute for Scotland 'B'. Although struggling to adapt to the different roles, he gave 100 per cent and was outstanding at Bristol City in April.
Queen's Park *(From juniors on 20/3/2001) SL 30+2 SLC 1 SC 2*
Dumbarton *(Free on 22/7/2002) SL 62+1/4 SLC 3 SC 2 Others 4*
Sunderland *(£25,000 on 13/8/2004) P/FL 14+4/1 FLC 2 FAC 4/1*
Hartlepool U *(Loaned on 12/8/2005) FL 22 FLC 2 Others 1*
Sheffield U *(Loaned on 18/2/2006) FL 2*
Wolverhampton W *(£150,000 on 2/11/2006) FL 54+7/5 FLC 1 FAC 5/1 Others 2*

COLLINS Samuel (Sam) Jason
Born: Pontefract, 5 June 1977
Height: 6'3" **Weight:** 14.0
Sam's career has been hampered by injuries in recent times. Having recovered from the previous season's serious knee injury, the Hull defender regained match-fitness early on in 2007-08 while on loan to Swindon, providing much-needed cover in defence. He played soundly and had a full part in the victory at Millwall before returning to his parent club. However, with Hull playing consistently in the Championship, Sam's final, and impressive, appearance for them was in the FA Cup third round defeat at Plymouth. The big central defender then joined Hartlepool in the January transfer window in a permanent deal and immediately stamped his authority on his new club, playing alongside his former Bury team-mate Michael Nelson. A suspension and an injury kept him out for short spells but he settled well.
Huddersfield T *(From trainee on 6/7/1994) FL 34+3 FLC 6+1 FAC 3*
Bury *(£75,000 on 2/7/1999) FL 78+4/2 FLC 5 FAC 0+2 Others 1*
Port Vale *(Free on 15/7/2002) FL 135/11 FLC 4 FAC 5 Others 5*
Hull C *(Signed on 3/11/2005) FL 23 FLC 2 FAC 2*
Swindon T *(Loaned on 28/9/2007) FL 3+1*
Hartlepool U *(Signed on 31/1/2008) FL 10/2*

COLLIS Stephen (Steve) Philip
Born: Harrow, 18 March 1981
Height: 6'2" **Weight:** 13.0
Once again, Steve started as Darryl Flahavan's deputy at Southend but when chosen to keep goal in the Carling Cup game against Cheltenham, he entered a match-winning performance. The game was level in the closing minutes when Steve saved a penalty to take the tie into extra-time and eventual victory. Flahavan then suffered a rare injury and Steve stepped up again, performing so admirably for 20 games that a returning Flahavan was confined to the bench. Steve kept his place until the New Year, when Flahavan took over. Has provided sterling back up for Southend but the acquisition of Scott Masters from Brentford in January made Steve's future uncertain and he was released in the summer.
Barnet *(From juniors on 27/8/1999)*
Nottingham F *(Free on 11/7/2000)*
Yeovil T *(Free on 6/8/2001) FL 41+2 FAC 0+1 Others 2*
Southend U *(Free on 3/7/2006) FL 20+1 FLC 2 FAC 3 Others 1*

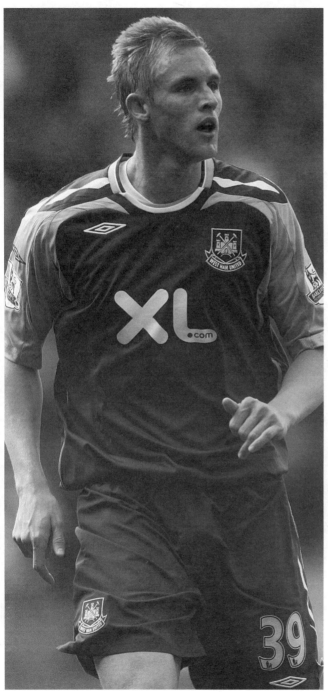

Jack Collison

COLLISON Jack David
Born: Watford, 2 October 1988
Height: 6'0" **Weight:** 13.10
International Honours: W: 2; U21-5
The tall central midfielder was made
reserve-team captain at West Ham
last season. Showing great leadership
qualities, he did well on his League
debut as a substitute against Arsenal and
started the game against Bolton. He was
chosen for Wales under-21s and scored a
stunning goal on his debut against Bosnia
in November.
West Ham U (From trainee on 10/8/2007)
PL 1+1

COMMINGES Miguel
Born: Les Abymes, Guadeloupe, 16
March 1982
Height: 5'9" **Weight:** 11.3
Arriving at Swindon from French club
Reims, Miguel proved to be a real find
and had a magnificent debut season
in the League. He is adaptable, able to
play on either wing, in defence or in
midfield. Used in a variety of positions,
he eventually settled at right-back, where
his pace and skill showed to great effect
as an attacking force. Selected for his
native Guadeloupe during the season, he
was a popular performer at the County
Ground and scooped every 'Player of
the Season' award. Unfortunately for
Swindon, Miguel decided to aim for a
higher sphere and was expected to sign
for Cardiff.
*Swindon T (Signed from Reims, France, ex
Amiens, on 10/8/2007) FL 32+8 FLC 1 FAC
4 Others 2*

COMMONS Kristian (Kris)
Arran
Born: Mansfield, 30 August 1983
Height: 5'6" **Weight:** 9.8
With his close control and excellent
technical ability, Kris can outwit most
defenders. In Nottingham Forest's
promotion campaign, he was happy to
play on either flank or just behind a main
striker. The high spot of his season was a
hat-trick against Cheltenham in October.
Kris struggled with a persistent groin
injury during the last three months of the
season, restricting his availability, but he
was always a valuable member of Forest's
team when fit. Named in the PFA League
One select side, he was out of contract at
the end of the season and reported to be
joining Derby.
*Stoke C (From trainee on 25/1/2001) FL
20+21/5 FLC 1+2 FAC 0+1 Others 1*
*Nottingham F (Free on 2/7/2004) FL
112+26/32 FLC 5+1 FAC 8+1/5 Others
4+2/1*

CONLON Barry John
Born: Drogheda, 1 October 1978
Height: 6'3" **Weight:** 13.7
International Honours: RoI: U21-7
Signed from Mansfield in the summer,
Barry worked hard for the Bradford cause
although he had to wait until Boxing Day
for his first goal from open play, bundling
in a stoppage-time winner against
Lincoln. The striker won the fans round
through his enthusiasm and commitment,
always giving his maximum.
*Manchester C (From trainee at Queens Park
R on 14/8/1997) FL 1+6 FLC 0+1*
*Plymouth Arg (Loaned on 26/2/1998) FL
13/2*
*Southend U (£95,000 on 4/9/1998) FL
28+6/7 FAC 1 Others 1*
*York C (£100,000 on 20/7/1999) FL
33+15/11 FLC 2+2 FAC 1 Others 0+1*

*Colchester U (Loaned on 9/11/2000) FL
23+3/8 FAC 1 Others 1*
*Darlington (£60,000 on 6/7/2001) FL
114+1/39 FLC 4 FAC 4/3 Others 2*
*Barnsley (Free on 5/7/2004) FL 25+10/7 FLC
3+1/1 FAC 1 Others 1*
*Rotherham U (Loaned on 14/10/2005) FL
3/1 Others 1*
*Darlington (Free on 24/7/2006) FL 12+7/6
FAC 1+1 Others 2*
*Mansfield T (Free on 12/1/2007) FL 16+1/6
Bradford C (Free on 18/7/2007) FL 21+21/7
FLC 1 FAC 0+2 Others 1*

CONNELL Alan John
Born: Enfield, 15 February 1983
Height: 5'11" **Weight:** 10.8
Known as a skilful and tricky striker, Alan
joined Brentford from Hereford in the
close season. He scored on his debut

Alan Connell

against Mansfield on the opening day
but was then in and out of the side until
a change of manager in December. Alan
scored twice at Wrexham in Andy Scott's
first game in charge and was a regular
until the end of the campaign, with 12
goals in total. Popular with the fans for
his effort as well as his ability, Alan prefers
playing alongside a big centre-forward.
*Bournemouth (From juniors at Ipswich T on
9/7/2002) FL 18+36/8 FLC 1+3/1 FAC 3+2/2
Others 0+1*
*Torquay U (Signed on 14/7/2005) FL
12+10/7 FLC 0+1 FAC 0+2 Others 1*
*Hereford U (Free on 1/8/2006) FL 33+11/9
FLC 0+1 FAC 4/1 Others 1*
*Brentford (Free on 3/7/2007) FL 35+7/12
FLC 1 FAC 1 Others 1*

CONNOLLY Adam James
Born: Manchester, 10 April 1986
Height: 5'9" **Weight:** 12.4
This hard-working midfield player made
a useful contribution to Cheltenham as
a regular member of the squad under
the management of first John Ward and
then Keith Downing. Adam was never
far from the first team, although he also
captained the reserves in 14 matches and
scored four goals. His first-team chances
tended to arrive when others were injured
and he started both in the centre and on
the right of midfield as well as making a
number of substitute appearances. When
an injury crisis threatened Cheltenham's
chances of staying in League One towards
the end of the season, Adam made some
important cameo appearances from the
bench. Was out of contract at the end of
the campaign.
*Cheltenham T (From trainee on 4/7/2005) FL
14+18/1 FAC 2 Others 3/1*

CONNOLLY David James
Born: Willesden, 6 June 1977
Height: 5'8" **Weight:** 11.4
Club Honours: Ch '07
International Honours: RoI: 41; U21
A Republic of Ireland international
striker, David's first-team opportunities
at Sunderland were severely restricted
last term as he made only one start and
four substitute appearances. A diminutive
forward with a real eye for goal, David
has been a consistent scorer at his many
clubs and will probably continue to be if,
as is expected, he leaves the Stadium of
Light in the summer.
*Watford (From trainee on 15/11/1994) FL
19+7/10 FLC 1 FAC 3+3/4 Others 1/1 (Free
to Feyenoord, Holland during 1997 close
season)*
*Wolverhampton W (Loaned on 21/8/1998)
FL 18+14/6 FLC 2 FAC 0+1*
Wimbledon (Free from Feyenoord, Holland

on 27/7/2001) FL 63/42 FLC 1 FAC 4
West Ham U (£285,000 on 8/8/2003) FL
37+2/10 FLC 2/2 FAC 4/2 Others 3
Leicester C (£500,000 on 22/7/2004) FL
48+1/17 FAC 3+2
Wigan Ath (£2,000,000 on 31/8/2005) PL
4+15/1 FLC 2+1/1 FAC 1/1
Sunderland (Signed on 31/8/2006) P/FL
31+8/13 FLC 0+1 FAC 1+1

CONNOLLY Matthew (Matt)
Thomas Martin
Born: Barnet, 24 September 1987
Height: 6'1" **Weight:** 11.3
International Honours: E: Yth
Proving to be a real find, Matt impressed
in the Championship early in the season
when Arsenal loaned him to Colchester
for three months. Colchester had already
decided the talented defender would be
most comfortable at centre-half, when he
spent the first part of the season at Layer
Road. He scored twice and was at ease on
the ball but his low point was a red card
for a foul on Charlton's former Colchester
striker Chris Iwelumo. Having returned to
Arsenal, he became part of the Queens
Park Rangers' revolution when he moved
across London in January. Despite his
youth, his game is incredibly mature and
he quickly established himself as a vital
part of the new-look Rangers' defence.
Originally played at full-back, it did not
take him long to make the switch to his
preferred centre-back position, where
he excelled alongside several different
partners.
Arsenal (From trainee on 1/7/2005) FLC 1+1
Bournemouth (Loaned on 23/11/2006) FL
3+2/1 FAC 2
Colchester U (Loaned on 16/7/2007) FL
13+3/2
Queens Park Rgrs (£1,000,000 on
2/1/2008) FL 18+2 FAC 1

CONNOLLY Paul
Born: Liverpool, 29 September 1983
Height: 6'0" **Weight:** 11.9
Club Honours: Div 2' 04
Paul was almost ever-present during the
season at right-back for Plymouth. Good
in the air and strong in the tackle, he
was one of the main reasons why the
Pilgrims' defence was among the meanest
in the Championship. He enjoys raiding
down the flank and provides dangerous
crosses to create scoring opportunities.
Paul scored his first goal in his 149th
appearance for the club with a header
in the victory over Norwich in November.
He then advised manager Paul Sturrock
that he would not be signing a further
contract at the end of the season and was
given a fond farewell by the supporters
after seven years at Home Park. It was

announced in May that Paul was to join
Derby on a free transfer.
Plymouth Arg (From trainee on 23/7/2002)
FL 156+6/1 FLC 5 FAC 9 Others 1

CONNOR Paul
Born: Bishop Auckland, 12 January 1979
Height: 6'1" **Weight:** 11.5
Club Honours: AMC '00, '06
Paul shouldered the responsibility of
leading Cheltenham's attack for much
of the season as the Robins battled to
retain their League One status. Although
sometimes criticised by supporters for
not scoring enough goals, Paul's all-
round contribution was considerable.
He set up two stoppage-time goals
in a dramatic win over Brighton and
discovered his scoring touch at just the
right time with three strikes in the last
seven games. His second-half goal against
Doncaster in the final game put to bed
any relegation fears. With a number of
different partners, Paul seemed to work
best alongside 16-goal striker Steven
Gillespie. His appearances were restricted
to the substitutes' bench during the
two-month loan of Steve Brooker but he
returned refreshed for the nail-biting last
few weeks.
Middlesbrough (From trainee on 4/7/1996)
Hartlepool U (Loaned on 6/2/1998) FL 4+1
Stoke C (Free on 25/3/1999) FL 18+18/7 FLC
3+3/3 FAC 0+1 Others 2+3
Cambridge U (Loaned on 9/11/2000) FL
12+1/5 FAC 1
Rochdale (£100,000 on 9/3/2001) FL
76+18/28 FLC 3 FAC 8+1/3 Others 0+2
Swansea C (£35,000 on 12/3/2004) FL
51+14/16 FLC 1 FAC 6/3 Others 3/1
Leyton Orient (£40,000 on 31/1/2006) FL
20+14/7 FLC 1 FAC 0+3 Others 1
Cheltenham T (£25,000 on 15/1/2007) FL
35+19/5 FLC 1 FAC 2 Others 2/1

CONSTABLE James Ashley
Born: Malmesbury, 4 October 1984
Height: 6'2" **Weight:** 12.12
Like Scott Bevan, James joined
Shrewsbury from Kidderminster in
January. The striker was in good form,
scoring 11 times in 20 outings for the
Harriers and was tracked by previous
Shrews' manager Gary Peters. James
is committed, useful in the air and can
hold the ball well. He made his debut
from the bench in the 2-1 home defeat
by Lincoln in February but a week later
scored the vital equaliser in the draw with
Brentford and followed that with two
more, including a stoppage-time equaliser
in the 3-3 draw with MK Dons. As new
manager Paul Simpson scanned his staff,
James made an equal number of starts
and substitute appearances, scoring four

times.
Walsall (£4,000 from Chippenham T on
21/11/2005) FL 9+14/3 FLC 1 FAC 0+1
Others 1+3/2 (Free to Kidderminster Hrs on
30/1/2007)
Shrewsbury T (Signed on 30/1/2008) FL
7+7/4

CONSTANTINE Leon
Born: Hackney, 24 February 1978
Height: 6'2" **Weight:** 11.10
Luck was in short supply for Leon after
he agreed to join Leeds from Port Vale
in the summer. Despite doubts that the
club would start the season, the striker
stuck with them, only to suffer an ankle
injury that kept him out for three months,
just as the League was about to kick-off.
He did not start until November, when
he scored after eight minutes in the
2-1 Johnstone's Paint Trophy defeat by
Bury. His only League One start for Leeds
came in the following month at Walsall
and his next outing, on New Year's Day,
summed up his bad luck. He went on at
half-time with Leeds trailing 3-0 at home
to Oldham, scored within a minute but
damaged a shoulder in doing so and
did not play for United again. Instead,
he joined Oldham, against whom he
was injured, on a one-month loan in
March to regain fitness. A powerful
physical presence who leads the line well,
Leon made eight appearances, scoring
against Millwall and Huddersfield, before
returning to Elland Road.
Millwall (Signed from Edgware T on
31/8/2000) FL 0+1 Others 1
Leyton Orient (Loaned on 27/8/2001) FL
9+1/3 Others 0+1
Partick T (Loaned on 11/1/2002) SL 2 SC 1
Brentford (Free on 8/8/2002) FL 2+15 FLC
1+1
Southend U (Free on 21/8/2003) FL 40+3/21
FAC 2+1 Others 6+1/4
Peterborough U (Free on 2/7/2004) FL
5+6/1 Others 1
Torquay U (Loaned on 29/10/2004) FL 4/3
FAC 1
Torquay U (£75,000 on 10/12/2004) FL
30+8/7 FLC 1 Others 0+1
Port Vale (£20,000 on 4/11/2005) FL
71+1/32 FLC 4/2 FAC 7/2 Others 2/2
Leeds U (Free on 9/8/2007) FL 1+3/1 FAC
0+2 Others 1/1
Oldham Ath (Loaned on 4/3/2008) FL 7+1/2

CONVEY Robert (Bobby)
Born: Philadelphia, Pennsylvania, USA,
27 May 1983
Height: 5'9" **Weight:** 11.4
Club Honours: Ch '06
International Honours: USA: 46
The season did not really come to life
for Bobby until the home Carling Cup
tie against Liverpool when, despite

Bobby Convey

assured. Lee started only four games and in one of them was substituted after four minutes, sacrificed for substitute goalkeeper Rob Elliot after Nicky Weaver was sent off at Plymouth. Is a skilful winger with a good left foot and an excellent crosser.
Watford *(Signed from Aylesbury U on 19/11/1999) FL 31+28/7 FLC 0+2 FAC 2+1*
York C *(Loaned on 2/10/2002) FL 7/1 Others 1/1*
Queens Park Rgrs *(Loaned on 20/12/2002) FL 13/1*
Queens Park Rgrs *(Free on 3/7/2004) FL 109+10/9 FLC 3+1/1 FAC 4*
Fulham *(£2,500,000 on 20/7/2007)*
Charlton Ath *(Loaned on 31/1/2008) FL 4+5*

COOKE Andrew (Andy) Roy
Born: Shrewsbury, 20 January 1974
Height: 6'0" **Weight:** 12.8
The season started well for Andy, with two goals in Shrewsbury's opening-day 4-0 victory at Lincoln. Three days later, the strong striker who holds up the ball well, suffered a bad hamstring injury in a Carling Cup tie against Colchester and was out until Boxing Day when, predictably, he scored against Stockport. His season continued to be ravaged by injury and although he scored five times, he was released in April. Andy will be remembered fondly at Shrewsbury.
Burnley *(Signed from Newtown on 1/5/1995) FL 134+37/52 FLC 8+2/6 FAC 7+3/2 Others 9+2/2*
Stoke C *(£350,000 on 1/12/2000) FL 71+17/21 FLC 1+1 FAC 2+2/1 Others 4+4/1 (Free to Busan Icons, South Korea on 22/7/2003)*
Bradford C *(Free on 7/1/2005) FL 30+7/5 FLC 1+1 FAC 2/1 Others 2*
Darlington *(Loaned on 14/2/2006) FL 11+3/3*
Shrewsbury T *(Free on 1/8/2006) FL 31+17/15 FLC 0+1 FAC 1+1 Others 1+2/2*

COOPER Kevin Lee
Born: Derby, 8 February 1975
Height: 5'7" **Weight:** 10.7
Unable to get a game at Cardiff, Kevin went on loan to Tranmere in October and started three games in 11 days before returning to Ninian Park after only three weeks. Allowed to leave Cardiff in January, he signed for Chesterfield on a short-term deal to bring an experienced and creative head to the left of midfield. However, a chronic lack of match fitness meant he could not hit the ground running and, consequently, he never had much of a look-in. Kevin came off the bench to score at Grimsby on his debut but started only twice after that and did not complete the full 90 minutes in either

Reading eventually losing 4-2, he fired in a cracking left-foot volley from the edge of the box. It was his only goal and in a generally frustrating year, he completed the full 90 minutes in only four of his 24 appearances. A series of niggling injuries limited his progress, although he showed flashes of his old dribbling skill and crossing ability from either flank while taking his total of Reading appearances past 100. A consolation for Bobby is that he remains part of the United States' squad.
Reading *(£850,000 from DC United, USA on 4/8/2004) P/FL 69+23/7 FLC 3+1/1 FAC 7*

COOK Anthony Lloyd Evans
Born: Hackney, 10 August 1989
Height: 5'8" **Weight:** 11.1
Arriving at Dagenham from Croydon Athletic early in the season, Anthony

put in some impressive performances in Daggers' reserves before being rewarded with a two-year contract. Having made his first League appearance as a substitute at Shrewsbury in December, the young defender looks to have a bright future as a sturdy ball-winner.
Dagenham & Redbridge *(Free from Croydon Ath on 31/8/2007) FL 0+1*

COOK Lee
Born: Hammersmith, 3 August 1982
Height: 5'9" **Weight:** 11.7
Lee was signed by Charlton on loan from Fulham in January for the remainder of the season to boost a promotion push. He was not fully fit, after recovering from knee and hip injuries, when he arrived at the Valley and with Jerome Thomas, Leroy Ambrose and Lloyd Sam competing for the two wing places, a start was not

match before moving on.
Derby Co *(From trainee on 2/7/1993) P/FL 0+2 FLC 0+2 Others 0+1*
Stockport Co *(£150,000 on 24/3/1997) FL 146+22/21 FLC 7+5/2 FAC 6 Others 1*
Wimbledon *(£800,000 + on 15/3/2001) FL 50+1/13 FLC 1 FAC 2*
Wolverhampton W *(£1,000,000 on 26/3/2002) P/FL 32+30/9 FLC 1 FAC 0+1 Others 2+1/1*
Sunderland *(Loaned on 6/1/2004) FL 0+1*
Norwich C *(Loaned on 19/3/2004) FL 6+4*
Cardiff C *(Signed on 2/8/2005) FL 31+9/2 FLC 2 FAC 1+1*
Yeovil T *(Loaned on 29/9/2006) FL 4*
Walsall *(Loaned on 23/2/2007) FL 8*
Tranmere Rov *(Loaned on 25/10/2007) FL 3+1*
Chesterfield *(Free on 8/2/2008) FL 2+5/1*

COOPER Shaun David
Born: Newport, Isle of Wight, 5 October 1983
Height: 5'10" **Weight:** 10.10
Shaun once again showed what a versatile player he is by taking up positions all along the back four for Bournemouth last season, as well as his usual midfield place. A consistent performer, who is extremely capable at set pieces, he cheered the Cherries with a terrific goal against Port Vale.
Portsmouth *(From trainee on 7/4/2001) FL 3+4*
Leyton Orient *(Loaned on 17/10/2003) FL 9*
Kidderminster Hrs *(Loaned on 24/9/2004) FL 10 FAC 1 Others 1*
Bournemouth *(Free on 5/8/2005) FL 95+11/1 FLC 3+1 FAC 6/1 Others 4*

COPPINGER James
Born: Middlesbrough, 10 January 1981
Height: 5'7" **Weight:** 10.6
Club Honours: AMC '07
International Honours: E: Yth
Playing on the right of midfield for Doncaster last season, his skilful ball play when going forward could be too much for many defenders. James worked hard to assist his defence and reached his best form when Paul Green was his midfield partner with James O'Connor behind him, forming a formidable trio going forward. He scored three League goals and two were contenders for 'Goal of the Season'. James hammered in tremendous shots from 30 yards in away games against Millwall and Tranmere. He reserved his best performance for the second leg of the play-off semi-final against Southend at the Keepmoat Stadium, scoring a stunning hat-trick in a 5-1 victory, and played in the Wembley final against Leeds as Rovers gained the victory to take them into the Championship.

Newcastle U *(£250,000 + from trainee at Darlington on 27/3/1998) PL 0+1*
Hartlepool U *(Loaned on 10/3/2000) FL 6+4/3 Others 1*
Hartlepool U *(Loaned on 25/1/2002) FL 14/2*
Exeter C *(Free on 2/8/2002) FL 35+8/5 FLC 1 FAC 3 Others 2*
Doncaster Rov *(£30,000 on 7/7/2004) FL 124+21/12 FLC 7+4/1 FAC 5+4 Others 9+1/3*

CORDEN Simon **Wayne**
Born: Leek, 1 November 1975
Height: 5'9" **Weight:** 11.3
Wayne started last season as Leyton Orient's first-choice left-winger. One of the most skilful players at the club, he can also play on the right and likes nothing better than to get on the ball and dribble past opponents. With his contract due to expire in the summer, he was allowed to join Notts County on loan in March. Wayne is at his most dangerous when cutting inside to fire in one of his spectacular shots and added width to the County attack as they battled to stay

clear of relegation from League Two. His experience was valuable, although he lost his place in the last few games when Myles Weston regained fitness.
Port Vale *(From trainee on 20/9/1994) FL 30+36/1 FLC 4 FAC 2+1/1*
Mansfield T *(Free on 3/7/2000) FL 173+19/35 FLC 8/2 FAC 9+1/1 Others 8*
Scunthorpe U *(Free on 18/2/2005) FL 8+9 FLC 1+1 FAC 1+1 Others 3*
Chester C *(Loaned on 13/1/2006) FL 2*
Leyton Orient *(Free on 23/3/2006) FL 61+15/5 FLC 2 FAC 4+1/2 Others 1*
Notts Co *(Loaned on 14/3/2008) FL 7+2*

CORK Jack Frank Porteous
Born: Carshalton, 25 June 1989
Height: 6'0" **Weight:** 10.12
International Honours: E: Yth
Chelsea midfielder Jack joined Championship side Scunthorpe on a season-long loan in August and left with all the club's main 'Player of the Year' awards. He had to be patient as he started only one match in the first

James Coppinger

two months of the campaign but once he won his place in the draw at Cardiff at the end of October, he started every other match apart from when serving a three-match ban following a controversial red card at home to Ipswich in March. A superbly talented ball player, he also deputised at right-back and always looked very comfortable on the ball, scoring his first two League goals during the season – both against Coventry. Jack also represented England under-19s during the campaign.

Chelsea *(From trainee on 5/7/2006)*
Bournemouth *(Loaned on 3/11/2006) FL 7 FAC 2*
Scunthorpe U *(Loaned on 17/8/2007) FL 32+2/2 FAC 1*

CORLUKA Vedran
Born: Derventa, Bosnia, 5 February 1986
Height: 6'3" **Weight:** 13.3
International Honours: Croatia: 23
Vedran was Sven-Goran Eriksson's sixth signing for Manchester City, on a five-year deal after attracting interest from several Premier League clubs. Capped by Croatia, he already had first-hand knowledge of what to expect in the Premier League, having played in the 2-0 victory over England in 2006 as well as facing Arsenal in a Champions' League qualifier in the same year. Born in Bosnia & Herzegovina when it was still part of the former Yugoslavia, Vedran played over 60 times for Dinamo Zagreb and gained loan experience at Inter Zapresic. Tall and commanding, Vedran showed his versatility during his first season at City, turning in some superb performances at right-back, centre-half and in a central midfield role. He was a key member of the Croatian side that prevented England from reaching Euro 2008 and Croatia manager Slaven Bilic calls him the best right-back in the world.

Manchester C *(£7,000,000 from Dinamo Zagreb, Croatia, ex Inter Zapresic - loan, on 10/8/2007) PL 34+1 FLC 3 FAC 3*

CORR Barry
Born: Wicklow, 2 April 1985
Height: 6'4" **Weight:** 12.8
International Honours: RoI: Yth
Barry had a dreadful time with injuries at Swindon. The striker had a delayed start after recovering from a back injury, then suffered a shoulder problem that brought his season to a premature end. He spent the last three months of 2006-07 on loan from Sheffield Wednesday, a deal that became permanent at the start of last season. Barry scored a late winner as a substitute against Tranmere in his first appearance in October and was

initially used sparingly from the bench. He netted from the spot in his first start against Hartlepool, following this with a New Year's Day winner at Yeovil and a well-taken brace at Bournemouth. His five goals from a limited number of appearances underline the undoubted ability of the gangling forward, good in the air but with a neat touch. If he can overcome his injury worries, he will be a handful for lower division defences.

Leeds U *(From trainee on 11/4/2002)*
Sheffield Wed *(Free on 18/4/2005) FL 7+10 FLC 1 FAC 1*
Bristol C *(Loaned on 27/10/2006) FL 1+2 Others 1/1*
Swindon T *(Signed on 19/3/2007) FL 15+10/8 FAC 2+1*

CORT Carl Edward Richard
Born: Southwark, 1 November 1977
Height: 6'4" **Weight:** 12.7
International Honours: E: U21-12
Carl is an imposing striker who arrived at the Walkers Stadium from Wolverhampton in the summer with a decent reputation but injury problems blighted his stay in Leicester, where opportunities were equally divided between the starting line-up and the bench. The undoubted highlight of his stay was a scoring performance at Stamford Bridge in a Carling Cup thriller but he eventually suffered from the managerial merry-go-round and was allowed to leave by mutual consent in January, subsequently making an unheralded move to lowly Spanish outfit Marbella, where David Pleat is the football consultant.

Wimbledon *(From trainee on 7/6/1996) PL 54+19/16 FLC 8+2/7 FAC 6+4/2*
Lincoln C *(Loaned on 3/2/1997) FL 5+1/1*
Newcastle U *(£7,000,000 on 6/7/2000) PL 19+3/7 FLC 3/1 FAC 2 Others 0+1*
Wolverhampton W *(£2,000,000 on 28/1/2004) P/FL 78+16/31 FLC 1 FAC 3+1/1*
Leicester C *(Signed on 9/8/2007) FL 7+7 FLC 1/1*

CORT Leon Terence Anthony
Born: Bermondsey, 11 September 1979
Height: 6'2" **Weight:** 13.4
The tall, commanding centre-half was Crystal Palace's 'Player of the Year' in 2006-07 and began last season, at a time when his house was seriously damaged by fire, in the heart of their defence. When Neil Warnock took over as the Palace manager Leon was allowed to go on loan to Stoke in November and the transfer was made permanent in the January window. Amazingly for a central defender, Leon has not been booked for four years. He slotted comfortably into the Stoke side alongside another loan

player, Ryan Shawcross, and was an ever-present for the remainder of the season. His eight goals, mainly from set pieces, went a long way to securing promotion to the Premiership for the Potters.

Millwall *(Free from Dulwich Hamlet on 23/1/1998)*
Southend U *(Free on 11/7/2001) FL 135+2/11 FLC 3 FAC 13/1 Others 8*
Hull C *(Free on 7/7/2004) FL 85+1/10 FLC 1 FAC 4*
Crystal Palace *(£1,250,000 on 6/7/2006) FL 49/7 FAC 1*
Stoke C *(£1,200,000 on 2/11/2007) FL 33/8 FAC 2*

COTTERILL David Rhys George Best
Born: Cardiff, 4 December 1987
Height: 5'10" **Weight:** 10.11
International Honours: W: 11; U21-11; Yth
A skilful winger who can play on either flank, David never found the consistency to be a regular choice at Wigan in 2007-08, being substituted in both his League starts and finding himself in the queue behind Antonia Valencia. David's best game for Wigan was in the FA Cup at Sunderland, where he scored with a stunning long-distance drive. A regular for Wales, who likes to take on defenders and is exciting to watch, in order to get some games under his belt he joined Sheffield United in the January transfer window, on loan to the end of the season. David was virtually ever-present for the Blades, playing on the right as an attacking midfielder. Fast and tricky, he was dangerous going forward, his searching crosses created opportunities and he worked hard at his defensive duties.

Bristol C *(From trainee on 5/11/2005) FL 48+14/8 FLC 1/1 FAC 1 Others 1+1*
Wigan Ath *(£2,000,000 on 31/8/2006) PL 7+11/1 FLC 1 FAC 1+1/1*
Sheffield U *(Loaned on 8/2/2008) FL 15+1*

COUGHLAN Graham
Born: Dublin, 18 November 1974
Height: 6'2" **Weight:** 13.6
Club Honours: S Div 1 '01; Div 3 '02; Div 2 '04
After Graham was freed by Sheffield Wednesday, his signing was a major coup for Rotherham as many other clubs had sought his signature and he was immediately made club captain. His experience of playing at a higher level was invaluable as he proved to be dominant at the centre of the back four, despite the fact that he had to play alongside a number of different partners. He could always be relied upon to look

Pablo Counago

Pablo returned to Ipswich during the summer on a free transfer from Malaga and it was as if he had never left. The forward was always a crowd favourite and a goal in the season's opener against Sheffield Wednesday rekindled the relationship. He does not possess great ability in the air but more than makes up for this with skill on the ground. This was amply demonstrated in the home game with Wolverhampton, when he received the ball near the by-line and dribbled past two defenders before placing it into the net.

Ipswich T *(Free from Celta Vigo, Spain on 19/7/2001) P/FL 51+49/31 FLC 7/2 FAC 4+2 Others 7+2/3 (Freed during 2005 close season)*

Ipswich T *(Signed from Malaga, Spain on 25/7/2007) FL 35+8/12 FLC 1 FAC 1*

COUSINS Mark Richard
Born: Chelmsford, 9 January 1987
Height: 6'2" **Weight:** 12.2

A product of Colchester's youth team, the young goalkeeper made his senior debut as an early substitute in the 2-2 home draw against Barnsley, the U's first home game, after Dean Gerken was sent off for a professional foul. His first touch of the ball was to pick it out of the net, when Brian Howard beat him from the ensuing penalty. He also appeared as a late substitute at Bristol City in January, after Gerken picked up an injury. Mark was rewarded in the summer with a new one-year contract.

Colchester U *(From trainee on 1/7/2006) FL 0+2*

COX Dean Arthur Edward
Born: Haywards Heath, 12 August 1987
Height: 5'4" **Weight:** 9.8

Although not quite reaching the same level of consistency that marked his initial season as a first-team regular, Dean maintained a reputation as the playmaker of the Brighton side, the one most likely to provide the killer pass. Operating wide on either wing or just behind the front two, he always looks for the opening that will create a scoring opportunity. Dean weighed in with another seven goals, including a delicate, curled lob against Millwall in September that was probably the highlight of his season, but it was during the latter part of the campaign that he really showed what he was capable of as Albion challenged for a place in the play-offs. A bubbly and occasionally irascible character, he will aim to continue his considerable progress.

Brighton & Hove A *(From trainee on 28/6/2006) FL 80+5/12 FLC 3/1 FAC 6/2 Others 7/2*

after his own game while encouraging those around him.

Blackburn Rov *(£100,000 from Bray W on 14/10/1995)*
Swindon T *(Loaned on 25/3/1997) FL 3*
Livingston *(Free on 29/3/1999) SL 53+3/2 SLC 4 SC 2 Others 5*
Plymouth Arg *(Free on 21/6/2001) FL 177/25 FLC 4 FAC 10 Others 2/1*
Sheffield Wed *(Signed on 15/7/2005) FL 47+4/5 FLC 2/1 FAC 3*
Burnley *(Loaned on 22/3/2007) FL 1+1*
Rotherham U *(Free on 19/7/2007) FL 45/1 FLC 1 FAC 2 Others 1*

COULSON Michael James
Born: Scarborough, 4 April 1988
Height: 5'10" **Weight:** 10.0

Michael had a loan spell with Northwich early in the season before returning to Barnsley. As the campaign developed, he became more involved and, after a number of substitute appearances, made his first League start. He is an energetic forward who can play either wide or down the middle, showing an eye for goal with an FA Cup winner against Blackpool. Unfortunately, a training-ground injury in April will rule him out for around six months but Michael signed a two-year extension to his contract.

Barnsley *(Free from Scarborough on 24/7/2006) FL 1+13 FLC 2+1 FAC 1+4/2*

COUNAGO Pablo
Born: Pontevedra, Spain, 9 August 1979
Height: 6'0" **Weight:** 11.6
International Honours: Spain: U21

COX Ian Gary
Born: Croydon, 25 March 1971
Height: 6'0" **Weight:** 12.2
International Honours: Trinidad & Tobago: 16
Veteran central defender Ian started the season as Gillingham's main lynchpin and held his place until the end of November. Ian was rarely called upon after a change of management and was released by the club in March. A player who gave sterling service to the Gills for almost five years, he looked like calling it a day as a full-time professional.
Crystal Palace (£35,000 from Carshalton Ath on 8/3/1994) P/FL 2+13 FAC 1+2/1
Bournemouth (Free on 28/3/1996) FL 172/16 FLC 14 FAC 10 Others 11/1
Burnley (£500,000 on 4/2/2000) FL 107+8/5 FLC 7 FAC 8+1
Gillingham (Free on 6/8/2003) FL 150+3/6 FLC 7 FAC 5 Others 2

COX Neil James
Born: Scunthorpe, 8 October 1971
Height: 6'0" **Weight:** 13.7
Club Honours: FLC '94; Div 1 '95
International Honours: E: U21-6
The most experienced player on the Crewe staff, whose career began at Scunthorpe in 1990, Neil took his total of League appearances past 500 last season. He captained Crewe, using his vast experience at a higher level either as a defender or the holding player in midfield, but had to undergo surgery on a shoulder injury during the season. After the final game, he announced his retirement at the age of 37.
Scunthorpe U (From trainee on 20/3/1990) FL 17/1 FAC 4 Others 4+1
Aston Villa (£400,000 on 12/2/1991) P/FL 26+16/3 FLC 5+2 FAC 4+2/1 Others 2
Middlesbrough (£1,000,000 on 19/7/1994) P/FL 103+3/3 FLC 14+1 FAC 5/1 Others 1+1
Bolton W (£1,200,000 on 27/5/1997) P/FL 77+3/7 FLC 9/1 FAC 1+1 Others 3
Watford (£500,000 on 5/11/1999) P/FL 215+4/20 FLC 18/1 FAC 11
Cardiff C (Free on 2/8/2005) FL 21+6/2 FLC 1 FAC 1
Crewe Alex (Free on 5/6/2006) FL 50+8/1 FLC 2 FAC 3/1 Others 1

COX Simon Richard
Born: Reading, 28 April 1987
Height: 5'10" **Weight:** 10.12
Simon had been a member of Reading's Academy since the age of ten and it was a matter of regret to many when he was transferred to Swindon, where he had previously been on loan. He made only two substitute appearances for Reading, at Swansea in the Carling Cup and at home to Tottenham in the FA Cup,

impressing both times, but it was easy to understand the talented young striker's desire for regular first-team football. Swindon's leading scorer initially arrived at the County Ground on loan and after a very productive spell, Town fans were delighted when he was signed on a permanent basis at the end of January. Having initially struggled to find his scoring form, once a full-time Swindon player he finished the season strongly and his 15-goal haul after missing almost two months augers well for the future. A busy striker, Simon is always dangerous around the box.
Reading (From trainee on 22/11/2005) P/FL 0+2 FLC 0+3 FAC 0+4
Brentford (Loaned on 11/9/2006) FL 11+2 FLC 1
Northampton T (Loaned on 22/3/2007) FL 6+2/3
Swindon T (Loaned on 31/8/2007) FL 18+1/8 Others 1+1/1
Swindon T (£200,000 on 31/1/2008) FL 17/7

COYNE Christopher (Chris) John
Born: Brisbane, Australia, 20 December 1978
Height: 6'1" **Weight:** 13.10
Club Honours: Div 1 '05
International Honours: Australia: U23; Yth
Having fully recovered from the previous season's injury, Chris took centre stage in the Luton defence alongside Chris Perry in 2007-08. Excellent in the air, good on the ground and brave in the tackle, he has a commanding presence. His height also makes him very useful in attacking situations and his influence on Jaroslaw Fojut and Keith Keane helped to turn them from raw talents into very capable centre-backs. Chris' performance in the FA Cup third round kept a strong Liverpool forward line under control and by the time of his sudden sale to Colchester in January he was at his best. After making an impressive debut in the 1-1 draw at promotion-chasing Bristol City, he thrilled the fans when scoring with an instinctive overhead kick in the exciting 4-3 defeat at West Bromwich at the end of March. Although the Australian was unable to prevent the U's from suffering relegation, he did help to tighten a leaky defence with a number of commanding performances and will be key to their bid to return to the Championship in 2008-09.
West Ham U (£150,000 from Perth SC, Australia on 13/1/1996) PL 0+1
Brentford (Loaned on 21/8/1998) FL 7 FLC 1
Southend U (Loaned on 25/3/1999) FL 0+1

Dundee (Free on 31/3/2000) SL 16+4 SLC 0+2 SC 4 Others 2
Luton T (£50,000 on 18/9/2001) FL 207+14/14 FLC 10/2 FAC 18/1 Others 3
Colchester U (£350,000 on 11/1/2008) FL 16/1

COYNE Daniel (Danny)
Born: Prestatyn, 27 August 1973
Height: 5'11" **Weight:** 13.0
International Honours: W: 16; B-1; U21-9; Yth; Sch
Tranmere signed Welsh international goalkeeper Danny from Burnley on a two-year contract in July for his second spell at the Birkenhead club, where he came up through the youth ranks and started his League career. Described by manager Ronnie Moore as the best goalkeeper in League One, he was virtually an ever-present in the side, missing only five games early in the season through injury. Danny has retained his sharpness and ability to read the game and is not reticent in organising the defence to his liking. A highly experienced but still enthusiastic player, he is especially good in dealing with crosses and shows no fear in diving in low among flailing boots to avert any danger to his goal.
Tranmere Rov (From trainee on 8/5/1992) FL 110+1 FLC 13 FAC 2 Others 2
Grimsby T (Free on 12/7/1999) FL 181 FLC 13 FAC 7
Leicester C (Free on 4/7/2003) PL 1+3 FLC 1
Burnley (£25,000 on 4/8/2004) FL 39+1 FLC 4
Tranmere Rov (Free on 17/7/2007) FL 41 FLC 1 FAC 4

CRADDOCK Jody Darryl
Born: Redditch, 25 July 1975
Height: 6'1" **Weight:** 12.4
With a burgeoning reputation as an artist away from football, the central defender missed Wolverhampton's first League game but scored with a brilliant first-time shot in the Carling Cup. Yet within a couple of days, Jody was surprisingly loaned to Stoke and his prospects looked bleak. He did an excellent job for Stoke as a stop-gap replacement for the departed Danny Higginbotham but played only four times before he was recalled to Molineux. Wolves' central defence had struggled in his absence and Jody briefly resumed his partnership with Gary Breen. He was forming another good understanding with Darren Ward when a groin injury put him out of action for two months. While his problems were not over, he defended well, particularly in an April visit to Charlton.

replacing Alex Nicholls in the final League game against Hartlepool.
Walsall (From trainee on 17/5/2008) FL 0+1

CRADDOCK Thomas (Tom)
Born: Darlington, 14 October 1986
Height: 5'11" **Weight:** 11.10
Club Honours: FAYC '04
Tom, a product of Middlesbrough's Academy, started his career as a defender but was successfully converted into a striker, scoring consistently when Boro lifted the FA Youth Cup in 2004. His first appearance was as a second-half substitute for Egyptian international Mohamed Shawky in the 2-0 Carling Cup defeat at Tottenham in September. But as injuries to key players mounted, he made his first senior start at Manchester City. With his contract running out in the summer, Tom agreed to join Hartlepool on loan in February to bolster their strike force after the departure of Ian Moore. Tom was with Pools for a month without creating a great impression and returned to the Riverside to finish the season in Middlesbrough's reserves.
Middlesbrough (From trainee on 4/7/2006) PL 1+3 FLC 0+1
Wrexham (Loaned on 26/10/2006) FL 1/1
Hartlepool U (Loaned on 14/2/2008) FL 1+3

CRAIG Tony Andrew
Born: Greenwich, 20 April 1985
Height: 6'0" **Weight:** 10.13
A Peter Taylor signing for Crystal Palace in the summer from local rivals Millwall, the left-back was a regular until Neil Warnock replaced him with Clint Hill. After a long spell out with injury he went back to Millwall on loan in March to help the club out in the last six crucial games of the season, as their injury list was alarming. Although a left-back for most of his career, the quality defender was drafted into the centre of defence and had some outstanding games. Tony has tremendous spirit and tackles hard but returned to Palace after scoring with a fine header in his final game against Carlisle.
Millwall (From trainee on 13/3/2003) FL 75+4/2 FLC 3+2 FAC 2 Others 1
Wycombe W (Loaned on 22/10/2004) FL 14 FAC 2 Others 2
Crystal Palace (£150,000 on 28/6/2007) FL 13 FLC 1
Millwall (Loaned on 27/3/2008) FL 5/1

CRAINEY Stephen Daniel
Born: Glasgow, 22 June 1981
Height: 5'9" **Weight:** 9.11
Club Honours: SPD '02
International Honours: S: 6; B-1; U21-7
Stephen was a revelation at Blackpool after signing on a free from Leeds. He

Tom Craddock

Cambridge U (Free from Christchurch on 13/8/1993) FL 142+3/4 FLC 3/1 FAC 6 Others 5
Sunderland (£300,000 + on 4/8/1997) P/FL 140+6/2 FLC 8+2 FAC 7+2 Others 3
Sheffield U (Loaned on 27/8/1999) FL 10
Wolverhampton W (£1,750,000 on 15/8/2003) P/FL 138+11/7 FLC 8/2 FAC 5+1 Others 2/1
Stoke C (Loaned on 17/8/2007) FL 4

CRADDOCK Joshua (Josh) Glynn
Born: Wolverhampton, 5 March 1991
Height: 5'11" **Weight:** 10.8
The young midfield player figured in the Walsall youth team that won the Puma Youth Alliance North-West Conference. Josh is rated highly at Walsall and stepped out for a brief five-minute debut when

cemented his place at left-back and only niggling injuries kept his League starts down to 37. His previous experience at Championship level with Leeds and Southampton shone through with solid defensives performances, the pick of them against Preston in December. He scored his first goal for Blackpool on Boxing Day against Sheffield United with a deflected free kick to level the game. Stephen picked up five awards at the club's end-of-season presentation night.

Glasgow Celtic (From juniors on 3/7/1997) SL 18+21 SLC 6+1/1 SC 2+3 Others 3+2
Southampton (£500,000 + on 31/1/2004) PL 5
Leeds U (£200,000 on 6/8/2004) FL 51+1 FLC 6 FAC 2 Others 2
Blackpool (Free on 11/7/2007) FL 37+3/1 FLC 2 FAC 1

CRANEY Ian Thomas William
Born: Liverpool, 21 July 1982
Height: 5'10" **Weight:** 12.7
Club Honours: FC '06
International Honours: E: SP-7

Ian returned to Accrington on loan from Swansea last September, having made just four appearances for the Swans in 2007-08, one of them being from the bench. Unfortunate to injure a hamstring in his second game, he was back in three weeks to score against Barnet. He turned down opportunities to join other clubs, either on loan or permanently, to sign for Stanley at a club record fee in January, marking his homecoming by scoring one goal and making the other two in the 3-3 home draw with Chester. The lynchpin of Stanley's midfield he also grabs vital goals, as demonstrated by his winners at Chester, in stoppage-time, and Rotherham.

Accrington Stanley (£17,500 from Altrincham on 22/6/2004) FL 18/5 FLC 2 FAC 1 Others 2/1
Swansea C (£150,000 on 23/11/2006) FL 24+4 FLC 2 Others 1
Accrington Stanley (£25,000 on 28/9/2007) FL 34/7

CRANIE Martin James
Born: Yeovil, 23 September 1986
Height: 6'0" **Weight:** 12.4
International Honours: E: U21-6; Yth

Martin signed for Portsmouth from Southampton in June and made his Premier League debut on the right side of defence in the first home game of the season against Manchester United. At half-time, he was replaced to allow a change of formation and his only full game for Pompey was against Leeds in the Carling Cup in August. In early October, he joined Queens Park Rangers

Richard Cresswell

on loan for three months and did well at Loftus Road until his season was cruelly cut short when he fractured a leg in his sixth Championship start, a 2-1 home defeat by Coventry, and played no more football in 2007-08.

Southampton *(From trainee on 29/9/2004)*
P/FL 11+5 FLC 2+1 FAC 3+2 Others 1
Bournemouth *(Loaned on 29/10/2004)*
FL 2+1
Yeovil T *(Loaned on 8/11/2006) FL 8*
Yeovil T *(Loaned on 3/3/2007) FL 3+1*
Portsmouth *(£150,000 on 5/7/2007) PL 1+1 FLC 1*
Queens Park Rgrs *(Loaned on 8/10/2007) FL 6*

CRESSWELL Richard Paul Wesley
Born: Bridlington, 20 September 1977
Height: 6'0" **Weight:** 11.8
International Honours: E: U21-4
Richard was signed from Leeds in the close season as a striker with a good goals record but found himself playing wide on Stoke's left for most of the season. He renewed a partnership with Ricardo Fuller that flourished at Preston and although not in his preferred position, knuckled down and did a superb job. He supported the two main strikers and scored 12 times, including the important goal at Colchester that took Stoke to the brink of promotion.

York C *(From trainee on 15/11/1995) FL 72+23/21 FLC 3+3 FAC 4+2/3 Others 4*
Mansfield T *(Loaned on 27/3/1997) FL 5/1*
Sheffield Wed *(£950,000 + on 25/3/1999) P/FL 7+24/2 FLC 1+1/1 FAC 0+3*
Leicester C *(£750,000 on 5/9/2000) PL 3+5 FLC 1 FAC 0+2/1 Others 0+2*
Preston NE *(£500,000 on 12/3/2001) FL 164+23/49 FLC 8+2/5 FAC 2+1/3 Others 4+2/1*
Leeds U *(£1,150,000 on 24/8/2005) FL 30+8/9 FLC 1+1/2 FAC 0+2 Others 0+2*
Stoke C *(Signed on 3/8/2007) FL 42+1/11 FLC 0+1/1 FAC 2*

CRESSWELL Ryan Anthony
Born: Rotherham, 22 December 1987
Height: 5'9" **Weight:** 10.5
Unable to get a game at Sheffield United last season, Ryan was loaned to Rotherham in September, making just one start, before moving on loan to Morecambe, against whom he had played a few weeks earlier. A solid debut at right-back against Chesterfield was followed by a move to the centre against Accrington before injury cut short his stay. The tall young central defender then spent the second half of the season at Macclesfield in the most successful of his three loans, providing much-needed height in the defence, dominating in

the air and attacking the ball. Ryan was a regular choice, usually in a back-four, although following the appointment of Keith Alexander, he played equally well in a back-five.

Sheffield U *(From trainee on 25/7/2006)*
Rotherham U *(Loaned on 21/9/2007) FL 1+2 Others 1*
Morecambe *(Loaned on 2/11/2007) FL 2*
Macclesfield T *(Loaned on 10/1/2008) FL 19/1*

CROFT Gary
Born: Burton-on-Trent, 17 February 1974
Height: 5'9" **Weight:** 11.8
International Honours: E: U21-4
Arriving at Lincoln from Grimsby in the summer, two suspensions and a serious calf injury sustained in a Boxing Day defeat at Bradford restricted the experienced full-back to just 21 appearances in his solitary season at Sincil Bank. The former England under-21 international was sent off in the games at Wrexham and Hereford and although he returned for the closing stages of the season, found himself one of four players released by manager Peter Jackson.

Grimsby T *(From trainee on 7/7/1992) FL 139+10/3 FLC 7 FAC 8+2/1 Others 3*
Blackburn Rov *(£1,700,000 on 29/3/1996) PL 33+7/1 FLC 6 FAC 4+2*
Ipswich T *(£800,000 on 21/9/1999) P/FL 20+9/1 FLC 3+1 FAC 1 Others 2+1*
Wigan Ath *(Loaned on 17/1/2002) FL 7*
Cardiff C *(Free on 28/3/2002) FL 65+12/3 FLC 2 FAC 3+2 Others 2+2*
Grimsby T *(Free on 5/8/2005) FL 52+9 FLC 2 FAC 2 Others 3+2*
Lincoln C *(Free on 1/8/2007) FL 20 FAC 2*

CROFT Lee David
Born: Wigan, 21 June 1985
Height: 5'9" **Weight:** 13.1
International Honours: E: Yth
An exciting Norwich right-winger in the traditional mould, Lee likes to use his pace and trickery to beat defenders on the outside to create opportunities for himself and his team-mates. Unfortunately, his composure in front of goal does not always match his build-up and he managed only one goal last season but his direct style will always take him into promising positions. The former Manchester City youth product is fast approaching his 100th game for the Canaries and remains a firm favourite with the fans.

Manchester C *(From trainee on 2/7/2002) PL 4+24/1 FLC 0+1 FAC 0+3*
Oldham Ath *(Loaned on 12/11/2004) FL 11+1 FAC 3/1 Others 2/1*
Norwich C *(£585,000 on 2/8/2006) FL 52+25/4 FLC 3+1 FAC 5+1*

CROFTS Andrew Lawrence
Born: Chatham, 29 May 1984
Height: 5'9" **Weight:** 10.8
International Honours: W: 12; U21-10; Yth
Once again a regular member of the Welsh squad, Andrew was made club captain at the start of the season by manager Ronnie Jepson. Strong in the tackle and good on the ball, he led by example in the latter part of the season when Gillingham were desperately trying to retain their League One status. He won the 'Goal of the Season' award for his tremendous strike at Brighton in a 4-2 defeat.

Gillingham *(From trainee on 6/8/2003) FL 155+10/17 FLC 4+3/2 FAC 3+2 Others 3*

CROOKS Lee Robert
Born: Wakefield, 14 January 1978
Height: 6'0" **Weight:** 12.1
International Honours: E: Yth
The experienced Lee appeared at centre-back in Rochdale's first two League games of last season and was on the bench several times before being injured against Shrewsbury. After a month out, he made a handful of further appearances but did not play after the turn of the year when manager Keith Hill put his faith in younger players. Lee was released in March to join Guiseley.

Manchester C *(From trainee on 14/1/1995) P/FL 52+24/2 FLC 5+2 FAC 5 Others 3*
Northampton T *(Loaned on 26/12/2000) FL 3*
Barnsley *(£190,000 on 2/3/2001) FL 50+17 FLC 2 FAC 2 Others 2*
Bradford C *(Free on 6/8/2004) FL 44+3/1 FLC 3 FAC 1/1 Others 2*
Notts Co *(Loaned on 9/1/2006) FL 18/1*
Rochdale *(Free on 3/8/2006) FL 31+9 FLC 1 FAC 1 Others 2*

CROSBY Andrew (Andy) Keith
Born: Rotherham, 3 March 1973
Height: 6'2" **Weight:** 13.7
Club Honours: Div 3 '01; Div 1 '07
Scunthorpe assistant manager/captain
Andy stepped up to Championship level for the first time in his career and had a solid season at the heart of the Iron's defence. He started 38 of the club's first 40 League games before sitting out the run-in with a knee problem. A strong, commanding centre-half, who is an excellent leader and organiser on the pitch, he netted three goals in September and added another in February after converting the rebound from the first penalty miss of his career.

Doncaster Rov *(From trainee at Leeds U on 4/7/1991) FL 41+10 FLC 1+1 FAC 2 Others 4+1/1*

Darlington (Free on 10/12/1993) FL 179+2/3 FLC 10 FAC 11/1 Others 9
Chester C (Free on 8/7/1998) FL 41/4 FLC 3 FAC 1 Others 1
Brighton & Hove A (£10,000 on 28/7/1999) FL 64+8/5 FLC 3 FAC 1+1 Others 7
Oxford U (Free on 13/12/2001) FL 109+2/12 FLC 5 FAC 4 Others 2/1
Scunthorpe U (Free on 2/8/2004) FL 155+8/15 FLC 5 FAC 10 Others 3+1/1

CROSSLEY Mark Geoffrey
Born: Barnsley, 16 June 1969
Height: 6'0" **Weight:** 16.0
International Honours: W: 8; B-1; E: U21-3
Still reliable, the veteran goalkeeper opted to delay his retirement plans and sign a new 12-month deal following a successful first season at Oldham after arriving from Fulham in the summer. After experiencing injury problems and loss of form early in the season, Mark went on to make 46 starts – the club's second-highest tally of appearance – and kept 13 clean sheets. Despite his advancing years, he impressed with his handling, positioning and organisation. The former Wales international, who spent most of his career at the highest level, is a UEFA A and B licensed coach, now tasked with steering the club's young talent through the ranks.
Nottingham F (From trainee on 2/7/1987) P/FL 301+2 FLC 39+1 FAC 32 Others 18
Millwall (Loaned on 20/2/1998) FL 13
Middlesbrough (Free on 25/7/2000) PL 21+2 FLC 5 FAC 3
Stoke C (Loaned on 29/11/2002) FL 1
Stoke C (Loaned on 6/3/2003) FL 11
Fulham (£500,000 on 14/8/2003) PL 19+1 FLC 4
Sheffield Wed (Loaned on 8/11/2006) FL 17/1 FAC 2
Oldham Ath (Free on 10/8/2007) FL 38 FLC 2 FAC 5 Others 1

CROUCH Peter James
Born: Macclesfield, 30 January 1981
Height: 6'7" **Weight:** 11.12
Club Honours: Div 1 '04; FAC '06; CS '06
International Honours: E: 28; B-1; U21-6; Yth
In 2006-07 the gangling Liverpool and England striker was at the peak of his career after top-scoring with 18 goals, many of rare quality. Last season, he found himself out of favour with manager Rafa Benitez and relegated to fourth choice behind Fernando Torres, Dirk Kuyt and Andriy Voronin. He started only nine Premiership games and had to wait until January to score his first Premiership goal, a very late equaliser that saved a point in the home game

against Aston Villa. He added four more in his infrequent appearances but was used more often in domestic Cup competitions and the Champions' League, in which he scored six more goals. It often appeared that Liverpool's best performances coincided with Peter's return, as in home victories over Toulouse (4-0), Besiktas (8-0) and Porto (4-1) in the Champions' League and, later in the season, the dramatic 4-2 victory over Arsenal in the quarter-final second leg. This was the only critical match that he was allowed to start and he was totally ignored, even as a substitute, for the semi-final matches against Chelsea, even though he terrorised their defence in the Premiership at Stamford Bridge two months earlier. His experience with England was equally frustrating. Passed over as a first-choice striker for England's early games of the season, probably due to his lack of games for Liverpool, he was brought back in November only because injuries exhausted manager Steve McClaren's options. Peter responded by scoring the only goal of a friendly in Austria and the equalising second goal in England's critical Euro 2008 qualifying match against Croatia at Wembley, taking his international record to 14 goals in 24 games. In other circumstances this goal, a perfectly-executed chest down and volley from David Beckham's pin-point cross, would have made him a national hero since a draw would have been sufficient to ensure England's qualification. Instead, it was soon forgotten as they stumbled to a humiliating defeat and were eliminated.
Tottenham H (From trainee on 2/7/1998)
Queens Park Rgrs (£60,000 on 28/7/2000) FL 38+4/10 FLC 1+1 FAC 3/2
Portsmouth (£1,250,000 on 11/7/2001) FL 37/18 FLC 1/1 FAC 1
Aston Villa (£4,000,000 + on 28/3/2002) PL 20+17/6 FLC 1+1 Others 4
Norwich C (Loaned on 8/9/2003) FL 14+1/4
Southampton (£2,000,000 on 14/7/2004) PL 18+9/12 FLC 1 FAC 5/4
Liverpool (£7,000,000 on 20/7/2005) PL 55+30/22 FLC 5/1 FAC 10+1/5 Others 23+10/14

CROW Daniel (Danny) Stephen
Born: Great Yarmouth, 26 January 1986
Height: 5'10" **Weight:** 11.4
Last season Danny made only two League starts for Peterborough and was used twice as a substitute. Although the striker scored two goals in these limited opportunities he was allowed to join Notts County on loan in October. He had the saddest of starts to his first loan spell,

when he broke a foot bone after an hour, but once fit he was back at Meadow Lane for the remainder of the season. A busy, quick-footed striker who likes to spin off the last defender, he found a number of scoring positions but was unlucky with his conversion rate. With increased physical strength and better luck he could add more goals. Was released by Peterborough at the end of the season.
Norwich C (From trainee on 29/9/2004) PL 0+3 FAC 0+1
Northampton T (Loaned on 15/2/2005) FL 4+6/2
Peterborough U (Free on 4/8/2005) FL 58+19/23 FLC 1+2 FAC 6/3 Others 3+1/3
Notts Co (Loaned on 9/10/2007) FL 13+1/2

CROWE Jason William Robert
Born: Sidcup, 30 September 1978
Height: 5'9" **Weight:** 10.9
Club Honours: Div 1 '03
International Honours: E: Yth
The Northampton wing-back enjoyed another excellent season. During an injury crisis, Jason was asked to play in central midfield and his accomplished performance concealed the fact it was not his regular position. Whether he is creating chances, scoring goals or stopping them, Jason always gives his maximum. This was underlined when Plymouth offered to buy him during the transfer window for a fee that would have broken the Cobblers' record sale of £265,000.
Arsenal (From trainee on 13/5/1996) FLC 0+2 FAC 0+1
Crystal Palace (Loaned on 10/11/1998) FL 8
Portsmouth (£750,000 + on 7/7/1999) FL 67+19/5 FLC 4 FAC 1+2
Brentford (Loaned on 12/9/2000) FL 9 FLC 2
Grimsby T (Free on 7/8/2003) FL 64+5/4 FLC 3 FAC 3 Others 1
Northampton T (Free on 7/7/2005) FL 128/9 FLC 5 FAC 8 Others 1+3

CROWELL Matthew (Matty) Thomas
Born: Bridgend, 3 July 1984
Height: 5'9" **Weight:** 10.12
Club Honours: AMC '05
International Honours: W: U21-7; Yth
Matty was given a short-term contract at Wrexham to prove his fitness and form at the start of the season but was always playing catch-up. The competitive midfield man played his last game against Rotherham just before Christmas and left soon afterwards to join Northwich in the Blue Square Premier, where Wrexham will feature in 2008-09.
Southampton (From trainee on 13/7/2001)
Wrexham (Free on 15/7/2003) FL 70+23/4 FLC 2+1 FAC 2 Others 8+2/1

CUDICINI Carlo
Born: Milan, Italy, 6 September 1973
Height: 6'1" **Weight:** 12.3
Club Honours: FAC '00; CS '00; FLC '05
International Honours: Italy: U21; Yth
Still a top 'keeper, the long-serving, loyal Carlo had another solid season and, as always, was an extremely reliable stand-in whenever goalkeeper Petr Cech was unavailable. The popular Italian started 18 matches and finished with a highly creditable ten clean sheets for a Chelsea total nudging the 100 mark. He was

a substitute at Schalke in November in a Champions' League group match when Cech limped off with a calf strain. Qualification was by no means assured at that stage but Carlo defied the German club's strikers and helped to secure a valuable point and progress to the next stage. He is widely regarded as the best second 'keeper in the Premier League and would have many more club and, perhaps, international honours were it not for the brilliant Czech Republic goalkeeper. Part of a club that has seen

revolutionary changes in the past five years, Carlo and John Terry are the only survivors from the managerial reign of Luca Vialli.
Chelsea (£160,000 from Castel di Sangro, Italy, ex AC Milan, Prato, Lazio, on 6/8/1999) PL 136+4 FLC 17 FAC 30 Others 23+2

CULLIP Daniel (Danny)
Born: Bracknell, 17 September 1976
Height: 6'1" **Weight:** 12.7
Club Honours: Div 3 '01; Div 2 '02
The rugged defender was one of several to fall victim to a change of management at Queens Park Rangers in 2007-08, making seven appearances for Rangers in the early stages but never featuring under Luigi De Canio. Released from his contract last December, Gillingham signed him in February and he immediately fitted into the back four with ease, making his presence felt by organising the defenders around him. Mark Stimpson was aiming to sign him on a long-term contract during the summer.
Oxford U (From trainee on 6/7/1995)
Fulham (Free on 5/7/1996) FL 41+9/2 FLC 8 FAC 2 Others 1
Brentford (£75,000 on 17/2/1998) FL 15 FLC 2
Brighton & Hove A (£50,000 on 17/9/1999) FL 216+1/7 FLC 8/1 FAC 11/2 Others 6/1
Sheffield U (£250,000 on 17/12/2004) FL 11 FAC 4/1
Watford (Loaned on 24/3/2005) FL 4
Nottingham F (Signed on 5/8/2005) FL 29+2 FLC 1 FAC 5+1 Others 1
Queens Park Rgrs (Free on 31/1/2007) FL 18+1 FLC 1
Gillingham (Free on 21/2/2008) FL 11

CUMBERS Luis Cosme
Born: Chelmsford, 6 September 1988
Height: 6'0" **Weight:** 11.10
Luis is a highly-rated midfield player or striker who, on his current progress, is set to be a regular member of the Gillingham side in years to come. Confident and a good reader of the game, he spent part of the season on loan at Grays in the Blue Square Premier to further his experience.
Gillingham (From trainee on 28/5/2008) FL 2+5 Others 0+1

CUMMINGS Warren Thomas
Born: Aberdeen, 15 October 1980
Height: 5'9" **Weight:** 11.8
International Honours: S: 1; U21-9
Warren, a long-serving Bournemouth left-back, recovered from an early season injury and returned to the kind of form that earns him so much respect from the Cherries' supporters. He was a regular in the side after regaining fitness and played a part in the brave fight to avoid

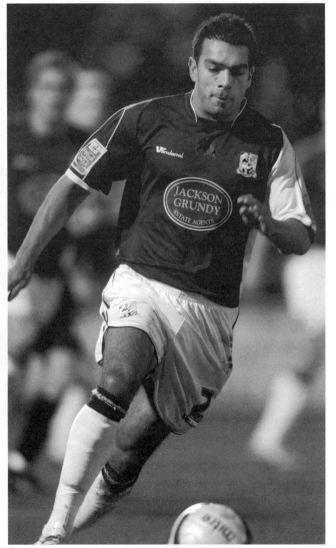

Jason Crowe

relegation.
Chelsea *(From trainee on 5/7/1999)*
Bournemouth *(Loaned on 20/10/2000) FL
10/1 Others 1*
West Bromwich A *(Loaned on 21/3/2001)
FL 1+2*
West Bromwich A *(Loaned on 25/7/2001)
FL 6+8 FLC 0+2*
Dundee U *(Loaned on 23/8/2002) SL 7+1
SLC 1*
Dundee U *(Loaned on 16/11/2002) SL 0+3*
Bournemouth *(Free on 3/2/2003) FL
149+6/6 FLC 4+1/1 FAC 9+1 Others 6*

CUMMINS Michael (Micky)
Thomas
Born: Dublin, 1 June 1978
Height: 6'0" **Weight:** 11.11
Club Honours: AMC '01
International Honours: RoI: U21-2; Yth
This experienced Darlington central
midfielder occupied this position for the
majority of the season and contributed
five goals, one more than in the previous
season. Four of these strikes came
in three consecutive games during
December, including a brace at Lincoln
on the Saturday before Christmas, but
sadly his scoring spree did not continue.
He always showed composure in his
play, with an eye for a good pass and an
opportunity to break forward towards
goal. Was released at the end of the
campaign.
Middlesbrough *(From trainee on 1/7/1995)
PL 1+1*
Port Vale *(Free on 17/3/2000) FL 247+6/31
FLC 7/1 FAC 11/1 Others 16/1*
Darlington *(Free on 21/7/2006) FL 69+10/10
FLC 1+2 FAC 3+1 Others 3+2*

CURETON Jamie
Born: Bristol, 28 August 1975
Height: 5'8" **Weight:** 10.7
International Honours: E: Yth
Jamie ended the season as Norwich's top
scorer with 14 goals in all competitions
following his return to Carrow Road
from Colchester in July, 11 years after
he left. The impish striker scored some
spectacular goals, including a deftly
lobbed volley to level the scores in Glenn
Roeder's first game in charge, at home
to Ipswich in November. A natural scorer
with predatory instincts, he has the ability
to sense where the ball will drop in the
penalty area and be there. He would
admit that he could have scored more
goals on his return to Norwich, but he
remains the prodigal son for Canary fans
and there are more to come from him.
Norwich C *(From trainee on 5/2/1993) P/FL
13+16/6 FLC 0+1 FAC 0+2*
Bournemouth *(Loaned on 8/9/1995) FL 0+5
Others 0+1*
Bristol Rov *(£250,000 on 20/9/1996) FL*

165+9/72 FLC 7+1/2 FAC 10/2 Others 6/3
Reading *(£250,000 on 21/8/2000) FL
74+34/50 FLC 4+1/1 FAC 5+2/2 Others 6+1/2*
*(Free to Busan Icons, South Korea during
2003 close season)*
Queens Park Rgrs *(£95,000 from Busan
Icons, South Korea on 2/2/2004) FL 20+23/6
FLC 2/1 FAC 1*
Swindon T *(Free on 5/8/2005) FL 22+8/7 FLC
0+1 Others 0+1*
Colchester U *(Loaned on 21/10/2005) FL
7+1/4 FAC 2/3*
Colchester U *(Free on 2/6/2006) FL 44/23
FLC 0+1 FAC 1/1*
Norwich C *(£750,000 on 2/7/2007) FL
29+12/12 FLC 2/2 FAC 2*

CURRAN Craig
Born: Liverpool, 23 August 1989
Height: 5'9" **Weight:** 11.9
Despite Craig bursting on the Tranmere
scene with a hat-trick in his home debut
at the end of the previous season, Ronnie
Moore chose to use him only sparingly
and mostly as a substitute in 2007-08,
allowing him to continue to learn his
trade in the reserves. This was not always
popular with supporters, who never
failed to greet his appearances with great
enthusiasm. Craig, who prefers to play
up front as an out-and-out striker, is
sufficiently versatile to perform in midfield
as well. This powerful and determined
player, still only 18 when the new season
starts, remains a great prospect and must
be hoping for a regular place.
Tranmere Rov *(From trainee on 29/8/2006)
FL 3+36/6 FLC 0+1 FAC 1+2 Others 1*

CURRIE Darren Paul
Born: Hampstead, 29 November 1974
Height: 5'11" **Weight:** 12.7
Freed by Ipswich in the summer, Darren
is a talented player whose close control
and ability to pass and cross accurately
make him look pure class on his day, as
he demonstrated by scoring on his Luton
debut against Hartlepool. He appeared
to flag late in games, being replaced 13
times in his 25 starts, but often gave a
fresh dimension to the game when used
as a substitute. With Luton being forced
back in the majority of their matches,
he was ready to help out in defence by
closing down oncoming forwards. Darren
was given a free transfer at the end of
the season.
West Ham U *(From trainee on 2/7/1993)*
Shrewsbury T *(Loaned on 5/9/1994) FL
10+2/2*
Shrewsbury T *(Loaned on 3/2/1995) FL 5*
Leyton Orient *(Loaned on 16/11/1995)
FL 9+1*
Shrewsbury T *(£70,000 on 7/2/1996) FL
46+20/8 FLC 2+1/1 FAC 3*
Plymouth Arg *(Free on 26/3/1998) FL 5+2*

Barnet *(Free on 13/7/1998) FL 120+7/19 FLC
5/1 FAC 3/2 Others 6*
Wycombe W *(£200,000 on 11/7/2001) FL
109+17/14 FLC 5 FAC 6+1/5 Others 5*
Brighton & Hove A *(Free on 5/8/2004) FL
21+1/2 FLC 1*
Ipswich T *(£250,000 on 10/12/2004) FL
64+19/9 FLC 2 FAC 2 Others 1+1*
Coventry C *(Loaned on 23/11/2006) FL 6+2*
Derby Co *(Loaned on 15/3/2007) FL 4+3/1
Others 0+1*
Luton T *(Free on 4/7/2007) FL 25+6/2 FLC
1+1 FAC 4+1*

CURTIS John Charles Keyworth
Born: Nuneaton, 3 September 1978
Height: 5'10" **Weight:** 11.9
Club Honours: FAYC '95; FLC '02
International Honours: E: B-1; U21-16;
Yth; Sch
Signed from Nottingham Forest in the
summer, John never really had a chance
to settle into the Queens Park Rangers'
side before the departure of John
Gregory, the man who brought him to
the club. John made four appearances at
right-back but his short Rangers' career
was finished by September and he left
Loftus Road in December. Looking to get
back into League football, he went on
trial at Preston.
Manchester U *(From trainee on 3/10/1995)
PL 4+9 FLC 5 Others 0+1*
Barnsley *(Loaned on 19/11/1999) FL 28/2
Others 1+1*
Blackburn Rov *(£2,250,000 on 1/6/2000)
P/FL 61 FLC 10 FAC 6 Others 1*
Sheffield U *(Loaned on 3/3/2003) FL 9+3
FAC 1 Others 3*
Leicester C *(Free on 15/8/2003) PL 14+1
FLC 1 FAC 1*
Portsmouth *(Free on 2/2/2004) PL 5+2*
Preston NE *(Loaned on 10/9/2004) FL 12*
Nottingham F *(Free on 3/2/2005) FL 76+3
FLC 1 FAC 8 Others 3*
Queens Park Rgrs *(Free on 3/8/2007) FL
3+1 FLC 0+1*

CURTIS Wayne John
Born: Barrow, 6 March 1980
Height: 6'0" **Weight:** 12.2
Wayne has been with Morecambe for ten
years and deservedly enters his testimonial
season. He is a versatile player who was
used either wide on the left or as a striker
in the first League season, although
he was in and out of the side. Big and
strong, Wayne always gave his maximum
and was a more than useful substitute for
manager Sammy McIlroy. He went close
with his strong shot several times but
managed only two goals and will look for
a better return.
Morecambe *(Free from Holker OB on
3/3/1998) FL 16+20/2 FLC 0+1 FAC 1 Others
2+2*

D

DABO Ousmane
Born: Laval, France, 8 February 1977
Height: 6'1" **Weight:** 13.4
International Honours: France: 3
The experienced French midfielder had a difficult time at Manchester City during 2007-08 and was never really part of Sven-Goran Eriksson's plans, finding first-team opportunities limited. After making just one appearance, in City's Carling Cup clash with Bristol City, Ousmane returned to Lazio in January on a free transfer.
Manchester C (Signed from SS Lazio, Italy, ex Stade Rennais, Inter Milan, Vicenza - loan, Parma, AS Monaco, Vicenza, Atalanta, on 7/7/2006) PL 10+3 FLC 0+1 FAC 4

DA COSTA Filipe Gui Paradela Maciel
Born: Lisbon, Portugal, 30 August 1984
Height: 5'11" **Weight:** 11.6
Filipe's debut for Leeds was delayed as United became embroiled in a contractual dispute between the Portuguese winger and his former club, Greek side Ionikos. After a flurry of appearances as a substitute he was sent off in his first start for Leeds, a 2-1 Johnstone's Paint Trophy home defeat by Bury. He did not figure again, even as an unused sub, and was released in April.
Leeds U (Free from Ionikos, Greece, ex Amora, Sporting Braga, Reggiana, US Tolentino - loan, AEL Larisa - loan, on 31/8/2007) FL 0+4 FAC 0+1 Others 1+1

DAGNALL Christopher (Chris)
Born: Liverpool, 15 April 1986
Height: 5'8" **Weight:** 11.9
Chris's season was split into two by a serious knee injury. After starting in fine form, including two goals against eventual champions MK Dons, the Rochdale striker damaged cruciate ligaments and had to have surgery to rebuild his knee, as did defender Gary Brown. Expected to miss all the remainder of the season, Chris was relying on his team-mates to keep Dale's season going to the play-offs. But in the event, with no prior match practice, he reappeared as a substitute against Rotherham at the end of March and, amazingly, hit a hat-trick in the last ten minutes. Chris scored in both legs of the play-off semi-final against Darlington as Dale won through to Wembley for the first time.
Tranmere Rov (From trainee on 11/7/2003) FL 18+21/7 FLC 0+1 FAC 0+1 Others 1+2
Rochdale (£25,000 on 13/1/2006) FL 54+18/27 FLC 3 FAC 2 Others 5/3

D'AGOSTINO Michael
Born: Vancouver, Canada, 7 January 1987
Height: 5'9" **Weight:** 11.4
International Honours: Canada: Yth
Wide-right player Michael joined Cheltenham on loan from Blackpool in November. The former University of Kentucky and Vancouver Whitecaps player signed for Blackpool at the start of the season and moved to Cheltenham to gain first-team experience. A tricky winger with pace and crossing ability, Michael made his League debut as a substitute at Leyton Orient shortly before Christmas. His loan was extended to the end of the season and he held down a regular place on the right of midfield for three months in the New Year as the Robins dragged themselves clear of the League One relegation zone.
Blackpool (Signed from Kentucky Wildcats, USA on 4/10/2007)
Cheltenham T (Loaned on 22/11/2007) FL 14+11

DAILLY Christian Eduard
Born: Dundee, 23 October 1973
Height: 6'0" **Weight:** 12.10
Club Honours: SC '94, '08
International Honours: S: 66; B-1; U21-34; Yth; Sch

On arriving at Southampton on loan from West Ham in September, Christian became the fifth man to start a match as centre-back for the Saints - after just eight games. He settled in quickly, impressing with his steady, assured defending, on the ground as well as in the air, and astute switching of play. Christian even made some appearances in midfield and his return to London was regretted, but in January he went home to Scotland and UEFA Cup football with Glasgow Rangers.
Dundee U (From juniors on 2/8/1990) SL 110+33/18 SLC 9/1 SC 10+2 Others 8+1/1
Derby Co (£1,000,000 on 12/8/1996) PL 62+5/4 FLC 6 FAC 4+1
Blackburn Rov (£5,300,000 on 22/8/1998) P/FL 60+10/4 FLC 5+1 FAC 4 Others 2
West Ham U (£1,750,000 on 18/1/2001) P/FL 133+25/2 FLC 8/1 FAC 14+6 Others 3+2/1
Southampton (Loaned on 21/9/2007) FL 11
Glasgow Rgrs (Loaned on 30/1/2008) SL 12/2 SLC 1 SC 4 Others 4+1

DALEY Omar
Born: Kingston, Jamaica, 25 April 1981
Height: 5'10" **Weight:** 11.0
International Honours: Jamaica: 52
Jamaican international Omar was used on both flanks by Bradford and even as a second striker, where his speed down the middle unsettled opposing defenders.

Omar Daley

As one of the most eye-catching players in League Two on his day, the Yorkshire club were keen to sign up Omar on a new contract in January to prevent rivals coming in.

Reading *(Loaned from Portmore U, Jamaica on 19/8/2003) FL 0+6 FLC 0+1*
Preston NE *(Loaned from Portmore U, Jamaica on 3/8/2004) FL 1+13 FLC 1+2/1*
Bradford C *(Signed from Charleston Battery, USA on 16/1/2007) FL 50+5/6 FLC 1 FAC 2*

DALY George Jeffrey
Born: Westminster, 25 October 1990
Height: 5'11" **Weight:** 10.11
At Wycombe since the age of 13 and a prolific scorer for the under-16s, George signed apprenticeship forms last summer. By Christmas he had scored three hat-tricks for the under-18s and was rewarded with substitute appearances at Brentford and Shrewsbury in late December. Still only 18, one of his biggest fans is former manager Paul Lambert.
Wycombe W *(Trainee) FL 0+2*

DANBY John Robert
Born: Stoke-on-Trent, 20 September 1983
Height: 6'2" **Weight:** 14.7
For the second successive season the Chester goalkeeper started every game despite the summer signing of the experienced Gavin Ward. John benefited from the early-season coaching of Ward and, despite a dip in form, was a consistent and reliable performer in a difficult season. John is a good shot-stopper and proved adept at saving

John Danby

penalties with excellent stops against Nottingham Forest and Bradford. His performance in the penultimate game of the season against Stockport was instrumental in keeping Chester in the League and John has now made more than 100 appearances for the Blues.
Kidderminster Hrs *(From juniors on 14/12/2001) FL 46+2 FLC 1 Others 1*
Chester C *(Free on 3/8/2006) FL 92 FLC 2 FAC 6 Others 4*

DANIEL Colin
Born: Nottingham, 15 February 1988
Height: 5'11" **Weight:** 11.6
A promising left-sided midfield player signed by Crewe from Eastwood in the summer despite offers from other clubs, he made just one substitute appearance, at Hartlepool in December. To further his football education, Colin went on loan to Grays and Leek. A fast, attacking player, Crewe hope that he will develop into a first-teamer before too long.
Crewe Alex *(£20,000 + from Eastwood T on 8/5/2007) FL 0+1*

DANIELS Charlie
Born: Harlow, 7 September 1986
Height: 5'10" **Weight:** 11.10
Charlie joined Leyton Orient on a season-long loan from Tottenham as cover for both left-back and the left of midfield. He has a powerful shot and scored a spectacular goal against Oldham at home from long range.
Tottenham H *(From trainee on 7/7/2005)*
Chesterfield *(Loaned on 9/3/2007) FL 2*
Leyton Orient *(Loaned on 4/8/2007) FL 24+7/2 FLC 1+1 FAC 2 Others 1+1*

DANN Scott
Born: Liverpool, 14 February 1987
Height: 6'2" **Weight:** 12.0
Club Honours: Div 2 '07
International Honours: E: U21-2
Having fulfilled the rich promise that he had shown at Walsall in the second half of 2006-07, Scott had become one of the top First Division central defenders by the time he signed for Coventry in last January's transfer window for a fee that, according to reports, could rise to £1-million. He looked a class player from his first appearance, as a substitute against Barnsley, and he was soon first choice at City alongside Elliott Ward. Cool in possession and able to start attacks with his long, accurate passes, Scott is also a potential goal threat at corners. With ex-Walsall team-mate Danny Fox and on-loan goalkeeper Kasper Schmeichel, Coventry's defence was far more secure and he fully deserved his selection for the England under-21 squad.

Scott Dann

Walsall *(From trainee on 6/8/2004) FL 52+7/7 FLC 1+1/1 FAC 7 Others 1*
Coventry C *(Signed on 31/1/2008) FL 14+2*

DANNS Neil Alexander
Born: Liverpool, 23 November 1982
Height: 5'9" **Weight:** 12.1
After making two Premier League appearances for Birmingham in October, the energetic and attack-minded right-sided midfielder was signed by Crystal Palace in January to replace the injured Paul Ifill. However, to Neil Warnock's frustration Neil suffered several spells out of the side through injury and the club were unable to see the best of him. A player who can score vital goals, he will be looking to come good at Palace in 2008-09.
Blackburn Rov *(From trainee on 3/7/2000) PL 1+2 FLC 2 FAC 1 Others 1*
Blackpool *(Loaned on 7/8/2003) FL 12/2 FLC 2 Others 1*
Hartlepool U *(Loaned on 12/3/2004) FL 8+1/1 Others 0+2*
Colchester U *(Signed on 9/9/2004) FL 70+3/19 FLC 3/1 FAC 5+1/5 Others 4+1/3*
Birmingham C *(£500,000 + on 26/6/2006) P/FL 11+20/3 FLC 5 FAC 0+3*
Crystal Palace *(£600,000 on 22/1/2008) FL 2+2*

DAVENPORT Calum Raymond Paul
Born: Bedford, 1 January 1983
Height: 6'4" **Weight:** 14.4
International Honours: E: U21-8; Yth
The West Ham centre-half, who had been a long-term target for Watford, was signed on loan in January and went straight into the side to play Charlton. Unfortunately, he broke a bone in his

neck in an accidental collision, a serious injury that led to him being stretchered off after only 50 minutes of football in a Watford shirt. In the circumstances, there was no alternative other than for him to return to Upton Park to recuperate.
Coventry C *(From trainee on 6/1/2000) P/FL 64+11/3 FLC 3 FAC 5+1*
Tottenham H *(£1,100,000 + on 31/8/2004) PL 9+6/1 FLC 2 FAC 1 Others 1+1*
West Ham U *(Loaned on 9/9/2004) FL 10*
Southampton *(Loaned on 4/1/2005) PL 5+2 FAC 4+1*
Norwich C *(Loaned on 12/9/2005) FL 14+1/1 FLC 1*
West Ham U *(£3,000,000 on 18/1/2007) PL 5+1*
Watford *(Loaned on 18/1/2008) FL 1*

DAVIDSON Callum lain
Born: Stirling, 25 June 1976
Height: 5'10" **Weight:** 11.8
Club Honours: S Div 1 '97
International Honours: S: 17; U21-2
Callum enjoyed his best season at Deepdale, adding goals to his well-established reputation for determined

Callum Davidson

tackling at left-back or in midfield and assured passing over a range of distances. He filled both roles in his first injury-free campaign for Preston and solved the club's penalty-taking crisis with two successful strikes in the final stages of the season to add to his brace at Cardiff. A vastly experienced professional, Callum ended the season on 349 club appearances and the hope is for many more.
St Johnstone *(From juniors on 8/6/1994) SL 39+5/4 SLC 1 Others 3*
Blackburn Rov *(£1,750,000 on 12/2/1998) P/FL 63+2/1 FLC 3+1 FAC 6 Others 1+1*
Leicester C *(£1,700,000 on 12/7/2000) P/FL 90+11/2 FLC 5+1 FAC 5+1 Others 0+1*
Preston NE *(Free on 6/8/2004) FL 93+8/9 FLC 1+1 FAC 7*

DAVIDSON Ross
Born: Burton-on-Trent, 6 September 1989
Height: 6'2" **Weight:** 11.5
This central midfield player graduated through the ranks at Port Vale. After biding his time in the youth team and the reserves, Ross deserved his chance and made his debut as a substitute for the last 20 minutes in a 6-0 defeat at Swindon in April. Fortunately, the experience did not deter him and he appeared from the bench in the next two games as the season closed. Strong and with an eye for goal, Ross is a good example of a box-to-box player and signed his first professional contract just before the end of the campaign.
Port Vale *(From trainee on 5/5/2008) FL 0+3*

DAVIES Andrew John
Born: Stockton, 17 December 1984
Height: 6'3" **Weight:** 14.8
International Honours: E: U21-1; Yth
Having been with Middlesbrough since the age of 13, Andrew started 2007-08 by playing in the first three Premiership games and the Carling Cup victory over Northampton. After that, he was used as a substitute and frustration at not holding a regular place persuaded him to accept the offer of a loan move to Southampton. In the black comedy that was Southampton's defence last season, it speaks volumes that Andrew was voted 'Player of the Year' after only 25 League and Cup appearances. Arriving from Middlesbrough in late October, his debut was delayed for a fortnight after he pulled a muscle in training but it did not take long to convince the faithful that he was worth the fee needed to make him a permanent fixture in January. The seventh of the ten players to feature at centre-back for Saints, it was not just his abundant ability that made him a favourite but his infectious enthusiasm, something that had been in short supply at St Mary's. Unfortunately, just when his partnership with Wayne Thomas was looking formidable, Andrew's season ended at Blackpool in March when he sustained a broken cheekbone.
Middlesbrough *(From trainee on 6/7/2002) PL 39+14 FLC 4+1 FAC 2+1 Others 4*
Queens Park Rgrs *(Loaned on 12/1/2005) FL 9*
Derby Co *(Loaned on 6/7/2005) FL 22+1/3 FAC 1*
Southampton *(£1,000,000 on 9/10/2007) FL 22+1 FAC 2*

DAVIES Arron Rhys
Born: Cardiff, 22 June 1984
Height: 5'9" **Weight:** 10.0
Club Honours: Div 2 '05
International Honours: W: 1; U21-14
After being a key member of the Yeovil team that destroyed Nottingham Forest's play-off bid the previous campaign, Arron moved to the City Ground last summer. Unfortunately, he suffered a serious ankle injury on the pre-season tour to Scotland

and was unable to make his Forest debut until the end of October. Arron is equally happy on either wing and had his best game in an impressive team performance against Crewe in November. He suffered a hamstring injury in March, ruling him out until the last two games, and hopes for a clear run ahead.

Southampton (From trainee on 11/7/2002)
Barnsley (Loaned on 13/2/2004) FL 1+3
Yeovil T (Signed on 16/12/2004) FL 76+25/22 FLC 2+1/1 FAC 2+4/2 Others 5/2
Nottingham F (Signed on 20/7/2007) FL 9+10/1 FAC 1+2

DAVIES Benjamin (Ben)
James
Born: Birmingham, 27 May 1981
Height: 5'6" **Weight:** 10.7
Club Honours: FC '04
A creative midfield player able to unlock the opposition, Ben can be deadly from free kicks and takes a good corner. Always committed and looking to take responsibility, he missed Shrewsbury's early games while recovering from the Achilles tendon injury suffered in the previous season's play-off at MK Dons. Ben had to wait until late November for his comeback but had a good spell the following month, his four goals making the difference in three victories. After Stewart Drummond left in January, he was made captain but struggled to be as influential as Shrewsbury stuttered badly.

Walsall (From trainee at Stoke C on 11/8/1999)
Kidderminster Hrs (Free on 1/3/2000) FL 11+1 FLC 1 Others 1
Chester C (Free on 7/5/2002) FL 80+9/9 FLC 1+1/1 FAC 6 Others 1+2
Shrewsbury T (Free on 6/6/2006) FL 69+1/18 FLC 1 FAC 2 Others 5

DAVIES Craig Martin
Born: Burton-on-Trent, 9 January 1986
Height: 6'2" **Weight:** 13.5
International Honours: W: 5; U21-8; Yth
Craig made a big impact at Oldham following his capture from Italian side Verona on a two-year contract last summer. The lightning-quick striker hit the goal trail soon after his arrival and finished as leading scorer, with 13 in all competitions. This rejuvenation earned him a recall to the Wales squad following an 18-month absence enforced by international suspension. At times a nightmare for defenders with his direct approach, Craig's main area for improvement would be to match his excellent approach play with greater end-product. It was a huge blow to the club's promotion hopes when he tore a hamstring in mid-February and did not

return until the final game. Craig looks set to play a crucial part in manager John Sheridan's plans.

Oxford U (From trainee on 17/2/2005) FL 23+25/8 FLC 1 FAC 1+2 Others 1+2 (£85,000 to Verona, Italy on 31/1/2006)
Wolverhampton W (Loaned from Verona, Italy on 4/8/2006) FL 6+17 FLC 1 FAC 3/2
Oldham Ath (Free on 20/7/2007) FL 31+1/10 FLC 2/1 FAC 5/1 Others 2/1

DAVIES Curtis Eugene
Born: Leytonstone, 15 March 1985
Height: 6'1" **Weight:** 11.13
Club Honours: Div 1 '05
International Honours: England: U21-3
Aston Villa signed the central defender on a year's loan from West Bromwich with a view to a permanent move. By his own admission, Curtis had a poor debut against Leicester in the Carling Cup in September, later describing himself as a 'pub player'. He came on more strongly after that and, to his surprise and pleasure, was in Fabio Capello's original 30-man England squad for the friendly against Switzerland. Curtis scored his first Villa goal at Wigan, his first Premier League start for the club, but at the beginning of March was ruled out for the rest of the season after rupturing an Achilles tendon.

Luton T (From trainee on 2/7/2004) FL 54+2/2 FLC 2 FAC 3 Others 0+1
West Bromwich A (£3,000,000 on 1/9/2005) P/FL 65/2 FLC 2 FAC 6
Aston Villa (Loaned on 31/8/2007) PL 9+3/1 FLC 1 FAC 1

DAVIES Gareth Michael John
Born: Chesterfield, 4 February 1983
Height: 6'1" **Weight:** 12.13
A broken toe in pre-season kept the versatile Chesterfield defender or midfielder out of the picture for three months. Although a loan spell at Stalybridge helped him return to fitness he was released not long after his one appearance of the season, as a substitute in the 2-1 win over Wrexham. A local lad, Gareth left with everyone's good wishes when joining Halifax in February.

Chesterfield (Free from Buxton on 20/8/2001) FL 73+43/2 FLC 2+2 FAC 3+3/2 Others 6

DAVIES Kevin Cyril
Born: Sheffield, 26 March 1977
Height: 6'0" **Weight:** 13.6
International Honours: E: U21-3; Yth
In yet another hugely impressive season, the target man confirmed again that he is absolutely vital to Bolton. Kevin's wholehearted commitment and will to

Kevin Davies

win saw him scoop a number of club awards at the end of the campaign. At times playing as a target man down the middle or sometimes on the right of a three-pronged attack, Kevin was at the heart of most of Bolton's attacking last season. He scored his first goal in the memorable 2-2 UEFA Cup draw at Bayern Munich in November and his first League goal soon followed in the 4-1 victory over Wigan. Kevin was a prominent figure in helping Bolton clamber their way to Premiership safety during the latter stages of the season, scoring the winner against West Ham in April and even playing with a broken hand to ensure the target was achieved.

Chesterfield *(From trainee on 18/4/1994) FL 113+16/22 FLC 7+2/1 FAC 10/6 Others 9+2/1*
Southampton *(£750,000 on 14/5/1997) PL 20+5/9 FLC 3+1/3 FAC 1*
Blackburn Rov *(£7,250,000 on 2/6/1998) P/FL 11+12/1 FLC 3 FAC 2/1 Others 1*
Southampton *(Signed on 18/8/1999) PL 59+23/10 FLC 3+2/1 FAC 3+5/2*
Millwall *(Loaned on 13/9/2002) FL 6+3/3*
Bolton W *(Free on 25/7/2003) PL 169+3/35 FLC 9+2/1 FAC 9/3 Others 12+1/1*

DAVIES Scott David
Born: Blackpool, 27 February 1987
Height: 6'2" **Weight:** 11.4
The young Morecambe goalkeeper came to the fore when the Shrimps won promotion to the League with their Wembley play-off victory. After being offered a new deal he started the season on trial at Gillingham but, failing to win a contract, returned to Morecambe and was third choice behind Joe Lewis and Steven Drench. Following some impressive performances in the reserves, he was given the chance to show his undoubted potential in a handful of starts towards the end of the season and earned several 'Man of the Match' awards.
Morecambe *(From juniors on 26/7/2005) FL 10 Others 3*

DAVIES Simon
Born: Haverfordwest, 23 October 1979
Height: 5'10" **Weight:** 11.4
International Honours: W: 50; B-1; U21-10; Yth
Simon is versatile and able to play in a number of midfield roles for Fulham but is at his most effective down the flanks, where he uses his close control and pace to go past opponents. He is an excellent dead-ball specialist, not afraid to try his luck from distance as he proved with long-range free kicks at Sunderland and West Ham. Another strike, this time in open play, was crucial to the home win over Aston Villa but perhaps his best

game of the season was at Reading, where his astute passes laid on both goals in a 2-0 win. Simon appeared regularly for Wales during the season.
Peterborough U *(From trainee on 21/7/1997) FL 63+2/6 FLC 4 FAC 3 Others 3*
Tottenham H *(£700,000 on 10/1/2000) PL 99+22/13 FLC 10+3/3 FAC 10+3/2*
Everton *(£3,500,000 on 26/5/2005) PL 35+10/1 FLC 3 FAC 1+1 Others 3*
Fulham *(£2,500,000 on 24/1/2007) PL 50+1/7 FLC 2 FAC 2+1*

DAVIES Steven (Steve) Gary
Born: Liverpool, 29 December 1987
Height: 6'1" **Weight:** 11.7
Despite a frustrating season, this versatile player remained a target for other clubs and Tranmere turned down several offers from Leeds for the winger before he suffered a cruciate knee-ligament injury in September. He completed a successful and comparatively rapid recovery from surgery and was back in the team towards the end of the campaign. Able to operate in attack or on the left, Steve is always a threat at set pieces and his talent has helped him to refine his game considerably. A valuable and rapidly-maturing asset to any team, he was out of contract at Rovers at the end of the season and there was strong interest from Derby.
Tranmere Rov *(From trainee on 28/7/2005) FL 30+30/5 FLC 2+1 FAC 3 Others 4+1*

DAVIS Claude
Born: Kingston, Jamaica, 6 March 1979
Height: 6'3" **Weight:** 14.4
International Honours: Jamaica: 47
Promotion-winning manager Billy Davies knew Claude from their days together at Preston and believed he could make an impact in the Premiership with Derby. In an unsettled season, the Jamaican centre-half struggled along with the rest of the team in 2007-08, although he has an imposing physical presence. Having suffered a last-day relegation to Sheffield United, Claude appeared to be attempting to tailor his game to the top level when all the Rams wanted was for him to impose himself on opposing strikers. Ironically, one his most dominant performance, at home to Middlesbrough in December after a shaky start, ended with him suffering a knee injury. Surgery was required and he missed the remainder of the season.
Preston NE *(Signed from Portmore U, Jamaica on 15/8/2003) FL 74+20/4 FLC 4 FAC 5 Others 5*
Sheffield U *(£2,500,000 + on 14/6/2006) PL 18+3 FLC 1*
Derby Co *(£3,000,000 on 25/7/2007) PL 19 FAC 2*

DAVIS Kelvin Geoffrey
Born: Bedford, 29 September 1976
Height: 6'1" **Weight:** 14.0
International Honours: E: U21-3; Yth
Kelvin started the season on the bench but two demoralising defensive displays into the season he was back in the Southampton goal, behind an improvised back four that would have undermined the confidence of less solid characters. In a three-manager season, Kelvin supported 24 different defensive combinations, changes largely forced by injuries, and remained first rate throughout until a broken finger sidelined him at the beginning of March. He returned to the bench at the end of the month only because there was no other fit goalkeeper in the squad.
Luton T *(From trainee on 1/7/1994) FL 92 FLC 7 FAC 2 Others 6*
Torquay U *(Loaned on 16/9/1994) FL 2 FLC 1 Others 1*
Hartlepool U *(Loaned on 8/8/1997) FL 2 FLC 1*
Wimbledon *(£600,000 + on 14/7/1999) FL 131 FLC 7 FAC 8*
Ipswich T *(Free on 6/8/2003) FL 84 FLC 2 FAC 3 Others 4*
Sunderland *(£1,250,000 on 1/7/2005) PL 33 FAC 2*
Southampton *(£1,000,000 on 21/7/2006) FL 73 FLC 3 FAC 5 Others 1*

Kelvin Davis

115

DAVIS Liam Lloyd
Born: Wandsworth, 23 November 1986
Height: 5'9" **Weight:** 11.7
The home-grown left-sided Coventry player with an excellent turn of pace and two good feet looked to be on the verge of a regular first-team place at the start of the season. A knee injury kept him out of contention and he did not have an opportunity until Christmas when, as a substitute against Ipswich, he set up Dele Adebola's goal with a blistering run. He made three starts, two at left-back because of an injury crisis, but did not appear after Chris Coleman's arrival as manager. Liam was released before the end of the season.
Coventry C (From trainee on 1/7/2006) FL 3+8 FAC 1
Peterborough U (Loaned on 15/9/2006) FL 7 FLC 1

DAVIS Sean
Born: Clapham, 20 September 1979
Height: 5'10" **Weight:** 12.0
Club Honours: Div 1 '01
International Honours: E: U21-11
For the first four months of last season, Sean was in irrepressible form for Portsmouth, arguably the best of his career. Between August and the end of November he missed only one Premier League game through suspension as he turned in one memorable performance after another while anchoring midfield. In the 7-4 defeat of Reading at the end of September the local Press were moved to describe him as playing "like a man possessed". In the system Pompey operated, Sean was able to fill the role he likes best, playing in a holding position. Then, from late November, a succession of niggling injuries sidelined him effectively until the end of January, when new arrivals increased the competition for places and he was unable to recover his pre-Christmas consistency and dominance. He was again linked with a summer move.
Fulham (From trainee on 2/7/1998) P/FL 128+27/14 FLC 9+5/3 FAC 15+2/2 Others 12/1
Tottenham H (£3,000,000 on 10/7/2004) PL 11+4 FLC 1+1
Portsmouth (Signed on 12/1/2006) PL 63+7/1 FLC 2 FAC 2+2/1

DAVIS Solomon (Sol) Sebastian
Born: Cheltenham, 4 September 1979
Height: 5'8" **Weight:** 11.0
Club Honours: Div 1 '05
During the early part of last season Sol was unavailable for Luton through injury and, along with four others who had formed the core of Mike Newell's League

One winning squad, seemed surplus to requirements. A loan to Peterborough never came off and the second most expensive player in Luton's history seldom featured, even in the reserves. After almost a year without a League appearance, Sol started in a 4-0 defeat at Hartlepool and completed 90 minutes to establish he was nearing full fitness. His run ended when he was sent off at Swansea and on his return, lacked his customary bite in the tackle, although he prefers to use his experience to deny space or intercept crosses and passes.
Swindon T (From trainee on 29/5/1998) FL 100+17 FLC 7 FAC 5+1 Others 1
Luton T (£600,000 + on 16/8/2002) FL 165+10/2 FLC 8+1 FAC 11 Others 4

DAVIS Steven
Born: Ballymena, 1 January 1985
Height: 5'7" **Weight:** 9.7
Club Honours: FAYC '02; SC '08
International Honours: NI: 28; U23-1; Yth; Sch
Arriving from Aston Villa last summer and going straight into the team for Fulham's opening game at Arsenal, he remained a first choice until a surprise loan move to Rangers in January led to a hectic time chasing four trophies. Steven works hard in midfield, decisive in the tackle and harrying opponents into conceding possession so that he can set up attacking moves, helped by his excellent passing. A regular in the Northern Ireland team, he continued to be selected throughout his time at Craven Cottage, where he is expected back.
Aston Villa (From trainee on 15/1/2002) PL 70+21/5 FLC 6/2 FAC 4+1/2
Fulham (Signed on 17/7/2007) PL 22 FLC 2 FAC 0+1
Glasgow Rgrs (Loaned on 31/1/2008) SL 11+1 SLC 1 SC 2+2 Others 8/1

DAVISON Aidan John
Born: Sedgefield, 11 May 1968
Height: 6'1" **Weight:** 13.12
Club Honours: AMC '98
International Honours: NI: 3; B-1
Age and injuries finally caught up with Aidan, one of the most experienced and reliable goalkeepers ever to play for Colchester. He began the season as reserve to Dean Gerken, having swapped his number one shirt for 13, and was also Gerken's goalkeeping coach. When Gerken was sent off during the first home match of the season, against Barnsley, Aidan was recalled for the trip to Preston. He contributed to a 3-0 victory at Deepdale, ironically one of Colchester's only two clean-sheets all season. Aidan played six times before

injury struck at the end of October. He struggled with shoulder problems and never made another appearance, either on the pitch or the bench, and announced his retirement at the end of the season.
Notts Co (Signed from Billingham Synthonia on 25/3/1988) FL 1
Bury (£6,000 on 7/10/1989)
Millwall (Free on 14/8/1991) FL 34 FLC 3 FAC 2 Others 2
Bolton W (£25,000 on 26/7/1993) P/FL 35+2 FAC 8 Others 4
Hull C (Loaned on 29/11/1996) FL 9 Others 1
Bradford C (Free on 14/3/1997) FL 10
Grimsby T (Free on 16/7/1997) FL 77 FLC 10 FAC 7 Others 10
Sheffield U (Free on 6/8/1999) FL 1+1
Bradford C (Free on 4/1/2000) P/FL 49+2 FLC 6 FAC 1 Others 2+1
Grimsby T (Free on 8/8/2003) FL 32 FLC 1 FAC 2 Others 1
Colchester U (Free on 12/7/2004) FL 99 FLC 2 FAC 7 Others 1

DAWSON Andrew (Andy) Stuart
Born: Northallerton, 20 October 1978
Height: 5'9" **Weight:** 10.2
Along with Ian Ashbee, Bo Myhill and Ryan France, Andy now stands on the verge of playing for Hull in all four divisions following their rise to the Premier League through the play-off win against Bristol City at Wembley. After being second choice to Damien Delaney at left-back for the most of the early months of the season, the brother of Tottenham's Michael Dawson was restored to the left of the Tigers' defence from December as they stormed up the table to equal their highest position of third. He filled in at right-back in the first League win of the season, against Norwich, and in the Carling Cup victory at Premier League Wigan. Andy scored a spectacular free-kick as a substitute to complete a 3-0 home win over Preston in November.
Nottingham F (From trainee on 31/10/1995) FLC 1
Scunthorpe U (£70,000 on 18/12/1998) FL 192+3/8 FLC 6 FAC 12/1 Others 12/2
Hull C (Free on 1/7/2003) FL 145+7/6 FLC 4+2 FAC 7/2 Others 3

DAWSON Michael Richard
Born: Northallerton, 18 November 1983
Height: 6'2" **Weight:** 12.12
Club Honours: FLC '08
International Honours: E: B-2; U21-13; Yth
The Tottenham central defender was struck by injury at the dawn of last season and then, most crucially for him, in February, thus missing the chance of

a Carling Cup winners' medal. Michael still started 38 games and came off the bench once but will now have to face competition from Jonathan Woodgate and a fit Ledley King. He continues to impress with his determination and telling long diagonal balls out of defence. While there were some lapses in concentration, he is still only 24 and has the mentality to apply himself and succeed in future seasons.

Nottingham F (From trainee on 23/11/2000) FL 82+1/7 FLC 5 FAC 2 Others 1
Tottenham H (Signed on 31/11/2005) PL 99+2/2 FLC 8+1 FAC 10 Others 15+1/1

DAWSON Stephen John
Born: Dublin, 4 December 1985
Height: 5'9" **Weight:** 11.2
International Honours: RoI: U21-1
Stephen signed a new contract for Mansfield just before the start of last season, after some haggling through the summer. His goals were rare but he scored a spectacular 25-yarder in the local derby with Chesterfield at Field Mill in September. He was a regular in the centre of the Stags' midfield, apart from injury and a one-match ban for a fifth booking at the turn of the year. Is a crowd pleaser who never gives less than 100 per cent.

Leicester C (From trainee on 15/7/2003)
Mansfield T (Free on 5/8/2005) FL 106+11/4 FLC 3+1 FAC 7+1 Others 2

DAY Christopher (Chris) Nicholas
Born: Walthamstow, 28 July 1975
Height: 6'3" **Weight:** 13.6
International Honours: E: U21-6; Yth (UEFA-U18 '93)
Chris, an able goalkeeper, started last season promisingly but after only a handful of games for Millwall was replaced by Rab Douglas and then Lenny Pidgeley. He never reclaimed his first-team spot. Although an excellent shot-stopper and good with crosses, he is still working on his kicking. Was released in the summer.

Tottenham H (From trainee on 16/4/1993) Others 4
Crystal Palace (£225,000 + on 9/8/1996) FL 24 FLC 2 FAC 2
Watford (£225,000 on 18/7/1997) P/FL 11 FLC 1 Others 1
Lincoln C (Loaned on 4/12/2000) FL 14 Others 4
Queens Park Rgrs (Free on 24/7/2001) FL 87 FLC 6 FAC 2 Others 5
Preston NE (Loaned on 23/2/2005) FL 6
Oldham Ath (Free on 2/8/2005) FL 30 FLC 1 FAC 4 Others 1
Millwall (Free on 6/7/2006) FL 9+1 FLC 2 Others 2

DAY Jamie Robert
Born: High Wycombe, 7 May 1986
Height: 5'9" **Weight:** 10.7
Jamie enjoyed his best season for Peterborough, starting all but four of the League games and becoming a free-kick expert after Christmas when finding the net three times from dead-ball situations. As an attacking left-back, he provided many dangerous crosses for United's forwards.

Peterborough U (From trainee on 19/8/2003) FL 78+14/5 FLC 4 FAC 6 Others 4+1

DEAN James
Born: Blackburn, 15 May 1985
Height: 5'11" **Weight:** 11.7
Signed from Northwich in the summer, James made six appearances for Bury before leaving to join Altrincham on loan in December. The tall striker was initially seen as the ball winner the Shakers needed to lead the line and his aerial threat was obvious. It was hoped his loan would develop his experience but his time with the Shakers did not work out as either party wished and he was released in January.

Bury (Signed from Northwich Victoria on 6/8/2007) FL 3+1 FLC 1 Others 1

DEENEY Troy
Born: Birmingham, 29 June 1988
Height: 5'11" **Weight:** 12.0
After one substitute appearance in 2006-07, Troy opened his Walsall scoring account with a last-minute winner at Millwall in September. There were no further goals, but whenever called upon last season he played tirelessly, whether in attack or midfield. Troy is an extremely positive youngster and could do well.

Walsall (Free from Chelmsley T on 27/2/2007) FL 16+20/1 FAC 2+2 Others 0+1

DEFOE Jermain Colin
Born: Beckton, 7 October 1982
Height: 5'7" **Weight:** 10.4
Club Honours: FLC '08
International Honours: E: 28; B-2; U21-23; Yth
Although a great favourite at Tottenham, Jermain found it hard to get past Dimitar Berbatov and Robbie Keane in 2007-08, especially with Darren Bent also in contention. He scored eight times in eight starts and 23 substitute appearances in all competitions, including two in the UEFA Cup thrashing of Anorthosis Famagusta and a vital first in the Carling Cup at Manchester City. Frustrated at being unable to hold down a first-team spot,

Jermain Defoe (right)

117

every Spurs' fan understood his desire for regular football and it came as no surprise when Portsmouth came in for him in the January transfer window. The move to Fratton Park, while not being settled formally until several days after the official 31 January deadline, was an instant success. As at his previous clubs, West Ham, Bournemouth and Tottenham, Jermain scored on his debut in a 1-1 draw with Chelsea and was on target in each of the next four home games. In so doing he broke Alan Biley's 1982-83 record of scoring in his first four home League games, and in his first eight appearances he averaged a goal a game. Had he stayed at Spurs he may well have won a Carling Cup winners' medal and was ineligible in the FA Cup as Pompey went on to win at Wembley, but Jermain knew that he had made the right choice. After appearing in two autumn England internationals and against the United States, at the end of May he scored twice in a 3-0 win for England over Trinidad & Tobago as he looked to secure a regular place in the side. Jermain is involved in the Portsmouth community initiative that aims to prevent crime by giving young people free weekly football.
West Ham U (£400,000 + from trainee at Charlton Ath on 15/10/1999) P/FL 62+31/29 FLC 6+1/6 FAC 4+1/6
Bournemouth (Loaned on 26/10/2000) FL 27+2/18 FAC 1/1 Others 1
Tottenham H (£7,000,000 + on 2/2/2004) PL 88+51/43 FLC 10+5/10 FAC 8+5/5 Others 4+6/6
Portsmouth (£9,000,000 on 31/1/2008) PL 12/8

DE LA CRUZ Bernardo **Ulises**
Born: Piqulucho, Ecuador, 8 February 1974
Height: 5'11" **Weight:** 11.12
International Honours: Ecuador: 90
Ulises played only one complete Premiership game for Reading, a battling 0-0 draw away to Manchester United on the first weekend. After that he made the occasional appearance in Cup games, was on the bench in a handful of League matches and did not even make the squad for the last three months of the campaign. It was little surprise, therefore, when he was given a free transfer during the summer. But he will be remembered with great respect and affection by Reading fans, who appreciated his commitment to the Funce-Cruz, a charity he set up to improve living standards in Piquiucho, an Afro-Ecuadorian community in one of Ecuador's poorest regions.
Hibernian (£700,000 from Liga Deportiva Universitaria, Ecuador on 18/6/2001) SL

25+7/2 SLC 2 SC 2+2/1 Others 2
Aston Villa (£1,500,000 on 2/8/2002) PL 66+23/1 FLC 6+2/1 FAC 2
Reading (Free on 25/8/2006) PL 12+3/1 FLC 4 FAC 6

DELANEY Damien Finbarr
Born: Cork, 20 July 1981
Height: 6'3" **Weight:** 13.10
International Honours: RoI: 2; U21-1; Yth
Having started 2007-08 as Hull's centre-back on the opening day against Plymouth, Damien was soon moved to a less familiar left-back position to accommodate the central pairing of Wayne Brown and Michael Turner. Although a regular with the Tigers, he was transferred to Queens Park Rangers in the January transfer window. Despite being thought of as a centre-back when Rangers signed him, Damien immediately stamped his authority at left-back, where his boundless energy and attacking verve quickly won over the Loftus Road crowd. His confident swagger often finds him causing problems in attack and he scored his first goal at Hillsborough after a typically energetic move. As in his previous five years, he gave total commitment and made his Republic of Ireland debut against Serbia on the day that Hull won the Championship play-off final.
Leicester C (£50,000 from Cork C on 9/11/2000) PL 5+3 FLC 1 FAC 1+1
Stockport Co (Loaned on 15/11/2001) FL 10+2/1
Huddersfield T (Loaned on 28/3/2002) FL 1+1
Mansfield T (Loaned on 6/9/2002) FL 7
Hull C (£50,000 on 18/10/2002) FL 220+4/5 FLC 7 FAC 8
Queens Park Rgrs (£600,000 + on 17/1/2008) FL 17/1

DELAP Rory John
Born: Sutton Coldfield, 6 July 1976
Height: 6'0" **Weight:** 12.10
Club Honours: AMC '97
International Honours: RoI: 11; B-1; U21-4
The midfield general and long-throw expert played a big part in Stoke's successful return to top-flight football. Rory was signed on loan from Sunderland in October 2006 but his leg was broken in two places during his home debut, ironically against his parent club. Stoke honoured an agreement to sign him on a permanent basis and were rewarded as Rory became one of their unsung heroes. He was captaining Stoke when promotion was achieved.
Carlisle U (From trainee on 18/7/1994) FL 40+25/7 FLC 4+1 FAC 0+3 Others 12+2

Derby Co (£500,000 + on 6/2/1998) PL 97+6/11 FLC 7/2 FAC 2+1
Southampton (£3,000,000 + on 21/7/2001) P/FL 118+14/5 FLC 9+1 FAC 7+1 Others 1+1
Sunderland (Free on 31/1/2006) P/FL 11+1/1 FLC 1
Stoke C (Free on 12/10/2006) FL 46/2 FLC 1 FAC 1

DELPH Fabian
Born: Bradford, 21 November 1989
Height: 5'7" **Weight:** 9.7
International Honours: E: Yth
It was a case of deja vu for promising teenage midfielder Fabian at Leeds. In 2006-07, he made his debut as a substitute in the final game and a year later, his only League One action was also in the last match of the regular season when he went on in the 2-1 victory against Gillingham. The England under-19 player turned professional in January and also tasted senior action as a replacement in the Carling Cup defeat at Portsmouth. He skippered United's reserves.
Leeds U (From trainee on 11/1/2008) FL 0+2 FLC 0+1

DE MERIT Jay Michael
Born: Green Bay, Wisconsin, USA, 4 December 1979
Height: 6'1" **Weight:** 13.5
International Honours: USA: 7
Jay was a commanding figure at centre-half for Watford and a steadying influence in defence. A natural leader, he became club captain in December after the departure of Gavin Mahon and led by example. However, he suffered a series of injury problems in the New Year and found it difficult to regain his place, having to be content with sporadic appearances in central defence or at right-back. On a happier note, Jay consolidated his place as a regular member of the United States' international squad during the season. Away from football, Jay, who graduated in design in the States, had a painting accepted for an exhibition in a London art gallery.
Watford (Free from Northwood, ex University of Illinois, Chicago Fire, on 13/8/2004) P/FL 108+15/8 FLC 9+1 FAC 9 Others 4+1/1

DEMETRIOU Jason
Born: Newham, 18 November 1987
Height: 5'11" **Weight:** 10.8
Jason was mainly used by Leyton Orient as cover for both central and left midfield places in 2007-08. He is equally at home breaking up attacks or starting them with his tricky wing play.
Leyton Orient (From trainee on 19/7/2006) FL 34+27/5 FLC 2/1 FAC 4+1 Others 2+3

DE MONTAGNAC Ishmel

Born: Newham, 15 June 1988
Height: 5'10" **Weight:** 11.5
Club Honours: Div 2 '07
International Honours: E: Yth
Although used mainly as a substitute in his third season, Ishmel was the one Walsall player capable of setting the crowd roaring with his speed, ability to go past an opponent, accurate crossing and occasional powerful shooting that won him the club's 'Goal of the Season' award.
Walsall (From trainee on 13/12/2005) FL 26+47/6 FLC 0+2 FAC 5+3/1 Others 3+1

DEMPSEY Clinton (Clint) Drew

Born: Nacogdoches, Texas, USA, 9 March 1983
Height: 6'1" **Weight:** 12.2
International Honours: USA: 41
A hard-working Fulham midfielder who can operate on either side of the pitch, he made several appearances in a more advanced position last season. Surprisingly left on the bench twice in the opening four matches, he quickly fought his way back into the team and gave several 'Man of the Match' performances, hitting three goals in a four-match spell. Fulham's leading Premiership scorer with six, his industrious style was much appreciated by team-mates and supporters alike. Clint continued to star for the United States, scoring in the early season friendly against Brazil.
Fulham (£1,500,000 from New England Revolution, USA, ex Dallas Texans, Furman University, on 19/1/2007) PL 30+16/7 FLC 2 FAC 2+2

DEMPSEY Gary William

Born: Wexford, 15 January 1981
Height: 5'9" **Weight:** 10.4
Having rejected a new deal with Scottish Premier League side Aberdeen, Gary signed a contract with Yeovil in the summer. A central

Clint Dempsey

midfielder, possessing good technical ability and physically strong with a good work ethic, the Irishman's season was unfortunately disrupted by a number of injuries. After making 18 appearances for Yeovil, he signed for St Patrick's Athletic in the January transfer window.
Dunfermline Ath (Signed from Waterford U, ex Bray W, on 1/6/2001) SL 48+32/7 SLC 5+1 SC 7+4/1 Others 1
Aberdeen (Signed on 1/4/2005) SL 37+17/2 SLC 3+1 SC 3
Yeovil T (Signed on 19/7/2007) FL 10+6/2 FAC 0+1 Others 1

[DENILSON] PEREIRA NEVES Denilson

Born: Sao Paulo, Brazil, 16 February 1988
Height: 5'10" **Weight:** 10.10
International Honours: Brazil: Yth
The young Brazilian spent last season somewhat overshadowed by his Arsenal team-mates and found a consistent spot only in the Carling Cup run. Denilson remains a useful understudy to Cesc Fabregas, although he does not yet have the all-round game to compete with the Spaniard for a regular berth. He does, though, have a good short-passing game and covers the pitch energetically. Denilson appeared in every competition, 13 times in the Premier League, four in the Champions' League, once in the FA Cup and five in the Carling Cup, in which he scored his two goals.
Arsenal (£3,400,000 from Sao Paulo, Brazil on 31/8/2006) PL 8+15 FLC 11/2 FAC 3 Others 4+1

DENNEHY Billy

Born: Tralee, 17 February 1987
Height: 5'8" **Weight:** 10.1
International Honours: RoI: U21-2
Despite the young wide-left player's loan from Sunderland being extended for a second month in December, he failed to gain a regular place at Accrington. Having made his debut as a substitute in the 2-1 home defeat by Rochdale and his full debut in the victory over Chesterfield, he picked up an injury and made only one more start before returning to Sunderland in January. Was out of contract in the summer and looking for a new club.
Sunderland (Signed from Shelbourne on 28/1/2005)
Accrington Stanley (Loaned on 22/11/2007) FL 2+5

DENNIS Kristian

Born: Manchester, 12 March 1990
Height: 5'11" **Weight:** 11.0
A prolific scorer for Macclesfield's youth

team last season, Kristian made just one appearance for the senior side, at Rotherham on New Year's Day for his League debut as a late substitute at a time when the two main strikers were unavailable for selection.
Macclesfield T (Trainee) FL 0+1

DERBYSHIRE Matthew (Matt) Anthony
Born: Great Harwood, 14 April 1986
Height: 5'10" **Weight:** 11.1
International Honours: E: U21-11
It was a frustrating season at Blackburn for Matt as, because of the competition for place up front, he slipped into the role of substitute. As always he was effective, scoring the winner in the first game of the season at Middlesbrough and denying the same club victory in the return fixture. However, it was his supremely clever finish for the only goal at Newcastle that was the highlight of his season. A player who can always be relied upon to run and run, he spent much of the season being sent on in a wide-right position and it may be that he needs more strength to play up the centre.
Blackburn Rov (Signed from Great Harwood T on 20/4/2004) PL 12+34/8 FLC 2+1/1 FAC 4+3/4 Others 3+5/2
Plymouth Arg (Loaned on 31/8/2005) FL 2+10 FLC 1
Wrexham (Loaned on 9/2/2006) FL 16/10

DE RIDDER Daniel Robin Frede
Born: Amsterdam, Holland, 6 March 1984
Height: 6'0" **Weight:** 10.12
International Honours: Holland: U21-30
Signed from Celta Vigo in the summer, Daniel proved to be a skilful, nippy winger whose dribbling skills caused opponents problems. He also has an eye for a pass and crossed the ball dangerously, playing on either flank, and was a model professional. After Steve Bruce left Birmingham, Daniel's chances were restricted and he did not figure again after shock FA Cup defeat by Huddersfield in January.
Birmingham C (Free from Celta Vigo, Spain, ex Ajax, on 2/8/2007) PL 6+4 FLC 1 FAC 1

DERRY Shaun Peter
Born: Nottingham, 6 December 1977
Height: 5'10" **Weight:** 10.13
Club Honours: Div 3 '98
Shaun became the third member of the Crystal Palace side to have a second spell at Selhurst Park when Neil Warnock took him on loan from Leeds last November. His form was so good that he was signed on a permanent basis in January. A busy, hard-tackling midfield player,

who did not miss a game to the end of the season, he did not add to his earlier goals for Palace.
Notts Co (From trainee on 13/4/1996) FL 76+3/4 FLC 4+1 FAC 6+1/1 Others 3
Sheffield U (£700,000 on 26/1/1998) FL 62+10 FLC 4 FAC 6/1
Portsmouth (£300,000 + on 16/3/2000) FL 48+1/1 FLC 4 FAC 1+1
Crystal Palace (£400,000 on 6/8/2002) P/FL 62+21/3 FLC 9 FAC 4 Others 1+2
Nottingham F (Loaned on 24/12/2004) FL 7 FAC 1
Leeds U (Signed on 18/2/2005) FL 71/3 FLC 0+2 FAC 1+1 Others 3
Crystal Palace (Signed on 19/11/2007) FL 30 Others 2

DEVANEY Martin Thomas
Born: Cheltenham, 1 June 1980
Height: 5'10" **Weight:** 11.12
Martin was again one of Barnsley's most dangerous players, his wide play offering a constant threat. Prime examples were his two crosses against Liverpool and Chelsea in the FA Cup that brought goals and famous victories. He can also be relied on to score his fair share of goals, with the winner at Southampton his highlight, although his output was less than the previous season.
Coventry C (From trainee on 4/6/1997)
Cheltenham T (Free on 5/8/1999) FL 154+49/37 FLC 5+1/1 FAC 6+3/2 Others 8+2/2
Watford (Free on 1/7/2005)
Barnsley (Free on 26/8/2005) FL 95+18/16 FLC 2+1/1 FAC 10+1/2 Others 4

DEVERA Joseph (Joe)
Born: Southgate, 6 February 1987
Height: 6'2" **Weight:** 12.0
In only his second full season with Barnet, Joe again went from strength to strength. Building on his success in the previous season, when he won the club's 'Young Player of the Year' award, Joe scooped both the 'Player of the Year' and 'Most Improved Player' awards, voted for by the fans. One of the Bees' most consistent performers, equally comfortable at right-back or in the centre of defence, Joe is firm favourite at Underhill.
Barnet (From juniors on 21/11/2005) FL 64+3 FLC 3 FAC 8+1 Others 3+1

DE VOS Jason Richard
Born: Ontario, Canada, 2 January 1974
Height: 6'4" **Weight:** 13.7
Club Honours: Div 2 '03
International Honours: Canada: 49; U23-14; Yth
Jason was the only Ipswich player to appear in every League game, occupying one of the central defensive positions. The

Jason De Vos

Canadian is strong in the air and uses his experience to anticipate likely attacking ploys of opposing forwards. He scored twice during the season, netting the opener in the defeat of Coventry when he headed in Owen Garvan's free kick, and added one against West Bromwich. After the final game of the season, he confirmed that he had retired from professional football and was returning to Canada, where he will be commentating on Toronto FC for CBS.
Darlington (Free from Montreal Impact, Canada on 29/11/1996) FL 43+1/5 FLC 3/1 FAC 4 Others 1
Dundee U (£400,000 on 12/10/1998) SL 91+2/2 SLC 5+1 SC 12
Wigan Ath (£500,000 on 8/8/2001) FL 87+3/15 FLC 6 FAC 2
Ipswich T (Free on 2/6/2004) FL 171/10 FLC 3/1 FAC 3 Others 2

DE VRIES Dorus
Born: Beverwijk, Holland, 29 December 1980
Height: 6'1" **Weight:** 12.8
Club Honours: Div 1 '08
International Honours: Holland: U21
Dorus signed for Swansea in the summer from relegated Scottish Premier League

side Dunfermline and after ousting Willy Gueret, went on to clinch the goalkeeping berth, with his consistency a great asset. He has the agility to make good saves and another strength is his excellent communication with the defence, adding greatly to City's stability.
Dunfermline Ath (Signed from ADO Den Haag, Holland, ex Stormvogels Telstar, on 1/7/2006) SL 27 SLC 2 SC 5
Swansea C (Signed on 1/8/2007) FL 46 FLC 2 FAC 4 Others 6

DE VRIES Mark Lyndon Patrick
Born: Paramaribo, Surinam, 24 August 1975
Height: 6'4" **Weight:** 13.5
The Dutch striker commanded a place in Martin Allen's early Leicester line-ups and scored in the August demolition of Watford before falling out of favour. Allowed to go out on loan to Leeds in October, due to their regular strikers Jermaine Beckford and Tresor Kandol being suspended at the same time, he netted a last-minute winner against Yeovil on his home debut after going on as substitute. Although he went back to the Foxes before his loan was up because of a broken toe, he returned to Leeds the following month prior to signing permanently for Dundee United during the January transfer window. Not only did he link up again with his former boss Craig Levein at Tannadice, he also rediscovered his scoring form.
Heart of Midlothian (Free from Dordrecht 90, Holland on 1/6/2002) SL 62+10/29 SLC 6/1 SC 3 Others 8+1/4
Leicester C (Signed on 16/1/2005) FL 34+17/8 FLC 4+2/2 FAC 3+3/1
Leeds U (Loaned on 1/10/2007) FL 1+5/1 Others 2

DE ZEEUW Adrianus (Arjan) Johannes
Born: Castricum, Holland, 16 April 1970
Height: 6'1" **Weight:** 13.11
Club Honours: Div 1 '03
Arjan joined Coventry from Wigan in the close season. The vastly experienced central defender was made club captain but did not seem fully fit early in the season and struggled in the heavy defeat at Ipswich. His fitness improved and there were glimpses of class, especially with solid performances in away wins at Stoke and Queens Park Rangers and the Carling Cup tie with West Ham. He was a regular after Christmas until the arrival of Chris Coleman and after the FA Cup embarrassment against West Bromwich, Arjan was dropped and later told he would be released at the end of the season.
Barnsley (£250,000 from Telstar, Holland,

ex Vitesse 22, on 3/11/1995) P/FL 138/7 FLC 12 FAC 14
Wigan Ath (Free on 2/7/1999) FL 126/6 FLC 8 FAC 6 Others 6
Portsmouth (Free on 3/7/2002) P/FL 103+3/5 FLC 6 FAC 6
Wigan Ath (£500,000 on 11/8/2005) PL 52 FLC 3+1 FAC 1
Coventry C (Free on 6/7/2007) FL 16+1 FLC 1 FAC 1

DIABY Vassiriki Abou
Born: Paris, France, 11 May 1986
Height: 6'3" **Weight:** 11.11
International Honours: France: 3; U21-1; Yth
Abou is probably one of those Arsenal players who did not make as much progress as expected during the course of last season. That said, he was yet another of the squad to be interrupted by injuries and, just as significantly, had to play wide in midfield rather than his chosen position in the centre. Tall and strong, he continues to be compared to former Gunners great Patrick Vieira but has a long way to go to emulate his exploits for Arsenal. With Mathieu Flamini's departure, Abou may have the chance to prove himself in his preferred role. He played 14 times in the Premier League, scoring once, six times in the Champions' League, adding a further couple of goals, twice in the FA Cup and on five occasions in the Carling Cup,

with another goal.
Arsenal (£2,000,000 from Auxerre, France on 20/1/2006) PL 27+12/3 FLC 8+2/1 FAC 4 Others 5+4/2

DIAGOURAGA Toumani
Born: Paris, France, 10 June 1987
Height: 6'2" **Weight:** 11.5
Signed on loan for last season from Watford, central-midfielder Toumani made a big contribution to Hereford's promotion campaign. From early on, his quality was evident with his rangy running style and extraordinary energy to carry him from box to box repeatedly earning him a reputation among Hereford fans as a sort of lower-division Patrick Vieira. Although his goals were rare, his early-season equaliser at Chester reinforced Hereford as front-runners and he more than made up for his low strike rate with the chances he provided for team-mates.
Watford (From trainee on 17/11/2004) P/FL 1 FLC 3 FAC 1+1
Swindon T (Loaned on 23/3/2006) FL 5+3
Rotherham U (Loaned on 12/1/2007) FL 4+3
Hereford U (Loaned on 9/8/2007) FL 41/2 FLC 2 FAC 6 Others 1

DIALLO Drissa
Born: Nouadhibou, Mauritania, 4 January 1973
Height: 6'1" **Weight:** 12.0
Club Honours: AMC '08; Div 2 '08
Drissa began the season by being sent

Drissa Diallo

off in the opening-day home defeat by Bury but returned to be the regular right-back for MK Dons, filling in well in his preferred central slot when either Sean O'Hanlon or Danny Swailes was missing. He hit a match-winning penalty in the Johnstone's Paint Trophy shoot-out at Gillingham but was forced to miss the Wembley final after damaging his shoulder the previous weekend, an injury that kept him out of action for the remainder of the season.
Burnley *(Free from KV Mechelen, Belgium, ex RC Tilleur, Sedan, AS Brevannes, on 9/1/2003) FL 14/1 FAC 4/1*
Ipswich T *(Free on 6/6/2003) FL 39+6 FLC 3 Others 1*
Sheffield Wed *(Free on 8/7/2005) FL 8+3 FLC 1*
MK Dons *(Free on 27/7/2006) FL 70/2 FLC 3 FAC 2 Others 6*

DIAO Salif Alassane
Born: Kedougou, Senegal, 10 February 1977
Height: 6'0" **Weight:** 11.7
Club Honours: FLC '03
International Honours: Senegal: 39
After a loan from Liverpool in 2006-07, Salif was expected back at Stoke. The midfield strongman then proved impossible to locate until he eventually signed an 18-month deal just before Christmas. Lack of form and fitness restricted the Senegalese international's appearances for Stoke and when he seemed back to full fitness, a further hamstring problem kept him out to the end of the campaign.
Liverpool *(£5,000,000 from Sedan, France, ex Monaco, on 9/8/2002) PL 19+18/1 FLC 7+1/1 FAC 1+1 Others 8+6/1*
Birmingham C *(Loaned on 18/1/2005) PL 2*
Portsmouth *(Loaned on 31/8/2005) PL 7+4 FLC 1 FAC 1*
Stoke C *(Signed on 13/10/2006) FL 35+3 FAC 1+2*

DIARRA Lassana
Born: Paris, France, 10 March 1985
Height: 5'8" **Weight:** 10.10
Club Honours: FLC '07; FAC '08
International Honours: France: 13; U21-15; Yth
The promising midfielder made his final Chelsea appearance as a substitute in the Community Shield against Manchester United in August but his growing impatience at a lack of chances led him to cross London and join the French enclave at Arsenal as a last-minute August deadline day signing. A versatile midfielder who can also operate at right-back, Lassana impressed on his debut in the Carling Cup at home to Newcastle and although featuring irregularly in the

Premier League, he played three times in the Champions' League and three times in the Carling Cup. However, by January he was bemoaning his inability to become a regular and, after requesting a move, joined Portsmouth for a fee that represented a quick profit for Arsenal. The French international's desire for regular involvement was satisfied by Pompey. Lassana, now a regular for France, is relatively diminutive compared with his domestic team-mates but is extremely powerful, combative and fiercely determined, driving the side forward from midfield with energy, controlled aggression and genuine skill. He scored his first goal in English football in Pompey's FA Cup fourth round victory over Plymouth at the end of January and ended the season where he had begun it, at Wembley. After giving a brilliant, dominant display in the FA Cup final against Cardiff, he fully deserved his winners' medal and manager Harry Redknapp continues to savour an outstanding signing.
Chelsea *(£2,800,000 from Le Havre, France on 22/7/2005) PL 9+4 FLC 2+1 FAC 6 Others 4+5*
Arsenal *(£2,000,000 on 31/8/2007) PL 4+3 FLC 3 Others 1+2*
Portsmouth *(£5,500,000 on 17/1/2008) PL 11+1/1 FAC 5/1*

DIATTA Lamine
Born: Dakar, Senegal, 2 July 1975
Height: 6'1" **Weight:** 13.0
International Honours: Senegal: 40
Lamine is a former captain of Senegal who bought out his contract at Besiktas and joined Newcastle on a short-term deal last March. He is a centre-back who is calm on the ball and good in the air but had little opportunity to make a mark when limited to two substitute appearances, in the 82nd minute against Reading, and in added-time at West Ham. He was not retained at the end of the season.
Newcastle U *(Free from Besiktas, Turkey, ex Toulouse, Marseille, Rennes, Lyon, St Etienne, on 11/3/2008) PL 0+2*

DICKER Gary
Born: Dublin, 31 July 1986
Height: 6'0" **Weight:** 12.2
International Honours: RoI: U21-1
Signed from League of Ireland side UCD in the summer, Gary began to settle into the Stockport side quietly until a ligament injury sidelined him for around two months. On his return, his cool, commanding displays in midfield helped the Hatters rocket up the table. Calm on the ball, he seems to create time for himself and, in his holding role, soaks up

pressure and intercepts well, traits seen at their best with a superb display in the play-off final against Rochdale.
Birmingham C *(Signed from UCD, Ireland on 31/1/2007)*
Stockport Co *(Free on 10/8/2007) FL 29+1 FLC 2 Others 4*

DICKINSON Carl Matthew
Born: Swadlincote, 31 March 1987
Height: 6'0" **Weight:** 12.0
Stoke's hard-running and strong-tackling left-back or central defender never lets them down. Carl is physically strong and displayed both courage and mental strength when he returned to the team only a couple of days after his father died suddenly. He dedicated a storming performance to his father's memory and is one for the future.
Stoke C *(From trainee on 3/8/2006) FL 28+18 FLC 2 FAC 1+1*
Blackpool *(Loaned on 20/10/2006) FL 7 FAC 2 Others 1*

DICKINSON Liam Michael
Born: Salford, 4 October 1985
Height: 6'4" **Weight:** 11.7
The bargain signing from neighbours Woodley Sports had an incredible season at Stockport in 2007-08. He scored County's first goal, the winner in the opening-day victory over Dagenham, and the Hatters' last one, their third, against Rochdale at Wembley to secure victory and promotion. It was his 21st goal of a campaign that saw the hard-working and popular striker pick up all the club's 'Player of the Year' awards.
Stockport Co *(Signed from Woodley Sports on 22/12/2005) FL 57+37/33 FLC 1+1 FAC 2 Others 8/2*

DICKOV Paul
Born: Livingston, 1 November 1972
Height: 5'6" **Weight:** 11.9
Club Honours: ECWC '94
International Honours: S: 10; U21-4; Yth; Sch
Although a cult-hero among Manchester City fans, the veteran striker found first-team opportunities scarce last season and had to go on loan for his football, first to Crystal Palace at the end of August and then to Blackpool in January. It was a season of two halves for the talented and experienced Scottish international striker. In the first part, at Crystal Palace for four months, Paul played in nine games, completed 90 minutes only once and did not score. Part two was at Blackpool, including a return visit to Selhurst Park. By the end of his time at Bloomfield Road in May, Paul had scored six goals in 11 appearances, including a run of five in

five games. Of all his goals for Blackpool, the brace at Hull will be most fondly remembered, especially the second, when lobbing the goalkeeper from the edge of the area. Was released in the summer.
Arsenal *(From trainee on 28/12/1990)* PL 6+15/3 FLC 2+2/3
Luton T *(Loaned on 8/10/1993)* FL 8+7/1
Brighton & Hove A *(Loaned on 23/3/1994)* FL 8/5
Manchester C *(£1,000,000 on 23/8/1996)* P/FL 105+51/33 FLC 9+4/5 FAC 5+4/1 Others 3/2
Leicester C *(Signed on 22/2/2002)* P/FL 81+8/32 FLC 4/2 FAC 4/3
Blackburn Rov *(£150,000 on 16/6/2004)* PL 44+6/14 FLC 3+1/2 FAC 7/1
Manchester C *(Free on 3/7/2006)* PL 9+7 FLC 0+2 FAC 0+1
Crystal Palace *(Loaned on 31/8/2007)* FL 6+3
Blackpool *(Loaned on 31/1/2008)* FL 7+4/6

DICKSON Christopher (Chris) Matthew
Born: Plumstead, 28 December 1984
Height: 5'11" **Weight:** 13.4
An exciting prospect, Chris made his Charlton debut in the Carling Cup at Swindon as a late substitute before being loaned out to Crewe, where he made three appearances without scoring. However, his loan to Gillingham was a big success and he hit 11 goals in 14 League and Cup appearances, enough for him to end the season as their leading scorer. Upon his return to the Valley, he made four further substitute appearances for Charlton and scored the equaliser in the FA Cup replay at West Bromwich. The young striker then sustained a knee injury in a freak accident in the hotel foyer before the home game against Stoke and was ruled out for the rest of the season. Chris is quick, strong and a distinct prospect.
Charlton Ath *(Signed from Dulwich Hamlet, ex Erith & Belvedere, on 12/3/2007)* FL 0+2 FLC 0+1 FAC 0+2/1
Crewe Alex *(Loaned on 17/8/2007)* FL 2+1
Gillingham *(Loaned on 21/9/2007)* FL 9+3/7 Others 2/4

DICKSON Ryan Anthony
Born: Saltash, 14 December 1986
Height: 5'10" **Weight:** 11.5
Ryan again struggled to find a way into Plymouth's side, making a solitary appearance in 2007-08 from the substitutes' bench against Wycombe in the Carling Cup in August. With a hankering for first-team football, the left-sided player initially joined Brentford on loan in November before signing a permanent deal in January. Although played at outside-left in his first few games, Ryan then appeared at left-back where he proved to be a strong defender,

good going forward and an excellent crosser of the ball. He did not miss a League game from the day he signed until the end of the season.
Plymouth Arg *(From trainee on 1/8/2005)* FL 2+3 FLC 0+1 FAC 0+1
Torquay U *(Loaned on 12/1/2007)* FL 7+2/1
Brentford *(Signed on 16/11/2007)* FL 30+1

DIMECH Luke Anthony
Born: Valletta, Malta, 11 January 1977
Height: 5'11" **Weight:** 12.6
International Honours: Malta: 56
Luke's ambition for a second term in English professional football was achieved when he signed for Macclesfield last summer, having previously been in Malta

with Marsaxlokk. A strong, hard-tackling centre-back, he went straight into the starting line-up in a back-four formation, missing matches only when he was called up by Malta. With a lack of height in the centre of the Macclesfield defence, Luke found himself on the substitutes' bench when the taller Ryan Cresswell was signed on loan in January and, towards the end of the season, made only occasional appearance. However, he continued to represent Malta, playing a part in their 7–1 record win against Liechtenstein. Was released at the end of the campaign.
Mansfield T *(Free from Shamrock Rov, ex Lincoln C trainee, Sliema, Birkirkara, on 7/8/2003)* FL 36+9/1 FLC 2 FAC 3+1 Others 2

Luke Dimech

123

Chester C *(Free on 6/7/2005) FL 27+3 FLC 1 FAC 4 (Freed during 2006 close season)*
Macclesfield T *(Free from Marsaxlokk, Malta, on 9/8/2007) FL 23+3 FLC 1 FAC 1 Others 1*

DINNING Tony

Born: Wallsend, 12 April 1975
Height: 6'0" **Weight:** 12.11
Club Honours: Div 2 '03; AMC '04
The experienced midfielder joined Chester at the start of October, following his release by Stockport, in a deal taking him through to the end of the season. After making his debut in the 3-1 victory over Shrewsbury, Tony scored his first goal, a winner from the penalty spot at Lincoln in November. Knee-ligament damage, sustained at Wrexham, forced him to miss three months in the middle of the season and when he returned to the side, he was unable to regain his earlier authority as Chester struggled at the wrong end of the table.
Newcastle U *(From trainee on 1/10/1993)*
Stockport Co *(Free on 23/6/1994) FL 159+32/25 FLC 12+5/3 FAC 4+7 Others 6+1/2*
Wolverhampton W *(£600,000 + on 22/9/2000) FL 35/6 FLC 1/1 FAC 1*
Wigan Ath *(£750,000 on 7/9/2001) FL 79+5/12 FLC 5 FAC 3*
Stoke C *(Loaned on 27/3/2002) FL 5 Others 3*
Walsall *(Loaned on 20/11/2003) FL 2+3*
Blackpool *(Loaned on 23/11/2004) FL 10/3 Others 3*
Ipswich T *(Loaned on 9/8/2004) FL 3+4 FLC 2*
Bristol C *(Free on 28/10/2004) FL 15+4 Others 1*
Port Vale *(Signed on 23/3/2005) FL 40+2/5 FLC 1 FAC 4 Others 1*
Stockport Co *(Free on 12/7/2006) FL 27+5/2 FLC 1 FAC 3 Others 2*
Chester C *(Free on 5/10/2007) FL 20/2 FAC 1 Others 1*

DIOP Pape Bouba

Born: Dakar, Senegal, 28 January 1978
Height: 6'4" **Weight:** 15.7
Club Honours: FAC '08
International Honours: Senegal: 38
Having spent three years with Fulham, where his presence was often the key to them holding the upper hand in midfield, Pape Bouba made only two substitute appearances in the first five games last season and that was the cue for Portsmouth to swoop. Three years after a trial at Fratton Park, they eventually got their man when he signed for them on the last day of the August transfer window. After making his debut a fortnight later in a 0-0 draw with Liverpool, he played regularly,

normally in central midfield, and missed games only through suspension or while away at the African Cup of Nations with Senegal. His form was a revelation with many storming, even inspirational, performances anchoring midfield, normally in a 4-5-1 formation. Although less happy playing wide on the right, he was still a major influence in Pompey's success.
Fulham *(Signed from RC Lens, France on 30/7/2004) PL 70+6/8 FLC 3+1 FAC 4/1*
Portsmouth *(Signed on 31/8/2007) PL 25 FLC 1+1 FAC 4+1*

DIOUF El Hadji Ousseynou

Born: Dakar, Senegal, 15 January 1981
Height: 5'11" **Weight:** 11.11
Club Honours: FLC '03
International Honours: Senegal: 41
In what was seemingly his last season as a Bolton player, El Hadji showed why he would be sorely missed. Beginning the season with a virtuoso performance in the 3-0 home win over Reading in August, he had to wait until December for his first League goal when he finished off a delightful move in the 4-2 defeat at Manchester City. He scored a famous winner in the home UEFA Cup victory over Atletico Madrid and, during the latter stages of the season, netted an exquisitely placed goal in the vital 2-0 victory against Sunderland that virtually sealed Bolton's Premiership survival. His form was a little patchy at times during the second half of the season but El Hadji signed off in considerable style. A real fans' favourite, this colourful, and at times controversial and, made his mark at the Reebok Stadium.
Liverpool *(£10,000,000 from RC Lens, France, ex Sochaux, Rennes, on 17/7/2002) PL 41+14/3 FLC 7/3 FAC 4 Others 9+5*
Bolton W *(£3,500,000 on 20/8/2004) PL 102+12/21 FLC 3+2 FAC 3+2 Others 6+6/3*

DISLEY Craig Edward

Born: Worksop, 24 August 1981
Height: 5'10" **Weight:** 11.0
Playing in the centre of Bristol Rovers' midfield, the former Mansfield man enjoyed another good season, with his tremendous workrate and accurate passing. Craig scored a finely created goal against Rushden in the FA Cup and followed it with vital winning penalties in shoot-out victories over Leyton Orient and Fulham, finishing the campaign with nine goals.
Mansfield T *(From trainee on 23/6/1999) FL 106+35/16 FLC 2 FAC 9+1 Others 5*
Bristol Rov *(Free on 13/7/2004) FL 138+21/22 FLC 4+1/1 FAC 14+1/3 Others 16/2*

DISTIN Sylvain

Born: Paris, France, 16 December 1977
Height: 6'4" **Weight:** 13.10
Club Honours: FAC '08
When Sylvain signed for Portsmouth in late May, Harry Redknapp described it as the best free transfer of the season. How prophetic those words were as he had a wonderfully consistent campaign in the middle of Pompey's defence. His partnership with Sol Campbell proved to be particularly effective, one of the best in the Premier League. In all competitions Pompey kept 23 clean sheets and they were together for 19 of them. Strong, powerful and commanding in the air, he missed only two games all season, both in the Premier League, and his total of 45 appearances was the highest in the squad. While he did not score in 2007-08 he likes to get forward as much as possible and those forward runs can prove very threatening in the opponents' last third. On this form he must consider himself very unlucky not to have any international caps. Was voted the 'Players' Player of the Year' and had an outstanding FA Cup final.
Newcastle U *(Loaned from Paris St Germain, France, ex Tours, Guegnon, on 14/9/2001) PL 20+8 FLC 2 FAC 5*
Manchester C *(£4,000,000 from Paris St Germain, France on 4/7/2002) PL 178/5 FLC 7 FAC 16/1 Others 5*
Portsmouth *(Free on 4/7/2007) PL 36 FLC 3 FAC 6*

DIXON Jonathan (Jonny) James

Born: Murcia, Spain, 16 January 1984
Height: 5'9" **Weight:** 11.2
A former Wycombe striker, Jonny was given a second opportunity in the League when Brighton signed him from Aldershot during the January window, but was almost immediately sidelined by an ankle injury and it was another month before he could even reach the bench. He went on to make two starting appearances in April in the absence of Nicky Forster but was unable to recapture the form that made him such a dangerous striker at Aldershot. Jonny will hope to have a good pre-season's training behind him in order to make a bigger impact.
Wycombe W *(From trainee on 14/2/2003) FL 21+52/7 FLC 1+4/1 FAC 1+1 Others 2+3/1 (£6,000 to Aldershot T on 11/1/2007)*
Brighton & Hove A *(Free on 30/1/2008) FL 2+2*

DJORDJIC Bojan

Born: Belgrade, Serbia, 6 February 1982
Height: 5'10" **Weight:** 11.5
International Honours: Sweden: U21-5

Johan Djourou-Gbadjere

January and was embroiled in their fight to avoid relegation. At St Andrews he defended manfully for City, usually alongside Liam Ridgewell, and had to adapt to being under constant pressure. He also played in the centre of midfield in a rare away win at Derby and impressed with his strength and tidy passing. On his return to Arsenal, he was selected for the Carling Cup semi-final first leg against Tottenham but was injured in a torrid first half and did not reappear after the interval. Johan was then out for a long period before returning for two Premier League games at the end of the campaign.
Arsenal *(From trainee on 28/8/2004) PL 25+5 FLC 9+1 FAC 3 Others 5*
Birmingham C *(Loaned on 10/8/2007) PL 13*

D'LARYEA Jonathan (Jon)
Amar
Born: Manchester, 3 September 1985
Height: 5'10" **Weight:** 12.2
An ankle injury that ended Jon's 2006-07 campaign early at Mansfield had not cleared by the time pre-season training started and an operation was necessary. Thus Jon's return to action was delayed until October when, with Town leading Macclesfield 5-0, he went on for the last 35 minutes. He was soon a regular in the side in his accustomed position, winning the ball in the centre of midfield. Was out of contract in the summer and looking for a new club.
Manchester C *(From trainee on 17/7/2003) FLC 1*
Mansfield T *(Signed on 21/10/2005) FL 89+6/1 FLC 3 FAC 6+1 Others 2*

D'LARYEA Nathan Amarkine
Born: Manchester, 3 September 1985
Height: 5'10" **Weight:** 10.0
The former Manchester City reserve-team skipper signed for Rochdale in the summer, making his debut as a substitute on the opening day. He made his full debut at centre-back in the Carling Cup victory over Stoke a few days later and with Dale missing several senior defenders could have looked forward to a significant run in the side, only to suffer a long-term injury himself. He played at right-back in the FA Cup against Southend, when Dale's three on-loan defenders were ineligible, but despite showing excellent form in the reserves Nathan was on the fringe of the squad until he was a late selection against Notts County in April when Dale's regular centre-backs were stuck in a traffic jam. A speedy, mobile defender, he made several further appearances before the end of the season and was Dale's right-back in the play-off final at Wembley.

Bojan made only two appearances for Plymouth Argyle during last season, as a 67th-minute substitute against Doncaster in the Carling Cup in August and a start against Cardiff in the televised clash at Home Park in September. The left-sided midfielder's contract was terminated by mutual consent in October and in the following month Bojan signed a two-year contract with Swedish Club AIK.
Manchester U *(£1,000,000 from Bromma Pojkama on 18/2/1999 on 18/2/1999) PL 0+1 FLC 1*
Sheffield Wed *(Loaned on 7/12/2001) FL 4+1*
Glasgow Rgrs *(Signed on 4/1/2005) SL 4 SC 1*
Plymouth Arg *(Free on 12/7/2005) FL 18+22/4 FLC 1+2 FAC 0+1*

DJOUROU-GBADJERE Johan
Danon
Born: Abidjan, Ivory Coast, 18 January 1987
Height: 6'3" **Weight:** 13.11
International Honours: Switzerland: 17; U21; Yth
Johan, a young Swiss defender, was loaned by Arsenal to Birmingham until

Manchester C *(From trainee on 17/7/2003)*
Macclesfield T *(Loaned on 19/1/2007) FL 1*
Rochdale *(Free on 17/7/2007) FL 2+4 FLC 1
FAC 1 Others 2*

DOBIE Robert **Scott**
Born: Workington, 10 October 1978
Height: 6'1" **Weight:** 12.8
International Honours: S: 6
Scott made only one League start for
Nottingham Forest, against Bournemouth
on the opening day of last season, before
the injury problems that hindered his City
Ground career soon returned. After a
training injury, he was unable to regain a
place and was transferred to Carlisle in the
January transfer window, thus returning to
the club where he began his professional
career. A more complete player than seven
years earlier, his all-round game gave an
added dimension to the United attack.
He also weighed in with a number of
goals, including the only score in the win
at Crewe and the last-minute strike that
overcame Yeovil. Scott is a very competitive
performer who is always committed and
the return to Brunton Park undoubtedly
gave a welcomed boost to his career.
Carlisle U *(From trainee on 10/5/1997) FL
101+35/24 FLC 2+6 FAC 4+1/2 Others 6+1*
Clydebank *(Loaned on 3/11/1998) SL 6*
West Bromwich A *(£125,000 + on
11/7/2001) P/FL 57+53/21 FLC 6+4/4 FAC 1+6*
Millwall *(£500,000 + on 10/11/2004) FL
15+1/3*
Nottingham F *(£525,000 on 25/2/2005) FL
20+21/3 FLC 1 FAC 0+4 Others 2+1/1*
Carlisle U *(Signed on 23/1/2008) FL 8+7/4
Others 2*

DOBSON Craig Gregory
Born: Chingford, 23 January 1984
Height: 5'7" **Weight:** 10.10
Club Honours: FAT '07
International Honours: Jamaica: 1
Signed during the January transfer
window from Stevenage, Craig's debut
for the MK Dons was delayed by injury
problems until the final game of the
season, when he started on the right-
wing against Morecambe. Part of the
squad that celebrated winning the League
Two title, his 45 minutes on the pitch
augured well for the future.
Cheltenham T *(From trainee at Crystal
Palace on 2/7/2003) FL 0+2 Others 0+1*
(Freed during 2004 close season)
MK Dons *(Free from Stevenage Borough,
ex Grays Ath, Barnet, Cambridge C, on
31/1/2008) FL 1*

DOBSON Michael William
Born: Isleworth, 9 April 1981
Height: 5'11" **Weight:** 12.4
Club Honours: Div 2 '07

Injury problems led to Michael handing
over the Walsall captaincy to Tommy
Mooney in his second season at the Banks'
Stadium. He came back to contribute his
usual incisive tackling in midfield in the
last few games of the season and scored
a picture goal in the final game against
Hartlepool but was released in May as
Walsall cleared the decks ready for a new
managerial appointment.
Brentford *(From trainee on 30/6/1999) FL
164+13/3 FLC 6+1 FAC 11+1/1 Others 15/4*
Reading *(Loaned on 24/11/2005) FL 0+1*
Walsall *(Free on 3/7/2006) FL 60+3/4 FLC
2 FAC 2+1*

DODDS Louis Bartholomew
Born: Leicester, 8 October 1986
Height: 5'11" **Weight:** 11.11
With Lincoln in 2007-08 on a season-long
loan from Leicester, Louis was a virtual
ever-present throughout the campaign,
scoring nine goals from his 44 League and
Cup appearances. A number of impressive
performances saw the Imps' fans take to
the young attacking midfielder and his
superbly executed goal against Wycombe
at Sincil Bank saw him pick up the 'Goal
of the Season' trophy at the end of the
season.
Leicester C *(From trainee on 15/7/2005)*
Rochdale *(Loaned on 20/2/2007) FL 6+6/2*
Lincoln C *(Loaned on 31/7/2007) FL 38+3/9
FLC 0+1 FAC 2*

DOHERTY Gary Michael Thomas
Born: Carndonagh, 31 January 1980
Height: 6'2" **Weight:** 13.1
International Honours: RoI: 34; U21-
7; Yth
In another consistent season at Norwich,
the former Tottenham defender went
about his duties with the minimum of
fuss. Solid and reliable, he is both good in
the air and brave in the challenge, often
throwing his body into tackles to block
shots. His only goal was a late equalizer
against Bury in the FA Cup at Carrow
Road which, as a former striker, was a
disappointing return for someone who
wins as many headers in the opposition
area as he does. He is only three
appearances short of 150 for the Canaries.
Luton T *(From trainee on 2/7/1997) FL
46+24/12 FLC 0+3/1 FAC 6+2/2 Others 1+1*
Tottenham H *(£1,000,000 on 22/4/2000) PL
45+19/4 FLC 3+3 FAC 7+1/4*
Norwich C *(Signed on 20/8/2004) P/FL
122+8/3 FLC 9+1 FAC 6+1/1*

DOHERTY Thomas (Tommy)
Edward
Born: Bristol, 17 March 1979
Height: 5'8" **Weight:** 9.13
Club Honours: AMC '03
International Honours: NI: 9

After Tommy made such a good
impression the previous season when on
loan from Queens Park Rangers, Wycombe
manager Paul Lambert was keen to sign
the skilful midfielder permanently last
summer. Unfortunately Tommy contracted
appendicitis, so his move did not take
place until October, the loan being made
permanent in January. Not until the end
of December was Tommy fully fit but
from then on he was a permanent fixture
in midfield. As the anchor-man, Tommy
displays an impressive array of ball skills,
with excellent close control under pressure,
and superb vision. Is also an effective and
clean tackler, on average just two fouls
a game committed, and his disciplinary
record was also much improved.
Bristol C *(From trainee on 8/7/1997) FL
155+33/7 FLC 9+1/1 FAC 7+1 Others 18+1/1*
Queens Park Rgrs *(Signed on 30/6/2005)
FL 14+1*
Yeovil T *(Loaned on 2/3/2006) FL 1*
Wycombe W *(Loaned on 15/9/2006) FL
23+3/2 FLC 3+1 Others 1*
Wycombe W *(Free on 22/10/2007) FL 21+3
Others 2*

DOIG Christopher (Chris) Ross
Born: Dumfries, 13 February 1981
Height: 6'2" **Weight:** 12.6
International Honours: S: U21-13;
Yth; Sch
The Northampton skipper and central
defender, Chris lost a great chunk of the
season to injury. He was injured against
Darlington in November and did not play in
the first team again until the meeting with
Southend in April. When he came back, it
was as if he had never been away, so sure
was he in halting the flow of attacks with
fine tackling and powerful heading.
Queen of the South *(Associated Schoolboy)
SL 2+2*
Nottingham F *(From trainee on 7/3/1998)
P/FL 62+15/1 FLC 7+2 FAC 7*
Northampton T *(Loaned on 15/9/2003) FL 9*
Northampton T *(Free on 7/7/2005) FL
90+2/3 FLC 3 FAC 8/1 Others 3*

DOLMAN Liam Edward Lewis
Born: Brixworth, 26 September 1987
Height: 6'0" **Weight:** 14.5
Liam won a place in the heart of the
Northampton defence with some dogged
displays at the back. He tackles well, is
good in the air and his distribution is
sound. Sadly, he lost his place for a spell
when injured in the act of scoring his first
goal for the club.
Northampton T *(From trainee on
11/7/2006) FL 28+3/1 FAC 4 Others 2*

DOMORAUD Wilfried
Born: Maisons-Alfort, France, 18 August
1988
Height: 6'1" **Weight:** 13.10

Having previously played for the Nancy 'B' side in France, the young striker signed a one-year contract for Yeovil at the end of August after scoring a hat-trick for the reserves. However, after being given his debut when coming off the bench at Brighton and making a further five substitute appearances without finding the net, Wilfried went loan to Weymouth in January and then Weston-super-Mare the following month. Able to play down the middle or in a wider position, he began to score regularly for Weston before being released by Yeovil at the end of the season.

Yeovil T (Free from Nancy, France on 31/8/2007) FL 0+5 Others 0+1

DONE Matthew (Matty)
Born: Oswestry, 22 June 1988
Height: 5'8" **Weight:** 10.7
Great things were expected of Matty on the left of midfield at Wrexham but playing in a struggling side inhibited his progress. He always excites when on the ball but perhaps does not live up to expectations and although his pace frightens defenders, the final ball is sometimes off course. Matty has the time and potential to succeed and was one of the few to be offered a new contract by manager Brian Little.

Wrexham (From trainee on 3/8/2006) FL 41+25/1 FLC 2+1/1 FAC 3 Others 2

DONG FANGZHUO
Born: Dalian, China, 23 January 1985
Height: 6'1" **Weight:** 11.9
International Honours: China: 13
A young Manchester United forward who arrived in the footsteps of Ji-Sung Park, Dong Fangzhuo's appearances where limited in the Reds' action-packed campaign. He made his first Champions' League appearance as a substitute in United's last match of the qualifying stages against AS Roma, replacing fellow striker Wayne Rooney, and earlier played in the Carling Cup defeat by Coventry at Old Trafford.

Manchester U (£500,000 + from Dalian Shide, China, ex Dalian Saidelong, before being immediately loaned to Royal Antwerp, Belgium until 15/1/2007, on 12/1/2004) PL 1 FLC 1 Others 0+1

DOOLAN John
Born: Liverpool, 7 May 1974
Height: 6'1" **Weight:** 13.0
Club Honours: Div 3 '04
The veteran Rochdale midfielder missed the start of last season through suspension but reappeared to help Dale recover from a poor start. After some time out injured, he again formed the

midfield axis with Gary Jones but when Dale suffered a disappointing run in February, he was left out as David Perkins took over the central role. His distribution remained as good as ever, though, and he had earlier made the pass of the season with a 50-yard ball to set up youngster Kallum Higginbotham for his first senior goal against Accrington. John reappeared for the final League game of the season and made one last cameo appearance at the end of Dale's play-off second leg match against Darlington. He ended his time with the club at Wembley, where he was a non-playing substitute, before joining Southport as player-coach.

Everton (From trainee on 1/6/1992)
Mansfield T (Free on 2/9/1994) FL 128+3/10 FLC 8/1 FAC 7/2 Others 4+1/1
Barnet (£60,000 on 13/11/1998) FL 132+2/7 FLC 5+1/1 FAC 4 Others 5
Doncaster Rov (Signed on 20/3/2003) FL 68+9/2 FLC 5/1 FAC 1 Others 1
Blackpool (Free on 1/7/2005) FL 15+4 FLC 2 FAC 1 Others 1+1
Rochdale (Free on 20/1/2006) FL 75+8/3 FLC 2/1 FAC 1/1 Others 2+2

DORNEY Jack Christopher
Born: Ashton-uner-Lyne, 9 January 1990
Height: 5'9" **Weight:** 10.2
Another of Bury's youth products, Jack is a versatile player who can feature wide on the right or left and up front. With three starts and a further four substitute appearances, Chris Casper's judgement was confirmed as Alan Knill continued to name Jack among his substitutes. He established himself as a good prospect.

Bury (From trainee on 8/12/2007) FL 3+4 FAC 0+2 Others 0+2

DOUGHTY Philip (Phil) Michael
Born: Kirkham, 6 September 1986
Height: 6'2" **Weight:** 13.2
Unable to get a game at Blackpool in 2007-08, Phil spent two months at Macclesfield, on loan to Luke Dimech's partner in the centre of defence, and although Macclesfield did not achieve a victory while he was involved, he proved a reliable defender. Nor did he have much luck in a second loan, when joining Accrington in January, his three games ending in defeat. It did not help that both clubs were having a bad time when he joined them and Phil will be looking to get back on course in the coming season after being released in the summer.

Blackpool (From trainee on 5/10/2004) FAC 0+1 Others 3
Macclesfield T (Loaned on 7/11/2007) FL 5+1
Accrington Stanley (Loaned on 18/1/2008) FL 3

DOUGLAS Jonathan
Born: Monaghan, 22 November 1981
Height: 5'10" **Weight:** 12.12
International Honours: RoI: 8; U21-1; Yth
Injury ruined much of Jonathan's season and his absence from the team coincided with a slump in Leeds' fortunes. He missed 17 games after United snatched a last-gasp draw at Walsall in December, when he was carried off in stoppage-time with a knee injury. Leeds won only five games while he was out and when he returned the club had a new manager, Gary McAllister. Once fit, Jonathan captained a side that picked up momentum to reach the play-offs, having a superb game as midfield anchorman in the Wembley-clinching 2-0 win at Carlisle. He was in good form earlier in the campaign, netting twice in the 4-2 victory over Millwall and being on target in the 4-0 thumping of Huddersfield, the week before his bad injury at the Banks' Stadium.

Blackburn Rov (From trainee on 10/2/2000) P/FL 14+2/1 FLC 1+2 FAC 1+4
Chesterfield (Loaned on 26/3/2003) FL 7/1
Blackpool (Loaned on 7/8/2003) FL 15+1/3 FLC 3 Others 1
Gillingham (Loaned on 10/3/2005) FL 10
Leeds U (Signed on 19/8/2005) FL 88+11/9 FLC 6+1 FAC 3 Others 5+1

DOUGLAS Robert (Rab) James
Born: Lanark, 24 April 1972
Height: 6'3" **Weight:** 14.12
Club Honours: S Div 3 '96; SPD '01, '02, '04; SLC '01, '04, '05;
International Honours: S:19
Recalled to the Leicester squad last February when Ben Alnwick was injured, Rab was an occasional substitute for the Foxes but used more as a goalkeeping coach between loan spells with Millwall, Wycombe and Plymouth. When Millwall had an injury crisis among their goalkeepers in September they took Rab for two months. During his time at the Den, the crowd really got behind him as he had some excellent games, proving to be strong in the air and an excellent shot-stopper. By his performances, the Scottish international added necessary experience to an essentially young side. Next stop was Wycombe, who also needed cover in October and the experienced goalkeeper made his debut in a 2-2 draw at Hereford in early December. With first-choice Frank Fielding facing a delay in the extension of his own loan, Rab made two more appearances in January, keeping clean sheets in both. The situation was even more pressing at Plymouth as Rab arrived for a week in March when Luke

McCormick was suspended. He made his solitary appearance for the Pilgrims in the 2-1 victory at Bristol City, having first met his team-mates at their pre-match meal in Taunton. Was released by Leicester at the end of the season.

Livingston (Free from Forth W on 26/10/1993) SL 72 SLC 1 SC 3 Others 1
Dundee (£1,000,000 on 1/8/1997) SL 117 SLC 8 SC 7 Others 1
Glasgow Celtic (£1,500,000 on 16/10/2000) SL 107+1 SLC 7 SC 17 Others 30
Leicester C (Free on 7/6/2005) FL 32 FLC 1 FAC 2
Millwall (Loaned on 14/9/2007) FL 7
Wycombe W (Loaned on 23/10/2007) FL 3
Plymouth Arg (Loaned on 14/3/2008) FL 1

DOUMBE Mathias Kouo
Born: Paris, France, 28 October 1979
Height: 6'1" **Weight:** 12.5
International Honours: France: Yth
Mathias, now a vastly experienced central-defender, had a frustrating season with Plymouth, making only ten League starts for the Pilgrims. When called upon, he again showed his pace, power and man-marking abilities. Despite his lack of first-team opportunities, Mathias agreed a further

two-year contract at the end of the season, making him Plymouth's longest-serving outfield player.
Hibernian (Signed from Paris St Germain, France, ex Nantes, on 26/10/2001) SL 44+1/2 SLC 5 SC 3
Plymouth Arg (Free on 8/6/2004) FL 106+4/3 FLC 3+1 FAC 4

DOWNES Aaron Terence
Born: Mudgee, New South Wales, Australia, 15 May 1985
Height: 6'3" **Weight:** 13.0
International Honours: Australia: U23; Yth
Aaron mysteriously suffered an uncertain season at the heart of Chesterfield's defence. A spate of early bookings suggested difficulty in getting to grips with the more direct forward play in League Two and trips around the world with Australia's Olympic team did not help him settle. The tidy defender who scooped the club's 'Player of the Year' awards in 2006-07 will, it is hoped, re-emerge when playing alongside the experienced Robert Page.
Chesterfield (Free from Frickley Ath on 29/7/2004) FL 110+6/7 FLC 5 FAC 2 Others 4/2

Aaron Downes

DOWNES Aidan
Born: Dublin, 24 July 1988
Height: 5'8" **Weight:** 11.7
International Honours: RoI: U21-3; Yth
The Everton Academy and reserve forward joined Yeovil in March, having scored on his debut for the Republic of Ireland under-21 team in October. Yet to make a first-team appearance for Everton, Aidan enjoyed a successful loan spell with Yeovil and scored the goal that made absolutely sure of League One safety. The winger-cum-striker left Everton at the end of the season when David Moyes released a number of young players, thus giving Yeovil manager Russell Slade the chance to clinch his signature.
Everton (£90,000 from Tolka Rov on 24/1/2006)
Yeovil T (Loaned on 27/3/2008) FL 3+2/1

DOWNING Stewart
Born: Middlesbrough, 22 July 1984
Height: 5'11" **Weight:** 10.6
Club Honours: FLC '04
International Honours: E: 18; B-2; U21-8; Yth
In another hectic season of progress and consolidation, Stewart was arguably the most consistent player at the Riverside. He started in all but one of Middlesbrough's 45 League and Cup games and was a playing substitute in the other, a 2-0 FA Cup victory at Mansfield. To the delight of the management, Stewart signed a new five-year deal in late February, immediately ending tiresome speculation that he was bound for Tottenham. During the season, he took his tally of England caps to 17 in away defeats by Russia and France and was named in Fabio Capello's 31-man squad for the summer friendlies against the United States and Trinidad & Tobago. To his personal satisfaction, Stewart was Middlesbrough's leading scorer with ten goals.
Middlesbrough (From trainee on 6/9/2001) PL 120+24/17 FLC 5+2/1 FAC 21+1/1 Others 17+1/1
Sunderland (Loaned on 29/10/2003) FL 7/3

DOWSON David
Born: Bishop Auckland, 12 September 1988
Height: 5'10" **Weight:** 12.1
Quick and direct, the Sunderland man improved Chesterfield's creativity after joining on loan in February. Although a striker by instinct, he was often played in a wide-left midfield berth and prospered, cutting in with purpose to score three times in nine starts. David's fourth-minute goal against Brentford in February

was reckoned to be the fastest by a Chesterfield player making his debut. He has yet to appear for Sunderland.
Sunderland *(From trainee on 12/7/2007)*
Chesterfield *(Loaned on 21/2/2008) FL 9+3/3*

DOYLE Colin Anthony
Born: Cork, 12 August 1985
Height: 6'5" **Weight:** 14.5
International Honours: RoI: 1; U21-4; Yth

Colin started the season as first-choice goalkeeper for Birmingham after the heroics in the Championship during 2006-07. He made his Premier League debut at Chelsea and participated in the next two home games before Steve Bruce opted to bring back the experienced Maik Taylor. Big and tall, Colin is aggressive and decisive when coming from his line.
Birmingham C *(From trainee on 2/7/2004) P/FL 22 FLC 3+1*
Chester C *(Loaned on 22/10/2004) Others 1*
Nottingham F *(Loaned on 3/12/2004) FL 2+1 FAC 1*
Millwall *(Loaned on 24/11/2005) FL 14*

DOYLE Kevin Edward
Born: Wexford, 18 September 1983
Height: 5'11" **Weight:** 12.6
Club Honours: Ch '06
International Honours: RoI: 18; U21-11

Although he was unable to repeat his scoring feats of the previous season, Kevin remained a vital member of Reading's attack. His total of six goals was scant reward for all his unselfish running up front, when he tried to take so much weight off the shoulders of his team-mates. He also played a number of games wide on the right of midfield as Reading tried to counter the loss through injury of orthodox winger Glen Little, but did not look especially comfortable. Kevin continued to be a regular choice for the Republic of Ireland squad and made his debut on the BBC television programme 'A Question of Sport'. Although there was speculation he might move on following Reading's relegation, he was quoted as saying he is happy to stay at the Madejski Stadium.
Reading *(£75,000 from Cork C on 5/8/2005) P/FL 103+10/37 FLC 2+2 FAC 1+3/1*

DOYLE Michael Paul
Born: Dublin, 8 July 1981
Height: 5'8" **Weight:** 11.0
International Honours: RoI: 1; U21-8
Coventry's combative central midfielder played in every game apart from four when he was suspended. His aggression

Michael Doyle

was more tempered last season and three of his suspended games were the result of an extremely unfortunate red card against West Bromwich in the FA Cup. Michael's strength is his energy – he runs miles in a game and closes down opponents. This was illustrated to great effect in the wins at Old Trafford and Blackburn. His passing ability, a delightful one setting up Jay Tabb's winner against Norwich, and he scored seven times, including two penalties and two in the home win over Plymouth. His best effort was the winner at home to Preston, a screamer from 25 yards. He lost the captaincy to Arjan De Zeeuw and later, having regained it, to Stephen Hughes, and was taken off penalties after a miss against Crystal Palace at Christmas.
Glasgow Celtic (From juniors on 1/8/1998) Coventry C (Free on 4/7/2003) FL 207+3/17 FLC 11/1 FAC 13

DOYLE Nathan Luke Robert
Born: Derby, 12 January 1987
Height: 5'11" **Weight:** 11.11
International Honours: E: Yth
Right-back Nathan had to wait until the final home game for his solitary League appearance of the season. He was outstanding in an unfamiliar left-back role following an injury to Henrik Pedersen early in the win against Crystal Palace that denied Hull's place in the play-offs. His end-of-season involvement became a fairy tale in the second leg of the Championship play-off semi-final against Watford. On the day that he became a father, Nathan's first senior goal in the last minute sparked wild celebrations at the KC Stadium and clinched the Tigers' first trip to Wembley, followed by promotion to the top flight for the first time in their history.
Derby Co (From trainee on 21/1/2004) FL 4+5 FAC 0+1
Notts Co (Loaned on 24/2/2006) FL 12
Bradford C (Loaned on 4/8/2006) FL 25+3 FLC 1 FAC 3 Others 1
Hull C (Signed on 31/1/2007) FL 1+1 FLC 1 FAC 1 Others 0+2/1

DOYLEY Lloyd Collin
Born: Whitechapel, 1 December 1982
Height: 6'0" **Weight:** 11.10
A polished defender, Lloyd claimed the right-back shirt for the first half of last season and was one of Watford's best players. Composed, reliable and determined, Lloyd also attacked with more conviction and claimed a number of assists early on. However, for some reason his form fell away at the turn of the year and he was relegated to the bench for

much of February and March. A former Watford trainee and local favourite, Lloyd is yet to score for Watford, his only club, despite making almost 200 first-team appearances.
Watford (From trainee on 8/3/2001) P/FL 157+24 FLC 12 FAC 3+4 Others 4

DRENCH Steven Mark
Born: Manchester, 11 September 1985
Height: 6'1" **Weight:** 12.9
International Honours: E: Sch
After breaking his arm in the previous season's Conference play-off, Steven was expected to start as Morecambe's first-choice goalkeeper. But Joe Lewis was signed on loan from Norwich and the former Blackburn man was mainly a substitute, limited to three League and three Cup appearances. He joined Southport on loan in January and helped them to clinch a place in the Unibond North play-offs before he was released by Morecambe.
Blackburn Rov (From trainee on 19/9/2002) Morecambe (Free on 24/11/2005) FL 3+1 FAC 1 Others 2

DROGBA Didier Yves Tebily
Born: Abidjan, Ivory Coast, 11 March 1978
Height: 6'2" **Weight:** 13.8
Club Honours: FLC '05, '07; PL '05, '06; CS '05
International Honours: Ivory Coast: 52
No other modern-day player divides public opinion like Didier, who could truly be said to have endured a season of highs and lows. His exploits the previous season saw him elected into the 'FIFPro World XI'. He became unsettled in September when his mentor Jose Mourinho left the club but let his prowess on the pitch do the talking with a string of inspired performances, scoring a series of spectacular goals including a brace against his favourite opposition Arsenal; a brilliant free-kick in the Carling Cup final at Wembley and the pair against Liverpool, in a bravura all-round performance, that clinched Chelsea's place in the Champions' League final. He can also play as an out-and-out right-winger as witnessed by his telling crosses for Michael Ballack to head home in successive matches against Manchester United and Newcastle. The African Cup of Nations fell away badly for his Ivory Coast side as, after a bright start, they were heavily defeated in the semi-finals by Egypt and again by Ghana in the third-place match. The Champions' League final was an awful disappointment for Didier as first he was denied a winner when his superb curling shot struck a post and then was

unnecessarily dismissed in extra-time, thus depriving the Blues of a penalty-taker.
Chelsea (£24,000,000 from Marseille, France, ex Levallois, Le Mans, Guingamp, on 23/7/2004) PL 87+23/50 FLC 7+4/6 FAC 10+2/4 Others 38+3/20

DRUMMOND Stewart James
Born: Preston, 11 December 1975
Height: 6'2" **Weight:** 13.8
International Honours: E: SP-13
Stewart thrived on responsibility at the New Meadow in 2007-08 and produced some commanding performances in 25 appearances, his most important goal being the equaliser at Bury in October that ended a slump in results. Having started the season as the Shrews' captain, although they were going through a difficult time it caused much surprise to the fans when he was allowed to rejoin his old club, Morecambe, in the January transfer window. Although he slotted immediately into the Morecambe midfield it took him time to settle into his old surroundings and just as he began to look more like his normal fluent self, an ankle injury caused him to miss the last four games. He was always a threat at corners and scored twice, to add to the three goals he collected for Shrewsbury.
Chester C (Free from Morecambe on 25/6/2004) FL 85+2/12 FLC 2 FAC 6/1 Others 1+2
Shrewsbury T (Free on 14/7/2006) FL 65+2/7 FLC 1 FAC 3 Others 4/1
Morecambe (£15,000 on 4/1/2008) FL 17+1/2 Others 1+1

DRURY Adam James
Born: Cambridge, 29 August 1978
Height: 5'10" **Weight:** 11.8
Club Honours: Div 1 '04
Adam managed just ten appearances for Norwich before a serious ankle injury ended his season in mid-October which, as well as being a real blow for the player, left a big gap in City's defence at a time when they were struggling for form and results. Recognised as one of the best defenders outside the Premiership, this tough-tackling left-back was in light training as the season drew to a close and will be chomping at the bit for a return to action.
Peterborough U (From trainee on 3/7/1996) FL 138+10/2 FLC 8 FAC 9 Others 10+1
Norwich C (£275,000 on 21/3/2001) P/FL 246+2/3 FLC 9 FAC 10 Others 3

D'SANE Roscoe Niquaye
Born: Epsom, 16 October 1980
Height: 5'7" **Weight:** 10.11
After arriving at Accrington from

Wimbledon in the summer, Roscoe was injured in pre-season and missed the first four games. Following an appearance from the bench against Peterborough, he scored in his first full game, a Johnstone's Paint Trophy tie against Oldham. He formed a useful partnership with Paul Mullin, scoring several important goals, and it was a surprise to many Stanley supporters when the striker was sold to Torquay in January.
Crystal Palace (From trainee on 29/6/1999. Freed during 2001 close season)
Southend U (Free from Slough T, ex Woking, on 8/11/2001) FL 1+1 (Free to Woking in January 2002)
Accrington Stanley (Free from AFC Wimbledon, ex Aldershot T, Wealdstone, on 5/7/2007) FL 18+4/7 FAC 1 Others 1/1

DUBERRY Michael Wayne
Born: Enfield, 14 October 1975
Height: 6'1" **Weight:** 13.6
Club Honours: FLC '98; ECWC '98; ESC '98
International Honours: E: U21-5
Michael began as first-choice Reading centre-back alongside Ivar Ingimarsson but injuries in the games against Chelsea and Fulham in the early part of the campaign cost him his place. He was not recalled for a run in the side until the last three games of the season, when the Wigan goalkeeper's brilliant save from Michael's header cost Reading a victory that might have kept them in the Premiership. Virtually unbeatable in the air and using his brain to save his legs, Michael has been offered a one-year extension to his current Reading contract.
Chelsea (From trainee on 7/6/1993) PL 77+9/1 FLC 8 FAC 12/2 Others 9
Bournemouth (Loaned on 29/9/1995) FL 7 Others 1
Leeds U (£4,000,000 + on 29/7/1999) P/FL 54+4/4 FLC 0+4 FAC 4+2 Others 9+1
Stoke C (Loaned on 15/10/2004) FL 15
Stoke C (Free on 3/3/2005) FL 80/1 FLC 2 FAC 5
Reading (£800,000 on 31/1/2007) PL 20+1 FLC 2 FAC 1

DUBLIN Dion
Born: Leicester, 22 April 1969
Height: 6'2" **Weight:** 12.4
Club Honours: Div 3 '91
International Honours: E: 4
Having just reached his 39th birthday, the immensely popular former England striker decided to hang up his boots at the end of the season after playing almost 750 competitive matches for his many clubs. His selection as Norwich's 'Player of the Season' was a fitting tribute to a great player and a true gentleman. Dion looked as if he could

continue for several seasons to come. His physical presence and clever use of the ball made him a match for the best defenders and he was on the end of crosses to score nine goals as well as creating numerous others. Occasionally used as a central defender, Dion will be very difficult to replace in the Canaries' squad and the warmth of many ovations for him at away grounds confirmed he had gained the respect of football fans across the country. He appears set to attain a career in the media following his retirement.
Norwich C (Free from Oakham U on 24/3/1988)
Cambridge U (Free on 2/8/1988) FL 133+23/52 FLC 8+2/5 FAC 21/10 Others 14+1/5
Manchester U (£1,000,000 on 7/8/1992) PL 4+8/2 FLC 1+1/1 FAC 1+1 Others 0+1
Coventry C (£2,000,000 on 9/9/1994) PL 144+1/61 FLC 11+2/4 FAC 13/7
Aston Villa (£5,750,000 on 6/11/1998) PL 120+35/48 FLC 13+2/7 FAC 5+2/1 Others 10+2/2
Millwall (Loaned on 28/3/2002) FL 5/2 Others 2/1
Leicester C (Free on 19/7/2004) FL 49+9/5 FLC 2 FAC 4+1/1
Glasgow Celtic (Free on 31/1/2006) SL 3+8/1 SLC 0+1/1
Norwich C (Free on 22/9/2006) FL 50+20/12 FLC 1+2/1 FAC 5+1/3

DUDFIELD Lawrence (Lawrie) George
Born: Southwark, 7 May 1980
Height: 6'1" **Weight:** 13.9
One of the most committed players in the Notts County squad, Lawrie is always prepared to chase lost causes and misplaced passes, of which there were a few, and run himself to a standstill. He never had the best of fortune in the penalty area and his lack of goals led to his release at the end of the season. Lawrie could be a good capture if he finds the right strike partner.
Leicester C (Signed from Kettering T on 6/6/1997) PL 0+2
Lincoln C (Loaned on 15/9/2000) FL 2+1
Chesterfield (Loaned on 14/12/2000) FL 4+10/3 Others 3+1/1
Hull C (£190,000 on 2/7/2001) FL 39+20/13 FLC 2 FAC 2/2 Others 3
Northampton T (Signed on 14/3/2003) FL 20+9/4 FLC 1+1 FAC 0+1 Others 0+2/2
Southend U (Signed on 5/2/2004) FL 29+20/9 FLC 1 Others 4+5/3
Northampton T (Free on 4/8/2005) FL 2+4/1 FLC 0+1
Boston U (Free on 31/8/2005) FL 21+15/5 FAC 1+2 Others 2
Notts Co (Free on 3/7/2006) FL 55+19/8 FLC 3+1/1 FAC 2+1/3 Others 2

Damien Duff

DUFF Damien Anthony
Born: Dublin, 2 March 1979
Height: 5'10" **Weight:** 12.0
Club Honours: FLC '02, '05; PL '05, '06; CS '05
International Honours: RoI: 68; B-1; Yth; Sch
Damien is a winger highly regarded at Newcastle, able to play on either flank, although preferring the left, and occasionally used in a more central role supporting the attack. A busy player with good close control and able to carry the ball when attacking with pace, he began the season recovering from surgery on an ankle injury incurred the previous April and had to wait until December to make his first appearance as a substitute in the home game with Derby. His skill excited the crowd and his display earned him a regular starting slot but when Kevin Keegan changed to a formation based on an attacking front three, Damien was largely confined to a role as substitute for the rest of the season, although he added a further Republic of Ireland international cap to his collection.
Blackburn Rov (Signed from Lourdes Celtic on 5/3/1996) P/FL 157+27/27 FLC 16+1/5 FAC 13+5/2 Others 4/1
Chelsea (£17,000,000 on 26/7/2003) PL 63+18/14 FLC 7+1/2 FAC 4+4 Others 21+7/3
Newcastle U (£5,000,000 on 26/7/2006) FL 32+6/1 FLC 1+1 FAC 3/1 Others 8+1

DUFF Michael James
Born: Belfast, 11 January 1978
Height: 6'1" **Weight:** 11.8
Club Honours: FAT '98; FC '99
International Honours: NI: 20
Michael scored Burnley's first goal of

the season in the opener against West Bromwich and for the first two months of the season showed all the defensive, and sometimes attacking, qualities that had made him one of the Clarets' star performers in 2006-07. He continued at right-back despite the arrival of Graham Alexander but suffered a serious knee injury against Crystal Palace at the end of September. Although expected to be out for the season, his recovery was faster than anticipated and following a successful run in the reserves, he returned for the final game, ironically at Palace.

Cheltenham T *(From trainee on 17/8/1996) FL 201/12 FLC 6 FAC 15 Others 9*
Burnley *(£30,000 on 8/7/2004) FL 126+9/3 FLC 10/1 FAC 3*

DUFF Shane Joseph
Born: Wroughton, 2 April 1982
Height: 6'1" **Weight:** 12.10
International Honours: NI: U21-1
Shane was again a mainstay of the Cheltenham defence, having recovered from a pre-season injury to begin his ninth campaign with the club in the centre of a new look back-four. He put in a series of notable performances before missing two months in the middle of the season with an Achilles injury. Ironically, this absence coincided with an upturn in the team's fortunes but Shane returned in February to replace the injured Gavin Caines and forged a new partnership with on-loan Bristol City defender Richard Keogh. A product of Town's youth policy, Shane has matured into a strong, well-organised defender and a senior professional at the club.

Cheltenham T *(From juniors on 20/10/2000) FL 155+7/2 FLC 2+1 FAC 8+1 Others 11/1*

DUFFY Ayden Stuart
Born: Kettering, 16 November 1986
Height: 5'8" **Weight:** 10.12
A goalkeeper who worked his way through the Lincoln youth set-up, Ayden was forced to wait until last April for his League bow when he replaced the injured Alan Marriott in a 2-1 win at Chester. Ayden retained the goalkeeping jersey for the remainder of the season and his form between the sticks was rewarded by the offer of a new one-year contract by manager Peter Jackson.

Lincoln C *(From trainee on 6/7/2006) FL 3+1*

DUFFY Darryl Alexander
Born: Glasgow, 16 April 1984
Height: 5'11" **Weight:** 12.1
Club Honours: S Div 1 '05; SLCC'04; Div 1 '08
International Honours: S: B-2; U21-8

Darryl signed a permanent contract with Swansea in the close season after impressing on loan from Hull towards the end of 2006-07. Despite starting in the first team, his lack of goals and a groin strain suffered at Leeds in September saw him struggle to claim a regular place for the remainder of the season.

Glasgow Rgrs *(From juniors on 1/7/2003) SL 0+1 SLC 0+1 Others 0+1*
Brechin C *(Loaned on 16/1/2004) SL 8/3*
Falkirk *(Signed on 25/6/2004) SL 55+2/27 SLC 5/4 SC 1 Others 5/6*
Hull C *(Signed on 11/11/2006) FL 9+15/3 FLC 0+3/1 FAC 0+1*
Hartlepool U *(Loaned on 3/11/2006) FL 10/5*
Swansea C *(Signed on 22/3/2007) FL 17+11/6 FLC 0+2 FAC 1+3 Others 3+2/1*

DUFFY Richard Michael
Born: Swansea, 30 August 1985
Height: 5'10" **Weight:** 10.4
International Honours: W: 13; U21-8; Yth
The young Portsmouth full-back returned for a fourth loan spell in three seasons at Coventry to fill a problem position but was injured at Watford in his second game and returned to Fratton Park. At his best Richard is an accomplished right-sided player with cool distribution and good positional play.

Swansea C *(From trainee on 3/9/2002) FL 16+2/1 FAC 3+1 Others 1*
Portsmouth *(£300,000 on 26/1/2004) PL 0+1 FLC 1*
Burnley *(Loaned on 24/9/2004) FL 3+4/1 FLC 2*
Coventry C *(Loaned on 27/1/2005) FL 14 FAC 1*
Coventry C *(Loaned on 1/7/2005) FL 30+2 FAC 2*
Coventry C *(Loaned on 23/10/2006) FL 13 FAC 1*
Swansea C *(Loaned on 11/1/2007) FL 8+3 FAC 1*
Coventry C *(Loaned on 21/3/2008) FL 2*

DUFFY Robert (Rob) James
Born: Swansea, 2 December 1982
Height: 6'1" **Weight:** 12.4
Club Honours: Div 1 '03
International Honours: W: Yth
Signed by Oxford in the Conference at the start of 2006-07, Rob was their top scorer. After breaking an arm in September, he recovered to sign on loan for Wrexham in the January transfer window. The target man was hardly used, coming off the bench only six times, all late in the game, in February and early March. He did not feature again and returned to Oxford in April. Is the brother of Richard Duffy, a Welsh international with Portsmouth.

Rushden & Diamonds *(From juniors on 7/7/2000) FL 8+21/1 FLC 0+1 FAC 3+1/3*

Others 1 (Freed during 2005 close season)
Wrexham *(Loaned from Oxford U, ex Cambridge U, Kettering T, Stevenage Borough, on 25/1/2008) FL 0+6*

DUGUID Karl Anthony
Born: Letchworth, 21 March 1978
Height: 5'11" **Weight:** 11.7
Colchester's club captain celebrated the 400th senior appearance of his career on the opening day at Sheffield United. Over the years, he has played all over the pitch for his one club, at right-back, left-back, right-wing, left-wing and up front. He started last season in defence, with Mark Yeates and Kevin McLeod as the regular wingers, but was later pushed up the right flank following Yeates' long-term injury. His performances were always full of energy and commitment. Transfer speculation in January came to nothing but he will be disappointed not to have scored and to have suffered the first relegation of a fine career.

Colchester U *(From trainee on 16/7/1996) FL 317+68/42 FLC 10+3 FAC 17+6/2 Others 12+5/1*

DUKE Matthew (Matt)
Born: Sheffield, 16 June 1977
Height: 6'5" **Weight:** 13.4
In the most successful season in Hull's history, as they reached the top flight for the first time with a Wembley play-off final victory, Matt was on an emotional roller coaster. Selected ahead of regular goalkeeper Bo Myhill for the Carling Cup tie at Crewe in August, he retained his place at Coventry, his first League start for 21 months. Matt's impressive performances meant he stayed for the next two games before he was cruelly sidelined by a thigh injury. Much worse was to follow in January when he was diagnosed with testicular cancer. Thankfully, successful removal of the tumour hastened his return to the KC Stadium. The esteem in which he is held was wonderfully demonstrated in April, when he received a standing ovation from supporters while warming up as an unused substitute in the home game against Watford.

Sheffield U *(Free from Alfreton T on 26/8/1999)*
Hull C *(£60,000 from Burton A on 23/7/2004) FL 5+3 FLC 2 Others 0+1*
Stockport Co *(Loaned on 5/8/2005) FL 3*
Wycombe W *(Loaned on 13/1/2006) FL 5*

DUNBAVIN Ian Stuart
Born: Huyton, 27 May 1980
Height: 6'2" **Weight:** 13.0
Freed by Halifax in the summer, Ian started last season as Accrington's

number-two goalkeeper, though he was called upon in September when first choice Kenny Arthur broke a leg. He had an unbroken run of 22 League matches before losing his place in February to a fit-again Arthur at a time when Stanley had suffered five defeats in six games. Stanley's poor defensive record was certainly not down to Ian alone and he was outstanding at times, especially in home defeats by Wycombe and Rotherham. Ian's displays certainly restricted the deficit and he deservedly collected 'Man of the Match' awards in both games.
Liverpool *(From trainee on 26/11/1998)*
Shrewsbury T *(Free on 17/1/2000) FL 91+5 FLC 3 FAC 6 Others 7 (Freed during 2004 close season)*
Accrington Stanley *(Free from Halifax T, following loan period at Scarborough, on 2/8/2006) FL 44+2 FLC 2 FAC 2 Others 1*

DUNCAN Derek Henry Junior
Born: Newham, 23 April 1987
Height: 5'9" **Weight:** 10.12
Wycombe snapped up this pacy winger in June after Grays agreed to his release, having signed him from Leyton Orient only four weeks earlier. He made his debut for the Chairboys as a 77th-minute substitute in the Johnstone's Paint Trophy tie at Swansea in December, his only appearance as it turned out. He was subsequently loaned to Lewes in November for two months. With a year left on his contract at Wycombe, Derek will hope for more first-team opportunities.
Leyton Orient *(From trainee on 1/8/2006) FL 6+14 FAC 0+3 Others 3+3/1*
Wycombe W *(Free on 3/7/2007) Others 0+1*

DUNCUM Samuel (Sam)
Born: Sheffield, 18 February 1987
Height: 5'9" **Weight:** 11.2
Sam came up through Rotherham's junior ranks and is a pacy winger who can cross the ball equally well with either foot. He was another player who struggled to earn a regular place and was loaned out to non-League football for much of the campaign. Was released in the summer.
Rotherham U *(From trainee on 3/8/2006) FL 2+5 FLC 0+1 Others 0+1*

DUNFIELD Terence (Terry)
Born: Vancouver, Canada, 20 February 1982
Height: 5'10" **Weight:** 11.3
International Honours: Canada: U23-1; Yth; E: Yth
Having been released by Worcester and living in Macclesfield, Terry sought a trial at the Moss Rose in the summer of 2007.

He made such an excellent impression in both the pre-season matches and in training that he was immediately awarded a contract. A midfield dynamo, Terry has been almost ever-present throughout the season, enthusiastically covering ground whatever the status of the game, and was given the responsibility of captaincy for a period. His one goal came from a well taken free-kick against Chester early in the season. Terry was voted 'Player of the Year' by the supporters.
Manchester C *(From trainee on 5/5/1999) PL 0+1*
Bury *(Loaned on 16/8/2002) FL 15/2 FLC 3*
Bury *(Free on 13/12/2002) FL 48+11/3 FLC 0+1 Others 3+1/1 (Freed during 2005 close season)*
Macclesfield T *(Free, following injury and a spell with Worcester C, on 31/7/2007) FL 40+1/1 FLC 1 FAC 1*

DUNN Christopher (Chris)
Michael
Born: Havering, 23 October 1987
Height: 6'4" **Weight:** 12.5

Chris made his debut for Northampton in the last League game of the season, a 2-1 victory over Tranmere Rovers. It was a good way to end a run of 78 consecutive League and Cup games as substitute goalkeeper. Chris grew in confidence as the match progressed and looks to have a bright future.
Northampton *(From trainee on 08/01/2007) FL 1*

DUNN David John Ian
Born: Great Harwood, 27 December 1979
Height: 5'10" **Weight:** 12.3
Club Honours: FLC '02
International Honours: E: 1; U21-20; Yth
David had a reasonable season for Blackburn when he was played in central midfield. His fitness levels improved, his tackling back was more certain and his ability on the ball continued to make him prominent. However, he would have liked to do better in the final third, often failing either to wriggle through and create chances for himself or slip the killer pass

David Dunn

to a team-mate. He ended the season struggling with niggling injuries.

Blackburn Rov (From trainee on 30/9/1997) P/FL 120+16/30 FLC 14+3/5 FAC 11+2/3 Others 3+1
Birmingham C (£5,500,000 on 9/7/2003) P/FL 46+12/7 FLC 2+3 FAC 5+1/1
Blackburn Rov (£2,200,000 on 17/1/2007) PL 32+10/1 FLC 3 FAC 2+1 Others 5+1

DUNNE Alan James
Born: Dublin, 23 August 1982
Height: 5'10" **Weight:** 12.0
Alan, a no-nonsense Millwall midfield player who is strong in the challenge and has an eye for goal, was unfortunately dogged by injury in 2007-08. Having to play a bit part for most of the season, he was sorely missed in the middle of the park, where his character shines through. An injury-free run would suit him and the club.

Millwall (From trainee on 17/3/2000) FL 108+15/12 FLC 7+1/2 FAC 7/2 Others 1

DUNNE Richard Patrick
Born: Dublin, 21 September 1979
Height: 6'1" **Weight:** 14.0
Club Honours: FAYC '98; Div 1 '02
International Honours: Rol: 42; B-1; U21-4; Yth (UEFA-U18 '98); Sc
For the fourth season in succession, Manchester City's official supporters' club selected Richard as their 'Player of the Year'. That unique achievement is confirmation enough of the City captain's magnificent form that has made him one of the most highly-rated and consistent centre-backs in the Premiership. The big Republic of Ireland defender developed his professionalism even further, leading by example and producing many fine performances at club and international level. Not least, of course, in City's splendid 2-1 victory in the Manchester derby. No wonder he's a fans' favourite.

Everton (From trainee on 8/10/1996) PL 53+7 FLC 4 FAC 8
Manchester C (£3,000,000 on 20/10/2000) P/FL 257+6/7 FLC 11 FAC 25 Others 3+1

DYER Alex Craig
Born: Knowsley, 1 June 1990
Height: 5'8" **Weight:** 11.7
Alex just muscled his way into a place in Northampton's midfield and celebrated by scoring a goal on his full debut. With the ability to get forward and bring others into the game, he is one for the future. He also joined the club's exclusive list of 17-year-old scorers.

Northampton T (From trainee on 8/11/2007) FL 3+3/1 FLC 1 FAC 0+1 Others 1

DYER Bruce Antonio Noel Emmanuel
Born: Ilford, 13 April 1975
Height: 6'0" **Weight:** 11.3
International Honours: E: U21-11
Bruce started fit and well at Doncaster after his injury problems of the previous season. Although taking a full part in the pre-season friendlies, his only competitive game was as a substitute against Bradford in the first round of the Johnstone's Paint Trophy. He went on loan to Rotherham, making three appearances, and was released by Doncaster shortly after his return. Bruce continued to train at Doncaster before ending his season on non-contract terms, linking well with other forwards in his three substitute appearances.

Watford (From trainee on 19/4/1993) FL 29+2/6 FLC 4/2 FAC 1 Others 2/1
Crystal Palace (£1,100,000 on 10/3/1994) P/FL 95+40/37 FLC 9+5/1 FAC 7+3/6 Others 3+2
Barnsley (£700,000 on 23/10/1998) FL 149+33/59 FLC 11+1/4 FAC 5+2/3 Others 2+1/3
Watford (Free on 10/7/2003) FL 39+29/12 FLC 6+2/2 FAC 1+2
Stoke C (Free on 4/8/2005) FL 2+9 FLC 1
Millwall (Loaned on 4/11/2005) FL 9+1/2
Sheffield U (Loaned on 27/1/2006) FL 3+2/1
Doncaster Rov (Free on 5/6/2006) FL 9+6/1 FAC 0+1 Others 1+1
Bradford C (Loaned on 31/1/2007) FL 2+3/1
Rotherham U (Loaned on 13/9/2007) FL 3
Chesterfield (Free on 27/3/2008) FL 0+3

DYER Kieron Courtney
Born: Ipswich, 29 December 1978
Height: 5'7" **Weight:** 9.7
International Honours: E: 33; B-3; U21-11; Yth
A summer signing from Newcastle, the West Ham midfielder is very quick and has good control and pace. On his debut at Birmingham, he caused their defence problems and was brought down for the penalty that eventually won the game for the Hammers. Disaster struck at Bristol Rovers in the Carling Cup when, after nine minutes, he suffered an horrific injury that resulted in a double fracture of his right leg. This forced him to miss the rest of the season but as the campaign ended, Kieron was running again and on course for a complete recovery.

Ipswich T (From trainee on 3/1/1997) FL 79+12/9 FLC 11/1 FAC 5 Others 5+1/2
Newcastle U (£6,000,000 on 16/7/1999) PL 169+21/23 FLC 6+3/3 FAC 17+1/5 Others 30+3/5
West Ham U (£6,000,000 on 16/8/2007) PL 2 FLC 1

DYER Lloyd Richard
Born: Birmingham, 13 September 1982
Height: 5'10" **Weight:** 11.4
Club Honours: AMC '08; Div 2 '08
Lloyd was one of a number of MK Dons players whose game stepped up several notches following the arrival of Paul Ince. A quick, left-footed winger, he thrived when playing on either side of the front three ,often favoured by the manager, and his precise shooting brought a double-figure goal return. Lloyd also set up numerous goals and chances with his accurate crossing, did his fair share of defensive tracking back and was unsurprisingly chosen in the PFA League Two select team.

West Bromwich A (Signed from juniors at Aston Villa on 9/7/2001) P/FL 2+19/2 FLC 2 FAC 0+2
Kidderminster Hrs (Loaned on 5/9/2003) FL 5+2/1
Coventry C (Loaned on 22/3/2005) FL 6
Queens Park Rgrs (Loaned on 27/9/2005) FL 15
Millwall (Free on 31/1/2006) FL 2+4
MK Dons (Free on 2/8/2006) FL 82+4/16 FLC 1+3 FAC 2 Others 3+2

DYER Nathan Antone Jonah
Born: Trowbridge, 29 November 1987
Height: 5'6" **Weight:** 9.0
After a tentative 2006–07 season at Southampton, Nathan showed some scintillating form until a tendon injury, requiring surgery, halted his progress in early December. A quick, tricky dribbler, Nathan passes and crosses well, is improving as a striker and tackles back to good effect. He was greatly missed but made a couple of cameo appearances from the bench at the end of the season, looking full of vim. By then, his year had been seriously marred by well-documented events.

Southampton (From trainee on 13/10/2005) FL 35+17/1 FLC 3+3/2 FAC 2+1
Burnley (Loaned on 28/10/2005) FL 4+1/2

DZEMAILI Blerim
Born: Tetovo, Macedonia, 12 April 1986
Height: 5'10" **Weight:** 11.7
International Honours: Switzerland: 7
Blerim joined Bolton in the summer with a fine pedigree, having captained FC Zurich at the age of 20. A member of the Swiss national team, he was a young player of whom big things were expected. However, with injury being a contributory factor, the skilful midfielder made only one appearance last season, as a substitute in the FA Cup defeat by Sheffield United.

Bolton W (Free from FC Zurich, Switzerland on 6/7/2007) FAC 0+1

E

EAGLES Christopher (Chris) Mark

Born: Hemel Hempstead, 19 November 1985
Height: 6'0" **Weight:** 10.8
Club Honours: FAYC '03
International Honours: E: Yth

A talented right-sided Manchester United midfielder who is highly regarded for his dribbling and close control, Chris made a flurry of Premiership appearances as a substitute at the start of the campaign, combined with a single Carling Cup outing against Coventry in October and a Champions' League appearance against AS Roma in December.
Manchester U (From trainee on 25/7/2003) PL 2+4/1 FLC 2+4 FAC 1 Others 2+2
Watford (Loaned on 21/1/2005) FL 10+3/1
Sheffield Wed (Loaned on 4/8/2005) FL 21+4/3
Watford (Loaned on 6/1/2006) FL 16+1/3 FAC 1 Others 0+1

EARDLEY Neal James

Born: Llandudno, 6 November 1988
Height: 5'9" **Weight:** 10.7
International Honours: W: 7; U21-4; Yth

Neal was Oldham's most-used player and also skippered the side on several occasions. Although it was only his second full campaign, the young right-back shows a maturity beyond his years and made history as Oldham's youngest-ever full international on his Wales debut in September. A solid defender and composed figure, he poses a huge threat when raiding forward with his deadly-accurate range of crossing. Unsurprisingly linked with several higher division clubs, Neal continues to hit new heights and was tried in central midfield towards the end of the season. He ended on a high with two excellent goals in the last-day win at Crewe, taking his tally for the season to six.
Oldham Ath (From trainee on 19/9/2006) FL 77+2/8 FLC 3 FAC 8 Others 2

EARNSHAW Robert

Born: Mulfulira, Zambia, 6 April 1981
Height: 5'8" **Weight:** 10.10
International Honours: W: 38; U21-10; Yth

After arriving from Norwich as Derby's record signing, Robert endured a frustrating season and, in March, lost his place in the Welsh squad. The striker has a good scoring record at Championship level but it was not easy to play in attack for Derby when so few chances were

Robert Earnshaw

created. Even so, Robert was not the only one to be puzzled by the fact that neither Billy Davies, who signed him, nor Paul Jewell gave him a sustained run in the side. Most of his appearances were from the bench and his first Derby goal was of scant consolation, coming in a crushing home defeat by Preston in the FA Cup. His first in the Premiership served only to prod Arsenal into further activity. Robert has good pace and is a lively forward but had to snatch at brief opportunities. Was transferred to Nottingham Forest for £2.6 million on 30 May.
Cardiff C *(From trainee on 4/8/1998) FL 141+37/85 FLC 6+2/10 FAC 11+2/9 Others 5+1/1*
Morton *(Loaned on 20/1/2000) SL 3/2 SC 1*
West Bromwich A *(£3,500,000 + on 1/9/2004) PL 22+21/12 FLC 2+1/2 FAC 3+1/3*
Norwich C *(£3,500,000 on 31/1/2006) FL 41+4/27 FLC 1 FAC 1*
Derby Co *(£3,500,000 on 29/6/2007) PL 7+15/1 FLC 1 FAC 0+2/1*

EASTER Jermaine Maurice
Born: Cardiff, 15 January 1982
Height: 5'8" **Weight:** 12.4
International Honours: W: 7; Yth
Wycombe's prolific striker began the season as first choice, scoring two penalties early on amid constant speculation about interest from other clubs. Plymouth had a bid turned down in August and the uncertainty began to affect his game. He was dropped at the end of September before Plymouth landed their man, on loan at the end of October and permanently, on a two-and-a-half year contract, when the transfer window opened in January. He is a powerful striker with pace to burn and his willingness to work, including defensive closing-down, impressed Plymouth fans. His early appearances were as a substitute and Jermaine notched his first goal with a clinical strike against West Bromwich. When he forced his way into the starting line-up, his output improved, with three goals in the final seven games. He remained in the Wales squad but a knee injury kept him out of the end-of-season games against Iceland and Holland.
Wolverhampton W *(From trainee on 6/7/2000)*
Hartlepool U *(Free on 17/3/2001) FL 0+27/2 Others 0+3*
Cambridge U *(Loaned on 6/2/2004) FL 25+14/8 FLC 1 FAC 1 Others 2/1*
Boston U *(Free on 15/3/2005) FL 5+4/3*
Stockport Co *(Free on 14/7/2005) FL 18+1/8 FLC 1 FAC 3/3*
Wycombe W *(£80,000 on 30/11/2006) FL 44+15/21 FLC 7/6 FAC 1/1 Others 2+1*
Plymouth Arg *(£210,000 on 26/10/2007) FL 20+12/6 FAC 2*

EASTON Clint Jude
Born: Barking, 1 October 1977
Height: 5'11" **Weight:** 10.8
Club Honours: Div 2 '98
International Honours: E: Yth
Arriving from Gillingham in the summer with a reputation as a left-back, Clint made his contribution to Hereford's promotion from the left of midfield. His ability to play a killer pass soon established him as an important member of the side and a remarkable number of early-season goals arrived with 'assist – Easton' marked against them. Clint also scored important goals – two against promotion

rivals Peterborough and Darlington – and his ability as one of Hereford's dead-ball specialists resulted in many more. His experience was crucial to a mainly youthful side during the tense run-in.
Watford *(From trainee on 5/7/1996) P/FL 50+14/1 FLC 4+4/1 FAC 3+1 Others 3*
Norwich C *(£200,000 on 19/6/2001) FL 41+9/5 FLC 2 FAC 0+2 Others 3*
Wycombe W *(Free on 20/7/2004) FL 69+8/2 FLC 3 FAC 1 Others 4+2/2*
Gillingham *(Free on 31/7/2006) FL 26+6/1 FLC 1 FAC 2 Others 1*
Hereford U *(Free on 30/7/2007) FL 36+3/3 FLC 2/1 FAC 2+1 Others 1*

Clint Easton

EASTON Craig
Born: Airdrie, 26 February 1979
Height: 5'10" **Weight:** 11.3
International Honours: S: U21-21; Yth
Having left Leyton Orient for Swindon in the summer, Craig had to settle for a place as an unused substitute in the opening game. He started the second game against Luton, scored the winner on his debut, and went on to make a useful contribution with his goals through the season. Craig is a real box-to-box performer with his strong, energetic running through midfield, usually in a central position. He played on the right against Huddersfield and celebrated with two goals.
Dundee U (From juniors on 31/8/1995) SL 162+44/12 SLC 15+4/4 SC 19+1/2
Livingston (Free on 1/7/2004) SL 24+6/3 SLC 3/1 SC 2/1
Leyton Orient (Free on 21/7/2005) FL 65+6/ 5 FLC 2 FAC 6/1 Others 2
Swindon T (Free on 10/8/2007) FL 40/6 FLC 1 FAC 3 Others 1

EASTWOOD Freddy
Born: Epsom, 29 October 1983
Height: 5'11" **Weight:** 12.0
Club Honours: Div 1 '06
International Honours: W: 9
Signed from Southend in the summer, Freddy is an exciting forward and had a wonderful start for Wolverhampton, scoring six times. This included two against Blackpool, when his willingness to take people on and shoot promised much. Freddy qualified for Wales through a grandparent and hit a fine goal on his debut in Bulgaria, scoring another in Slovakia. It all went sour when he found himself out of the Wolverhampton team after a lacklustre display against Hull. On a rare start, he missed a penalty at Ipswich and hit the woodwork in other matches. Freddy did not begin a club game in 2008, despite some useful contributions as substitute and two more goals for Wales, and was placed on the transfer list in May.
Southend U (Signed from Grays Ath, ex trainee at West Ham U, on 4/10/2004) FL 106+9/53 FLC 4+1/4 FAC 6/3 Others 7+2/5
Wolverhampton W (£1,500,000 on 13/7/ 2007) FL 10+21/3 FLC 2/1 FAC 0+2

EBANKS-BLAKE Sylvan
Augustus
Born: Cambridge, 29 March 1986
Height: 5'10" **Weight:** 13.4
Club Honours: FAYC '03
Sylvan started well with a great strike for Plymouth's winner in the 3-2 victory at Hull on the opening day and cemented his status as a fans' favourite and top

prospect, scoring 11 League goals by the New Year. His main attributes are his pace, strength in holding off defenders and clinical eye for goal. His form persuaded Wolverhampton to bid £1.5-million in the January transfer window, thereby triggering a clause in his contract. He looked the sort of young striker Wolves needed and did not take long to get off the mark but he had only two goals after seven appearances. A winner at Colchester and a brace at home to Southampton showing his knack in front of goal and of his two at Charlton one, after a brilliant run, was voted second-best goal of the season in the League. That made it seven in seven games and his final total of 12 made him top scorer for a club he only joined in January. Sylvan was the leading Championship scorer with 23 and seems to have the right attitude to make the most of his ability.
Manchester U (From trainee on 24/2/2005) FLC 1+1/1
Plymouth Arg (£200,000 + on 18/7/2006) FL 49+17/21 FLC 4/1 FAC 3+1/1
Wolverhampton W (£1,500,000 on 10/1/2008) FL 20/12

EBOUE Emmanuel (Manu)
Born: Abidjan, Ivory Coast, 4 June 1983
Height: 5'10" **Weight:** 11.3
International Honours: Ivory Coast: 23
Manu remained something of an enigma at Arsenal. Originally signed as a right-back, he has been ousted from that spot by Bacary Sagna. He played on the right of midfield for most of the campaign but contributed no goals and very little in the way of quality wing play. Yet he was a constant starter as he made 23 Premier League appearances despite missing several games when with the Ivory Coast at the African Cup of Nations. Manu was involved ten times in the Champions' League as well as three appearances in domestic Cups.
Arsenal (£1,540,000 from Beveren, Belgium, ex ASEC Mimosas Abidjan, on 1/1/2005) PL 54+12 FLC 5+2/1 FAC 7 Others 23+4/1

ECHANOMI Efe
Born: Nigeria, 27 September 1986
Height: 5'7" **Weight:** 11.7
Efe returned to the Leyton Orient first team having missed most of the previous season through injury. Used mainly as cover for Adam Boyd and Wayne Gray, Efe made various substitute appearances during the season, scoring the only goal in the Johnstone's Paint Trophy game at Notts County. He was out of contract during the summer.
Leyton Orient (From trainee on 19/7/2006) FL 4+47/8 FLC 2+1 FAC 0+2 Others 2+1/1

ECKERSLEY Adam James
Born: Worsley, 7 September 1985
Height: 5'9" **Weight:** 11.13
International Honours: E: Yth
The left-back had two spells with Port Vale, one on loan. He first appeared on loan from Manchester United in October but was sent off on his debut against Brighton. Only one more game followed before a bad leg injury in training put him out for ten weeks, so he returned to Old Trafford. In January, Adam joined the Vale until the end of the season on a free transfer and became a regular in the side. A strong tackler with a sharp turn of pace, he scored one goal, a rocket shot from 30 yards against Yeovil. At the end of the season, he was a victim of the fall-out from relegation and released on a free transfer along with a number of others.
Manchester U (From trainee on 2/7/2004) FLC 1
Barnsley (Loaned on 8/11/2007) FL 6
Port Vale (Signed on 12/10/2007) FL 18/1

Manu Eboue

EDDS Gareth James
Born: Sydney, Australia, 3 February 1981
Height: 5'11" **Weight:** 10.12
International Honours: Australia: U23-2; Yth
In and out of the MK Dons' starting team for the first few months of the campaign, Gareth then had to sit out the beginning of 2008 because of injury, returning just in time to be an unused substitute in the Johnstone's Paint Trophy final success. Whenever called upon, he showed great enthusiasm, whether at right-back or in midfield, and remained popular with the growing band of supporters. Was released at the end of the campaign.
Nottingham F (From trainee on 19/2/1998) FL 11+5/1 FAC 1
Swindon T (Free on 9/8/2002) FL 8+6 FLC 0+1 FAC 1 Others 2
Bradford C (Free on 14/7/2003) FL 19+4 FLC 1
MK Dons (Free on 23/7/2004) FL 97+25/10 FLC 6+2 FAC 9+1/2 Others 6+1

EDGAR David Edward
Born: Ontario, Canada, 19 May 1987
Height: 6'2" **Weight:** 12.0
International Honours: Canada: Yth
David is a Newcastle centre-back and the son of former club goalkeeper Eddie. Tall and composed for his age, his leadership skills were recognised at club level when he was appointed captain of the reserves and at international level when he captained Canada in the FIFA under-20 World Championships played in his native country in July 2007. He was called into the full national squad for a match against Iceland in August but did not feature. He made an early-season substitute appearance for Newcastle but after a number of selections as an unused substitute, had to wait until late March before setting foot on the pitch again. After that, he played in most of the remaining games, impressing with his calmness under pressure.
Newcastle U (From trainee on 20/9/2006) PL 4+4/1 FLC 0+1 FAC 1

EDGHILL Richard Arlon
Born: Oldham, 23 September 1974
Height: 5'9" **Weight:** 11.5
International Honours: E: B-1; U21-3
This extremely experienced defender moved to Macclesfield from Bradford in the summer. In the early part of the season Richard regularly appeared out of position in the centre of the defence in a back-four formation. Despite his lack of height, Richard drew on his vast experience to defend solidly but moved to his more accustomed right-back position when Dave Morley regained full fitness.

Unfortunately Richard broke two ribs in the home match against Brentford at the beginning of November and only made one further appearance because younger defenders were preferred. Was out of contract in the summer and looking for a new club.
Manchester C (From trainee on 15/7/1992) P/FL 178+3/1 FLC 17 FAC 8+1 Others 3
Birmingham C (Loaned on 14/11/2000) FL 3
Wigan Ath (Free on 21/10/2002) Others 1
Sheffield U (Free on 17/1/2003) FL 0+1
Queens Park Rgrs (Free on 22/8/2003) FL 28+12 FLC 3 FAC 1 Others 1+1
Bradford C (Free on 12/8/2005) FL 39+4/1 FLC 2 FAC 3/1 Others 2
Macclesfield T (Free on 17/7/2007) FL 13+2 FLC 1

EDMAN Erik Kenneth
Born: Huskvarna, Sweden, 11 November 1978
Height: 5'10" **Weight:** 12.6
International Honours: Sweden: 53
Recruited by Wigan from Rennes in the January transfer window, the full-back played only five League games before a knee injury, that happened when he made a goal-line clearance at Blackburn, ended his season. Composed and assured at left-back, Erik is a stylish player possessing an effective tackle and with a good turn of pace. Combined with his close control, this enables him to raid down the wing and supply dangerous crosses. He made his Blues' debut in the home win over Derby and became an instant favourite with the fans. Sadly, after tearing anterior cruciate ligaments in his left knee, he would miss Sweden's involvement in the Euro 2008 finals and the start of Wigan's fourth season in the Premier League.
Tottenham H (£1,300,000 from SC Heerenveen, Holland, ex Helsingborg, on 5/8/2004) PL 31/1 FAC 2+1 (Transferred to Rennes, France on 31/8/2005)
Wigan Ath (£500,000 from Rennes, France on 23/1/2008) PL 5

[EDUARDO] DA SILVA Eduardo Alves
Born: Rio de Janeiro, Brazil, 25 February 1983
Height: 5'9" **Weight:** 11.0
International Honours: Croatia: 22; U21
The Croatian international joined Arsenal from Dinamo Zagreb in the summer, having impressed both against the club in the previous season's Champions' League qualifier, where he became the scorer of the first-ever competitive goal at the Emirates Stadium, and against England in a Euro 2008 qualifying tie. He is possibly the most natural finisher at the club and is

clinical when bearing down on goal, but is more than just a striker. He has a great range of passing and is also very quick, in both thought and movement. Eduardo was just starting to forge a promising partnership in attack with Emmanuel Adebayor when he suffered an horrific ankle injury at the start of the Premier League game against Birmingham. Sadly, he will be out of action for a minimum of nine months and his loss coincided with Arsenal's slide in form and ultimate disappointment at the end of the season. All Arsenal fans wish him a speedy and successful recovery.
Arsenal (£10,000,000 from Dinamo Zagreb, Croatia, ex Nova Kennedy, Bangu - loan, Inker Zapresic - loan, on 3/8/2007) PL 13+4/4 FLC 3+2/4 FAC 2+1/1 Others 4+2/3

EDWARDS Carlos Akenhaton
Born: Port of Spain, Trinidad, 24 October 1978
Height: 5'11" **Weight:** 11.9
Club Honours: AMC '05; Ch '07
International Honours: Trinidad & Tobago: 57
Sunderland's flying right-winger was again hampered by injuries, picking up hamstring trouble at Birmingham in the second match of last season and suffering a broken leg against Derby in December. A Trinidad and Tobago international, Carlos is an excellent crosser, capable of shooting from long range with either foot and can skip past defenders with ease. His return to the first team in March coincided with a run of positive results that enabled Sunderland to secure their Premier League status.
Wrexham (£125,000 from Defence Force, Trinidad on 8/8/2000) FL 144+22/23 FLC 4+2/1 FAC 3 Others 6/1
Luton T (Free on 1/8/2005) FL 64+4/8 FLC 4+1 FAC 1
Sunderland (£1,400,000 on 4/1/2007) P/FL 26+2/5 FAC 0+1

EDWARDS David Alexander
Born: Pontesbury, 3 February 1986
Height: 5'11" **Weight:** 11.2
International Honours: W: 5; U21-8; Yth
David was Kevin Blackwell's first signing for Luton, from Shrewsbury at a fee set by tribunal. The captain of the Welsh under-21 team is a product of Shrewsbury's youth academy and comfortably made the transition to League One after his debut in the opening game. A right-sided midfield player, equally at home in a holding role, he tackles well and passes accurately. His constant running makes him both a provider as well as a scorer, with goals in successive games against

Tranmere and Bristol Rovers. David made his full international debut for Wales as a substitute against the Republic of Ireland and started against Germany four days later. In the last minute of his final game, he was close to a winner in the FA Cup third round against Liverpool but a few days later the administrator sold him to Wolverhampton and he scored within nine minutes of his debut. His surging runs enlivened games and he often threatened further goals. He added another appearance for Wales after his move but was injured just as he was settling in. When he returned against Ipswich, he hurt a knee early on and his season was curtailed.
Shrewsbury T (From trainee on 5/1/2004) FL 82+21/12 FLC 2 FAC 5/2 Others 3+2/1
Luton T (£250,000 + on 7/8/2007) FL 18+1/4 FLC 2 FAC 4 Others 1
Wolverhampton W (£675,000 on 14/1/2008) FL 10/1

EDWARDS Michael (Mike)
Born: Hessle, 25 April 1980
Height: 6'1" **Weight:** 12.0
Victim of a dreadful freak injury in pre-season, Mike had to rebuild his fitness until early 2008 before he could resume playing. He was sadly missed, being simply the best player at Notts County. A cool and consistent central defender, he always reads the game and his opponents well. It is hoped he will enjoy better fortune and again be the first name on the team sheet.
Hull C (From trainee on 16/7/1998) FL 165+13/6 FLC 8+1 FAC 11/2 Others 9+1
Colchester U (Free on 27/3/2003) FL 3+2
Grimsby T (Free on 7/8/2003) FL 32+1/1 FAC 2 Others 1
Notts Co (Free on 2/7/2004) FL 116+3/11 FLC 7/1 FAC 3 Others 1

EDWARDS Paul
Born: Manchester, 1 January 1980
Height: 5'11" **Weight:** 10.12
The tricky left-sided player joined Port Vale on a free transfer from Oldham and made his debut as a substitute against Wrexham in the Carling Cup before establishing a regular place. He scored one of the club's goals of the season against Cheltenham after a mazy run in a 3-0 victory. He can bamboozle defences with dazzling wing play on his day and filled in at left-back a number of times. His one-footedness was sometimes exploited by opponents, leading to a spell out of the team under new manager Lee Sinnott. Paul complained in the Press and was recalled against Yeovil, heading a goal in a 2-2 draw. A leg injury against Tranmere ended his season early.

Doncaster Rov (Free from Ashton U on 2/2/1998) FL 5+4 (Freed during 1998 close season)
Swindon T (Free from Leigh RMI, ex Knutsford T, Altrincham, on 17/8/2001) FL 14+6 FLC 0+1 FAC 1/1 Others 1
Wrexham (Free on 12/7/2002) FL 73+6/4 FLC 3 FAC 0+1 Others 3
Blackpool (Free on 26/7/2004) FL 22+6/3 FAC 1 Others 2
Oldham Ath (Free on 5/8/2005) FL 39+21 FLC 1+1 FAC 2+2 Others 1+1
Port Vale (Free on 19/7/2007) FL 17+8/2 FLC 0+1 FAC 2 Others 1

EDWARDS Philip Lee
Born: Bootle, 8 November 1985
Height: 5'10" **Weight:** 11.9
Club Honours: FC '06
As in the previous season, Philip did not start as first choice at Accrington but as a defender well capable of filling any of the back four positions. He more than proved his capability when Peter Cavanagh suffered a long-term injury and was frequently Stanley' best defender. Several times he was moved into the centre of defence to shore up what had been a problem position for Stanley all season. One of the few successes of a difficult campaign came against Dagenham in April and Philip marked his 100th Stanley appearance by scoring the only goal of the game – and his only one of the season. In the latter stages of the campaign, he was easily Stanley's best player, being truly outstanding at times, and deservedly collected the 'Players' Player of the Year' award.
Wigan Ath (From trainee on 7/7/2005)
Accrington Stanley (Free on 31/7/2006) FL 57+7/2 FLC 1+1 FAC 1 Others 3+1

EDWARDS Preston Matthew
Born: Cheshunt, 5 September 1989
Height: 6'0" **Weight:** 12.7
International Honours: E: Yth
Preston is a highly-rated Millwall goalkeeper who has already been capped by England at under-18 level. He made his home League debut against Doncaster, going on as substitute to replace the injured Rhys Evans. For one so young, he commands his area with authority and Millwall have high hopes for him.
Millwall (From trainee on 4/11/2006) FL 0+1 Others 0+1

EDWARDS Robert (Rob) Owen
Born: Telford, 25 December 1982
Height: 6'1" **Weight:** 12.0
International Honours: W: 15; Yth
Rob had been injured at the end of 2006-07 and went on as substitute in the first match, his 100th appearance for

Wolverhampton. The versatile defender played in the Carling Cup but injury again ruled him out and he had to wait until Boxing Day for his first League start. Things improved slightly and his first goal for the club was a well-taken effort against Stoke. The March fixture against Queens Park Rangers was only his seventh start and an ankle injury meant he lasted only a few minutes. That was his campaign over.
Aston Villa (From trainee on 4/1/2000) PL 7+1 FAC 1
Crystal Palace (Loaned on 21/11/2003) FL 6+1/1
Derby Co (Loaned on 9/1/2004) FL 10+1/1
Wolverhampton W (£150,000 + on 26/7/2004) FL 82+18/1 FLC 6 FAC 2+3

EDWORTHY Marc
Born: Barnstaple, 24 December 1972
Height: 5'8" **Weight:** 11.10
Club Honours: Div 1 '04
Apart from an emergency outing as a central defender in a heavy home defeat by West Ham, Marc was largely ignored by manager Billy Davies in the first part of Derby's season. When Paul Jewell took over as manager, Marc was more in the picture in his normal right-back slot, especially when loan signing Danny Mills was ruled out by injury. As always, he brought his solid professionalism to a difficult situation and did his best to hold the fort. Sadly, a cracked rib hampered him towards the end of a frustrating season and he left when his contract expired.
Plymouth Arg (From trainee on 30/3/1991) FL 52+17/1 FLC 5+2 FAC 5+2 Others 2+2
Crystal Palace (£350,000 on 9/6/1995) P/FL 120+6 FLC 8+1/1 FAC 8 Others 8
Coventry C (£850,000 + on 28/8/1998) P/FL 62+14/1 FLC 5 FAC 4
Wolverhampton W (Free on 23/8/2002) FL 18+4 FLC 1
Norwich C (Free on 8/8/2003) P/FL 69+2 FLC 2+1 FAC 2
Derby Co (Free on 6/7/2005) P/FL 75+2 FLC 1+1 FAC 4 Others 0+1

EHIOGU Ugochuku (Ugo)
Born: Hackney, 3 November 1972
Height: 6'2" **Weight:** 14.10
Club Honours: FLC '96, '04
International Honours: E: 4; B-1; U21-15
Ugo joined Sheffield United from Glasgow Rangers on an 18-month contract during the January transfer window, rejoining his former Middlesbrough boss Bryan Robson. Due to the form of Chris Morgan and Matt Kilgallon, Ugo's opportunities were limited but when called upon he used his experience and ability to read the game to compensate for his lack of

speed. Very good in the air and accurate in the tackle, he showed his worth particularly in United's ten-man defeat of Hull in April.

West Bromwich A *(From trainee on 13/7/1989) FL 0+2*
Aston Villa *(£40,000 on 12/7/1991) P/FL 223+14/12 FLC 22+1/1 FAC 22+2/1 Others 18/1*
Middlesbrough *(£8,000,000 on 20/10/2000) PL 122+4/7 FLC 7 FAC 9+2/1 Others 4+3*
Leeds U *(Loaned on 23/11/2006) FL 6/1*
Glasgow Rgrs *(Free on 25/1/2007) SL 9/1 SLC 1 Others 2*
Sheffield U *(Free on 18/1/2008) FL 5+5*

EL-ABD Adam Mohamad

Born: Brighton, 11 September 1984
Height: 5'11"   **Weight:** 13.9
Continuing to show his versatility in the Brighton side, Adam turned out at right-back, left-back, central defence and central midfield and acquitted himself admirably in all positions. A combative, no-nonsense player who can also pass the ball better than he is sometimes given credit for, Adam appeared in every game bar one, through suspension, until suffering a knee injury at Huddersfield in March that sidelined him for the rest of the season. Nevertheless, he will count the past campaign as a personal success, with the highlight being his well-taken goal in a 4-2 victory over Gillingham in March.

Brighton & Hove A *(From trainee on 22/12/2003) FL 113+20/2 FLC 3/1 FAC 7/1 Others 9*

[ELANO] BLUMER Elano Ralph

Born: Iracemapolis, Brazil, 14 June 1981
Height: 5'10"   **Weight:** 10.5
International Honours: Brazil: 28
An attacking midfielder who likes to play in a wide position, he appeared four times for Brazil in their winning 2007 Copa America campaign. Sven-Goran Eriksson then made his move for the 26-year-old playmaker, who became his seventh Manchester City signing of the summer. Following the arrival of Geovanni, Elano was only City's second-ever Brazilian player. His trickery, quick feet and clever passing gave the club an added dimension, starting with a debut assist for the opening goal of the season against West Ham at Upton Park. A virtuoso performance against Newcastle in September was capped by his first goal, an arrow of a free-kick to wrap up a 3-1 victory.

Manchester C *(£8,000,000 from Shakhtar Donetsk, Ukraine, ex Guarani, Internacional, Santos, on 9/8/2007) PL 29+5/8 FLC 2/1 FAC 2/1*

ELDER Nathan John

Born: Hornchurch, 5 April 1985
Height: 6'1"   **Weight:** 11.9
Powerfully-built and blessed with pace, Nathan has great aerial ability but his work on the ground is still somewhat raw and he never quite managed to force his way in at Brighton, where he became almost a perpetual substitute. In January he scored his second goal for the club, a last-minute equaliser at Oldham, but moved to Brentford on the day the January transfer window closed. He proved an imposing target-man who won plenty of balls in the air and scored on his debut at Mansfield. It was the first of only four goals, all in away games, but was hampered by a knee injury that kept him out of the last two matches.

Brighton & Hove A *(£10,000 from Billericay T, ex Hornchurch, Aveley, on 1/1/2007) FL 2+20/2 FAC 0+2 Others 1+2*
Brentford *(£35,000 on 31/1/2008) FL 16+1/4*

ELDING Anthony Lee

Born: Boston, 16 April 1982
Height: 6'1"   **Weight:** 13.10
Club Honours: FC '02
A fine season for the striker included his first League hat-trick, two of them penalties, in Stockport's 3-1 victory at Brentford. After what was cited as a "potential breach of contract" kept him out of the team against Darlington, Anthony got his head down on his return, worked hard and the goals continued to flow. As a Leeds' fan, Anthony completed a dream move to Elland Road just before the January transfer window closed but the man who signed him, Dennis Wise, never got to play him as he moved to Newcastle just days later. Anthony was prolific at Edgeley Park but took time to settle at Leeds, his only League One goal coming in the 2-1 home defeat by Cheltenham. An injury to top-scorer Jermaine Beckford let Anthony in to start the last three games of the regular season as Leeds secured their place in the play-offs and he will be looking to make more of an impact this coming season.

Boston U *(From juniors on 6/7/2001) FL 3+5 FAC 0+1 Others 0+1 (Transferred to Stevenage Borough, via loan spell at Gainsborough Trinity, on 12/2/2003)*
Boston U *(Signed from Kettering T on 16/8/2006) FL 18+1/5 FAC 0+1 Others 0+1*
Stockport Co *(Signed on 4/1/2007) FL 38+7/24 FLC 2/1 FAC 2 Others 3/1*
Leeds U *(Signed on 31/1/2008) FL 4+5/1*

ELITO Medy Efoko

Born: DR Congo, 20 March 1990
Height: 6'0"   **Weight:** 10.6
International Honours: E: Yth

Great things are expected of this flying winger, who prefers to play on the left. Medy had already represented England under-17s and under-18s before breaking into the Colchester first team during March. He started his first game in the home draw against Cardiff, and crowned his third start with a thunderous goal in the dramatic 4-3 defeat at West Bromwich. A product of the U's youth team, he has already been tracked by a number of bigger clubs.

Colchester U *(From trainee on 6/8/2007) FL 7+4/1*

ELLINGTON Nathan Levi Fontaine

Born: Bradford, 2 July 1981
Height: 5'10"   **Weight:** 12.10
Club Honours: Div 2 '03
Nathan made five appearances for West Bromwich at the start of last season and scored once, against Peterborough in the Carling Cup, before becoming Watford's record signing. Nathan took time to settle and had to be content with substitute appearances during the first half of the season, when he appeared to lack match fitness and sharpness. Marlon King's departure in January gave him the opportunity to start regularly and he scored his first Watford goal against Charlton, ending the season with a modest total of four. A striker with plenty of natural ability, Nathan's form was disappointing and at the end of the season he agreed to join Derby on a season's loan with a view to a free transfer.

Bristol Rov *(£150,000 from Walton & Hersham on 18/2/1999) FL 76+40/35 FLC 7/2 FAC 6+1/4 Others 6+1/3*
Wigan Ath *(£750,000 + on 28/3/2002) FL 130+4/59 FLC 6+1/6 FAC 3+1/2 Others 0+1*
West Bromwich A *(£3,000,000 on 15/8/2005) P/FL 34+34/15 FLC 6/5 FAC 3+1 Others 0+3*
Watford *(£3,250,000 on 30/8/2007) FL 18+16/4 FAC 1+1 Others 2*

ELLIOT Robert (Rob)

Born: Chatham, 30 April 1986
Height: 6'3"   **Weight:** 14.10
Club Honours: FC '06
Rob started last season as Charlton's third-choice goalkeeper behind Nicky Weaver and Darren Randolph but moved up to the bench when Randolph joined Bury on loan in January. Earlier, he had turned down the chance of a loan, hoping to impress at Charlton, and had his chance when Weaver was sent off after only two minutes at Plymouth in April. Rob took over and played brilliantly, helping the ten men

Nathan Ellington

earn a deserved victory and making a superb reflex save near the end. He was unfortunate not to start the next game but manager Alan Pardew recalled Randolph and, unwisely as it transpired, gave him the nod. Powerfully built and agile, Rob signed a new two-year contract and with his undoubted ability could challenge for the number-one spot.

Charlton Ath *(From trainee on 27/1/2005)* FL 0+1
Notts Co *(Loaned on 28/1/2005)* FL 3+1
Accrington Stanley *(Loaned on 31/7/2006)* FL 7 FLC 0+1 Others 3

ELLIOTT Marvin Conrad
Born: Wandsworth, 15 September 1984
Height: 5'11" **Weight:** 12.2
Had it not been for the great form of the Bristol City goalkeeper Adriano Basso the midfield player, signed on a free transfer from Millwall, would surely have been the Ashton Gate 'Player of the Season'. He had to make do with the Bristol City supporters' 'Young Player of the Year' award, in addition to being recognised by his fellow professionals with a place in the PFA 'Championship Select' team. Marvin's energy never flags and some of his goals, such as his volleyed winner against Blackpool at Ashton Gate, were out of the top drawer. It was his tackling that most impressed, often appearing double-jointed as he contorted his body. Billy Wedlock, the great Bristol City and England centre-half, was called the 'India Rubber Man' and perhaps Marvin's limbs are of a similar quality. He was much missed in the middle in the play-off final at Wembley when Bradley Orr's first-half injury required him to switch to right-back.

Millwall *(From trainee on 6/2/2002)* FL 119+25/3 FLC 5+1/1 FAC 7+3 Others 3+1
Bristol C *(Signed on 31/7/2007)* FL 44+1/5 FLC 2/1 FAC 1 Others 3

ELLIOTT Robert (Robbie) James
Born: Gosforth, 25 December 1973
Height: 5'10" **Weight:** 11.6
International Honours: E: U21-2; Yth
Signed from Leeds in the close season by Hartlepool manager Danny Wilson to add class and experience to his newly promoted League One side, the skilful defender started as first-choice left-back but initially struggled in his new surroundings and was in and out of the side. Unable to claim a regular place, he was given a short run in mid-season but was subsequently mainly limited to the role of non-playing substitute and was released at the end of the season.

141

Newcastle U *(From trainee on 3/4/1991)*
P/FL 71+8/9 FLC 5 FAC 7+3 Others 5+1
Bolton W *(£2,500,000 + on 2/7/1997)* P/FL
71+15/5 FLC 4+1/2 FAC 5 Others 5+2
Newcastle U *(Free on 11/7/2001)* PL 55+8/2
FLC 4+1 FAC 5+1 Others 13+1/1
Sunderland *(Free on 4/8/2006)* FL 7 FLC 1
Leeds U *(Signed on 1/1/2007)* FL 5+2 FAC 1
Hartlepool U *(Free on 9/7/2007)* FL 14+1
Others 1

ELLIOTT Stephen William
Born: Dublin, 6 January 1984
Height: 5'8" **Weight:** 11.8
Club Honours: Ch '05, '07
International Honours: Rol: 9; U21-
10; Yth
Arriving from Sunderland in the summer,
the striker played in Wolverhampton's
opening game but injury put him out of
the next four. He was then involved in the
next seven, scoring twice, at Sheffield and
Plymouth, while his first goal at Molineux
secured three points against Colchester.
Stephen's industry appealed to manager
Mick McCarthy and he was very much
a team player. In the New Year, he was
used on the right in place of the injured
Michael Kightly and again worked hard,
although injuries continued to hamper
his progress.
Manchester C *(From trainee on 17/1/2001)*
PL 0+2
Sunderland *(Signed on 6/8/2004)* P/FL
55+26/22 FLC 1+3/1 FAC 3
Wolverhampton W *(Signed on 20/7/2007)*
FL 18+11/4 FAC 1+1/1

ELLIOTT Steven (Steve)
William
Born: Derby, 29 October 1978
Height: 6'1" **Weight:** 14.0
Club Honours: AMC '04
International Honours: E: U21-3
A central defender, Steve signed a new
contract after Bristol Rovers gained
promotion in 2006-07 and responded
well with some solid performances. He
injured knee ligaments in the FA Cup
replay victory over Fulham in January and
was missing for two months. Although
scoring the winner at Walsall, his best
goal was a superb 28-yard left-footed
volley against Gillingham at the Memorial
Stadium.
Derby Co *(From trainee on 26/3/1997)* P/FL
58+15/1 FLC 8+1 FAC 3+2
Blackpool *(Free on 14/11/2003)* FL 28
Others 5
Bristol Rov *(Free on 5/7/2004)* FL 157+1/12
FLC 6 FAC 12 Others 15+1

ELLIOTT Stuart
Born: Belfast, 23 July 1978
Height: 5'10" **Weight:** 11.9
International Honours: NI: 39; U21-3

Stuart achieved the rare distinction of
playing for two clubs that won Wembley
play-off finals in the same season. Having
been a key figure in Hull's rise to the
Championship, the attacking left-sided
midfielder retained an influence despite
becoming an increasingly peripheral
figure. Stuart's volleyed goal at Wigan in
the Carling Cup second round provided
the Tigers with their first win against
Premier League opposition for ten years.
His continued involvement with
Northern Ireland means that he is
headed only by Jamaica's Theo Whitmore
in the list of Hull's most-capped players.
Stuart joined Doncaster in January,
on loan to the end of the season. He
made only one start, the rest of his
appearances being as a substitute on
the left, where he showed his pace and
ability to run at defences. Was released
in the summer.
Motherwell *(£100,000 from Glentoran on
20/7/2000)* SL 50+20/22 SLC 2+1 SC 1+1/1
Hull C *(£175,000 on 12/7/2002)* FL
156+37/65 FLC 6+3/1 FAC 4+4/1 Others
0+1/1
Doncaster Rov *(Loaned on 31/1/2008)* FL
1+9

ELLIOTT Thomas (Tom)
Joshua
Born: Leeds, 9 September 1989
Height: 5'10" **Weight:** 11.0
England under-17 striker Tom had just
one senior outing for Leeds, starting the
1-0 Carling Cup victory at Macclesfield at
the beginning of the season. Most of his
time was spent with the Academy under-
18 side and the reserves, for whom he
finished top scorer.
Leeds U *(Trainee)* FL 0+3 FLC 1

ELLIOTT Wade Patrick
Born: Eastleigh, 14 December 1978
Height: 5'9" **Weight:** 11.1
International Honours: E: Sch
For most observers Burnley's 'Player of
the Season', Wade continued to turn
in eye-catching performances on the
Clarets' right-wing and was a model of
consistency, appearing in every League
game and starting in all but one. He
always had pace and the ability to take
the ball past his man but has added
greater accuracy with the final pass and,
although scoring only two goals himself,
was the provider of many more. Both his
goals were special, the long-range effort
against Charlton a contender for Turf
Moor's 'Goal of the Season'. Manager
Owen Coyle acted early to extend
Wayne's stay at the club in advance of
his contract expiring at the end of the
season.

Bournemouth *(£5,000 from Bashley on
4/2/2000)* FL 178+42/31 FLC 6+1 FAC 19/5
Others 9+2/1
Burnley *(Free on 4/7/2005)* FL 108+16/9 FLC
2+1 FAC 3

ELLISON Kevin
Born: Liverpool, 23 February 1979
Height: 6'1" **Weight:** 12.8
Kevin rejoined Chester from Tranmere
during the summer and ended the season
as City's leading scorer with 11 goals. A
left-sided attacking midfielder, Kevin was
always looking to get in the box and was
often switched to a more central role
alongside John Murphy as Chester found
goals hard to come by in the second half
of the campaign. After a steady rather
than spectacular first half of the season
Kevin was not helped by persistent
transfer speculation and a series of
niggling injuries as City struggled. A
strong left-footed player, he can be a real
match winner as he proved by scoring
twice in victories over Mansfield and
Barnet. He also held his nerve to score an
injury-time penalty to give City a crucial
point at Hereford.
Leicester C *(£50,000 + from Altrincham on
13/2/2001)* PL 0+1
Stockport Co *(£55,000 on 30/11/2001)* FL
33+15/2 FLC 1 FAC 1 Others 2
Lincoln C *(Loaned on 12/3/2004)* FL 11
Others 2
Chester C *(Free on 6/8/2004)* FL 60/20 FLC 2
FAC 4/1 Others 3/1
Hull C *(£100,000 on 12/1/2005)* FL 26+13/2
FLC 1 FAC 1
Tranmere Rov *(Signed on 28/6/2006)* FL
26+8/4 FLC 1 FAC 1 Others 2

ELOKOBI George Nganyuo
Born: Cameroon, 31 January 1986
Height: 6'0" **Weight:** 13.2
The no-nonsense left-back reached a
new level. Having gradually improved
over the years at Colchester, following
his step-up from non-League, he started
the first 14 games in his favoured
position, having had few chances the
previous season because of the presence
of Chris Barker on loan. George lost his
place during the autumn and as a result
requested a transfer, which prompted an
adverse reaction from some supporters.
He eventually secured his big move to
Wolverhampton at the end of January,
made his debut at Blackpool and soon
established himself in the team. He was
prone to some errors in the early games
but showed enough ability to keep his
place. George has a knack of getting in
deep, accurate crosses from awkward
positions, one of which helped bring a
goal against Southampton.

Tommy Elphick

Colchester U *(Free from Dulwich Hamlet on 12/7/2004) FL 35+4/2 FLC 1+1 FAC 1 Others 4/1*
Chester C *(Loaned on 27/1/2005) FL 4+1*
Wolverhampton W *(Signed on 31/1/2008) FL 15*

ELPHICK Thomas (Tommy)

Born: Brighton, 7 September 1987
Height: 5'11" **Weight:** 11.7
After impressing in a handful of appearances at the end of the previous campaign, Tommy went into the Brighton side for the second game of the season and never looked back. His exceptional first term as the regular centre-half was interrupted only by a hernia problem in November and December, and he went on to win the supporters' 'Player of the Season' award at the age of 20, with fewer than 50 senior appearances to his name. Sound in the air and swift on the ground, Tommy also notched two goals and could be the bedrock of Brighton's defence for several years.
Brighton & Hove A *(From trainee on 8/6/2006) FL 41+2/2 FLC 1 FAC 2 Others 2*

EL ZHAR Nabil

Born: Ales, France, 27 August 1986
Height: 5'7" **Weight:** 10.3
International Honours: Morocco: 2; Yth. France: Yth
A French-born winger or striker of Moroccan parentage, Nabil made only three appearances for Liverpool last season, starting as a right-winger in the Carling Cup match against Cardiff in October, when he hit a stunning 25-yard goal to open the scoring, as a substitute in the same competition at Chelsea in December and again as substitute in the FA Cup third round tie at Luton in January. In March, Nabil made his international debut for Morocco in Belgium and scored a goal in his team's startling 4-1 victory.
Liverpool *(Signed from St Etienne, France, ex OAC Ales, Nimes Olympique, on 31/8/2005) PL 0+3 FLC 1+1/1 FAC 0+1*

EMANUEL Lewis James

Born: Bradford, 14 October 1983
Height: 5'8" **Weight:** 11.12
International Honours: E: Yth; RoI: B-1
Lewis was thought to be an emerging talent when he signed for Luton in 2006. Naturally left sided and quick, his penetrating runs from defence made him a useful weapon, especially with his ability to shoot from distance. The signing of new players and uncertainty affected his form but a loan to Brentford helped him. Having made an excellent debut at left-back for the Bees against Lincoln, his quick thinking setting up the

Michael Essien

winner, he was injured in his third game and returned to Luton. He seemed to be on his way to Yeovil until manager Mick Harford intervened with the administrator. Lewis had his first appearance of the season as a substitute at Leyton Orient and started at left-back against Bournemouth. Then he found a niche on the left of midfield, in front of Sol Davis and looked like his old self.

Bradford C (From trainee on 5/7/2001) FL 102+37/4 FLC 5 FAC 5+1 Others 2+1
Luton T (£100,000 on 27/7/2006) FL 54+3/4 FLC 1 FAC 2 Others 1
Brentford (Loaned on 25/10/2007) FL 3

EMERTON Brett Michael
Born: Sydney, Australia, 22 February 1979
Height: 6'1" **Weight:** 13.5
International Honours: Australia: 64; U23; Yth
International duty with Australia prevented Brett appearing in the Inter Toto Cup for Blackburn and there was a belief that he might lose his right-back position, with Andre Ooijer available. By the second game of the season, he had regained his place and proved one of the unsung members of the team. A natural athlete, strong and determined, he overlaps well and is positionally sound. He never complained when the club moved him to wide right midfield and finished the season playing in the centre of midfield, his performance against Manchester United being as good as any for Rovers in that area all season.

Blackburn Rov (£2,200,000 from Feyenoord, Holland, ex Sydney Olympic, on 21/7/2003) PL 144+27/8 FLC 6+5/2 FAC 10+4 Others 11+1/1

[EMRE] BELOZOGLU Emre
Born: Istanbul, Turkey, 7 September 1980
Height: 5'7" **Weight:** 10.10
International Honours: Turkey: 58
A long-term ankle injury delayed the start of the season for Turkish international midfielder Emre and thereafter he struggled to gain a regular starting place for Newcastle, his cause hampered by a string of further niggling injuries. Although he is a busy little player, who always makes himself available to colleagues in possession, is difficult to knock off the ball, and an accurate passer with his left foot, most of his appearances were from the bench. His standing with his country is such that he continued to add to his caps for Turkey. Emre's only goal was in the home game against Everton, a delightful drive into the bottom corner.

Newcastle U (£3,800,000 from Inter Milan, Italy, ex Galatasaray, on 25/7/2005) PL 46+12/5 FLC 4+1 FAC 2+2 Others 11+2/1

ENCKELMAN Peter
Born: Turku, Finland, 10 March 1977
Height: 6'2" **Weight:** 12.5
International Honours: Finland: 11; U21-15
The Finnish international goalkeeper joined Cardiff on loan from Blackburn last January. Peter played a major role in City's run to the FA Cup final, his ability to command his area being crucial. Followed David Forde, Ross Turnbull, Kasper Schmeichel and Mike Oakes in trying to establish himself as number one and did well enough to be offered a two-year contract as he was a free agent this summer. Cardiff have signed Manchester United reserve goalkeeper Tom Heaton on a season-long loan for 2008-09 and Peter was offered the chance to battle it out with the young newcomer.

Aston Villa (£200,000 from TPS Turku, Finland on 1/2/1999) PL 51+1 FLC 6 FAC 1 Others 7+1
Blackburn Rov (£150,000 on 7/11/2003) PL 2 FLC 1
Cardiff C (Loaned on 10/1/2008) FL 15+1 FAC 4

[ENRIQUE] SANCHEZ DIAZ Jose Enrique
Born: Valencia, Spain, 23 January 1986
Height: 6'0" **Weight:** 12.0
International Honours: Spain: U21-3
Nicknamed 'The Bull' in his native Spain for his aggressive style of play, Enrique is a highly-rated young left-back for whom Sam Allardyce paid big money to Villarreal to sign him for Newcastle against competition from a number of Premier League rivals. Strong and sturdy, he is difficult to knock off the ball and a feature of his game is his surging attacking down the wing in support of his forwards. He took time to settle in the Premier League and his form was variable in his two spells in the side, in October and again in January, but under new manager Kevin Keegan he became a regular starter and his game continued to improve as the season wore on, providing hope that there will be more performances to match his reputation.

Newcastle U (£6,500,000 from Villarreal, Spain, ex Levante, Valencia, Celta Vigo - loan, on 17/8/2007) PL 18+5 FLC 2 FAC 3

EPHRAIM Hogan
Born: Holloway, 31 March 1988
Height: 5'9" **Weight:** 11.0
International Honours: E: Yth
After a productive three-month loan spell from West Ham ended in November, Queens Park Rangers made sure that the switch became permanent once the transfer window opened in January.

Hogan is one of the few players at Loftus Road to figure under all three Rangers' managers and still be at the club. He made his debut for John Gregory on the opening day, excelled under Mick Harford and was signed permanently by Luigi De Canio after scoring the first goal of the new manager's Rangers' career. Deployed mainly on the left flank, he has gone a long way to filling the void left by the departure of Lee Cook last summer and, at only 20, has a bright future.

West Ham U (From trainee on 15/4/2005) FLC 0+1
Colchester U (Loaned on 23/11/2006) FL 5+16/1
Queens Park Rgrs (£800,000 on 10/8/2007) FL 20+9/3 FAC 1

ESAJAS Etienne
Born: Amsterdam, Holland, 4 November 1984
Height: 5'7" **Weight:** 10.4
Signed from Dutch side Vitesse Arnhem just after the start of the season, Etienne has not been able to force himself into the Sheffield Wednesday side on a regular basis. A fast, tricky winger, strong on his left side, he operates very directly and likes to run at players with the ball. He lifts supporters to their feet but unfortunately picked up a foot injury in January, thus halting his progress. He needs to force himself into Brian Laws' plans and a goal or two would help.

Sheffield Wed (Signed from Vitesse Arnhem, Holland on 31/8/2007) FL 5+13 FAC 1

ESSIEN Michael
Born: Accra, Ghana, 3 December 1982
Height: 5'10" **Weight:** 12.3
Club Honours: PL '06; FLC '07
International Honours: Ghana: 40
This high-octane midfielder had another outstanding season for club and country in 2007-08. Michael was an influential figure as Chelsea finished runners-up in three competitions and skippered the hosts Ghana to third place in the African Cup of Nations. His athleticism and versatility make him comfortable in any area of the pitch, from emergency central defender to supporting the front players, from where he scored six goals with his explosive shooting, including two in four days against Wigan and Everton that kept the Premier League dreams alive. A further example of his versatility came in the critical Champions' League semi-finals and final when he was switched to right-back to counter the attacking threat and to surge down the flank as an attacking outlet. As Chelsea face yet more upheaval, the dynamic Michael will be a pivotal figure in their future.

Chelsea *(£24,400,000 from Lyon, France on 19/8/2005) PL 83+8/10 FLC 10+1/1 FAC 8+3/1 Others 29+1/2*

ESSON Ryan John

Born: Aberdeen, 19 March 1980
Height: 6'1" **Weight:** 12.7
International Honours: S: U21-7; Yth
Following an-injury ravaged season in 2006-07, the Shrewsbury goalkeeper knew that he would be second choice and played only in two Carling Cup games before he was released in January. Always keen to fight for his place, he saved a late penalty against Colchester to set up a second round meeting with Fulham. Ryan signed for Hereford late in the season as cover for injured back-up 'keeper Mike Ingham. He waited for his chance and showed his talents in the final match, a clean sheet helping the Bulls to a last-day victory.
Aberdeen *(Signed from Parkvale on 23/1/1996) SL 85+4 SLC 4 SC 5 Others 2*
Shrewsbury T *(Free on 27/7/2006) FL 6 FLC 2*
Hereford U *(Free on 17/3/2008) FL 1*

ETHERINGTON Matthew (Mattie)

Born: Truro, 14 August 1981
Height: 5'10" **Weight:** 11.2
International Honours: E: U21-3; Yth
The West Ham left-sided midfielder started last season on top form. Combining well with George McCartney, he was a constant threat to defenders. At Reading in September he was superb, linking up well with Craig Bellamy and scoring twice in the second half. He scored again at Derby in November to add a new dimension to his game. After a spell in which consistency tended to desert him, perhaps because of so many enforced changes in the team, Mattie played against Birmingham in February and suffered a groin injury that forced him to miss the remainder of the season.
Peterborough U *(From trainee on 15/8/1998) FL 43+8/6 FLC 1+1 FAC 2+1 Others 2*
Tottenham H *(£500,000 on 10/1/2000) PL 20+25/1 FLC 3+1 FAC 1+1/1*
Bradford C *(Loaned on 23/10/2001) FL 12+1/1*
West Ham U *(£1,000,000 on 8/8/2003) P/FL 143+9/14 FLC 6+1 FAC 13+1/1 Others 6+1/1*

ETUHU Dickson Paul

Born: Kano, Nigeria, 8 June 1982
Height: 6'2" **Weight:** 13.4
Club Honours: Div 1 '02
International Honours: Nigeria: 5
A tall powerhouse in central midfield, Dickson was signed by Sunderland from Norwich during the close season and

impressed with his competitive nature, boundless energy and aerial prowess at set pieces. He missed part of the campaign while representing Nigeria in the African Cup of Nations. Dickson served a suspension in September, having quickly collected five yellow cards, and struck his only goal against Wigan in February with a typical bullet header.
Manchester C *(From trainee on 23/12/1999) FL 11+1 FLC 1*
Preston NE *(£300,000 on 24/1/2002) FL 100+34/17 FLC 8 FAC 4/1 Others 0+3*
Norwich C *(£450,000 on 11/11/2005) FL 57+5/6 FLC 2+1/1 FAC 5*
Sunderland *(£1,500,000 on 17/7/2007) PL 18+2/1 FLC 1*

ETUHU Kelvin

Born: Kano, Nigeria, 30 May 1988
Height: 5'11" **Weight:** 11.2
International Honours: E: Yth
Kelvin became the 24th Academy graduate to reach Manchester City's first team when making his debut as a substitute in the Carling Cup victory over Norwich and setting up the winner for Georgios Samaras with a fine through pass. December was good for Kelvin, with his first Premier League appearance, again as a substitute at Wigan, followed by a start at Tottenham. Best of all, he was a half-time substitute with City trailing 2-1 to Bolton, set up the equaliser and scored his first senior goal in stoppage-time to wrap up a 4-2 victory. The speedy right-winger was a late loan-signing for Leicester manager Ian Holloway. His Foxes' career effectively lasted a fortnight before an injury, coupled with his lack of experience, marked him as a square peg in Leicester's round relegation-threatened hole.
Manchester C *(From trainee on 9/11/2005) PL 2+4/1 FLC 0+1 FAC 0+1*
Rochdale *(Loaned on 5/1/2007) FL 3+1/2*
Leicester C *(Loaned on 5/3/2008) FL 2+2*

EUELL Jason Joseph

Born: Lambeth, 6 February 1977
Height: 6'0" **Weight:** 11.6
International Honours: Jamaica: 3; E: U21-6; Yth
Signed from Middlesbrough on the August transfer deadline day, Jason quickly became a considerable presence at Southampton because of his athleticism, impressive fitness and powerful running. A Southampton midfield that was rarely the sum of its parts was a problem three managers failed to resolve but none held Jason responsible and he remained a constant selection. Intriguingly, his effectiveness was enhanced in February after Nigel Pearson took over the team and began playing him alongside Inigo Idiakez and/or Mario Licka, neither of

whom had been prominent until the change of management.
Wimbledon *(From trainee on 1/6/1995) P/FL 118+23/41 FLC 15+2/4 FAC 14+5/2 Others 2+2*
Charlton Ath *(£4,750,000 on 16/7/2001) PL 102+37/34 FLC 4+3/1 FAC 5+4/2*
Middlesbrough *(Signed on 31/8/2006) PL 9+8 FLC 0+1 FAC 0+2*
Southampton *(Free on 31/8/2007) FL 31+7/3 FAC 3*

EUSTACE John Mark

Born: Solihull, 3 November 1979
Height: 5'11" **Weight:** 12.12
A combative, hard-tackling midfielder with boundless enthusiasm and energy, John was made captain of Stoke early in the season following Danny Higginbotham's transfer to Sunderland. Popular with the crowd, it was a surprise to most supporters when he was sold to rivals Watford in January but he slotted in seamlessly at Vicarage Road and was an influential figure in midfield. He successfully snuffs out opposing attacks and links well with forward players when Watford attack. John was sent off against former club Stoke in March, costing him a four-game suspension. Although sent off again in the first play-off match against Hull the decision was rescinded, enabling him to turn out in the second match at the KC Stadium. A natural leader, John refused the chance to captain Watford until he was better established but led the team towards the end of the season.
Coventry C *(From trainee on 5/11/1996) P/FL 62+24/7 FLC 6+2/2 FAC 3+2/1*
Dundee U *(Loaned on 17/2/1999) SL 8+3/1 SC 2*
Middlesbrough *(Loaned on 17/1/2003) PL 0+1*
Stoke C *(Free on 4/8/2003) FL 55+19/5 FLC 3+1 FAC 5+1/1*
Hereford U *(Loaned on 13/10/2006) FL 8*
Watford *(£250,000 + on 31/1/2008) FL 13 Others 2*

EVANS Chedwyn (Ched) Michael

Born: Rhyl, 28 December 1988
Height: 6'0" **Weight:** 12.0
International Honours: W:2; U21-8
Ched made his Manchester City debut as a substitute against Norwich in the Carling Cup. Following that appearance in September, Norwich kept an eye on the Wales under-21 striker and subsequently took him on loan until January. On the eve of his spell at Carrow Road, Ched scored a memorable hat-trick for Wales under-21s as they saw off France at Ninian Park. Goals and impressive performances at Norwich built up a reputation and Glenn Roeder persuaded City to allow

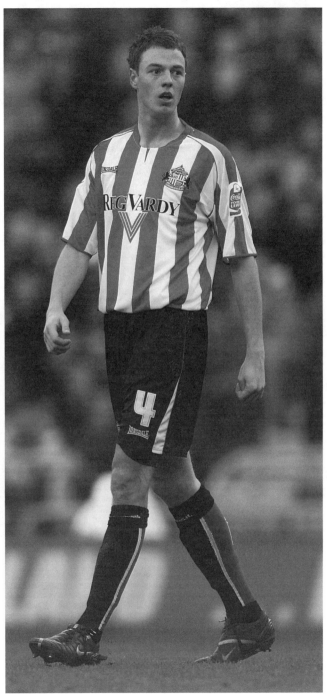

Jonny Evans

a further loan until February. Ched had an instant impact at Norwich, scoring ten goals in 28 League appearances for the Canaries. A strong running striker who never allows defenders a moment's peace, he possesses a hammer of a right foot and scored some spectacular goals, including Norwich's 'Goal of the Season' from 35 yards at Cardiff in February. He netted regularly for Wales in their UEFA under-21 qualifying campaign and scored with a cute flick when he won his first full cap in Iceland. Glenn Roeder has already expressed his desire to have Ched back at Carrow Road next season.
Manchester C *(From trainee on 3/7/2007) FLC 0+1*
Norwich C *(Loaned on 22/11/2007) FL 20+8/10*

EVANS Gareth Charles
Born: Stockport, 26 April 1988
Height: 6'0" **Weight:** 12.8
Gareth moved to Macclesfield from Crewe during the close season to provide cover for the first-choice strikers and made his League debut as a substitute in the opening match of the season at Bradford. Most of his appearances in the first half of the season were off the bench but in the second half he was more often than not a starter. Ever improving and gaining in strength, Gareth scored seven goals, including the winning strike in the penultimate match that ensured Town's retention of League status.
Macclesfield T *(From trainee at Crewe Alex on 28/8/2007) FL 20+22/7 FLC 0+1 FAC 1 Others 0+2*

EVANS Gareth David
Born: Wrexham, 10 January 1987
Height: 6'1" **Weight:** 12.12
Gareth impressed in 2006-07, his debut season, and played himself into the Wrexham side at home to Barnet in late October. He has much to prove but may have an important part to play in central defence in the Blue Square Premier. Because of chopping and changing as Wrexham sought a winning formula, Gareth never had chance to establish himself and was loaned to Tamworth in mid-season.
Wrexham *(From trainee on 5/8/2006) FL 19+6 FLC 0+2 FAC 1*

EVANS Jonathan (Jonny) Grant
Born: Belfast, 3 January 1988
Height: 6'2" **Weight:** 12.2
Club Honours: Ch '07
International Honours: NI: 10; U21-3; Yth
Jonny, a young Manchester United defender, appeared as a late substitute

for Gerard Pique in the Champions' League qualifier at home to Dynamo Kiev in November and helped to secure qualification to the knock-out stages. In January, Jonny rejoined Sunderland on loan for the second time and was immediately drafted into the squad. He played 90 minutes in his first game, a 3-0 FA Cup defeat by Wigan. Jonny renewed his central defensive partnership with Nyron Nosworthy that was so successful in Sunderland's Championship promotion. A regular for Northern Ireland, he is a left-sided defender whose poise on the ball, reading of the game, aerial ability and excellent distribution belie his relative inexperience. It was no coincidence that his return to Wearside coincided with an upturn in defensive performances as the Black Cats secured their Premier League status. Sunderland fans hope that Roy Keane can persuade Sir Alex Ferguson to part with him on a permanent basis but Jonny has expressed a wish to stay at Old Trafford.

Manchester U *(From trainee on 12/4/2005) FLC 1 Others 1+1*
Sunderland *(Loaned on 4/1/2007) FL 18/1 FAC 1*
Sunderland *(Loaned on 4/1/2008) PL 15 FAC 1*

EVANS Paul Simon
Born: Oswestry, 1 September 1974
Height: 5'8" **Weight:** 11.6
Club Honours: Div 3 '94, '99
International Honours: W: 2; U21-4; Yth
Freed by Swindon during the summer, the former Welsh international re-signed for Bradford. A bustling central midfielder, Paul featured regularly during the first half of the season when his commitment to the cause was summed up by an appalling head injury suffered in a collision at Barnet. Packing a powerful free kick and always willing to have a shot anywhere around the box, Paul will be looking for a new club in the summer.

Shrewsbury T *(From trainee on 2/7/1993) FL 178+20/26 FLC 12+2/4 FAC 12+1/2 Others 12/4*
Brentford *(£110,000 on 3/3/1999) FL 130/31 FLC 8 FAC 3 Others 13/3*
Bradford C *(Free on 9/8/2002) FL 36+6/5 FLC 2 FAC 1*
Blackpool *(Loaned on 17/11/2003) FL 10/1*
Nottingham F *(Signed on 25/3/2004) FL 42+5/4 FLC 3 FAC 3*
Rotherham U *(Loaned on 18/11/2005) FL 4 Others 1/1*
Swindon T *(Free on 3/8/2006) FL 11+4/3 FLC 1/1 FAC 1*
Bradford C *(Free on 3/8/2007) FL 19+6 FLC 1 FAC 2*

EVANS Raphale (Rapha) Mondale
Born: Manchester, 7 May 1990
Height: 6'0" **Weight:** 14.7
A second-year scholar at Rochdale, Rapha was a regular in the reserves' defence and was called into the first-team squad for a Johnstone's Paint Trophy game, though remaining on the bench. With Dale fielding a settled defence in the second half of the season as they chased a play-off spot, Rapha had to wait until the final day, when Keith Hill rested several of his regulars, to make his senior debut at left-back against Shrewsbury. The same evening he won Rochdale's 'Youth Player of the Year' award and was rewarded with a first professional contract.
Rochdale *(Trainee) FL 1*

EVANS Rhys Karl
Born: Swindon, 27 January 1982
Height: 6'1" **Weight:** 12.2
International Honours: E: U21-2; Yth; Sch
The goalkeeper was unable to force himself into Blackpool's team in 2007-08, with Paul Rachubka appearing in every League game, and after only two starts, both in the Carling Cup, he joined Bradford on a month's loan in October. Rhys' started well enough at Valley Parade but after four appearances he had to return to Blackpool early when he damaged a shoulder against Grimsby. Allowed to join Millwall in January on a free transfer, he went into the side to face Nottingham Forest and quickly proved to be an excellent shot-stopper with the command in the air that gives any defence confidence. Rhys also has the ability and vision to change defence into attack with regularity. The only blip to his ever-present record was caused by an injury against Doncaster but, although replaced, he was back in goal for the next game. Was out of contract in the summer and looking for a new club.
Chelsea *(From trainee on 8/2/1999)*
Bristol Rov *(Loaned on 25/2/2000) FL 4*
Queens Park Rgrs *(Loaned on 6/11/2001) FL 11*
Leyton Orient *(Loaned on 10/8/2002) FL 7*
Swindon T *(Free on 28/7/2003) FL 118 FLC 2+1 FAC 4 Others 3*
Blackpool *(Free on 5/7/2006) FL 32 FLC 3 FAC 5 Others 1*
Bradford C *(Loaned on 5/10/2007) FL 4*
Millwall *(Free on 22/1/2008) FL 21 FAC 1*

EVANS Steven (Steve) James
Born: Wrexham, 26 February 1979
Height: 6'4" **Weight:** 12.2
International Honours: W: 6
Along with the team, Steve's form for Wrexham suffered badly and he was not the commanding figure in the centre of the defence of the previous campaign. Steve is a big presence at the back and always a threat at set pieces, scoring in a 2-0 win over Darlington at the Racecourse and earning a point at home to fellow Blue Square Premier-bound Mansfield with another goal in April. John Toshack continues to include Steve in Welsh squads.
Wrexham *(Signed from TNS on 3/8/2006) FL 64+2/5 FLC 2 FAC 3 Others 2*

EVATT Ian Ross
Born: Coventry, 19 November 1981
Height: 6'3" **Weight:** 13.11
Another good season for Ian was halted by a nasty injury picked up in the home fixture against Colchester. The knee and ankle damage caused by a tackle left him sidelined for two months, meaning he only made 27 League starts. A tall and commanding centre-back who joins the attack at set pieces, he did not score in the season but his presence created room for others. When in the side, his partnership with Kaspars Gorkss flourished and should continue into the coming season.
Derby Co *(From trainee on 3/12/1998) P/FL 19+15 FLC 0+2/1 FAC 1*
Northampton T *(Loaned on 10/8/2001) FL 10+1 FLC 2*
Chesterfield *(Free on 4/8/2003) FL 84/9 FLC 2 FAC 2/1 Others 1+1*
Queens Park Rgrs *(£150,000 + on 6/6/2005) FL 21+6 FLC 1*
Blackpool *(Free on 3/8/2006) FL 69+4 FLC 3 FAC 6/1 Others 4*

EVRA Patrice
Born: Dakar, Senegal, 15 May 1981
Height: 5'8" **Weight:** 11.13
Club Honours: FLC '06; PL '07, '08; CS '07; UEFACL '08
International Honours: France: 13
A quick, athletic and attack-minded Manchester United and France full-back, Patrice continued to be a key figure for United throughout the season. A regular performer in the Premiership, he missed only five games all season and contributed much to United's quest for honours. In the Champions' League too, he figured prominently despite being injured in the warm-up before the group game against Dynamo Kiev. His defensive qualities and surging runs down the flank took United all the way to Moscow for the final against Chelsea in May. Playing also in all rounds of the FA Cup, Patrice is one of Sir Alex Ferguson's most valued assets in an outstanding defence.
Manchester U *(£5,500,000 from AS Monaco, France on 12/1/2006) PL 62+6/1 FLC 1+2 FAC 7+2 Others 15+3/1*

F

FABIANSKI Lukasz
Born: Kostrzyn nad Odra, Poland, 18 April 1985
Height: 6'3" **Weight:** 13.0
International Honours: Poland: 8; U21
The young Polish goalkeeper joined Arsenal in the summer from Legia Warsaw and had to be content with being third choice for most of the campaign. The Carling Cup afforded him a chance of regular action and he appeared in all five of the ties, keeping two clean sheets. He was also given a late run in the Premier League, starting the last three League fixtures and registering two more clean sheets. He is a brave goalkeeper and is certainly not afraid to come for the ball in a crowded penalty area as well as being a solid shot-stopper. With Jens Lehmann leaving the club, Lukasz will feel he has the opportunity to push himself nearer the first team on a consistent basis.
Arsenal (£2,000,000 from Legia Warsaw, Poland, ex Lubuszanin Drezdenko, Sparta Brodnica, Mieszko Gniezno, Lech Poznan, on 6/7/2007) PL 3 FLC 5

FABREGAS Francesc (Cesc)
Born: Barcelona, Spain, 4 May 1987
Height: 5'9" **Weight:** 10.8
Club Honours: CS '04; FAC '05
International Honours: Spain: 32; U21; Yth
Cesc started last season in blistering fashion for Arsenal, scoring 11 goals by the end of October. The Spanish midfielder formed an excellent partnership with Mathieu Flamini that allowed him to play a more attacking role than had previously been possible. Cesc has a tremendous range of passing, can tackle and is good at set pieces. Having now added goals to his game, he is already looking the complete midfield player at just 21 years of age and after achieving an amazing total of 23 assists, 19 of those coming in the Premier League, he was named as the 'Young Player of the Premier League Season' and also selected in the PFA 'Premier League Team of the Season'. As a member of the Spanish side that won the European Championship final in June, Cesc excelled in the semis when he came on for the injured David Villa after 34 minutes and was the driving force in a 3-0 win over Russia.
Arsenal (From trainee on 14/9/2004) PL 120+18/14 FLC 6+4/1 FAC 8+2 Others 35+5/11

FACEY Delroy Michael
Born: Huddersfield, 22 April 1980
Height: 5'11" **Weight:** 13.10
A bright, energetic striker with plenty of pace and good in the air for his height, Delroy signed for Gillingham after being freed by Rotherham at the end of the previous campaign. In and out of the team for most of the season, he moved on loan to Wycombe to try and help them reach the play-offs. With his bustling style, Delroy gave Wycombe's attack a much stronger physical presence. He is a classic target-man, strong in the air and good at holding up the ball. His two goals included an important strike in the play-off semi-final against Stockport. Capitalising on a poor clearance, he outpaced and out-muscled a defender before skilfully steering the ball past the advancing goalkeeper. In his short stay, Delroy was popular with the fans, who would clearly like the signing to be permanent.
Huddersfield T (From trainee on 13/5/1997) FL 40+35/15 FLC 1+1 FAC 1+2 Others 2
Bolton W (Signed on 4/7/2002) PL 1+9/1
FAC 4
Bradford C (Loaned on 8/11/2002) FL 6/1
Burnley (Loaned on 1/9/2003) FL 12+2/5 FLC 2
West Bromwich A (£100,000 on 30/1/2004) FL 2+7
Hull C (Free on 1/7/2004) FL 12+9/4 FLC 1 FAC 2/2 Others 1
Huddersfield T (Loaned on 26/2/2005) FL 4
Oldham Ath (Free on 24/3/2005) FL 1+8 FLC 1
Tranmere Rov (Free on 31/8/2005) FL 30+7/8 FAC 1 Others 3/1
Rotherham U (Free on 3/8/2006) FL 37+3/10 FLC 1 FAC 1 Others 1/1
Gillingham (Signed on 1/8/2007) FL 27+5/3 FLC 0+1 FAC 1 Others 1
Wycombe W (Loaned on 27/3/2008) FL 4+2/1 Others 2/1

FAE Emerse
Born: Nantes, France, 24 January 1984
Height: 5'8" **Weight:** 11.0
International Honours: Ivory Coast: 17
Reading paid a club record fee to sign Emerse from French club Nantes in pre-season, ostensibly to replace departed

Delroy Facey

midfielder Steve Sidwell. The player declared himself very happy to join the Royals but that feeling did not last long. Had a ten-match spell in the first-team squad without looking particularly special, then contracted malaria while playing for the Ivory Coast in the African Cup of Nations. He was eventually back in the Reading team for a couple of substitute appearances near the end of the season but was suspended and fined two weeks wages after refusing to play for the reserves.

Reading (£2,500,000 from Nantes, France on 17/8/2007) PL 3+5 FLC 2 FAC 1

FAGAN Craig Anthony

Born: Birmingham, 11 December 1982
Height: 5'11" **Weight:** 11.12
Although he can also play as a central striker, Craig was generally used by Derby on the right of midfield. He suffered an early-season suspension when an incident in a heavy defeat at Liverpool was judged retrospectively and this did not help him to settle in the Premiership. His all-action style always earned him a place but a lack of goals hampered him, his only successful strike came against Blackpool in the Carling Cup. Fourteen months after leaving Hull to join Derby's successful assault on the Championship play-offs, Craig returned to the KC Stadium on loan in March to repeat the feat by helping to take the Tigers in to the top flight for the first time in their history as the Rams moved in the opposite direction. Although niggling injuries hampered his attempts to recapture his earlier outstanding form, the lively right-sided front runner can never be accused of giving less than total commitment. Especially given the need for a larger squad, reports suggested that Craig would make a permanent return to the Tigers.

Birmingham C (From trainee on 20/12/2001) PL 0+1 FLC 0+2 FAC 0+1
Bristol C (Loaned on 16/1/2003) FL 5+1/1 Others 1
Colchester U (Free on 5/8/2003) FL 55+8/17 FLC 5/3 FAC 10/4 Others 4
Hull C (Signed on 28/2/2005) FL 67+13/15 FLC 2+1 FAC 1
Derby Co (£750,000 on 12/1/2007) P/FL 29+10/1 FLC 1/1 FAC 3 Others 3
Hull C (Loaned on 7/3/2008) FL 4+4 Others 0+3

FALLON Rory Michael

Born: Gisborne, New Zealand, 20 March 1982
Height: 6'2" **Weight:** 11.10
International Honours: E: Yth
Rory started the season well by scoring

with a diving header in Plymouth's opening-day victory at Hull. After that, he struggled to maintain his starting place and most of his appearances were as a substitute. Rory went exactly a year after he signed without a competitive goal at Home Park before he scored a second-half equaliser against Southampton. The tall, powerful striker continues to be optimistic that he can become a regular and, in March, scored twice against Bristol City to help record an important victory and boost his chances at Home Park.

Barnsley (From trainee on 23/3/1999) FL 33+19/11 FLC 2+1 FAC 1 Others 2
Shrewsbury T (Loaned on 14/12/2001) FL 8+3
Swindon T (£60,000 on 14/11/2003) FL 43+32/21 FLC 1+2 FAC 2+2/1 Others 5+2/3
Yeovil T (Loaned on 22/2/2005) FL 2+4/1
Swansea C (£300,000 on 26/1/2006) FL 34+7/12 FLC 1 FAC 2+1 Others 3/1
Plymouth Arg (£300,000 on 19/1/2007) FL 18+26/8 FLC 0+2 FAC 1

FARQUHARSON Nicholas (Nick) Augustus

Born: Coventry, 7 September 1988
Height: 5'10" **Weight:** 12.10
A strong and aggressive midfielder with an eye for goal, Nick is a product of Crewe's youth system and progressed through the ranks in 2007-08 to make his debut in the Johnstone's Paint Trophy at Chester. With a view to adding experience, he was sent out on loan to Northwich in November, Nantwich in January and Nuneaton in March, but was not retained at the end of the campaign.

Crewe Alex (From trainee on 10/5/2007) Others 1

FAUBERT Julien

Born: Le Havre, France, 1 August 1983
Height: 5'10" **Weight:** 11.12
International Honours: France: 1
The flying French winger was signed by West Ham from Bordeaux in the summer but was injured on their pre-season tour. Playing in Austria, he ruptured an Achilles tendon and, after an extensive rehabilitation programme, finally made his debut as a substitute against Fulham in January. Unfortunately, he then suffered a niggling calf injury that forced him to miss games. He came back for a few matches and played particularly well against Newcastle in April, when he was superb with fast powerful running and direct crosses. Hammers fans look forward to seeing a fully-fit Julien.

West Ham U (£6,000,000 From Bordeaux, France, ex AS Cannes, on 13/7/2007) PL 4+3 FAC 0+1

FAYE Abdoulaye Diagne

Born: Dakar, Senegal, 26 February 1978
Height: 6'2" **Weight:** 13.10
International Honours: Senegal: 12
Abdoulaye made his only Bolton appearance in the opening-day defeat by Newcastle and it came as no surprise when Sam Allardyce returned to his former club to take this highly rated and versatile defender or midfielder to Tyneside just as the August transfer window closed. Expected to be used to stiffen Newcastle's midfield, most of his appearances were as a central defender, a position for which his aggression, power, and ability in the air are well suited. He was a regular starter until suffering a calf injury at Sunderland in December, a problem he aggravated on his return three weeks later, and was absent again during the African Cup of Nations when he appeared for Senegal. Returning at the end of February, when he scored his only goal in the home defeat by Manchester United, Abdoulaye became a fixture in the heart of the defence.

Bolton W (Signed from RC Lens, France on 3/8/2005) PL 53+7/3 FLC 2 FAC 3 Others 7
Newcastle U (£2,500,000 on 31/8/2007) PL 20+2/1 FLC 1 FAC 1

FAYE Amdy Mustapha

Born: Dakar, Senegal, 12 March 1977
Height: 6'1" **Weight:** 12.4
International Honours: Senegal: 13
Amdy made only one start for Charlton in 2007-08, against Stockport in the Carling Cup, and one substitute appearance against Sheffield Wednesday before being loaned to Glasgow Rangers for the remainder of the season in an attempt to cut the wage bill after relegation from the Premiership. Amdy can play in midfield or central defence, is good in the air and a strong tackler.

Portsmouth (£1,500,000 from Auxerre, France on 14/8/2003) PL 44+3 FLC 2 FAC 2+1
Newcastle U (£2,000,000 on 25/1/2005) PL 22+9 FLC 1+1 FAC 3 Others 9
Charlton Ath (£2,000,000 on 10/8/2006) P/FL 25+4/1 FLC 3+1 FAC 1
Glasgow Rgrs (Loaned on 31/8/2007) SL 2+2 SLC 1 Others 0+1

FEATHERSTONE Nicky Lee

Born: Goole, 22 September 1988
Height: 5'9" **Weight:** 11.7
Despite only six substitute appearances in Hull's highly successful Championship campaign, it was another season of solid progress for the locally-born youngster. Nicky made his full debut in the Carling Cup win at Crewe in August, in midfield rather than his usual attacking role. He was again in midfield for the victory at

Wigan in the next round as the Tigers beat Premier League opposition for the first time in a decade. Nicky's efforts were rewarded with a contract extension in September, up to June 2010.
Hull C (From trainee on 18/12/2006) FL 0+8 FLC 2+1 FAC 0+1

FEDERICI Adam
Born: Nowra, Australia, 31 January 1985
Height: 6'2" **Weight:** 14.2
International Honours: Australia: U21; Yth
The Australian goalkeeper had little opportunity to show his ability as he had to occupy the bench throughout every one of Reading's 38 Premiership games, such was the consistency of first-choice Marcus Hahnemann. Adam made four appearances, two each in the Carling and FA Cups, and was a regular in the Premiership Reserve League side, showing himself to be a reliable and brave goalkeeper. His work on the training ground with goalkeeping coach Sal Bibbo was sound, although he must be getting anxious for regular first-team football. He was in the limelight during the summer as a member of the Australian soccer squad bound for the Olympic Games in Beijing.
Wolverhampton W (Free from Australian Institute of Sport, via trial at Bolton W, on 27/2/2003. Freed during 2003 close season)
Reading (Free from Sardenga, Italy, following trial at Leeds U, on 20/1/2005) PL 0+2 FLC 2 FAC 6

FEENEY Warren James
Born: Belfast, 17 January 1981
Height: 5'10" **Weight:** 11.6
International Honours: NI: 24; U21-8; Yth; Sch
Signed from Luton in the summer, having been at Cardiff on loan towards the end of the previous season, the hard-running Irish striker was soon pushed out of the Cardiff front line by the arrival of big signings Robbie Fowler and Jimmy Floyd Hasselbaink. Allowed to join Swansea on loan just before the August transfer window closed, the Northern Ireland international striker followed in the footsteps of his grandfather Jim, who played at full-back for the Swans when they won the Third Division South title in 1948-49. Warren took some time to convince a minority of fans but before rupturing ankle ligaments against Southend, an injury that sidelined him for three months, his consistency and link-up play helped to establish the Swans as genuine promotion contenders. Although Swansea's manager Roberto Martinez was keen to keep him, the injury saw Warren returning to Cardiff in order to regain

fitness. Then, after almost recovering he damaged a knee and was out for the rest of the season. Even if fit, Warren could not have played in Cardiff's FA Cup run because he had already appeared for Swansea in the competition.
Leeds U (Signed from St Andrew's BC on 26/1/1998)
Bournemouth (Free on 22/3/2001) FL 83+25/36 FLC 1+1 FAC 6+4 Others 3+2/1
Stockport Co (Free on 29/7/2004) FL 31/15 FAC 2/2
Luton T (£175,000 on 24/3/2005) FL 45+32/8 FLC 4/2 FAC 1+1/1
Cardiff C (Signed on 23/2/2007) FL 5+6 FLC 1
Swansea C (Loaned on 31/8/2007) FL 7+3/5 FAC 1+1/1 Others 0+1

FEILHABER Benny
Born: Rio de Janeiro, Brazil, 19 January 1985
Height: 5'9" **Weight:** 10.10
International Honours: USA: 16
Arriving from SV Hamburg, like Robert Earnshaw Benny was a significant purchase given little chance to prove himself with Derby. He started only once, at Reading in October, but in his substitute appearances showed a tidy touch in midfield. He remained a regular in the United States' squad, despite a frustrating time at club level. Possible transfers to Israel and Major League Soccer were mooted but Benny was not interested in the moves. In his limited number of substitute appearances, he

always looked a sound player and passed accurately, which was seldom a feature of County's play.
Derby Co (£1,000,000 from SV Hamburg, Germany, ex UCLA, on 17/8/2007) PL 1+9

FENTON Nicholas (Nick) Leonard
Born: Preston, 23 November 1979
Height: 5'10" **Weight:** 10.4
International Honours: E: Yth
Nick was to prove one of Grimsby's most consistent performers, the central defender showing great form at both ends of the pitch. Town's main threat at set pieces, his best game among many was the Mariners' 4-1 Johnstone's Paint Trophy success over Huddersfield, Nick scoring once and claiming two assists in addition to solid defensive duties in a 'Man of the Match' display. His contribution in the back line was all the more creditable given that he had several defensive partners in a number of different formations.
Manchester C (From trainee on 26/11/1996) FL 15 FLC 3+1 Others 1
Notts Co (Loaned on 7/10/1999) FL 13/1 Others 1
Bournemouth (Loaned on 23/3/2000) FL 8
Bournemouth (Loaned on 11/8/2000) FL 4+1
Notts Co (£150,000 on 18/9/2000) FL 153+2/9 FLC 7 FAC 12/2 Others 4
Doncaster Rov (Free on 27/7/2004) FL 58+5/3 FLC 7 FAC 5/1 Others 4
Grimsby T (Signed on 25/8/2006) FL 77+3/6 FLC 1 FAC 5 Others 9/1

Nick Fenton

FERDINAND Anton Julian
Born: Peckham, 18 February 1985
Height: 6'0" **Weight:** 11.0
International Honours: E: U21-17; Yth
Anton was superb at the centre of the
West Ham defence, where he and Matty
Upson formed an excellent partnership.
In October, Anton sustained a hamstring
injury at Coventry and this forced him
to miss eight weeks of the season. He
returned against Manchester United in
December to head a fine goal in the 2-1
victory and followed this three games
later with the winner against Fulham.
Now too old for the England under-21
side, Anton is rapidly maturing and
looking towards the senior squad.
West Ham U (From trainee on 15/8/2002)
P/FL 118+20/5 FLC 6+1 FAC 14 Others 4

FERDINAND Rio Gavin
Born: Peckham, 7 November 1978
Height: 6'2" **Weight:** 12.1
Club Honours: PL '03, '07, '08; CS '03,
'07; FLC '06; UEFACL '08
International Honours: E: 68; B-1;
U21-5; Yth
A consummate Manchester United and
England central defender who combines
great strength in the air with neat skills
on the ground, Rio assumed the mantle
of captain in the absence of Gary Neville
with great aplomb. He started last season
in inspiring form, playing a major part
in a United defence that managed to
keep six consecutive clean sheets in
the Premiership before conceding an
early goal to Aston Villa at Villa Park in
October. It was also in this game that Rio
scored his first goal of the season. Three
days later, he notched his first European
Champions' League goal for the Reds
against Dynamo Kiev with a superb
header as United dominated to win 4-2.
He bagged a second Premiership goal
in the 6-0 drubbing of Newcastle at Old
Trafford and in United's FA Cup quarter-
final against Portsmouth in March, Rio
made a rare appearance as a goalkeeper
after Edwin Van Der Sar had left the pitch
with a groin injury and his replacement,
Tomasz Kuszczak, was sent off after
conceding a penalty. Unfortunately Rio
was unable to save Sulley Muntari's spot
kick and United's dream of a domestic
double ended. As the season reached
its climax, Rio shook off a couple of
injury scares to lead the Reds to their
ninth Premiership title and to success in
the European Champion's League final
against Chelsea in Moscow. Linked with
an early-season move to Barcelona, he
signed a bumper five-year contract that
will keep him at Old Trafford until 2013.

West Ham U (From trainee on 27/11/1995)
PL 122+5/2 FLC 11+1 FAC 9 Others 9
Bournemouth (Loaned on 8/11/1996) FL
10 Others 1
Leeds U (£18,000,000 on 27/11/2000) PL
54/2 FLC 2 FAC 3 Others 14/1
Manchester U (£29,100,000 + on
22/7/2002) PL 183+1/6 FLC 9+1 FAC 20+1
Others 51+1/1

FERENCZI Istvan
Born: Gyor, Hungary, 14 September 1977
Height: 6'3" **Weight:** 13.1
International Honours: Hungary: 9
Istvan again put every bit of energy into
playing in Barnsley's attack, leading the
line with physical strength and no little
skill. If his goal output was down on the
previous season, that in no way reflected
lack of effort. His partnership with Jon
Macken brought the Reds a number
of victories in their best League period,
leading up to Christmas, and Istvan was
usually on the bench in the second half of
the season.
Barnsley (£250,000 from Zalaegerszeg,
Hungary, ex Gyori Nosza, Tatabanyai SC,
MATAV Sopron, Zalaegerszeg, Verbroedring
Geel, Gyori ETO, Levski Sofia, VfL Osnabr on
31/1/2007) FL 39+14/11 FLC 0+1/1 FAC 4

[FERNANDES] TAVARES
FERNANDES Manuel Henriques
Born: Lisbon, Portugal, 5 February 1986
Height: 5'9" **Weight:** 10.12
International Honours: Portugal: 3;
U21-4; Yth
After a permanent deal fell through
during the summer, the Portuguese
under-23 international returned to
Everton on loan from Valencia in January.
Although obviously gifted, the midfielder
struggled initially through a shortage of
match-fitness and showed only glimpses
of his undoubted talent before finishing
the season strongly. A fine ball player with
the eye for a killer pass, his long-term
future at Everton was uncertain at the
end of the campaign.
Portsmouth (Loaned from Benfica, Portugal
on 31/8/2006) PL 7+3 FLC 2/1
Everton (Loaned from Benfica, Portugal on
31/1/2007) PL 8+1/2
Everton (Loaned from Valencia, Spain on
11/1/2008) PL 9+3 FLC 1 Others 1+1

FERNANDES Gelson
Born: Praia, Cape Verde, 2 September
1986
Height: 6'0" **Weight:** 11.3
International Honours: Switzerland:
11; U21-4
Gelson is a combative midfielder who
moved to Manchester City from Swiss

side FC Sion in July. As captain of the
Switzerland under-21 side, he attracted
the interest of a number of other
Premier League clubs, including Bolton
and Newcastle. He made his debut in
the Carling Cup win over Bristol City in
August and quickly followed that with his
first full cap, against Holland. He started
in the Premier League for the first time
against Portsmouth in November and
his all-action style looked well suited to
the demands of English football. Gelson
netted his first goal for the Blues in the
impressive 2-0 victory over Newcastle
at St James' Park in January, a decisive
blow for Sam Allardyce. His second was
in City's home defeat by Arsenal, Gelson
popping up in the penalty area to drag
the score back to 2-1. Having continued
to be a regular in his national side, playing
in their defeat by England at Wembley
in February, he also held down a regular
place at City.
Manchester C (Signed from Sion,
Switzerland on 20/7/2007) PL 21+5/2 FLC
2+1 FAC 1+2

FERREIRA Renato Paulo
Born: Cascais, Portugal, 18 January 1979
Height: 6'0" **Weight:** 11.13
Club Honours: FLC '05, '07; PL '05, '06;
CS '05
International Honours: Portugal: 51
It was a mixed campaign for Chelsea's
Portuguese right-back Paulo. The
departures of Geremi and Glen Johnson
ensured that Paulo would be undisputed
first choice at right-back but that
situation soon changed with the arrival
of Juliano Belletti from Barcelona, whose
long-range shooting added another
dimension to Chelsea's play. Paulo was
restricted to fitful appearances before
wresting the position back from Belletti
towards the end of the season but even
this upturn in fortune had a sting in
the tail as Michael Essien was preferred
to both players for crucial Champions'
League matches, including the final.
Paulo has endeared himself to Chelsea
fans with his wholehearted enthusiasm
and attacking dashes down the right,
something that was recognised in April
by the offer of a new five-year contract,
that was accepted with alacrity. The
season finished with yet more twists as
shortly before Paulo's omission from the
Champions' League final, Chelsea signed
another right-back, Jose Bosingwa for
a hefty fee. Ironically, Bosingwa was
Paulo's successor with both FC Porto and
Portugal.
Chelsea (£13,200,000 from FC Porto,
Portugal on 20/7/2004) PL 80+12 FLC 9+1
FAC 8+4/1 Others 23+3

FIELDING Francis (Frank) David

Born: Blackburn, 4 April 1988
Height: 6'1" **Weight:** 11.11
International Honours: E: Yth
When Wycombe lost both their permanent goalkeepers to injury within six weeks of the start of the season, Frank was signed from Blackburn as an emergency loan until January, making his professional debut in the 1-0 win at Bradford at the end of September. Clean sheets became a byword for Frank, keeping 15 in his 39 games, while proving to be an absolute rock in defence. He commands his area well, catches cleanly and is a particularly good shot-stopper, bringing off numerous breathtaking saves. He had to return to Rovers in January to sign a new contract with them but was soon back on loan until the end of the season.
Blackburn Rov (From trainee on 10/7/2006)
Wycombe W (Loaned on 28/9/2007) FL 36 FAC 1 Others 2

FIGUEROA Maynor

Born: Jutiapa, Honduras, 2 May 1983
Height: 5'11" **Weight:** 13.4
International Honours: Honduras: 51
The Honduran international was secured by Wigan on a six-month loan spell in the January transfer window after impressing in a three-week trial at Christmas. Recruited from Deportivo Olimpio, the same club from which the Latics signed Wilson Palacios, Maynor is a left-back who is quick, athletic and attack-minded. He had a difficult start to his Premier League career in trying to establish himself as a challenger to Erik Edman and Kevin Kilbane and his only appearance was as a last-minute substitute in the home match against Birmingham.
Wigan Ath (Loaned from Deportivo Olimpia, Honduras, ex Deportivo Victoria, on 22/1/2008) PL 1+1

FINLAY Matthew (Matt) James

Born: Salisbury, 25 January 1990
Height: 6'2" **Weight:** 12.0
A versatile left-sided Bournemouth youth player who can occupy a number of positions both in defence and attack, Matt was drafted into the first-team squad during an injury crisis last season. He went on as a substitute for the last 13 minutes against Tranmere in an assured debut but was released at the end of the season.
Bournemouth (Trainee - Brockenhurst College) FL 0+1

FINNAN Stephen (Steve) John

Born: Limerick, 20 April 1976
Height: 5'10" **Weight:** 11.6
Club Honours: Div 3 '98; Div 2 '99; Div 1 '01; UEFACL '05; ESC '05; FAC '06; CS '06
International Honours: RoI: 50; B-1; U21-8
Voted 'Player of the Year' by Liverpool supporters at the end of 2006-07, Steve signed a new two-year contract in the summer, seemingly at the peak of his career. It was a surprise, therefore, to find that his hold on the right-back slot was considerably loosened by Alvaro Arbeloa last season. The first warning came in December when he lost his place for six games, perhaps a factor in his announcing his retirement from international football in January. He returned to first-team duty at Christmas but lost his place again in March, initially and rather strangely to Jamie Carragher, and played in only the less important Premiership games thereafter, with Arbeloa as the first choice in the critical Champions League semi-final matches against Chelsea. Steve has been a model of consistency, if underrated, over five seasons at Anfield and it is unclear why he fell out of favour with Rafa Benitez unless the manager felt that, at 32, the Irishman lacked the pace of the younger Spaniard. For the Republic, Steve scored only his second international goal, a very late face-saver in a disappointing 1-1 draw with Cyprus in November in his penultimate appearance for the national team. Since the Republic failed to qualify for Euro 2008 in dismal fashion and feeling that he would be too old to play in the 2010 World Cup, he decided to retire although in May the new Irish manager, Giovanni Trappatoni, asked him to reconsider.
Birmingham C (£100,000 from Welling U on 12/6/1995) FL 9+6/1 FLC 2+2 Others 2+1
Notts Co (Loaned on 5/3/1996) FL 14+3/2 Others 3/1
Notts Co (£300,000 on 31/10/1996) FL 71+9/5 FLC 4 FAC 7/1 Others 1
Fulham (£600,000 on 13/11/1998) P/FL 171+1/6 FLC 10+1 FAC 18/1 Others 6
Liverpool (£3,500,000 on 30/6/2003) PL 134+11/1 FLC 5+1 FAC 12+1 Others 49+4

FINNIGAN John Francis

Born: Wakefield, 29 March 1976
Height: 5'8" **Weight:** 10.11
The Cheltenham captain's season was ended early by a troublesome combination of heel and ankle injuries that required an operation in February. It began positively enough for him with two goals in the opening nine games and

some trademark performances of midfield industry. His partnership with David Bird in central midfield offered much promise but the injury surfaced in a 2-0 defeat at Doncaster in September. He started two more games but was substituted in both and a New Year comeback in the reserves lasted less than 15 minutes. The medical staff took a long-term view and opted for surgery that should result in a return early in the new season.
Nottingham F (From trainee on 10/5/1993)
Lincoln C (£50,000 on 26/3/1998) FL 139+4/3 FLC 7 FAC 8+1/1 Others 7
Cheltenham T (Free on 7/3/2002) FL 197+6/19 FLC 6+1/1 FAC 10+1/1 Others 11+1/4

FLAHAVAN Darryl James

Born: Southampton, 9 September 1977
Height: 5'10" **Weight:** 12.1
Club Honours: Div 1 '06
Having started last season as Southend's first-choice goalkeeper, Darryl lost his place to Steve Collis in early September and did not return until January. Although small in stature, Darryl again showed his class between the posts, playing a major part in Southend's end of season charge to the play-offs. Having improved his one weak point, coming off his line for crosses, Darryl will look forward to another season as Southend's number-one.
Southampton (From trainee on 14/5/1996. Free to Woking on 13/8/1998)
Southend U (Free from Chesham U on 16/10/2000) FL 289+2 FLC 9 FAC 23 Others 28

FLAMINI Mathieu

Born: Marseille, France, 7 March 1984
Height: 5'10" **Weight:** 11.12
International Honours: France: 2; U21
Mathieu had the chance to operate in his favoured central midfield berth at Arsenal because of Gilberto's absence at the Copa America and seized it with aplomb. His energetic displays allowed his midfield partner Cesc Fabregas to venture further forward and score goals. Mathieu not only works hard defensively but also attacks with ability and contributed three goals in his 30 Premier League appearances. He also featured in eight of the club's Champions' League ties but injury in the last of these, against Liverpool in the Anfield quarter-final, brought his season to a premature end. Despite his insistence on wanting to stay with Arsenal, Mathieu would not commit to a new contract and in May it was confirmed that he had chosen instead to move on a free transfer to AC Milan. His

departure was a huge disappointment and although he managed only one really consistent season in an Arsenal shirt, his loss will be felt keenly.
Arsenal *(Signed from Olympique Marseille, France on 11/8/2004) PL 67+35/7 FLC 7+2 FAC 10+1 Others 25+6/1*

FLEMING Andrew (Andy) Lee
Born: Liverpool, 18 February 1989
Height: 6'1" **Weight:** 12.0
Following on from his debut the previous season, Andy impressed Wrexham's coaching staff with his attitude and displays for the reserves. A neat and tidy front man with some good touches, Andy was brought into the starting line-up late in the season with so many others misfiring and could do well in the Blue Square Premier.
Wrexham *(From trainee on 30/7/2007) FL 3+3*

FLETCHER Carl Neil
Born: Camberley, 7 April 1980
Height: 5'10" **Weight:** 11.7
International Honours: W: 29
Carl started last season as the Crystal Palace club captain under Peter Taylor and scored a fine goal against Sheffield United. The talented midfield player then scored his first international goal for Wales against Norway in February, a game that marked his 27th appearance for his country. Carl has now passed 300 League games since starting with Bournemouth in 1998.
Bournemouth *(From trainee on 3/7/1998) FL 186+7/19 FLC 6 FAC 15+1/1 Others 9+1/3*
West Ham U *(£250,000 on 31/8/2004) P/FL 32+12/3 FLC 0+1 FAC 4+3 Others 1*
Watford *(Loaned on 16/9/2005) FL 3*
Crystal Palace *(£400,000 on 2/8/2006) FL 50+15/4 FAC 3*

FLETCHER Darren Barr
Born: Dalkeith, 1 February 1984
Height: 6'0" **Weight:** 13.5
Club Honours: FAC '04; FLC '06; PL '07, '08; CS '07; UEFACL '08
International Honours: S: 36; B- 1; U21-2
An elegant Manchester United and Scotland midfield player, who has an excellent touch and passing skills, Darren faced a new threat to his place following the arrival of Owen Hargreaves from Bayern Munich. Used mainly as a substitute through the Premiership campaign - he made only five starts – he figured more in the highly successful Champions' League run to final victory in Moscow. Also making a rare start in the FA Cup run, he came into contention for the fifth round against Arsenal at

Old Trafford and scored two goals as the Reds knocked out the Gunners 4-0. In April, he played his part as a second-half substitute as United beat Barcelona at Old Trafford to earn their place in the Champions' League final against Chelsea.
Manchester U *(From trainee on 3/2/2001) PL 79+28/7 FLC 10 FAC 11+7/2 Others 26+11*

FLETCHER Steven (Steve) Mark
Born: Hartlepool, 26 June 1972
Height: 6'2" **Weight:** 14.9
After leaving Bournemouth in the summer, the imposing forward performed wholeheartedly to lead Chesterfield's attack, easily surviving the hurly-burly of League Two to hold the ball and bring team-mates into the game with deft flicks. He also weighed in with his highest goal return since 2004. The fans took to the big man, but Steve found travelling from his south coast home difficult and regretfully declined Chesterfield's offer of a contract for 2008-09.
Hartlepool U *(From trainee on 23/8/1990) FL 19+13/4 FLC 0+2/1 FAC 1+2 Others 2+2/1*
Bournemouth *(£30,000 on 28/7/1992) FL 446+47/87 FLC 30/4 FAC 31+2/9 Others 19+3/5*
Chesterfield *(Free on 11/7/2007) FL 23+15/5 FAC 1*

FLINDERS Scott Liam
Born: Rotherham, 12 June 1986
Height: 6'4" **Weight:** 14.0
International Honours: E: Yth
Scott's only appearances in Crystal Palace's goal last season were in Cup competitions and with Neil Warnock not naming a substitute 'keeper for the bench, he had two spells on loan, to Yeovil in February and to Blackpool in March. Signed by Yeovil as a replacement for the injured Steve Mildenhall, the towering goalkeeper played nine times, keeping two clean sheets in difficult times, and was solid as Town battled for League One safety. Back at Selhurst Park, with Julian Speroni still blocking his way to first-team football and in a bid to further his experience, Scott was next allowed to move to Blackpool but did not play for the first team.
Barnsley *(From trainee on 2/4/2005) FL 14 FLC 2 FAC 2 Others 1*
Crystal Palace *(Signed on 17/7/2006) FL 7+1 FLC 2 FAC 3*
Gillingham *(Loaned on 8/9/2006) FL 9 Others 1*
Brighton & Hove A *(Loaned on 20/2/2007) FL 12*
Yeovil T *(Loaned on 11/2/2008) FL 9*

FLO Tore Andre
Born: Stryn, Norway, 15 June 1973
Height: 6'4" **Weight:** 13.8
Club Honours: FLC '98; ECWC '98; ESC '98; FAC '00; CS '00; SLC '02; SC '02
International Honours: Norway: 75; U21
Star Norwegian striker Tore Andre brought the curtain down on his illustrious career when he announced his retirement in March. Leeds had hoped to get plenty of football out of the former Chelsea man but a succession of injuries restricted him to four League One starts. When he did play, however, his class was obvious, as he left the bench to score late goals in wins over Southend, Port Vale and Huddersfield, all at Elland Road. A superb reader of the game, he was a model professional and true gentleman who reached the highest level of the game.
Chelsea *(£300,000 from Brann Bergen, Norway, ex Sogndal, Tromso, on 4/8/1997) PL 59+53/34 FLC 7+2/3 FAC 5+5/1 Others 23+9/12*
Glasgow Rgrs *(£12,000,000 on 23/11/2000) SL 44+9/29 SLC 2+1/1 SC 5/4 Others 10+1/4*
Sunderland *(£6,750,000 on 30/8/2002) P/FL 23+6/4 FLC 2/2 FAC 1+1 (Transferred to Siena, Italy on 28/8/2003)*
Leeds U *(Free from Valerenga, Norway on 3/1/2007) FL 5+18/4 FAC 0+1*

FLYNN Matthew
Born: Preston, 10 May 1989
Height: 6'0" **Weight:** 11.8
Matthew, a full-back, was awarded his first professional contract in the summer, having progressed through the ranks at Macclesfield. His senior debut came in the first round Johnstone's Paint Trophy victory at Wrexham, when he went on as a substitute in the final moments for what turned out to be his sole senior appearance. Matthew spent a month on loan at non-League side Warrington.
Macclesfield T *(From trainee on 21/2/2008) Others 0+1*

FLYNN Michael (Mike) John
Born: Newport, 17 October 1980
Height: 5'10" **Weight:** 12.10
Club Honours: Div 2 '03
International Honours: W: SP
Mike signed on a free in the summer following two years at Gillingham, where he was top scorer with 12 goals from central midfield and club captain. His time at Blackpool was not as successful as that but he still managed to make 20 starts in the League and score three goals, his first against Scunthorpe in a 1-1 draw. He played in both derbies against Preston

but dropped out of the side when Keith Southern returned and was released at the end of the season.
Wigan Ath (£50,000 from Barry T, ex Newport Co, on 25/6/2002) FL 5+33/2 FLC 0+4 FAC 1+2/1 Others 2
Blackpool (Loaned on 20/8/2004) FL 6 FLC 1
Gillingham (Signed on 3/2/2005) FL 90+7/19 FLC 4 FAC 3/2 Others 1
Blackpool (Free on 6/7/2007) FL 20+8/3 FLC 3 FAC 1

FOGDEN Wesley (Wes) Keith
Born: Brighton, 12 April 1988
Height: 5'9" **Weight:** 11.6
Having recovered from the health problems which threatened his career, Wes will be pleased to have established himself as a member of the squad at Brighton, where his versatility – he can play at right-back or as a right-winger – comes in useful. After a lengthy loan at Dorchester, he made his debut at right-back in a Johnstone's Paint Trophy tie at Swansea and acquitted himself admirably, doing much to negate the considerable threat offered by the eventual League One champions. As captain of the reserves, Wes lifted the Sussex Senior Cup at the end of the season.
Brighton & Hove A (From trainee on 28/6/2006) FL 1+2 Others 1

FOJUT Jaroslaw
Born: Legionowo, Poland, 17 October 1987
Height: 6'2" **Weight:** 13.0
International Honours: Poland: Yth
After impressing several top European clubs as a schoolboy playing in youth tournaments, the Polish centre-back signed for Bolton at 17 on a two-year contract. He joined Luton on loan and made his debut in the Johnstone's Paint Trophy against Northampton, looking solid and capable before earning a League debut as a substitute against Bristol Rovers. Confident in Jaroslaw's ability, manager Kevin Blackwell rested Chris Coyne for the Carling Cup game at home to Charlton to give him his first start. His performance then and in subsequent games belied his age and when Coyne returned, Chris Perry was moved to left-back. Brave, skilful and good in the air, Jaroslaw played in 11 consecutive matches and when he added goals to his game, became a player to rely on, as was evident when he was missing with a slight injury. The time on loan improved his game so he was disappointed that, as a result of Luton going into administration, the FA and League refused to sanction an extension.

Bolton W (From trainee on 6/7/2006) PL 0+1 FLC 1+1 FAC 0+1
Luton T (Loaned on 31/8/2007) FL 15+1/2 FLC 2 FAC 3/1 Others 2

FOLAN Caleb Colman
Born: Leeds, 26 October 1982
Height: 6'1" **Weight:** 12.12
Caleb, a tall striker with a languid style, speed and deft skill, started only once for Wigan in the Premier League, on the opening day. Days after featuring in Wigan's Carling Cup defeat by Hull in August, he swapped sides to become the Tigers' first £1-million signing. He had been at Hull on loan in 2001 and soon made a vastly bigger impact than in his previous 22-minute substitute appearance against Oxford. His second City debut ended with a night in a Blackpool hospital after suffering a neck injury. Although he was also hampered by a niggling foot injury, Caleb was soon playing a crucial part in the rise to the Premier League through the Championship play-off final. Often used to great effect from the bench, he enjoyed an especially potent strike partnership with Manchester United loanee Fraizer Campbell.
Leeds U (From trainee on 2/11/1999)
Rushden & Diamonds (Loaned on 5/10/2001) FL 1+5 Others 1
Hull C (Loaned on 30/11/2001) FL 0+1
Chesterfield (Free on 14/2/2003) FL 57+45/15 FLC 3+1/3 FAC 1+1 Others 2/1
Wigan Ath (£500,000 on 26/1/2007) PL 9+6/2 FLC 1
Hull C (£1,000,000 on 31/8/2007) FL 18+11/8 FAC 1 Others 0+3/1

FOLEY David John
Born: South Shields, 12 May 1987
Height: 5'4" **Weight:** 8.9
Able to play in midfield or as a striker, the skilful young Hartlepool player had long shown promise and early in the season it looked as if David was about to make the big breakthrough. As a second-half substitute in the Carling Cup tie at Scunthorpe, he scored two late goals to seal a great 2-1 win and also scored in a Johnstone's Paint Trophy tie, but a League goal still eludes him. A useful squad member he was on the substitutes' bench in 31 of the 46 League games.
Hartlepool U (From trainee on 4/7/2006) FL 17+56 FLC 0+5/2 FAC 0+1 Others 1+3/2

FOLEY Kevin Patrick
Born: Luton, 1 November 1984
Height: 5'9" **Weight:** 11.2
Club Honours: Div 1 '05
International Honours: RoI: B-1; U21-9
A surprise signing from Luton at the beginning of last season, Kevin immediately made the Wolverhampton right-back place his own. He even scored a fine goal, chesting the ball down against Norwich and lashing it in. Kevin played in 36 consecutive games and seemed an early candidate for 'Player of the Season'. Although he suffered a slight dip in form, with some mixed performances, he continued to give his all and produced a fine display when moved up to central midfield against Ipswich in April.
Luton T (From trainee on 8/3/2004) FL 143+8/3 FLC 3+2/2 FAC 8 Others 1+1
Wolverhampton W (£700,000 on 14/8/2007) FL 42+2/1 FLC 2 FAC 3

Kevin Foley

155

FOLLY Yoann
Born: Paris, France, 6 June 1985
Height: 5'11" **Weight:** 11.0
International Honours: France: U21
Leaving Sheffield Wednesday to join
his old boss Paul Sturrock at Plymouth
in January seemed like a good move
for the young French midfielder. Yoann
never established himself at Hillsborough.
Although skilful and, when in the mood,
able to cover ground to good effect, his
inconsistency counted against him. He
scored against Hartlepool in the Carling
Cup but handed in a transfer request and
joined Sturrock for the third time in his
career on a two-and-a-half year deal. A
central midfielder who can also play out
wide or at full-back, his opportunities at
Plymouth were restricted by a mystery
virus. Yoann made only one starting
appearance for the Pilgrims, against
Ipswich in January, and aimed to regain
full fitness in summer.
*Southampton (£250,000 from St Etienne,
France on 31/7/2003) P/FL 12+2 FLC 2+1
FAC 0+1*
*Nottingham F (Loaned on 7/1/2005) FL 0+1
FAC 1/1*
Preston NE (Loaned on 14/3/2005) FL 0+2
*Sheffield Wed (Signed on 31/1/2006) FL
41+12 FLC 0+1/1 FAC 0+1*
*Plymouth Arg (£200,000 on 11/1/2008) FL
1+3 FAC 0+1*

FONTAINE Liam Vaughan Henry
Born: Beckenham, 7 January 1986
Height: 6'3" **Weight:** 12.2
Club Honours: Div 2 '05
International Honours: E: Yth
This wholehearted defender had another
good season at Ashton Gate but
possibly suffers through his versatility.
He impressed when deputising at the
back for Jamie McAllister as Bristol City
embarked on a six-match unbeaten
run following a goalless draw at Hull.
His highlight was a first-ever goal
when he netted City's equaliser at
Wolverhampton, a feat that caused
manager Gary Johnson to back-track
over his bet to bare his backside in
Burton's window until TV AM obliged
him to stage the stunt in a dignified
manner. To his surprise, Liam played a
full part in City's defeat by Hull in the
play-off final because Jamie McCombe
was laid low by a stomach bug the
previous night.
*Fulham (From trainee on 5/3/2004) PL 0+1
FAC 1*
*Yeovil T (Loaned on 13/8/2004) FL 15 FLC
2 Others 1*
*Kilmarnock (Loaned on 28/1/2005) SL 3
SC 2*

*Yeovil T (Loaned on 31/8/2005) FL 10 FLC
1 FAC 0+1*
*Bristol C (Signed on 16/1/2006) FL 69+14/1
FLC 3 FAC 4+1/1 Others 5+3*

FONTE Jose Miguel da Rocha
Born: Penafiel, Portugal, 22 December
1983
Height: 6'2" **Weight:** 12.8
International Honours: Portugal: U21-3
The brother of Arsenal's Rui Fonte, the
tall young Portuguese central defender
was signed by Crystal Palace from Benfica
on a year's loan in June when Peter
Taylor was manager. Although starting as
fourth choice, Jose ended the season as
the regular partner to Mark Hudson and
scored a brilliant 20-yard volley in a 2-1
victory over Stoke, his only goal of the
campaign.
*Crystal Palace (Loaned from Benfica,
Portugal, ex Vitoria Setubal, Pacos de Ferreira
- loan, Estrela Amadora - loan, on 31/7/2007)
FL 17+5/1 FLC 1 FAC 1 Others 1+1*

FORAN Richard (Richie)
Born: Dublin, 16 June 1980
Height: 6'1" **Weight:** 12.9
International Honours: RoI: U21-2
Struggling to hold a place in the Southend
squad, Richie was consigned to the bench
except for a lone start in the Johnstone's
Paint Trophy tie against Dagenham,
when he was played out of position in
left midfield. It was still something of a
surprise that he was loaned out to League
Two side Darlington in October, a move
that was extended for the remainder
of the season in the January transfer
window. He returned to Roots Hall at the
end of the campaign nursing a serious
knee injury. Darlington used Richie as a
striker, to exploit his strength in the air, as
well as in left midfield. A series of niggling
injuries restricted him to just 11 starts
and after being sent off against Bradford
in late March, a knee injury ended his
season. He contributed three goals,
including a crucial match-winning penalty
at Mansfield in January.
*Carlisle U (£20,000 from Shelbourne on
31/8/2001) FL 84+7/25 FLC 1 FAC 6/2 Others
7+2/2*
Oxford U (Loaned on 9/1/2004) FL 3+1
*Motherwell (Free on 16/6/2004) SL
76+14/23 SLC 10+2/11 SC 3/1*
*Southend U (£200,000 on 31/1/2007) FL
9+12/1 FLC 0+1 Others 1/1*
*Darlington (Loaned on 14/11/2007) FL
11+1/2*

FORBES Adrian Emmanuel
Born: Ealing, 23 January 1979
Height: 5'8" **Weight:** 11.10
Club Honours: AMC '06
International Honours: E: Yth

Unable to make the step up from
League One to the Championship with
Blackpool, the right-winger started only
one Carling Cup game and made two
substitute appearances in the League
before being transferred to Millwall in
January. Having signed an 18-month
contract for the Lions, this versatile
player proved he could play anywhere
on the field with confidence. Very
quick and hard working with a great
engine, Adrian was like a little terrier
in the middle of the park but found it
hard to regain his place after an injury.
Recognised as an asset, he was an
important player to have on the bench.
*Norwich C (From trainee on 21/1/1997) FL
66+46/8 FLC 1+4 FAC 2+2*
*Luton T (£60,000 on 16/7/2001) FL
39+33/14 FLC 1 FAC 5/6 Others 0+1*
*Swansea C (Free on 2/7/2004) FL 48+21/11
FLC 1 FAC 5+1 Others 6+4/1*
*Blackpool (Free on 5/7/2006) FL 26+10/1
FLC 1 FAC 5 Others 4*
*Millwall (Signed on 4/1/2008) FL 6+5 FAC
2+1*

FORBES Kieron Emerson
Born: Wembley, 17 August 1990
Height: 5'5" **Weight:** 11.3
A central midfield player in his second
year as a Watford Academy scholar,
Kieron made his first-team debut at
the age of 16 as a substitute against
Gillingham in the Carling Cup. He
continued to make regular appearances in
the reserves and youth teams but was not
retained at the end of the season.
Watford (Trainee) FLC 0+1

FORBES Terrell Dishan
Born: Southwark, 17 August 1981
Height: 6'0" **Weight:** 12.8
Club Honours: FAYC '99
The centre-back's second season with
Yeovil raised his status amongst fans even
higher as his fantastic tackling and pace
helped to shore up the defence when
most needed. Terrell's style of closing his
opponents down quickly and giving them
little time proved highly successful and
when coupled with composure and the
ability to use both feet, provided Yeovil
with a strong, reliable defender.
West Ham U (From trainee on 2/7/1999)
*Bournemouth (Loaned on 18/10/1999) FL
3 FAC 1*
*Queens Park Rgrs (Free on 24/7/2001) FL
113+1 FLC 6 FAC 3+1 Others 6*
*Grimsby T (Free on 15/9/2004) FL 33
Others 1*
*Oldham Ath (Free on 4/7/2005) FL 33+6 FLC
1 FAC 3 Others 1*
*Yeovil T (Free on 21/7/2006) FL 87 FLC 2
FAC 2 Others 7*

FORDE David

Born: Galway, 20 December 1979
Height: 6'2" **Weight:** 13.7
Although ending 2006-07 as Cardiff's first-choice goalkeeper, the Irishman was unable to make the team last season and joined Luton on loan in August. He had an immediate debut against Gillingham as Luton's three other registered 'keepers were all injured. David is powerfully built, handles safely and positions himself intelligently. After a clean sheet in the Carling Cup against Sunderland, there was speculation that his loan might become a permanent move but manager Kevin Blackwell did not pursue his interest. Instead, David joined Bournemouth on an emergency loan in March. After a couple of games in which he gained much needed match-time, he excelled in the dramatic final run in as Bournemouth won seven of the final nine games, with the highlight being a brilliant penalty save against Millwall. Was released at the end of the campaign.
West Ham U *(£75,000 from Barry T on 1/2/2002. Freed during 2004 close season)*
Cardiff C *(Signed from Derry C on 2/1/2007) FL 7*
Luton T *(Loaned on 24/8/2007) FL 5 FLC 1*
Bournemouth *(Loaned on 7/3/2008) FL 11*

FORRESTER Jamie Mark

Born: Bradford, 1 November 1974
Height: 5'6" **Weight:** 11.0
Club Honours: FAYC '93
International Honours: E: Yth (UEFA-U18 '93); Sch
Having finished his first season at Sincil Bank as Lincoln's leading scorer, the experienced striker was once again a regular on the score sheet in 2007-08 with his 44 League and Cup outings yielding 14 goals. His intelligent and unselfish play saw him link up well with Ben Wright, with the duo playing a major part in the Imps' recovery from the bottom of the League to a respectable mid-table finish. At the end of his contract, Jamie agreed a move to Notts County.
Leeds U *(£60,000 from Auxerre, France on 20/10/1992) PL 7+2 FAC 1+1/2*
Southend U *(Loaned on 1/9/1994) FL 3+2*
Grimsby T *(Loaned on 10/3/1995) FL 7+2/1*
Grimsby T *(Signed on 17/10/1995) FL 27+14/6 FLC 0+1 FAC 3+1/3*
Scunthorpe U *(Signed on 21/3/1997) FL 99+2/37 FLC 6/1 FAC 7/4 Others 7 (Free to FC Utrecht, Holland on 1/6/1999)*
Walsall *(Loaned on 30/12/1999) FL 2+3*
Northampton T *(£150,000 from FC Utrecht, Holland on 21/3/2000) FL 109+12/45 FLC 5/1 FAC 7/2 Others 3/2*
Hull C *(Signed on 22/11/2003) FL 17+15/7 FAC 0+1 Others 1/1*

Bristol Rov *(Free on 5/7/2004) FL 23+29/9 FAC 0+1 Others 3+1/2*
Lincoln C *(Signed on 23/3/2006) FL 85+5/35 FLC 2/1 FAC 3/1 Others 4+2*

FORSSELL Mikael Kaj

Born: Steinfurt, Germany, 15 March 1981
Height: 6'1" **Weight:** 12.8
International Honours: Finland: 55; U21-8; Yth
Ended last season as Birmingham's top-scorer with nine goals and bagged Blues' first top-flight hat-trick since 1981, against Tottenham in March. Mikael came into own after Alex McLeish was appointed as manager and could never be faulted for his effort. When the ball is played into the penalty area, he has a habit of finding space or being on the end of things and finishing clinically. He also showed great discipline in dropping deep as required by the manager when the team were defending. Was released in the summer.
Chelsea *(Free from HJK Helsinki, Finland on 18/12/1998) PL 6+27/5 FLC 1+4/2 FAC 3+6/5 Others 2+4*
Crystal Palace *(Loaned on 23/2/2000) FL 13/3*
Crystal Palace *(Loaned on 30/6/2000) FL 31+8/13 FLC 8/2 FAC 1+1*

Birmingham C *(Loaned on 29/8/2003) PL 32/17 FLC 0+1 FAC 3+1/2*
Birmingham C *(Loaned on 1/7/2004) PL 4*
Birmingham C *(£3,000,000 on 4/7/2005) P/FL 34+31/13 FLC 5+1/2 FAC 5+1/3*

FORSTER Nicholas (Nicky) Michael

Born: Caterham, 8 September 1973
Height: 5'10" **Weight:** 11.5
International Honours: E: U21-4
A good number of Brighton fans were surprised when Nicky, then 33, was signed from Hull on a three-year contract but it proved to be good business for the Sussex side. It was three months into the season before the experienced striker got into his stride following a thigh injury and a bout of sickness but Nicky never looked back and ended the campaign with 19 goals, including two in a match six times. Still blessed with considerable pace, he showed himself to be a whole-hearted player, never afraid to defend from the front by closing down defenders. In January he assumed the captaincy and inspired others with his effort, vocal encouragement and on-pitch coaching before finishing as runner-up to Tommy Elphick in the 'Player of the

Terrell Forbes

157

Season' award.

Gillingham *(Signed from Horley T on 22/5/1992) FL 54+13/24 FLC 3+2 FAC 6/2*
Brentford *(£100,000 on 17/6/1994) FL 108+1/39 FLC 11/3 FAC 8/1 Others 7+1/4*
Birmingham C *(£700,000 on 31/1/1997) FL 24+44/11 FLC 2+2/1 FAC 3+1*
Reading *(£650,000 on 23/6/1999) FL 157+30/60 FLC 10+1/4 FAC 7+1/2 Others 5+4/2*
Ipswich T *(Free on 1/8/2005) FL 21+3/8 FLC 1*
Hull C *(£250,000 on 31/8/2006) FL 26+9/5 FAC 1+1/1*
Brighton & Hove A *(£75,000 on 6/7/2007) FL 39+2/15 FLC 1 FAC 4/2 Others 2/2*

FORTE Jonathan Ronald James
Born: Sheffield, 25 July 1986
Height: 6'2"   **Weight:** 12.2
Club Honours: AMC '07
International Honours: Barbados: 1
Signed from Sheffield United in the summer, Jonathan suffered an inconsistent first season with Championship side Scunthorpe, drifting in and out of the starting line-up before enjoying five successive starts for the first time in the closing five games of the season. Very quick with silky skills, he was employed as a winger on either flank or up front, doing particularly well when asked to play as a lone striker in the away matches at Charlton and Sheffield United. He scored four times during a campaign in which he was also called up to make his international debut for Barbados in a World Cup qualifier.

Sheffield U *(From trainee on 7/7/2004) FL 2+28/1 FLC 3+2 FAC 0+4*
Doncaster Rov *(Loaned on 31/8/2005) FL 6+2/4 Others 1*
Doncaster Rov *(Loaned on 19/11/2005) FL 3+2 Others 1*
Rotherham U *(Loaned on 9/1/2006) FL 8+3/4*
Doncaster Rov *(Loaned on 21/7/2006) FL 31+10/5 FLC 3/3 FAC 4 Others 3/1*
Scunthorpe U *(Signed on 16/7/2007) FL 18+20/4 FLC 0+1 FAC 0+1*

FORTUNE Clayton Alexander
Born: Forest Gate, 10 November 1982
Height: 6'3"   **Weight:** 13.10
Clayton returned for pre-season from a dislocated shoulder only to suffer the same injury during a Leyton Orient warm-up game at Grays. Frustratingly, he came back only to suffer the injury again during training. This required an operation to correct the problem. Clayton appeared before the end of the season as a substitute against Cheltenham but was out of contract during the summer.

Bristol C *(From trainee at Tottenham H on 22/3/2001) FL 29+24 FLC 2+2 FAC 1 Others 5+2*

Port Vale *(Loaned on 10/11/2005) FL 20+5/2 FAC 4*
Leyton Orient *(Free on 3/8/2006) FL 9+1 FLC 1*
Port Vale *(Loaned on 23/11/2006) FL 11+2 FAC 1 Others 1*

FORTUNE Jonathan (Jon) Jay
Born: Islington, 23 August 1980
Height: 6'2"   **Weight:** 11.4
Jon started last season as Charlton's first-choice central defender, alongside Madjid Bougherra and then Sam Sodje. Having been sent off, after the final whistle, against Ipswich in December, he was unable to regain his position from the impressive Paddy McCarthy when his ban was served. He made only a handful of appearances after that and none after the away defeat at Blackpool, in which he scored the third goal in a 5-3 defeat. He also scored in the 2-1 defeat at Stoke in August. Jon is an accomplished central defender, quick, strong, good in the air and keen to go up for free kicks and corners.

Charlton Ath *(From trainee on 2/7/1998) P/FL 123+26/7 FLC 12+2/1 FAC 10+1/2*
Mansfield T *(Loaned on 18/2/2000) FL 4*
Mansfield T *(Loaned on 31/8/2000) FL 14*
Stoke C *(Loaned on 31/1/2007) FL 4*
Stoke C *(Loaned on 7/3/2007) FL 10/1*

FOSTER Benjamin (Ben) Anthony
Born: Leamington Spa, 3 April 1983
Height: 6'2"   **Weight:** 12.6
Club Honours: AMC '05
International Honours: E: 1
A young Manchester United goalkeeper who has rocketed to prominence since his transfer from Stoke, Ben made his Premiership debut in March against Derby when Edwin Van Der Sar and Tomasz Kuszczak were injured and suspended respectively, Kuszczak having been sent off against Portsmouth in the FA Cup the previous Saturday. United won 1-0, with Ben making two crucial saves on the way to keeping a clean sheet. Despite that promising start, he was back to reserve duty again but is strongly tipped to figure in the future.

Stoke C *(Signed from Racing Club Warwick on 25/4/2001)*
Kidderminster Hrs *(Loaned on 29/10/2004) FL 2*
Wrexham *(Loaned on 24/1/2005) FL 17 Others 4*
Manchester U *(£1,000,000 on 22/7/2005) PL 1*
Watford *(Loaned on 2/8/2005) FL 44 FAC 1 Others 3*
Watford *(Loaned on 10/8/2006) PL 29 FLC 1 FAC 3*

FOSTER Daniel (Danny)
Born: Enfield, 23 September 1984
Height: 5'10"   **Weight:** 12.10
Club Honours: FC '07
International Honours: E: SP-3
Danny suffered for most of the season with a groin injury and need pain-killing injections to survive the first half of the campaign. At that stage, Dagenham's right-back feared that he would need an operation, but a rest in early December helped and he continued to play until March before undergoing minor surgery. Danny netted a rare goal in the victory over Hereford at the end of February.

Tottenham H *(From trainee on 25/7/2002)*
Dagenham & Redbridge *(Free on 1/7/2004) FL 31+1/1 FLC 1 FAC 3*

FOSTER Stephen
Born: Mansfield, 3 December 1974
Height: 6'1"   **Weight:** 12.0
Club Honours: FAT '97; Div 3 '04; Div 1 '07
Signed from Scunthorpe during the close season, Stephen was the rock upon which the Darlington defence was based and he missed only four games all season. Significantly, the Quakers did not win in his absence. He is strong in the air and his vast experience allows him to read the game so well as to make his performances seem effortless. He was made club captain by Dave Penney, who had managed him at Doncaster, and very much led by example. Stephen contributed two goals to the campaign but more important were the countless numbers he prevented with his timely interventions at the back and confident organising of his fellow defenders.

Mansfield T *(From trainee on 15/7/1993) FL 2+3 FLC 2 (Free to Telford U on 22/1/1994)*
Bristol Rov *(£150,000 from Woking on 23/5/1997) FL 193+4/7 FLC 14 FAC 13 Others 11*
Doncaster Rov *(Free on 1/8/2002) FL 95/2 FLC 7 FAC 3 Others 3*
Scunthorpe U *(Free on 19/1/2006) FL 62 FLC 2 FAC 3 Others 1*
Darlington *(Free on 18/7/2007) FL 42/2 FLC 1 FAC 2 Others 3*

FOSTER Stephen (Steve) John
Born: Warrington, 10 September 1980
Height: 5'11"   **Weight:** 11.8
International Honours: E: Sch
Steve made only one appearance in Burnley's colours, in the Carling Cup victory at Grimsby, before moving to Barnsley in the August transfer window. The sheer weight of competition for places in defence at Turf Moor limited his opportunities for progress there. Barnsley signed him on a two-year contract and

he made his debut a day later in the victory over Plymouth. As the season developed, Steve became one their most consistent performers. He started at right-back and when Lewin Nyatanga went back to Derby, successfully switched to centre-back. Such was his form that when Nyatanga returned to Oakwell, Steve continued at centre-back and was a leading performer in the FA Cup run, scoring crucial equalisers against both Blackpool and Liverpool. He was voted 'Player of the Season' by the supporters.
Crewe Alex *(From trainee on 19/9/1998) FL 200+18/15 FLC 9+1/2 FAC 10+1/1 Others 4*
Burnley *(Free on 2/8/2006) FL 7+10 FLC 2 FAC 1*
Barnsley *(£100,000 on 24/8/2007) FL 41/1 FAC 5/2*

FOTHERINGHAM Mark McKay
Born: Dundee, 22 October 1983
Height: 5'7" **Weight:** 12.0
International Honours: S: B-1; U21-3; Yth
The former Glasgow Celtic midfielder ended the campaign firmly ensconced as Norwich's captain, having missed much of the first half of the season through an ankle injury. A committed and vocal leader, his enthusiasm and passion for the game are unquestionable. He likes to dictate the pattern of play from midfield, distributing passes, long and short, to all areas while also looking to get forward at every opportunity. The popular Scot, who has also played professionally in Germany and Switzerland, was offered a new contract for 2008-2009 and beyond.
Glasgow Celtic *(From juniors on 1/8/1999) SL 2+1*
Dundee *(Free on 29/8/2003) SL 39+12/4 SLC 3+2 SC 2 Others 0+1 (Free to SC Freiburg, Germany during 2005 close season)*
Norwich C *(Signed from FC Aarau, Switzerland on 31/1/2007) FL 35+7/2 FLC 1/1 FAC 2+1*

FOWLER Robert (Robbie) Bernard
Born: Liverpool, 9 April 1975
Height: 5'11" **Weight:** 11.10
Club Honours: FLC '95, '01; FAC '01; UEFAC '01; ESC '01
International Honours: E: 26; B-1; U21-8; Yth (UEFA-U18 '93)
Robbie and Jimmy Floyd Hasselbaink were Cardiff's big-name strikers and both signed one-year contracts with one-year options that could be triggered

by appearances or by the club. Robbie scored six goals but suffered badly with injury problems and eventually flew to America for surgery to resolve a long-standing hip injury. Although he regained fitness before the end of the season, Robbie was not quite ready to earn a place in the FA Cup final squad. Cardiff manager Dave Jones insists that Robbie still has 20-plus goals a season in him after a full pre-season programme and talks were progressing on a pay-as-you-play contract.
Liverpool *(From trainee on 23/4/1992) PL 210+26/120 FLC 32/27 FAC 21+3/12 Others 26+12/11*
Leeds U *(£11,000,000 on 30/11/2001) PL 24+6/14 FAC 1+1 Others 0+1*
Manchester C *(£3,000,000 + on 30/1/2003) PL 63+17/21 FLC 3/2 FAC 5/4 Others 4/1*
Liverpool *(Free on 30/1/2006) PL 15+15/8 FLC 3/2 Others 2+4/2*
Cardiff C *(Free on 24/7/2007) FL 10+3/4 FLC 3/2*

FOX Daniel (Danny)
Born: Winsford, 29 May 1986
Height: 6'0" **Weight:** 12.6
Club Honours: Div 2 '07
International Honours: E: U21-1
Danny was a key figure on the left of the defence as Walsall moved into a play-off position in the first half of the season. His powerful shooting further enhanced his game and his move to Coventry in January left fans reflecting on what might have been had he stayed. Along with his Walsall team-mate Scott Dann, the young left-back made a big impression at Coventry after joining at the end of January. His skill on the ball and tackling qualities were evident from his debut at Hull and he impressed the home fans a few days later in the big home win over Barnsley. A yellow card earned him a one-game suspension but otherwise he was ever-present in the League until the end of the season. Danny's dead-ball delivery was superb and he created several goals, including Elliott Ward's header against Wolverhampton. His own first goal, threatened for a while, was a beautifully flighted curling shot at Colchester. Apparently, the former Everton apprentice was already earmarked for the England under-21 side before his move and made his debut against Poland in March.
Everton *(From trainee on 10/7/2004)*
Walsall *(Free on 1/7/2005) FL 98+1/6 FLC 4 FAC 11 Others 4*
Coventry C *(£300,000 on 28/1/2008) FL 18/1*

FOX David Lee
Born: Leek, 13 December 1983
Height: 5'9" **Weight:** 12.2
International Honours: E: Yth
David, a central midfielder, had limited Championship opportunities at Blackpool. He is an expert passer, with the ability to create chances, and it was expected that he would have more of an impact. He scored twice, an equaliser in 1-1 draw at home to Crystal Palace and in the FA Cup against Barnsley. When in the side, David continued to take the corners and free kicks.
Manchester U *(From trainee on 18/12/2000)*
Shrewsbury T *(Loaned on 8/10/2004) FL 2+2/1 Others 1*
Blackpool *(Free on 20/1/2006) FL 53+19/6 FLC 5 FAC 6/1 Others 0+2*

FRAMPTON Andrew (Andy) James Kerr
Born: Wimbledon, 3 September 1979
Height: 5'11" **Weight:** 10.10
Andy signed for Millwall from Brentford in the summer and the versatile defender played in both a central position and at left-back, where his fierce tackling was appreciated by the fans. He prefers left-back but performed well when injuries to the central defenders caused problems, slotting in with ease. He likes to get forward and this paid off with his first Millwall goal, against Walsall.
Crystal Palace *(From trainee on 8/5/1998) FL 19+9 FLC 3+1 FAC 2*
Brentford *(Free on 28/10/2002) FL 121+13/4 FLC 2 FAC 15+2/2 Others 11/1*
Millwall *(Signed on 27/6/2007) FL 28+2/1 FLC 1 FAC 3 Others 1*

FRANCE Ryan
Born: Sheffield, 13 December 1980
Height: 5'11" **Weight:** 11.11
Sidelined until January as he continued his recovery from the previous February's ruptured cruciate knee ligaments, Ryan returned to his status as a valuable squad member at Hull and continued his remarkable rise up the football pyramid. Having played in the Northern Counties East League as recently as 2002, versatile right-sided player joins fellow Tigers Ian Ashbee, Andy Dawson and Bo Myhill in having the opportunity to appear in all four divisions for the club following Hull's promotion to the top flight for the first time. Ryan established his own niche in City's record books by surpassing Stuart Elliott and Neil Mann for the most substitute appearances.
Hull C *(£15,000 from Alfreton T on 24/9/2003) FL 75+56/6 FLC 4+1/1 FAC 4+2/1 Others 2/1*

FRANCIS Damien Jerome
Born: Wandsworth, 27 February 1979
Height: 6'1" **Weight:** 11.2
Club Honours: Div 1 '04
International Honours: Jamaica: 1
Damien spent the first part of the season at
Watford recovering from a serious cruciate
knee ligament injury sustained the previous
April. He returned to first-team action in
December but by January the knee had
swollen up again and he was forced to go
back to the treatment room. A combative
and energetic midfield player with an
excellent scoring record, Damien will hope
for better things this coming season.
*Wimbledon (From trainee on 6/3/1997)
P/FL 80+17/15 FLC 7+4 FAC 9*
*Norwich C (Signed on 23/7/2003) P/FL
71+2/14 FLC 3 FAC 2*
*Wigan Ath (£1,500,000 on 10/8/2005) PL
16+4/1 FLC 1 FAC 3*
*Watford (£1,000,000 + on 13/7/2006) P/FL
34+9/5 FLC 2/1 FAC 6/1*

FRANCIS Simon Charles
Born: Nottingham, 16 February 1985
Height: 6'0" **Weight:** 12.6
International Honours: E: Yth
Having started last season as second-
choice right-back behind Lewis Hunt,
Simon seized his chance in January and
secured the position with a number of
assured displays. With an excellent first
touch and fine distribution, by the end
of the season he had recaptured the
form he initially showed when joining
the Shrimpers from Sheffield United and
was rewarded with a one-year contract
extension.
*Bradford C (From trainee on 3/5/2003) FL
49+6/1 FLC 1 FAC 1*
*Sheffield U (£200,000 on 16/3/2004) FL
6+6 FLC 2 FAC 0+1*
*Grimsby T (Loaned on 26/9/2005) FL 5
Others 1*
*Tranmere Rov (Loaned on 18/11/2005)
FL 16+1/1*
*Southend U (£70,000 on 16/6/2006) FL
56+11/3 FLC 4+3 FAC 4/1 Others 2*

FRANKS Billy Robert
Born: Shoreham, 26 November 1989
Height: 6'2" **Weight:** 12.7
The tall Bournemouth youth-team
centre-half had been on the bench on a
couple of occasions before being handed
a debut when starting against Tranmere.
The youngster rose to the challenge
superbly and played a big part in the
victory. He can play across the back line
and does not only make a tackle but
always tries to use the ball intelligently
when in possession.
*Bournemouth (Trainee - Brockenhurst
College) FL 1*

FRASER Thomas (Tommy)
Francis Peter
Born: Brighton, 5 December 1987
Height: 5'11" **Weight:** 12.6
Although starting for Brighton on fewer
occasions than in 2006-07, Tommy may
have enjoyed the past campaign more
as he was allowed to operate in his
preferred position as a combative central
midfielder rather than on the wing.
When he did so he showed himself to
be a player of some ability but he was
largely confined to fill-in roles when
more senior players were unavailable.
With another 12-month contract earned,
Tommy hopes to break through as an
automatic choice.
*Brighton & Hove A (From trainee on
28/6/2006) FL 33+19/1 FLC 2 FAC 6+1
Others 5+2*

FRECKLINGTON Lee Craig
Born: Lincoln, 8 September 1985
Height: 5'8" **Weight:** 11.0
International Honours: RoI: B-1
While Lee's form in 2007-08 did not
match that of the previous season, the
energetic midfielder remained one of
Lincoln's most consistent performers
and was a constant threat whenever in
possession. After the Imps turned down
two bids for him from Peterborough, he
put pen-to-paper on a contract extension
in February, a deal that will see him
remaining at the club until the summer
of 2011.
*Lincoln C (From trainee on 3/8/2005) FL
72+25/14 FLC 2/1 FAC 3/1 Others 5+3*

**FREEDMAN Douglas
(Dougie)** Alan
Born: Glasgow, 21 January 1974
Height: 5'9" **Weight:** 11.2
International Honours: S: 2; B-1; U21-
8; Sch
The Crystal Palace legend signed a
new two-year contract in the close
season but was used as a substitute
for most games and was reserve team
manager for a spell. He scored his
only goal against Stoke in October
and has a testimonial match to come
before the new season. Dougie proved
the missing piece of the jigsaw as
manager Gary McAllister steered Leeds
to the League One play-offs. When
the promotion push threatened to
fall apart, McAllister persuaded the
former Scotland international to Elland
Road on loan. Palace's longest-serving
current player, he provided the vital link
between midfield and attack as Leeds

adapted to McAllister's preferred passing
style. He netted five goals in nine starts
- doubles against Port Vale and Carlisle
- and the only goal at Yeovil that sealed
United's place in the play-offs. It was his
96th-minute strike against Carlisle that
triggered battling United's remarkable
comeback. They trailed 2-0 at Elland
Road until his goal and he had a hand in
both Jonny Howson's goals at Brunton
Park, turning the tie on its head.
*Queens Park Rgrs (From trainee on
15/5/1992)*
*Barnet (Free on 26/7/1994) FL 47/27 FLC
6/5 FAC 2 Others 2*
*Crystal Palace (£800,000 on 8/9/1995) P/FL
72+18/31 FLC 3+2/1 FAC 2+1 Others 3+2/2*
*Wolverhampton W (£800,000 on
17/10/1997) FL 25+4/10 FAC 5+1/2*
*Nottingham F (£950,000 on 12/8/1998)
P/FL 50+20/18 FLC 8+1/4 FAC 3+1/1*
*Crystal Palace (£600,000 on 23/10/2000)
P/FL 141+96/64 FLC 14+1/9 FAC 5+5/1
Others 1+2*
*Leeds U (Loaned on 7/3/2008) FL 9+2/5
Others 3/1*

FREEMAN Luke
Born: Dartford, 22 March 1992
Height: 5'9" **Weight:** 11.0
When introduced for the last ten minutes
of Gillingham's FA Cup tie against
Barnet, Luke became the youngest
player to appear in the competition
proper, at 15 years and 133 days. He
made two more substitute appearances
for the Gills before Arsenal stepped in
and paid a tidy sum in January to take
Luke to the Emirates Stadium on a
three-year scholarship deal. The positive
left-footed striker has pace to burn from
a wide position and Arsene Wenger
was impressed enough to say that he
thought him a very interesting prospect.
An England under-16 international, Luke
scored on his debut against Japan.
*Gillingham (Associated Schoolboy) FL 0+1
FAC 0+1 Others 0+1*
Arsenal (£200,000 as trainee on 26/1/2008)

FRIEDEL Bradley (Brad)
Howard
Born: Lakewood, Ohio, USA, 18 May
1971
Height: 6'3" **Weight:** 14.7
Club Honours: FLC '02
International Honours: USA: 82
Despite being 37 years old, Brad was
the only player to appear for every
minute of the Blackburn season. One
of the rocks on which the team is built,
it was surprising that the national Press
appeared to recognise him only near the

Simon Francis

end of the season, when his second-half wonder show almost defied Manchester United. In truth, this was little more than he had been doing all season and he is one of the reasons Blackburn have been able to survive in the Premiership. Technically competent in all aspects, he has a rare ability to change direction, against all laws of momentum, and this, coupled with strong arms and wrists, enables him to make some astonishing saves at point-blank range.
Liverpool (£1,000,000 from Columbus Crew, USA on 23/12/1997) PL 25 FLC 4 Others 1+1
Blackburn Rov (Free on 7/11/2000) P/FL 288/1 FLC 20 FAC 29 Others 20

FROST Stefan (Stef)
Born: Eastwood, 3 July 1989
Height: 6'2" **Weight:** 11.5
The talented local youngster first appeared in senior football with Notts County two years earlier. His progress was not as dynamic as hoped and he has suffered from a lack of regular football. Eventually he was loaned out to non-League Matlock and had the misfortune to break a leg late in the season. Quick and skilful on the ball, he usually plays down the right of the attack but has also performed usefully in central midfield. Was out of contract in the summer and looking for a new club.
Notts Co (From trainee on 4/7/2006) FL 0+6 Others 0+1

FRYATT Matthew (Matty)
Charles
Born: Nuneaton, 5 March 1986
Height: 5'10" **Weight:** 12.4
International Honours: E: Yth
Seemingly in and out of favour at Leicester during 2007-08, Matty not surprisingly failed to discover his best scoring form and frequently had to settle for a late appearance from the bench when many supporters would have liked to see him start more often. His most notable contribution was the goal that toppled Martin O'Neill's Aston Villa from the Carling Cup on their home soil but once Ian Holloway took over City's managerial reins, his chances became strictly limited.
Walsall (From trainee on 28/4/2003) FL 49+21/27 FLC 0+1 FAC 3/2 Others 3+1/1
Carlisle U (Loaned on 18/12/2003) FL 9+1/1
Leicester C (Signed on 10/1/2006) FL 60+21/11 FLC 3+1/1 FAC 3/1

FULLER Barry Marc
Born: Ashford, 25 September 1984
Height: 5'10" **Weight:** 11.10
Club Honours: FAT '07
International Honours: E: SP-1
Comfortable at right-back or in midfield, Barry has yet to gain a regular first-team spot at Gillingham but will be pushing his claims in the season ahead. He was signed from Stevenage in January and although small in stature he gets up really well and has good awareness of those around him.
Charlton Ath (From trainee on 15/7/2004. Free to Stevenage Borough on 2/1/2006)
Barnet (Loaned on 14/1/2006) FL 15/1
Gillingham (Free on 28/1/2008) FL 9+1

FULLER Ricardo Dwayne
Born: Kingston, Jamaica, 31 October 1979
Height: 6'3" **Weight:** 13.3
International Honours: Jamaica: 33
Fast and tricky, Ricardo made his name as a striker at Preston and Southampton. On his day he is a real handful for defenders, as he proved by finishing Stoke's top scorer with 15 goals. His only drawback is a volatile temperament but he worked to keep it in check through the promotion season. Ricardo is enormously popular with the fans and now looks forward to increasing his goals tally in the Premier League.
Crystal Palace (£1,000,000 from Tivoli Gardens, Jamaica on 19/2/2001) FL 2+6
Heart of Midlothian (Loaned on 19/10/2001) SL 27/8 SC 2/2
Preston NE (£500,000 on 1/7/2002) FL 57+1/27 FLC 2+1/2 FAC 2/2
Portsmouth (£200,000 + on 27/8/2004) PL 13+18/1 FLC 3+1 FAC 1+1
Southampton (£340,000 on 5/8/2005) FL 22+9/9 FLC 0+1 FAC 0+1
Ipswich T (Loaned on 24/2/2006) FL 3/2
Stoke C (Signed on 30/8/2006) FL 64+8/25 FAC 3+1/1

FULOP Marton
Born: Budapest, Hungary, 3 May 1983
Height: 6'6" **Weight:** 14.7
International Honours: Hungary: 15; U21-1
Marton is a goalkeeper who has represented Hungary at under-21 and full international level. His solitary appearance for Sunderland in 2007-08 was in a 1-0 home defeat by Arsenal on the final day. He spent the early part of the season on loan at Leicester and has announced that he wishes to leave

the Stadium of Light in the summer in order to play regular first-team football. Marton may well have been a contender for 'Player of the Season' at Leicester had Sunderland not recalled him midway through the campaign. Commanding in the air and a good shot-stopper, he was beaten by Nottingham Forest 'keeper Paul Smith in the re-staged Carling Cup tie as Leicester allowed the home team to restore the status quo from the initial abandonment. There were high hopes of a permanent transfer in January but Roy Keane effectively priced Marton out of the market, forcing the Foxes to look elsewhere. He was Hungary's regular custodian during his Walkers Stadium loan.
Tottenham H (Signed from MTK Hungaria, Hungary on 8/6/2004)
Chesterfield (Loaned on 11/3/2005) FL 7
Coventry C (Loaned on 28/10/2005) FL 31 FAC 2
Sunderland (£500,000 on 23/11/2006) P/FL 6
Leicester C (Loaned on 17/8/2007) FL 24 FLC 3

FURLONG Paul Anthony
Born: Wood Green, 1 October 1968
Height: 6'0" **Weight:** 13.8
Club Honours: FAT '88
International Honours: E: SP-5
A veteran of 586 League and Cup games and scorer of 178 goals, Paul became the oldest player ever to sign for Luton, at 38 years and 280 days, when he arrived from Queens Park Rangers in the summer. In October, when he lined up against Northampton aged 39 years and 15 days, he broke Fred Hawkes' 87-year-old record as the oldest Hatter, by one day. Signed for his experience, he was inevitably slower with age but compensated by his reading of the game and craft in the penalty area. Manager Kevin Blackwell intended to use him as a late substitute but injuries to Sam Parkin and Paul Peschisolido meant he started. In his richest form for four seasons, Paul notched up double strikes in the Cups against Sunderland and Gillingham, giving him ten goals. Although not as consistent in the second half of the campaign, adding only two to his total in all in all competitions, he finished as joint top scorer. Paul works hard on his fitness and made it known in the local media that he wanted to play for Luton in the coming season, but was released in the summer.
Coventry C (£130,000 from Enfield on 31/7/1991) FL 27+10/4 FLC 4/1 FAC 1+1 Others 1

Watford (£250,000 on 24/7/1992) FL 79/37 FLC 7/4 FAC 2 Others 3
Chelsea (£2,300,000 on 26/5/1994) PL 44+20/13 FLC 3+1 FAC 5+5/1 Others 7/3
Birmingham C (£1,500,000 on 17/7/1996) FL 104+27/50 FLC 11+2/3 FAC 5/3 Others 4
Queens Park Rgrs (Loaned on 18/8/2000) FL 3/1
Sheffield U (Loaned on 8/2/2002) FL 4/2
Queens Park Rgrs (Free on 8/8/2002) FL 137+31/56 FLC 3+1 FAC 2+1 Others 4+1/1
Luton T (Free on 7/8/2007) FL 24+8/8 FLC 3+1/2 FAC 1+1 Others 1/2

FUSEINI Ali
Born: Accra, Ghana, 7 December 1988
Height: 5'9" **Weight:** 12.11
Injuries among senior players opened the way for Ali, a product of the Millwall Academy, to make one of the midfield positions his own last season. He grabbed the chance eagerly and maintained a fine level of quality for one so young. Ali is an energetic, quick-thinking attacking midfielder who has gone from strength to strength and shows much promise for the future.
Millwall (From trainee on 27/9/2006) FL 36+8/2 FAC 4+2

FUTCHER Benjamin (Ben) Paul
Born: Manchester, 20 February 1981
Height: 6'4" **Weight:** 12.4
Released by Peterborough in the summer, the giant defender was taken to Bury by director of football Keith Alexander to strengthen the defence. His obvious aerial threat is matched by an ability to use both feet, making him a solid all-round centre half. His height was used to great effect in the Johnstone's Paint Trophy tie against Leeds when he headed in Bury's equaliser. Having been comfortable in Chris Casper's five-man defence, Ben was less happy in the four-man set-up under Alan Knill until he formed a formidable partnership with loan signing Efe Sodje.
Oldham Ath (From trainee on 5/7/1999) FL 2+8 FAC 0+1 (Free to Stalybridge Celtic on 3/1/2000)
Lincoln C (Free from Doncaster Rov on 7/8/2002) FL 119+2/13 FLC 3 FAC 4/1 Others 14/2
Boston U (Free on 8/7/2005) FL 13+1 FAC 3/1 Others 2
Grimsby T (Signed on 12/1/2006) FL 15+4/2 FLC 1 Others 1+2/1
Peterborough U (Signed on 25/8/2006) FL 22+3/3 FAC 3 Others 2
Bury (Free on 16/7/2007) FL 40 FLC 1 FAC 4/1 Others 2/1

G

GABBIDON Daniel (Danny) Leon
Born: Cwmbran, 8 August 1979
Height: 6'1" **Weight:** 11.2
International Honours: W: 40; U21-17; Yth
The Welsh centre-back had a frustrating season at West Ham as, after beginning a run of games in October, he suffered a bad groin injury in December that ended his season. Danny is excellent in the air and has a salmon-like leap. At Chelsea in December, he was the rock of the defence that kept Didier Drogba quiet. It was unfortunate that he was injured, especially when the Hammers' squad was severely weakened by similar problems. Danny again played for Wales when fit.
West Bromwich A (From trainee on 3/7/1998) FL 20 FLC 4+1 FAC 2
Cardiff C (£175,000 + on 10/8/2000) FL 194+3/10 FLC 8 FAC 11 Others 3
West Ham U (Signed on 5/7/2005) PL 57+3 FLC 4+1 FAC 8 Others 2

GAIN Peter Thomas
Born: Hammersmith, 11 November 1976
Height: 6'1" **Weight:** 11.0
International Honours: RoI: U21-1; Yth
Peter joined Dagenham from Peterborough on an 18-month deal during the January transfer window. Unfortunately, a virus delayed his debut for two weeks but after that, his ability to hold the ball in midfield and hit passes through to the strikers excited the fans. He scored with a terrific long-range shot against Morecambe in March.
Tottenham H (From trainee on 1/7/1995)
Lincoln C (Loaned on 31/12/1998) FL 0+3 Others 1
Lincoln C (£15,000 on 26/3/1999) FL 195+29/21 FLC 7+1 FAC 9+1/1 Others 14+2
Peterborough U (Free on 4/7/2005) FL 63+8/9 FLC 2+1 FAC 2+2 Others 2
Dagenham & Redbridge (Free on 17/1/2008) FL 18/1

GALL Kevin Alexander
Born: Merthyr Tydfil, 4 February 1982
Height: 5'9" **Weight:** 11.1
Club Honours: Div 2 '05
International Honours: W: U21-8; Yth; Sch
Despite his pace and eye for goal, Kevin was seldom at his best for Carlisle last season. Outstanding at Walsall in the first match, most of his starts were in the early weeks, after which he was more often used as a substitute. A loan to Darlington was followed by a brief excursion to

Major League Soccer club Toronto before his surprise return to Brunton Park. He was made available for transfer but arrived at Darlington with a bang. He hit the bar 25 seconds into his debut with Tommy Wright following up to net the only goal of the game. Although Kevin did not score for Darlington, he impressed with his non-stop running and rapid closing down of opponents. Despite his loan being extended, he was recalled by Carlisle just before Easter after eight appearances.
Newcastle U (From trainee on 29/4/1999)
Bristol Rov (Free on 22/3/2001) FL 28+22/5 FLC 2 FAC 2+2 Others 2+2
Yeovil T (Free on 4/2/2003) FL 80+43/13 FLC 3+2/1 FAC 9+2/1 Others 3+1/1
Carlisle U (Free on 3/8/2006) FL 54+12/9 FLC 2+1 FAC 3 Others 1+2/2
Darlington (Loaned on 28/1/2008) FL 7+1

GALLAGHER Paul
Born: Glasgow, 9 August 1984
Height: 6'1" **Weight:** 12.0
International Honours: S: 1; B-1; U21-11
Paul was a regular for Preston during a three-month loan from Blackburn

early last season, missing only four games before returning to Ewood Park in January. Following that, he arrived at Stoke for his second loan spell of the season on the last day of transfer dealings. A popular front runner or left-sided midfielder, Kevin was signed to supplement the squad as the Championship promotion challenge reached a climax. However, he could not claim a regular place in the side and played only a handful of games, mostly as a substitute.
Blackburn Rov (From trainee on 5/2/2003) PL 19+41/6 FLC 0+2/1 FAC 5+2/1 Others 2+2
Stoke C (Loaned on 29/8/2005) FL 32+5/11 FAC 3/1
Preston NE (Loaned on 31/8/2007) FL 15+4/1
Stoke C (Loaned on 31/1/2008) FL 2+5

GALLAS William
Born: Paris, France, 17 August 1977
Height: 6'1" **Weight:** 12.7
Club Honours: FLC '05; PL '05, '06; CS '05
International Honours: France: 65; U21; Yth

William Gallas

William was the surprise choice to succeed Thierry Henry as club captain in the 2007 close season and soon had the chance to lift silverware as Arsenal won both the inaugural Emirates Cup and the Amsterdam Tournament. William is a fine centre-back and for the majority of the season demonstrated his leadership qualities as Arsenal suffered only one defeat in their first 30 Premier League games. He provided several important goals, including the stoppage-time leveller at home to Manchester United and what must have been a particularly satisfying winner against Chelsea. William notably suffered a very public moment of frustration at Birmingham but hopes to retain the armband for another campaign. Was a key part of France's Euro 2008 squad.

Chelsea (£6,200,000 from Olympique Marseille, France, ex SM Caen, on 4/7/2001) PL 147+12/12 FLC 13 FAC 17/1 Others 36/1
Arsenal (Signed on 31/8/2006) PL 52/7 FLC 1 FAC 4 Others 14

GALLEN Kevin Andrew
Born: Chiswick, 21 September 1975
Height: 5'11" **Weight:** 12.10
Club Honours: AMC '08; Div 2 '08
International Honours: E: U21-4; Yth (UEFA-U18 '93); Sch
Released by Queens Park Rangers in the summer, Kevin became Paul Ince's first signing for MK Dons. An experienced striker, he soon proved to be capable of fitting in with whatever system was being adopted. He led the line particularly well when playing as a lone striker, holding up the ball well to bring supporting players into the equation. He scored nine goals despite missing several games through injury and worthily played his part in Johnstone's Paint Trophy and League Two title double success.

Queens Park Rgrs (From trainee on 22/9/1992) P/FL 126+45/36 FLC 9+3/2 FAC 6+2/2
Huddersfield T (Free on 10/8/2000) FL 30+8/10 FAC 1
Barnsley (Free on 27/7/2001) FL 8+1/2 FLC 0+1
Queens Park Rgrs (Free on 20/11/2001) FL 183+11/54 FLC 7+1/3 FAC 2+1 Others 5+2
Plymouth Arg (Loaned on 12/1/2007) FL 6+7/1 FAC 3/1
MK Dons (Free on 6/8/2007) FL 15+9/8 FLC 1+1/1 FAC 1 Others 4

GALLINAGH Andrew (Andy) Anthony
Born: Sutton Coldfield, 16 March 1985
Height: 5'8" **Weight:** 11.8
Andy broke into the Cheltenham team with a series of assured performances at either full-back or central defence. The former youth-team player had to wait patiently for his chance, having started only twice in the two previous seasons. When the Robins lost three central defenders to injury in the final pre-season friendly, Andy was pressed into action for the opening game against Gillingham. His concentration, positional sense and steely determination earned him a regular place and after a handful of games at right and left-back, he was given a run in central defence alongside Gavin Caines. This partnership coincided with the team's best defensive sequence, only one goal conceded in six games. Not surprisingly, Andy's form earned him a new two-year contract at the end of the season.

Cheltenham T (Signed from Stratford T on 30/9/2004) FL 25+3 FLC 1 Others 2+1

GARCIA Richard
Born: Perth, Australia, 4 September 1981
Height: 6'1" **Weight:** 11.2
Club Honours: FAYC '99
International Honours: Australia: U23; Yth
Having followed Colchester team-mate Wayne Brown to Hull in the summer, Richard played a leading role in the most successful season in their history as they

Ricardo Gardner

won promotion to the top flight for the first time. He was a regular on the right of midfield, developing an impressive partnership with right-back Sam Ricketts as they dovetailed in attacking and defensive duties. The popular Australian provided valuable and often spectacular goals. His 35-yard strike against Burnley at the KC Stadium in March was Hull's 'Goal of the Season'. Richard displayed his character by recovering from a shoulder injury that threatened his involvement in the Championship play-offs adventure and in coping with the sad loss of his father in February. Only the third Aussie Tiger, after Danny Allsopp and Jason Van Blerk, his admirable efforts meant he was on the verge of a call-up to the Australian national team.
West Ham U *(From trainee on 16/9/1998) P/FL 4+12 FLC 0+5 FAC 0+1*
Leyton Orient *(Loaned on 11/8/2000) FL 18/4 FLC 3*
Colchester U *(Signed on 3/9/2004) FL 62+20/16 FLC 2+1 FAC 7+2/2 Others 5/3*
Hull C *(Free on 5/7/2007) FL 35+3/5 FLC 1+1/1 FAC 0+1 Others 3/1*

GARDNER Anthony Derek
Born: Stone, 19 September 1980
Height: 6'5" **Weight:** 13.8
International Honours: E: 1; U21-1
The Tottenham centre-back's chances were again limited, in part through injury but more because other players were picked ahead of him. Anthony played in the first four games, when Ledley King and Michael Dawson were absent, and although Spurs made a losing start, he scored in their second game with a downward header from a corner. He featured in UEFA Cup games under Martin Jol but failed to win selection under Juande Ramos. Loaned to Everton in January, he did not manage an appearance for the Toffees before returning to White Hart Lane.
Port Vale *(From trainee on 31/7/1998) FL 40+1/4 FLC 2 FAC 1*
Tottenham H *(£1,000,000 on 28/1/2000) PL 94+20/2 FLC 13/1 FAC 11+3 Others 3*

GARDNER Craig
Born: Solihull, 25 November 1986
Height: 5'10" **Weight:** 11.13
International Honours: E: U21-6
Craig came through the youth ranks at Aston Villa and is a good all-rounder, defending well and getting forward to score the occasional goal. He has two good feet, vision and passing ability, while being versatile enough to play at right-back or further forward in midfield. Is a tough competitor in midfield and strong in the tackle. Craig scored his

first goal for Villa in their 4-4 draw at Tottenham but suffered a thigh strain playing for England under-21s in March, leading to a short absence. It was a mixed season for the youngster, who made 16 starts and nine appearances as a substitute. Awarded an England under-21 debut in a friendly against Romania in August, he also played twice against Poland.
Aston Villa *(From trainee on 2/2/2005) PL 29+15/5 FLC 1 FAC 0+2*

GARDNER Ricardo Wayne
Born: St Andrew, Jamaica, 25 September 1978
Height: 5'9" **Weight:** 11.0
International Honours: Jamaica: 58
Despite missing the first five games because of injury, Ricardo returned to reclaim the Bolton left-back position he has made his own over the past ten years. He scored his only goal of the

season in the memorable UEFA Cup 2-2 draw at Bayern Munich in November and continued to impress as the season progressed, with his trademark energetic and pacy displays. However, a broken rib sustained in the home draw against Manchester City in March effectively brought Ricardo's season to a premature end.
Bolton W *(£1,000,000 from Harbour View, Jamaica on 17/8/1998) P/FL 247+36/15 FLC 17+4/2 FAC 16+4 Others 17/3*

GARDNER Scott Andrew
Born: Luxembourg, 1 April 1988
Height: 5'9" **Weight:** 11.4
International Honours: E: Yth
Right-back Scott impressed for Leeds in a pre-season friendly against Wigan at Elland Road and he made his debut in the Carling Cup victory at Macclesfield in August, a week after signing his first professional contract. Capped by England

Glyn Garner

at under-16 and under-18 level, he had a spell on loan with United's Blue Square Premier neighbours Farsley Celtic. He showed up well in his League One debut against Gillingham in the final game of the regular season.
Leeds U (From trainee on 4/4/2006) FL 1 FLC 1

GARGAN Samuel (Sam) Joseph
Born: Hurstpierpoint, 24 June 1988
Height: 6'3" **Weight:** 11.12
After scoring a considerable number of goals on loan at Worthing, Bognor Regis and Welling, as well as for Brighton's reserves, Sam was recalled in April to make his League debut as a late substitute in the penultimate game at Bristol Rovers. A tall, strong striker with aerial ability and a decent touch, Sam will be hoping to carry his prolific form from youth and non-League level forward to the senior game.
Brighton & Hove A (From trainee on 27/6/2007) FL 0+1

GARNER Glyn
Born: Pontypool, 9 December 1976
Height: 6'2" **Weight:** 13.6
International Honours: W: 1
Glyn joined Shrewsbury from Leyton Orient last summer and was immediately given the goalkeeper's jersey, making his debut in the opening day 4-0 victory at Lincoln. He probably played his most effective games in the early part of the season with some important point-winning saves, notably in the 1-0 home win against Bradford. Glyn divided supporters' opinions at the New Meadow, especially when Shrewsbury began to struggle. He made 41 consecutive appearances before new manager Paul Simpson gave Scott Bevan an opportunity.
Bury (Free from Llanelli on 7/7/2000) FL 124+2 FLC 5 FAC 3 Others 4+1
Leyton Orient (Free on 14/7/2005) FL 86 FLC 2 FAC 8 Others 1+1
Shrewsbury T (Free on 7/8/2007) FL 41 FAC 1

GARNER Joseph (Joe) Alan
Born: Blackburn, 12 April 1988
Height: 5'10" **Weight:** 11.13
International Honours: E: Yth; Sch
Following a successful loan spell at Brunton Park in 2006-07, Joe became Carlisle's record signing when he arrived from Blackburn at the start of last season. A natural scorer, he netted, on average, once every other game. His clinical finish at Southend in October put United top of the table and in a

spell before Christmas he scored in four consecutive matches. His form was attracting the attention of bigger clubs but an injury at Crewe in February brought his season to a premature end. United fans were left wondering if his presence might have made the difference between automatic promotion and defeat in the play-offs.
Blackburn Rov (From trainee on 16/4/2005)
Carlisle U (£140,000 on 19/1/2007) FL 47+2/19 FLC 1 FAC 2 Others 0+1

GARRETT Robert (Robbie)
Born: Belfast, 5 May 1988
Height: 5'6" **Weight:** 10.4
International Honours: NI: U21-10; Yth
The all-action midfield competitor was on loan from Stoke in the previous season and impressed the Racecourse faithful with his wholehearted displays for Wrexham. Robbie joined the Dragons, again on loan, in late September and was heavily involved until mid-December. He found it hard to impose himself in a struggling team but remained a regular for the Northern Ireland under-21 side. Was released at the end of the campaign.
Stoke C (From trainee on 27/6/2006) FL 0+2
Wrexham (Loaned on 30/1/2007) FL 10
Wrexham (Loaned on 28/9/2007) FL 9+3 FAC 1

GARRIDO Javier
Born: Irun, Spain, 15 March 1985
Height: 5'10" **Weight:** 11.11
International Honours: Spain: U21-4
Javier is a left-back who, despite being only 22, had nearly three full seasons in La Liga under his belt by the time he moved to Manchester City from Real Sociedad last August. Javier made his debut in the opening game against West Ham, looking immediately at home in the Premier League, and kept Michael Ball out of the starting line-up for the early part of the campaign. Ball eventually became the first-choice left back but Javier continued to make the occasional appearance off the bench to keep his rival on his toes. An ability to fill in on the left of midfield meant that Sven-Goran Eriksson had the option to use him in place of Martin Petrov if needed.
Manchester C (£1,500,000 from Real Sociedad, Spain on 3/8/2007) PL 21+6 FLC 2

GARRY Ryan Felix Mayne
Born: Hornchurch, 29 September 1983
Height: 6'2" **Weight:** 13.0
Club Honours: FAYC '01
International Honours: E: Yth
Signed from Arsenal in the summer

after a long time out injured, the Bournemouth defender showed his pedigree as he immediately grabbed a first-team place before sustaining shin splints against Northampton in September. That proved to be Ryan's last start for the Cherries but he regained fitness to make a number of brief substitute appearances late in the season.
Arsenal (From trainee on 2/7/2001) PL 1 FLC 0+1
Bournemouth (Free on 10/8/2007) FL 6+2 FLC 0+1

GARVAN Owen
Born: Dublin, 29 January 1988
Height: 6'2" **Weight:** 10.8
International Honours: RoI: U21-4; Yth
Owen continues to be the mainstay of Ipswich's midfield with his ability to move the ball around the pitch by accurate passing, long or short. Pops up with a goal now and then, as against Charlton when his cross-cum-shot from the left wing deceived the 'keeper and went in off the far post. He was included in the Republic of Ireland's senior squad for the first time for their close season tour.
Ipswich T (From trainee on 27/5/2005) FL 92+10/6 FLC 1+1/1 FAC 2+2

GATTING Joseph (Joe) Stephen
Born: Brighton, 25 November 1987
Height: 5'11" **Weight:** 12.4
Joe's career suffered a stall last season, as he made only nine appearances in Brighton's first team, all as a substitute. A consistent scorer in the reserves, notching another ten goals, Joe spent three months on loan at Woking, scoring eight times, but he has found it hard to make the step up to League One level.
Brighton & Hove A (From trainee on 15/4/2006) FL 15+29/4 FLC 0+1 FAC 0+3 Others 2+2

GAYNOR Ross Leon
Born: Drogheda, 9 September 1987
Height: 5'10" **Weight:** 11.12
An Ireland under-21 player and a product of the Millwall Academy, Ross had a brief first-team chance for the club when he made his League debut from the substitutes' bench against Walsall. A left-sided player, with good pace and vision, he was out of contract in the summer.
Millwall (From trainee on 5/5/2006) FL 1+2 FAC 2+1

GEARY Derek Peter
Born: Dublin, 19 June 1980
Height: 5'6" **Weight:** 10.8
Derek continued to be a popular player

at Sheffield United, having signed a contract extension till 2010. Hard-working, fast with good anticipation, he tackled well and was dangerous going forward, although his final ball was not always the best. He often saved the day with a well-judged final clearance, interception or tackle. His season was disrupted first by a sending off at Scunthorpe and then by a long lay-off following a knee operation but, returning earlier than expected, he continued where he had left off. Runner-up in the supporters' 'Player of the Year' award, many feel he is overdue for a Republic of Ireland cap.
Sheffield Wed *(Signed from Rivermount Boys Club on 17/11/1997) FL 95+9 FLC 12+2 FAC 4 Others 5*
Stockport Co *(Free on 2/8/2004) FL 12+1 FLC 1 Others 1*
Sheffield U *(£25,000 on 22/10/2004) P/FL 77+9/1 FLC 6+1 FAC 9+1*

[GEOVANNI] DEIDERSON GOMEZ Geovanni Mauricio
Born: Aciaca, Brazil, 11 January 1980
Height: 5'9" **Weight:** 10.10
International Honours: Brazil: 4
Attacking midfielder Geovanni arrived at Manchester City on a one-year Bosman deal in July, becoming the first Brazilian to sign for the Blues. Having been freed by Cruzeiro, City stole a march by snapping up the 27-year-old just days after he had scored for Portsmouth in a pre-season friendly. The former Brazilian international was an instant hit with the fans, scoring the second goal of the opening day win over West Ham at Upton Park before his stunning strike saw the Blues pick up a memorable derby win over United. A player with a great range of passing skills, to go with his shooting ability, it was not clear where he would be at the start of 2008-09.
Manchester C *(Free from Cruzeiro, Brazil, ex Cruzeiro, America Brazil, Barcelona, Benfica, on 26/7/2007) PL 2+17/3 FLC 2+1 FAC 0+1*

GERA Zoltan
Born: Pecs, Hungary, 22 April 1979
Height: 5'11" **Weight:** 11.3
Club Honours: Ch '08
International Honours: Hungary: 53
Zoltan had another fine season, his ten goals including a crucial winner in the Black Country derby against arch-rivals Wolverhampton that took West Bromwich back to the top of the Championship with three games remaining. He soon followed up with what proved to be the clincher in a 2-1

victory at Norwich. Although Zoltan suffered his fair share of leg and ankle injuries, his never-say-die attitude hardly waned and his superb skill, enthusiasm and heading ability were vital to Albion as they battled away in the League and FA Cup. The Hungarian international was recognised again by his country, passing 50 caps and scoring his 16th goal.
West Bromwich A *(£1,500,000 from Ferencvaros, Hungary ex Harkany, Pecsi MFC, on 9/8/2004) P/FL 104+32/21 FLC 2+2/1 FAC 8+4/3 Others 2+1*

[GEREMI] N'JITAP FOTSO Geremi Sorele
Born: Bafoussam, Cameroon, 20 December 1978
Height: 5'11" **Weight:** 12.8
Club Honours: PL '05, '06; CS '05; FLC '07
International Honours: Cameroon: 68
Having signed for Newcastle from Chelsea during a summer in which he applied for British citizenship, Geremi was appointed club captain, operating mainly on the right of midfield, although he is also a capable right-back as he demonstrated against Liverpool in November. For a player of his pedigree his performances were disappointing and he lost both his place and the club captaincy in December. He played in the Cameroon side that reached the final of the African Cup of Nations and was chosen in the 'Team of the Tournament' but was out of favour on his return to Tyneside. Recalled in March, he began to display the qualities expected of him and, although he tended to flit in and out of matches, his contributions were often telling, with a number of key assists. His only goal in the season was against West Ham, only the second headed goal of his career, the first being for Middlesbrough against Newcastle.
Middlesbrough *(Loaned from Real Madrid, Spain, ex Racing Baffousam, Cerro Porteno, Genclerbirligi, on 31/7/2002) PL 33/7 FAC 1*
Chelsea *(£7,000,000 from Real Madrid, Spain on 1/8/2003) PL 48+24/4 FLC 8 FAC 8+1 Others 10+10*
Newcastle U *(Free on 14/7/2007) PL 24+3/1 FLC 1*

GERKEN Dean Jeffery
Born: Southend, 22 May 1985
Height: 6'3" **Weight:** 13.0
It proved a difficult season for the highly-rated goalkeeper, not least because he was playing behind the leakiest defence in the Championship. He was kept busy every match and did not celebrate his first clean-sheet of the season until April, ironically against East Anglian rivals

Ipswich. It was Colchester's first shut-out in 40 games. An early sending-off and a loss of form held Dean back during the first three months but he was ever-present from the beginning of November.
Colchester U *(From trainee on 12/7/2004) FL 86+2 FLC 4 FAC 5 Others 5*

GERRARD Anthony
Born: Liverpool, 6 February 1986
Height: 6'2" **Weight:** 13.1
Club Honours: Div 2 '07
International Honours: RoI: Yth
The central defender had an excellent third campaign at the heart of the Walsall defence and was voted 'Player of the Season' by both fans and team-mates. Anthony missed only three games and was always a menace when going forward for set pieces, snatching three goals. He is a cousin of the Liverpool and England midfield star Steven.
Everton *(From trainee on 10/7/2004)*
Walsall *(Free on 24/3/2005) FL 115+6/4 FLC 2 FAC 8+1 Others 4*

GERRARD Steven George
Born: Huyton, 30 May 1980
Height: 6'2" **Weight:** 12.4
Club Honours: FLC '01, '03; FAC '01, '06; UEFAC '01; ESC '01; UEFACL '05; CS '06
International Honours: E: 67; U21-4; Yth
Liverpool's talismanic midfield dynamo enjoyed another outstanding season, as good as, if not better than, his superlative 2005-06 campaign. Yet while he capped that season with a thunderbolt 30-yard volley to save the 2006 FA Cup final, for all of his efforts last season Liverpool finished in a distant fourth in the Premier League and had to be content with a third Champions' League semi-final appearance in four years. Steven was the club's second highest scorer with 21 goals, six from the penalty spot, and including many of his trademark volleys and drives from outside the penalty box, starting with a superb free kick against Aston Villa on the opening day of the season. Strangely, he had to wait until October for his second, a mere consolation in the disastrous defeat by Besiktas in Turkey that nearly ended his Champions' League campaign early. He followed this with goals in nine of the next ten games, remarkable for a midfielder, and soon afterwards a hat-trick in the FA Cup third round replay against Luton. His most important goal was the 90th-minute effort that gave Liverpool a decisive 2-0 advantage over Inter Milan in the Champions' League first leg at Anfield in February, a diagonal

167

Dean Gerken

shot lacking his customary power but so accurate that it eluded the Inter 'keeper and rolled in off the far post. Almost as important was his coolly converted 86th-minute penalty in the quarter-final second leg with Arsenal, only a minute after the Gunners had scored a second away goal to seemingly win the tie. In the latter weeks of the season manager Rafa Benitez moved Steven forward to a support striker role behind Fernando Torres. While this tactical switch enabled Liverpool to finish the season strongly in the Premiership, warding off the challenge of city rivals Everton for fourth place, it did not work in the crucial match at Old Trafford against Manchester United nor in the second leg Champions' League semi-final clash with Chelsea. If Steven's performances for Liverpool can fairly be described as world-class, he remains an enigma in an England shirt. Hopefully, the new England manager Fabio Capello can find him a role in the England team that enables him to reproduce his Liverpool form.

Liverpool *(From trainee on 26/2/1998) PL 278+24/55 FLC 17+2/7 FAC 19+4/8 Others 86+9/26*

GHALY Hossam El Sayed
Born: Kafr-el-Sheikh, Egypt, 15 December 1981
Height: 5'11" **Weight:** 12.4
International Honours: Egypt: 21
Hossam fell completely out of favour with Tottenham and after a summer move to Birmingham broke down, he returned to Egypt to train with his former club Al-Ahly. An extended loan to Derby last January gave him a chance to resurrect his career and he accepted it eagerly. He declared himself unavailable for the African Cup of Nations in order to concentrate on club football. Crisp and tidy in midfield, Hossam is a player who wants the ball at his feet and uses it intelligently. Playing in a struggling side did not help him, although his class was obvious in flashes, but Paul Jewell decided against pursuing a permanent deal.

Tottenham H *(Signed from Feyenoord, Holland, ex Al-Ahly, on 31/1/2006) PL 17+4/1 FLC 2+1 FAC 2+2/1 Others 3+3/1*
Derby Co *(Loaned on 11/1/2008) PL 13+2 FAC 1*

GIANNAKOPOULOS Stilianos (Stelios)
Born: Athens, Greece, 12 July 1974
Height: 5'8" **Weight:** 11.0
Club Honours: Div 2 '04
International Honours: Greece: 76
A perennial crowd favourite at Bolton, Stelios made his first appearance of last

season as a substitute in the Carling Cup win at Fulham, when he scored the winner. Despite having been a key contributor in previous years, the Greek International had fewer opportunities last season, making his first League appearance as a substitute in the home defeat by Chelsea in October. Many of his subsequent appearances came from the bench, with his only League start in the 2-1 defeat by Blackburn in January. Despite this, Stelios still scored some vitally important goals, including the 93rd-minute equaliser against Derby, a goal against Tottenham with his first touch of the ball in April and the 93rd-minute equaliser in the UEFA Cup tie against his fellow Greeks, Aris Thessaloniki. An agile and busy attacking midfielder, he always gave his all to Bolton. Was out of contract in the summer and looking for another club.

Bolton W *(Free from Olympiakos, Greece on 15/7/2003) PL 86+51/20 FLC 10+4/3 FAC 12/3 Others 10+4/2*

GIBB Alistair (Ali) Stuart
Born: Salisbury, 17 February 1976
Height: 5'9" **Weight:** 11.7
The experienced Hartlepool right-winger, who can also play at right-back, made only occasional appearances and with little chance of regular football, went on loan to Notts County for the remainder of the season. Manager Ian McParland recruited Ali as the potential solution to the lack of a natural wide-right midfielder and he went straight into the team, producing steady but unspectacular performances, before losing some confidence. He had to be sacrificed as County had too many loan players following the late emergency signing of goalkeeper Russell Hoult and was not subsequently involved. At the end of 2007-08, he was released by Hartlepool on a free transfer.

Norwich C *(From trainee on 1/7/1994)*
Northampton T *(Loaned on 22/9/1995) FL 9/1 Others 2*
Northampton T *(£30,000 on 5/2/1996) FL 51+71/3 FLC 8+4 FAC 5+3 Others 4+3*
Stockport Co *(£50,000 on 18/2/2000) FL 157+8/1 FLC 6 FAC 6 Others 3*
Bristol Rov *(Free on 25/3/2004) FL 45+19/1 FLC 2 FAC 3+1/1*
Hartlepool U *(Free on 31/8/2006) FL 16+15 FLC 1+1 FAC 2+1 Others 1+2*
Notts Co *(Loaned on 11/1/2008) FL 9*

GIBBS Kieran James Ricardo
Born: Lambeth, 26 September 1989
Height: 5'10" **Weight:** 10.2
International Honours: E: Yth
Kieran started for Arsenal in the Emirates

Cup and was a revelation on the wing. He featured twice in the Carling Cup and continued to score from midfield for the reserves, the FA Academy under-18 side and in the FA Youth Cup. A regular member of the England under-19s, this technically gifted, but slightly built, midfielder was allowed by Arsene Wenger to join Norwich on loan in January. He made seven appearances for the Canaries in their successful fight against relegation from the Championship and showed enough qualities for Glenn Roeder to state publicly that he would like him to return next season. Composed in possession, he is adept at breaking forward to support his strikers.

Arsenal *(From trainee on 14/9/2007) FLC 1+1*
Norwich C *(Loaned on 31/1/2008) FL 6+1*

GIBSON Darron Thomas Daniel
Born: Derry, 25 October 1987
Height: 6'0" **Weight:** 12.4
International Honours: Rol: 2; U21-1; Yth
Signed on loan from Manchester United, Darron had a fine first half for Wolverhampton at home to Charlton, his first game. He scored with a clean strike at home to Burnley but had almost three months without starting for Wolverhampton until a little spell towards the end of the season. He put in some strong attempts on goal and almost scored with a low drive against West Bromwich.

Manchester U *(From trainee on 12/8/2005) FLC 0+1*
Wolverhampton W *(Loaned on 19/10/2007) FL 15+6/1 FAC 1+2*

GIDDINGS Stuart James
Born: Coventry, 27 March 1986
Height: 6'0" **Weight:** 11.8
International Honours: E: Yth
Stuart joined Oldham on a one-month loan in August because of a defensive injury crisis at Boundary Park. The Coventry man made three starts at left-back but his stay was unfortunately curtailed when he had to return to his parent club for treatment on an ankle injury. Stuart was subsequently released by new Coventry manager Chris Coleman in March.

Coventry C *(From trainee on 16/6/2004) FL 12+4 FLC 2 FAC 1*
Oldham Ath *(Loaned on 10/8/2007) FL 2 FLC 1*

GIGGS Ryan Joseph
Born: Cardiff, 29 November 1973
Height: 5'11" **Weight:** 10.9
Club Honours: ESC '91; FAYC '92; FLC

'92, '06; PL '93, '94, '96, '97, '99, '00, '01, '03, '07, '08; CS '93, '94, '96, '97, '03, '07; FAC '94, '96, '99, '04; UEFACL '99, '08
International Honours: W: 64; U21-1; Yth; E: Sch
An outstanding, naturally talented Manchester United and Wales left-winger, who can play equally as well as a front-line striker, Ryan's adaptability in Sir Alex Ferguson rotation system made him the favoured choice for the early clash with Chelsea at Old Trafford in September, a 2-0 win for the Reds. How Chelsea must hate seeing Ryan on the wing. He had already played a starring role in the Community Shield opener against the Blues at Wembley. Signing a new contract extension that will keep him at Old Trafford until the end of 2008-09, Ryan celebrated that landmark with his first goal of the campaign, waltzing past two defenders and netting a deflected shot in the 4-1 romp at Aston Villa in October. The goal put the Welshman in an exclusive club of two, as only he and Gary Speed have scored in every Premiership season since its inception in 1992. In December, he scored his 100th League goal for the Reds in the resounding 4-1 win over Derby at Old Trafford - a remarkable feat for a winger. As Ryan homed in on Sir Bobby Charlton's appearance record, he figured heavily in Sir Alex Ferguson's plans. In April he was a second-half substitute in United's successful European Champions' League semi-final against Barcelona at Old Trafford. With Sir Alex believing Ryan can carry on playing for United beyond 2008-09, what better way for him to repay his manager than with the goal that clinched the title at Wigan on the final day of the Premiership season. Appropriately, he equalled Sir Bobby's all-time appearance record (758) for the Reds that day before surpassing it in the Champions' League final. More club records will follow this most celebrated of Manchester United footballers.

Manchester U *(From trainee on 1/12/1990) P/FL 469+66/101 FLC 25+5/7 FAC 55+7/10 Others 120+12/26*

GILBERT Kerrea Kuche
Born: Willesden, 28 February 1987
Height: 5'6" **Weight:** 11.3
International Honours: E: Yth
A small but athletic full back, Kerrea joined Southend on loan from Arsenal before the start of last season, having impressed manager Steve Tilson on a previous loan spell to Cardiff. Despite starting the campaign as first-choice right-back, Kerrea lacked consistency and

at the end of the month's loan at Roots
Hall, Tilson decided against an extension.
Arsenal (From trainee on 1/7/2005) PL 2 FLC
3+1 FAC 2 Others 0+1
Cardiff C (Loaned on 27/7/2006) FL 21+3
FAC 2
Southend U (Loaned on 8/8/2007) FL 5
FLC 1

GILBERT Eric **Peter**
Born: Newcastle, 31 July 1983
Height: 5'9" **Weight:** 12.13
International Honours: W: U21-12
Last season was a disappointing one for
the Sheffield Wednesday left-back, as a
series of injuries and Tommy Spurr's fine
form restricted Peter's appearances. He
would benefit from being more forceful
when given a chance and continues to
work on his attacking play. Peter is at his
most effective as part of a back four and
has good positional play.
Birmingham C (From trainee on 1/7/2002)
Plymouth Arg (Signed on 8/7/2003) FL 78/1
FLC 2 FAC 2 Others 2/1
Leicester C (£200,000 on 3/8/2005) FL 4+1
Sheffield Wed (Free on 24/11/2005) FL
31+2 FLC 1
Doncaster Rov (Loaned on 9/1/2007) FL 4
Others 1

[GILBERTO] DA SILVA MELO Gilberto
Born: Rio de Janeiro, Brazil, 25 April 1976
Height: 5'11" **Weight:** 12.4
International Honours: Brazil: 23
Brazil's international left-back was signed
in January by Tottenham from Hertha
Berlin. Gilberto had an inauspicious
debut at home against PSV Eindhoven,
when his mistake led to the only goal
by the visitors, but redeemed himself
with a goal against West Ham as a
substitute. Although having limited
first-team opportunities, playing seven
games in all, he gained confidence as the
season closed, demonstrating competent
ball-winning and retention skills, with
enough pace and penetration to give the
opposition defence problems. Gilberto
was a regular for Brazil in the Copa
America 2007, playing five times games
for them.
Tottenham H (£2,000,000 from Hertha
Berlin, Germany, ex America Brazil,
Flamengo, Cruzeiro, Inter Milan, Vasco da
Gama, Gremio, Sao Caetano, on 31/1/2008)
PL 3+3/1 Others 1

[GILBERTO] SILVA Gilberto
Born: Lagoa da Prata, Brazil, 7 October
1976
Height: 6'2" **Weight:** 12.4
Club Honours: CS '02, '04; FAC '03,
'05; PL '04
International Honours: Brazil: 63

Jerry Gill

The Brazilian captain returned from his country's Copa America success to find he had been overlooked for Arsenal's captaincy and lost his place to Mathieu Flamini. In truth it was a frustrating campaign for him and on the rare occasions he did feature he looked somewhat off the pace. Although he played 23 times in the Premier League, 11 of these appearances were as a substitute and he scored once. He featured on seven occasions in the Champions' League and three times each in the FA Cup and Carling Cups. For a long period it looked likely that Gilberto would leave Arsenal at the end of the season but with Flamini's departure, he would appear to have a role still to play.

Arsenal *(£4,500,000 from Atletico Mineiro, Brazil, ex America-MG, on 9/8/2002)* PL 153+17/17 FLC 8/1 FAC 12+3 Others 40+11/6

GILL Benjamin (Ben) David
Born: Harrow, 4 October 1987
Height: 5'9" **Weight:** 10.11
Versatile midfield player Ben joined Cheltenham from Watford at the start of the season and made a handful of appearances for the Robins, including a start on the right of midfield at Brighton in an FA Cup replay. Ben also made 20 appearances and scored two goals for the reserves, sometimes operating as a central defender. His preferred position is in central midfield and although he was unable to force his way into the first team, Ben will hope to establish himself as a more regular selection.
Watford *(From trainee on 2/3/2006)* FLC 0+2 FAC 0+1
Cheltenham T *(Free on 8/8/2007)* FL 0+2 FLC 0+1 FAC 1 Others 0+2

GILL Jeremy (Jerry) Morley
Born: Clevedon, 8 September 1970
Height: 5'7" **Weight:** 11.0
International Honours: E: SP-1
Veteran right-back Jerry enjoyed another highly consistent season as a key member of the Cheltenham back four, fighting off the challenge posed by young defender Andy Gallinagh and new signing Andy Lindegaard to make 47 starts in all competitions. Most of his games were at right-back, although he made a handful of appearances on the left as cover for the injured Alan Wright. A very reliable player and model professional, he has worked hard to prolong his career into his late 30s and was offered a further one-year contract. His positional sense and organisational qualities stem from years of experience but, while he demonstrated a keenness to get forward and shoot from distance, he is still awaiting his

first senior goal since 1996-97. Off the field, Jerry is building a reputation as a businessman and took over the franchise of the Cheltenham club shop at the end of the season.
Leyton Orient *(Free from Trowbridge T on 16/12/1988. Free to Weston-super-Mare on 1/7/1990)*
Birmingham C *(£30,000 from Yeovil T on 14/7/1997)* FL 43+17 FLC 11+1 FAC 3 Others 1
Northampton T *(Free on 9/8/2002)* FL 41 FLC 1 FAC 2 Others 2
Cheltenham T *(Free on 27/2/2004)* FL 170+5 FLC 4+2 FAC 11 Others 9+1

GILLESPIE Keith Robert
Born: Larne, 18 February 1975
Height: 5'10" **Weight:** 11.3
Club Honours: FAYC '92; FLC '02
International Honours: NI: 81; U21-1; Yth; Sch
Having signed a new two-year deal in July, Keith was a regular in the Sheffield United side at the start of the season, playing on the right of midfield. Working hard and effectively in his defensive duties he was less influential than in the previous season, particularly with his crosses. From January he lost his place to Dave Carney and then loanee David Cotterill and nearly all Keith's subsequent appearances were from the bench. He continued to play for Northern Ireland.
Manchester U *(From trainee on 3/2/1993)* PL 3+6/1 FLC 3 FAC 1+1/1
Wigan Ath *(Loaned on 3/9/1993)* FL 8/4 Others 2
Newcastle U *(£1,000,000 on 12/1/1995)* PL 94+19/11 FLC 7+1/1 FAC 9+1/2 Others 11+5
Blackburn Rov *(£2,250,000 on 18/12/1998)* P/FL 67+46/5 FLC 8+3 FAC 6+4/1 Others 0+3
Wigan Ath *(Loaned on 1/12/2000)* FL 4+1 FAC 2
Leicester C *(Free on 9/7/2003)* P/FL 26+16/2 FLC 0+2 FAC 4
Sheffield U *(Free on 5/8/2005)* P/FL 58+38/4 FLC 2+1 FAC 2+1

GILLESPIE Steven
Born: Liverpool, 4 June 1984
Height: 5'9" **Weight:** 11.5
Steven enjoyed by far his most successful season to date for Cheltenham. Despite enduring a mixed opening game, in which he scored and was sent off, Steven went on to fulfil some of the undoubted promise shown since he first joined the Robins on loan from Bristol City in 2005. A clever forward with an eye for goal and the knack of finding himself a crucial yard in the penalty area, he hit 16 goals in all competitions including a spectacular effort to earn a 1-0 win over Leeds at Whaddon Road and a double in the 2-0 win at Hartlepool. Forced to miss eight

games with a hip injury in September and October, Steven returned to forge profitable striking partnerships with first Paul Connor and then on-loan Bristol City target-man Steve Brooker. He made the occasional appearance wide on the right of midfield and contributed three further goals as the Robins battled to League One survival, his goal in the final game setting up a dramatic win over promotion-chasing Doncaster.
Bristol C *(From trainee at Liverpool on 6/8/2004)* FL 4+8/1 FLC 0+1 FAC 0+2 Others 1+1
Cheltenham T *(Loaned on 11/1/2005)* FL 10+2/5
Cheltenham T *(Signed on 11/11/2005)* FL 52+22/24 FLC 0+1 FAC 2/2 Others 5+1/2

GILLET Kenny Lego
Born: Bordeaux, France, 3 January 1986
Height: 5'10" **Weight:** 12.4
Kenny enjoyed a fine first season in English football, having arrived at Barnet following a spell with French Second Division side Caen. A close friend of Arsenal's Gael Clichy, who acted as his translator when Kenny was in talks with Barnet, he made the left-back slot his own and caught the eye with his neat first touch, good distribution and fine all-round technical ability.
Barnet *(Free from SM Caen, France on 30/8/2007)* FL 30+1 FAC 6

GILLETT Simon James
Born: Oxford, 6 November 1985
Height: 5'6" **Weight:** 11.7
In a less torrid season, Simon, a Southampton Academy graduate, might have expected a run or two in the first team but his experience remains confined to loan periods and three cameos from the bench. He is a clever and industrious midfielder, who at present looks destined to make his mark elsewhere despite the club offering him a new contract at the end of the campaign. To keep match-fit, Simon arrived at Yeovil on a two-month loan in September and made his debut in a 2-1 win at Brighton, lasting 67 minutes. During his stay, the diminutive midfielder played on both flanks and showed himself to be both skilful in possession and a player who never gives up.
Southampton *(From trainee on 8/11/2003)* FL 0+2 FAC 0+1
Walsall *(Loaned on 30/9/2005)* FL 2
Blackpool *(Loaned on 9/8/2006)* FL 13+1/1 Others 1/1
Bournemouth *(Loaned on 22/11/2006)* FL 7/1
Blackpool *(Loaned on 31/1/2007)* FL 7+10 Others 0+2
Yeovil T *(Loaned on 21/9/2007)* FL 3+1 Others 0+1

GILLIGAN Ryan James
Born: Swindon, 18 January 1987
Height: 5'10" **Weight:** 11.7
Midfielder Ryan turned in sound
performances over the season, whether
asked to play wide, in the centre of
Northampton's midfield, or up front. His
speed is one of his biggest assets as are his
bravery and consistency. He earned a few
goals this season and manager Stuart Gray
has earmarked him as one for the future.
*Northampton T (From trainee at Watford
on 12/8/2005) FL 46+39/8 FLC 1+3 FAC 3+1
Others 0+2*

GIVEN Seamus (Shay) John
James
Born: Lifford, Ireland, 20 April 1976
Height: 6'1" **Weight:** 13.4
Club Honours: Div 1 '96
International Honours: RoI: 86; U21-
5; Yth
This was another injury-hampered
season for Shay as persistent groin
problems ruined his normal record as
a virtual ever-present in the Newcastle
goal. Injured in a pre-season friendly
against Sampdoria, he missed the start
of the Premier League and, apart from a
Carling Cup appearance against Barnsley
at the end of August, had to wait until
replacing the injured Steve Harper in the
late-September Carling Cup tie against
Arsenal for an opportunity to re-establish
himself. Although a further groin problem

Shay Given

caused him to miss a couple of games
in November, he remained first choice
until the problem resurfaced at Aston
Villa in February. He was replaced,
returned for the following game at
home to Manchester United and had to
be substituted again. His season ended
prematurely as he went to Germany for
surgery. Shay remains one of the Premier
League's best 'keepers, very agile with
quick reflexes, although he did score a
bizarre own goal at home to Everton
in October. When fit he continued
to represent the Republic of Ireland,
becoming the country's most capped
goalkeeper when playing against Slovakia
in September. Now very much at home on
Tyneside, he was chosen to switch on the
city's Christmas lights.
*Blackburn Rov (From juniors at Glasgow
Celtic on 8/8/1994) PL 2 FLC 0+1*
Swindon T (Loaned on 4/8/1995) FL 5
Sunderland (Loaned on 19/1/1996) FL 17
*Newcastle U (£1,500,000 on 14/7/1997) PL
332 FLC 10+1 FAC 32 Others 62*

GLEESON Stephen Michael
Born: Dublin, 3 August 1988
Height: 6'2" **Weight:** 11.0
International Honours: RoI: 2; U21-4; Yth
Although the midfielder scored both goals
for the Republic of Ireland under-21 side
in a 2-2 draw with Germany in August,
at club level Stephen was restricted to
45 minutes for Wolverhampton in the
Carling Cup. An injury forced him back
to Ireland for recuperation but he made
further under-21 appearances despite
being out of the frame at Wolves.
Allowed out on loan to Hereford in
February, Stephen never found his true
form there despite a promising debut
in a victory at Shrewsbury. He was
then shifted from his preferred central
midfield position out to the right against
Stockport and never looked comfortable
before losing his place and returning
to Molineux. Stockport fans had been
disappointed when Stephen went to
Hereford but manager Jim Gannon
monitored the situation and moved
quickly to bring the teenager back to
Edgeley Park on loan for a second time
in the March window. Although his form
was uneven, the talented midfielder hit
the crucial late equaliser at Wycombe
in the play-off semi-final first leg with a
quite magnificent volley.
*Wolverhampton W (From trainee on
5/7/2006) FL 0+3 FLC 1 Others 0+1*
*Stockport Co (Loaned on 3/11/2006) FL
14/2 FAC 3*
Hereford U (Loaned on 21/2/2008) FL 3+1
*Stockport Co (Loaned on 27/3/2008) FL 4+2
Others 2+1/1*

GLENNON Matthew (Matty)
William
Born: Stockport, 8 October 1978
Height: 6'2" **Weight:** 14.9
Huddersfield's number-one goalkeeper
made great strides during his second year
with the club and only a sending-off in
the away defeat by Southend stopped
him from being ever-present. Matty made
his 50th appearance for the club on the
opening day, not only a victory but a
well-deserved clean sheet. His campaign
was marked by a succession of matches in
which he made great saves and collected
dangerous crosses. The calm and
confident shot-stopper was vociferous as
he marshalled the defence and made sure
he dominated his area. Matty marked the
penultimate game of the season with his
100th appearance and did not concede
a goal in the final five games, a feat not
achieved by any Town goalkeeper since
1982-83.
Bolton W (From trainee on 3/7/1997)
Bristol Rov (Loaned on 15/9/2000) FL 1
*Carlisle U (Loaned on 10/11/2000) FL 29
FAC 3 Others 1*
*Hull C (£50,000 on 20/6/2001) FL 35 FLC 3
FAC 2 Others 2*
*Carlisle U (Free on 18/10/2002) FL 76 FLC 1
FAC 4 Others 10*
Falkirk (Free on 20/7/2005) SL 21 SC 2
St Johnstone (Signed on 27/1/2006) SL 12/1
*Huddersfield T (Free on 29/6/2006) FL 91
FLC 2 FAC 6 Others 2*

GLOVER Daniel (Danny)
Born: Crewe, 24 October 1989
Height: 6'0" **Weight:** 11.3
After graduating through Port Vale's
youth team, the striker made his debut as
a substitute in a Johnstone's Paint Trophy
tie at Morecambe. Unfortunately, Danny
missed the crucial penalty in a shoot-out
defeat. He helped the youth team to
reach the quarter-finals of the FA Youth
Cup and became a regular member of
the squad. A skilful player, he battled his
way into a starting role and scored his
first senior goal with a low shot in a 2-2
draw against Northampton. This was a
slice of history as he and his father Dean,
the assistant manager, are now the only
father and son pairing to score League
goals for Vale.
*Port Vale (From trainee on 27/7/2007) FL
9+6/1 Others 0+1*

GNAPKA Claude
Born: Marseille, France, 9 June 1983
Height: 6'0" **Weight:** 13.10
Freed by Swindon in the summer, having
been unable to break into their team,
Claude was mostly used at full-back by
Peterborough but can also play in the

centre of defence. Having won a year's contract at the clubs pre-season training camp, he played in over half the games and proved an enthusiastic defender, sometimes too keen as ten bookings proved. Although offered a new contract at the end of the season he chose not to sign it and left the club.
Swindon T (Free from Vaduz, Liechtenstein, ex Montpellier, Racing Santander, Deportivo Alaves, on 22/3/2007)
Peterborough U (Free on 19/7/2007) FL 25+3 FAC 2+1 Others 1

GOLBOURNE Scott Julian
Born: Bristol, 29 February 1988
Height: 5'8" **Weight:** 11.8
International Honours: E: Yth
An injury to Nicky Shorey while he was on England duty gave Scott the chance of his Premiership debut for Reading last season and he acquitted himself well in the left-back position at Bolton before being replaced by Bobby Convey in a tactical switch. Reading lost 3-0 but did better in Scott's only other appearance, this time as an extra-time substitute in the 1-0 Carling Cup victory at Swansea. Looking to keep match fit, the attacking right-back was

one of four Reading players to spend time on loan at Bournemouth during the season, moving there in November. He made five starts in the League after signing and scored an excellent goal against Barrow in the FA Cup but after being replaced against Oldham he did not appear again before returning to Reading at the end of the year.
Bristol C (From trainee on 5/3/2005) FL 11+3 FLC 1/1
Reading (£150,000 on 3/1/2006) P/FL 1+1 FLC 0+1 FAC 1
Wycombe W (Loaned on 18/8/2006) FL 13+2/1 FLC 3 Others 1
Wycombe W (Loaned on 12/1/2007) FL 18+1 FLC 1
Bournemouth (Loaned on 6/11/2007) FL 5 FAC 2/1 Others 1

GOODALL Alan Jeffrey
Born: Birkenhead, 2 December 1981
Height: 5'9" **Weight:** 11.6
Signed from Rochdale in the summer, Alan is a classic utility player who, according to Luton manager Kevin Blackwell, can play in several positions. Making a scoring debut when netting Luton's second goal against Hartlepool,

Alan was used as an attacking full-back, where his speed allows him to put over useful crosses and hassle opponents. When he was sent off at Brighton after 14 consecutive games, he found it difficult to regain a place until he returned on the left. He made a heroic comeback in the 1-1 draw at Bristol Rovers, in which three players were sent off. Included in manager Mick Harford's first four games in charge, he was dropped after a 1-0 home defeat by Swindon. Harford preferred other players at full-back and Alan's only opportunities were two games in central defence. His last appearance was in a 2-0 defeat at Southend and he did not figure again before being given a free transfer.
Rochdale (Signed from Bangor C on 30/7/2004) FL 110+10/8 FLC 2 FAC 4 Others 5
Luton T (Free on 24/7/2007) FL 25+4/1 FLC 3 FAC 2+1 Others 1

GOODISON Ian De Souza
Born: St James, Jamaica, 21 November 1972
Height: 6'3" **Weight:** 12.10
International Honours: Jamaica: 100

Craig Gordon

The former Jamaican international captain and the current Tranmere skipper, Ian once again excelled in every game played and was voted Rovers' 'Player of the Season' by the supporters for the second year running. His strength and steadiness were in evidence all season and it was noticeable that the team was not as effective when he was absent through a four-match ban after being sent off at Crewe on New Year's Day. Rovers invariably look more solid and assured when the vastly experienced 35-year-old centre-back is at the heart of the defence. Remaining free of serious injury all season, Ian turned down the chance to add to his collection of Jamaican caps in order to stay with the club over the Easter weekend.
Hull C (Free from Olympic Gardens, Jamaica on 22/10/1999) FL 67+3/1 FLC 2 FAC 6+1 Others 5 (Free to Seba U, Jamaica during 2002 close season)
Tranmere Rov (Free from Seba U, Jamaica on 20/2/2004) FL 169+7/2 FLC 4 FAC 7 Others 8+2

GOODWIN James (Jim)
Born: Waterford, 20 November 1981
Height: 5'9" **Weight:** 12.2
Club Honours: Div 1 '07
International Honours: RoI: 1; U21-14
Scunthorpe midfielder Jim was a first choice in their Championship side, missing only a handful of games all season. A highly-committed, strong-tackling player, he anchored the midfield well, proving a good contrast to the silky skills of on-loan Chelsea youngster Jack Cork. He scored three goals, including a stunning individual effort against Burnley in the opening home match but was surprisingly released at the end of the season.
Glasgow Celtic (Signed from Tramore on 25/11/1997) SL 1
Stockport Co (Free on 7/6/2002) FL 81+22/7 FLC 3 FAC 6/1 Others 7/1
Scunthorpe U (Free on 3/8/2005) FL 74+10/6 FLC 0+1 FAC 0+3 Others 3+1/1

GOODWIN Lee Jon
Born: Stepney, 5 September 1978
Height: 6'1" **Weight:** 13.12
After a year out with a knee injury, the midfielder was expected to return in February but the operation to grow a cartilage outside his knee and inject it back in, proved unsuccessful and he has now retired from football. He went on for the last minute of Dagenham's final game to give him one League appearance and has been offered a youth coaching position at the club.
West Ham U (From trainee on 9/7/1997)
Dagenham & Redbridge (Free on 1/8/1998) FL 0+1

GORDON Craig Anthony
Born: Edinburgh, 31 December 1982
Height: 6'4" **Weight:** 12.2
Club Honours: SC '06
International Honours: S: 31; U21-5
Craig arrived at Sunderland from Heart of Midlothian in the summer at a record fee between British clubs for a goalkeeper and made a dream start to his new career in England, keeping a clean sheet in the victory over Tottenham on the opening day. A key member of the Scotland side that unluckily missed out on qualification for Euro 2008, Craig cuts a commanding figure. His agility and lightning reflexes were given a tough examination last term as the Black Cats fought an ultimately successful battle against relegation. Craig was rested for three games in December following a confidence-denting 7-1 defeat at Everton, although none of the seven goals could be directly attributed to him. However, he returned to complete the campaign and, with a busy Premier League debut year under his belt, it is expected that he will go on to perform consistently well at this level.
Heart of Midlothian (From juniors on 1/8/2000) SL 138+1 SLC 8 SC 15 Others 14
Cowdenbeath (Loaned on 31/8/2001) SL 13 SLC 1
Sunderland (£9,000,000 on 10/8/2007) PL 34 FAC 1

GORKSS Kaspars
Born: Riga, Latvia, 6 November 1981
Height: 6'3" **Weight:** 13.5
International Honours: Latvia: 15
Making a big impression in his second season at Blackpool, the Latvian international forced his way into the first team. Kaspars went on to score nine goals, an impressive tally for a centre-back, and netted twice in the 2-2 Carling Cup draw with Derby, a game Blackpool won on penalties. At international level, Kaspars scored against Denmark in a Euro qualifier, although Latvia lost 3-1. He was runner-up in the annual Latvian 'Player of the Year' awards and has since been linked with a move away from Blackpool.
Blackpool (Signed from FK Ventspils, Latvia, ex FK Auda, Osters IF, Assyriska FF, on 2/1/2007) FL 47+3/5 FLC 3+1/2 FAC 1+2

GOSLING Daniel (Dan)
Born: Brixham, 2 February 1990
Height: 5'10" **Weight:** 11.3
International Honours: E: Yth
Dan, a product of Plymouth's youth system, was a versatile member of the squad, playing in a variety of positions including right-back and the right of

midfield. Extremely comfortable on the ball, he passes well and in January it was announced that he would be signing for Premier League Everton in a deal that could rise to £2-million. Manager David Moyes spoke of his belief that Dan will soon challenge for a place at Everton, either at right-back or the midfield holding position. Dan was a valuable member of the England under-17 World Youth Cup team that reached the quarter-final stage after an impressive win against Brazil.
Plymouth Arg (From trainee on 20/2/2007) FL 13+9/2 FAC 2
Everton (£1,000,000 on 14/1/2008)

GOWARD Ryan Lee
Born: Mansfield, 1 November 1989
Height: 5'9" **Weight:** 11.8
A 17-year-old local lad who made his first-team bow in Mansfield's County Cup win over Notts County at the end of 2006-07, Ryan's League debut came as a substitute in the draw at Barnet last October, when he stepped in at left-back in place of Dan Martin. Nominally a midfielder, he filled in well for the final few minutes of the game. At the end of the season he was named the Stags' 'Youth Team Player of the Year'.
Mansfield T (Trainee) FL 0+2

GOWER Mark
Born: Edmonton, 5 October 1978
Height: 5'11" **Weight:** 11.12
Club Honours: FLC '99, Div 1 '06
International Honours: E: SP-4; Yth; Sch
Another stalwart of Southend, Mark's season was one of the best he has produced in the blue of the Shrimpers. Equally at home with either foot, his quality delivery from midfield and his finishing were a joy to behold at times and many of Southend's goals owed much to his guile. Rumoured to be a transfer target of promoted Swansea, Southend fans will hope that Mark decides he belongs in the South-East and that he continues to contribute to the resurgence of the Shrimpers.
Tottenham H (From trainee on 1/4/1997) FLC 0+2
Motherwell (Loaned on 12/3/1999) SL 8+1/1
Barnet (£32,500 on 19/1/2001) FL 10+4/1 Others 1/1
Southend U (£25,000 on 25/7/2003) FL 189+14/35 FLC 8/1 FAC 14/3 Others 17+1/2

GOWLING Joshua (Josh)
Anthony Izaac
Born: Coventry, 29 November 1983
Height: 6'3" **Weight:** 12.9

It was another season of good progress for Bournemouth's stylish central defender. Despite missing a number of games through niggling injuries, Josh was solid and reliable, strong in the air as well as on the ground. He forged an excellent partnership with Jason Pearce in the final run-in, when Bournemouth conceded only five goals in the final seven games in a brave attempt to overcome the ten-point deduction for entering administration.

Bournemouth *(Free from Herfolge, Denmark, ex West Bromwich A trainee, on 1/8/2005) FL 72+11/1 FLC 3 FAC 4 Others 4*

GRABBAN Lewis James
Born: Croydon, 12 January 1988
Height: 6'0" **Weight:** 11.3
Last season was one of mixed fortunes for the tall, strong striker who, after making a substitute appearance for Crystal Palace against Bristol Rovers in the Carling Cup, was loaned to Motherwell in the Scottish Premier League without scoring in his six games as a substitute. Lewis returned to Selhurst Park, going on twice more from the bench, before signing for local rivals Millwall in January. He joined Millwall initially on a short-term basis but after some excellent performances it was hoped he will be with them next season. Lewis scored three goals in ten games, and would have played more but for niggling injuries. For a young player, he has great vision and is clinical in front of goal.

Crystal Palace *(From trainee on 28/7/2006) FL 0+10/1 FLC 0+3*
Oldham Ath *(Loaned on 16/8/2006) FL 1+8 FLC 1*
Motherwell *(Loaned on 31/8/2007) SL 0+5 SLC 0+1*
Millwall *(£150,000 on 21/1/2008) FL 10+3/3 FAC 1*

GRADEL Max-Alain
Born: Abidjan, Ivory Coast, 30 November 1987
Height: 5'8" **Weight:** 12.3
The young winger joined Bournemouth in August on loan from Leicester and stayed for the whole season, winning a legion of admirers with his exciting play and terrific eye for goal. Throughout the campaign he was dogged by personal problems that meant he had compassionate leave but invariably returned to give 100 per cent. Max-Alain was one of the most popular loan players ever to wear a Bournemouth shirt.

Leicester C *(Signed from Lewisham College, via trials at West Ham U, on 21/9/2005)*
Bournemouth *(Loaned on 9/8/2007) FL 31+3/9 FLC 1 FAC 2/1 Others 1*

Josh Gowling

GRAHAM Daniel (Danny)
Anthony William
Born: Gateshead, 12 August 1985
Height: 5'11" **Weight:** 12.5
International Honours: E: Yth
Signed from Middlesbrough in the summer, having been on loan at Carlisle since January 2007, Danny had a season to remember, not just for his goals but for his selfless contribution to the success of the team. His best performance came in the victory at Nottingham Forest, where he battled tirelessly for much of the match in his customary role as a lone striker. Yet, when the chance came, he grabbed the only goal of the game with an impressive first-time finish. It was a microcosm of his displays throughout the campaign. Still in his early 20s, Danny will hope to build on this achievement in the coming season.
Middlesbrough (From trainee on 6/3/2004) PL 1+14/1 FLC 0+2/1 FAC 0+2 Others 1+1
Darlington (Loaned on 19/3/2004) FL 7+2/2
Derby Co (Loaned on 24/11/2005) FL 11+3
Leeds U (Loaned on 23/3/2006) FL 1+2
Blackpool (Loaned on 2/8/2006) FL 1+3/1
Carlisle U (Free on 1/1/2007) FL 50+6/21 FLC 2/1 FAC 2 Others 4/2

GRAHAM David Baillie
Born: Edinburgh, 6 October 1978
Height: 5'10" **Weight:** 11.5
International Honours: S: U21-8
Arriving at Gillingham from Sheffield Wednesday just before the start of the season, he soon showed his ability, not only through his scoring prowess but for holding the ball and bringing other players into the game. He scored twice in a 3-1 win over Orient and once in the 3-2 defeat of Bristol Rovers before being released at the end of January.
Glasgow Rgrs (From juniors on 1/7/1995) SL 0+3 Others 1+1
Dunfermline Ath (Signed on 15/11/1998) SL 17+23/4 SLC 1 SC 3/1 Others 0+1
Inverness CT (Loaned on 5/1/2001) SL 0+2 SC 0+2
Torquay U (Free on 22/3/2001) FL 103+17/47 FLC 3+1/2 FAC 4 Others 1+1
Wigan Ath (£215,000 on 26/7/2004) FL 13+17/1 FLC 1 FAC 1
Sheffield Wed (£250,000 on 12/8/2005) FL 19+9/2 FLC 2/1
Huddersfield T (Loaned on 23/1/2006) FL 15+1/9 Others 2
Bradford C (Loaned on 29/7/2006) FL 17+5/3 Others 1
Torquay U (Loaned on 21/3/2007) FL 7
Gillingham (Free on 9/8/2007) FL 7+9/3 FLC 1 FAC 1/1 Others 0+1

GRAHAM Richard (Richie)
Stephen
Born: Newry, 5 August 1979
Height: 5'10" **Weight:** 12.3
Club Honours: FC '05
International Honours: NI: U21-15; Yth
Having signed for Dagenham from Barnet in the summer, the winger's season was hampered by a series of groin injuries and Richie made only a handful of substitute appearances as a result. He had a minor operation in January and fears that he would require a further hernia operation were put to rest when he played in the reserves for the final month. He obviously hopes for an injury-free run.
Queens Park Rgrs (From trainee on 8/8/1996) FL 0+2 (Freed in March 2002)
Barnet (Free from Kettering T, ex Chesham U, on 10/7/2004) FL 35+14/3 FLC 2 FAC 2 Others 0+1
Dagenham & Redbridge (Free on 7/8/2007) FL 4+3 Others 0+1

GRAND Simon
Born: Chorley, 23 February 1984
Height: 6'1" **Weight:** 10.12
International Honours: E: SP
Handed a one-year deal by Morecambe after being released by Grimsby in the summer, Simon was looking forward to the new campaign with optimism. However, the central defender failed to capture a regular place, although making several fleeting appearances and scoring a superb goal from 25 yards at Chesterfield to seal a 2-2 draw. He was an integral member of the all-conquering reserve side and a popular member of the squad but was released at the end of the season.
Rochdale (From trainee on 3/7/2002) FL 33+7/2 FLC 1 FAC 7 Others 1
Carlisle U (Free on 1/7/2004) FL 3+9/2 FLC 2 FAC 0+1 Others 2+3/1
Grimsby T (Signed on 9/1/2007) FL 4+3
Morecambe (Free on 3/8/2007) FL 4+2/1 FLC 0+1 FAC 1 Others 3+1

GRANQVIST Andreas
Born: Helsingborg, Sweden, 16 April 1985
Height: 6'4" **Weight:** 13.3
International Honours: Sweden: 3: U21
After a year on loan with Wigan, in which he appeared only in an FA Cup tie, Andreas moved permanently on a two-year deal from his home-town club Helsingborg IF in the summer. The Swedish international captained his former club and is rated as one of the best defenders in the country. He made his Premier League debut in the opening match and played in 12 of the next 15. Tall, strong and athletic, with a good turn of pace, he has the equipment to make a class centre-half. Following a change of management, Andreas found it difficult to hold down a place and, hoping to be involved for Sweden in Euro 2008,

was allowed to return to Helsingborg on six months loan in the January transfer window.
Wigan Ath (Free from Helsingborgs IF, Sweden on 3/1/2007) PL 13+1 FLC 1 FAC 2

GRANT Anthony (Tony) James
Born: Liverpool, 14 November 1974
Height: 5'10" **Weight:** 10.5
Club Honours: CS '95
International Honours: E: U21-1
The vastly experienced former England under-21 international joined Chester from Accrington during the summer and was an integral part of the City midfield that began the season in such fine style. Unfortunately, after starting the first 11 games, Tony struggled with a series of niggling injuries and made only sporadic appearances over the rest of the season without ever experiencing a sustained run in the side. In the early part of the campaign, Tony added the creativity that was missing from Chester's midfield later in the season and scored his only goal in the excellent 2-1 win at Rochdale in August. He was released at the end of the season.
Everton (From trainee on 8/7/1993) PL 43+18/2 FLC 5+1 FAC 4+4 Others 2+2/1
Swindon T (Loaned on 18/1/1996) FL 3/1
Tranmere Rov (Loaned on 2/9/1999) FL 8+1 FLC 1/1
Manchester C (£450,000 on 24/12/1999) P/FL 11+10 FLC 1 FAC 2+1
West Bromwich A (Loaned on 1/12/2000) FL 3+2
Burnley (£250,000 on 11/10/2001) FL 121+20/3 FLC 9+1 FAC 15
Bristol C (Free on 19/8/2005) FLC 1
Crewe Alex (Free on 12/1/2006) FL 13+1 FAC 1
Accrington Stanley (Free on 31/1/2007) FL 6
Chester C (Free on 30/7/2007) FL 15+4/1 FLC 1 FAC 1 Others 1

GRANT Anthony Paul Shaun
Andrew Daure
Born: Lambeth, 4 June 1987
Height: 5'11" **Weight:** 11.3
International Honours: E: Yth
Following a trial game with Luton reserves, Tony was signed from Chelsea on loan but what should have been three months but was reduced to less than one when Town went into administration. He is a versatile midfield player, good at holding the ball but was booked for dissent in his debut as a substitute against Southend. He was used mainly from the bench, effectively against Nottingham Forest in the FA Cup second round when he carried out orders to keep possession to the letter. He was one of three players sent off in the only game he started and

Andreas Granqvist

the ban ended his time at Luton. The combative right-sided midfielder next joined Southend on a 93-day loan. Tony made several useful contributions from the bench during the run to the play-offs before his loan ended. Strong in the tackle and with decent distribution, although he was unable to dislodge Tommy Black from his starting place he also played well for the reserves, often filling in selflessly at right-back. Tony inadvertently broke a club record, almost 20 years old, for the most number of substitute appearances without actually starting a game for Southend. Was released at the end of the season.
Chelsea *(From trainee on 1/7/2005) PL 0+1*
Oldham Ath *(Loaned on 13/1/2006) FL 2*
Wycombe W *(Loaned on 1/8/2006) FL 39+1 FLC 5 FAC 2 Others 1+1*
Luton T *(Loaned on 16/11/2007) FL 1+3 FAC 0+1*
Southend U *(Loaned on 31/1/2008) FL 0+10*

GRANT Lee Anderson
Born: Hemel Hempstead, 27 January 1983
Height: 6'2" **Weight:** 13.4
International Honours: E: U21-4; Yth
Signed by Sheffield Wednesday from Derby in the summer, Lee established himself as the number-one goalkeeper at Hillsborough. His start to the season was reasonable but lapses of concentration in several games appeared to drain his confidence. However, in the second half he really excelled and helped the defence to become a much more solid unit. Has time on his side to mature further as a goalkeeper.
Derby Co *(From trainee on 17/2/2001) FL 69+5 FLC 3 FAC 2*
Burnley *(Loaned on 15/11/2005) FL 1*
Oldham Ath *(Loaned on 31/1/2006) FL 16*
Sheffield Wed *(Free on 24/7/2007) FL 44 FLC 2 FAC 2*

GRANT Robert
Born: Liverpool, 1 July 1990
Height: 5'11" **Weight:** 12.0
Having made his debut for Accrington the previous season, Robert may have been disappointed that he was restricted to a few appearances as substitute until late in the season, when he started against Dagenham. Following that, he kept his place for the last five games, playing in his usual position on the left of midfield. However, his potential was well recognised by the club in January when he was rewarded with his first professional contract. Thereafter, he trained with the first team and played regularly in the reserves. In February he

was presented with the Football League 'Apprentice of the Month' award.
Accrington Stanley *(From trainee on 8/2/2008) FL 6+2*

GRANVILLE Daniel (Danny) Patrick

Born: Islington, 19 January 1975
Height: 5'11" **Weight:** 12.5
Club Honours: FLC '98, ECWC '98; Div 1 '02
International Honours: E: U21-3

Danny, an experienced defender, was involved in the first half of Colchester's difficult season in the Championship, following his arrival last summer from Crystal Palace. He played ten games in a row in October and November, but otherwise was more of a peripheral figure. He operated at both full-back and centre-half, but was restricted to a couple of substitute appearances in the New Year. His bad luck was summed up by a late own goal at home to Norwich, when under pressure from former U's striker Jamie Cureton. A groin problem kept him out during the closing weeks and he was released during the last week of the season.

Cambridge U *(From trainee on 19/5/1993) FL 89+10/7 FLC 3+2 FAC 2+2 Others 4+2*
Chelsea *(£300,000 + on 21/3/1997) PL 12+6 FLC 3 Others 4+1/1*
Leeds U *(£1,600,000 on 8/7/1998) PL 7+2 FLC 1 FAC 3 Others 0+1*
Manchester C *(£1,000,000 on 7/8/1999) P/FL 56+14/3 FLC 1+4 FAC 5*
Norwich C *(Loaned on 27/10/2000) FL 6*
Crystal Palace *(£500,000 on 28/12/2001) P/FL 117+5/9 FLC 6/1 FAC 4+3 Others 3*
Colchester U *(Free on 9/8/2007) FL 14+5 FLC 1*

GRAVESEN Thomas

Born: Vejle, Denmark, 11 March 1976
Height: 5'10" **Weight:** 13.6
International Honours: Denmark: 56; U21-6

The Danish international arrived at Everton on a season's loan from Glasgow Celtic but a combination of injuries and the good form of others limited the midfielder's opportunities in his second spell at the club. Thomas made only three starts before departing from Goodison for a second time in front of an appreciative crowd against Newcastle on the final day. He remains a top-class midfield player, whether sitting in front of the defence or driving ahead to join the forwards.

Everton *(£2,500,000 from SV Hamburg, Germany, ex Vejle BK, on 9/8/2000) PL 131+10/11 FLC 6/1 FAC 6+2 (£2,500,000 to Real Madrid, Spain on 14/1/2005)*
Glasgow Celtic *(Signed from Real Madrid,*

Spain on 30/8/2006) SL 18+4/6 SLC 1 SC 0+4 Others 4+2
Everton *(Loaned on 31/8/2007) PL 1+7 FLC 0+1 FAC 1 Others 1+2*

GRAY Andrew (Andy) David

Born: Harrogate, 15 November 1977
Height: 6'1" **Weight:** 13.0
International Honours: S: 2; B-3; Yth

With five goals in the first five games, Andy started like a house on fire at Burnley and maintained a healthy strike-rate to remain one of the Championship's top marksmen up to Christmas. A forward with most of the assets, he is adept at holding up play and perfectly complemented the more flamboyant skills of Robbie Blake while rarely passing up a scoring chance. He remained ever-present in the League until his January move, in controversial circumstances, to Charlton but the efforts of Ade Ainbiyi and the on-loan Andrew Cole ensured that the loss was not too badly felt. Great things were expected from the striker when he signed for Charlton, initially on loan, before the deal was made permanent. Despite his record at Burnley, Andy went 14 games without scoring before heading in Charlton's equaliser from a Lee Cook free kick against Southampton. He added another in the final game, a 4-1 win over Coventry. Andy was used by Charlton mainly as a target-man, due to his ability to hold the ball up, and he replaced Chris Iwelumo, who did so well in the first half of the season.

Leeds U *(From trainee on 1/7/1995) PL 13+9 FLC 3+1 FAC 0+2*
Bury *(Loaned on 11/12/1997) FL 4+2/1*
Nottingham F *(£175,000 on 2/9/1998) P/FL 34+30/1 FLC 3+4 FAC 4+1*
Preston NE *(Loaned on 23/2/1999) FL 5*
Oldham Ath *(Loaned on 25/3/1999) FL 4*
Bradford C *(Free on 9/8/2002) FL 77/20 FLC 2 FAC 2/1*
Sheffield U *(Signed on 27/2/2004) FL 56+2/25 FLC 2/2 FAC 5/1*
Sunderland *(£1,100,000 on 10/8/2005) PL 13+8/1 FAC 0+1*
Burnley *(£750,000 + on 17/3/2006) FL 68+1/28 FLC 2+1/2 FAC 1*
Charlton Ath *(£1,500,000 + on 1/1/2008) FL 10+6/2*

GRAY David Peter

Born: Edinburgh, 4 May 1988
Height: 6'0" **Weight:** 12.10

A promising youngster on Manchester United's staff, David arrived at Crewe on loan last November and played in the away League game at Nottingham Forest. Unable to play in the FA Cup at the request of United, he made just the one appearance for Crewe before returning to Old Trafford. He is a quick, right-sided

player who can operate either at full-back or further up the pitch.
Manchester U *(From trainee on 17/8/2005) FLC 1*
Crewe Alex *(Loaned on 22/11/2007) FL 1*

GRAY Julian Raymond

Born: Lewisham, 21 September 1979
Height: 6'1" **Weight:** 11.10

Signed from Birmingham by Iain Dowie in the close season, Julian had a dream debut for Coventry at Barnsley, scoring an excellent goal in the 4-1 victory. He suffered a knee ligament injury after four League games but was back in October and performed more consistently, giving the team much needed width on the left. Just as his season looked set to take off, he was injured against West Ham and for the remainder of the season was in and out of the first team. On his day he can cause havoc with his full-back through skill and crossing ability but is too often a peripheral player. His best display was in the 4-0 win over Barnsley, when he made a goal for Leon Best and scored one himself.

Arsenal *(From trainee on 13/7/1998) PL 0+1*
Crystal Palace *(£250,000 + on 21/7/2000) FL 100+25/10 FLC 5+6/1 FAC 6/2 Others 2*
Cardiff C *(Loaned on 13/10/2003) FL 5+4*
Birmingham C *(Free on 24/6/2004) P/FL 38+22/3 FLC 7/1 FAC 6/1*
Coventry C *(Free on 10/7/2007) FL 20+6/3 FLC 2 FAC 1*

GRAY Kevin John

Born: Sheffield, 7 January 1972
Height: 6'0" **Weight:** 14.0
Club Honours: Div 2 '06

Kevin was brought in for one season after leaving Carlisle to add steel and know-how to a youthful Chesterfield defence and was made club captain. After a training injury in December, he never recovered the level of match-fitness necessary to challenge for a regular place. Kevin still used his experience to good effect, coaching and helping with match preparation before his release at the end of the season.

Mansfield T *(From trainee on 1/7/1990) FL 129+12/3 FLC 8/1 FAC 6+1 Others 13+2/2*
Huddersfield T *(Signed on 18/7/1994) FL 214+16/6 FLC 12+1 FAC 15 Others 11*
Stockport Co *(Loaned on 11/8/2000) FL 1*
Tranmere Rov *(Free on 8/7/2002) FL 11+1/1 FLC 1 FAC 1+1 Others 2+1*
Carlisle U *(Free on 25/11/2003) FL 96+4/9 FLC 1 FAC 2/1 Others 5*
Chesterfield *(Free on 11/7/2007) FL 10+5 FAC 1 Others 1*

GRAY Michael

Born: Sunderland, 3 August 1974
Height: 5'7" **Weight:** 10.10
Club Honours: Div 1 '96, '99
International Honours: E: 3

Michael was signed from Sunderland in the summer as a left-back and took time to find his true form and fitness at Wolverhampton. He was then injured against Coventry and out for almost two months. From then on he was a regular and when the club signed another left-back, Michael was simply given a more advanced role. Scored with a beautiful curling shot at Crystal Palace and, after a fortuitous goal at Burnley, hit a splendid winner at home to Scunthorpe, making it three in five appearances. Michael continued to give energetic performances that belied his age and delighted the crowd. Was released at the end of the campaign.
Sunderland (From trainee on 1/7/1992) P/FL 341+22/16 FLC 23+4 FAC 17+1/1 Others 2
Glasgow Celtic (Loaned on 31/8/2003) SL 2+5 SLC 1 Others 1+1
Blackburn Rov (Free on 28/1/2004) PL 63+1 FLC 6 FAC 1 Others 2
Leeds U (Loaned on 3/2/2005) FL 10
Leeds U (Loaned on 22/3/2007) FL 6
Wolverhampton W (Free on 1/8/2007) FL 29+4/3 FLC 1 FAC 2+1

GRAY Wayne William
Born: Camberwell, 7 November 1980
Height: 5'10" **Weight:** 12.10
Club Honours: Div 1 '06
Wayne rejoined Leyton Orient in the summer from Yeovil, having previously been on loan in 2001-02. At Brisbane Road he soon formed a good understanding with Adam Boyd and is a very pacy forward who can also play on the right wing if required.
Wimbledon (From trainee on 10/2/1999) P/FL 33+42/6 FLC 1+1 FAC 1+7/1
Swindon T (Loaned on 3/3/2000) FL 8+4/2
Port Vale (Loaned on 6/10/2000) FL 2+1
Leyton Orient (Loaned on 30/11/2001) FL 13+2/5 FAC 2/1
Brighton & Hove A (Loaned on 27/3/2002) FL 3+1/1
Southend U (Free on 8/7/2004) FL 56+27/20 FLC 1+1 FAC 1+1 Others 7+4/2
Yeovil T (Free on 8/7/2006) FL 24+22/11 FLC 1/1 FAC 1 Others 4
Leyton Orient (Signed on 20/7/2007) FL 30+8/8 FLC 2 FAC 2/2 Others 1

GRAZIOLI Giuliano Stefano Luigi
Born: Marylebone, 23 March 1975
Height: 5'11" **Weight:** 12.11
Club Honours: FC '05
Sadly, Guiliano did not register a goal in his fifth and final season with Barnet. The striker was limited to only two League starts but put in a number of hard-working displays from the substitutes' bench and remained a firm favourite among the Bees' fans. They gave him a

hero's reception in his final League game at Underhill, against Stockport, where he went on as a late substitute.
Peterborough U (Signed from Wembley on 19/10/1995) FL 23+18/16 FLC 1+2 FAC 0+3/1 Others 0+2
Swindon T (Free on 15/7/1999) FL 45+33/18 FLC 3+4 FAC 1+1 Others 1
Bristol Rov (Free on 2/7/2002) FL 28+6/11 FLC 1 FAC 3/1
Barnet (Signed on 8/7/2003) FL 36+21/9 FLC 4/1 FAC 1+3

GREEN Dominic Ashley
Born: Newham, 5 July 1989
Height: 5'7" **Weight:** 11.5
A product of a West Ham local community involvement scheme, Dominic signed a contract with Dagenham before last season. As a young midfielder with a bright future, he was used sparingly but his pace and ability to go past full-backs make him an exciting prospect. Dominic went on loan to Thurrock in February in an effort to give him some better class football than in the reserves.
Dagenham & Redbridge (From West Ham U/Thames Gateway Football Partnership Scheme on 7/8/2007) FL 2+10

GREEN Francis (Franny) James
Born: Nottingham, 25 April 1980
Height: 5'9" **Weight:** 11.4
Freed by Boston, Franny arrived at Macclesfield in the summer 2007 and went straight into the team, being a regular apart from a short spell in January when he was recovering from an abdominal injury. Over the season he was paired with different strike partners but ably adjusted his game accordingly and always played with enthusiasm and pace. Franny completed the season as Town's top-scorer with 11 goals, five of which were winning strikes, although one of his best performances came in the home draw against MK Dons when he scored twice.
Peterborough U (£25,000 + from Ilkeston T on 2/3/1998) FL 51+57/14 FLC 4+3 FAC 5 Others 3+4/2
Lincoln C (£7,500 on 16/9/2003) FL 79+21/18 FLC 2+1/1 FAC 1+2 Others 5+5/1
Boston U (Loaned on 22/11/2005) FL 5+1/1
Boston U (Free on 2/8/2006) FL 35+4/4 FAC 1
Macclesfield T (Free on 10/8/2007) FL 35+6/11 FLC 1 FAC 0+1 Others 1

GREEN Jamie Paul
Born: Rossington, 18 August 1989
Height: 5'7" **Weight:** 10.7
Yet another of Rotherham's home-grown youngster, Jamie broke through to the first team towards the end of the season.

Unfortunately, it was at the time when the club had gone into administration but he displayed his versatility by featuring both at left-back and on the left of midfield. Is one for the future.
Rotherham U (From trainee on 29/6/2007) FL 6+3/1

GREEN Matthew (Matty) James
Born: Bath, 2 January 1987
Height: 5'5" **Weight:** 10.6
Matty made only one appearance for Cardiff last season, in the Carling Cup, being unable to break through at City following the arrival of Robbie Fowler and Jimmy Floyd Hasselbaink before joining Darlington on loan in October. A fast and direct forward, he made an impressive debut against Leeds in the Johnstone's Paint Trophy, hitting the post late in the second half of the 1-0 defeat. However, he could not match this first performance in two other starts and two substitute outings and returned to Ninian Park. With no prospect of making a breakthrough at Cardiff, towards the end of November he was allowed to spend time on loan at Oxford United in the Conference and was still there at the end of the campaign. Out of contract with Cardiff and released, Matty was offered a deal by Oxford.
Cardiff C (£10,000 from Newport Co on 31/1/2007) FL 0+6 FLC 0+1
Darlington (Loaned on 8/10/2007) FL 3+1 Others 0+1

GREEN Paul Jason
Born: Pontefract, 10 April 1983
Height: 5'11" **Weight:** 12.0
Club Honours: Div 3 '04; AMC '07
Paul could not get in the Doncaster team in the first half of last season and occupied a regular seat on the substitutes' bench. Then, just before Christmas, he received the call when Mark Wilson was injured and seized the chance with both feet to renew his partnership with James Coppinger on the right, becoming one of the midfield mainstays in his tenth season with the club, having come through the youth set-up. Paul won many 'Man of the Match' awards for his non-stop, box-to-box work, scoring six goals in all competitions, and ran himself into the ground at Wembley in the play-off final against Leeds in his quest to help Rovers win promotion. A free agent in the summer, Paul declined Rovers' offer of an improved contract to join Derby.
Doncaster Rov (From trainee on 16/8/2000) FL 161+37/25 FLC 8+3/1 FAC 7+3 Others 11+4/1

179

GREEN Paul Michael
Born: Birmingham, 15 April 1987
Height: 5'11" **Weight:** 12.0
An energetic full-back, Paul capped
his first full season with Lincoln in style
with his enthusiastic and consistent
performances seeing him claim both the
players' and the supporters' 'Player of
the Season' awards. His overlapping runs
and excellent delivery caused problems
for a number of opposing defences, most
notably Morecambe in the Imps' final
away game, which saw Paul score a fine
first goal of the season.
Aston Villa (From trainee on 19/4/2005)
Lincoln C (Free on 23/11/2007) FL 47+5/2 FLC
1 FAC 2 Others 3

GREEN Robert Paul
Born: Chertsey, 18 January 1980
Height: 6'2" **Weight:** 12.2
Club Honours: Div 1 '04
International Honours: E: 1; B-1; Yth
It was a terrific season for the West Ham
goalkeeper, who played in every League
game. He is reassuring, commands his
box and throughout the campaign made
many brilliant stops as well as saving
penalties against Reading, Portsmouth
and Tottenham. He was 'Man of the
Match' on many occasions and arguably
the most in-form goalkeeper in the
country, with many observers endorsing
his claim to be in the England squad.
Robert deservedly won the annual
'Hammer of the Year' award, voted for
by the fans.
Norwich C (From juniors on 3/7/1997) P/FL
222+1 FLC 7 FAC 8 Others 3
West Ham U (£2,000,000 on 18/8/2006) PL
64 FLC 2 FAC 2

GREEN Ryan Michael
Born: Cardiff, 20 October 1980
Height: 5'8" **Weight:** 11.6
International Honours: W: 2; U21-16;
Yth
The former Welsh international started
last season as first-choice right-back at
Bristol Rovers but after 12 appearances
he sustained a broken jaw in an off-field
incident in November and was sidelined
for two months. Ryan subsequently
suffered a groin problem that required
surgery and kept him out for the
remainder of the campaign.
Wolverhampton W (From trainee on
25/10/1997) FL 6+2 FLC 2 FAC 0+2
Torquay U (Loaned on 2/3/2001) FL 10
Millwall (Free on 19/10/2001) FL 12+1
Cardiff C (Free on 14/8/2002) Others 1
Sheffield Wed (Free on 27/11/2002) FL 4
(Free to Hereford U on 8/8/2003)
Bristol Rov (Free from Hereford U on
7/6/2006) FL 41+4 FAC 1 FAC 2+1 Others 7

GREEN Stuart
Born: Whitehaven, 15 June 1981
Height: 5'10" **Weight:** 11.4
Although starting the Crystal Palace
2007-08 season with two goals from
free kicks against Leicester and Coventry,
the midfield player was transfer listed by
Neil Warnock and returned north when
signing for Blackpool on the January
transfer deadline day. Having signed an
18-month contract at Blackpool, Stuart
found his chances limited, his only start
being in a 3-0 defeat by Plymouth, but he
will be looking for more opportunities in
the coming season.
Newcastle U (From trainee on 8/7/1999)
Carlisle U (Loaned on 14/12/2001) FL 16/3
Hull C (£150,000 on 3/7/2002) FL
111+26/24 FLC 2+1 FAC 4+1/1 Others 1/1
Carlisle U (Loaned on 19/2/2003) FL 9+1/2
Others 3
Crystal Palace (£75,000 on 31/8/2006) FL
12+12/4 FLC 1 FAC 2
Blackpool (Free on 31/1/2008) FL 1+5

**GREENACRE Christopher
(Chris)** Mark
Born: Halifax, 23 December 1977
Height: 5'11" **Weight:** 12.8
A centre-forward in the traditional
mould and predatory in the box, Chris
finished last season as Tranmere's
leading scorer for the third consecutive
season. Although a total of 14 League
and Cup goals was comparatively low
by his previous standards, a spell on the
sidelines through injury in mid-season
contributed to this. Very popular with the
supporters, he is a consistent and hard-
working team player who relishes every
chance to capitalize on opposition errors.
In addition, Chris adapts easily to any
formation and forms an understanding
quickly with fellow strikers and wingers.
He netted his 50th goal for Rovers in
March.
Manchester C (From trainee on 1/7/1995) FL
3+5/1 FAC 0+1
Cardiff C (Loaned on 22/8/1997) FL 11/2
Blackpool (Loaned on 5/3/1998) FL 2+2
Scarborough (Loaned on 10/12/1998) FL
10+2/2 Others 1
Mansfield T (Free on 5/11/1999) FL
120+1/49 FLC 5/3 FAC 5/6 Others 2+1
Stoke C (Free on 8/7/2002) FL 44+31/7 FLC
2 FAC 5+1/2
Tranmere Rov (Free on 18/7/2005) FL
120+9/44 FLC 3 FAC 5/6 Others 4+1/1

GREENING Jonathan
Born: Scarborough, 2 January 1979
Height: 5'11" **Weight:** 11.7
Club Honours: UEFACL '99; FLC '04;
Ch '08
International Honours: E: U21-18; Yth
Jonathan was outstanding throughout

the season, pulling the strings in all
four midfield positions, choosing to
play on the left most of the time. West
Bromwich's only ever-present in the
Championship, he took over the captaincy
from Paul Robinson. As the promotion
race began to hot up after the turn of
the year, his experience, know-how,
skill and commitment shone through.
Surprisingly, Jonathan scored only once,
a real cracker in the 5-1 televised home
League win over Queens Park Rangers in
September. As skipper, he was particularly
disappointed to lose to Portsmouth
in the FA Cup semi-final at Wembley.
Jonathan who, along with team-mates
Paul Robinson and Kevin Phillips, was in
the PFA Championship select team, starts
the new Premiership campaign with 298
career League appearances under his belt
and 347 overall.
York C (From trainee on 23/12/1996) FL
5+20/2 FLC 0+1 Others 1
Manchester U (£500,000 + on 25/3/1998)
PL 4+10 FLC 6 FAC 0+1 Others 3+3
Middlesbrough (£2,000,000 on 9/8/2001)
PL 91+8/4 FLC 5 FAC 4+1
West Bromwich A (£1,250,000 on
30/7/2004) P/FL 155+5/5 FLC 5+3/1 FAC 13
Others 3

GREER Gordon
Born: Glasgow, 14 December 1980
Height: 6'2" **Weight:** 12.5
International Honours: S: B-1
Gordon, a centre-half who had been
released by Kilmarnock, was signed
by Doncaster in the close season after
impressing in the pre-season friendlies.
He began in the first team but suffered a
setback before Christmas when he was
injured. It was April before he regained
fitness and was able to rejoin the squad
as the campaign reached its climax.
Clyde (Free from Port Glasgow on
28/6/2000) SL 27+3 SLC 0+1 SC 1 Others 1
Blackburn Rov (£200,000 on 23/5/2001)
FLC 1
Stockport Co (Loaned on 27/3/2003) FL
4+1/1
Kilmarnock (Signed on 31/8/2003) SL
102+5/4 SLC 8/1 SC 5
Doncaster Rov (Free on 25/7/2007) FL
10+1/1 FLC 1+1 FAC 2 Others 2

GREGAN Sean Matthew
Born: Guisborough, 29 March 1974
Height: 6'2" **Weight:** 14.7
Club Honours: Div 2 '00
Sean was appointed Oldham's captain
last summer and was widely expected
to be the defensive lynchpin. However,
following an accidental kick on his heel
at Huddersfield in October, he endured a
lengthy battle for fitness before learning
he needed an operation to repair Achilles

...amage. A vastly experienced centre-back, dominant in the air and boasting excellent distribution, his organisational skills were sorely missed. Sean did not return for the Latics until early April, the longest injury lay-off his career, and his absence was a huge blow to League One play-off aspirations. He will be chomping at the bit to lead the club to success.

Darlington *(From trainee on 20/1/1991) FL 29+7/4 FLC 8 FAC 7 Others 10+1/1*
Preston NE *(£350,000 on 29/11/1996) FL 106+6/12 FLC 14 FAC 15/1 Others 10*
West Bromwich A *(£1,500,000 on 5/8/2002) P/FL 76+3/2 FLC 4 FAC 2*
Leeds U *(£500,000 on 17/9/2004) FL 63+1 FLC 6 FAC 1 Others 3*
Oldham Ath *(Free on 8/11/2006) FL 42 FLC 2 FAC 2/1 Others 4*

GRIFFIN Adam
Born: Salford, 26 August 1984
Height: 5'7" **Weight:** 10.5
Adam failed to show the form of previous seasons, despite playing in most of Stockport's games in the first half of the campaign. In the second half, players returning from injury and the emergence of fellow left-winger Tommy Rowe meant he played little football and he was released at the end of the campaign.
Oldham Ath *(From trainee on 9/8/2003) FL 58+4/3 FLC 2 FAC 4+1 Others 4+1/1*
Oxford U *(Loaned on 10/11/2005) FL 8+1 FAC 2 Others 2*
Stockport Co *(Signed on 20/1/2006) FL 58+23/6 FLC 2+1 FAC 4 Others 1*

GRIFFIN Andrew (Andy)
Born: Billinge, 7 March 1979
Height: 5'9" **Weight:** 10.10
International Honours: E: U21-3; Yth
Andy was freed by Portsmouth and signed in the summer to add experience to Derby's defence after their promotion to the Premiership. He did a workmanlike job at left or right-back but the chance to rejoin Stoke in January, his first club and the one where he spent 2006-07 on loan, was too tempting to reject. A good tackler, he reads the game well and when the captain, Dominic Matteo, was injured Andy took over his responsibilities. He can play in either of the full-back positions but before he suffered a hamstring injury towards the end of the season was used exclusively on the right flank as the Potters mounted their successful challenge for promotion.
Stoke C *(From trainee on 5/9/1996) FL 52+5/2 FLC 4+1 FAC 2*
Newcastle U *(£1,500,000 + on 30/1/1998) PL 63+13/2 FLC 8 FAC 6 Others 14/1*
Portsmouth *(Free on 2/7/2004) PL 38+6 FLC 3+1 FAC 1*

Scott Griffiths

181

Stoke C (Loaned on 9/9/2006) FL 32+1/2
FAC 1
Derby Co (Signed on 1/8/2007) PL 13+2
Stoke C (£300,000 on 11/11/2008) FL 15

GRIFFITHS Leroy Henerica Septon
Born: Lambeth, 30 December 1976
Height: 5'11" Weight: 13.5
Having done the rounds of non-League clubs, Leroy joined Gillingham on a short-term contract from Fisher Athletic in November. A hard worker and always lively, the striker was seen at his best when he appeared as a substitute in order to run at defences late in matches. He is also comfortable in a wide left position.
Queens Park Rgrs (£40,000 from Hampton & Richmond Borough, ex Corinthian Casuals, on 30/5/2001) FL 26+10/3 FAC 1 (Free to Farnborough T during 2003 close season)
Gillingham (Free from Fisher Ath, ex Grays Ath, Aldershot T - loan, on 12/11/2007) FL 4+20/2 Others 0+1

GRIFFITHS Scott Robert
Born: Westminster, 27 November 1985
Height: 5'9" Weight: 11.2
Club Honours: FC '07
International Honours: E: SP-2
Another great season for the left-back ended with him named as runner-up for Dagenham's 'Player of the Year'. He took a month to get used to the pace of the League but his game improved with every step he made. His ability to get down the left flank, together with his defensive skills, had him watched by a number of bigger clubs. Scott signed an extension to his contract before last season started.
Dagenham & Redbridge (Free from Aveley on 12/8/2004) FL 41 FLC 1 FAC 3 Others 3

GRITTON Martin Francis
Born: Glasgow, 1 June 1978
Height: 6'1" Weight: 12.2
Martin made the move from Lincoln to Macclesfield last summer as he wanted the opportunity to feature on a regular basis. Achieving his objective in the first half of the season he scored on his debut at the Moss Rose against MK Dons only three minutes after going on as a substitute. He went on to score a further eight goals in all competitions, most of which were typical striker's goals from short range, and also played a vital part when defending set pieces. Martin struggled with injury in the second half of the season, severely restricting his appearances, but finished as second-top scorer.
Plymouth Arg (Free from Porthleven on 7/8/1998) FL 15+29/7 FLC 2+2/1 FAC 0+4 Others 3/1

Torquay U (Signed on 8/8/2002) FL 72+21/23 FLC 2 FAC 2+1/3 Others 2
Grimsby T (£5,000 on 24/12/2004) FL 29+20/6 FLC 0+2 FAC 0+1 Others 1
Lincoln C (Signed on 31/1/2006) FL 9+18/3 Others 1+2
Mansfield T (Loaned on 12/1/2007) FL 14+5/6
Macclesfield T (Free on 3/7/2007) FL 27+4/8 FAC 1/1 Others 2

GROUNDS Jonathan Martin
Born: Thornaby, 2 February 1988
Height: 6'1" Weight: 12.3
Jonathan graduated from Middlesbrough's Academy just before the season and, at one point, the club seriously considered releasing him before handing him a one-year contract instead. Both Andrew Taylor and Manny Pogatetz were injured so Jonathan had his break at left-back, making his debut at the Riverside in the 1-1 draw against Liverpool in January. A string of impressive displays over the following weeks saw him rewarded with a new two-year contract in March.
Middlesbrough (From trainee on 6/7/2007) PL 5 FAC 2

GROVES Matthew (Matt)
Born: Bristol, 11 December 1988
Height: 6'3" Weight: 13.10
A young striker, Matt made his debut for Bristol Rovers as a substitute in the FA Cup against Rushden and his League debut in the following match at Huddersfield. He ended the season with a two-month loan spell at Chippenham to obtain further experience.
Bristol Rov (From Filton College on 5/6/2007) FL 0+1 FAC 0+1

GUDJONSSON Johannes (Joey) Karl
Born: Akranes, Iceland, 25 May 1980
Height: 5'8" Weight: 11.5
International Honours: Iceland: 34; U21-10; Yth
Something of a forgotten man in the early part of the season, Joey's opportunities in Burnley's Championship side increased after the arrival of Owen Coyle as manager in November. His impact was immediate, with his first goal for the club in the fine win at Watford, and he had a decent run in the side in the New Year. A hard-working midfield man, the Icelandic international has yet to find reward for one of his trademark bullet free-kicks.
Aston Villa (Loaned from Real Betis, Spain, ex IA Akranes, KRC Genk, MVV Maastricht, RKC Waalwijk, on 27/11/2003) PL 9+2/2
Wolverhampton W (Loaned from Real Betis, Spain on 29/8/2003) PL 5+6 FLC 3/1

FAC 1+1
Leicester C (Free from Real Betis, Spain on 11/8/2004) FL 66+11/10 FLC 5/2 FAC 7/1 (Freed during 2006 close season)
Burnley (£150,000 from AZ Alkmaar, Holland on 22/1/2007) FL 22+17/1 FLC 1 FAC 0+1

GUERET Willy July
Born: St Claude, Guadeloupe, 3 August 1973
Height: 6'1" Weight: 13.5
Club Honours: AMC '06, '08; Div 2 '08
One of the main reasons why MK Dons missed out on promotion in 2006-07 was their lack of a quality goalkeeper but there was no such problem once Willy arrived on the scene after being released by Swansea last summer. From the opening game against Bury, he was a commanding presence, particularly in the air, and as the season wore on it became clear that his shot-stopping ability was another major asset. A penalty save in the Johnstone's Paint Trophy area final shoot-out win over Swansea helped take the Dons to Wembley and a first-half penalty save in the final contributed greatly to the victory over Grimsby. The fact that he played every minute of every League game shows just how important he was in lifting the title.
Millwall (Free from Le Mans, France on 31/7/2000) FL 13+1 FAC 3 Others 2
Swansea C (Free on 5/8/2004) FL 132 FLC 3 FAC 10 Others 10
MK Dons (Signed on 10/8/2007) FL 46 Others 6

GUINAN Stephen (Steve) Anthony
Born: Birmingham, 24 December 1975
Height: 6'1" Weight: 13.7
International Honours: E: SP-4
Freed by Cheltenham in the summer, Steve began last season as one of Hereford's first-choice strikers and his hard-working, thoughtful and intelligent play created space and chances for others. A two-goal performance at Notts County earned an important win for the side before a dismissal against MK Dons interrupted him. He had just re-established himself when a serious calf injury, also in a match against Notts County, sidelined him for three months. Steve was back to play a useful role in the final matches of Hereford's countdown to promotion.
Nottingham F (From trainee on 7/1/1993) P/FL 2+5 FLC 2/1
Darlington (Loaned on 14/12/1995) FL 3/1
Burnley (Loaned on 27/3/1997) FL 0+6
Crewe Alex (Loaned on 19/3/1998) FL 3

Halifax T *(Loaned on 16/10/1998) FL 12/2*
Plymouth Arg *(Loaned on 24/3/1999) FL 11/7*
Scunthorpe U *(Loaned on 10/9/1999) FL 2+1/1*
Cambridge U *(Free on 24/12/1999) FL 4+2 FAC 0+2 Others 1*
Plymouth Arg *(Free on 23/3/2000) FL 15+15/3 FLC 2 FAC 2 Others 0+1*
Shrewsbury T *(Free on 28/3/2002) FL 4+1 (Free to Hereford U on 15/8/2002)*
Cheltenham T *(Free from Hereford U on 17/5/2004) FL 79+13/13 FLC 3/1 FAC 8/1 Others 5+3/3*
Hereford U *(Free on 25/1/2007) FL 36+8/10 FLC 0+2 FAC 0+2*

GUNNARSSON Brynjar Bjorn

Born: Reykjavik, Iceland, 16 October 1975
Height: 6'1" **Weight:** 11.12
Club Honours: Ch '06
International Honours: Iceland: 65; U21-8; Yth

Brynjar was a permanent fixture in Reading's midfield for the first half of last season, winning more than his fair share of crunching tackles and setting up chances for the strikers with some incisive passing. Then, on Boxing Day, he was sent off after half-an-hour in the 1-1 draw at West Ham for a two-footed tackle on Hayden Mullins. Brynjar was suspended, lost his place in the team and played only once more, at centre-back in the 3-1 defeat at Aston Villa. He had a series of injuries in training and the arrival of Marek Matejovsky meant that his Premiership opportunities were always likely to be limited. But he has a year left on his contract and will be hoping to make more of an impression.
Stoke C *(£600,000 from Orgryte IS, Sweden on 4/1/2000) FL 128+3/16 FLC 7/1 FAC 7/2 Others 12+1/1*
Nottingham F *(Free on 1/8/2003) FL 9+4 FAC 1*
Stoke C *(Free on 19/3/2004) FL 1+2*
Watford *(Free on 2/7/2004) FL 34+2/3 FLC 5 FAC 1+1*
Reading *(Signed on 22/7/2005) P/FL 47+25/7 FLC 2+1 FAC 6/1*

GUNTER Christopher (Chris) Ross

Born: Newport, 21 July 1989
Height: 5'11" **Weight:** 11.2
International Honours: W: 6; U21-7; Yth

Newport-born Chris grew up as a Cardiff supporter, spending ten years in the youth development system, and travelled away on supporters' buses before signing as a professional. After breaking into the Cardiff side at right-back, Chris

Danny Guthrie

struggled to establish himself but John Toshack picked him for Wales and his progress was such that he was signed by Tottenham in January. Able to play at left or right-back, most of his Spurs' football was in the reserves and although he made a debut in their FA Cup win at Reading he featured in only four first-team games in his first half-season. Never a candidate for Carling Cup success because he had already played for Cardiff in the competition, the teenager continued to represent Wales, at full and under-21 level and is clearly regarded as an investment for the future by Spurs.

Cardiff C *(From trainee on 25/10/2006) FL 20+8 FLC 3+2*
Tottenham H *(£2,000,000 + on 4/1/2008) PL 1+1 FAC 1+1*

GUTHRIE Daniel (Danny) Sean

Born: Shrewsbury, 18 April 1987
Height: 5'9" **Weight:** 11.6
International Honours: E: Yth; Sch
Sammy Lee used his Liverpool connections to sign Danny, a highly-regarded prospect, for Bolton on a season-long loan before the start of last season. Making his first start in the Carling Cup tie at Fulham, he scored his first goal in Bolton colours, a rocket of a 20-yard strike. His first League appearance was in the home defeat by Chelsea and Danny proceeded to hold down a place for much of what was left of the season. A driving and skilful midfielder, Danny has all the attributes required to become a successful Premiership performer. He clearly prefers to play in the centre of midfield, where many of his best performances came, although he was used on many occasions as a right-winger. Despite losing his starting place towards the end of the season, Danny was still highly respected by all who followed him on a regular basis.

Liverpool *(From trainee on 8/12/2004) PL 0+3 FLC 1+2 Others 1*
Southampton *(Loaned on 5/3/2007) FL 8+2 Others 2*
Bolton W *(Loaned on 5/7/2007) PL 21+4 FLC 2/1 FAC 1 Others 6+1*

GUTTRIDGE Luke Horace

Born: Barnstaple, 27 March 1982
Height: 5'5" **Weight:** 9.7
Club Honours: Div 1 '06
Luke, a hard-working midfielder, never had much of a look-in at Colchester after being recruited from Leyton Orient

during the summer. He started only once before Christmas, a 1-0 defeat at Shrewsbury in the Carling Cup. He had a run of six consecutive games, starting with a Boxing Day draw against Southampton, but after January made only a couple more brief appearances as a substitute. Luke was always behind the likes of Johnnie Jackson, Dean Hammond and Kem Izzet in the pecking order. Was out of contract in the summer and looking for a new club.

Torquay U *(Trainee) FL 0+1*
Cambridge U *(Free on 15/8/2000) FL 127+9/17 FLC 1+3 FAC 6+1/1 Others 9+3/2*
Southend U *(Signed on 18/3/2005) FL 59+4/5 FLC 1+1 FAC 1+3 Others 0+3*
Leyton Orient *(Loaned on 23/11/2006) FL 7/1*
Leyton Orient *(Signed on 30/1/2007) FL 8+2*
Colchester U *(Free on 11/7/2007) FL 5+9 FLC 1 FAC 1*

GUY Jamie Lesley

Born: Barking, 1 August 1987
Height: 6'1" **Weight:** 13.0
The Colchester striker never really got out of first gear in 2007-08. He had some joy in his first season at Championship level, with three goals, but he did not even manage a start this time, being restricted to 12 outings as a substitute, and always behind the likes of Kevin Lisbie, Clive Platt and Teddy Sheringham. Jamie will hope for more joy in League One over the coming year, because he is strong and a slick finisher.

Colchester U *(From trainee on 31/7/2006) FL 1+46/3 FLC 1 FAC 0+2 Others 1+3*

GUY Lewis Brett

Born: Penrith, 27 August 1985
Height: 5'10" **Weight:** 10.8
Club Honours: AMC '07
International Honours: E: Yth
A Doncaster forward with pace, who causes concern among defenders when he runs at them, particularly when used as a substitute against tired legs. Lewis works hard up front but has stiff competition in the attacking department at Rovers. He was out for some time in the latter part of the season with a viral illness but was back on the bench to influence the play-offs as a playing substitute.

Newcastle U *(From trainee on 3/8/2002) Others 0+1*
Doncaster Rov *(Free on 3/3/2005) FL 54+51/16 FLC 9+1 FAC 6+3/1 Others 8+5/5*

GUYETT Scott Barry

Born: Ascot, Australia, 20 January 1976
Height: 6'2" **Weight:** 13.2
Club Honours: FC '04; Div 2 '05
International Honours: E: SP-4
The giant centre-back cemented a regular place in Russell Slade's Yeovil defence last season with a string of brilliant displays. Scott's strong heading ability helped the side both defensively and from set pieces in the Glovers' attack and he was a vital player in the relegation fight with some spectacular displays in the heart of the defence. Partnered by Terry Skiverton and Terrell Forbes, the Australian proved a valuable player for Yeovil.

Oxford U *(Free from Southport, ex Brisbane C, Gresley Rov, on 9/7/2001) FL 20+2 FLC 1 FAC 1 Others 1 (Free to Chester C on 2/8/2002)*
Yeovil T *(Free from Chester C on 30/7/2004) FL 73+16/2 FLC 1 FAC 6 Others 6*

GWYNNE Samuel (Sam) Luke

Born: Hereford, 17 December 1987
Height: 5'8" **Weight:** 11.3
Hereford-born Sam's patience finally paid off with an extended run for the Bulls in mid-season. After coming through the youth ranks and making a brief debut in Hereford's Conference-promotion season, Sam had to wait until Lionel Ainsworth's departure to Watford for a chance. Although by inclination a central midfielder, Sam slotted in comfortably on the right of midfield around Christmas and the New Year, showing plenty of promise before again having to be content with a squad place.

Hereford U *(From juniors on 24/6/2006) FL 9+6 FAC 2+1 Others 0+1*

GYEPES Gabor

Born: Budapest, Hungary, 26 June 1981
Height: 6'3" **Weight:** 13.1
International Honours: Hungary: 22
Central defender Gabor must have thought his career was over when he was released by Wolverhampton after a leg injury had caused him to miss almost two years of football. Given a short-term contract at Northampton, Gabor worked his way back to fitness and into the Cobblers' first team. He added stability to the defence and put in so many excellent performances he was offered a further one-year contract before the end of the season.

Wolverhampton W *(Signed from Ferencvaros, Hungary on 5/8/2005) FL 19+1 FLC 2 FAC 2 (Freed on 24/4/2007)*
Northampton T *(Free, following long term injury and trial at Queens Park Rgrs, on 25/11/2008) FL 13*

H

HACKETT Christopher (Chris) James
Born: Oxford, 1 March 1983
Height: 6'0" **Weight:** 11.6
A speedy and tricky Millwall winger with a rasping shot, Chris started last season well but suffered a bad injury barely a month into it and spent the rest of the campaign in the treatment-room. He has great attacking flair and can also be used as part of a three-pronged attack. Like many at the New Den, he hopes to steer clear of further injuries.
Oxford U (From trainee on 20/4/2000) FL 72+53/9 FLC 0+3 FAC 3+3 Others 4+4
Heart of Midlothian (£20,000 on 24/1/2006) SL 1+1
Millwall (Free on 3/8/2006) FL 22+17/3 FLC 1 FAC 2 Others 3/1

HACKNEY Simon John
Born: Stockport, 5 February 1984
Height: 5'8" **Weight:** 10.3
Club Honours: Div 2 '06
Having missed much of the previous term through injury, 2007-08 was much more successful for one of the fans' favourite Carlisle players. Simon loves to attack defenders down his favourite left flank and can often beat them through sheer speed before putting in a telling cross. His left-footed shooting is devastating and his powerful strike against Leeds that inspired Carlisle to inflict a first defeat of the campaign on the visitors was voted as the club's 'Goal of the Season'.
Carlisle U (Signed from Woodley Sports on 16/2/2005) FL 62+29/16 FLC 4+1 FAC 2+1 Others 6+6

HADFIELD Jordan Michael
Born: Swinton, 12 August 1987
Height: 5'9" **Weight:** 11.11
Club Honours: Div 2 '08
This hard-working central midfielder found it impossible to force his way into Macclesfield's team on a regular basis last season when more experienced players were preferred. He made two late appearances from the substitutes' bench in League matches and played for the full 90 minutes in two Johnstone's Paints Trophy matches before moving to MK Dons on loan in November. There he quickly showed his capacity for hard graft in midfield. His loan was extended until the end of the season and he put in a number of solid performances, either when starting or leaving the bench in the late stages of games.
Stockport Co (Trainee) FL 1

Macclesfield T (Free on 7/7/2006) FL 30+9/1 FLC 0+1 FAC 3+1 Others 3
MK Dons (Loaned on 16/11/2007) FL 6+7

HAGEN Erik Bjornstad
Born: Verne, Norway, 20 July 1975
Height: 6'1" **Weight:** 13.3
International Honours: Norway: 28
Erik, a formidable presence at centre-half, joined Wigan at the start of the year, becoming Steve Bruce's fifth and final January transfer-window capture in a loan for the remainder of the season from Russian Club Zenit St Petersburg. A wholehearted and powerful player who dominates in the air, he is a tough-tackling defender. He was the first Norwegian to play in Russia and went on as substitute for Zenit in the UEFA Cup tie against Everton. Erik made his only appearance for Wigan when starting at Portsmouth after suspensions forced Paul Scharner to switch to midfield. After that, the regular Norwegian international failed to make a further appearance and was expected to return to Russia.
Wigan Ath (Loaned from Zenit St Petersburg, Russia, ex Jevnaker, Liv Fossekallen, Valerenga, on 31/1/2008) PL 1

HAGGERTY David Patrick
Born: Sheffield, 28 March 1991
Height: 6'2" **Weight:** 13.7
Recognised as a highly promising young central defender, David made his Rotherham debut in the closing stages of the last game of the season, having been a regular in the reserves. He is good in the air, tackles and passes confidently, so his aim in the season ahead is to put pressure on senior players and earn a regular place.
Rotherham U (Trainee) FL 0+1

Marcus Hahnemann

185

HAHNEMANN Marcus Stephen
Born: Seattle, Washington, USA, 15 June 1972
Height: 6'3" **Weight:** 16.2
Club Honours: Ch '06
International Honours: USA: 7
Marcus was the only Reading player to be on the field for every minute of the 38 Premiership games, being statistically the busiest Premiership goalkeeper when making a total of 152 saves. He recovered from a serious hand injury at the end of the previous campaign to be, again, a brave and consistent last line of a Reading defence that was regularly under pressure and produced many outstanding performances, especially towards the end of the season as Reading struggled to hold on to their Premiership status. After 20 appearances he was guaranteed a one-year extension to his contract and kept his 100th clean sheet for the Royals in the 0-0 draw at Wigan. Marcus remains a member of the United States' international squad and contributed a weekly column to the Daily Mail newspaper.
Fulham (£80,000 from Colorado Rapids, USA on 9/7/1999) FL 2 FLC 2
Rochdale (Loaned on 12/10/2001) FL 5 Others 2
Reading (Loaned on 14/12/2001) FL 6
Reading (Free on 14/8/2002) P/FL 244 FLC 8+1 FAC 7 Others 2

HALDANE Lewis Oliver
Born: Trowbridge, 13 March 1985
Height: 6'0" **Weight:** 11.13
International Honours: W: U21-1
Bristol Rovers used Lewis' outstanding pace down the left-hand side of midfield but he found it difficult to score and had a disappointing time. His only goal of the season was important, an injury-time winner against Millwall. Lewis suffered an injury against Carlisle over Christmas and in the second half of the season only made sporadic appearances, usually from the bench.
Bristol Rov (From trainee on 13/10/2003) FL 90+57/15 FLC 2+1 FAC 5+7 Others 9+5/2

HALFORD Gregory (Greg)
Born: Chelmsford, 8 December 1984
Height: 6'4" **Weight:** 13.10
International Honours: E: Yth
Greg was signed by Sunderland from Reading in the summer and figured at right-back in three of the first four games. At 6'5", he is an imposing figure and is a superb crosser of the ball. An aggressive competitor, he collected two red cards by late October and these enforced absences saw him lose ground at the Stadium of

Light. Greg was allowed to join Charlton on loan during the January transfer window to replace Danny Mills, who had returned to Manchester City. He made his debut at right-back in the home win over Crystal Palace and was ever present from then on. Although his defensive qualities seemed patchy at times, his real strength was going forward and his extremely long throws brought another dimension to Charlton's game. Always a threat when attacking, he scored in consecutive games, against West Bromwich, when he headed in Darren Ambrose's free kick, and Wolverhampton, a volley from Jerome Thomas' cross. Greg is strong in the air and mobile, with good passing ability.
Colchester U (From trainee on 8/8/2003) FL 132+4/18 FLC 4+1/1 FAC 13/5 Others 8+1
Reading (£2,000,000 + on 30/1/2007) PL 2+1
Sunderland (£2,500,000 on 11/6/2007) PL 8 FLC 1
Charlton Ath (Loaned on 31/1/2008) FL 16/2

HALL Asa Philip
Born: Dudley, 29 November 1986
Height: 6'2" **Weight:** 11.9
International Honours: E: Yth
As a central midfielder who can also play at full-back, Asa was signed on loan by Shrewsbury from Birmingham in January. He had previous League experience at Boston and was keen to be on the ball in all areas of the pitch. Asa scored goals in Birmingham's reserves and took only four minutes to show he could do it at Shrewsbury with the opener his debut against Morecambe. A bout of illness restricted his involvement but as the season ended there were discussions about him joining Shrews after his contract came to an end at Birmingham.
Birmingham C (From trainee on 24/11/2004)
Boston U (Loaned on 6/1/2006) FL 5+7
Shrewsbury T (Loaned on 16/1/2008) FL 13+2/3

HALL Daniel (Danny) Andrew
Born: Ashton-under-Lyne, 14 November 1983
Height: 6'2" **Weight:** 12.7
Danny is most comfortable as a defensive midfield player, although he can play both as a full-back and a central defender. Despite finishing the previous season strongly, Danny struggled to hold a regular starting place with Shrewsbury. Probably his most effective contribution came in the 2-1 New Year's Day defeat at Peterborough, but he moved to Gretna later that month.
Oldham Ath (From trainee on 7/8/2003) FL

57+7/1 FLC 1 FAC 7+1 Others 6
Shrewsbury T (Free on 1/7/2006) FL 28+14 FLC 1+1 FAC 2 Others 6

HALL Fitz
Born: Leytonstone, 20 December 1980
Height: 6'1" **Weight:** 13.4
Effective in the air and a powerful presence at centre-half, Fitz made only two Premier League appearances for Wigan following the summer signings of Titus Bramble and Andreas Granquist. His only start was in the Carling Cup against Hull and he showed his versatility by playing right-back after an injury to Mario Melchiot in the game at Manchester United. Keen for regular first-team football, he was allowed to join Queens Park Rangers in the January transfer window and had a baptism of fire in the FA Cup against Chelsea at Stamford Bridge. Despite the narrow defeat, Fitz immediately showed what he is capable of and played his part in restricting the all-star Chelsea line-up to a single goal. After that, he was considered a first choice in the back four but his appearances were limited by nagging groin injuries.
Oldham Ath (£20,000 + from Chesham U, ex Staines T, on 15/3/2002) FL 44/5 FLC 4 FAC 3/1 Others 2+1
Southampton (£250,000 + on 14/7/2003) PL 7+4 FLC 1
Crystal Palace (£1,500,000 on 12/8/2004) P/FL 75/3 FLC 2 FAC 2 Others 2
Wigan Ath (£3,000,000 on 30/6/2006) PL 22+3 FLC 2 FAC 1
Queens Park Rgrs (£700,000 on 4/1/2008) FL 14 FAC 1

HALL Marcus Thomas Jackson
Born: Coventry, 24 March 1976
Height: 6'1" **Weight:** 12.2
International Honours: E: B-1; U21-8
Marcus' days as first-choice left-back were over last summer when Coventry signed Gary Borrowdale, but he started the season as Elliott Ward's central defensive partner and put in solid performances as City set off like a train. At the end of November, having been out injured, he was recalled at left-back and starred in victories at Stoke and Queens Park Rangers before losing his place to Borrowdale. Marcus, who is approaching 300 games for the Sky Blues, was offered a new contract.
Coventry C (From trainee on 1/7/1994) P/FL 113+19/2 FLC 14+1/2 FAC 8+2
Nottingham F (Free on 7/8/2002) FL 1
Southampton (Free on 30/8/2002)
Stoke C (Free on 6/12/2002) FL 76+3/1 FLC 3 FAC 5
Coventry C (Signed on 21/2/2005) FL 103+4 FLC 3+1 FAC 5

HALL Paul Anthony
Born: Manchester, 3 July 1972
Height: 5'9" **Weight:** 11.0
Club Honours: Div 3 '03
International Honours: Jamaica: 41
Arriving from Chesterfield in the summer, Paul began his second spell with Walsall as his 35th birthday approached and gave some useful displays in midfield in the first half of the season, netting a late winner at Hartlepool in September. In the New Year he was loaned to Wrexham at the same time as team-mate Danny Sonner made the same move on a free transfer. Brian Little hoped they could help to resurrect an ailing, free-falling Wrexham outfit. Paul added strength up front and scored what might have been a vital goal in the fight against relegation from the Football League against local rivals Chester in March. A recurrence of a leg injury curtailed his rescue act and Wrexham were unable to survive. Was released at the end of the campaign.
Torquay U *(From trainee on 9/7/1990) FL 77+16/1 FLC 7 FAC 4+1/2 Others 5+1/1*
Portsmouth *(£70,000 on 25/3/1993) FL 148+40/37 FLC 10+3/1 FAC 7+1/2 Others 5+2/2*
Coventry C *(£300,000 on 10/8/1998) PL 2+8 FLC 2+1/1*
Bury *(Loaned on 18/2/1999) FL 7*
Sheffield U *(Loaned on 17/12/1999) FL 1+3/1*
West Bromwich A *(Loaned on 10/2/2000) FL 4*
Walsall *(Free on 17/3/2000) FL 46+6/10 FLC 4+1 FAC 3/1 Others 3*
Rushden & Diamonds *(Free on 11/10/2001) FL 106+6/26 FLC 3 FAC 4+2 Others 4+2/3*
Tranmere Rov *(Free on 25/3/2004) FL 49+6/13 FLC 2 FAC 1 Others 5/1*
Chesterfield *(Free on 5/7/2005) FL 84+7/20 FLC 5 FAC 3 Others 2/1*
Walsall *(Free on 5/7/2007) FL 7+12/1 FLC 1 FAC 2+1 Others 1*
Wrexham *(Loaned on 11/1/2008) FL 7+4/1*

HALL Ryan Marcus Leon
Born: Dulwich, 4 January 1988
Height: 5'10" **Weight:** 10.5
A young Academy wide midfield player who had scored four goals in the reserves, Ryan made his debut for Crystal Palace as a substitute against Queens Park Rangers in November. This was his only taste of League action and there was another sub appearance against Watford in the FA Cup before he went on loan to Dagenham in January, making his debut at Morecambe. The fast right-winger was unfortunate in that his arrival saw a change in style that did not involve wingers in the starting line-up. Instead, he was a regular on the bench, scoring

three goals in his two months at Victoria Road. Following his time at Dagenham, Ryan took in a final loan spell in March at Crawley in the Blue Square Premier League. Was released in the summer.
Crystal Palace *(From trainee on 5/8/2005) FL 0+1 FAC 0+1*
Dagenham & Redbridge *(Loaned on 10/1/2008) FL 2+6/2*

HALLS John
Born: Islington, 14 February 1982
Height: 6'0" **Weight:** 11.4
Club Honours: FAYC '00
International Honours: E: Yth
Scoring Reading's second equaliser in the Carling Cup tie against Liverpool was the highlight of John's 2007-08 season with the Royals. That game was eventually lost, as was his only Premiership appearance, as an 83rd-minute substitute at Bolton. His only other outing was in the Carling Cup victory at Swansea, in which he was booked then substituted in extra-time. The consistency of other players, especially in the full-back positions, meant that his chances would always be limited and he was allowed on a number of loans before being released by Reading at the end of the campaign. At the beginning of November John helped Preston over an injury crisis, making four impressive appearances at right-back and in January he joined Crystal Palace to replace the injured Danny Butterfield, the first of his five starts being a fine 3-0 win at Wolverhampton. Then, in March, John joined Sheffield United on a month's loan, later extended to the end of the season. He was new manager Kevin Blackwell's only signing, acquitting himself well when covering at right wing-back for the injured Derek Geary and also impressing as a central defender in an emergency. Is a strong tackler who can be a threat when coming forward to produce searching crosses.
Arsenal *(From trainee on 18/7/2000) FLC 0+3*
Colchester U *(Loaned on 18/1/2002) FL 6*
Stoke C *(£100,000 on 4/10/2003) FL 67+2/2 FLC 2 FAC 3*
Reading *(£250,000 on 19/1/2006) P/FL 1+1/1 FLC 4/1 FAC 2*
Preston NE *(Loaned on 1/11/2007) FL 4*
Crystal Palace *(Loaned on 10/1/2008) FL 5*
Sheffield U *(Loaned on 14/3/2008) FL 5+1*

HALMOSI Peter
Born: Szombathely, Hungary, 25 September 1979
Height: 6'0" **Weight:** 11.9
International Honours: Hungary: 18
Peter joined Plymouth on a permanent deal from Hungarian club Debreceni

VSC after impressing while on loan in 2006-07. Peter is a highly gifted midfield player with a fantastic left foot and has wonderful ability from set pieces. He continued to be a member of the Hungarian national squad, having won more than 15 caps. An extremely popular player, with some supporters going as far to call him the most naturally talented footballer to play for the Pilgrims in the modern era. He can hurt opponents and scored some important goals during the season, including the winner against Ian Holloway's Leicester at the Walkers Stadium in February. Towards the end of the season, Peter struggled to recover from a knee injury suffered in the home game against Watford in March.
Plymouth Arg *(£400,000 from Debreceni, Hungary, ex Haldas Szombatheley, Grazer AK, on 12/1/2007) FL 55+4/12 FLC 2 FAC 3+2/1*

HAMANN Dietmar (Didi)
Born: Waldsasson, Germany, 27 August 1973
Height: 6'3" **Weight:** 12.2
Club Honours: FLC '01; FAC '01, '06; UEFAC '01; ESC '01, '05; CS '01; UEFACL '05
International Honours: Germany: 59; U21; Yth
Didi's unusual transfer from Bolton in 2006 has paid dividends for Manchester City. He never turned out for Bolton after joining them from Liverpool but is known throughout football as a cultured defensive midfielder. A Champions' League winner with Liverpool in their 2005 victory over Milan, Didi brought a cool-head and much-needed experience to the City squad, helping to encourage further development of the Blues' young players. Last season was undoubtedly his best for City so far, with many assured and solid performances in a system more suited to his style.
Newcastle U *(£4,500,000 from Bayern Munich, Germany, ex Wacker Munchen, on 5/8/1998) PL 22+1/4 FLC 1 FAC 7/1*
Liverpool *(£8,000,000 on 23/7/1999) PL 174+17/8 FLC 8+4 FAC 15+1/1 Others 56+8/2*
Bolton W *(Free on 11/7/2006)*
Manchester C *(£400,000 on 12/7/2006) PL 38+7 FLC 3 FAC 4+1*

HAMER Benjamin (Ben) John
Born: Chard, 20 November 1987
Height: 5'11" **Weight:** 12.4
Ben joined Brentford on loan from Reading at the start of the season. The young goalkeeper had a brilliant debut on the opening day, making five outstanding saves against Mansfield. A month later he

Peter Halmosi

was left out of the side before returning to Reading. Ben rejoined Brentford for a second spell later in the season, resuming at Dagenham. His shot-stopping ability helped the Bees rise up the table and his performance at Barnet in February was particularly impressive. He kept the experienced Simon Brown out of the side until March and returned for the last two matches.
Reading (From trainee on 5/7/2006)
Brentford (Loaned on 10/8/2007) FL 20 FLC 1

HAMILTON-OMOLE Marvin
Dolapo Ananda Daniel
Born: Leytonstone, 8 October 1988
Height: 6'0" **Weight:** 11.3
A tall rangy left-back or central defender, Marvin signed a one-year deal at the start of the season and made his senior debut for Gillingham early in the

campaign. Among his attributes is a massive long throw. Marvin enjoyed a successful loan with Folkestone Invicta before being released by the Gills and joining Dover in April.
Gillingham (From trainee on 10/8/2007) FL 3+2 Others 1

HAMMELL Steven (Steve)
Born: Rutherglen, 18 February 1982
Height: 5'9" **Weight:** 11.3
International Honours: S: 1; U21-11
Steve missed the start of Southend's campaign in 2007-08 after being injured by a terrible tackle in a pre-season match at Crawley. When fit, he returned at left-back, where his attacking tendencies and excellent delivery from set pieces provided a major boost. He scored a brilliant free kick in the home game against Cheltenham. Since moving from Scotland, Steve's family struggled to

settle in the area and during the January transfer window, Southend accepted a bid from his former club Motherwell.
Motherwell (Signed from Bearsden BC on 31/8/1999) SL 210+5/2 SLC 15 SC 12
Southend U (Free on 3/7/2006) FL 54+1/3 FLC 5/1 FAC 7

HAMMILL Adam James
Born: Liverpool, 25 January 1988
Height: 5'11" **Weight:** 11.7
Club Honours: FAYC '06
International Honours: E: Yth
Nifty and confident, this talented winger came to Southampton on loan from Liverpool, having spent the previous season at Dunfermline. He was confined to substitute performances by the early form of Nathan Dyer but delivered some classy, crowd-pleasing football before grabbing a regular place in December. Despite looking impressive he struggled to make an impact in a midfield that rarely played to its potential and managed only one start after Nigel Pearson took over as manager in February.
Liverpool (From trainee on 31/1/2006)
Dunfermline Ath (Loaned on 18/1/2007) SL 9+4/1 SC 5
Southampton (Loaned on 16/7/2007) FL 12+13 FAC 2+1

HAMMOND Dean John
Born: Hastings, 7 March 1983
Height: 6'0" **Weight:** 12.4
Although lacking the consistency of his 2006-07 campaign, Dean was still an enormously influential character at Brighton until his transfer in January. A determined, forward-looking midfielder, he was the captain and already had six goals to his name but his last few weeks at the Withdean Stadium were disappointing. Sidelined by a knee strain, he was sent off in his comeback at Oldham, his last game for the club. Following an unseemly debate in the media on a new contract offer, Dean was sold to Colchester on the last day of the January window. Dean moved to enjoy life in the Championship rather than League One, but his stay in the second tier was only short as the U's were relegated. Although frustrated by injury on his arrival after a couple of appearances as a substitute he started 11 games on the bounce before missing the final fixture at Scunthorpe due to illness. He settled into his favoured role in central midfield, after a stint on the right, proving to be a big danger in the air with a fierce shot. Will hope to make a big impression for the U's in their new stadium over the coming year.

Brighton & Hove A *(From trainee on 10/6/2002) FL 122+14/21 FLC 5/1 FAC 7/2 Others 5+2/2*
Leyton Orient *(Loaned on 17/10/2003) FL 6+2 FAC 1*
Colchester U *(£250,000 on 31/1/2008) FL 11+2*

HAMSHAW Matthew (Matt) Thomas
Born: Rotherham, 1 January 1982
Height: 5'9" **Weight:** 11.12
International Honours: E: Yth; Sch
Started last season for Mansfield in his customary role wide on the right of midfield and had a wonderful game against his old club, Stockport, at Field Mill early in the campaign when the Stags picked up their first win. Over Christmas, he was switched to the left flank to cover for injuries but was not quite so effective. Back on the right he ended in fine form when the battle against relegation was at its height. Was out of contract in the summer and looking for a new club.
Sheffield Wed *(From trainee on 5/1/1999) FL 35+39/2 FLC 6+3/2 FAC 2+1/2 Others 2*
Stockport Co *(Free on 5/8/2005) FL 35+4/5 FLC 1 FAC 3 Others 1*
Mansfield T *(Free on 3/8/2006) FL 83+2/6 FLC 2 FAC 7/1 Others 2*

HAND Jamie
Born: Uxbridge, 7 February 1984
Height: 5'11" **Weight:** 11.10
International Honours: E: Yth
The right-sided midfielder did not fit in to Bobby Williamson's plans at Chester in 2007-08 and left the Deva Stadium for Lincoln in August after only one start, in the Carling Cup, against Nottingham Forest and a substitute's appearance against Chesterfield. A combative midfielder, Jamie was a regular in the first team until a change of management saw Peter Jackson take charge at Sincil Bank. Loaned out to Oxford United in February 2008, he left the Imps by mutual consent shortly after the season came to a close.
Watford *(From trainee on 17/4/2002) FL 40+15 FLC 1+2 FAC 1+2*
Oxford U *(Loaned on 27/8/2004) FL 11 Others 1/1*
Livingston *(Loaned on 6/1/2005) SL 5+2 SC 1+1*
Peterborough U *(Loaned on 23/9/2005) FL 9 Others 1/1*
Northampton T *(Loaned on 14/2/2006) FL 8+3*
Chester C *(Free on 5/7/2006) FL 43+1/2 FLC 2 FAC 5/1 Others 1/1*
Lincoln C *(Signed on 17/8/2007) FL 19+6 Others 1*

HANGELAND Brede Paulsen
Born: Houston, Texas, USA, 20 June 1981
Height: 6'5" **Weight:** 14.7
International Honours: Norway: 44; U21-12
Signed by Fulham from FC Copenhagen during the January transfer window, the American-born Norwegian central defender was voted 'Man of the Match' following a solid performance on his debut at Bolton in the same month. At 6'5", Brede naturally dominates opponents in the air but is also deceptively skilful on the ground, often bringing the ball out of defence calmly before making a telling pass. He produced a number of assured performances, notably in the 2-0 away win at Reading, where he was unlucky not to open his scoring account for Fulham. He was one of three players denied by the bar that afternoon. Brede was selected for Norway against Montenegro in March.
Fulham *(£2,500,000 from FC Copenhagen, Denmark, ex FK Vidar, Viking Stavanger, on 22/1/2008) PL 15*

HARBAN Thomas (Tom) John
Born: Barnsley, 12 November 1985
Height: 6'0" **Weight:** 11.12
A right-back or central defender, Tom joined Bradford on loan from Barnsley for the first six months of the season and made seven appearances when Darren Williams was injured. He joined Halifax in January.
Barnsley *(From trainee on 6/7/2005)*
Bradford C *(Loaned on 25/7/2007) FL 6 Others 1*

HARDING Daniel (Dan) Andrew
Born: Gloucester, 23 December 1983
Height: 6'0" **Weight:** 11.11
International Honours: E: U21-4
Started the season as first choice left-back and held that position for the first half of the season, opening his scoring account for Ipswich with a spectacular long-range effort at Hull. Dan lost his place when the management team tried different personnel in a bid to improve the club's poor away record. He reclaimed his position in February but a lack of consistency meant he was out again as the season drew to a close.
Brighton & Hove A *(From trainee on 28/7/2003) FL 56+11/1 FLC 1+2 FAC 1 Others 4+1*
Leeds U *(£850,000 on 4/6/2005) FL 20 FLC 1*
Ipswich T *(Signed on 4/8/2006) FL 69+3/1 FLC 2 FAC 4*

HARDY Aaron
Born: South Elmsall, 26 May 1986
Height: 5'8" **Weight:** 11.4

Aaron made his first appearance of the season as a substitute in Huddersfield's Carling Cup defeat at Blackpool and started at centre-half in the home win over Bournemouth. The Academy product made an encouraging start with some strong tackles and accurate passing. A move to his favoured right-back berth for a further four games was cut short by a groin injury that kept him on the sidelines until the latter part of the season. Aaron was one of the crop of young players released at the end of the season.
Huddersfield T *(From trainee on 8/7/2005) FL 10+5 FLC 0+1 Others 3*

HAREWOOD Marlon Anderson
Born: Hampstead, 25 August 1979
Height: 6'1" **Weight:** 11.0
Marlon, who signed for Aston Villa from West Ham in the summer, is a powerful striker who causes a threat to any defence. He uses his strength and speed to create chances for himself and others and scored on his full debut for Villa against Wrexham in the Carling Cup, following it up with the 100th League goal of his career at Blackburn in November. Marlon became the 'super-sub' for Villa, starting only three times and making most of his appearances from the bench.
Nottingham F *(From trainee on 9/9/1996) P/FL 124+58/51 FLC 12+4/3 FAC 3+2/1 Others 2*
Ipswich T *(Loaned on 28/1/1999) FL 5+1/1*
West Ham U *(£500,000 on 25/11/2003) P/FL 123+19/47 FLC 6/3 FAC 13+1/5 Others 7+1/1*
Aston Villa *(£4,000,000 on 19/7/2007) PL 1+22/5 FLC 2/1*

HARGREAVES Owen Lee
Born: Calgary, Canada, 20 January 1981
Height: 5'11" **Weight:** 11.7
Club Honours: PL '08; UEFACL '08
International Honours: E: 42; B-1; U21-3
An outstanding England midfield player, Owen finally joined Manchester United from Bayern Munich in May after almost a year of rumours and negotiation around the transfer. He first played for United in a pre-season friendly against Peterborough and made his Premiership bow in the third game of the season against local rivals Manchester City at Eastlands. It proved to be a real baptism of fire as the Reds lost 1-0. With only fleeting appearances in the Premiership, he scored his first goal against Fulham in March with a well-taken free-kick from outside the penalty area. He then notched the all-important winner in a vital Premiership match against Arsenal in April with another free kick. During his

six years at Bayern Munich, Owen was an integral part of their run of success. Now at Old Trafford he is helping his new club do the same. Though somewhat similar in style to Michael Carrick, his first season at Old Trafford goes down as an unqualified success.

Manchester U *(£17,000,000 from Bayern Munich, Germany, ex Calgary Foothills, on 4/7/2007) PL 16+7/2 FAC 2+1 Others 5+3*

HARLEY Jonathan (Jon)
Born: Maidstone, 26 September 1979
Height: 5'9" **Weight:** 10.3
Club Honours: FAC '00
International Honours: E: U21-3; Yth
Previously a guaranteed starter at left-back for Burnley, Jon was regarded as second choice to new arrival Stephen Jordan by manager Steve Cotterill and started last season in an unfamiliar midfield role. Although he performed well enough there, he drifted out of the first-team picture until the arrival of new boss Owen Coyle in November. Coyle immediately restored him to his former role, and Jon remained there, performing as solidly as ever, virtually until the end of the season when illness ruled him out. He left Turf Moor after rejecting the new terms offered on the expiry of his contract.

Chelsea *(From trainee on 20/3/1997) PL 22+8/2 FLC 0+1 FAC 7 Others 1+3*
Wimbledon *(Loaned on 20/10/2000) FL 6/2*
Fulham *(£3,500,000 on 8/8/2001) PL 19+6/1 FLC 2 FAC 4+1 Others 4*
Sheffield U *(Loaned on 30/10/2002) FL 8+1/1 FLC 2*
Sheffield U *(Loaned on 16/9/2003) FL 5*
West Ham U *(Loaned on 16/1/2004) FL 15/1 FAC 1*
Sheffield U *(Free on 4/8/2004) FL 48/2 FLC 3 FAC 5*
Burnley *(£75,000 on 26/8/2005) FL 116+3/3 FLC 3+1 FAC 3*

HARPER James Alan John
Born: Chelmsford, 9 November 1980
Height: 5'10" **Weight:** 11.7
Club Honours: Ch '06
A model of consistency and professionalism, James was in the Reading squad for every one of the 42 Premiership and Cup games, the only one in which he did not play being the 2-2 FA Cup draw at Tottenham. Making his 300th appearance for the Royals in the home game against Fulham he worked hard throughout the season to hold together a midfield that suffered from incessant changes in personnel. He scored vital goals too, including a last-minute winner at home to Wigan, an excellent individual effort in the historic 3-1 win against

Liverpool and an added-time winner in the 1-0 victory at Middlesbrough to ensure Reading's first away win of the campaign. James has now been appointed the club's 'Ambassador for Children' and is an excellent role-model on and off the field.

Arsenal *(From trainee on 8/7/1999)*
Cardiff C *(Loaned on 29/12/2000) FL 3*
Reading *(£400,000 on 28/2/2001) P/FL 254+21/24 FLC 11+2/1 FAC 13 Others 4+2*

HARPER Stephen (Steve) Alan
Born: Seaham, 14 March 1975
Height: 6'2" **Weight:** 13.0
Goalkeeper Steve is Newcastle's longest-serving player and while he has long been frustrated by the excellence of Shay Given, injuries to the latter enabled him to record his highest total of League appearances for a season. A fine 'keeper in his own right, with safe hands and quick feet, his skill with the ball was acknowledged when he made a 12-minute cameo appearance as an outfield player in the pre-season friendly against Glasgow Celtic. An injury to Shay gave Steve a place in the opening game at Bolton, where a fine performance helped earn a point and kept him as first choice until an injury allowed Shay to reclaim the jersey in September. However, when Shay's problems escalated in late February, Steve returned to the side and remained until the end of the season, delivering such a series of fine performances that Shay was not missed.

Newcastle U *(Free from Seaham Red Star on 5/7/1993) PL 65+7 FLC 12 FAC 9+1 Others 15+2*
Bradford C *(Loaned on 18/9/1995) FL 1*
Hartlepool U *(Loaned on 29/8/1997) FL 15*
Huddersfield T *(Loaned on 18/12/1997) FL 24 FAC 2*

HARRIS James (Jay) William
Born: Liverpool, 15 April 1987
Height: 5'7" **Weight:** 11.6
Voted Accrington's 'Young Player of the Year', he was a regular in the midfield, and, as in the previous season, missed very few games. Jay's tenacious style of play was off-putting to opponents and, on occasions, to referees. Very popular with supporters, as demonstrated by his collecting six 'Man of the Match' awards, this was countered by ten yellow cards for a full range of offences and a sending-off at Shrewsbury. Although James failed to score all season, his combative midfield play compensated. Was released in the summer.

Everton *(From trainee on 20/7/2005)*
Accrington Stanley *(Free on 3/8/2006) FL 64+9/2 FLC 2 FAC 2 Others 1+1*

HARRIS Neil
Born: Orsett, 12 July 1977
Height: 5'11" **Weight:** 12.9
Club Honours: Div 2 '01
Neil is a Millwall legend and thoroughly deserves the accolade and all the tributes paid to him. Having appeared in over 250 games in his two spells and set the club's all-time League scoring record, he is admired by Lions' players and fans alike, although he had an in-and-out season with injuries and management changes. A quick-thinking centre-forward with a great eye for a goal, Neil was used in many positions but always got on with the job in his normal professional way, a great example to the young players.

Millwall *(£30,000 from Cambridge C on 26/3/1998) FL 186+47/93 FLC 6+1 FAC 13+2/2 Others 13+1/3*
Cardiff C *(Loaned on 3/12/2004) FL 1+2/1*
Nottingham F *(Free on 22/12/2004) FL 16+17/1 FLC 2 FAC 1+3 Others 0+2*
Gillingham *(Loaned on 28/8/2005) FL 28+8/6 FAC 1 Others 1+1*
Millwall *(Free on 9/11/2007) FL 40+8/8 FLC 1 FAC 1+1*

HARRISON Daniel (Danny) Robert
Born: Liverpool, 4 November 1982
Height: 5'11" **Weight:** 12.5
Arriving in the summer from Tranmere, Danny's all-action style in midfield made him an automatic choice in his first season at Rotherham. He passes well and is always willing to join in the attack with the strikers. He likes to test opposing 'keepers and if he deserved more than his handful of goals, he more than made up for that by creating many chances for his colleagues. Danny was equally invaluable when defending.

Tranmere Rov *(From trainee on 16/5/2002) FL 89+35/5 FLC 2+1 FAC 8+1 Others 8+3/2*
Rotherham U *(Free on 1/7/2007) FL 44/4 FLC 1/1 FAC 2 Others 2*

HARRISON Lee David
Born: Billericay, 12 September 1971
Height: 6'2" **Weight:** 12.7
Lee passed 300 appearances for Barnet, including their time in the Conference, during last season and the goalkeeper again gave fine service. He was ever-present in the first half of the season but in and out of the side from the turn of the year, because of injuries and as the emergence of Rob Beckwith. Lee is still a key player for the Bees and his advancing years are nothing for a 'keeper.

Charlton Ath *(From trainee on 3/7/1990)*
Fulham *(Loaned on 18/11/1991) Others 1*
Gillingham *(Loaned on 24/3/1992) FL 2*
Fulham *(Free on 18/12/1992) FL 11+1 FAC 1 Others 6*

Jay Harris

Barnet *(Free on 15/7/1996) FL 183 FLC 9 FAC 3 Others 12*
Peterborough U *(Loaned on 12/12/2002) FL 12*
Leyton Orient *(Signed on 14/3/2003) FL 59+1 FLC 1 FAC 3+1 Others 1*
Peterborough U *(Free on 2/8/2005) FL 6 Others 2*
Barnet *(Free on 5/8/2006) FL 65+1 FLC 1 FAC 7 Others 1*

HARROLD Matthew (Matt)
James
Born: Leyton, 25 July 1984
Height: 6'1" **Weight:** 11.10
A tall centre-forward, Matt started as first-choice striker at Southend last season but a combination of frequent changes of partner and a lack of goals meant he lost his place. He scored three goals, all in Cup ties and two of them penalties, but Steve Tilson was unconvinced and scoured the market for replacements. From the New Year, Matt was in the reserves, struggling even to win a place on the first-team bench.
Brentford *(Free from Harlow T on 12/8/2003) FL 11+21/2 FAC 2+3/3 Others 2*
Grimsby T *(Loaned on 4/3/2005) FL 6/2*
Yeovil T *(Signed on 15/7/2005) FL 30+17/9 FLC 1+2/1 FAC 1+2 Others 1*
Southend U *(£90,000 on 31/8/2006) FL 25+27/3 FLC 2/2 FAC 2+2/1 Others 1*

HARSLEY Paul
Born: Scunthorpe, 29 May 1978
Height: 5'9" **Weight:** 11.10
Paul is a workmanlike midfield player or full-back and was a regular in Port Vale's side, taking over the captaincy midway through the campaign. He scored his only goal from open play in a 3-2 defeat at Carlisle, exactly as he had in 2006-07, but this time he followed it with two successful penalties. Luke Rodgers was the previous captain and penalty taker but after he missed two, Paul pulled rank. A good organiser, he has a defensive role in midfield, winning the ball for the playmakers. He can fit in well at right-back, a position Vale had trouble with, and even filled in at centre-back once. Worthily named 'Player of the Year', he was offered a new contract.
Grimsby T *(From trainee on 16/7/1996)*
Scunthorpe U *(Free on 7/7/1997) FL 110+18/5 FLC 6 FAC 4+2/1 Others 5+1*
Halifax T *(Free on 1/7/2001) FL 45/11 FLC 1 FAC 3/1 Others 1*
Northampton T *(Free on 8/7/2002) FL 46+13/2 FLC 2 FAC 3+2/1 Others 2+2*
Macclesfield T *(Free on 13/2/2004) FL 105+2/11 FLC 3 FAC 5 Others 11/2*
Port Vale *(Free on 13/7/2006) FL 68+5/6 FLC 4 FAC 3 Others 2*

Neil Harris

he was picked for the Carling Cup tie at Bristol City, making a world-class save when the game was still finely balanced. After another run-out in the same competition, Joe started in the Premier League in the 3-1 win at home to Newcastle and, following some impressive performances, Sven-Goran Eriksson made him his number-one 'keeper just before Christmas. After a wonderful season, Joe is regarded as one of the country's best young 'keepers and was rewarded with a call to the full England squad.

Shrewsbury T *(From trainee on 10/8/2004) FL 52 FLC 2 FAC 2*
Manchester C *(£600,000 on 31/5/2006) PL 27 FLC 3 FAC 3*
Tranmere Rov *(Loaned on 1/1/2007) FL 6*
Blackpool *(Loaned on 8/4/2007) FL 5*

HART Michael
Born: Bellshill, 10 February 1980
Height: 5'10" **Weight:** 11.6
Signed from Aberdeen in January, Michael had first to overcome injury and then wait for his chance in Preston's defence. An early end to Billy Jones' season gave Michael the chance to show his qualities at right-back in the last two games and he showed enough of the determination and experience that convinced Alan Irvine to sign him. He took part in Aberdeen's European adventure before his move south.

Aberdeen *(From juniors on 1/8/1997) SL 6+10 SLC 0+2 SC 1*
Livingston *(Loaned on 8/3/2000) SL 3*
Livingston *(Loaned on 26/9/2000) SL 16+6 Others 1+1*
Livingston *(Signed on 1/7/2001) SL 24+8 SLC 2 SC 2 Others 1+1*
Aberdeen *(Signed on 24/1/2003) SL 102+5 SLC 5 SC 7+1 Others 5*
Preston NE *(£100,000 on 31/1/2008) FL 2*

HARTE Ian Patrick
Born: Drogheda, 31 August 1977
Height: 6'0" **Weight:** 12.4
International Honours: RoI: 64; U21-3
An experienced former Republic of Ireland international, Ian arrived at Sunderland as a free agent from Spanish club Levante last August. A renowned dead-ball expert, Ian's three starts for the Black Cats resulted in a draw and two defeats, the last of which was a 7-1 mauling at Everton in November. It was announced at the end of the campaign that Ian would not be retained by Sunderland.

Leeds U *(From trainee on 15/12/1995) PL 199+14/28 FLC 10+2/2 FAC 16+2/3 Others 45/6 (Transferred to Levante, Spain on 12/7/2004)*
Sunderland *(Free on 29/8/2007) PL 3+5*

HART Danny Gary
Born: Hendon, 26 April 1989
Height: 5'9" **Weight:** 11.5
Locally-born Danny was signed on a two-year deal by the Bees on the eve of the new season, arriving from non-League Borehamwood. The midfield player was limited to two first-team outings, both from the bench, but has been earmarked by Bees' manager Paul Fairclough as one for the future. Danny enjoyed two successful loan spells during the season, at Northwood and Wivenhoe Town, but hopes to establish himself in Barnet's team in the months ahead.

Barnet *(Free from Borehamwood on 14/8/2007) FL 0+2*

HART Gary John
Born: Harlow, 21 September 1976
Height: 5'9" **Weight:** 12.8
Club Honours: Div 3 '01; Div 2 '02
Despite a testimonial season, his tenth as a professional at Brighton, Gary will not look back fondly on 2007-08, when he was a peripheral figure. Ever willing and hard-working, he had to settle for two starts at right-back in March and a handful of appearances as a substitute. The nadir came when he was sent off at home to Huddersfield in January. After a hernia problem earlier in the season, Gary went on loan to Havant & Waterlooville before his swansong, and then succumbed to a knee injury. He was still unable to play when his release was announced but will be remembered at Brighton for his total commitment over the last decade.

Brighton & Hove A *(£1,000 from Stansted on 18/6/1998) FL 290+52/44 FLC 9+3 FAC 10+1 Others 8+5/1*

HART Charles Joseph (Joe) John
Born: Shrewsbury, 19 April 1987
Height: 6'3" **Weight:** 12.9
International Honours: E: 1; U21-12; Yth
Having made his debut for Manchester City in 2006-07, a finger injury in early August pushed the young goalkeeper down the pecking order slightly before

Joe Hart

HARTLEY Peter
Born: Hartlepool, 3 April 1988
Height: 6'0" **Weight:** 12.6
The young Sunderland defender joined Chesterfield on loan in February and settled into the left-back position. Always giving 100 per cent, Peter showed good close control, an effective tackle and an eye for going forward, while doing his share of talking and organising. He is able to cover well at centre-half, and this versatility may persuade the Spireites to offer terms on his release by Sunderland, where he has yet to make an appearance.
Sunderland (From trainee on 25/7/2006) FL 0+1
Chesterfield (Loaned on 21/2/2008) FL 12

HARTSON John
Born: Swansea, 5 April 1975
Height: 6'1" **Weight:** 14.6
Club Honours: SPD '02, '04, '06; SLC '06; SC '05
International Honours: W: 51; U21-9; Yth
Immediately before his retirement from professional football, the vastly experienced Welsh international striker made four appearances for Norwich on loan from West Bromwich. Although lacking the mobility of his youth, he revealed several moments of class and could easily have netted a hat-trick in the first 20 minutes of his debut, at home to Bristol City.
Luton T (From trainee on 19/12/1992) FL 32+22/11 FLC 0+1 FAC 3+3/2 Others 2
Arsenal (£2,500,000 on 13/1/1995) PL 43+10/14 FLC 2+4/1 FAC 2+1/1 Others 8+1/1
West Ham U (£3,200,000 + on 14/2/1997) PL 59+1/24 FLC 6/6 FAC 7/3
Wimbledon (£7,000,000 on 15/1/1999) P/FL 46+3/19 FLC 7/2 FAC 1
Coventry C (Signed on 8/2/2001) PL 12/6
Glasgow Celtic (£6,000,000 on 2/8/2001) SL 125+21/88 SLC 10+1/7 SC 11+1/8 Others 25+7/6
West Bromwich A (£500,000 on 12/7/2006) FL 14+7/5 FLC 1+1 FAC 1/1
Norwich C (Loaned on 15/10/2007) FL 2+2

HARTY Ian McGuinness
Born: Airdrie, 8 April 1978
Height: 5'8" **Weight:** 10.7
Ian arrived from Airdrie in the summer but played only 37 minutes of football for Darlington in two substitute appearances at Barnsley and Macclesfield, so the home fans never saw him in action. The tricky midfielder

had his contract cancelled in November for personal reasons and returned north of the border.
Albion Rov (From juniors at Heart of Midlothian on 8/8/1996) SL 15+12/2 SLC 1 SC 3+1 Others 0+1
Stranraer (Free on 1/7/1998) SL 139+13/51 SLC 7+2/4 SC 13+1/7 Others 9/6
Clyde (Free on 1/7/2003) SL 63+5/31 SLC 3+1 SC 6/2 Others 3/1
Hamilton Academical (Free on 30/8/2005) Stranraer (Free on 1/3/2006) SL 3+2 Others 1+1
Raith Rov (Free on 1/8/2006) SL 9+2/4 SLC 1 Others 1
Stirling A (Free on 12/1/2007) SL 1
Ayr U (Free on 31/1/2007) SL 1
Airdrie U (Free on 16/2/2007) SL 7+4/3 Others 3/2
Darlington (Free from Airdrie U on 7/8/2007) FL 0+1 FLC 0+1

HASLAM Steven (Steve) Robert
Born: Sheffield, 6 September 1979
Height: 5'11" **Weight:** 11.0
Arriving from Halifax in the summer, the utility player missed the first nine games, as knee and back problems persisted, before making his debut against Lincoln at right-back in place of Andy Parrish. Injuries at the centre of the defence saw Steve moved between sweeper and centre-back but he showed his true ability in the second half against Morecambe in November in the centre of midfield. Although Steve came in for some criticism from Alan Knill in February, the new manager stuck by him for 15 games before illness kept him out at Barnet in April.
Sheffield Wed (From trainee on 12/9/1996) P/FL 115+29/2 FLC 10+1 FAC 9+1 Others 5+1 (Free to Halifax T on 13/8/2004)
Northampton T (Free on 27/8/2004) FL 2+1 (Free to Halifax T on 12/10/2004)
Bury (Free on 5/7/2007) FL 37/1 FAC 5 Others 3

HASSELBAINK Jerrel (Jimmy Floyd)
Born: Surinam, 27 March 1972
Height: 6'2" **Weight:** 13.4
Club Honours: CS '00
International Honours: Holland: 23
The Bluebirds signed two big-name strikers in Jimmy Floyd and Robbie Fowler in the summer and there is no doubt that Jimmy Floyd proved the bigger success after Robbie missed most of the season through injuries. Both signed a one-year deal with a one-year option and the former Chelsea man showed moments of brilliance. He fired nine goals, including a cracker in the

2-0 FA Cup win over Wolverhampton. However, he had a disappointing FA Cup final against Portsmouth and, as the season ended, it seemed Fowler looked more likely to stay with Cardiff than the former Dutch international.
Leeds U (£2,000,000 from Boavista, Portugal, ex Campomaiorense, on 18/7/1997) PL 66+3/34 FLC 5/2 FAC 9/5 Others 4/1 (£12,000,000 to Atletico Madrid, Spain on 20/8/1999)
Chelsea (£15,000,000 from Atletico Madrid, Spain on 12/7/2000) PL 119+17/69 FLC 10/7 FAC 16/7 Others 11+4/4
Middlesbrough (Free on 12/7/2004) PL 48+10/22 FLC 3/1 FAC 7+1/3 Others 17+3/7
Charlton Ath (Free on 14/7/2006) PL 11+14/2 FLC 2+1/2 FAC 1
Cardiff C (Free on 16/8/2007) FL 33+3/7 FLC 3/1 FAC 4+1/1

HASSELL Robert (Bobby) John Francis
Born: Derby, 4 June 1980
Height: 5'9" **Weight:** 12.6
Bobby missed the start of Barnsley's season because of a knee injury and did not feature until the Christmas period. After a couple of appearances in his favourite right-back position, Bobby took on an unfamiliar role as a holding player in midfield because of Anderson's serious injury. Bobby took to the position comfortably and having demonstrated that he could win the ball, became more of an all-round player as his confidence grew.
Mansfield T (From trainee on 3/7/1998) FL 151+9/3 FLC 6+1 FAC 9 Others 4
Barnsley (Free on 5/7/2004) FL 116+10/4 FLC 3 FAC 12 Others 5

HATCH Liam Morris Adam
Born: Hitchin, 3 April 1982
Height: 6'2" **Weight:** 12.3
Club Honours: FC '05
After a number of seasons in which Liam struggled to score on a regular basis for Barnet, he found his goal touch in style in the first half of last season. With goals in the first and second rounds of the FA Cup for the Bees among his tally, it was enough to convince Peterborough manager Darren Ferguson to buy the striker at the start of the January transfer window. Due his chances being limited by the outstanding form of Peterborough's twin strikers, Liam started only one game for Posh but did score twice in his ten substitute appearances.
Barnet (Free from Gravesend & Northfleet on 23/7/2003) FL 49+38/11 FLC 1+2 FAC 4+2/2 Others 0+4
Peterborough U (£150,000 on 3/1/2008) FL 1+10/2

Karl Hawley

HAVERN Gianluca
Born: Manchester, 24 September 1988
Height: 6'1" **Weight:** 13.0
Gianluca waited patiently for an opportunity to impress and was finally given a chance in Stockport's last League game. Although a centre-back, he played at right-back and rounded off a hugely impressive performance with the only goal of the game to clinch the 'Man of the Match' award. The former youth-team skipper signed a new one-year deal in May to keep him at Edgeley Park for another season.
Stockport Co *(From trainee on 25/4/2007) FL 1/1*

HAWKINS Colin Joseph
Born: Galway, 17 August 1977
Height: 6'1" **Weight:** 13.6
International Honours: RoI: U21-9; Yth
The Irish central defender who impressed so much at the end of the previous season for Coventry was hampered by injuries in 2007-08. After appearing in the Carling Cup against Notts County in August he suffered a serious Achilles tear that required major surgery and was out for most of the season. At the end of March, he went on loan to Chesterfield and was informed by the Coventry management that he would be released at the end of the season. A change of management as well as the tendon problem led to City's decision, but Colin appeared to be just the sort of player Chesterfield needed at the heart of a young defence. His composure and ability to marshal others was immediately seen and he enjoys pressing forward with the ball at his feet.
Coventry C *(Signed from Salthill Devon on 25/11/1995. Freed during 1997 close season)*
Coventry C *(Signed from Shelbourne, ex St Patrick's Ath, Doncaster Rov, Bohemians, on 29/1/2007) FL 13 FLC 1*
Chesterfield *(Loaned on 27/3/2008) FL 5*

HAWLEY Karl Leon
Born: Walsall, 6 December 1981
Height: 5'7" **Weight:** 12.0
Club Honours: Div 2 '06
International Honours: E: SP
Paul Simpson signed Karl for Preston last summer but the former Carlisle striker had to wait for his debut, then found himself in and out of the side all season. A regular scorer in previous years, the highlight for Karl came with two first-half goals in the FA Cup triumph at Derby. Only three League goals in 25 appearances suggest he is still adapting to the demands of the Championship and he will aim to consolidate on his first campaign.

*Walsall (From trainee on 26/1/2001) FL 0+1
FAC 0+1 Others 0+2*
*Raith Rov (Loaned on 9/8/2002) SL 15+2/7
SLC 1 SC 1+2/1*
*Raith Rov (Loaned on 29/8/2003) SL 4+5/2
SLC 1*
*Carlisle U (Free on 3/8/2004) FL 76+2/34
FLC 2+1 FAC 2 Others 7/4*
*Preston NE (Free on 1/8/2007) FL 20+5/3
FLC 0+1 FAC 3/2*

HAYES Jonathan (Jonny)
Born: Dublin, 9 July 1987
Height: 5'7" **Weight:** 11.0
International Honours: RoI:
U21-3
Brought to Leicester from Reading
during the summer by Martin Allen, the
diminutive Jonny impressed with some
direct wing play and dangerous crossing
during a handful of cameo appearances
from the bench before going to
Northampton to further his experience.
He gave some spirited performances
when called upon by Town, not only as
an out-and-out winger but unafraid to
put in a tackle when required to defend.
He should have a future in the League.
Reading (From trainee on 14/7/2004)
*MK Dons (Loaned on 11/1/2007) FL 0+11
Others 2*
*Leicester C (Free on 7/8/2007)
FL 1+6*
*Northampton T (Loaned on 8/1/2008)
FL 5+6*

HAYES Paul Edward
Born: Dagenham, 20 September
1983
Height: 6'0" **Weight:** 12.2
A summer switch back to Scunthorpe
from Barnsley saw Paul play a big part
in the club's Championship season.
Virtually an ever-present until mid-
February, he was asked to play either
in the hole just behind a front striker or
occasionally on the right side of midfield
but it was in the final three games,
when he was utilised as an out-and-out
centre-forward, that he looked happiest,
banging in five goals in those three
games to end the season with eight.
A strong player, he is very skilful and
good at linking play between attack and
midfield.
*Scunthorpe U (From trainee at Norwich C
on 22/3/2003) FL 68+31/28 FLC 2+1/2 FAC
6+2/4 Others 3+3/1*
*Barnsley (£150,000 on 11/7/2005) FL
63+12/11 FLC 1+2 FAC 7/5 Others
3+1/2*
*Huddersfield T (Loaned on 23/2/2007)
FL 4/1*
*Scunthorpe U (Free on 17/7/2007) FL
32+8/8 FLC 1 FAC 1*

HAYLES Barrington (Barry) Edward
Born: Lambeth, 17 May 1972
Height: 5'9" **Weight:** 13.0
Club Honours: GMVC '96; Div 2 '99;
Div 1 '01
International Honours: Jamaica: 10;
E: SP-2
In Paul Wotton's continued absence,
Barry was honoured to be named as
Plymouth's captain during the first
few months of the season. This vastly
experienced centre-forward proved a
constant menace to the opposition,
never letting defenders settle on the
ball, and he scored two goals for the
Pilgrims before following ex-manager
Ian Holloway to Leicester. Initially signed
on emergency loan forms in December,
it was converted to a permanent signing
in January. He found the net twice
in his first four outings but then the
goals completely dried up as the team
struggled against relegation. Barry
eventually divided his time between the
starting line-up and the bench, either as
a striker or wide in midfield, but all to
no avail.
*Bristol Rov (£250,000 from Stevenage
Borough on 4/6/1997) FL 62/32 FLC 4/1 FAC
5/2 Others 3+2/1*
*Fulham (£2,100,000 on 17/11/1998) P/FL
116+59/44 FLC 10+2/5 FAC 12+7/6 Others
2+5/2*
Sheffield U (Free on 26/6/2004) FL 4 FLC 1
*Millwall (Signed on 1/9/2004) FL 49+6/16
FLC 4/1 FAC 1*
*Plymouth Arg (£100,000 on 1/8/2006) FL
58+4/15 FLC 1 FAC 2+1/1*
*Leicester C (£150,000 on 1/1/2008) FL
9+9/2 FAC 1*

HAYNES Daniel (Danny) Lewis
Born: Peckham, 19 January 1988
Height: 5'11" **Weight:** 11.11
Club Honours: FAYC '05
International Honours: E: Yth
Although Danny made the most starts
of his Ipswich career during the season,
there were still more appearances as
a substitute. He tends to have a good
20 or 30 minutes during a game and
needs to develop this so that he has an
influential 90 minutes on a regular basis.
Many of his starts were in a wide-right
midfield attacking role, where he could
use his pace to pressurise defenders.
Scored his customary goal against
Norwich and also notched one against
his former club Charlton, with a stunning
volley following a corner.
*Ipswich T (From trainee on 2/2/2006) FL
28+63/17 FLC 1+1 FAC 4+2*
Millwall (Loaned on 26/9/2006) FL 5/2

HAYTER James Edward
Born: Sandown, Isle of Wight, 9 April
1979
Height: 5'9" **Weight:** 11.2
James joined Doncaster in the summer for
a club record fee, after spending ten years
at Bournemouth. Rejoining his former
manager Sean O'Driscoll at the Keepmoat
Stadium, he was the leading scorer at the
club until a hernia operation in February
kept him out of the side until near the
end of the season. James regained his
place in the play-off semi-finals against
Southend and wrote himself into Rovers'
history when he scored the only goal at
Wembley, a great header against Leeds to
take the Rovers into the Championship.
*Bournemouth (From trainee on 7/7/1997)
FL 305+53/94 FLC 9+3/4 FAC 18+3/5 Others
12+4/5*
*Doncaster Rov (£200,000 on 25/6/2007) FL
21+13/7 FLC 2/1 FAC 2/2 Others 2+2/1*

HAZELL Reuben Daniel
Born: Birmingham, 24 April 1979
Height: 5'11" **Weight:** 12.0
Without a club last summer after his
release by Chesterfield, the experienced
defender joined Oldham for two months
on non-contract terms. His form in the
back four was impressive enough for
him to be awarded a contract until the
summer of 2009. Reuben operated in
both full-back positions but it was in
his usual central defensive role where
he looked most accomplished, quick,
powerful and a great reader of the game.
A personal highlight came when the
Latics ended Leeds' ten-month unbeaten
home record on New Year's Day. Reuben
netted his only goal with a stunning
25-yard half-volley in a display that
earned Oldham the League Managers'
Association 'Performance of the Week'
award.
Aston Villa (From trainee on 20/3/1997)
*Tranmere Rov (Free on 5/8/1999) FL 38+4/1
FLC 8 FAC 3 Others 1*
*Torquay U (Free on 10/1/2002) FL 77+7/2
FLC 1 FAC 2 Others 1*
Kidderminster Hrs (Free on 1/8/2004)
*Chesterfield (Free on 2/8/2005) FL 69+3/2
FLC 4 FAC 2 Others 2*
*Oldham Ath (Free on 14/9/2007) FL 32+2/1
FAC 3+1 Others 1*

HEALY David Jonathan
Born: Downpatrick, 5 August 1979
Height: 5'8" **Weight:** 11.0
International Honours: NI: 64; B-1;
U21-8; Yth; Sch
The much-rumoured transfer from Leeds
was completed in summer and the
Northern Ireland international took just
50 seconds of his Fulham debut to find

the net, taking advantage of a slip by the Arsenal goalkeeper. He was again on the mark in his second game against Bolton but goals at club level then dried up a little, despite a number of hard-working performances. He linked well with Brian McBride but was initially out of favour following the arrival of Roy Hodgson as Fulham manager. The Northern Ireland international always looks liable to score whenever he receives the ball around the box and this was certainly true at international level. His goal against Denmark in November was his 13th of the Euro 2008 qualifying campaign, setting a new scoring record.

Manchester U (From trainee on 28/11/1997) PL 0+1 FLC 0+2

Port Vale (Loaned on 25/2/2000) FL 15+1/3

Preston NE (£1,500,000 on 29/12/2000) FL 104+35/44 FLC 7+1 FAC 7+1 Others 3/1

Norwich C (Loaned on 30/1/2003) FL 5/1

Norwich C (Loaned on 13/3/2003) FL 5+3/1

Leeds U (Signed on 29/10/2004) FL 82+29/29 FLC 3+1 FAC 3+1/2 Others 1+1

Fulham (£1,500,000 on 16/7/2007) PL 15+15/4 FLC 1+1/1 FAC 2/1

HEATH Matthew (Matt) Philip
Born: Leicester, 1 November 1981
Height: 6'4" **Weight:** 13.13
Big centre-back Matt netted Leeds' first goal of an eventful League One season, heading the equaliser from a well-worked free-kick in the opening day 2-1 victory at Tranmere. It was his only goal of the campaign but he featured in 30 successive games as Leeds made light of their 15-point deduction to mount a serious promotion bid. By the turn of the year the Elland Road club had brought in Lubo Michalik from Bolton and Matt found himself out of the starting line-up. He joined Championship battlers Colchester on loan and immediately fitted into the U's defence, which had previously been looking shaky. Lacking a little match-fitness, Matt also missed a couple of games with a groin problem but formed a good partnership with Chris Coyne. He returned from injury to play the final game at Scunthorpe, and although his back-header let in a late equaliser in a 3-3 draw, he did enough to earn a permanent contract, signing shortly after the season ended.

Leicester C (From trainee on 17/2/2001) P/FL 42+9/6 FLC 3 FAC 5+2

Stockport Co (Loaned on 24/10/2003) FL 8 Others 1

Coventry C (£200,000 on 12/7/2005) FL 30+2/1 FLC 2/1

Leeds U (Free on 9/11/2006) FL 51+1/4 FLC 2 FAC 3 Others 1+1

Colchester U (Loaned on 14/3/2008) FL 5

HECKINGBOTTOM Paul
Born: Barnsley, 17 July 1977
Height: 5'11" **Weight:** 12.0
Left-back Paul returned for his second spell at Bradford, initially on loan before signing permanently from Barnsley in January. A solid and dependable defender, he also possesses a long throw that proved to be a dangerous weapon around the penalty area.

Sunderland (From trainee at Manchester U on 14/7/1995)

Scarborough (Loaned on 17/10/1997) FL 28+1 Others 1

Hartlepool U (Loaned on 25/9/1998) FL 5/1

Darlington (Free on 25/3/1999) FL 111+4/5 FLC 4 FAC 8/1 Others 8

Norwich C (Free on 5/7/2002) FL 7+8 FLC 0+1

Bradford C (Free on 17/7/2003) FL 87 FLC 2 FAC 2 Others 1

Sheffield Wed (Free on 12/7/2004) FL 41+1/4 FLC 1 FAC 1/2 Others 3

Barnsley (Signed on 13/1/2006) FL 45+4/1 FAC 1 Others 3

HEFFERNAN Paul
Born: Dublin, 29 December 1981
Height: 5'10" **Weight:** 10.7
Club Honours: AMC '07
International Honours: RoI: U21-3
Paul found it hard to score goals for Doncaster last season, managing seven in the League and nine in total. However, he suffered a bad ankle injury at Port Vale in November and was out until February. It took five games as a substitute before he regained a starting place but went on to score most of his goals before losing out in early April. He started in the last match at Cheltenham before blotting his copybook at Southend in the first leg of the play-off semi-final when he was sent off. That was the end of his season.

Notts Co (Signed from Newtown, Co Wicklow on 22/10/1999) FL 74+26/36 FLC 2+3/1 FAC 2+2/1 Others 2+3

Bristol C (£125,000 + on 16/7/2004) FL 10+17/5 FLC 0+1 FAC 1/1 Others 2/1

Doncaster Rov (£125,000 on 8/6/2005) FL 63+19/26 FLC 5+4/4 FAC 4+3/4 Others 10+1/10

HEGARTY Nicholas (Nick) Ian
Born: Hemsworth, 25 June 1986
Height: 5'10" **Weight:** 11.0
A season of two halves saw Nick out of favour at Grimsby until November, during which time he had a loan spell at York. His first three Mariners' outings saw him in three different positions – on the left of midfield, left-wing and left wing-back – before regular selection in the last role. He excelled with pace, accurate centres and confidence to shoot from distance.

Awarded a new three-year contract prior to Grimsby's Johnstone's Paint Trophy final trip to Wembley, Nick's first senior goal, against Accrington, was ironically scored with his right foot.

Grimsby T (From trainee on 11/1/2006) FL 36+12/4 FAC 3+1 Others 7+1

HELGUSON Heidar
Born: Akureyri, Iceland, 22 August 1977
Height: 6'0" **Weight:** 12.2
International Honours: Iceland: 40; U21-6; Yth
Signed in the summer from Fulham, the Icelandic striker made his Bolton debut as a substitute in the opening day defeat by Newcastle. His first start came soon after, against his former club, and although on the losing side, Heidar opened his scoring account. A series of knee and ankle problems led to him missing almost six months of the season, though he did return to start the vital 2-0 win at Reading in February. Continual injury problems restricted Heidar to just a handful of appearances last season but his goals to games ratio was impressive and bodes well for the future.

Watford (£1,500,000 from SK Lillestrom, Norway, ex Throttur, on 7/12/2000) P/FL 132+42/55 FLC 8+7/5 FAC 8+2/4

Fulham (£1,100,000 on 7/7/2005) PL 31+26/12 FLC 3/3 FAC 3

Bolton W (Signed on 20/7/2007) PL 3+3/2 Others 2

HENDERSON Darius Alexis
Born: Sutton, 7 September 1981
Height: 6'0" **Weight:** 12.8
Darius seemed likely to leave Watford in pre-season but was persuaded to stay and ended up signing a new four-year contract last September. The archetypal Championship striker, he was an ideal partner for Marlon King. Hard-working, willing to take the knocks up front and ready to come back to defend, he was very popular with the fans who appreciated his wholehearted commitment. His qualities were never better demonstrated than against Leicester, when he scored the winner and played alone up front for the whole of the second half after Watford had been reduced to ten men. Darius was the club's leading scorer with 13 goals, despite missing penalties in consecutive matches in March. He was sent off on the last day of the season at Blackpool and subsequently missed the first leg of the play-offs, returning to score Watford's only goal in the second leg.

Reading (From trainee on 15/12/1999) FL 5+66/11 FLC 2+2/2 FAC 1+2 Others 4+1/2

Brighton & Hove A (Loaned on 8/8/2003)

Darius Henderson

FL 10/2

Gillingham *(£25,000 on 2/1/2004) FL 31+5/ 9 FAC 2+1/1*

Swindon T *(Loaned on 20/8/2004) FL 6/5*

Watford *(£450,000 on 4/8/2005) P/FL 85+20/29 FLC 3 FAC 5+1 Others 3+1/2*

HENDERSON Ian

Born: Bury St Edmunds, 24 January 1985
Height: 5'8" **Weight:** 10.10
Club Honours: Div 1 '04
International Honours: E: Yth
After being freed by Norwich in the summer and joining Northampton, the striker had an in-and-out season. With the forward line changing throughout the campaign, first-team opportunities were limited but, despite that, he showed some neat touches when called upon. Having collected his share of goals for the reserves, his opener for the senior team should not be too far away.

Norwich C *(From trainee on 3/2/2003) P/FL 26+42/6 FLC 4+3 FAC 1+3*

Rotherham U *(Loaned on 12/1/2007) FL 18/1*

Northampton T *(Free on 17/7/2007) FL 9+14 FLC 2 FAC 1+1*

HENDERSON Paul John

Born: Sydney, Australia, 22 April 1976
Height: 6'1" **Weight:** 12.6
A goalkeeper who was sidelined by the arrival of loanees Marton Fulop and Ben Alnwick, Paul eventually regained his Leicester place for the crucial latter stages of the season. Although making a string of fine saves, including a couple of penalties, to keep the Foxes in with a chance of survival until the very last day, it was not enough to stave off relegation.

Bradford C *(Signed from Northern Spirit, Australia, ex Sutherland, on 10/8/2004) FL 40 FLC 1 FAC 1 Others 1*

Leicester C *(Free on 4/8/2005) FL 56+1 FLC 5 FAC 3*

HENDERSON Stephen

Born: Dublin, 2 May 1988
Height: 6'2" **Weight:** 13.10
International Honours: RoI: U21-1
The close-season signing from Aston Villa, did not have long to wait for his debut in Bristol City's goal. When Adriano Basso injured his ribs in the opening game against Queens Park Rangers,

Stephen went on at half-time and pulled off a brilliant save to help City draw. He was not beaten until the dying seconds. During the season he spent time on loan with Blue Square Premier clubs York and Weymouth.

Aston Villa *(From trainee on 5/5/2006)*

Bristol C *(Free on 25/7/2007) FL 0+1*

HENDERSON Wayne

Christopher Patrick
Born: Dublin, 16 September 1983
Height: 5'11" **Weight:** 12.2
Club Honours: FAYC '02
International Honours: RoI: 6; U21-13; Yth
Wayne started the season as Preston's first-choice goalkeeper but suffered a serious back injury that ended his season prematurely. Prior to his injury, Wayne looked likely to retain his position for the season, despite an uncharacteristic lapse that gifted Morecambe the winner in the Carling Cup tie. It is hoped the Eire international will return to display his excellent shot-stopping along with ability to command the area and organise the defensive unit.

Aston Villa *(From trainee on 27/9/2000)*

Wycombe W *(Loaned on 23/4/2004) FL 3*

Notts Co *(Loaned on 9/8/2004) FL 9 Others 1*

Notts Co *(Loaned on 3/12/2004) FL 2 Others 1*

Brighton & Hove A *(£20,000 on 5/8/2005) FL 52 FAC 2 Others 3*

Preston NE *(£150,000 on 31/1/2007) FL 7 FLC 1*

HENDON Ian Michael

Born: Ilford, 5 December 1971
Height: 6'0" **Weight:** 12.10
Club Honours: FAYC '90; CS '91; Div 3 '98; FC '05
International Honours: E: U21-7; Yth
In his new role as Barnet's assistant manager, the veteran defender was used last season only when the Bees were struggling with injuries at the back. Ian still put in some good displays and led by example, both on and off the pitch, where he has made a notably good impression as Paul Fairclough's assistant. He could have a promising career, possibly in management, when he decides to hang up his boots permanently.

Tottenham H *(From trainee on 20/12/1989) FL 0+4 FLC 1 Others 0+2*

Portsmouth *(Loaned on 16/1/1992) FL 1+3*

Leyton Orient *(Loaned on 26/3/1992) FL 5+1*

Barnsley *(Loaned on 17/3/1993) FL 6*

Leyton Orient *(£50,000 on 9/8/1993) FL 130+1/5 FLC 8 FAC 7 Others 12/1*

Birmingham C *(Loaned on 23/3/1995) FL 4*

*Notts Co (£50,000 on 24/2/1997) FL 82/6
FLC 5/1 FAC 8+1
Northampton T (£30,000 on 25/3/1999) FL
60/3 FLC 4 FAC 1/1 Others 1
Sheffield Wed (£40,000 + on 12/10/2000)
FL 49/2 FLC 2 FAC 2
Peterborough U (Free on 24/1/2003) FL 7/1
Barnet (Free on 1/7/2003) FL 61+4/8 FLC 4
FAC 3/1 Others 1*

HENDRIE Lee Andrew

Born: Birmingham, 18 May 1977
Height: 5'10" **Weight:** 10.3
International Honours: E: 1; B-1; U21-
13; Yth
Signed by new Sheffield United manager
Bryan Robson from Aston Villa on a
three-year deal, Lee was dogged by
injury during his first few months at
Bramall Lane. After five games in early
autumn, he was sidelined until December
before coming back to make a few
substitute appearances. Although he
made the starting line-up, with the Blades
struggling for consistency the crowd got
on Lee's back. In January he was loaned
to Leicester and the highly-rated and
hard-working midfielder looked to be an
inspirational signing by Ian Holloway. His
sole strike was an exquisitely curled effort
to see off Scunthorpe but an injury picked
up at Barnsley caused him to miss City's
final two fixtures. That may well have
been the difference between survival and
relegation in a tightly-fought campaign.
*Aston Villa (From trainee on 18/5/1994) PL
202+49/27 FLC 15+3/3 FAC 12+8 Others
14+5/2
Stoke C (Loaned on 29/9/2006) FL 17/3
Stoke C (Loaned on 29/1/2007) FL 9+2
Sheffield U (Free on 27/7/2007) FL 7+5/1
FLC 1/1 FAC 1
Leicester C (Loaned on 28/2/2008) FL 9/1*

HENNESSEY Wayne Robert

Born: Anglesey, 24 January 1987
Height: 6'0" **Weight:** 11.6
International Honours: W: 10; U21-5;
Yth
Injury to Matt Murray gave Wayne
a chance to establish himself at
Wolverhampton and he took it with both
hands. The tall goalkeeper also became a
regular for Wales. He pulled off a number
of tremendous saves during the season
and even when he made an error at
home to Burnley, did not allow it to shake
his confidence. Wayne kept a clean sheet
when Wales played in Germany and was
an ever-present in League matches for
Wolverhampton. He was selected for the
PFA 'Championship Team of the Season'.
*Wolverhampton W (From trainee on 7/4/
2005) FL 46 FAC 3 Others 2
Stockport Co (Loaned on 12/1/2007) FL 15*

HENRY James

Born: Reading, 10 June 1989
Height: 6'1" **Weight:** 11.11
International Honours: S: Yth. E: Yth
Having played only once for Reading in
2007-08, when substituting for John
Halls in the last ten minutes of the Carling
Cup tie against Liverpool, James is a
confident, tricky and fast right-winger
as evidenced by his continuing selection
for the England under-19 team. Loan
spells at Bournemouth, where he was
one of a quartet of Reading youngsters
on loan during the season, and Norwich,
gave James his best chance of first-team
football. On loan to Bournemouth in
November, James had a sensational
debut when he scored both goals in a
2-0 win at Bristol Rovers, while his last
few appearances came from the bench
and also proved to be highly effective.
Also enjoying a brief spell with Norwich
in February, making three appearances
before returning to Reading, James has
proved to be quick and neat on the ball
and looks set for a bright future as long
as he can also add physical strength to his
attributes.
*Reading (From trainee on 12/6/2006) FLC
0+1
Nottingham F (Loaned on 22/3/2007) FL
0+1
Bournemouth (Loaned on 2/11/2007) FL
8+3/4
Norwich C (Loaned on 31/1/2008) FL
1+2*

HENRY Karl Levi Daniel

Born: Wolverhampton, 26 November
1982
Height: 6'1" **Weight:** 10.13
International Honours: E: Yth
Karl, a locally-born midfielder, did not
start the first couple of League games
for Wolverhampton but once in the
team resumed his partnership with Seyi
Olofinjana, having a run of 25 games
and usually playing in a holding role.
He did venture forward on occasions,
scoring the winner at home to Preston
with a low drive. Karl was perhaps not
as consistent as in the previous season
but did not hide when things were
running against him. This was typified
at Charlton, where he missed an easy
chance but still made a long run to slide
in a late winner. He suffered a knee
injury there and missed five games,
returning for the final fixture.
*Stoke C (From trainee on 30/11/1999) FL
63+57/1 FLC 4+1 FAC 7+2 Others 1+1
Cheltenham T (Loaned on 13/1/2004) FL
8+1/1
Wolverhampton W (£100,000 on
3/8/2006) FL 72+2/6 FLC 2+1 FAC 5*

HENRY Paul Nicholas

Born: Liverpool, 28 January 1988
Height: 5'9" **Weight:** 11.5
Paul signed his second professional
contract with Tranmere in July
after another season of impressive
performances as captain of the reserves.
The nephew of former Rover's favourite
Nick Henry, he is able to play in the centre
of midfield or in defence and made
his first appearance as a substitute at
Doncaster in November. Paul was handed
his first start a month later at Luton but
was out of contract again in the summer.
*Tranmere Rov (From trainee on 16/5/2006)
FL 1+1*

HERD Benjamin (Ben)
Alexander

Born: Welwyn Garden City, 21 June 1985
Height: 5'9" **Weight:** 10.12
Ben is rated as a defender by both
managers at Shrewsbury last season and
missed only one League game. Always
dependable, committed and keen to get
forward, Ben spent much of the first half
of the season in midfield when Darren
Moss was preferred at right-back. He
created a number of goals, notably in
victories over Lincoln and Grimsby, but
is most effective at full-back and played
there regularly after the turn of the year.
*Watford (From trainee on 8/5/2003)
Shrewsbury T (Free on 6/6/2005) FL 116+6/
3 FLC 4 FAC 4+1 Others 4+2*

HERD Christopher (Chris)

Born: Perth, Australia, 4 April 1989
Height: 5'8" **Weight:** 12.0
The wholehearted midfield player joined
Port Vale on loan from Aston Villa in
January. He played on the right and
had an excellent debut against Millwall,
looking as if he had been playing for
years, rather that taking a first step at
League level. With a turn of pace and
always committed he was unluckily sent
off in the last minute of a defeat at Bristol
Rovers. When he returned at Hartlepool
he scored twice to give the Vale a 2-0
lead in the first 15 minutes before they
folded to lose 3-2. His final appearance
was in a 2-0 victory at local rivals Crewe
before he was recalled by Villa and then
sent to Wycombe on loan for a month.
Had Chris stayed longer, he may well have
won Vale's 'Player of the Year' award.
Going straight into the Wanderers' side
at Hereford he gave an eye-catching
performance on the right, taking on
and beating defenders and twice nearly
scoring. He started the next two games
before ending his spell with a substitute
appearance. Wycombe have a tradition of
receiving high-class loan players from Villa

and Chris was no exception.
Aston Villa (From trainee on 3/7/2007)
Port Vale (Loaned on 10/1/2008) FL 11/2
Wycombe W (Loaned on 14/3/2008) FL 3+1

HESKEY Emile William Ivanhoe
Born: Leicester, 11 January 1978
Height: 6'2" **Weight:** 13.12
Club Honours: FLC '97, '00, '01, '03;
FAC '01; UEFAC '01; ESC '01; CS '01
International Honours: E: 45; B-1; U21-
16; Yth
Emile enjoyed another outstanding
season for Wigan, leading the line
with great panache and returning to
international football. A powerful target-
man with a fantastic turn of pace, he is a
hard-working and willing centre-forward.
Emile scored in the home game against
Sunderland and his form led to a recall for
England, playing alongside Michael Owen
in the European Championship wins over
Israel and Russia at Wembley. He broke
a metatarsal bone in his foot against
Fulham in September and missed two
months. Emile scored the winner in an
important victory over Bolton and his best
goal came from a Jason Koumas cross
to snatch a last-minute equaliser against
Chelsea. Consistently driving forward near
the end of the campaign as the Latics
avoided relegation, he played on despite
niggling groin injuries. His all-round play
and commitment could not be faulted, as
his strength allied to good use of the ball
in the air caused nightmares for some of
the Premiership's best defenders.
Leicester C (From trainee on 3/10/1995) P/FL
143+11/40 FLC 25+2/6 FAC 11 Others 5
Liverpool (£11,000,000 on 10/3/2000) PL
118+32/39 FLC 7+5/2 FAC 9+5/6 Others
42+5/13
Birmingham C (£3,500,000 + on 2/7/2004)
PL 68/14 FLC 5/1 FAC 5/1
Wigan Ath (£5,500,000 on 14/7/2006) PL
60+2/12 FLC 0+1 FAC 3

HESSEY Sean Peter
Born: Whiston, 19 September 1978
Height: 5'10" **Weight:** 12.6
Chester's Sean spent most of the season
on loan at Macclesfield and was a regular
in the in the centre of the defence in a
back-four formation, although that often
became a back-five after the appointment
of Keith Alexander as manager. Then Sean
acted as sweeper on occasions. A hard
tackling player, his excellent partnership
with Ryan Cresswell gave the back line a
more solid appearance in the latter part
of the season. His performances and
leadership were recognized when he was
appointed team captain in March before
being released by Chester in the summer.
Leeds U (From juniors at Liverpool on

Tony Hibbert

15/9/1997)
Wigan Ath (Free on 24/12/1997)
Huddersfield T (Free on 12/3/1998) FL
7+4 FAC 1
Kilmarnock (Free on 31/8/1999) SL 38+6/1
SLC 2 SC 1
Blackpool (Free on 12/2/2004) FL 4+2
Others 0+1
Chester C (Free on 2/7/2004) FL 70+9/1 FLC
2 FAC 6 Others 5/1
Macclesfield T (Loaned on 9/11/2007)
FL 26

HEYWOOD Matthew (Matt)
Stephen
Born: Chatham, 26 August 1979
Height: 6'2" **Weight:** 14.0
The tall, commanding centre-half was
out of favour at Brentford at the start
of the season. He deputised for the
injured John Mackie for four games
in September and was recalled to play
alongside him in October. Matt went
from strength to strength and took
over as team captain in December. His
no-nonsense defending won over the
Brentford fans and he proved to be an
inspiring leader. After suffering a rib
injury at Chesterfield in February, his
seven-game absence coincided with a
poor run of results. Matt was offered a
new contract for 2008-09.
Burnley (From trainee on 6/7/1998) FL
11+2 FAC 1 Others 1
Swindon T (Free on 22/1/2001) FL 176+7/8
FLC 5+1 FAC 9/1 Others 10/1
Bristol C (Free on 1/7/2005) FL 22+2/2
FAC 0+1
Brentford (Signed on 28/7/2006) FL 55+5/2
FLC 2 FAC 2 Others 3

HIBBERT Anthony (Tony)
James
Born: Liverpool, 20 February 1981
Height: 5'8" **Weight:** 11.3
Club Honours: FAYC '98
Now an established part of Everton's
squad, the full-back had a generally
sound season. Although usually second
choice to Phil Neville on the right side
of the Blues' defence, Tony still played
in two-thirds of the Toffees' Premiership
matches. The former Everton youth
player is a tigerish tackler, far happier
when facing an orthodox winger, and
his best two best performances of the
season were at Manchester City and
Arsenal, marking Martin Petrov and Theo
Walcott, respectively, with considerable
aplomb. The defender finished the
season just short of 200 appearances
for the Goodison side, having signed an
extension to his contract.
Everton (From trainee on 1/7/1998) PL
153+11 FLC 10+1 FAC 10 Others 8+4

HIBBERT David (Dave) John
Born: Eccleshall, 28 January 1986
Height: 6'2" **Weight:** 12.6
A young and athletic striker signed from
Preston last summer, Dave opened his
Shrewsbury account on the first day
with a goal in a 4-0 win at Lincoln. He
had the distinction of scoring the first
League goal at the New Meadow in a
1-0 victory over Bradford. An excellent
early spell brought him six goals in his
first eight games and he had ten by the
turn of the year. Dave is good in the air
but as Shrewsbury began to struggle,
goals became more elusive, probably not
helped by frequent changes of striking
partners. Even so, he ended as leading
scorer with 12.
Port Vale (Trainee) FL 2+7/2 Others 1
Preston NE (Free on 6/7/2005) FL 0+10
FAC 1+2
Rotherham U (Loaned on 5/8/2006) FL
12+9/2 FLC 0+1
Bradford C (Loaned on 5/1/2007) FL 4+4
Shrewsbury T (Signed on 18/6/2007) FL
36+8/12 FLC 1+1

HIGGINBOTHAM Daniel
(Danny) John
Born: Manchester, 29 December 1978
Height: 6'1" **Weight:** 12.6
With money needed to be raised to
fund prospective purchases, the previous
season's Stoke captain played only one
League and one Carling Cup match
before being transferred to Sunderland
in August. The money received ultimately
allowed manager Tony Pulis to sign
Leon Cort, Ryan Shawcross and Glenn
Whelan as he reorganised his promotion
chasing squad. Danny endeared himself
to all Black Cats' fans with derby goals
against Newcastle in November and
Middlesbrough in April, both towering
headers. His usefulness at set pieces was
again put to good use against Aston Villa
in December with another goal. Able to
operate in central defence or at left-back,
Danny was used solely as a stopper by
Roy Keane and soon established himself
in the side before a broken toe sustained
in January, coupled with the return of
Jonny Evans, restricted his appearances.
However, he did return to action before
the end of the campaign.
Manchester U (From trainee on 10/7/1997)
PL 2+2 FLC 1 Others 1+1
Derby Co (£2,000,000 on 12/7/2000) P/FL
82+4/3 FLC 7+1/1 FAC 3+1
Southampton (Signed on 31/1/2003) P/FL
84+10/4 FLC 4 FAC 7 Others 1
Stoke C (£225,000 on 4/8/2006) FL 45/7
FLC 1 FAC 2
Sunderland (£2,500,000 on 30/8/2007)
PL 21/3

HIGGINBOTHAM Kallum
Michael
Born: Salford, 15 June 1989
Height: 5'11" **Weight:** 10.10
With Salford City as a junior, Kallum had
scored a hat-trick for Oldham's youth
team against Rochdale in the Lancashire
Youth Cup final at the end of 2006-07
and was one of manager Keith Hill's
first summer signings for Dale. Brought
in as one for the future, he made a
string of exciting substitute appearances
and earned himself a regular position
on Dale's right flank from November
onwards, though he briefly figured in his
youth-team role as a central striker later
in the season. He netted his first senior
goal when ten-man Dale came back
from a goal down to win at Accrington
and scored in successive games against
Dagenham and Barnet as the club closed
in on a play-off place. Kallum ended
his first season in senior football with a
Wembley appearance.
Oldham Ath (Free from Salford C on
1/8/2006)
Rochdale (Free on 19/6/2007) FL 22+11/3
FAC 1 Others 3+1

HIGGS Shane Peter
Born: Oxford, 13 May 1977
Height: 6'2" **Weight:** 12.12
Cheltenham's goalkeeper played in all 51
matches and his assured displays won him
the 'Players' Player of the Year' award
for the second season running. During
January, Shane kept goal for 446 minutes
without conceding a goal as the Robins
hauled themselves out of the bottom four
in League One. Tall and strong but agile
with sharp reflexes, his value to the team
was considerable and his performance
in the nail-biting final-day match against
Doncaster was a big factor in Cheltenham
staying up while denying their opponents
automatic promotion. Has worked
diligently at his game over the nine years
he has spent at Town and is justifiably
regarded as one of the finest goalkeepers
in the lower divisions.
Bristol Rov (From trainee on 17/7/1995)
FL 10 Others 2 (Free to Worcester C on
11/7/1998)
Cheltenham T (£10,000 from Worcester
C on 21/6/1999) FL 225+2 FLC 6 FAC 13
Others 16

[HILARIO] SAMPAIO Henrique
Hilario Alves
Born: Sao Pedro da Cova, Portugal, 21
October 1975
Height: 6'2" **Weight:** 13.5
Club Honours: FLC '07
International Honours: Portugal: B; U21
The second season of Chelsea's

Portuguese number-three goalkeeper was a carbon copy of his first, stepping into the breach after injuries and surpassing all expectations to maintain the hunt for honours. Hilario went on at Blackburn in December to replace hip-injury victim Petr Cech and immediately pulled off a plunging save to seal the points in a hard-fought encounter. A run of four matches, and three clean sheets, followed before he was again thrust into the spotlight in April during the tense Champions' League quarter-final against Fenerbahce. This time it was Carlo Cudicini, with a groin strain, who limped off and again Hilario stood firm as the Turkish club swarmed forward looking for the precious away goal that would have sent them through. He pulled off a string of vital saves to ensure Chelsea's passage to the titanic semi-final against Liverpool. In his two seasons at Chelsea Hilario has had a somewhat eccentric career, mixing high-profile appearances with periods of obscurity when playing in front of a handful of supporters in reserve matches. But 'cometh the hour, cometh the man': he has never let Chelsea down!
Chelsea (Free from CD Nacional, Portugal, ex Naval, Academica Coimbra, Porto, Estrela Amadoro, Porto, Varzim, Academica Coimbra, on 10/7/2006) PL 13+1 FLC 4 FAC 2 Others 3+1

HILL Clinton (Clint) Scott
Born: Huyton, 19 October 1978
Height: 6'0" **Weight:** 11.6
Just when this popular defender had clawed his way back to fitness after a couple of seasons of injury problems at Stoke, he was allowed to join Crystal Palace, initially on loan, in an exchange deal for Leon Cort. Having started the season in Stoke's reserve side he was missed by the fans, who had enjoyed his no-nonsense style of play. At Palace, the experienced left-back scored three goals in his loan spell before signing a full contract in January and becoming a member of the best defence in the Championship, as the club reached the play-offs.
Tranmere Rov (From trainee on 9/7/1997) FL 138+2/16 FLC 18/3 FAC 11+1/1
Oldham Ath (Signed on 16/7/2002) FL 17/1 FLC 4 FAC 2 Others 2
Stoke C (£120,000 on 22/7/2003) FL 71+9/3 FLC 2 FAC 2
Crystal Palace (Free on 6/11/2007) FL 28/3 FAC 0+1 Others 2

HILL Matthew (Matt) Clayton
Born: Bristol, 26 March 1981
Height: 5'7" **Weight:** 12.6
Club Honours: AMC '03

Matt was usually second-choice left-back in the latter part of the season, making only four starts after the turn of the year following some uncharacteristically shaky performances as the team adapted to Alan Irvine's new methods. Prior to that, he seemed to have regained his place and form after playing only once in the first month. Usually a solid defender with a surprisingly good spring for a small man, he is always keen to overlap and put in a telling cross. Matt ended the season with a standing ovation at former club Bristol City but still seeks his first Preston goal after over 100 matches.
Bristol C (From trainee on 22/2/1999) FL 182+16/6 FLC 8 FAC 15 Others 19+5
Preston NE (£100,000 on 10/1/2005) FL 93+11 FLC 3 FAC 6+1 Others 3

HILLS John David
Born: Blackpool, 21 April 1978
Height: 5'9" **Weight:** 11.2
Club Honours: AMC '02
After being released by Sheffield Wednesday in the summer, John joined Blackpool for the third time. The left-back's career started at Blackpool before he moved on to Everton and returned to Blackpool after three years. This time round he was unable to force his way into the team, with the impressive Stephen Crainey holding down the left-back place. However, in the few appearances he made it was clear that John had lost none of his pace and attacking instincts. He was released at the end of the season.
Blackpool (From trainee on 27/10/1995)
Everton (£90,000 on 4/11/1995) PL 1+2
Swansea C (Loaned on 30/1/1997) FL 1/1
Swansea C (Loaned on 22/8/1997) FL 7/1
Blackpool (£75,000 on 16/1/1998) FL 146+16/16 FLC 5 FAC 12/1 Others 13+1/2
Gillingham (Free on 6/8/2003) FL 47+5/2 FLC 3/1 FAC 2
Sheffield Wed (Free on 6/7/2005) FL 41+2 FLC 2+1
Blackpool (Free on 11/7/2007) FL 1+3 FLC 3 FAC 1

HILLS Lee Mark
Born: Croydon, 13 April 1990
Height: 5'10" **Weight:** 11.11
International Honours: E: Yth
Another player developed by the Crystal Palace Academy, Lee, a gifted left-back with a dangerous long throw, was one of the many youngsters to be given an opportunity under Neil Warnock last season. Lee made his debut against Watford in November and scored his first goal in the live television game at Bristol City. He signed a two-year contract with Palace in January and is an England under-19 international. An exciting

prospect, he came third in Wickes' 'Young Apprentice of the Year'.
Crystal Palace (From trainee on 1/2/2008) FL 6+6/1 FAC 1

HINDS Richard Paul
Born: Sheffield, 22 August 1980
Height: 6'2" **Weight:** 11.0
Club Honours: Div 1 '07
Richard proved to be a good team player after arriving from Scunthorpe in the summer. Manager Brian Laws knew him from Glanford Park and despite a slow start he became a valuable player for Sheffield Wednesday, the club he also supports. Richard played at right-back, mainly in the absence of Frank Simek, but also in midfield and in his favoured position as a central defender. He can consider himself to have made the step-up to Championship level very competently.
Tranmere Rov (From juniors on 20/7/1998) FL 42+13 FLC 3+5 FAC 5 Others 1
Hull C (Free on 1/7/2003) FL 40+5/1 FLC 1 FAC 1 Others 1+1
Scunthorpe U (Free on 17/3/2005) FL 85+8/8 FLC 3/1 FAC 6 Others 2+1
Sheffield Wed (Free on 5/7/2007) FL 30+8/2 FLC 2 FAC 2

HINES Sebastian (Seb) Tony
Born: Wetherby, 29 May 1988
Height: 6'2" **Weight:** 12.4
International Honours: E: Yth
Seb, who has played for England at under-19 level, sampled Premiership football for the first time in mid-August at Fulham, when he substituted for another substitute, Dong-Gook Lee, with just a minute of the 2-1 victory remaining. A defender of outstanding promise, Seb was one of a quartet of junior players - Graeme Owens, Rhys Williams and Jonathan Grounds were the others - who were handed their first professional contracts after graduating through the Academy. He had a further taste of senior action with the whole 120 minutes of the FA Cup replay against Sheffield United at the Riverside in February.
Middlesbrough (From trainee on 2/7/2005) PL 0+1 FLC 0+1 FAC 3/1

HINES Zavon
Born: Jamaica, 27 December 1988
Height: 5'10" **Weight:** 10.7
Zavon joined Coventry on loan from West Ham in March after an abortive attempt to sign Freddy Eastwood from Wolverhampton on a similar basis. While he never started for the Sky Blues, Zavon was a useful substitute with young, fresh legs giving defenders a hard time in the last ten or 15 minutes.

Alexander Hleb

His one goal, at Hillsborough, promised to be a valuable winner until Sheffield Wednesday equalised in stoppage-time. On his showing for Coventry, Zavon could have a bright future.
West Ham U *(From trainee on 6/7/2007)*
Coventry C *(Loaned on 27/3/2008) FL 0+7/1*

HINSHELWOOD Adam
Born: Oxford, 8 January 1984
Height: 5'10" **Weight:** 12.10
Adam surely hoped that the persistent knee problems that have plagued him since March 2005 were behind him, but it proved not to be. After making a promising comeback in the reserves in September, the tenacious Brighton defender made just one brief appearance in the first team, as an 89th-minute substitute in the defeat at Gillingham, before further complications with his injury. Yet another operation was required, meaning he missed the rest of the season, but the club stood by this dogged player and will give him a chance to prove his fitness in the new campaign.
Brighton & Hove A *(From trainee on 28/7/2003) FL 77+8/1 FLC 3 FAC 4 Others 4+1*

HINTON Craig
Born: Wolverhampton, 26 November 1977
Height: 6'0" **Weight:** 12.0
Club Honours: FC '00
The Bristol Rovers' central defender had to be patient as he waited for an opportunity to play first-team football in the first three months of last season, but he certainly grasped the chance when recalled. He scored five goals, including a powerful header at Premiership Fulham in the FA Cup. These were his first goals in over 100 appearances for the club.
Birmingham C *(From trainee on 5/7/1996) FL 172+1/3 FLC 5 FAC 10 Others 8*
Bristol Rov *(Free on 20/7/2004) FL 116+12/2 FLC 3 FAC 14+2/3 Others 13*

HIRD Adrian Samuel (Sam)
Born: Askern, 7 September 1987
Height: 6'0" **Weight:** 12.0
Sam was signed by Doncaster in the summer after being released by Leeds. A right-back or preferably a centre-half, he could not break into the first team because of the competition in front of him, which comprised Adam Lockwood, Steve Roberts, Gordon Greer and Matthew Mills in the centre-half positions and the consistent James O'Connor at right-back. To keep match

fit Sam went out on loan to Grimsby in November. The loan was so successful that it was eventually extended to three months, a permanent move only breaking down due to wage demands. He showed ability as an attacking wing-back in a 3-5-2 formation, playing his part in an unbeaten run of ten league games to help lift the Mariners away from the relegation zone. Recalled by Doncaster towards the end of the season when injuries began to take their toll, Sam made a good impression when appearing in all the play-off games, including the final at Wembley against his old club Leeds.
Leeds U *(From trainee on 13/9/2005)*
Doncaster Rov *(Free on 8/2/2007) FL 3+6 Others 4+1*
Grimsby T *(Loaned on 20/11/2007) FL 17 FAC 1*

HLEB Alexander
Born: Minsk, Belarus, 1 May 1981
Height: 5'10" **Weight:** 10.12
International Honours: Belarus: 41
Alexander made an immediate impact at the start of last season when he scored the last-gasp winner against Fulham as Arsenal came back from a goal down to win 2-1. The Belarus midfield player enjoyed by far his most consistent season to date as he played either wide on the right or, to greater effect, in the 'hole' behind the spearhead striker. If there is one criticism that can still be levelled at him, it is a lack of goals, although he is marvellously creative on the ball and possesses astonishingly quick feet. His season finished with a suspension, while he was linked with a summer move to Inter Milan.
Arsenal *(£8,000,000 + from VfB Stuttgart, Germany on 5/8/2005) PL 73+16/7 FLC 4+2 FAC 5+1 Others 27+2/3*

HOBBS Jack
Born: Portsmouth, 18 August 1988
Height: 6'3" **Weight:** 13.4
Club Honours: FAYC '06
International Honours: E: Yth
Jack is a young central defender who was signed by Liverpool manager Rafa Benitez in 2005 from Lincoln, where he had made a single substitute appearance at the age of 16 years, five months – the Imps' youngest ever debutant. Following two seasons in Liverpool's youth team and reserves, Benitez introduced him to the first team in the Carling Cup, as a substitute at Reading and starting against Cardiff in the next round. Following a Premiership debut as a substitute for Jamie Carragher in a 4-0 victory over Bolton in December, he was

surprisingly handed a start in the next match at Reading, where Benitez fielded a weakened team in an unfamiliar 4-3-3 formation before a crucial Champions' League match in Marseille. Liverpool suffered a shock 3-1 defeat, their first of the season in the Premier League, to a team eventually relegated. Jack was not at fault for any of the Reading goals and lasted the full 90 minutes. He also played in the Carling Cup fifth round defeat at Chelsea, but in the New Year was farmed out to Scunthorpe for more regular experience. Jack joined the Championship strugglers in January on loan until the end of the season and immediately impressed in the heart of the defence, looking comfortable on the ground and dominant in the air. He celebrated his first goal in the defeat at Stoke before being switched to cover at right-back prior to returning to Anfield.
Lincoln C *(Trainee) FL 0+1*
Liverpool *(£750,000 on 19/8/2005) PL 1+1 FLC 2+1*
Scunthorpe U *(Loaned on 25/1/2008) FL 7+2/1*

HODGE Bryan Johnstone
Born: Hamilton, 23 September 1987
Height: 5'11" **Weight:** 11.7
International Honours: S: Yth
An exciting midfield player, Bryan was signed on loan from Blackburn in November and fitted in well at Millwall, making ten League appearances at a time when the injury list at the Den appeared endless. A hard-working, composed midfielder, who is a good passer of the ball and as much at home when attacking as well as defending, he next had a loan spell at Darlington in early February and made his debut against Barnet at the Arena. He slotted into the team comfortably and was only once on the losing side in his seven games for the Quakers.
Blackburn Rov *(From trainee on 2/11/2004)*
Mansfield T *(Loaned on 22/2/2007) FL 9*
Millwall *(Loaned on 2/11/2007) FL 10 FAC 3*
Darlington *(Loaned on 8/2/2008) FL 7*

HODGES Lee Leslie
Born: Epping, 4 September 1973
Height: 6'0" **Weight:** 12.1
Club Honours: Div 3 '02; Div 2 '04
International Honours: E: Yth
Lee started last season from the substitutes' bench but managed to regain his left-back position during October and then went on to make 19 consecutive League appearances for Plymouth. Now an Argyle veteran of

seven seasons, he continued to be the model professional and an example to younger players. It was announced in April that Lee was to be released when his contract expired and he was given a rousing reception when he appeared as a late substitute in the final game at Home Park to thank him for his tremendous service to Argyle.

Tottenham H *(From trainee on 29/2/1992)* PL 0+4
Plymouth Arg *(Loaned on 26/2/1993)* FL 6+1/2
Wycombe W *(Loaned on 31/12/1993)* FL 2+2 FAC 1 Others 1
Barnet *(Free on 31/5/1994)* FL 94+11/26 FLC 6+1 FAC 6+1/4 Others 4+1
Reading *(£100,000 on 29/7/1997)* FL 58+21/10 FLC 7+3 FAC 7+1/1 Others 0+2
Plymouth Arg *(Free on 17/8/2001)* FL 162+33/11 FLC 5/1 FAC 10+2 Others 2+1

HODGKISS Jared

Born: Stafford, 15 November 1986
Height: 5'8" **Weight:** 11.3
Reserve to right-back Carl Hoefkens, Jared never let down West Bromwich when called into action and produced some fine displays, including solid performances in the 4-2 home League win over Charlton, when he was up against a very useful winger, and the FA Cup tie against Bristol Rovers.
West Bromwich A *(From trainee on 16/1/2006)* P/FL 3+7 FLC 4 FAC 2

HOEFKENS Carl

Born: Lier, Belgium, 6 October 1978
Height: 5'11" **Weight:** 11.9
Club Honours: Ch '08
International Honours: Belgium: 21
Arriving from Stoke during the summer, Carl proved to be a fine acquisition for West Bromwich. His powerful overlapping runs from right-back gave Albion another attacking dimension and he defended with durability, aggression and skill, making around a dozen last-ditch tackles well inside his penalty area. Carl was never given the run-around by an opposing winger and his attitude and commitment were first-class despite having several cracks on the head, three in quick time in the Good Friday game at Charlton. Close to a recall by Belgium, he was Albion's man of the match in the FA Cup semi-final defeat by Portsmouth at Wembley.
Stoke C *(Signed from Germinal Beerschot, Belgium on 29/7/2005)* FL 86+3/5 FLC 1 FAC 6
West Bromwich A *(£750,000 on 7/8/2007)* FL 42 FAC 5

Danny Hollands

HOLDSWORTH Andrew (Andy)
Born: Pontefract, 29 January 1984
Height: 5'9" **Weight:** 11.2
The dependable Huddersfield defender was deservedly named 'Player of the Season' by supporters and his team-mates. Andy played regularly in midfield, a position that gave him greater freedom than his normal full-back role. Cool, calm and covering ground effectively, he carried out much unsung work in attack and defence. He crosses well and his incisive passing earned him many assists. A home-grown talent, he made the 200th-career appearance for his only club in the New Year's Day defeat by Nottingham Forest. Goals in three of the last four home games showed his ability going forward, the last being a wonderful header goal in the victory over local rivals Leeds.
Huddersfield T (From trainee on 6/12/2003) FL 184+13/6 FLC 6/1 FAC 11/1 Others 8+1

HOLLAND Matthew (Matt) Rhys
Born: Bury, 11 April 1974
Height: 5'9" **Weight:** 10.12
International Honours: Rol: 49; B-1
Matt missed the early part of 2007-08 because of a knee injury in pre-season and on his return, injured a calf in Charlton's Carling Cup defeat at Luton. He returned in late November and, after a couple of substitute appearances, replaced Jose Semedo in the centre of midfield and stayed there, taking over as captain when Andy Reid moved to Sunderland. Matt built up a good understanding with Zheng Zhi and was a model of consistency, crowning a fine season by winning the 'Player of the Year' award from Charlton supporters. A strong tackler with good positional sense, Matt is comfortable on the ball and passes well, always giving his best. He can be relied upon to pop up with the occasional goal, as he did at Cardiff when he was on the end of Andy Reid's corner to open the scoring. Was out of contract in the summer and looking for a new club.
West Ham U (From trainee on 3/7/1992)
Bournemouth (Signed on 27/1/1995) FL 97+7/18 FLC 6 FAC 3 Others 3
Ipswich T (£800,000 on 31/7/1997) P/FL 259/38 FLC 23+1/6 FAC 12 Others 17+2/2
Charlton Ath (£750,000 on 17/6/2003) P/FL 144+13/12 FLC 7+1 FAC 11+1/1

HOLLANDS Daniel (Danny) Timothy
Born: Ashford, Middlesex, 6 November 1985
Height: 5'11" **Weight:** 12.11

This stylish Bournemouth midfielder came to the fore during last season and his efforts were rewarded when he won the 'Player of the Year' award. A player who likes to shoot on sight, he scored several excellent goals during the campaign and, despite his tender years, captained the side on a number of occasions.
Chelsea (From trainee on 12/11/2003)
Torquay U (Loaned on 9/3/2006) FL 10/1
Bournemouth (Free on 6/7/2006) FL 51+19/5 FLC 0+1 FAC 6/2 Others 3+1

HOLMES Derek
Born: Lanark, 18 October 1978
Height: 6'0" **Weight:** 13.2
Club Honours: Div 2 '06
Derek is a tall experienced striker, commanding in the air, and added physical strength to Rotherham after joining them last summer from Carlisle. He netted a rare hat-trick against Lincoln, with shots from either foot and a header. Derek had to play alongside a number of different colleagues, so it was difficult for him to build up real understanding but he could always be relied upon to give opposing defences plenty to think about.
Heart of Midlothian (From juniors on 5/1/1995) SL 1+6/1 SLC 0+2/2 Others 0+3/1
Cowdenbeath (Loaned on 21/11/1997) SL 13/5
Raith Rov (Loaned on 8/1/1999) SL 13+1/6
Ross Co (Free on 15/10/1999) SL 39+19/14 SLC 1+1/1 SC 1+1 Others 3
Bournemouth (£40,000 on 14/9/2001) FL 63+52/16 FLC 2+3 FAC 2+7/2 Others 5+2
Carlisle U (Signed on 23/2/2005) FL 38+38/10 FLC 2/1 FAC 2 Others 8/2
Rotherham U (Free on 19/7/2007) FL 33+4/11 FLC 1 Others 1+1

HOLMES Ian David
Born: Ellesmere Port, 27 June 1985
Height: 6'0" **Weight:** 12.5
Seen as a prospect, the 22-year-old Matlock forward was signed by Mansfield on the last day of the transfer window in August. It was a big step up for Ian and while being groomed for the future, he scored his first goal for the club in the 3-0 win over Lewes in the FA Cup. With the injury to Micky Boulding, Ian had an extended run in the side and did well. However, with Boulding's return to fitness and the arrival of Jefferson Louis he slipped down the pecking order and was allowed out on loan to Telford in March until the end of the season. Was released in the summer.
Mansfield T (Signed from Matlock T on 31/8/2007) FL 4+12/1 FAC 1+1/2 Others 1

HOLMES Lee Daniel
Born: Mansfield, 2 April 1987
Height: 5'7" **Weight:** 10.6
International Honours: E: Yth
Signed on loan from Derby, the skilful left-sided midfielder was one of the bright spots in the second half of Walsall's season and enjoyed an inspired spell in February with four goals in as many games. Lee was released by Derby at the end of his contract and Walsall fans were hoping his move to the Banks' Stadium might be made permanent, before it was reported that he had signed for Southampton.
Derby Co (From trainee on 15/5/2004) FL 26+20/2 FLC 2 FAC 1+3
Swindon T (Loaned on 22/12/2004) FL 14+1/1 Others 1
Bradford C (Loaned on 4/8/2006) FL 16 FLC 1 FAC 1 Others 1
Walsall (Loaned on 11/1/2008) FL 19/4

HOLMES Peter James
Born: Bishop Auckland, 18 November 1980
Height: 5'10" **Weight:** 10.6
Club Honours: Div 1 '05
International Honours: E: Yth; Sch
Although a cultured player in Rotherham's midfield, Peter struggled to carve out a regular place after he was signed from Luton last summer. Whenever called upon, he proved to be one of the most accurate passers of the ball in the club. He is accurate from dead-ball situations and was perhaps unlucky not to have played the number of games his experience probably warranted.
Sheffield Wed (From trainee on 2/12/1997)
Luton T (Free on 1/8/2000) FL 67+38/11 FLC 6+3 FAC 5+2 Others 5+1/1
Chesterfield (Loaned on 12/1/2007) FL 10/1
Lincoln C (Loaned on 22/3/2007) FL 5
Rotherham U (Free on 6/7/2007) FL 19+5/2 FLC 1 FAC 0+1 Others 1

HOLNESS Marcus Lewis
Born: Swinton, 8 December 1988
Height: 6'0" **Weight:** 12.2
Marcus, captain of Oldham's youth side, was loaned out to Ossett at the start of last season but then signed on loan for Rochdale in October, when they had six first-team defenders out of action. He made his debut in a Johnstone's Paint Trophy match against Bury and played his first League game the following weekend in a victory at Grimsby. His performances as a substitute earned him a regular spot in the centre of the Dale's defence over the following month and Keith Hill made his transfer permanent

in the January window. When Nathan Stanton returned to the side, Marcus was mostly used on the bench, but produced solid performances all along the back four whenever called upon. He was a non-playing substitute in the play-off final at Wembley.
Oldham Ath (From trainee on 3/7/2007)
Rochdale (Free on 2/10/2007) FL 13+6 Others 1+1

HOLROYD Christopher (Chris)
Born: Macclesfield, 24 October 1986
Height: 5'11" **Weight:** 12.3
The young striker started the season on the bench for Chester and scored his first goal as a substitute in the Johnstone's Paint Trophy tie at Carlisle. Following four successive starts at the end of October, Chris seemed to grow in confidence after replacing Glenn Rule at Morecambe on Boxing Day, when he scored once and was unlucky not to add to his tally. He followed this with two well-taken goals at Accrington in January, when he acted as a lone-striker. A nippy, hard-working player who likes to run at defenders, Chris will hope to make further progress, having had his contract extended.
Chester C (From trainee at Crewe Alex on 5/7/2006) FL 21+26/4 FLC 0+2 FAC 0+1 Others 0+2/1

HOLT Andrew (Andy)
Born: Stockport, 21 May 1978
Height: 6'1" **Weight:** 12.7
Club Honours: AMC '05
Northampton's wide midfield player had several players behind him at left-back last season but formed the best understanding with Daniel Jones. Andy was a real asset in attack with his ability to provide passes for team-mates following excellent wing play.
Oldham Ath (From trainee on 23/7/1996) FL 104+20/10 FLC 8 FAC 6+4 Others 3
Hull C (£150,000 on 15/3/2001) FL 45+26/3 FLC 1 FAC 1 Others 5+1
Barnsley (Loaned on 15/8/2002) FL 4+3 FLC 1
Shrewsbury T (Loaned on 27/3/2003) FL 9
Wrexham (Free on 3/8/2004) FL 80+1/9 FLC 3 FAC 2/1 Others 7
Northampton T (Free on 11/7/2006) FL 62+9/4 FLC 2 FAC 6+1 Others 1

HOLT Gary James
Born: Irvine, 9 March 1973
Height: 6'0" **Weight:** 12.11
Club Honours: SC '98; Div 1 '04
International Honours: S: 10
Wycombe eagerly snapped up this experienced Scottish international central

midfielder last summer, on his release from Nottingham Forest. Almost ever-present, he quickly became the heart of the midfield, putting in prodigious amounts of work. Whether quickly closing down opponents, winning the ball in the air or setting up attacks, Gary was involved everywhere. He is a true box-to-box player, often the most mobile of the team towards the end of games. Team-mates came to rely on him to clean up in midfield.
Stoke C (From Glasgow Celtic N/C on 20/10/1994)
Kilmarnock (Free on 18/8/1995) SL 138+13/9 SLC 10+1 SC 13 Others 8
Norwich C (£100,000 on 22/3/2001) P/FL 161+7/3 FLC 5 FAC 6 Others 3
Nottingham F (Signed on 4/7/2005) FL 53+12/1 FLC 2 FAC 8/1 Others 4/1
Wycombe W (Free on 18/7/2007) FL 42+1/2 FAC 1 Others 2

HOLT Grant
Born: Carlisle, 12 April 1981
Height: 6'1" **Weight:** 12.7
Grant was unable to reproduce his 2006-07 'Player of the Season' form for Nottingham Forest in 2007-08 but still gave maximum effort, despite being often played out of position on either wing as the management decided to use only one main forward. In a rare start as the main striker against Orient in January, he gave his best performance and scored twice. Although still in the squad, Grant was allowed to move on loan to Blackpool in March but could not force his way into their team, making only four substitute appearances before returning to Forest at the end of the season. Will be looking for better this coming term.
Halifax T (Signed from Workington on 16/9/1999) FL 0+6 FLC 1/1 Others 1 (Free to Barrow during 2001 close season)
Sheffield Wed (Free from Barrow on 27/3/2003) FL 12+12/3 FLC 0+1 FAC 2/1 Others 1+2
Rochdale (Signed on 30/1/2004) FL 75/35 FLC 2/1 FAC 4/5 Others 2/2
Nottingham F (Signed on 12/1/2006) FL 74+22/21 FLC 1+2 FAC 5+1/1 Others 3+1/3
Blackpool (Loaned on 20/3/2008) FL 0+4

HONE Daniel Joseph
Born: Croydon, 15 September 1989
Height: 6'2" **Weight:** 12.0
Having started the season as a regular for Lincoln's reserves and the under-18 side, centre-back Danny was thrust onto the first-team scene in Peter Jackson's initial game in charge, coming on as a substitute for the injured Lee Beevers. Danny, who joined City as an under-11,

tackled the transition between reserve and League football with maturity beyond his fledgling years and was rewarded with a professional contract that will run until the summer of 2010. He also shared the 'Young Player of the Season' award with striker Lenell John-Lewis.
Lincoln C (From trainee on 6/12/2007) FL 20+3/1 FAC 2

HOOLAHAN Wesley (Wes)
Born: Dublin, 10 August 1983
Height: 5'6" **Weight:** 10.3
International Honours: RoI: 1; U21-12
After being on loan from Livingston during the previous season, Wes signed for Blackpool on a more permanent basis. Still considered one the best midfielders in the Championship, he made his international debut as a substitute for the Republic of Ireland against Colombia in a friendly in May. Playing predominantly on the left, his close control, skill and dribbling ability attracted increased attention from potential buyers. He scored six goals in the season, among them penalties in two derby games, against Burnley in the 2-2 draw at Turf Moor and against Preston in the 1-0 win at Deepdale, a cheeky chip from the spot.
Livingston (Signed from Shelbourne on 1/1/2006) SL 14+2 SLC 1 SC 0+2
Blackpool (Signed on 24/7/2006) FL 80+7/13 FLC 2+3/1 FAC 3+1/1 Others 3/1

HOOPER Gary
Born: Loughton, 26 January 1988
Height: 5'9" **Weight:** 11.2
Club Honours: FAT '05
A small, mobile centre-forward, Gary struggled for opportunities at Southend before taking over from Matt Harrold as a strike partner with Leon Clarke for an extended spell. A shortage of goals and an apparent lack of confidence cost him his place. Despite a scoring return in January at Bournemouth, Gary was loaned out to League Two side Hereford and played a major part in their promotion in his productive three-month stay. His pace, enthusiasm and hard work were much appreciated at Edgar Street but it was his ability in front of goal that caught the eye. His talent at spotting a scoring opportunity, with right foot or left, brought him 11 goals in just 19 appearances and his selfless work produced many goals for others.
Southend U (Free from Grays Ath on 10/8/2006) FL 12+20/2 FLC 3+4/2 FAC 2+2 Others 0+1
Leyton Orient (Loaned on 15/3/2007) FL 2+2/2
Hereford U (Loaned on 28/1/2008) FL 19/11

HOPE Richard Paul
Born: Stockton, 22 June 1978
Height: 6'2" **Weight:** 12.6
Richard moved to Wrexham in June, just days after playing for Shrewsbury in the first play-off final of a reconstructed Wembley. The Reds moved quickly to sign him on a three-year deal but Richard was unable to produce his best form in the centre of defence and was put on transfer list in May, with two years of his contract to run.
Blackburn Rov *(From trainee on 9/8/1995)*
Darlington *(Free on 17/1/1997) FL 62+1/1 FLC 3 FAC 1 Others 0+1*
Northampton T *(Signed on 18/12/1998) FL 113+22/7 FLC 3 FAC 5+3 Others 7+1*
York C *(Free on 8/8/2003) FL 36/2 FLC 1 FAC 1 Others 1*
Chester C *(Free on 30/7/2004) FL 26+2 FAC 2 Others 1+2/1*
Shrewsbury T *(Free on 12/8/2005) FL 75/2 FLC 3 FAC 2/1 Others 4*
Wrexham *(Free on 18/7/2007) FL 33 FLC 1 FAC 1 Others 1*

HORLOCK Kevin
Born: Erith, 1 November 1972
Height: 6'0" **Weight:** 12.0
Club Honours: Div 2 '96; Div 1 '02
International Honours: NI: 32; B-2
Having been released by Doncaster in January, the experienced former Northern Ireland international was signed by Mansfield's new manager Paul Holland in March, having earlier had a trial with Scunthorpe. Needed to add experience and some steel to Town's midfield, Kevin was desperately short of match practice on his arrival and was used only sparingly from the bench.
West Ham U *(From trainee on 1/7/1991)*
Swindon T *(Free on 27/8/1992) P/FL 151+12/22 FLC 15+2/1 FAC 12/3 Others 5+2*
Manchester C *(£1,250,000 on 31/1/1997) P/FL 184+20/37 FLC 15+1/3 FAC 9/1 Others 3/1*
West Ham U *(£300,000 on 15/8/2003) FL 23+4/1 FLC 2 FAC 4*
Ipswich T *(Free on 9/7/2004) FL 46+12 FLC 1+1 FAC 1 Others 1*
Doncaster Rov *(Free on 10/2/2006) FL 15/1*
Scunthorpe U *(Free on 8/1/2008)*
Mansfield T *(Loaned on 21/3/2008) FL 0+5*

HORSFIELD Geoffrey (Geoff) Malcolm
Born: Barnsley, 1 November 1973
Height: 5'10" **Weight:** 11.0
Club Honours: FC '98; Div 2 '99
With the arrival of Bryan Robson as Sheffield United's manager, Geoff hoped for a fresh start at Bramall Lane in 2007-08 but after a few pre-season games he made just two Carling Cup appearances as a substitute, scoring his first goal for

the Blades at MK Dons. To keep match-fit, the experienced target-man joined Championship strugglers Scunthorpe at the end of January, on loan until the end of the season. He had an immediate impact, inspiring a victory against Charlton on his debut and proving a handful for defences. Eventually, he struggled to offer any real goal threat and dropped out of the team once the club's relegation was confirmed in April. Was released at the end of the campaign.
Scarborough *(From juniors on 10/7/1992) FL 12/1 FAC 1 Others 0+2 (Free to Halifax T on 31/3/1994)*
Halifax T *(Free from Witton A on 8/5/1997) FL 10/7 FLC 4/1*
Fulham *(£325,000 on 12/10/1998) FL 54+5/ 22 FLC 6/6 FAC 8+1/3*
Birmingham C *(£2,000,000 + on 12/7/ 2000) P/FL 75+33/23 FLC 10+1/3 FAC 1+1 Others 5/2*
Wigan Ath *(Signed on 6/9/2003) FL 16/7 FLC 1*
West Bromwich A *(£1,000,000 on 18/12/2003) P/FL 48+19/14 FLC 2/1 FAC 2+2*
Sheffield U *(Loaned on 13/2/2006) FL 1+2*
Sheffield U *(Signed on 3/7/2006) FLC 0+2/1*
Leeds U *(Loaned on 4/8/2006) FL 11+3/2 FLC 1*
Leicester C *(Loaned on 31/1/2007) FL 9+4/2*
Scunthorpe U *(Loaned on 31/1/2008) FL 11+1*

HORWOOD Evan David
Born: Billingham, 10 March 1986
Height: 6'0" **Weight:** 11.2
Freed by Gretna last January, Evan came into the Carlisle side in early February and from then on was a fixture at left-back. One of the younger members of the side, his game rapidly developed as the season progressed and he produced a series of confident performances.
Sheffield U *(From trainee on 12/11/2004) FLC 0+1*
Stockport Co *(Loaned on 11/3/2005) FL 10*
Chester C *(Loaned on 31/11/2006) FL 1*
Darlington *(Loaned on 13/10/2006) FL 2*
Darlington *(Loaned on 1/1/2007) FL 18 Others 1*
Gretna *(Loaned on 31/8/2007) SL 15/1 SC 1/1*
Carlisle U *(Signed on 17/1/2008) FL 19 Others 2*

HOSKINS William (Will) Richard
Born: Nottingham, 6 May 1986
Height: 5'11" **Weight:** 11.2
International Honours: E: Yth
A talented striker, especially when used in a withdrawn role with the ball to his feet, Will found it hard to settle at Watford in 2007-08 and went on loan to Millwall

in September. Able to turn defences and link up play, he did the Lions proud in his short stay by scoring four goals in 12 appearances. On his return, he did not feature at Watford and agreed another loan, this time to his home-town club Nottingham Forest. After only a couple of games he suffered a back injury that ended his season in February. Before the injury, Forest had agreed a fee with Watford.
Rotherham U *(From trainee on 16/2/2005) FL 35+38/23 FLC 2+1/1 FAC 1+2 Others 1+1/1*
Watford *(Signed on 5/1/2007) P/FL 4+6 FLC 2*
Millwall *(Loaned on 18/9/2007) FL 9+1/2 FAC 2/2*
Nottingham F *(Loaned on 8/2/2008) FL 2*

HOULT Russell
Born: Ashby-de-la-Zouch, 22 November 1972
Height: 6'3" **Weight:** 14.9
After being signed by Stoke to understudy Steve Simonsen and being often used as such, Russell eventually made his League debut in City's goal at Plymouth in December. Unfortunately, he was sent off for a professional foul and never appeared in the first team again, signing for Notts County on loan in February. The move came about after the regular 'keeper, Kevin Pilkington, suffered a broken ankle and Russell quickly settled in with a series of solid performances. Dominating his area, showing a clean pair of hands, he conceded only one goal in the last six home games to help save County from the drop and his reliability spread confidence to those in front of him. Was out of contract in the summer and looking for a new club.
Leicester C *(From trainee on 28/3/1991) FL 10 FLC 3 Others 1*
Lincoln C *(Loaned on 27/8/1991) FL 2 FLC 1*
Bolton W *(Loaned on 3/11/1993) FL 3+1 Others 1*
Lincoln C *(Loaned on 12/8/1994) FL 15 Others 1*
Derby Co *(£300,000 on 17/2/1995) P/FL 121+2 FLC 8 FAC 7*
Portsmouth *(£300,000 + on 21/1/2000) FL 40 FLC 4*
West Bromwich A *(£500,000 on 5/1/2001) P/FL 189+1 FLC 10 FAC 11 Others 2*
Nottingham F *(Loaned on 16/9/2005) FL 8*
Stoke C *(Free on 31/1/2007) FL 1 FLC 1*
Notts Co *(Loaned on 22/2/2008) FL 14*

HOWARD Brian Richard William
Born: Winchester, 23 January 1983
Height: 5'8" **Weight:** 11.1
International Honours: E: Yth
Having signed a new two-year contract

before the season began, Brian went on to enjoy an outstanding campaign for Barnsley. He celebrated his appointment as club captain by leading through example and from his central midfield position was able to prompt the rest of his team. Brian is an excellent passer and showed throughout the season his ability to time his arrival in the penalty area and find the target. The obvious highlight was his stoppage-time winner against Liverpool at Anfield in the great FA Cup upset. He had a 100 per cent record from the penalty spot and was deservedly voted into the PFA Championship select team.
Southampton *(From trainee on 27/1/2000)*
Swindon T *(Free on 6/8/2003) FL 49+21/9*

FLC 3+1 FAC 4/1 Others 4+1
Barnsley *(Free on 6/7/2005) FL 108+6/26*
FLC 1 FAC 10/1 Others 4

HOWARD Charlie Sydney
Born: Southwark, 26 November 1989
Height: 6'0"   **Weight:** 13.7
A talented Gillingham midfielder, he was captain of the successful youth team and made his League debut in the 2-1 defeat at Port Vale on Easter Monday. A hard-working, terrier type of player with good skills, he is one for the future and was voted Gillingham's 'Young Player of the Year'.
Gillingham *(From trainee on 10/12/2007) FL 1 Others 1+1*

HOWARD Michael (Mike) Anthony
Born: Birkenhead, 2 December 1978
Height: 5'9"   **Weight:** 11.13
Club Honours: Div 3 '00
Mike's chances as Morecambe's left-back were restricted by Danny Adams' consistency and he started only twice in the League. He played in the early rounds of the Johnstone's Paint Trophy but was allowed out on loan for the second half of the season and appeared regularly for Oxford United before returning to Christie Park. The popular squad member will again be challenging Adams.
Tranmere Rov *(From trainee on 9/7/1997)*
Swansea C *(Free on 6/2/1998) FL 221+7/2 FLC 9 FAC 15 Others 8*
Morecambe *(Free on 29/7/2004) FL 2+2 Others 3+1*

HOWARD Steven (Steve) John
Born: Durham, 10 May 1976
Height: 6'2"   **Weight:** 14.6
Club Honours: Div 1 '05
International Honours: S: B-1
Goals were elusive in Steve's first crack at the Premiership, his only success for Derby coming against Manchester United at Old Trafford. His effort never flagged, although he could have wished for better service. Leicester came in with a good offer and Steve left with the good wishes of supporters, who appreciated his honest approach. The powerful striker had one glorious afternoon at West Bromwich where he became the first Foxes' marksman to collect a hat-trick on opposition turf since the days of Gary Lineker. His body language during the rest of the campaign rather betrayed his thoughts on the lack of suitable service, the same problem he had at Derby, and he will be hoping for better in 2008-09.
Hartlepool U *(Free from Tow Law on 8/8/1995) FL 117+25/26 FLC 7+1/1 FAC 5/2 Others 7/3*
Northampton T *(£120,000 on 22/2/1999) FL 67+19/18 FLC 4 FAC 2+1 Others 2*
Luton T *(£50,000 on 22/3/2001) FL 209+3/95 FLC 7/2 FAC 8/5 Others 1*
Derby Co *(£1,000,000 on 27/7/2006) P/FL 57+6/17 FLC 2+1/1 FAC 3 Others 3/2*
Leicester C *(£1,500,000 on 1/1/2008) FL 20+1/6 FAC 1*

HOWARD Timothy (Tim) Matthew
Born: North Brunswick, New Jersey, USA, 6 March 1979
Height: 6'3"   **Weight:** 14.12
Club Honours: CS '03; FAC '04; FLC '06
International Honours: USA: 29; U21
Tim had an excellent season with Everton

Brian Howard

and established himself as one of the most consistent goalkeepers in the top-flight. The American international was an integral part of the Blues' excellent campaign, one in which he set a new club record by becoming the first Everton 'keeper to concede less than a goal a game in his first 50 matches. His personal highlight was a brave performance in the UEFA Cup tie against Fiorentina. A feisty competitor and excellent shot-stopper with a good command of his area, Tim enjoyed a near flawless campaign.
Manchester U *(£2,300,000 from New York/ New Jersey Metrostars, USA on 22/7/2003) PL 44+1 FLC 8 FAC 10 Others 14*
Everton *(Signed on 5/7/2006) PL 72 FLC 4 FAC 1 Others 8*

HOWE Jermaine **Renee (Rene)**
Born: Bedford, 22 October 1986
Height: 6'0" **Weight:** 14.3
Rene was signed from non-League Kettering as a striker but was only a fringe player at Peterborough before joining Rochdale on loan in January. After a slow start, he scored in successive games and formed a productive partnership with the smaller Adam Le Fondre. He really came to the fore towards the end of the season, netting six times in six games, including a hat-trick as a substitute against Grimsby. Having scored the goal against Morecambe that ensured a place in the play-offs, Rene signed off from his spell at Rochdale with an appearance at Wembley.
Peterborough U *(Signed from Kettering T, ex Bedford T, on 19/7/2007) FL 2+13/1 FAC 0+2 Others 1*
Rochdale *(Loaned on 8/1/2008) FL 19+1/9 Others 2+1*

HOWELL Luke Alexander
Born: Heathfield, 5 January 1987
Height: 5'10" **Weight:** 10.5
Club Honours: AMC '08
Signed just before the season, having impressed MK Dons while on trial following his release by Gillingham, Luke is a versatile right-sided player who had few chances to shine in the first half of the season through a combination of his injuries and the team's winning form. He eventually earned a starting place at right-back in the win at Notts County on Boxing Day and played in the next six games before falling out of contention. He was recalled for the final home game against Morecambe, picking up the sponsors' 'Man of the Match' award for a determined central midfield display.

Gillingham *(From trainee on 25/7/2006) FL 0+1 Others 1*
MK Dons *(Free on 11/8/2007) FL 8 FLC 1 Others 2*

HOWELLS Jake Thomas
Born: St Albans, 18 April 1991
Height: 5'9" **Weight:** 11.8
Having played three successful Luton reserve games in three weeks at left-back, Jake earned a surprise call into the first-team squad, as a reward for his performances, in the final game of last season. He made his debut as a substitute, replacing fellow left-back Sol Davis, and did well in a very poor game. Afterwards he told the local media that

he had turned down an offer to sign for Fulham to join Luton.
Luton T *(Trainee) FL 0+1*

HOWLAND David
Born: Ballynahinch, 17 September 1986
Height: 5'11" **Weight:** 11.8
International Honours: NI: U21-4
David signed on loan from Birmingham in January until the end of the season. The central midfield player made his Port Vale debut in a 3-1 home defeat by Bournemouth but did well enough to become a regular. A wholehearted player with good stamina, his enthusiasm endeared him to the fans. A Northern Ireland under-21 international, winning

Jonny Howson

four caps, he scored once for the Vale, a last-minute winner against Leyton Orient. His season ended three games early through a leg injury and he returned to Birmingham, but they gave him a free transfer and he was immediately offered a contract by Vale.
Birmingham C (From trainee on 19/11/2004)
Port Vale (Loaned on 23/1/2008) FL 17/1

HOWSON Jonathan (Jonny) Mark

Born: Morley, 21 May 1988
Height: 5'11" **Weight:** 12.1
Local lad Jonny wrote himself into Leeds' folklore with the goals that took them to Wembley. Voted the 'Young Player of the Season', he scored twice at Carlisle in the League One play-off second leg, the winner coming in stoppage-time. Dougie Freedman's late goal in the first leg gave United a lifeline that the youngster seized dramatically. He was one of the major successes at the club in a season that ultimately ended in the disappointment of defeat by Doncaster at Wembley. He built on the promise shown in the previous campaign with a string of impressive displays and was carefully nurtured by manager Dennis Wise, who tipped him for a bright future. Jonny blossomed in new boss Gary McAllister's passing style of play, scoring United's goal in the 1-1 draw at Northampton and opening his Elland Road account in the crucial 3-2 victory over promotion rivals Carlisle in April.
Leeds U (From trainee on 10/7/2006) FL 27+8/4 FLC 2+1 FAC 3 Others 5/2

HOYTE Justin Raymond

Born: Leytonstone, 20 November 1984
Height: 5'11" **Weight:** 10.10
Club Honours: CS '04
International Honours: E: U21-18; Yth
Justin was rarely in Arsenal's first team and had to make do with appearances in the club's run to the Carling Cup semi-finals. With the arrival of Bacary Sagna, Justin was relegated to third choice right-back and while his commitment cannot be faulted, it is difficult to see him breaking through to become a regular Arsenal player. He played all five Carling Cup ties along with five Premier League games, two in the Champions' League and three in the FA Cup.
Arsenal (From trainee on 1/7/2002) PL 24+10/1 FLC 14 FAC 4+4 Others 8+4
Sunderland (Loaned on 31/8/2005) PL 27/1 FLC 1 FAC 2

HREIDARSSON Hermann

Born: Reykjavik, Iceland, 11 July 1974
Height: 6'1" **Weight:** 13.1
Club Honours: Div 3 '99; FAC '08
International Honours: Iceland: 75; U21-6
Hermann signed for Portsmouth at the end of May after exercising a clause in his contract that allowed him to leave Charlton on a free transfer if they were relegated. A tall, powerful, quick and very experienced defender, he slotted in superbly and contributed to Pompey's extremely frugal defence that kept 22 clean sheets in all competitions last season. Normally playing on the left of the back four, he also figured in the centre of defence when required. He likes to get forward when the opportunity arises and scored three Premier League goals. It is a testimony to him that he is almost certainly one of the first names on the team-sheet each week. He was voted Iceland's 'Footballer of the Year' for the third time and is an Icelandic international with 75 caps, making him the third most capped Icelander of all time. He needs six more caps to move into second place. His wife is also a footballer and captained the Icelandic national team while Hermann, away from the pitch, is noted for his Elvis Presley-like performances.
Crystal Palace (Signed from IBV, Iceland on 9/8/1997) P/FL 32+5/2 FLC 5/1 FAC 4 Others 2
Brentford (£850,000 on 24/9/1998) FL 41/6 FLC 2 FAC 2/1 Others 3/1
Wimbledon (£2,500,000 on 14/10/1999) P/FL 25/1 FAC 2
Ipswich T (£4,000,000 + on 19/8/2000) P/FL 101+1/2 FLC 11 FAC 6 Others 9/1
Charlton Ath (£500,000 + on 27/3/2003) PL 130+2/3 FLC 8/1 FAC 9
Portsmouth (Free on 1/6/2007) PL 30+2/3 FLC 0+1 FAC 6

HUBERTZ Poul

Born: Roskilde, Denmark, 21 September 1976
Height: 6'5" **Weight:** 14.9
After arriving on a free transfer from Millwall in the summer, the tall striker showed amazing dribbling skills and an ability to hold up the ball for Northampton's runners. Often he would be forced into a corner by defenders only to turn and send the ball into the penalty area. His goal against Nottingham Forest at Sixfields was unforgettable, converted with an agile overhead kick. Good in the air and clever on the floor, Poul makes up with skill what he lacks in pace. He was released at the end of the season but went out with a bang by scoring

the winner in the last match against Tranmere.
Millwall (Signed from Aalborg BK, Denmark, ex Roskilde, Frem, Farum, Frem - loan, Herfolge, on 2/8/2006) FL 14+20/9 FLC 1+1/1 FAC 0+2
Northampton T (Free on 8/8/2007) FL 33+7/13 FLC 2 FAC 4 Others 1

HUCKERBY Darren Carl

Born: Nottingham, 23 April 1976
Height: 5'10" **Weight:** 11.12
Club Honours: Div 1 '02, '04
International Honours: E: B-1; U21-4
The season ended with the news that Darren was not to be offered a new contract at Norwich, creating a considerable stir among Canary fans who will always remember him for his match-winning displays in the four-and-a-half years he spent with the Canaries. Possessing exciting acceleration, he often terrorises defences with his pace and direct running. Preferring to operate off the left flank, cutting in to use his stronger right foot, he ended his Norwich career with 48 goals and countless assists. It remains to be seen where Darren will pursue his career next but it looks possible that he may enjoy a season or two in Major League Soccer before retiring to his Norfolk home.
Lincoln C (From trainee on 14/7/1993) FL 20+8/5 FLC 2 Others 1/2
Newcastle U (£400,000 on 10/11/1995) PL 0+1 FAC 0+1
Millwall (Loaned on 6/9/1996) FL 6/3
Coventry C (£1,000,000 on 23/11/1996) PL 85+9/28 FLC 2 FAC 12/6
Leeds U (£4,000,000 on 12/8/1999) PL 11+29/2 FLC 1+1/2 FAC 1+2 Others 1+11/2
Manchester C (£2,250,000 + on 29/12/2000) P/FL 44+25/22 FLC 2+3/6 FAC 6+1/2 Others 1/1
Nottingham F (Loaned on 24/2/2003) FL 9/5 Others 2
Norwich C (£750,000 on 12/9/2003) P/FL 177+13/41 FLC 5/2 FAC 8/5

HUDDLESTONE Thomas (Tom) Andrew

Born: Nottingham, 28 December 1986
Height: 6'3" **Weight:** 14.12
Club Honours: FLC '08
International Honours: E: U21-26; Yth
Tottenham's Tom was the subject of a widely-reported story to the effect that new coach Juande Ramos had ordered him to lose about a stone in weight. Absent from the team for a while, he clearly responded well and once he won back his place in the squad in December, continued to play a full part in the season, earning a Carling Cup winners' medal off the bench.

Tom Huddlestone

Tom is a magnificent passer of the ball, short or from distance, and opens up defences many times with his precision. His height perhaps prevents him being quite so influential in midfield, when other attributes are required, such as consistent ball-winning, pace and the ability to turn quickly. Tom can cover at centre-back but mainly played in Tottenham's midfield last season, as he did in his England under-21 appearances. He was named in Fabio Capello's 30-man full England squad for the two end-of-season friendlies.
Derby Co *(From trainee on 27/2/2004)* FL 84+4 FLC 2 FAC 3 Others 2
Tottenham H *(£1,000,000 on 1/7/2005)* PL 33+20/4 FLC 5+4/3 FAC 3+2 Others 11+4
Wolverhampton W *(Loaned on 25/10/2005)* FL 12+1/1

HUDSON Mark
Born: Bishop Auckland, 24 October 1980
Height: 5'10" **Weight:** 11.3
Freed by Huddersfield in the close season, Mark signed for Rotherham after several other clubs had been after him but he missed the early games when picking up an injury in pre-season. Once fully fit, he was virtually an automatic choice in midfield and scored a number of vital goals, many coming from strikes around the edge of the penalty area. He also provided vital passes for those around him and has a good vision of the game.
Middlesbrough *(From trainee on 5/7/1999)* PL 0+5 FAC 0+1
Chesterfield *(Loaned on 13/8/2002)* FL 15+1/1 FLC 1 FAC 0+1 Others 0+1
Carlisle U *(Loaned on 10/12/2002)* FL 14+1/1
Chesterfield *(Free on 21/3/2003)* FL 72+5/8 FLC 1 FAC 1 Others 3
Huddersfield T *(Free on 7/7/2005)* FL 55+6/6 FLC 1+1 FAC 4 Others 2
Rotherham U *(Free on 9/7/2007)* FL 30+1/9 FAC 2

HUDSON Mark Alexander
Born: Guildford, 30 March 1982
Height: 6'3" **Weight:** 12.6
The Crystal Palace central defender, who took over as club captain in February, had a great season, missing only one game. Palace had the best defensive record in the Championship, conceding only 42 goals in the 46 matches, and Mark was one of the prime reasons for that comforting solidity. With excellent heading ability at both ends of the pitch, he was disappointed to score only two goals in the campaign. Was out of contract in the summer.
Fulham *(From trainee on 6/4/1999)* FLC 2+1
Oldham Ath *(Loaned on 25/8/2003)* FL 15 Others 1
Crystal Palace *(£550,000 on 16/1/2004)* P/FL 112+8/7 FLC 8 FAC 6 Others 2

HUGHES Aaron William
Born: Cookstown, 8 November 1979
Height: 6'0" **Weight:** 11.2
International Honours: NI: 59; B-2; Yth
One of the most consistent players to wear a Fulham shirt last season, he usually played as a central defender. Aaron seemed to form defensive partnerships with ease though his best form came alongside Norwegian Brede Hangeland. A composed never-say-die defender who is solid in the tackle and an excellent distributor of the ball, Aaron joined Fulham from Aston Villa in the summer, though a pre-season injury delayed his debut until mid-September. Once selected, he remained an integral part of the team, missing out only during a short injury spell around the turn of the year. Having proved a capable captain at international level, it came as no surprise when Aaron was chosen to lead Fulham during much of Brian McBride's absence. He continued to add to his Northern Ireland caps.
Newcastle U *(From trainee on 11/3/1997)* PL 193+12/4 FLC 9+1 FAC 15+4/1 Others 39+5/1
Aston Villa *(£1,500,000 on 6/8/2005)* PL 50+4 FLC 5 FAC 5
Fulham *(£1,000,000 on 5/7/2007)* PL 29+1 FLC 1 FAC 1

HUGHES Andrew (Andy) John
Born: Manchester, 2 January 1978
Height: 5'11" **Weight:** 12.1
Club Honours: Div 3 '98

Mark Hudson (Crystal Palace)

On the same day that Leeds' 15-point deduction was confirmed just before the start of the season, manager Dennis Wise swooped to sign versatile Andy from Norwich in time to play in the opening victory at Tranmere. Leeds' supporters enjoyed Andy's 100-per-cent commitment, although it earned him ten yellow cards, and ability to fill a variety of positions, often switching several times within a game. Central midfield and left-back were his best positions and he captained the side on a few occasions. His only goal was in United's penultimate away game of the season, a 2-0 win at Millwall.
Oldham Ath *(From trainee on 20/1/1996)* FL 18+15/1 FLC 1+1 FAC 3+1 Others 1+2
Notts Co *(£150,000 on 29/1/1998)* FL 85+25/17 FLC 6+1/1 FAC 10/2 Others 2
Reading *(Free on 16/7/2001)* FL 157+9/18 FLC 7/1 FAC 6+1 Others 3
Norwich C *(£500,000 on 21/7/2005)* FL 63+9/2 FLC 4 FAC 2+1
Leeds U *(Signed on 10/8/2007)* FL 32+8/1 FAC 1 Others 0+2

HUGHES Bryan
Born: Liverpool, 19 June 1976
Height: 5'9" **Weight:** 11.2
Bryan's Hull debut, after he was their major summer signing from Charlton, was his 500th career appearance. Mainly because of the outstanding form of Dean Marney, Bryan spent much of the campaign on the left of midfield and made a telling contribution as Hull

equalled their highest League position, third in the Championship. Comfortable on the ball with a fine array of passing, his earlier experiences with Birmingham brought a significant shift when he was restored to his preferred central midfield role for the play-off matches that led to Wembley and promotion to the top flight for the first time. Despite a career record of 72 goals, Bryan's only strike of the season was the fifth in a 5-0 win against Southampton in March.
Wrexham *(From trainee on 7/7/1994)* FL 71+23/12 FLC 2 FAC 13+3/7 Others 6+1/1
Birmingham C *(£750,000 + on 12/3/1997)* P/FL 197+51/34 FLC 17+5/3 FAC 8+5/4 Others 6+2/1
Charlton Ath *(Free on 2/7/2004)* PL 47+27/5 FLC 5+2 FAC 8/5
Hull C *(Free on 30/6/2007)* FL 26+9/1 FLC 1 Others 3

HUGHES Jeffrey (Jeff) Edward
Born: Larne, N Ireland, 29 May 1985
Height: 6'1" **Weight:** 11.0
International Honours: NI: 2; U21-7
The young Northern Ireland left-back was signed for Crystal Palace by Peter Taylor in July 2007 from Lincoln. However, with Tony Craig taking the number three shirt Jeff played more in midfield or on the left wing before being put on the transfer list soon after Neil Warnock's arrival as manager. This resulted in loan moves to Peterborough in November and Bristol Rovers in March. Jeff's best game for Peterborough, a 3-1 FA Cup win at Colchester, was also his last as a training injury prevented his debut for the Pirates and ended his season.
Lincoln C *(Free from Larne on 24/8/2005)* FL 55+8/8 FLC 1 Others 4/3
Crystal Palace *(£250,000 on 5/7/2007)* FL 4+6
Peterborough U *(Loaned on 22/11/2007)* FL 2+5/1 FAC 1+1

HUGHES Jerahl
Born: Brighton, 10 August 1989
Height: 5'7" **Weight:** 11.9
After being unable to win a professional contract at Crystal Palace, despite starring in the FA Youth Cup side that reached the fifth round, Jerahl signed for Yeovil in the summer following an impressive trial. A pacy winger able to play on either flank, Jerahl has the ability to go past defenders and has an eye for goal. Unfortunately, he was unable to break through, making just two substitute appearances before being released.
Yeovil T *(From trainee at Crystal Palace on 25/7/2007)* FL 0+1 Others 0+1

HUGHES Lee
Born: Smethwick, 22 May 1976
Height: 5'10" **Weight:** 11.6
International Honours: E: SP-4
Lee joined Oldham in controversial
circumstances last September following
his release from prison after a well-
publicised court case. Despite the national
media attention and pressure focussed
around his return to the professional
game, Lee began to make a big impact
after he finally regained full match-fitness.
He netted his first goals for the club in
a 3-0 away win at Bournemouth in late
November and went on to hit seven in
15 League starts. Still a powerful leader
of the line and a predatory finisher, his
contribution was disappointingly cut short
after January following a series of groin
problems that eventually required surgery.
*West Bromwich A (£250,000 + from
Kidderminster Hrs on 19/5/1997) FL
137+19/78 FLC 10+3/4 FAC 6/2 Others 2/1*
*Coventry C (£5,000,000 on 9/8/2001) FL
38+4/15 FLC 1+1*
*West Bromwich A (£2,500,000 on
30/8/2002) P/FL 35+20/11 FLC 2+3/2 (Freed
during 2004 close season)*
*Oldham Ath (Free, time away from football,
on 28/8/2007) FL 15+3/7 FAC 3/1*

HUGHES Liam John
Born: Stourbridge, 11 September 1988
Height: 6'2" **Weight:** 11.9
Liam was signed by Bury on the deadline
day on loan from Wolverhampton and
started once, entering from the bench
on a further three occasions. The young
forward, who can also play wide, showed
good pace and technique for the Shakers
as well as a willingness to try his luck at
goal from any range.
*Wolverhampton W (From trainee on
2/3/2007)*
*Bury (Loaned on 22/11/2007) FL 1+3 FAC
0+1*

HUGHES Mark Anthony
Born: Dungannon, 16 September 1983
Height: 5'10" **Weight:** 12.4
International Honours: NI: 2; U23-1;
U21-12; Yth
The hard-working midfielder was given
the chance to resurrect his League
career when he moved to Chester from
Stevenage Borough during the summer.
Mark started last season in excellent form
and was a key figure in the centre of
Chester's midfield as the Blues challenged
for a play-off place in the early part of the
campaign. However, like many members
of the team, he struggled to impose
his authority after Christmas as Chester
only won two more games in 2008. The
former Northern Ireland international

contributed four goals for the Blues,
including almost identical long-range
efforts in successive home games against
Peterborough and Bury.
Tottenham H (From trainee on 12/7/2001)
Northampton T (Loaned on 27/8/2004) FL 3
*Oldham Ath (Free on 19/11/2004) FL
55+5/1 FLC 1 FAC 7 Others 2+3 (Free to
Thurrock on 3/11/2006)*
*Chesterfield (Free from Thurrock on
3/11/2006) FL 2/1 FAC 1 (Free to Stevenage
Borough on 19/1/2007)*
*Chester C (Free on 10/8/2007) FL 39+4/4
FLC 1 FAC 1 Others 2*

HUGHES Mark Anthony
Born: Kirkby, 9 December 1986
Height: 6'2" **Weight:** 13.0
Vice-captain Mark helped bottle up the
centre of Northampton's defence last
season with some sterling performances.
A good header of the ball and not afraid
to put in a tackle despite flying boots,
Mark unfortunately missed the last few
games through injury.
*Everton (From trainee on 21/12/2004) PL
0+1 FLC 1+1*
Stockport Co (Loaned on 13/2/2006) FL 3/1
*Northampton T (Signed on 31/1/2007) FL
51+1/3 FLC 2 FAC 4 Others 1*

HUGHES Michael Eamonn
Born: Larne, 2 August 1971
Height: 5'7" **Weight:** 10.13
International Honours: NI: 71; U23-2;
U21-1; Yth; Sch
A free-transfer signing by Iain Dowie
from his former club Crystal Palace in
the summer, Michael was given a one-
year contract at Coventry. The vastly
experienced midfield player suffered with
thigh strains and found it hard to get up
a head of steam. After an early-season
injury, he played only one more game
before December but returned at West
Bromwich and was a major influence
in the 4-2 victory. Rarely squandering
possession Michael may not be the fastest
midfield player at Coventry but was the
one capable of the killer pass. He was
recalled in February when Michael Doyle
was suspended and put in several good
performances in a defence-shielding
role. With a contract option relying on a
number of appearances, he disappeared
but Chris Coleman recalled him at
Colchester and he marshalled the midfield
superbly. Was released in the summer.
*Manchester C (From trainee on 17/8/1988)
FL 25+1/1 FLC 5 FAC 1 Others 1 (£450,000 to
RS Strasbourg, France on 3/8/1992)*
*West Ham U (Loaned from RS Strasbourg,
France on 29/11/1994) PL 15+2/2 FAC 2*
*West Ham U (Loaned from RS Strasbourg,
France on 2/10/1995) PL 28 FLC 2 FAC 3/1*

*West Ham U (Free from RS Strasbourg,
France on 12/8/1996) PL 33+5/3 FLC 5 FAC 2*
*Wimbledon (£1,600,000 on 25/9/1997) P/FL
99+16/13 FLC 5+1/2 FAC 8+1/2*
Birmingham C (Loaned on 28/3/2002) FL 3
*Crystal Palace (Free on 14/8/2003) P/FL
110+16/7 FLC 6/2 FAC 4/1 Others 5*
*Coventry C (Free on 10/7/2007) FL 16+2
FAC 2*

HUGHES Richard Daniel
Born: Glasgow, 25 June 1979
Height: 5'9" **Weight:** 9.12
International Honours: S: 5; U21-9; Yth
Richard, an Italian-raised Scot, continued
to be 'Mr Reliable' or 'Mr Backup'. As the
depth of Portsmouth's squad increased he
did not normally figure regularly, except
around Christmas and the New Year.
However, when injuries or international
calls depleted playing resources, or for
tactical reasons, Richard could always
be expected to fill the breach admirably.
A combative player who never stops
working for the team, he has excellent
ball-winning capacity and distribution. In
his six years with the club he has never let
Pompey down.
*Arsenal (Free from Atalanta, Italy on
11/8/1997)*
*Bournemouth (£20,000 on 5/8/1998) FL
123+8/14 FLC 9+1 FAC 8/2 Others 5*
*Portsmouth (£100,000 on 13/6/2002) P/FL
65+25 FLC 6+2 FAC 7+4/1*
Grimsby T (Loaned on 21/2/2003) FL 12/1

HUGHES Stephen John
Born: Reading, 18 September 1976
Height: 6'0" **Weight:** 12.12
Club Honours: FAYC '94; PL '98; CS '98
International Honours: E: U21-8; Yth;
Sch
Stephen, the Sky Blues' captain, divides
Coventry fans. Goals from the talented
midfielder were again rare, although
against Millwall in the FA Cup he netted
his first at the Ricoh Arena in three years
with a superb free-kick, following a similar
dead-ball goal at Ipswich earlier. Stephen
played a more defensive midfield role
last season and gave some wholehearted
displays with solid tackling. After Chris
Coleman's arrival, Stephen was restored
to the captaincy but when asked to play
a more forward role towards the end of
the season, appeared to lack the pace to
hurt the opposition. He was in the wars
again, a depressed cheekbone against
Watford and concussion against Leicester
after being hit by a fierce clearance by
Marcus Hall. Stephen was out of contract
this summer.
*Arsenal (From trainee on 15/7/1995) PL
22+27/4 FLC 5+3/1 FAC 7+6/1 Others 2+4/1*
Fulham (Loaned on 26/7/1999) FL 3 FLC 1

Everton (£500,000 + on 10/3/2000) PL 27+2/1 FLC 1+1 FAC 2/1
Watford (Free on 12/7/2001) FL 11+4 FLC 2
Charlton Ath (Free on 14/8/2003)
Coventry C (Free on 6/7/2004) FL 125+8/6 FLC 7/1 FAC 4/1

HUKE Shane

Born: Reading, 2 October 1985
Height: 5'11" **Weight:** 12.7
Shane joined Dagenham in the summer from Peterborough and played in his normal central midfield position as well as covering at right-back. He scored Dagenham's first away goal in the League, enough to earn what proved an important 1-0 victory at Mansfield. A battling midfielder, Shane radiates energy but missed the February programme with an ankle injury.
Peterborough U (From trainee on 10/10/2003) FL 18+11/1 FLC 0+1 FAC 3 Others 2
Dagenham & Redbridge (Free on 9/7/2007) FL 31+5/2 FLC 0+1 FAC 3/1 Others 3

HULBERT Robin James

Born: Plymouth, 14 March 1980
Height: 5'9" **Weight:** 10.5
International Honours: E: Yth; Sch
Robin began as a Port Vale regular but as results deteriorated, the tough-tackling midfielder became a victim of the changes. His job was to win the ball for others and he did that to good effect, but ankle injuries limited his appearances and he was used spasmodically in the New Year. Probably his best game was in the 3-3 home draw with Leeds when he powered forward to help Vale recover from 2-0 and then 3-2 behind. His final appearance was in the 2-1 home win over Gillingham on Easter Monday and he was released at the end of the season.
Swindon T (From trainee on 25/9/1997) FL 12+17 FLC 1+1 FAC 2
Bristol C (£25,000 on 23/3/2000) FL 21+18 FLC 1+4 Others 5+3 (Free to Telford U on 21/11/2003)
Shrewsbury T (Loaned on 27/3/2003) FL 4+3
Port Vale (Free from Telford U on 29/7/2004) FL 54+13/1 FLC 1 FAC 1+1 Others 2

HULSE Robert (Rob) William

Born: Crewe, 25 October 1979
Height: 6'1" **Weight:** 11.4
Just over nine months after his horrific broken leg, Rob went on as a Sheffield United substitute at Cardiff. Because of an injury to James Beattie, Rob made the starting line-up sooner than expected and worked hard as a target-man. On several occasions he was unlucky not to score, probably affected by the long lay-off. When Beattie was fit, Rob's contributions

were mainly from the bench and, with pre-season games under his belt, he will hope to challenge for a starting place.
Crewe Alex (From trainee on 25/6/1998) FL 97+19/46 FLC 6+1/2 FAC 5+1 Others 2/4
West Bromwich A (£750,000 + on 8/8/2003) P/FL 29+9/10 FLC 5+1/3 FAC 1+1
Leeds U (£800,000 + on 8/2/2005) FL 45+7/18 FLC 1+1 FAC 2/1 Others 3/1
Sheffield U (£2,200,000 + on 31/7/2006) P/FL 38+12/8 FAC 0+3

HUME Iain Edward

Born: Brampton, Canada, 31 October 1983
Height: 5'7" **Weight:** 11.2
International Honours: Canada: 21; Yth
A diminutive striker, sometimes used in a wide or free role, whose wholehearted efforts kept him in the forefront of the Leicester fans' affections. Iain managed to finish as City's leading marksman for the third successive season. Generally scoring in bursts, and almost managing to stave off relegation single-handedly during the closing fixtures, he was the only player to find the net in the last five games. His early strike against Watford was selected as the players' 'Goal of the Season' and he added to his tally of Canadian caps during the season.
Tranmere Rov (From juniors on 6/11/2000) FL 100+50/32 FLC 4+4 FAC 8+2/3 Others 6+3/2
Leicester C (£500,000 on 31/8/2005) FL 101+21/33 FLC 6/1 FAC 4

HUMPHREY Christopher (Chris) Charles

Born: Shrewsbury, 19 September 1987
Height: 5'11" **Weight:** 11.6
Chris has blistering pace as a right-winger but is still learning in his second year at Shrewsbury. Always exciting to watch as he runs at opponents, Chris has work to do on the final product. He was used mainly from the bench and played four times on loan at Stafford in the Blue Square Premier to help boost his confidence. In his most effective games Chris provided opportunities, including the home 3-1 win over Stockport and the 3-3 draw with MK Dons. The Shrewsbury crowd like him and the future could be bright.
Shrewsbury T (From trainee at West Bromwich A on 6/9/2006) FL 7+30 FLC 2 Others 3+3

HUMPHREYS Richard (Ritchie) John

Born: Sheffield, 30 November 1977
Height: 5'11" **Weight:** 14.6
International Honours: E: U21-3; Yth
In another memorable season for the inspirational Hartlepool player, Ritchie

made occasional appearances in midfield, but was usually employed at left-back. With Micky Barron out of action, he took over as captain and during the season reached a personal milestone of 300 League appearances for the club. In February it was announced that he was one of six Hartlepool players, past or present, who would have a street named in their honour. He was voted 'Player of the Season' by supporters and was also named the Hartlepool 'Player of the Century'.
Sheffield Wed (From trainee on 8/2/1996) P/FL 34+33/4 FLC 4+2 FAC 5+4/5
Scunthorpe U (Loaned on 13/8/1999) FL 6/2
Cardiff C (Loaned on 22/11/1999) FL 8+1/2 FAC 1 Others 1
Cambridge U (Free on 2/2/2001) FL 7/3
Hartlepool U (Free on 18/7/2001) FL 306+7/30 FLC 9 FAC 19/1 Others 14+2/1
Port Vale (Loaned on 8/9/2006) FL 5+2

HUNT David John

Born: Dulwich, 10 September 1982
Height: 5'11" **Weight:** 11.9
After joining Shrewsbury from Northampton last summer, David established himself as a strong central midfield player able to take effective free kicks and corners or launch a bullet-like throw into the penalty area, all providing Town's goals. His first goal was from a free kick in the 4-3 home defeat by Rochdale in September and the other, a fine volley, in the 2-0 victory against Macclesfield in December. He may be disappointed with that return and injury at Macclesfield in March kept him out of the run-in. He will hope to be more involved in the season ahead.
Crystal Palace (From trainee on 9/7/2002) FL 2 FLC 0+1
Leyton Orient (Signed on 11/7/2003) FL 57+8/1 FLC 2 FAC 3/1 Others 3+1
Northampton T (Free on 24/3/2005) FL 57+16/3 FLC 1 FAC 5+2 Others 2+1
Shrewsbury T (Free on 7/8/2007) FL 22+5/2 FLC 1+1

HUNT James Malcolm

Born: Derby, 17 December 1976
Height: 5'8" **Weight:** 10.3
This tough midfielder was a regular starter for Grimsby, having arrived from Bristol Rovers in the summer, usually in a holding role in front of the defence. James took the eye in a 2-1 defeat at Rotherham where, despite a line-up hit by injuries and a dismissal, his hard-working display for the ten-man Mariners saw him voted Town's 'Man of the Match'. The solid tackler's consistency also earned him a spell as team captain before Christmas.
Notts Co (From trainee on 15/7/1994) FL

15+4/1 FAC 0+1 Others 2+2/1
Northampton T *(Free on 7/8/1997) FL
150+22/8 FLC 8+2 FAC 7+3/1 Others 10+1/1*
Oxford U *(Free on 12/7/2002) FL 75+5/3
FLC 4/1 FAC 3*
Bristol Rov *(Free on 5/7/2004) FL 93+2/6
FLC 3 FAC 5 Others 5*
Grimsby T *(Free on 15/1/2007) FL 47+5/2
FLC 1 FAC 3 Others 5*

HUNT Lewis James
Born: Birmingham, 25 August 1982
Height: 5'11" **Weight:** 12.8
Club Honours: Div 1 '06
The adaptable defender or midfielder
completed his fifth season at Southend.
After Kerrea Gilbert was dropped,
manager Steve Tilson called on his utility
man to slot in at right-back. Lewis stayed
in the side until the end of January, also
deputising at centre-back and even
left-back three times. He lost his place,
through injury, to Simon Francis, could
not regain it and had to be content with
bench duty. Reliable when used and an
athletic performer, Lewis finished on the
sidelines when he underwent a double
hernia operation. Was released at the end
of the campaign.
Derby Co *(From trainee on 17/2/2001) FL
8+3 FLC 0+2*
Southend U *(Free on 28/10/2003) FL
126+20/2 FLC 7+2/1 FAC 14 Others 10+1*

HUNT Nicholas (Nicky) Brett
Born: Westhoughton, 3 September 1983
Height: 6'1" **Weight:** 13.8
International Honours: E: U21-10
Despite starting as Bolton's first-choice
right-back, a season of further injury
problems and increased competition from
Joey O'Brien and Gretar Steinsson led
to fewer appearances than Nicky would
have hoped. Nicky was unfortunate to
be part of a defence that simply could
not keep a clean sheet at the beginning
of the season, though he quite clearly
improved the attacking side of his game,
showing himself to be a very effective
crosser of the ball when advancing further
upfield. Spending much of the season
flitting in and out of the starting line-up,
he unfortunately dislocated his shoulder
for the sixth time in five years in the home
defeat by Arsenal in March, an injury that
ended his campaign.
Bolton W *(From trainee on 7/7/2001) P/FL
113+15/1 FLC 11 FAC 9+3 Others 10*

HUNT Stephen James
Born: Southampton, 11 November 1984
Height: 6'1" **Weight:** 13.0
Stephen is a tall left-sided defender who
has played mainly in the centre of Notts
County's defence but latterly at left-back.

Young, strong and determined, he is
developing with the benefit of regular
senior football and shows composure in
possession.
Colchester U *(From trainee at Southampton
on 19/7/2004) FL 16+6/1 FLC 2 FAC 1+1
Others 1*
Notts Co *(Free on 31/7/2006) FL 60+9/3 FLC
4 FAC 1 Others 2*

HUNT Stephen Patrick
Born: Port Laoise, Ireland, 1 August 1980
Height: 5'7" **Weight:** 12.6
Club Honours: Ch '06
International Honours: RoI: 11; B-1;
U21-1
A regular for Reading throughout last
season, missing only the Carling Cup tie
at Swansea and the Premiership games
at Arsenal, Stephen spent the majority
of the campaign playing wide on the left
of midfield, although he had a run of
games on the opposite flank when Bobby
Convey came into the starting line-up.
It was during this spell that he scored
in three consecutive games, against
Liverpool, Birmingham and Sunderland.
He impressed the last club so much

that a reported bid of £5-million was
made for his services, which Reading
rejected. Stephen's contract ties him to
the Madejski Stadium for some time to
come but speculation continues about his
immediate future, especially as he remains
a member of the Republic of Ireland
team. Was voted 'Player of the Season'
by readers of the Reading Chronicle
newspaper.
Crystal Palace *(From trainee on 29/6/1999)
FL 0+3*
Brentford *(Free on 6/8/2001) FL 126+10/25
FLC 2+2 FAC 8+3/2 Others 9/3*
Reading *(Free on 30/6/2005) P/FL 68+42/11
FLC 6+1 FAC 5+2/3*

HUNTER Garry Paul
Born: Morecambe, 1 January 1985
Height: 6'0" **Weight:** 12.3
The Morecambe-born midfielder is one
of the smallest players in the League but
what he lacks in height he more than
makes up for in talent and determination.
He worked hard to stop rival midfielders
being comfortable in possession and also
showed that he can spot a pass, with
some clever through balls for his strikers.

Stephen Hunt (Reading)

He scored only one League goal, a rare header at that, which was perhaps a disappointment for a player who used to be regularly on target in the reserves.
Morecambe *(From juniors on 7/5/2003) FL 19+19/1 FLC 0+3 FAC 0+1 Others 5/1*

HUNTINGTON Paul David
Born: Carlisle, 17 September 1987
Height: 6'3" **Weight:** 12.8
International Honours: E: Yth
Leeds snapped up former England youth international Paul from Newcastle after relegation to League One. He made his first start with the winner in a Johnstone's Paint Trophy tie at Darlington but had to bide his time. The chance came when fellow centre-back Rui Marques was away with Angola in the African Cup of Nations. Paul, a good distributor of the ball, took his chance with some assured displays and chipped in with vital away goals in the 1-1 draw at Luton and 2-0 success at Leyton Orient. He was runner-up to Jonny Howson as 'Young Player of the Year' and finished the season as first-choice centre-back alongside Lubo Michalik.
Newcastle U *(From trainee on 20/6/2005) PL 10+1/1 FLC 1 FAC 2 Others 1+1*
Leeds U *(Signed on 31/8/2007) FL 12+5/1 FAC 2 Others 5/1*

HURST Glynn
Born: Barnsley, 17 January 1976
Height: 5'10" **Weight:** 11.10
Ever popular, Glynn began last season aiming to prove his fitness. Unfortunately, goals did not flow for the striker who seemed bemused by Bury's 5-3-2 formation. The fans never lost faith and his intense workrate was always appreciated. Two goals in the Johnstone's Paint Trophy win at Rochdale showed that he still knew where the back of the net was. Glynn's form rose markedly with the arrival of Alan Knill and the change to 4-4-2. Although he shared the task of partnering Andy Bishop with loan-signing Adam Rooney, goals against Brentford, Wrexham and Notts County gave glimpses of how good he can be.
Barnsley *(From trainee at Tottenham H on 13/7/1994) FL 0+8 FLC 1 (Freed on 27/3/1997)*
Swansea C *(Loaned on 15/12/1995) FL 2/1*
Mansfield T *(Loaned on 18/11/1996) FL 5+1 Others 0+1*
Ayr U *(£30,000 from Emley on 23/3/1998) SL 78/49 SLC 6/2 SC 10 Others 1+2*
Stockport Co *(£150,000 on 16/2/2001) FL 22+4/4 FLC 0+1*
Chesterfield *(Free on 14/12/2001) FL 77+7/29 FLC 1 FAC 0+1*

Notts Co *(Free on 5/7/2004) FL 51+8/23 FLC 2 FAC 4+1 Others 1/1*
Shrewsbury T *(Free on 1/1/2006) FL 15+1/3*
Bury *(Signed on 22/9/2006) FL 61+16/17 FLC 1 FAC 4+1/1 Others 2+1/2*

HURST Kevan James
Born: Chesterfield, 27 August 1985
Height: 6'0" **Weight:** 11.7
Club Honours: Div 1 '07
Having completed a summer move to Championship side Scunthorpe, the winger was a key part of the Iron's squad during the first half of the season. A skilful player who delivers a large number of crosses in each game, he quickly became marked as one of the club's danger men. His confidence dropped in the second half of the season and he lost his place for a month but returned on the right-wing in April and celebrated with his first goal for the club in the 3-2 win over Cardiff.
Sheffield U *(From trainee on 24/3/2004) P/FL 0+1 FLC 0+3 FAC 1*
Boston U *(Loaned on 25/3/2004) FL 3+4/1*
Stockport Co *(Loaned on 18/2/2005) FL 14/1*
Chesterfield *(Loaned on 18/8/2005) FL 30+7/4 FLC 1/1 FAC 1+1/1 Others 1*
Chesterfield *(Loaned on 26/7/2006) FL 25/3 FLC 4 Others 1*
Scunthorpe U *(Signed on 31/1/2007) FL 42+4/1 FLC 1 FAC 1*

HURST Paul Michael
Born: Sheffield, 25 September 1974
Height: 5'4" **Weight:** 9.4
Club Honours: AMC '96
Despite struggling to maintain a regular place, this loyal one-club stalwart played enough games to beat Rotherham's all-time appearances record, leaving him just short of the 500 mark. Paul could always be relied upon to give his utmost for the club, both on the left of midfield and in activities off the field, although this may prove to be his last campaign as he was out of contract in the summer. If so, he will be sadly missed for his exemplary attitude.
Rotherham U *(From trainee on 12/8/1993) FL 382+51/13 FLC 11+3 FAC 24+3/3 Others 18+2*

HUSBANDS Michael Paul
Born: Birmingham, 13 November 1983
Height: 5'9" **Weight:** 9.13
Club Honours: FAYC '02
Michael joined Macclesfield from Port Vale in the summer of 2007, starting the first three matches in his accustomed role of striker. He only made one further appearance in the first round of the Johnstone's Paint Trophy at Wrexham,

when he scored the winning goal from the penalty spot. A groin injury kept him out of contention for much of September and October, after which he spent time on loan at Telford. Michael's contract was cancelled by mutual agreement at the end of January 2008.
Aston Villa *(From trainee on 2/4/2002)*
Southend U *(Free on 31/7/2003) FL 3+8 FLC 1 FAC 0+2 Others 0+2*
Walsall *(Free, via trial at Bristol Rov, on 9/9/2005) FL 1+3*
Port Vale *(Free on 13/10/2005) FL 9+38/5 FLC 0+3 FAC 4+1/1 Others 1+1*
Macclesfield T *(Free on 1/8/2007) FL 2 FLC 1 Others 1/1*

HUTCHINGS Stephen (Steve) Henry
Born: Portsmouth, 13 December 1990
Height: 6'0" **Weight:** 12.0
Steve is a Bournemouth second-year youth-team striker who, after appearing regularly for the reserves during last season, was handed a place on the bench. A promising youngster, he gained a debut when going on as a substitute against Millwall and held up the ball effectively to help the side to a 2-0 win.
Bournemouth *(Trainee - Brockenhurst College) FL 0+1*

HUTCHINSON Benjamin (Ben) Lloyd Phillip
Born: Nottingham, 27 November 1987
Height: 5'11" **Weight:** 12.10
Ben, a super-confident player whose pace and strength would unsettle most defenders, played all his games for Middlesbrough last season as a regular contributor from the substitutes' bench. In early October he replaced Tom Craddock on the hour against Manchester City and scored on his debut. Boro were losing 3-1 at Eastlands when Tuncay's shot was parried by City 'keeper Joe Hart straight to Ben. With Ben out of contract at the end of 2007-08 and with both player and club failing to come to an agreement, Ben signed a three-and-a-half year pre-contract agreement with Glasgow Celtic on 26 January. However, when the Scottish giants came back with the offer of a nominal fee to allow the transfer to go through on the closing day of the transfer window the deal was done. Although Gordon Strachan emphasised that Ben would be groomed as one for the future he decided to blood him by giving him eight minutes as a substitute over two Scottish Premier games at Parkhead, against Hearts and Motherwell.
Middlesbrough *(Signed from Arnold T on 31/1/2006) PL 0+8/1 FAC 1*

HUTCHISON Donald (Don)

Born: Gateshead, 9 May 1971
Height: 6'1" **Weight:** 11.8
International Honours: S: 26; B-2

As the last of Luton manager Kevin Blackwell's signings to be given a full League debut, having arrived from Coventry, Don's experience and class were shown in the early rounds of the Cups. He scored the opening goal in the Johnstone's Paint Trophy against Northampton and played occasionally in his preferred central midfield position, although more often used as a substitute to hold the ball late in games. When Chris Coyne was sold, Don moved to the centre of defence. His reading of the game, tackling and ability in the air were outweighed by a lack of speed and new manager Mick Harford's decided Keith Keane was a better partner for Chris Perry. When Perry moved to Southampton; Don returned for the final weeks of the season alongside Keane and although the partnership started well with a draw and a win, the whole team suffered a collective meltdown in form from then on. Was out of contract in the summer and looking for a new club.

Hartlepool U (From trainee on 20/3/1990) FL 19+5/2 FLC 1+1 FAC 2 Others 1
Liverpool (£175,000 on 27/11/1990) P/FL 33+12/7 FLC 7+1/2 FAC 1+2 Others 3+1/1
West Ham U (£1,500,000 on 30/8/1994) PL 30+5/11 FLC 3/2 FAC 0+1
Sheffield U (£1,200,000 on 11/1/1996) FL 70+8/5 FLC 3+2 FAC 5/1 Others 2+1
Everton (£1,000,000 + on 27/2/1998) PL 68+7/10 FLC 4+1/1 FAC 9
Sunderland (£2,500,000 on 19/7/2000) PL 32+2/8 FLC 2/2 FAC 3
West Ham U (£5,000,000 on 31/8/2001) P/FL 36+27/5 FLC 2+1 FAC 3+1 Others 0+1
Millwall (Free on 5/8/2005) FL 7+4/2 FLC 1+2
Coventry C (Free on 24/11/2005) FL 13+25/4 FAC 2
Luton T (Free on 7/8/2007) FL 15+6 FLC 1 FAC 2 Others 2/1

HUTH Robert

Born: Berlin, Germany, 18 August 1984
Height: 6'3" **Weight:** 12.12
Club Honours: PL '05, '06
International Honours: Germany: 17; U21-2; Yth

Persistent injury problems curtailed Robert's appearances and his second season at Middlesbrough proved to be as frustrating as his first. He made an impressive return in early December at Reading and Jonathan Woodgate's surprise departure to Tottenham in the January transfer window gave Robert the ideal opportunity to consolidate his

Middlesbrough place. He immediately struck up an understanding with his defensive partner David Wheater and scored against Newcastle at St James' Park to earn a much-needed, last-gasp draw for Boro. Robert was recalled to the Germany squad for a friendly international in Switzerland but an ankle injury was discovered at the training camp and he returned to England. Middlesbrough fans are looking forward to a full season of play from him, just as he is.

Chelsea (From trainee on 23/8/2001) PL 23+19 FLC 2 FAC 4+3/1 Others 3+8/1
Middlesbrough (£6,000,000 on 31/8/2006) PL 17+8/2 FLC 1 FAC 3+1

HUTTON Alan

Born: Glasgow, 30 November 1984
Height: 6'1" **Weight:** 11.6
Club Honours: SPD '05
International Honours: S: 7; U21-7

The right-back was subject to some 'will he, won't he?' speculation when Tottenham first approached Glasgow Rangers for his transfer. Alan may have missed out on a UEFA Cup losers' medal but the consolation was helping to win the Carling Cup in only his third game. Although ineligible for Tottenham's UEFA Cup challenge, he played 15 times after his January signing, quickly winning over the demanding fans who recognised the 23-year-old Scot as a winner. Tall, strong, fast and direct, he is good in the air and on the ground, and apart from his defensive duties was an integral part of attacks down the right. Alan has yet to score for Tottenham but he has a decent shot, while his crossing and passing more than make up for any shortage of goals. A Scottish international, Alan played six times, including the famous victory over France in Paris in September while still at Ibrox.

Glasgow Rgrs (From juniors on 1/8/2002) SL 89+5/2 SLC 4 SC 3/1 Others 19+1/1
Tottenham H (£9,000,000 on 30/1/2008) PL 14 FLC 1

HYDE Micah Anthony

Born: Newham, 10 November 1974
Height: 5'9" **Weight:** 11.5
Club Honours: Div 2 '98
International Honours: Jamaica: 16

As Peterborough's club captain, Micah was the stabilizing factor in the successful League Two promotion push. Always on hand to help out in the midfield, prompting and organising, he typifies the modern box-to-box player. Despite getting into good shooting positions, he is happy to lay the ball off to those better placed.

Cambridge U (From trainee on 19/5/1993) FL 89+18/13 FLC 3 FAC 7+2 Others 4+1
Watford (£225,000 on 21/7/1997) P/FL 235+18/24 FLC 16+1/4 FAC 13 Others 3
Burnley (Free on 23/7/2004) FL 95+7/1 FLC 6+1 FAC 5/1
Peterborough U (£75,000 on 11/1/2007) FL 51+4 FLC 1 FAC 3 Others 2

HYYPIA Sami

Born: Porvoo, Finland, 7 October 1973
Height: 6'4" **Weight:** 13.5
Club Honours: FLC '01, '03; FAC '01, '06; UEFAC '01; ESC '01, '05; CS '01; UEFACL '05
International Honours: Finland: 90; U21-27; Yth

Prior to the start of last season, the future of the veteran Liverpool and Finnish international central defender seemed uncertain following the emergence of the young Daniel Agger. However, an early season injury to Agger meant that Sami played a fuller part in Liverpool's campaign than manager Rafa Benitez had intended, feeling that the Finn lacked the pace to play more than one game a week. In the event, Sami did not let the side down, resuming his partnership with Jamie Carragher and maintaining his place even after Benitez signed Martin Skrtel in the January transfer window to increase his central defensive options, with Carragher switched to right-back in a number of games. Sami scored four goals, none more important than his equaliser in the Champions' League quarter-final second leg against Arsenal in April. Probably the best goal of his career, he directed a powerful header from a corner into the top of the net in the 30th-minute. It gave Liverpool a foothold after they had been outplayed by the Gunners and a springboard for eventual triumph, although no one could have scripted the dramatic denouement of the game when the advantage swung from one side to the other. Although not selected to start for the semi-final with Chelsea he came on as a substitute in the second leg after Skrtel's injury and was unfortunate to concede the penalty that gave Chelsea a 2-1 advantage in extra-time. Ironically a few minutes later he was brought down in the Chelsea area but no penalty was given. As a reward for his efforts Sami was awarded a new one-year contract in April and while it is unlikely that he will play many games this coming season, his experience will be invaluable and his place in the pantheon of great Liverpool central defenders is assured.

Liverpool (£2,600,000 from Willem II, Holland, ex MyPa, on 7/7/1999) PL 298+4/21 FLC 17/2 FAC 28/2 Others 97+1/8

I

IBEHRE Jabo Oshevire
Born: Islington, 28 January 1983
Height: 6'2" **Weight:** 12.10
Jabo missed the start of last season for
Leyton Orient because he picked up an
ankle injury in pre-season. A big, strong
forward who likes to get the ball down
and run at opposing defenders with pace,
Jabo was used mainly as cover for Adam
Boyd and Wayne Gray. He was out of
contract in the summer.
Leyton Orient (From trainee on 18/7/2001)
FL 112+97/36 FLC 3+3/2 FAC 11+5/1 Others
11+1/2

IDE Charlie Joe
Born: Sunbury, 10 May 1988
Height: 5'8" **Weight:** 10.6
An exciting, diminutive Brentford striker
or outside-right, Charlie had an extremely
disappointing season. A regular until the
end of December, he scored just one
goal, at Luton in the FA Cup, and was
already short on confidence when he
suffered a groin injury. Once fit, he joined
Lewes on loan in March before being
transfer listed at the end of the campaign.
Brentford (From trainee on 27/6/2006) FL
40+6/7 FLC 1+1 FAC 3/1 Others 1+2

IDIAKEZ Inigo
Born: San Sebastian, Spain, 8 November
1973
Height: 6'0" **Weight:** 12.2
International Honours: Spain: U21
This gifted and experienced midfielder,
with a sweet right foot, has not
had much luck since arriving at
Southampton. Injury clouded his initial
season, part of which was spent on
loan to Queens Park Rangers, and an
Achilles tendon problem kept him out
for much the last campaign. Just before
George Burley departed to become
Scotland's manager in January, Inigo
found himself playing alongside Youseff
Safri in midfield and looking far more
comfortable. During the run-in, Nigel
Pearson returned to the same central-
midfield combination and it was effective
as Saints staved off relegation at the last
gasp. Was out of contract in the summer
and looking for a new club.
Derby Co (Signed from Rayo Vallecano,
Spain, ex Real Sociedad, Real Oviedo, on
27/7/2004) FL 86+2/20 FLC 1+1/1 FAC 5/1
Others 1
Southampton (£250,000 on 31/8/2006) FL
26+9/2 FAC 1+1 Others 0+1
Queens Park Rgrs (Loaned on 10/3/2007)
FL 4+1/1

Jabo Ibehre

IDRIZAJ Besian
Born: Baden bei Wien, Austria, 12
October 1987
Height: 6'2" **Weight:** 12.4
The Austrian striker, who joined Crystal
Palace on loan from Liverpool last season,
failed to score in his few appearances,
most of them as a substitute. Before
Christmas, the Eagles tried to cancel his
loan agreement but Liverpool refused.
Although Besian was then sent out on
loan to Oldham, he failed to arrive at
Boundary Park and returned home to
Wacker Tirol in January.
*Liverpool (Signed from LASK Linz, Austria,
ex Admira Linz, on 30/8/2005)*
Luton T (Loaned on 16/3/2007) FL 3+4/1
*Crystal Palace (Loaned on 31/8/2007) FL
3+4*

IFIL Jerel Christopher
Born: Wembley, 27 June 1982
Height: 6'1" **Weight:** 12.11
Despite a mid-term loss of form taking
some of the shine off Jerel's season at
Swindon, overall impressions remain
positive. At his best he is one of the top
central defenders in the lower divisions,
fast, strong and good in the air. He has
played successfully at full-back in the past
and, as one of the longest-serving players,
remains a firm favourite at the County
Ground. He netted a rare headed goal to
secure Town an equally infrequent away
win at Millwall at the end of September.

Watford (From trainee on 8/2/2000) FL 10+1
*Huddersfield T (Loaned on 28/3/2002) FL
1+1 Others 2*
Swindon T (Loaned on 30/1/2003) FL 5+4
Swindon T (Loaned on 4/9/2003) FL 6
Swindon T (Loaned on 14/11/2003) FL 10
*Swindon T (£70,000 on 14/7/2004) FL
144+7/2 FLC 5 FAC 9/1 Others 5*

IFIL Philip (Phil) Nathan
Born: Willesden, 18 November 1986
Height: 5'9" **Weight:** 10.8
International Honours: E: Yth
A youthful, skilful, solid and versatile
defender, at his best at right wing-
back, Phil impressed on his loan with
Southampton, linking especially well
with Nathan Dyer when attacking down
the flank. The Tottenham man's only
shortcoming was lack of experience and
it would have been interesting to see
him mature at St Mary's had his tenure
been extended. It was not and the Saints
never found an adequate replacement.
With Spurs agreeing to transfer Phil
on his return to White Hart Lane, he
grabbed the chance of regular football at
Colchester when signing in the January
transfer window. Showing improving
form over the next three months,
although he blotted his copy-book with
two own-goals inside four days in the
defeats at Plymouth and Crystal Palace,
he was never afraid to get forward at
every opportunity to deliver telling crosses

from the right flank. Dreadfully unlucky
to be sent off for an innocuous challenge
on Fraizer Campbell against Hull, the red
card was rescinded, which allowed him to
be ever-present for United after his move.
*Tottenham H (From trainee on 19/11/2004)
PL 3 FLC 1+1*
Millwall (Loaned on 12/9/2005) FL 13 FLC 1
Millwall (Loaned on 20/1/2006) FL 3
*Southampton (Loaned on 28/9/2007) FL
11+1*
Colchester U (Signed on 10/1/2008) FL 20

IFILL Paul
Born: Brighton, 20 October 1979
Height: 6'0" **Weight:** 12.10
Club Honours: Div 2 '01
International Honours: Barbados: 8
Fast and tricky, and a player who can
operate both flanks, Paul's season at
Crystal Palace in 2007-09 was plagued by
injuries. However, things looked better for
him when he was reunited with his old
Sheffield United manager Neil Warnock,
who took over at Selhurst Park in
October. Paul managed two goals when
appearing as a substitute at Coventry and
Watford and will be hoping for better
fortunes in the final year of his contract.
*Millwall (From trainee on 2/6/1998) FL
188+42/40 FLC 5/1 FAC 15/2 Others 9+2*
*Sheffield U (£800,000 on 24/5/2005) P/FL
31+11/9 FLC 2 FAC 1*
*Crystal Palace (£750,000 on 5/1/2007) FL
11+15/4 FAC 0+1 Others 0+2*

IGOE Samuel (Sammy) Gary
Born: Staines, 30 September 1975
Height: 5'6" **Weight:** 10.0
While Bristol Rovers could always rely on
the experienced midfielder to contribute,
mostly from substitute appearances, they
allowed him to join Hereford on loan for
the final stages of the season. Although
a late arrival, Sammy still had a key part
to play in the Bulls' promotion campaign.
Slotting in on the right of midfield for a
handful of matches, his quality quickly
showed through and his ability to play
a killer pass produced a clutch of crucial
goals. More powerful than his slight
stature suggests, his ability to win the
ball and bring others into the action was
a feature of his play. Was released in the
summer.
*Portsmouth (From trainee on 15/2/1994) FL
100+60/11 FLC 7+5 FAC 2+3*
*Reading (£100,000 on 23/3/2000) FL
53+34/7 FLC 4+1 FAC 4+2 Others 6+1*
Luton T (Loaned on 27/3/2003) FL 2
*Swindon T (Free on 14/7/2003) FL 75+4/9
FLC 3+1 FAC 3 Others 3+1*
Millwall (Free on 5/8/2005) FL 3+2 FLC 2
*Bristol Rov (Loaned on 13/1/2006) FL
10+1/1*

Jerel Ifil

Phil Ifil

clean sheet against Yeovil before the Bulls went out on penalties. His season closed prematurely when he ruptured a finger ligament in training, keeping him out of the action for the final six weeks. Was released at the end of the campaign.
Sunderland *(£30,000 from Cliftonville on 28/7/1999) P/FL 1+1 FLC 2*
Carlisle U *(Loaned on 1/10/1999) FL 7*
Stockport Co *(Loaned on 23/8/2002) FLC 1*
Darlington *(Loaned on 22/11/2002) FL 3*
York C *(Loaned on 24/1/2003) FL 17*
Wrexham *(Loaned on 16/3/2004) FL 11*
Doncaster Rov *(Loaned on 2/11/2004) FL 1 Others 1*
Wrexham *(Free on 11/7/2005) FL 71 FLC 3 FAC 4 Others 2*
Hereford U *(Free on 17/8/2007) Others 1*

INGIMARSSON Ivar
Born: Reykjavik, Iceland, 20 August 1977
Height: 6'0" **Weight:** 12.7
Club Honours: Ch '06
International Honours: Iceland: 30; U21-14; Yth
Ivar contributed another season of near-impeccable performances for Reading, and was the captain during the absence through injury of Graeme Murty. His displays were all the more praiseworthy as he was partnered at centre-back by six different team-mates during the campaign and because the Royals' defence was under constant pressure in most matches. A dependable and resolute defender, if not a flamboyant one, he also found time to venture up field and netted twice, in the 2-1 home win over Sunderland and in the extraordinary 6-4 defeat at Tottenham. Ivar made his 200th appearance for Reading during the season and although now nearing the veteran stage of his career, looks as committed and fit as ever. He has retired from the international scene, however, after winning 29 caps for Iceland.
Torquay U *(Loaned from IBV Vestmannaeyjar, Iceland on 21/10/1999) FL 4/1*
Brentford *(£150,000 from IBV Vestmannaeyjar, Iceland on 18/11/1999) FL 109+4/10 FLC 6 FAC 3 Others 13/1*
Wolverhampton W *(Free on 2/7/2002) FL 10+3/2 FLC 2*
Brighton & Hove A *(Loaned on 10/2/2003) FL 15*
Reading *(£100,000 + on 23/10/2003) P/FL 184+3/10 FLC 9 FAC 11/1*

INSUA Emiliano
Born: Buenos Aires, Argentina, 7 January 1989
Height: 5'10" **Weight:** 12.8
International Honours: Argentina: U23; Yth

Bristol Rov *(Free on 1/8/2006) FL 44+17/1 FLC 1+1 FAC 8+3 Others 7+2/4*
Hereford U *(Loaned on 27/3/2008) FL 4*

INCE Clayton
Born: Arima, Trinidad, 13 July 1972
Height: 6'3" **Weight:** 14.2
Club Honours: Div 2 '07
International Honours: Trinidad & Tobago: 64
Clayton was an ever-present in his second season at Walsall and kept a total of 19 clean sheets. As his 36th birthday approached, his safe handling, agility and bravery were as good as ever and at 6'3" the Trinidad and Tobago goalkeeper cuts an imposing figure, especially in a one-on-one situation. Clayton has become a Walsall star.

Crewe Alex *(£50,000 from Defence Force, Trinidad on 21/9/1999) FL 120+3 FLC 6 FAC 8*
Coventry C *(Free on 11/7/2005) FL 1 FLC 2 FAC 1*
Walsall *(Free on 10/7/2006) FL 91 FLC 3 FAC 7 Others 2*

INGHAM Michael (Mike) Gerard
Born: Preston, 7 September 1980
Height: 6'4" **Weight:** 13.12
International Honours: NI: 3; U21-4; Yth
Having been released by Wrexham during the summer, Mike was a cheerful substitute at Hereford, patiently watching Wayne Brown's excellent goalkeeping. His only chance of action was in the Johnstone's Paint Trophy, when he kept a

Despite being signed in January 2007, Emiliano played no part in Liverpool's 2007-08 campaign until the last two weeks of the season when, after a substitute appearance at Birmingham, he started the last two Premier League games, against Manchester City and Tottenham, showing good composure. It remains to be seen if he is the long-term answer to the left-back problem at Anfield but with the probable departure of John Arne Riise in the summer he could receive more opportunities this coming term.

Liverpool *(Signed from Boca Juniors, Argentina on 31/1/2007) PL 4+1*

IRELAND Stephen James

Born: Cobh, 22 August 1986
Height: 6'0" **Weight:** 11.5
International Honours: RoI: 6; Yth
Stephen is yet another product of Manchester City's exceptional Academy run by former Bury player Jim Cassell. He came of age last season, with definite improvements made in all aspects of his game, whether in a wide, central or attacking midfield position. He has presence in the tackle and skill on the ball. A last-minute thunderbolt against Reading in November to seal the points for City was celebrated by Stephen unceremoniously removing his shorts to reveal his now trademark Superman underwear.

Manchester C *(From trainee on 14/9/2004) PL 59+22/5 FLC 4+1 FAC 8+2/2*

IRIEKPEN Ezomo (Izzy)

Born: Newham, 14 May 1982
Height: 6'1" **Weight:** 12.4
Club Honours: FAYC '99
International Honours: E: Yth
Arriving from Swansea in the summer, the centre-half's first season at Scunthorpe United got off to a flying start when he was 'Man of the Match' and scorer in the 1-1 draw at Charlton on the opening day. But a groin injury in the second game against Burnley led to a frustrating six months out of the first team as suspension and then a knee operation followed. Returning to the starting line-up at the beginning of March for ten of the last 12 games, he ended the season captaining the team. A quick, commanding defender, who also filled in at right-back, he is very strong in the air and is expected to have a big role to play in the future.

West Ham U *(From trainee on 25/5/1999)*
Leyton Orient *(Loaned on 22/10/2002) FL 5/1 FAC 1 Others 2/1*
Cambridge U *(Loaned on 28/2/2003) FL 13/1*

Swansea C *(Free on 22/8/2003) FL 121+2/7 FLC 1 FAC 10+1/1 Others 0+2*
Scunthorpe U *(Free on 24/7/2007) FL 12+5/1 FLC 1*

ISAKSSON Andreas

Born: Trelleborg, Sweden, 3 October 1981
Height: 6'6" **Weight:** 13.12
International Honours: Sweden: 59; U21
Following his move from French side Rennes the giant Swedish goalkeeper's start to his Manchester City career was dogged by injuries in 2006-07, but having recovered his form and confidence Andreas expected to consolidate his position last season. His chances were limited by the form of City's two emerging young goalkeepers, Kasper Schmeichel and Joe Hart. Given a run of five games in November and December by Sven-Goran Eriksson, Andreas made way for Hart before coming back into the side thrashed 8-1 by Middlesbrough. Capped five times by Sweden during the campaign, he is expected to move on.

Manchester C *(£2,000,000 from Stade Rennais, France, ex Trelleborg, Juventus, Djurgaarden, on 17/8/2006) PL 17+2 FLC 1*

ITANDJE Charles Hubert

Born: Paris, France, 2 November 1982
Height: 6'4" **Weight:** 13.0
International Honours: France: U21
A former French under-21 international goalkeeper signed by Liverpool in the summer as cover for Pepe Reina following the departures of Scott Carson, on loan to Aston Villa, and Jerzy Dudek, Charles came with a good pedigree having played 170 games for RC Lens in the French Championship over nine seasons. However, it seems likely that he was signed as a stop-gap pending the emergence of one of Liverpool's younger 'keepers. His seven games of the season were in the Carling Cup and FA Cup, Rafa Benitez having guaranteed him some first-team action, but with the Reds' relatively early exit from both competitions, he did not have much chance to shine against top quality opposition.

Liverpool *(Signed from RC Lens, France, ex Red Star 93, on 10/8/2007) FLC 3 FAC 4*

IWELUMO Christopher (Chris) Robert

Born: Coatbridge, 1 August 1978
Height: 6'3" **Weight:** 13.8
International Honours: S: B-1
With seven strikers on Charlton's books, it was not certain that Chris, who arrived in the summer from Colchester,

would have a regular place in 2007-08. However, that is exactly what he achieved, featuring in every League game. Chris was top scorer with ten goals, all in games that he started. Coming off the bench for the first two games, Chris started the next 24 League fixtures, his nine goals in that time including last-minute headers to win consecutive away games at Southampton and Bristol City. Playing many times as a lone striker suited his style as he is big, strong in the air, and has the awareness to bring others into the game. He also has a fierce shot, as seen with two home goals against Sheffield Wednesday. When manager Alan Pardew changed the system mid-season to play two up front, Luke Varney and Andy Gray were preferred. Chris was left out and, unluckily many thought, started only eight more times, scoring once.

St Mirren *(From juniors on 5/8/1996) SL 7+19 SLC 0+3/1 SC 1+1/1 Others 0+2 (Free to Aarhus Fremad, Denmark during 1998 close season)*
Stoke C *(£25,000 from Aarhus Fremad, Denmark on 1/3/2000) FL 40+44/16 FLC 2+4/ 2 FAC 6+2/4 Others 4+1/1*
York C *(Loaned on 10/11/2000) FL 11+1/2 FAC 4/1*
Cheltenham T *(Loaned on 13/2/2001) FL 2+2/1*
Brighton & Hove A *(Signed on 16/3/2001) FL 10/4 Others 3 (Freed during 2004 close season)*
Colchester U *(Free from Alemania Aachen, Germany on 6/7/2005) FL 87+5/35 FLC 2 FAC 6/2 Others 2+1*
Charlton Ath *(Free on 9/8/2007) FL 32+14/ 10 FLC 0+2 FAC 0+2*

IZZET Kemal (Kem)

Born: Whitechapel, 29 September 1980
Height: 5'8" **Weight:** 10.5
Kem suffered his most frustrating season for several years. The central midfielder missed only one of Colchester's first 23 League games, that through a one-match suspension. But he lost form and confidence as the season progressed, although he could never be faulted for lack of effort or endeavour. His best work was defensive, halting opposing attacks with well-timed blocks or brave tackles. But his shooting let him down and he will be disappointed not to have scored. He was on the bench for the last couple of months before starting the final game at Scunthorpe.

Charlton Ath *(From trainee on 11/1/1999)*
Colchester U *(Signed on 22/3/2001) FL 229+27/17 FLC 7+1/1 FAC 11+1 Others 10+1/2*

J

JAASKELAINEN Jussi
Born: Vaasa, Finland, 19 April 1975
Height: 6'3" **Weight:** 12.10
International Honours: Finland: 42;
U21-14; Yth

In a frustrating end to the season, Jussi was ruled out of action after sustaining a back injury as Bolton warmed up for the UEFA Cup tie against Sporting Lisbon in March. He subsequently missed his first Premier League game, at Wigan, in over three years, ending a run of 121 consecutive appearances since his previous absence, on New Year's Day 2005. Before that, Jussi was maintaining his own high standards with some match-winning performances to enhance his lofty and justified reputation as one of the Premiership's top goalkeepers. Having spent ten years as a Bolton player, Jussi was out of contract at the end of the season and his future was unclear, with a number of clubs vying for his signature.
Bolton W *(£100,000 + from VPS Vassa, Finland, ex MPS, on 14/11/1997) P/FL 344+1 FLC 16 FAC 14 Others 13*

JACKMAN Daniel (Danny)
James
Born: Worcester, 3 January 1983
Height: 5'5" **Weight:** 10.2

Freed by Gillingham last summer, the defender excelled in every position Northampton asked him to occupy. At wing-back he used space well to feed the forwards and sprayed passes around with ease from central midfield. Danny scored a pleasing first goal for the Cobblers, a volley from the edge of the area in the 4-1 defeat of champions Swansea and capped his campaign by winning the 'Player of the Year' award.
Aston Villa *(From trainee on 4/4/2001)*
Cambridge U *(Loaned on 14/2/2002) FL 5+2/1 Others 1+1*
Stockport Co *(£70,000 on 31/10/2003) FL 51+9/4 FLC 1 FAC 1 Others 4*
Gillingham *(Signed on 5/8/2005) FL 65+8/1 FLC 3+1 Others 0+2/1*
Northampton T *(Free on 30/7/2007) FL 34+5/1 FLC 1 FAC 4*

JACKSON Jamie Noel Emmanuel
Donnelly
Born: Sheffield, 1 November 1986
Height: 5'6" **Weight:** 10.4

Jamie emerged from Chesterfield's youth team as a speedy forward and crisp finisher of promise, but his career stalled against the canny and more physically imposing defenders in League football.

Danny Jackman

Unable to embrace a midfield role fully, much of his season was spent on loan at Matlock and Gainsborough before Chesterfield released him.
Chesterfield (From trainee on 5/7/2006) FL 1+19 FAC 0+1 Others 1+1

JACKSON John (Johnnie)

Born: Camden, 15 August 1982
Height: 6'1" **Weight:** 13.0
International Honours: E: Yth
Johnnie had the distinction of playing every minute of every game for Colchester, emulating former U's defender Wayne Brown's achievement in the previous campaign. The classy midfielder's efforts were recognised at the 'Player of the Year' presentations. Often played on the left of midfield and, while Johnnie freely admits that he prefers to play in the centre, he buckles down and does an excellent job. He contributed seven goals, many from long-range free-kicks and some helped by deflections off the defensive wall. Johnnie scored three goals inside a week in mid-February, helping to earn five points.
Tottenham H (From trainee on 23/3/2000) PL 12+8/1 FLC 1 FAC 1+2
Swindon T (Loaned on 13/9/2002) FL 12+1/1 FAC 2 Others 2/1
Colchester U (Loaned on 11/3/2003) FL 8
Coventry C (Loaned on 21/11/2003) FL 2+3/2
Watford (Loaned on 23/12/2004) FL 14+1
Derby Co (Loaned on 16/9/2005) FL 3+3
Colchester U (Free on 31/7/2006) FL 70+8/9 FLC 1 FAC 1+1

JACKSON Matthew (Matt)

Alan
Born: Leeds, 19 October 1971
Height: 6'1" **Weight:** 12.12
Club Honours: FAC '95; Div 2 '03
International Honours: E: U21-10; Sch
Joining Watford on a free transfer from Wigan before the start of last season, Matt is an experienced and much-travelled centre-half who compensates for any lack of pace with his organisational and leadership qualities. In October, he moved to Blackpool on loan for a month to improve his match fitness, arriving at Bloomfield Road to cover for Ian Evatt, who had picked up an injury. He started two League games and made one substitute appearance, slotting in comfortably until he was recalled by Watford due to a number of injuries suffered at Vicarage Road. Although enjoying a run of matches at the turn of the year, he remained on the fringe thereafter and concentrated on guiding the young players in the reserves.

Luton T (From juniors on 4/7/1990) FL 7+2 FLC 2 Others 0+1
Preston NE (Loaned on 27/3/1991) FL 3+1 Others 1
Everton (£600,000 on 18/10/1991) P/FL 132+6/4 FLC 9 FAC 14/2 Others 4
Charlton Ath (Loaned on 26/3/1996) FL 8 Others 2
Queens Park Rgrs (Loaned on 20/8/1996) FL 7
Birmingham C (Loaned on 31/10/1996) FL 10
Norwich C (£450,000 on 24/12/1996) FL 158+3/6 FLC 6 FAC 5
Wigan Ath (Free on 19/10/2001) P/FL 157+10/4 FLC 13 FAC 7+2 Others 2
Watford (Free on 14/6/2007) FL 6 FLC 2
Blackpool (Loaned on 5/10/2007) FL 2+1

JACKSON Michael (Mike)

James
Born: Runcorn, 4 December 1973
Height: 6'0" **Weight:** 13.8
Club Honours: Div 2 '97, '00
International Honours: E: Yth
The experienced Blackpool centre-back and club captain made a healthy contribution considering his age and started 23 times in the League despite being second choice behind Kaspars Gorkss and Ian Evatt. Always likely to score the odd goal, Mike grabbed a stoppage-time winner in 2-1 Carling Cup win over Southend. After picking up an injury in April, he was unable to break back into the team and was released at the end of the season.
Crewe Alex (From trainee on 29/7/1992) FL 5 FLC 1 FAC 1 Others 2
Bury (Free on 13/8/1993) FL 123+2/9 FLC 9/1 FAC 3 Others 12
Preston NE (£125,000 on 26/3/1997) FL 237+8/17 FLC 16/2 FAC 14 Others 8
Tranmere Rov (Loaned on 18/12/2002) FL 6
Tranmere Rov (Free on 2/7/2004) FL 84/8 FLC 2 FAC 2 Others 8
Blackpool (Free on 5/7/2006) FL 65+3/1 FLC 4+1/1 FAC 6/1 Others 3

JACKSON Richard

Born: Whitby, 18 April 1980
Height: 5'8" **Weight:** 10.12
A full-back capable of playing on either flank, Richard joined Luton at the start of last season, having found opportunities difficult to come by at Derby. A neat, hard-working player, he proved a good reader of the game, timing his tackles and blocking shots, crosses and passes. At the start, he was preferred to the popular Sol Davis but injuries were never far away. On returning from an enforced lay-off, he played on the right and gave glimpses of the form he showed earlier in his career. He was not included in

Mick Harford's first two line-ups but was brought back for the Leeds game, was then in and out until he settled at left-back before the emergence of Ed Asafu-Adjaye and the revival of Sol Davis cost him his place. Richard played in the final game after being told his contract would not be renewed.
Scarborough (From trainee on 27/3/1998) FL 21+1 FLC 2
Derby Co (£30,000 + on 25/3/1999) P/FL 98+20 FLC 5 FAC 2 Others 2
Luton T (Free on 9/8/2007) FL 27+2 FLC 3 FAC 4 Others 1

JACKSON Simeon Alexander

Born: Kingston, Jamaica, 28 March 1987
Height: 5'8" **Weight:** 11.0
International Honours: Canada: Yth
Signed from Rushden and Diamonds last January, Simeon took time to become accustomed to the pace of League football but showed he has the ability and alertness in the penalty area to make himself a name as a striker in Gillingham's colours. Once turned down by the Gills, he is a Canadian youth international.
Rushden & Diamonds (From trainee on 28/4/2006) FL 8+9/5
Gillingham (£150,000 on 31/1/2008) FL 14+4/4

JACOBSON Joseph (Joe) Mark

Born: Cardiff, 17 November 1986
Height: 5'11" **Weight:** 12.6
International Honours: W: U21-14; Yth
Having been on loan at Bristol Rovers in 2006-07, the deal became permanent in the summer when Joe moved from Cardiff. Holding down a regular place at left-back, he could always be relied upon to deliver accurate crosses when he joined the attack. Joe captained the Welsh under-21 side that qualified for the European Championships.
Cardiff C (From trainee on 5/7/2006) FL 0+1 FLC 1
Accrington Stanley (Loaned on 23/11/2006) FL 6/1 Others 1
Bristol Rov (Signed on 15/2/2007) FL 43+8/1 FLC 1+1 FAC 7 Others 2

JAGIELKA Philip (Phil)

Nikodem
Born: Manchester, 17 August 1982
Height: 5'11" **Weight:** 12.8
International Honours: E: 1; B-1; U21-6; Yth
Those who voiced doubts on Everton's decision to sign the versatile player from Sheffield United in the summer were soon silenced as, after a shaky start both at full-back and in midfield, the Manchester-born player – who was released by Everton as a 15- year-

old youngster – established himself as a bedrock in the centre of defence, showing impressive commitment, sound leadership and a great ability to read the game. Apart from the odd blemish, Phil was splendidly consistent and made a major contribution to Everton's season, also scoring vital goals against AZ67 in the UEFA Cup and Reading in the Premier League. At the end of the campaign, he was deservedly selected in the full England squad.

Sheffield U *(From trainee on 8/5/2000) P/FL 231+23/18 FLC 16/2 FAC 14/2 Others 3*
Everton *(£4,000,000 on 5/7/2007) PL 27+7/1 FLC 5 FAC 1 Others 7+2/1*

JAIDI Radhi Ben Abdelmajid

Born: Tunis, Tunisia, 30 August 1975
Height: 6'4" **Weight:** 14.0
International Honours: Tunisia: 99
Radhi was given a chance by Birmingham in the winter and, after a run in the team that was interrupted by the African Cup of Nations, in which he represented Tunisia, he returned and was a strong figure during the run-in, showing great heart, determination and physical presence. The defender was threatening at set pieces, often going close or having headers saved, and earned some notoriety by jumping up and down at free-kicks to hamper the goalkeeper.

Bolton W *(Free from Esperance de Tunis, Tunisia on 14/7/2004) PL 35+8/8 FLC 3 FAC 2+1 Others 3*
Birmingham C *(£2,000,000 on 4/8/2006) P/FL 56/6 FLC 4 FAC 2*

JALAL Shwan Saman

Born: Baghdad, Iraq, 14 August 1983
Height: 6'2" **Weight:** 14.2
International Honours: E: SP-5
Although Shwan started last season as Peterborough's goalkeeper, he spent the second half of it on loan to Morecambe and, on returning, was released by Posh. He was one of five 'keepers used by Morecambe after arriving in January, a move that many thought would end with a permanent transfer. Unfortunately for the former Woking man, things didn't really go to plan. He made some good saves but all too often his kicking let him down and he lost his place to Scott Davies. To give him credit, Shwan performed superbly in the reserves and was their hero in a Pontin's League Cup final penalty shoot-out victory before starting the final game against MK Dons.

Tottenham H *(Signed from Hastings T on 5/7/2001. Freed in April 2004)*
Peterborough U *(Signed from Woking on 10/1/2007) FL 8 FLC 2 Others 1*
Morecambe *(Loaned on 11/1/2008) FL 12*

JAMES David Benjamin

Born: Welwyn Garden City, 1 August 1970
Height: 6'5" **Weight:** 14.5
Club Honours: FAYC '89; FLC '95; FAC '08
International Honours: E: 39; B-2; U21-10; Yth
It is easy to run out of superlatives when describing David's truly wonderful season. In the form of his life and, until a calf

David James

muscle injury forced him out of the last three Premier League games, he missed only two early round Carling Cup ties, when he was rested but still named on the bench Portsmouth kept a club record 23 clean sheets and David was in goal for 20 one of them. He has now kept a total of 159 clean sheets in 511 Premier League appearances. So, in almost a third of his Premier League games he has not conceded a goal – a staggering statistic.

Between January 2004 and late April 2008 he made 166 consecutive Premier League appearances and now needs another 25 appearances to overtake Gary Speed's record of 535. Along with Sol Campbell and four other players, David has appeared in all 16 of the Premier League seasons. His superb club form deservedly led to an England recall for the friendly internationals against Germany, Switzerland and France and the squad for the summer games against the United States and Trinidad & Tobago. He was short-listed for the PFA's 'Player of the Year' award and included in the PFA's 'Premier League Team of the Season'. For the second year running he was voted 'Player of the Season' by Pompey fans as well as winning all the supporters' clubs awards. He capped his season with his first FA Cup winners' medal when Pompey beat Cardiff 1-0. Earlier in the season his penalty save at Preston in the fifth round was a huge contribution to this. He writes a fortnightly column for the Observer Sport and has become a passionate environmentalist.
Watford (From trainee on 1/7/1988) FL 89 FLC 6 FAC 2 Others 1
Liverpool (£1,000,000 on 6/7/1992) PL 213+1 FLC 22 FAC 19 Others 22
Aston Villa (£1,800,000 on 23/6/1999) PL 67 FLC 5 FAC 8 Others 4
West Ham U (£3,500,000 on 17/7/2001) P/FL 91 FLC 5 FAC 6
Manchester C (£1,300,000 + on 14/1/2004) PL 93 FLC 1 FAC 6
Portsmouth (£1,200,000 on 15/8/2006) PL 73 FLC 2 FAC 8

JARMAN Nathan George
Born: Scunthorpe, 19 September 1986
Height: 5'10" **Weight:** 12.8
After being freed by Barnsley during the summer and showing promise on his brief substitute outings for Grimsby, Nathan's initial monthly contract was eventually extended to the season's end, the young striker ending with a senior run as a lone forward. Nathan also helped the Mariners progress to the Johnstone's Paint Trophy final, being on target in a penalty shoot-out to defeat holders Doncaster in round three. His persistence was rewarded with a new one-year deal in May.
Barnsley (From trainee on 10/5/2005) FL 1+14 FLC 2 FAC 0+2
Bury (Loaned on 25/11/2006) FL 1+1
Grimsby T (Free on 20/9/2007) FL 5+2 Others 0+1

JARRETT Jason Lee Mee
Born: Bury, 14 September 1979
Height: 6'0" **Weight:** 12.4
Club Honours: Div 2 '03
The midfield man had a short loan with

Queens Park Rangers from Preston, starting once and making a single appearance off the bench. On Preston's transfer list, Jason fared better at Oldham when he joined them in January and after an impressive debut in the 2-0 home win over Carlisle, the deal was immediately extended until the end of the season. A quality passer and all-action presence in central midfield, he made 15 League One appearances in total for the Boundary Park club. Despite being dogged by an ankle problem, Jason netted three goals in two games in late March before returning early to Deepdale for treatment on the injury. Latics manager John Sheridan reportedly declared his interest in securing Jason on a permanent deal.
Blackpool (From trainee on 3/7/1998) FL 2 FAC 0+1 Others 1
Wrexham (Free on 8/10/1999) FL 1
Bury (Free on 13/7/2000) FL 45+17/4 FLC 0+1 FAC 2+2 Others 3/1
Wigan Ath (£75,000 on 27/3/2002) FL 67+28/1 FLC 7/2 FAC 3 Others 1+1/1
Stoke C (Loaned on 7/11/2005) FL 2 FAC 1
Norwich C (Free on 4/7/2005) FL 6+5 FLC 2+1 FAC 1
Plymouth Arg (Loaned on 24/11/2005) FL 7
Preston NE (Signed on 7/3/2006) FL 12+3/1 FLC 1 Others 1
Hull C (Loaned on 3/11/2006) FL 3
Leicester C (Loaned on 8/2/2007) FL 13
Queens Park Rgrs (Loaned on 2/10/2007) FL 1+1
Oldham Ath (Loaned on 29/1/2008) FL 12+3/3

JARVIS Matthew (Matt) Thomas
Born: Middlesbrough, 22 May 1986
Height: 5'8" **Weight:** 11.7
Having arrived at Wolverhampton from Gillingham in the summer, a hip injury meant that Matt was not seen until October and then only as substitute. His full debut finally came in December and that month produced his first goal, against Leicester. He was gradually becoming more involved, showing his ability to beat a player and hit a dangerous cross. As a substitute at home to Scunthorpe, Matt helped turn the game in Wolverhampton's favour. Although left-sided, he can play on either wing and only the end of the season halted his most sustained run in the team.
Gillingham (From trainee on 13/5/2004) FL 78+32/12 FLC 4+1/1 FAC 3+1/1 Others 3/2
Wolverhampton W (Signed on 5/7/2007) FL 17+9/1 FAC 2

JARVIS Paul Alfred
Born: Weston-super-Mare, 26 May 1989
Height: 5'11" **Weight:** 11.0

Another graduate from Morecambe's youth system, Paul was given a one-year deal after finishing his 'A' levels. A left-sided midfielder, he was on the bench for two Johnstone's Paint Trophy games and was involved in the win over Port Vale. He was released at the end of the season.
Morecambe (From juniors on 24/7/2007) Others 0+1

JARVIS Rossi
Born: Fakenham, 11 March 1988
Height: 6'0" **Weight:** 11.3
International Honours: E: Yth
Younger brother of Ryan, the tough-tackling and combative midfielder made only five starts for Norwich and failed to figure under new manager Glenn Roeder. A regular member of the England age group set-up over the years, Rossi found it tough even to earn a place on the bench during the second half of the season and was given a free transfer in May. A strong character with the ability to play in defence if required, his versatility and positive attitude should secure him a club.
Norwich C (From trainee on 5/1/2006) FL 4+3 FLC 2+1 FAC 1
Torquay U (Loaned on 26/1/2007) FL 2+2
Rotherham U (Loaned on 13/3/2007) FL 10

JARVIS Ryan Robert
Born: Fakenham, 11 July 1986
Height: 5'11" **Weight:** 11.0
Club Honours: Div 1 '04
International Honours: E: Yth
Ryan spent time on loan to Kilmarnock from Norwich during the first half of the season, scoring once in the Scottish Premier League. A second loan took the former England under-19 international to Notts County in January and the capable, hard-working striker quickly gained popularity with the fans. His non-stop running was always appreciated but it was sometimes to his own detriment as he did not get himself into scoring positions as often as he would have liked. In his last few games he played on the right, performing with credit, and although it was clearly not his position, he helped County to retain their League status. A skilful striker with quick feet and great awareness, he never fulfilled his potential at Carrow Road but his end of season free transfer was as disappointing to Canary fans as it was to Ryan himself.
Norwich C (From trainee on 5/8/2003) P/FL 5+24/3 FLC 5/2 FAC 1+3
Colchester U (Loaned on 24/3/2005) FL 2+4
Leyton Orient (Loaned on 16/2/2007) FL 14/6
Kilmarnock (Loaned on 24/8/2007) SL 4+5/1 SLC 1+1
Notts Co (Loaned on 31/1/2008) FL 17/2

JEFFERS Francis
Born: Liverpool, 25 January 1981
Height: 5'9" **Weight:** 11.0
Club Honours: FAYC '98
International Honours: E: 1; U21-16;
Yth; Sch
A major signing from Blackburn in the summer, Francis suffered a frustrating first season at Hillsborough for a quality striker. He never got into an early stride because of injury and scored just two goals from open play, one of them, against Hull, enough to win the game for Sheffield Wednesday. Just as he was coming into something like his best form, he sustained a bad injury at Stoke and was out for the rest of the season, apart from a brief attempt at a comeback. He was sorely missed as the Owls battled, successfully in the end, to retain their Championship status.
Everton (From trainee on 20/2/1998) PL 37+12/18 FLC 2+2/1 FAC 6+1/1
Arsenal (£8,000,000 + on 27/6/2001) PL 4+18/4 FLC 1/1 FAC 7+1/3 Others 1+7
Everton (Loaned on 1/9/2003) PL 5+13 FLC 1 FAC 0+3/2
Charlton Ath (£2,600,000 on 12/8/2004) PL 9+11/3 FLC 2/1 FAC 2/1
Glasgow Rgrs (Loaned on 31/8/2005) SL 4+4 SLC 1+1 Others 2+2
Blackburn Rov (Free on 29/7/2006) PL 3+7 FLC 0+1 FAC 0+1 Others 0+3/1
Ipswich T (Loaned on 2/3/2007) FL 7+2/4
Sheffield Wed (£700,000 on 10/8/2007) FL 7+3/2 FLC 1 FAC 1

JELLEYMAN Gareth Anthony
Born: Holywell, 14 November 1980
Height: 5'10" **Weight:** 10.6
International Honours: W: U21-1; Yth
Mansfield's regular left-back at the start of last season, Gareth can also play in midfield or the centre of defence. Picked up an ankle injury in September and was out of the side for several weeks before coming back in midfield, the left-back berth having been taken by Dan Martin. Then, with the squad particularly stretched on Boxing Day, he appeared at centre-back against his former club Peterborough. Injured in April, he missed crucial games during the run-in.
Peterborough U (From trainee on 5/8/1998) FL 80+21 FAC 7+2 Others 12+1
Boston U (Loaned on 6/8/2004) FL 3
Mansfield T (Free on 21/11/2005) FL 123+4/1 FLC 6/1 FAC 9/1 Others 1+1

JENAS Jermaine Anthony
Born: Nottingham, 18 February 1983
Height: 5'11" **Weight:** 11.2
Club Honours: FLC '08
International Honours: E: 19; B-1;
U21-9; Yth

Still only 25, Jermaine continues to be a mainstay of the Tottenham team and served as such under both Martin Jol and Juande Ramos. Although suffering one or two injuries during last season, he still managed to play in 45 games. Jermaine scored six goals in all competitions, the most memorable being at home and away against Arsenal in the Carling Cup semi-final victory. Such was his form during this period that Fabio Capello gave him a start in England's friendly against Switzerland. He still makes the England squad regularly but faces stiff competition for a midfield place. Jermaine's athleticism and speed play a big part in his game and he often makes vital contributions at either end of the pitch.
Nottingham F (From trainee on 19/2/2000) FL 29/4 FLC 2 FAC 2
Newcastle U (£5,000,000 on 5/2/2002) PL 86+24/9 FLC 3/1 FAC 6+1/1 Others 28+4/1
Tottenham H (£7,000,000 on 31/8/2005) PL 82+2/16 FLC 8/2 FAC 6/2 Others 12+1/1

JENNINGS James Ryan
Born: Manchester, 2 September 1987
Height: 5'10" **Weight:** 11.2
For much of last season opportunities were limited for James at Macclesfield, with only two appearances in the Johnstone's Paint Trophy in the early months. Anxious for regular football he spent time on loan at Blue Square Premier side Altrincham, making nine appearances. However, he was recalled by Keith Alexander on his appointment as manager and started his first match in charge against Notts County at the beginning of March. A left-sided player, James had only previously played at full-back or centre-back but was assigned a central midfield role, where he gave an assured performance, and went on to feature there regularly for the remainder of the season.
Macclesfield T (From trainee on 24/7/2006) FL 10+10 FAC 0+2 Others 1+1

JENNINGS Steven (Steve) John
Born: Liverpool, 28 October 1984
Height: 5'7" **Weight:** 11.7
Having been sent out on loan to Hereford during the previous season, Steve forced his way into the Tranmere side from the very start of the last campaign and impressed immediately with his hard work and determination to stay there. A solid midfielder with a lot of potential, happy to win the ball from a holding role, he remained on merit and but for games lost due to a sending off and a couple of minor injuries, would probably have been an ever-present. Steve is immensely

popular with Rovers' supporters, who voted him their 'Young Player of the Season', but is out of contract at Prenton Park in the close season.
Tranmere Rov (From trainee on 28/10/2002) FL 68+28/3 FLC 2+2 FAC 6/2 Others 6+2/2
Hereford U (Loaned on 18/1/2007) FL 11

JENSEN Brian
Born: Copenhagen, Denmark, 8 June 1975
Height: 6'1" **Weight:** 12.4
A goalkeeper who divides opinion amongst Burnley fans but who remains a cult figure for many, Brian barely had a look-in before Christmas, Blackpool's last-minute equaliser costing him the chance of a sustained run in the side. A change of manager brought him back into favour, though, and from January on he was clearly Owen Coyle's first choice between the sticks. Capable of fine reflex saves and generally a commanding presence in his area, Burnley's longest-serving player was offered a further extension to his contract at the end of the season.
West Bromwich A (£100,000 from AZ Alkmaar, Holland, ex B93, Hvidovre, on 3/3/2000) FL 46 FLC 4
Burnley (Free on 18/7/2003) FL 159+3 FLC 9 FAC 9

JEROME Cameron Zishan
Born: Huddersfield, 14 August 1986
Height: 6'1" **Weight:** 13.5
International Honours: E: U21-10
In his first-ever Premier League season, Cameron finished second top-scorer with seven goals, five away from home. His blistering speed and movement meant that defenders found him a real handful. He scored the quickest goal of the season, at Derby after 33 seconds, and although out of the starting line-up, and used primarily as a substitute by Alex McLeish he always added a dangerous dimension through his pace and mobility.
Cardiff C (Signed, following trials at Huddersfield T, Grimsby, Sheffield Wed, Middlesbrough, on 14/1/2004) FL 65+8/24 FLC 2+2/2 FAC 2/1
Birmingham C (£3,000,000 + on 2/6/2006) P/FL 41+30/14 FLC 4/2 FAC 2+1

JEVONS Philip (Phil)
Born: Liverpool, 1 August 1979
Height: 5'11" **Weight:** 11.10
Club Honours: FAYC '98; Div 2 '05
Despite scoring twice for goal-shy Bristol City in a 3-0 Carling Cup win at Brentford, the striker had few opportunities at Ashton Gate last season. He joined Huddersfield on loan and signed permanently in January, enjoying a fruitful FA Cup debut with two goals in

the victory over Grimsby. He showed neat footwork, deft touches when linking with others around him and once fully match-fit, enlivened the front line and stayed among the goals. Phil is industrious and among his goals were two well-taken penalties in the same match at Swindon. A calf injury ended his run but he returned as a scoring substitute in the final game against Luton.

Everton *(From trainee on 10/11/1997)* PL 2+6 FLC 1
Grimsby T *(£150,000 + on 26/7/2001)* FL 46+17/18 FLC 4/2 FAC 3/1
Hull C *(Loaned on 5/9/2002)* FL 13+11/3 FLC 1 FAC 1
Yeovil T *(Free on 21/7/2004)* FL 80+4/42 FLC 3 FAC 7/3 Others 1
Bristol C *(Free on 19/7/2006)* FL 31+12/11 FLC 2+1/2 FAC 5/4 Others 3+1/2
Huddersfield T *(Signed on 22/11/2007)* FL 17+4/7 FAC 3+1/2

JOACHIM Julian Kevin
Born: Boston, 20 September 1974
Height: 5'6" **Weight:** 12.2
International Honours: E: U21-9; Yth; (UEFA-U18 '93)

After being Darlington's most expensive buy at the start of the previous season, Julian was joined by another record-breaking striker when Pawel Abbott arrived from Swansea. Julian was deployed almost solely as a right-winger, where his lightning pace and good close control troubled the majority of defences, with his accurate crosses producing many chances for others. He was a model of consistency, seldom lost the ball and usually managed to find a telling pass. The only slight downside was that he contributed only six goals because of his position out on the right. Was released at the end of the campaign.

Leicester C *(From trainee on 15/9/1992)* P/FL 77+22/25 FLC 7+2/3 FAC 4+1/1 Others 4+2/2
Aston Villa *(£1,500,000 on 24/2/1996)* PL 90+51/39 FLC 9+1/3 FAC 8+4/2 Others 6+3/1
Coventry C *(Signed on 11/7/2001)* FL 41+15/11 FLC 1 FAC 4/3
Leeds U *(Free on 2/7/2004)* FL 10+17/2 FLC 3 FAC 0+1
Walsall *(Loaned on 24/3/2005)* FL 8/6
Boston U *(Free on 5/8/2005)* FL 44+2/17 FLC 1 FAC 3/2 Others 1
Darlington *(£100,000 on 15/8/2006)* FL 66+10/13 FLC 3/3 FAC 2+1 Others 5

JOHN Collins
Born: Zwedru, Liberia, 17 October 1985
Height: 6'0" **Weight:** 12.11
International Honours: Holland: 2; U21; Yth

Julian Joachim

Collins spent much of the season on loan from Fulham, first at Leicester and then Watford. Gary Megson signed the experienced striker just days before he left Leicester to manage Bolton. Under caretaker Frank Burrows, he scored in a couple of successive fixtures but was allowed to return to Craven Cottage by Ian Holloway. A long-term transfer target for Watford, Collins joined them on loan from Fulham in January with a view to a permanent deal. Much was expected of the Dutch international but, arriving with a hamstring strain that delayed his Watford debut, he neither made a significant impact nor scored any goals in his five appearances. Injury ended his stay in April and he was back at Craven Cottage in the final weeks of the season for surgery.

Fulham (£600,000 from Twente Enschede, Holland on 31/1/2004) PL 41+54/20 FLC 1+5 FAC 2+5/3

Leicester C (Loaned on 23/10/2007) FL 7+4/2

Watford (Loaned on 25/1/2008) FL 3+2

JOHN Stern
Born: Tunapuna, Trinidad, 30 October 1976
Height: 6'1" **Weight:** 12.12
Club Honours: Ch '07
International Honours: Trinidad & Tobago: 100
This powerful striker made his final appearance for Sunderland in August at Birmingham as a late substitute and scored an added-time equaliser that, in hindsight, turned out to be a pivotal goal to both clubs' Premier League campaigns. A makeweight in the deal that saw Kenwyn Jones off to Sunderland in August, it was not until October that Stern established himself in the starting line-up at Southampton. After that, he hit the back of the net regularly and although not the most mobile of players, does have great control and excels at knocking the ball down, laying it off for team-mates, or holding it until one should happen along. His volleying sparks memories of Matthew Le Tissier and, already popular, his immortality was guaranteed with two tremendous goals on the last day of the season when Saints beat Sheffield United 3–2 at St Mary's to secure their place in the Championship.

Nottingham F (£1,500,000 + from Columbus Crew, USA on 22/11/1999) FL 49+23/18 FLC 3/2 FAC 4+1

Birmingham C (Free on 8/2/2002) P/FL 42+35/16 FLC 2/3 FAC 1+2/1 Others 3/1

Coventry C (£200,000 on 14/9/2004) FL 65+13/26 FLC 3 FAC 6+1/3

Derby Co (Loaned on 16/9/2005) FL 6+1

Sunderland (£250,000 on 29/1/2007) P/FL 10+6/5

Southampton (Signed on 30/8/2007) FL 35+5/19 FAC 1+1

JOHN-BAPTISTE Alexander (Alex) Aaron
Born: Sutton-in-Ashfield, 31 January 1986
Height: 5'11" **Weight:** 11.7
After much speculation over moves to a higher division during the summer, Alex signed a new contract with Mansfield, much to the delight of everyone at the club. He began last season at right-back and performed with his usual aplomb but after an injury to Martin McIntosh he returned to his usual position in the centre of the defence. Troubled by a back injury, he missed the Christmas and New Year games and did not return to action until mid-March.

Mansfield T (From trainee on 5/2/2003) FL 170+4/5 FLC 6 FAC 9/1 Others 8+1

JOHN-LEWIS Lenell (Lenny) Nicholas
Born: Hammersmith, 17 May 1989
Height: 5'10" **Weight:** 11.10
The teenage striker was six months into his second year as a scholar at Lincoln when he was offered a professional contract by manager Peter Jackson. It took Lenny just three games to chalk up his first League goal, with his winner at Stockport leading to a regular first-team role, mainly on the right side of attack. Although a stomach injury ruled him out of the closing stages of the season, his form was rewarded as he shared the 'Young Player of the Season' award with Danny Hone.

Lincoln C (From trainee on 21/12/2007) FL 15+6/3 FAC 0+2

JOHNSON Adam
Born: Sunderland, 14 July 1987
Height: 5'9" **Weight:** 9.11
Club Honours: FAYC '04
International Honours: E: U21-7; Yth

Alex John-Baptiste

A naturally left-footed England under-21 international, Adam was frustrated by his lack of first-team opportunities at Middlesbrough last season and enjoyed a most successful three months on loan with Watford, making a huge impact with his class and composure. Full of skill and guile, he made an eye-catching debut as a substitute against Southampton and was ever-present thereafter. He proved to be an excellent dead-ball kicker and crosser and a useful scorer, weighing in with five goals. It was no coincidence that Watford lost only one of the 12 matches Adam played in during his stay at Vicarage Road. Not surprisingly, Watford were keen to extend the loan to the end of the season but Middlesbrough's need was the greater. Because of an ever-growing list of injuries, he was recalled in November but had to settle, more often than not, for a place on the bench, making only five starts, two of them in the FA Cup. He ended the season as a second-half substitute for Julio Arca and scored his only Boro goal of the campaign in the 8-1 Riverside mauling of Manchester City. Adam was a regular member of England's under-21 squad.

Middlesbrough (From trainee on 12/5/2005) PL 14+30/2 FLC 3 FAC 4+4 Others 2+2
Leeds U (Loaned on 17/10/2006) FL 4+1
Watford (Loaned on 14/9/2007) FL 11 +1/5

JOHNSON Andrew (Andy)

Born: Bedford, 10 February 1981
Height: 5'9" **Weight:** 9.7
International Honours: E: 8; Yth
Andy had a consistent season for Everton without scoring the goals his overall performances deserved. After successful surgery on a troublesome foot injury, the England international started the season as first choice but a subsequent spell on the bench and the arrival of Ayegbeni Yakubu resulted in a spell on the bench. Then, often deployed late in the game against tiring defenders, the pacy striker's goals tally reached double figures by March as he regained a first-team spot, but the Toffees' moderate late form meant he failed to add to his bag. The hard-working forward is a firm favourite at Goodison and it is hoped that next season will bring greater rewards.

Birmingham C (From juniors on 11/3/1998) FL 44+39/8 FLC 6+9/5 FAC 1 Others 1+3
Crystal Palace (£750,000 on 5/8/2002) P/FL 134+6/74 FLC 7/7 FAC 8/2 Others 5/1
Everton (£6,000,000 on 2/6/2006) PL 52+9/17 FLC 4 FAC 2/1 Others 6+1/4

JOHNSON Andrew (Andy) James

Born: Bristol, 2 May 1974
Height: 6'0" **Weight:** 13.0
Club Honours: Div 1 '98
International Honours: W: 15; E: Yth
Andy signed in July after his release by Leicester and made his Barnsley debut on the first day of the season. The hard-working defensive midfielder played in the opening few games before Anderson arrived on loan. From then on, Andy was in the reserves and never again featured in the senior team. He was made available for transfer in January but stayed at Oakwell until the season ended.

Norwich C (From trainee on 4/3/1992) P/FL 56+10/13 FLC 6+1/2 FAC 2
Nottingham F (£2,200,000 on 4/7/1997) P/FL 102+17/9 FLC 6+1/1 FAC 2
West Bromwich A (£200,000 on 19/9/2001) P/FL 121+11/7 FLC 4+1 FAC 7/1
Leicester C (Free on 7/7/2006) FL 21+1/1
Barnsley (Free on 25/6/2007) FL 4 FLC 1

JOHNSON Bradley (Brad) Paul

Born: Hackney, 28 April 1987
Height: 6'0" **Weight:** 12.10
Brad carried on in 2007-08 where he left off the previous season, controlling Northampton's midfield and powering his way through opposing defences. He made the first team under the club's previous manager John Gorman but current manager Stuart Gray developed his game. The powerfully-built midfielder turned down an approach from Leicester to join Leeds in the January transfer window, sitting out the Cobblers' 3-0 defeat at Elland Road as he had already agreed terms. Still only 21, he shows bags of potential. Big and strong, with excellent fitness and packing a punch with his shooting, he became a regular in the Leeds' midfield, although he was given a run at left-back in an experimental United line-up in their final game of the League One season, a 2-1 win over Gillingham when he smacked in a thunderous volley. That was in sharp contrast to his only other goal for Leeds when he walked the ball into an empty net in a 2-0 win against Bournemouth after a defensive mix-up. He kept the left-back spot for all three play-off games.

Cambridge U (From juniors on 17/11/2004) FL 0+1
Northampton T (Free on 23/5/2005) FL 44+9/8 FLC 3/1 FAC 2+1/1 Others 2
Leeds U (£250,000 on 9/1/2008) FL 18+3/3 Others 3

JOHNSON Brett

Born: Hammersmith, 15 August 1985
Height: 6'1" **Weight:** 13.0

A central defender, Brett was hampered by injuries last season, restricting his Northampton appearances to just a handful. With competition for places in central defence keener than in other departments at the club, he was released at the end of the campaign.

Northampton T (Free from Aldershot T on 7/7/2005) FL 14+12 FLC 1+3 FAC 0+1 Others 0+1

JOHNSON Damien Michael

Born: Lisburn, 18 November 1978
Height: 5'9" **Weight:** 11.2
Club Honours: FLC '02
International Honours: NI: 48; U21: 11; Yth
Damien missed most of the first-half of the season because of hamstring trouble but once back in the Birmingham side, as the captain, he led by example from central midfield. A great fetcher and carrier of the ball, his persistent running and tackling set the side's tempo. After he was sent off at Wigan in April, his three-game absence was keenly felt as Blues struggled to avoid relegation.

Blackburn Rov (From trainee on 2/2/1996) P/FL 43+17/3 FLC 12+3/1 FAC 3+4 Others 0+1
Nottingham F (Loaned on 29/1/1998) FL 5+1
Birmingham C (Signed on 8/3/2002) P/FL 176+7/4 FLC 5+2 FAC 12 Others 1

JOHNSON Edward (Eddie)

Born: Bunnell, Florida, USA, 31 March 1984
Height: 6'0" **Weight:** 12.10
International Honours: USA: 34
Eddie joined Fulham from Kansas City Wizards in the January transfer window. After proving his fitness, the striker was a substitute against West Ham and was unlucky not to score within minutes of joining the action but did enough to encourage Roy Hodgson to give him his first start the following week against Manchester United. A bustling forward who works hard off the ball, he linked well up front with fellow countryman Brian McBride. An established United States international he appeared against Poland in March after his arrival at Craven Cottage.

Fulham (£3,000,000 from Kansas City Wizards, USA, ex Dallas Burn, on 30/1/2008) PL 4+2

JOHNSON Edward (Eddie) William

Born: Chester, 20 September 1984
Height: 5'10" **Weight:** 13.7
Club Honours: FAYC '03
International Honours: E: Yth

Beginning last season for Bradford in central midfield, the club also used him as a centre-forward later on when goals were hard to come by. He scored his goals in clutches, including one at each end at Barnet in September. The former Manchester United player was laid low for two months in mid-season with a back complaint and was released during the summer.

Manchester U *(From trainee on 4/10/2001) FLC 0+1*
Coventry C *(Loaned on 16/7/2004) FL 20+6/5 FLC 1+1 FAC 0+1*
Crewe Alex *(Loaned on 6/7/2005) FL 16+6/5 FLC 0+1*
Bradford C *(Free on 21/7/2006) FL 47+17/7 FLC 2/1 FAC 4 Others 1*

JOHNSON Glen McLeod

Born: Greenwich, 23 August 1984
Height: 6'0" **Weight:** 12.0
Club Honours: FLC '05; PL '05; FAC '08
International Honours: E: 8; U21-14; Yth
After featuring in Chelsea's first three matches in 2007-08, including the Community Shield against Manchester United, Glen lost his place to new arrival Juliano Belletti and joined Portsmouth, where he had enjoyed a successful season-long loan in 2006-07. Having signed a four-year contract with Portsmouth at the end of August, Glen made the right-back position his own, turning in consistently excellent displays and missing only an occasional game through injury or illness. Apart from his constantly improving defensive play he enjoys going forward, a quality amply demonstrated at Wigan when he scored after a mazy run from the half-way line. His form was rewarded by a recall to the England squad two-and-a-half years after his last appearance, and he played the final half-hour of England's defeat by France in March before being involved against the United States and Trinidad & Tobago. Glen ended the season where he began it, at Wembley for the FA Cup final, and is arguably now the best right-back in the Premier League.

West Ham U *(From trainee on 25/8/2001) PL 14+1 FAC 0+1*
Millwall *(Loaned on 17/10/2002) FL 7+1*
Chelsea *(£6,000,000 on 22/7/2003) PL 35+7/3 FLC 5+1 FAC 8 Others 13+3/1*
Portsmouth *(Loaned on 11/7/2006) PL 25+1 FAC 2*
Portsmouth *(£4,000,000 on 31/8/2007) PL 29/1 FLC 1 FAC 6*

JOHNSON Jemal Pierre

Born: Paterson, New Jersey, USA, 3 May 1984
Height: 5'8" **Weight:** 11.5
Club Honours: AMC '08; Div 2 '08

Glen Johnson

231

As a quick and alert striker capable of playing anywhere across the front line, Jemal proved a very shrewd addition to the MK Dons' squad by manager Paul Ince after being picked up from Wolverhampton in the summer. He made his debut in unfortunate circumstances as the Dons tossed away a late lead to lose at Rochdale in early September but it was not long before he scored in a win at Brentford and from then on was used equally as a starter and off the bench, scoring some vital match-winning goals along the way.
Blackburn Rov *(From trainee on 10/5/2002) PL 0+6 FAC 1+3/1*
Preston NE *(Loaned on 28/10/2005) FL 2+1/1*
Darlington *(Loaned on 10/3/2006) FL 9/3*
Wolverhampton W *(Signed on 17/8/2006) FL 14+6/3 FLC 0+1 FAC 0+3*
Leeds U *(Loaned on 20/2/2007) FL 3+2*
MK Dons *(Signed on 31/8/2007) FL 17+22/5 FAC 1/1 Others 6/2*

JOHNSON Jermaine
Born: Kingston, Jamaica, 25 June 1980
Height: 5'9" **Weight:** 11.5
International Honours: Jamaica: 40
Over the season, Jermaine's pace and directness on the right wing tore some teams apart, most notably city rivals United at Hillsborough. He needs to become more consistent in both his crossing and shooting to confirm his ability. His versatility helped Sheffield Wednesday and he filled in a few times at full-back when injuries made selection difficult for Brian Laws.

Jermaine Johnson

Bolton W *(£750,000 from Tivoli Gardens, Jamaica on 19/9/2001) PL 4+8 FLC 3 FAC 1+1*
Oldham Ath *(Free on 28/11/2003) FL 31+8/9 FLC 2 FAC 1/1 Others 1 (Freed during 2005 close season)*
Bradford C *(Free from Tivoli Gardens, Jamaica on 24/7/2006) FL 26+1/4 FLC 1 FAC 3*
Sheffield Wed *(£500,000 on 30/1/2007) FL 35+7/3 FLC 3 FAC 2*

JOHNSON Josh Thor
Born: Carenage, Trinidad, 16 April 1981
Height: 5'5" **Weight:** 10.7
International Honours: Trinidad & Tobago: U21; Yth
Somewhat surprisingly, the pacy Wrexham winger, who can also play in midfield, did not start all season in 2007-08 and was used only in late stages when leaving the bench. He played well for the reserves but had been signed for the first team and was released at the end of the season. A good crosser of the ball, the Trinidad & Tobago international suffered a disappointing time at the Racecourse.
Wrexham *(Signed from San Juan Jabloteh, Trinidad on 7/8/2006) FL 10+19/1 FLC 1+2 FAC 1+1 Others 1*

JOHNSON Lee David
Born: Newmarket, 7 June 1981
Height: 5'6" **Weight:** 10.7
Club Honours: FAT '02; FC '03; Div 2 '05
International Honours: E: SP-5
Perhaps because he is the son of the manager or maybe because goals were scarce, a number of Bristol City fans questioned Lee's right to a place. Then injury ruled him out for all but two of the last eight League games. This coincided with City's worst form of the season and a golden opportunity of automatic promotion slipped away as the range of skills that mark him as a footballer of rare ability were sorely missed. Lee was a first-half substitute in the play-off final at Wembley, when Bradley Orr suffered a fractured cheekbone, and linked play well as City continued to take the game to Hull.
Watford *(From trainee on 3/10/1998)*
Brighton & Hove A *(Free on 4/9/2000) Others 1/1*
Brentford *(Free on 22/3/2001)*
Yeovil T *(Free on 12/7/2001) FL 115/14 FLC 5/3 FAC 11/2 Others 3+1*
Heart of Midlothian *(£20,000 on 11/1/2006) SL 1+3 SC 1*
Bristol C *(Signed on 9/8/2006) FL 80+2/6 FLC 2 FAC 7 Others 4+4*

JOHNSON Leon Dean
Born: Shoreditch, 10 May 1981
Height: 6'0" **Weight:** 12.4

A free transfer from Gillingham last summer, Leon is a big, strong central defender who quickly became a key member of the Wycombe defence, playing in all but one game, when he was rested, and forming two great partnerships, firstly with David McCracken and then Mike Williamson. He has the ability to dominate attackers without fouling them and was rewarded for his good performances by winning the supporters' 'Player of the Year' award.
Southend U *(From trainee on 17/11/1999) FL 43+5/3 FLC 1 FAC 1+3 Others 8*
Gillingham *(Free on 15/8/2002) FL 80+18/2 FLC 3 FAC 3+1 Others 3*
Wycombe W *(Free on 3/7/2007) FL 44+1 FLC 1 FAC 1 Others 3*

JOHNSON Michael
Born: Urmston, 3 March 1988
Height: 6'0" **Weight:** 12.7
International Honours: E: Yth
At 18, Michael became the 20th graduate from Manchester City's highly productive Academy to break into the first team. A composed, creative midfielder, Michael started last season as he had ended the previous one, despite a new manager taking the helm and new players joining the club. His determination to hold down a place was rewarded with his first City goal in the second game of the season against Derby and he followed that with a string of assured performances, including another goal against Aston Villa which, like the one against Derby, was decisive in bringing victory. Unfortunately, his season was disrupted by a nagging abdominal injury that eventually forced him to miss around two months in the middle of the campaign. However, he showed no ill-effects when he returned, immediately finding the form that he shown earlier.
Manchester C *(From trainee on 5/1/2006) PL 33/2 FLC 2*

JOHNSON Michael Owen
Born: Nottingham, 4 July 1973
Height: 5'11" **Weight:** 11.12
Club Honours: AIC '95
International Honours: Jamaica: 14
The way Michael was frozen out at Derby earlier in the season was one of several mysteries because, although 34 when the campaign started, he remained one of the most intelligent and committed defenders on the books. And keeping out goals was not one of Derby's strongest suits. Loaned to Sheffield Wednesday in September, he made a tremendous impact at Hillsborough as a strong, experienced centre-half who was outstanding in a back four. As the defensive organiser it was no coincidence that the Owls' first

League win came on his debut. He stayed for three months and was given a terrific ovation when he played his last home game against Watford. Only the Owls' lack of finance stopped a permanent deal. Needed back at Pride Park, when Derby faced Wednesday in the FA Cup third round, Michael warmed up before going on as substitute and was given a welcome by both sets of fans. Allowed to go on loan to Notts County in February, Michael was keen to help their cause because they had treated him well when he started his career. In his home city, his contribution to the relegation fight into which he was thrust was immense. He used his defensive intelligence and vast experience to influence those around him, rallying the team and galvanising the supporters. When Derby released him, he quickly signed a one-year deal at Meadow Lane.

Notts Co (From trainee on 9/7/1991) FL 102+5 FLC 9 FAC 4 Others 15+1
Birmingham C (£225,000 on 1/9/1995) P/FL 227+35/13 FLC 25+6/5 FAC 6+4 Others 11
Derby Co (Signed on 15/8/2003) P/FL 127+11/4 FLC 2/1 FAC 7+2 Others 1
Sheffield Wed (Loaned on 21/9/2007) FL 13
Notts Co (Loaned on 29/2/2008) FL 11+1/1

JOHNSON Roger
Born: Ashford, Middlesex, 28 April 1983
Height: 6'3" **Weight:** 11.0
Cardiff's 'Player of the Season', Roger earned the supporters' club award and showed he has adapted to life in the Championship. Alongside Glenn Loovens, he formed a formidable central defensive partnership and kept club captain Darren Purse out of the team. He is an aggressive, no-nonsense player who scored a number of crucial goals for the Bluebirds. Roger had a particularly good game at Wembley in the FA Cup final against Portsmouth, marshalling the troops well and making last-ditch tackles.

Wycombe W (From trainee on 10/7/2001) FL 146+11/19 FLC 6/1 FAC 6/1 Others 11+3/1
Cardiff C (£275,000 on 13/7/2006) FL 67+7/7 FLC 5/1 FAC 6/1

JOHNSON Simon Ainsley
Born: West Bromwich, 9 March 1983
Height: 5'9" **Weight:** 12.0
International Honours: E: Yth
Simon was a peripheral figure in the early season for Hereford, having arrived from Darlington in the summer, but a cameo appearance as a substitute at Wycombe, where he played a leading part in a fight-back from two-down and scored the equaliser, ensured that he would be a key member of the squad for the remainder of the season. Either on the left or right of midfield, with an occasional

opportunity to lead the attack, Simon produced flashes of brilliance and scored some important goals, none more so than the spectacular strike to win the FA Cup third round replay with Tranmere.

Leeds U (From trainee on 7/7/2000) P/FL 3+8 FLC 1
Hull C (Loaned on 12/8/2002) FL 4+8/2 FLC 0+1
Blackpool (Loaned on 13/12/2003) FL 3+1/1 FAC 0+1
Sunderland (Loaned on 10/9/2004) FL 1+4
Doncaster Rov (Loaned on 6/12/2004) FL 8+3/3
Barnsley (Loaned on 24/2/2005) FL 10+1/2
Darlington (Free on 29/7/2005) FL 43+23/9 FLC 3/1 FAC 3 Others 3+1
Hereford (Free on 9/8/2007) FL 22+11/5 FLC 0+1 FAC 3+1/1 Others 1

JONES Bradley (Brad)
Born: Armidale, Australia, 19 March 1982
Height: 6'3" **Weight:** 12.3
Club Honours: AMC '04
International Honours: Australia: 1; U23-4; Yth
After waiting so long for the opportunity to play in his first international for Australia, Brad was given his chance in early June 2007 against Uruguay in a friendly in Sydney. With his contract about to expire in the summer and with West Bromwich showing an interest, Middlesbrough persuaded Brad to sign a new two-year deal. Brad tore a thigh muscle during a reserve game against Everton, an injury that kept him out for three months. He played only three times, in Carling Cup games against Northampton and Tottenham and the 3-2 Premiership defeat by Sunderland at the Stadium of Light.

Middlesbrough (From trainee on 26/3/1999) PL 18 FLC 2 FAC 5+1 Others 4
Stockport Co (Loaned on 13/12/2002) FL 1
Blackpool (Loaned on 4/11/2003) FL 5 Others 2
Blackpool (Loaned on 5/11/2004) FL 12
Sheffield Wed (Loaned on 4/8/2006) FL 15

JONES Daniel Jeffrey
Born: Rowley Regis, 14 July 1986
Height: 6'2" **Weight:** 13.0
Daniel is a neat left-sided player but made no starts for Wolverhampton. He was used as a substitute at home to Sheffield Wednesday in January and looked lively enough but his season was based around two extended loans at Northampton. At Sixfields, the wing-back gave evidence of being a player with a future, regularly having supporters on their feet with his speedy runs, pinpoint centres and specialist free kicks. Town were so impressed that they negotiated a second

loan in March and would clearly like to sign him on a permanent basis.
Wolverhampton W (From trainee on 2/2/2006) FL 9+1
Northampton T (Loaned on 7/8/2007) FL 17+6/3 FLC 1+1 FAC 1+2 Others 1
Northampton T (Loaned on 7/3/2008) FL 10

JONES David Frank Llwyd
Born: Southport, 4 November 1984
Height: 5'11" **Weight:** 10.10
Club Honours: FAYC '03
International Honours: E: U21-1; Yth
In Derby's promotion season, David appeared to be one of the players most likely to flourish in the Premiership in 2007-08 because of his passing ability. As it turned out, he struggled to earn a place, starting only three times under Billy Davies. Soon after the change of management, he underwent a double hernia operation, so needed to make an impression as the season neared its end. He scored against Chelsea at Stamford Bridge, scant consolation in a 6-1 defeat, and began to show his potential when given a run of games. The midfield blend needs to be right, as tackling is not his strength, and he should have been given more opportunities with free kicks.

Manchester U (From trainee on 18/7/2003) FLC 2+1 FAC 1
Preston NE (Loaned on 3/8/2005) FL 21+3/3 FLC 1
Derby Co (£1,000,000 on 17/11/2006) P/FL 38+4/7 FLC 1 FAC 2 Others 0+2

JONES Gary Roy
Born: Birkenhead, 3 June 1977
Height: 5'10" **Weight:** 12.0
The Rochdale skipper was again their key man in midfield last season, driving his team on by example with his non-stop running. During the campaign, he overtook Graham Smith's 34-year-old club record for senior appearances and also passed the milestone of 300 League games for Dale. He would have equalled Smith's League appearance record but was rested for the last game of the season ahead of the play-offs. Gary bagged seven goals with his powerful shooting, including two against Mansfield on the day he broke the appearance record, making him the first midfielder ever to score 50 senior goals for the club. Unsurprisingly, he won both the supporters' and the players' 'Player of the Season' awards. On his 361st senior appearance for the club, he became the first Dale skipper to lead his side out at Wembley.

Swansea C (Signed from Caernarfon T on 11/7/1997) FL 3+5 FLC 0+1
Rochdale (Free on 15/1/1998) FL 123+17/22

FLC 4+1 FAC 6+3 Others 7+2/3
Barnsley *(£175,000 on 30/11/2001) FL 56/2 FLC 1*
Rochdale *(Free on 13/11/2003) FL 176+1/26 FLC 4 FAC 8 Others 9*

JONES Gary Steven
Born: Chester, 10 May 1975
Height: 6'3" **Weight:** 14.0
To his credit Gary played through the season despite an ankle problem, postponing an operation to aid both Grimsby's fight against relegation and progress in the Johnstone's Paint Trophy. Although not as prolific as in the past, the forward nevertheless contributed some vital strikes, his presence and experience as a target-man securing single goal victories in December over Brentford, Mansfield and Lincoln. A Wembley substitute against MK Dons, Gary also scored the only goal in Grimsby's FA Cup first round success over Carlisle, his curling shot from outside the box capping a 'Man of the Match' performance. Was out of contract in the summer and looking for a new club.
Tranmere Rov *(From trainee on 5/7/1993) FL 117+61/28 FLC 17+4/3 FAC 9+2/3 Others 1+1*
Nottingham F *(Free on 3/7/2000) FL 24+12/2 FLC 1+1 FAC 1*
Tranmere Rov *(Free on 29/8/2002) FL 81+11/16 FLC 4 FAC 9+1/2 Others 4+1/2*
Grimsby T *(Free on 1/8/2005) FL 78+37/25 FLC 4+1/1 FAC 5/2 Others 6+4/2*

JONES Kenwyne Joel
Born: Point Fortin, Trinidad, 5 October 1984
Height: 6'2" **Weight:** 13.6
International Honours: Trinidad & Tobago: 64; U21
There were great expectations of Kenwyne at St Mary's at the start of Southampton's season in 2007-08 but no sooner had it begun than he was gone to Sunderland, with Stern John travelling in the opposite direction. A fantastic signing by manager Roy Keane, Kenwyne was regarded as a bargain when he arrived at the end of August. A powerfully-built centre-forward who has been likened to Chelsea's Didier Drogba, he has immense strength, pace and superb aerial ability, combined with an excellent first touch for such a big man. A Trinidad & Tobago international, Kenwyne was off to a great start with a goal on his home debut, an excellent left-footed drive into the bottom corner. His heading power was best exemplified by the goals he registered at West Ham in October and at home to Bolton in December, and his spectacular celebrations were almost as big a hit as

the goals. Named 'Players' Player of the Year' at the Stadium of Light, there was concern when he was injured against England in Trinidad at the beginning of June.
Southampton *(Signed from W Connection, Trinidad on 20/5/2004) P/FL 44+27/19 FLC 4/1 FAC 2+2/2 Others 1*
Sheffield Wed *(Loaned on 17/12/2004) FL 7/7*
Stoke C *(Loaned on 14/2/2005) FL 13/3*
Sunderland *(£6,000,000 + on 30/8/2007) PL 33/7*

JONES Luke Joseph
Born: Darwen, 10 April 1987
Height: 5'9" **Weight:** 11.9
Luke spent the early part of the season recovering from a knee injury sustained in the warm-up before the previous season's play-off final. Shrewsbury's right-sided central defender, who can also play at full-back, had his first taste of action in the 1-0 home win over Barnet in November and had an excellent game. After a difficult first half at Accrington in December, he was substituted and lost his place. Luke went on loan to Kidderminster in January and although recalled by new manager Paul Simpson, was released at the end of the season.
Blackburn Rov *(From trainee on 8/7/2005)*
Shrewsbury T *(Free on 10/11/2006) FL 10+4 FAC 0+1 Others 4*

JONES Mark Alan
Born: Wrexham, 15 August 1984
Height: 5'11" **Weight:** 10.10
Club Honours: AMC '05
International Honours: W: 2; U21-4
A talented Wrexham midfielder, Mark's game sadly went backwards in a struggling side. He was unable to impose himself and his explosive shooting from distance was not seen. Wrexham's dismal form in the last two years contributed. Mark was out with hamstring problems in January, but did not feature even when fit again and was released in summer.
Wrexham *(From trainee on 9/7/2003) FL 102+26/22 FLC 4+1/1 FAC 4+1/1 Others 9+2/4*

JONES Michael
Born: Liverpool, 3 December 1987
Height: 6'3" **Weight:** 13.0
It had been expected that Michael would be a serious contender for Wrexham's goalkeeping spot but his chances were again limited last season and he was third choice behind Anthony Williams and Gavin Ward. Included in the two Carling Cup ties, he played twice more, both in the League. On the bench numerous times before going to Hinckley on loan in January, he was recalled for the end of season match against Accrington when relegation was confirmed. Unfortunate to concede a bizarre goal, he was one of

Kenwyne Jones

many released at the end of season. **Wrexham** *(From trainee on 3/8/2006) FL 9+2 FLC 2*

JONES Michael (Mike) David
Born: Birkenhead, 15 August 1987
Height: 5'8" **Weight:** 10.8
As a mainstay of the Tranmere reserve side, Mike can play either on the right or in the centre of midfield. Having started last season as one of the regular substitutes, he was handed his first League start in the home game against Crewe in October and then remained on the fringes of the team for the rest of the campaign. An excellent crosser of the ball, he netted his first senior goal at Oldham in March and grew in confidence with each appearance, showing some assured touches when in possession. Out of contract, Mike left Rovers at the end of the season.
Tranmere Rov *(From trainee on 21/4/2006) FL 5+5/1 FAC 0+2 Others 0+1*
Shrewsbury T *(Loaned on 8/1/2007) FL 3+10/1 Others 0+1*

JONES Nathan Jason
Born: Rhondda, 28 May 1973
Height: 5'7" **Weight:** 10.12
Club Honours: Div 3 '01
The experienced left-back's third season at Yeovil was unfortunately cut short after he suffered a broken arm against Oldham but his performances up to February were nothing short of remarkable. His tireless running on the left became an invaluable source of attack for Town and his sound defensive awareness kept the defence organised. The Welshman's signature step-over drew massive applause from the Glovers' faithful and his motivational influence rallied his fellow players to raise their game.
Luton T *(£10,000 from Merthyr Tydfil on 30/6/1995. Freed on 20/12/1995)*
Southend U *(Free from Numancia, Spain on 5/8/1997) FL 82+17/2 FLC 6+2 FAC 3+1/1 Others 0+3*
Scarborough *(Loaned on 25/3/1999) FL 8+1*
Brighton & Hove A *(Free on 7/7/2000) FL 109+50/7 FLC 5+3/1 FAC 6+1 Others 8+1*
Yeovil T *(Free on 6/7/2005) FL 108+8/2 FLC 4 FAC 5 Others 6+1*

JONES Richard (Richie) Glynn
Born: Manchester, 26 September 1986
Height: 6'0" **Weight:** 11.0
Club Honours: FAYC '03; FLC '06
International Honours: E: Yth
Richie joined Yeovil on loan from Manchester United in August as the club looked to strengthen in midfield and stayed until the New Year, starting seven times and coming off the bench

on a further four occasions. At Huish Park, he looked a classy midfielder, with good tackling and distribution who could play either wide or in a central position. Having shown the fans just what he was capable of, he returned to Old Trafford and reserve team football to continue his education.
Manchester U *(From trainee on 4/11/2004) FLC 2+2 FAC 1*
Colchester U *(Loaned on 27/10/2006) FL 0+6*
Barnsley *(Loaned on 12/2/2007) FL 1+3*
Yeovil T *(Loaned on 14/8/2007) FL 6+3 Others 1+1*

JONES Stephen (Steve) Graham
Born: Derry, 25 October 1976
Height: 5'4" **Weight:** 10.9
International Honours: NI: 29
Only one League start for Burnley last season showed Steve's difficulty in breaking into the Clarets' side, his usual left-wing berth being regularly occupied by Kyle Lafferty. An exciting player at his best, his pace a threat to any defence, he had to be content with a regular spot on the bench before being loaned out to his former club Crewe for the closing stages of the season. Although the Northern Ireland international started only two League games for Crewe, he showed the Gresty Road crowd that he retains a good turn of speed.
Blackpool *(Free from Chadderton on 30/10/1995)*
Bury *(Free on 23/8/1996. Free to Sligo Rov during 1997 close season)*
Crewe Alex *(£75,000 + from Leigh RMI, ex Bray W, Chorley, on 4/7/2001) FL 122+37/39 FLC 5+1/4 FAC 4+1/1 Others 2+2/1*
Rochdale *(Loaned on 5/2/2002) FL 6+3/1*
Burnley *(Free on 1/8/2006) FL 38+20/6 FLC 3+1 FAC 1+1*
Crewe Alex *(Loaned on 27/3/2008) FL 2+2/1*

JONES William (Billy)
Born: Shrewsbury, 24 March 1987
Height: 5'11" **Weight:** 13.0
International Honours: E: Yth
A summer signing from Crewe, Billy replaced Graham Alexander as Preston's regular right-back in September and proved to be an astute purchase. Vastly experienced for such a young player, his class became ever more evident once surgery resolved a niggling hernia problem that kept him out through January. Solid and dependable at the back, he showed an increasing willingness to overlap, giving him the chance to demonstrate his powerful shooting. A nasty ankle-gash ended his season two games early.

Crewe Alex *(From trainee on 13/7/2004) FL 127+5/8 FLC 5 FAC 2/1 Others 4*
Preston NE *(Signed on 12/7/2007) FL 28+1 FLC 1 FAC 1*

JONES William (Billy) Kenneth
Born: Chatham, 26 March 1983
Height: 6'0" **Weight:** 11.5
One of the Crewe's summer signings when arriving from Exeter, Billy proved to be a solid and reliable defender in 2007-08. He settled quickly at left-back and held the position on a regular basis until he was injured at Huddersfield in December. Was unable to resume training until April but was pleased and relieved to play in the final game against Oldham.
Leyton Orient *(From trainee on 10/7/2001) FL 68+4 FLC 2 FAC 3+1 Others 0+1*
Kidderminster Hrs *(Free on 7/1/2005) FL 10+2 (Free to Exeter C on 6/7/2005)*
Crewe Alex *(£65,000 on 29/5/2007) FL 22 FLC 1 FAC 2 Others 1*

JORDAN Michael William
Born: Cheshunt, 7 April 1986
Height: 6'2" **Weight:** 13.2
Michael made only one appearance in goal, despite Chesterfield conceding three more goals than in the previous season's relegation. Although competent and reassuringly unflamboyant, he was unable to put worthwhile pressure on Barry Roche for the position and was released shortly before the season's end.
Arsenal *(From trainee on 2/7/2004)*
Chesterfield *(Free on 2/8/2006) FL 7*

JORDAN Stephen Robert
Born: Warrington, 6 March 1982
Height: 6'0" **Weight:** 11.13
Stephen was signed for Burnley from Manchester City by Steve Cotterill in the summer and was immediately installed as first-choice left-back. He remained ever-present in the League until Cotterill's departure in November, after which a combination of injury and new boss Owen Coyle's clear preference for Jon Harley kept him largely on the sidelines. A capable defender who sometimes looked happier going forward than at the back, his Clarets' prospects may improve following Harley's departure.
Manchester C *(From trainee on 11/3/1999) PL 49+4 FLC 1+3 FAC 7*
Cambridge U *(Loaned on 4/10/2002) FL 11 Others 3*
Burnley *(Free on 23/7/2007) FL 20+1 FLC 3*

JORGENSEN Claus Bech
Born: Holstebro, Denmark, 27 April 1979
Height: 5'11" **Weight:** 11.0
International Honours: Faroe Islands: 10
The experienced central midfielder made

a massive contribution to Blackpool last season, his previous Championship experience with Coventry shining through. From 30 League starts, he scored four goals, the most important being the opener in the 2-1 win over Sheffield Wednesday late in the season at Bloomfield Road. A box-to-box midfielder, his ability to break up play kept him in the side ahead of new signing Mike Flynn. Claus was offered a new contract by Blackpool at the end of the season.
Bournemouth *(Free from AC Horsens, Denmark on 12/7/1999) FL 77+10/14 FLC 6/1 FAC 6 Others 1+1*
Bradford C *(Free on 23/7/2001) FL 41+9/12 FLC 2+1 FAC 1*
Coventry C *(Free on 5/8/2003) FL 30+22/6 FLC 3+2 FAC 0+5*
Bournemouth *(Loaned on 23/1/2004) FL 16+1*
Blackpool *(Signed on 31/8/2006) FL 51+17/6 FAC 1+4 Others 4*

JOSEPH Marc Ellis
Born: Leicester, 10 November 1976
Height: 6'0" **Weight:** 12.10
Early-season injuries and illness restricted Marc's appearances for Rotherham after he arrived from Blackpool but once he had shaken them off he became a regular in defence, figuring mainly at right- back. He was willing to play wherever asked and proved equally competent in the centre of defence or at left-back. Marc's all-round contribution was further emphasised by his four goals, some from spectacular strikes.
Cambridge U *(From trainee on 23/5/1995) FL 136+17 FLC 7 FAC 5+2 Others 7+1*
Peterborough U *(Free on 3/7/2001) FL 60+1/2 FLC 3 FAC 6 Others 3*
Hull C *(£40,000 on 22/11/2002) FL 81+8/1*

FLC 2 FAC 3 Others 1
Bristol C *(Loaned on 10/11/2005) FL 3*
Blackpool *(Signed on 10/1/2006) FL 18+6 Others 1*
Rotherham U *(Free on 8/7/2007) FL 34+2/4 FLC 0+1 Others 1*

JOYCE Ben Patrick
Born: Plymouth, 9 September 1989
Height: 5'8" **Weight:** 11.4
A member of Swindon's youth set-up, having arrived from Boston in the summer, Ben scored on his League debut with a well-taken goal against Port Vale. He did not look out of his depth on his introduction to League football and gave another couple of lively performances off the bench in the last two games. A slightly-built striker with good pace and an eye for goal, he was offered a professional contract.
Swindon T *(From trainee on 22/2/2008) FL 0+3/1*

JOYCE Luke James
Born: Bolton, 9 July 1987
Height: 5'9" **Weight:** 11.4
After some impressive displays in the previous season, resulting in his being voted Carlisle's most improved player, the new campaign proved to be more problematic. One of a number of players competing for a midfield berth, Luke was given few opportunities to perform. Yet when he came off the bench for his first appearance of the season, he scored within two minutes, a goal that sparked United's 3-2 victory over Port Vale, despite being two goals down at half-time.
Wigan Ath *(Trainee) FAC 0+1*
Carlisle U *(Free on 23/3/2006) FL 8+11/2*

JOYNES Nathan
Born: Hoyland, 7 August 1985
Height: 6'1" **Weight:** 12.0
Although a willing runner for the Barnsley cause, the young striker started last season on loan at Bradford. Nathan made his debut at Shrewsbury in August but then hardly featured and five months later joined Halifax, where he had enjoyed a successful loan spell the previous term.
Barnsley *(From trainee on 18/2/2005) FL 0+1*
Boston U *(Loaned on 31/1/2007) FL 9+1/1*
Bradford C *(Loaned on 27/7/2007) FL 1+1 Others 0+1*

JUPP Duncan Alan
Born: Haslemere, 25 January 1975
Height: 6'0" **Weight:** 12.12
Club Honours: Div 1 '06
International Honours: S: U21-9
An attack-minded right-back who can also defend efficiently, Duncan again suffered from injuries during the course of the season, appearing only spasmodically before leaving Gillingham in December to join Bognor Regis Town. At his best, he is a reliable defender, capable of playing right across the back line.
Fulham *(From trainee on 12/7/1993) FL 101+4/2 FLC 10+2 FAC 9+1/1 Others 9+1/2*
Wimbledon *(£125,000 + on 27/6/1996) P/FL 23+7 FLC 8+2 FAC 3+2*
Notts Co *(Free on 8/11/2002) FL 6+2 FAC 0+1*
Luton T *(Free on 28/2/2003) FL 2+3*
Southend U *(Free on 17/7/2003) FL 96+4 FLC 2 FAC 3 Others 12/1*
Gillingham *(Free on 31/7/2006) FL 28+1 FLC 1 FAC 2 Others 2*

JUTKIEWICZ Lukas Isaac Paul
Born: Southampton, 20 March 1989
Height: 6'1" **Weight:** 12.11
In January, Lukas was signed by Plymouth on loan from Everton until the end of the season. He moved to Goodison from Swindon the previous May and was three times an unused substitute in UEFA Cup games before rejoining his former manager Paul Sturrock. Lukas made his debut for the Pilgrims three days later in their 3-2 FA Cup victory over Hull City as an 85th-minute substitute. The young striker struggled to make an impact, mainly appearing in the reserves, including a four-goal haul in January, but has already decided his international future. He opted for Poland, where his grandfather was born, being also eligible for Lithuania and the Republic of Ireland.
Swindon T *(From trainee on 28/7/2006) FL 16+22/5 FAC 0+3 Others 1*
Everton *(£500,000 + on 14/5/2007)*
Plymouth Arg *(Loaned on 1/1/2008) FL 1+2 FAC 0+2*

Claus Jorgensen

K

KABBA Steven (Steve)
Born: Lambeth, 7 March 1981
Height: 5'10" **Weight:** 11.12
Steve was a regular and hard-working member of the Watford first-team squad but struggled to impose himself on his rare starts. A versatile forward, he played both as an orthodox striker and wide on the right, and scored his first goal in two years against Wolverhampton in February. However, he failed to find the net for the rest of the season.
Crystal Palace (From trainee on 29/6/1999) FL 2+8/1 FLC 0+1
Luton T (Loaned on 28/3/2002) FL 0+3
Grimsby T (Loaned on 23/8/2002) FL 13/6 FLC 1
Sheffield U (£250,000 on 15/11/2002) P/FL 46+32/18 FLC 1 FAC 6/4 Others 1+2/1
Watford (£500,000 on 26/1/2007) P/FL 13+12/1 FLC 1 FAC 3+1

KABOUL Younes
Born: St-Julien-en-Genevois, France, 4 January 1986
Height: 6'4" **Weight:** 13.9
Club Honours: FLC '08
International Honours: France: U21-10
Arriving from Auxerre in the summer and with Ledley King and Michael Dawson ahead of him in Tottenham's pecking order, he was clearly signed with a view to the future. However, early-season injuries meant that Younes was pushed in at the deep end and made his debut in the opening game at Sunderland. Younes is a skilful player, and likes to get forward as much as possible. His tendency to be a little too elaborate in crucial defensive positions can cause problems but at the other end he scored four goals, including the memorable last-minute equaliser in a dramatic 4-4 draw against Aston Villa, a match chosen to celebrate the club's 125-year history. At the end of the season, he appeared to be out of favour with Juande Ramos.
Tottenham H (£8,000,000 from Auxerre, France on 12/7/2007) PL 19+2/3 FLC 3+1 FAC 1 Others 3/1

KAEBI Hossein
Born: Ahvaz, Iran, 23 September 1985
Height: 5'6" **Weight:** 10.2
International Honours: Iran: 57
Nicknamed the 'Prince of Persia' in the media when he arrived from the Iranian side Persepolis, complete with entourage, Hossein looked nimble and skilful but a touch lightweight on the few occasions he was thrust into first-team action with

Leicester. Eventually, his failure to learn English prevented him fully integrating into the squad and, by the time he was released in January, he had made more starts for Iran during the season than he had with the Foxes. His international appearances included a game against Costa Rica in Tehran that had to be staged behind closed doors when the low temperatures froze up all the water pipes in the national stadium, requiring fans to be locked out on safety grounds.
Leicester C (Signed from Persepolis, Iran, ex Foolad, Al-Sadd, Foolad, Emirates, on 22/8/2007) FL 2+1

KALOU Salomon
Born: Oume, Ivory Coast, 5 August 1985
Height: 5'9" **Weight:** 10.10
Club Honours: FLC '07
International Honours: Ivory Coast: 8
Chelsea's exciting young striker had an excellent season for club and country. Salomon became a virtual automatic selection for the Blues ahead of more illustrious and expensive fellow strikers and played more matches up front than anyone else. Most frequently used on the left of a front three, he caused defences no end of problems by cutting inside on his stronger right foot to create chances for the central strikers or curl shots into the opposite corner. He was used through the middle whenever Blues' managers made a tactical readjustment. A total of 11 goals represented an excellent return and he formed a formidable strike partnership with club colleague Didier Drogba for the Ivory Coast in the African Cup of Nations. The Elephants set off at a blistering pace but had to settle for fourth place with Salomon and Drogba finishing as the country's joint-top scorers with three goals apiece. The striking positions at Chelsea are now up for grabs and Salomon has a great opportunity to be the main man.
Chelsea (£8,000,000 from Feyenoord, Holland, ex Excelsior - loan, on 13/7/2006) PL 43+20/14 FLC 5+5/3 FAC 3+7/2 Others 7+16/1

KAMARA Diomansy Mehdi
Born: Paris, France, 8 November 1980
Height: 6'0" **Weight:** 11.5
International Honours: Senegal: 35
Purchased from West Bromwich, Diomansy was the most expensive of Laurie Sanchez's summer signings for Fulham. A strong player with pace and power he mostly featured up front but on occasions played wide if a 4-5-1 formation was used. Initially he featured on the bench before making his first Premier League start against Tottenham

in September, when he scored with a spectacular overhead kick late in the game to earn a draw. A regular in the first half of the season he was absent during January, when he featured for Senegal in the African Cup of Nations. On his return he found himself in and out of the side before showing some of his best form in the final games, netting vital goals at Derby and Manchester City.
Portsmouth (Loaned from Modena, Italy on 1/9/2004) PL 15+10/4 FLC 2/2 FAC 2
West Bromwich A (£1,500,000 from Modena, Italy on 5/8/2005) P/FL 54+6/21 FLC 3+2/1 FAC 3+1/2 Others 3/1
Fulham (£6,000,000 on 16/7/2007) PL 17+11/5 FLC 1+1/1

KAMARA Malvin Ginah
Born: Southwark, 17 November 1983
Height: 5'11" **Weight:** 13.7
International Honours: Sierra Leone: 1
Signed from Port Vale in the close season, the attacking winger established himself in the Huddersfield side, either wide on the flanks or as a striker. Quick and dangerous when running at opposing defences, he proved a useful outlet when he took up some great scoring positions. He worked hard on his defensive duties and grew stronger as the season progressed when linking with his fellow midfielders. With his deft touches and turn of pace he struck many vital crosses into the danger areas. A two-goal haul in the FA Cup first round victory over Accrington and the winner at Swansea were the highlights in a haul of five goals.
Wimbledon/MK Dons (From trainee on 17/7/2003) FL 37+40/5 FLC 0+2/1 FAC 2+3 Others 2+2
Cardiff C (Free on 5/7/2006) FL 3+12/1 FLC 1
Port Vale (Signed on 17/1/2007) FL 14+4/1
Huddersfield T (Free on 4/7/2007) FL 33+10/3 FLC 1 FAC 3+2/2 Others 1

KAMUDIMBA KALALA Jean-Paul
Born: Luburbashi, DR Congo, 16 March 1982
Height: 5'10" **Weight:** 12.1
International Honours: DR Congo: 8
Congolese central midfielder Jean-Paul joined Oldham from Yeovil in the summer. A bustling, box-to-box player, he began well, including a goal in only his second appearance, against Mansfield in the Carling Cup. However, Jean-Paul found himself squeezed out of the starting line-up by on-loan Neil Kilkenny and a rejuvenated Gary McDonald. He returned to play a starring role in the giant-killing FA Cup win at Everton in January but started only five more senior games. In April, despite having a year

left on his contract, he was informed by manager John Sheridan that he could leave on a free transfer if another club showed interest.

Grimsby T *(Free from OGC Nice, France on 25/7/2005) FL 14+7/5 FLC 3/1 FAC 1*
Yeovil T *(Free on 20/7/2006) FL 35+3/1 FLC 1 Others 0+3*
Oldham Ath *(Free on 3/7/2007) FL 14+6 FLC 2/1 FAC 2 Others 2*

KANDOL Tresor Osmar

Born: Banga, DR Congo, 30 August 1981
Height: 6'2" **Weight:** 11.7
International Honours: DR Congo: 1
Tresor got Leeds' early season bandwagon rolling with a late opening-day winner at Tranmere and celebrated with a spectacular back-flip. His partnership with Jermaine Beckford up front was a key factor in Leeds winning the first seven League One games as they rapidly wiped out their 15-point deduction. That run ended at Gillingham, where both Leeds' strikers were sent off and the nine men were denied victory by a last-minute goal. Tresor hit the winner at Brighton and added a double at Bournemouth in November but the goals dried up for him, although he was picked in the DR Congo squad for the first time for a friendly against Algeria in March. Despite giving way to Dougie Freedman when the Palace man arrived on loan, Tresor finished as he started, with a late winner in the 2-1 victory over Gillingham to take his League One tally to 11.

Luton T *(From trainee on 26/9/1998) FL 9+12/3 FLC 3+1/2 Others 0+1*
Cambridge U *(Free on 24/8/2001) FL 2+2*
Bournemouth *(Free on 12/10/2001) FL 3+9 FAC 0+2 Others 1/1 (Freed during 2002 close season)*
Darlington *(Loaned from Dagenham & Redbridge on 11/11/2005) FL 6+1/2*
Barnet *(£50,000 from Dagenham & Redbridge, ex Chesham U, Purfleet, Thurrock, on 30/1/2006) FL 27+2/10 FLC 1+1/2 FAC 0+1/2 Others 2/3*
Leeds U *(£200,000 on 23/11/2006) FL 43+16/12 FLC 2 FAC 2 Others 0+3*

KANU Nwankwo

Born: Owerri, Nigeria, 1 August 1976
Height: 6'4" **Weight:** 13.3
Club Honours: CS '99; FAC '02, '03, '08; PL '02, '04
International Honours: Nigeria: 73; U23 (OLYM '96); Yth (World-U17)
What an enigma! Because of his ageing bones Nwankwo has to be rested, rotated, wrapped in cotton wool, even mothballed sometimes and then used sparingly as a substitute but is still an absolute joy to watch. Not a ball-winner

by any means, he is rarely dispossessed as he shields the ball as if it were a sphere of gold on the end of a piece of string. His passing and distribution are elegant, delightful even, with rarely a ball wasted. Although his season with Portsmouth was disrupted by knee and hamstring injuries and absence on African Cup of Nations duty with Nigeria, he was still able to turn in several 'Man of the Match' performances. He earned his permanent place in Pompey's folklore by scoring the only goal of the FA Cup final against Cardiff, having also scored the only goal of the semi-final against West Bromwich, one of his former clubs. He is the only player to win the Champions League, UEFA Cup, Premier League, FA Cup and an Olympic gold medal. He actively promotes the building of hospitals in Africa through the Kanu Heart Foundation and is about to establish his own football foundation to set up football academies in Africa.

Arsenal *(£4,500,000 from Inter Milan, Italy, ex Fed Works, Iwuanyanwu National, Ajax, on 4/2/1999) PL 63+56/30 FLC 8/4 FAC 5+11/3 Others 28+26/7*
West Bromwich A *(Free on 30/7/2004) PL 38+15/7 FLC 1+1/1 FAC 3/1*
Portsmouth *(Free on 18/8/2006) PL 45+16/14 FLC 0+1/1 FAC 5+2/4*

KANYUKA Patrick Elamenji

Born: Kinshasa, DR Congo, 19 July 1987
Height: 6'2" **Weight:** 13.10
The tall young central defender joined Swindon from Queens Park Rangers in January and made his debut in a 1-0 victory at Luton, where he demonstrated his bravery by continuing to win everything in the air despite suffering a head injury. He also showed good form in his next appearance at Oldham but a groin injury 15 minutes into his home debut against Leeds seemed to bring an early end to his season. He recovered well to appear as a substitute right-back in the last game of the season.

Queens Park Rgrs *(From juniors on 19/7/2004) FL 8+4 FLC 1+1 FAC 1*
Swindon T *(Free on 18/1/2008) FL 3+1*

KAPO Obou Narcisse Olivier

Born: Abidjan, Ivory Coast, 27 September 1980
Height: 6'0" **Weight:** 12.2
International Honours: France: 9
Having announced himself with a stunning goal for Birmingham at Chelsea on the opening day, Olivier has so much natural ability that the game looked too easy for him at times. Despite being tall, his ball control was sublime and he was hardly ever dispossessed. Olivier became

a big player for the Blues and when he was on song the team was infinitely more threatening. He scored winning goals against Wigan and Bolton but an eight-week spell out through injury from February deprived the team significantly of his languid, creative talents when coming in off the left flank.

Birmingham C *(£3,000,000 from Juventus, Italy, ex Auxerre, AS Monaco - loan, Levante - loan, on 13/7/2007) PL 22+4/5*

KARACAN Jem Paul

Born: Lewisham, 21 February 1989
Height: 5'10" **Weight:** 11.6
Without a senior appearance for Reading, the young midfielder joined Bournemouth on loan last October and became a popular figure, with a great work ethic. Scoring arguably the goal of the season against Leeds at Dean Court, Jem was a regular in the side before returning to Reading and then moving to Millwall on loan in March. The hard-working, spirited midfielder worked wonders for the Lions and although he did not score he had a hand in many of Millwall's goals as they battled successfully to steer clear of relegation.

Reading *(From trainee on 6/7/2007)*
Bournemouth *(Loaned on 18/10/2007) FL 11+2/1 FAC 3/1 Others 1*
Millwall *(Loaned on 20/3/2008) FL 7*

KAVANAGH Graham Anthony

Born: Dublin, 2 December 1973
Height: 5'10" **Weight:** 12.11
Club Honours: AMC '00; Ch '07
International Honours: Rol: 16; B-1; U21-9; Yth; Sch
A combative central midfield player, Graham made a solitary appearance for Sunderland, in an FA Cup defeat by Wigan in January, between two separate loan spells with Sheffield Wednesday. Graham first arrived at Hillsborough in September and it was no coincidence that his debut against Hull, along with Michael Johnson's first appearance, brought Wednesday their first League victory. Although in the twilight of his career, his drive, enthusiasm and cajoling of others around him spurred the team. He rejoined the Owls in January until the end of the season and although the second spell was interrupted by injury, his tenacious play in midfield and tactical know-how served the club brilliantly. A permanent transfer would certainly suit the Wednesday fans.

Middlesbrough *(Signed from Home Farm on 16/8/1991) P/FL 22+13/3 FLC 1 FAC 2+2/1 Others 7*
Darlington *(Loaned on 25/2/1994) FL 5*
Stoke C *(£250,000 + on 13/9/1996) FL 198+8/35 FLC 16+2/7 FAC 6 Others 15/4*

Cardiff C *(£1,000,000 on 6/7/2001) FL
140+2/28 FLC 6+1 FAC 11/3 Others 5*
Wigan Ath *(Signed on 4/3/2005) P/FL 43+5
FLC 4+1 FAC 1+1*
Sunderland *(£500,000 on 31/8/2006) P/FL
10+4/1 FAC 1*
Sheffield Wed *(Loaned on 21/9/2007) FL
7/1 FLC 1*
Sheffield Wed *(Loaned on 31/1/2008) FL
14+2/1*

KAY Antony Roland
Born: Barnsley, 21 October 1982
Height: 5'11" **Weight:** 11.8
International Honours: E: Yth
Signed for Tranmere from Barnsley for two
years on a free transfer in June, Antony
is a versatile member of Ronnie Moore's
squad and although his preferred position
is at centre-back, his manager is convinced
that he has greater potential as a right-
back and even gave him a experimental
short run in the centre of midfield at the
end of last season. Powerfully built, he
possesses enviable timing, finishes well
and knows instinctively how to find good
positions, scoring seven goals to finish as
the second-highest scorer, ahead of more
conventional forwards. The variety of his
goals tells you that Antony is more than
just a big man who can convert crosses
and corners.
Barnsley *(From trainee on 25/10/1999) FL
156+18/11 FLC 6 FAC 9/1 Others 8*
Tranmere Rov *(Free on 18/7/2007) FL 30+8/
6 FAC 4/1 Others 1*

KAZIMIERCZAK Przemsylaw (Prez)
Born: Lodz, Poland, 22 February 1988
Height: 6'0" **Weight:** 12.2
Prez was signed as an emergency loan in
September from Bolton after Wycombe's
two first-choice goalkeepers were
injured. Second fiddle to the Chairboys'
other loanee Frank Fielding, his only
appearance was in the 2-0 Johnstone's
Paint Trophy defeat at Swansea. Back at
Bolton, Darlington signed him on loan
in January as cover for David Stockdale,
Andy Oakes being ruled out for the
season with a shoulder injury. After
warming the bench for three months,
he finally made his Darlington debut on
the last day at Peterborough when he
replaced Stockdale after 12 minutes and
kept a clean sheet with a competent
performance in a 2-0 victory against
already promoted Posh.
Bolton W *(From trainee on 14/7/2006)*
Accrington Stanley *(Loaned on 31/1/2007)
FL 7+1*
Wycombe W *(Loaned on 28/9/2007)
Others 1*
Darlington *(Free on 31/1/2008) FL 0+1*

Antony Kay

KEANE Keith Francis

Born: Luton, 20 November 1986
Height: 5'9" **Weight:** 11.1
Club Honours: Div 1 '05
International Honours: Rol: U21-4; Yth
Having established himself as a useful utility player in the previous campaign at Luton, Keith started last season on the fringes. His first appearance was in the Carling Cup at Dagenham and his next in the Johnstone's Paint Trophy, in central defence. That was followed by his first League appearance at left-back in a 1-0 defeat at Cheltenham. Two weeks later, he was a substitute for Alan Goodall in the most gruelling game of the season, with three players, including captain Chris Coyne, sent off against Bristol Rovers. Keith emerged as a hero when Town picked up a point and with Coyne out for three games, he was right-back in a defence that won two consecutive games and held Liverpool to a draw in the FA Cup. When Luton could not extend Jaroslaw Fojut's loan, Keith was drafted into the centre of defence or occasionally as a right-back. Mick Harford finally settled on him as Chris Perry's central defensive partner at Southend. Succeeding Perry as captain for the Cheltenham home game, at 21, he led by example and his defensive displays earned him the 'Player of the Year' award and selection for the Republic of Ireland under-21 end-of-season tour.
Luton T (From trainee on 23/8/2004) FL 74+15/4 FLC 5+2 FAC 3+3 Others 3

KEANE Robert (Robbie) David

Born: Dublin, 8 July 1980
Height: 5'9" **Weight:** 11.10
Club Honours: FLC '08
International Honours: Rol: 81; B-1; Yth (UEFA-U18 '98)
In the absence of club captain Ledley King for much of the season, Robbie was an able deputy as captain of Tottenham and continued to lead the Republic of Ireland. Robbie was voted as Tottenham's 'Player of the Season' by a massive majority, having finished as level top-scorer with Dimitar Berbatov, 15 in the Premier League and 23 in all competitions as he appeared in 54 games. Robbie lifted the Carling Cup alongside Ledley King and reached another special landmark with his 100th goal for Spurs, against Sunderland in January. As well as his scoring prowess, he is liable to contribute all round the pitch, even making a goal-line clearance, such is his all-round football skill. Robbie was often switched into midfield to accommodate an additional striker such as Darren Bent. His best goal of the season was surely a 25-yard curler from

the edge of the penalty box that levelled the scores at home against Chelsea in a dramatic 4-4 thriller. Robbie became the 15th player in Tottenham's history to reach 100 League and Cup goals and after adding seven more in the remainder of the season, stands 12th in the all-time list. Having committed himself until 2012, Robbie clearly has 100 League goals for Spurs within his sights to join an elite group of only eight previous players for the club.
Wolverhampton W (From trainee on 26/7/1997) FL 66+7/24 FLC 7+2/3 FAC 3+2/2
Coventry C (£6,000,000 on 20/8/1999) PL 30+1/12 FAC 3 (£13,000,000 to Inter Milan, Italy on 31/7/2000)
Leeds U (£12,000,000 from Inter Milan, Italy on 22/12/2000) PL 28+18/13 FLC 2/3 FAC 2 Others 6/3
Tottenham H (£7,000,000 on 31/8/2002) PL 158+39/80 FLC 14+5/7 FAC 15+4/11 Others 15+4/9

KEATES Dean Scott

Born: Walsall, 30 June 1978
Height: 5'6" **Weight:** 10.10
Club Honours: Div 2 '07
Dean, a diminutive midfielder, took time to settle in at Peterborough after leaving Walsall in the summer but once he found his feet he proved what a battler he is. Tigerish in midfield and never knowing when beaten, he surprised everyone, including opponents, by scoring three of his five goals with his head - not bad at 5'6".
Walsall (From trainee on 14/8/1996) FL 125+34/9 FLC 15+1/1 FAC 10+4 Others 14+1/3
Hull C (Free on 23/8/2002) FL 45+5/4 FLC 1+1 Others 2
Kidderminster Hrs (Signed on 10/2/2004) FL 48+1/7 FLC 1 FAC 1 Others 1
Lincoln C (Free on 3/8/2005) FL 19+2/4 FLC 2 FAC 1
Walsall (Free on 31/1/2006) FL 50+3/15 FLC 2 FAC 2
Peterborough U (Free on 12/7/2007) FL 33+7/5 FLC 1+1 FAC 2+1

KEBE Jimmy Boubou

Born: Vitry-sur-Seine, France, 19 January 1984
Height: 6'2" **Weight:** 11.7
International Honours: Mali: 8
A gap in the Reading squad on the right of midfield persuaded them to pay French Second Division club Lens a fee in the region of £400,000 to bring Jimmy to the Madejski Stadium. The Mali international, who holds Malian and French passports, had to wait for his Royals' debut but almost scored an equaliser at Everton after being introduced as an 80th-minute

substitute in Reading's 1-0 defeat. His appearances were sparse thereafter, as John Oster was preferred. But Jimmy has signed a two-and-a-half-year contract, so more will be expected of him as Royals return to the Championship.
Reading (Signed from RC Lens, France, ex Chateauroux - loan, Boulogne - loan, on 31/1/2008) PL 1+4

KELLER Kasey C

Born: Olympia, Washington, USA, 27 November 1969
Height: 6'2" **Weight:** 13.12
Club Honours: FLC '97
International Honours: USA: 102
An experienced goalkeeper signed from Borussia Monchengladbach in August, Kasey went straight into the Fulham team at Aston Villa but suffered an injury and was out of action until restored for a three-game spell, during which he gave an outstanding display at Chelsea. Further injury problems to an arm meant a lengthy spell on the sidelines but he was recalled for the trip to Blackburn and went on to feature in the final ten games of the season. An excellent shot-stopper, he also displays great positional sense and judgement in whether to catch or punch out a cross. As the summer approached there was some doubt as to whether the former United States international would remain at the club.
Millwall (Free from Portland University on 20/2/1992) FL 176 FLC 14 FAC 8 Others 4
Leicester C (£900,000 on 17/8/1996) PL 99 FLC 16 FAC 8 Others 2 (Signed for Rayo Vallecano, Spain during 1999 close season)
Tottenham H (Free on 16/8/2001) PL 85 FLC 10 FAC 4 (Freed on 15/1/2005)
Southampton (Loaned on 12/11/2004) PL 4
Fulham (Signed from Borussia Moenchengladbach, Germany on 24/8/2007) PL 13 FLC 1

KELLY Ashley Craig

Born: Ashton-under-Lyne, 22 December 1988
Height: 5'7" **Weight:** 11.0
As a product of Oldham's youth system, Ashley penned his first professional contract last summer. The energetic midfield player went on loan to Leigh RMI and Barrow before returning to Boundary Park just before Christmas. An injury crisis then saw him spend several games on the bench before he made his bow as a late substitute in a 2-0 home win over Leyton Orient in April. However, those 12 minutes proved to be Ashley's only first-team action and his contract was not renewed.
Oldham Ath (From juniors on 3/7/2007) FL 0+1

KELLY Shaun David
Born: Liverpool, 11 December 1988
Height: 6'1" **Weight:** 11.4
After graduating through the Chester Academy, Shaun spent the early part of last season on loan at Blue Square North side Vauxhall Motors. Having made his Chester debut at the end of 2006-07, Shaun's first League appearances of the season was as a substitute at Accrington in January, replacing the injured Paul Butler. A promising centre-half, Shaun became a regular on the bench following Simon Davies' appointment as manager and was given further opportunities towards the end of the campaign when he again replaced Butler alongside Paul Linwood. Shaun was rewarded with an extension to his contract.
Chester C (From juniors on 23/1/2007) FL 7+5

KELLY Stephen Michael David
Born: Dublin, 6 September 1983
Height: 5'11" **Weight:** 12.4
International Honours: RoI: 11; U21-17; Yth
The only Premier League outfield player to play in every single minute of every game, Stephen is a reliable, highly disciplined Birmingham right-back who covers his centre-halves brilliantly. He made several goal-saving tackles and blocks throughout the season and proved to be a great athlete, becoming more adventurous as the season progressed. A consistently excellent performer, his doggedness and reading of the game were impressive.
Tottenham H (From juniors on 11/9/2000) PL 29+8/2 FLC 1 FAC 6
Southend U (Loaned on 30/1/2003) FL 10
Queens Park Rgrs (Loaned on 27/3/2003) FL 7 Others 2
Watford (Loaned on 24/9/2003) FL 13
Birmingham C (£750,000 on 18/7/2006) P/FL 73+1 FLC 4+1 FAC 2

KELTIE Clark Stuart
Born: Newcastle, 31 August 1983
Height: 6'0" **Weight:** 12.7
Clark's seventh season at Darlington was marred by a series of injuries and he added only 23 starts to his career total. His steady influence in midfield, strong tackling and long crossfield passes were greatly missed in the second half of the campaign as Darlington's promotion challenge fell away. He possesses a strong shot but managed to add only five goals, three of them from the penalty spot, to his club total. Was released in the summer.
Darlington (Free from Walker Central on 19/9/2001) FL 129+32/9 FLC 3 FAC 8+1/1 Others 5+1/1

KEMPSON Darran Kaya
Born: Blackpool, 6 December 1984
Height: 6'2" **Weight:** 12.13
International Honours: E: SP-2
Signed from Crewe immediately prior to 2007-08 getting underway, the central defender made his Shrewsbury debut on the opening day, giving an assured performance in the 4-0 victory at Lincoln. Darran scored once, the only goal in the Carling Cup victory over Colchester, to earn a second round tie with Premiership Fulham. Hard-working, strong and a no-nonsense defender, he had a mixed season, being involved in 23 League games as Shrewsbury sought their strongest central defensive partnership. Loaned to Accrington in February, he made an immediate impact, playing all his eight games in the centre of defence and being consistently one of Stanley's best players. His only goal was immensely satisfying to him, scored in the victory against his former club, Morecambe. He collected 'Man of the Match' awards in his last two games at the Fraser Eagle Stadium before being recalled by the Shrews' new manager Paul Simpson. Back at the New Meadow he gave some of his best performances as the club battled successfully for the points to retain League status.
Crewe Alex (Free from Morecambe, ex trainee at Preston NE, on 14/7/2006) FL 6+1 FLC 0+1 FAC 0+1 Others 1
Bury (Loaned on 23/2/2007) FL 12
Shrewsbury T (Free on 7/8/2007) FL 18+5 FLC 2/1 Others 1
Accrington Stanley (Loaned on 29/2/2008) FL 8/1

KENNEDY Callum Ewan
Born: Chertsey, 9 November 1989
Height: 6'0" **Weight:** 12.6
Showing good form, the second-year Swindon scholar made his debut at left-back in the Johnstone's Paint Trophy victory over Brentford. An adaptable left-footed player with plenty of pace, who can perform equally well in defence or midfield, Callum signed a professional contract in February.
Swindon T (From trainee on 22/2/2008) Others 1

KENNEDY Jason Brian
Born: Stockton, 11 September 1986
Height: 6'1" **Weight:** 11.10
Club Honours: FAYC '04
This tall, combative midfielder arrived at Darlington on loan from Middlesbrough at the beginning of March and bolstered midfield with his strong aerial presence and bursts forward into the penalty area. He scored his only goal in the crucial

comeback against Morecambe at the Arena on Easter Monday and remained at the club until the end of the season, making a dozen appearances in all. Was released by Boro in the summer.
Middlesbrough (From trainee on 3/2/2005) PL 1+3 Others 1+2
Boston U (Loaned on 3/11/2006) FL 13/1
Bury (Loaned on 2/3/2007) FL 12
Livingston (Loaned on 1/8/2007) SL 18/2 SLC 2 SC 1 Others 1
Darlington (Loaned on 29/2/2008) FL 13/2 Others 2/1

KENNEDY Mark John
Born: Dublin, 15 May 1976
Height: 5'11" **Weight:** 11.9
International Honours: RoI: 34; U21-7; Yth; Sch
A much-travelled Republic of Ireland international, Mark started last season in fine form for Crystal Palace before injuries severely limited his time. As a result, two spells of four games apiece made up his total for the campaign. An experienced left-sided midfield player who, at his best, was capable of dominating games, Mark's contract was not renewed at the end of the season.
Millwall (From trainee on 6/5/1992) FL 37+6/9 FLC 6+1/2 FAC 3+1/1
Liverpool (£1,500,000 on 21/3/1995) PL 5+11 FLC 0+2 FAC 0+1 Others 0+2
Queens Park Rgrs (Loaned on 27/1/1998) FL 8/2
Wimbledon (£1,750,000 on 27/3/1998) 11+10 FLC 4+1/1 FAC 2
Manchester C (£1,000,000 + on 15/7/1999) P/FL 56+10/8 FLC 5+4/3 FAC 2
Wolverhampton W (£1,800,000 on 6/7/2001) P/FL 157+10/12 FLC 3+1 FAC 12/1 Others 3+1/1
Crystal Palace (Free on 12/7/2006) FL 42+4/1 FAC 1+1

KENNEDY Thomas (Tom) Gordon
Born: Bury, 24 June 1985
Height: 5'10" **Weight:** 11.1
One of Rochdale's key summer signings, Tom arrived from Bury as a replacement for the departed Alan Goodall and immediately made himself a fixture at left-back, becoming a big favourite with the Dale fans. With a string of injuries to other Dale defenders, he even had a short spell at centre-back, excelling despite his lack of inches. Highlights of his season included a last-gasp winner from the penalty spot against rivals Wycombe and a brilliant solo goal against Chester a couple of weeks later. Like his uncle Alan, of Liverpool fame, he proved a cool head in a penalty shoot-out, being one of Dale's five successful penalty converters

in the play-off semi-final victory over Darlington.

Bury (From trainee on 2/11/2002) FL 131+12/5 FLC 2+1 FAC 7+1/1 Others 3+1
Rochdale (Free on 5/7/2007) FL 43/2 FLC 2 FAC 1 Others 4

KENNY Patrick (Paddy) Joseph

Born: Halifax, 17 May 1978
Height: 6'1" **Weight:** 14.6
International Honours: Rol: 7
Paddy signed a contract extension to 2010 and started last season as Sheffield United's first-choice goalkeeper but was prone to more misjudgements than usual. He lost his place through injury in October and, when fit, did not return until Ian Bennett was injured in turn. From that point, Paddy was in excellent form, much more confident with crosses and making some tremendous saves. He was very unlucky to concede an FA Cup goal at Middlesbrough in the way he did.

Bury (£10,000 + from Bradford PA on 28/8/1998) FL 133 FLC 5 FAC 7 Others 5
Sheffield U (Free on 26/7/2002) P/FL 232 FLC 14 FAC 17 Others 3

KENTON Darren Edward

Born: Wandsworth, 13 September 1978
Height: 5'9" **Weight:** 11.11
An experienced defender who battled

back into contention after not figuring in Martin Allen's plans at Leicester, he failed to establish a regular place and was allowed by Ian Holloway to move to Leeds in the January transfer window. Darren's experience was added to the Leeds' squad as cover for Rui Marques, who was away on African Cup of Nations duty, in a loan move that became permanent four games later. Although his debut was at centre-half in a 1-0 win at Crewe in January, the bulk of his appearances for the Elland Road club were at left-back, a problem position for Leeds throughout the season. Defensively strong, he also has a good spring, enabling him to win aerial battles against much taller opponents. Was out of contract in the summer and looking for a new club.

Norwich C (From trainee on 3/7/1997) FL 142+16/9 FLC 9+1 FAC 2+2 Others 3
Southampton (Free on 19/5/2003) P/FL 24+5 FLC 3 FAC 1/1
Leicester C (Loaned on 3/3/2005) FL 9+1 FAC 1
Leicester C (Free on 31/7/2006) FL 26+7/2 FLC 2+2 FAC 1
Leeds U (Free on 11/1/2008) FL 16

KEOGH Andrew (Andy) Declan

Born: Dublin, 16 May 1986
Height: 6'0" **Weight:** 11.7

Club Honours: Div 1 '07
International Honours: Rol: 7; B-1; U21-9; Yth
Andy scored a fine 25-yarder against Norwich and the striker teamed up well with a variety of partners at Wolverhampton. He had four games for the Republic of Ireland by October, including one against Germany in the European Championship qualifier but, by Christmas, Andy remained on one League goal before converting a header at Norwich. He hit two in the 4-1 FA Cup win at Watford and in the League began to form an understanding with new signing Sylvan Ebanks-Blake. The goals were more frequent and there were another two in the 3-3 draw with Queens Park Rangers, quickly followed by a goal for the Eire under-21 side, while a diving header against Cardiff made it 11 for Wolves.

Leeds U (From trainee on 20/5/2003) FLC 0+1
Scunthorpe U (Loaned on 6/8/2004) FL 9+3/2
Bury (Loaned on 14/11/2005) FL 4/2
Scunthorpe U (Signed on 14/2/2005) FL 69+17/19 FLC 2 FAC 7/3 Others 2/1
Wolverhampton W (£600,000 on 23/1/2007) FL 50+10/13 FLC 2/1 FAC 3/2 Others 2

KEOGH Richard John

Born: Harlow, 11 August 1986
Height: 6'0" **Weight:** 11.11
International Honours: Rol: U21-8
Strangely, the highly-rated defender did not have much of a look-in at Bristol City in 2007-08, although he captained the Republic of Ireland under-21s for the second time, against Montenegro. Richard went on loan to three clubs and was perhaps surprised to be offered another City contract at the end of the season. Huddersfield was his first stop at the end of August and he began with a faultless 'Man of the Match' display in the victory at Millwall, with some great blocking challenges and towering headers. Marking his home debut with a wonderful 30-yard strike in the defeat by Cheltenham, such was his commitment in the centre of defence that he was kept for a further month. Next came a month on loan with Carlisle in November. There was talk of the move becoming permanent but nothing ensued and he returned to Ashton Gate in January. Tall and powerful, Richard joined Cheltenham in March and was thrust straight into the team at Leeds, despite having met his new team-mates for the first time on the coach heading to Elland Road. He fitted straight in and produced an authoritative performance alongside Shane Duff as

Paddy Kenny

the Robins scored a notable 2-1 victory.
The loan was extended to the end of the
season and he played an important part
in helping Cheltenham retain their League
One status.
Stoke C (From trainee on 6/1/2005)
Bristol C (Free on 26/7/2005) FL 24+16/3
FLC 2 FAC 5+1/1 Others 3+2/1
Wycombe W (Loaned on 10/11/2005) FL
2+1
Huddersfield T (Loaned on 31/8/2007) FL
9/1 Others 1
Carlisle U (Loaned on 22/11/2007) FL 7
Cheltenham T (Loaned on 10/3/2008) FL 10

KERR Scott Anthony
Born: Leeds, 11 December 1981
Height: 5'9" **Weight:** 10.12
The Lincoln team captain in 2007-08,
Scott overcame a frustrating start to
the season, that saw him begin on
the substitutes' bench before going
on to become a regular in the Imps'
midfield. Unlucky to be sent off on a
couple of occasions, which restricted
his appearances further, the second of
these suspensions came at the end of the
season and coincided with the birth of his
first child. Is tenacious in the tackle and
an essential cog of the City midfield.
Bradford C (From trainee on 4/7/2000) PL
0+1 FLC 0+1 Others 1
Hull C (Signed on 20/6/2001) Others 1 (Free
to Scarborough on 7/3/2003)
Lincoln C (Free from Scarborough on 3/8/
2005) FL 118+3/6 FLC 4/1 FAC 5 Others 6

KERRY Lloyd
Born: Chesterfield, 22 January 1988
Height: 6'2" **Weight:** 12.4
Locally born, Lloyd joined Chesterfield
on loan in February and was happy to
extend the agreement to the end of the
season. As a busy, eye-catching midfielder
with a competitive tackle and decent
ball-holding skills, he finishes moves with
a powerful shot that brought goals in the
4-1 win over Lincoln in March. Lloyd's
aim was to earn a Chesterfield contract
when his Sheffield United one expired in
the summer.
Sheffield U (From trainee on 25/7/2006)
Torquay U (Loaned on 16/2/2007) FL 6+1/1
Chesterfield (Loaned on 15/2/2008) FL
8+5/2

KEWELL Harold (Harry)
Born: Sydney, Australia, 22 September
1978
Height: 6'0" **Weight:** 11.10
Club Honours: FAYC '97; UEFACL '05;
FAC '06
International Honours: Australia: 36;
Yth
In the history of Liverpool, no player has

been more unlucky with injuries than the
unfortunate Australian international left-
winger. In five seasons at Anfield, he has
spent more time in the treatment room
or in recuperation than in training or on
the field of play. In 2006-07, he returned
only in the final week but at the start of
the new season was again unavailable
due to a recurrence of a perennial groin
strain in pre-season. Returning to fitness
in November, he was eased back into the
first team but despite making nine starts,
was only a shadow of the player that
Leeds once saw and never completed a
full 90 minutes. When he went on as a
substitute in the FA Cup debacle against
Barnsley in February, it was not only his
final appearance of the season but his
last in a Liverpool shirt. It has to be said
that manager Rafa Benitez has shown
more patience and sympathy to him than
Reds' supporters. He was offered a new
contract, albeit on reduced terms, but
Harry wisely declined and will seek a fresh
start elsewhere, possibly in his native
country. One can only wish him well after
his disappointing stay at Anfield when,
without the injuries, he would probably
be regarded as the most talented
Australian footballer of all time.
Leeds U (Signed from the Australian
Academy of Sport on 23/12/1995) PL
169+12/45 FLC 8/4 FAC 16/6 Others 34+3/8
Liverpool (£5,000,000 on 9/7/2003) PL
81+12/12 FLC 2+3/1 FAC 7+3 Others
19+12/3

KHIZANISHVILI Zurab
Born: Tbilisi, Georgia, 6 October 1981
Height: 6'1" **Weight:** 12.8
Club Honours: SPD '05
International Honours: Georgia: 51
The Georgian suffered from the desire
to pair Chris Samba and Ryan Nelsen at
centre-back for Blackburn. He did not get
on the field in a Premiership game until
October and did not start until December,
when he was superb as an emergency
measure against Chelsea. A torrid game,
when he played right-back at Manchester
City and was undone by Martin Petrov's
pace, was put behind him and whenever
called upon he appeared a technically
sound centre-back whose only problem is
lack of genuinely dominating stature.
Dundee (Signed from Lokomotiv Tbilisi,
Georgia on 8/3/2001) SL 39+3 SLC 3 SC 5
Glasgow Rgrs (Signed on 30/6/2003) SL
39+4 SLC 4+1 SC 2 Others 14
Blackburn Rov (Signed on 31/8/2005) PL
51+6/1 FLC 6+1/1 FAC 6+2 Others 6+1

KIELY Dean Laurence
Born: Salford, 10 October 1970
Height: 6'0" **Weight:** 12.5

Club Honours: Div 2 '97; Div 1 '00;
Ch '08
International Honours: RoI: 10; B-1; E:
Yth; Sch
Dean, one of the oldest goalkeepers ever
to play for West Bromwich at senior level,
had another fine season. He had erratic
moments but his displays between the
posts were as good as ever, saving Albion
from defeat several times, especially
in League games at Bristol City and
Crystal Palace and in home clashes with
Wolverhampton and Sheffield United.
Dean earned the Baggies victories or
draws with some fantastic saves against
Blackpool and Watford at the Hawthorns
and away to Sheffield Wednesday,
Wolverhampton and Norwich, helping
Albion win the last three games as they
headed for the title. During 2007-08
Dean reached the personal milestone
of 650 League appearances and is now
fast approaching 750 club appearances.
He was unlucky with the goal that beat
Albion in the FA Cup semi-final.
Coventry C (From trainee on 30/10/1987)
York C (Signed on 9/3/1990) FL 210 FLC 9
FAC 4 Others 17
Bury (£125,000 on 15/8/1996) FL 137 FLC
13 FAC 4 Others 3
Charlton Ath (£1,000,000 on 26/5/1999)
P/FL 222 FLC 12 FAC 14
Portsmouth (£500,000 on 25/1/2006) PL 15
FLC 1 FAC 1
Luton T (Loaned on 23/11/2006) FL 11
West Bromwich A (Free on 30/1/2007) FL
61 FLC 3 FAC 8 Others 3

KIGHTLY Michael John
Born: Basildon, 24 January 1986
Height: 5'9" **Weight:** 9.12
Club Honours: FAT '06
International Honours: E: U21-3
Michael made a slow start to the
season before getting into the groove
with some dynamic performances
for Wolverhampton. He made three
appearances for England at under-
21 level, while his first brace for
Wolverhampton helped them win 3-2 at
Cardiff. The right-winger was still in good
form in November, when he suffered
an ankle injury. Michael went on as
substitute a couple of times in January,
turning the game when Wolverhampton
faced an embarrassing FA Cup exit to
Cambridge United, but the ankle was still
not right and he required keyhole surgery
in February. He finally returned in April
and celebrated his first full appearance
for nearly five months by scoring
against Cardiff. Michael was voted the
Championship's 'Young Player of the
Season'.
Southend U (From trainee on 12/12/2003)

Kevin Kilbane

FL 2+11 FAC 1+2 Others 2+1/1 (Freed during
2005 close season)
Wolverhampton W (Signed from Grays Ath
on 17/11/2006) FL 44+1/12 FLC 1+1 FAC
0+2/1 Others 2

KILBANE Kevin Daniel
Born: Preston, 1 February 1977
Height: 6'0" **Weight:** 12.10
International Honours: RoI: 87; U21-11
A consistent performer since joining
Wigan, Kevin enjoyed arguably his best
season yet. Following the sale of Leighton
Baines to Kevin's former club Everton
in summer, he played the majority of
games at left-back. Having moved from
his usual midfield slot, he enhanced
his reputation as a fine professional,
flourishing in defence as one of Wigan's
most consistent performers. His natural
attacking instincts and turn of pace
ensured that he was as much of a
threat to opponents as a defensive rock.
Powerful in the air, he netted his only
goal with a brilliant header in the home
win over West Ham. Kevin continues
to be a vital member of the Republic of
Ireland team, used in a more central role.
Preston NE (From trainee on 6/7/1995) FL
39+8/3 FLC 4 FAC 1 Others 1+1
West Bromwich A (£1,000,000 on 13/6/
1997) FL 105+1/15 FLC 12/2 FAC 4/1
Sunderland (£2,500,000 on 16/12/1999)
P/FL 102+11/8 FLC 4 FAC 3+4/1
Everton (£750,000 on 2/9/2003) PL 86+18/4
FLC 3 FAC 10/1 Others 3+1
Wigan Ath (Signed on 31/8/2006) PL 59+7/
2 FLC 2 FAC 3

KILBEY Thomas (Tom)
Charles
Born: Waltham Forest, 19 October 1990
Height: 6'3" **Weight:** 13.8
As a product of Millwall's youth
programme, Tom had a first-team chance
against Swansea in the Johnstone's Paint
Trophy, going on as substitute. A left-
sided midfield player, he showed such
promise that several clubs began to sit up
and take notice. Eventually, Tom signed
for Portsmouth, which should be a good
move for such a talented player.
Millwall (Trainee) Others 0+1
Portsmouth (£400,000 on 6/2/2008)

KILGALLON Matthew (Matt)
Shaun
Born: York, 8 January 1984
Height: 6'1" **Weight:** 12.5
International Honours: E: U21-5; Yth
Following a somewhat shaky start to his
Sheffield United career in 2006-07, Matt
made a steady if unspectacular start to his
second season. However, as the campaign
progressed, Matt's performances in the

centre of defence improved and he was particularly impressive during the second half of the season. Excellent anticipation is backed by strength in the air and accurate tackling. Despite missing few games, he received only one booking and was runner-up in the supporters' 'Player of the Year' poll.
Leeds U (From trainee on 10/1/2001) P/FL 73+7/3 FLC 6+1 FAC 4 Others 3+1
West Ham U (Loaned on 23/8/2003) FL 1+2 FLC 1
Sheffield U (£1,750,000 + on 8/1/2007) P/FL 45+1/2 FLC 3 FAC 3

KILKENNY Neil Martin
Born: Enfield, 19 December 1985
Height: 5'8" **Weight:** 10.8
International Honours: Australia: 1; U23. E: Yth
After a three-year gap, the talented central midfielder rejoined Oldham on loan from Birmingham on the eve of last season. The midfield dynamo's initial impact was checked by a torn thigh muscle but, once fit, he began to shine again in the play-making role that previously made him such a crowd favourite. Neil went on to net three times in 25 appearances and Oldham tried to sign him on a permanent basis in January. Following a starring role in Latics' victory at Leeds on New Year's Day, the final game of the Australian international's time, he was successful competition from Elland Road for his services, Leeds beating Oldham and promotion rivals Doncaster for Neil's signature. Although recruited by Dennis Wise, his excellent use of the ball was ideally suited to new manager Gary McAllister's passing game. He continually caught the eye by pulling the strings in midfield and opened his Leeds' scoring account with a thumping drive from the edge of the box in the 2-0 home win over Bournemouth in March. After Leeds' play-off defeat by Doncaster at Wembley he was scheduled to join the Australian squad for the Beijing Olympics.
Birmingham C (From trainee at Arsenal on 27/1/2004) P/FL 6+20 FLC 3+3 FAC 1+6
Oldham Ath (Loaned on 19/11/2004) FL 24+3/4 FAC 3 Others 4/1
Oldham Ath (Loaned on 10/8/2007) FL 19+1/1 FLC 1/1 FAC 3/1 Others 1
Leeds U (Signed on 4/1/2008) FL 16/1 Others 3

KILLOCK Shane Adam
Born: Huddersfield, 12 March 1989
Height: 6'0" **Weight:** 12.4
Having shown much promise, the 18-year-old Huddersfield Academy product

was a surprise addition to the back four in the away defeat by Crewe. Cool and calm, the youngster made a positive start to his Town career. Strong in the air and in the tackle, Shane remained involved around the first team before being loaned to Hyde in the Blue Square North to gain experience.
Huddersfield T (From trainee on 16/1/2008) FL 1

KIM Do-Heon
Born: Dongducheon, South Korea, 14 July 1982
Height: 5'9" **Weight:** 11.7
International Honours: South Korea: 48
Midfield playmaker with a terrific engine, Do-Heon played for South Korea in the 2004 Olympic Games and 2006 World Cup. He had 32 caps and six goals to his credit when he joined West Bromwich on loan in January. Do-Heon scored nine goals in 106 appearances for Bluewings, with whom he won the South Korean League in 2004, and struck eight times in 35 starts for Chunma. He made his Albion debut as a substitute in the 5-0 FA Cup win at Coventry and netted his first goal in England with a close-range header in the last match 2-0 League win at Queens Park Rangers that clinched the Championship for Albion.
West Bromwich A (Signed from Seongnam Ilhwa Chunma, South Korea, ex Suwon Samsung Bluewings, on 31/1/2008) FL 1+3/1 FAC 0+3

KING Andrew (Andy) Philip
Born: Barnstaple, 29 October 1988
Height: 6'0" **Weight:** 11.10
International Honours: W: U21-1; Yth
Andy is a highly-rated young Leicester midfielder who broke through from nowhere to make a handful of appearances last season, as well as being elevated to the Welsh under-21 squad. His only goal of the campaign, a stunning 25-yarder against Southampton, was voted the 'Goal of the Season' by the Foxes' Supporters' Club.
Leicester C (From trainee on 23/5/2007) FL 5+6/1 FAC 0+1

KING Gary Ian
Born: Grimsby, 27 January 1990
Height: 5'10" **Weight:** 11.4
A young striker, Gary was one of nine outfield products of Lincoln's youth set-up to appear in the League during 2007-08 and he marked his full debut in April with a goal in the 3-1 home win over Brentford. Gary, who joined the Imps as an under-nine, had earlier the same day agreed a one-year professional contract. According to reports he is a positive and

determined youngster who chases half chances and has been described within the club as a rising star.
Lincoln C (Trainee) FL 3+3/1

KING Ledley Brenton
Born: Stepney, 12 October 1980
Height: 6'2" **Weight:** 13.6
Club Honours: FLC '08
International Honours: E: 19; B-1; U21-12; Yth
The Tottenham captain continues to suffer with long-term knee problems and was restricted to ten games last season. In fact, he managed only five full games but thankfully these included all 120 minutes of the memorable Carling Cup final victory over Chelsea. So Ledley's dream was fulfilled, a just reward for his dedication and loyalty, when he climbed the Wembley steps to lift and parade the club's first trophy of the 21st Century. Ledley also played in the home and away legs of the semi-final against Arsenal and the crucial UEFA Cup game against PSV Eindhoven. When fit, he is an immaculate defender, worthy of international recognition. This was again offered in 2007-08 but turned down because of his injury problems. He was rested at the end of the season in the hope that his career can be renewed.
Tottenham H (From trainee on 22/7/1998) PL 194+3/7 FLC 18/1 FAC 17+1/3 Others 8

KING Liam
Born: Rainworth, 31 December 1987
Height: 5'9" **Weight:** 10.2
Liam, another Rotherham player who had come through the junior ranks, failed to make his mark at senior level, with just one substitute appearance, and spent much of the season on loan in non-League football. Was released at the end of the campaign.
Rotherham U (From trainee on 3/8/2006) FL 4+3

KING Mark
Born: Liverpool, 6 June 1988
Height: 5'10" **Weight:** 12.0
Signed in January after being freed by Blackburn, Mark played his first two games for Accrington at left-back and was then moved into midfield for two games, all of them ending in defeat. He was dropped to the bench for two games and after that called upon only rarely, even as a substitute. It was a disappointing time for the young player. Was released in the summer.
Blackburn Rov (From trainee on 8/10/2007)
Accrington Stanley (Free on 11/1/2008) FL 4+2

Simon King

KING Marlon Francis

Born: Dulwich, 26 April 1980
Height: 6'1" **Weight:** 11.12
International Honours: Jamaica: 13
Fully fit after his previous injury-blighted season in the Premiership and with an improved contract, great things were expected of Marlon at Watford in 2007-08. A skilful and hard-working striker with an excellent scoring record, he made a slow start but enjoyed a purple patch in October with seven goals in eight matches, taking him to the landmark of 100 League goals. In January, Marlon was set to join Fulham but the deal broke down and he ended up at Wigan. Marlon made his Blues' debut in a three-man attack against Middlesbrough, alongside Emile Heskey and Marcus Bent, and netted his only goal at Blackburn, converting a penalty. Used at the end of the season as a substitute, he never stopped running and his upper-body strength makes him a formidable opponent. Marlon is also an excellent team player, with his unselfishness in holding the ball and providing openings for colleagues.
Barnet (From trainee on 9/9/1998) FL 36+17/ 14 FLC 0+2 FAC 0+1 Others 2+2
Gillingham (£255,000 on 28/6/2000) FL 82+19/40 FLC 6+3/4 FAC 5+1/3
Nottingham F (£950,000 on 27/11/2003) FL 40+10/10 FLC 3/3 FAC 3+1/2

Leeds U (Loaned on 4/3/2005) FL 4+5
Watford (£500,000 on 12/7/2005) P/FL 77+4/36 FAC 2+1 Others 3/1
Wigan Ath (£5,000,000 on 25/1/2008) PL 8+7/1

KING Simon Daniel Roy

Born: Oxford, 11 April 1983
Height: 5'11" **Weight:** 12.4
Club Honours: FC '05
International Honours: E: SP
A highly-rated central defender who arrived at Gillingham from Barnet in the summer, Simon was initially used at left-back but when switched to the centre of the defence soon began to show his true worth with some commanding performances. He was runner-up in the 'Player of the Year' voting.
Oxford U (From trainee on 13/12/2000) FL 3+1
Barnet (Signed on 15/7/2003) FL 74+1/2 FLC 3/1 FAC 5 Others 2
Gillingham (£200,000 on 30/7/2007) FL 39+3 FLC 1 FAC 1 Others 3

KINGSON Richard Paul Franck

Born: Accra, Ghana, 13 June 1978
Height: 6'0" **Weight:** 13.0
International Honours: Ghana: 56
Arriving from Ankaraspor in the summer, Richard made one Premier League appearance, in Eric Black's only game as caretaker manager at Birmingham, and let in a soft goal against Portsmouth but in two Carling Cup games the goalkeeper was highly impressive. Agile, with a good spring and sharp reflexes, he knocked himself out at Blackburn after colliding with a post when making a brave save and had to be taken to hospital. Richard impressed for Ghana at the African Cup of Nations. Was released in the summer.
Birmingham C (Free from Ankaraspor, Turkey, ex Great Olympics, Sakaryaspor, Goztepe Izmir, Antalyaspor, Elazigspor, Ankaraspor, Galatasaray, Hammarby, on 1/8/2007) PL 1 FLC 2

KIRALY Gabor Ferenc

Born: Szombathely, Hungary, 1 April 1976
Height: 6'3" **Weight:** 13.6
International Honours: Hungary: 70
Clearly signed as Burnley's first-choice goalkeeper, Gabor arrived at Turf Moor from Crystal Palace in the pre-season and quickly established himself as a capable shot-stopper and generally reliable presence in the area. Although he was almost ever-present until January when Owen Coyle gave second-choice Brian Jensen his chance, it was to prove virtually the end for Gabor, as one further brief run in the side ended with a disappointing

display against Wolverhampton before he was made available for transfer at the end of the season.
Crystal Palace (Free from Hertha Berlin, Germany on 12/8/2004) P/FL 104 FLC 1 FAC 4 Others 2
Aston Villa (Loaned on 15/12/2006) PL 5 FAC 1
Burnley (Free on 30/7/2007) FL 27 FLC 1 FAC 1

KIRK Andrew (Andy) Robert

Born: Belfast, 29 May 1979
Height: 5'11" **Weight:** 11.7
International Honours: NI: 8; U21-9; Yth; Sch
Manager Stuart Gray took the striker off Northampton's transfer list at the start of 2007-08 and the confidence was repaid with nine goals in his first 12 games. However, when the goals dried up in what was an uneven period for Andy, Yeovil offered him terms during the January transfer window. Russell Slade clinched the signing and the Ulsterman scored some crucial goals during the end of season run-in to help the Glovers avoid relegation. He quickly became a fans' favourite and although left out for the final few games, still has another year on his contract with the Glovers.
Heart of Midlothian (£50,000 from Glentoran on 19/2/1999) SL 64+50/30 SLC 5+4/2 SC 5+2 Others 1+3
Boston U (Signed on 22/7/2004) FL 25/18 FLC 1 FAC 4/2 Others 0+1
Northampton T (£125,000 on 11/3/2005) FL 82+24/30 FLC 3/3 FAC 5+4/2 Others 4+1/1
Yeovil T (Free on 18/1/2008) FL 15+4/4

KIRKLAND Christopher (Chris) Edmund

Born: Barwell, 2 May 1981
Height: 6'6" **Weight:** 11.7
Club Honours: FLC '03
International Honours: E: 1; U21-8; Yth
Chris is regarded as one of the best all-round goalkeepers in the Premiership and was vital to Wigan throughout last season. Having suffered with injuries during his career, he missed only one League game. Tremendously agile for his height, with safe hands and ever-growing confidence, he is rated as one of England's best young goalkeepers. A terrific shot-stopper, he fills the goal and his presence adds stability to the defence. He produced many 'Man of the Match' performances in the quest to preserve Wigan's Premiership status, his best probably coming in the away match against Chelsea. Named in Fabio Capello's first England squad for the friendly against Switzerland, he was also

Wigan's 'Players' Player of the Year'. The final game of the season was his 150th career appearance.
Coventry C (From trainee on 6/5/1998) P/FL 24 FLC 3+1 FAC 1
Liverpool (£6,000,000 + on 31/8/2001) PL 25 FLC 6 FAC 3 Others 11
West Bromwich A (Loaned on 18/7/2005) PL 10 FAC 2
Wigan Ath (Signed on 22/7/2006) PL 63 FAC 1

KISHISHEV Radostin Prodanov
Born: Burgas, Bulgaria, 30 July 1974
Height: 5'10" **Weight:** 12.4
International Honours: Bulgaria: 78
Signed from Charlton, the experienced midfielder seemed to be a key Martin Allen signing during the summer but he failed to fit in at Leicester and was allowed to link up with Leeds in October for a second loan spell. The Bulgarian international was welcomed with open arms at Elland Road, as he starred for Leeds when on loan from Charlton the previous season in their fruitless battle to avoid the drop from the Championship. This time round, injuries prevented him from performing at his best and he returned to his parent club. Back at Leicester, Radostin never progressed beyond the reserves under Ian Holloway, despite obvious shortcomings and injury problems in the first-team midfield, and will look to be back on an even keel this coming term.
Charlton Ath (£300,000 + from Liteks Lovech, Bulgaria, ex Neftokhimik Burgas, Bursapor, on 14/8/2000) PL 149+30/2 FLC 7+2 FAC 11+1
Leeds U (Loaned on 2/3/2007) FL 10
Leicester C (Free on 7/8/2007) FL 2+5 FLC 2
Leeds U (Loaned on 23/10/2007) FL 5+2

KISNORBO Patrick Fabio Maxime
Born: Melbourne, Australia, 24 March 1981
Height: 6'2" **Weight:** 11.9
International Honours: Australia: 14; U23; Yth
A consistent Leicester central defender, who was voted as the supporters' 'Player of the Season' for the second successive year, Patrick was not quite as prolific as in previous campaigns but his presence helped to turn the Foxes' defence into one of the meanest in the division, despite relegation. He suffered a cruciate ligament knee injury in the vital 'six-pointer' against Sheffield Wednesday, an incident that may well have tipped the relegation pendulum against City, and is likely to be out of football for around six months. The injury will have repercussions for Australia's World Cup campaign.

Heart of Midlothian (Signed from South Melbourne, Australia on 2/7/2003) SL 45+3/1 SLC 4 SC 2+1 Others 9/1
Leicester C (Free on 15/7/2005) FL 117+1/9 FLC 6+2/1 FAC 3+1/1

KITCHEN Ashley James
Born: Edwinstowe, 10 October 1988
Height: 5'11" **Weight:** 11.6
Ashley was called into action for Mansfield during an injury crisis last October, filling in at right-back, and despite not being fully fit he slotted in quite well. In December, needing match practice, he was sent for a one-month loan to Gainsborough.
Mansfield T (From trainee on 12/7/2007) FL 5 FAC 0+1

KITSON David (Dave) Barry
Born: Hitchin, 21 January 1980
Height: 6'3" **Weight:** 12.11
Club Honours: Ch '06
Just after Christmas, it was rumoured in the media that Dave might receive a surprise call-up to Fabio Capello's England squad as he was the leading English scorer in the Premiership, with eight to his credit. And this after becoming the quickest Reading substitute to be red-carded, just 37 seconds after being introduced to the 0-0 draw at Old Trafford on the first weekend of the season. But the call never came and the goals dried up as the lanky striker often found himself ploughing the proverbial lone furrow as Reading were forced to employ a defensive 4-5-1 formation. He often had to come deep to find the ball and also defended with enthusiasm, especially at set pieces. His only goals in the second half of the season came in the 2-0 home win over Manchester City and on the last day of the Premiership, when a 4-0 win at Derby was not enough to save the Royals from relegation.
Cambridge U (Signed from Arlesey T on 16/3/2001) FL 97+5/40 FLC 4/1 FAC 9/2 Others 7+1/4
Reading (£300,000 on 30/12/2003) P/FL 111+24/54 FLC 5+1/4 FAC 5+1/2

KLEIN-DAVIES Joshua (Josh) David
Born: Bristol, 6 July 1989
Height: 6'2" **Weight:** 14.7
International Honours: W: Yth
Josh, a former Bristol City Academy striker, was on loan at Yate, where he scored five goals, before being recalled by Bristol Rovers over Christmas. After making his debut as a substitute late in the match against Carlisle, Josh scored his first League goal against Huddersfield and completed the season with a number of

promising substitute appearances.
Bristol Rov (From trainee at Bristol C on 19/7/2007) FL 2+8/1

KNIGHT David Sean
Born: Houghton-le-Spring, 15 January 1987
Height: 6'0" **Weight:** 11.7
International Honours: E: Yth
The former Middlesbrough goalkeeper joined Swansea just before the August transfer window closed. David's only first-team opportunities came in the FA Cup first round victory over Billericay and the FA of Wales Premier Cup tie at Newport. He injured ankle ligaments in November but was back in the squad within a couple of weeks. Was out of contract in the summer and looking for a new club.
Middlesbrough (From trainee on 3/2/2005)
Darlington (Loaned on 30/12/2005) FL 3
Oldham Ath (Loaned on 25/8/2006) FL 2
Swansea C (Free on 31/8/2007) FAC 1

KNIGHT Leon Leroy
Born: Hackney, 16 September 1982
Height: 5'4" **Weight:** 9.10
Club Honours: AMC '06; Div 2 '08
International Honours: E: Yth
Pint-sized striker Leon was the man MK Dons felt would replace departed leading scorer Izzy McLeod but although he scored a couple of cracking goals in a mid-October televised home game against Lincoln, he generally failed to impress and was sold to Wycombe in January. Initially having to settle for a place on the substitutes' bench, Leon replaced John Sutton in attack in February and formed a good partnership with Scott McGleish, including a spell of three goals in four games. Against Darlington, he scored with a remarkable overhead kick and the following week bagged a spectacular 25-yard effort against Wrexham. Leon has good close control and a nose for finding the right place, benefiting from the excellent support supplied by McGleish.
Chelsea (From trainee on 17/9/1999) Others 0+1
Queens Park Rgrs (Loaned on 9/3/2001) FL 10+1
Huddersfield T (Loaned on 23/10/2001) FL 31/16 FAC 2/1 Others 4
Sheffield Wed (Loaned on 8/7/2002) FL 14+10/3 FLC 2 FAC 0+1
Brighton & Hove A (£100,000 on 24/7/2003) FL 98+10/34 FLC 4 FAC 2 Others 6/2
Swansea C (£125,000 on 6/11/2006) FL 20+8/15 Others 5+2/4
Barnsley (Loaned on 23/11/2006) FL 6+3
MK Dons (Signed on 22/1/2007) FL 22+11/5 FLC 1/1 Others 0+2
Wycombe W (£50,000 on 5/1/2008) FL 12+8/5 Others 0+2

KNIGHT Zatyiah (Zat)

Born: Solihull, 2 May 1980
Height: 6'6" **Weight:** 13.8
International Honours: E: 2; U21-4
Zat began the season at Fulham, featuring in the first four Premier League games before moving to Aston Villa, against whom he featured in his final match for the Craven Cottage club. A towering central defender who is dominant in the air and an excellent reader of the game, enabling him to time last-ditch tackles to perfection, Zat joined Villa, the team he has always supported, at the end of August and scored on his debut with a header against Chelsea. He lost his place to Curtis Davies at the turn of the year after being sent off against Chelsea on Boxing Day and missed ten games. The big plus was his good relationship with Martin Laursen in the centre of Villa's defence that produced a string of consistent performances during the season.
Fulham *(Signed from Rushall Olympic on 19/2/1999) P/FL 140+10/3 FLC 9 FAC 15+2/1 Others 3+2*
Peterborough U *(Loaned on 25/2/2000) FL 8*
Aston Villa *(£4,000,000 on 29/8/2007) PL 25+2/1 FLC 1*

KNIGHTS Darryl James

Born: Ipswich, 1 May 1988
Height: 5'7" **Weight:** 10.1
Club Honours: FAYC '05
International Honours: E: Yth
Arriving at Yeovil on a permanent basis in the summer, having previously been on loan from Ipswich, Darryl showed glimpses of his lightning pace in the pre-season friendlies. However, after making only four substitute appearances early in the campaign and suffering personal problems, the striker went on loan to Blue Square Premier Cambridge in October. He followed with another loan at Kidderminster in January and, having done well and scored four goals, signed for them after being released by Yeovil at the end of the season.
Ipswich T *(From trainee on 20/5/2005) FL 0+1*
Yeovil T *(Free on 24/2/2007) FL 0+7 Others 0+2*

KONCHESKY Paul Martyn

Born: Barking, 15 May 1981
Height: 5'10" **Weight:** 10.12
International Honours: E: 2; U21-15; Yth
Paul made Fulham his fourth London club when he moved from West Ham last summer. A left-sided defender, he is strong in the tackle and composed on

the ball, often calmly bringing it from defence to set up an attacking move. An excellent crosser of the ball, he was rarely out of the side, missing only a few games through suspension. Paul was the regular left-back except for one occasion when he was on the left of midfield. Although he failed to find the net he can shoot effectively from distance and was particularly unlucky not to open his account in the home game against Wigan.
Charlton Ath *(From trainee on 25/5/1998) P/FL 91+58/5 FLC 5+4/1 FAC 8+3*
Tottenham H *(Loaned on 1/9/2003) PL 10+2 FLC 2+1*
West Ham U *(£1,500,000 on 5/7/2005) PL 58+1/1 FLC 1+1 FAC 7/1 Others 2*
Fulham *(£2,000,000 on 16/7/2007) PL 33 FLC 2 FAC 2*

KONSTANTOPOULOS Dimitrios (Dimi)

Born: Kalamata, Greece, 29 November 1978
Height: 6'4" **Weight:** 12.2
International Honours: Greece: U21-9
Signed by Iain Dowie from Hartlepool last summer after keeping a record number of clean sheets, the giant Greek goalkeeper had an unhappy time at Coventry and

Paul Konchesky

kept only one clean sheet in 23 games. That was at Cardiff early in the season when he pulled off five superb saves. He had other moments, including an excellent game at Blackburn in the FA Cup. After Chris Coleman's arrival he went on loan to Nottingham Forest but was injured before playing a game and returned to Coventry.
Hartlepool U *(Free from Deportivo Farense, Portugal on 22/1/2004) FL 117 FLC 5 FAC 10 Others 7*
Coventry C *(Free on 10/7/2007) FL 21 FAC 2*

KOREN Robert

Born: Ljubljana, Slovenia, 20 September 1980
Height: 5'9" **Weight:** 11.3
Club Honours: Ch '08
International Honours: Slovenia: 30; U21-12
Proving to be the perfect partner for Jonathan Greening in West Bromwich's midfield, Robert had an outstanding season, producing hard-working displays and scoring his share of goals, ten in total, including excellent strikes in League games against Southampton (away), Bristol City (home) and Scunthorpe (home). He also came close to equalizing in the FA Cup semi-final against Portsmouth, when his shot struck the bar. Robert improves by the game and it is important that he stays fit for the new season.
West Bromwich A *(Free from Lillestrom, Norway, ex NK Drovograd, NK Publikum, on 5/1/2007) FL 53+5/10 FLC 0+1 FAC 6+3/1 Others 3*

KOUMAS Jason

Born: Wrexham, 25 September 1979
Height: 5'10" **Weight:** 11.0
International Honours: W: 29
Jason joined Wigan from West Bromwich in the close season and immediately seemed to be the creative midfielder they were seeking. He was used either on the left or in central midfield but was most effective in the middle, just behind the strikers. Very comfortable on the ball, his passing was at times outstanding and the only surprise was that he managed only one League goal, becoming one of four different Wigan players to score from the penalty spot. Possessing exceptional skill and technique, he demonstrated the adaptability and workrate required for the physical intensity of the Premiership. A regular for Wales, Jason twice scored two goals in each of the internationals against the Republic of Ireland and Norway.
Tranmere Rov *(From trainee on 27/11/1997) FL 96+31/25 FLC 9+5/2 FAC 9/5*
West Bromwich A *(£2,500,000 on*

PFA FOOTBALLERS' WHO'S WHO

29/8/2002) P/FL 103+20/23 FLC 6 FAC 8+1
Others 3
Cardiff C (Loaned on 2/8/2005) FL 42+2/12
FLC 2+1/1
Wigan Ath (£5,600,000 + on 10/7/2007) PL
21+9/1 FLC 0+1 FAC 1+1

KOVACS Janos
Born: Budapest, Hungary, 11 September
1985
Height: 6'4" **Weight:** 14.10
International Honours: Hungary: Yth
The imposing Hungarian centre-
half turned in powerful displays for
Chesterfield. His obvious passion for the
game struck a chord with the fans, who
took him to their hearts. Janos has the
potential to go a long way in the League
and he has already cemented a place with
Chesterfield. The highlight was probably
his first senior goal, scored against Lincoln
in November and celebrated with simple,
uncoordinated joy.
Chesterfield (Free from MTK Hungaria,
Hungary on 11/8/2005) FL 55+2/2 FLC 2 FAC
1 Others 2

KOZLUK Robert (Rob)
Born: Mansfield, 5 August 1977
Height: 5'8" **Weight:** 11.7
International Honours: E: U21-2
Rob was released by Sheffield United
during the summer and made an
opening-day Barnsley debut. After a
number of games in his favourite right-
back position, he found himself out of
the starting line-up but came back for
his longest and most consistent spell
in the team for the last three months
of the season. A dependable full-back,
his experience saved the Reds in many
dangerous situations.
Derby Co (From trainee on 10/2/1996) PL
9+7 FLC 3 FAC 2+1
Sheffield U (Signed on 12/3/1999) P/FL
193+20/2 FLC 8+1 FAC 11 Others 3
Huddersfield T (Loaned on 7/9/2000) FL 14
Preston NE (Loaned on 6/1/2005) FL 0+1
FAC 1
Barnsley (Free on 17/7/2007) FL 24 FLC 2
FAC 3+1

KRANJCAR Niko
Born: Vienna, Austria, 13 August 1984
Height: 6'1" **Weight:** 13.3
Club Honours: FAC '08
International Honours: Croatia: 44;
U21-3
Some observers wondered whether Niko
would be capable of withstanding the
rigours of a full English Premier League
season. A foot injury sidelined him during
August but after that, he went from
strength to strength, proved the sceptics
completely wrong and became a fixture

on the left of Portsmouth's midfield,
contributing regular 'Man of the Match'
performances. He has all the qualities
in his locker and has added strength
and stamina to go with his exceptional
technical ability. Niko has genuine vision
and perception along with an exquisite
right foot. While he scored only five goals
for Pompey, some of those have been
screamers from 25-yard free kicks. He
played regularly for Croatia and most
English fans will remember him opening
the scoring with a shot from 30 yards as
Croatia beat England 3-2 at Wembley
in November to prevent the home team
from qualifying for the final stages of the
2008 European Championships.
Portsmouth (£3,500,000 from Hajduk Split,
Croatia, ex Dynamo Zagreb, on 31/8/2006) PL
42+16/6 FLC 4 FAC 8/1

KUDJODJI Ebenezer (Ben)
Joseph Tettley
Born: Dunstable, 23 April 1989
Height: 6'0" **Weight:** 11.11
Another local product of the Crystal
Palace Academy, Ben is a tall, busy striker
who was a regular in the reserves and
youth team last season, impressing many
with his ability. He made his debut as a

last-minute substitute against Barnsley in
March and was a non-playing sub in the
next game before being released in the
summer.
Crystal Palace (From trainee on 5/7/2007)
FL 0+1

KUIPERS Michel
Born: Amsterdam, Holland, 26 June 1974
Height: 6'2" **Weight:** 14.10
Club Honours: Div 3 '01; Div 2 '02
After three seasons of injury problems
and playing second-fiddle to other
goalkeepers, Michel finally regained the
Brighton jersey and had an excellent
campaign. A good, all-round goalkeeper
with particularly sharp reactions, the
former Dutch Marine was the only
ever-present player as Albion made a late
dash for the play-offs and may consider
himself unlucky to have finished only
third in the 'Player of the Season' poll.
Now approaching the veteran stage,
Michel was consistent throughout,
probably saving his best display in the
goalless draw at Nottingham Forest. As
the only remaining player to have served
the returning manager Micky Adams at
Withdean previously, he will be doing all
he can to keep his place.

Michel Kuipers

Bristol Rov *(Free from SDW Amsterdam, Holland on 20/1/1999) FL 1*
Brighton & Hove A *(Free on 4/7/2000) FL 198+1 FLC 7 FAC 12 Others 10*
Hull C *(Loaned on 29/8/2003) FL 3*
Boston U *(Loaned on 24/11/2005) FL 4*
Boston U *(Loaned on 16/2/2006) FL 11*

KUQI Shefki

Born: Vuqitern, Kosovo, 10 November 1976
Height: 6'2" **Weight:** 13.10
International Honours: Finland: 52
An out-and-out striker who is a handful for any opposing defence and a constant threat in the air, Shefki was among the substitute for Crystal Palace's first three games last August before going to Premiership Fulham in a surprise loan signing. Spending the first half of the season at Craven Cottage and impressing with his commitment, most of his ten appearances were from the bench. It was in this role that he gave his finest display in the home win over Reading in November, setting up a goal for Clint Dempsey. He returned to Selhurst Park when a full transfer fell through but a breach of club rules resulted in Shefki being transfer listed before going to his old club Ipswich on loan in March. Having received a tremendous welcome from the crowd when he appeared as a substitute against Charlton, his comeback did not last long as he was stretchered off after just ten minutes with a hamstring problem. Initially it was thought that he would miss the rest of the season but he recovered well and featured in the final two games. Shefki has indicated he would like to make his return permanent. Despite a lack of first-team exposure, he continued to feature for Finland and scored in a Euro 2008 qualifier against Azerbaijan.
Stockport Co *(£300,000 from FC Jokerit, Finland, ex HJK Helsinki, on 31/1/2001) FL 32+3/11 FLC 2/1 FAC 1*
Sheffield Wed *(£700,000 + on 11/1/2002) FL 58+6/19 FLC 3 FAC 1*
Ipswich T *(Free on 26/9/2003) FL 69+10/30 FLC 0+2 FAC 2+1/1 Others 3+1/1*
Blackburn Rov *(Free on 1/6/2005) PL 15+19/7 FLC 4+2/1 FAC 1+1*
Crystal Palace *(£2,500,000 on 31/8/2006) FL 26+17/7 FLC 1 FAC 1+1/1*
Fulham *(Loaned on 31/8/2007) PL 3+7*
Ipswich T *(Loaned on 14/3/2008) FL 2+2*

KUSZCZAK Tomasz

Born: Krosno Odrzanskie, Poland, 20 March 1982
Height: 6'3" **Weight:** 13.3
Club Honours: UEFACL '08
International Honours: Poland: 6

Signed from West Bromwich in the summer, following a year's loan, the highly-rated Polish international was again the goalkeeping understudy to Edwin Van Der Sar at Manchester United. Making only fleeting appearances in the side, he enjoyed a four-match unbroken run in the Premiership during December and played three times in the Champions' League. Having replaced Van Der Sar in United's FA Cup quarter-final against Portsmouth at Old Trafford, Tomasz was shown a red card for a foul on Milan Baroš that resulted in the penalty that won the game for Pompey. Remaining positive whilst playing second fiddle to Van Der Sar, Tomasz says he wants to become the number-one goalkeeper at Old Trafford. Depending on Van Der Sar's ambitions and the emergence of Ben Foster already being tipped as the eventual successor Tomasz may have only another season to impress the Old Trafford faithful.
West Bromwich A *(Free from Hertha Berlin, Germany on 2/8/2004) PL 30+1 FLC 3 FAC 0+1*
Manchester U *(Signed on 11/8/2006) PL 14+1 FLC 3 FAC 5+1 Others 3+2*

KUYT Dirk

Born: Katwijk, Holland, 22 July 1980
Height: 6'0" **Weight:** 12.1
International Honours: Holland: 42
When Rafa Benitez signed the Dutch international striker in 2006, it was assumed that he would be the consistent scorer Liverpool's lacked but after a promising debut season, the goals dried up for Dirk in 2007-08, at least in the Premiership. In fairness it must be recorded that he was deeply affected by the death of his father in the summer and Benitez kept faith because of his wholehearted commitment to the team ethic. Of his three Premiership goals in 24 starts, two were from penalties in the same game, the local derby against Everton at Goodison Park in October. The winner came in the 90th-minute, with the Dutchman showing great composure to convert the penalty. He was fortunate to have the opportunity following an uncharacteristic two-footed tackle on Phil Neville for which he received a caution rather than a merited red card. Despite his dearth of Premiership goals, he was prolific in the Champions' League, with seven from ten starts, many of which kept their European adventure on the road, notably in an undeserved 1-1 draw in Porto, the vital 85th-minute opener in the 2-0 home victory over Inter Milan, the vital away goal at Arsenal in the quarter-final and the first in the home match

against Chelsea in the semi-final. Most of his goals were scored from close range and were often scrappy, the result of being in the right place at the right time. In the closing weeks of the season Benitez switched Dirk to the right of midfield with Steven Gerrard pushed forward as a support striker. While the new formation worked well, with Liverpool finishing the season strongly, Dirk can never be faulted for commitment and enthusiasm, Howerver, it seemed odd that a once prolific striker should end up as a makeshift winger.
Liverpool *(£9,000,000 from Feyenoord, Holland, ex Quick Boys, FC Utrecht, on 18/8/2006) PL 51+15/15 FLC 0+2 FAC 3+2/2 Others 20+3/8*

KYLE Kevin Alistair

Born: Stranraer, 7 June 1981
Height: 6'3" **Weight:** 13.7
International Honours: S: 9; B- 3; U21-12
The tall striker had an excellent start at Coventry last season, scoring with a trademark header in the 4-1 win at Barnsley, but played only one more game before hip and ankle injuries sidelined him. On his return at the end of October, he was subjected to booing from a section of the Coventry crowd despite a gutsy and hard-working display against Watford. His finest moment came at Queens Park Rangers when, as a late substitute, he headed in the winner in stoppage-time, but he continued to be the butt of the crowd. Joining Wolverhampton on loan until the end of the season, Kevin was to be the big target-man that Wolves sometimes needed. He began as a substitute, then started the next three games. Kevin was then on the bench again, scoring with a strong drive at Crystal Palace, and also made a noticeable impact at Charlton after coming on for the last ten minutes. He twice went close before setting up the winner with a slide rule centre.
Sunderland *(Free from Ayr Boswell on 25/9/1998) P/FL 59+32/11 FLC 4+2/5 FAC 8+2/1 Others 2/2*
Huddersfield T *(Loaned on 8/9/2000) FL 0+4*
Darlington *(Loaned on 1/11/2000) FL 5/1 FAC 3/1*
Rochdale *(Loaned on 26/1/2001) FL 3+3*
Coventry C *(£600,000 on 25/8/2006) FL 25+19/5 FLC 0+1 FAC 2*
Wolverhampton W *(Loaned on 31/1/2008) FL 3+9/1 FAC 1*

L

LACZKO Zsolt
Born: Szeged, Hungary, 18 December 1986
Height: 6'0" **Weight:** 12.8
International Honours: Hungary: U21
The enthusiastic Hungarian winger impressed during a trial at Leicester in December and again in his early first-team outings, especially against Coventry at the Walkers Stadium. Gradually, though, the physical demands of the Championship seemed to wear him down and he became less effective, especially away from home, before dropping out of the picture during the latter stages of the season.
Leicester C (Loaned from Olympiakos, Greece, ex Ferencvaros, Levadiakos - loan, on 9/1/2008) FL 5+4

LAFFERTY Kyle
Born: Enniskillen, 16 September 1987
Height: 6'4" **Weight:** 11.0
International Honours: NI: 16; U21-2; Yth
By now probably Burnley's most high-profile player through his Northern Ireland exploits, Kyle remains something of a work in progress. A striker possessing most of the obvious assets, height, pace, aggression and enthusiasm, he spent virtually the whole of the season employed on the Clarets' left wing, ostensibly because of the wide choice of front men available, although Kyle certainly offered attributes that his rivals lacked. That said, he enjoyed a fine season playing out wide, with few Championship defenders able to live with his speed. He finally got his chance in the centre near the end of the campaign and celebrated with a superb goal against Barnsley. It is to be hoped he remains at Turf Moor long enough for the fans to see more of the same.
Burnley (From trainee on 2/12/2005) FL 52+31/10 FLC 3+1 FAC 1+1
Darlington (Loaned on 6/1/2006) FL 9/3

LAIRD Marc James Peter
Born: Edinburgh, 23 January 1986
Height: 5'11" **Weight:** 12.12
A central midfield player who joined Port Vale on loan from Manchester City in November, Marc made an impressive debut in the club's FA Cup victory at Morecambe and his array of passing skills helped him to hold a regular place. He did particularly well in the 2-1 victory at Gillingham and then scored a superb goal against Walsall. That alerted Millwall to

Kyle Lafferty

Rickie Lambert

vie for his services and the young Scot signed on a two-and-a-half-year deal in January, fitting into Millwall's midfield with ease. Energetic and hard-working, Marc began to form a formidable partnership with Ali Fuseini and scored his first Millwall goal against his earlier team-mates at Port Vale with a stunning right-footed strike.

Manchester C *(From trainee on 23/1/2004)*
Northampton T *(Loaned on 26/1/2007)*
FL 2+4
Port Vale *(Loaned on 8/11/2007) FL 7/1 FAC 3*
Millwall *(Free on 9/1/2008) FL 16+1/1*

LAIRD Scott Benjamin

Born: Taunton, 15 May 1988
Height: 5'9"   **Weight:** 11.8
Despite being born in England, Scott chose to represent Scotland and was called up to their under-19 squad. Initially recognised as a centre-back, Scott can also play at left-back and on the left of midfield. After making his one and only appearance for Plymouth in the Carling

Cup win over Wycombe in August, he joined Blue Square Premier sides Torquay on loan in September and Stevenage in December. The Stevenage move was made permanent the following month.
Plymouth Arg *(From trainee on 4/7/2006)*
FLC 1

LALLANA Adam David

Born: St Albans, 10 May 1988
Height: 5'8"   **Weight:** 11.6
International Honours: E: Yth
Joining Bournemouth on loan from Southampton last October was a dream move for the attacking midfielder as he supported them as a boy and he impressed in the few appearances he managed to make before an injury took him back to St Mary's. An outstanding prospect in attack as well as midfield, Adam is fast, has superior ball control and dribbling skills and is hard to stop, squirming through packed defences being something of a speciality. He returned from loan to play a sensational part in Saints' Championship survival campaign,

leaving the bench during the penultimate game, a 1-1 draw at West Bromwich, to score the opening goal with a poise that belied his youth.
Southaman *(From trainee on 6/12/2005)*
FL 1+5/1 FLC 1
Bournemouth *(Loaned on 9/10/2007) FL 2+1 Others 1*

LAMBERT Rickie Lee

Born: Liverpool, 16 February 1982
Height: 5'10"   **Weight:** 11.2
Rickie led the Bristol Rovers' forward line well, held down a regular place alongside a number of different striking partners and scored a spectacular goal at Luton from almost 40 yards that was nominated nationally as 'Goal of the Season'. His free-kick strike proved to be the winner over Southampton and ensured Rovers of their first FA Cup quarter-final appearance for 50 years. He was Rovers' top scorer with 20 League and Cup goals.
Blackpool *(From trainee on 17/7/2000)*
FL 0+3
Macclesfield T *(Free on 2/3/2001) FL 36+8/8 FAC 4/2 Others 1*
Stockport Co *(£300,000 on 30/4/2003) FL 88+10/18 FLC 3 FAC 2+1 Others 5+1/1*
Rochdale *(Signed on 17/2/2005) FL 61+3/28 FLC 1 FAC 1 Others 2*
Bristol Rov *(£200,000 on 31/8/2006) FL 70+12/22 FLC 1+1 FAC 12+1/6 Others 9/2*

LAMPARD Frank James

Born: Romford, 20 June 1978
Height: 6'0"   **Weight:** 12.6
Club Honours: FLC '05, '07; PL '05, '06; CS '05
International Honours: E: 61; B-1; U21-19; Yth
Last season, a mixture of highs and lows, both on and off the pitch, saw that modern-day rarity, the absence of the durable Frank from Chelsea's team and how desperately they missed him in their own version of Black September, when they failed to score in the Premier League, suffered two defeats and underwent a change of management. His recovery from a groin strain prompted a return to normal service for the Blues and, by his own admission, the finest form of his career. He masterminded the six-goal demolition of Manchester City and, three days later, followed it with his second Chelsea hat-trick to rescue them from a surprise Carling Cup defeat by Leicester. He broke the 100-goal barrier for Chelsea with two against Huddersfield in the FA Cup fifth round to become their highest-scoring midfield player and only the eighth centurion in the club's history. Frank reached another landmark when he scored four goals in a match

for the first time, hapless Derby being the victims. In the wake of the untimely death of his mother, Frank showed great character to step up and slot home the decisive penalty in the Champions' League semi-final against Liverpool, effectively putting the Blues into their first European Cup final. Again, his scoring instinct came to the fore in Moscow with an opportunist equaliser, the 20th goal of yet another top-scoring season, a phenomenal achievement for a midfield player. Following the ramifications of the penalty shoot-out defeat and yet another managerial change, Frank's contract extension remained in the air with Chelsea fans desperately hoping for a positive outcome to the negotiations.

West Ham U (From trainee on 1/7/1995) PL 132+16/23 FLC 14+1/8 FAC 13/2 Others 10/4
Swansea C (Loaned on 6/10/1995) FL 8+1/1 Others 1+1
Chelsea (£11,000,000 on 3/7/2001) PL 241+6/71 FLC 17+8/9 FAC 28+4/13 Others 62+3/17

LANDZAAT Denny
Domingoes
Born: Amsterdam, Holland, 6 May 1976
Height: 5'10" **Weight:** 11.0
International Honours: Holland: 37
As a busy midfielder with an eye for goal, the Dutch international did not really make the anticipated progress with Wigan and struggled at times to adapt to the Premiership, putting in a handful of solid but unspectacular performances. Comfortable in possession and strong in the tackle, he is a versatile player and although his primary position is in central midfield, he also played on the right-wing and in a defensive role. On target from a penalty against Sunderland, he followed with a goal at Bolton and a beautifully-taken effort at home to Blackburn. Following the appointment of Steve Bruce, Denny was allowed to return to Holland, signing for his boyhood idols Feyenoord during the January transfer window.

Wigan Ath (£2,500,000 from AZ Alkmaar, Holland, ex MVV Maastricht, Willem II Tilburg, on 21/7/2006) PL 48+4/5 FLC 1 FAC 1

LANGFORD Andrew (Andy)
James
Born: Manchester, 3 July 1988
Height: 5'11" **Weight:** 12.5
The young Morecambe reserve team captain won the second string's 'Player of the Year' award for some fine displays at the back. He made one substitute appearance in the Johnstone's Paint

Trophy win at Tranmere and was released at the end of the season.
Morecambe (From juniors on 18/7/2006) Others 0+1

LANGLEY Richard Barrington Michael
Born: Harlesden, 27 December 1979
Height: 5'10" **Weight:** 11.4
International Honours: Jamaica: 12; E: Yth
Unfortunately, a pre-season knee ligament injury virtually put an end to Richard's season. Luton's PFA representative fought back and by April was ahead of schedule when turning out for the reserves and putting together his customary short and long-passing game. Richard was a substitute for Darren Currie for the final 15 minutes of the League season and will hope to pick his career up wherever he is playing in 2008-09, having been released in the summer.

Queens Park Rgrs (From trainee on 31/12/1996) FL 123+10/18 FLC 6/2 FAC 7 Others 2/1
Cardiff C (£250,000 on 15/8/2003) FL 63+6/8 FAC 3
Queens Park Rgrs (Signed on 31/8/2005) FL 22+11/3 FAC 1
Luton T (Free on 13/7/2006) FL 18+12/1 FLC 0+1 FAC 3

LANGMEAD Kelvin Steven
Born: Coventry, 23 March 1985
Height: 6'1" **Weight:** 13.6
Shrewsbury's striker turned central defender, Kelvin always gave strong performances. He found his second season as a defender harder going as manager Gary Peters struggled to find the right pairing in a side that generally underachieved. Kelvin had to adjust to five partners but, as 'Mr Consistent', he played in 39 League games before a knee injury cut his season short, doing especially well in November and December. Despite his presence when joining the attack, he scored only once, inspiring a recovery when Shrewsbury were 3-0 down to MK Dons and hit back to draw 3-3. Now Town's longest-serving player, he captained the side occasionally.

Preston NE (From trainee on 26/2/2004) FL 0+1
Carlisle U (Loaned on 27/2/2004) FL 3+8/1
Kidderminster Hrs (Loaned on 4/9/2004) FL 9+1/1 Others 1
Shrewsbury T (Signed on 26/11/2004) FL 137+17/16 FLC 1+2 FAC 3+1 Others 7+1

LANSBURY Henri George
Born: Enfield, 12 October 1990
Height: 6'2" **Weight:** 10.10
International Honours: E: Yth

Henri is a fine home-grown prospect for Arsenal and while he played only once for the first team, as a substitute in the Carling Cup tie at Sheffield United, Arsène Wenger has already said that Henri will feature much more prominently in the squad next season. He played five times for the reserves and scored five goals in eight games for the FA Academy under-18 side, along with a hat-trick in the FA Youth Cup.
Arsenal (Trainee) FLC 0+1

LAPPIN Simon
Born: Glasgow, 25 January 1983
Height: 5'11" **Weight:** 9.6
Club Honours: S Div 1 '06
International Honours: S: U21-10
A versatile left-sided Norwich player, Simon, who is equally at home at left-back or in his preferred role on the left of midfield, is a cultured player with an elegant left foot. He is also a player who can pick out incisive passes over short and long distances and has superb delivery from dead-ball situations. Simon made an excellent start to the season with the Canaries before falling out of favour following Peter Grant's replacement by Glenn Roeder. He scored a superb goal against Barnet in the Carling Cup and always gave of his best when asked to play in the more defensive role. An extended loan with Motherwell in the Scottish Premier League rejuvenated his season and he played a full part in their relative successes this season, including a winning goal against Celtic.

St Mirren (From juniors on 1/7/1999) SL 136+16/9 SLC 6+1/1 SC 9+2 Others 7+1/2
Norwich C (£100,000 on 31/1/2007) FL 29/2 FLC 3/1 FAC 1
Motherwell (Loaned on 31/1/2008) SL 7+7/2 SC 0+1

LARKIN Colin
Born: Dundalk, 27 April 1982
Height: 5'9" **Weight:** 10.4
International Honours: RoI: Yth
After being released by Chesterfield in summer, it was a frustrating season for the striker at Northampton. Colin spent a lot of time on the bench because of frequent changes made in attack and injury also took its toll. Colin's three goals were all in 1-1 draws and away from home.

Wolverhampton W (From trainee on 19/5/1999) FL 1+2 FLC 0+1/1
Kidderminster Hrs (Loaned on 14/9/2001) FL 31+2/6 Others 1+1/1
Mansfield T (£135,000 on 9/8/2002) FL 61+31/25 FLC 1 FAC 5+1/1 Others 3+4
Chesterfield (Free on 1/7/2005) FL 58+22/11 FLC 4/2 FAC 3 Others 1+2
Northampton T (Free on 5/7/2007) FL 14+19/2 FLC 0+2 FAC 4/1 Others 1

LARRIEU Romain

Born: Mont-de-Marsan, France, 31 August 1976
Height: 6'4" **Weight:** 13.11
Club Honours: Div 3 '02
International Honours: France: Yth

Now in his eighth season with Plymouth, Romain continued to battle with Luke McCormick to be the Pilgrims' goalkeeper. Despite starting the campaign as first choice, Romain lost his place and shortly afterwards joined League One side Yeovil on a month's loan in September. Yeovil needed Romain when Steve Mildenhall was injured and he served them well, keeping two clean sheets and being on the losing side only twice in seven appearances. Back at Home Park, he regained his place in November and went on to make 12 consecutive appearances, including a 'Man of the Match' display at home to Bristol City, when he pulled off a string of top-quality saves. Unfortunately Romain suffered a health scare during the season but is now on the road to a full recovery.

Plymouth Arg (Free from ASOA Valence, France, ex Montpellier, on 30/11/2000) FL 197+1 FLC 3 FAC 10 Others 3
Gillingham (Loaned on 22/11/2007) FL 14
Yeovil T (Loaned on 21/9/2007) FL 6 Others 1

LARSSON Sebastian Benet

Born: Eskilstuna, Sweden, 6 June 1985
Height: 5'10" **Weight:** 11.4
International Honours: Sweden: 5; U21-10

Hugely popular and influential, Birmingham's Sebastian won both the 'Player of the Season' and the 'Players' Player of the Season' after working the right wing relentlessly, passing the ball incisively and delivering brilliant crosses and corners throughout the campaign. Scored a stunning 30-yard winner in stoppage-time at Tottenham in Alex McLeish's first game in charge and was an expert at free kicks, his ability to curl the ball up and over the wall out of reach of the goalkeeper being unrivalled. It was no surprise when he was given an international debut for Sweden, having raised his game at City. He always tried to inspire others around him by example when the chips were down.

Arsenal (From trainee on 1/7/2002) PL 2+1 FLC 4+3 FAC 0+1 Others 1
Birmingham C (£500,000 on 4/8/2006) P/FL 59+19/10 FLC 5/2 FAC 4/3

[LAUREN] BISAN-ETAME MAYER Laureano

Born: Lodhji Kribi, Cameroon, 19 January 1977

Sebastian Larsson

Height: 5'11" **Weight:** 11.4
Club Honours: FAC '02, '03, '05; PL
'02, '04; CS '02; '04
International Honours: Cameroon: 25;
(ANC '00, '02; OLYM '00)
Injury and illness disrupted the first six
weeks of Lauren's season at Portsmouth,
although he did appear in several
Premier League games in August and
early September. After Glen Johnson's
signing in late August, he found it
difficult to claim his favoured right-
back berth and rarely featured before
Christmas. Very mild mannered off
the pitch he is extremely strong and
determined on it, qualities that were
used excellently when first-choice
defenders were unavailable in the second
half of the season. He enjoys sparring
with the Pompey kit-man.
*Arsenal (£7,200,000 from Real Mallorca,
Spain, ex Cant Sevilla, Utrera, Sevilla,
Levante, on 16/6/2000) PL 152+7/6 FLC 2
FAC 23/2 Others 50+7/1*
*Portsmouth (£1,500,000 on 18/1/2007) PL
20+5 FLC 1 FAC 2+1*

LAURSEN Martin
Born: Silkeborg, Denmark, 26 July 1977
Height: 6'2" **Weight:** 12.5
International Honours: Denmark: 49;
U21-14; Yth
A composed and authoritative central
defender, Martin was a key performer for
Aston Villa and at last enjoyed an injury-
free time in 2007-08 to put a regular
run of games under his belt. He missed
only two matches during the season and
was a valuable addition to the defence
because he plays with thought as well
as total commitment. Also dangerous at
the other end of the field as a constant
threat in the air at set pieces, Martin
enjoyed his best spell of fitness and,
therefore, best form for Villa. He also
played for Denmark.
*Aston Villa (£3,000,000 from AC Milan,
Italy, ex Silkeborg, Verona, Parma, on
1/7/2004) PL 63+2/7 FLC 1 FAC 1*

LAW Joshua (Josh) Neil
Born: Nottingham, 19 August 1989
Height: 5'11" **Weight:** 11.6
The son of former Chesterfield manager
Nicky Law and the brother of another
Nicky Law, of Sheffield United, Josh
spent most of the season on loan at
Alfreton, his father's current club. Able to
play on the right of midfield or full-back,
Josh's Chesterfield career amounted to
35 minutes in one substitute appearance.
His release in May sparked interest from
several local clubs.
*Chesterfield (From trainee on 11/7/2007)
Others 0+1*

LAW Nicholas (Nicky)
Born: Plymouth, 29 March 1988
Height: 5'10" **Weight:** 11.6
International Honours: E: Yth
Nicky scored his first goal for Sheffield
United in the Carling Cup at MK Dons
prior to going on loan to Bradford in
October. The midfield player arrived
at Bradford, where his father of the
same name had managed, to gain
experience. His arrival coincided with
an upturn in City's fortunes as his runs
behind the strikers gave them an added
attacking option and he scored twice in
a 4-1 win at Dagenham. Returning to
Bramall Lane Nicky was a regular in the
reserves, making one further substitute
appearance for the first team in April.
*Sheffield U (From trainee on 17/11/2005)
P/FL 2+3 FLC 3+1/1 FAC 0+1*
Yeovil T (Loaned on 16/2/2007) FL 5+1
Bradford C (Loaned on 6/10/2007) FL 10/2

LAWRENCE Dennis William
Born: Port of Spain, Trinidad, 1 August
1974
Height: 6'7" **Weight:** 12.7
Club Honours: AMC '05; Div 1 '08
International Honours: Trinidad &
Tobago: 69
Dennis is a Trinidad and Tobago centre-
back who, during the season, announced
his retirement from international football
but continued to be one of the first
names on the Swansea team sheet. His
one spell on the sidelines was the result
of a knee injury at Crewe in February and
his only goals last season had particular
value, helping to achieve away wins at
Bournemouth and Bristol Rovers.
*Wrexham (£100,000 from Defence Force,
Trinidad on 10/3/2001) FL 190+8/14 FLC 3
FAC 4+1/1 Others 10/1*
*Swansea C (£75,000 on 17/8/2006) FL
77+2/7 FLC 2 FAC 6 Others 4+1*

LAWRENCE Liam
Born: Retford, 14 December 1981
Height: 5'10" **Weight:** 11.3
Club Honours: Ch '05, '07
Stoke's versatile midfielder was in top
form all season and is able to play on
either wing or through the middle, with
a preference for the right side. Liam
scooped the awards at the 'Player of the
Year' night and his 15 goals, including
a hat-trick against Barnsley, went a long
way to ensuring the Potters' return to
the top flight of English football. He is
still awaiting his first cap for the Republic
of Ireland but his form suggested it
cannot be far away.
*Mansfield T (From trainee on 3/7/2000) FL
120+16/34 FLC 3 FAC 8/5 Others 4+2*
Sunderland (Signed on 5/8/2004) P/FL

49+24/10 FLC 3+2 FAC 2
*Stoke C (£500,000 on 18/11/2006) FL
67+1/19 FLC 1 FAC 3/1*

LAWRENCE Matthew (Matt)
James
Born: Northampton, 19 June 1974
Height: 6'1" **Weight:** 12.12
Club Honours: Div 2 '01
International Honours: E: Sch
An experienced and versatile Crystal
Palace defender, Matt set off at right-
back before replacing Leon Cort in the
centre of defence in the early stages
of the campaign. His consistently good
form was one of the reasons why Palace
went on to attain the best defensive
record in the Championship. Having
signed an extension to his contract in
September, the former Millwall favourite
was awarded the vice-captaincy and
celebrated a few months later with his
first goal since January 2000, at Sheffield
Wednesday in March.
*Wycombe W (£20,000 from Grays Ath on
19/1/1996) FL 13+3/1 FLC 4 FAC 1 Others
0+1*
Fulham (Free on 7/2/1997) FL 57+2 FLC 4+1

Liam Lawrence

FAC 2 Others 5
Wycombe W *(£86,000 + on 2/10/1998) FL
63/4 FLC 4 FAC 6 Others 3*
Millwall *(£200,000 on 21/3/2000) FL
213+11 FLC 9+1 FAC 19 Others 8*
Crystal Palace *(Signed on 3/8/2006) FL
67+4/1 FLC 1+1 FAC 3 Others 1+1*

LAWRIE James

Born: Belfast, 18 December 1990
Height: 6'0" **Weight:** 12.5
International Honours: NI: Yth
James is a promising striker who
graduated through Port Vale's youth team
and made his debut as a substitute in the
FA Cup first round at Morecambe, thus
becoming the club's youngest player in
the competition for over 60 years. He has
a good awareness on the ball and made
a further five substitute appearances as
Vale nursed him carefully. James played a
prominent part in Vale's progress to the
quarter-finals of the FA Youth Cup and is
a Northern Ireland under-18 international.
He was courted by other clubs before
signing his first professional contract with
the Vale.
Port Vale *(From trainee on 12/2/2008) FL
0+6 FAC 0+1*

LEACOCK Dean Graham

Born: Croydon, 10 June 1984
Height: 6'2" **Weight:** 12.4
International Honours: E: Yth
Adaptability was the key to Dean's season
at Derby in 2007-08. He is most at home
as a central defender but was also called
up as a defensive midfield player and
at right-back. Although a number of
niggling injuries limited his development,
not to mention Derby's vain struggle
to come to terms with the Premiership,
Dean made some progress. He is an
accomplished footballer who likes to play
the ball out from the back but needs to
beef up the physical side of his game.
Fulham *(From trainee on 17/7/2002) PL
8+1 FLC 4*
Coventry C *(Loaned on 10/9/2004) FL 12+1
FLC 1 FAC 1+1*
Derby Co *(£375,000 on 11/8/2006) P/FL
58+6 FLC 1 FAC 2 Others 3*

LEADBITTER Grant

Born: Chester-le-Street, 7 January 1986
Height: 5'9" **Weight:** 10.3
Club Honours: Ch '07
International Honours: E: U21-3; Yth;
Sch
As a central midfielder at Sunderland,
Grant's progress in 2007-08 was curtailed
by various injuries, including hamstring
problems in August and a broken toe in
January. Grant is a thoughtful player, who
is capable of producing a range of telling

passes over long and short distances.
He is also an excellent striker of the ball
and his two goals last season were both
crisp drives against Middlesbrough and
Blackburn in successive matches, the
second homing in from 25 yards.
Sunderland *(From trainee on 9/1/2003) P/FL
49+38/9 FLC 3+1 FAC 1+1*
Rotherham U *(Loaned on 23/9/2005) FL
3+2/1 FAC 1 Others 1*

LEARY Michael Antonio

Born: Ealing, 17 April 1983
Height: 5'11" **Weight:** 12.3
International Honours: RoI: Yth
Signed in the summer following his
release by Luton, an injury at Norwich
in the Carling Cup in August led to
his missing much of the first half of
Barnet's season. Sent off twice over
the course of the campaign, Michael
answered his critics brilliantly in the Bees'
final few games, where he took on an
unfamiliar position at centre-back and
was appointed captain in the absence of
Ismail Yakubu. He showed his versatility
by slotting into the centre-half spot with a
number of fine displays.
Luton T *(From juniors on 3/8/2001) FL 9+13/
2 FLC 1+1 FAC 1+1 Others 3+2/1*
Bristol Rov *(Loaned on 31/8/2005) FL 12+1
Others 1*
Walsall *(Loaned on 6/1/2006) FL 12+3/1
FAC 3/1*
Torquay U *(Loaned on 3/11/2006) FL 0+2
FAC 1*
Brentford *(Loaned on 4/1/2007) FL 17*
Barnet *(Free on 12/7/2007) FL 19+3/1 FLC
1 FAC 3+1*

LEDGISTER Aaron Turone

Born: Birmingham, 9 October 1987
Height: 5'9" **Weight:** 12.8
A wide midfielder or striker, Aaron joined
Cheltenham on a two-year contract from
Bristol City in the summer. Aaron was a
Scholarship player at Ashton Gate and
played in three trial matches for Town
reserves before being offered a deal by
former manager John Ward. His only
appearance was as a substitute in the
Carling Cup first round at Southend and
he gained further experience in loans to
Weston-super-Mare and Bath.
Cheltenham T *(From trainee at Bristol C on
24/7/2007) FLC 0+1*

LEDLEY Joseph (Joe)
Christopher

Born: Cardiff, 23 January 1987
Height: 6'0" **Weight:** 11.7
International Honours: W: 22; U21-5;
Yth
The Welsh international was the target
for a seven-figure transfer bid by

Wolverhampton during last season but it
was turned down. Joe wanted to stay and
Cardiff wanted to keep him. Premiership
Everton were also keen on the wide
midfield player. Having already made
more than 150 League appearances for
the Bluebirds, he has insisted he wants
to play in the Premiership for his home-
city club. Joe was yet another of the
Championship side who did not look out
of place at Wembley in the FA Cup 1-0
final defeat by Portsmouth.
Cardiff C *(From trainee on 29/10/2004) FL
146+11/18 FLC 6+3/1 FAC 7+1/1*

LEE Alan Desmond

Born: Galway, 21 August 1978
Height: 6'2" **Weight:** 13.9
International Honours: RoI: 10; U21-5
Alan continued to lead the line for
Ipswich and his ability in the air makes
him a good target man, while his turn of
speed can catch out defenders. He took
no end of punishment from opposing
defenders and many felt he might have
received more protection from referees.
Alan had the distinction of scoring the
first and last goals of Ipswich's campaign.
In the opening game against Sheffield
Wednesday, he converted a second-
minute penalty to set up a convincing
victory and in the final match against Hull
headed the winner soon after joining the
action as a substitute.
Aston Villa *(From trainee on 21/8/1995)*
Torquay U *(Loaned on 27/11/1998) FL 6+1/
2 Others 2/1*
Port Vale *(Loaned on 2/3/1999) FL 7+4/2*
Burnley *(£150,000 on 8/7/1999) FL 2+13
FLC 1+1 FAC 0+2 Others 1/1*
Rotherham U *(£150,000 on 21/9/2000) FL
105+6/37 FLC 5/2 FAC 4+1/1 Others 1/1*
Cardiff C *(£850,000 + on 15/8/2003) FL
47+39/10 FLC 6/1 FAC 2+2/1*
Ipswich T *(Signed on 10/1/2006) FL 89+11/
31 FLC 1/1 FAC 3+1/1*

LEE Charlie

Born: Whitechapel, 5 January 1987
Height: 5'10" **Weight:** 11.7
Freed by Tottenham in the summer, the
young midfielder enjoyed a successful
first season at Peterborough and became
a hero on the London Road terraces.
Although mainly used in a battling, hard-
tackling midfield role, Charlie was equally
at home in central defence. He has a
vicious shot, as he demonstrated when
successful from long range on several
occasions.
Tottenham H *(From trainee on 15/7/2005)*
Millwall *(Loaned on 16/11/2006) FL 4+1
Others 1*
Peterborough U *(Free on 27/7/2007) FL
32+10/6 FLC 1+1 FAC 3+1/1 Others 1+1/1*

LEE Dong-Gook
Born: Pohang, South Korea, 29 April 1979
Height: 6'1" **Weight:** 12.8
International Honours: South Korea: 71
It was a disappointing and forgettable final season at Middlesbrough for the enigmatic South Korean international. Although he scored in the Carling Cup against Northampton and FA Cup against Mansfield, his only senior goals for the club, he failed to establish himself as a Premiership player during his 15 months at the Riverside. He rejected the opportunity to return to his former club Pohang Steelers on transfer deadline day and was, as expected, released by Gareth Southgate at the end of the season.
Middlesbrough *(Free from Pohang Steelers, South Korea, ex Pohang Steelers, Werder Bremen - loan, Gwangju, on 9/1/2007) PL 8+15 FLC 2/1 FAC 1+3/1*

LEE Graeme Barry
Born: Middlesbrough, 31 May 1978
Height: 6'2" **Weight:** 13.7
Club Honours: AMC '07
Graeme had a difficult season in 2007-08, with injuries keeping him out of the Doncaster side in the first part of the campaign. Regaining fitness by the end of January he was loaned out to Hartlepool, his original club, for match practice. Still highly regarded at Victoria Park, Graeme jumped at the chance but it was a difficult time and, still lacking full fitness, he was unable to win a regular place before returning to his parent club and going out on loan to Shrewsbury in March. A commanding and experienced player, he was signed by new Shrewsbury manager Paul Simpson to add much-needed stability to the defence and following an excellent debut in the 1-1 draw at Dagenham he was equally influential in the 0-0 draw against Notts County two days later. Back at Doncaster, as injuries took their toll on Rovers' central defence, he was recalled but made only one appearance as a substitute before being released in the summer.
Hartlepool U *(From trainee on 2/7/1996) FL 208+11/19 FLC 7+2/1 FAC 8+1 Others 13+2/2*
Sheffield Wed *(Free on 2/7/2003) FL 63+4/5 FLC 1/1 FAC 4 Others 3/1*
Doncaster Rov *(£50,000 on 13/1/2006) FL 56+4/5 FLC 1 FAC 3 Others 5+1/1*
Hartlepool U *(Loaned on 14/2/2008) FL 3*
Shrewsbury T *(Loaned on 19/3/2008) FL 4+1*

LEE Jason Benedict
Born: Forest Gate, 9 May 1971
Height: 6'3" **Weight:** 13.8
Club Honours: Div 2 '98

A traditional big English centre-forward, Jason is recognised as being one of he fittest players at Notts County despite his age. Manager Ian McParland says he trains like an 18-year-old trying to force his way into the team. Sadly, after finishing the previous season as leading scorer, his goal touch deserted him and a broken arm in training interrupted him in mid-season. It was slow to mend and although he returned to action, he was released at the end of the season.
Charlton Ath *(From trainee on 2/6/1989) FL 0+1 Others 0+2*
Stockport Co *(Loaned on 6/2/1991) FL 2*
Lincoln C *(£35,000 on 1/3/1991) FL 86+7/21 FLC 6 FAC 2+1/1 Others 4*
Southend U *(Signed on 6/8/1993) FL 18+6/3 FLC 1 FAC 1 Others 5+3/3*
Nottingham F *(£200,000 on 4/3/1994) P/FL 41+35/14 FLC 4+3/1 FAC 0+5 Others 4+2*
Charlton Ath *(Loaned on 5/2/1997) FL 7+1/3*
Grimsby T *(Loaned on 27/3/1997) FL 2+5/2*
Watford *(£200,000 on 16/6/1997) FL 36+1/1 11 FLC 4 FAC 4 Others 1*
Chesterfield *(£250,000 on 28/8/1998) FL 17+11/1 FAC 0+2 Others 0+2*
Peterborough U *(£50,000 on 3/1/2000) FL 49+29/17 FAC 5/1 Others 2+2/1*
Falkirk *(Free on 1/8/2003) SL 27+2/8 SC 1+1/1 Others 1*
Boston U *(Free on 6/8/2004) FL 43+13/11 FLC 3/1 FAC 5+1/2 Others 0+2*
Northampton T *(Signed on 9/1/2006) FL 8+3/1*
Notts Co *(Free on 27/6/2006) FL 59+10/16 FLC 3/1 FAC 1+1*

LEE Kieran Christopher
Born: Stalybridge, 22 June 1988
Height: 6'1" **Weight:** 12.0
This versatile young player made his debut against Chelsea in the FA Cup at Stamford Bridge after joining Queens Park Rangers on loan from Manchester United. Kieran is capable of playing almost anywhere across midfield and in either full-back berth but has mainly been used as an attacking wide player, much of his action coming off the bench. Was released at the end of the campaign.
Manchester U *(From trainee on 6/7/2006) PL 1 FLC 0+2/1*
Queens Park Rgrs *(Loaned on 2/1/2008) FL 2+5 FAC 0+1*

LEE Richard Anthony
Born: Oxford, 5 October 1982
Height: 6'0" **Weight:** 12.8
International Honours: E: Yth
Richard started last season as Watford's second-string goalkeeper but had his opportunity when Mart Poom was injured and was first choice for the

remainder of the campaign. He took his chance with a series of assured and confident performances and was one of Watford's most consistent players, giving outstanding displays against Stoke, Southampton and West Bromwich. Having saved a penalty against Gillingham in the Carling Cup, he was unhappy when palming the ball into his own net for a Barnsley winner. Richard, who has been at Watford since the age of ten, is a notably articulate and mature character away from football and when captain Jay De Merit was injured, he had the rare honour – for a goalkeeper – of leading the team and seemed to relish the responsibility. He also received the club's 'Community Ambassador' award.
Watford *(From trainee on 7/3/2000) P/FL 80+2 FLC 9 FAC 4 Others 2*

LEE Thomas (Tommy) Edward
Born: Keighley, 3 January 1986
Height: 6'2" **Weight:** 12.0
Tommy was Macclesfield's first choice goalkeeper until the end of November, when he injured a hand and made only one further appearance from the substitutes' bench because of Jonny Brain's fine form. Although he kept only a handful of clean sheets, this was a reflection of the team's indifferent form rather than his performances, in which he showed an overall improvement in all aspects of his game. When Keith Alexander was appointed manager, he elected not to include a substitute 'keeper, allowing Tommy to spend the final weeks of the season on loan at Rochdale, whose two senior goalkeepers were injured. Though beaten in his first game, he played a large part in the ten-match unbeaten run that ensured Dale's fifth-place finish, Tommy winning the supporters' 'Player of the Month' award for April. In the play-off semi-final second leg, he made the save in the penalty shoot-out that took Rochdale to Wembley for the first time. Was out of contract in the summer and looking for a new club.
Manchester U *(From trainee on 6/7/2005)*
Macclesfield T *(Loaned on 18/1/2006) FL 11 Others 1*
Macclesfield T *(Free on 26/7/2006) FL 51+1 FLC 1 FAC 2*
Rochdale *(Loaned on 21/3/2008) FL 11 Others 3*

LEE Young-Pyo
Born: Hong Chung, South Korea, 23 April 1977
Height: 5'9" **Weight:** 10.6
Club Honours: FLC '08
International Honours: South Korea: 96
His season at Tottenham was hampered

Adam Le Fondre

by injury and the arrival and emergence of other players at left-back. Lee continued to represent South Korea, playing in a friendly against Turkmenistan in February and a World Cup qualifier against North Korea in March. At Tottenham, Young-Pyo has mostly been deployed at left-back, despite a preference for his right foot, but is a fast defender, who makes plenty of valuable tackles and interceptions. He was linked with a summer move back to his former club PSV Eindhoven, having played his last Tottenham game in January.
Tottenham H *(£1,360,000 from PSV Eindhoven, Holland on 31/8/2005) PL 68+2 FLC 6 FAC 7 Others 10*

LEE-BARRETT Arran
Born: Ipswich, 28 February 1984
Height: 6'2" **Weight:** 12.10
International Honours: E: SP-1
Arran joined Hartlepool from Coventry in the close season with goalkeeper Dimi Konstantopoulos travelling in the opposite direction. Arran began as United's first-choice 'keeper but an uncertain start saw him immediately replaced by another new signing, Jan Budtz. He had a long spell in the background but remained patient until given another chance in the second half of 2007-08. More successful this time, he was able to retain the position until the end of the season.
Cardiff C *(From trainee at Norwich C on 23/5/2003. Free to Weymouth on 12/7/2005)*
Coventry C *(Free on 12/1/2007)*
Hartlepool U *(Free on 3/7/2007) FL 18 Others 1*

LE FONDRE Adam
Born: Stockport, 2 December 1986
Height: 5'10" **Weight:** 11.4
As the signing that Rochdale manager Keith Hill and the Dale fans were keenest to make after his spell on loan the previous term, Hill finally managed to persuade Stockport to part with Adam in August. He was brought in to share the scoring load with Chris Dagnall and Glenn Murray. Dagnall's long-term injury absence and Murray's transfer to Brighton in January piled much of the onus on Adam to keep Dale's play-off push on track. The live-wire striker responded in style with 17 goals, including a second-half hat-trick against Accrington that re-ignited Dale's run to the play-off places after a poor February and several goal of the season contenders as Dale went all the way to Wembley for the first time.
Stockport Co *(From trainee on 18/2/2005) FL 29+34/17 FLC 1+1/1 FAC 1+4 Others 1+2/1*
Rochdale *(Loaned on 19/1/2007) FL 7/4*
Rochdale *(Signed on 3/7/2007) FL 30+16/16 FLC 0+2 FAC 1/1 Others 2+2*

LEGWINSKI Sylvain
Born: Clermont-Ferrand, France, 6 October 1973
Height: 6'3" **Weight:** 11.7
International Honours: France: B-3; U21
The foot injury that curtailed Sylvain's 2006-07 season for Ipswich continued to cause him problems in pre-season and he spent the first few matches of the new campaign on the bench. Had a run of games in October and November but was unable to reproduce his form of the previous season and drifted out of the first-team picture. He made his last appearance in January and was not offered a new contract.
Fulham (£3,500,000 from Bordeaux, France, ex AS Monaco, on 22/8/2001) PL 116+12/8 FLC 4+2/1 FAC 18/1 Others 10+2/2
Ipswich T (Free on 31/8/2006) FL 40+7/7 FLC 0+1 FAC 4

LEHMANN Jens
Born: Essen, Germany, 10 November 1969
Height: 6'3" **Weight:** 13.10
Club Honours: PL '04; CS '04; FAC '05
International Honours: Germany: 61
Jens lost his place in the Arsenal side in 2007-08 after two well-publicised mistakes, at home to Fulham and away to Blackburn, the first coming in the opening minute of the season. The German international goalkeeper had to content himself with a place on the bench most of the time, although he featured in all three of Arsenal's FA Cup ties and three matches in the Champions' League. Jens made only seven appearances in the Premier League, frustrating for him after a long career at the top level. The Emirates crowd showed what they felt when he made his last appearance as a substitute against Everton. It had been confirmed that he would leave Arsenal in summer and he was accorded a wonderful reception as players and supporters took the chance to say an emotional good-bye to each other. Jens went into the European Championships as Germany's first choice before deciding whether to play on for a new club.
Arsenal (£1,250,000 from Borussia Dortmund, Germany, ex SW Essen, Schalke 04, AC Milan, on 5/8/2003) PL 146+1 FAC 13 Others 39

LEIGERTWOOD Mikele Benjamin
Born: Enfield, 12 November 1982
Height: 6'1" **Weight:** 13.11
Mikele played a full part in Sheffield United's pre-season but after just four appearances, new manager Bryan Robson allowed him to move to Queens Park Rangers, where he became the first signing of the Flavio Briatore era in August. Mikele stamped his authority on a midfield lacking leaders at the time and played some fine football during a generally poor time for Rangers. Not only did he contribute good defensive displays but also showed an assured touch in front of goal, all his five goals being absolute belters. His first secured a vital point at Leicester, he scored in Luigi De Canio's first match in charge and bagged two in an excellent 3-0 home win over Stoke.
Wimbledon (From trainee on 29/6/2001) FL 55+1/2 FLC 4/1 FAC 5
Leyton Orient (Loaned on 19/11/2001) FL 8 FAC 2
Crystal Palace (£150,000 on 2/2/2004) P/FL 41+18/1 FLC 3 FAC 2 Others 4
Sheffield U (£600,000 on 1/7/2006) P/FL 17+4 FLC 2
Queens Park Rgrs (Signed on 31/8/2007) FL 33+7/5

LENNON Aaron Justin
Born: Leeds, 16 April 1987
Height: 5'5" **Weight:** 9.12
International Honours: E: 9; B-2; U21-3; Yth
Under Juande Ramos' management at Tottenham there was more to Aaron's game than pure wing play. While he remains one of the fastest players around and an exciting winger who can feature on the right or left, he was required to track back more under Ramos and even became the last line of defence when making a goal-line clearance. Unfortunate to suffer minor injuries at the wrong times, not helping his international aspirations, he gained some assurance in the spring when he played in England's vital under-21 game against the Republic of Ireland. Aaron scored three times last season and knows that better finishing and a more consistent end product with his passes and crosses are required.
Leeds U (Trainee) P/FL 19+19/1 FLC 1+2 FAC 1+1
Tottenham H (£1,000,000 on 1/7/2005) PL 68+14/7 FLC 7+3/1 FAC 8+2/1 Others 15+2/1

LENNON Neil Francis
Born: Lurgan, 25 June 1971
Height: 5'9" **Weight:** 12.2
Club Honours: FLC '97, '00; SPD '01, '02, '04, '06, '07; SC '01, '04, '05, '07; SLC '01, '06
International Honours: NI: 40; B-1; U23-1; U21-2; Yth
When the Glasgow Celtic legend announced he was leaving Parkhead in May, a host of clubs battled for his signature before Neil agreed to join Nottingham Forest on a one-year deal, starting the season as a holding midfielder, linking play. After being ever-present in the first 12 League games, he was replaced against Luton in October in a poor team performance and shortly afterwards returned to Scotland for family reasons. On his return he failed to re-establish himself, making only a handful of further appearances. Being surplus to requirements at Forest, he linked up with former Celtic team-mate Paul Lambert at Wycombe on the January deadline day, signing until the end of the season. Lambert had tried to sign him in the summer but Neil was unwilling to drop to League Two at that time. Neil slotted into the Wycombe midfield in his usual holding role and although not as mobile these days, his experience and judgement proved useful. However, his stay was cut short when Gordon Strachan persuaded him to accept a coaching role at Celtic.
Manchester C (From trainee on 26/8/1989) FL 1
Crewe Alex (Free on 9/8/1990) FL 142+5/15 FLC 8+1/1 FAC 16/1 Others 15+1
Leicester C (£750,000 on 23/2/1996) P/FL 169+1/6 FLC 23/3 FAC 8 Others 7
Glasgow Celtic (£5,750,000 on 8/12/2000) SL 212+2/3 SLC 10+1 SC 26 Others 52+1
Nottingham F (Free on 7/7/2007) FL 15+3 FLC 2 FAC 1 Others 0+1
Wycombe W (Free on 31/1/2008) FL 8+1

LEON-AYARZA Diego
Born: Palencia, Spain, 16 January 1983
Height: 5'8" **Weight:** 10.10
A January signing from Grasshopper Zurich, Diego made his Barnsley debut as a substitute ten days later against Norwich but took time to settle into the English game. He was seen in his early matches as a wide-left player but moved to central midfield in two crucial away wins late in the season, with a wonderful 25-yard free kick in the second of them. Diego has a fine left foot and together with his passing and ability to beat a man, is already a favourite with Barnsley fans, who expect a lot of him in the season ahead.
Barnsley (Free from Grasshoppers Zurich, Switzerland, ex Real Madrid, Arminia Bielefeld, on 9/1/2008) FL 16+2/1 FAC 1+1

LESCOTT Aaron Anthony
Born: Birmingham, 2 December 1978
Height: 5'8" **Weight:** 10.9
International Honours: E: Sch
The Bristol Rovers' full-back, the older brother of Everton's Joleon, enjoyed his best season at the club with performances that were both impressive and consistent. When switched from right to left-back, he

proved a highly dependable defender and linked up well with his attack.
Aston Villa (From trainee on 5/7/1996) FAC 0+1
Lincoln C (Loaned on 14/3/2000) FL 3+2
Sheffield Wed (£100,000 on 3/10/2000) FL 19+18 FLC 3+1 FAC 2
Stockport Co (£75,000 on 14/11/2001) FL 65+7/1 FLC 2+1 FAC 2+1 Others 2+1
Bristol Rov (Free on 25/3/2004) FL 131+8 FLC 3+2 FAC 15 Others 10

LESCOTT Joleon Patrick
Born: Birmingham, 16 August 1982
Height: 6'2" **Weight:** 13.0
International Honours: E: 5; B-1; U21-2; Yth
Voted Everton's 'Player of the Season' by some distance, the classy defender confirmed his reputation as one of the best signings from the Championship in recent years, given further weight when he became a regular member of the England defence. Equally comfortable at centre-half or left-back, the former Wolverhampton player also provided the added bonus of ten goals as a potent threat from set pieces. Cool and calm on the ball, Joleon was at his best from left-back when breaking forward, as sheer strength makes him difficult to shake off the ball. At centre-half, he is strong in the air and an assured reader of the game. The greatest tribute to his consistency is that at the end of the season he had appeared in every Everton first-team match since signing in the summer of 2006.
Wolverhampton W (From trainee on 18/8/1999) FL 206+6/13 FLC 7+1 FAC 10 Others 5
Everton (£5,000,000 on 12/6/2006) PL 73+3/10 FLC 8 FAC 1+1 Others 10/2

LESLIE Steven William
Born: Glasgow, 5 November 1987
Height: 5'9" **Weight:** 10.12
Steven scored his first goal for Shrewsbury as they opened their season with a 4-0 victory at Lincoln. The young left-sided midfield player is equally at home at left-back and has a great turn of speed with a good quality ball into the box. After some good contributions, including a substitute appearance that changed the game at Bury to help win a point, his contract was extended for another year. He continued to build on his early season performances, giving manager Paul Simpson something to think about.
Shrewsbury T (From juniors on 1/7/2006) FL 11+12/1 FLC 2+1 FAC 1 Others 1+1

LESTER Jack William
Born: Sheffield, 8 October 1975
Height: 5'10" **Weight:** 11.8
Club Honours: AMC '98
International Honours: E: Sch

Chesterfield pulled off a remarkable coup when landing the scheming striker on a free from Nottingham Forest and were rewarded for their endeavour by a scoring return that no other Spireites' player had matched 50 years. Goals are not all you get with Jack, because he provides a fine link between midfield and attack, retaining possession as the boots fly in and looking for the killer pass to a fellow forward. Jack was voted the PFA Fans' 'Player of the Year' for League Two and made a clean sweep of the awards at the club's 'Player of the Year' dinner in May.
Grimsby T (From juniors on 8/7/1994) FL 93+40/17 FLC 13+4/6 FAC 8+1/2 Others 4+4
Doncaster Rov (Loaned on 20/9/1996) FL 5+6/1
Nottingham F (£300,000 on 28/1/2000) FL 73+26/21 FLC 3/3 FAC 1 Others 0+1
Sheffield U (Free on 1/8/2003) FL 26+18/12 FLC 3+1/3 FAC 2/1
Nottingham F (£50,000 on 26/11/2004) FL 42+34/12 FLC 0+1 FAC 1+5 Others 5/1
Chesterfield (Free on 1/8/2007) FL 35+1/23 FLC 1/1 FAC 1/1

LETHEREN Kyle Charles
Born: Llanelli, 26 December 1987
Height: 6'2" **Weight:** 12.2
International Honours: W: U21-1
Kyle made his Barnsley debut as a second-half substitute for Heinz Muller in the FA Cup tie against Blackpool. He was a regular in the reserves throughout the season and proved good shot-stopper, before being released at the end of the season.
Barnsley (From trainee at Swansea C on 4/8/2006) FAC 0+1

LETO Sebastian Eduardo
Born: Alejandro Korn, Argentina, 30 August 1986
Height: 6'2" **Weight:** 12.4
Sebastian is a 21-year-old left-winger signed by Liverpool manager Rafa Benitez in summer from a little known Argentine team, Lanus FC. Although said to be highly rated in his native country and wanted by the biggest Argentine clubs, he had not been capped at youth or under-20 level. He made his Liverpool debut early in the season in the second leg of the Champions' League tie against Toulouse that Liverpool won 4-0 and also started in Carling Cup matches against Reading and Cardiff. More surprisingly, he played in the Champions' League match at home to Marseille, in which a miserable defeat put future progress in the competition at risk. Sebastian made little impact and was dropped from the first-team squad in November for the remainder of the season. It is difficult to

assess his future at Anfield although he was reportedly called up to the Argentine under-23 squad in May.
Liverpool (£1,850,000 from Lanus, Argentina on 17/8/2007) FLC 2 Others 2

LEVEN Peter McDonald
Born: Glasgow, 27 September 1983
Height: 5'11" **Weight:** 12.13
Released by Kilmarnock last summer, the crafty midfielder turned down a contract with a Scottish Premier side to try his luck in English football. He can play on the left but is better in a central role, where his eye for a defence-splitting pass can turn a game. Peter's value soon soared and Chesterfield reportedly turned down a £100,000 bid for him on transfer deadline day, feeling he was integral to their play-off push.
Glasgow Rgrs (From juniors on 1/8/2000)
Kilmarnock (Free on 10/7/2004) SL 53+12/5 SLC 7/1 SC 3
Chesterfield (Signed on 7/8/2007) FL 42/6 FLC 1 FAC 1

LEWINGTON Dean Scott
Born: Kingston, 18 May 1984
Height: 5'11" **Weight:** 11.2
Club Honours: AMC '08: Div 2 '08
One of the most solid and consistent left-backs in the lower divisions, Dean again proved to be a cornerstone of the MK Dons' defence. Quite tall for his position, Dean tackles well, is strong in the air and likes to shoot from distance at every opportunity. He failed to find the net during the campaign but his precise delivery from corners led to several headed goals and he was deservedly voted into the PFA League Two team of the season. As the only senior player left from the club's old Wimbledon days, he took particular delight in helping the Dons to a Wembley final win as well as the League Two title.
Wimbledon/MK Dons (From trainee on 17/7/2003) FL 205+1/5 FLC 5 FAC 13 Others 12/1

LEWIS Edward (Eddie) James
Born: Cerritos, California, USA, 17 May 1974
Height: 5'9" **Weight:** 11.12
International Honours: USA: 77
Two games into last season, Eddie switched from Leeds in League One to the Premiership with Derby, signing a two-year deal. Both his outings for Leeds, where he was reigning 'Player of the Year', had been at left-back but he generally featured further forward for the Rams. A jump of two divisions was too tempting for Eddie to resist and he provided Derby with experience on the

Dean Lewington

left of midfield, also playing at left-back. He has no great pace but can deliver the ball from wide positions and has a good knowledge of the game. After joining Derby, Eddie added to his impressive tally of United States caps, including a substitute appearance at Wembley, and established himself as a sound professional, also taking part in charity work.
Fulham *(£1,300,000 from San Jose Clash, USA on 17/3/2000) P/FL 8+8 FLC 6/1*
Preston NE *(Signed on 5/9/2002) FL 97+14/ 15 FLC 5+1/1 FAC 4 Others 3*
Leeds U *(Free on 4/7/2005) FL 83+2/8 FLC 4+1 FAC 3 Others 3/1*
Derby Co *(£275,000 on 20/8/2007) PL 22+2 FAC 2+1*

LEWIS Joseph (Joe) Peter
Born: Bury St Edmunds, 6 October 1987
Height: 6'5" **Weight:** 11.12
International Honours: E: U21-1; Yth
Joe joined Morecambe in August as a relatively unknown goalkeeper on loan from Norwich. But the 6'5" giant soon made his mark with some sensational performances that made him a firm favourite. As well as being a fine shot-stopper, he is a brave 'keeper, suffering a head wound that required more than 20 stitches, in a game against Rotherham in October and then breaking his nose in another clash when back in the side. His displays earned him a place in Stuart Pearce's England under-21 squad and a move to Peterborough, who became one of the promoted teams, after twice starring against Darren Ferguson's side. On becoming Peterborough's record signing when he arrived from Norwich in the mid-season transfer window, days after starring for Morecambe in a 3-2 win over Posh, he went straight into the side, dislodging long-standing favourite Mark Tyler, and producing a number of displays that showed his potential. He crowned a particularly fine display at Chesterfield with a last-minute penalty save and completed a memorable season by travelling as cover with the full England team for their match against Trinidad & Tobago.
Norwich C *(From trainee on 27/10/2004)*
Stockport Co *(Loaned on 22/3/2007) FL 5*
Morecambe *(Loaned on 1/8/2007) FL 19 FLC 3*
Peterborough U *(£400,000 on 7/1/2008) FL 22 FAC 1*

LEWIS Stuart Allan
Born: Welwyn Garden City, 15 October 1987
Height: 5'10" **Weight:** 11.6
International Honours: E: Yth

A young midfield player who joined Gillingham from Stevenage in January and on the few occasions that he appeared showed the ability that could make him a regular in the season ahead. Calm on the ball, with good footwork, and a neat passer of the ball, he will be hoping to confirm good impressions in 2008-09.
Tottenham H (From trainee on 19/7/2005. Freed on 31/1/2007)
Barnet (Free on 31/11/2007) FL 2+2 (Free to Stevenage Borough on 20/3/2007)
Gillingham (Free on 28/1/2008) FL 6+4

LICKA Mario
Born: Ostrava, Czech Republic, 30 April 1982
Height: 5'10" **Weight:** 11.11
As the forgotten man of St Marys'. Mario, despite his skill and pace, had not played since January 2007 and not even reached the bench last season until Nigel Pearson's appointment as Southampton manager in February. The multi-lingual Mario, who speaks French, Italian and English in addition to his native Czech, responded well, proving an ebullient figure in a Saints' midfield that functioned, if not to the sum of its parts, at least more tellingly than it had been doing. Was out of contract in the summer and looking for a new club.
Southampton (Free from FC Slovacko, Czech Republic, ex Banik Ostrava, Livorno - loan, on 4/8/2006) FL 17+10/1 FLC 2+1 FAC 0+2

LIDDELL Andrew (Andy) Mark
Born: Leeds, 28 June 1973
Height: 5'7" **Weight:** 11.6
Club Honours: AMC '99; Div 2 '03
International Honours: S: U21-12
The vastly-experienced right-winger was appointed Oldham's club captain last summer but endured a frustrating time in his third season at Boundary Park. After making 17 appearances and netting three times, he suffered problems with an Achilles tendon, the result of wear and tear from 600-plus games said the experts. Surgery was eventually required in the New Year and he was sidelined until April. Despite his advancing years, Andy subsequently accepted a new one-year contract, with manager John Sheridan highlighting his knowledge as essential in the development of the club's younger talent.
Barnsley (From trainee on 6/7/1991) P/FL 142+56/34 FLC 11+4/3 FAC 5+7/1 Others 2+1
Wigan Ath (£350,000 on 15/10/1998) FL 206+11/70 FLC 11/1 FAC 7/1 Others 14+1

Sheffield U (Free on 7/7/2004) FL 26+7/3 FLC 1 FAC 5/3
Oldham Ath (Free on 29/6/2005) FL 89+4/21 FLC 3+1 FAC 8/1 Others 5/3

LIDDLE Gary Daniel
Born: Middlesbrough, 15 June 1986
Height: 6'1" **Weight:** 12.6
Club Honours: FAYC '04
International Honours: E: Yth
Having been hailed as a great signing in 2006-07, Gary was seen as a key player when Hartlepool took their place in a higher division after promotion. A consistent performer, he has an enthusiastic approach and likes to go for goal by unleashing long-range shots. He acquitted himself well in League One and was almost ever-present in what was a season of consolidation for Hartlepool. Can also play in defence.
Middlesbrough (From trainee on 14/7/2003)
Hartlepool U (Signed on 18/8/2006) FL 83/5 FLC 4 FAC 3+1/1 Others 3/1

LILLIS Joshua (Josh) Mark
Born: Derby, 24 June 1987
Height: 6'0" **Weight:** 12.8
Scunthorpe's reserve goalkeeper Josh found his opportunities restricted to just five appearances. His two starts came in the Carling Cup defeat by Hartlepool and the 3-0 loss at Plymouth in December, when he deputised for suspended first-choice Joe Murphy. A good shot-stopper, he came in for praise following his display as a second-half substitute in the draw at Cardiff in October.
Scunthorpe U (From trainee on 2/8/2006) FL 2+2 FLC 1 FAC 0+1 Others 0+1

LINDEGAARD Andrew (Andy) Rindom
Born: Taunton, 10 September 1980
Height: 5'8" **Weight:** 11.4
Club Honours: FAT '02; FC '03; Div 2 '05
Arriving in the summer from Yeovil, Andy proved a capable and versatile player, who operated in a number of different positions for Cheltenham. He earned a two-year contract after some impressive performances in pre-season and started as first choice on the right of midfield in a 4-4-2 formation. Andy missed three games through suspension and a further four with a hamstring strain in autumn but returned to score in an important 1-0 win over Luton in November. He switched to the left for a run of 13 games in the New Year, coinciding with a sudden upturn in the team's fortunes, and played at right-back in a 1-0 win over Bournemouth. Andy scored his second goal in a 1-1 draw with Hartlepool and ended with a

series of important contributions from the bench as the Robins battled to avoid relegation from League One.
Yeovil T (Signed from Westlands Sports on 5/6/2002) FL 57+32/3 FLC 0+1 FAC 3+2 Others 4
Cheltenham T (Free on 24/7/2007) FL 31+11/2 FLC 1

LINDFIELD Craig Anthony
Born: Birkenhead, 7 September 1988
Height: 6'0" **Weight:** 11.0
Club Honours: FAYC '06, '07
International Honours: E: Yth
Craig caused quite a stir when he joined Notts County on loan from Liverpool and early in his debut at Accrington, crashed in a superb opening goal. That was his only goal and after a mere handful of games he returned to Liverpool. County soon encountered him again after the striker joined Chester on a month's loan in the middle of January and made his debut as a substitute against them at Meadow Lane. The gangling youngster played up front alongside the experienced John Murphy and, facing some canny League Two defenders, showed useful skills and proved difficult to shake off the ball. Unfortunately, he failed to find the back of the net in his seven appearances for Chester.
Liverpool (From trainee on 9/8/2006)
Notts Co (Loaned on 2/11/2007) FL 3/1 FAC 1
Chester C (Loaned on 18/1/2008) FL 5+2

LINES Christopher (Chris) John
Born: Bristol, 30 November 1985
Height: 6'2" **Weight:** 12.0
A young central midfielder, Chris finally made the vital breakthrough in the Bristol Rovers' first team, his ball-winning skills and accurate passing being appreciated by the supporters. He played the majority of his games on the left flank.
Bristol Rov (From juniors on 26/11/2004) FL 30+8/3 FAC 6+2 Others 1+2

LINWOOD Paul Anthony
Born: Birkenhead, 24 October 1983
Height: 6'2" **Weight:** 12.8
One of the successes of a disappointing campaign for Chester, the left-sided central defender was a consistent performer. Forming a strong partnership with Paul Butler at the start of the season, he was also solid playing alongside youngsters Kevin Roberts and Shaun Kelly. Fearsome in the tackle and strong in the air, Paul showed his leadership qualities when he took over as captain later in the season. A difficult player to shake off the ball, he scored one goal for the

Blues, in the 3-3 draw at Accrington. Paul deservedly won the 'Player of the Year' award at the Deva Stadium.
Tranmere Rov (From trainee on 3/4/2002) FL 34+10 FAC 4+1 Others 4
Wrexham (Loaned on 26/8/2005) FL 8+1
Chester C (Free on 4/8/2006) FL 75+4/2 FLC 2 FAC 2+1 Others 3/1

LISBIE Kevin Anthony
Born: Hackney, 17 October 1978
Height: 5'9" **Weight:** 10.12
International Honours: Jamaica: 10; E: Yth
Signed from Charlton in the summer, the front runner enjoyed an outstanding season in a struggling side. Although Colchester finished bottom of the Championship, Kevin poached a remarkable 17 goals. He was the envy of most other Championship clubs, especially Charlton, against whom he scored three goals in the two meetings, including a brace in the 2-1 win at the Valley on New Year's Day. His goals at least gave the U's hope of beating the drop until the final few weeks of the season. Kevin's best spell was six goals in seven matches from early February. His pace caught out many defenders and his finishing was often deadly.
Charlton Ath (From trainee on 24/5/1996) P/FL 62+93/16 FLC 4+9/3 FAC 2+6
Gillingham (Loaned on 5/3/1999) FL 4+3/4
Reading (Loaned on 26/11/1999) FL 1+1
Queens Park Rgrs (Loaned on 1/12/2000) FL 1+1
Norwich C (Loaned on 9/9/2005) FL 4+2/1
Derby Co (Loaned on 24/2/2006) FL 7/1
Colchester U (Free on 10/8/2007) FL 39+3/17 FAC 1

LITA Leroy Halirou
Born: Kinshasa, DR Congo, 28 December 1984
Height: 5'9" **Weight:** 11.2
Club Honours: Ch '06
International Honours: E: U21-9
There were nine months between Leroy's first and second goals for Reading in 2007-08. He scored an extra-time winner in the Carling Cup tie at Swansea in August and netted the club's last Premiership goal, at least for the time being, in the final minute of the 4-0 demolition of Derby in May. In between, the England under-21 striker was a peripheral figure at Reading, completing 90 minutes on only four occasions before joining Charlton on loan in March as Alan Pardew's team attempted to reach the Championship play-offs. Brought in to bolster Charlton's strike force, Leroy was immediately put into the side that lost to Preston at the Valley, alongside Luke

Varney. He was tried with Andy Gray and even on his own before teaming up with Chris Iwelumo, when things seemed to click as he scored three goals in two games, including a brace at Plymouth, Charlton's first win in seven attempts. Although not that tall, Leroy is good in the air and scored two of his three Charlton goals with headers. He has good pace, reads the game well and has a good first touch.
Bristol C (From trainee on 6/3/2003) FL 44+41/31 FLC 2+1/2 FAC 1+4/3 Others 4+3/2
Reading (£1,000,000 on 15/7/2005) P/FL 54+19/19 FLC 5+2/5 FAC 6+2/7
Charlton Ath (Loaned on 5/3/2008) FL 8/3

LITTLE Glen Matthew
Born: Wimbledon, 15 October 1975
Height: 6'3" **Weight:** 13.0
Club Honours: Ch '06
In what was a frustrating season for him, Glen had to spend most of his time in the treatment room at Reading under the supervision of physio Jon Fearn or in the gym as he attempted to recover from the Achilles injury that forced him to spend almost a year out of the game. He made slow but patient and steady progress, joined in a series of training ground friendlies and reserve fixtures, then made a long-awaited first-team return as a second-half substitute in the games against Fulham and Wigan. Despite only playing a total of 51 Premiership minutes, he showed flashes of his old brilliance as an orthodox wide-right player. Glen has another year on his contract and will make an important contribution to Reading's attempt to make an immediate return to the top flight.
Crystal Palace (From trainee on 1/7/1994). Free to Glentoran on 11/11/1994)
Burnley (£100,000 from Glentoran on 29/11/1996) FL 211+35/32 FLC 11+4 FAC 11+6/3 Others 4+1/1
Reading (Loaned on 27/3/2003) FL 6/1 Others 1
Bolton W (Loaned on 1/9/2003) PL 0+4
Reading (Free on 24/5/2004) P/FL 81+15/5 FLC 3+2 FAC 3+3

LITTLE Mark Daniel
Born: Worcester, 20 August 1988
Height: 6'1" **Weight:** 12.11
International Honours: E: Yth
Injury delayed Mark's beginning to last season at Wolverhampton and he was unavailable until October. After a substitute appearance at Ipswich, the full-back could not find a place at Molineux and went on loan to Northampton. By the time he left Sixfields, Mark was regarded as a hero, having put in many

top-notch performances. Whether he played at full-back or in the middle of defence, he seemed to absorb attacks with ease. Good in the air, difficult to knock off the ball and good distribution marked him as a player with a good future.
Wolverhampton W (From trainee on 26/8/2005) FL 19+8 FLC 1 FAC 3 Others 0+1
Northampton T (Loaned on 10/1/2008) FL 17

LIVERMORE David
Born: Edmonton, 20 May 1980
Height: 5'11" **Weight:** 12.1
Club Honours: Div 2 '01
David is a hugely respected model professional, who provided reliable cover for Hull's midfield in the first half of their Championship campaign last season, being particularly valuable in the absence of captain Ian Ashbee. Reportedly due to a clause in his contract that would have triggered a new Tigers' deal if he played two more games, the left-sided midfielder was allowed to go on loan to League One Oldham as the January transfer window closed. During his stay at Boundary Park, he operated manfully in a variety of positions, including left-back and centre-back and left and centre midfield, making ten appearances. Having also netted a rare goal in the Latics' 2-2 home draw with Swindon he decided against extending his loan for a third month and opted to return to the KC Stadium. Back at City David played once more, at centre-back, in place of the injured Wayne Brown for the crucial promotion clash at Sheffield United in April. Was released at the end of the campaign.
Arsenal (From trainee on 13/7/1998)
Millwall (£30,000 on 30/7/1999) FL 269+4/12 FLC 14/2 FAC 18 Others 7
Leeds U (£400,000 on 21/7/2006)
Hull C (£400,000 on 2/8/2006) FL 33+12/5 FLC 4 FAC 3
Oldham Ath (Loaned on 31/1/2008) FL 10/1

LIVERMORE Jake Cyril
Born: Enfield, 14 November 1989
Height: 5'9" **Weight:** 11.10
This tall and powerful central midfielder joined MK Dons on loan from Tottenham and during his month with the club played a valuable role late in games, going on to shore up the central area in each of his five unbeaten appearances. He showed good promise and, on the evidence of his contribution, may be more suited to defensive than attacking roles.
Tottenham H (From trainee on 23/11/2007)
MK Dons (Loaned on 29/2/2008) FL 0+5

Freddie Ljungberg

LIVESEY Daniel (Danny) Richard

Born: Salford, 31 December 1984
Height: 6'2" **Weight:** 13.0
Club Honours: Div 2 '06

Selection for the PFA League One team was no more than Danny deserved for his outstanding form at Carlisle last season. Virtually ever-present at the heart of the United defence, he produced a whole series of gutsy performances that made a crucial contribution to Carlisle's successful season. Whenever the opportunity arises, particularly at set pieces, Danny loves to move forward and he bagged a number of valuable goals. He also took on the added responsibility of captaincy for much of the season, due to Paul Thirlwell's absence through injury.

Bolton W *(From trainee on 17/8/2002) PL 0+2 FLC 1 FAC 3*
Notts Co *(Loaned on 5/9/2003) FL 9+2 Others 1*
Rochdale *(Loaned on 6/2/2004) FL 11+2*
Blackpool *(Loaned on 4/8/2004) FL 1*
Carlisle U *(Free on 24/12/2004) FL 108+4/11 FLC 5 FAC 3+1 Others 10*

LJUNGBERG Karl Fredrik (Freddie)

Born: Halmstad, Sweden, 16 April 1977
Height: 5'9" **Weight:** 11.6
Club Honours: CS '99; PL '02, '04; FAC '02, '03, '05
International Honours: Sweden: 75; U21-12; Yth

Signed from Arsenal in the summer, it was a tough start to life with West Ham when he was forced to endure a series of niggling injuries in the early months of the season. It was not until January that the Swede began to return to his best form, surging down the right flank and making dangerous runs. Freddie scored his first goal against Birmingham in February and soon followed with another at Sunderland. In April, there were further setbacks as first he sustained hamstring trouble then, against Newcastle, was carried off after cracking ribs, bringing an end to his season. He continued to add to his caps for Sweden and was looking forward to appearing in the European championships

Arsenal *(£3,000,000 from BK Halmstad, Sweden on 17/9/1998) PL 188+28/46 FLC 3 FAC 28+5/11 Others 66+10/15*
West Ham U *(£3,500,000 on 25/7/2007) PL 22+3/2 FLC 2 FAC 1*

LLEWELLYN Christopher (Chris) Mark

Born: Swansea, 29 August 1979
Height: 5'11" **Weight:** 11.6
Club Honours: AMC '05
International Honours: W: 6; B-1; U21-14; Yth; Sch

As has been the case throughout his Wrexham career, Chris keeps himself fit and missed few games, again being top of the appearances list. Last season was not one of his best, despite strong

running and high workrate. Chris, never an out-and-out striker, prefers to come from deep but is a grafter and chases players down. Released along with a host of others in May, the door was left ajar for him.

Norwich C *(From trainee on 21/1/1997) FL 103+39/17 FLC 7+3 FAC 3+3/1*
Bristol Rov *(Loaned on 21/2/2003) FL 14/3*
Wrexham *(Free on 6/8/2003) FL 91/15 FLC 2+1/1 FAC 3/1 Others 8+1/3*
Hartlepool U *(Signed on 12/7/2005) FL 24+5 FLC 0+1 FAC 1/1 Others 1*
Wrexham *(Free on 4/8/2006) FL 77+2/12 FLC 4/2 FAC 3 Others 2*

LLOYD Paul Laurence

Born: Preston, 26 March 1987
Height: 5'8" **Weight:** 10.13

The speedy young Morecambe winger started only one League game but always impressed in the reserves and gave a fine display in a Johnstone's Paint Trophy win at Hartlepool, scoring a penalty in the shoot-out victory. Has a good turn of pace and can put it in useful crosses. The potential is there and having been offered a new deal at the end of the season, he will look to get more opportunities.

Morecambe *(From juniors on 26/7/2005) FL 1+6 Others 1+2*

LOACH Scott James

Born: Nottingham, 27 May 1988
Height: 6'1" **Weight:** 13.2

A young goalkeeper signed on loan from Watford after Joe Lewis' loan spell was up, Scott made two League starts for Morecambe and one in the Johnstone's Paint Trophy, showing a good deal of promise. After a losing debut on New Year's Day against Stockport, he made some fine saves, including one from a penalty, in a victory over Macclesfield. Back at Watford as the third-choice 'keeper, Scott joined Bradford on loan in January, distinguishing himself straight away by saving a penalty and then brilliantly turning away the follow-up in a win at Macclesfield. Ironically, he had saved another Macclesfield penalty a month earlier on behalf of Morecambe.

Watford *(From trainee at Lincoln C on 30/5/2006)*
Morecambe *(Loaned on 1/1/2008) FL 2 Others 1*
Bradford C *(Loaned on 30/1/2008) FL 20*

LOCKWOOD Adam Brian

Born: Wakefield, 26 October 1981
Height: 6'0" **Weight:** 12.7
Club Honours: FAT '02; FC '03; AMC '07
International Honours: E: SP-2

Adam took over as Doncaster captain at

the beginning of the season, with Graeme Lee out injured. He led the side by example with consistently good performances at centre-back before suffering a nasty foot injury at home to Leeds in March. That looked as if it would end his season but Adam made a surprise return as a substitute in the play-off final at Wembley against Leeds and jointly lifted the Cup, as club captain, with Brian Stock.
Reading (From trainee on 19/3/1999)
Yeovil T (Free on 17/10/2001) FL 67+6/4 FLC 2+1 FAC 3 Others 2
Torquay U (Loaned on 18/11/2005) FL 9/3 FAC 3
Doncaster Rov (Free on 3/7/2006) FL 81+2/ 5 FLC 5 FAC 6 Others 6+2

LOCKWOOD Matthew (Matt) Dominic
Born: Southend, 17 October 1976
Height: 5'9" **Weight:** 10.12
Matt signed for Nottingham Forest from Leyton Orient last summer and made his debut at left-back against Bournemouth on the opening day. Unfortunately, he suffered an ankle injury that kept him out until December. On his return, he enjoyed his best spell with five consecutive games before he was again hit by injury. Julian Bennett's excellent form meant there was no way back and Matt was used as cover for the remainder of the season.
Queens Park Rgrs (From trainee at Southend U on 2/5/1995)
Bristol Rov (Free on 24/7/1996) FL 58+5/1 FLC 2+1 FAC 6 Others 4+2
Leyton Orient (Free on 7/8/1998) FL 319+9/ 50 FLC 15/2 FAC 25/2 Others 25/3
Nottingham F (Signed on 20/7/2007) FL 11 FAC 1

LOFT Douglas (Doug) James
Born: Maidstone, 26 December 1986
Height: 6'0" **Weight:** 12.1
Something of an enigma at the Withdean Stadium, Doug made just two starting appearances for Brighton and a further 15 as a substitute but that was enough to earn him another year's contract. A slight, energetic midfielder, he always looks to get forward and threaten the opposing goal. At Luton in April, he was employed as a forward after coming off the bench and performed well but the highlight of his season was undoubtedly his last-minute equaliser in the FA Cup at Cheltenham.
Brighton & Hove A (Free from Hastings U on 19/1/2006) FL 6+21/2 FLC 0+2 FAC 0+3/1 Others 1

LOGAN Conrad Joseph
Born: Letterkenny, 18 April 1986
Height: 6'2" **Weight:** 14.0
International Honours: RoI: Yth

The Irishman, who arrived at Stockport during the summer on a season-long loan from Leicester, immediately held down the goalkeeper spot before a mistake against Bury when he rolled the ball out unaware that Efe Sodje was behind him, leading to a red card and a suspension. County boss Jim Gannon moved quickly to bring in Everton's John Ruddy, who subsequently kept Conrad out of the team. He was recalled for the second play-off semi-final and made the most of his opportunity to keep his place for the Wembley victory over Rochdale.
Leicester C (From trainee on 15/7/2003) FL 18 FLC 2
Boston U (Loaned on 24/12/2005) FL 10
Boston U (Loaned on 20/4/2006) FL 3
Stockport Co (Loaned on 10/8/2007) FL 34 FLC 2 Others 5

LOGAN Shaleum Narval
Born: Wythenshawe, 29 January 1988
Height: 6'1" **Weight:** 12.7
After making a fine start to last season, Shaleum signed a three-year contract with Manchester City and, a day later, made his debut in the Carling Cup win over Bristol City. He followed with another Carling Cup appearance against Norwich before embarking on a series of loans to gain experience. Although he was not on the winning side as a Grimsby player, having arrived there in October, Shaleum impressed during his month at Blundell Park. An attacking, quick full-back, the teenager netted after just 18 minutes of his debut against Rochdale following a solo run and struck from distance in the 1-1 draw with Bradford. Shaleum's next move was to Scunthorpe in November and he impressed on his debut at Blackpool, when showing a willingness to get forward during his four appearances before returning to Eastlands. Shaleum could well have appeared for Stockport in the League Two play-off final at Wembley but for Manchester City recalling the youngster because of an injury crisis at Eastlands. The lightning-quick defender was hugely popular during a spell in Stockport that began with a 'Man of the Match' performance on his debut at Accrington in February.
Manchester C (From trainee on 3/7/2006) FLC 2
Grimsby T (Loaned on 11/10/2007) FL 5/2
Scunthorpe U (Loaned on 9/11/2007) FL 4
Stockport Co (Loaned on 22/2/2008) FL 6+1

LOKANDO Mbive (Peggy)
Born: DR Congo, 18 September 1989
Height: 5'11" **Weight:** 12.0
International Honours: E: Yth. DR Congo

A former Arsenal trainee, Peggy came to Southend in the summer and featured in several pre-season friendlies. Despite his tender years, he was offered a two-year deal within six months of his arrival, Southend fending off interest from other clubs. His form in the reserves earned promotion, Peggy making his debut as a late substitute for Alan McCormack in the Carling Cup tie against Watford. It was his only taste of first-team action but much is expected of the slightly built central midfielder. Although capped at youth level by England, he was selected for the Democratic Republic of Congo in their March friendlies in France and won his first cap as a substitute against Gabon in a match staged at Aubervilliers.
Southend U (From trainee at Arsenal on 10/8/2007) FLC 0+1

LOMAS Stephen (Steve) Martin
Born: Hanover, Germany, 18 January 1974
Height: 6'0" **Weight:** 12.8
International Honours: NI: 45; B-1; Yth; Sch
After joining Gillingham from Queens Park Rangers immediately prior to 2007-08 getting underway, the highly experienced midfielder had the misfortune to become only the fourth Gills player to be sent off on his debut, at Cheltenham on the opening day of the season. An excellent passer of the ball with neat skills, he was released by the new manager, Mark Stimson, in January.
Manchester C (From trainee on 22/1/1991) P/FL 102+9/8 FLC 15/2 FAC 10+1/1
West Ham U (£1,600,000 on 26/3/1997) P/ FL 179+8/10 FLC 13/2 FAC 10+3/1 Others 13
Queens Park Rgrs (Free on 31/8/2005) FL 44+11/2 FAC 2
Gillingham (Free on 10/8/2007) FL 8 FAC 1

LOMAX Kelvin
Born: Bury, 12 November 1986
Height: 5'11" **Weight:** 12.3
The Oldham youth product looked set to start 2007-08 at left-back only to be injured in the final pre-season friendly. When fit, Kelvin found loan-players Stuart Giddings and Ryan Bertrand blocking his path and joined neighbours Rochdale on loan. Dale needed him as no fewer than five potential right-backs were injured and he made ten League appearances, helping them to recover from a shaky start. Back at Oldham, he had to be patient until January before making a memorable first start as the Latics beat Everton 1-0 at Goodison in the FA Cup third round. Kelvin made a vital double goal-line clearance from James McFadden

and went on to make 17 further starts to leave himself well placed to press his claims in the coming season ahead. He also agreed a new three-and-half year contract.

Oldham Ath *(From trainee on 12/7/2005) FL 27+13 FAC 2+1 Others 3+2*
Rochdale *(Loaned on 13/9/2007) FL 10*

LONERGAN Andrew (Andy)

Born: Preston, 19 October 1983
Height: 6'4" **Weight:** 13.2
International Honours: RoI: Yth; E: Yth
Preston's young goalkeeper regained his regular starting place after Wayne Henderson's early-season injury and held it for the next 46 games. A couple of uncharacteristic but costly errors in the New Year could have seen him replaced but he battled back to demonstrate the superb shot-stopping ability for which he is best known. After two seasons out through injury, he was glad to reach 100 senior games since his debut as a 16-year-old. Preston spent most of the season near the foot of the Championship, so his 12 clean sheets were vital in staving off relegation. Andy will hope for a less busy time ahead.

Preston NE *(From trainee on 21/10/2000) FL 88/1 FLC 3 FAC 6*
Darlington *(Loaned on 20/12/2002) FL 2*
Wycombe W *(Loaned on 6/10/2005) FL 2*
Swindon T *(Loaned on 3/11/2006) FL 1*

Andy Lonergan

LONG Shane Patrick

Born: Kilkenny, 22 January 1987
Height: 5'10" **Weight:** 11.2
International Honours: RoI: 8; B-1; U21-1; Yth
As in the previous two seasons, Shane was used more frequently by Reading as a second-half substitute than in the starting line-up. In a generally difficult campaign for Reading strikers, he scored only three goals, the most notable of these being the decider in the 2-1 home win against Newcastle. Shane netted with his second touch of the ball just ten seconds after making his entrance, chesting down a free kick from Nicky Shorey before rifling the ball into the top of the visitors' net. He also scored at Portsmouth in Reading's incredible 7-4 defeat and in the 2-0 win over Manchester City. Relatively young in terms of big-match practice, Shane is an emerging talent, though he is adding to his experience by remaining a member of the Republic of Ireland squad along with Royals' team-mates Kevin Doyle and Stephen Hunt.

Reading *(Signed from Cork C on 19/8/2005) P/FL 17+44/8 FLC 3/1 FAC 7/2*

LOOVENS Glenn

Born: Doetinchem, Holland, 22 September 1983
Height: 6'1" **Weight:** 12.11
International Honours: Holland: U21; Yth

Dutch defender Glenn looked a class act through the season, his partnership with Roger Johnson at the heart of Cardiff's defence being a crucial factor in the club's run to the FA Cup final. Glenn has been tipped for a Premiership future. Cardiff signed him from Feyenoord and he has blossomed as a central defender who is strong in the tackle and rarely loses aerial challenges.

Cardiff C *(£250,000 from Feyenoord, Holland on 4/8/2005) FL 98+1/3 FLC 3 FAC 9*

LOUIS Jefferson Lee

Born: Harrow, 22 February 1979
Height: 6'2" **Weight:** 13.0
International Honours: Dominica: 1
A big, strong forward, Jefferson signed for Mansfield until the end of the season in January after being released by Weymouth. He made an immediate impression, scoring on his debut against Brentford and hitting the net three times in his first four appearances. Difficult to knock off the ball, he led the line and held up the ball well, adding new options to the Stags' front line and taking some of the pressure off Micky Boulding. He missed the Easter game at Bury as he was on international duty with Dominica.

Oxford U *(Free from Thame U, ex Aylesbury U, on 4/3/2002) FL 18+38/8 FLC 1+2/1 FAC 1+3/1 Others 2 (Transferred to Forest Green Rovers on 24/9/2004)*
Bristol Rov *(Signed from Woking on 5/5/2005) FL 3+6 FLC 1 (Freed during October 2005)*
Mansfield T *(Free from Weymouth, ex Hemel Hempstead, Worthing, Lewes, Stevenage Borough, Eastleigh, Yeading, Havant & Waterlooville, on 30/1/2008) FL 14+4/4*

LOW Joshua (Josh) David

Born: Bristol, 15 February 1979
Height: 6'1" **Weight:** 12.0
International Honours: W: U21-4; Yth
Josh scored Peterborough's first goal of the season but that was just about as good as it got for the midfielder. He found his chances limited and was released at the end of the season. As a strong, right-sided midfielder he still has plenty to offer.

Bristol Rov *(From trainee on 19/8/1996) FL 11+11 FLC 0+2 FAC 2+2 Others 2*
Leyton Orient *(Free on 27/5/1999) FL 2+3/1 FLC 1*
Cardiff C *(Free on 20/11/1999) FL 54+21/6 FLC 1+1 FAC 2+3 Others 3+1*
Oldham Ath *(Free on 12/8/2002) FL 19+2/3 FLC 2 FAC 2/1 Others 2*
Northampton T *(£165,000 on 8/8/2003) FL 90+12/15 FLC 5/1 FAC 8+1/2 Others 8/1*

Leicester C (Free on 28/7/2006) FL 12+4 FLC 2+1
Peterborough U (£100,000 on 5/1/2007) FL 26+8/3 FLC 2 FAC 2+2 Others 1

LOWE Keith Stephen

Born: Wolverhampton, 13 September 1985
Height: 6'2" **Weight:** 13.3
Club Honours: AMC '06
Keith was on loan to Port Vale from Wolverhampton for the season but took time to settle in the centre of defence as the team constantly changed. Strong in the air, he was sometimes beaten for pace but never conceded defeat. His personal highlight was the home game against Millwall in which he scored two headers, his first goals for the Vale. He scored again soon afterwards as his form improved under new manager Lee Sinnott and appeared at right-back in some games before returning to Wolves. Was released in the summer.
Wolverhampton W (From trainee on 24/11/2004) FL 14 FLC 1+1
Burnley (Loaned on 26/8/2005) FL 10+6 FLC 2/1
Queens Park Rgrs (Loaned on 31/1/2006) FL 1
Swansea C (Loaned on 10/3/2006) FL 4 Others 2
Cheltenham T (Loaned on 8/9/2006) FL 7+1 FLC 1 Others 1
Cheltenham T (Loaned on 9/1/2007) FL 7+1/1
Port Vale (Loaned on 19/7/2007) FL 24+4/3 FLC 1 FAC 2

LOWE Ryan Thomas

Born: Liverpool, 18 September 1978
Height: 5'11" **Weight:** 11.10
After a good season with Crewe in 2006-07, Ryan found it hard to retain a regular place in 2007-08, despite being able to occupy a variety of positions in attack and continuing to contribute to the goals tally. Jim Gannon, who had been chasing Ryan for more than two years, finally got his man when he arrived at Stockport on loan in the March transfer window. Unfortunately, a shoulder injury just ten minutes into his debut against Darlington did not help him and probably explains why he did not make the kind of impact expected.
Shrewsbury T (Free from Burscough on 25/7/2000) FL 81+56/23 FLC 2+2 FAC 4+2 Others 7+2/4
Chester C (Free on 22/3/2005) FL 36+4/14 FAC 2/3
Crewe Alex (Free on 2/5/2006) FL 47+17/12 FLC 2/1 FAC 2 Others 6/4
Stockport Co (Loaned on 27/3/2008) FL 4

LOWNDES Nathan Peter

Born: Salford, 2 June 1977
Height: 5'11" **Weight:** 11.6
Club Honours: Div 2 '04
It proved a difficult campaign for Nathan at Chester as he struggled with injuries after moving to the Deva Stadium from Port Vale in the summer. Although the striker started the first three games, he picked up an injury at Rochdale and on his return had to be content with a place on the bench. A hard-working player, he returned for a six-game run in November but the recurrence of a back injury sustained with Port Vale saw him miss the reminder of the campaign after the game against Bury in December. As the season drew to a conclusion, Nathan's contract was paid up and he left the club.
Leeds U (From trainee on 1/4/1995)
Watford (£40,000 on 3/10/1995) FL 1+6 FLC 0+1 FAC 1+1 Others 1
St Johnstone (£50,000 on 21/8/1998) SL 30+34/14 SLC 2+2/2 SC 4+2 Others 2+1
Livingston (Free on 20/7/2001) SL 7+14/3 SLC 0+2 SC 0+2
Rotherham U (Loaned on 28/3/2002) FL 2
Plymouth Arg (Free on 23/7/2002) FL 25+28/10 FLC 1 FAC 0+1 Others 3+1/2
Port Vale (Free on 5/11/2004) FL 38+21/6 FLC 1 FAC 4+2/1 Others 1
Chester C (Free on 4/7/2007) FL 8+4 FLC 1 FAC 1 Others 0+1

LOWRY Jamie

Born: Newquay, 18 March 1987
Height: 6'0" **Weight:** 12.0
Jamie has progressed more rapidly than anyone could have hoped at Chesterfield. The likeable young man is developing into a composed defender, bringing mobility, tenacity and important height. He can also play with creativity and power on the right of midfield. Jamie has the knack of turning up in the right place to accept chances and the popular Cornishman has a promising future in the game.
Chesterfield (From trainee on 5/7/2006) FL 47+3/6 FLC 1+2 FAC 1 Others 2

LUA LUA Kazenga

Born: Kinshasa, DR Congo, 10 December 1990
Height: 5'11" **Weight:** 12.1
Newcastle right-winger Kazenga is the younger brother of the former club striker Lomana and although very much his own player, does possess many of the ball skills with which Lomana often delighted the home fans. Kazenga displays a welcome confidence in his ability and a willingness to take on opponents with his good close control. Clearly one for the future, he was limited to a few substitute appearances in

January and in the last game, at Everton. Playing for the reserves he scored the goal against Blyth Spartans that took the final of the Northumberland Senior Cup to penalties and converted his spot-kick to help bring the trophy to St James' Park.
Newcastle U (From trainee on 2/5/2008) PL 0+2 FAC 0+3

[LUCAS] PEZZINI-LEIVA Lucas

Born: Dourados, Brazil, 9 January 1987
Height: 5'8" **Weight:** 11.7
International Honours: Brazil: 2; U20-9
Lucas is a highly talented Brazilian midfielder signed by Liverpool manager Rafa Benitez in the summer from Brazilian team Gremio. He was voted best player in the Brazilian Campeanato in 2006 and shortly after joining the Reds had his full international debut for Brazil. Despite this pedigree, he took some time to make his mark at Anfield. His debut was in late August, as a substitute against Toulouse in the Champions' League, and he started in the Carling Cup against Reading the following month. After a few more substitute outings, he made his first Premiership start at home to Newcastle in October and went on to make 12 more starts, standing in for Javier Mascherano or Xabi Alonso. It may be significant that Liverpool won eight and drew four of those games, in which he provided five assists, so he is clearly an influential player. His first goal for the Reds came in the traumatic FA Cup tie with non-Leaguers Havant & Waterlooville when he scored the first equaliser with a curling 25-yard shot. It is still not clear whether his best position will be as a holding midfielder or a box-to-box player, such as Steven Gerrard, but he is in a squad containing three other top-class internationals in that department so may have to wait for the automatic slot that would be his right at many other Premiership clubs.
Liverpool (Signed from Gremio, Brazil, on 26/7/2007) PL 12+6 FLC 3 FAC 3+1/1 Others 2+5

LUCAS David Anthony

Born: Preston, 23 November 1977
Height: 6'2" **Weight:** 13.10
International Honours: E: Yth
David had little opportunity to show his goalkeeping skills in his first full season at Leeds after arriving from Barnsley because of the consistency of Casper Ankergren. He kept a clean sheet on his United debut in the Johnstone's Paint Trophy win at Darlington, but was on the losing side in each of his three League One appearances, defeats at Cheltenham and Southend and a home loss to Tranmere.

Preston NE *(From trainee on 12/12/1994) FL 117+5 FLC 10 FAC 7 Others 11*
Darlington *(Loaned on 14/12/1995) FL 6*
Darlington *(Loaned on 3/10/1996) FL 7*
Scunthorpe U *(Loaned on 23/12/1996) FL 6 Others 2*
Sheffield Wed *(Loaned on 1/10/2003) FL 17 Others 1*
Sheffield Wed *(£100,000 on 14/6/2004) FL 52 FLC 4 FAC 2 Others 4 (Freed during 2006 close season)*
Barnsley *(Free, following long-term injury, on 4/1/2007) FL 2+1*
Leeds U *(Free on 11/9/2007) FL 3 FAC 0+1 Others 2*

LUCKETTI Christopher (Chris) James
Born: Rochdale, 28 September 1971
Height: 6'0" **Weight:** 13.6
Club Honours: Div 2 '97
Despite talk of Chris leaving Sheffield United last summer he signed a one-year deal, but the form of other central defenders limited his opportunities. On his few appearances, he used his experience and ability to read the game to make up for a lack of pace and scored his first goal for the club at MK Dons in the Carling Cup. Loaned on the March deadline day to Southampton, a club with defensive deficiencies largely due to an injury plague, Chris, partnered by Chris Perry, became the tenth centre-back of the season to start for Saints. Despite the lack of familiarity, the veterans settled in quickly and defensive performances improved markedly. Chris amply demonstrated that experience has added to, rather than diminished, his strengths as a canny and effective stopper.
Rochdale *(Trainee) FL 1*
Stockport Co *(Free on 23/8/1990)*
Halifax T *(Free on 12/7/1991) FL 73+5/2 FLC 2/1 FAC 2 Others 4*
Bury *(£50,000 on 1/10/1993) FL 235/8 FLC 16 FAC 11/1 Others 15/1*
Huddersfield T *(£750,000 + on 14/6/1999) FL 68/1 FLC 7/1*
Preston NE *(£750,000 on 23/8/2001) FL 184+5/10 FLC 8 FAC 8+2 Others 3*
Sheffield U *(£300,000 on 8/3/2006) P/FL 14+3 FLC 3+1/1*
Southampton *(Loaned on 27/3/2008) FL 4*

LUMSDON Christopher (Chris)
Born: Newcastle, 15 December 1979
Height: 5'7" **Weight:** 10.6
Club Honours: Div 2 '06
Playing mostly in a defensive midfield role, Chris had probably his best season to date for Carlisle. Always willing to chase and harry to break up opposition attacks, he produced a number of 'Man of the

Match' displays despite the unspectacular role he was asked to perform. He is one of a number of United players who have risen with the club from the Conference to the brink of the Championship, all of whom enhanced their reputations in the past 12 months.
Sunderland *(From trainee on 3/7/1997) P/FL 2 FLC 1+1*
Blackpool *(Loaned on 3/2/2000) FL 6/1*
Crewe Alex *(Loaned on 11/9/2000) FL 14+2*
Barnsley *(£350,000 on 8/10/2001) FL 70+15/13 FLC 2+1 FAC 3+3 Others 2+1*
Carlisle U *(Free on 12/8/2004) FL 111+6/9 FLC 3 FAC 4 Others 12*

LUNT Kenneth (Kenny) Vincent
Born: Runcorn, 20 November 1979
Height: 5'10" **Weight:** 10.0
International Honours: E: Yth; Sch
It was a very disappointing season for Kenny. The midfield player was not a regular at the start of the season and not even in Sheffield Wednesday's 16 after Christmas before taking the chance to restart his career on loan to his old club Crewe in February. Kenny was still a big favourite at Crewe, having earlier joined them after attending the FA school at Lilleshall, and playing more than 400 games before joining Wednesday. Playing his first game back against Leeds, Kenny went on to prove that he is still a talented midfield player who creates good opportunities for others.
Crewe Alex *(From trainee on 12/6/1997) FL 343+30/35 FLC 21+4/1 FAC 15+1 Others 4/1*
Sheffield Wed *(Free on 25/7/2006) FL 33+8 FLC 3+1 FAC 2+1*
Crewe Alex *(Loaned on 19/2/2008) FL 14*

LYNCH Joel John
Born: Eastbourne, 3 October 1987
Height: 6'1" **Weight:** 12.10
International Honours: E: Yth
Although his season at Brighton was disrupted by two severe injuries, Joel will be pleased with his continued progress. Confident on the ball – sometimes too confident – the young defender reads the game well and is blessed with the pace that allows him to make tackles when he seems to be beaten. While the highlight of his season was probably the late winner at home to Cheltenham in February, Joel looks destined to be a part of the Albion defence, either in the centre or at left-back, for several years.
Brighton & Hove A *(From trainee on 3/3/2006) FL 68+9/2 FLC 3 FAC 5+1 Others 4+2*

LYNCH Mark John
Born: Manchester, 2 September 1981
Height: 5'11" **Weight:** 11.5
Club Honours: Ch '05

Chris Lumsdon

After an injury-plagued season in 2006-07, Mark looked to get his career back on track by regaining his place in the Yeovil side. Although not a regular, the versatile defender slotted into both full-back positions when required by Yeovil and his solid performances towards the end of the campaign helped Russell Slade's threadbare squad maintain their League One status. Despite that, Mark was released in the summer.
Manchester U *(From trainee on 3/7/2001) Others 1*
St Johnstone *(Loaned on 25/10/2001) SL 20*
Sunderland *(Signed on 26/7/2004) FL 5+6 FLC 2*
Hull C *(Free on 16/6/2005) FL 15+1 FAC 0+1*
Yeovil T *(Free on 22/8/2006) FL 29+2 FLC 2 FAC 1+1 Others 2+1*

LYNCH Ryan Patrick
Born: Solihull, 13 March 1987
Height: 5'11" **Weight:** 11.9
A young midfielder or defender signed from Coventry in the close season, Ryan made one full appearance for Crewe at left-back in the League against Tranmere at the beginning of January before going out on loan to Stafford three days later. He had another loan spell, this time with Altrincham, before being released at the end of the season.
Crewe Alex *(From trainee at Coventry C on 1/8/2007) FL 1+1 Others 0+1*

M

McALISKEY John James
Born: Huddersfield, 2 September 1984
Height: 6'5" **Weight:** 12.7
International Honours: RoI: U21-1
A very tall striker who moved from
Huddersfield to Mansfield in the summer
with centre-half Martin McIntosh,
John settled in well and scored Town's
second goal in their pre-season win over
Derby. He had to wait until September
to open his account in the League at
Peterborough and was in and out of the
side after this until injury at MK Dons
on New Year's Day forced a longer lay-
off. Deemed surplus to requirements
on transfer deadline day in March, his
contract was paid up and he left the club
before signing with Alfreton until the end
of the season.
*Huddersfield T (From trainee on 1/5/2004)
FL 15+28/7 FLC 0+1 Others 1+3/1*
Torquay U (Loaned on 30/9/2005) FL 3
Wrexham (Loaned on 19/9/2006) FL 3 FLC 1
*Mansfield T (Free on 12/7/2007) FL 9+7/2
FLC 1 FAC 0+2 Others 1*

McALLISTER James (Jamie)
Reynolds
Born: Glasgow, 26 April 1978
Height: 5'11" **Weight:** 11.0
Club Honours: SLC '04
International Honours: S: 1
Many Bristol City fans found it surprising
that the left-sided defender was not in
the frame to add to his solitary Scottish
cap. Perhaps it was because of his
wandering tendencies but it was another
distinguished campaign for the cultured
and tenacious player. In the play-off final
at Wembley he was good in defence but
was unable to get forward enough as the
side failed in their attempt to reach the
Premiership.
*Queen of the South (Signed from Bellshill
BC on 10/7/1996) SL 17+14 SLC 0+1 SC 2/1
Others 0+2*
*Aberdeen (Signed on 26/5/1999) SL 103+14
SLC 5+3 SC 13+2/1 Others 3+1*
*Livingston (Free on 28/6/2003) SL 34/1 SLC
5/1 SC 4*
*Heart of Midlothian (Free on 2/6/2004) SL
31+16 SLC 5 SC 5+2/2 Others 6*
*Bristol C (Signed on 4/8/2006) FL 69+3/1
FLC 3 FAC 7 Others 5+1*

McALLISTER Sean Brian
Born: Bolton, 15 August 1987
Height: 5'8" **Weight:** 10.7
Sean had hoped to make the big
breakthrough into the Sheffield
Wednesday first team last season, but

was sent out on loan to Mansfield in
September to gain more experience. As
a wholehearted young and energetic
midfielder who had come up through the
Owls' youth system, the 20-year-old Sean
made a confident start at Peterborough
and improved during his two-month stay,
taking in another month before returning
to Hillsborough when the Stags' injury
crisis eased. He was next sent on loan to
Bury in November, but failed to make it
off the bench prior to his recall. Eventually
he got into to the Owls' side and was
doing well until an injury put him out for
all but the last game of the campaign.
*Sheffield Wed (From trainee on 17/7/2006)
FL 6+10/1 FLC 1*
Mansfield T (Loaned on 8/9/2007) FL 5+2

McANUFF Joel (Jobi) Joshua
Frederick
Born: Edmonton, 9 November 1981
Height: 5'11" **Weight:** 11.10
International Honours: Jamaica: 1
As a long-term Watford target, Jobi finally
moved to Vicarage Road from Crystal
Palace during the summer. A two-footed
winger with plenty of pace and skill, he
started last season on Watford's left flank
but lost his place in September following
the arrival of Adam Johnson on loan
from Middlesbrough. This setback may
have done him a favour, because when
Johnson returned to the Riverside, Jobi
regained his first-team spot and was
noticeably more focused and effective
in the second half of the season. The

Jobi McAnuff

Jamaican international scored only two goals but the second, a swerving drive that rescued a point against Cardiff on Boxing Day, was voted Watford's 'Goal of the Season'.
Wimbledon (From trainee on 11/7/2000) FL 76+20/13 FLC 2/1 FAC 4+2/1
West Ham U (£300,000 on 4/2/2004) FL 4+9/1 Others 0+1
Cardiff C (£250,000 on 13/8/2004) FL 42+1/2 FLC 3 FAC 2/1
Crystal Palace (£600,000 + on 7/6/2005) FL 66+9/12 FLC 2 FAC 4/2 Others 2
Watford (£1,750,000 + on 5/6/2007) FL 31+8/2 FAC 2 Others 2

McARDLE Rory Alexander
Born: Sheffield, 1 May 1987
Height: 6'1" **Weight:** 11.5
International Honours: NI: U21-19; Yth
Rory, who celebrated his 21st birthday on the last day of the regular season, was the mainstay of Rochdale's back four throughout, as their most experienced central defender while Nathan Stanton was recovering from injury. Later in the season, they were able to resume their outstanding partnership from 2006-07. Dominant in the air, Rory was also a threat from set pieces in a side with few tall men, his biggest moment coming when his towering header gave Dale the lead in the play-off final at Wembley. He was also a regular for Northern Ireland under-21s in the European Championship qualifiers.
Sheffield Wed (From trainee on 15/7/2005) FL 0+1
Rochdale (Loaned on 26/7/2005) FL 16+3/1 FAC 1
Rochdale (Signed on 7/11/2006) FL 67+1/2 FLC 2 FAC 2 Others 3/1

McAULEY Gareth
Born: Larne, 5 December 1979
Height: 6'3" **Weight:** 13.0
International Honours: NI: 10; B-1; Sch
The commanding Leicester central defender featured for Northern Ireland, under former Foxes' boss Nigel Worthington, as well as being a mainstay of City's mean rearguard. He managed only a couple of strikes during the season, and will probably be best remembered in City folklore for the header that came back off the woodwork in the vital final-day encounter at the Britannia Stadium, the moment that could have brought survival for the Foxes.
Lincoln C (£10,000 from Coleraine, ex Linfield, Crusaders, on 5/8/2004) FL 65+7/8 FLC 3 FAC 2 Others 7/2
Leicester C (Free on 7/6/2006) FL 70+4/5 FLC 7/1 FAC 3/1

McBRIDE Brian Robert
Born: Arlington Heights, Illinois, USA, 19 June 1972
Height: 6'1" **Weight:** 12.7
International Honours: USA: 95
A Fulham striker whose attitude and commitment makes him a model professional, he suffered the agony of missing much of the season after dislocating a knee while scoring his first goal of the season against Middlesbrough in August. Having undergone an operation, Brian immediately buckled down to regaining his fitness and returned for the West Ham game in February. After that, the central striker missed only one match. He leads the line well, is particularly effective in the air and scored a number of vital goals as Fulham clawed their way out of relegation trouble, notably a typically brave header to open the score against Birmingham.
Preston NE (Loaned from Columbus Crew, USA, ex St Louis University, VFL Wolfsburg, on 15/9/2000) FL 8+1/1 FLC 1 FAC 1
Everton (Loaned from Columbus Crew, USA on 5/2/2003) PL 7+1/4
Fulham (£600,000 from Columbus Crew, USA on 27/1/2004) PL 102+38/32 FLC 2+3/4 FAC 7+2/4

McBRIDE Kevin
Born: Airdrie, 14 June 1981
Height: 5'10" **Weight:** 10.8
Arriving from Motherwell in the summer, the tricky, ball-playing midfielder failed to make any impact at Darlington despite scoring on his debut against Wrexham on the opening day. After starting the first four games he made only three more substitute outings before being released to return north of the border with Falkirk.
Glasgow Celtic (From juniors on 7/7/1998)
Motherwell (Signed on 10/8/2004) SL 49+14/6 SLC 6+2/2 SC 1 Others 2
Darlington (Free on 6/6/2007) FL 3+3/1 FLC 1

McCAMMON Mark Jason
Born: Barnet, 7 August 1978
Height: 6'5" **Weight:** 14.5
Club Honours: AMC '07
International Honours: Barbados: 2
Mark began last season as a semi-permanent occupier of the substitutes' bench for Doncaster but gained a regular starting place at the turn of the year. He holds the ball well and, with his height and weight, is a forward who ruffles a few feathers in opposing defences. A playing substitute in the play-off final against Leeds at Wembley, he helped Rovers gain promotion to the Championship.
Cambridge U (Free from Cambridge C on 31/12/1996) FL 1+3 FAC 0+1 Others 1

Charlton Ath (Free on 17/3/1999) FL 1+3 FLC 0+1
Swindon T (Loaned on 3/1/2000) FL 4
Brentford (£100,000 + on 18/7/2000) FL 46+29/10 FLC 4/1 FAC 3+1/1 Others 3+5/3
Millwall (Free on 27/3/2003) FL 15+7/2 FLC 0+1 FAC 0+1 Others 0+1
Brighton & Hove A (Free on 16/12/2004) FL 19+6/3 FLC 1/1 FAC 0+1
Bristol C (Loaned on 17/2/2006) FL 8+3/4
Doncaster Rov (Free on 2/8/2006) FL 37+17/6 FLC 1+2/3 FAC 5/2 Others 4+4/2

McCANN Henry Austin
Born: Alexandria, 21 January 1980
Height: 5'9" **Weight:** 11.13
Austin performed solidly and consistently for Notts County as an orthodox left-back. He is often underrated but it came as a surprise when he was demoted to third choice after being a regular through the previous season. Austin decided to return to Scotland after losing his place and being out of contract in the summer.
Airdrie (From trainee at Wolverhampton W on 31/7/1997) SL 80+14/7 SLC 7+1/1 SC 2+1/1 Others 8+1
Heart of Midlothian (Signed on 16/2/2001) SL 35+4/1 SLC 0+1 SC 4 Others 0+1
Clyde (Free on 1/4/2004) SL 6
Boston U (Free on 7/8/2004) FL 76+4/1 FLC 3 FAC 6 Others 1
Notts Co (Free on 3/7/2006) FL 56+9 FLC 3 FAC 1 Others 1

McCANN Christopher (Chris) John
Born: County Meath, 21 July 1987
Height: 6'1" **Weight:** 11.11
International Honours: RoI: Yth
Now established as a regular in the centre of Burnley's midfield, Chris had a generally solid season, his highs including several goals to maintain his fine scoring record from the engine room, and lows including a needless dismissal in the home defeat by Preston. A fine playmaker, his aerial prowess was often crucial in the middle of the park, while his versatility again enabled him to stand in at the back or out wide when needed. A first full cap for the Republic of Ireland will surely come his way before long.
Burnley (From trainee on 5/1/2006) FL 73+23/12 FLC 4+1 FAC 3

McCANN Gavin Peter
Born: Blackpool, 10 January 1978
Height: 5'11" **Weight:** 11.0
International Honours: E: 1
In what proved to be a very astute signing, Gavin joined Bolton from Aston Villa in the summer and, despite being seen by many as a squad player at best, proved to be a vital asset as the season

progressed. He made his Bolton debut in the opening-day defeat by Newcastle and scored a vital first goal for the club in the 1-0 UEFA Cup victory at Red Star Belgrade. Gavin featured in the team with greater frequency as the season progressed, his tough tackling, experience and tireless workrate proving invaluable. Scoring what proved to be a massively important first League goal in the 1-0 win at Middlesbrough in April, Gavin was certainly an unsung hero in the battle against relegation and will be looking to continue his fine run of form into the new season.

Everton *(From trainee on 1/7/1995) PL 5+6*
Sunderland *(£500,000 on 27/11/1998) P/FL 106+10/8 FLC 4+3/2 FAC 11+1/3*
Aston Villa *(£2,250,000 on 31/7/2003) PL 108+2/3 FLC 12/2 FAC 7*
Bolton W *(£1,000,000 on 13/6/2007) PL 21+10/1 FLC 2 Others 8/2*

McCANN Grant Samuel
Born: Belfast, 14 April 1980
Height: 5'10" **Weight:** 12.0
International Honours: NI: 16; U21-11
The central or left-sided midfield player was a regular in the Barnsley squad last season and in the starting line-up during September and October, his highlight being a pair of superb free kicks at Southampton that produced the two opening goals. On New Year's Day, he scored with a volley at Scunthorpe and impressed them so much that he joined them 14 days later on a two-and-a-half-year contract. As a regular in central midfield for the Iron, after missing three matches for being sent off in the opening ten minutes of the draw at Sheffield United he returned to show good passing and a willingness to get forward from midfield, celebrating his first goal with an excellent free-kick at Queens Park Rangers in March. Grant continued to be selected in the Northern Ireland squad.

West Ham U *(From trainee on 6/7/1998) PL 0+4*
Livingston *(Loaned on 27/8/1999) SL 0+4*
Notts Co *(Loaned on 11/8/2000) FL 2 FLC 1*
Cheltenham T *(Loaned on 17/10/2000) FL 27+3/3 FAC 2 Others 1*
Cheltenham T *(£50,000 on 4/10/2002) FL 162+1/32 FLC 6/3 FAC 8/4 Others 12/4*
Barnsley *(£100,000 on 23/11/2006) FL 28+13/4 FLC 1+1 FAC 1*
Scunthorpe U *(£100,000 on 15/1/2008) FL 12+2/1*

McCARTHY Benedict (Benni)
Saul
Born: Cape Town, South Africa, 12 November 1977
Height: 6'0" **Weight:** 12.8

Benni McCarthy

International Honours: South Africa: 70
Benni had a disappointing season for
Blackburn, unsettled, as he admitted, by
the denial of a move to Chelsea. Almost
half of his 11 goals were penalties and
he eventually lost his place to Jason
Roberts. Apart from an explosive goal at
Tottenham, he could not match his first
season but Blackburn appear content to
nurse him through his lean patch and
have awarded him a new long-term
contract. At his best Benni is a free-
scoring striker who can net with both
head and foot from all ranges and angles.
*Blackburn Rov (£2,500,000 from Porto,
Portugal, ex Seven Stars, Cape Town Spurs,
Ajax Cape Town, Ajax, Celta Vigo, on 2/8/
2006) PL 57+10/26 FLC 2+1/1 FAC 4+2/3
Others 10+2/5*

McCARTHY Patrick (Paddy)
Richard
Born: Dublin, 31 May 1983
Height: 6'1" **Weight:** 12.8
International Honours: RoI: B-1; U21-
7; Yth
After signing from Leicester in the
summer it was a strange season for
Paddy, who started four of Charlton's
first five League games and then did
not feature until late December, after
which he was ever-present. Paddy did
not look comfortable in the early games
alongside Jon Fortune in defence, losing
his place to Madjid Bougherra and later
Sam Sodje. He was a substitute against
Hull at the Valley in December, started
the next game and stayed there. A strong
and uncompromising central defender,
Paddy won over the crowd with his no-
nonsense approach and aerial ability. He
scored three goals, one in the last minute
securing a point at his old club Leicester.
*Manchester C (From trainee on 14/6/2000)
Boston U (Loaned on 22/11/2002) FL 11+1
Notts Co (Loaned on 23/3/2003) FL 6
Leicester C (£100,000 on 4/3/2005) FL
69+3/3 FLC 3+2/1 FAC 4+1
Charlton Ath (£650,000 on 10/8/2007) FL
27+2/2 FLC 2/1 FAC 2*

McCARTNEY George
Born: Belfast, 29 April 1981
Height: 6'0" **Weight:** 12.6
Club Honours: Ch '05
International Honours: NI: 25; U21-5;
Yth; Sch
As dependable as ever, the left-back
had a terrific season at West Ham, being
ever-present in all matches. He was one
of the most consistent performers at
the club, nullifying the threat down the
right flank and providing good options in
the attacking third of the pitch. Against
Bolton in November he scored a stunning

volley and was 'Man of the Match'
for his defensive qualities. During the
season he added to his caps for Northern
Ireland and was runner-up in the annual
'Hammer of the Year' awards.
*Sunderland (From trainee on 28/5/1998)
P/FL 117+17 FLC 6+2 FAC 10+3 Others 2
West Ham U (£600,000 on 8/8/2006) PL
54+6/1 FLC 5 FAC 4*

McCLEARY Garath James
Born: Oxford, 15 May 1987
Height: 5'10" **Weight:** 12.6
A pacy young winger, Garath joined
Nottingham Forest in January from
Bromley after a short trial. He immediately
impressed with a stunning goal in his
first game for the reserves, against
Shrewsbury, and continued to gain
fitness at that level until his League debut
against Carlisle in March. He was used
chiefly as a substitute for the remainder
of the campaign and was impressive
enough to hope for more chances in his
first full year.
*Nottingham F (Signed from Bromley, ex
Oxford C, Slough T, on 31/1/2008) FL 3+5/1*

McCLENAHAN Trent James
Born: Sydney, Australia, 4 February 1985
Height: 5'9" **Weight:** 11.0
International Honours: Australia: U23-
1; Yth
Maintaining his progress, the young
Australian right-back became a key player
in Hereford's promotion push last season.
Although out for two short spells early
in the campaign, when he went home
to assist Australia's under-23 side in their
successful qualification bid for the Beijing
Olympics, he was soon back in the side on
his return to Hereford and was an ever-
present from early November until the
end of the season. Strong in the tackle,
Trent reads the game well and is keen to
help his attack with powerful overlapping
runs. He goes down as one of Hereford's
most improved players.
*West Ham U (From trainee on 6/1/2005) FL
0+2 FLC 1
MK Dons (Loaned on 24/3/2005) FL 7+1
MK Dons (Loaned on 18/8/2005) FL 24+5
FLC 1 FAC 4
Hereford U (Free on 4/8/2006) FL 62+2/2
FLC 4 FAC 4+1 Others 2*

McCOMBE Jamie Paul
Born: Pontefract, 1 January 1983
Height: 6'5" **Weight:** 12.6
Injury ruled the giant central defender out
of the early season games for Bristol City
and it took him some time to rediscover
his old stirring form when he eventually
regained his place. From the turn of the
year, however, he was back to his best

and knocked in the occasional goal,
none better than the overhead kick that
secured the points against Hull at Ashton
Gate in March. Unfortunately, he was
unavailable to face the Tigers in the
Championship play-off final as he was
laid low by a stomach bug on the night
before the game and his aerial threat at
set pieces was sorely missed.
*Scunthorpe U (From trainee on 28/11/2001)
FL 42+21/1 FLC 1 FAC 5+1/2 Others 4+1/1
Lincoln C (Free on 11/3/2004) FL 83+4/7 FAC
3/1 FAC 2 Others 7+1
Bristol C (Signed on 26/5/2006) FL 63+12/7
FAC 5/2 Others 5*

McCOMBE John Paul
Born: Pontefract, 7 May 1985
Height: 6'2" **Weight:** 12.10
Arriving from Huddersfield in the summer,
John was seen as a cover centre-back for
the early part of the season but grabbed
his chance with both hands when first
Dean Beckwith and then Karl Broadhurst,
Hereford's preferred centre-back pairing,
were injured. He held his place on merit
for much of the season, combining ability
in the air with a talent to bring the ball
out of defence and use it accurately. An
important goal in an FA Cup second-
round tie against Hartlepool cemented his
reputation with Hereford fans before he
was surprisingly released in the summer.
*Huddersfield T (From trainee on
5/7/2004) FL 4+4 FLC 1 FAC 1 Others 4
Hereford U (Free on 24/7/2007) FL 23+4
FAC 3+1/1 Others 1*

McCORMACK Alan
Born: Dublin, 10 January 1984
Height: 5'8" **Weight:** 10.8
International Honours: RoI: Yth; Sch
The tigerish midfielder had an
outstanding season for Southend in
2007-08. A regular in central midfield,
although manager Steve Tilson would
occasionally use him wide on the right
to accommodate Nicky Bailey and
captain Kevin Maher. Once Maher left
for Gillingham, Bailey and Alan formed
a formidable partnership, both being
tenacious tacklers with an eye for goal.
Alan's aggressive style of play incurs the
wrath of referees and opponents, so
red and yellow cards stack up, but his
workrate, energy and skill make him vital
to Southend. His bursts into opposition
penalty areas are a major contribution,
as is his relentless tracking back to help
defenders.
*Preston NE (Signed from Stella Maris BC on
14/8/2002) FL 2+9 FLC 0+1
Leyton Orient (Loaned on 29/8/2003) FL
8+2 Others 1
Southend U (Loaned on 17/3/2005) FL*

5+2/2 Others 0+1
Motherwell (Loaned on 29/7/2005) SL 24/2
SLC 3 SC 1
Southend U (£30,000 on 18/11/2006) FL
62+2/11 FLC 3 FAC 7 Others 3/1

McCORMICK Luke Martin
Born: Coventry, 15 August 1983
Height: 6'0" **Weight:** 13.12
Club Honours: Div 2 '04
Proving yet again to be a confident
goalkeeper, Luke had another solid season
with Plymouth, making many top-class
saves behind one of the meanest defences
in the Championship. He started the
season as back up to Romain Larrieu
but soon regained his place. His displays
included match-winning stops throughout
but especially against Leicester at the
Walkers Stadium to frustrate former Argyle
manager Ian Holloway. Luke signed an
extended contract at the end of the season
to keep him at Home Park until 2010.
Plymouth Arg (From trainee on 9/7/2002)
FL 137+1 FLC 7 FAC 8 Others 4
Boston U (Loaned on 22/10/2004) FL 2

McCRACKEN David
Born: Glasgow, 16 October 1981
Height: 6'2" **Weight:** 11.6
International Honours: S: U21-5
After making more than 200 appearances
in seven years at Dundee United, David
signed a two-year contract for Wycombe
last summer. He was immediately made
club captain and formed an effective
partnership with Leon Johnson in the
centre of defence. An injury at Hereford
in March saw him lose his place to a fit
again Mike Williamson and, thereafter, he
was mainly called on from the bench. His
single goal was a valuable headed winner
against Rotherham in February.
Dundee U (From juniors on 30/6/1998) SL
166+13/8 SLC 13+1 SC 8+1 Others 1
Wycombe W (Signed on 9/8/2007) FL 35+2/
1 FLC 1 FAC 1 Others 1

McCREADY Christopher (Chris) James
Born: Ellesmere Port, 5 September 1981
Height: 6'0" **Weight:** 11.11
International Honours: E: Sch
Returning to the fold in the summer after
spending 2006-07 with Tranmere on a
12-month contract, Chris quickly slipped
into gear with Crewe as though he had
never been away. Still a reliable defender
who can fill a variety of positions at the
back and is always comfortable on the
ball, he netted his first goal for Crewe
in the FA Cup first round tie against MK
Dons in November.
Crewe Alex (From trainee on 30/5/2000) FL
59+17 FLC 1+1 FAC 1+1

Tranmere Rov (Free on 1/8/2006) FL 42/1
FLC 1 FAC 2 Others 2
Crewe Alex (Free on 1/7/2007) FL 32+2/1
FLC 1 FAC 2/1

McCUNNIE Jamie Patrick
Born: Airdrie, 15 April 1983
Height: 5'11" **Weight:** 11.0
International Honours: S: U21-20
Jamie is a utility player who, in recent
seasons, built up a great reputation
in Scottish football. Signing from
Dunfermline in the close season, he
was seen as the sort of quality player
Hartlepool needed if they were to
establish themselves back in League One.
Used mainly at right-back, he turned in
solid and wholehearted performances and
was more than capable in midfield. Out
for a lengthy spell in mid-season with a
knee injury, he subsequently struggled to
regain to his best form.
Dundee U (From juniors on 30/6/1998) SL
166+13/8 SLC 13+1 SC 8+1 Others 1
Dunfermline Ath (Signed on 29/8/2005) SL
26+10 SLC 3/1 SC 4+1
Hartlepool U (Signed on 17/7/2007) FL
23+6/1 FLC 2 FAC 2 Others 2+1

McDAID Sean Andrew
Born: Harrogate, 6 March 1986
Height: 5'8" **Weight:** 10.12
Club Honours: AMC '07
Sean deputised for Gareth Roberts in his
normal position at left-back for Doncaster
last season but also played on the left
of midfield in a number of games, from
where he scored his first League goal
for Rovers, against Swindon in April.
Unfortunately, in a practice match in late
April, he dislocated a kneecap in a tackle
and was sidelined for the rest of the
campaign.
Leeds U (From trainee on 6/3/2003)
Doncaster Rov (Free on 28/7/2005) FL
65+14/1 FLC 7+1 FAC 3 Others 6

McDERMOTT David Anthony
Born: Stourbridge, 6 February 1988
Height: 5'5" **Weight:** 10.0
A diminutive and skilful midfielder,
David always looked lively during
regular substitute appearances but was
released at the end of the campaign. As
the youngest-ever first-team player for
Walsall, David will now hope to continue
his football elsewhere, having been at the
club since a schoolboy.
Walsall (From trainee on 3/7/2006) FL 1+13
FLC 0+1 FAC 1+1 Others 1+1

McDERMOTT Neale Terence
Born: Newcastle, 8 March 1985
Height: 5'11" **Weight:** 11.2
International Honours: E: Sch

One of a number of candidates for a
midfield role at Carlisle in 2007-08, Neale
featured in only one first team game
before leaving the club by mutual consent
in spring. A box-to-box midfielder, he is
the son of Terry McDermott, the former
Newcastle, Liverpool and England star.
Newcastle U (From trainee on 18/5/2002)
Fulham (Free on 31/1/2003)
Swindon T (Loaned on 31/8/2005) FL 9+4/2
FAC 1 Others 1+1
Darlington (Loaned on 13/2/2006) FL 1+2
Carlisle U (Free on 3/8/2006) FL 6+9/3 FLC
1+2

MacDONALD Alexander (Alex)
Born: Warrington, 14 April 1990
Height: 5'7" **Weight:** 11.4
As a product of Burnley's youth
development scheme, Alex impressed
sufficiently in the reserves to be given his
first-team chance, with appearances from
the bench in each of the last two games
of the season before being offered his
first professional contract. Not tall, but
solidly built, speedy and clearly relishing
a challenge, he looks capable of pushing
for a place on the left of midfield or on
the wing in the seasons to come.
Burnley (Trainee) FL 0+2

MacDONALD Charles (Charlie) Lea
Born: Southwark, 13 February 1981
Height: 5'8" **Weight:** 12.10
Having joined Southend from Blue Square
Premier side Ebbsfleet in the summer,
Charlie never managed to cement a
permanent place, although the striker was
a regular member of the 16-man squad.
Small in stature, Charlie made up for his
lack of height with an amazing workrate
and contributed five goals, including two
in a 3-0 FA Cup win over Oxford United
in December. Perhaps the new season
will see his goal-poaching skills used more
regularly.
Charlton Ath (From trainee on 10/11/1998)
P/FL 1+7/1 FLC 0+3 FAC 1+1/1 (Freed during
2002 close season)
Cheltenham T (Loaned on 16/3/2001) FL
7+1/2
Torquay U (Loaned on 15/2/2002) FL 5
Colchester U (Loaned on 27/3/2002) FL
2+2/1
Southend U (Free from Gravesend &
Northfleet, ex Margate, Stevenage Borough,
Crawley T, Weymouth, on 15/6/2007) FL
11+14/1 FLC 2+1/1 FAC 2+2/3 Others 0+2

McDONALD Gary Matthew
Born: Irvine, 10 April 1982
Height: 6'0" **Weight:** 12.7
International Honours: S: B-1

Injuries and a loss of form saw the central midfielder in and out of favour during his second season with Oldham. Gary's great strength remains his forward runs into the opposition penalty area and the highlight of his campaign was the match-winning 25-yard strike to knock out Everton in the FA Cup third round at Goodison Park, the supporters' choice as 'Goal of the Season'. In April, Gary rejected the offer of a new deal and signed a pre-contract agreement with Scottish Premier League side Aberdeen. He bade farewell on a high, signing off with his sixth goal of the season in the final-day win at Crewe.
Kilmarnock (From juniors on 1/7/2001) SL 80+26/11 SLC 3+1/1 SC 5+1/2
Oldham Ath (Free on 3/7/2006) FL 70+8/11 FLC 1+1 FAC 9/2 Others 2+1

MacDONALD Shaun Benjamin
Born: Swansea, 17 June 1988
Height: 6'0" **Weight:** 11.4
Club Honours: AMC '06
International Honours: W: U21-12; Yth
Shaun missed the start of the season through injury and was included as substitute in the early Cup games, making his only start for Swansea in the FA of Wales Premier Cup tie at Newport in December. Along with substitute appearances in both legs of the Johnstone's Paint Trophy area final games against MK Dons, he remained a regular in the Wales under-21 side aiming for a first appearance in the European finals, with a 'Man of the Match' performance against France in Cardiff.
Swansea C (From trainee on 8/4/2006) FL 5+11 FLC 0+1 FAC 2 Others 6+3

MacDONALD Sherjill
Born: Amsterdam, Holland, 20 November 1984
Height: 6'0" **Weight:** 12.8
International Honours: Holland: U21
After making 14 substitute appearances for West Bromwich between August and January, Sherjill went out on loan to Hereford last February. There, his exceptional pace and talent were quickly in evidence when he took just eight minutes to score when leading the attack for the Bulls. Two goals on his debut were followed by a memorable first-half hat-trick at Rochdale in his second appearance and six goals in his month at Edgar Street, along with his excellent all-round play, were a big bonus in Hereford's successful push for promotion. Back at the Hawthorns, and one substitute appearance later, a cartilage operation ended Sherjill's season prematurely.

James McFadden

West Bromwich A (£200,000 from AGOW Apeldoen, Holland, ex Anderlecht, Heracles Almelo, SV Hamburg, on 29/1/2007) FL 0+19 FLC 0+2 FAC 0+4 Others 0+1
Hereford U (Loaned on 8/2/2008) FL 7/6

McEVELEY James (Jay) Michael
Born: Liverpool, 11 February 1985
Height: 6'1" **Weight:** 12.11
International Honours: S: 3; B-1. E: U21-1
For the first half of last season, Jay played in every Derby match, either starting or as a substitute. During that time, he made his debut for Scotland, on a grandpaternal qualification, against South Africa, and stayed in the squad. He also scored his first competitive goal for the Rams with a fine strike in the narrow Boxing Day defeat by Liverpool. Injured knee ligaments at Bolton in the first game of the New Year put him out of contention for six weeks and the absence appeared to affect his confidence. He is still learning at left-back but has the strength and presence to carve out a good career.
Blackburn Rov (From trainee on 8/7/2002) PL 17+1 FLC 4+1 FAC 3 Others 1
Burnley (Loaned on 15/12/2003) FL 0+4 FAC 1
Gillingham (Loaned on 10/3/2005) FL 10/1

Ipswich T (Loaned on 30/8/2005) FL 17+2/1
Derby Co (£600,000 on 29/1/2007) P/FL 36+8/2 FLC 1 Others 3

McEVILLY Lee Richard
Born: Liverpool, 15 April 1982
Height: 6'0" **Weight:** 13.0
International Honours: NI: 1; U23-1; U21-9
Re-signed from Wrexham during the summer, Lee's second spell at Accrington was far less successful than his first, mainly because he was unable to establish himself. He started by playing up front with Paul Mullin but after being sent off in the fourth game, never again started. Loaned to Rochdale in November, Lee was an instant success, scoring the winner against Mansfield and netting twice more in his month back at Spotland. Although the Dale boss Keith Hill would have liked to have extended his loan negotiations fell through. Back at Stanley, he made just one substitute appearance before going on loan again, this time to Cambridge United. Spending the rest of the season at the Abbey Stadium, despite a spell out injured, he helped United to the Blue Square Premier play-off final. Was out of contract in the summer and looking for a new club.
Rochdale (£20,000 from Burscough on 24/12/2001) FL 55+30/25 FAC 5+2/1 Others 3/1

'Free to Accrington Stanley on 22/7/2004)
Wrexham *(Signed from Accrington Stanley on 11/7/2005) FL 33+18/14 FAC 2+1/2 Others 0+1*
Accrington Stanley *(Free on 30/7/2007) FL 3+8 FLC 1 FAC 0+1*
Rochdale *(Loaned on 21/11/2007) FL 3+4/3*

McFADDEN James Henry
Born: Glasgow, 14 April 1983
Height: 5'10" **Weight:** 10.10
International Honours: S: 37; B-1; U21-7

In the first half of last season, the Glaswegian was mostly used as a substitute at Everton, only sporadically showing his rich potential, although he did score a crucial goal in the away UEFA Cup win in Kharkiv. Transferred to Birmingham in the January window, James made a big difference to the City attack, his calm, classy play and ability to keep the ball or beat a man helping pep up Alex McLeish's side. He scored twice in the dramatic 2-2 draw at home to Arsenal, keeping his nerve to drive in the equaliser from the penalty spot in the fifth minute of stoppage-time. Undoubtedly, James' knee injury in March hurt the Blues' chances of avoiding relegation. Typically, the highlight of his campaign was a quite stupendous winning goal for Scotland in Paris in September and he continued to save some of his best form for his country.
Motherwell *(From juniors on 31/7/1999) SL 52+11/26 SLC 1/1 SC 5+1/5*
Everton *(£1,250,000 on 8/9/2003) PL 53+56/11 FLC 12/3 FAC 7+2/3 Others 7+2/2*
Birmingham C *(£5,750,000 on 18/1/2008) PL 10+2/3*

McFAUL Shane
Born: Dublin, 23 May 1986
Height: 6'1" **Weight:** 12.2
International Honours: RoI: U21-1; Yth

Plucked from the University College Dublin club in January following a trial, Shane hoped to make more progress during his time at Brighton. A tall midfielder, he looked comfortable on the ball for the reserves, finding his colleagues well, but his first-team experience was limited to one appearance as a last-minute substitute. He was called up for the Republic of Ireland under-21 squad in February but was not offered fresh terms at the end of the season.
Notts Co *(From trainee on 28/2/2004) FL 19+11 FAC 2+1 Others 1 (Freed on 6/10/2005)*
Brighton & Hove A *(Free form University College Dublin, ex Virginia Beach, on 16/1/2008) FL 0+1*

McGIVERN Leighton Terence
Born: Liverpool, 2 June 1984
Height: 5'8" **Weight:** 11.1

Sadly for Leighton, last season was similar to the previous campaign, in that a run of injuries prevented him from ever establishing himself in the Accrington side. Most of his appearances were as a substitute and, in fact, he made fewer starts than in 2006-07, his only goal coming in the 3-1 win at Dagenham in October. He ended the campaign as the reserves' leading scorer before being released in the summer.
Rochdale *(Free from Vauxhall Motors on 30/7/2004) FL 2+23/1 FLC 0+1 FAC 0+2 Others 0+2 (Freed during 2005 close season)*
Accrington Stanley *(Free from Vauxhall Motors on 9/11/2006) FL 5+14/2 FAC 0+1 Others 0+2*

McGLEISH Scott
Born: Barnet, 10 February 1974
Height: 5'9" **Weight:** 11.3

Scott had a truly memorable season at Wycombe, scoring 25 goals, all in the League, and surpassing Sean Devine's club record of 23. The many highlights included a four-goal haul at Mansfield in January and Wycombe's official 'Goal of the Season' when he volleyed in a 30-yard shot at MK Dons in April. The goals came in equal measure from both feet and, despite not being the tallest of front-men, several from his head. He has an excellent football brain but what really makes him so special is his endless running and all-round team play, always willing to track back and defend when needed.
Charlton Ath *(Free from Edgware T on 24/5/1994) FL 0+6*
Leyton Orient *(Loaned on 10/3/1995) FL 4+2/1 Others 1/1*
Peterborough U *(Free on 4/7/1995) FL 3+10 FLC 0+1 FAC 0+1 Others 3+1/2*
Colchester U *(Loaned on 23/2/1996) FL 1+5/2*
Colchester U *(Loaned on 28/3/1996) FL 9/4 Others 2*
Cambridge U *(Loaned on 2/9/1996) FL 10/7 FLC 1*
Leyton Orient *(£50,000 on 22/11/1996) FL 36/7 FLC 3/1 FAC 1 Others 1*
Barnet *(£70,000 on 1/10/1997) FL 106+28/36 FLC 5/4 FAC 3 Others 7+2/2*
Colchester U *(£15,000 on 11/1/2001) FL 118+26/38 FLC 4 FAC 9+1/2 Others 7+2/7*
Northampton T *(Free on 8/7/2004) FL 106+5/42 FLC 4/2 FAC 10/7 Others 6+1/3*
Wycombe W *(Signed on 26/1/2007) FL 56+4/30 FLC 0+1 FAC 1 Others 2*

McGOLDRICK David James
Born: Nottingham, 29 November 1987
Height: 6'1" **Weight:** 11.10

A lively and talented striker, David is one of a handful of young players at Southampton who might have expected their careers to progress in 2007-08 but following an early sub appearance in the Carling Cup, David joined Port Vale on a half-season loan in August and made a promising debut in a 1-0 victory at Bournemouth, where he spent time on loan the previous season. Unfortunately, being in a struggling side did not bring the best out of him and he took a few games to settle. He scored his first goal against Cheltenham, followed with a cracking shot at Northampton in the next game. A change of manager and a restriction on finance prompted by the club's relegation battle led to his return to St Mary's early in the New Year and he figured in the side on ten occasions.
Notts Co *(Associated Schoolboy) FL 2+2*
Southampton *(From trainee on 19/9/2005) FL 4+14 FLC 0+3/1 FAC 2+2*
Notts Co *(Loaned on 23/9/2005) FL 4+2 Others 0+1*
Bournemouth *(Loaned on 16/2/2007) FL 12/6*
Port Vale *(Loaned on 31/8/2007) FL 15+2/2 Others 1*

McGOVERN Jon-Paul
Born: Glasgow, 3 October 1980
Height: 5'7" **Weight:** 9.6
Club Honours: SLC '04

Having been unceremoniously left out of MK Dons' line-up for the second leg of the previous season's play-off semi-final, Jon-Paul began 2007-08 as a starter for new manager Paul Ince but after showing his customary skill on the ball in the opening games was sold to Swindon as the August transfer period came to an end. Jon-Paul made his Swindon debut in the Johnstone's Paint Trophy victory over Brentford and scored on his full League debut at Hartlepool with an exquisite chip, earning his side a point. Involved throughout the season, usually wide in midfield, he is a hard-working player who can deliver a telling cross. He also played in the centre of midfield a number of times and filled in at right-back for the last game of the season.
Glasgow Celtic *(From juniors at Heart of Midlothian on 8/6/2000)*
Sheffield U *(Loaned on 13/8/2002) FL 11+4/1 FLC 2/1 FAC 1/1*
Livingston *(Free on 1/7/2003) SL 12+15 SLC 0+3 SC 0+2*
Sheffield Wed *(Free on 3/6/2004) FL 49+4/6 FLC 3 FAC 1 Others 4/2*
MK Dons *(Free on 4/8/2006) FL 42+5/3 FLC 4+1/1 FAC 3 Others 2*
Swindon T *(Signed on 31/8/2007) FL 34+7/2 FAC 3/1 Others 2*

McGRAIL Christopher (Chris) Francis

Born: Preston, 25 February 1988
Height: 6'0" **Weight:** 13.5

Returning to Accrington on loan from Preston last August, the young striker went on as a substitute in the home game against Darlington and also appeared from the bench against Oldham in the Johnstone's Paint Trophy. Unfortunately, Chris had to return to Deepdale after suffering a recurrence of a back injury.

Preston NE *(From trainee on 1/7/2007)*
Accrington Stanley *(Loaned on work experience scheme on 16/11/2007) FL 0+2*
Accrington Stanley *(Loaned on 21/8/2007) FL 0+1 Others 0+1*

McGREGOR Mark Dale Thomas

Born: Ellesmere Port, 16 February 1977
Height: 5'11" **Weight:** 11.5

Mark, a vastly experienced defender, began as Port Vale's right-back but filled in at centre-half when required. Never afraid to go in where it hurts, he was a regular in the first half of the campaign but as results suffered, the team was chopped and changed. When new manager Lee Sinnott signed some loan players, Mark was out in the cold in the New Year. He knuckled down in the reserves and was a role model for Vale's highly-rated youngsters, who looked up to him as an elder statesman. He was released on a free transfer three weeks before the end of the season.

Wrexham *(From trainee on 4/7/1995) FL 237+7/11 FLC 9 FAC 24+1 Others 11*
Burnley *(Free on 20/7/2001) FL 46+8/2 FLC 4/1 FAC 5+2*
Blackpool *(Free on 30/7/2004) FL 52+7 FLC 3 FAC 5 Others 2/1*
Port Vale *(Free on 18/1/2006) FL 58+8 FLC 3 FAC 2+1*

McGUGAN Lewis Shay

Born: Long Eaton, 25 October 1988
Height: 5'9" **Weight:** 11.6
International Honours: E: Yth

Lewis had a late start to the campaign because of injury but carried on his heroics of the previous season with some eye-catching performances in the centre of the Nottingham Forest midfield. Despite his tender years, he always makes himself available and is equally comfortable with short or long passing. He scored a number of key goals, including the club's 'Goal of the Season'.

Nottingham F *(From trainee on 15/11/2006) FL 35+11/8 FAC 3+1/1 Others 2+2*

McINDOE Michael

Born: Edinburgh, 2 December 1979
Height: 5'8" **Weight:** 11.0
Club Honours: FAT '02; FC '03; Div 3 '04

International Honours: S: B-2

Many mocked when the close-season signing from Wolverhampton remarked that he joined Bristol City as he considered them to be a better prospect for promotion than his old side. As it turned out in an exciting campaign, the left-winger was proved correct as City pipped Wolves for the play-offs. A tricky, combative player well able to resist heavy tackling, he has a tendency to wander all over the pitch. Michael topped off his season with a brilliant 30-yard free kick in stoppage-time in the play-off semi-final against Crystal Palace. Unfortunately, in the big game at Wembley he was, despite much unflagging energy, unable to break through.

Luton T *(From trainee on 2/4/1998) FL 19+20 FLC 4+1 FAC 0+3 Others 1 (Free to Hereford U on 20/7/2000)*
Doncaster Rov *(£50,000 from Yeovil T on 5/8/2003) FL 117+5/28 FLC 10/4 FAC 6/3 Others 4*
Derby Co *(Loaned on 8/3/2006) FL 6+2*
Barnsley *(£125,000 on 13/7/2006) FL 18/4 FLC 0+2/1*
Wolverhampton W *(£250,000 on 23/11/2006) FL 25+2/3 FAC 3 Others 2*
Bristol C *(Signed on 25/7/2007) FL 45/6 FLC 1 Others 3/1*

McINTOSH Martin Wyllie

Born: East Kilbride, 19 March 1971
Height: 6'2" **Weight:** 12.0
International Honours: S: B-2; Sch

Arriving from Huddersfield in the summer, Martin initially added some very welcome experience to Mansfield's back line, his organisational skills helping to marshal the defence. He scored with a spectacular free-kick in the season's first win over Stockport in September before an injury later in that month ruled him out for eight weeks. During his time out, the overall performances of the side improved and he found it difficult to claim a regular place when fit again. When he did get back, he was harshly sent off in the home fixture with Accrington and served a suspension. A hamstring injury he sustained in December ended both his season and his time at Field Mill as he was released in March without regaining full fitness.

St Mirren *(From trainee at Tottenham H on 30/11/1988) SL 2+2*
Clydebank *(Signed on 17/8/1991) SL 59+6/10 SLC 2 SC 4+1/1 Others 3/1*
Hamilton Academical *(Signed on 1/2/1994) SL 99/12 SLC 5 SC 5 Others 5/1*
Stockport Co *(£80,000 on 15/8/1997) FL 96+3/5 FLC 5+1 FAC 4*
Hibernian *(£250,000 on 10/2/2000) SL 13 SLC 3 SC 2*

Rotherham U *(£125,000 on 17/8/2001) FL 122/16 FLC 6 FAC 4*
Huddersfield T *(Free on 7/7/2005) FL 44+4/4 FLC 1 FAC 1 Others 2*
Grimsby T *(Loaned on 17/8/2006) FL 4*
Mansfield T *(Free on 7/8/2007) FL 9+2/1 FLC 1*

McINTYRE Kevin

Born: Liverpool, 23 December 1977
Height: 5'11" **Weight:** 12.2
Club Honours: FC '04

A left-sided player, Kevin was Macclesfield's left-back in the first half of last season, only occasionally moving to midfield following the late introduction of substitutes. Although a very capable defender and set-piece expert, he was unable to achieve his usual consistently high level of performance and signed for Shrewsbury in January. As a creative central midfield player who can also play at full-back, Kevin delivered telling corners and free kicks, notably a pinpoint corner for Kelvin Langmead to begin a fight back off the first goal after Town trailed 3-0 to MK Dons. Took some time to settle in but gradually became more influential, scoring his first goal in the 4-1 defeat at Chesterfield in April and his second against Wrexham a week later to set up a vital win.

Tranmere Rov *(From trainee on 6/11/1996) FL 0+2 (Free to Doncaster Rov on 19/11/1999)*
Chester C *(Free from Doncaster Rov on 15/5/2002) FL 9+1 FLC 1 FAC 1+1 Others 3*
Macclesfield T *(Free on 24/12/2004) FL 130+4/16 FLC 2 FAC 7/11 Others 10*
Shrewsbury T *(£50,000 on 4/1/2008) FL 22/2*

MACKAIL-SMITH Craig

Born: Watford, 25 February 1984
Height: 6'3" **Weight:** 12.4
Club Honours: FC '07
International Honours: E: SP-7

Injury kept Craig out of the Peterborough team during the first two months of last season but once fit, there was no holding him. He scored 12 League goals but just as important was his tireless running that created numerous chances for others. His pace will be a factor in the return to League One.

Peterborough U *(Signed from Dagenham & Redbridge, ex Arlesey T, on 29/11/2007) 47+4/20 FAC 4/7 Others 0+1*

MACKAY Malcolm (Malky) George

Born: Bellshill, 19 February 1972
Height: 6'1" **Weight:** 11.7
Club Honours: Div 1 '04
International Honours: S: 5

Having semi-retired after a distinguished

playing career to join Watford's coaching staff, the former battle-hardened centre-back came back to make just one appearance for Watford, against Wolverhampton in the FA Cup. He continued to turn out for the reserves when required, showing his leadership qualities and helping to bring the younger players along.

Queen's Park *(From juniors on 8/12/1989)* *SL 68+2/6 SLC 3/2 SC 2 Others 2*
Glasgow Celtic *(Signed on 6/8/1993) SL 32+5/4 SLC 5+1 SC 4/1 Others 4+1*
Norwich C *(£350,000 on 18/9/1998) FL 198+14/15 FLC 8+1 FAC 8 Others 3/1*
West Ham U *(£300,000 on 10/9/2004) FL 17+1/2 FLC 1 FAC 3*
Watford *(Free on 18/8/2005) P/FL 48+4/3 FLC 1+1 FAC 4/2 Others 3*

MACKAY Michael
Born: Durham, 11 October 1982
Height: 6'0" **Weight:** 11.6
It was a promising first full season for the striker signed by Hartlepool from non-League football late in 2006-07. He started down the pecking order but when brought into the senior squad showed himself to be a capable performer. Michael is a fine opportunist scorer, with a couple of his efforts being Hartlepool 'Goal of the Season' contenders. With Richie Barker injured he stepped up at the end of the season.

Hartlepool U *(Signed from Consett, ex Birtley, Durham C, on 8/2/2007) FL 10+15/5 FAC 1+1 Others 1+2/1*

MACKEN Jonathan (Jon) Paul
Born: Manchester, 7 September 1977
Height: 5'10" **Weight:** 12.8
Club Honours: Div 2 '00
International Honours: RoI: 1; E: Yth
Jon returned from a successful loan at Barnsley to make four substitute appearances when Derby were troubled by injuries last season. Unluckily as it turned out, one of them was for five minutes in the FA Cup third round against Sheffield Wednesday, thus ruling him out of Barnsley's journey to the semi-finals after he joined them on a permanent basis in January. Jon originally moved to Oakwell on a two-month loan in November and showed his talent as a leader of the line by playing with his back to goal and bringing in other players. As his sharpness increased by playing regularly, he became more of a goal threat and netted three times in his last two appearances. In his first game as a full-time Barnsley player, he scored the winner against Colchester and remained first-choice striker.

Manchester U *(From trainee on 10/7/1996)*

Paul McKenna

Preston NE *(£250,000 on 31/7/1997) FL 155+29/63 FLC 12+2/8 FAC 10+5/2 Others 9+3/1*
Manchester C *(£4,000,000 + on 5/3/2002) P/FL 27+24/7 FLC 1+1/3 FAC 2+2/2 Others 1+1*
Crystal Palace *(£1,100,000 on 22/6/2005) FL 14+11/2 FLC 2 FAC 0+2 Others 0+1*
Ipswich T *(Loaned on 31/8/2006) FL 13+1/4*
Derby Co *(Free on 31/1/2007) P/FL 4+7 FAC 0+2 Others 2*
Barnsley *(Loaned on 1/11/2007) FL 11/3*
Barnsley *(£100,000 on 28/11/2008) FL 17+1/5*

McKENNA Paul Stephen
Born: Chorley, 20 October 1977
Height: 5'7" **Weight:** 11.12
Club Honours: Div 2 '00
Preston's longest-serving player took over as captain when he finally overcame a long-term groin injury to open his season

in October. The battling midfielder was sorely missed up to that point and it took him time to settle back into his former style, but he missed only one game for the rest of the campaign. He continues to be an inspiration to team-mates and fans alike and Alan Irvine's first match in charge was Paul's 350th league game for his only club. Four matches later he joined the select band with 400 appearances for North End.

Preston NE *(From trainee on 2/2/1996) FL 356+22/28 FLC 16 FAC 18+2/2 Others 11+2*

MacKENZIE Christopher (Chris) Neil
Born: Northampton, 14 May 1972
Height: 6'0" **Weight:** 12.6
Chris began the season as Shrewsbury's goalkeeping coach, with two 'keepers in front of him making it difficult to break into the first team. He made one

appearance in the Johnstone's Paint Trophy at Yeovil before going on loan to Kidderminster and signing for them in January.
Hereford U *(£15,000 from Corby T on 20/7/1994) FL 59+1/1 FLC 2 FAC 4 Others 8 (Free to Farnborough T in 1997 close season)*
Leyton Orient *(Free on 17/10/1997) FL 30 FLC 3 FAC 5 Others 2 (Free to Nuneaton Borough on 1/8/1999)*
Chester C *(Free from Telford U on 2/7/2004) FL 53+1 FLC 1 FAC 4 Others 2*
Shrewsbury T *(Free on 2/8/2006) FL 20 FLC 1 Others 5*

McKENZIE Leon Mark
Born: Croydon, 17 May 1978
Height: 5'11" **Weight:** 11.2
Club Honours: Div 1 '04
Leon's first full season at Coventry was expected to be a major success and he set off with a sixth-minute header at Barnsley on the opening day. Injuries wrecked his season and he started only nine games. Playing alongside Kevin Kyle, he was 'Man of the Match' against Hull and scored with a header. His selfless running and ability to take a man on won him many fans but he suffered a knee injury and was out for two months. His best game was at West Bromwich where he played on the left of a three-pronged attack and superbly set up the second goal in the 4-2 win. In the following game he created Jay Tabb's goal against Southampton but a dead leg turned into a serious thigh injury requiring surgery. It was his last appearance of the season.
Crystal Palace *(From trainee on 7/10/1995) P/FL 44+41/7 FLC 5+2/1 FAC 2+4*
Fulham *(Loaned on 3/10/1997) FL 1+2*
Peterborough U *(Loaned on 13/8/1998) FL 4/3*
Peterborough U *(Loaned on 30/11/1998) FL 10/5 Others 1/1*
Peterborough U *(Free on 13/10/2000) FL 83+7/45 FLC 2 FAC 7+1/1 Others 3/4*
Norwich C *(£325,000 on 15/12/2003) P/FL 47+32/20 FLC 2/2*
Coventry C *(£600,000 on 31/8/2006) FL 32+10/9 FAC 2/1*

MacKENZIE Neil David
Born: Birmingham, 15 April 1976
Height: 6'1" **Weight:** 12.4
Club Honours: AMC '02; Div 1 '07
Having arrived from Scunthorpe in the summer Neil was intended to be the playmaker and architect of Notts County from central midfield but showed the same inconsistency as many of his colleagues and was also interrupted by injury. Capable of producing match-winning passes but so often denied the opportunity to express himself in the

cut and thrust of League Two, Neil is a dead-ball specialist and was several times unlucky with direct free kicks.
Stoke C *(From trainee at West Bromwich A on 9/11/1995) FL 15+27/1 FLC 1+1 FAC 0+1 Others 0+1*
Cambridge U *(Loaned on 24/3/1999) FL 3+1/1*
Cambridge U *(£45,000 on 14/10/1999) FL 20+8 FLC 1+1 FAC 5 Others 0+1*
Kidderminster Hrs *(Free on 24/11/2000) FL 20+3/3 FAC 0+1 Others 2*
Blackpool *(Free on 9/7/2001) FL 6+8/1 FLC 1+1 FAC 1+3/1 Others 3/2*
Mansfield T *(Free on 6/8/2002) FL 50+21/4 FLC 2+1 FAC 6/3 Others 4+3*
Macclesfield T *(Free on 26/11/2004) FL 20+4/1 FLC 1/1*
Scunthorpe U *(Free on 24/11/2005) FL 22+16/4 FAC 2 Others 3*
Hereford U *(Loaned on 27/10/2006) FL 7*
Notts Co *(Free on 4/7/2007) FL 24+5/6 FLC 1 FAC 2 Others 1*

McKEOWN James Karl
Born: Sutton Coldfield, 24 July 1989
Height: 6'2" **Weight:** 14.0
Released by Walsall last summer, the young goalkeeper joined Peterborough and made a substitute appearance, looking confident and assured. The club have high hopes for him, which is why they allowed long-serving Mark Tyler out on loan after buying Joe Lewis.
Peterborough U *(From trainee at Walsall on 25/7/2007) FL 0+1*

MACKIE James (Jamie) Charles
Born: Dorking, 22 September 1985
Height: 5'8" **Weight:** 11.2
Plymouth secured Jamie's transfer from Devon rivals Exeter during the January window after he handed in a transfer request, expressing a desire to move to Home Park. The pacy forward, who can also play in wide positions, made an electrifying start. In his first appearance for the Pilgrims, as a substitute against Barnsley, Jamie scored within 11 seconds of his arrival on the pitch, thus breaking the Plymouth record for the fastest debut goal. Towards the end of the season Jamie forced his way into the starting line-up and impressed with his wholehearted performances.
Wimbledon/MK Dons *(Signed from Leatherhead on 9/11/2004) FL 8+8 FAC 2+1 Others 1 (Freed during 2005 close season)*
Plymouth Arg *(£145,000 from Exeter C on 28/1/2008) FL 4+9/3*

MACKIE John George
Born: Whitechapel, 5 July 1976
Height: 6'0" **Weight:** 12.6

Freed by Leyton Orient, the centre-half joined Brentford in the close season and was immediately appointed captain. However, John struggled to impose himself and suffered hamstring, leg and head injuries. A change of management led to his contract being cancelled in January, following which he joined Hornchurch.
Reading *(Free from Sutton U on 5/11/1999) FL 61+10/3 FLC 3+1 FAC 5+2 Others 1+2*
Leyton Orient *(Free on 13/1/2004) FL 119+3/11 FLC 1 FAC 7/1 Others 5*
Brentford *(Free on 3/7/2007) FL 14 FLC 1 FAC 1*

MACKIN Levi Alan
Born: Chester, 4 April 1986
Height: 6'1" **Weight:** 12.0
International Honours: W: U21-1
The Welsh under-21 international midfielder found it difficult to break into the Wrexham side last season. Although starting the early games, he failed to regain a place after injury and was loaned out to Blue Square Premier side Droylsden. Recalled in April after Brian Little lost faith with the previous incumbents, although too late to make any difference, Levi returned with renewed energy. He played in the final four games and scored with a header in Wrexham's last League game for at least 15 months, at Lincoln. A player who likes to be involved, he is direct and purposeful.
Wrexham *(From trainee on 11/7/2005) FL 18+27/1 FLC 2+4 FAC 0+1 Others 0+1*

MACKLIN Lloyd Joshua
Born: Camberley, 2 August 1991
Height: 5'9" **Weight:** 12.3
Lloyd made his Swindon debut as a late substitute in the Johnstone's Paint Trophy win over Brentford in September. He progressed through Town's Centre of Excellence and although still a first-year scholar, has been offered a professional contract. Lloyd is a wide midfield player with a great deal of pace.
Swindon T *(Trainee) Others 0+1*

McLACHLAN Fraser Malcolm
Born: Knutsford, 9 November 1982
Height: 5'11" **Weight:** 12.7
It was tough for the hard-working Morecambe midfielder, who suffered a broken leg in the first week of the campaign at Preston. As a result, he made only one League start, in the final game at MK Dons. The ex-Mansfield player will be hoping for better luck ahead.
Stockport Co *(From trainee on 11/7/2001) FL 43+10/4 FLC 1 FAC 2 Others 0+1*
Mansfield T *(Signed on 11/11/2004) FL 23+6 FLC 1 FAC 1 Others 1*
Morecambe *(Free on 23/3/2006) FL 1 FLC 1*

McLAREN Paul Andrew
Born: High Wycombe, 17 November 1976
Height: 6'0" **Weight:** 13.4
Recognised at Tranmere as a skilled holding midfielder, Paul prefers to play on the right of the middle, using his vast experience to flourish as an anchorman. He has a reputation as a dead-ball specialist and contributed four goals from free kicks to Rovers' total. Always reliable and industrious, he remained injury-free throughout the last season but his enthusiastic style of play earned him ten yellow cards. But for the ensuing suspensions, he would surely have been an ever-present for the Birkenhead club. Picked up the 'Players' Player of the Season' award from his team-mates but was out of contract at the end of the campaign.
Luton T (From trainee on 5/1/1994) FL 137+30/4 FLC 10+4/1 FAC 11/1 Others 9
Sheffield Wed (Free on 11/6/2001) FL 83+13/8 FLC 6+1/1 FAC 2 Others 1
Rotherham U (Free on 2/8/2004) FL 67+5/4 FLC 2 FAC 2/2 Others 1
Tranmere Rov (Free on 3/7/2006) FL 85/5 FLC 1 FAC 6

McLEAN Aaron
Born: Hammersmith, 25 May 1983
Height: 5'6" **Weight:** 10.8
Club Honours: FAT '06
International Honours: E: SP-5
Known as the goal machine, Aaron became a Peterborough hero by scoring 29 League goals, along with four in Cup competitions, to lead Posh to promotion. With his pace, fast feet and ability in the air he is a formidable attacking force. The partnership with Craig Mackail-Smith produced 52 goals, a fact that will not be lost on League One defences.
Leyton Orient (From trainee on 9/7/2001) FL 5+35/2 FAC 0+3 Others 1+1/1 (Free to Aldershot T on 28/3/2003)
Peterborough U (£150,000 from Grays Ath on 31/10/2006) FL 61/36 FLC 2 FAC 8/6 Others 3/1

MacLEAN Steven (Steve)
Born: Edinburgh, 23 August 1982
Height: 5'10" **Weight:** 11.1
International Honours: S: U21-4
Following the arrival of Robbie Fowler and Jimmy Floyd Hasselbaink, life became tough for a number of Cardiff strikers, including Steve, who had arrived at Ninian Park in the summer after being out of contract with Sheffield Wednesday. He also suffered injury problems and left Cardiff in January to sign a three-and-a-half-year deal with Plymouth, where he was reunited with his former Wednesday

manager Paul Sturrock. Having become the record signing for Argyle, the skilful striker, who is often involved in the build-up play by coming off defenders, provided excellent link-up play with the midfield. Steve scored his first Argyle goal against Barnsley at Home Park in February but will be looking to improve his goals ratio in the season ahead.
Glasgow Rgrs (From juniors on 17/9/1998) SL 0+3 SC 0+1
Scunthorpe U (Loaned on 6/8/2003) FL 37+5/23 FLC 1+1/1 FAC 5 Others 3/1
Sheffield Wed (£125,000 on 27/7/2004) FL 60+23/32 FLC 2 FAC 3/1 Others 1+1/2
Cardiff C (Free on 1/7/2007) FL 6+9/1 FLC 1+1 FAC 1
Plymouth Arg (£500,000 on 18/1/2008) FL 14+3/3

McLEOD Izale (Izzy) Michael
Born: Birmingham, 15 October 1984
Height: 6'0" **Weight:** 11.2
International Honours: E: U21-1
Good things were expected of Izzy when Charlton signed him from MK Dons at the start of last season. Unfortunately he never really got going, with only two starts in the League and numerous late cameos from the substitutes' bench. A tall, lean striker who is extremely quick and good in the air, his exceptional pace often takes him well clear of defenders. Four of the five penalties awarded to Charlton during the season were for fouls on Izzy, who finally broke his scoring duck in the 4-2 defeat at West Bromwich in December. He was allowed to go on loan to Colchester in February but misfortune struck when his spell at Layer Road was ended in the cruellest fashion by a serious knee injury in the 4-1 defeat at Plymouth. It was only his second appearance and having gone on as a substitute he was stretchered off shortly afterwards and set to be out for several months. It was a big blow, not least because he was looking forward to teaming up with his old MK Dons strike partner Clive Platt.
Derby Co (From trainee on 7/2/2003) FL 24+15/4 FLC 1+1
Sheffield U (Loaned on 12/3/2004) FL 1+6
MK Dons (£100,000 on 4/8/2004) FL 105+11/54 FLC 4+1/3 FAC 8+1/3 Others 5
Charlton Ath (£1,100,000 + on 10/8/2007) FL 2+16/1 FLC 3 FAC 2
Colchester U (Loaned on 29/2/2008) FL 0+2

McLEOD Kevin Andrew
Born: Liverpool, 12 September 1980
Height: 5'11" **Weight:** 11.3
Club Honours: AMC '06
Enjoying a good start to 2007-08, having benefited from a strict pre-season fitness regime, the left-winger duly scored on

the opening day at Sheffield United. He and fellow winger Mark Yeates gave United good width but both faded as the season wore on. Kevin managed only one more goal, in the 1-1 home draw against Norwich, before being hampered by injury and illness during the last couple of months. He made a glorious return for the final game at Scunthorpe, saving his best for last by scoring twice in a 3-3 draw to earn the 'Man of the Match' award. At his best, he can provide lethal ammunition from the left flank and also has a knack of ghosting into the box from wide positions.
Everton (From trainee on 24/9/1998) PL 0+5 FLC 1 FAC 0+1
Queens Park Rgrs (Loaned on 21/3/2003) FL 8/2 Others 3
Queens Park Rgrs (Signed on 18/8/2003) FL 30+29/4 FLC 3+1/1 FAC 2 Others 1/1
Swansea C (Signed on 16/2/2005) FL 32+12/7 FLC 2 FAC 1 Others 3+1
Colchester U (Free on 30/8/2006) FL 34+18/7 FLC 1 FAC 2

McMAHON Anthony (Tony)
Born: Bishop Auckland, 24 March 1986
Height: 5'10" **Weight:** 11.6
Club Honours: FAYC '04
International Honours: E: Yth
The Middlesbrough player's long haul on the road to full recovery following a catalogue of injuries - broken leg, dislocated shoulder, ankle, medial knee ligaments et al - overlapped into 2007-08. In a bid to achieve match-fitness, manager Gareth Southgate sanctioned a month's loan to Blackpool in November. He played the full 90 minutes of his debut at right-back for the Seasiders against Scunthorpe but picked up a hamstring strain after only quarter-of-an-hour in his second game at Southampton, ending the loan. Tony received a big boost to his confidence when he was rewarded with a year's extension to the contract that was due to end in the summer. His season for Boro started and ended with a 15-minute appearance when he replaced Luke Young in the 8-1 demolition of Manchester City at the Riverside in the final game. It was an emotional moment as all his team-mates applauded him on to the pitch in appreciation of his dedication and commitment.
Middlesbrough (From trainee on 7/2/2005) PL 15+2 FLC 1+1 FAC 1+1 Others 4
Blackpool (Loaned on 9/11/2007) FL 2

McMANUS Paul James
Born: Liverpool, 22 April 1990
Height: 5'6" **Weight:** 10.4
This diminutive striker made his Chester debut at the age of 17, as a substitute

for Richie Partridge in the home win over Shrewsbury at the start of October. Another product of Chester's flourishing youth policy, Paul is an exciting prospect with his pace and close control and will become more effective as he gains match experience. Towards the end of the season, he started more regularly up front alongside big John Murphy and was duly rewarded for his efforts when he netted his first City goal with an excellent finish against Lincoln. Paul's contract was extended at the end of the season.
Chester C *(From trainee on 2/10/2007) FL 9+10/1 FAC 0+1 Others 1*

McNAMEE Anthony
Born: Kensington, 13 July 1984
Height: 5'6" **Weight:** 10.0
International Honours: E: Yth
Anthony moved to Swindon in January with many Watford fans feeling he had failed to fulfil his potential only through lack of opportunity. Diminutive but hugely talented, he has great ball skill and a dangerous cross but can be inconsistent. Before his departure, Anthony gave a reminder of his capabilities with outstanding wing-play for Watford against Gillingham in the Carling Cup. Although taking some time to get into his stride, through a lack of match-fitness, Anthony made a big impact towards the end of the season at Swindon. A small left-winger, quick as well as skilful, he produced a string of outstanding performances, especially at the County Ground, and provided a host of scoring chances. He also showed that he can take them himself, scoring against Port Vale and netting a deflected winner against Millwall in the final game. An extended run could see him develop into a very dangerous player.
Watford *(From trainee on 17/4/2002) P/FL 34+57/2 FLC 6+2 FAC 3+1/1*
Crewe Alex *(Loaned on 21/3/2007) FL 5*
Swindon T *(Signed on 18/1/2008) FL 18+1/2*

McNAMEE David Kenneth
Born: Glasgow, 10 October 1980
Height: 5'11" **Weight:** 11.2
Club Honours: SLC '04
International Honours: S: 4; B-1
Last season was yet another frustrating campaign for the Scottish full-back, with hamstring problems limiting him to just 13 starts for Coventry. After his first appearance, as a late substitute at Old Trafford, he made one start at right-back in place of the injured Isaac Osbourne before reverting to the bench. His next start, on the right of midfield against Watford, was not a success and for the following game Iain Dowie switched him

Kevin McNaughton

and Osbourne, David giving his usual committed performances at right-back. He set up Michael Mifsud's winner against Colchester and played his part in away wins at Stoke and Queens Park Rangers but hamstring problems always lurked and an injury against Crystal Palace on Boxing Day ruled him out of the second half of the season.
St Mirren *(From juniors on 1/8/1997) SL 23+1 SLC 1 SC 1*
Blackburn Rov *(£300,000 on 19/2/1999)*
Livingston *(Signed on 31/8/2002) SL 82+3/4 SLC 10+1 SC 7 Others 1*
Coventry C *(£100,000 on 16/6/2006) FL 28+1 FLC 1+1*

McNAUGHTON Kevin Paul
Born: Dundee, 28 August 1982
Height: 5'10" **Weight:** 10.6
International Honours: S: 4; B-1; U21-1
A huge hit with Cardiff fans, Kevin completed his season by earning a call into the Scotland squad, playing against Croatia in a friendly. Is an extremely quick

full-back who loves to get forward and support attacks. His pace also enables him to cover inside and he scored a couple of cracking goals, including a volley in the FA Cup win at Hereford. Part of a strong Scottish contingent at City last season, along with Gavin Rae and Steve Thompson, he produced a storming display in the FA Cup final as City went down to Portsmouth.
Aberdeen *(From juniors on 1/8/1999) SL 165+10/3 SLC 9 SC 13 Others 5*
Cardiff C *(Free on 6/7/2006) FL 74+3/1 FLC 2 FAC 8/1*

McNEIL Matthew (Matty)
Born: Manchester, 14 July 1976
Height: 6'5" **Weight:** 14.3
The former non-League journeyman was signed from Macclesfield in the summer. A tough, old-style centre forward, most of his goals came in Cup matches and he even turned out a number of times at centre-half, looking an accomplished defender. Playing through much of the

season with a hernia, Matty picked up a knee-ligament injury at Bradford, missing the rest of the season before going on as a substitute for the final minute of County's play-off final victory over Rochdale.

Macclesfield T (Free from Hyde U, ex Stalybridge Celtic, Runcorn, on 2/3/2006) FL 41+6/6 FAC 2+2 Others 1+1/1
Stockport Co (Free on 10/8/2007) FL 17/2 FLC 2/1 FAC 2/2 Others 1+1/1

McNULTY James (Jimmy)
Born: Runcorn, 13 February 1985
Height: 6'2" **Weight:** 12.0
International Honours: S: Yth
In the first half of last season at Macclesfield, Jimmy played out of position as a central defender rather than in his normal role of left-back. He coped extremely well, using his height to good advantage, but lost his place when two central defenders were signed on loan. Having turned down the offer of a new contract with Macclesfield and opting to sign for Stockport at the beginning of January, Jimmy was engaged by County primarily as a left-back. The Merseysider showed his versatility with several impressive performances as a left-sided centre-back for Stockport and was only a whisker away from scoring the club's first goal in the play-off final before the ball bounced off Rochdale defender Nathan Stanton and into the net.
Wrexham (Trainee) Others 0+1 (Freed during 2004 close season)
Macclesfield T (Free from Caernarfon T on 1/8/2006) FL 28+6/1 FLC 1 FAC 2+1/1 Others 3
Stockport Co (Free on 7/1/2008) FL 11 Others 2+1

McPHAIL Stephen John Paul
Born: Westminster, 9 December 1979
Height: 5'10" **Weight:** 12.0
Club Honours: FAYC '97
International Honours: RoI: 10; B-1; U21-7; Yth (UEFA-U18 '98)
This cultured player was a crucial figure in Cardiff's midfield and took over the captaincy when Darren Purse lost his starting place, leading out the team in the FA Cup final against Portsmouth at Wembley. Rarely giving away possession, Stephen is a player who can set the tempo for City through the middle. The main area he will be looking to improve on in 2008-09 is in goalscoring, but he did come up with a couple of crackers last season.
Leeds U (From trainee on 23/12/1996) PL 52+26/3 FLC 2+4 FAC 3 Others 15+5
Millwall (Loaned on 14/3/2002) FL 3
Nottingham F (Loaned on 27/8/2003) FL

13+1 FLC 2
Barnsley (Free on 5/7/2004) FL 66+4/4 FLC 2+1 FAC 2 Others 4
Cardiff C (Free on 4/7/2006) FL 85+1/3 FLC 4 FAC 7

McPHEE Stephen
Born: Glasgow, 5 June 1981
Height: 5'7" **Weight:** 10.8
International Honours: S: U21-1
After two injury-plagued years at the KC Stadium, Stephen finally broke his Hull duck in the Carling Cup win at Crewe in August. The tricky forward continued to be a regular substitute during the first half of the Tigers' campaign and went on to add further goals against Charlton and Cardiff. With Hull having increased their attacking options, Stephen was transferred to Championship rivals Blackpool in the January transfer window, becoming the club's record signing. He quickly kick-started his new career, scoring four goals in 16 League starts as a striker, the first coming against Charlton in a 5-3 home win, two more against Norwich and another at Queens Park Rangers. With pace, good finishing and effort, Stephen became the first-choice striker.
Coventry C (From juniors on 19/11/1998)
St Mirren (Loaned on 3/3/2001) SL 6+1
Port Vale (Free on 30/7/2001) FL 125+5/39 FLC 4/2 FAC 6/1 Others 7/2 (Freed during 2004 close season)
Hull C (£200,000 from Beira Mar Aveira, Portugal on 19/5/2005) FL 18+17/2 FLC 3/1 FAC 2
Blackpool (£300,000 on 8/1/2008) FL 16+3/4

McQUOID Joshua (Josh)
Born: Southampton, 15 December 1989
Height: 5'9" **Weight:** 10.10
International Honours: NI: Yth
Josh continued his progress from the previous season and made his full debut for Bournemouth against Tranmere, keeping his place in the side against Millwall. A versatile youth-team player, effective in midfield or just behind the front two, he was offered a full-time contract at the end of the season.
Bournemouth (Trainee - Brockenhurst College) FL 2+5 FAC 0+2 Others 0+1

McSHANE Paul David
Born: Wicklow, 6 January 1986
Height: 5'11" **Weight:** 11.5
Club Honours: FAYC '03
International Honours: RoI: 12; U21-6; Yth
Paul arrived at Sunderland from West Bromwich and is a wholehearted defender who can operate at right-back

or centre-half. His enthusiastic and combative style can land him in hot water and he picked up a red card at Arsenal last October. The young Irishman was in and out of the treatment room in August after suffering a shoulder injury at Liverpool, followed by a head wound, requiring ten stitches, at Wigan. He struck up a useful central-defensive partnership with another new arrival, Danny Higginbotham. Paul was capped by the Republic of Ireland against Cyprus and Wales before the turn of the year.
Manchester U (From trainee on 13/1/2003)
Walsall (Loaned on 23/12/2004) FL 3+1/1
Brighton & Hove A (Loaned on 4/8/2005) FL 38/3 FLC 1 FAC 1
West Bromwich A (Free on 10/8/2006) FL 31+1/2 FLC 3 FAC 4/1 Others 3
Sunderland (£1,500,000 + on 27/7/2007) PL 20+1 FAC 1

McSHEFFREY Gary
Born: Coventry, 13 August 1982
Height: 5'8" **Weight:** 10.10
International Honours: E: Yth
Showed great willingness and a tremendous work ethic up and down the left flank for Birmingham last season and even kept the supremely talented Olivier Kapo on the sidelines for a spell. He never shirked responsibility to accept the ball and try to make things happen, although moves did not always come off and his potency in front of goals dipped from his free-scoring Championship days. Gary put away key penalties in wins at Tottenham and over Manchester City, despite the pressure.
Coventry C (From trainee on 27/8/1999) P/FL 108+35/44 FLC 7+2/5 FAC 8+2/4
Stockport Co (Loaned on 30/11/2001) FL 3+2/1
Luton T (Loaned on 22/8/2003) FL 18/9 FLC 1/1
Luton T (Loaned on 18/9/2004) FL 1+4/1
Birmingham C (£3,000,000 on 17/8/2006) P/FL 64+8/16 FLC 2+1/3 FAC 4/1

McSTAY Henry Matthew Patrick
Born: Armagh, 6 March 1985
Height: 6'0" **Weight:** 11.12
International Honours: RoI: U21. NI: Yth
Another versatile Morecambe defender, Henry can play at right-back or as a central defender. He was recommended by Warren Joyce at Royal Antwerp and made his debut as a substitute in a victory at Mansfield in February. As his fitness improved, he won a place at centre-half and started the last ten games. Although not the tallest, he was rarely beaten in the air and brought extra pace to Morecambe's back line. His best

performance came near the end of the campaign in a narrow defeat at Rochdale and he earned a two-year contract.
Leeds U (From trainee on 12/3/2002. Free to Halifax T on 31/3/2005)
Morecambe (Free from Royal Antwerp, Belgium, ex Portadown, on 30/1/2008) FL 12+1 Others 1

McSWEENEY Leon
Born: Cork, 19 February 1983
Height: 6'1" **Weight:** 11.3
Arriving in the January transfer window from Cork, during the Irish off-season, Leon settled in well at Stockport, scoring the only goal of the game at Dagenham with an absolute peach of a volley. He suffered a hernia problem at the beginning of March that required surgery, but returned in time to help County win promotion via the play-offs.
Leicester C (Signed from Cork C on 10/8/2001. Freed during 2003 close season)
Stockport Co (Free from Cork C, ex Scarborough, Hucknall T, Hednesford T, Hucknall T, Hednesford T, Ilkeston T, on 4/1/2008) FL 5+6/1 Others 1+3

McVEIGH Paul Francis
Born: Belfast, 6 December 1977
Height: 5'6" **Weight:** 10.5
Club Honours: Div 1 '04
International Honours: NI: 20; U21-11; Yth; Sch
Signed as a squad player from Norwich in the summer, Paul made his Luton debut as a substitute in the opening game. He arrived with a reputation for clever ball control, a good body swerve and an eye for goal. A prolific scorer in the reserves, apart from one 90-minute appearance he was either replaced or used as a substitute in all his other League games. Six weeks into Mick Harford's reign as manager, he was called up for the home game against Walsall and although he never lasted a full match, started a 12-game run. In a struggling side, he was unable to produce his best form and was not offered a new contract.
Tottenham H (From trainee on 10/7/1996) PL 2+1/1
Norwich C (Free on 23/3/2000) P/FL 148+68/36 FLC 3+5 FAC 7+1/2 Others 3/1
Burnley (Loaned on 22/3/2007) FL 6+2/3
Luton T (Free on 10/8/2007) FL 15+10 FLC 1+3 FAC 0+2 Others 1+1

MADDEN Simon Francis
Born: Dublin, 1 May 1988
Height: 5'9" **Weight:** 11.10
International Honours: RoI: Yth
Simon, a 20-year-old right-back, made his Leeds' debut in a 2-1 home defeat by Bury in the Johnstone's Paint Trophy in

November. It was the Republic of Ireland under-19 player's only senior appearance and he was released from his contract in April shortly after having an unsuccessful trial with Cheltenham.
Leeds U (From trainee on 10/5/2006) Others 1

MADINE Gary Lee
Born: Gateshead, 24 August 1990
Height: 6'2" **Weight:** 11.10
Gary came to prominence as part of the Carlisle side that reached the quarter-final of the FA Youth Cup. Following his first-team debut in early March, he featured in most of United's games, usually as a substitute, during the end of season run-in. A striker who has already plundered goals at youth and reserve level, he is willing to take responsibility and is a player full of promise.
Carlisle U (From juniors on 13/12/2007) FL 1+10 Others 0+1

MADJO Guy Bertrand
Born: Douala, Cameroon, 1 June 1984
Height: 6'0" **Weight:** 13.5
Guy was given a second chance in the League by Cheltenham, who signed him on loan from Blue Square Premier club Crawley in November. The striker trained with the Cameroon squad before the African Cup of Nations and made his first appearance for the Robins as a substitute in the 1-0 win over Leeds. Guy

Kevin Maher

started twice before joining Shrewsbury in a permanent deal when the January transfer window opened, after his 11 goals in 17 outings for Crawley had caught Shrewsbury's eye, and he made his debut in a 3-1 reverse at Hereford. Lively and holding the ball up well, Guy scored his first League goal a week later in the 2-0 defeat against Morecambe and another in the 1-1 draw at Grimsby, a vital point as Shrewsbury became drawn into the relegation battle. When Paul Simpson became manager, there were fewer starting opportunities for Guy as the search was on for the most effective striking partnership.
Bristol C (Free from Petersfield T on 16/9/2005) FL 1+4 Others 0+1/1 (Free to Forest Green Rov on 18/1/2006)
Cheltenham T (Loaned from Crawley T, ex Stafford Rgrs, on 22/11/2007) FL 2+3
Shrewsbury T (£20,000 from Crawley T on 11/1/2008) FL 10+5/3

MAHER Kevin Andrew
Born: Ilford, 17 October 1976
Height: 6'0" **Weight:** 12.5
Club Honours: Div 1 '06
International Honours: RoI: U21-4
In the previous season Kevin was voted Southend's 'Player of the Year' but football is fickle and the captain was out of favour for much of 2007-08. He started in his usual central midfield berth, with new arrival Nicky Bailey alongside him and Alan McCormack on the right. Manager Steve Tilson decided his team lacked natural width and bought McCormack in alongside Bailey as his preferred midfield option. Kevin could not dislodge them so, after ten years, was confined to occasional appearances on the bench. A proposed transfer to Swindon in the January transfer window did not materialise and he eventually accepted an offer from former Southend team-mate Mark Stimson to go on loan to Gillingham for the rest of the season. Kevin was stranded on 454 appearances for Southend, third in the club's all-time list behind Alan Moody and Sandy Anderson, and although he remained strong and determined in the Gillingham midfield the club were unable to avoid relegation from League One.
Tottenham H (From trainee on 1/7/1995)
Southend U (Free on 23/1/1998) FL 375+8/22 FLC 18/1 FAC 27/1 Others 25+1/1
Gillingham (Loaned on 7/3/2008) FL 7

MAHER Stephen John
Born: Dublin, 3 March 1988
Height: 5'10" **Weight:** 11.0
International Honours: RoI: Yth
Having made just one substitute

appearance in 2006-07, the central midfielder was given an opportunity to prove his worth in his second season with Yeovil. Although he received a red card after just one minute of his first outing for Town, he showed his promise and potential in six matches after the suspension but was among several released by Glovers' boss Russell Slade.
Yeovil T (Signed from Dublin C on 1/8/2006) FL 4+3 Others 0+1

MAHON Alan Joseph
Born: Dublin, 4 April 1978
Height: 5'10" **Weight:** 11.5
Club Honours: FLC '02
International Honours: RoI: 2; U21-18; Yth; Sch
Still seemingly unable to make the breakthrough to regular first-team football at Burnley, Alan's season was badly disrupted by injury. When he did play, it was usually in a central-midfield role from which he frequently displayed his not inconsiderable passing skills and willingness to shoot. He lacked consistency, though, and too often seemed to drift out of games. If his talents were fully exploited, he could yet become one of the Clarets' stars.
Tranmere Rov (From trainee on 7/4/1995) FL 84+36/13 FLC 12+6/1 FAC 4+2 (Free to Sporting Lisbon, Portugal on 1/7/2000)
Blackburn Rov (£1,500,000 from Sporting Lisbon, Portugal on 14/12/2000) P/FL 25+11/1 FLC 4+3 FAC 10
Cardiff C (Loaned on 24/1/2003) FL 13+2/2
Ipswich T (Loaned on 5/9/2003) FL 7+4/1 FLC 1
Wigan Ath (Free on 6/2/2004) P/FL 39+8/9 FLC 6 FAC 3/1
Burnley (£200,000 on 23/3/2006) FL 30+29/3 FLC 3+1 FAC 0+1

MAHON Gavin Andrew
Born: Birmingham, 2 January 1977
Height: 6'0" **Weight:** 13.2
Club Honours: Div 3 '99
After seven seasons and more than 200 matches for Watford, Gavin moved to Queens Park Rangers in January. The midfielder, a popular and influential club captain at Vicarage Road, gave loyal and exemplary service to the Hornets in a largely unsung role and deserved the chance of a new challenge. Gavin was almost ever present at Watford before his transfer to Rangers and after a debut in the FA Cup defeat at Chelsea, had to play second fiddle to Mikele Leigertwood for some weeks. Once settled into the side in the later months of the campaign, he demonstrated why Watford had valued him so highly with a string of committed and professional performances.

Wolverhampton W (From trainee on 3/7/1995)
Hereford U (Free on 12/7/1996) FL 10+1/1 FLC 4
Brentford (£50,000 + on 17/11/1998) FL 140+1/8 FLC 8 FAC 5 Others 12
Watford (£150,000 + on 4/3/2002) P/FL 180+9/6 FLC 10 FAC 12+1/1 Others 3
Queens Park Rgrs (£200,000 on 1/1/2008) FL 11+5/1 FAC 1

MAIN Curtis Lee
Born: South Shields, 20 June 1992
Height: 5'9" **Weight:** 12.2
The 15-year-old schoolboy striker became the youngest player ever to appear for Darlington when he went on as an 83rd-minute substitute at Peterborough in the final game of the season. The club had to seek permission from South Shields Community School to play him as his apprenticeship does not officially start until next season, after he has turned 16. He broke Dale Anderson's record for the youngest-ever Quaker by some margin as Dale was 16 years and 254 days old when he appeared 21 years ago, at Chesterfield in May 1987.
Darlington (Associated Schoolboy) FL 0+1

MAKELELE Claude
Born: Kinshasa, DR Congo, 18 February 1973
Height: 5'7" **Weight:** 10.12
Club Honours: FLC '05, '07; PL '05, '06; CS '05
International Honours: France: 71; B-4; U21
Rarely can a contemporary player have given his name to a position within the game, but the 'holding, Makelele role' has become staple fare for television commentators and pundits these past few years. The original is still the best. The iconic midfielder was used sparingly in the Premier League as John Obi Mikel appeared to be groomed for the part, but Claude's importance in the big matches was exemplified by his performances in the Champions' League. He was imperious in his usual fashion, sitting in front of the back four, mopping up attacks and allowing attacking midfielders Frank Lampard and Michael Ballack to inflict damage further forward. Claude was particularly effective against Premier League rivals Liverpool and Manchester United in the later stages of the competition. Yet again, he failed to score but his value was recognised with a contract extension.
Chelsea (£16,600,000 from Real Madrid, Spain, ex Brest Armorique, Nantes, Olympique Marseille, Celta Vigo, on 1/9/2003) PL 132+12/2 FLC 12+2 FAC 9 Others 48+2

MAKIN Christopher (Chris) Gregory
Born: Manchester, 8 May 1973
Height: 5'10" **Weight:** 11.2
Club Honours: Div 1 '99; Ch '06
International Honours: E: U21-5; Yth; Sch
Injuries and suspensions saw Chris, a steady, experienced and accomplished full-back, thrust into the centre of the Southampton's defence at the beginning of the season. The experiment may have worked if Chris had played in a less makeshift rearguard but this was not the case and the team struggled. With two fit centre-backs available, Chris lost his place and a hip injury sustained in September ensured that he never had an outing in his favoured positions. He announced his retirement in April, an anti-climactic conclusion to a distinguished career.
Oldham Ath (From trainee on 2/11/1991) P/FL 93+1/4 FLC 7 FAC 11 Others 1+1 (Transferred to Olympique Marseille, France during 1996 close season)
Wigan Ath (Loaned on 28/8/1992) FL 14+1/2
Sunderland (£500,000 from Olympique Marseille, France on 5/8/1997) P/FL 115+5/1 FLC 13 FAC 7+1 Others 1+1
Ipswich T (£1,250,000 on 7/3/2001) P/FL 78 FLC 4 FAC 2 Others 7+1
Leicester C (Free on 2/8/2004) FL 21 FLC 1 FAC 1
Derby Co (Signed on 16/2/2005) FL 13
Reading (Free on 3/8/2005) FL 11+1 FLC 2+1 FAC 4
Southampton (Free on 16/8/2006) FL 24+3 FLC 3 FAC 1 Others 1

MALBRANQUE Steed
Born: Mouscron, Belgium, 6 January 1980
Height: 5'8" **Weight:** 11.7
Club Honours: FLC '08
International Honours: France: U21
The Tottenham midfielder played in more games than any other squad member last season, starting no less than 52 and being used as substitute in three others. Steed is widely recognised as one of the hardest-working players in the squad but there are more facets to his game. He scored seven times in all competitions, including the 90th-minute goal that sealed Tottenham's 5-1 victory over rivals Arsenal to reach the Carling Cup final and was a member of the Wembley side. Throughout the campaign, Steed played predominantly on the left but was occasionally given a freer role across midfield. He is a determined ball-winner, often coming to the rescue of his defence, and a perceptive passer over short distances. Steed remains a

great favourite of the fans and will surely remain a vital part of the squad.

Fulham (£5,000,000 from Lyon, France on 14/8/2001) PL 160+12/32 FLC 6+2/2 FAC 17/7 Others 12+2/3

Tottenham H (£2,000,000 on 31/8/2006) PL 53+9/6 FLC 9/2 FAC 7+2/1 Others 13+3/3

MALCOLM Robert (Bob)
Born: Glasgow, 12 November 1980
Height: 5'11" **Weight:** 12.2
Club Honours: SPD '03, '05; SC '03; SLC '05
International Honours: S: B-1; U21-1
Never able to reproduce the form shown when he first joined Derby from Glasgow Rangers, Bob made only one Premiership appearance, in a 6-0 defeat by Liverpool at Anfield, before moving to Queens Park Rangers on loan in November. Despite something of a baptism of fire on his debut, he went on to settle into the side under caretaker boss Mick Harford and his efforts went a long way towards stabilising the defence after John Gregory's departure. His time at Loftus Road came to an end in December and after problems off the field his Derby contract was cancelled in January and he returned to Scotland with Motherwell.

Glasgow Rgrs (From juniors on 1/7/1997) SL 66+22/3 SLC 7 SC 9+3 Others 7+1

Derby Co (Free on 5/9/2006) P/FL 7+3 FLC 2 FAC 2

Queens Park Rgrs (Loaned on 15/11/2007) FL 10+1

MALONEY Shaun Richard
Born: Mirri, Malaysia, 24 January 1983
Height: 5'7" **Weight:** 10.2
Club Honours: SPD '02, '04, '06; SLC '06
International Honours: S: 11; B-1; U21-21
Although Shaun is predominantly a midfield player, he is also capable of operating in a more advanced role and is particularly dangerous with his free kicks. In some ways, it was a disappointing season for him, in that he was unable to secure a regular place for Aston Villa, making 13 starts and 12 appearances from the bench. Shaun scored against the Faeroe Islands when playing for Scotland and was further involved in their gallant attempt to reach the European Championship finals.

Glasgow Celtic (From juniors on 7/7/1999) SL 51+53/26 SLC 9+2/8 SC 4+4/1 Others 5+10/2

Aston Villa (£1,000,000 on 31/1/2007) PL 16+14/5 FLC 2/2 FAC 0+1

MALOUDA Florent Johan
Born: Cayenne, French Guiana, 13 June 1980

Steed Malbranque

Height: 5'11" **Weight:** 11.10
International Honours: France: 41
One of the key factors in FC Lyon's domination of Ligue 1 in recent years was the dazzling wing play of Florent, being instrumental in Lyon's hat-trick of League titles and impressive Champions' League runs. A World Cup runner-up with France in 2006, he reunited with former team-mates Michael Essien (Lyon) and Didier Drogba (Guingamp) in July and although he had the difficult task of replacing crowd-favourite Arjen Robben, settled in quickly, striking up a good partnership with Ashley Cole. His performances in his first few matches had Blues' fans drooling with beautifully taken goals against Manchester United in the Community Shield and Birmingham in the opening Premier League match. Unaccountably, he faded from the scene owing to a string of niggling injuries; stamina concerns and the outstanding form of Shaun Wright-Phillips and Joe Cole. Just as he was being written off in some quarters, he made a remarkable resurgence to figure prominently at the sharp end of the season. He scored his second Premier League goal in the penultimate match at Newcastle, nine months after his first, and featured in both Champions' League semi-finals and the final. Overall, Florent's initial season in England can be classed as a slight disappointment but if he can continue where he left off Chelsea fans could be in for a treat.

Chelsea (£13,500,000 from Lyon, France, ex Chateauroux, Guingamp, on 16/7/2007) PL 16+5/2 FLC 2+1 FAC 2 Others 9+3/2

MANCIENNE Michael Ian
Born: Feltham, 8 January 1988
Height: 5'10" **Weight:** 11.7
International Honours: E: U21-4; Yth
After enjoying a productive season on loan from Chelsea in 2006-07, Michael returned for a second spell. Once again, he featured mainly at right-back and, despite being a natural centre-half, made the position his own and capped another fine season by being named Queens Park Rangers' 'Young Player of the Season'. Over the latter half of the campaign his committed and determined displays made

a massive contribution to Rangers' vastly improved defensive record.

Chelsea *(From trainee on 11/1/2006)*
Queens Park Rgrs *(Loaned on 17/10/2006) FL 26+2 FAC 2*
Queens Park Rgrs *(Loaned on 9/8/2007) FL 26+4 FLC 1*

MANGAN Andrew (Andy) Francis

Born: Liverpool, 30 August 1986
Height: 5'9" **Weight:** 10.4
Club Honours: FC '06
Freed by Accrington in the summer, the quick forward joined Bury, proving that he had an eye for goal, and gave manager Chris Casper a valuable option. Although his first goal came in the disappointing defeat by Chesterfield his next, in a home defeat by Accrington, set him on a run of three goals in six games, including a superb effort against local rivals Rochdale. Andy's chances were limited by Andy Bishop's return to fitness. After a groin injury had kept him out over Christmas, in a bid to improve his fitness, new Bury boss Alan Knill allowed him to join former club Accrington on loan in February. Andy's time back at Stanley was not a huge success as he spent much of it on the bench, as in his first spell. However, he scored the vital second goal in the 3-2 win over Morecambe and remained popular with Stanley supporters before a recurrence of his injury. Was released by Bury in the summer.

Blackpool *(Trainee) FL 0+2*
Accrington Stanley *(Free on 12/8/2005) FL 6+28/4 FAC 1 Others 2+1*
Bury *(Free on 17/7/2007) FL 7+13/4 FLC 0+1 FAC 1+2 Others 0+2*
Accrington Stanley *(Loaned on 22/2/2008) FL 3+4/1*

MANNIX David Christopher

Born: Winsford, 24 September 1985
Height: 5'8" **Weight:** 11.6
International Honours: E: Yth
Arriving back from Norwegian club Ham-Kam in January, David's signing created a good deal of excitement at Accrington after the great impression he made in the previous season when on loan from Liverpool. He went straight into midfield and although he played competently, retaining his place for most games until the end of the season, he never quite produced that something special. Perhaps the anticipation had been too great.

Liverpool *(From trainee on 12/6/2003. Freed on 29/1/2007)*
Accrington Stanley *(Loaned on 23/11/2006) FL 1*
Accrington Stanley *(Free from Ham-Kam, Norway, on 31/1/2008) FL 9+3*

MARIAPPA Adrian Joseph

Born: Harrow, 3 October 1986
Height: 5'11" **Weight:** 12.2
Bearing in mind his fine performances in the previous season, it was surprising that Adrian was unable to command a regular place in Watford's first team in 2007-08. He filled in at both centre-half and right-back when other players were injured or as a substitute and continued to impress with his skill, composure and ability in the air. Adrian is a natural leader and a potential future captain.

Watford *(From trainee on 4/7/2005) P/FL 31+16 FLC 4+1 FAC 5+2 Others 1*

MARNEY Dean Edward

Born: Barking, 31 January 1984
Height: 5'9" **Weight:** 10.7
International Honours: E: U21-1
Following an initial settling-in campaign in 2006-07, Dean's increasing influence in the centre of midfield last season matched the amazing improvements in Hull's fortunes as they equalled their highest League position, earned a first trip to Wembley in the Championship play-offs and reached the top flight for the first time. Described as an absolute workaholic, this was amply demonstrated with his last-minute goal against Barnsley in October when a lung-bursting run the length of the KC Stadium ended with a cool finish to clinch another victory. After a slight dip in form following a mid-season illness, Dean returned to his earlier high standard and resumed his midfield engine-room partnership with captain Ian Ashbee to guide the Tigers into uncharted territory.

Tottenham H *(From trainee on 3/7/2002) PL 4+4/2 FAC 0+3*
Swindon T *(Loaned on 24/12/2002) FL 8+1*
Queens Park Rgrs *(Loaned on 16/1/2004) FL 1+1 Others 1*
Gillingham *(Loaned on 5/11/2004) FL 3*
Norwich C *(Loaned on 2/8/2005) FL 12+1 FLC 2*
Hull C *(£1,000,000 on 18/7/2006) FL 61+17/ 8 FLC 3+2 FAC 2 Others 0+1*

MARPLES Simon James

Born: Sheffield, 30 July 1975
Height: 5'10" **Weight:** 11.11
Club Honours: Div 3 '04
International Honours: E: SP-2
The experienced right-sided defender struggled to get into Chester's side at the start of the campaign but injury to James Vaughan gave him an opportunity in September. A reliable performer, Simon likes to push forward when given the chance and linked well with Richie Partridge on the right as City pressed for a play-off place before Christmas. Simon

lost his place as Chester's form declined in December and Vaughan was fit again. He made his final appearance in the defeat at Brentford at the end of the year before being released at the season's end.

Doncaster Rov *(Free from Stocksbridge Park Steels on 13/9/1999) FL 40+3 FLC 3 FAC 1+1 Others 1*
Chester C *(Free on 1/8/2006) FL 40+6 FAC 4 Others 2*

MARRIOTT Alan

Born: Bedford, 3 September 1978
Height: 6'1" **Weight:** 12.5
As the longest-serving member of Lincoln's squad in 2007-08, the season turned out to be goalkeeper Alan's last for the Imps as he was one of four players to be released by manager Peter Jackson in May. Having started the season as the first-choice 'keeper, Alan found himself dropped to the substitutes' bench for nine games to accommodate loanee Ben Smith, whilst an injury sustained at Chester towards the end of the campaign saw Ayden Duffy take over between the sticks.

Tottenham H *(From trainee on 3/7/1997)*
Lincoln C *(Free on 5/8/1999) FL 351 FLC 10 FAC 13 Others 21*

MARSHALL Andrew (Andy) John

Born: Bury St Edmunds, 14 April 1975
Height: 6'2" **Weight:** 13.7
International Honours: E: U21-4; Yth (UEFA-U18 '93)
Despite being the 'Player of the Year' for 2006-07, Andy was Coventry's second-choice goalkeeper behind Dimi Konstantopoulos at the start of the season. Andy was selected for the Carling Cup ties and kept three successive clean sheets, including an excellent performance in the victory over Manchester United at Old Trafford. After that, he took over from the Greek for the first of three brief League spells. He always performed with his usual quiet confidence and City's defence was better when he was in the side. After a run of eight games he was replaced by loanee Kasper Schmeichel, allegedly because a back problem needed surgery. The operation was held over until the end of the season and Andy sat on the bench for the last nine games before signing a new one-year deal.

Norwich C *(From trainee on 6/7/1993) P/FL 194+1 FLC 18 FAC 5+1*
Bournemouth *(Loaned on 9/9/1996) FL 11*
Gillingham *(Loaned on 21/11/1996) FL 5 FLC 1 Others 1*
Ipswich T *(Free on 4/7/2001) P/FL 53 FLC 2 FAC 4 Others 6*

Wolverhampton W (Loaned on 18/11/2003) FLC 1
Millwall (Signed on 28/1/2004) FL 66+1 FLC 2 FAC 6
Coventry C (Free on 17/7/2006) FL 57 FLC 5 FAC 1

MARSHALL David James

Born: Glasgow, 5 March 1985
Height: 6'3" **Weight:** 13.0
Club Honours: SPD '04; SC '04
International Honours: S: 2; U21-10
After a loan spell at Norwich was cut short by injury in the previous season, David completed a transfer from Glasgow Celtic in July. A regular member of the full Scottish squad, the goalkeeper was Norwich's only ever-present, producing an excellent level of consistency that earned him third place in the 'Player of the Season' voting. Still only 23, he is inexperienced in goalkeeping terms but his fantastic shot-stopping displays won admiration from many neutral observers as well as Norwich fans. Brave and excellent in one-on-one situations, he is sure to develop into one of the best 'keepers in the country and will give Craig Gordon a run for the Scottish number-one jersey.
Glasgow Celtic (From juniors on 1/8/2002) SL

David Marshall

34+1 SLC 2 SC 3+1 Others 8+1
Norwich C (£1,000,000 on 17/1/2007) FL 48 FLC 3 FAC 5

MARTIN Christopher (Chris) Hugh

Born: Beccles, 4 November 1988
Height: 5'10" **Weight:** 11.7
International Honours: E: Yth
As is often the case, Chris found his first season as a full professional more difficult than his startling entry to the first team in 2006-07. A product of Norwich's Academy, he is a clever striker with an unusual style. He uses his intelligence and awareness to create openings for himself and can manipulate the ball in tight situations to get strikes at goal when little or no opportunity appears to be there. Still learning his trade, he had limited impact but his time is sure to come again and he will need to work hard to ensure that he maintains a regular place in the Norwich squad.
Norwich C (From trainee on 17/4/2007) FL 16+9/4 FLC 1+1 FAC 1+2/1

MARTIN Christopher (Chris) Joseph

Born: Mansfield, 21 July 1990
Height: 6'0" **Weight:** 13.5

Port Vale's reserve goalkeeper progressed through the club's youth system. Tall and commanding, Chris was a member of the successful team that reached the quarter-finals of the FA Youth Cup and a regular non-playing substitute before injury to Joe Anyon gave him his chance in the first team. Unfortunately, Vale lost 6-0 at Swindon on his debut in April, but he played the next game, a 2-2 home draw with Northampton. He is held in high regard and signed his first professional contract just before the end of the season.
Port Vale (From trainee on 18/4/2008) FL 2

MARTIN Daniel (Dan) Ashley

Born: Derby, 24 September 1986
Height: 6'1" **Weight:** 12.13
International Honours: W: U21-1
Having been signed from neighbouring Notts County in the summer, Dan added a touch of class to the Mansfield side, initially in midfield. However, following an injury to Gareth Jelleyman, Dan filled in at left-back to such good effect that he retained the position until losing his place through injury in February. Was released in the summer.
Derby Co (From trainee on 16/10/2004)
Notts Co (Free on 19/7/2005) FL 28+23/8 FLC 2+2/1 Others 1
Mansfield T (Free on 24/7/2007) FL 21+5 FLC 1 FAC 4 Others 0+1

MARTIN David (Dave) John

Born: Erith, 3 June 1985
Height: 5'9" **Weight:** 10.10
A raw, raiding left-winger, Dave was a squad player at Crystal Palace in 2007-08 but following the appointment of Neil Warnock as manager he was given two starts before being sold to Millwall in January. An asset to Millwall, especially in the final part of the season, Dave got right into the thick of things and his mazy runs through defences were a delight to see. With a good eye for a scoring opportunity, had it not been for injuries he would have played more games and Lions' fans hope that he will be free from injury in the coming season.
Crystal Palace (£25,000 from Dartford, ex Slade Green, on 23/1/2007) FL 2+12 FLC 1
Millwall (£50,000 + on 31/1/2008) FL 7+4/2

MARTIN Joseph (Joe) John

Born: Dagenham, 29 November 1988
Height: 6'0" **Weight:** 13.0
Seeking to gain experience, the Tottenham youngster was loaned to Blackpool on transfer deadline day. While Joe's father, Alvin Martin, was a West Ham defender and his brother David is a goalkeeper at Liverpool, Joe is a

Javier Mascherano

midfielder and made his senior debut in the final game against Watford, playing on the right-wing. He impressed the home fans with his crossing and pace and it is thought that manager Simon Grayson could try to secure Joe's services on an extended loan.

Tottenham H *(From trainee on 5/12/2005)*
Blackpool *(Loaned on 27/3/2008) FL 1*

MARTIN Lee Robert
Born: Taunton, 9 February 1987
Height: 5'10" **Weight:** 10.3
International Honours: E: Yth
Expected to move up a gear after spending the previous season on loan at Glasgow Rangers, the highly-rated Manchester United midfielder made one appearance for the Reds, in the Carling Cup defeat by Coventry in October, before going on loan to Plymouth the same month. Skilful and tricky when used on the wing by Argyle, Lee scored his first goal for the club in the 1-0 victory over Coventry, which was his full debut, but was interrupted by a hamstring injury. Lee later returned to the team but it was decided that he would go back to Old Trafford at the end of his three months. He was soon off on another loan, this time to Sheffield United in January. Lee's first appearance for the Blades, after serving a one-match ban, was in the Sheffield derby. Fast and with good control, he played mainly wide on the left of midfield but occasionally on the right. After settling into the side he injured a knee in the FA Cup at Middlesbrough when making a block tackle and recovered only towards the end of the season before injuring an ankle.

Manchester U *(From trainee on 15/2/2005)* FLC 2
Glasgow Rgrs *(Loaned on 11/8/2006) SL 4+3 SLC 0+2 Others 1*
Stoke C *(Loaned on 26/1/2007) FL 4+9/1 FAC 1*
Plymouth Arg *(Loaned on 5/10/2007) FL 10+2/2*
Sheffield U *(Loaned on 11/1/2008) FL 5+1 FAC 2+1*

MARTIN Russell Kenneth Alexander
Born: Brighton, 4 January 1986
Height: 6'0" **Weight:** 11.8
Russell continued as the first-choice right-back for Wycombe and probably had his best season. He is now an accomplished defender, strong in the tackle with good covering abilities. Is also very effective bringing the ball forward, has great stamina, and is always available to deliver a dangerous right-wing cross. In fact, he provided most goal assists of all the team and likes to have a pop at goal from any

distance. Out of contract at the end of the season, the extremely popular Russell declined the club's offer to stay in favour of a three-year deal with Peterborough.
Wycombe W *(Free from Lewes on 4/8/2004) FL 88+28/5 FLC 7+1 FAC 5 Others 12+1*

MARTINS Obafemi (Oba) Akinwunmi
Born: Lagos, Nigeria, 28 October 1984
Height: 5'7" **Weight:** 11.0
International Honours: Nigeria: 21
Although playing for most of last season in a Newcastle side short of midfield creativity, the striker still delivered a creditable goals return. Blessed with electric pace and a powerful shot in both feet, Oba's spring makes him surprisingly dangerous in the air. In the season's opener at Bolton, he demonstrated his athleticism by scoring with a scissors kick and continued to find the net at regular intervals, whether starting or entering as a substitute, until he left to play for Nigeria in the African Cup of Nations. He returned with an ankle injury and on his recovery was used as a substitute for a couple of matches until Kevin Keegan introduced a new formation, with Oba in an attacking role largely on the left flank. It was so successful that Newcastle went on a seven-game unbeaten run and banished the threat of relegation.
Newcastle U *(£10,160,000 from Inter Milan, Italy, ex Reggiana, on 25/8/2006) PL 55+9/20 FLC 3+1/1 FAC 2 Others 7+2/6*

MARTIS Shelton
Born: Willemstad, Curacao, Netherlands Antilles, 29 November 1982
Height: 6'1" **Weight:** 12.11
International Honours: Dutch Antilles: 1
Signed from Hibernian in the summer, Shelton was a reserve for West Bromwich and made only two senior appearances in 2007-08, at right-back in a 2-1 League win at Leicester and at left-back in the Carling Cup defeat by Cardiff. In a bid to keep him match fit he joined Scunthorpe on a month's loan in January and made his first appearance in the FA Cup defeat at Preston. In fact, all four of his appearances for the Iron ended in defeat before he was recalled to the Hawthorns. Despite that, Shelton had looked assured on the ball when coming forward from centre-half.
Darlington *(Free from FC Eindhoven, Holland, ex Feyenoord, Excelsior, on 5/8/2005) FL 41+1/2 FLC 1 FAC 1 Others 1*
Hibernian *(Free on 10/8/2006) SL 27 SLC 4+1 SC 2*
West Bromwich A *(£50,000 on 13/7/2007) FL 2 FLC 1*
Scunthorpe U *(Loaned on 4/1/2008) FL 3 FAC 1*

MARTOT David
Born: Fecamp, France, 1 February 1981
Height: 5'10" **Weight:** 11.2
Other than a brief hiatus at the turn of the year, David spent the entire season from the end of August on loan at Brighton from Le Havre. A nippy midfielder who can play in the centre or out wide, he was in and out of the side, often alternating with Jake Robinson as the pair tried to find the consistency that would establish one or other. As a useful squad player it was slightly surprising that David was not offered terms at the end of the campaign, although he will have been disappointed with a return of two goals from 31 appearances.
Brighton & Hove A *(Loaned from Le Havre, France on 31/8/2007) FL 17+9/1 FAC 0+2 Others 2+1/1*

MASCHERANO Javier Alejandro
Born: Santa Fe, Argentina, 8 June 1984
Height: 5'10" **Weight:** 12.1
International Honours: Argentina: 36
Few players have made such an immediate impact at a new club as the Argentine international midfielder who, in the previous season, went from a West Ham misfit to Liverpool's 'Man of the Match' in the Champions' League final. He simply carried on where he had left off. One of the finest holding midfielders in the world, Javier's razor sharp tackles, covering, interceptions, marking and short passing ensured that Liverpool not only won the ball but retained it. Every successful team needs such a player and whilst Momo Sissoko performed that role with distinction for two years, the unfortunate Mali international was totally eclipsed after Javier's arrival. Liverpool formalised his status at the club in February by paying a fee of £18.6-million to MSI, the agency that owned the player and had initially loaned him. In March he scored his first goal for the Reds, a cracking 25-yard shot on the run after carrying the ball out of defence for 50 yards. For colleagues and supporters alike there were few more popular scorers all season. Sadly, burgeoning confidence ran away with him in the next match, a critical Premiership meeting at Manchester United, and he was sent off late in the first half when, after receiving a earlier caution, he raced across the pitch to remonstrate with the referee over a booking for Fernando Torres. He compounded the offence by refusing to leave the pitch immediately and, as a result, a one-match suspension was raised to three plus a £15,000 fine. Fortunately, this applied only to the Premiership

and he was free to play in the climactic Champions' League matches against Arsenal and Chelsea.

West Ham U *(Loaned from Corinthians, Brazil, ex River Plate, on 31/8/2006) PL 3+2 Others 2*
Liverpool *(£18,600,000 from Corinthians, Brazil on 31/1/2007) PL 32/1 FLC 0+1 FAC 1+1 Others 17*

MASTERS Clark John

Born: Hastings, 31 May 1987
Height: 6'3" **Weight:** 13.12

Clark started last season on loan to Welling but on returning to Brentford was a regular on the bench. The goalkeeper made his first appearance of the season at Peterborough in October, following Simon Brown's first-minute dismissal, and despite conceding seven goals, was Brentford's 'Man of the Match'. He appeared in the next game before Brown returned and joined Southend in the January transfer window. Following that, he was immediately loaned to Stevenage for the rest of the season.

Brentford *(From trainee on 27/6/2006) FL 11+1 FAC 2 Others 2*
Southend U *(Signed on 11/1/2008)*

MATEJOVSKY Marek

Born: Brandys nad Labem, Czech Republic, 20 December 1981
Height: 5'10" **Weight:** 11.3
International Honours: Czech Republic: 8

Marek joined Reading from Czech minnows Mlada Boleslav in a deal worth more than £1-million and was given a three-and-a-half-year contract. A Czech international with six caps to his credit when he arrived, he immediately slotted into Royals' midfield and made a huge impression with the accuracy and perception of his passing. More than any other player in the squad, he has the ability to split the opposing defence with one touch of the ball. His one goal in 14 appearances, a 20-yard screamer that flew into the top of the Liverpool net at Anfield, was a contender for the BBC's 'Goal of the Month' and won Match magazine's accolade for the same title in March. Marek was selected as a member of the Czech Republic's squad for the Euro 2008 championships.

Reading *(£1,400,000 from Mlada Boleslav, Czech Republic, ex Mlada Boleslav, Jablonec, on 11/1/2008) PL 10+4/1*

MATTEO Dominic

Born: Dumfries, 28 April 1974
Height: 6'1" **Weight:** 11.12
International Honours: S: 6; E: B-1; U21-4; Yth

The midfield dynamo originally joined Stoke on a short-term deal that was extended into last season, with a one-year contract and the captaincy of the club. Unfortunately, a foot injury ruled Dominic out and he did not make another appearance for City after Christmas. As Stoke surged on to promotion without him, Dominic's future was left in the balance before being released in the summer.

Liverpool *(From trainee on 27/5/1992) PL 112+15/1 FLC 9 FAC 6+2/1 Others 10+1*
Sunderland *(Loaned on 24/3/1995) FL 1*
Leeds U *(£4,750,000 on 24/8/2000) PL 115/2 FLC 2 FAC 6 Others 23/2*
Blackburn Rov *(Free on 7/6/2004) FAC 5/1*
Stoke C *(Free on 19/1/2007) FL 23/1 FAC 1*

MATTIS Dwayne Antony

Born: Huddersfield, 31 July 1981
Height: 6'1" **Weight:** 10.10
International Honours: RoI: U21-2; Yth

Dwayne had few chances at Barnsley in 2007-08, although he produced his best display at Newcastle in the Carling Cup. The tall midfielder joined Walsall on a month's loan in September and showed up well in four autumn games, three of which were won and the other drawn, before a broken leg brought to an end to what had been a highly promising spell. After returning to Oakwell to recuperate, Dwayne played a couple of reserve games towards the end of the season and was a substitute at Cardiff on the final day.

Huddersfield T *(From trainee on 8/7/1999) FL 50+19/2 FLC 1+2 FAC 3+1 Others 4/1*
Bury *(Free on 30/7/2004) FL 93+4/11 FLC 4/1 FAC 8/5*
Barnsley *(£50,000 + on 11/1/2007) FL 3+1 FLC 1*
Walsall *(Loaned on 28/9/2007) FL 4*

MATTOCK Joseph (Joe) William

Born: Leicester, 15 May 1990
Height: 5'11" **Weight:** 12.5
International Honours: E: U21-4; Yth

An outstanding young prospect at left-back for Leicester, and used occasionally as a left-sided midfielder, Joe impressed sufficiently in a struggling team to earn England under-21 honours as the second-youngest ever to play at that level, behind Theo Walcott. Not surprisingly, he was voted the club's 'Young Player of the Season' by the Supporters' Club. City turned down a reportedly substantial bid from a Premiership club for Joe in mid-season but he will surely further his career at that level before too long.

Leicester C *(From trainee on 25/4/2007) FL 29+6 FLC 2*

MAWENE Youl

Born: Caen, France, 16 July 1979
Height: 6'2" **Weight:** 12.6

After Youl missed all 2006-07 through injury, everyone at Deepdale was delighted to see him back in the centre of Preston's defence in August. He remained there apart from four games over Christmas, when a family illness took priority. The quality of Youl's partnerships with Liam Chilvers and Sean St Ledger was not reflected by the tide of goals conceded. A couple of uncharacteristic errors late in the season suggested his long lay-off was taking its toll but the Frenchman is back in the right rhythm and added three goals to double his tally for the club.

Derby Co *(£500,000 from RC Lens, France, ex Caen, on 4/8/2000) P/FL 54+1/1 FLC 2 FAC 4*
Preston NE *(Free on 3/8/2004) FL 108+6/6 FLC 4 FAC 8 Others 5*

MAY Benjamin (Ben) Steven

Born: Gravesend, 10 March 1984
Height: 6'1" **Weight:** 12.6

Out of favour with League One Millwall, Ben made a surprise switch to Championship side Scunthorpe on loan in September, doing well during his month at Glanford Park. After being recalled to the New Den, Scunthorpe went back in January and signed him on a permanent basis, using him largely as a substitute during the rest of the season. A giant target-man, he looked good at holding up the ball and celebrated his first goal in the defeat at home by Ipswich in March.

Millwall *(From juniors on 10/5/2001) FL 43+35/14 FLC 4+1/1 FAC 7+2/2 Others 2+1/2*
Colchester U *(Loaned on 27/3/2003) FL 4+2*
Brentford *(Loaned on 25/8/2003) FL 38+3/7 FAC 1 Others 1*
Colchester U *(Loaned on 6/8/2004) FL 5+9/1 FLC 0+2/1*
Brentford *(Loaned on 3/12/2004) FL 7+3/1 FAC 4+2*
Scunthorpe U *(Loaned on 28/9/2007) FL 0+5*
Scunthorpe U *(£100,000 on 18/1/2008) FL 6+10/1*

MAY Daniel (Danny) William

Born: Watford, 19 November 1988
Height: 5'8" **Weight:** 10.9

Full-back Danny did not have many opportunities last season because of the number of defenders on the books at Northampton. He gave some excellent displays for the reserves and played his part when promoted to League One. He was released after the end of the season.

Northampton T *(From trainee on 5/7/2007) FL 2+3 Others 1*

MAYBURY Alan Paul
Born: Dublin, 8 August 1978
Height: 5'11" **Weight:** 11.12
Club Honours: FAYC '97
International Honours: RoI: 10; B-1; U21-8; Yth

A gritty full-back who can operate on both flanks, Alan is an experienced defender who did not figure in Martin Allen's plans for Leicester at the start of last season. He had one isolated outing in December under Ian Holloway but took up the offer of a loan back to Scotland with Aberdeen, where family commitments were easier to handle. Was released at the end of the campaign.

Leeds U (Free from St Kevin's BC on 17/8/ 1995) PL 10+4 FLC 1 FAC 2 Others 1
Reading (Loaned on 25/3/1999) FL 8
Crewe Alex (Loaned on 8/10/2000) FL 6
Heart of Midlothian (£100,000 on 12/10/ 2001) SL 110+2/4 SLC 7 SC 5 Others 10
Leicester C (£100,000 on 6/1/2005) FL 83+2/3 FLC 6+2 FAC 8+1
Aberdeen (Loaned on 31/1/2008) SL 13 SC 3+1 Others 2

MAYNARD Nicholas (Nicky) David
Born: Winsford, 11 December 1986
Height: 5'11" **Weight:** 11.0

Nicky, Crewe's second highest scorer in 2006-07 with 19 goals, had the misfortune to break a leg in the opening game against Brighton. He worked his way back to the first team, scoring in the home game against Gillingham in December, and recovered his form on a regular basis. A composed striker, he finished with 14 goals, including a first League hat-trick against Cheltenham and pairs at home to Hartlepool and at Yeovil. A fit Nicky makes a big difference to Crewe.

Crewe Alex (From trainee on 9/6/2005) FL 52+7/31 FLC 3/2 FAC 0+1 Others 2+2/1

MAYO Kerry
Born: Haywards Heath, 21 September 1977
Height: 5'10" **Weight:** 13.4
Club Honours: Div 3 '01; Div 2 '02

Kerry's career as a professional at Brighton finally came to an end after 12 years and a season in which he became only the eighth Albion player to pass 400 appearances. The burly left-back was dropped after defeat at Crewe on the opening day, making way first for Sam Rents and then the on-loan Matt Richards. However, with both Richards and Rents injured, Kerry returned to the starting line-up in March and held his place with some vintage performances until Richards recovered. In the final

game, Kerry went on for a last-minute cameo to say farewell to the Withdean crowd.

Brighton & Hove A (From trainee on 3/7/ 1996) FL 329+37/12 FLC 11+1 FAC 13+6/2 Others 9+4

MAYO Paul
Born: Lincoln, 13 October 1981
Height: 5'11" **Weight:** 11.9

Paul was recruited from Lincoln in the summer by then manager Steve Thompson to add more attacking options on the left for Notts County. As a strong-tackling left-back who likes to get forward and join his attack, he lacked consistency early on and was allowed to join Darlington on loan in January. With injury problems in defence, the Quakers needed him as cover and he enjoyed a good spell there, scoring on his debut against Bury at the Arena. When he returned to County towards the end of the season, he only made intermittent appearances and will be looking to put things right in 2008-09. He can also play on the left of midfield.

Lincoln C (From trainee on 6/4/2000) FL 92+14/6 FLC 4 FAC 5+1/1 Others 9/2
Watford (£100,000 on 8/3/2004) FL 25 FLC 2
Lincoln C (Free on 3/8/2005) FL 53+9/4 FLC 1+1 FAC 2/1 Others 1+2
Notts Co (Free on 3/7/2007) FL 27+2 FAC 2 Others 1
Darlington (Loaned on 8/1/2008) FL 7/1

MEARS Tyrone
Born: Stockport, 18 February 1983
Height: 5'11" **Weight:** 11.10

Signed from West Ham on a more permanent basis in the summer after his tremendous performance in the Wembley play-off final, Tyrone made a bright start in Derby's return to the Premiership, showing his pace and willingness to attack from right-back. Unfortunately, his form began to suffer as he battled against a shin injury that had troubled him on and off since his time with Preston. It was decided in January that surgery was the only answer and Tyrone was expected to miss the remainder of the season. His work in rehabilitation was so determined that he returned as a substitute by the end of March. A start against Aston Villa was an unhappy occasion, a 6-0 home defeat, but Tyrone was happy to be playing on the right of midfield and enjoyed a goal against his previous club, West Ham, as he continued in that position.

Manchester C (From juniors on 5/7/2000) FL 0+1
Preston NE (£175,000 on 10/7/2002) FL

50+20/4 FLC 2+2 FAC 5+2 Others 2
West Ham U (£1,000,000 + on 5/7/2006) PL 3+2 Others 1
Derby Co (£1,000,000 on 31/1/2007) P/FL 30+8/2 FAC 2 Others 3

MEDLEY Luke Anthony Cleve
Born: Greenwich, 21 June 1989
Height: 6'1" **Weight:** 13.5

The former Tottenham trainee made a sensational start with Bradford when he scored with his first touch in senior football. Luke came off the bench against Wrexham and had been on the pitch for less than two minutes when he lashed in a vicious drive from the side of the penalty area. A striker with height, skill and physical presence, he is expected to make the step up.

Bradford C (From trainee at Tottenham H on 2/7/2007) FL 1+8/2

MEITE Abdoulaye
Born: Paris, France, 6 October 1980
Height: 6'0" **Weight:** 12.12
International Honours: Ivory Coast: 20

Having enjoyed a successful first season, Abdoulaye again set out at the heart of Bolton's defence. He was a permanent fixture during the first half of the campaign, even notching his first Bolton goal in the UEFA Cup draw away to Macedonian team FK Rabotnicki Kometal. On returning from duty with the Ivory Coast in the African Cup of Nations, Abdoulaye found the solid defensive partnership of Gary Cahill and Andy O'Brien prevented him from regaining his place. Sporadic appearances followed until the much publicised disagreement with Gary Megson at half-time during the 2-0 defeat at Manchester United effectively put an end to his season.

Bolton W (£1,000,000 from Olympique Marseille, France, ex Red Star 93, on 10/8/ 2006) PL 56 FLC 4 FAC 3+1/1 Others 5+1/1

MELCHIOT Mario
Born: Amsterdam, Holland, 4 November 1976
Height: 6'2" **Weight:** 11.11
Club Honours: FLC '00; CS '00
International Honours: Holland: 22; U21-13; Yth

Currently the club captain at Wigan, Mario was recruited at the start of last season on a three-year deal from French side Rennes. He was one of Wigan's star performers, his attacking forays a feature of the team's style. He was encouraged to get forward and relished the freedom it gave him. His link with Antonio Valencia created countless chances down the right but he did not neglect his defensive duties, his strong tackling and sense of

anticipation make him one of the most reliable defenders in the top flight. A fans' favourite and a permanent fixture in the side when fit, he was voted by the young supporters 'JJ's Player of the Year'. Against Newcastle in December, he made the 200th Premier League appearance of his career.

Chelsea *(Free from Ajax, Holland on 5/7/1999) PL 117+13/4 FLC 9 FAC 14+2 Others 9+1/1*
Birmingham C *(Free on 19/7/2004) PL 55+2/2 FLC 3 FAC 7 (Freed during 2006 close season)*
Wigan Ath *(Free from Rennes, France on 5/7/2007) PL 31 FLC 1 FAC 1*

MELLBERG Erik **Olof**
Born: Gullspang, Sweden, 3 September 1977
Height: 6'1" **Weight:** 12.10
International Honours: Sweden: 85; U21

Olof is a powerful presence in the heart of Aston Villa's defence, his strong tackling and sense of anticipation making him one of the most reliable defenders in the Premier League and a permanent fixture when fit. Commanding in the air, Olof is predominantly a centre-back but spent most of the season at right-back. He missed only four games but was sent off, for the first time in his Villa career, at Portsmouth, for two bookable offences. It was Olof's final season at Villa Park and he signed a three-year contract with Juventus. He has been a virtually immovable presence in defence since

Mario Melchiot

he joined Villa in 2001 and made more than 250 starts in claret and blue while continuing to represent Sweden. This excellent player will be sorely missed.
Aston Villa *(£5,000,000 from Racing Santander, Spain, ex Degerfors, AIK Solna, on 25/7/2001) PL 231+1/8 FLC 17 FAC 9 Others 5*

MELLIGAN John **(JJ)** James
Born: Dublin, 11 February 1982
Height: 5'9" **Weight:** 11.4
Club Honours: Div 3 '04
International Honours: RoI: U21-1; Yth

JJ joined Leyton Orient during the summer on a free transfer from Cheltenham and was used mainly a right-winger. He can play equally well as an attacking midfielder, just behind the main strikers, and scored one of the goals of the season with his curling shot at Crewe, bent in at the near post to deceive the goalkeeper.
Wolverhampton W *(From trainee on 11/7/2000) FL 0+2*
Bournemouth *(Loaned on 30/11/2001) FL 7+1 FAC 1*
Kidderminster Hrs *(Loaned on 13/9/2002) FL 10/5 Others 2/2*
Kidderminster Hrs *(Loaned on 3/12/2002) FL 18+1/5 Others 1*
Kidderminster Hrs *(Loaned on 3/10/2003) FL 5/1 Others 1*
Doncaster Rov *(Loaned on 17/11/2003) FL 21/2*
Cheltenham T *(£25,000 on 13/7/2004) FL 101+13/15 FLC 4/1 FAC 9/1 Others 8/1*
Leyton Orient *(Free on 27/7/2007) FL 25+7/3 FLC 2 FAC 1+1 Others 2*

MELLOR Neil Andrew
Born: Sheffield, 4 November 1982
Height: 6'0" **Weight:** 13.7
Club Honours: FLC '03

Neil was on course to set a new Preston record for substitute appearances in a season until he started the final six games. Despite scoring 15 goals for the reserves, he was unable to transfer his undoubted scoring talents to the first team until a late run took him to double figures. Fast and a fine natural finisher, he had to convince himself that he had the necessary levels of fitness to complete a match. Five goals in the last six games showed Neil's capabilities and his partnership with Chris Brown promises great things.
Liverpool *(From trainee on 8/2/2002) PL 7+5/2 FLC 6/3 FAC 1+1 Others 1+1/1*
West Ham U *(Loaned on 7/8/2003) FL 8+8/2 FLC 1+1 FAC 0+3*
Wigan Ath *(Loaned on 19/1/2006) PL 3/1 FLC 1 FAC 1*
Preston NE *(Signed on 31/8/2006) FL 14+27/10 FLC 1 FAC 1+4/1*

MENDES Miguel **Pedro** Dasilva
Born: Guimaraes, Portugal, 26 February 1979
Height: 5'10" **Weight:** 12.4
Club Honours: FAC '08
International Honours: Portugal: 2; U21

Pedro, a player with tremendous natural ability and an excellent passer of the ball, found himself in a peripheral role for a large part of the season as the depth of Portsmouth's squad affected him as much as, if not more than, anyone else. A minor injury early in the season also restricted his appearances so that the bulk of his 18 Premier League games were in midwinter and spring as injuries to others and international calls depleted resources. Injured in mid-April, he returned to the team for the last Premier League game and retained his place in the FA Cup winning team. He is still highly popular with the fans, who will always remember the goal against Manchester City in 2005-06 that sparked Pompey's Premier League survival, but a move abroad in the summer appears to be on the cards.
Tottenham H *(£2,000,000 from FC Porto, ex Vitoria Guimaraes, on 16/7/2004) PL 25+5/1 FLC 2+2 FAC 2*
Portsmouth *(Signed on 12/1/2006) PL 53+5/5 FLC 3 FAC 6*

MEREDITH James Gregory
Born: Albury, New South Wales, Australia, 4 April 1988
Height: 6'1" **Weight:** 11.7

A young Australian left-back who can also play in midfield, James joined Shrewsbury from Sligo, having been freed by Derby last summer. He impressed manager Gary Peters in a reserves trial and was signed on a full-time contract, making his debut in February in the 2-1 home defeat by Hereford. His three appearances showed potential and he will look to develop further.
Derby Co *(From trainee on 19/7/2006. Freed on 31/7/2007)*
Chesterfield *(Loaned on 20/2/2007) FL 1*
Shrewsbury T *(Free from Sligo Rov on 18/1/2008) FL 3*

MERIDA Francisco **(Fran)**
Born: Barcelona, Spain, 4 March 1990
Height: 5'11" **Weight:** 13.0
International Honours: Spain: Yth

Fran has followed the same route to Arsenal that was previously trodden by Cesc Fabregas and if he goes anywhere near emulating his achievements in a Gunners' shirt, will be some player. A midfielder who, like Cesc, loves to control the centre ground with a fine range of passing, he has the ability to tackle and score goals in equal measure. He played

three times in the Carling Cup, along with five reserve games and one for the FA Academy League under-18 side.
Arsenal *(From trainee on 19/3/2007) FLC 0+3*

MICHALIK Lubomir (Lubo)
Born: Cadca, Slovakia, 13 August 1983
Height: 6'4" **Weight:** 13.0
International Honours: Slovakia: 4
Lubo made his first start of the season in Bolton's Carling Cup victory over Fulham and followed it with a League start in the December defeat by Liverpool. After the towering centre-half's chances were further limited by the signing of Gary Cahill, he was transferred to Leeds on the final day of the January window. Lubo had shone for Leeds the previous season, while on loan from the Trotters, and the United boss Dennis Wise had made several attempts to sign him before he left to become Newcastle's Executive Director of Football. The deal he set up still went through and Lubo played the remaining 17 games of the League One season under new boss Gary McAllister. Despite dropping down a couple of divisions he was in Slovakia's squad to face Iceland in Zilina in March, although he did not play.
Bolton W *(Signed from FC Senec, Slovakia, ex Cadca, on 31/1/2007) PL 8+3/1 FLC 1+1 FAC 1 Others 3*
Leeds U *(Loaned on 9/3/2007) FL 7/1*
Leeds U *(£500,000 on 31/1/2008) FL 17 Others 3*

[MIDO] AHMED HOSSAM Abdel Hamid
Born: Cairo, Egypt, 23 February 1983
Height: 6'0" **Weight:** 12.10
International Honours: Egypt: 44
In the summer, Tottenham's Egyptian international Mido was a wanted man. Birmingham and Sunderland were willing to pay the £6-million asking price but he could not agree personal terms with either club. Middlesbrough, going through a serious crisis with player injuries, joined the race and signed him on a four-year-deal in August. Mido was off to a great start when he scored on his debut against Fulham and also on his home debut against Newcastle but, in November, he suffered a stress fracture of the pubic bone that kept him out for more than three months. He was sent off in the 80th minute against Arsenal at the Emirates Stadium in March before being ruled out for the remainder of the season by a hernia operation on a long-standing injury.
Tottenham H *(Loaned from AS Roma, Italy, ex KAA Gent, Ajax, Celta Vigo, Olympique Marseille, on 26/1/2005) PL 4+5/2 FAC 0+2/1*

Tottenham H *(Loaned from AS Roma, Italy on 1/7/2005) PL 24+3/11*
Tottenham H *(£4,500,000 from AS Roma, Italy on 15/9/2006) PL 7+5/1 FLC 2+2/3 FAC 2+1/1 Others 2+2*
Middlesbrough *(£7,000,000 on 16/8/2007) PL 8+4/2 FLC 0+1 FAC 2+2*

MIFSUD Michael
Born: Pieta, Malta, 17 April 1981
Height: 5'5" **Weight:** 9.11
International Honours: Malta: 56
The diminutive Coventry striker made an instant impression and in early December led the Championship scorers with 13 League and Cup goals from 13 starts, including four braces, with both goals in the shock Carling Cup victory over Manchester United. Pace was his weapon and he caused palpitations for Championship defences, notably Stoke and West Bromwich. His finishing before Christmas was devastating but the goals dried up, especially in the League where he went 25 games without one before scoring in the final game at Charlton. He continued to score in the FA Cup, netting twice at Blackburn, winning the 'Player of the Round' award, and scoring against Millwall. In the home League game against West Bromwich, he was unfortunately sent off after ten minutes and was suspended for three games. Some argued that playing wide right was not helping him, others suggested that talk of a Premiership move - Wigan and Bolton were mentioned - was behind the slump. Big, tough defenders sometimes got the better of him but he was a breath of fresh air for the Sky Blues. In March Michael scored five for Malta against Liechtenstein, cementing his celebrity status on the island where he was voted 'Sports Personality of the Year'.
Coventry C *(Free from Lillestrom, Norway, ex Sliema W, Kaiserslautern, Sliema W, on 12/1/2007) FL 46+14/14 FLC 3/4 FAC 3/3*

MIKAELSSON Tobias Lars
Born: Ljungskile, Sweden, 17 November 1988
Height: 5'9" **Weight:** 12.3
After joining Port Vale on loan from Aston Villa in January, the tall striker made his debut as a substitute in a defeat at Swansea before starting the next five games. He scored plenty of goals for Villa reserves but found League football harder and took time to settle. He improved with each game, using his height to good effect, and although he did not score, was instrumental in helping the team to ten goals in his five starts. His best game was at Hartlepool when Vale stormed into a 2-0 lead but, after Tobias left the field

Michael Mifsud

with an ankle injury, folded to lose 3-2. The injury was bad enough to cut short his loan and he returned to Villa Park.
Aston Villa *(Signed from Ljungskile SK, Sweden on 18/11/2005)*
Port Vale *(Loaned on 18/1/2008) FL 5+1*

MIKEL Jon Obi
Born: Jos, Nigeria, 22 April 1987
Height: 5'11" **Weight:** 12.8
Club Honours: FLC '07
International Honours: Nigeria: 19
When Lassana Diarra left Chelsea, a vacancy arose in the midfield ranks for a 'young Claude Makelele' to be groomed and take the stage while the veteran French international rested his ageing legs. The precocious Jon Obi blossomed in a more deep-lying role and is fulfilling the earlier potential that saw Chelsea and Manchester United locked in a bitter struggle for his signature. He was virtually an automatic choice for the Premier League campaign while Makelele was saved for Champions' League ties. Jon Obi always seems to have an abundance

of time and space in the hurly-burly of midfield, the sign of a quality player. He stands out with his languid style, getting the ball under perfect control and knocking short, accurate passes to feet. The only blemishes on an excellent season were, as in his first campaign, two dismissals for tackles that were mistimed rather than malicious. Although he failed to score during the season, his positional sense in front of the back four allowed midfield colleagues to surge forward and notch plenty between them.

Chelsea *(£12,000,000 + from Lyn Oslo, Norway, via Manchester U, on 18/7/2006) PL 31+20 FLC 6+1 FAC 7+1/2 Others 8+7*

MILDENHALL Stephen (Steve) James
Born: Swindon, 13 May 1978
Height: 6'4" **Weight:** 14.0
The goalkeeper was ever-present at Yeovil in 2006-07 and was going well last season before suffering a serious knee injury in February. Out of action for a couple of months, Steve returned to feature as Yeovil battled their way clear of relegation, maintaining his consistent performances and giving individual moments of brilliance that added to his status as a fans' favourite. The towering 'keeper also deputised as captain when Terry Skiverton was unavailable.

Swindon T *(From trainee on 19/7/1996) FL 29+4 FLC 2 FAC 2 Others 1*
Notts Co *(£150,000 on 16/7/2001) FL 75+1 FLC 5/1 FAC 6 Others 3*
Oldham Ath *(Free on 1/12/2004) FL 6*
Grimsby T *(Free on 6/7/2005) FL 46 FLC 3 FAC 1 Others 4*
Yeovil T *(Free on 7/7/2006) FL 75 FLC 2 FAC 2 Others 6*

MILES (formerly PLUCK) Colin Ian
Born: Edmonton, 6 September 1978
Height: 6'0" **Weight:** 13.10
Club Honours: FAT '02; FC '03; Div 2 '05
Injuries ruined Colin's season as a left-sided defender with Port Vale. The only full 90 minutes he completed was in a 2-0 home defeat by Hartlepool. A strong tackler, equally at home at left-back or centre-half, ankle and calf injuries meant that he could never string games together. His final game was against Walsall on Boxing Day when he appeared as a 35th-minute substitute only to limp off ten minutes later. He made a few appearances for the reserves before the end of the season but he was released on a free transfer.

Watford *(From trainee on 13/2/1997) FL 1 Others 1*
Morton *(Free on 4/2/2000) SL 3+1 (Free to*

Stevenage Borough on 1/3/2000)
Yeovil T *(Free from Dover Ath, ex Hayes, on 30/7/2001) FL 74+13/4 FLC 1 FAC 9/3 Others 3*
Port Vale *(Free on 8/7/2006) FL 24+8 FLC 1+1 FAC 2+1 Others 1*

MILES John Francis
Born: Bootle, 28 September 1981
Height: 5'10" **Weight:** 12.9
Club Honours: Div 2 '08
Turning down the chance to follow Paul Ince to MK Dons, John joined Accrington from Macclesfield in the summer and played in the first eight League and Cup games, mainly on the right of midfield. After that he was in and out of the team, with most of his appearances as a substitute, until December when he had a run of five games. In January, he joined MK Dons on loan for the rest of the season, and made a number of telling contributions as the season came to its conclusion. John, who is neat and skilful on the ball, fitted into the team easily and although fairly unheralded when he arrived he certainly played his part in the late unbeaten run that brought the title to the Dons.

Liverpool *(From trainee on 27/4/1999)*
Stoke C *(Free on 28/3/2002) FL 0+1*
Crewe Alex *(Free on 16/8/2002) FL 0+5/1 FLC 1 FAC 2 Others 0+2*
Macclesfield T *(Signed on 27/3/2003) FL 75+47/21 FLC 4 FAC 3+3/1 Others 3+4*
Accrington Stanley *(Free on 16/7/2007) 12+4 FLC 1 FAC 0+1 Others 1*
MK Dons *(Loaned on 24/1/2008) FL 7+5*

MILLAR Christian Dale
Born: Stoke-on-Trent, 27 November 1989
Height: 5'11" **Weight:** 11.0
A member of Macclesfield's successful youth team, Christian made his League debut in January against Morecambe at the Moss Rose, when he replaced Jamie Tolley in the centre of midfield, and was denied a goal by the Morecambe 'keeper early in the second half. Christian's only other senior appearance came in the following match at Peterborough, a 90th-minute entry from the bench.

Macclesfield T *(Trainee) FL 0+2*

MILLER Adam Edward
Born: Hemel Hempstead, 19 February 1982
Height: 5'11" **Weight:** 11.6
Club Honours: FAT '07
Signed from Stevenage in January, having been on loan since November, Adam proved to be an enthusiastic midfield player who added greater mobility to that department of Gillingham's team. He is

much more suited to playing in a free role just behind the front two but struggled in the latter part of the season with a hernia problem.

Queens Park Rgrs *(£50,000 from Aldershot on 15/11/2004) FL 10+5 FLC 1*
Peterborough U *(Loaned on 23/9/2005) FL 2 (Free to Stevenage Borough on 23/1/2006)*
Gillingham *(Signed from Stevenage Borough on 22/11/2007) FL 26+2/3*

MILLER Ian Jonathan
Born: Colchester, 23 November 1983
Height: 6'2" **Weight:** 12.2
Ian returned to Darlington, initially on loan from Ipswich, at the beginning of the season and later signed permanently. He was used mainly as cover when either of the regular centre-backs, Steve Foster or Alan White, was out injured or suspended. Commanding in the air and a good reader of the game, showing great pace with his timely interceptions, he went on to make 18 starts and 11 substitute appearances, weighing in with three goals.

Ipswich T *(Signed from Bury T on 23/9/2006) FL 0+1*
Boston U *(Loaned on 3/11/2006) FL 12*
Darlington *(Loaned on 9/2/2007) FL 7/1*
Darlington *(Signed on 31/7/2007) FL 18+10/2 Others 0+1/1*

MILLER Ishmael Anthony
Born: Manchester, 5 March 1987
Height: 6'3" **Weight:** 14.0
Club Honours: Ch '08
Having initially signed on loan from Manchester City, Ishmael made a terrific start, scoring a wonder goal seven minutes into his West Bromwich debut as a substitute against Preston in August. He went on to form a lethal partnership with Kevin Phillips, netting nine times in 15 appearances before being sidelined with a knee injury, suffered against Wolverhampton in November. The 21-year-old powerhouse, who signed a permanent deal in January, duly regained full fitness and netted the first hat-trick of his career as Albion beat Bristol Rovers 5-1 to book a place in their 2008 FA Cup semi-final. A fortnight later Ishmael was named in England's under-21 squad with his Baggies' strike partner Luke Moore.

Manchester C *(From trainee on 9/3/2005) PL 3+14 FLC 0+1 FAC 0+2*
West Bromwich A *(Signed on 15/8/2007) FL 24+10/9 FLC 1/2 FAC 3+2/5*

MILLER Justin James
Born: Johannesburg, South Africa, 16 December 1980
Height: 6'0" **Weight:** 11.10
An attacking right-back, Justin began

last season with Port Vale after being signed from Leyton Orient in the summer and made his debut against Hartlepool, instantly becoming a regular. His foraging runs down the right offered an extra attacking option and he was dangerous in the air from free kicks. He scored his first goal with a trademark header in a 2-2 draw in the Johnstone's Paint Trophy, a game lost on penalties. As the team struggled, Justin was left out following a change of manager. His final game was in an unfamiliar left-back position in a 3-0 defeat at Millwall and in early April he was given a free transfer after reaching a settlement.

Ipswich T (From juniors on 26/11/1999)
Leyton Orient (Loaned on 13/9/2002) FL 13 FLC 1 FAC 2 Others 2
Leyton Orient (Free on 31/1/2003) FL 138+12/5 FLC 4 FAC 9+1/1 Others 3+1/1
Port Vale (Free on 30/7/2007) FL 12+2 FAC 1 Others 1/1

MILLER Kenneth (Kenny)

Born: Edinburgh, 23 December 1979
Height: 5'9" **Weight:** 10.9
Club Honours: SPD '07
International Honours: S: 37; B-1; U21-7

Having been signed from Glasgow Celtic on the final day of the August transfer window, Kenny's stunning goal on his debut against Newcastle last September, giving Derby their only victory of the Premiership season, was not the start of better times for club or player. As the Rams floundered ever deeper into trouble, Kenny, despite his apparently urgent running, found further goals elusive. Nobody started more games for Derby, so a final tally of four successful strikes in the Premiership was a disappointing return, although he seldom had much support. Kenny played an important part in Scotland's valiant bid to reach the European Championship finals and was widely expected to return to Glasgow Rangers.

Hibernian (Signed from Hutchison Vale BC on 22/5/1996) SL 29+16/12 SLC 1+2/1 SC 5/1
Stenhousemuir (Loaned on 25/11/1998) SL 11/8
Glasgow Rgrs (£2,000,000 on 16/7/2000) SL 12+18/8 SLC 1/1 SC 2+1/1 Others 3+2/1
Wolverhampton W (Loaned on 7/9/2001) FL 3+2/2
Wolverhampton W (£3,000,000 on 14/12/2001) P/FL 128+34/50 FLC 6+1/5 FAC 10+2/5 Others 3+2/1
Glasgow Celtic (Signed on 1/7/2006) SL 21+12/7 SLC 0+1 SC 2+2/1 Others 5+3/3
Derby Co (£2,250,000 on 31/8/2007) PL 30/4 FAC 3/2

MILLER Liam William Peter

Born: Cork, 13 February 1981
Height: 5'8" **Weight:** 10.6
Club Honours: SPD '04; Ch '07
International Honours: RoI: 18; U21-15

Liam found Sunderland's midfield congested last season and was by no means the first choice of Roy Keane, who made him available for transfer in February. He notched a spectacular last-minute equaliser at neighbours Middlesbrough in September and added to his tally of Republic of Ireland caps against Wales in November. However, he was sent off at Chelsea in December and despite a run of games at the turn of the year, was largely out of favour for the remainder of the campaign, making a brief return near the end. Liam has a good football brain, excellent stamina and the ability to deliver an incisive pass.

Glasgow Celtic (Signed from Ballincollig AFC on 28/10/1997) SL 13+13/2 SLC 1+1 SC 0+1 Others 5+10/3
Manchester U (Free on 13/7/2004) PL 3+6 FLC 3/2 FAC 2+2 Others 3+3
Leeds U (Loaned on 4/11/2005) FL 26+2/1 FAC 2 Others 3
Sunderland (Free on 31/8/2006) P/FL 40+14/3 FLC 1 FAC 1

MILLER Shaun Robert

Born: Alsager, 25 September 1987
Height: 5'10" **Weight:** 11.8

In his second season at senior level for Crewe, Shaun was yet another of their attacking options who was unable to hold down a regular place in 2007-08. Injuries have to some extent limited his availability and it is to be hoped that he can come back stronger to fulfil the hopes Crewe have for him as a front-line player.

Crewe Alex (From trainee on 3/7/2006) FL 7+15/4 FLC 1 FAC 0+1 Others 0+1

MILLER Thomas (Tommy) William

Born: Easington, 8 January 1979
Height: 6'1" **Weight:** 11.12

Tommy returned in the summer, after being released by Sunderland, to start a third spell in Ipswich's midfield. He took time to settle back in the side and had to wait until October for his first goal, a penalty against Preston. They are probably his favourite opponents because he also scored at Deepdale, making eight goals in nine appearances, none of which have brought defeat, against them. He is something of a dead-ball specialist, never having missed a penalty, and scored some vital goals from direct free kicks, notably in the 94th minute at Wolverhampton, when he curled his shot round the wall to earn his side a valuable point.

Hartlepool U (From trainee on 8/7/1997) FL 130+7/35 FLC 6/3 FAC 5/1 Others 12/5
Ipswich T (£800,000 + on 16/7/2001) P/FL 101+16/30 FLC 5+2/2 FAC 3+2/3 Others 7+3/2
Sunderland (Free on 2/7/2005) P/FL 30+3/3 FAC 2
Preston NE (Loaned on 14/11/2006) FL 4+3
Ipswich T (Free on 7/8/2007) FL 32+5/5 FLC 1

MILLS Daniel (Danny) John

Born: Norwich, 18 May 1977
Height: 5'11" **Weight:** 11.9
Club Honours: FLC '04
International Honours: E: 19; U21-14; Yth

As a former Charlton player, Danny went back to the Valley last August, on loan from Manchester City, as cover for injured right-back Yazz Moutaouakil. Thrown straight in against Crystal Palace at Selhurst Park, he was one of the best players in a 1-0 victory. The uncompromising right-back kept his place for the next 17 games, starting one as an emergency left-back, before serving a one-match ban after his fifth yellow card. He was sent off in the next game, at home to Hull, and it was decided not to take up the option of an extension until the end of the season. It was a pity because Danny added some steel to Charlton's defence. Paul Jewell hoped to add extrovert qualities to Derby's struggling team when he signed Robbie Savage and the on-loan Manchester City man in January. The former England full-back began promisingly but, in only his third game, suffered a knee injury that required surgery. With a strong chance that Danny would be out for the remainder of the season Derby wanted to cancel the loan but City declined, the Premiership upholding their stance.

Norwich C (From trainee on 1/11/1994) FL 46+20 FLC 3+2/1 FAC 2
Charlton Ath (£350,000 on 19/3/1998) P/FL 45/3 FLC 3 FAC 1 Others 2
Leeds U (£4,370,000 on 1/7/1999) PL 96+5/3 FLC 4/1 FAC 6+1 Others 27+2
Middlesbrough (Loaned on 22/8/2003) PL 28 FLC 7 FAC 2
Manchester C (Free on 13/7/2004) PL 47+4/1 FLC 2 FAC 1
Hull C (Loaned on 14/9/2006) FL 9
Charlton Ath (Loaned on 31/8/2007) FL 19
Derby Co (Loaned on 4/1/2008) PL 2 FAC 1

MILLS Matthew Claude

Born: Swindon, 14 July 1986
Height: 6'3" **Weight:** 12.12
International Honours: E: Yth

Matthew joined Doncaster on loan from Manchester City as a right-back or centre-

back and played in both positions for the club. He was injured in late November and returned to his parent club but was brought back by Rovers in January upon his return to fitness. Matthew was an excellent acquisition, as he proved in the play-off final at Wembley against Leeds.
Southampton *(From trainee on 16/7/2004)*
FL 3+1 FLC 2
Coventry C *(Loaned on 18/9/2004) FL 4 FLC 1*
Bournemouth *(Loaned on 21/2/2005) FL 12/3*
Manchester C *(£750,000 on 31/1/2006) PL 1+1*
Colchester U *(Loaned on 26/1/2007) FL 8+1*
Doncaster Rov *(Loaned on 14/8/2007) FL 29+5/3 FLC 1 Others 6*

MILLS Pablo Simeon Ishmael
Born: Birmingham, 27 May 1984
Height: 6'0" **Weight:** 11.6
International Honours: E: Yth
Pablo spent the early part of the season on loan to Crawley in the Blue Square Premier before returning to Rotherham with a refreshing attitude. The powerful player turned in a number of outstanding displays in midfield, although he had previously been regarded mainly as a defender. Pablo may well have netted more than his single goal but brilliant saves and the woodwork thwarted him a number of times.
Derby Co *(From trainee on 16/7/2002) FL 40+18 FLC 1 FAC 5 Others 0+1*
MK Dons *(Loaned on 31/8/2005) FL 16/1 Others 3/1*
Walsall *(Loaned on 10/2/2006) FL 14*
Rotherham U *(Free on 3/8/2006) FL 59+5/2 FLC 2 FAC 2 Others 1*

MILNER James Philip
Born: Leeds, 4 January 1986
Height: 5'9" **Weight:** 11.0
International Honours: E: U21-36; Yth
Winger James was one of the few successes in a difficult season for Newcastle, operating primarily on the right flank and occasionally on the left. Strong and difficult to shake off the ball, he uses his fine control to raid down the wing at pace and his good awareness enables him to deliver inviting crosses or subtle short passes. He scored Newcastle's 500th Premier League goal in the win over Spurs in October and was a regular in the team until a foot injury suffered at Liverpool in March ended his season early. James set a record for England under-21 caps when appearing against Montenegro in September. His wholehearted, skilful performances led to him collecting a string of supporters' branches 'Player of the Year' awards as well as being voted

the North-East 'Young Player of the Year' at the Prince's Trust Awards in October.
Leeds U *(From trainee on 12/2/2003) PL 28+20/5 FLC 1 FAC 1+4*
Swindon T *(Loaned on 4/9/2003) FL 6/2*
Newcastle U *(£3,600,000 on 7/7/2004) PL 70+22/6 FLC 5 FAC 5+3/2 Others 17+11/2*
Aston Villa *(Loaned on 31/8/2005) PL 27/1 FLC 3/2 FAC 3*

MILSOM Robert (Rob) Steven
Born: Redhill, 2 January 1987
Height: 5'10" **Weight:** 11.5
A tigerish left-footed midfield ball-winner, Rob joined Brentford on a month's loan from Fulham in February. Instantly recognisable with his ginger hair, he worked hard but struggled to impose himself in League Two. He can also play in defence.
Fulham *(From trainee on 7/12/2005)*
Brentford *(Loaned on 11/2/2008) FL 5+1*

MINTO-ST AIMIE Kieron Lloyd Junior
Born: Wembley, 4 May 1989
Height: 6'1" **Weight:** 13.0
The former youth-team prospect made just one appearance for Queens Park Rangers in 2007-08, in the Carling Cup defeat by Leyton Orient, before the club terminated his contract in January. Kieron, who had a loan spell at Oxford United earlier in the season, thought long and hard as to where he should kick-start

his career before signing permanently for Barnet. The form of Jason Puncheon and Albert Adomah on the wings limited Kieron's chances but, when called upon, he showed promise and next year could be important for him.
Queens Park Rgrs *(From trainee on 19/5/2007) FL 0+1*
Barnet *(Free on 31/1/2008) FL 5+5*

MIRFIN David Matthew
Born: Sheffield, 18 April 1985
Height: 6'2" **Weight:** 14.5
David, a commanding Huddersfield centre-half, started in his regular berth before a knee injury kept him out for four games. A great physical presence, he soon returned when fully fit, showing great strength, pace and linking well with other players. Usually a consistent performer, David found himself sacrificed as tactics dictated selection. Never one to let anyone down in a full-blooded tussle, his work was rewarded with a goal in the away defeat by Oldham. After a change of management, the reliable defender returned to the side on a more regular basis.
Huddersfield T *(From trainee on 6/12/2003) FL 141+20/9 FLC 4 FAC 6+2 Others 5+1/3*

MITCHELL Andrew (Andy) John
Born: Liverpool, 18 April 1990
Height: 5'8" **Weight:** 10.7

Pablo Mills

Yet another graduate from the Chester Academy, Andy was given his debut last March as substitute for Paul Rutherford at Darlington at the tender age of 17. A right-winger, he was given further substitute appearances by manager Simon Davies, who had been key to Andy's development through the youth system at the Deva Stadium. His confidence grew with each appearance and he will be looking to progress further after being awarded a professional contract in the summer.

Chester C (Trainee) FL 0+4

MITCHELL Scott Andrew
Born: Ely, 2 September 1985
Height: 5'11" **Weight:** 12.0
Scott signed on loan from Livingston in mid-season and showed fine form during his brief stay at Peterborough. A hard-working and industrious midfielder with good tackling skill, he also proved to be a neat user of the ball.
Ipswich T (From trainee on 5/3/2004) FL 0+2 FLC 1 FAC 1
Livingston (Signed on 1/8/2006) SL 41/4 SLC 3 SC 2 Others 2
Peterborough U (Signed on 24/1/2008) FL 1+4 FAC 0+1

MKANDAWIRE Tamika Paul
Born: Malawi, 28 May 1983
Height: 6'0" **Weight:** 12.3
Joining Leyton Orient during the summer on a free transfer from Hereford, Tamika proved to be a good quality centre-half who, while not the biggest, was excellent both in the air and on the ground. He also chipped in with his share of goals during the season.
West Bromwich A (From trainee on 18/5/2002)
Hereford U (Free on 14/7/2004) FL 39/2 FLC 2 FAC 4 Others 1
Leyton Orient (Free on 27/7/2007) FL 35/3 FLC 2 FAC 2 Others 1

MOHAMED Kaid
Born: Cardiff, 23 July 1984
Height: 5'11" **Weight:** 12.6
The pacy Welsh striker signed for Swindon in the summer following a successful trial, having been at Carmarthen. He made his debut as a late substitute in the opening game at Northampton and was introduced from the bench a couple of times before his first start in the Johnstone's Paint Trophy defeat by Cheltenham. His first League start was at Southend in December and his pace and direct style troubled the home defence. He put in another good performance on the left in the New Year's Day victory at Yeovil but his appearances

became limited to the bench after this, although a late run and shot nearly brought an FA Cup victory over Barnet. Kaid went on loan to Torquay in the Blue Square Premier and was released at the end of the season.
Swindon T (Signed from Carmarthen T, ex Cwmbran T, Llanelli, Carmarthen T, Cwmbran T, Llanelli, on 10/8/2007) FL 3+8 FAC 0+1 Others 1+1

MOKOENA Aaron Teboho
Born: Johannesburg, South Africa, 25 November 1980
Height: 6'2" **Weight:** 12.6
International Honours: South Africa: 57
Although seldom appreciated, Aaron held Mark Hughes' confidence for his ability to patrol in front of the back four and stop opponents creating problems for the defence. Often brought on by Blackburn to defend a lead, he was preferred before Christmas to Robbie Savage but lost his place when he went to the African Cup of Nations with South Africa and Steven Reid came into the side. Although he is not a natural on the ball, he attends to the basics, covers well and spots danger. His lack of involvement towards the end of the season raised speculation that he may leave Ewood Park.
Blackburn Rov (£300,000 from KRC Genk, Belgium on 4/1/2005) PL 46+37 FLC 3+4 FAC 13+1/1 Others 5+5

MOLONEY Brendon Anthony
Born: Killarney, 18 January 1989
Height: 6'1" **Weight:** 11.12
This Nottingham Forest right-back, who displays much class for one so young, was a surprise inclusion in the first two League games of last season before arriving at Chesterfield on loan in January to further his experience. He is also very confident and determined. Although he defends strongly he also likes to get forward and the highlight of his time at Chesterfield was his goal against Hereford, in front of the Sky cameras in January, when he crashed home a shot after a run from his own half. When his time was up at Saltergate, Brendon returned to the City Ground to continue learning his trade in the reserves.
Nottingham F (From trainee on 3/3/2006) FL 2+1
Chesterfield (Loaned on 11/1/2008) FL 8+1/1

MONCUR Thomas James
Born: Hackney, 23 September 1987
Height: 5'10" **Weight:** 12.8
Fulham centre-half Thomas made his League debut on loan for Bradford at Notts County and provided the long pass

for City's first goal. A quick and mobile defender, he can also operate at right-back where his pace is a real asset.
Fulham (From trainee on 30/9/2005)
Bradford C (Loaned on 29/1/2008) FL 6+1

MONK Garry Alan
Born: Bedford, 6 March 1979
Height: 6'0" **Weight:** 13.0
Club Honours: AMC '06; Div 1 '08
After missing nearly all the previous season with a knee injury, Garry returned to action at centre-back and produced a high level of consistency. He was an influential figure at the heart of the Swansea defence, giving a stable platform for players in front of him. A back injury on the training field in March saw the skipper sidelined for a dozen matches but he was able to savour the last home game against Leyton Orient, when promotion was already assured. Garry was one of five from Swansea in the PFA 'League One Team of the Season'.
Torquay U (Trainee) FL 4+1
Southampton (Signed on 23/5/1997) PL 9+2 FLC 1 FAC 0+1
Torquay U (Loaned on 25/9/1998) FL 6
Stockport Co (Loaned on 9/9/1999) FL 2 FLC 2
Oxford U (Loaned on 12/1/2001) FL 5
Sheffield Wed (Loaned on 13/12/2002) FL 15
Barnsley (Free on 21/11/2003) FL 14+3 FAC 4/1
Swansea C (Free on 2/7/2004) FL 101/2 FLC 3 FAC 7 Others 17/1

MONKHOUSE Andrew (Andy) William
Born: Leeds, 23 October 1980
Height: 6'1" **Weight:** 11.6
Andy is an attacking left-sided midfielder who made such a big impression at Hartlepool in 2006-07 as the club gained promotion that it was inevitable he would struggle to repeat his achievements. The season started badly with him serving a suspension and he was later out for long periods through injury. He showed glimpses of his best form but it was only towards the end of the season that he had a long unbroken run of first-team football.
Rotherham U (From trainee on 14/11/1998) FL 68+60/9 FLC 7/3 FAC 2+6 Others 3+1/1
Swindon T (Free on 24/7/2006) FL 9+1/2 Others 0+1
Hartlepool U (Signed on 23/11/2006) FL 47+4/9 FLC 0+1 FAC 0+2

MONTAGUE Ross
Born: Twickenham, 1 November 1988
Height: 6'0" **Weight:** 11.4
A young Brentford target-man, Ross started the season with loan spells

at Sutton in August and Welling the following month. Returning to Griffin Park, he had a run of games in December and January, impressing as Brentford's fortunes improved. He scored his first goal with a header against Chester but in February he suffered a back injury that kept him out for the rest of the season.
Brentford *(From trainee on 26/6/2007) FL 7+7/1*

MONTGOMERY Gary Stephen
Born: Leamington Spa, 8 October 1982
Height: 6'1" **Weight:** 13.8
Freed by Rotherham in the summer, Gary had an unfortunate start to his Grimsby debut against Bradford. Called from the bench on 90 minutes to replace dismissed goalkeeper Phil Barnes, he saved a free kick with his first touch only to concede a stoppage-time penalty for the equaliser. Given his full bow a week later at old club Rotherham, he proved a capable 'keeper when selected and was responsible for Town's first clean sheet of the campaign, at Barnet.
Coventry C *(From trainee on 31/1/2001) FL 8 FLC 1*
Kidderminster Hrs *(Loaned on 28/3/2002) FL 2*
Rotherham U *(Free on 14/7/2003) FL 33+2 FLC 0+1 FAC 1 Others 1*
Grimsby T *(Free on 5/7/2007) FL 4+1 FAC 2*

MONTGOMERY Nicholas (Nick) Anthony
Born: Leeds, 28 October 1981
Height: 5'9" **Weight:** 11.8
International Honours: S; B-1; U21-2
Having signed a contract extension until 2010 with Sheffield United, Nick suffered a season punctuated and ended early by injuries. He made a late start while recovering from the previous season's shoulder injury, followed by a hernia operation and a bout of pleurisy. He finally established himself in the side at the end of October and played with his usual energy and enthusiasm, tackling and harrying in midfield. Under new manager Bryan Robson, Nick played a more forward role than in the past but his final ball and finishing were not his strongest points. After playing through several games with a painful foot, examination revealed a broken bone so his season ended in January.
Sheffield U *(From trainee on 7/7/2000) P/FL 165+62/7 FLC 11+3/2 FAC 13+4*

MOONEY Thomas (Tommy) John
Born: Billingham, 11 August 1971
Height: 5'10" **Weight:** 12.6
Club Honours: Div 2 '98

On his arrival from Wycombe in the summer, Walsall became the battling striker's 12th League club and he belied his 36 years by playing in 40 games and scoring 13 goals. Tommy, who showed his experience by being able to hold the ball to bring team-mates into the game, was still going strong during the last month of the season when converting a penalty at Cheltenham and scoring an opportunist goal against Hartlepool. After being released by Walsall he seemed likely to move into Spanish football during the summer.
Aston Villa *(From trainee on 23/11/1989)*
Scarborough *(Free on 1/8/1990) FL 96+11/ 30 FLC 11+2/8 FAC 3 Others 6/2*
Southend U *(£100,000 on 12/7/1993) FL 9+5/5 FLC 1+1 Others 2+3*
Watford *(Signed on 17/3/1994) P/FL 221+29/60 FLC 22/3 FAC 11+1/2 Others 4*
Birmingham C *(Free on 1/7/2001) P/FL 29+5/13 FLC 1/2 FAC 1 Others 3*
Stoke C *(Loaned on 13/9/2002) FL 11+1/3*
Sheffield U *(Loaned on 17/1/2003) FL 2+1 FLC 0+1 FAC 2/1*
Derby Co *(Loaned on 19/3/2003) FL 7+1*
Swindon T *(Free on 21/7/2003) FL 41+4/19 FLC 0+1/1 FAC 1 Others 2*
Oxford U *(Free on 30/7/2004) FL 42/15 FLC 1 FAC 1 Others 1*
Wycombe W *(Free on 27/7/2005) FL 85+2/ 29 FLC 7/2 FAC 3 Others 4/1*
Walsall *(Free on 11/7/2007) FL 36/11 FLC 1 FAC 3/1*

MOORE Byron Curtis
Born: Stoke-on-Trent, 24 August 1988
Height: 6'0" **Weight:** 10.10
Byron came through Crewe's youth system to make his senior debut in the opening game of last season against Brighton. A hard-working front player, usually deployed on the left, he did well in his first campaign in League One and scored his first goal at Oldham in September.
Crewe Alex *(From trainee on 2/5/2007) FL 25+8/3 FLC 1 FAC 2*

MOORE Christopher (Chris)
Born: Hammersmith, 13 January 1980
Height: 5'9" **Weight:** 11.5
Club Honours: FC '07
International Honours: W: SP
Chris did not have the continuous run he hoped for in the Dagenham team. He was the fourth-choice striker and spent most of the time on the bench, going on for bit parts. He claimed the club's second League goal and had the personal satisfaction of scoring against Brentford, who released him in January 2007. The left-footed front man was also on the mark minutes from the end at Southend,

taking the Johnstone's Paint Trophy tie into a penalty shoot-out. Was out of contract in the summer.
Brentford *(Free from Dagenham & Redbridge, ex Northwood, on 12/7/2006) FL 8+8/2 FLC 1+1 FAC 0+1 Others 1*
Dagenham & Redbridge *(Free on 30/1/ 2007) FL 13+13/2 FLC 1 FAC 2 Others 1+2/1*

MOORE Darren Mark
Born: Birmingham, 22 April 1974
Height: 6'2" **Weight:** 15.6
International Honours: Jamaica: 3
Had more players matched Darren's integrity, Derby may not have been so hopelessly marooned at the foot of the Premiership at the end of 2007-08. Although a pillar of the previous season's promotion in the centre of defence, it is probable that he did not expect to figure so frequently in the top flight. Darren is physically imposing but there were times when he struggled against international strikers. He was not alone in a porous defence but, however games went, nobody could ever reproach him for lack of effort or concentration. Passing was never his strength and nobody expected him to be a playmaker. Putting the ball to safety was his priority and his genuine approach, along with his good works off the field, make him immensely popular within the club, who named him as their 'Player of the Year'.
Torquay U *(From trainee on 18/11/1992) FL 102+1/8 FLC 6 FAC 7/1 Others 8/2*
Doncaster Rov *(£62,500 on 19/7/1995) FL 76/7 FLC 4 FAC 1 Others 3/1*
Bradford C *(£310,000 + on 18/6/1997) P/FL 62/3 FLC 6/1 FAC 2*
Portsmouth *(£500,000 + on 15/11/1999) FL 58+1/2 FLC 5 FAC 2*
West Bromwich A *(£750,000 on 15/9/ 2001) P/FL 93+11/6 FLC 4 FAC 8*
Derby Co *(£500,000 on 26/1/2006) P/FL 71+9/3 FLC 2/1 FAC 4+1 Others 3/1*

MOORE Ian Ronald
Born: Birkenhead, 26 August 1976
Height: 5'11" **Weight:** 12.0
International Honours: E: U21-7; Yth
A much-travelled striker, Ian was signed from Leeds in the close season by Hartlepool manager Danny Wilson to strengthen his newly promoted League One side and he fitted in well, rediscovering his scoring boots when playing in attack alongside target-man Richie Barker. Ian requested a move to his native North-West after admitting that he was having difficulties with the amount of travelling involved and was transfer listed in mid-season. He signed for Tranmere, the club where he started his career and where his father Ronnie is manager, on

transfer deadline day, diverting from his journey to Oldham where he was due to undergo a medical. Speedy in attack, he is still able to get behind defences and found the net three times for the Birkenhead club, including a goal on a dream Rovers' debut at one of his previous clubs, Leeds.

Tranmere Rov *(From trainee on 6/7/1994)* FL 41+17/12 FLC 3+2/1 FAC 1+1 Others 0+1
Bradford C *(Loaned on 13/9/1996)* FL 6
Nottingham F *(£1,000,000 on 15/3/1997)* P/FL 3+12/1 FLC 0+2 FAC 1
West Ham U *(Loaned on 26/9/1997)* PL 0+1
Stockport Co *(£800,000 on 31/7/1998)* FL 83+10/20 FLC 8/2 FAC 3/1
Burnley *(£1,000,000 on 20/11/2000)* FL 170+22/37 FLC 6+1/1 FAC 17/12
Leeds U *(£50,000 + on 24/3/2005)* FL 20+39/2 FLC 3+2/3 FAC 1
Hartlepool U *(Free on 12/7/2007)* FL 22+2/6 FLC 2/1 FAC 2/1 Others 2/1
Tranmere Rov *(Free on 31/1/2008)* FL 17/3

MOORE Luke Isaac

Born: Birmingham, 13 February 1986
Height: 5'11" **Weight:** 11.13
Club Honours: FAYC '02
International Honours: E: U21-5; Yth
An exciting young striker with an incredible burst of pace, Luke struggled to get into the Aston Villa side following the emergence of Gabriel Agbonlahor. He then joined West Bromwich Albion, in February, on loan until the end of the season with a view to a permanent transfer. Signed by manager Tony Mowbray to add some sparkle to Albion's attack as the promotion race hotted up, he is a smart, fast, direct forward who made his Baggies' debut as a substitute against Hull soon after signing. On his return to the side after injury, he made his first start a month later but was sent off before half-time in the home game against Leicester that Albion eventually lost 4-1. Luke gained his fifth England under-21 cap while at the Hawthorns, against Poland in March.

Aston Villa *(From trainee on 13/2/2003)* PL 36+51/14 FLC 2+4/1 FAC 3+2
Wycombe W *(Loaned on 11/12/2003)* FL 6/4
West Bromwich A *(Loaned on 22/2/2008)* FL 3+7

MOORE Samuel (Sammy) Leslie

Born: Deal, 7 September 1987
Height: 5'8" **Weight:** 9.0
The diminutive, right-footed, wide midfielder joined Brentford at the start of the season on five-months loan from Ipswich. Sammy worked hard and always gave maximum effort as he played mostly on the right. In December he reverted to a substitute role before returning to Ipswich the following month, after which he was transferred to Blue Square Premier side Stevenage.

Ipswich T *(From trainee on 8/7/2006)* FL 0+1
Brentford *(Loaned on 25/7/2007)* FL 13+7/2 FLC 1 FAC 2 Others 1

MOORE Stefan

Born: Birmingham, 28 September 1983
Height: 5'10" **Weight:** 11.0
Club Honours: '02
International Honours: E: Yth
One of the casualties of the Queens Park Rangers' revolution, Stefan made just 12 appearances in 2007-08 before moving to Walsall in February, scoring only once. It was an important strike as it helped to earn Rangers secure a vital 1-1 home draw with Watford in September at a time when points were scarce. Although Stefan made an excellent start to his Walsall career by scoring the winning goal within a few minutes of his debut at Luton, he took some time to settle and will hope for better this coming season.

Aston Villa *(From trainee on 9/10/2000)* PL 9+13/2 FLC 2+3 FAC 0+1 Others 0+2
Chesterfield *(Loaned on 27/10/2001)* FL 1+1 Others 1
Millwall *(Loaned on 6/8/2004)* FL 3+3 Others 1
Leicester C *(Loaned on 11/3/2005)* FL 2+5
Queens Park Rgrs *(Free on 14/6/2005)* FL 19+20/3 FLC 2 FAC 0+1
Port Vale *(Loaned on 30/8/2006)* FL 6+2/1 FLC 0+1
Port Vale *(Loaned on 23/11/2006)* FL 2+2 FAC 1 Others 0+1
Walsall *(Free on 29/2/2008)* FL 3+2/1

MORGAN Christopher (Chris) Paul

Born: Barnsley, 9 November 1977
Height: 5'10" **Weight:** 12.9
Having signed an extension to his contract, the Sheffield United captain began last season as first choice but after about a dozen games he lost his place to the on-loan Gary Cahill. With Cahill's departure Chris returned but was injured in his first game and it was not until the end of January that he re-established himself. He then produced his usual solid and fearless performances, being very good in the air and solid in the tackle, with no-nonsense clearances when under pressure and an aerial threat in the opposition penalty area. His season ended early as a result of two sendings-off, both for two yellow cards.

Barnsley *(From trainee on 3/7/1996)* P/FL 182+3/7 FLC 14/1 FAC 9 Others 4
Sheffield U *(Free on 1/8/2003)* P/FL 155+6/9 FLC 9/1 FAC 10/1

MORGAN Craig

Born: St Asaph, 18 June 1985
Height: 6'1" **Weight:** 12.7
Club Honours: AMC '05
International Honours: W: 8; U21-12; Yth
At the age of 22, Craig broke into the Welsh team during the season on the back of some fine displays in the centre of Peterborough's defence. Once again he proved a formidable opponent for forwards, his tough tackling being more than a match for the majority of them. Craig has a fine left foot, is sound in the

Chris Morgan

air and a good organiser.
Wrexham (From trainee on 10/7/2003) FL
33+19/1 FLC 1/1 FAC 1+1 Others 9
MK Dons (Signed on 5/7/2005) FL 41+2 FLC
2 FAC 4 Others 2
Wrexham (Loaned on 16/10/2006) FL 1
Others 1
Peterborough U (Free on 23/11/2006) FL
63+1/3 FLC 1 FAC 6+1

MORGAN Dean Lance
Born: Enfield, 3 October 1983
Height: 5'11" **Weight:** 11.2
The influx of nine new players in 2007-08
left a question mark over Dean's future at
Luton. He did well enough in the reserves
to be named as a substitute and, after
his first appearance at Tranmere, played
in the next three games, in midfield or
attack, without completing a full 90
minutes. Having joined Southend on a
three-month loan in November Dean
was employed occasionally as a wide-left
player but more usually as an out-and-
out forward. Possessing an excellent
turn of pace, although sometimes letting
himself down with his first touch, his best
performance in a Southend shirt was in
his final match when he scored twice in
a 5-2 FA Cup victory over Dagenham. He
returned to Luton amid speculation of a
permanent move to Leeds, which did not
materialise, in time to be a substitute in
Mick Harford's first game as manager.
Harford selected him for the next game
at Bournemouth and was repaid with a
goal before Dean left for another loan
spell, this time at Crewe, in March. After
making his Crewe debut in the home
game against Port Vale and recording his
first goal at Gillingham, the season ended
as it began, with his future in doubt.
Colchester U (From trainee on 8/8/2001) FL
23+48/6 FLC 1 FAC 0+3 Others 1+1
Reading (Free on 28/11/2003) FL 13+18/3
FLC 0+1 FAC 1+2
Luton T (Free on 21/7/2005) FL 54+34/11
FLC 8+1/1 FAC 1+2 Others 0+1
Southend U (Loaned on 16/11/2007) FL
6+2 FAC 3/3
Crewe Alex (Loaned on 7/3/2008) FL 7+2/1

MORGAN Mark **Paul** Thomas
Born: Belfast, 23 October 1978
Height: 6'0" **Weight:** 11.5
International Honours: NI: U21-1
Recruited from Lincoln last summer
to play as the sweeper in Bury's back
five, Paul started the season well in
his favoured position. A back injury in
November sidelined him for three games
and although he returned as sweeper,
injury to Dave Challinor meant he moved
forward to centre-half. Having taken time
to fit into this a return to sweeper was

welcomed. Unfortunately, a combination
of a thigh strain and a hernia meant he
did not feature in the second half of the
season. His calmness and ability to read
a game were missed and Bury quickly
rejected an inquiry from Macclesfield
regarding Paul.
Preston NE (From trainee on 9/5/1997)
FLC 1
Lincoln C (Free on 17/7/2001) FL 203+9/2
FLC 6 FAC 5+1 Others 14
Bury (Free on 16/7/2007) FL 20 FLC 1 FAC 1

MORGAN Westley (Wes)
Nathan
Born: Nottingham, 21 January 1984
Height: 6'2" **Weight:** 14.0
Alongside Kelvin Wilson, Wes formed one
of the best central defensive partnerships
in League One, contributing to
Nottingham Forest's excellent defensive
record. Wes is a crowd favourite and
always starts the roars when he brings
the ball out of defence. He is the longest-
serving member of the City Ground
squad, with more than 200 appearances
since his debut in August 2003.
Nottingham F (Signed from Central
Midlands League side, Dunkirk, on 5/7/2002)
FL 181+17/6 FLC 11 FAC 14 Others 4+2/1
Kidderminster Hrs (Loaned on 27/2/2003)
FL 5/1

MORGAN-SMITH Amari
Aaron
Born: Wolverhampton, 3 April 1989
Height: 6'0" **Weight:** 13.6
Signed by Stockport after an innovative,
reality show-style week of trials held in
the summer, Amari was given a one-year
contract. The former Crewe youngster
played a number of reserve matches,
impressing in the Manchester Senior Cup,
and was rewarded with an appearance
off the bench against Brentford at the
end of the season but was not offered a
further contract.
Stockport Co (From trainee at Crewe Alex
on 31/8/2007) FL 0+1

MORLEY David (Dave)
Thomas
Born: St Helens, 25 September 1977
Height: 6'3" **Weight:** 13.8
Club Honours: Div 3 '04
Macclesfield's tall central defender missed
the start of last season following an
summer ankle operation. He returned for
the first round Johnstone's Paint Trophy
victory at Wrexham and scored a bullet
90th-minute header in the home League
win, also against Wrexham. Dave was
unable to force his way into the starting
line-up on a regular basis and his contract
was cancelled by mutual consent towards

the end of October. Soon afterwards, he
signed for Blue Square North side Hyde.
Manchester C (From trainee on 3/1/1996)
FL 1+2/1
Ayr U (Loaned on 14/3/1998) SL 4
Southend U (Signed on 28/8/1998) FL
63+13 FLC 6 FAC 0+2 Others 2
Carlisle U (Free on 26/1/2001) FL 37+4/1 FLC
1 FAC 1 Others 1
Oxford U (Free on 14/12/2001) FL 16+2/3
Doncaster Rov (Free on 5/7/2002) FL 24+6/
1 FLC 2 FAC 3 Others 3
Macclesfield T (£15,000 on 14/1/2005) FL
101+2/7 FLC 2 FAC 4 Others 11

MORRELL Andrew (Andy)
Jonathan
Born: Doncaster, 28 September 1974
Height: 5'11" **Weight:** 12.0
After finishing as Blackpool's top scorer
in 2006-07 with 20 goals Andy found
opportunities limited last season in the
Championship, spending much of the
second half of the campaign on the
substitutes' bench. Still as willing as ever
and persistent up front, he managed five
goals, most importantly a 90th-minute
equalizer in a 2-2 draw against Burnley.
Andy was offered a new contract at the
end of the season.
Wrexham (Free from Newcastle Blue Star on
18/12/1998) FL 76+34/40 FLC 3/1 FAC 1+2
Others 2+3/2
Coventry C (Free on 2/7/2003) FL 53+45/17
FLC 5+1/2 FAC 4+3
Blackpool (Signed on 16/8/2006) FL 57+21/
21 FLC 2+3 FAC 4+1/3 Others 3/1

MORRIS Glenn James
Born: Woolwich, 20 December 1983
Height: 6'0" **Weight:** 11.3
Glenn started the season at Leyton Orient
as reserve goalkeeper but regained his
place in the first team in the New Year.
An excellent shot-stopper who commands
his area positively, Glenn was out of
contract during the summer.
Leyton Orient (From trainee on 4/3/2003)
FL 85+2 FLC 3+1 FAC 3 Others 11

MORRIS Ian
Born: Dublin, 27 February 1987
Height: 6'0" **Weight:** 11.2
Club Honours: Div 1 '07
International Honours: RoI: U21-4
Republic of Ireland under-21 midfielder
Ian suffered a knee ligament injury
pre-season and did not win a place in
Scunthorpe's starting line-up until mid-
December but featured regularly during
the second half of the campaign. After
playing the previous season mainly as a
left-winger, Ian looked far more effective
in a central role, either in midfield or just
behind the strikers. A good passer of the

ball, he is building up a reputation for his long-range shooting, confirmed by a stunning 30-yard strike in the draw against Sheffield Wednesday in April.
Leeds U *(From trainee on 4/3/2005)*
Blackpool *(Loaned on 23/9/2005) FL 21+9/3 Others 1*
Scunthorpe U *(Signed on 31/8/2006) FL 38+15/6 FLC 1 FAC 3*

MORRIS Lee
Born: Blackpool, 30 April 1980
Height: 5'10" **Weight:** 11.2
International Honours: E: U21-1; Yth
Following his play-off heroics for Yeovil against Nottingham Forest in the previous campaign, Lee was regarded as one of Russell Slade's key players for 2007-08. Unfortunately, the striker's career was cruelly blighted by injuries yet again and his season started in the worst possible way when he tore cruciate knee ligaments after just two appearances. Released from his contract in March due to his injuries, Lee was planning to do his pre-season work under Nigel Clough at Burton.
Sheffield U *(From trainee on 24/12/1997) FL 14+12/6 FAC 1+5/2 Others 0+1*
Derby Co *(£1,800,000 + on 15/10/1999) P/FL 62+29/17 FLC 1+4/1 FAC 2+2*
Huddersfield T *(Loaned on 8/3/2001) FL 5/1*
Leicester C *(£120,000 on 2/2/2004) FL 2+8*
Yeovil T *(Free on 3/8/2006) FL 23+11/5 FLC 1+1 FAC 1 Others 3/1*

MORRISON Clinton Hubert
Born: Wandsworth, 14 May 1979
Height: 6'1" **Weight:** 11.2
International Honours: RoI: 36; U21-2
The Republic of Ireland international striker, now well into his second spell at Crystal Palace after signing from Birmingham, opened last season on 97 goals for the club. Although he added two more early on, he had to wait until November before scoring his 100th, but by the end of the campaign was leading scorer with 16 in the League. Clinton, now the fourth highest scorer in Palace history, had a mid-season spell of 11 goals in 13 games.
Crystal Palace *(From trainee on 29/3/1997) P/FL 141+16/62 FLC 16+3/9 FAC 4/1 Others 0+1*
Birmingham C *(£4,250,000 + on 3/8/2002) PL 56+31/14 FLC 2+1/1 FAC 6+1/1*
Crystal Palace *(£2,000,000 on 26/8/2005) FL 96+28/41 FLC 2+2 FAC 3+1 Others 3*

MORRISON James Clark
Born: Darlington, 25 May 1986
Height: 5'10" **Weight:** 10.5
Club Honours: FAYC '04; Ch '08

International Honours: S:1. E: Yth
James joined West Bromwich on a four-year contract and may soon see his price rise by a further £700,000, depending on appearances. His former club, Middlesbrough, are due 15 per cent of any sell-on fee but Albion have no desire to lose the talented wide man, who had a fine first season with the Baggies, scoring six goals and making several more for his strike colleagues. Possessing a powerful shot, he enjoyed shooting from distance but his workrate frequently earned praise from his manager.
Middlesbrough *(From trainee on 14/7/2003) PL 40+27/3 FLC 3+1/1 FAC 6+7/1 Others 11+3/3*
West Bromwich A *(£1,500,000 on 9/8/2007) FL 25+10/4 FLC 2 FAC 5+1/2*

MORRISON Sean Joseph
Born: Plymouth, 8 January 1991
Height: 6'4" **Weight:** 14.0
Sean made his Swindon debut as a first-half substitute in the late-season draw at Gillingham when still on a first-year youth contract. He quickly overcame any nerves and claimed an assist, heading on for Hasney Aljofree's late equaliser. The youngster proved this performance was no accident with a starring display in the last game of the season, against Millwall. A central defender with physical strength and presence, good in the air, composed on the ball and not afraid to tackle, Sean was offered a professional contract and looks to have a bright future.
Swindon T *(From trainee on 22/2/2008) FL 1+1*

MOSES Adrian (Adie) Paul
Born: Doncaster, 4 May 1975
Height: 5'10" **Weight:** 12.8
International Honours: E: U21-2
A number of injury problems restricted the Lincoln central defender's appearances to just 21 in 2007-08. Although he was unable to hold down a regular first-team place, Adie's experience during his second season at Sincil Bank will hopefully have proved vital to the younger members of the squad who were given their chance to impress by manager Peter Jackson. Adie was one of four players to be released at the end of the season.
Barnsley *(From juniors on 2/7/1993) P/FL 137+14/3 FLC 15+1 FAC 15*
Huddersfield T *(£225,000 on 20/12/2000) FL 63+6/1 FLC 1 FAC 2+1/1 Others 5*
Crewe Alex *(Free on 8/7/2003) FL 46+11 FLC 4 FAC 2*
Lincoln C *(Free on 19/7/2006) FL 42+8/1 FLC 2 FAC 3*

MOSES Victor
Born: Lagos, Nigeria, 12 December 1990
Height: 5'10" **Weight:** 11.12
International Honours: E: Yth
Victor is a highly-rated Crystal Palace youngster who continued to make rapid progress. A locally born player of Nigerian descent, he made his debut against Cardiff in November as a 72nd-minute substitute and scored his first Championship goal when hitting an equaliser at West Bromwich. He went on to make appearances in the League, FA Cup and both play-off games and scored two more goals, at Watford and at home to Burnley. A player who can perform to a good standard in any number of positions, he has been used so far at Palace wide on the left. Having played for England at under-16 and under-17 levels, his performances are being monitored by several Premiership scouts.
Crystal Palace *(From trainee on 27/12/2007) FL 9+4/3 FAC 0+1 Others 1+1*

MOSS Darren Michael
Born: Wrexham, 24 May 1981
Height: 5'10" **Weight:** 11.6
International Honours: W: U21-4; Yth
Darren, a right-back who can also play in midfield, signed for a second spell at Shrewsbury after being released by Crewe. A keen, hard-working competitor who likes to get forward, he is popular with the Shrewsbury faithful. Despite a pre-season injury, he played well on the opening day at Lincoln and had a significant hand in one of the four goals. Darren dipped in form as Shrewsbury struggled to find the right blend and was cast in a variety of roles but ended the season strongly in midfield, scoring a vital goal in the 3-0 defeat of Wrexham as points became important to secure League status.
Chester C *(From trainee on 14/7/1999) FL 33+9 FLC 1+1 FAC 4 Others 1*
Shrewsbury T *(Free on 24/7/2001) FL 84+13/10 FLC 1+1 FAC 4 Others 8/1*
Crewe Alex *(Free on 2/3/2005) FL 54+5/2 FLC 1 FAC 1 Others 2/1*
Shrewsbury T *(Free on 7/8/2007) FL 28+3/2 FLC 1 FAC 1 Others 1*

MOSS Neil Graham
Born: New Milton, 10 May 1975
Height: 6'2" **Weight:** 13.10
It was a highly frustrating campaign for the popular Bournemouth goalkeeper. Having been kept out of the side by on-loan Asmir Begovic at the start of the season, he then sustained a serious facial injury against MK Dons in the Johnstone's Paint Trophy. Recovering,

he found a place on the bench but then broke his wrist in the warm-up at Cheltenham in January and required an operation that sidelined him for the rest of the season.
Bournemouth *(From trainee on 29/1/1993)* FL 21+1 FLC 1 FAC 3+1 Others 2
Southampton *(£250,000 on 20/12/1995)* PL 22+2 FLC 2
Gillingham *(Loaned on 8/8/1997)* FL 10 FLC 2
Bournemouth *(Free on 13/9/2002)* FL 162 FLC 6 FAC 14 Others 11

MOSTTO Miguel Angel
Born: Ica, Peru, 11 November 1979
Height: 5'9" **Weight:** 12.0
International Honours: Peru: 10
Signed from Peruvian club Cienciano on a two-year contract last summer, Miguel made his Barnsley debut on the opening day. Although a prolific scorer in his native country, he struggled to come to terms with the English game. He has a good touch and can link up play but managed only one goal, a poacher's finish against Burnley. Miguel fell out of the picture with the arrival of Jon Macken and Danny Nardiello but remained in the Peruvian squad and returned to his native country in January, joining Coronel Bolognesi on loan until the end of the season.
Barnsley *(£400,000 from Ciencaino, Peru, ex Coronel Bolognesi, on 15/6/2007)* FL 7+7/1 FLC 2 FAC 1

MOUSINHO John
Born: Isleworth, 30 April 1986
Height: 6'1" **Weight:** 12.7
Brentford's midfield ball-winner started last season in the side and scored his first ever goals against Barnet and Dagenham before a knee injury in October caused him to miss 15 games. After two substitute appearances on his return, he suffered a thigh injury in February and was out for another five games. Once over that, John was a regular in the squad for the remainder of the campaign, impressing with his surging forward runs.
Brentford *(Free from Notre Dame University, USA on 7/10/2005)* FL 45+19/2 FLC 3 FAC 2 Others 2+1

MOUSSA-NYINZAPA Franck
Born: Brussels, Belgium, 24 July 1989
Height: 5'8" **Weight:** 10.8
International Honours: Belgium: Yth
Very highly rated at Roots Hall, the Belgian under-18 international became a fixture in the squad at Southend as a regular on the bench last season. He started some matches when suspensions or injuries hit and had a short starting

run in an unfamiliar position wide on the right. A skilful dribbler, strong in the tackle, with a good eye for the right pass, Franck has a bright future in midfield and was rewarded with an extended contract. Steve Tilson had no qualms about naming him to start the second leg of the play-off semi-final against Doncaster.
Southend U *(From trainee on 8/3/2007)* FL 8+13 FLC 2+1 FAC 1+1 Others 1

MOUTAOUAKIL Yassin (Yazz)
Born: Nice, France, 18 July 1986
Height: 5'11" **Weight:** 11.7
International Honours: France: U21-5; Yth
Arriving from Chateauroux in the summer, Yazz started 2007-08 as Charlton's first-choice right-back. Unfortunate to injure an ankle in only his third game, he was unable to regain his place because Danny Mills signed on loan. He was recalled at home against Plymouth, Mills switching to the left, but apart from a handful of substitute appearances he had to wait until January, when Mills had returned to Manchester City. After starting half a dozen games he lost his place to another loan signing, Greg Halford, and did not feature again. Good in the air and comfortable on the ball, Yazz crosses well and is exciting in full flight. He was sent off in a reserve game against Wycombe in April and the three-match ban rules him out of the 2008-09 opener.
Charlton Ath *(£400,000 from Chateauroux, France on 5/7/2007)* FL 7+3 FLC 2 FAC 2

MPENZA Emile
Born: Brussels, Belgium, 4 July 1978
Height: 5'10" **Weight:** 11.9
International Honours: Belgium: 54
Experienced Belgian international striker Emile joined Manchester City on loan in February 2007 until the end of the season. His efforts for City in the run-in at the end of that season were rewarded with a permanent contract, including an option to stay for a possible three years. He started last season brightly with three goals in his first nine appearances but a niggling injury limited his opportunities to shine and he was released in the summer.
Manchester C *(Signed from Al-Rayyan, Qatar, ex KV Kortrijk, Racing Excelsior Mouscron, Standard Liege, Schalke 04, Standard Liege, SV Hamburg, on 31/1/2007)* PL 17+8/5 FLC 1+1/1 FAC 1+1

MUAMBA Fabrice Ndala
Born: Kinshasa, DR Congo, 6 April 1988
Height: 6'1" **Weight:** 11.10
International Honours: E: U21-8; Yth

In his first full season at Premier League level after his loan from Arsenal to Birmingham was made permanent in the summer, Fabrice's energy and enthusiastic habit of breaking up play were highly impressive. A tall, long-legged frame made him a difficult opponent to avoid in midfield, although passing and composure came under severe scrutiny. Scored his first professional goal with a close-range volley at Portsmouth and expertly headed Blues' last goal of the campaign in the ill-fated 4-1 win over Blackburn. Earned an England under-21 call-up.
Arsenal *(From trainee on 8/4/2006)* FLC 2
Birmingham C *(£2,000,000 on 2/8/2006)* P/FL 67+4/2 FLC 3+1 FAC 4

MUGGLETON Carl David
Born: Leicester, 13 September 1968
Height: 6'2" **Weight:** 13.4
International Honours: E: U21-1
Now in the twilight of his career, Carl signed a new one-year contract to remain at Mansfield as cover for Jason White and also to coach the club's young goalkeepers. However, when White hit a bad spell Carl came back into the side and performed very well until he was afflicted by a groin injury in March and forced out for a couple of weeks. He is the oldest ever Stags' goalkeeper and their third oldest player of all time. Carl helped out as assistant manager following the managerial changes in March. Was released at the end of the campaign.
Leicester C *(From apprentice on 17/9/1986)* FL 46 FAC 3 Others 5
Chesterfield *(Loaned on 10/9/1987)* FL 17 Others 2
Blackpool *(Loaned on 1/2/1988)* FL 2
Hartlepool U *(Loaned on 28/10/1988)* FL 8 Others 2
Stockport Co *(Loaned on 1/3/1990)* FL 4
Stoke C *(Loaned on 13/8/1993)* FL 6 FLC 1 Others 2
Glasgow Celtic *(£150,000 on 11/1/1994)* SL 12 SC 1
Stoke C *(£150,000 on 21/7/1994)* FL 148+1 FLC 17 FAC 5 Others 6
Rotherham U *(Loaned on 1/11/1995)* FL 6 Others 1
Sheffield U *(Loaned on 28/3/1996)* FL 0+1
Mansfield T *(Loaned on 9/9/1999)* FL 9
Chesterfield *(Loaned on 9/12/1999)* FL 5
Cardiff C *(Loaned on 15/3/2001)* FL 6
Cheltenham T *(Free on 1/7/2001)* FL 7 FLC 1
Bradford C *(Loaned on 28/12/2001)* FL 4 FAC 1
Chesterfield *(Free on 9/7/2002)* FL 112 FLC 5 FAC 3 Others 4
Mansfield T *(Free on 3/8/2006)* FL 52 FLC 1 FAC 7 Others 2

MUIRHEAD Benjamin (Ben) Robinson
Born: Doncaster, 5 January 1983
Height: 5'9" **Weight:** 10.5
International Honours: E: Yth
Like Adam Le Fondre a successful loanee from the previous season, Ben joined Rochdale from Bradford in the summer. Unable to fully reproduce his earlier form, although initially first choice on the right-wing, he lost his place in mid-season with the emergence of Kallum Higginbotham. However, he returned to figure, at least on the bench, in almost all the games from the middle of January and became a Dale legend when he converted the final penalty in the shoot-out that settled the play-off semi-final against Darlington to take Rochdale to Wembley.
Manchester U *(From trainee on 7/1/2000)*
Bradford C *(Free on 6/3/2003) FL 70+42/4 FLC 3+1 FAC 4+2 Others 1+2*
Rochdale *(Loaned on 8/2/2007) FL 12/3*
Rochdale *(Free on 5/7/2007) FL 18+13 FLC 2 Others 0+3*

MULGREW Charles (Charlie) Patrick
Born: Glasgow, 6 March 1986
Height: 6'3" **Weight:** 13.1
International Honours: S: U21-10; Yth
At Wolverhampton in 2007-08, Charlie was restricted to Carling Cup appearances, either at left-back or in midfield, despite being a regular for the Scotland under-21 team, scoring against Finland in September and Lithuania in October. In order to get more games under his belt, Charlie went out on loan to Southend in the January transfer window. It was a vital time for Southend, with their regular left-back Steve Hammell leaving for Motherwell and Che Wilson a long-term injury victim. After an indifferent start, Charlie proved to be an outstanding acquisition once settled in the side, making up for a relative lack of agility with a good touch and excellent distribution. His set pieces were a major benefit and his vicious balls into the penalty box were hard to defend, while his goal from a free kick at Carlisle precipitated a rare success at Brunton Park in the run towards the play-offs.
Glasgow Celtic *(From juniors on 1/7/2005)*
Dundee U *(Loaned on 6/1/2006) SL 13/2 SC 1*
Wolverhampton W *(Signed on 25/8/2006) FL 5+1 FLC 2 Others 0+1*
Southend U *(Loaned on 31/1/2008) FL 18/1 Others 2*

MULLER Heinz
Born: Frankfurt, Germany, 30 May 1978
Height: 6'5" **Weight:** 15.4
International Honours: Germany; Yth

Barnsley brought Heinz from Lillestrom in August on a three-year contract and he made his debut in the Carling Cup win over Darlington five days later. From his first game until injury ruled him out, Heinz was an immense presence in goal. He is fine shot-stopper and, because of his size, good at dealing with crosses. The German saved more than his fair share of penalties but his season ended in late January when he damaged knee ligaments. Heinz became an even bigger hero then because he stayed on for an hour after suffering the injury and kept a clean sheet.
Barnsley *(Signed from Lillestrom, Norway, ex FSV Frankfurt, Hannover 96, Arminia Bielfeld, St Pauli, Jahn Regensburg, Odd Grenland, on 14/8/2007) FL 28 FLC 2 FAC 2*

MULLIGAN David (Dave) James
Born: Bootle, 24 March 1982
Height: 5'8" **Weight:** 9.13
Club Honours: Div 3 '04; Div 1 '07
International Honours: New Zealand: 16; Yth
Unable to hold down a first-team place at Scunthorpe in 2007-08, Dave was loaned to Grimsby a week or so into the season and had an unusual start to his time at Town, making his debut as a substitute against Shrewsbury before being replaced for tactical reasons 27 minutes later. The stocky, experienced full-back was a regular choice throughout his stay with the Mariners and provided an option at free kicks in attacking situations. Back at Glanford Park, and without a game, Dave joined Port Vale on a free transfer in January and made an impressive debut in a 3-1 home victory over Millwall. Dave's overlapping and dead-ball expertise added a new dimension to the Vale in what had become a struggling season. It is fair to say he struggled against nippy wingers, which is what he came up against at Swansea and Swindon, but overall his experience helped the Vale defence. He scored once, from a direct free kick in the final game at Southend. Towards the end of the season there was talk of him being offered a spell in New Zealand, for whom he plays his international football, after being released on a free transfer.
Barnsley *(From trainee on 18/10/2000) FL 59+6/1 FLC 1 FAC 3 Others 1*
Doncaster Rov *(Free on 16/2/2004) FL 63+14/4 FLC 2+2 FAC 3/2 Others 3+1*
Scunthorpe U *(Free on 2/8/2006) FL 20+4/1 FLC 2/1 FAC 0+1 Others 2*
Grimsby T *(Loaned on 30/8/2007) FL 4+2 Others 1*
Port Vale *(Free on 9/1/2008) FL 10+3/1*

MULLIGAN Gary Thomas
Born: Dublin, 23 April 1985
Height: 6'1" **Weight:** 12.3
International Honours: RoI: Yth
An old fashioned striker who leads the Gillingham line well, holding up the ball and bringing others into play, Gary has a great workrate and never gives up a cause as lost when he tries to close down defenders. A former Irish youth international, his ability to drag defenders out of position to make room for his team-mates does not go unnoticed, despite a shortage of goals.
Wolverhampton W *(From trainee on 9/7/2002) FL 0+1*
Rushden & Diamonds *(Loaned on 13/10/2004) FL 12+1/3*
Sheffield U *(Free on 6/7/2005) FLC 1+1*
Port Vale *(Loaned on 23/9/2005) FL 8+2/1 FAC 1 Others 1*
Gillingham *(Free on 31/1/2006) FL 62+19/13 FLC 1+1 FAC 2+1/1 Others 2+1/1*

MULLIN John Michael
Born: Bury, 11 August 1975
Height: 6'0" **Weight:** 11.10
John endured a frustrating season, making most of his appearances for Tranmere as a substitute. Although an operation in September on a long-standing ankle injury was a success, it also revealed significant ligament damage and the rehabilitation after this latter injury sidelined him until early December. Described by Rovers' boss Ronnie Moore as having a good engine, John prefers to operate in central midfield, but does relish any opportunity to push forward and can turn in a more than adequate performance as an emergency striker if required. Is out of contract at the end of the season.
Burnley *(From trainee on 18/8/1992) FL 7+11/2 FAC 2*
Sunderland *(£40,000 + on 12/8/1995) P/FL 23+12/4 FLC 5+1 FAC 2+1*
Preston NE *(Loaned on 13/2/1998) FL 4+3 Others 1*
Burnley *(Loaned on 26/3/1998) FL 6*
Burnley *(Free on 20/7/1999) FL 38+39/8 FLC 2+1 FAC 5+1/1 Others 1*
Rotherham U *(£150,000 on 5/10/2001) FL 159+21/12 FLC 7+1 FAC 5/2 Others 2*
Tranmere Rov *(Free on 27/6/2006) FL 43+7/5 FLC 1 FAC 1+2 Others 1+1*

MULLIN Paul Bernard
Born: Burnley, 16 March 1974
Height: 6'3" **Weight:** 14.6
Club Honours: FC '06
Paul was Accrington's top scorer for the seventh time in eight seasons, though his tally was not as high as usual, and was the 'Player of the Year' for the sixth

time in that period. Once again he was seldom absent. In fact he has missed only a dozen Unibond Premier, Conference and League games in eight years and in March became the first Stanley player ever to make 400 appearances. However, he is much more than just a scorer, as he tackles back, distributes well and is adept at bringing other players into the game. In January, he turned down the opportunity to move to Shrewsbury and instead signed an extension to his contract, to the relief of everyone at Stanley.
Accrington Stanley *(Signed from Radcliffe Borough, ex Accrington Stanley, Darwen, Trafford, Clitheroe, on 24/8/2000) FL 89/26 FLC 3/1 FAC 2/1 Others 3/1*

MULLINS Hayden Ian
Born: Reading, 27 March 1979
Height: 6'0" **Weight:** 11.12
International Honours: E: U21-3
Hayden became known as 'Mr Reliable', so steady was he in West Ham's midfield throughout the season. On countless occasions, he broke up opposing attacks with timely interventions and was superb when in possession, hardly misplacing a pass. Hayden is one of those players who does his job in a calm manner and is missed when not in the side.
Crystal Palace *(From trainee on 28/2/1997) FL 219+3/18 FLC 24/2 FAC 9 Others 2*
West Ham U *(£600,000 on 22/10/2003) P/FL 147+16/3 FLC 8 FAC 14+1/3 Others 6*

Paul Mullin

MULLINS John (Johnny) Christopher
Born: Hampstead, 6 November 1985
Height: 5'11" **Weight:** 12.7
Johnny began last season as a regular on the Mansfield bench, with Alex John-Baptiste being moved over from the centre to fill his regular right-back berth. However, through injury and suspensions to others he was soon back in the starting line-up, but more usually at right-back but occasionally filling in at centre-back and proving to be accomplished in either position. His consistent performances helped Johnny to win the fans' 'Player of the Year' award.
Reading *(From trainee on 17/12/2004)*
Kidderminster Hrs *(Loaned on 17/12/2004) FL 21/2*
Mansfield T *(Free on 5/6/2006) FL 81+5/4 FLC 3/1 FAC 5+1 Others 2*

MUNTARI Sulley Ali
Born: Konongo, Ghana, 27 August 1984
Height: 5'11" **Weight:** 12.7
Club Honours: FAC '08
International Honours: Ghana: 39
Sulley joined Portsmouth from Udinese for a club record fee at the end of May. A strong and powerful Ghanaian central midfielder, with formidable technique, he contributed greatly to Pompey's successful season, becoming a fixture in the side. He missed games only through suspension or being away on African Cup of Nations duty with Ghana. In that competition, he played in all their six matches, scoring three times, including the opening goal in a 4-2 win over the Ivory Coast in the third place final, and was voted an 'All-Star Player'. Domestically, he scored two excellent long-range left-footed goals in the 3-1 win at Aston Villa and the only goal of the game from the penalty spot when Pompey won at Old Trafford in the quarter-finals of the FA Cup.
Portsmouth *(£7,000,000 from Udinese, Italy on 6/7/2007) PL 27+2/4 FAC 4/1*

MURDOCK Colin James
Born: Ballymena, 2 July 1975
Height: 6'2" **Weight:** 13.0
Club Honours: Div 2 '00
International Honours: NI: 34; B-3; Yth
Released by Rotherham, the experienced central defender joined Shrewsbury after a pre-season trial. Colin is strong in the air, reads the game and is a cultured distributor. After a debut at left-back in the first game, the remainder of his 29 appearances were in central defence. In a difficult season, Colin was never able to form a settled partnership but his two goals included an important point-saver

at Wycombe. Always committed and a significant help to less experienced players, he performed well when points were vital to ensure League status but was released at the end of the season.
Manchester U *(From juniors on 21/7/1992)*
Preston NE *(£100,000 on 23/5/1997) FL 163+14/6 FLC 13+1 FAC 9+2 Others 10*
Hibernian *(Free on 17/1/2003) SL 37/3 SLC 6/1 SC 1 Others 1*
Crewe Alex *(Free on 31/1/2005) FL 15+1*
Rotherham U *(Free on 1/8/2005) FLC 1+1 FAC 1 Others 0+1*
Shrewsbury T *(Free on 3/8/2007) FL 29/2 FLC 1 FAC 1*

MURPHY Daniel (Danny) Benjamin
Born: Chester, 18 March 1977
Height: 5'10" **Weight:** 11.0
Club Honours: FLC '01, '03; FAC '01; UEFAC '01; ESC '01; CS '01
International Honours: E: 9; U21-5; Yth; Sch
Signed from Tottenham on the final day of the August transfer window, Danny was initially used as a squad player at Fulham until established as a first choice. A tenacious, ball-winning midfielder who harries opponents into conceding possession and often makes timely interceptions, he is an excellent passer of the ball with good positional awareness. This was displayed to devastating effect with an inch-perfect pass to set up Diomansy Kamara's last-minute goal at Manchester City, a team he scored against earlier in the season, with a perfectly-timed forward run. Danny's most important contribution came on the final day at Portsmouth, when his header from Jimmy Bullard's free kick proved to be the goal that kept Fulham in the Premiership. Never afraid to take responsibility, he netted twice from the penalty spot.
Crewe Alex *(From trainee on 21/3/1994) FL 110+24/27 FLC 7 FAC 7/4 Others 15+2/4*
Liverpool *(£1,500,000 + on 17/7/1997) PL 114+56/25 FLC 15+1/11 FAC 11+4/3 Others 38+10/5*
Crewe Alex *(Loaned on 12/2/1999) FL 16/1*
Charlton Ath *(£2,500,000 on 12/8/2004) PL 54+2/7 FLC 4+1/2 FAC 2+1/1*
Tottenham H *(£2,000,000 on 31/1/2006) PL 7+15/1 FLC 3 FAC 1 Others 2+1*
Fulham *(Signed on 31/8/2007) PL 28+5/5 FLC 1 FAC 1/1*

MURPHY Daryl
Born: Waterford, 15 March 1983
Height: 6'0" **Weight:** 12.13
Club Honours: Ch '07
International Honours: RoI: 8; U21-1
A left-sided striker who can operate on

the wing or through the middle, Daryl scored Sunderland's most memorable goal last season when he headed home a stoppage-time winner at the Stadium of Light against Middlesbrough to guarantee Sunderland's place in the Premier League. He scored an almost identical goal at Bolton a week later but into his own net, giving him a rare and almost certainly unique double of goals that kept two sides in the Premiership in successive weeks. Daryl netted Sunderland's undoubted 'Goal of the Season' in February when his raking 25-yarder found the back of Wigan's net. He continued to raise his tally of Republic of Ireland caps.
Luton T *(Signed from Southend U, Waterford on 14/11/2000. Freed on 18/4/2002)*
Sunderland *(£100,000 from Waterford U on 2/6/2005) P/FL 52+32/14 FLC 2+1 FAC 2+1*
Sheffield Wed *(Loaned on 24/11/2005) FL 4*

MURPHY David Paul
Born: Hartlepool, 1 March 1984
Height: 6'1" **Weight:** 12.3
International Honours: E: Yth
Brought in from Hibernian during the January window, David's cool, assured and steady performances at left-back for Birmingham impressed initially. A good user of the ball, who took up good defensive positions, and even when he came under intense pressure from some of the best wide men in the Premier League showed grit to dig in and give as good as he got. Scored his first Blues' goal with a speculative 25-yarder that stayed low against Blackburn on the final day of the season.
Middlesbrough *(From trainee on 20/7/2001) PL 4+9 FLC 2/1 FAC 0+1*
Barnsley *(Loaned on 12/3/2004) FL 10/2*
Hibernian *(Free on 29/7/2004) SL 107/4 SLC 9/1 SC 12/1 Others 6/1*
Birmingham C *(£1,500,000 on 18/1/2008) PL 14/1*

MURPHY John James
Born: St Helens, 18 October 1976
Height: 6'2" **Weight:** 14.0
Club Honours: AMC '02, '04
When John rejoined Chester from Macclesfield during the summer, he was returning to the club that gave him his League debut back in 1994. The big centre-forward was always the first name on the team sheet but never had the chance to form an effective partnership as a number of strikers were tried with varying degrees of success. A first-class professional, John is a handful

for any defender and his aerial ability helped create opportunities that often went begging. John finished the season as second-highest scorer at the Deva Stadium, behind Kevin Ellison, with nine goals, and his experience and knowledge benefited youngsters Chris Holroyd and Paul McManus.
Chester C *(From trainee on 6/7/1995) FL 65+38/20 FLC 7+3/1 FAC 1+2 Others 3+1*
Blackpool *(Signed on 6/8/1999) FL 229+23/83 FLC 9+2/5 FAC 16/5 Others 16+3/11*
Macclesfield T *(Free on 27/10/2006) FL 25+4/7 FAC 3/2*
Chester C *(Free on 2/7/2007) FL 39/9 Others 1*

MURPHY Joseph (Joe)
Born: Dublin, 21 August 1981
Height: 6'2" **Weight:** 13.6
Club Honours: Div 1 '07
International Honours: RoI; U21-14; Yth (UEFA-U16 '98)
Scunthorpe's first-choice goalkeeper had another good season between the posts despite his side's relegation from the Championship. A good shot-stopper and excellent kicker of the ball, his performances led to a recall for the full Republic of Ireland squad. Joe missed only one League game during the campaign, when he served a suspension following a red card in the draw at Coventry at the end of November.
Tranmere Rov *(From trainee on 5/7/1999) FL 61+2 FLC 8 FAC 3 Others 1*
West Bromwich A *(Signed on 17/7/2002) P/FL 3+2 FLC 1*
Walsall *(Loaned on 8/10/2004) FL 25 Others 2*
Sunderland *(Free on 11/8/2005)*
Walsall *(Loaned on 21/10/2005) FL 14 Others 2*
Scunthorpe U *(Free on 2/8/2006) FL 90 FLC 2 FAC 4 Others 2*

MURPHY Kieran Thomas
Born: Kingston, 21 December 1987
Height: 5'11" **Weight:** 11.0
International Honours: RoI: U21-2
Kieran made his League debut for MK Dons in the opening-day home defeat by Bury and also figured at Macclesfield in a tumultuous 3-3 draw. The arrival of Danny Swailes from Macclesfield then limited his opportunities and after being loaned to Blue Square Premier club Crawley in mid-November, he remained with them for the rest of the campaign, gaining experience both at right-back and in his preferred central defensive position. Was released in the summer.
MK Dons *(From trainee on 6/7/2006) FL 1+2 FLC 2 Others 1*

MURPHY Peter James
Born: Liverpool, 13 February 1990
Height: 6'0" **Weight:** 11.10
Peter is in his second season as a scholar at Accrington and usually plays at full-back, although he has appeared in several positions for the youth team. Last season he was a regular in the reserves and spent time in the Unibond League with Prescot Cables on work experience. He made his first-team debut in April at Wrexham, playing in the centre of defence and giving a very confident display. Peter has been offered professional terms for the coming season.
Accrington Stanley *(Trainee) FL 2*

MURPHY Peter Michael
Born: Dublin, 27 October 1980
Height: 5'11" **Weight:** 12.10
Club Honours: Div 2 '06
International Honours: RoI: 1; U21-2; Yth
Carlisle's longest serving player, Peter notched up his 300th senior appearance during last season. His best position is generally regarded as being in central defence, where his ability to read and control the game is seen to best advantage. Is an accomplished footballer who in the last close season became only the second player in the club's history, following Eric Welsh, to win a full international cap, when he made his debut for the Republic of Ireland. Though not a frequent goalscorer, he netted three times late in the campaign, illustrating his undoubted knack of being in the right place at the right time at both ends of the pitch.
Blackburn Rov *(From trainee on 15/7/1998)*
Halifax T *(Loaned on 26/10/2000) FL 18+3/1 FAC 1 Others 2*
Carlisle U *(Free on 10/8/2001) FL 221+14/10 FLC 5+1 FAC 10 Others 18/1*

MURRAY Adam David
Born: Birmingham, 30 September 1981
Height: 5'8" **Weight:** 10.10
Club Honours: Div 2 '06
International Honours: E: Yth
Adam partnered Terry Dunfield in the centre of Macclesfield's midfield during the first half of last season, when his workrate could not be faulted, but he was prone to unforced errors that often led to lost possession. At the beginning of January he informed the club that he could no longer give 100 per cent to the cause and did not wish to play at League Two level, resulting in his contract being cancelled. Adam immediately signed for Blue Square Premier side Oxford.
Derby Co *(From trainee on 7/10/1998) P/FL 25+31 FLC 3+1 FAC 4 (Free to Solihull*

Peter Murphy

Borough on 12/11/2003)
Mansfield T *(Loaned on 26/2/2002) FL 13/7*
Kidderminster Hrs *(Loaned on 29/8/2003)
FL 3*
Notts Co *(Free from Burton A on
27/11/2003) FL 1+2 FAC 0+1*
Kidderminster Hrs *(Free on 9/1/2004) FL
16+3/3*
Mansfield T *(Free on 7/7/2004) FL 27+5/5
FLC 1 FAC 1+1 Others 2*
Carlisle U *(Free on 27/3/2005) FL 29+8/1 FLC
1/1 Others 4/1*
Torquay U *(£10,000 on 31/8/2006) FL 21
FAC 3 Others 1*
Macclesfield T *(£17,500 on 10/1/2007) FL
30+4 FLC 1 FAC 1*

MURRAY Glenn
Born: Maryport, 25 September 1983
Height: 6'2" **Weight:** 12.7
Club Honours: Div 2 '06
Glenn made a slow start for Rochdale
after an exceptional scoring season in
2006-07 but Dale manager Keith Hill
kept faith in him. The striker regained top
form towards the end of the year and
scored six times in seven appearances. His
form was good enough for Brighton to
sign him in January, the largest sum paid
by the club for a player since 1981, and
Glenn quickly impressed the Withdean
faithful with two goals on his home
debut. Although giving a false impression
at times, he has beautiful balance, silky
ball control and is at home with the ball
on the ground or in the air. Drifting into
some great positions, he scored nine
goals for Albion to add to his Rochdale
total and the lanky forward looks set to
knock them in alongside the experienced
Nicky Forster in the years to come.
Carlisle U *(Free from Barrow on 17/12/2004)
FL 3+24/3 FLC 1 FAC 0+1 Others 1+6/1*
Stockport Co *(Loaned on 2/8/2006) FL 11/3*
Rochdale *(Signed on 20/10/2006) FL 50+4/
25 FLC 2/1 FAC 3 Others 1*
Brighton & Hove A *(£300,000 on 25/1/
2008) FL 20+1/9*

MURRAY Ian William
Born: Edinburgh, 20 March 1981
Height: 6'0" **Weight:** 10.11
International Honours: S: U21-15
The former Hibernian captain joined
Norwich on a free transfer from Glasgow
Rangers in August. A versatile player who
prefers to operate in central midfield, his
short stay at Carrow Road saw him used
more often as a left-back or in central
defence. An excellent reader of the game
and a competitive character on the field,
he did not figure in Glenn Roeder's plans
after a November defeat at Plymouth
and when the chance came to rejoin
Hibernian on a free transfer in January he

jumped at the opportunity.

Hibernian *(From juniors at Dundee U on 13/7/1999) SL 127+14/13 SLC 8/2 SC 13+2/2 Others 2*
Alloa Ath *(Loaned on 29/12/2000) SL 2*
Glasgow Rgrs *(Signed on 9/6/2005) SL 38+5 SLC 2 SC 3 Others 11+1*
Norwich C *(Signed on 23/8/2007) FL 8+1 FLC 2*

MURRAY Scott George
Born: Aberdeen, 26 May 1974
Height: 5'10" **Weight:** 11.0
Club Honours: AMC '03
International Honours: S: B-2
This popular Scottish winger did not have many starting opportunities for Bristol City last season, despite a superb 25-yard goal against Queens Park Rangers in the opening game. By putting away a rebound the following week at Blackpool, he prevented the Seasiders from notching up their 13th straight victory, when City's and Manchester United's record of 14 successive wins was coming under threat. Consolation of sorts for the effervescent Scott came by captaining City's reserves to a League and Cup double. He was offered a new one-year contract and no doubt his positive attitude in the dressing room contributed to that.
Aston Villa *(£35,000 from Fraserburgh on 16/3/1994) PL 4*
Bristol C *(£150,000 on 12/12/1997) FL 193+31/46 FLC 10+3 FAC 13+1/7 Others 18+2/8*
Reading *(£650,000 on 9/7/2003) FL 25+9/5 FLC 3+1 FAC 1*
Bristol C *(£500,000 on 25/3/2004) FL 91+36/28 FLC 6 FAC 7+2/2 Others 7+3/1*

MURTAGH Conall Francis
Born: Belfast, 29 June 1985
Height: 6'0" **Weight:** 11.11
After spells with Heart of Midlothian and Raith on loan, Conall began a university course in Manchester and played part-time with Connahs Quay and Rhyl in the Welsh Premier League. The midfield player, who is good on the ball, was spotted by Wrexham and joined them in summer, having a baptism of fire against Aston Villa at the Racecourse. Loaned to Droylsden in January, he returned in April to end the season in the first team. Conall remains at university and has another year on his Wrexham contract.
Heart of Midlothian *(Free from Crusaders, ex Ballymena U, on 1/7/2003. Freed on 31/5/2005)*
Raith Rov *(Loaned on 21/11/2005) SL 10+1/1*
Wrexham *(Free from Rhyl, ex Sligo Rov, Altrincham, Connah's Quay Nomads, on 18/7/2007) FL 3+1 FLC 1+1*

MURTY Graeme Stuart
Born: Saltburn, 13 November 1974
Height: 5'10" **Weight:** 11.10
Club Honours: Ch '06
International Honours: S: 4; B-1
Leaving the pitch at Derby with tears in his eyes signalled the end of Graeme's tenth and most difficult season at Reading. The club captain led his team with quiet dignity on and off the pitch but could not prevent relegation on the last day of the season, thus ending Royals' two-year sojourn in the Premiership. Graeme played in the majority of the games, leading his side in the right-back position, and although he is now considered a veteran by many commentators, his desire to overlap and support the attack has not dimmed. He trained with the Scotland squad but was not able to add to his international caps. A regular Monday morning spot on local radio, plus occasional appearances as a studio pundit on BBC's 'Match of the Day' programme could lead to a media career when football is no longer an option. Meanwhile, a well-deserved testimonial beckons in the new season.
York C *(From trainee on 23/3/1993) FL 106+11/7 FLC 10/2 FAC 5+1 Others 6+2*
Reading *(£700,000 on 10/7/1998) P/FL 295+11/2 FLC 9 FAC 14+1 Others 6+2*

MVUEMBA Makengo Arnold
Born: Alencon, France, 28 January 1985
Height: 5'7" **Weight:** 10.7
International Honours: France: U21
Arnold made his move from Rennes permanent in July but the depth of Portsmouth's squad again limited his opportunities. Although the French under-21 international midfielder started a Carling Cup tie in September he had to wait until January for his next appearance of any kind, an FA Cup tie at Ipswich followed by a Premier League game a week later. Cameo substitute appearances followed over the next few months until he played twice in the very late stages of the season. A very skilful player, it is nevertheless difficult to see him holding down a regular place in the months ahead.
Portsmouth *(Signed from Rennes, France on 16/1/2007) PL 4+11/1 FLC 1+1 FAC 1+1*

MYHILL Glyn (Bo) Oliver
Born: Modesto, California, USA, 9 November 1982
Height: 6'3" **Weight:** 14.6
International Honours: W: 1. E: Yth
Following an inauspicious start, Bo recovered to further enhance his already admirable reputation. Dropped for

a League game for the first time in four years as Hull's goalkeeper for the opener at Coventry, an unfortunate injury to his able deputy Matt Duke gave Bo the opportunity he required. He took it with both hands as the Tigers rose to their highest-ever final League position and won promotion through the Championship play-offs. He achieved two notable personal landmarks. At the relatively young age of 25, in the February match against Norwich Bo became only the ninth 'keeper to make 200 appearances for Hull. A month later, the American-born former England youth international made his full international debut for Wales against Luxembourg, alongside fellow Tiger Sam Ricketts. Bo's mother was born in Llangollen.
Aston Villa *(From trainee on 28/11/2000)*
Bradford C *(Loaned on 22/11/2002) FL 2*
Macclesfield T *(Loaned on 8/8/2003) FL 15 FLC 1*
Stockport Co *(Loaned on 22/11/2003) FL 2 Others 1*
Hull C *(£50,000 on 12/12/2003) FL 202 FLC 5 FAC 7 Others 4*

MYRIE-WILLIAMS Jennison
Born: Lambeth, 17 May 1988
Height: 5'11" **Weight:** 12.8
A wide player with pace, Jennison joined Cheltenham on loan from Bristol City shortly before the start of last season, spending three months at Whaddon Road operating either on the left of midfield or as a striker, and scoring in the 3-1 Johnstone's Paint Trophy win at Swindon. Cheltenham manager Keith Downing wanted to keep him for longer but was prevented from doing so by the regulations regarding loan players. Following that, the promising left-winger signed a one-month loan deal with Tranmere in November, which was eventually extended until the end of the season. A versatile player, who is also able to perform up front where his lightning pace can always trouble opposing defences, Jennison was openly happy to have regular football and contributed three goals to Tranmere's total, including a second-half screamer against Leeds at Elland Road.
Bristol C *(From trainee on 22/4/2006) FL 15+1/2 FLC 0+1 FAC 1+4 Others 3+1*
Cheltenham T *(Loaned on 10/8/2007) FL 7+5 Others 1/1*
Tranmere Rov *(Loaned on 28/11/2007) FL 21+4/3 FAC 1*

N

NAFTI Mehdi
Born: Toulouse, France, 28 November 1978
Height: 5'9" **Weight:** 11.3
International Honours: Tunisia: 41
Mehdi played some of the best football of his Birmingham career, bringing his experience and neat and tidy use of possession to the table. He worked well alongside Fabrice Muamba in the centre of the park and was also an important and popular influence in the dressing room, due to his humour and linguistic skills. His highlight came when he turned the home game against Fulham as a second-half substitute, when Blues were trailing, through his tackling, urgency and determination to drive the team forward.
Birmingham C (£1,000,000 + from Racing Santander, Spain, ex Toulouse, on 31/1/2005) P/FL 45+24 FLC 2 FAC 0+1

NALIS Lilian Bernard Pierre
Born: Paris, France, 29 September 1971
Height: 6'1" **Weight:** 13.3
Lilian is a cultured Plymouth central midfielder with a great workrate. He is strong in the tackle and good in the air, very rarely giving the ball away, and makes simple but effective passes. Blessed with great experience and positional sense, the popular Frenchman was honoured to be given the captaincy when Barry Hayles left. He scored a solitary goal, against Burnley at Home Park in February. Was released at the end of his contract and given a great reception by Home Park fans after the final home game.
Leicester C (Free from Chievo, Italy, ex SM Caen, Laval, Guingamp, Le Havre, Bastia, on 16/7/2003) P/FL 43+16/6 FLC 2 FAC 1+4
Sheffield U (Free on 6/7/2005) FL 3+1 FLC 1 FAC 1
Coventry C (Loaned on 14/10/2005) FL 5+1/2
Plymouth Arg (Free on 13/1/2006) FL 94+8/6 FLC 2 FAC 7

[NANI] ALMEIDA DA CUNHA Luis Carlos
Born: Praia, Cape Verde, 17 November 1986
Height: 5'9" **Weight:** 10.7
Club Honours: CS '07; PL '08; UEFACL '08
International Honours: Portugal: 16; U21-10
A superb young Manchester United winger with an abundance of skills, Nani made his debut in the Community Shield against Chelsea at Wembley.

Mehdi Nafti

Easing into Premiership action at home to Reading in August, he scored his first goal, a 30-yard winner, against Tottenham and celebrated with his trademark somersault. After setting up crucial Premiership goals for Louis Saha and Nemanja Vidic against Sunderland and Everton respectively, he returned to face his previous club, Sporting Lisbon, in a Champions' League qualifier in September. His Portuguese team-mate Ronaldo stole the limelight by scoring the only goal but Nani set up Wayne Rooney to score against AS Roma in the second match of the group. He was on target in the 4-1 drubbing of Middlesborough at Old Trafford and his reputation as scorer and provider was further enhanced when he netted one and had a hand in three others in the 4-0 FA Cup victory over Arsenal. His other goal arrived in March, the last in the 3-0 defeat of Liverpool at Old Trafford only five minutes after entering as a substitute. Sent off against West Ham in the last home Premiership game, Nani scored one of the penalties in the Champions' League final shoot-out as United lifted the trophy for the third time.
Manchester U (£15,000,000 from Sporting Lisbon, Portugal on 3/7/2007) PL 16+10/3 FLC 1 FAC 2/1 Others 7+5

NARDIELLO Daniel (Danny) Antony
Born: Coventry, 22 October 1982
Height: 5'11" **Weight:** 11.4
International Honours: W: 3; E: Yth; Sch
A John Gregory signing who barely had

a chance to flourish before being moved on, Danny made his Queens Park Rangers' debut at Bristol City on the opening day of 2007-08 but failed to find the net in his eight appearances. After he had left for Rangers at the start of the season, it was a major surprise when Danny rejoined Barnsley, on loan to the end of the campaign, in January. He started again in the FA Cup tie at Southend, made a number of starts and, at his best, was a real handful as his performance and goal against West Bromwich showed. As the season came to its conclusion, he was on the bench too often for his liking.
Manchester U (From trainee on 1/11/1999) FLC 1+2 Others 0+1
Swansea C (Loaned on 24/10/2003) FL 3+1 Others 1/1
Barnsley (Loaned on 27/1/2004) FL 14+2/7
Barnsley (Free on 16/7/2004) FL 41+51/21 FLC 1+2 FAC 2+3 Others 4+1/3
Queens Park Rgrs (Free on 3/8/2007) FL 4+4
Barnsley (Loaned on 24/1/2008) FL 8+3/1 FAC 2

NASH Carlo James
Born: Bolton, 13 September 1973
Height: 6'5" **Weight:** 14.1
Club Honours: Div 1 '02
Manager Tony Pulis needed an experienced goalkeeper to keep Steve Simonsen on his toes for the last stage of Stoke's season and turned to Wigan to sign Carlo on loan. Playing in the last ten matches on the way to promotion he did more than press Simonsen. He is a good shot-stopper, gathers crosses cleanly and has the agility to pull out important saves. Carlo did not appear for Wigan in 2007-08.
Crystal Palace (£35,000 from Clitheroe on 16/7/1996) FL 21 FLC 1 Others 3
Stockport Co (Free on 7/6/1998) FL 89 FLC 5 FAC 4
Manchester C (£100,000 on 12/1/2001) P/FL 37+1 FLC 2 FAC 1
Middlesbrough (£150,000 on 14/8/2003) PL 3 FLC 2
Preston NE (£175,000 on 24/3/2005) FL 82 FLC 2 FAC 5 Others 5
Wigan Ath (£300,000 on 28/6/2007)
Stoke C (Loaned on 4/3/2008) FL 10

NAVARRO Alan Edward
Born: Liverpool, 31 May 1981
Height: 5'9" **Weight:** 12.6
Club Honours: AMC '08; Div 2 '08
Alan was not known to many MK Dons' supporters when he arrived before the season on a free transfer from Macclesfield, despite more then 100 League games to his credit, and missed the first few games through injury. Once

in the team, there he stayed, showing great consistency in anchoring midfield. A strong tackler who distributes the ball simply but effectively, he was rarely caught out of position and although not a prolific scorer, took great delight in netting one of the goals in the win at Stockport that guaranteed the Dons promotion back into League One.
Liverpool (From trainee on 27/4/1999)
Crewe Alex (Loaned on 22/3/2001) FL 5+3/1
Crewe Alex (Loaned on 9/8/2001) FL 7 FLC 2
Tranmere Rov (£225,000 on 9/11/2001) FL 35+10/1 FAC 4+2/1 Others 0+1 (Freed on 13/5/2005)
Chester C (Loaned on 20/8/2004) FL 3 FLC 1
Macclesfield T (Loaned on 16/12/2004) FL 11/1
Macclesfield T (Free from Accrington Stanley on 11/10/2005) FL 55+4/2 FLC 1 FAC 6 Others 5
MK Dons (Free on 10/8/2007) FL 38+1/3 FLC 2 FAC 1 Others 5

NAYLOR Richard Alan
Born: Leeds, 28 February 1977
Height: 6'1" **Weight:** 13.7
It was another season in which injuries curtailed Richard's appearances for Ipswich, restricting him to a mere six starts in February and March. Prior to that he needed surgery for a cartilage problem and when he was just about ready to return, sustained a slipped disc in his neck. The neck problem recurred in March and ended his season.
Ipswich T (From trainee on 10/7/1995) P/FL 212+89/37 FLC 11+10/1 FAC 8+6/1 Others 7+6/1
Millwall (Loaned on 29/1/2002) FL 2+1
Barnsley (Loaned on 4/3/2002) FL 7+1

NAYSMITH Gary Andrew
Born: Edinburgh, 16 November 1978
Height: 5'7" **Weight:** 11.8
Club Honours: SC '98
International Honours: S: 40; B-1; U21-22; Sch
Signed by new manager Bryan Robson from Everton in the summer on a three-year deal, Gary was a regular in the Sheffield United side throughout last season, being captain in the absence of Chris Morgan, and continuing to gain caps for Scotland. Playing as a left wing-back, he concentrated on his defensive duties, being good in the tackle and using his experience and anticipation to compensate for a lack of pace. He produced a series of solid performances at right-back and, if anything, improved towards the end of the season.

Heart of Midlothian (Signed from Whitehill Welfare on 17/6/1996) SL 92+5/3 SLC 5/1 SC 10 Others 7/1
Everton (£1,750,000 on 20/10/2000) PL 113+21/6 FLC 6+1/1 FAC 11+3
Sheffield U (£1,000,000 on 10/7/2007) FL 38 FLC 2 FAC 3

N'DOUR Alassane
Born: Dakar, Senegal, 12 December 1981
Height: 6'2" **Weight:** 11.7
International Honours: Senegal
Brought in on loan from FC Troyes in the close season, Alassane, who played for Senegal in the 2002 World Cup finals, netted in his full Walsall debut against Tranmere at the beginning of April but made only two more appearances in midfield before going home.
West Bromwich A (Loaned from St Etienne, France on 2/9/2003) FL 2 FLC 1
Walsall (Loaned from Troyes, France on 8/2/2008) FL 3+6/1

N'DUMBU-NSUNGU Guylain (Guy)
Born: Kinshasa, DR Congo, 26 December 1982
Height: 6'1" **Weight:** 12.8
International Honours: DR Congo: U21
The striker joined Bradford on loan from Gillingham for the first half of the season and scored on his debut against Macclesfield, when he followed up a saved penalty. Guy scored six goals for the Yorkshire club, including two in his best game at Hereford. The popular Congolese striker made a surprise return to Darlington, the club he served for the latter part of 2005, when he re-signed in January and picked up where he had left off, scoring in his first two starts. Guy is strong in the air, with clever footwork in and around the box, but unfortunately a couple of niggling injuries limited his contribution. Even so, he maintained his impressive record of almost a goal a game, measured by his starts in two spells for the Quakers. Was released at the end of the campaign.
Sheffield Wed (Signed from Amiens, France on 9/9/2003) FL 24+11/10 FLC 0+1 FAC 1+1/1 Others 5+1
Preston NE (Loaned on 28/9/2004) FL 4+2
Colchester U (Free on 20/1/2005) FL 2+6/1 FAC 0+1
Darlington (Free on 4/8/2005) FL 11+10/10 FAC 0+1 Others 1/1
Cardiff C (Free on 9/1/2006) FL 4+7
Gillingham (Free on 26/7/2006) FL 14+18/3 FLC 1 FAC 0+2/2 Others 1
Bradford C (Loaned on 9/8/2007) FL 17+1/6 FLC 0+1 FAC 2
Darlington (Free on 29/1/2008) FL 4+4/3 Others 0+2

NEAL Lewis Ryan
Born: Leicester, 14 July 1981
Height: 6'0" **Weight:** 11.2
Despite starting only nine games and appearing as a substitute in nine others, Lewis was rewarded with a 12-month contract extension by Preston. Predominantly left-footed, the winger remains a fans' favourite despite his lack of opportunities and his free-ranging style was seen to good effect in the reserves. A good crosser with a powerful shot, he has the ability to beat his man on either side, although he can over-elaborate at times. Both his goals came after leaving the bench, with his first touch against Hull and a last-minute winner at Southampton.
Stoke C (From juniors on 17/7/1998) FL 29+41/2 FLC 2+1 FAC 3+3 Others 1+2/1
Preston NE (Signed on 3/8/2005) FL 24+41/5 FLC 1 FAC 5+2

NEILL Lucas Edward
Born: Sydney, Australia, 9 March 1978
Height: 6'1" **Weight:** 12.0
Club Honours: Div 2 '01
International Honours: Australia: 41; U23-12; Yth
The West Ham captain led by example as he rallied the team and, due to the many injuries, had to play in all positions in the back four. Lucas was consistent throughout the season and in top form against Derby and Tottenham in November. A strong tackler and good in the air, he always looked for ways to go forward with runs down the right flank. He remains a regular in the Australian team and was with them for the World Cup qualifying matches in June.
Millwall (Free from Australian Academy of Sport on 13/11/1995) FL 124+28/13 FLC 6+1 FAC 4 Others 11+1
Blackburn Rov (£1,000,000 on 7/9/2001) PL 184+4/5 FLC 12/1 FAC 17/1 Others 10/1
West Ham U (£1,500,000 on 23/1/2007) PL 45 FLC 4 FAC 3

NELSEN Ryan William
Born: Christchurch, New Zealand, 18 October 1977
Height: 6'1" **Weight:** 14.0
International Honours: New Zealand: 34
Ryan returned to action with Blackburn after undergoing surgery to cure a hamstring injury. However, he was seriously affected by problems with scar tissue and twice had sustained spells of absence so that it could settle down. By the end of the season he was playing better and admitted that he probably should have remained out of action longer after the operation. The problem

Lucas Neill

limited his ability to accelerate from a standing start and he was caught flat-footed several times in the first half of the season. Still there is his inherent toughness, competitive ability and perception of danger that sees him in the right place in the penalty area to clear dangerous crosses.

Blackburn Rov *(Free from DC United, USA on 10/1/2005) PL 80 FLC 7 FAC 9+2 Others 7*

NELSON Michael John
Born: Gateshead, 28 March 1980
Height: 6'2" **Weight:** 13.12
Hartlepool's dependable central defender enjoyed another successful season. He was again one of Pool's key players and missed few games. Unfortunately, circumstances dictated that he had to play with a number of different partners in central defence, which at times led to misunderstandings. He always gives 100 per cent and has made over 200 League appearances for Hartlepool in five seasons.

Bury *(Free from Bishop Auckland on 22/3/2001) FL 68+4/8 FLC 4 FAC 3 Others 5*
Hartlepool U *(£70,000 on 10/7/2003) FL 209+4/9 FLC 10 FAC 15/1 Others 13*

NELSON Stuart James
Born: Stroud, 17 September 1981
Height: 6'1" **Weight:** 12.12
Stuart joined Leyton Orient on a free transfer from Brentford in the summer and started last season as first-choice goalkeeper before losing his place in the New Year to Glenn Morris. A confident 'keeper who commands his area well, Stuart was out of contract in the summer.

Millwall *(Signed from Cirencester T on 6/10/2000. Free to Des Moines University, USA during 2001 close season)*
Brentford *(£10,000 from Hucknall T, ex Oxford C, Doncaster Rov, on 2/2/2004) FL 115+1 FLC 4 FAC 15 Others 4*
Leyton Orient *(Free on 16/7/2007) FL 30 FLC 2 FAC 1*

NELTHORPE Craig Robert
Born: Doncaster, 10 June 1987
Height: 5'10" **Weight:** 11.0
As a member of Doncaster's squad, Craig was kept on the sidelines at the beginning of last season by Martin Woods. After a loan to Gateshead, he appeared twice as a substitute in the League and once each in the FA Cup and Johnstone's Paint Trophy. As a fast raiding left-winger with a tremendous shot, he is equally at home at left-back. In the later stages of the season he went on loan to Blue Square Premier side Halifax and then to Darlington in League Two, where Craig was reunited with his

former boss Dave Penney in March. He made a surprise debut against Bradford after Guy Ndumbu-Nsungu was injured in the warm-up and went on to start three further games on the left.
Doncaster Rov (From trainee on 28/6/2006) FL 3+7/1 FAC 0+1 Others 0+3
Darlington (Loaned on 27/3/2008) FL 4+3 Others 0+1

NEVILLE Gary Alexander
Born: Bury, 18 February 1975
Height: 5'11"　**Weight:** 12.8
Club Honours: FAYC '92; PL '96, '97, '99, '00, '01, '03, '07; FAC '96, '99, '04; CS '96; EC '99; FLC '06
International Honours: E: 85; Yth (UEFA-U18 '93)
A hard-tackling Manchester United right-back, who is equally as effective as a central defender, Gary needed the majority of the season to recover from an injury suffered against Bolton in March 2007. On his return in a reserve game against Everton in January, he scored a rare goal in the 21st minute, helping United to a 2-2 draw. In April, he made his long-awaited return to the first team against AS Roma in the Champions' League quarter-final at Old Trafford. His arrival as an 81st-minute substitute for Anderson earned him a standing ovation and he was promptly given the captain's armband. It was Gary's 99th Champions' League appearance. Despite the promise of that night, Gary remained outside the main action as the Reds attacked the double prize of Premiership and European Cup.
Manchester U (From trainee on 29/1/1993) PL 349+15/5 FLC 16+1 FAC 41+3 Others 108+8/2

NEVILLE Philip (Phil) John
Born: Bury, 21 January 1977
Height: 5'11"　**Weight:** 12.0
Club Honours: FAYC '95; PL '96, '97, '99, '00, '01, '03; FAC '96, '99, '04: CS '96, '97, '03; EC '99
International Honours: E: 59; B-1; U21-7; Yth; Sch
Phil continued to set a fine example both on and off the pitch as Everton captain and had another consistent season. The complete professional, the England international remains the Goodison club's first-choice right-back, although also employed on occasions in the centre of midfield. Phil is an excellent defender but his best work was when regularly raiding down the right flank, from where he is capable of producing accurate crosses. In midfield, he is a capable ball-winner in the holding role and scored a couple of goals as an extra bonus.

Manchester U (From trainee on 1/6/1994) PL 210+53/5 FLC 16+1 FAC 25+6/1 Others 50+25/2
Everton (£3,500,000 on 4/8/2005) PL 106/3 FLC 7+1 FAC 5 Others 12

NEVLAND Erik
Born: Stavanger, Norway, 10 November 1977
Height: 5'10"　**Weight:** 11.9
International Honours: Norway: 6; U21-2
The Norwegian international striker signed for Fulham late in January from Dutch club FC Groningen. A forward with a direct style and a keen eye for the half-chance, he started the first two games after his arrival but took time to settle and featured in a couple of reserve games to reach full match-fitness. In the latter stages of the season he gave a number of impressive performances as a substitute, scoring vital goals against Reading and Birmingham. Still a regular international, he featured for Norway against Montenegro in March.
Manchester U (Signed from Viking Stavanger, Norway on 15/7/1997) PL 0+1 FLC 0+2/1 FAC 2+1 (Transferred to Viking Stavanger, Norway on 6/1/2000)
Fulham (£1,800,000 from Groningen, Holland on 31/1/2008) PL 2+6/2

NEWBY Jonathan (Jon) Philip Robert
Born: Warrington, 28 November 1978
Height: 6'0"　**Weight:** 12.4
Club Honours: FAYC '96
The well-travelled former Liverpool striker was handed a one-year deal by Morecambe after leaving Southport and, having impressed in pre-season, was quick to make his mark at Christie Park as he scored the Shrimps' first ever League goal, against Wrexham. Regarded by many as the club's best finisher, his goal ratio was the best at Morecambe but he made only 15 starts to the disappointment of supporters. Despite a shortage of opportunities he scored ten goals in all competitions, including the club's only hat-trick in a 5-1 win over Rotherham. He can finish with either foot and is a decent header of the ball, so will have been disappointed to learn of his release.
Liverpool (From juniors on 23/5/1997) PL 0+1 FLC 0+1 FAC 0+2
Crewe Alex (Loaned on 3/3/2000) FL 5+1
Sheffield U (Loaned on 4/8/2000) FL 3+10
Bury (£100,000 on 2/2/2001) FL 109/21 FLC 4/1 FAC 3 Others 6/2
Huddersfield T (Free on 7/8/2003) FL 10+4 FLC 1
York C (Loaned on 25/3/2004) FL 6+1

Bury (Free on 6/8/2004) FL 21+25/5 FLC 1+1 FAC 0+2 Others 1
Wrexham (Free on 17/8/2006) FL 2+9 FLC 0+1 Others 0+1 (Freed on 14/12/2006)
Morecambe (Free from Southport on 4/8/2007) FL 11+21/6 FLC 0+1/1 FAC 1 Others 3+2/3

NEWEY Thomas (Tom) William
Born: Huddersfield, 31 October 1982
Height: 5'10"　**Weight:** 10.6
In a season when he passed 100 games for Grimsby, Tom once again showed his importance to the side with several goal assists when supporting the attack. On target with a stunning free-kick to end promoted Hereford's unbeaten away record, tactical changes saw Tom figure at both left-back and as part of a three-man central defence, showing good positioning and heading ability. Appointed team captain after Christmas, Tom had the honour of leading out the Mariners at Wembley in the Johnstone's Paint Trophy Final.
Leeds U (From trainee on 4/8/2000)
Cambridge U (Loaned on 14/2/2003) FL 6 Others 1
Darlington (Loaned on 27/3/2003) FL 7/1
Leyton Orient (Free on 8/8/2003) FL 34+2/0 3 FLC 1+1 FAC 2+2 Others 3
Cambridge U (Free on 21/1/2005) FL 15+1
Grimsby T (Free on 28/7/2005) FL 119+4/3 FLC 3 FAC 5 Others 10

Tom Newey

NEWMAN Robert (Rob) Nigel

Born: Bradford-on-Avon, 13 December 1963
Height: 6'1" **Weight:** 13.2
Club Honours: AMC '86
Having been out of action for a considerable time, Bournemouth's assistant manager was called into the squad during an injury crisis. Formerly a top-class defender with Bristol City, Norwich and Southend, Rob became Bournemouth's oldest ever debutant, at 44 years of age, when he appeared as a late substitute at Bristol Rovers in the Johnstone's Paint Trophy.
Bristol C (From apprentice on 5/10/1981) FL 382+12/52 FLC 29+1/2 FAC 27/2 Others 36/5
Norwich C (£600,000 on 15/7/1991) P/FL 181+24/14 FLC 22+2/2 FAC 13/1 Others 7
Motherwell (Loaned)
Wigan Ath (Loaned on 26/3/1998) FL 8
Southend U (Free on 28/7/1998) FL 63+9/11 FLC 4/1 FAC 4 Others 5 (Freed on 3/3/2003)
Bournemouth (From retirement, ex Chelmsford C, Cambridge U, on 21/9/2007) Others 0+1

NEWSHAM Marc Anthony

Born: Hatfield, Yorkshire, 24 March 1987
Height: 5'10" **Weight:** 9.11
Rotherham fielded a number of young, home-grown players and Marc was another given the opportunity to carve out a regular place. He has an eye for goal but had to be content with a place on the bench more often than a starting role. Marc proved to be accurate from the penalty spot in the reserves and is another of the players on whom the future of the club could well depend.
Rotherham U (From trainee on 3/8/2006) FL 14+34/7 FLC 0+1 FAC 1+1 Others 3+2/1

NEWTON Adam Lee

Born: Grays, 4 December 1980
Height: 5'10" **Weight:** 11.6
Club Honours: FAYC '99
International Honours: St Kitts; E: U21-1
A speedy, wide attacker who was again used mainly as a defender at Peterborough, Adam has grown into the role but shows what he can do when pushing forward. He is one of the club's longest-serving players and appears to have a few more years left in him.
West Ham U (From trainee on 1/7/1999) PL 0+2 Others 0+1
Portsmouth (Loaned on 2/7/1999) FL 1+2 FLC 2
Notts Co (Loaned on 22/11/2000) FL 13+7/1 FAC 2
Leyton Orient (Loaned on 8/3/2002) FL 10/1
Peterborough U (Free on 8/7/2002) FL 191+27/8 FLC 6+1 FAC 13+2/1 Others 7+2

NEWTON Sean Michael

Born: Liverpool, 23 September 1988
Height: 6'0" **Weight:** 12.0
Sean was another product of the Chester youth policy to be given a first-team opportunity by Bobby Williamson. After spending the early part of the season on loan at Blue Square North side Southport, he was given his debut at Grimsby on New Year's Day on the left of Chester's four-man defence. He retained his place the following week with an assured performance at Accrington before being sent out on loan to Droylsden in February to gain further experience. Sean's contract with Chester was extended at the end of the season.
Chester C (From juniors on 24/1/2007) FL 2

NEWTON Shaun O'Neill

Born: Camberwell, 20 August 1975
Height: 5'8" **Weight:** 11.7
Club Honours: Div 1 '00
International Honours: E: U21-3
Having been on loan from West Ham since the previous March, the deal was firmed up in the summer. However, despite the veteran midfielder being given opportunities at Leicester by an assortment of managers during the first half of the season, he failed to establish a regular place. He was released during the January transfer window.
Charlton Ath (From trainee on 1/7/1993) P/FL 189+51/20 FLC 19+1/3 FAC 11+6/2 Others 7+1/2
Wolverhampton W (£850,000 + on 8/8/2001) P/FL 115+15/12 FLC 5+2/1 FAC 8+1 Others 4+1
West Ham U (£10,000 on 11/3/2005) P/FL 19+21/1 FLC 1+1 FAC 2+2 Others 2+1
Leicester C (Free on 9/3/2007) FL 16+3/1 FLC 1

N'GOTTY Bruno

Born: Lyon, France, 10 June 1971
Height: 6'1" **Weight:** 13.8
International Honours: France: 6; B-10; U21; Yth
Freed by Birmingham in the close season, Bruno arrived at Leicester as an imposing and experienced defender who operated at various times in the centre of the back line or at right-back, and even occasionally as a midfield anchor. Generally regarded as solid and dependable, if unspectacular as age begins to slow him to an extent. Though he was not always a first choice, he still played in the vast majority of fixtures and certainly never let anyone down.
Bolton W (Signed from Olympique Marseille, France, ex Lyon, Paris St Germain, AC Milan, Venezia, on 11/9/2001) PL 143+5/4 FLC 8+2/1 FAC 7 Others 6+1/1

Birmingham C (Free on 19/7/2006) FL 25/1 FAC 2/1
Leicester C (Free on 9/8/2007) FL 30+8 FLC 4 FAC 0+1

N'GUESSAN Diombo (Dany)

Born: Paris, France, 11 August 1987
Height: 6'1" **Weight:** 12.3
An enigmatic Frenchman, Dany spent the 2007-08 season flitting between a starting place and the substitutes' bench in what was generally a frustrating first full season at Lincoln for the former Glasgow Rangers' forward. Although more than capable of playing in a central striking role he mainly found himself operating on the flank and weighed in with seven goals, two coming in a match-winning performance against Hereford at Sincil Bank.
Glasgow Rgrs (Signed from Auxerre, France on 7/7/2005)
Boston U (Loaned on 19/8/2006) FL 13+10/5 FLC 1 FAC 1 Others 0+1
Lincoln C (Free on 24/1/2007) FL 27+19/7 FLC 1 FAC 1+1 Others 0+1

NICHOLAS Andrew (Andy) Peter

Born: Liverpool, 10 October 1983
Height: 6'2" **Weight:** 12.8
Swindon's longest-serving player had a frustrating time. A stress fracture of the heel in pre-season training delayed his participation until October and he found it hard to break into the side when other players were already established. A tall, left-sided defender able to play at full-back or in the centre of defence, Andy is deceptively quick and likes to get forward. He was released at the end of the season.
Swindon T (From trainee at Liverpool on 21/7/2003) FL 105+21/4 FLC 2/1 FAC 5 Others 7+1/1
Chester C (Loaned on 18/3/2005) FL 5

NICHOLLS Alexander (Alex)

Born: Stourbridge, 9 December 1987
Height: 5'10" **Weight:** 11.0
After missing out on any first-team appearances in 2006-07, Alex was in and out of the Walsall side for most of last season but at his best added pace and enthusiasm to the front line. His three goals were all scored in away games, including a splendid opportunist effort in a fine win on a windswept night at Yeovil in February.
Walsall (From trainee on 3/7/2006) FL 11+16/2 FLC 0+1 FAC 2+5/1 Others 1+2/1

NICHOLLS Kevin John Richard

Born: Newham, 2 January 1979
Height: 6'0" **Weight:** 11.0

311

Club Honours: Div 1 '05
International Honours: E: Yth
Kevin will probably look back on his
first season with Preston with some
disappointment, as he failed to retain
a regular starting spot after the change
of management at Deepdale and then
sustained an injury that ended his season
early. Signed from Leeds in the summer to
add bite to midfield, Kevin was appointed
captain after Graham Alexander's move
to Burnley and appeared in 18 of the
first 19 games. His endeavour was never
in question but he could not match the
standards he showed as a visiting player
for Luton and had only one minute
of first-team football after the end of
November.
*Charlton Ath (From trainee on 29/1/1996)
FL 4+8/1 FLC 2+2*
*Brighton & Hove A (Loaned on 26/2/1999)
FL 4/1*
*Wigan Ath (£250,000 + on 22/6/1999) FL
19+9 FLC 2 Others 4/1*
*Luton T (£25,000 + on 3/8/2001) FL 173+2/
31 FLC 6/1 FAC 5/2 Others 1*
*Leeds U (£700,000 on 1/8/2006) FL 12+1
FLC 1 FAC 1*
*Preston NE (£700,000 on 6/7/2007) FL 17+1
FLC 1 FAC 0+1*

NICHOLSON Stuart Ian
Born: Newcastle, 3 February 1987
Height: 5'10" **Weight:** 11.7
International Honours: E: Yth
Stuart made only one substitute
appearance for West Bromwich, against
Bournemouth in the Carling Cup, before
going on loan to Shrewsbury and later
to Wrexham. The young striker made his
Shrewsbury debut at home to Bradford
in August, showing some nice touches,
but scored his only goal in the 2-0 home
victory over Accrington. What was to be a
season-long loan did not work out for him
and he agreed a three-month deal with
Wrexham in January as one of Brian Little's
hoped-for rescue squad in the fight against
the drop. Stuart impressed with his pace
and enthusiasm in his first start against MK
Dons at the Racecourse but was unable
to score and was demoted to the bench.
Stuart's last game, also against MK Dons,
was a 4-1 defeat that virtually sealed
relegation from the League and on going
back to West Bromwich he was released.
*West Bromwich A (From trainee on 16/1/
2006) P/FL 0+6 FLC 2+1/2 FAC 0+1*
*Bristol Rov (Loaned on 16/11/2006) FL
8+2/2 Others 1/1*
*Bristol Rov (Loaned on 31/1/2007) FL 4+8/4
Others 0+3*
*Shrewsbury T (Loaned on 16/8/2007) FL
6+8/1 FAC 1 Others 1*
Wrexham (Loaned on 18/1/2008) FL 9+4

NICOLAU Nicky George
Born: St Pancras, 12 October 1983
Height: 5'8" **Weight:** 10.8
Club Honours: FAYC '01
A U-turn by Paul Fairclough led to Nicky
re-signing for Barnet, days after initially
being released last summer. Fairclough
clearly made a good decision as Nicky
had a solid season operating on the left
for the Bees, either at left-back or on the
left of midfield. He gets forward well and
showed this particularly when he scored
a late winner away at one of his former
clubs, Hereford, in January. Was released
at the end of the campaign.
Arsenal (From trainee on 1/7/2002)
*Southend U (Free on 25/3/2004) FL 24+7/1
FLC 1 Others 5+2/1*
*Swindon T (Free on 5/8/2005) FL 3+2 FLC
0+1*
*Barnet (Free on 1/8/2006) FL 48+12/3 FLC
2+1 FAC 7+2 Others 3*

NIEMI Antti
Born: Oulu, Finland, 31 May 1972
Height: 6'1" **Weight:** 13.9
Club Honours: SLC '99
International Honours: Finland: 66;
U21-17; Yth
Antti was again Fulham's first-choice
goalkeeper for much of the season,
although injury plagued the Finnish
international. An excellent shot-stopper
with reflexes that enable him to reach
shots that seem to have beaten him, he
is never afraid to leave his line and meet
an opponent on the edge of the box.
His kicking is also an asset and set up
a number of promising attacks. Having
previously retired from international
football he returned for Finland against
Spain as they came close to qualification
for Euro 2008 but missed much of the
latter part of the season through injury.
*Glasgow Rgrs (Signed from FC
Copenhagen, Denmark, ex HJK Helsinki, on
22/7/1997) SL 13 SLC 1 Others 7+1*
*Heart of Midlothian (£400,000 on 17/12/
1999) SL 89 SLC 4 SC 9 Others 4*
*Southampton (£2,000,000 on 28/8/2002)
P/FL 106 FLC 7 FAC 9 Others 1*
*Fulham (£1,000,000 on 12/1/2006) PL 62
FAC 1*

NIVEN Derek Dunbar
Born: Falkirk, 12 December 1983
Height: 6'1" **Weight:** 11.2
Derek passed the milestone of 200 first-
team appearances for Chesterfield in
April. Determined and competitive, he
breaks up opposing moves and provides
drive to the midfield, leading the charge
forward with a good turn of pace. Many
visiting sides employed five-man midfields
to stifle the Spireites but Derek did not

shy from the challenge, posting an
impressive workrate in every game. He is
the club's longest-serving professional.
*Raith Rov (From juniors at Stenhousemuir
on 10/7/2000) SL 0+1*
Bolton W (Signed on 29/11/2001)
*Chesterfield (Free on 12/12/2003) FL 185/13
FLC 7/2 FAC 5 Others 4/1*

NIX Kyle Ashley
Born: Sydney, Australia, 21 January 1986
Height: 5'6" **Weight:** 9.10
International Honours: E: Yth
Signed by Bradford boss Stuart McCall
after impressing in a pre-season trial, the
former Sheffield United midfielder was a
bundle of energy. Left-footed Kyle is most
effective in a five-man midfield, although
he can also play on the wing, and chipped
in with some valuable goals.
Aston Villa (From trainee on 24/1/2003)
Sheffield U (Free on 8/4/2005) FLC 0+2
*Bradford C (Free on 2/8/2007) FL 31+9/6
FLC 1/1 FAC 2 Others 1/1*

NOBLE David James
Born: Hitchin, 2 February 1982
Height: 6'0" **Weight:** 12.4
Club Honours: FAYC '00
International Honours: S: B-1; U21-2;
E: Yth
It was the late show from the skilful
former Arsenal and Boston player. He
had few chances to shine early on but
came into his own towards the end of
the season. A fantastic 30-yard winner
against Crystal Palace in the first leg of
the play-off semi-final at Selhurst Park
proved to be Bristol City's most important
goal of the season. After a muted
Championship play-off final at Wembley,
David was replaced by Ivan Sproule in the
63rd minute.
Arsenal (From trainee on 13/3/2001)
*Watford (Loaned on 10/7/2001) FL 5+10/1
FLC 3*
*West Ham U (Free on 31/1/2003) FL 0+3
FLC 1*
*Boston U (Free on 27/2/2004) FL 54+3/5 FLC
2 FAC 2+2/1*
*Bristol C (Signed on 23/11/2005) FL 57+19/6
FLC 1 FAC 3/1 Others 6/1*

NOBLE Mark James
Born: West Ham, 8 May 1987
Height: 5'11" **Weight:** 12.0
International Honours: E: U21-10; Yth
The talented West Ham midfielder
established himself in the team
last season following some spirited
performances. A local lad, he is adored
by the fans for his all-round performances
and enthusiasm, as well as showing a
cool head when taking crucial penalties
against Birmingham and Liverpool. At the

end of November, Mark was forced to miss games following a hernia operation but when back in the side he was brilliant against Manchester United as he set up both goals, from a free kick and a corner. He was in similar form against Liverpool as he harried, tackled and used the ball superbly. Mark was a regular member of the England under-21 side.

West Ham U *(From trainee on 1/7/2004) P/FL 49+10/5 FLC 2+4 FAC 6/1 Others 0+3*
Hull C *(Loaned on 10/2/2006) FL 4+1*
Ipswich T *(Loaned on 18/8/2006) FL 12+1/1*

NOLAN Edward (Eddie) William
Born: Waterford, 5 August 1988
Height: 6'0" **Weight:** 13.5
International Honours: RoI: U21-8
Eddie is a promising young defender with Blackburn. He started last season well as a member of the side that were Lancashire Senior Cup winners. Restricted to reserve football at Ewood Park, he joined Hartlepool on loan and in two months acquitted himself well with a good run at right-back.

Blackburn Rov *(From trainee on 12/9/2005) Others 0+1*
Stockport Co *(Loaned on 16/3/2007) FL 2+2*
Hartlepool U *(Loaned on 22/11/2007) FL 11 FAC 1*

NOLAN Kevin Anthony Jance
Born: Liverpool, 24 June 1982
Height: 6'0" **Weight:** 14.0
International Honours: E: U21-1; Yth
Despite starting the first eight League games of last season, Kevin was surprisingly axed from the 16 in the home defeat by Chelsea in October. Despite that minor setback, he returned to the team as captain in Gary Megson's first game in charge and kept his place for much of the remainder of the campaign. Publicly praised by his new manager on numerous occasions, Kevin retained the captain's armband and scored a number of goals as he found his form of old, most notably with a deft finish in the 4-2 defeat at Manchester City. A stalwart in the centre of the park and a prominent figure in the UEFA Cup campaign, Kevin provides the inspiration and leadership that Megson hopes will push Bolton back to the upper reaches of the Premiership.

Bolton W *(From trainee on 22/1/2000) P/FL 237+39/40 FLC 10+4/3 FAC 12+7/4 Others 11+3/2*

NORRIS David Martin
Born: Stamford, 22 February 1981
Height: 5'7" **Weight:** 11.6
Club Honours: Div 2 '04
The popular, hard-working midfielder

began last season well for Plymouth, scoring on the opening day in the 3-2 victory at Hull. Once again David produced many 'Man of the Match' performances, playing in the centre of midfield as well as his usual role on the right. His early-season form was noted by many Championship clubs and, after he handed in a transfer request in January, Ipswich swooped to sign him for a record incoming fee received by the Pilgrims. He took time to settle but did much better when he took on a central-midfield role, as he seems to like being in the thick of the action. Opened his account with a goal at Southampton but a heel injury early in the home game against Charlton prevented him playing again and he underwent an operation in a bid to be fit for the new season. David is a possible candidate for the captaincy following the retirement of Jason De Vos.

Bolton W *(£50,000 from Boston U on 2/2/2000) FLC 3+1 FAC 1/1*
Hull C *(Loaned on 4/3/2002) FL 3+3/1*
Plymouth Arg *(Free on 8/10/2002) FL 216+10/27 FLC 5 FAC 11/1 Others 0+1*
Ipswich T *(£2,000,000 on 31/1/2008) FL 9/1*

NORTH Daniel (Danny) Jamie
Born: Grimsby, 7 September 1987
Height: 5'9" **Weight:** 12.2
Danny's first goal of the season, against Burnley in the Carling Cup, was notable as it was Grimsby's 7,000th in all competitions. The young forward then suffered with form and fitness problems before a successful recall in November saw him going on to be voted 'Powerade Player of the Month' for League Two in January when his four goals helped the Mariners to an unbeaten month. Possessing both a powerful shot and awareness for the half-chance, Danny subsequently made the required number of appearances to earn a new two-year contract.

Grimsby T *(From trainee on 2/7/2006) FL 33+16/15 FLC 0+1/1 FAC 4 Others 6+2*

NORVILLE Jason
Born: Trinidad, 9 September 1983
Height: 5'11" **Weight:** 11.2
International Honours: Trinidad & Tobago: 1
Jason was originally released by Barnet at the end of 2006-07, after struggling with a number of injuries, but Paul Fairclough gave him a second chance by signing him on a non-contract basis at the end of August. However, the striker struggled to hold down a place and left in January for Blue Square Premier club Woking, where he went on to net several goals.

Watford *(From trainee on 17/4/2002) FL*

6+8/1 FLC 0+1
Barnet *(Free on 6/8/2005) FL 13+20/3 FLC 0+3 FAC 1 Others 3/1*

NOSWORTHY Nyron Paul Henry
Born: Brixton, 11 October 1980
Height: 6'0" **Weight:** 12.0
Club Honours: Ch '07
Nyron is a hugely popular defender at Sunderland, equally at home at right-back or centre-half. A muscular player and a strong tackler, his pace can be used to good effect right across the back four. He was selected by Jamaica during last season but unfortunately a number of games scheduled to take place in England were cancelled, denying him the opportunity of a first cap. His partnership with Jonny Evans at the centre of defence went a long way towards securing Sunderland's Premier League status. Nyron is the vice-captain at Sunderland and led the side when Dean Whitehead was sidelined through injury.

Gillingham *(From trainee on 30/12/1998) FL 151+23/5 FLC 6+2/1 FAC 7+7 Others 1+2*
Sunderland *(Free on 2/7/2005) P/FL 80+8 FLC 3 FAC 1*

NOWLAND Adam Christopher
Born: Preston, 6 July 1981
Height: 5'11" **Weight:** 11.6
An attacking midfielder, Adam was unable to get into the Preston side last season and had a second spell on loan with Gillingham in September before returning to Deepdale after appearing in only a handful of games. A second loan from Preston took Adam to Stockport in November but despite playing well in County's biggest win of the season, 6-0 against Wycombe, he did not stay after four appearances and was released by his parent club in January. Was playing his football for Lancaster when the campaign ended.

Blackpool *(From trainee on 15/1/1999) FL 18+51/5 FLC 1+5/1 FAC 2+2/1 Others 0+2*
Wimbledon *(Signed on 29/6/2001) FL 35+21/5 FLC 2+1 FAC 2/2*
West Ham U *(£75,000 on 28/1/2004) FL 5+10/1 FLC 2*
Gillingham *(Loaned on 29/9/2004) FL 3/1*
Nottingham F *(£250,000 on 5/11/2004) FL 5 FAC 0+1*
Preston NE *(Free on 27/8/2005) FL 9+5/3*
Gillingham *(Loaned on 21/9/2007) FL 4+1 Others 0+1*
Stockport Co *(Loaned on 9/11/2007) FL 4*

NUGENT David James
Born: Liverpool, 2 May 1985
Height: 5'11" **Weight:** 12.13
Club Honours: FAC '08

International Honours: E: 1; U21-14; Yth

David joined Portsmouth in July after a successful two-and-a-half years at Preston. His transition to Premier League football was hampered by a long-standing groin injury that required surgery at the end of January and sidelined him for two months, causing him to miss seven matches. He did not score in his limited Premier League appearances but set Pompey on the way in their successful FA Cup campaign by hitting the only goal of the game at Ipswich in the third round and appeared as a late substitute in the FA Cup final. Linked with failed loan moves to Ipswich and Stoke in late season, David's fitness holds the key to his future success.

Bury (From trainee on 8/3/2003) FL 58+30/18 FLC 2+1 FAC 3+1/1 Others 3+4/1

Preston NE (Signed on 11/1/2005) FL 83+11/33 FLC 2 FAC 5+1/2 Others 5/2

Portsmouth (£6,000,000 on 11/7/2007) PL 5+10 FLC 2+1/2 FAC 1+3/1

NURSE Jonathan (Jon) David

Born: Bridgetown, Barbados, 1 March 1981

Height: 5'10" **Weight:** 12.6

International Honours: Barbados: 2

Arriving at Dagenham from Stevenage at the end of 2006-07, the forward suffered a hamstring injury after the third game and in his comeback a month later, pulled up again ten minutes after going on as a substitute. Although he did not score many goals, he played his part up front by forging a partnership with Ben Strevens. Jon won his first caps for Barbados in their World Cup qualifier in Dominica and the return.

Dagenham & Redbridge (Free from Stevenage Borough, ex Sutton U, Woking - loan, on 9/7/2007) FL 23+7/1 FLC 1 FAC 1+1/1 Others 0+2

NUTTER John Robert William

Born: Taplow, 13 June 1982

Height: 6'2" **Weight:** 12.10

Club Honours: FAT '05, '06, '07

Signed from Stevenage in January, having been on loan at Gillingham since November, John proved himself to be an aggressive left-back, with a superb first touch, linked to good passing ability. He also puts that left foot to good use with flighted corners and free kicks.

Wycombe W (Trainee) FL 1

Gillingham (Signed from Stevenage Borough, ex Aldershot T, St Albans C - loan, Grays Ath, on 22/11/2007) FL 23+1/1 Others 1

NYATANGA Lewin John

Born: Burton-on-Trent, 18 August 1988

Height: 6'2" **Weight:** 12.8

International Honours: W: 21; U21-10

Although continuing as a regular for Wales, Lewin was unable to make progress with Derby and went on an extended loan to Barnsley at the start of the season, becoming first choice in the heart of their defence. A commanding figure, who is good in the air both in defence and in attack at set plays, he formed a fine partnership with Dennis Sousa, their styles complementing each other. Lewin is also a good reader of the game and stopped problems early. Arriving back at Derby in early January, the defender scored in his first Premiership appearance, at Portsmouth, and played at left-back for County in two FA Cup ties, being sent off in the home defeat by Preston. This ruled him out of Barnsley's FA Cup adventure after he rejoined the Reds on loan for the remainder of the season, showing his versatility at left-back on a number of occasions. When the Championship season ended, he was with Derby again in time for another of their defensive disasters in the final game against Reading.

Derby Co (From trainee on 10/9/2005) P/FL 30+3/3 FLC 3 FAC 4 Others 0+1

Sunderland (Loaned on 19/10/2006) FL 9+2

Barnsley (Loaned on 13/2/2007) FL 10/1

Barnsley (Loaned on 27/7/2007) FL 24+1 FLC 2

Barnsley (Loaned on 31/1/2008) FL 16/1

NYGAARD Marc

Born: Copenhagen, Denmark, 1 September 1976

Height: 6'5" **Weight:** 14.5

International Honours: Denmark: 6; U21-6; Yth

The big Danish striker made 20 appearances for Queens Park Rangers last season, scoring once in a 1-1 home draw with Ipswich before leaving Loftus Road for his native Denmark in February. In his later months, Marc's command of languages was put to good use when he acted as translator for Rangers' new Italian manager Luigi De Canio during his settling-in period.

Queens Park Rgrs (Signed from Brescia, Italy on 23/7/2005) FL 43+26/13 FLC 2/1 FAC 1

N'ZOGBIA Charles

Born: Le Havre, France, 28 May 1986

Height: 5'7" **Weight:** 11.0

International Honours: France: U21; Yth

Lewin Nyatanga

Charles started last season in fine form for Newcastle, scoring three times in the first seven matches, but did not find the net again all season despite being a regular until March, when Kevin Keegan introduced a new attacking formation that cost him his place. He is most effective as an attacking midfielder on the left, where he can use his pace and fine control to offer a direct threat. Charles also appeared at left-back, a position from where he could launch dangerous raids but, at the same time, exposed his lack of defensive experience. He made his French under-21 debut against Wales in September and was called up by the Congo DR for their 'B' team match with France in February, an invitation he turned down as he was unsure of the best direction for his international future.

Newcastle U (Signed from Le Havre, France on 3/9/2004) PL 72+28/8 FLC 5+1 FAC 6+2 Others 13+5/1

O

OAKES Andrew (Andy) Mark
Born: Northwich, 11 January 1977
Height: 6'4" **Weight:** 12.4
The experienced goalkeeper started
2007-08 as Darlington's first choice after
arriving from Swansea in the summer
but was unfortunately sent off for a
professional foul after 63 minutes of the
opening game against Wrexham and
replaced by David Stockdale. He returned
for six more games in September and
October, proving to be a good shot-
stopper before being injured and out for
a lengthy spell. When fit again, he was
unable to regain his place as the younger
Stockdale was performing so well. Yet
another shoulder injury, sustained in
training, ruled him out for the remainder
of the season to compound a miserable
time for him at Darlington.
*Hull C (Signed from Winsford U, ex trainee
at Burnley, trial with Bury, Macclesfield T, on
8/12/1998) FL 19 Others 1*
*Derby Co (£460,000 on 7/6/1999) P/FL 43
FLC 2 FAC 1*
Bolton W (Loaned on 31/8/2004) PL 1
*Walsall (Free on 18/3/2005) FL 34 FLC 1 FAC
3 Others 1*
Swansea C (Free on 3/8/2006) FL 4 Others 1
Darlington (Free on 18/7/2007) FL 6 Others 1

OAKES Michael (Mike)
Christian
Born: Northwich, 30 October 1973
Height: 6'2" **Weight:** 14.7
Club Honours: FLC '96
International Honours: E: U21-6
Freed by Wolverhampton in the summer,
the veteran goalkeeper became a valuable
squad member for Cardiff last season
as understudy to Ross Turnbull, Kasper
Schmeichel and Peter Enckelman, while
starting 11 League games himself. Always
supportive and a leading squad member
whether he was starting or not. Out of
contract and released at the end of the
season, he was an unused substitute
for City's 1-0 FA Cup final defeat at the
hands of Portsmouth, thus picking up a
medal.
*Aston Villa (From juniors on 16/7/1991) PL
49+2 FLC 3 FAC 2 Others 5*
*Scarborough (Loaned on 26/11/1993) FL
1 Others 1*
*Wolverhampton W (£400,000 + on 29/10/
1999) P/FL 198+1 FLC 9+1 FAC 9 Others 2*
*Cardiff C (Free on 10/7/2007) FL 11 FLC 2
FAC 2*

OAKES Stefan Trevor
Born: Leicester, 6 September 1978
Height: 5'11" **Weight:** 12.4
Club Honours: FLC '00
Stefan was once again a key member of
the Wycombe midfield, in his favoured
wide left or left-central position. His
four goals were, naturally, anything but
ordinary, all in the 25 yards plus range,
perhaps the best at Morecambe pushing
35 yards. It is not just his trusty left foot
that impresses as he is comfortable on
the ball, able to keep possession in the
tightest of spots and a strong tackler.
He is a main outlet in midfield and able
to deliver pinpoint out-swinging crosses.
Stefan had a particularly strong second
half of the season and was considering a
new contract offer.
*Leicester C (From trainee on 3/7/1997) P/FL
39+25/2 FLC 7+1/2 FAC 5+2*
Crewe Alex (Loaned on 17/3/2003) FL 3+4
Walsall (Free on 18/7/2003) FL 1+4
*Notts Co (Free on 17/2/2004) FL 42+3/5 FLC
0+1 FAC 2+1/1*
*Wycombe W (Free on 6/7/2005) FL 83+23/5
FLC 9/3 FAC 4/1 Others 2+3*

OAKLEY Matthew (Matt)
Born: Peterborough, 17 August 1977
Height: 5'10" **Weight:** 12.1
International Honours: E: U21-4
Again proving an admirable captain, Matt
was one of the few Derby players able to
cope with elevation to the Premiership
last season. He was also more likely than
most to produce a goal and remained
joint leading scorer in the League, with
three, until overtaken in May. It came as
a surprise, to him as well as supporters,
when he was sold to Leicester in January.
The classy midfielder appeared to be
a vital signing when Leicester tempted
him to cross the East Midlands but after
a storming start he suffered from a loss
of confidence as the team struggled and
was decidedly less effective in the later
weeks after skipper Stephen Clemence
was sidelined with injury.
*Southampton (From trainee on 1/7/1995)
P/FL 238+23/14 FLC 21+2/2 FAC 22+3/4
Others 1*
*Derby Co (Free on 4/8/2006) P/FL 55+1/9
FLC 1 FAC 2 Others 3*
Leicester C (£500,000 on 11/1/2008) FL 20

O'BRIEN Andrew (Andy)
James
Born: Harrogate, 29 June 1979
Height: 6'3" **Weight:** 12.4
International Honours: RoI: 26; U21-8;
E: U21-1; Yth
As bargain signing from Portsmouth,
Andy was perhaps the most astute
capture of Sammy Lee's short reign as
Bolton manager. His first start came
in the 1-0 defeat at Birmingham in
September and Andy retained his place
for much of the rest of the season,
forging an excellent central defensive
partnership with Gary Cahill from January
onward. A series of consistently excellent

Stefan Oakes

performances were greatly appreciated by the Bolton faithful and Andy's no-nonsense style and wholehearted approach quickly won them over. Strong in the tackle and possessing great awareness, Andy made one of the centre-half berths his own and will surely continue in that position in the coming months.

Bradford C *(From trainee on 28/10/1996) P/FL 113+20/3 FLC 5 FAC 8 Others 4*
Newcastle U *(£2,000,000 on 28/3/2001) PL 114+6/6 FLC 4+1 FAC 7+3/1 Others 32+5*
Portsmouth *(£2,000,000 on 7/7/2005) PL 30+2 FLC 3 FAC 2*
Bolton W *(Signed on 14/8/2007) PL 31+1 FLC 1 FAC 1 Others 7+1*

O'BRIEN Burton

Born: Johannesburg, South Africa, 10 June 1981
Height: 5'10" **Weight:** 10.12
Club Honours: SLC '04
International Honours: S: U21-6; Yth
A good, steadying, left-sided midfielder, Burton proved to be a valuable member of the Sheffield Wednesday squad. He plays mainly as an attacking arm of a midfield four but also performs well as an orthodox winger. He works hard, has a nice touch, but should be taking up scoring positions more often. Although much of his work goes unnoticed, he is always a busy team player. Was released at the end of the campaign.

St Mirren *(From juniors on 11/6/1998) SL 17+9/1 SC 2*
Blackburn Rov *(£300,000 on 19/2/1999) FLC 0+1*
Livingston *(Signed on 31/8/2002) SL 88+11/14 SLC 8+1 SC 10/1 Others 1*
Sheffield Wed *(Free on 15/7/2005) FL 73+26/6 FLC 2+1 FAC 2*

O'BRIEN Joseph (Joey) Martin

Born: Dublin, 17 February 1986
Height: 5'11" **Weight:** 10.13
International Honours: RoI: 3; U21-6; Yth
Eager to put the 2006-07 injury nightmare behind him, when a tendon problem in his right knee led to him missing the entire season, Joey made his first appearance for Bolton after a 15-month lay-off as a substitute in the away UEFA Cup tie against Macedonian side FK Rabotnicki Kometal in September. His first League start came in the following game, at home to Tottenham, and he was re-established as a very valuable squad member. Equally adept at right-back or in the centre of midfield, Joey carried out both roles with equal aplomb as the season progressed. An energetic and versatile performer, Joey's return to

fitness and form led to him regaining a place in the Republic of Ireland team for two Euro 2008 qualifiers.

Bolton W *(From trainee on 17/11/2004) PL 37+6 FLC 3+1 FAC 4 Others 10+1*
Sheffield Wed *(Loaned on 3/12/2004) FL 14+1/2*

O'BRIEN Luke

Born: Halifax, 11 September 1988
Height: 5'9" **Weight:** 11.7
Teenage left-back Luke is the understudy to Paul Heckingbottom at Bradford. Chances were limited but he came in for an FA Cup tie against Tranmere when Heckingbottom was suspended and made a solid League debut at Brentford in April, clearing off the line to deny Nathan Elder.

Bradford C *(From trainee on 4/7/2007) FL 2 FAC 1 Others 0+1*

O'CALLAGHAN George

Born: Cork, 5 September 1979
Height: 6'1" **Weight:** 11.5
International Honours: RoI: Yth
George made only one appearance for Ipswich early in the season and went on loan to Brighton at the end of August, having rejected terms for a permanent transfer. Playing very deep for Brighton, George was happy to make himself available for colleagues, passed well and seemed to be the creative midfielder they had sought for some time. The lanky Irishman was a consistent performer for three months, although he was sent off at home to Carlisle in November, but tensions over his future culminated with an outburst in the local media and George quickly returned to Ipswich before rejoining Cork City.

Port Vale *(From trainee on 10/7/1998) FL 22+12/4 FLC 2 FAC 1+2 Others 0+1 (Freed on 30/3/2002)*
Ipswich T *(Signed from Cork C on 17/1/2007) FL 4+8/1 FAC 1*
Brighton & Hove A *(Loaned on 31/8/2007) FL 13+1 FAC 1 Others 2*

O'CEARUILL Joseph (Joe) Delpesh

Born: Edmonton, 9 February 1987
Height: 5'11" **Weight:** 12.11
International Honours: RoI: 2; U21-9; Yth
The young defender was with Barnet for the first half of last season after his release by Arsenal, but his appearances were limited by virtue of the fine form displayed by centre-backs, Sagi Burton-Godwin and Ismail Yakubu. Before leaving for his native Ireland to join St Patrick's Athletic, Joe signed off in style by scoring a crucial penalty in Barnet's FA Cup third round replay shoot-out triumph

against League One side Swindon.

Arsenal *(From trainee at Watford, ex trainee at Leyton Orient, on 11/7/2006)*
Brighton & Hove A *(Loaned on 5/1/2007) FL 6+2 FAC 1 Others 0+1*
Barnet *(Free on 24/8/2007) FL 9+5 FAC 1+2 Others 1*

O'CONNOR Garreth

Born: Dublin, 10 November 1978
Height: 5'7" **Weight:** 11.0
Unable to secure a place at Burnley, Garreth was loaned to his former club Bournemouth at the start of last season to the delight of Cherries' fans. Unfortunately, the midfielder's lack of match fitness showed and he failed to do himself justice in his short spell at Dean Court. On his return to Burnley he could not get going, with just one brief appearance as a substitute, and having never quite lived up to his initial goal-strewn impact at Turf Moor, he was released at the end of the season.

Bournemouth *(Free from Bohemians on 5/6/2000) FL 109+59/24 FLC 4+2/1 FAC 14+4/1 Others 11+1/2*
Burnley *(Free on 29/7/2005) FL 26+12/7 FLC 3 FAC 1+1/2*
Bournemouth *(Loaned on 10/8/2007) FL 5+1 FLC 1 Others 1+1*

O'CONNOR Garry Lawrence

Born: Edinburgh, 7 May 1983
Height: 6'1" **Weight:** 12.2
International Honours: S: 15; U21-8
Garry got off to a good start for Birmingham after signing from Lokomotiv Moscow in the summer when scoring on his debut against Sunderland as a substitute. He was also on the spot to stun Arsenal with the equaliser away from home in January but had to make do with a diet of action coming off the bench for the most part. Has an accomplished knack of holding up the ball, used his presence to good effect to link play and worked hard for the team tactically.

Hibernian *(From Salvesen BC on 1/7/1999) SL 115+23/46 SLC 9+2/5 SC 9+5/6 Others 3/1 (Transferred to Lokomotiv Moscow, Russia on 7/3/2006)*
Peterhead *(Loaned on 25/8/2000) SL 4/2 Others 1*
Birmingham C *(£2,700,000 from Lokomotiv Moscow, Russia on 17/7/2007) PL 5+18/2 FLC 2/1 FAC 1/1*

O'CONNOR James Francis Edward

Born: Birmingham, 20 November 1984
Height: 5'10" **Weight:** 12.5
Club Honours: FAYC '02; AMC '07
A consistent performer at right-back for Doncaster, James played a number of

James O'Connor (Doncaster Rovers)

games in the middle of last season with a hernia problem but never allowed his standards to drop. He eventually had an operation in early March but was soon back in the team as if he had never been away. His form was good enough to win the 'Man of the Match' award in the play-off final against Leeds at Wembley.
Aston Villa *(From trainee on 24/4/2004)*
Port Vale *(Loaned on 3/9/2004)* FL 13 Others 2
Bournemouth *(Free on 18/2/2005)* FL 43+2/ 1 FLC 1 FAC 1 Others 1+1
Doncaster Rov *(£130,000 on 19/5/2006)* FL 79+1/1 FLC 5 FAC 5 Others 8

O'CONNOR James Kevin
Born: Dublin, 1 September 1979
Height: 5'8" **Weight:** 11.6
Club Honours: AMC '00
International Honours: RoI: U21-9; Yth
It was very much a season of two halves for James. A virtual forgotten man prior to December, he was unaccountably given barely a whiff of Burnley first-team action prior to Steve Cotterill's departure. New boss Owen Coyle soon restored him to his familiar central-midfield role and James responded with a series of top-drawer displays that made his earlier absence all the more mysterious. Ever industrious, he was often the essential link between defence and attack and weighed in with his usual goals quota.
Stoke C *(From trainee on 5/9/1996)* FL 176/ 16 FLC 9/3 FAC 8+1 Others 16+1/3
West Bromwich A *(Signed on 8/8/2003)* P/FL 27+3 FLC 5+1 FAC 1+1
Burnley *(Loaned on 29/10/2004)* FL 12+1
Burnley *(£175,000 on 24/3/2005)* FL 117+9/ 11 FLC 6+1 FAC 3

O'CONNOR Kevin Patrick
Born: Blackburn, 24 February 1982
Height: 5'11" **Weight:** 12.0
International Honours: RoI: U21-6
Brentford's longest-serving player appeared primarily in a central-midfield role, playing in every game apart from the nine he missed after suffering a hamstring injury in February. He did his job quietly, blocking the opposition with tackles and interceptions before setting up opportunities for his colleagues. Kevin scored a wonderful goal from a free kick at Mansfield in February.
Brentford *(From trainee on 4/3/2000)* FL 240+33/25 FLC 8+1/4 FAC 19+2/3 Others 10+5/1

O'CONNOR Michael Joseph
Born: Belfast, 6 October 1987
Height: 6'1" **Weight:** 11.8
International Honours: NI: 1; U21-3; Yth

317

A Northern Ireland youth international, Michael was awarded his first senior cap for his country in March. Having made his Crewe debut in August 2006 at Scunthorpe, injuries kept him out of the side for several spells last season but the tough-tackling midfielder with an eye for goal is expected to do well in the game.
Crewe Alex (From trainee on 27/7/2005) FL 42+12 FLC 2/1 Others 3

ODEJAYI Olukayode (Kayode)

Born: Ibadon, Nigeria, 21 February 1982
Height: 6'2" **Weight:** 12.2
International Honours: Nigeria: 1
Kayode made his Barnsley debut as a substitute on the opening day of the season after he was signed from Cheltenham. The big centre-forward found it hard to adapt at the higher level but became an Oakwell legend when he netted the winner against Chelsea in the great FA Cup tie. Kayode's power made him a handful for even the best defenders, with strong running and heading strength his greatest assets. He would like more goals in the forthcoming season.
Bristol C (From trainee on 17/7/2000) FL 0+6 Others 1 (Free to Forest Green Rov on 28/9/2002)
Cheltenham T (£25,000 from Forest Green Rov on 5/6/2003) FL 100+48/30 FLC 5+1/1 FAC 7+3/2 Others 7+3/1
Barnsley (£200,000 on 5/6/2007) FL 23+16/3 FLC 1 FAC 3+2/1

ODHIAMBO Eric Geno Sije

Born: Oxford, 12 May 1989
Height: 5'9" **Weight:** 11.2
A graduate of Leicester's Academy, the young striker appeared from the bench in the Tigers' Carling Cup tie at Accrington before joining Southend on loan in September. He started twice alongside fellow loanee Leon Clarke but, slightly built, struggled to adapt to the physical side of League One and manager Steve Tilson did not pursue his interest. Returning to Leicester at the end of his month, Eric then went on loan to Dundee United, under former City boss Craig Levein, for experience.
Leicester C (From trainee on 20/2/2007) FLC 0+2
Southend U (Loaned on 31/8/2007) FL 2+3 Others 1
Dundee U (Loaned on 1/1/2008) SL 1+3 SC 0+3

O'DONNELL Daniel (Danny)

Born: Rainford, 10 March 1986
Height: 6'2" **Weight:** 11.11
Having spent 2006-07 on loan at Crewe,

Danny's move to Gresty Road was made permanent in the summer when Liverpool accepted a six-figure fee for him. The promising defender, who has played in several different positions at the back for Alexandra, is big, strong and reliable. Many good judges see him as one of the cornerstones that the club will build on in the years ahead.
Liverpool (From trainee on 25/11/2004)
Crewe Alex (Signed on 8/8/2006) FL 40+12/2 FLC 1+2 FAC 1 Others 3

O'DONNELL Richard Mark

Born: Sheffield, 12 September 1988
Height: 6'2" **Weight:** 13.5
The third-choice Sheffield Wednesday goalkeeper enjoyed his first taste of League action after initially joining Oldham on an emergency seven-day loan in March. With Mark Crossley injured, Richard was unexpectedly thrown into a 3-0 reverse at Luton hours after meeting his new team-mates. However, he made several superb saves as the Latics' defence had a collective bad day. His loan was extended to the end of the season and he made two more impressive starts before going on at Crewe for the final half-hour of the campaign.
Sheffield Wed (From trainee on 5/7/2007)
Oldham Ath (Loaned on 14/3/2008) FL 3+1

O'DONOVAN Roy Simon

Born: Cork, 10 August 1985
Height: 5'7" **Weight:** 10.4
International Honours: Rol: B-2; U21-9
A young striker who arrived at Sunderland from Cork City, Roy was mainly as a substitute in 2007-08 when his pace could be employed to good effect against tiring defenders. An excellent team player, Roy linked well with whoever was up front alongside him and was desperately unlucky on a number of occasions not to break his scoring duck for the Black Cats.
Coventry C (From trainee on 13/8/2002. Freed on 1/12/2004)
Sunderland (£500,000 + from Cork C on 10/8/2007) PL 4+13 FLC 0+1 FAC 1

O'GRADY Christopher (Chris) James

Born: Nottingham, 25 January 1986
Height: 6'1" **Weight:** 12.8
International Honours: E: Yth
An automatic choice for most of the season at Rotherham, Chris is a speedy player up front with several of his goals coming from distance. Even if he feels that his tally of goals should be higher, he has the consolation that his pace helped to create chances for others. Signed for Oldham on 28 May.
Leicester C (From trainee on 3/8/2004) FL

6+18/1 FLC 1/1
Notts Co (Loaned on 24/9/2004) FL 3+6 FAC 0+1 Others 1
Rushden & Diamonds (Loaned on 12/8/2005) FL 20+2/4 FLC 1 Others 2
Rotherham U (£65,000 on 19/1/2007) FL 46+5/13 FLC 1 FAC 2/1 Others 1/1

O'HALLORAN Stephen Edward

Born: Cork, 29 November 1987
Height: 6'0" **Weight:** 11.7
International Honours: Rol: 2; U21-9
Brought to Southampton on loan from Aston Villa to provide much-needed defensive cover, the young Republic of Ireland international left-back played 26 minutes as a substitute, replacing Gregory Vignal against Norwich in January. He was soon on his way back to Villa Park, caretakers John Gorman and Jason Dodd preferring to field Vignal with his arm in a splint. He did manage a 90-minute stint at St Mary's when he represented the Irish Republic in an under-21 match against England in February.
Aston Villa (From trainee on 30/11/2005)
Wycombe W (Loaned on 20/10/2006) FL 9+2 FLC 2 Others 1
Southampton (Loaned on 17/1/2008) FL 0+1

O'HANLON Sean Philip

Born: Southport, 2 January 1983
Height: 6'1" **Weight:** 12.5
Club Honours: AMC '08; Div 2 '08
International Honours: E: Yth
A commanding right-sided MK Dons central defender, Sean's back-four partnership with Danny Swailes was one of the main reasons why the Dons conceded only 37 goals in their title-winning campaign. A fine reader of the game and no slouch at covering ground, Sean tackled strongly, passed the ball without fuss and rarely missed a header all season. His aerial prowess brought him several key goals, including one at Wembley in the Johnstone's Paint Trophy final win, and his commitment was shown late in the campaign, when he continued playing despite a broken nose.
Everton (From trainee on 26/2/2000)
Swindon T (£150,000 on 23/11/2004) FL 97+2/9 FLC 1+1 FAC 5/1 Others 5+1
MK Dons (Free on 27/7/2006) FL 74+5/8 FLC 3 FAC 3 Others 9/1

O'HARA Jamie Darryl

Born: Dartford, 25 September 1986
Height: 5'11" **Weight:** 12.4
Club Honours: FLC '08
International Honours: E: U21-2; Yth
Still not quite ready for the Tottenham first team, Jamie arrived at Millwall on

a three-month loan last August and became an instant favourite with the crowd, his enthusiasm and tireless performances from the middle of the park being outstanding. It did not take Spurs long to recognise the young midfielder's improvement and, instead of extending the loan, they recalled him to White Hart Lane. Given a debut by Juande Ramos, Jamie made an immediate impact from the bench at Portsmouth, playing a key part in the winning goal. A left-footed midfielder, with good dead-ball abilities he was also an effective substitute in the Carling Cup at Manchester City and started the Premier League game at Arsenal. Not only can he be used on the left and in the centre of midfield but is also confident at left-back. In that position, with Steed Malbranque's assistance, he did a great job in the first half of an FA Cup tie at Old Trafford against Manchester United's Ronaldo but his best performances were in midfield. Jamie scored twice in his 25 games for Spurs and was unlucky not to be selected for the Carling Cup final. His achievements brought England under-21 recognition against Poland and Wales and he ended the campaign as the 'Young Player of the Season' to go with the Spurs Trust's 'Breakthrough' award. He was also rewarded with a new three-year contract.
Tottenham H (From trainee on 29/9/2004) PL 9+8/1 FLC 1+1 FAC 1+1 Others 1+3/1
Chesterfield (Loaned on 13/11/2006) FL 19/5
Millwall (Loaned on 24/8/2007) FL 10+4/2 Others 1

O'HARE Alan Patrick James
Born: Drogheda, 31 July 1982
Height: 6'2" **Weight:** 12.2
International Honours: RoI: Yth
While Chesterfield employed several left-backs last season, Alan did not get the opportunities that his experience and form prior to injury in 2006-07 might have merited. A fine ambassador for the club, Alan was popular for his work on and off the field in his six years and most fans were sorry to see him released.
Bolton W (From trainee on 24/11/2001)
Chesterfield (Loaned on 25/1/2002) FL 19
Chesterfield (Free on 9/10/2002) FL 107+28/3 FLC 5 FAC 2 Others 8+1

OJI Samuel (Sam) Udoka
Born: Westminster, 9 October 1985
Height: 6'0" **Weight:** 13.0
Sam joined Leyton Orient initially on loan from Birmingham as cover for the O's centre-halves before signing a six-month contract during the January window. With the ability to read the game well and time his tackles to perfection, Sam

can also play right-back if required.
Birmingham C (From trainee at Arsenal on 16/5/2004) FAC 0+1
Doncaster Rov (Loaned on 24/11/2005) FL 1+3 FLC 0+1
Bristol Rov (Loaned on 16/2/2007) FL 5
Leyton Orient (Free on 28/8/2007) FL 9+4 Others 2

OKOCHA Augustine (Jay Jay) Azuka
Born: Enugu, Nigeria, 14 August 1973
Height: 5'8" **Weight:** 11.0
International Honours: Nigeria: 75
Over recent editions of the 'PFA Footballers' Who's Who', the title of Hull's biggest-ever signing has been revised several times. The bar was lifted to a new level in September when Jay Jay agreed to become a Tiger and confirm them as genuine promotion contenders. After a year playing for Qatar Sports Club, arguably the most gifted African footballer of all-time was persuaded to return to England by City manager Phil Brown, his former coach at Bolton. He soon displayed his outstanding skill, notably receiving a standing ovation from all four sides of the ground when substituted late in his debut at Wolverhampton. A series of niggling injuries disrupted Jay Jay's season, as did a sending-off against Burnley in March, the first red card of his illustrious career. Otherwise, it was no fluke that Jay Jay's arrival coincided with the Tigers' highest final League position, their first visit to Wembley and promotion to the Premier League. Was out of contract at the end of the campaign.
Bolton W (Free from Paris St Germain, France, ex Enugu R, B.Nuenkirchen, Eintracht Frankfurt, Fenerbahce, on 3/8/2002) PL

106+18/14 FLC 7+2/4 FAC 4+1 Others 6+1 (Freed during 2006 close season)
Hull C (Free from Qatar SC on 6/9/2007) FL 10+8 FLC 1

OKUONGHAE Magnus
Born: Nigeria, 16 February 1986
Height: 6'3" **Weight:** 13.4
Magnus joined Dagenham during the close season from Crawley and was one of five centre-backs at the club. Having just started to become a regular, he suffered a groin injury in the warm-up at Notts County when he jumped to head a ball and was out for more than two months. In March, he joined Blue Square Premier side Weymouth on loan to regain fitness but returned three weeks later after dislocating a shoulder.
Rushden & Diamonds (From trainee on 6/7/2005) FL 15+7/1 FLC 0+1 Others 0+1 (Free to Aldershot T on 15/8/2006)
Dagenham & Redbridge (Free from Crawley T, ex St Albans C, on 9/7/2007) FL 9+1 Others 1

O'LEARY Kristian (Kris) Denis
Born: Port Talbot, 30 August 1977
Height: 6'0" **Weight:** 13.4
Club Honours: Div 3 '00; AMC '06
International Honours: W: Yth
Experienced campaigner Kris was in his testimonial season with Swansea and was a regular starter in midfield during the first half of the season. He played as centre-back in one game, at Huddersfield, and is a useful man to have in any squad, given his ability to play in defence or midfield.
Swansea C (From trainee on 1/7/1996) FL 238+46/10 FLC 13 FAC 15+3/1 Others 21+2
Cheltenham T (Loaned on 23/11/2006) FL 5/1

Jay Jay Okocha

O'LEARY Stephen Michael
Born: Barnet, 12 February 1985
Height: 5'10"   **Weight:** 11.8
Club Honours: Div 1 '05
International Honours: RoI: Yth
After Stephen's patient wait for an extended run with Luton, there was some reward when he played in the final three games of 2006-07 but the signing of nine players in the summer set him back again. He replaced Steve Robinson in the 5-0 FA Cup third round replay defeat at Liverpool and played as well as anybody but manager Mick Harford put him on the bench in his second game in charge, at Bournemouth. A central or right-sided midfielder, Stephen works hard on and off the ball, with clever runs and accurate passes. Given his first start at the end of February, at home to Millwall, he played in the centre of midfield but when David Bell went on loan to Leicester he successfully moved into a more defensive role. He acquitted himself well with his tackling and clever marking in eight consecutive games.
Luton T (From trainee on 3/8/2004) FL 30+15/3 FLC 2+1 FAC 2+2 Others 2+1
Tranmere Rov (Loaned on 21/10/2005) FL 19+2/3 Others 1

OLEMBE Rene **Saloman**
Born: Yaounde, Cameroon, 8 December 1980
Height: 5'7"   **Weight:** 10.6
International Honours: Cameroon: 60
The Cameroon international defender signed for Wigan shortly after the transfer deadline last September on a one-year deal, having been released by Marseille earlier in the summer. A left-back with Premier League experience for Leeds during the 2003-04 season, he showed his versatility when playing on the left of midfield in his Wigan debut at Manchester United. Always giving good defensive cover to the full-back, his only other Premiership start was at Arsenal. Out of contract at the end of the season, he was expected to join team-mate Julius Aghahowa at Turkish club Kayserispor.
Leeds U (Loaned from Olympique Marseille, France, ex Nantes, on 31/8/2003) PL 8+4 FLC 2
Wigan Ath (Free from Olympique Marseille, France on 6/9/2007) PL 2+6 FAC 1

OLI Dennis Chiedozie
Born: Newham, 28 January 1984
Height: 6'0"   **Weight:** 12.2
Club Honours: FAT '05, '06
International Honours: E: SP-5
Hard-working striker Dennis joined Gillingham from Grays, initially on loan, and celebrated by scoring two superb

goals in the 2-1 defeat of Hartlepool in November. He eventually struck up an excellent partnership with Simeon Jackson and having impressed the management as a player who will continue to improve, signed a full contract in February designed to keep him at Priestfield Stadium until 2010. While not a prolific scorer his pace, especially when coming in from wide positions, keeps defenders on their toes.
Queens Park Rgrs (From juniors on 24/10/2001) FL 8+15 FLC 0+1 FAC 1+2 Others 2+1
Swansea C (Free on 6/8/2004) FL 0+1
Cambridge U (Free on 9/9/2004) FL 4/1 Others 1 (Freed on 24/11/2004)
Gillingham (Signed from Grays Ath on 12/11/2007) FL 17+5/4 Others 0+1/1

OLOFINJANA Seyi George
Born: Lagos, Nigeria, 30 June 1980
Height: 6'4"   **Weight:** 11.10
International Honours: Nigeria: 20
Seyi scored Wolverhampton's first goal

of the season, neatly taken. Some inspired performances helped him clinch a contract extension but a second goal eluded him. He was not having the same impact on games, although he missed only one in the League up to January, when he represented Nigeria in the African Cup of Nations. Seyi seemed tired on his return, not making a first-team start for some time, but a well-taken goal at Burnley showed he was recovering form and his third goal came on the final day.
Wolverhampton W (£1,700,000 from SK Brann Bergen, Norway on 6/8/2004) FL 123+12/16 FLC 3+1 FAC 6/1 Others 2/1

**O'LOUGHLIN Charles
(Charlie)** Michael P
Born: Birmingham, 17 March 1989
Height: 6'1"   **Weight:** 13.2
The tall central defender appeared for a total of 63 minutes in Port Vale's team

Seyi Olofinjana

last season and half of them were spent in attack. His League debut was as a substitute for the final eight minutes of a defeat at Cheltenham, when he was thrown up front to cause havoc, which he did. The same thing happened in the next game when Vale were 3-2 down at Carlisle, this time for 27 minutes, and he almost scored with a header. He spent a month on loan with Hinckley in the Blue Square North. A wholehearted player, he never managed to hold down a first-team berth and was released on a free transfer after his final substitute appearance at Southend.
Port Vale *(From trainee on 27/7/2007) FL 0+3*

OLSSON Martin Tony Waikwa
Born: Sweden, 17 May 1988
Height: 5'7" **Weight:** 12.11
International Honours: Sweden: U21
Profiting from an injury to Bruno Berner, Martin was given his Blackburn debut in the Carling Cup game against Birmingham. A small but fast and skilful left-back, he would have been on the substitutes' bench more often had he not lost two months in the New Year for surgery on an ankle. He was back in action in the last home game of the season and demonstrated that he has the skill to play left midfield if required.
Blackburn Rov *(Signed from Hogaborgs BK, Sweden on 31/1/2006) PL 0+2 FLC 1 Others 0+1*

OMOZUSI Elliott
Born: Hackney, 15 December 1988
Height: 5'11" **Weight:** 12.9
International Honours: E: Yth
The talented young Fulham defender made several appearances at right-back during a two-month period late in 2007. Composed and effective both in the air and on the ground, he was outstanding in the 3-1 win over Reading in early November and despite receiving a late red card in that game, returned to the side at Old Trafford a month later. In the second half of the season, Elliott spent time in the reserves where he was sometimes asked to play in a more central defensive role. He did so without fuss and, already capped at under-19 level by England, looks to have a good future.
Fulham *(From juniors on 20/12/2005) PL 8 FLC 0+2 FAC 1*

O'NEIL Gary Paul
Born: Bromley, 18 May 1983
Height: 5'10" **Weight:** 11.0
Club Honours: Div 1 '03
International Honours: E: U21-7; Yth
A niggling ankle injury meant Gary missed

Portsmouth's first two League games of the 2007-08 season. Shrugging this off, he played well in the next two games but appeared only as a substitute in a Carling Cup match against Leeds in late August. This turned out to be his last appearance in a Pompey shirt as, to the dismay of many fans, the club's longest-serving player was transferred to Middlesbrough, having been the subject of a surprise swoop by manager Gareth Southgate on August transfer deadline day. It was a close run thing as he failed the medical because of a long-standing ankle problem but Boro pressed ahead, signing Gary on a five-year deal and a fee dependent on appearances. Later, in the last game of the old year, he set up the only goal when his new club visited Fratton Park. The versatile and energetic midfield player can play in a central role or wide on either flank but appeared mainly on the right for Middlesbrough. Gary's season, steady and unspectacular, ended prematurely when he suffered knee-ligament damage in the closing stages at Tottenham in April but immediate corrective surgery was successful and he is expected to be ready for action for the start of the new season.
Portsmouth *(From trainee on 5/6/2000) P/FL 142+33/16 FLC 7+4/1 FAC 7+1*
Walsall *(Loaned on 26/9/2003) FL 7*
Cardiff C *(Loaned on 24/9/2004) FL 8+1/1*
Middlesbrough *(£5,000,000 on 31/8/2007) PL 25+1 FAC 2+1*

ONIBUJE Folawiyo (Fola)
Born: Lagos, Nigeria, 25 September 1984
Height: 6'5" **Weight:** 14.9
Fola signed for Shrewsbury on non-contract terms last August to see if he could establish himself after being released by Wycombe and he made his debut in the Carling Cup victory over Colchester, looking to be a useful target-man. Fola's only other appearance was as a substitute against Fulham in the Carling Cup and he moved on without earning a full contract. It was also on a non-contract basis that he joined Macclesfield in March, making his one and only appearance in Keith Alexander's first match in charge as a late substitute in the home draw against Notts County. He was then injured in training and left the club in April.
Preston NE *(From juniors at Charlton Ath on 13/11/2002)*
Huddersfield T *(Loaned on 21/11/2003) FL 0+2*
Barnsley *(Free on 21/7/2004) FL 0+3 FAC 0+1*
Peterborough U *(Free on 24/3/2005) FL 0+2 (Freed during 2005 close season)*
Swindon T *(Signed from Cambridge U on*

1/7/2006) FL 6+8/2 FLC 1 Others 0+1
Brentford *(Loaned on 10/11/2006) FL 0+2 FAC 1*
Wycombe W *(Free on 1/1/2007) FL 1+4*
Shrewsbury T *(Free on 9/8/2007) FLC 1+1 (Freed on 1/9/2007)*
Macclesfield T *(Free, following spell out of the game after appearing for St Albans C, on 29/2/2008) FL 0+1*

ONUOHA Chinedum (Nedum)
Born: Warri, Nigeria, 12 November 1986
Height: 6'2" **Weight:** 12.4
International Honours: E: U21-14; Yth
Another product of Manchester City's prolific Academy, Nedum is a strong, intelligent young right-back who is also comfortable playing in the centre of defence. Having made his City debut back in October 2004, he has gone on to force his way into regular contention. His progress is a real highpoint for City fans who love to watch talented youngsters develop and the City-supporting youngster has received international recognition with England under-21s. Unfortunately, injuries hampered Nedum's season but a handful of excellent performances, including a wonderful first goal to seal the points against Tottenham in March, were reminders that he has a bright future.
Manchester C *(From trainee on 16/11/2004) PL 47+14/1 FLC 4+1 FAC 4*

OOIJER Andre Antonius Maria
Born: Amsterdam, Holland, 11 July 1974
Height: 6'0" **Weight:** 12.0
International Honours: Holland: 40
Andre returned at the start of the season for Blackburn, having suffered a broken leg at Christmas in the previous campaign. Completely recovered, there is a case for considering him the club's best defender. Cool and an organiser, he suffered a little from his versatility that saw him play at right-back as well as in central defence. He was constantly switched and the obvious preference for the pairing of Christopher Samba and Ryan Nelsen limited his appearances. A born competitor, the Dutchman was never one to surrender without a fight, no matter how badly the game was going.
Blackburn Rov *(£2,000,000 from PSV Eindhoven, Holland, ex SDZ, FC Volendam, Roda JC Kerkrade, on 25/8/2006) PL 43+4 FLC 1 FAC 1 Others 12*

ORLANDI Andrea
Born: Barcelona, Spain, 3 August 1984
Height: 6'0" **Weight:** 12.2
Signed by Swansea on a free from Spanish side Alaves on transfer deadline

day, the left-sided wide midfielder had been on a two-year loan from Barcelona's 'B' team. A talented player on the ball, with excellent crossing ability, he suffered sprained medial knee ligaments against Brighton in a Johnstone's Paint Trophy tie in January, an injury that kept him out of action for three months.

Swansea C *(Free from Deportivo Alaves, Spain, ex Barcelona - loan, Aris Salonika, on 31/8/2007) FL 1+7 FAC 2+2 Others 3*

ORMEROD Brett Ryan
Born: Blackburn, 18 October 1976
Height: 5'11" **Weight:** 11.4
Club Honours: AMC '02
Brett started Preston's first three games of the season but never managed a longer run as first choice. Chances were few and far between for the busy, hard-working forward and he made only nine starts and 11 appearances from the bench. Brett's only goal was an early strike in the home win over Plymouth and frustration at only five brief substitute appearances from December persuaded him to move on loan to Nottingham Forest in March. There he was consistently in the side as Forest made a late surge to seal automatic promotion to the Championship. Brett is a forward who never gives defenders a moment's peace and is always willing to chase lost causes.

Blackpool *(£50,000 from Accrington Stanley on 21/3/1997) FL 105+23/45 FLC 8/4 FAC 5+1/5 Others 7+2/8*
Southampton *(£1,750,000 on 7/12/2001) P/FL 62+37/12 FLC 6+1/6 FAC 6+4/1*
Leeds U *(Loaned on 23/9/2004) FL 6*
Wigan Ath *(Loaned on 18/3/2005) FL 3+3/2*
Preston NE *(Free on 30/1/2006) FL 37+25/13 FLC 1 FAC 1+2/1 Others 2*
Nottingham F *(Loaned on 7/3/2008) FL 13/2*

ORR Bradley James
Born: Liverpool, 1 November 1982
Height: 6'0" **Weight:** 11.12
Many Bristol City fans wondered about the ability of the defender when he joined on a free from Newcastle in 2004. None could doubt his commitment and he is now good enough to be picked by fellow professionals in the PFA 'Championship Select' team. Bradley has worked hard and, having much improved his distribution, must now surely rate as one of City's best ever right-backs. As in the previous season, he weighed in with some important goals, although his winner at Scunthorpe was perhaps fortunate. Sadly, his season ended on a low when he suffered a depressed fracture of his cheekbone, ending his involvement in the Championship play-off final at Wembley in the 40th minute. He was sorely missed

as not only had he been playing well but it disrupted the City team.
Newcastle U *(From trainee on 12/7/2001)*
Burnley *(Loaned on 29/1/2004) FL 1+3*
Bristol C *(Free on 30/7/2004) FL 129+23/9 FLC 3+1/1 FAC 8 Others 8*

OSBORNE Junior
Born: Watford, 12 February 1988
Height: 5'10" **Weight:** 10.12
Having failed to make an appearance for Watford in 2006-07, last season saw Junior on the team sheet just once, when he came off the bench in the Carling Cup. The young full-back again proved very unlucky with injuries, requiring operations on both knees. A pacy player with good touch, Junior will be desperate to get going this coming season.
Watford *(From trainee on 4/7/2005) FL 1+1 FLC 0+2*

OSBORNE Karleigh Anthony Jonathan
Born: Southall, 19 March 1988
Height: 6'2" **Weight:** 12.8
The Brentford centre-back, who is reasonably quick and prefers to play alongside a big centre-half, could not nail down a regular place despite having three spells in the defence during the campaign and clocking up over 30 appearances. He was most impressive when he partnered Matt Heywood and he captained the

side in Matt's absence in February. He scored his first Brentford goal against Shrewsbury in January.
Brentford *(From trainee on 27/6/2006) FL 44+8/1 FLC 2+1 FAC 0+1 Others 3*

OSBOURNE Isaac Samuel
Born: Birmingham, 22 June 1986
Height: 5'10" **Weight:** 11.12
Isaac was given Coventry's problem right-back shirt at the start of the season following David McNamee's calf injury and did an excellent job. When McNamee returned in October, Isaac moved to midfield, normally wide right where his combative tackling and energetic running showed to good effect. At Christmas McNamee was injured again and Isaac reverted to right-back where, other than two games from loanee Richard Duffy, he stayed. Chris Coleman made it clear that he wanted to bring in a right-back, so it seems that Isaac will have to fight for a midfield place.
Coventry C *(From trainee on 10/7/2003) FL 69+13 FLC 6 FAC 5*
Crewe Alex *(Loaned on 20/10/2006) FL 2 FLC 1 Others 1*

OSBOURNE Isaiah
Born: Birmingham, 5 November 1987
Height: 6'2" **Weight:** 12.7
Isaiah is a centre-back or holding midfielder. A local boy, developed through

Karleigh Osborne

Aston Villa's youth system, he continues to show some promise but has started only three games and was mainly used as a substitute in 2007-08. Was on the verge of joining Leicester on loan in January until the deal was blocked because of mounting injury concerns at Villa Park.
Aston Villa *(From trainee on 11/11/2005)* PL 7+12 FLC 3 FAC 1

OSEI-KUFFOUR Jonathan (Jo)
Born: Edmonton, 17 November 1981
Height: 5'7" **Weight:** 10.6
Club Honours: FAYC '00
Signed from Brentford in the summer, the striker enjoyed a tremendous second half to last season and despite off-field problems, managed to become the equal highest scorer at Bournemouth. Jo is a highly talented player with deceptive speed and an uncanny ability to hold the ball under pressure. He can also play behind a front two to great effect.
Arsenal *(From trainee on 18/7/2000)*
Swindon T *(Loaned on 24/8/2001)* FL 4+7/2 FLC 1 Others 1
Torquay U *(Free on 18/10/2002)* FL 111+37/ 29 FLC 2+1/1 FAC 5+1/1 Others 3+1/2
Brentford *(Free on 6/7/2006)* FL 38+1/12 FLC 2/1 FAC 1 Others 2/1
Bournemouth *(Free on 3/7/2007)* FL 37+5/ 12 FLC 1 FAC 2 Others 3/1

O'SHEA John Francis
Born: Waterford, 30 April 1981
Height: 6'3" **Weight:** 11.12
Club Honours: PL '03, '07, '08; CS '03, '07; FAC '04; FLC '06; UEFACL '08
International Honours: Rol: 45; U21-13; Yth (UEFA-U16 '98)
A highly talented Manchester United central defender who has presence, great composure and silky defensive skills, John's versatility remains a key part of United's game. Used as an emergency striker because of injury problems, John thus gained the distinction of having played in every position for United, including goalkeeper. Although he made more appearances as a substitute than as a starter in the Premiership, he is regarded by Sir Alex Ferguson as a hugely important player. Ferguson went on record to say: "John O'Shea is perhaps the most important cog in the Manchester United wheel". That is high praise indeed, coming from a man who is notoriously hard to please. "I rate John O'Shea as one of my greatest ever signings," Sir Alex added. With a new contract signed in November, John is expected to stay at the club until 2012.

Manchester U *(Signed from Waterford U on 2/9/1998)* PL 138+53/9 FLC 18+1/1 FAC 15+5/1 Others 44+14/1
Bournemouth *(Loaned on 18/1/2000)* FL 10/1 Others 1

OSMAN Leon
Born: Billinge, 17 May 1981
Height: 5'8" **Weight:** 11.0
Club Honours: FAYC '98
International Honours: E: Yth; Sch
The diminutive midfielder had arguably the finest season of his Everton career, despite missing the middle two months of the campaign with a broken toe. The former Academy player was deployed either in central midfield or out wide but also played as an auxiliary striker. Among his personal highlights were stunning strikes against Larissa and SK Brann in the UEFA Cup. Technically, Leon is among the most gifted in the Everton squad, with good, quick feet and an active football brain. To widespread satisfaction, he extended his contract to 2012.
Everton *(From trainee on 18/8/1998)* PL 112+20/17 FLC 8+3/1 FAC 7+1/2 Others 8+1/2
Carlisle U *(Loaned on 4/10/2002)* FL 10+2/1 Others 3/2
Derby Co *(Loaned on 26/1/2004)* FL 17/3

OSTER John Morgan
Born: Boston, 8 December 1978
Height: 5'9" **Weight:** 10.8
Club Honours: Ch '06
International Honours: W: 13; B-1; U21-9; Yth
A fringe player at Reading for most of last season, John was a candidate for the wide-right midfield position during the final three months of the campaign. Frequently substituted, he completed the full 90 minutes in only two of his 18 appearances, one of these being Reading's last Premiership game at Derby. A tricky, clever winger with the ability to beat a player and deliver a telling cross, John was handicapped by the tendency to be closed down. Having made more substitute appearances (47) than any other member of the current squad, he was told at the end of the season that his contract would not be renewed.
Grimsby T *(From trainee on 11/7/1996)* FL 21+3/3 FAC 0+1/1
Everton *(£1,500,000 on 21/7/1997)* PL 22+18/1 FLC 4+1/1 FAC 2+3/1
Sunderland *(£1,000,000 on 6/8/1999)* P/FL 48+20/5 FLC 9+2/1 FAC 7+3 Others 2
Barnsley *(Loaned on 19/10/2001)* FL 2
Grimsby T *(Loaned on 1/11/2002)* FL 10/5
Grimsby T *(Loaned on 21/2/2003)* FL 7/1
Leeds U *(Loaned on 5/11/2004)* FL 8/1

Burnley *(Free on 28/1/2005)* FL 12+3/1 FAC 2+1
Reading *(Free on 2/8/2005)* P/FL 29+47/2 FLC 6/1 FAC 8

OSTLUND Alexander
Born: Akersberga, Sweden, 2 November 1978
Height: 5'11" **Weight:** 12.1
International Honours: Sweden: 22; U21
Alexander, long-haired and bearded, cuts a distinctive figure, on the right of the Southampton back four – when he plays. Despite being a Swedish international, he failed to convince any of the three management teams at St Mary's in the past season that he should hold down a regular place, despite the fact he is an uncompromising tackler and works effectively down the flank. He lost his place to Jermaine Wright early in the season and tore a hamstring in October. On recovery he was kept out of the team by the on-loan Phil Ifil. Further minor injuries impeded his reintroduction and, during the nail-biting finale, he was not even among the substitutes. Out of contract in the summer, he is looking for a new club.
Southampton *(Signed from Feyenoord, Holland on 30/1/2006)* FL 35+9 FLC 1 FAC 3 Others 1

O'TOOLE John (John-Joe) Joseph
Born: Harrow, 30 September 1988
Height: 6'2" **Weight:** 13.7
International Honours: Rol: U21-4
John-Joe was Watford's find of last season, claiming a regular place in midfield after making his full League debut against Hull in October. A product of the Watford Academy, he is a mobile and combative player who tackles strongly and has the priceless knack of timing his late runs into opposing penalty areas, which resulted in four goals. He was controversially sent off against Leicester in February but the decision was subsequently rescinded. Although born in Harrow, John-Joe has an Irish grandfather and this connection enabled him to make a scoring debut for the Republic of Ireland under-21 team at the age of 19. At the end of the season he was voted Watford's 'Young Player of the Year'.
Watford *(From trainee on 27/9/2007)* FL 23+12/3 FLC 0+1 FAC 1/1 Others 0+1

OTSEMOBOR Jon
Born: Liverpool, 23 March 1983
Height: 5'10" **Weight:** 12.7
International Honours: E: Yth
The former Liverpool and Crewe right-

back joined Norwich on a free transfer in summer and played in all but four of City's games. He possesses all the attributes to perform at the very highest level but occasionally suffered lapses of concentration that took the shine off his excellent progress. Jon is incredibly quick, loves to go on swashbuckling runs down the right to bolster his side's attacking options and was a bit unfortunate to end the season with only one goal. He has a tremendous range of passing, as might be expected of a Liverpool and Crewe graduate, and tremendous upper body strength to knock opponents off the ball. This was his first full season at Championship level and he has the ability to become an even better player in the years ahead.

Liverpool *(From trainee on 23/3/2000) PL 4 FLC 2*
Hull C *(Loaned on 13/3/2003) FL 8+1/3*
Bolton W *(Loaned on 2/2/2004) PL 1*
Crewe Alex *(Loaned on 30/9/2004) FL 14/1 FLC 1*
Rotherham U *(Free on 1/8/2005) FL 4+6 FLC 1+1/1 Others 2*
Crewe Alex *(Free on 18/1/2006) FL 43 FLC 3 FAC 1 Others 3*
Norwich C *(Free on 3/7/2007) FL 41+2/1 FLC 3 FAC 0+1*

[OUBINA] MELENDEZ Borja Oubina

Born: Vigo, Spain, 17 May 1982
Height: 6'0" **Weight:** 11.11
International Honours: Spain: 2
Signed on a season-long loan from Celta Vigo, the classy midfielder played a total of only 16 minutes for Birmingham because of a serious knee injury. In his second game and first start, at Liverpool in September, he got his leg tangled in a tackle with Dirk Kuyt and suffered cruciate ligament damage. His loan was cancelled and he underwent rehabilitation back in his native Spain. Cited as a major loss by the club as they felt he would have been their midfield lynchpin, sitting deep to take the ball and bring others into the game with a range of intelligent passing.

Birmingham C *(Loaned from Celta Vigo, Spain, on 31/8/2007) PL 1+1*

OWEN Gareth David

Born: Cheadle, 21 September 1982
Height: 6'1" **Weight:** 11.6
International Honours: W: Yth
Purchased from Oldham in the summer, having spent the previous season on loan at Edgeley Park, the big Stockport defender had a commanding season at the back, alongside long-time defensive partner Ashley Williams. Although

Williams' injuries and eventual move meant that Gareth had several other partners at centre-half, he settled well beside each one. A cheekbone injury against Wycombe in the second leg of the play-off semi-final failed to keep him out and he played in the final against Rochdale with a special protective mask, eventually captaining his side to victory and promotion.

Stoke C *(From trainee on 5/7/2001) FL 1+4*
Oldham Ath *(Loaned on 16/1/2004) FL 15/1*
Torquay U *(Loaned on 1/7/2004) FL 2+3 FLC 1*
Oldham Ath *(£50,000 on 19/3/2005) FL 26 FLC 1 FAC 2+1*
Stockport Co *(Signed on 4/7/2006) FL 74+1 FLC 3 FAC 3 Others 5*

OWEN Michael James

Born: Chester, 14 December 1979
Height: 5'9" **Weight:** 11.2
Club Honours: FAYC '96; FLC '01, '03; FAC '01; UEFAC '01; ESC '01; CS '01
International Honours: E: 89; B-2; U21-1; Yth; Sch
Michael's Newcastle career continued to be plagued by injuries, beginning with a thigh problem that delayed his start to last season as he missed the opener. He made two substitute appearances before his first start against Barnsley in the Carling Cup but within a month was in Germany for double groin surgery, returning eight days later as a scoring substitute against Everton. He then tore a thigh muscle in England's friendly against Austria in November, putting him out of the decisive Euro 2008 qualifier against Croatia. Back at the turn of the year, he was ever-present to the end of the season, his longest run in a black and white shirt, and his importance to the club was acknowledged when he was appointed team captain by new manager Kevin Keegan. A series of injuries have robbed Michael of the cutting-edge pace he once had, and recognising this, Keegan introduced a new attacking formation with Michael playing slightly behind the front line, which seemed to suit him well. He retains his world-class striker's instinct for space and timing. Arriving from a deeper position made him difficult for defences to pick up, resulting in a return of seven goals in the last nine games that helped pull the club away from relegation worries. The role also exploits his excellent distribution - his pass completion rate for the season was an impressive 83 per cent - and his contribution is growing into more than that of a pure striker. His goal against Fulham in March meant he has now

scored more times for Newcastle than against them.

Liverpool *(From juniors on 18/12/1996) PL 193+23/118 FLC 12+2/9 FAC 14+1/8 Others 48+4/23 (£11,000,000 to Real Madrid, Spain on 20/8/2004)*
Newcastle U *(£16,000,000 from Real Madrid, Spain on 31/8/2005) PL 37+6/18 FLC 1/1 FAC 3/1*

OWENS Graeme Adam

Born: Cramlington, 1 June 1988
Height: 5'10" **Weight:** 11.5
Capable of playing on either wing, Graeme was a member of Middlesbrough's 2004 FA Youth Cup winning side at the tender age of 15. He made his senior debut as a substitute in the Carling Cup against eventual winners Tottenham, playing the final 14 minutes. His progress continued with some good performances in the reserves and in order to advance himself he joined Chesterfield on the March deadline day, showing great promise in taking the difficult step from reserve football to harder stuff in League Two. Highly rated, he has a huge reserve of pace and good close control to torment defenders. He also enjoys cutting in to mix it in the penalty area.

Middlesbrough *(From trainee on 4/7/2007) FLC 0+1*
Chesterfield *(Loaned on 27/3/2008) FL 2+2*

OWUSU Lloyd Magnus

Born: Slough, 12 December 1976
Height: 6'1" **Weight:** 14.0
Club Honours: Div 3 '99
International Honours: Ghana: 2
The big target-man, signed from Brentford in the summer, ended last season as Yeovil's top scorer. Imposing in the air and equally good with his feet, Lloyd scored 11 goals after setting out with five in his first nine games. He gained quite a fan following for the unique dances to celebrate his goals and is very much a team player. Lloyd had a relatively injury-free season and will be looking to add more goals.

Brentford *(£25,000 from Slough T on 29/7/1998) FL 148+16/64 FLC 3+4/3 FAC 8/2 Others 13+3/4*
Sheffield Wed *(Free on 8/7/2002) FL 24+28/9 FLC 2+1 FAC 3/1 Others 1+1*
Reading *(Signed on 23/12/2003) FL 25+16/10 FLC 1+1 FAC 0+3*
Brentford *(Free on 29/7/2005) FL 43+6/12 FAC 6/2*
Yeovil T *(Free on 8/8/2007) FL 31+12/9 FLC 1/1 FAC 1 Others 3/1*

P

PAGE Robert John
Born: Rhondda, 3 September 1974
Height: 6'0" **Weight:** 12.5
Club Honours: Div 2 '98
International Honours: W: 41; B-1;
U21-6; Yth; Sch
Less than a year after signing a contract extension until 2009, Robert was out of favour with Coventry manager Iain Dowie and restricted to two Carling Cup games against lower division opposition. Despite some excellent performances for the reserves, he was never in contention for a League start, and following interest from several clubs Robert plumped for Huddersfield in January. From first kick to last, the experienced defender stamped his authority on games and other Huddersfield players. Robert's no-nonsense approach brought a winning start against Oldham in the FA Cup and he bossed the team to three consecutive League victories without conceding a goal. Strong in the air and equally capable in the tackle, he organised Town so well that he was made captain. Robert is a born leader and Huddersfield kept ten clean sheets in the 20 games he started, but with his contract expiring in the summer he missed the final match to negotiate a move to Chesterfield.
Watford (From trainee on 19/4/1993) P/FL 209+7/2 FLC 17 FAC 12+1 Others 6/1
Sheffield U (£350,000 on 8/8/2001) FL 106+1/1 FLC 7 FAC 11 Others 3
Cardiff C (Free on 3/7/2004) FL 8+1
Coventry C (Free on 22/2/2005) FL 69+1/1 FLC 3 FAC 3
Huddersfield T (Free on 22/1/2008) FL 18/1 FAC 2

PAINTER Marcos
Born: Sutton Coldfield, 17 August 1986
Height: 5'11" **Weight:** 12.4
Club Honours: Div 1 '08
International Honours: RoI: U21-7; Yth
A foot injury soon after the start of the season saw the solid, dependable left-back sidelined but on his return to action, Marcos displayed a good level of consistency until March, when a hamstring injury forced an unwanted rest. He returned to action in early April as Swansea claimed promotion to the Championship.
Birmingham C (From trainee on 14/7/2005)

Wilson Palacios

P/FL 3+2 FLC 2+1 FAC 2+1
Swansea C (£50,000 on 16/11/2006) FL 51+2 FLC 1 FAC 2+1 Others 4

PALACIOS Wilson Roberto
Born: La Ceiba, Honduras, 29 July 1984
Height: 5'10" **Weight:** 11.3
International Honours: Honduras: 46
Signed on loan from Honduran side Olimpia after a recommendation from Arsene Wenger, Wilson was finding his feet at Birmingham when his brother, Edwin Rene, was kidnapped and manager Steve Bruce left for Wigan. City's new manager Alex McLeish had not seen enough of him to commit to a £700,000 signing but his abrasive style, allied to running power and shrewd passing, was ultimately missed. A dominant force in the Wigan engine room, the Honduran international was signed on a three-and-a-half year deal in the January transfer window. Nicknamed 'The Magician' in his country, Wilson is a tough, aggressive midfielder, difficult to dispossess and a brave tackler. After his Wigan debut at Derby, Wilson's high workrate quickly made him a fans' favourite and with Michael Brown playing the holding role he was encouraged to get forward, often making dangerous runs into the box, although failing to score.
Birmingham C (Loaned from Olimpia, Honduras, ex Deportivo Victoria, on 31/8/2007) PL 4+3 FLC 0+1
Wigan Ath (£1,000,000 from Olimpia, Honduras on 11/1/2008) PL 16 FAC 1

PALETHORPE Philip (Phil) John
Born: Birkenhead, 17 September 1986
Height: 6'2" **Weight:** 11.5
Phil started the season as Chester's third-choice goalkeeper and in November joined Blue Square North side Tamworth on loan. Following the departure of Gavin Ward in January, Phil was recalled from the Lamb and became a regular on the bench at the Deva Stadium. He made his City debut, and only appearance, as a late substitute in the home game against Darlington following a head injury to John Danby. Was released at the end of the campaign.
Tranmere Rov (From trainee on 19/9/2003)
Chester C (Free on 18/8/2006) FL 0+1

PALMER Aiden Witting
Born: Enfield, 2 January 1987
Height: 5'8" **Weight:** 10.4
Aiden started the season at Leyton Orient as reserve to Charlie Daniels at left-back before regaining his first-team place and signing a new contract. This occurred when a clause was triggered

after he had played the requisite number of senior games during the season. He is comfortable on the ball and takes every opportunity possible to join up with the attack.
Leyton Orient (From trainee on 19/7/2006) FL 35+2 FLC 3 Others 3

PALMER Christopher (Chris) Louis
Born: Derby, 16 October 1983
Height: 5'7" **Weight:** 10.12
Chris is a popular attacking left-back or left-winger at Wycombe and although competition for those places increased in summer, it was still a surprise when he went on loan to Darlington in August. Starting the first five games of the season for Darlington on the left, either in midfield or on the wing, he showed good pace with an ability to put in telling crosses on the run. Chris was due to stay until January but returned early in October, unable to settle. Following his return he had to be content with a place in the reserves until a surprise start at Notts County in the penultimate League game, his only appearance, before being released.
Derby Co (From trainee on 3/7/2003)
Notts Co (Free on 2/7/2004) FL 48+6/5 FLC 1/1 FAC 4+1 Others 0+1
Wycombe W (Free on 1/8/2006) FL 23+10 FLC 2+3 FAC 1+1 Others 2
Darlington (Loaned on 9/8/2007) FL 4 FLC 1

PALMER Marcus James
Born: Gloucester, 6 January 1988
Height: 6'0" **Weight:** 11.7
The young striker remained on the fringes of the Hereford side until a five-goal performance in a county cup-tie moved him up the pecking order last season. After a solitary substitute appearance, the pacy youngster went on loan to Gloucester where a hat-trick on his debut confirmed his eye for goal. Although he returned to Hereford, he was unable to challenge again for a first-team place.
Hereford U (From trainee at Cheltenham T on 31/8/2006) FL 1+3

PAMAROT Louis Noe
Born: Paris, France, 14 April 1979
Height: 6'2" **Weight:** 13.0
Club Honours: FAC '08
As in the previous season, Noe was not initially first choice in Portsmouth's defence but, from the end of August, featured regularly until a hamstring injury in mid-December kept him sidelined for a month. On his return he played in five further Premier League games and an FA Cup tie before a medial knee ligament injury, sustained in the win at Bolton,

again disrupted his season. By preference a central defender, he appeared in various positions in the back four and played his part in ensuring Pompey kept so many clean sheets. He scored three goals, two of which helped defeat Leeds 3-0 in a Carling Cup tie. His other one, a contender for 'Goal of the Season', was a stunning 30-yard left-footed volley to open the scoring in a 4-1 defeat of Newcastle at St James' Park. He made his comeback in a reserve game at the end of April, turned in an excellent performance, played in the final Premier League game and was an unused substitute in the FA Cup final.
Portsmouth (Loaned from OGC Nice, France, ex Paris St Germain, Martigues, on 7/9/1999) FL 1+1 FLC 0+1
Tottenham H (£1,700,000 from OGC Nice, France on 24/8/2004) PL 23+2/1 FLC 3 FAC 2/1
Portsmouth (Signed on 12/1/2006) PL 39+10/3 FLC 5/2 FAC 1

PANTSIL John
Born: Berekum, Ghana, 15 June 1981
Height: 5'10" **Weight:** 10.10
International Honours: Ghana: 43
The versatile West Ham defender was unable to establish himself as a regular member of the side but endeared himself to the fans with his all-action style. He was magnificent against Manchester United in December, when he went on as a substitute and played on the right flank to have a big part in the 2-1 victory. During the season he represented Ghana, adding to his many caps.
West Ham U (£1,000,000 from Hapoel Tel Aviv, Israel, ex Berekum Arsenal, Liberty Professionals, Berekum Arsenal, Maccabi Tel Aviv, on 7/8/2006) PL 7+12 FLC 1+2 FAC 1+1

PARK Ji-Sung
Born: Seoul, South Korea, 25 February 1981
Height: 5'9" **Weight:** 11.0
Club Honours: FLC '06; PL '07, '08
International Honours: South Korea: 70
An outstanding Manchester United midfielder who can play equally as well on either flank, Ji-Sung's appearances were severely limited, having had surgery in America on a recurring knee injury at the end of the previous campaign. He made a welcome return as a substitute in the Boxing Day fixture against Sunderland at Old Trafford. And what a return it was as United beat the Black Cats 4-0. Making his first start against Birmingham on New Year's Day, he scored his first Premiership goal of the season against Fulham in March. Though his lack of appearances for the Reds causes controversy in South

Korea, Ji-Sung takes things in his stride and proved his worth with an assist for Wayne Rooney in the Champions' League quarter-final against Roma in April. Saving arguably his best performance of the season for Barcelona at Old Trafford, Ji-Sung became the only Asian footballer to take part in the Champions' League semi-finals on three occasions, for PSV Eindhoven in 2005 and United in 2007 and 2008.
Manchester U (£4,000,000 from PSV Eindhoven, Holland, ex Kyoto Purple Sanga, on 11/7/2005) PL 39+20/7 FLC 3/1 FAC 7+2 Others 4+7

PARKER Benjamin (Ben) Brian Colin
Born: Pontefract, 8 November 1987
Height: 5'11" **Weight:** 11.6
International Honours: E: Yth
Although Leeds had made it to Wembley, Ben missed out, having gone out on loan to Darlington in February after appearing 15 times for the Elland Road side in 2007-08. However, the former England under-18 international reached the League Two play-offs with the Quakers and also looked to be heading for Wembley, only to injure a hamstring in the semi-final first leg draw against Rochdale and be forced out of the return. Although Ben was farmed out to the Quakers after spending the previous season on loan to Bradford, Leeds' boss Gary McAllister said that he has a future at Elland Road. Always willing to supplement the attack from left-back to deliver telling crosses, he also featured at centre-back. Before joining Darlington, Ben played for Leeds against them at the Arena in the Johnstone's Paint Trophy. A classy left-back, he shows great composure on the ball, distributes it intelligently and links well when attacking down the left.
Leeds U (From trainee on 16/11/2004) FL 6+3 FLC 2 FAC 2 Others 2
Bradford C (Loaned on 28/7/2006) FL 35+4 FAC 1 Others 1
Darlington (Loaned on 27/2/2008) FL 13 Others 1

PARKER Keigan
Born: Livingston, 8 June 1982
Height: 5'7" **Weight:** 10.5
International Honours: S: U21-1; Yth
Keigan was unable to make the step up from League One with Blackpool and following his 16 goals in 2006-07, failed to hit the net in ten League starts and 11 substitute appearances. The pacy striker started the season as first choice but by December was out of the team, with Ben Burgess and Andy Morrell being preferred. Keigan, very

much a confidence player, made only two appearances from the bench after the turn of the year and rejected a new contract. In May, the Scot joined League One side Huddersfield.

St Johnstone (From juniors on 1/8/1998) SL 80+44/23 SLC 7+3 SC 3+3 Others 3+1/2
Blackpool (Free on 21/7/2004) FL 96+45/34 FLC 6+2/1 FAC 6+2/2 Others 7+1/4

PARKER Scott Matthew

Born: Lambeth, 13 October 1980
Height: 5'7" **Weight:** 10.7
Club Honours: Div 1 '00; FLC '05
International Honours: E: 3; U21-12; Yth; Sch

Arriving from Newcastle in the summer, he was injured on the pre-season tour and unable to put together a decent run in the West Ham team until March. There were earlier appearances where the tough midfield player was able to show the Hammers what they had been missing, his grit and drive enabling him to go on surging runs through the middle. A creative player who uses the ball intelligently, he was superb at Middlesbrough in December when inspiring the team with a fine all-round performance and scoring the winner. A further injury brought more disruption before he was able to resume where he left off, giving a series of 'Man of the Match' performances.

Charlton Ath (From trainee on 22/10/1997) P/FL 104+24/9 FLC 8+2/1 FAC 4+3
Norwich C (Loaned on 31/10/2000) FL 6/1
Chelsea (£10,000,000 on 30/1/2004) PL 8+7/1 FLC 3 FAC 1 Others 7+2
Newcastle U (£6,500,000 on 15/6/2005) PL 54+1/4 FLC 4/1 FAC 3/1 Others 9+2
West Ham U (£7,000,000 on 7/6/2007) PL 17+1/1 FLC 2

PARKES Jordan David

Born: Hemel Hempstead, 26 July 1989
Height: 6'0" **Weight:** 12.0
International Honours: E: Yth

The highly regarded England under-19 left-back made two starts for Watford in the Carling Cup but suffered a setback in September after sustaining a broken metatarsal in training. Once he had recovered, he twice went out on loan, to Brentford and Barnet, to further his experience. Jordan made only one appearance for Brentford, as a substitute in midfield at Mansfield, but had more chances when he went to Barnet in March, featuring regularly at right-back in the Bees' final games and showing his potential in a number of solid performances.

Watford (From trainee on 5/2/2007) FLC 3
Brentford (Loaned on 17/11/2008) FL 0+1
Barnet (Loaned on 14/3/2008) FL 7+3

PARKIN Jonathan (Jon)

Born: Barnsley, 30 December 1981
Height: 6'4" **Weight:** 13.12

After being a hit in the previous season when on loan from Hull, Jon became manager Tony Pulis' first signing of the close season for Stoke. He had a battle to keep down his weight and spent most of the campaign sitting on the bench as Ricardo Fuller and Mama Sidibe filled the two striking roles. With further loan signings in January, Jon gradually lost his place as a substitute and his future was uncertain.

Barnsley (From trainee on 5/1/1999) FL 8+2 FLC 1+1 FAC 0+1
Hartlepool U (Loaned on 7/12/2001) FL 0+1
York C (Free on 7/2/2002) FL 64+10/14 FAC 2 Others 2/1
Macclesfield T (Free on 20/2/2004) FL 63+2/30 FLC 1/1 FAC 4+1/1 Others 7/4
Hull C (Signed on 12/1/2006) FL 40+7/11 FLC 1+2 FAC 2/1
Stoke C (Loaned on 10/3/2007) FL 5+1/3
Stoke C (£250,000 on 3/7/2007) FL 4+25/2 FLC 1 FAC 1+1

PARKIN Samuel (Sam)

Born: Roehampton, 14 March 1981
Height: 6'2" **Weight:** 13.0
International Honours: S: B-1; E- Sch

Sam's long-term ankle injuries took another turn for the worse when he

Scott Parker

was substituted after another knock on it in the Carling Cup first round against Dagenham last season. He was out until January, when he made his first tentative steps in the reserves, but injuries to Paul Furlong and Paul Peschisolido pushed him back into first-team action two weeks later, as a substitute for Calvin Andrew against Leeds. Sam repaid Mick Harford's faith with a stoppage-time goal, earning the manager his first point. Even when he was not fully fit, Harford persevered with him ahead of Andrew. Paired for the first time with the emerging talent of Ryan Charles against Cheltenham, the partnership worked well and as Sam's form and effectiveness returned, so did the goals - three in three games, his best run since he left Swindon.

Chelsea (From juniors on 21/8/1998)
Millwall (Loaned on 12/9/2000) FL 5+2/4
Wycombe W (Loaned on 24/11/2000) FL 5+3/1 FAC 0+3/1 Others 2/1
Oldham Ath (Loaned on 22/3/2001) FL 3+4/3
Northampton T (Loaned on 4/7/2001) FL 31+9/4 FLC 2/1 FAC 0+2 Others 2
Swindon T (Signed on 8/8/2002) FL 120+4/67 FLC 4+1/3 FAC 6 Others 5+2/3
Ipswich T (£450,000 on 29/7/2005) FL 17+5/5
Luton T (£325,000 on 25/8/2006) FL 19+8/6 FLC 1

PARKINSON Andrew (Andy) John

Born: Liverpool, 27 May 1979
Height: 5'8" **Weight:** 10.12
Andy has always been used as a right-sided midfielder-cum-striker at Notts County and has never really settled to that position. He is a skilful and experienced professional with an eye for goal. Rather underused last season but always enthusiastic, his reaction when summoned from the substitutes' bench is always exemplary as he joined the contest to do his best to influence the game. Was released in the summer.

Tranmere Rov (From trainee at Liverpool on 12/4/1997) FL 102+62/18 FLC 15+9/5 FAC 12+2/2 Others 1
Sheffield U (Free on 18/7/2003) FL 3+4 FLC 1 FAC 1+1
Notts Co (Loaned on 15/1/2004) FL 5/3
Notts Co (Loaned on 19/3/2004) FL 5+4
Grimsby T (Free on 30/7/2004) FL 75+10/12 FLC 4+1/1 FAC 2 Others 3
Notts Co (Free on 22/6/2006) FL 51+17/5 FLC 2 FAC 2 Others 0+1

PARNABY Stuart

Born: Bishop Auckland, 19 July 1982
Height: 5'11" **Weight:** 11.4
Club Honours: FLC '04
International Honours: E: U21-4; Yth; Sch

After joining Birmingham from Middlesbrough in the summer and with Stephen Kelly an ever-present at right-back, Stuart had to make do with bit parts, coming off the substitutes' bench usually for tactical reasons. Filled in as a defender or in midfield and was always diligent and eager to make his mark. His willingness to chase a lost cause won a dramatic late penalty at home to Arsenal and being quick over the ground was adept at taking up the correct position at either right or left-back, he did well for City.

Middlesbrough (From trainee on 21/7/1999) PL 73+18/2 FLC 5+3 FAC 11+1/1 Others 13+3/1
Halifax T (Loaned on 23/10/2000) FL 6
Birmingham C (Free on 3/7/2007) PL 4+9 FLC 2

PARRINELLO Tommaso (Tom) Salvatore

Born: Stoke Gifford, 11 November 1989
Height: 5'5" **Weight:** 10.12
The young Filton Academy left-back made his debut for Bristol Rovers as a substitute for the last five minutes of the FA Cup home victory over Rushden. Tom is expected to carry over his improvement to the coming season.

Bristol Rov (From Filton College on 26/7/2006) FAC 0+1

PARRISH Andrew (Andy) Michael

Born: Bolton, 22 June 1988
Height: 6'0" **Weight:** 11.0
Andy started at right-back in Bury's back five and played the first nine games of the season. Although he briefly lost his place to the returning Steve Haslam, injuries to other members of the defence meant that Andy was soon reinstated. This lasted only until Alan Knill took over and reverted to a back four. The loan signing of Efe Sodje saw him slip down the pecking order before being released in the summer.

Bury (From juniors at Bolton W on 23/9/2005) FL 29+14/1 FLC 1+1 FAC 3 Others 5

PARRY Paul Ian

Born: Chepstow, 19 August 1980
Height: 5'11" **Weight:** 11.12
International Honours: W: 11
Paul made the switch from winger to striker with good effect at Cardiff last season. Given freedom to roam and playing off the lead striker, mainly Jimmy Floyd Hasselbaink, he added extra zip and pace to the front line. Put his Welsh international career on hold for undisclosed personal reasons, although manager John Toshack said he would be back in when he was ready. Played at

Wembley in City's FA Cup final defeat at the hands of Portsmouth and was not found wanting as Cardiff battled away.
Cardiff C (£75,000 from Hereford U on 9/1/2004) FL 115+36/22 FLC 8+4 FAC 5/1

PARTINGTON Joseph (Joe) Michael

Born: Portsmouth, 1 April 1990
Height: 5'11" **Weight:** 12.0
International Honours: W: Yth
A young Bournemouth midfielder who represented Wales at under-19 level and also captained the side, Joe made his debut at Luton last season and went on to have several more appearances from the bench, scoring his first goal in the memorable victory at Swansea. He was among a number of young players to be offered a professional contract at the end of the campaign.

Bournemouth (Trainee - Brockenhurst College) FL 0+6/1

PARTRIDGE Richard (Richie) Joseph

Born: Dublin, 12 September 1980
Height: 5'8" **Weight:** 10.10
International Honours: RoI: U21-8; Yth (UEFA U18?98)
Richie, a long-time transfer target for Chester, signed from Rotherham in the summer and had an excellent first half of the season. A player with a great turn of pace who can play on either wing and is capable of delivering pinpoint crosses, he is also dangerous when cutting inside defenders and shooting from distance. This was shown to best effect at Stockport, when he scored both City goals with stunning long-range efforts in a 2-1 victory. For Richie, the latter half of the campaign was hampered by a series of injuries that saw him miss games and struggle to regain his momentum. However, on his day, Richie can be one of the best players in the division and a real match-winner.

Liverpool (From trainee on 16/9/1997) FLC 1+2
Bristol Rov (Loaned on 22/3/2001) FL 4+2/1
Coventry C (Loaned on 27/9/2002) FL 23+4/4 FLC 2 FAC 2
Sheffield Wed (Free on 5/8/2005) FL 6+9 FLC 1/1 FAC 1
Rotherham U (Free on 3/8/2006) FL 30+3/3 FLC 1/1 FAC 1 Others 1
Chester C (Signed on 2/7/2007) FL 34+2/5 Others 2/2

PATERSON James (Jim) Lee

Born: Airdrie, 25 September 1979
Height: 5'11" **Weight:** 13.6
International Honours: S: U21-9
Jim was signed by Plymouth from

Motherwell on a three-and-a-half year deal in January for an undisclosed fee, thought to be around £250,000. He is a hard-tackling left-back who loves to get forward to provide dangerous crosses and can also play on the left side of midfield, where he made his debut at Leicester in February. Jim scored his first goal in the victory at Southampton later that month but injury interrupted his season. He will be hoping to cement his first-team place at Home Park in the season ahead.

Dundee U (From juniors on 3/7/1996) SL 64+37/4 SLC 6+4/1 SC 4+6/2
Motherwell (Free on 14/7/2004) SL 91+17/5 SLC 9+1/1 SC 5+4
Plymouth Arg (Signed on 31/1/2008) FL 7+1/1

PATERSON Martin Andrew
Born: Tunstall, 13 May 1987
Height: 5'9" **Weight:** 11.5
International Honours: NI: 2; U21-2; Yth
Record signing Martin enjoyed a great first season with Championship side Scunthorpe, finishing as top scorer with 14 goals. A quick, hard-working player, who came in from Stoke, he netted in his first four starts for the club and didn't look back in the first half of the campaign. Attracted interest from a number of clubs during the January transfer window but stopped at Glanford Park and saved his best goal for last when he curled in a 25-yarder against Coventry at the start of March. His form was recognised with his first international caps for Northern Ireland but he missed the final match of the season after having a hernia operation.
Stoke C (From trainee on 27/6/2006) FL 2+13/1 FLC 0+1
Grimsby T (Loaned on 23/11/2006) FL 15/6
Scunthorpe U (Signed on 9/8/2007) FL 34+6/13 FLC 1/1 FAC 1

PATTERSON Marlon Anthony
Born: Southwark, 24 June 1983
Height: 5'8" **Weight:** 11.6
The left-back joined Dagenham in summer from Yeading and made his debut at Chester, showing great ability to go forward and deliver telling crosses. As a non-contract player, Marlon was always second choice and joined Welling for a month in December before spending the final two months at Grays in the Blue Square Premier.
Dagenham & Redbridge (Free from Yeading on 8/8/2007) FL 5+1

PATTISON Matthew (Matty) Joseph
Born: Johannesburg, South Africa, 27 October 1986
Height: 5'8" **Weight:** 12.4

Matty became Glenn Roeder's first permanent signing as Norwich manager in January following an earlier loan from Newcastle. Naturally left-sided, he prefers to play in central midfield from where he can break forward in support of his strikers and use his tenacious tackling to break up opposition attacks. He provides an excellent set-play delivery, particularly with crosses whipped in from the right with his left foot. Matty has yet to break his scoring duck but finds good positions and will surely be among the goals in future seasons. He hopes to break into the full South African squad now he has emerged as a first-team regular.
Newcastle U (From trainee on 21/12/2005) PL 4+6 FAC 2 Others 0+3
Norwich C (Signed on 15/11/2007) FL 22+5 FAC 2

PAYNTER William (Billy) Paul
Born: Liverpool, 13 July 1984
Height: 6'1" **Weight:** 12.0
The well-built striker made an immediate impact for Swindon after his arrival from Southend, hitting the first hat-trick of his career on his full League debut against Bournemouth during September, and soon following up with another brace against Gillingham. After that, his best form deserted him for a time and the goals dried up. Billy continued to work hard and could feel satisfied with a double figure goal return from all competitions, although he was used mainly from the bench towards the end of the season.
Port Vale (From trainee on 1/7/2002) FL 119+25/30 FLC 2+1 FAC 4+2/3 Others 5/1
Hull C (£150,000 on 9/11/2005) FL 11+11/3 FAC 1
Southend U (£200,000 on 5/8/2006) FL 5+4 FLC 2/1
Bradford C (Loaned on 31/1/2007) FL 15/4
Swindon T (Signed on 31/8/2007) FL 23+13/8 FAC 3+1/2

PEACOCK Lee Anthony
Born: Paisley, 9 October 1976
Height: 6'0" **Weight:** 12.8
Club Honours: AMC '97, '03
International Honours: S: U21-1; Yth
It was another successful season at Swindon for the hard-working Scot, who appears happy to play in any position. He began in midfield, having previously been recognised as a forward, but towards the end of the season was again used in attack, proving his effectiveness with a goal against Oldham in April. Whether as a forward or in midfield, Lee always plays with total commitment and can be relied upon to weigh in with a few goals.
Carlisle U (From trainee on 10/3/1995) FL

52+24/11 FLC 2+3 FAC 4+1/1 Others 6+4
Mansfield T (£90,000 on 17/10/1997) FL 79+10/29 FLC 4/1 FAC 4 Others 4/2
Manchester C (£500,000 on 5/11/1999) FL 4+4 FAC 1+1
Bristol C (£600,000 on 10/8/2000) FL 131+13/54 FLC 4/3 FAC 11/1 Others 16/5
Sheffield Wed (Free on 2/7/2004) FL 37+14/6 FLC 2+1/2 Others 3/1
Swindon T (Free on 20/1/2006) FL 87+7/18 FLC 1 FAC 5

PEAD Craig George
Born: Bromsgrove, 15 September 1981
Height: 5'9" **Weight:** 11.6
Club Honours: Div 2 '07
International Honours: E: Yth
Freed by Walsall in the summer, the competent right-back or central midfielder joined Brentford but missed the opening weeks through injury. He had a spell as a regular substitute before a disappointing run in midfield, after which he took over at right-back at the end of the year. Finding his right position, he was a regular for the rest of the season, looking the part and linking well with his colleagues. Craig was surprisingly transfer listed at the end of the campaign.
Coventry C (From trainee on 17/9/1998) FL 24+18/3 FLC 1 FAC 2
Notts Co (Loaned on 10/9/2004) FL 4+1 Others 1
Walsall (Free on 23/3/2005) FL 72+16 FLC 3 FAC 5 Others 4
Brentford (Free on 3/7/2007) FL 27+5 FAC 2 Others 0+1

PEARCE Alexander (Alex) James
Born: Wallingford, 9 November 1988
Height: 6'0" **Weight:** 11.10
International Honours: S: U21-1; Yth
Alex joined Reading's Academy at the age of ten and has developed into a powerful yet constructive centre-back. After making three appearances for Reading last season, in the Carling Cup at Swansea, and the FA Cup tie and replay against Tottenham, Alex broadened his experience through loans at Bournemouth and Norwich. The tall centre-half joined Bournemouth in November and, despite his tender years, showed himself to be a true leader on the field, settling well into the rigours of League One football before returning to Reading. A series of mature and forceful displays for Norwich in the second half of the season earned widespread praise. Powerful in the air and determined in the tackle, he was not afraid to play his way constructively out of defence rather than just launching the ball forward at the first opportunity. An outstanding prospect, he was selected

for the Scotland under-21 squad at the end of the season and has committed his future to Reading on a long-term contract.
Reading *(From trainee on 19/10/2006) FLC 0+1 FAC 1+2*
Northampton T *(Loaned on 9/2/2007) FL 15/1*
Bournemouth *(Loaned on 2/11/2007) FL 11 Others 1*
Norwich C *(Loaned on 31/1/2008) FL 8+3*

PEARCE Ian Anthony
Born: Bury St Edmunds, 7 May 1974
Height: 6'3" **Weight:** 14.4
Club Honours: PL '95
International Honours: E: U21-3; Yth
The central defender spent much of the season at Fulham battling against injury, his only Premier League appearance coming as a substitute at Aston Villa in August. That was followed by a start in the Carling Cup tie at Shrewsbury, where his resolute defending helped Fulham to a 1-0 success. After two further reserve appearances, he joined Southampton on loan in February and became the eighth player of the season to begin a game for the Saints at centre-back when he lined up alongside Andrew Davies at Scunthorpe. That proved to be his entire Southampton career as a recurring groin injury haunted the rest of his one-month loan from Fulham. Was released at the end of the campaign.
Chelsea *(From juniors on 1/8/1991) P/FL 0+4 Others 0+1*
Blackburn Rov *(£300,000 on 4/10/1993) PL 43+19/2 FLC 4+4/1 FAC 1+2 Others 6+1*
West Ham U *(£1,600,000 + on 19/9/1997) P/FL 135+7/9 FLC 8 FAC 10+1/1 Others 1+1*
Fulham *(£400,000 + on 23/1/2004) PL 55+2/1 FLC 3 FAC 2*
Southampton *(Loaned on 22/2/2008) FL 1*

PEARCE Jason Daniel
Born: Hillingdon, 6 December 1987
Height: 5'7" **Weight:** 11.3
A versatile defender who, after a good run of games, showed his true potential in the second half of last season. Jason initially joined Bournemouth on trial from Portsmouth with a view to a loan signing, but made the move permanent before 2007-08 got underway. He scored his first senior goal at Southend.
Portsmouth *(From trainee on 4/7/2006)*
Bournemouth *(Signed on 10/8/2007) FL 30+3/1 FLC 1 FAC 2+1 Others 1*

PEARCE Krystian Mitchell Victor
Born: Birmingham, 5 January 1990
Height: 6'1" **Weight:** 12.0
International Honours: E: Yth

Stephen Pearson

This colossus of a young centre-half joined Notts County on loan from Birmingham in November and quickly established himself as a regular with some remarkable performances. Strong and tall, Krystian demonstrated the attributes of a much older player, completely dominant in the air and quick in the tackle. It was a huge disappointment to all at Meadow Lane when the loan was not extended for the full season. His second loan took him to Port Vale in January, where he made an impressive debut as a second-half substitute at Bristol Rovers before being sent off in his second full game, at Hartlepool, after two yellow cards. Good in the air and cool on the ball for one so young, he showed a great appetite for Vale's fight against relegation. Although a regular member of teenage England squads, he chose to pull out of an under-19 game against Russia to play for the Vale against Gillingham as he thought it would be of more benefit in the long run. His loan ended a couple of games early following a knee injury against Huddersfield and he was badly missed in the next game as Vale lost 6-0 at Swindon. Krystian will hope to continue his education at Championship level in 2008-09.
Birmingham C *(From trainee on 2/3/2007)*
Notts Co *(Loaned on 8/11/2007) FL 8/1 FAC 2*
Port Vale *(Loaned on 31/1/2008) FL 11+1*

PEARSON Michael (Mike) Thomas
Born: Bangor, North Wales, 19 January 1988
Height: 5'9" **Weight:** 12.11
Originally on Liverpool's books as a schoolboy, Mike progressed through Oldham's youth ranks to become reserve-team skipper with glowing reports. He began as a striker but is now an accomplished midfield prospect. He was expected to be more involved after penning a one-year deal last summer but his ambition was hampered by a hernia injury and he made a solitary substitute appearance, plus a loan to Farsley, before being told that his contract would not be renewed.
Oldham Ath *(From trainee on 5/7/2006) FL 0+2*

PEARSON Stephen Paul
Born: Lanark, 2 October 1982
Height: 6'0" **Weight:** 11.1
Club Honours: SPD '04, '06, '07; SC '04
International Honours: S: 10; B-1; U21-8

The scorer of the Wembley goal that earned Derby promotion was a regular in midfield as they set out in the Premiership and did not miss a game until the turn of the year. A collision with his own defender Darren Moore in the Boxing Day defeat by Liverpool left Stephen with a shoulder injury that kept him out for four weeks. He was at his best when running through the centre of midfield but at times had to occupy a wide position. Involved in Scotland's brave bid to reach the European Championship finals, Derby supporters were surprised when he joined Stoke on loan in March to cover for Richard Cresswell, as Stoke continued their successful push for promotion from the Championship.
Motherwell *(From juniors on 1/8/2000) SL 68+12/12 SLC 3/1 SC 4+1 Others 1*
Glasgow Celtic *(£350,000 on 9/1/2004) SL 22+34/6 SLC 3+1 SC 5+1 Others 6+4/1*
Derby Co *(£750,000 on 11/1/2007) P/FL 29+4 FLC 0+1 FAC 3 Others 3/1*
Stoke C *(Loaned on 27/3/2008) FL 3+1*

PEDERSEN Henrik
Born: Copenhagen, Denmark, 10 June 1975
Height: 6'1" **Weight:** 13.5
International Honours: Denmark: 3
Although Henrik was still recovering from the previous season's Achilles injury, Hull manager Phil Brown had no concerns about adding him to the KC Stadium ranks in the summer, having been his long-term coach at Bolton. Teaming up with former Reebok colleague Jay Jay Okocha, he diligently worked his way back to full fitness and his efforts were rewarded with two goals on his full debut in a 3-1 win over Ipswich. Unfortunately, Henrik was soon sidelined again with a recurrence of a knee injury in a reserve game. Usually played on the left of midfield, he was equally sound at left-back and his return coincided with the Tigers' rise to their highest final League position on the way to promotion through the play-offs. A calf injury ruled Henrik out of the later stages of the campaign.
Bolton W *(£650,000 from Silkeborg, Denmark on 11/7/2001) PL 93+50/22 FLC 7+7/4 FAC 7+4/3 Others 2+1*
Hull C *(Free on 14/8/2007) FL 18+3/4 FLC 1*

PEDERSEN Morten Gamst
Born: Vadso, Norway, 8 September 1981
Height: 5'11" **Weight:** 11.0
International Honours: Norway: 40; U21-18; Yth
Morten Gamst had a poor season by his lofty standards and at one point lost his Blackburn place. He did not score a

League goal until the end of February, but ended with four, and his touch and crossing were often wayward. However, when Blackburn left him out in September and October, his absence was keenly felt for no player runs further or tackles more than the Norwegian. His ability to track back and make vital tackles, not only on the left but sometimes coming across behind the centre-backs, was exceptional. If his attacking play was sometimes whimsical, there was no evidence of that when he was defending.
Blackburn Rov *(£1,500,000 from Tromso, Norway on 27/8/2004) PL 121+5/23 FLC 8+2/ 3 FAC 13+2/5 Others 11+2/1*

PEJIC Shaun Melvyn
Born: Hereford, 16 November 1982
Height: 6'1" **Weight:** 12.3
Club Honours: AMC '05
International Honours: W: U21-6; Yth

Shaun Pejic

Shaun is another player who should by now have established himself as a permanent fixture in the heart of Wrexham's defence but suffered from the general malaise at the club in recent times. At 25, he has time on his side and is calm and always comfortable on the ball. With further experience, he will impose himself more on his co-defenders.
Wrexham *(From trainee on 9/8/2002) FL 161+13 FLC 9 FAC 6+1 Others 7+2/1*

[PELE] CARDOSO MONTEIRO Pedro Miguel
Born: Albufeira, Portugal, 2 May 1978
Height: 6'1" **Weight:** 13.8
Club Honours: Ch '08
International Honours: Cape Verde
Pele became West Bromwich's ninth summer signing when he joined them from Southampton in August. The Portuguese defender, who can operate at centre-half, full-back and as a midfield

anchorman, penned a two-year contract with the Baggies, with a year's option in the club's favour. He was never a regular but always gave his maximum when selected.
Southampton (Signed from Belenenses, Portugal, ex Imortal, Deportivo Farense, on 27/7/2006) FL 34+3/1 FLC 3 FAC 2 Others 2
West Bromwich A (£1,000,000 on 9/8/2007) FL 13+8 FLC 2 FAC 2+1

PELTIER Lee Anthony
Born: Liverpool, 11 December 1986
Height: 5'10" **Weight:** 12.0
After a successful loan spell at Hull in 2006-07, Lee's capture on loan from Liverpool in time for the start of the season represented a transfer coup by Yeovil manager Russell Slade. The defender or midfield player was an instant success and the fans appreciated the promising youngster's ability. Yeovil managed to seal a permanent deal for Lee in the January transfer window, with the right-back's consistently good performances attracting admiring glances. Noted for his mobility and enthusiasm, Lee looks set for a bright future.
Liverpool (From trainee on 25/11/2004) FLC 3 Others 1
Hull C (Loaned on 16/3/2007) FL 5+2
Yeovil T (Signed on 7/8/2007) FL 34 FLC 1 FAC 1 Others 2

PEMBLETON Martin John
Born: Scunthorpe, 1 June 1990
Height: 5'7" **Weight:** 10.9
A diminutive midfielder, who can play wide or central, Martin was the last of nine outfield products of Lincoln's youth set-up to appear in the League during 2007-08 and he did not disappoint with his six appearances late on seeing him receive some well-deserved praise from the Imps' management team. With the club since he was nine years old, Martin has proved to be both tricky in possession and determined to get the ball. Having agreed to a one-year professional contract prior to the penultimate home game of the season, he was later ruled out of the remaining fixture after suffering a knee injury.
Lincoln C (Trainee) FL 4+2

PENFORD Thomas (Tom) James
Born: Leeds, 5 January 1985
Height: 5'10" **Weight:** 11.3
Tom has always been regarded as one of the best ball players at Bradford and the midfielder added a creative touch when he won a place in the side towards the end of the season. He turned in an outstanding display against Rotherham on Easter

Saturday, setting up a goal for Joe Colbeck with a superb pass. Was released in the summer.
Bradford C (From trainee on 1/7/2006) FL 26+12/1 FLC 0+1 FAC 0+1 Others 0+1

PENNANT Jermaine Lloyd
Born: Nottingham, 15 January 1983
Height: 5'6" **Weight:** 10.0
Club Honours: FAYC '00, '01; CS '04, '06
International Honours: E: U21-24; Yth; Sch
The inconsistency of Liverpool's right-winger proved his downfall in the last campaign. In the opening weeks his form was so good that manager Rafa Benitez was recommending his inclusion in the England squad. His decline started with a totally unnecessary sending off in the Champions' League match at Porto in September, which reduced his team to ten men for the final half-hour. Ironically, Liverpool then played with more discipline and composure than they had previously shown and held out for a 1-1 draw their overall display did not merit. A few weeks later, he suffered a stress fracture of the right tibia that sidelined him for ten weeks before his return in early January in a dreary home draw with Wigan. Thereafter, he played only in Premiership games deemed less important by Benitez and scored two goals, at home to Newcastle and away to Fulham at the end of the season. His goal against Newcastle was a total fluke. A defender's clearance struck him on the shoulder and the rebound looped over the helpless goalkeeper. His goal at Fulham was more impressive, as he burst inside from the right wing and finished with a strong shot that the Fulham 'keeper appeared to assume was going wide. He also inspired Liverpool's comeback from a 2-0 deficit at Birmingham with a run and a cross for Peter Crouch to score. This burst of form may have influenced Benitez to use him as a substitute in the Champions' League semi-final second leg ahead of the more obvious choices, Crouch and Ryan Babel.
Notts Co (Associated Schoolboy) FAC 0+1 Others 0+1
Arsenal (From trainee on 16/03/2000, having been signed for £1,500,000 on 14/1/1999) PL 2+10/3 FLC 8+1 FAC 1 Others 1+3
Watford (Loaned on 10/1/2002) FL 9/2
Watford (Loaned on 15/11/2002) FL 12 FAC 2/1
Leeds U (Loaned on 20/8/2003) PL 34+2/2
Birmingham C (£500,000 + on 31/1/2005) PL 47+3/2 FLC 4/1 FAC 6
Liverpool (£6,700,000 + on 27/7/2006) PL 34+18/3 FLC 2 FAC 3 Others 12+8

PERCH James Robert
Born: Mansfield, 29 September 1985
Height: 5'11" **Weight:** 11.5
James maintained his utility-man tag by appearing in both full-back positions and all across midfield for Nottingham Forest. A hard worker who is able to pick a long or short pass, he did a good job wherever he was asked to play. Despite this, James never managed more than four consecutive games.
Nottingham F (From trainee on 9/11/2002) FL 113+23/8 FLC 2+2/1 FAC 10+2 Others 6/1

PERICARD Vincent de Paul
Born: Efok, Cameroon, 3 October 1982
Height: 6'1" **Weight:** 13.8
Club Honours: Div 1 '03
The striker, who has been in and out of the Stoke team since his arrival from Portsmouth, never really pushed Ricardo Fuller or Mama Sidibe for a place in attack last season and received a setback when he was jailed for a motoring offence before Christmas. On his release, he played with an electronic tag on an ankle and was allowed to join Southampton on loan just before the transfer window closed in March. No doubt looking to add some height and presence to the attack, new manager Nigel Pearson signed Vincent but he was unable to cement a place. After starting once for Southampton, he made regular late forays from the bench without getting the breaks.
Portsmouth (£400,000 from Juventus, Italy on 22/7/2002) P/FL 21+23/9 FLC 2+1/1 FAC 1+1
Sheffield U (Loaned on 16/9/2005) FL 3+8/2
Plymouth Arg (Loaned on 10/2/2006) FL 14+1/4
Stoke C (Free on 21/7/2006) FL 19+15/2 FLC 1/1 FAC 1+1
Southampton (Loaned on 14/3/2008) FL 1+4

PERKINS David Philip
Born: Heysham, 21 June 1982
Height: 6'2" **Weight:** 12.0
International Honours: E: SP-9
In his second season in the League, David became one of the mainstays of the Rochdale side, chiefly as Gary Jones' partner in the centre of midfield, though he also figured at left-back and on the left-wing. He scored his first senior goal in the Carling Cup victory over Stoke and sensationally netted a hat-trick away to close rivals Chesterfield in the League. His stunning strike in the second leg of the play-off semi-final kept Dale in the game but sadly, with two previous red cards and suspensions during the season, he was harshly sent off in extra-time and had to

miss the trip to Wembley when the red card was upheld, a decision his chairman branded as 'outrageous'.

Rochdale (Signed from Morecambe on 22/1/2007) FL 54+4/4 FLC 1/1 FAC 1 Others 3/1

PERRETT Russell (Russ)

Born: Barton-on-Sea, 18 June 1973
Height: 6'3" **Weight:** 13.2
Club Honours: Div 1 '05

Russ joined Bournemouth from Luton before the start of the season and in early games it was clearly apparent that he was still a stylish centre-half. He showed all his experience before he sustained a hamstring injury against Northampton in September and struggled to regain his fitness. Then, after fighting his way back and starting to forge a good central defensive partnership with Josh Gowling, Russ began to suffer from breathing problems a few days after the home match against Doncaster in February. That proved to be his final outing and he announced his retirement at the end of the season.

Portsmouth (Signed from Lymington on 30/9/1995) FL 66+6/2 FLC 5 FAC 4
Cardiff C (£10,000 on 21/7/1999) FL 28+1/1 FAC 5/1 Others 1
Luton T (Free on 10/8/2001) FL 89+10/9 FLC 3+1 FAC 4 Others 0+1
Bournemouth (Free on 20/7/2007) FL 10 Others 1

PERRY Christopher (Chris)
John

Born: Carshalton, 26 April 1973
Height: 5'9" **Weight:** 11.1

Chris, a small but vastly experienced central defender, joined Luton in summer after being released by West Bromwich. A good reader of the game, and a quick and a firm tackler; he went straight in to the side as Chris Coyne's partner. Three consecutive defeats raised doubts about their effectiveness and defender Jaroslaw Fojut joined the defence on loan. At times, Chris played left-back and looked more than useful, scoring his only goal against Nottingham Forest. After Coyne picked up a red card at Bristol Rovers, Chris returned to central defence and was left as Luton's only natural defender when Coyne was sold and Fojut's loan expired. Chris was briefly captain and formed, with Keith Keane, the smallest central defensive partnership in the division before joining Southampton on loan at the end of the March window. Experienced, sharp, constructive and effective in the air, it beggars belief that Chris is just 5'9". He became Saints' ninth central defender of the season when introduced from the financially

compromised Luton where, it was reported, he had not been paid for two months. He found an instant rapport in the middle of the back four with centre-back number ten, Chris Lucketti, also on loan, forming a partnership that was highly influential in staving off relegation.

Wimbledon (From trainee on 2/7/1991) PL 158+9/2 FLC 21 FAC 24/1
Tottenham H (£4,000,000 on 7/7/1999) PL 111+9/3 FLC 13 FAC 9 Others 4/1
Charlton Ath (£100,000 on 1/9/2003) PL 69+7/3 FLC 3 FAC 4+1
West Bromwich A (Free on 1/8/2006) FL 23 FLC 1 Others 3
Luton T (Free on 6/7/2007) FL 35/1 FLC 3 FAC 4 Others 2
Southampton (Loaned on 27/3/2008) FL 6

PERRY Kyle Blain

Born: Wolverhampton, 5 March 1986
Height: 6'4" **Weight:** 14.5

A wholehearted striker, Kyle clinched a move to Port Vale in January after helping to knock them out of the FA Cup. He began the season with Chasetown, scoring six goals in 11 games and helping them to reach the FA Cup third round. His burst down the wing set up the winner in their second round victory over Vale and he gave up his job as a graphic designer to turn professional. He made his senior bow at Swansea as a substitute and continued to progress, going close to a first goal against Oldham when he hit a post and the bar. Towards the end of the season, he played wide on the left and showed a fine turn of pace. A leg injury threatened to end his campaign early but he battled through to appear in the final two games.

Port Vale (Free from Chasetown, ex Telford U, on 11/1/2008) FL 9+7

PESCHISOLIDO Paolo (Paul)
Pasquale

Born: Scarborough, Canada, 25 May 1971
Height: 5'7" **Weight:** 10.12
Club Honours: Div 2 '99
International Honours: Canada: 53; U23-1; Yth

Paul was signed in the summer, after being released by Derby, for his experience and ability as a natural goal poacher alongside Paul Furlong and Sam Parkin. Because of injuries, he partnered Parkin for only a few minutes and Furlong four times. The only glimpse of his capabilities was a goal against Northampton in the Johnstone's Paint Trophy when he replaced Drew Talbot. A torn Achilles tendon necessitated several operations, one of them said to be pioneering, and he was unable regain

his fitness. Paul was released at the end of the season and returned to Canada to coach youngsters while considering offers.

Birmingham C (£25,000 from Toronto Blizzards, Canada on 11/11/1992) FL 37+6/16 FLC 2/1 FAC 0+1 Others 1+1
Stoke C (£400,000 on 1/8/1994) FL 59+7/19 FLC 6/3 FAC 3 Others 5+1/2
Birmingham C (£400,000 on 29/3/1996) FL 7+2/1
West Bromwich A (£600,000 on 24/7/1996) FL 36+9/18 FLC 4+1/3 FAC 1
Fulham (£1,100,000 on 24/10/1997) FL 69+26/24 FLC 7+1/4 FAC 9+1/2 Others 2
Queens Park Rgrs (Loaned on 3/11/2000) FL 5/1
Sheffield U (Loaned on 19/1/2001) FL 4+1/2
Norwich C (Loaned on 22/3/2001) FL 3+2
Sheffield U (£150,000 + on 10/7/2001) FL 35+44/17 FLC 3+5/2 FAC 3+5/2 Others 0+2/1
Derby Co (Signed on 12/3/2004) FL 38+53/20 FLC 3+1 FAC 2+3/4 Others 3
Luton T (Free on 7/8/2007) FL 2+2 Others 0+1/1

PETERS Jaime Bryant

Born: Pickering, Ontario, Canada, 4 May 1987
Height: 5'8" **Weight:** 11.6
International Honours: Canada: 15

International duty with Canada meant that Jaime missed some of Ipswich's pre-season training and this restricted his opportunities because his fitness lagged behind the other players. He had a run of substitute appearances in September but to gain experience and match fitness the club eventually sent him out on loan to Yeovil in January. The winger's darting runs and lightning pace were essential to Town in their battle to steer clear of relegation in the last three months of the season and a series of superb performances saw his popularity with the Yeovil fans rise as they ensured League One safety.

Ipswich T (Signed from Kaiserslautern, Germany on 6/8/2005) FL 24+17/2 FLC 1 FAC 3+1
Yeovil T (Loaned on 30/1/2008) FL 12+2/1

PETERS Ryan Vincent

Born: Wandsworth, 21 August 1987
Height: 5'8" **Weight:** 10.8

At his best a pacy Brentford outside-right, who loves running at defenders, Ryan made six early season substitute appearances without being able to make an impact and dropped out of first-team contention. He joined Margate on loan in October before the move became permanent in January.

Brentford (From trainee on 4/7/2005) FL 2+34/2 FLC 2+1 FAC 0+3 Others 3+2

PETROV Martin Petiov
Born: Vratsa, Bulgaria, 15 January 1979
Height: 5'11" **Weight:** 12.1
International Honours: Bulgaria: 74
The speedy Bulgarian winger joined
Manchester City from Atletico Madrid
in July and was first choice on the left
flank from the start of the season,
opening his goal account with two fine
strikes against Fulham in late September.
His first goal at home came a week
later in the impressive 3-1 victory over
Newcastle, proving that he has a real eye
for a chance as well as setting up team-
mates. An excellent season saw Martin
build up a real rapport with the City
fans who will be expecting more wing
wizardry.
*Manchester C (£4,700,000 from Atletico
Madrid, Spain, ex CSKA Sofia, Servette, VfL
Wolfsburg, on 3/8/2007) PL 34/5 FLC 1 FAC 3*

PETROV Stilian Alypshev
Born: Sofia, Bulgaria, 5 July 1979
Height: 5'9" **Weight:** 12.1
Club Honours: SPD '01, '02, '04, '06;
SLC '01, '06; SC '02, '04, '05
International Honours: Bulgaria: 78
Aston Villa's Stilian is an intelligent user
of the ball and can find a way through
packed defences. Known for his solid
performances, he is strong in the tackle
and astute with his distribution. At the
start of last season, he struggled to justify
the big fee paid to Glasgow Celtic a year
earlier, to the point that he was dropped.
He subsequently regained his place and
his performances were reminiscent of
those that made him such an influential
player under Martin O'Neill at Parkhead.
Stilian can play either as a winger or a
box-to-box central midfielder, where he
has the qualities to break up opposition
play as well as create chances for others.
His only goal, at Derby, was sensational.
He was on the edge of the centre circle,
roughly 45 yards from goal, when in one
delightful movement he chested down
goalkeeper Roy Carroll's errant clearance
and hit a superbly controlled half-volley
with the outside of his left boot to send
the ball dipping under the bar and into
the corner of the net.
*Glasgow Celtic (£2,000,000 from CSKA
Sofia, Bulgaria on 29/7/1999) SL 215+13/55
SLC 9+5 SC 15+3/5 Others 49+2/4
Aston Villa (£6,500,000 on 30/8/2006) PL
52+6/3 FLC 4+1 FAC 2*

PETTIGREW Adrian Robert
James
Born: Hackney, 12 November 1986
Height: 6'0" **Weight:** 13.1
The centre-back joined Brentford from
Chelsea on a month's loan in August that

was twice extended by a further month.
He started in his recognised position in
August but was then moved to play as
a defensive midfield shield as Brentford
struggled. After impressing in the early
games, he found it more difficult as
time went on and was dropped after the
defeat by Dagenham at the beginning
of October. His final month was spent as
a substitute. Adrian had a second loan,
to Rotherham in January, but failed to
carve out a regular starting place at left-
back and that, along with the difficult
financial position at Millmoor, brought
about an early return to Chelsea. Was
out of contract in the summer and
looking for a new club.
*Chelsea (From trainee on 23/3/2005)
Wycombe W (Loaned on 2/3/2007) FL 1
Brentford (Loaned on 10/8/2007) FL 9+2
FLC 1 FAC 1 Others 1
Rotherham U (Loaned on 30/1/2008) FL
3+1*

PHELAN Scott Richard
Born: Liverpool, 13 March 1988
Height: 5'7" **Weight:** 10.7
Signed by Bradford from Everton
reserves last summer, Scott's small
frame and tigerish manner in midfield
were reminiscent of manager Stuart
McCall. His best run in the side came
before Christmas, when he started four
successive games, but he scarcely figured
after the turn of the year. Was released
at the end of the campaign.
*Everton (From trainee on 26/7/2005)
Bradford C (Free on 7/8/2007) FL 8+5 FAC
1+1 Others 1*

PHILLIPS Demar Constantine
Born: Kingston, Jamaica, 23 September
1983
Height: 5'6" **Weight:** 9.7
International Honours: Jamaica: 27
Seen as a player for the future, Demar
joined Stoke from Waterhouse in
August on the recommendation of
fellow Jamaican Ricardo Fuller. So far,
the winger has made two substitute
appearances as the club concentrate on
building his frame in the reserves.
*Stoke C (Signed from Waterhouse, Jamaica
on 31/8/2007) FL 0+2*

PHILLIPS Kevin Mark
Born: Hitchin, 25 July 1973
Height: 5'7" **Weight:** 11.0
Club Honours: Div 1 '99; Ch '08
International Honours: E: 8; B-1
Named in the PFA Championship select
side and also voted Championship
'Player of the Year', Kevin had another
superb season for West Bromwich,
netting his 200th League goal and

also bagging Albion's 100th of the
campaign, a penalty in a vital 3-1 win
at Blackpool in April. He was the club's
leading marksman with 24 goals and at
least half were extra-special, including
brilliant home efforts against Ipswich,
Queens Park Rangers, Bristol City and
Scunthorpe, a point-saver at Charlton,
and a last-ditch headed winner at
Sheffield Wednesday. And he also
created chances for colleagues, laying on
the vital winner for Zoltan Gera against
Wolverhampton at Molineux. Despite his
34 years, Kevin is as sprightly and alert
as ever. Although plagued by niggling
injuries, he battled away gamely and
along with Ishmael Miller and Roman
Bednar, always proved a handful for
opposing defenders. The evergreen
Kevin will start 2008-09 knowing he is
well on his way to reaching 500 club and
international appearances.
*Watford (£10,000 from Baldock on
19/12/1994) FL 54+5/24 FLC 2/1 FAC 2
Others 0+2
Sunderland (£325,000 + on 17/7/1997)
P/FL 207+1/113 FLC 9+1/5 FAC 14/10
Others 3/2
Southampton (£3,250,000 on 14/8/2003)
PL 49+15/22 FLC 2/1 FAC 4+1/2 Others 2/1
Aston Villa (£750,000 + on 6/7/2005) PL
20+3/4 FLC 1+1/1 FAC 1+1
West Bromwich A (£700,000 on
22/8/2006) FL 60+11/38 FLC 1 FAC 4+2/5
Others 3/3*

PHILLIPS Matthew (Matt)
Born: Aylesbury, 13 March 1991
Height: 6'0" **Weight:** 12.10
With Wycombe since the age of eight,
17-year-old right-winger Matt was given
a surprise debut in the penultimate game
as a late substitute at Notts County
and did enough to earn a start in the
following game, at home to Bradford,
winning the 'Man of the Match' award
for his exciting attacking display. He laid
on the first goal, his corner led to the
second and he was deservedly included
in the League Two 'Team of the Week'.
The only true winger in the squad, Matt
will clearly be pushing for a first-team
spot this coming season.
Wycombe W (Trainee) FL 1+1 Others 0+1

PHILLIPS Steven (Steve)
John
Born: Bath, 6 May 1978
Height: 6'1" **Weight:** 11.10
Club Honours: AMC '03
An experienced former Bristol City
goalkeeper, Steve continued to hold
down a regular place in the Bristol
Rovers' side and his confidence proved
significant in creating a tight rearguard.

Along with captain Stuart Campbell, Steve was an ever-present and has missed only two matches in his two seasons at the club.
Bristol C *(Signed from Paulton Rov on 21/11/1996)* FL 254+3 FLC 12 FAC 17 Others 23
Bristol Rov *(Free on 25/7/2006)* FL 90 FLC 3 FAC 13 Others 10

PICKEN Philip (Phil) James
Born: Droylsden, 12 November 1985
Height: 5'9" **Weight:** 10.7
Phil worked hard to consolidate a place for Chesterfield as a versatile defender. He completed 100 League games for the Spireites and was selected to skipper the side towards the end of the season. Phil marks well and shows a good awareness that allows him to get forward frequently in support of the midfield, without neglecting his defensive duties.
Manchester U *(From trainee on 2/7/2004)*
Chesterfield *(Free on 19/8/2005)* FL 104+4/ 2 FLC 4 FAC 1 Others 2+1

PIDGELEY Leonard (Lenny) James
Born: Twickenham, 7 February 1984
Height: 6'4" **Weight:** 13.10
International Honours: E: Yth
This tall, experienced Millwall goalkeeper started last season with an injury but worked his way back to fitness and regained his first-team place. His shot-stopping is his main strength but he has quality in all other areas, especially coming out for crosses. After a lean spell over Christmas, he lost his place to Rhys Evans.
Chelsea *(From trainee on 11/7/2003)* PL 1+1
Watford *(Loaned on 16/9/2003)* FL 26+1 FAC 2
Millwall *(Loaned on 28/11/2005)* FLC 1
Millwall *(Signed on 12/6/2006)* FL 55 FLC 1 FAC 8 Others 1

PIENAAR Steven
Born: Johannesburg, South Africa, 17 February 1982
Height: 5'10" **Weight:** 10.6
International Honours: South Africa: 21
A pleasant surprise for Everton fans was the form of the South African winger, who came to Goodison on loan for Borussia Dortmund before the deal was made permanent later in the season. After initially appearing as a substitute, the South African soon made himself a key ingredient in the Toffees' fine form before Christmas, adding craft and ingenuity to midfield. Having appeared in the African Cup of Nations in the New Year, he returned to England with an ankle injury that kept him out for

Steven Pienaar

three weeks. On his return the midfielder continued to play an important part without hitting the heights of the first half of the campaign but still provided more assists than any other Everton player in an excellent first season in English football.
Everton (£2,000,000 from Borussia Dortmund, Germany, ex Ajax Cape Town, Ajax, on 25/7/2007) PL 25+3/2 FLC 3 FAC 1 Others 8

PILKINGTON Anthony Neil James
Born: Manchester, 3 November 1987
Height: 5'11" **Weight:** 12.0
It was an excellent season for Anthony, with a number of goals and eventual promotion for the young Stockport winger. While a knock on the head in County's FA Cup exit at Staines kept him out for a month and a dead leg caused him to miss a few weeks in January, his consistent form made him one of the first names on the team-sheet throughout the season. His personal highlight came in the re-arranged evening game at Bury, in which he scored twice in a 3-2 victory, including a thunderous volley that was nominated for 'Goal of the Season'. He finished off his memorable year with a goal in the play-off final against Rochdale at Wembley, helping County win an entertaining match 3-2.
Stockport Co (Free from Atherton Collieries on 19/12/2006) FL 41+12/11 FLC 0+2 FAC 0+1 Others 4+1/2

PILKINGTON George Edward
Born: Rugeley, 7 November 1981
Height: 5'11" **Weight:** 11.6
International Honours: E: Yth
Port Vale's excellent central defender was as dependable as ever, missing only one game and giving his all in the vain attempt to prevent relegation. George scored three goals, one against Morecambe in the FA Cup, and was team captain in the first half of the season until new manager Lee Sinnott decided to make a change. George will admit that he did not match his previous standards but took his total of appearances past 250 in five years, a measure of his consistency. At the end of the season he was released on a free transfer and should find another club.
Everton (From trainee on 18/11/1998)
Exeter C (Loaned on 1/11/2002) FL 7 FAC 4 Others 1
Port Vale (Free on 1/7/2003) FL 223+1/11 FLC 8 FAC 14/1 Others 6+1

PILKINGTON Kevin William
Born: Hitchin, 8 March 1974
Height: 6'1" **Weight:** 13.0
Club Honours: FAYC '92
International Honours: E: Sch

Kevin had an outstanding season at Notts County with a succession of excellent performances in a difficult time. As a goalkeeper, he had plenty of opportunity to shine as County struggled near the foot of League Two. He was voted 'Player of the Season' by the supporters and his team-mates. Always a highly capable 'keeper and an excellent professional.
Manchester U (From trainee on 6/7/1992) PL 4+2 FLC 1 FAC 1
Rochdale (Loaned on 2/2/1996) FL 6
Rotherham U (Loaned on 22/1/1997) FL 17
Port Vale (Free on 1/7/1998) FL 23 FLC 1 FAC 1 (Freed during 2000 close season)
Mansfield T (Free from Aberystwyth T on 8/9/2000) FL 167 FLC 4 FAC 11 Others 7
Notts Co (Free on 4/7/2005) FL 116 FLC 2 FAC 5

PIPE David Ronald
Born: Caerphilly, 5 November 1983
Height: 5'9" **Weight:** 12.4
International Honours: W: 1; U21-12; Yth
Signed from Notts County in the summer, the former Welsh international wide player quickly established himself as a firm favourite at Bristol Rovers, with supporters admiring his versatility. Playing consistently well on the right-wing, and at times at right-back, David's workrate, ability to beat a defender and delivery of accurate crosses were well received. He scored with a spectacular volley at Gillingham.
Coventry C (From trainee on 8/11/2000) FL 11+10/1 FLC 1+2 FAC 0+1
Notts Co (Free on 15/1/2004) FL 138+3/4 FLC 5 FAC 7 Others 1
Bristol Rov (£50,000 on 30/7/2007) FL 37+3/2 FLC 2 FAC 7 Others 1

PIQUE Gerard
Born: Barcelona, Spain, 2 February 1987
Height: 6'3" **Weight:** 12.10
Club Honours: FLC '06
International Honours: Spain: Yth
A technically gifted Manchester United central defender and grandson of a former Barcelona vice-president, Gerard returned to United following his spell at Real Zaragoza and scored on his first start in the Champions' League group stage against Dynamo Kiev at Old Trafford in November. In doing so, he became the 450th United player to score at least one goal for the club. He followed up with a flurry of Champions' League and Premiership appearances.
Manchester U (From trainee on 3/2/2005) PL 6+6 FLC 2+2 FAC 3 Others 3+1/2

PIRES Loick Muamba
Born: Lisbon, Portugal, 20 November 1989
Height: 6'2" **Weight:** 13.4
Loick was rewarded with first-team squad place following good performances for both the Leyton Orient youth team and reserves. Making his debut as a substitute at home to Carlisle, Loick can play both in the centre of attack or as a winger. He was due to sign a professional contract at the end of the season.
Leyton Orient (Trainee) FL 0+1

PITMAN Brett Douglas
Born: Jersey, 31 January 1988
Height: 6'0" **Weight:** 11.4
The young Bournemouth striker continued to develop well during last season, playing in a number of forward roles, including just behind the front two. Always involved in the first-team squad, the vast majority of his appearances came from the bench and he frequently had a considerable effect on games. He also came up with a number of important goals and assists.
Bournemouth (Signed from St Paul's on 1/7/2005) FL 26+61/12 FLC 0+3 FAC 2+3 Others 2+3/1

PIZARRO Claudio Miguel
Born: Callao, Peru, 3 October 1978
Height: 6'0" **Weight:** 12.6
International Honours: Peru: 53
One of the mysteries of football is how transfers can have such contrasting fortunes for former team-mates. Claudio and Roque Santa Cruz left Bayern Munich to try their luck in the English Premier League and while the latter thrived at Blackburn, Claudio had a frustrating time as he tried to acclimatise at Chelsea. With Michael Ballack, another former team-mate at Bayern, Claudio established a formidable reputation in German football, scoring over 100 goals in the Bundesliga after his arrival in 1999. Indeed, his career in England got off to the best possible start with a goal in his Premier League debut against Birmingham but, incredibly, that was it until scoring the only goal of the game against the same opposition 32 matches and five months later. These were the only goals of a particularly disappointing season and Claudio's options were further limited by the arrival of Nicolas Anelka in January, throwing his long-term future at Chelsea into considerable doubt.
Chelsea (Free from Bayern Munich, Germany, ex Deportivo Pesquero, Alianza Lima, Werder Bremen, on 12/6/2007) PL 4+17/2 FLC 3+1 FAC 2+2 Others 1+2

PLATT Clive Linton
Born: Wolverhampton, 27 October 1977
Height: 6'4" **Weight:** 13.0
The big target man negotiated the step up from League One to the Championship, having been recruited from MK Dons last summer. A red card in pre-season meant that he was forced to sit out three of Colchester's first five games but he made an impact on the opening day by heading a late equaliser at Sheffield United. Clive formed a good partnership with Kevin Lisbie and contributed seven goals before the turn of the year, but he only managed one more as he and the team struggled for form. He is a wholehearted performer who sets up more goals than he scores.
Walsall (From trainee on 25/7/1996) FL 18+14/4 FLC 1+2/1 FAC 0+1 Others 1+6
Rochdale (£70,000 + on 5/8/1999) FL 151+18/30 FLC 5/1 FAC 13/5 Others 7/1
Notts Co (Free on 7/8/2003) FL 19/3 FLC 3 FAC 3/3
Peterborough U (Free on 7/1/2004) FL 35+2/6 FLC 1 FAC 1
MK Dons (Free on 13/1/2005) FL 91+11/27 FLC 2+1 FAC 6+1/2 Others 1
Colchester U (£300,000 on 12/7/2007) FL 34+7/8 FLC 1

PLESSIS Damien
Born: Neuville-aux-Bois, France, 5 March 1988
Height: 6'3" **Weight:** 12.1
International Honours: France: Yth
Damien is a young holding midfield player signed by Liverpool manager Rafa Benitez in the summer from French champions Lyon. Given his youth and surfeit of central midfield talent at Anfield, he was not expected to make his bow before next season. However, after showing outstanding form in the reserves Benitez threw him in at the deep end in the Premiership match at Arsenal in April in front of 60,000 spectators when several first teamers were rested ahead of the second leg of the Champions' League quarter-final against the same opposition. He then made his second appearance in similar circumstances at Birmingham a few weeks later. Claudio showed remarkable composure in both games and although not ready for regular first-team football, Liverpool fans will be glad to know that there is a more than capable deputy for Javier Mascherano waiting in the wings.
Liverpool (Signed from Lyon, France on 31/8/2007) PL 2

POGATETZ Emanuel (Manny)
Born: Steinbock, Austria, 16 January 1983
Height: 6'2" **Weight:** 12.13
International Honours: Austria: 30
Austrian international Manny, who drives a Mini Cooper with a Union Jack on the roof, is thoroughly enjoying his life in the English Premiership. He featured in Middlesbrough's friendlies against Schalke and Darlington but soon underwent cartilage operations on both knees and was allowed to return to Austria for rehabilitation. He had to wait until November for his first Premiership appearance of the season in a goalless draw at Bolton. Always a big favourite with the fans, his scintillating form led him to be a near-automatic choice in Gareth Southgate's team and he led the side in the final ten games. Manny was made captain for the next season. With Austria co-hosting the Euro 2008 finals, Manny ended 17 months of international exile in February when he featured in Austria's 3-0 friendly home defeat by Germany.
Middlesbrough (£1,800,000 from Bayer Leverkusen, Germany, ex Grazer AK, on 28/6/2005) PL 79+4/3 FLC 2+1 FAC 17 Others 9

POKE Michael Harold
Born: Staines, 21 November 1985
Height: 6'1" **Weight:** 12.3
Having been associated with Southampton since the age of ten, Michael made his debut at Wolverhampton in March, aged 22. Recalled from loan at Torquay in February because second-choice goalkeeper Bartosz Bialkowski was sidelined, he replaced the injured Kelvin Davis and looked likely to hold his place until he sustained an ankle injury in the warm-up before the Hull match, his third start. As the alternative was to blood 16-year-old Andrej Pernecky, he played, practically on one foot. Saints lost 5–0 and Michael, a brave and athletic shot stopper, was then out of contention.
Southampton (From trainee on 9/1/2004) FL 3+1
Northampton T (Loaned on 18/10/2005) Others 2

POLLITT Michael (Mike) Francis
Born: Farnworth, 29 February 1972
Height: 6'4" **Weight:** 14.0
As Wigan's longest-serving player, the reliable and experienced goalkeeper was restricted to one Premier League start, at Arsenal, following an illness to Chris Kirkland. A solid performer who

Manny Pogatetz

commands his area well, Mike found himself on the bench for the whole of the campaign due to the impressive form of Kirkland. When called on in the Carling Cup tie against Hull and the FA Cup tie against Sunderland, he was his usual confident self, making difficult saves look easy with his tremendous positioning and quick reflexes. Out of contract at the end of the season, he was expected to accept a new one-year deal.

Manchester U *(From trainee on 1/7/1990)*
Bury *(Free on 10/7/1991)*
Lincoln C *(Loaned on 24/9/1992) FL 5 FLC 1*
Lincoln C *(Free on 1/12/1992) FL 52 FLC 4 FAC 2 Others 4*
Darlington *(Free on 11/8/1994) FL 55 FLC 4 FAC 3 Others 5*
Notts Co *(£75,000 on 14/11/1995) FL 10 Others 2*
Oldham Ath *(Loaned on 29/8/1997) FL 16*
Gillingham *(Loaned on 12/12/1997) FL 6*
Brentford *(Loaned on 22/1/1998) FL 5*
Sunderland *(£75,000 on 23/2/1998)*
Rotherham U *(Free on 14/7/1998) FL 92 FLC 4 FAC 7 Others 5*
Chesterfield *(Free on 15/6/2000) FL 46 FLC 3 FAC 1 Others 4*
Rotherham U *(£75,000 on 29/5/2001) FL 175 FLC 11 FAC 6*
Wigan Ath *(£200,000 on 30/6/2005) PL 26+2 FLC 8 FAC 2*
Ipswich T *(Loaned on 15/11/2006) FL 1*
Burnley *(Loaned on 11/1/2007) FL 4*

POOK Michael David

Born: Swindon, 22 October 1985
Height: 5'11" **Weight:** 11.10
Michael set out as a regular in Swindon's midfield but as the season progressed he was increasingly out of the picture, with only one appearance on the bench as an unused substitute in the last third of the campaign. His appearance total triggered an offer of a further contract with his home-town club but it remains to be seen whether he remains at the County Ground, although he is a strong runner with a good attitude.

Swindon T *(From trainee on 5/8/2005) FL 74+21/3 FLC 1+2/1 FAC 5+2 Others 4+1*

POOLE David Andrew

Born: Manchester, 25 November 1984
Height: 5'8" **Weight:** 12.0
Club Honours: FAYC '03
It was a mixed season at Stockport for David. Although he made a good enough start, the right-winger's campaign was curtailed by a back injury picked up against Rotherham. Just two games into his comeback he injured ligaments, leading to an operation and a six-week absence. Despite scoring a late equaliser at Bradford and the winner at Lincoln,

many of his appearances were from the bench and he was eventually released at the end of the season.

Manchester U *(From trainee on 2/7/2002)*
Yeovil T *(Free on 6/7/2005) FL 21+8/2*
Stockport Co *(£10,000 on 15/9/2006) FL 43+10/6 FLC 1 FAC 2+1/1 Others 2+1*

POOLE Glenn Stephen

Born: Barking, 3 February 1981
Height: 5'7" **Weight:** 11.4
Club Honours: FAT '06
Brentford's left-sided midfielder enjoyed a tremendous first League campaign after signing from Grays in the close season. Glenn was top scorer with 14 goals, most of which were spectacular long-range shots from his explosive left foot. The pick of them was a volley from outside the penalty area following a corner against Wycombe on Boxing Day. He scored twice in matches against Dagenham, in January, and Barnet the following month, missing only one League game when he was an unused substitute.

Rochdale *(Loaned from Grays Ath, ex trainee at Tottenham H, Yeovil T, Thurrock, on 22/3/2007) FL 1+5*
Brentford *(Free on 29/5/2007) FL 42+3/14 FAC 2 Others 1*

POOM Mart

Born: Tallinn, Estonia, 3 February 1972
Height: 6'4" **Weight:** 13.6
Club Honours: Ch '05
International Honours: Esthonia: 118
Mart joined Watford on a free transfer from Arsenal during the summer. A very experienced goalkeeper with over 100 international caps for Estonia, his sound handling and good anticipation promised well and he was outstanding in the 2-1 victory at Cardiff. Unfortunately, he suffered a back injury while on international duty in September and lost his club place to Richard Lee. A consummate professional, he continued to provide reliable back-up for the remainder of the season.

Portsmouth *(£200,000 from FC Wil, Switzerland, ex Flora, on 4/8/1994) FL 4 FLC 3 (Signed by Tallinn SC, Estonia on 9/5/1996)*
Derby Co *(£500,000 from Tallinn SC, Estonia on 26/3/1997) P/FL 143+3 FLC 12 FAC 8*
Sunderland *(£2,500,000 on 23/11/2002) P/FL 58/1 FLC 1+1 FAC 6 Others 2*
Arsenal *(Signed on 31/8/2005) PL 1 FLC 0+1*
Watford *(Signed on 8/8/2007) FL 12*

POPE Thomas (Tom) John

Born: Stoke-on-Trent, 27 August 1985
Height: 6'3" **Weight:** 11.3
With four substitute appearances for Crewe in the League to his credit in 2006-07, Tom quickly made his mark last

season, either starting or on the bench on a regular basis. He also added goals, his first being at Bristol Rovers in the first away game of the campaign. The tall striker is beginning to make excellent progress in the centre of the attack and hopes to make his place in the side more permanent.

Crewe Alex *(Free from Biddulph Victoria on 4/10/2005) FL 15+15/7 FLC 1 Others 1*

PORTER Joel William

Born: Adelaide, Australia, 25 December 1978
Height: 5'9" **Weight:** 11.13
International Honours: Australia: 4
A hard-working striker, always popular with Hartlepool supporters, Joel was able to recover his best form after two seasons badly affected by injuries. An instinctive scorer, he went on as substitute in the Johnstone's Paint Trophy tie at Lincoln and hit a hat-trick as Pool won 5-2. His brilliant solo effort against Gillingham was voted by supporters as Hartlepool's 'Goal of the Season'. At the end of the campaign, he was linked with New Zealand side Wellington Phoenix.

Hartlepool U *(Free from Olympic Sharks, Australia on 27/11/2003) FL 98+37/34 FLC 3+3/1 FAC 6+2/3 Others 8+5/5*

PORTER Levi Roger

Born: Leicester, 6 April 1987
Height: 5'3" **Weight:** 9.8
International Honours: E: Yth
This diminutive Leicester winger made the odd early appearance in 2007-08 before a cruciate ligament injury, suffered in the Carling Cup tie at Chelsea, brought a premature end to his season. Levi had made a highly promising breakthrough into the first team during the previous campaign and his return to action is eagerly awaited.

Leicester C *(From trainee on 15/7/2005) FL 27+11/3 FLC 2+1 FAC 2*

PORTER Max

Born: Hornchurch, 29 June 1987
Height: 5'10" **Weight:** 12.4
Max was given his chance at Barnet by Paul Fairclough when he was snapped up for an undisclosed fee from Bishops Stortford last summer. A hard-working young player, he filled in at right-back on a number of occasions, aside from his normal role in central midfield. He scored once, in the comfortable 5-2 home win over Lincoln.

Barnet *(Signed from Bishops Stortford, ex trainee at Southend U, Cambridge U, on 8/8/2007) FL 26+4/1 FLC 0+1 FAC 3+1 Others 1*

POTTER Alfie James
Born: Hackney, 9 January 1989
Height: 5'7" **Weight:** 9.6
Although he made three substitute appearances for Peterborough last season, the wide midfielder will mainly be remembered for his goal against Liverpool at Anfield when on loan to Havant & Waterlooville. Alfie had other loans, to Grays and AFC Wimbledon, to gain experience.
Peterborough U (From Millwall juniors on 19/7/2007) FL 0+2 FLC 0+1

POTTER Darren Michael
Born: Liverpool, 21 December 1984
Height: 6'1" **Weight:** 12.0
International Honours: Rol: 5; B-1; U21-11; Yth
Darren was Wolverhampton's captain at the end of 2006-07 but lost that role after much speculation. He started the first four games of the season and also appeared for the Republic of Ireland. Darren was then used only as a substitute for Wolverhampton, although he nearly created a goal against Bristol City with a defence-splitting pass. His fifth start finally came in late November and he was more involved in the spring, adding two more games for Eire, including a substitute appearance against Brazil. The tidy midfielder dropped out of the first-team picture in April.
Liverpool (From trainee on 18/4/2002) PL 0+2 FLC 4+1 FAC 1 Others 5+4
Southampton (Loaned on 27/1/2006) FL 8+2 FAC 1+1
Wolverhampton W (£250,000 on 17/8/2006) FL 46+10 FLC 2+1 FAC 6/1 Others 2

POWELL Christopher (Chris) George Robin
Born: Lambeth, 8 September 1969
Height: 5'10" **Weight:** 11.7
Club Honours: Div 1 '00
International Honours: E: 5
The veteran left-back returned to Charlton in the summer for his third spell, having been freed by Watford. Chris was expected to be used only in emergency but with Ben Thatcher injured he started eight consecutive League games in August and September before an ankle injury at Wolverhampton put him out for seven games. He started at home against Burnley and played another eight in succession before losing his place to Kelly Youga, who was recalled from a loan at Scunthorpe. Chris made one last cameo appearance in the final game against Coventry at the Valley, when he went on for the last six minutes in midfield and almost immediately scored Charlton's

fourth - and only his third goal in 270 appearances for the Addicks. It was a fitting end to his final game and he was given a tremendous send-off by the fans. He will be missed.
Crystal Palace (From trainee on 24/12/1987) FL 2+1 FLC 0+1 Others 0+1
Aldershot (Loaned on 11/11/1990) FL 11
Southend U (Free on 30/8/1990) FL 246+2/3 FLC 13 FAC 8 Others 21
Derby Co (£750,000 on 31/1/1996) P/FL 89+2/1 FLC 5 FAC 5/1
Charlton Ath (£825,000 on 1/7/1998) P/FL 190+10/1 FLC 8+1 FAC 8/1
West Ham U (Free on 10/9/2004) FL 35+1 FAC 3 Others 3
Charlton Ath (Free on 16/7/2005) PL 25+2 FLC 2 FAC 5
Watford (Free on 4/7/2006) PL 9+6 FAC 2+1
Charlton Ath (Free on 9/8/2007) FL 16+1/1 FLC 2

POWELL Darren David
Born: Hammersmith, 10 March 1976
Height: 6'3" **Weight:** 13.2
Club Honours: Div 3 '99
A commanding and combative presence in the centre of the Southampton defence, Darren's absences have been more significant for the Saints than his appearances as, for the second year in succession, injuries dominated his season. Even when he played, he rarely looked fully match-fit but he managed 90 useful minutes at St Mary's as Saints dragged themselves out of the relegation zone at the 11th hour by defeating Sheffield United 3–2. Was released at the end of the campaign.
Brentford (£15,000 from Hampton on 27/7/1998) FL 128/6 FLC 7 FAC 4 Others 10+1/2
Crystal Palace (£400,000 on 8/8/2002) P/FL 53+2/2 FLC 9+1/1 FAC 3 Others 4+1
West Ham U (Loaned on 19/11/2004) FL 5/1
Southampton (Free on 4/7/2005) FL 42+1/2 FAC 6

POWER Alan Thomas Daniel
Born: Dublin, 23 January 1988
Height: 5'7" **Weight:** 11.6
International Honours: Rol: U21-1
Alan was the latest youngster to come off the Nottingham Forest production line and made his debut against Peterborough in the Johnstone's Paint Trophy in September. He is a right or central midfielder and moved on loan to Grays in November to gain valuable experience. He returned to the City Ground and captained the reserves as they claimed the title. Was released in the summer.
Nottingham F (From trainee on 10/4/2006) Others 1

PRATLEY Darren Antony
Born: Barking, 22 April 1985
Height: 6'0" **Weight:** 10.13
Club Honours: Div 1 '08
Superbly fit, Darren is a box-to-box central midfielder who contributed some vital goals to Swansea's successful season. Overcoming a slight hamstring tear in late January, he was a vital component in the promotion squad that broke numerous records during the season, either in support of the attack or in defence. His red card in the penultimate home game against Yeovil saw him miss the finale against Leyton Orient.
Fulham (From trainee on 29/4/2002) PL 0+1 FLC 0+1
Brentford (Loaned on 22/2/2005) FL 11+3/1 Others 2
Brentford (Loaned on 30/8/2005) FL 25+7/4 FAC 4 Others 2
Swansea C (£100,000 on 23/6/2006) FL 64+6/6 FLC 1/1 FAC 5/1 Others 4+2

PRENDERGAST Rory
Born: Pontefract, 6 April 1978
Height: 5'8" **Weight:** 11.13
Rory was a regular on the bench for Rochdale in the early part of last season, coming on to score in the Carling Cup victory over Stoke. He also netted a late equaliser at Darlington but was unable to dislodge Adam Rundle from the left-wing spot and was released at the end of his contract in January, subsequently joining Farsley Celtic.
Barnsley (From trainee on 8/4/1997)
York C (Free on 6/8/1998) FL 1+2 FLC 0+1 FAC 0+1 (Freed on 26/3/1999)
Blackpool (Signed from Accrington Stanley, ex Oldham Ath - N/C, Northwich Victoria, Gainsborough Trinity, Bradford Park Avenue, on 22/7/2005) FL 22+7 FLC 3 FAC 0+1 Others 0+1
Rochdale (Free on 22/11/2007) FL 6+13/2 FLC 0+2/1 FAC 0+1 Others 1/1
Darlington (Loaned on 22/3/2007) FL 5+3

PRICA Rade
Born: Ljungby, Sweden, 30 June 1980
Height: 6'1" **Weight:** 12.8
International Honours: Sweden: 14; U21
The Swedish international striker joined Sunderland from Danish club Aalborg last January. Rade was off to a dream start on Wearside with a debut goal as a substitute against Birmingham and was desperately unlucky to have a second ruled out soon afterwards. Good in the air and an excellent leader of the line, Rade is a strong and aggressive forward who looked as if he was the answer to Sunderland's search for a regular partner for Kenwyne Jones. Unfortunately, a

succession of niggling injuries meant that Sunderland fans had to wait to see the best of him.

Sunderland (£2,000,000 from Aalborg BK, Denmark, ex Ljungby IF, Helsingborgs IF, Hansa Rostock, on 25/11/2008) PL 0+6/1

PRICE Jason Jeffrey

Born: Pontypridd, 12 April 1977
Height: 6'2" **Weight:** 11.5
Club Honours: Div 3 '00; AMC '07
International Honours: W: U21-7

Jason was out of the Doncaster team at the beginning of last season because of a ruptured Achilles received in the final of the Johnstone's Paint Trophy at the Millenium Stadium in April 2007. He made his comeback from the bench in the middle of September but it was the end of October before he started a first-team game. His return to the side provided the punch and goals that the attack needed, projecting the team on a successful run that took them to second spot in League One. A bad ankle injury, suffered at Tranmere on the first day of March, kept him out of the team for another month. Jason returned to start in attack in the play-offs and proved a thorn in the side of the opposition as the Rovers won their way to the Championship.

Swansea C (Free from Aberaman on 17/7/1995) FL 133+11/17 FLC 10/1 FAC 4/1 Others 4+1/1
Brentford (Free on 6/8/2001) FL 15/1 FLC 2 Others 1
Tranmere Rov (Free on 8/11/2001) FL 34+15/11 FAC 5/4
Hull C (Free on 17/7/2003) FL 45+30/13 FLC 3/1 FAC 3+1/1 Others 2/1
Doncaster Rov (Signed on 24/1/2006) FL 48+23/17 FLC 2+1 FAC 3+3 Others 9+1/5

PRICE Lewis Peter

Born: Bournemouth, 19 July 1984
Height: 6'3" **Weight:** 13.6
International Honours: W: 6; U21-10; Yth

Having been signed from Ipswich in the summer as goalkeeping back-up, Lewis was thrust into an emergency Derby debut against Liverpool on Boxing Day. Steve Bywater was named to keep goal but, during the warm-up, suffered an adverse reaction to the shoulder he injured three days earlier. Lewis performed creditably for nine games, despite some wayward kicking, and starred in an FA Cup penalty shoot-out victory over Sheffield Wednesday. He was considered unfortunate to lose his place as soon as Roy Carroll was signed and did his reputation no harm. Lewis added to his Welsh caps during the season and intends to compete for the senior role

at Derby, boosted by the club's vote as 'Young Player of the Year'.

Ipswich T (From juniors at Southampton on 9/8/2002) FL 67+1 FLC 4 FAC 3
Cambridge U (Loaned on 19/11/2004) FL 6
Derby Co (£200,000 on 27/7/2007) PL 6 FAC 3

PRISKIN Tamas

Born: Komarno, Slovakia, 27 September 1986
Height: 6'2" **Weight:** 13.3
International Honours: Hungary: 17

The Hungarian international striker spent another frustrating season at Watford in 2007-08, again being unable to claim a regular place. A predatory box player with an excellent international scoring record, Tamas seemed to have difficulty in dealing with the physical aspects of Championship football and although he scored a belated first League goal for Watford, against Colchester in December, his inconsistency cost him further chances. In March the lanky striker went on a month's loan to Preston, playing five games and scoring twice, while making a telling contribution to the battle against relegation.

Watford (Signed from Gyori ETO, Hungary on 1/8/2006) P/FL 14+16/3 FLC 5/2 FAC 3+2 Others 0+2
Preston NE (Loaned on 7/3/2008) FL 4+1/2

PROCTOR Andrew (Andy) John

Born: Blackburn, 13 March 1983
Height: 6'2" **Weight:** 12.4

Apart from a slight dip in form around the turn of the year, Andy had his best season since joining Accrington as a teenager. His strong and powerful midfield play was recognised when he was voted the League Two 'Player of the Month' in both August and February and his goals tally improved dramatically, being higher than for the previous four seasons combined. Although perhaps not as dominant towards the end of the season, he could always be found in the thick of things.

Accrington Stanley (Free from Great Harwood T on 21/2/2002) FL 78+8/13 FLC 2 FAC 1 Others 3/1

PROCTOR Michael Anthony

Born: Sunderland, 3 October 1980
Height: 5'11" **Weight:** 12.7

On loan from Hartlepool in 2006-07, Michael was signed by Wrexham on a permanent basis in the summer. Although the leading scorer, he had an up-and-down campaign, not helped by the fact that he never had a regular partner up front. Always alive to the half-chance, he had two braces at home against

Morecambe and Chester. Despite being on the bench a number of times, Michael came back with a bang in March and was on target in four successive games, including a spectacular overhead kick against Chester. Was a victim of Brian Little's end of season cull and told he could leave, although still under contract.

Sunderland (From trainee on 29/10/1997) P/FL 15+23/3 FLC 3+1 FAC 4+2/2
Halifax T (Loaned on 14/3/2001) FL 11+1/4
York C (Loaned on 9/8/2001) FL 40+1/14 FLC 1 FAC 6 Others 1
Bradford C (Loaned on 23/8/2002) FL 10+2/4
Rotherham U (Signed on 6/2/2004) FL 32+13/7 FLC 2/1 FAC 1
Swindon T (Loaned on 23/2/2005) FL 4/2
Hartlepool U (Free on 12/7/2005) FL 23+5/5 FLC 2+1/2 FAC 0+1
Wrexham (Free on 22/3/2007) FL 32+17/13 FLC 2/1 Others 0+1

PROSSER Luke Barrie

Born: Enfield, 28 May 1988
Height: 6'2" **Weight:** 12.4

Luke broke through to Port Vale's first team towards the end of last season. The central defender is good in the air and organises those around him, having made good use of his youth-team apprenticeship. To gain experience, he went on loan to Leigh RMI in the Blue Square North but returned of his own accord in an attempt to impress manager Lee Sinnott. He made his debut as a last-minute substitute at Brighton but his first start was in a 6-0 defeat at Swindon. He recovered well from that in the next game against Northampton and was offered his first professional contract.

Port Vale (From trainee on 1/7/2006) FL 3+2

PROUDLOCK Adam David

Born: Telford, 9 May 1981
Height: 6'0" **Weight:** 13.0
International Honours: E: Yth

Having arrived at Stockport in the summer after being released by Ipswich, Adam chipped in with ten goals, although much of his season was spent on the bench. The County faithful had a glimpse of his undoubted talent when he hit a hat-trick against Wycombe, including a goal from the half-way line, just before Christmas. Unfortunately, he could not reproduce this form consistently and the crowd favourite was released at the end of the campaign.

Wolverhampton W (From trainee on 15/7/1999) FL 42+29/13 FLC 4+2/2 FAC 2+3/2 Others 0+2
Clyde (Loaned on 1/8/2000) SL 4/4 SLC 2/1
Nottingham F (Loaned on 19/3/2002) FL 3

Tranmere Rov (Loaned on 25/10/2002) FL 5 Others 1
Sheffield Wed (Loaned on 13/12/2002) FL 3+2/2
Sheffield Wed (Signed on 6/9/2003) FL 37+13/9 FLC 1+2/2 FAC 3/3 Others 5+1/3
Ipswich T (Free on 10/10/2005) FL 3+6
Stockport Co (Free on 17/8/2006) FL 32+24/11 FLC 2/1 FAC 2+2/3 Others 1+1/1

PROVETT Robert **James (Jim)**
Born: Stockton, 22 December 1982
Height: 6'0" **Weight:** 13.4
After being released by Hartlepool, Jim was offered a contract by Chris Casper when impressing in a pre-season trial at Bury. Although some questioned his height for a goalkeeper, he answered with several match-winning performances, the best in the Johnstone's Paint Trophy victory over Leeds when he kept Bury in the game with a string of fine saves. New manager Alan Knill's arrival saw Jim fall behind loan-signing Darren Randolph as first choice. When Randolph was recalled by Charlton, Jim featured in the remaining games. Was out of contract in the summer and looking for a new club.
Hartlepool U (From trainee on 3/4/2002) FL 66 FLC 3 FAC 4 Others 5
Bury (Free on 6/8/2007) FL 32 FLC 1 FAC 5 Others 3

PRUTTON David Thomas
Born: Hull, 12 September 1981
Height: 6'1" **Weight:** 11.10
International Honours: E: U21-25; Yth
Having been signed from Nottingham Forrest in the summer, the midfield player became a cult figure among Leeds' fans, who dubbed him 'Jesus', a reference to his flowing locks. He also let his football flow, being one of the most consistent midfielders in the United engine room. Despite the future of Leeds being in doubt, David stuck with them in pre-season and signed a short-term deal that was later extended. The former England under-21 international scored his first goal in the 2-0 victory over Swansea in September, the seventh successive League One win for Leeds. Hard-grafting and skilful, David generally played on the right under Dennis Wise but had some games in a more central position when Gary McAllister took over.
Nottingham F (From trainee on 1/10/1998) FL 141+2/7 FLC 7 FAC 5
Southampton (£2,500,000 on 31/1/2003) P/FL 65+17/3 FLC 4+1/1 FAC 6+1/1
Nottingham F (Loaned on 30/1/2007) FL 11+1/2 Others 0+1
Leeds U (Free on 10/8/2007) FL 38+5/4 FLC 2 Others 4

PRYCE Ryan James
Born: Salisbury, 20 September 1989
Height: 6'0" **Weight:** 11.10
Ryan was handed his Bournemouth debut last season when Gareth Stewart was forced off against Southend and soon afterwards was given another opportunity when Stewart broke his ankle. With Neil Moss also out of action, the young goalkeeper made his full debut against Luton in January and played in the next game at Port Vale, being on the winning side both times. He was offered a full-time contract at the end of the season.
Bournemouth (Trainee - Brockenhurst College) FL 2+2

PUGH Andrew (Andy) John
Born: Gravesend, 28 January 1989
Height: 5'9" **Weight:** 12.5
A consistent scorer for the youth team, Andy signed his first professional contract for Gillingham last summer. Unable to break into the first team on a regular basis, with three substitute appearances during the campaign, he enjoyed successful loan spells at Welling and Maidstone.
Gillingham (From trainee on 5/7/2007) FL 0+5 FLC 0+1

PUGH Daniel (Danny) Adam
Born: Manchester, 19 October 1982
Height: 6'0" **Weight:** 12.10
Danny started Preston's first five games

on the left of midfield, scoring a solitary goal in the home Carling Cup defeat by Morecambe, but soon dropped out of the reckoning, making only one further start at left-back before joining Stoke in November, initially on loan. The former Manchester United youngster settled quickly as Stoke's left-back but also played in the centre of midfield and wide on the left, his favoured position. Comfortable on the ball, and a good crosser, Danny made a number of goals in his third attempt at promotion before losing his place to Carl Dickinson as the season reached a climax. Having signed on a permanent basis for Stoke in the January window, he will surely be back.
Manchester U (From trainee on 18/7/2000) PL 0+1 FLC 2 FAC 0+1 Others 1+2
Leeds U (Signed on 20/7/2004) FL 34+16/5 FLC 6/1 FAC 0+1
Preston NE (£250,000 on 6/7/2006) FL 50+2/4 FLC 2/1 FAC 3
Stoke C (£500,000 on 2/11/2007) FL 27+3 FAC 2

PUGH Marc Anthony
Born: Bacup, 2 April 1987
Height: 5'11" **Weight:** 11.5
A young right-winger signed from Bury, Marc can also play on the left or up front and loves to run at defenders. He started brightly for Shrewsbury, doing especially well in a 2-0 victory over Accrington, but never quite recaptured the same form

David Prutton

after a hamstring problem in October. The most important of his four goals was an equaliser at Morecambe to earn a point when Shrewsbury were in danger of becoming involved in the relegation battle. Is a popular player who excites the crowd.

Bury *(From trainee on 1/7/2006) FL 30+11/4 FLC 0+1 FAC 4/1 Others 1*
Shrewsbury T *(Signed on 20/7/2007) FL 27+10/4 FAC 1*

PULIS Anthony (Tony) James
Born: Bristol, 21 July 1984
Height: 5'10" **Weight:** 11.10
International Honours: W: U21-5
The midfielder son of the Stoke manager, who has spent most of his time at the club either in the reserves or out on loan, made only one substitute appearance last season before going on loan to Bristol Rovers. It was not a success. His Rovers' career lasted 15 minutes as a substitute at Doncaster in February, during which he was cautioned and conceded a penalty.

Portsmouth *(From trainee on 26/3/2003) FLC 0+1*
Stoke C *(Free on 23/12/2004) FL 0+2 FLC 2 FAC 0+2*
Torquay U *(Loaned on 24/12/2004) FL 1+2*
Plymouth Arg *(Loaned on 10/3/2006) FL 0+5*
Grimsby T *(Loaned on 23/11/2006) FL 9*
Bristol Rov *(Loaned on 8/2/2008) FL 0+1*

PUNCHEON Jason David Ian
Born: Croydon, 26 June 1986
Height: 5'8" **Weight:** 12.2
Once again, the Barnet winger claimed many plaudits and a number of goals. Known as a long-range specialist, Jason won the club's 'Goal of the Season' for the second time in succession for a superb free kick in a 2-1 win over Bradford at Underhill. He was also selected in the PFA League Two 'Team of the Year', on the left of midfield. His time at Barnet has constantly been filled with speculation about a move to a higher division, with several clubs obviously keeping tabs on his progress.

Wimbledon/MK Dons *(From trainee on 16/10/2004) FL 15+19/1 FLC 2+1 FAC 1+1 Others 2+1 (Freed on 20/1/2006)*
Barnet *(Free from Lewes, ex Fisher Ath, on 3/8/2006) FL 71+7/15 FLC 3/1 FAC 9/1 Others 3*

PURCHES Stephen (Steve) Robert
Born: Ilford, 14 January 1980
Height: 5'11" **Weight:** 12.0
Steve joined Leyton Orient during the summer on a free transfer from Bournemouth, going on to become the first-choice right-back and also the team

captain. Unfortunate to suffer from an injury during the early part of the season, he came back strongly to prove what a good acquisition he had been.

West Ham U *(From trainee on 6/7/1998)*
Bournemouth *(Free on 4/7/2000) FL 221+23/10 FLC 6 FAC 16+1 Others 11/2*
Leyton Orient *(Free on 25/7/2007) FL 35+2/1 FAC 2 Others 0+1*

PURDIE Robert (Rob) James
Born: Wigston, 28 September 1982
Height: 5'8" **Weight:** 11.2
As a Darlington signing from Hereford during the summer, Rob proved to be an energetic and skilful utility man who was deployed at full-back and midfield on both sides of the field. He is a player who enjoys getting forward and running with the ball, always exhibiting great enthusiasm for the game, but although he made over 40 appearances throughout the season, he is still looking for his first Darlington goal.

Hereford U *(From trainee at Leicester C on 7/8/2002) FL 43+1/6 FLC 2/1 FAC 4/2 Others 0+1*
Darlington *(Free on 18/7/2007) FL 30+9 FLC 1 FAC 2 Others 3*

PURSE Darren John
Born: Stepney, 14 February 1977
Height: 6'2" **Weight:** 12.8
International Honours: E: U21-2
It was a mixed season for the big central defender. Darren is Cardiff's club captain but struggled to keep a regular spot with Glenn Loovens and Roger Johnson in exceptional form. Remained supportive from his place on the bench and took the captain's armband whenever he was on the pitch. Moved his family to South Wales from the Midlands and, with a year left on his contract, was keen to stay with the Bluebirds. Was an unused substitute for the FA Cup final as Cardiff took on Premiership Portsmouth.

Leyton Orient *(From trainee on 22/2/1994) FL 48+7/3 FLC 2 FAC 1 Others 7+1/2*
Oxford U *(£100,000 on 23/7/1996) FL 52+7/5 FLC 10+1/2 FAC 2*
Birmingham C *(£800,000 on 17/2/1998) P/ FL 143+25/9 FLC 17+2/2 FAC 6 Others 6+1*
West Bromwich A *(£500,000 + on 18/6/2004) FL 2 FAC 2*
Cardiff C *(£750,000 on 2/8/2005) FL 82+6/10 FLC 6/2 FAC 3*

Jason Puncheon

Q

QUEUDRUE Franck
Born: Paris, France, 27 August 1978
Height: 6'0" **Weight:** 12.4
Club Honours: FLC '04
International Honours: France: B
Signed from Fulham in the summer,
Franck proved to be a solid, aggressive
performer at left-back for Birmingham,
who passed the ball sweetly and
accurately. Lost his place to new signing
David Murphy in January after a change
in manager but came back to turn in
an excellent performance at centre-half
in the 3-1 win over Manchester City,
before being sent off for denying a
scoring opportunity. A good professional
and a team man even when he was not
included, Franck might have kept the
position for the final six weeks but for the
suspension.
*Middlesbrough (£2,500,000 from RC Lens,
France, ex Meaux, on 12/10/2001) PL 145+5/
11 FLC 11+1/1 FAC 14 Others 18+5*
*Fulham (£2,000,000 on 28/7/2006) PL
28+1/1 FAC 3*
*Birmingham C (£2,000,000 on 3/8/2007) PL
14+2 FAC 1*

QUINN Alan
Born: Dublin, 13 June 1979
Height: 5'9" **Weight:** 11.7
International Honours: RoI: 8; U21-8;
Yth (UEFA-U18 '98)
Alan had few opportunities under
new Sheffield United manager Bryan
Robson, although the midfielder always
played with his customary energy and
enthusiasm. With hopes of a regular
place looking slim, he signed for Ipswich
in January and scored his first goal for
them on his return to Sheffield, across
the city against Wednesday. Alan also
delivered the cross that Alan Lee headed
in to enable Ipswich to register their first
away win of the season. Although never
troubling the scorers again, he took over
many of the dead-ball situations, his free
kicks and corners providing chances for
his team-mates.
*Sheffield Wed (Signed from Cherry Orchard
on 6/12/1997) P/FL 147+10/16 FLC 14/1 FAC
6+1 Others 2*
Sunderland (Loaned on 3/10/2003) FL 5+1
*Sheffield U (Free on 7/7/2004) P/FL 76+21/
11 FLC 6+2 FAC 3+1*
*Ipswich T (£400,000 on 19/1/2008) FL
14+2/1*

QUINN Stephen
Born: Dublin, 4 April 1986
Height: 5'6" **Weight:** 9.8

Franck Queudrue

International Honours: RoI: U21-9

Stephen was involved in a few games for Sheffield United in September and October before regaining a more regular place in late January, playing either in midfield or wide on the left. An energetic player who does not shirk a tackle, he can show good vision with through passes to forwards, while able to take on and beat his man down the flank before producing searching crosses. A good striker of the ball, he scored with an excellent volley against Hull, but missed six games towards the end of the season and took time to regain his place following a red card. He also played for the Republic of Ireland under-21s.

Sheffield U *(From trainee on 6/7/2005) P/FL 30+4/4 FLC 4+1 FAC 4+1*
MK Dons *(Loaned on 23/9/2005) FL 6 Others 0+1*
MK Dons *(Loaned on 11/11/2005) FL 7+2 FAC 1 Others 0+2*
Rotherham U *(Loaned on 21/1/2006) FL 16*

Alan Quinn

R

RACCHI Daniel (Danny) Craig
Born: Elland, 22 November 1987
Height: 5'8" **Weight:** 10.4
Danny was used at various stages of the season, predominately as a late substitute to add pace to the right side of Huddersfield's midfield. The speedy right-winger showed a skilful touch and good distribution to create chances but the Academy product was among those released.
Huddersfield T (From trainee on 1/7/2006) FL 0+6

RACHUBKA Paul Stephen
Born: San Luis Obispo, California, USA, 21 May 1981
Height: 6'1" **Weight:** 13.5
International Honours: E: Yth
Ever-present in the League, Paul continued where he left off in the previous season with the Blackpool number-one spot, having been signed on a permanent basis from Peterborough during the summer. Such is their confidence in him that manager Simon Grayson did not even name a substitute goalkeeper for the bench. An excellent shot-stopper, Paul worked hard last season on his handling of crosses and corners. He did, however, concede a goal in the last minute to hand Sheffield United a point but it was his only mistake in an otherwise excellent season in which he often saved Blackpool from defeat.
Manchester U (From trainee on 7/7/1999) PL 1 FLC 0+1 Others 0+1
Oldham Ath (Loaned on 23/11/2001) FL 16 Others 1
Charlton Ath (Signed on 20/5/2002)
Huddersfield T (Loaned on 2/3/2004) FL 13 Others 3
MK Dons (Loaned on 6/8/2004) FL 4
Northampton T (Loaned on 3/9/2004) FL 10 FLC 1
Huddersfield T (Free on 5/11/2004) FL 63 FLC 2 FAC 3 Others 3+1
Peterborough U (Loaned on 22/12/2006) FL 4
Blackpool (Free on 31/1/2007) FL 54 FLC 2 FAC 1 Others 3

RACON Therry Norbert
Born: Villeneuve-St-Georges, 1 May 1984
Height: 5'10" **Weight:** 10.7
Therry was signed by manager Alan Pardew from French side Guingamp on the eve of the new season to add strength to Charlton's central midfield. Comfortable on the ball and with good passing ability, it was surprising that more

wasn't seen of him. The early season form of Jose Semedo kept him out and he was further away when Matt Holland returned after injury. Starting only one League game, the victory at Bristol City, and a couple of games in the Carling Cup, his season was otherwise restricted to the occasional substitute appearance. In March, he joined Brighton on loan until the end of the season, having scored for Charlton's reserves against them in October. As a replacement for the injured Adam El-Abd, Therry performed well in a central-midfield position and he showed good passing skill and stamina in the Albion side that drew at Nottingham Forest and Leeds. Unable to maintain such a high level throughout his stay on the South Coast, his time there ended with one match remaining when he was recalled to the Valley.
Charlton Ath (Signed from Guingamp, France, ex Marseille, Lorient, on 24/8/2007) FL 1+3 FLC 2
Brighton & Hove A (Loaned on 20/3/2008) FL 8

RAE Gavin Paul
Born: Aberdeen, 28 November 1977
Height: 5'11" **Weight:** 10.7
International Honours: S: 13; U21-6
Arriving at Ninian Park from Glasgow Rangers in the summer, Gavin made more appearances than any other Cardiff player. As an energetic, box-to-box midfield player, he grew in stature as the season progressed. Cardiff badly missed the influential Riccy Scimeca, who spent most of last season injured, but Gavin formed a solid partnership with Stephen McPhail in central midfield. He went on to play almost the entire 90 minutes in the FA Cup final before being replaced in the dying moments.
Dundee (Signed from Hermes on 1/8/1996) SL 174+17/23 SLC 9+1 SC 16/2 Others 6/1
Glasgow Rgrs (£250,000 on 1/1/2004) SL 16+12/3 SLC 2 SC 2 Others 4+3
Cardiff C (Free on 6/7/2007) FL 40+5/4 FLC 4 FAC 5

RAINFORD David (Dave) John
Born: Stepney, 21 April 1979
Height: 6'0" **Weight:** 12.4
Club Honours: FC '07
Nine years after playing in the League on loan at Scarborough, Dave appeared as Dagenham entered the League at Stockport. A stomach injury kept him out of the side around Christmas but he returned to play an influential midfield role, scoring a number of important goals, both from open play and penalties. Last season Dave combined League football with a teaching job but following

a promotion at his school and needing to revert to part-time football, he was released from his contract.
Colchester U (From trainee on 30/7/1997) FL 0+1 (Freed during 1999 close season)
Scarborough (Loaned on 31/12/1998) FL 0+2 Others 1
Dagenham & Redbridge (Free from Bishops Stortford, ex Slough T, Grays Ath, Heybridge Swifts, on 4/7/2006) FL 28+1/8 FLC 1 FAC 1 Others 3

RAMAGE Peter Iain
Born: Whitley Bay, 22 November 1983
Height: 6'1" **Weight:** 12.2
Peter is a tall, strong Newcastle defender, able to play anywhere along the back four, but when appearing from the bench at Middlesbrough in late August tore a cruciate ligament, an injury so serious it needed a total knee reconstruction. He returned to action for the reserves in March and made a substitute appearance for the first team in the final game of the season at Everton. In May he turned down the offer of a new deal, preferring a move to secure regular first-team football, and signed for Queens Park Rangers.
Newcastle U (From trainee on 15/7/2003) PL 45+6 FLC 4+1 FAC 4+1 Others 6+2

RAMSDEN Simon Paul
Born: Bishop Auckland, 17 December 1981
Height: 6'0" **Weight:** 12.4
Simon suffered a couple of early season injuries but after returning to the Rochdale side at the end of November, he again became the automatic choice at right-back. His reappearance coincided with the start of a run of seven unbeaten games that enabled Dale to climb into the top ten for the first time in the season. Simon went on to miss just one game in the remainder of the campaign as the side clinched a play-off place and ended the season at Wembley, where he was moved into midfield to cover for the suspended David Perkins.
Sunderland (From trainee on 7/8/2000) FAC 0+1
Notts Co (Loaned on 16/8/2002) FL 21+11 FLC 1 FAC 1
Grimsby T (Free on 2/8/2004) FL 31+6 FLC 2 FAC 0+1 Others 1
Rochdale (Free on 30/1/2006) FL 82+2/6 FLC 3 Others 5

RAMSEY Aaron
Born: Caerphilly, 26 December 1990
Height: 5'9" **Weight:** 10.7
Signed as a professional from the youth ranks on his 17th birthday, teenager Aaron became the hottest prospect in

British football last season. Burst into the Cardiff team at 16, becoming the youngest first-team player in the club's history and beating John Toshack's record. The Welsh-speaking 'Rambo', from Caerphilly, near Cardiff, was the subject of written offers from Liverpool, Arsenal, Manchester United and Everton in the summer with a valuation of around £5m. Aaron was still under contract to Cardiff but they came under severe pressure because of the stature of clubs making the offers and the sums involved. Given the opportunity to come on for the final 30 minutes at Wembley in the FA Cup final, Aaron was unlucky not to level the score before Portsmouth won 1-0.
Cardiff C (From trainee on 3/1/2008) FL 11+5/1 FLC 0+1 FAC 3+2/1

RANDALL Mark Leonard
Born: Milton Keynes, 28 September 1989
Height: 6'0" **Weight:** 12.12
After appearing in two Carling Cup ties and being an unused substitute in the FA Cup third round at Burnley, as well as scoring against the Clarets in the FA Youth Cup, this Arsenal midfielder joined Burnley on loan in January. Although it was immediately apparent that here was a talent in the making, as he showed the skills on the ball expected from an Emirates graduate as well as a measure of aggression in the midfield battle area, he was given relatively little chance to develop his abilities with only two starts plus a few relatively brief outings from the bench. Back at Arsenal, Mark played in the last Premier League game at Sunderland and was a little unlucky to have a goal ruled out for offside. Following his added experience, Arsene Wenger confirmed that Mark will be more involved with the Arsenal first team this coming season.
Arsenal (From trainee on 7/2/2007) PL 0+1 FLC 1+3
Burnley (Loaned on 31/1/2008) FL 2+8

RANDOLPH Darren Edward
Born: Dublin, 12 May 1987
Height: 6'1" **Weight:** 12.3
Club Honours: FC '06
International Honours: RoI: B; U21-10
Having made his Premiership debut in the final game of the previous season and with Scott Carson returning to Liverpool after his loan, it was expected that Darren would be the number one goalkeeper at Charlton in 2007-08. However, the signing of the experienced Nicky Weaver meant that he was restricted to only three appearances, two of them in the Carling Cup. Frustrated by his lack of opportunities, he was allowed to go on

loan to Bury in February, being one of Alan Knill's first recruits after taking over as manager. Being both tall and broad, Darren is also athletic and agile, while his shot-stopping ability is matched by long, accurate kicking that can turn defence turned into attack. Although prone to the occasional mistake, Darren came to the Shakers' rescue more than once and a string of fine saves helped them to a vital win over Shrewsbury in March as they dragged themselves away from the relegation zone. Having made 14 appearances for Bury, Darren was recalled in controversial circumstances in April when Nicky Weaver had been suspended for one match and Rob Elliot, who had deputised competently for 86 minutes at Plymouth the previous week, was dropped. Although Darren played against Southampton at the Valley, only to make an error after just ten minutes, he put it behind him and got on with the game. During what was a difficult season he was still impressive enough to earn another five Republic of Ireland under-21 caps.
Charlton Ath (From trainee on 24/12/2004) P/FL 2 FLC 2
Gillingham (Loaned on 18/8/2006) FL 3 FLC 1
Bury (Loaned on 8/2/2008) FL 14

RANGEL Angel
Born: Tortosa, Spain, 28 October 1982
Height: 5'11" **Weight:** 11.9
Club Honours: Div 1 '08
Angel was an outstanding close season capture from Spanish Third Division side Terrassa FC and was an ever-present for Swansea going into April. Unfortunately, the attacking right-back suffered a groin injury just when promotion had been assured. He was one of five Swans players nominated in the PFA League One select team of the season.
Swansea C (Signed from Terrassa, Spain on 10/8/2007) FL 42/2 FLC 1 FAC 4 Others 4

RANKIN Isaiah
Born: Edmonton, 22 May 1978
Height: 5'10" **Weight:** 11.6
Isaiah began the campaign as Grimsby's lone striker in a 4-5-1 formation, but was unfortunate that his hard work in attack failed to bring the goals it deserved. While his pace proved a handful for opponents, his scoring attempts usually brought fine saves from goalkeepers or defensive blocks on the line. He did manage to find the net against Huddersfield in the Johnstone's Paint Trophy, only to then suffer a stomach injury and leave for Stevenage in the January transfer window.
Arsenal (From trainee on 12/9/1995) PL 0+1

Colchester U (Loaned on 25/9/1997) FL 10+1/5 Others 1
Bradford C (£1,300,000 on 14/8/1998) P/FL 15+22/4 FLC 2/1 FAC 0+2 Others 1+1/1
Birmingham C (Loaned on 19/1/2000) FL 11+2/4
Bolton W (Loaned on 11/8/2000) FL 9+7/2 FLC 2
Barnsley (£350,000 on 19/1/2001) FL 18+29/8 FLC 1+2/1 FAC 2+1/1 Others 1+1
Grimsby T (Signed on 12/2/2004) FL 12/4
Brentford (Free on 2/7/2004) FL 64+14/15 FLC 0+1 FAC 10+4/4 Others 2+2
Grimsby T (Free on 1/7/2006) FL 27+10/2 FLC 2 FAC 0+1 Others 2/1
Macclesfield T (Loaned on 22/3/2007) FL 1+3

RASIAK Grzegorz
Born: Szczecin, Poland, 12 January 1979
Height: 6'3" **Weight:** 13.3
International Honours: Poland: 37
Awkward looking but erratically brilliant in the penalty area, as a target-man and a striker, Grzegorz found it difficult to earn a regular start in Southampton's attack last season. With his prospects of making it into the Poland squad for the European Championship finals looking doubtful and George Burley vacating the manager's office for the Scotland job at the end of January, he was loaned to Bolton in January. A surprise signing when many were expecting a relatively big-name replacement for the recently departed Nicolas Anelka, Grzegorz's first Bolton appearances came from the substitutes' bench, with little success. He was given the nod over El Hadji Diouf to lead the line in two League games in April when Kevin Davies was suspended but failed to make the most of his opportunity and left the club at the end of the season, having failed to hit the target.
Derby Co (Free from Groclin Dyskobolia, Poland on 24/9/2004) FL 41/18 FLC 0+1 FAC 2/1 Others 1
Tottenham H (Signed on 31/8/2005) PL 4+4 FAC 1
Southampton (£2,000,000 on 8/2/2006) FL 57+18/28 FLC 2/1 FAC 4/3 Others 0+2/1
Bolton W (Loaned on 31/1/2008) PL 2+5

RAVEN David Haydn
Born: West Kirby, 10 March 1985
Height: 6'0" **Weight:** 11.6
International Honours: E: Yth
David was a virtual ever-present for Carlisle, playing mainly at right-back, although featuring occasionally in central defence. He is a solid and steady performer for whom defence is very much the first priority in his game. Having said that, the manner in which he scored his first senior goal in the victory at Leyton

Orient received widespread and justified acclaim.

Liverpool (From trainee on 20/5/2002) PL 0+1 FLC 2 FAC 1

Tranmere Rov (Loaned on 31/1/2006) FL 11

Carlisle U (Free on 3/8/2006) FL 79/1 FLC 2 FAC 3 Others 3

David Raven

RAVENHILL Richard (Ricky) John
Born: Doncaster, 16 January 1981
Height: 5'11" **Weight:** 11.3
Club Honours: Div 3 '04
The tenacious, hard-tackling Darlington midfielder never really established himself in the side and despite starting just over half the games in the League never had a run of more than five in succession. Ricky is more of a ball winner than a scorer but did contribute three goals on his forays forward into the box.

Barnsley (From trainee on 29/6/1999)

Doncaster Rov (Free on 18/1/2002) FL 58+40/9 FLC 6+3/1 FAC 5+1 Others 4

Chester C (Loaned on 9/7/2006) FL 1+2

Grimsby T (Free on 31/8/2006) FL 15+2/2 FAC 0+1 Others 2

Darlington (Signed on 16/1/2007) FL 38+12/4 FLC 1 FAC 1 Others 3

RAYNES Michael Bernard
Born: Wythenshawe, 15 October 1987
Height: 6'4" **Weight:** 12.0
A recurrence of his hamstring problem

kept Michael out of the Stockport side until October. His return coincided with an injury to first-choice centre-half Ashley Williams, though, and he settled at the back well. Even Williams' return didn't stop him making appearances, either at right-back or off the bench. Sadly, his hamstring nightmare returned when he limped off in the play-off semi-final at Wycombe, causing him to miss the second leg and the victorious final.

Stockport Co (From trainee on 8/3/2005) FL 65+15/1 FLC 0+1 FAC 5+1 Others 4+1

REAY Sean
Born: Jarrow, 20 May 1989
Height: 6'1" **Weight:** 12.0
Sean had to wait until the final home game before featuring in Darlington's first team when he was a 19th-minute substitute for the injured Pawel Abbot. His direct running and willingness to chase long balls characterise his game and he was rewarded with his first goal, against Dagenham, as the League curtain came down at the Arena, when he darted through on a return pass and found the net. Was released at the end of the season.

Darlington (From trainee on 2/11/2006) FL 1+3 Others 0+1

REECE Charles (Charlie) Thomas
Born: Birmingham, 8 September 1988
Height: 5'11" **Weight:** 12.0
The young central midfielder, who had once been on Aston Villa's books, was a regular in Bristol Rovers' reserve side. Developing consistently, game by game, he made his League debut for Rovers in a home match against Carlisle. Charlie is expected to challenge strongly for a first-team place in the future.

Bristol Rov (From Filton College on 5/6/2007) FL 0+1

REET Daniel (Danny) Steven
Born: Sheffield, 31 January 1987
Height: 6'0" **Weight:** 13.9
Manager Billy Dearden stated publicly that he was concerned about Danny's weight and he therefore started the season as a fixture on the Mansfield bench. Needing regular football, and with the Stags not having a reserve team, by mid-September Danny was sent out on three months loan to Alfreton. In December, the loan was extended until the end of the season and Danny's time at Field Mill ended in March when new manager Paul Holland terminated his contract.

Sheffield Wed (From juniors on 8/7/2005)

Bury (Loaned on 4/11/2005) FL 6/4 FAC 1+1

Mansfield T (£25,000 on 13/1/2006) FL 24+17/11 FLC 0+1/1 FAC 0+2 Others 0+2

Rochdale (Loaned on 22/3/2007) FL 0+6

REGAN Carl Anthony
Born: Liverpool, 14 January 1980
Height: 6'0" **Weight:** 11.5
International Honours: E: Yth
In the first half of the season, Carl was Macclesfield's regular right-back, missing only a few matches through illness, always ready to press forward and performing consistently. Despite that, he became another of Town's players to follow Paul Ince to MK Dons, joining them on the last day of the January transfer window, two days after playing against them. He quickly became a valuable member of the title-winning squad, being versatile enough to fill in either at right-back or in central defence depending on the circumstances, and scored a key goal early on in the important April victory at Lincoln. In nine appearances for the Dons, Carl did not taste defeat.

Everton (From trainee on 19/1/1998)

Barnsley (£20,000 on 15/6/2000) FL 31+6 FLC 5

Hull C (Free on 15/8/2002) FL 33+5 FLC 1 FAC 1 Others 1 (Freed on 25/3/2004)

Chester C (Free from Droylsden on 18/3/2005) FL 43+4 FLC 1 FAC 4

Macclesfield T (Free on 4/7/2006) FL 54+4/2 FLC 2 FAC 4 Others 1+1

MK Dons (Signed on 31/1/2008) FL 8+1/1

REHMAN Zeshan (Zesh)
Born: Birmingham, 14 October 1983
Height: 6'2" **Weight:** 12.12
International Honours: E: Yth. Pakistan: 6
Zesh, a Pakistan international, enjoyed something of a revival following the appointment of Luigi De Canio as manager at Queens Park Rangers. Despite never settling into a regular spot in the starting line-up, his all-round game improved dramatically under the Italian's influence and he stepped up admirably to cover injuries across the back four. He was also honoured by Rangers at the end of the season, scooping the 'Community Commitment Award' in recognition of his tireless and outstanding work in the local area.

Fulham (From trainee on 7/6/2001) PL 18+3 FLC 6+1/1 FAC 2

Brighton & Hove A (Loaned on 29/9/2003) FL 6/2 Others 1

Brighton & Hove A (Loaned on 14/11/2003) FL 3+2 Others 1

Norwich C (Loaned on 31/1/2006) FL 5

Queens Park Rgrs (Free on 8/8/2006) FL 40+6 FLC 2 FAC 1

Brighton & Hove A (Loaned on 22/3/2007) FL 8

REID Andrew (Andy) Matthew
Born: Dublin, 29 July 1982
Height: 5'7" **Weight:** 11.12
International Honours: RoI: 27; U21-15;
Yth (UEFA-U16 '98)
If any one factor had a real bearing on
Charlton's inability to gain automatic
promotion or indeed make the play-
offs, it was the sale of skipper Andy to
Sunderland at the end of January, the
club winning only four games after his
departure. Comfortable on the ball and
able to read the game well, with great
passing ability, Andy scored six goals for
Athletic last season, although four were
from the penalty spot. The two from open
play saw him score a great individual goal
against Sheffield Wednesday, when he
jinked past a defender before blasting
a shot into the bottom corner, and a
tremendous volley against Burnley. Andy
was used mainly in central midfield and
featured in every League game until a
knee injury at West Bromwich in mid-
December. It turned out to be his last
game before moving north. The left-sided
midfielder made an immediate impact
at Sunderland, his first goal being a
brilliantly volleyed 95th-minute winner
against West Ham in March that instantly
endeared him to the Black Cats' fans. His
crosses and deliveries into the penalty
area from corners and free kicks was
something that Sunderland had been
crying out for all season.
*Nottingham F (From trainee on 16/8/1999)
FL 121+23/21 FLC 6+2/1 FAC 6/2 Others 2/1*
*Tottenham H (Signed on 31/1/2005) PL
20+6/1 FLC 1*
*Charlton Ath (£3,000,000 on 17/8/2006)
P/FL 36+2/7 FLC 2/1*
*Sunderland (£4,000,000 on 31/1/2008)
PL 11+2/1*

REID Craig Kevin
Born: Coventry, 17 December 1985
Height: 5'10" **Weight:** 11.10
The young striker made a handful of
appearances for Cheltenham having been
top scorer for the reserves the previous
season. He made his full debut against
Southend in the Carling Cup and scored
his first goal against Swindon in the
Johnstone's Paint Trophy. Craig started
League games against Nottingham Forest
and Walsall in the first half of the season
but his appearances were restricted to the
bench after the turn of the year. A hard-
working forward with an eye for goal,
Craig maintained his scoring touch with
seven goals in a youthful reserve team,
including a hat-trick against Swansea.
Was released in the summer.
*Coventry C (From trainee at Ipswich T on
2/7/2004. Freed during 2006 close season)*

*Cheltenham T (Free, following trials at St
Mirren and Dunfermline Ath, on 12/1/2007)
FL 2+12 FLC 1 FAC 0+2 Others 1/1*

REID Izak George
Born: Stafford, 8 July 1987
Height: 5'5" **Weight:** 10.6
Izak is a versatile young player who is
equally capable of playing on the right
side of midfield or at right-back. There
were few opportunities for him in the
first half of the season at Macclesfield
as he was kept out of the side by his
elder brother, Levi, in midfield and Carl
Regan at full-back. However, on Regan's
departure, Izak was called into the
side and was ever-present either in the
starting line-up or as a substitute. There
were times when he and his brother
covered the right flank together. Despite
his lack of height, Izak is a strong
player who is rarely pushed off the ball
and makes good use of his pace. He
scored twice last season, his strike at
Peterborough in January being his first
senior goal.
*Macclesfield T (From trainee on 4/7/2006)
FL 19+14/2 Others 1+1*

REID Kyel Romaine
Born: Deptford, 26 November 1987
Height: 5'10" **Weight:** 12.5
International Honours: E: Yth
A pacy left-winger who failed to establish
a starting place at West Ham last season,
Kyel was used as a substitute and did well
in the limited time available to him. In
the game against Plymouth in the Carling
Cup, it was his cross that brought the
winning goal. On joining Crystal Palace
in March until the end of the season,
he became one of Neil Warnock's last-
minute loan signings for the club but
made only two substitute appearances
during his time there.
*West Ham U (From trainee on 2/12/2004) PL
1+2 FLC 1+2 FAC 0+1*
*Barnsley (Loaned on 23/11/2006) FL
12+14/2*
*Crystal Palace (Loaned on 27/3/2008) FL
0+2*

REID Levi Stanley Junior
Born: Stafford, 19 January 1983
Height: 5'5" **Weight:** 11.4
Signing for Macclesfield during the
summer from non-League Stafford, Levi
went straight into the starting line-up and
was ever present until newly appointed
manager Keith Alexander's change of
formation left him on the substitutes'
bench. Levi is a committed right-sided
midfielder who is a consistent performer,
strong in the challenge and hard-working
in an undemonstrative manner. There was

family satisfaction when he and younger
brother Izak guarded the right flank and
both of Levi's two goals ensured a share
of the points for Town. Was released at
the end of the campaign.
*Port Vale (From trainee on 1/7/2003) FL
28+14 FLC 1 FAC 5/1 Others 1 (Freed during
2005 close season)*
*Macclesfield T (Free from Stafford Rgrs, ex
Hinckley U, on 3/8/2007) FL 29+2/2 FLC 1
FAC 1 Others 2*

REID Paul James
Born: Sydney, Australia, 6 July 1979
Height: 5'10" **Weight:** 10.10
International Honours: Australia: Yth
After suffering a cruciate knee ligament
injury in 2006-07, Paul hoped for
better last season but it was not to
be. Still plagued by various knee and
groin problems, the popular Australian,
who became a British citizen during
the campaign, was confined to four
appearances for Brighton and another
five as a substitute. On his day a versatile
player able to perform at right-back,
central midfield or wide right, Paul helped
Albion reserves lift the Sussex Senior Cup
in what was his final game for the club,
as he was not offered new terms.
*Bradford C (Free from Wollongong Wolves,
Australia on 7/9/2002) FL 7+1/2*
*Brighton & Hove A (Free on 25/3/2004) FL
86+8/5 FLC 3+1/1 FAC 2+1 Others 2+1*

REID Paul Mark
Born: Carlisle, 18 February 1982
Height: 6'2" **Weight:** 12.4
International Honours: E: Yth
Having signed a two-year extension to his
contract before the start of the season,
it was a frustrating time for the defender
and Barnsley captain. He started the
first three games, scoring the winner
against Darlington in the Carling Cup,
but after being sent off at Colchester he
never got back into the team as firstly his
replacement Lewin Nyatanga and then
injury kept him out. Made available for
transfer in January, Paul finally moved on
loan to Carlisle on transfer deadline day,
eight years after his last appearance for
his home-town club. Returning to boost
Carlisle's drive for promotion and playing
in central defence he was, unfortunately,
only able to feature for half the game on
his debut before being sidelined by injury.
*Carlisle U (From trainee on 19/2/1999) FL
17+2 Others 3*
Glasgow Rgrs (£200,000 on 1/7/2000)
Preston NE (Loaned on 29/1/2002) FL 0+1/1
*Northampton T (Loaned on 31/12/2002)
FL 19*
*Northampton T (£100,000 on 19/6/2003)
FL 33/2 FLC 2 FAC 3 Others 2+2*

*Barnsley (Signed on 19/7/2004) FL 107+7/3
FLC 4/2 FAC 6/1 Others 4/1*
Carlisle U (Loaned on 27/3/2008) FL 1

REID Reuben James
Born: Bristol, 26 July 1988
Height: 6'0" **Weight:** 12.2
Reuben is an interesting prospect with
good pace and played in Plymouth's first
two Carling Cup games before being
loaned to League Two Wycombe at the
end of August. Although used mostly
from the bench, the young striker scored
on his debut when he went on seven
minutes from time at Macclesfield, riding
a tackle to convert the chance smartly.
On returning early to Home Park he was
told by new manager Paul Sturrock that
he would be released at the end of the
season. Reuben then went out on loan
to Brentford for the last three months of
the season, being used sparingly, starting
once and usually introduced as a late
substitute. He scored once, at Darlington.
*Plymouth Arg (From Millfield School on
18/1/2006) FL 1+6 FLC 1+2 FAC 2*
Rochdale (Loaned on 26/1/2006) FL 0+2
Torquay U (Loaned on 22/3/2007) FL 4+3/2
*Wycombe W (Loaned on 31/8/2007) FL
1+10/1 Others 1*
Brentford (Loaned on 31/1/2008) FL 1+9/1

REID Steven John
Born: Kingston, 10 March 1981
Height: 6'1" **Weight:** 12.4
Club Honours: Div 2 '01
International Honours: RoI: 20; U21-2;
E: Yth
Despite tearing a cruciate ligament when
in rehabilitation from a broken bone
in his back, Steven entered the season
in a state of recovery and by the time
he joined Blackburn's first team in the
games leading up to Christmas he was
short of match-fitness. Naturally athletic,
he gained a place in central midfield but
although appearing strong, he struggled
to be influential when playing the last
four games at right-back, a position in
which he has experience.
*Millwall (From trainee on 18/5/1998) FL
115+24/18 FLC 5+2 FAC 10/1 Others 10+1*
*Blackburn Rov (£1,800,000 + on 30/7/
2003) PL 86+19/6 FLC 4+2/1 FAC 3+4 Others
1+1*

REINA Jose (Pepe) Manuel
Born: Madrid, Spain, 31 August 1982
Height: 6'2" **Weight:** 13.8
Club Honours: ESC '05; FAC '06; CS '06
International Honours: Spain: 10
Once again the Liverpool and Spanish
international goalkeeper enjoyed another
consistent and high-quality campaign,
playing in every Premiership and

Pepe Reina

Champions' League game, with his deputy Charles Itandje brought in for the domestic Cup competitions, and keeping a total of 24 clean sheets. His 18 shut-outs in the Premiership campaign led to him winning the 'Golden Glove' award for the third consecutive year and in March he reached 50 clean sheets in the quickest time at Liverpool, 92 games, thus beating a record long held by Ray Clemence. An excellent shot-stopper and distributor of the ball, while there were no penalty shoot-out heroics to compare with the previous season he had the satisfaction of one penalty save, from Portsmouth's Nwankwo Kanu in an early season goalless draw. Pepe is now acknowledged to be one of the top 'keepers in the world, along with Petr Cech and Edwin Van Der Sar, but still remains the second choice for Spain, behind Real Madrid's Iker Casillas.
Liverpool (£6,000,000 from Villareal, Spain on 6/7/2005) PL 106 FLC 1 FAC 5 Others 44

RENDELL Scott David
Born: Ashford, Middlesex, 21 October 1986
Height: 6'1" **Weight:** 12.5
Striker Scott joined Peterborough on loan from local rivals Cambridge United at the end of February, in a deal that became permanent on 22 May. He had limited chances because of the form of the attacking players at the club but managed three goals and is one for the future.
Peterborough U (£115,000 from Cambridge U, ex Aldershot T, Forest Green Rov, Hayes, Crawley T, on 18/2/2008) FL 3+7/3

RENTS Samuel (Sam) David
Born: Brighton, 22 June 1987
Height: 5'11" **Weight:** 12.8
Given scant opportunities to show his worth, Sam was confined to four starts and four appearances as a substitute for Brighton as he fell in the pecking order behind Matt Richards, Kerry Mayo, Joel Lynch and the right-footed Adam El-Abd. Capable of delivering a delightful cross, the locally-born left-back was unfortunate to be injured at the same time as Richards, which did little to help his cause. After showing promise in previous seasons, it was a disappointment not to be offered a new contract.
Brighton & Hove A (From trainee on 28/6/2006) FL 23+7 FLC 0+1 FAC 1+3/1 Others 1+1

REO-COKER Nigel Shola Andre
Born: Thornton Heath, 14 May 1984
Height: 5'8" **Weight:** 10.5
International Honours: E: U21-23; Yth

Signed by Aston Villa from West Ham in time for 2007-08, Nigel is an industrious central midfield player who formed an excellent partnership with Gareth Barry. He missed only two games and scored his only goal against Wrexham in the Carling Cup. Playing in a much deeper role than he had for West Ham, he had to adjust to a holding position, even playing right-back on a few occasions. Nigel's aggressive style resulted in two suspensions. He was sent off, for the first time in his career, in the home game against Manchester United and picked up another one-match ban after accumulating five yellow cards. Apart from those absences, Nigel was ever-present for Villa and solid performances throughout established him as a shrewd capture by Martin O'Neill.
Wimbledon (From trainee on 15/7/2002) FL 57+1/6 FLC 2+1 FAC 2+1
West Ham U (£575,000 on 23/1/2004) P/FL 113+7/11 FLC 4 FAC 9+1 Others 5+3
Aston Villa (£8,500,000 on 16/7/2007) PL 36 FLC 2/1 FAC 1

REVELL Alexander (Alex) David
Born: Cambridge, 7 July 1983
Height: 6'3" **Weight:** 12.0
Despite missing five weeks of last season with a hernia problem, Alex had hit seven goals for Brighton by the time he was sold to Southend in January. That move came four weeks after the ever-willing forward hit his first senior hat-trick in the home game against Bournemouth, undoubtedly the highlight of his career. Unfortunately he lasted only three matches at the start of his Southend career before the hernia injury recurred and an operation left him on the sidelines until April. A willing worker, Alex had only a brief spell to show the United fans his striking skills but his aerial strength should be valuable to the Shrimpers and while still needing to work on his finishing he is guaranteed to win over supporters wherever he plays because of his all-out effort.
Cambridge U (From trainee on 21/4/2001) FL 19+38/5 FLC 0+1 FAC 0+2 Others 1+5 (Freed during 2004 close season)
Brighton & Hove A (Free from Braintree T on 17/7/2006) FL 48+11/13 FLC 3 FAC 4/3 Others 4+1/2
Southend U (£150,000 on 30/1/2008) FL 5+3 Others 0+2

RHODES Alexander (Alex) Graham
Born: Cambridge, 23 January 1982
Height: 5'9" **Weight:** 10.4
The former Brentford left-winger enjoyed an excellent debut for Bradford against

Macclesfield but then saw his progress jolted by several hamstring injuries. Alex was often most effective coming off the bench and his best game was as a scoring substitute against Notts County.
Brentford (Signed from Newmarket T on 13/11/2003) FL 17+40/5 FLC 2 FAC 1+3/1 Others 2
Swindon T (Loaned on 10/10/2006) FL 0+4
Bradford C (Free on 10/8/2007) FL 11+17/3 FLC 0+1 FAC 0+1

RHODES Jordan Luke
Born: Oldham, 5 February 1990
Height: 6'1" **Weight:** 11.3
Jordan is a product of the Ipswich Academy, having joined them when his father took over as the club's goalkeeping coach, and earned rave reviews during the season for his performances in the reserves and youth team by scoring over 40 goals. He had a loan spell at Oxford United and made his Ipswich debut as a substitute in the home game against Burnley. The striker is yet to start but did score his first senior goal after going on a substitute against Cardiff, tucking away a loose ball with aplomb.
Ipswich T (From trainee on 22/8/2007) FL 0+8/1

RICE Robert (Robbie) Anthony
Born: Hendon, 23 February 1989
Height: 5'8" **Weight:** 11.11
Previously with Fulham, Robbie is a right-sided defender or midfielder who has steadily progressed through the youth system at Wycombe. After a loan spell at Wealdstone in January, he made his debut for Wycombe at Notts County at the end of April as a late substitute in the right-back position. Highly rated by Wycombe's then manager Paul Lambert, Robbie signed a new contract at the end of the season.
Wycombe W (From trainee on 3/7/2007) FL 0+1

RICHARDS Garry
Born: Romford, 11 June 1986
Height: 6'3" **Weight:** 13.0
A tall centre-back acquired in the summer from Essex rivals Colchester, Garry was unable to gain a starting place at Southend due to the form of resident centre-backs Adam Barrett and Peter Clarke. He stepped in for a dozen games early in the season when an injury crisis forced manager Steve Tilson to play Barrett in an unfamiliar left-back role. Commanding in the air and a tough tackler, Garry was red carded at Oldham, although the dismissal was successfully contested. With no regular football in prospect at Roots Hall, Garry was sold

to Gillingham in the January transfer window and settled in well at the heart of their defence alongside Danny Cullip, proving to be be is a forceful player who takes no prisoners.
Colchester U (From trainee on 4/7/2005) FL 15+5/1 FAC 1 Others 3
Brentford (Loaned on 9/2/2007) FL 10/1
Southend U (£50,000 on 10/8/2007) FL 8+2 FLC 2 FAC 1 Others 1
Gillingham (£70,000 on 25/1/2008) FL 12+2/1

RICHARDS Marc John
Born: Wolverhampton, 8 July 1982
Height: 6'0" **Weight:** 12.7
International Honours: E: Yth
The experienced striker joined Port Vale in the summer after being freed by Barnsley. A hernia operation in pre-season limited his early mobility and he never had a long run in the team. As he neared fitness at Christmas he turned an ankle at Cheltenham, bringing another six weeks on the sidelines. A strong striker who can hold the ball well and bring others into the game, he began to hit his true form in March and scored his first Vale goal in a 2-1 win over Gillingham. That began a purple patch of five goals in six games, including two in a 3-2 victory at Brighton, arguably his and the team's best performance of the season. Marc hopes for an injury-free season in League Two.
Blackburn Rov (From trainee on 12/7/1999) FLC 1+1
Crewe Alex (Loaned on 10/8/2001) FL 1+3 FLC 0+1/1
Oldham Ath (Loaned on 12/10/2001) FL 3+2 Others 1/1
Halifax T (Loaned on 12/2/2002) FL 5
Swansea C (Loaned on 22/11/2002) FL 14+3/7
Northampton T (Free on 7/7/2003) FL 35+18/10 FLC 3 FAC 0+4/2 Others 4+2/1
Rochdale (Loaned on 24/3/2005) FL 4+1/2
Barnsley (Free on 31/8/2005) FL 51+18/18 FLC 1 FAC 5+2 Others 4
Port Vale (Free on 8/8/2007) FL 19+10/5 FLC 0+1 FAC 0+1 Others 1

RICHARDS Matthew (Matt) Lee
Born: Harlow, 26 December 1984
Height: 5'8" **Weight:** 11.0
International Honours: E: U21-1
After joining Brighton on loan from Ipswich in September, Matt spent the next three months at the Withdean Stadium and returned in January until the end of the season, although a torn hamstring kept him out for five weeks in the spring. Matt took some weeks to throw off the rustiness brought about by a lack of games but eventually settled

down to make the left-back slot his own. Always looking to get forward, Matt embarked on a brilliant run through midfield to set up Glenn Murray for the winner against Oldham in February.
Ipswich T (From trainee on 31/1/2002) FL 117+30/8 FLC 5+1 FAC 6+2/1 Others 4+2
Brighton & Hove A (Loaned on 21/9/2007) FL 28 FAC 3 Others 2

RICHARDS Micah Lincoln
Born: Birmingham, 24 June 1988
Height: 5'11" **Weight:** 13.0
International Honours: E: 11; U21-3
A product of Manchester City's excellent youth system and a player who, at 17 years of age, became England's youngest-ever international defender,

Micah Richards

Micah improved all aspects of his game, including his versatility. He gave excellent performances at right-back, centre-back and in midfield despite missing the last three months of the season through injury. Given his pace and terrific strength, he may well settle in the centre of defence and is one of the country's most exciting young talents, admired by leading clubs.
Manchester C (From trainee on 4/7/2005) PL 64+2/1 FLC 3 FAC 10/1

RICHARDSON Frazer
Born: Rotherham, 29 October 1982
Height: 5'11" **Weight:** 12.1
International Honours: E: Yth
Leeds' longest-serving current player,

Frazer passed 100 League starts during 2007-08. For many years, the defender was kept out of the picture by Gary Kelly's consistency, but has now made the right-back slot his own after the Republic of Ireland international's retirement. His 39 League appearances represented his best tally to date and his only goal was a real cracker, cutting in from the right to unleash a powerful drive that opened the scoring in a 3-0 win over Northampton in January. Frazer also had a few outings at left-back and on the right of midfield.
Leeds U (From trainee on 2/11/1999) P/FL 101+25/3 FLC 8/1 FAC 3 Others 6+1/1
Stoke C (Loaned on 10/1/2003) FL 6+1
Stoke C (Loaned on 8/11/2003) FL 6/1

RICHARDSON Kieran Edward
Born: Greenwich, 21 October 1984
Height: 5'9" **Weight:** 10.11
Club Honours: FAYC '03; FLC '06; PL '07
International Honours: E: 8; U21-12
Kieran was a big money signing by Roy Keane for Sunderland when he joined from West Bromwich in the summer. Unfortunately, a spate of injuries, including a fractured bone in his back in August, meant that supporters did not have the chance to see much of him. At home mainly on the left side of midfield or operating purely as a winger, where his pace and trickery are especially useful, Kieran opened his goal account against Bolton in December and fired home two superb efforts against Portsmouth in January in a live televised game. A hamstring injury the same month further disrupted his season and the hope is that he will have a fully-fit campaign.
Manchester U (From trainee on 21/8/2003) PL 20+21/2 FLC 11+2/3 FAC 8+2/4 Others 5+12/2
West Bromwich A (Loaned on 29/1/2005) PL 11+1/3
Sunderland (£5,500,000 on 16/7/2007) PL 15+2/3 FAC 1

RICHARDSON Leam Nathan
Born: Leeds, 19 November 1979
Height: 5'7" **Weight:** 11.4
Club Honours: AMC '04; FC '06
Leam played most of the first half of last season for Accrington in his usual full-back position but was later used as a wing back and in midfield, performing soundly in different areas of the field. He completed his third season as Stanley's most experienced professional, with the exception of Graham Branch. In February, Leam scored the only goal of the game against Brentford, his first for Stanley in his 112th appearance. In fact, it was his first ever in the League and the first he had scored since an FA Cup goal for

Blackpool in December 2003. He missed the last game of the season, having undergone a hernia operation, but will be ready to go again.
Blackburn Rov (From trainee on 31/12/1997) FLC 1
Bolton W (£50,000 on 13/7/2000) P/FL 5+8 FLC 3+1 FAC 1
Notts Co (Loaned on 9/11/2001) FL 20+1 FAC 1
Blackpool (Loaned on 20/12/2002) FL 20 FAC 1
Blackpool (Free on 15/7/2003) FL 44+7 FLC 2 FAC 1/1 Others 7+2
Accrington Stanley (Free on 12/8/2005) FL 67+8/1 FLC 3 FAC 2 Others 3

RICHARDSON Marcus Glenroy
Born: Reading, 31 August 1977
Height: 6'2" **Weight:** 13.2
Having left Blue Square Premier side Crawley, Marcus did enough in pre-season to earn a one-month contract and a chance to prove himself further. Unfortunately, the big striker lasted only 45 minutes of Bury's opening game against MK Dons and did not feature again for the Shakers. His contract ended at the beginning of October.
Cambridge U (Free from Harrow Borough on 16/3/2001) FL 7+9/2 FLC 1
Torquay U (£5,000 on 18/9/2001) FL 21+18/8 FLC 0+1 FAC 1 Others 0+1
Hartlepool U (Free on 1/10/2002) FL 23+4/5 FAC 2/1
Lincoln C (Loaned on 22/8/2003) FL 9+3/4 Others 1/1
Lincoln C (Free on 8/12/2003) FL 32+8/10 FLC 0+1 FAC 1 Others 2
Rochdale (Loaned on 17/2/2005) FL 1+1
Yeovil T (Free on 23/3/2005) FL 2+2
Chester C (Free on 6/7/2005) FL 22+12/4 FAC 3+1/2 Others 1 (Freed during 2007 close season)
Macclesfield T (Loaned on 23/3/2006) FL 8/3
Bury (Free from Crawley T, ex Weymouth, Cambridge U, on 10/8/2007) FL 1

RICHMAN Simon Andrew
Born: Ormskirk, 2 June 1990
Height: 5'11" **Weight:** 11.12
The promising right-sided midfield player was a regular in Port Vale's run to the FA Youth Cup quarter-finals, although he was injured for the ultimate defeat by Chelsea. Simon was rewarded for his good form with a first-team call against Leyton Orient in March, having a good debut and keeping his place before making another five starts. He took to League football as if he had been involved for years and earned a couple of 'Man of the Match' awards. He has a bright turn of pace, can beat a man on the run and

signed his first professional contract just before end of the season.
Port Vale (From trainee on 17/4/2008) FL 6

RICKETTS Donovan Damon
Born: Kingston, Jamaica, 7 June 1977
Height: 6'4" **Weight:** 14.7
International Honours: Jamaica: 46
This towering Jamaican international had been Bradford's first-choice goalkeeper but suffered a frustrating season after losing his place in October. Donovan found himself replaced at various times by two loan signings before his campaign was cut short at the end of March over a problem with his work-permit. That meant he had to return home to Kingston.
Bradford C (Signed from Village U, Jamaica on 28/8/2004) FL 108 FLC 2 FAC 7 Others 1

RICKETTS Michael Barrington
Born: Birmingham, 4 December 1978
Height: 6'2" **Weight:** 11.12
Club Honours: FLC '04
International Honours: E: 1
Michael, a much-travelled former England international, joined Oldham last summer after being released by Preston and made a dream start on his debut, netting a penalty awarded after just 40 seconds against Swansea on the opening day. However, he subsequently failed to settle and after netting only once in 11 more appearances, agreed a three-month loan at his first club, Walsall, in early November. Over 11 years after first signing for Walsall, Michael returned and although he was not quite the same player who won an England cap in his Bolton days, he scored some useful goals. He fell out of contention early in the New Year and, with doubts about his fitness, the Saddlers did not offer him a permanent deal. After becoming a free agent in January and having an unsuccessful trial at Southampton, Michael headed to the United States for more trials with MLS clubs Columbus Crew and San Jose Earthquakes.
Walsall (From trainee on 13/9/1996) FL 31+45/14 FLC 2+4 FAC 2+2 Others 3+1/1
Bolton W (£500,000 on 17/7/2000) P/FL 63+35/37 FLC 0+4/3 FAC 4+3/4 Others 1+2/2
Middlesbrough (£2,200,000 on 31/1/2003) PL 12+20/3 FLC 3+2/1 FAC 2
Leeds U (Free on 8/7/2004) FL 10+15 FLC 3+1/2
Stoke C (Loaned on 22/2/2005) FL 1+10
Cardiff C (Loaned on 31/8/2005) FL 17/5
Burnley (Loaned on 30/11/2005) FL 12+1/2
Southend U (Signed on 27/7/2006) FL 0+2
Preston NE (Free on 12/1/2007) FL 7+7/1 FAC 2

Oldham Ath (Free on 10/7/2007) FL 8+1/2 FLC 2 Others 1
Walsall (Loaned on 2/11/2007) FL 12/3 FAC 4/2

RICKETTS Rohan Anthony

Born: Clapham, 22 December 1982
Height: 5'9" **Weight:** 11.0
Club Honours: FAYC '01
International Honours: E: Yth
Another to make a Barnsley debut on the first day of the season, Rohan signed a two-year contract in July after being released by Wolverhampton. Rohan began the season in midfield and played in a number of positions but soon found himself on the fringes of the first team. Even a place on the bench proved elusive and after being told by manager Simon Davey that he was surplus to requirements, Rohan joined Major League Soccer side Toronto FC in April.
Arsenal (From trainee on 8/9/2001) FLC 0+1
Tottenham H (Free on 11/7/2002) PL 17+13/1 FLC 4+2/1
Coventry C (Loaned on 15/10/2004) FL 5+1
Wolverhampton W (Free on 15/3/2005) FL 35+16/1 FLC 1+1 FAC 3
Queens Park Rgrs (Loaned on 22/3/2007) FL 0+2
Barnsley (Free on 19/7/2007) FL 2+8 FLC 2 FAC 1

RICKETTS Samuel (Sam) Derek

Born: Aylesbury, 11 October 1981
Height: 6'0" **Weight:** 11.12
Club Honours: AMC '06
International Honours: W: 28. E: SP-4
In the season when Hull matched their highest final League position and made their first appearance at Wembley to win promotion through the Championship play-offs, Sam was one of their most consistent performers. Continuing his progress from 2006-07, he would have been ever-present at right-back but for suspension following an early-season red card at Coventry. Allied to his solid defensive qualities, Sam also provided a constant attacking threat with a ready supply of incisive crosses. The son of former show-jumper Derek Ricketts continued to transfer his outstanding club form to the international stage and is now the Tigers' most-capped Welshman, despite usually being employed on the left of the Principality's defence.
Oxford U (From trainee on 20/4/2000) FL 32+13/1 FLC 1 Others 2 (Free to Telford U on 7/7/2003)
Swansea C (Free from Telford U on 22/6/2004) FL 85+1/1 FLC 2 FAC 6 Others 11/2
Hull C (£300,000 on 18/7/2006) FL 84/1 FLC 4+1 FAC 2 Others 3

RIDGEWELL Liam Matthew

Born: Bexley, 21 July 1984
Height: 5'10" **Weight:** 11.0
Club Honours: FAYC '02
International Honours: E: U21-8; Yth
Liam, who became the first player to move from Aston Villa to Birmingham on a permanent basis since 1983, was made captain in Damien Johnson's absence and was direct, aggressive and never backed down at the heart of the defence. Scored an own goal in the St Andrew's Villa derby after heading the first Blues' strike in a key 3-2 win over Wigan two games earlier. Making more clearances than anyone in the Premier League and never letting any mishaps upset him, his wholehearted approach went down well with the fans. During the course of the season, Liam formed good partnerships with Johan Djourou-Gbadjere and later Radhi Jaidi.
Aston Villa (From trainee on 26/7/2001) PL 66+13/6 FLC 6+3 FAC 3+2
Bournemouth (Loaned on 11/10/2002) FL 2+3
Birmingham C (£2,000,000 on 3/8/2007) PL 35/1 FLC 1 FAC 1

RIDLEY Lee

Born: Scunthorpe, 5 December 1981
Height: 5'9" **Weight:** 11.2
Club Honours: Div 1 '07
Signed by Cheltenham from Scunthorpe in the summer of 2007 as a replacement for the departed Craig Armstrong, the left-back made his first-team debut against Gillingham on the opening day of the season, ironically with Armstrong in the opposition team, and went on to play in the next eight League matches. Following the departure of manager John Ward in October, his replacement Keith Downing brought in former Aston Villa and Blackburn Rovers left-back Alan Wright and Lee made a handful of appearances for the reserves before heading out for loan spells with first Darlington and then Lincoln. Arriving at Darlington in November, Lee was one of a succession of left-backs brought in by the Quakers during the season due to the long-term injury of the usual incumbent and played steadily throughout December and over the holiday period, totalling six games, before returning to Scunthorpe. On loan at Lincoln in January, he spent the final four months of the campaign producing a number of consistent performances and his arrival coincided with an upturn in the Imps' fortunes as they lifted themselves from the bottom of the table to a 15th-place finish.
Scunthorpe U (From trainee on 3/7/2001) FL 87+13/2 FLC 1+1 FAC 6+2/1 Others 5+2

Cheltenham T (Signed on 24/7/2007) FL 8 FLC 1 Others 1
Darlington (Loaned on 22/11/2007) FL 6
Lincoln C (Loaned on 4/1/2008) FL 15

RIGG Sean Michael

Born: Bristol, 1 October 1988
Height: 5'10" **Weight:** 10.2
A left-sided striker, Sean was a consistent squad member at Bristol Rovers and gained valuable experience playing alongside a variety of different partners. He scored only once, against Northampton at the Memorial Stadium, when he turned well on the edge of the penalty area and hooked in a fine goal. He has signed a new contract that will keep him with Rovers for the foreseeable future.
Bristol Rov (Free from Forest Green Rov on 2/6/2006) FL 15+34/2 FLC 0+2 FAC 2+5 Others 1+5/1

RIGGOTT Christopher (Chris) Mark

Born: Derby, 1 September 1980
Height: 6'3" **Weight:** 12.2
Club Honours: FLC '04
International Honours: E: U21-8; Yth
Acknowledged as a quality centre-back by his manager Gareth Southgate, Chris injured a foot in Middlesbrough's pre-season friendly at Burnley but was passed fit for the opening day. However, with Robert Huth, David Wheater and Jonathan Woodgate around, he found himself to be fourth choice and his season was limited to less than a dozen games. Not having played a first-team game for Boro since mid-November, Chris, frustrated by the lack of involvement, was allowed to join Tony Pulis' Championship promotion hopefuls Stoke on loan in February until the end of the season. With his wealth of Premiership experience, Chris held Stoke's defence together as the promotion push came to a climax but after being moved to right-back when Andy Griffin was injured he was unexpectedly recalled by Middlesbrough just before the end of the season and missed Stoke's vital promotion-clinching game against Leicester. With two Premiership games remaining, Chris marked his return to Boro by scoring their first goal against Portsmouth in a 2-0 victory but made sure he was at the Britannia Stadium to watch Stoke clinch promotion the following day. For the final game he was in an unchanged side for the 8-1 Riverside rout of Manchester City and ended the season with a philosophical comment: "As for what happens next and whether I've got a future at Boro, we'll see what happens in the summer".

Derby Co (From trainee on 5/10/1998) P/FL 87+4/5 FLC 7/1 FAC 2/1
Middlesbrough (£1,500,000 + on 31/1/2003) PL 74+7/5 FLC 9+1 FAC 8+1/1 Others 21/2
Stoke C (Loaned on 29/2/2008) FL 9

RIGTERS Maceo

Born: Amsterdam, Holland, 22 January 1984
Height: 5'10" **Weight:** 13.0
International Honours: Holland: U21-9
The young Dutchman had a disappointing 2007-08 season for Blackburn after being signed in the summer from NAC Breda, when struggling on the infrequent occasions he was introduced to the team. An explosive player, whose game is based on speed and power, Maceo seldom had anybody capable of threading the ball through or dinking it over the top and the chances that came his way were mainly headers. Going out on loan to Norwich in March he made only two fleeting appearances as a substitute before tearing a hamstring and returning to Ewood Park for treatment. Hopefully, the coming season will see the Dutch under-21 international striker, who top-scored in the UEFA under-21 championships, find his feet in the Premiership. As a willing worker, his running off the ball and ability to find space should bring him goals.
Blackburn Rov (Signed from NAC Breda, Holland, ex SC Heerenveen, FC Dordrecht, on 12/7/2007) PL 0+2 FLC 0+1 FAC 1 Others 1+2
Norwich C (Loaned on 19/3/2008) FL 0+2

RIISE John Arne

Born: Molde, Norway, 24 September 1980
Height: 6'1" **Weight:** 12.6
Club Honours: ESC '01, '05; CS '01, '06; FLC '03; UEFACL '05; FAC '06
International Honours: Norway: 71; U21-17; Yth
In his seventh and final season with Liverpool, the Norwegian international left-back endured a disappointing and inconsistent time, possibly due to domestic worries, and first lost his place to Alvaro Arbeloa then, for much of the season, found himself rotated with Fabio Aurelio for the left-back slot, with the Brazilian player gradually gaining the ascendancy as the manager's choice for the big Premiership and Champions' League games. Always renowned for his explosive shooting, John Arne remained goalless all season, a drought stretching back to the Champions' League victory in Barcelona in February 2007, but could not be faulted for effort with 36 recorded goal attempts during the season, either

missing the target or blocked by opposing 'keeper and defenders. The nadir of his season came in the Champions' League semi-final first leg against Chelsea in April when he was on for the injured Aurelio in the second half. Deep into stoppage-time with Liverpool leading, 1-0 John Arne faced an apparently harmless cross from Salomon Kalou that he could have hacked to safety with either foot. Instead, he stooped to head the ball clear and it flew off his head into Pepe Reina's net to hand Chelsea a precious away goal they had never looked like scoring. He has been an outstanding servant to Liverpool for seven years and should not be blamed for Liverpool's subsequent exit from the competition in the second leg. His error was cancelled out by Fernando Torres' equaliser at Stamford Bridge and Liverpool's eventual defeat was due to an overcautious approach to the second leg and a failure to seize the initiative once they had equalised.
Liverpool (£3,770,000 from AS Monaco, France, ex Aalesund, on 26/7/2001) PL 196+38/21 FLC 9+4/2 FAC 16+1/3 Others 75+9/5

RINALDI Douglas

Born: Erval Seco, Brazil, 10 February 1984
Height: 6'0" **Weight:** 12.3
The Brazilian midfield player signed a permanent contract during the summer after being at Watford on loan in 2006-07. He scored on his first appearance of the season against Gillingham in the first round of the Carling Cup and was included again in the second round tie at Southend. Unfortunately, he was injured soon after and failed to make any further appearances. A dead-ball specialist with a good touch and an eye for a pass, his lack of opportunities was a disappointment.
Watford (Signed from Veranopolis, Brazil on 31/1/2007) P/FL 6+1/1 FLC 2/1

RIX Benjamin (Ben)

Born: Wolverhampton, 11 December 1982
Height: 5'10" **Weight:** 11.11
Now one of the longest-serving players at Crewe, having come through the youth ranks into the senior side in 2001-02, Ben has been unlucky with injuries. A midfield player who forced his way back into the first team last season, he was a regular until mid-February when he had to undergo surgery. It must be hoped that he will be back, fit and strong, in time for the coming campaign.
Crewe Alex (From trainee on 6/2/2001) FL 87+41/4 FLC 5+1 FAC 7+4/2 Others 6+1
Bournemouth (Loaned on 31/1/2006) FL 7+4

ROBERT Laurent Pierre

Born: Saint-Benoit, Reunion, 21 May 1975
Height: 5'8" **Weight:** 10.13
International Honours: France: 9; B-4; Yth
Laurent had been out of football since his release by Spanish club Levante when Paul Jewell took a gamble on him last January as he tried to reshape an ailing Derby team. It was asking a great deal as Laurent had little time to gain match-fitness and he was unable to make much impression: he was not alone in that. Once a much-feared left winger who could beat his man and whip in dangerous crosses, his contract was cancelled in April, allowing him to join Toronto.
Newcastle U (£10,500,000 from Paris St Germain, France, ex Montpellier, Nancy, on 10/8/2001) PL 110+19/22 FLC 6+1/2 FAC 10/3 Others 29+6/5 (Transferred to Benfica, Portugal on 5/1/2006)
Portsmouth (Loaned on 7/7/2005) PL 13+4/1
Derby Co (Free from Levante UD, Spain on 11/1/2008) PL 3+1

ROBERTS Anthony (Tony) Mark

Born: Holyhead, 4 August 1969
Height: 6'0" **Weight:** 12.0
Club Honours: FC '07
International Honours: W: 2; B-2; SP: U21-2; Yth
Tony re-entered the League after Dagenham reached a financial agreement with an insurance company to pay back an amount of the settlement Tony received in 1999, when a knuckle injury forced him to leave Millwall. Despite his 37 years, the goalkeeper was a rock for Dagenham in their first League season and convincingly won their 'Player of the Year' and supporters' club awards. He was contacted in October by the Welsh FA, enquiring if he was available to represent them when they had a goalkeeping crisis. Tony is also a goalkeeping coach at Arsenal, training their young hopefuls on a daily basis.
Queens Park Rgrs (From trainee on 24/7/1987) P/FL 122 FLC 11 FAC 10+1 Others 2
Millwall (Free on 6/8/1998) FL 8 (Free to St Albans C on 7/4/1999)
Dagenham & Redbridge (Free from Atlanta Silverbacks, USA on 12/7/2000) FL 43 FLC 1 FAC 3 Others 3

ROBERTS Christian John

Born: Cardiff, 22 October 1979
Height: 5'10" **Weight:** 12.8
Club Honours: AMC '03
International Honours: W: U21-1; Yth

Christian scored the penalty at Northampton that earned Swindon a point on the opening day of last season and converted a late penalty against Bristol Rovers at the end of November, after which he was sidelined by a knee injury. He struggled to find his best form after returning in January, although he scored the winner at Luton the same month. He was later diagnosed with a micro-fracture to his right knee, which required surgery. It brought his season to an early end and could delay his return until well into next season. Talented and skilful, he can play as a striker but seems to have accepted that his best position is on the wing.

Cardiff C (From trainee on 8/10/1997) FL 6+17/3 FLC 2 FAC 2+3 Others 0+2
Exeter C (Free on 24/7/2000) FL 67+12/18 FLC 2+1 FAC 2+1 Others 2
Bristol C (Signed on 26/3/2002) FL 65+29/20
FLC 5+1 FAC 4+2/4 Others 10+2/2
Swindon T (£20,000 on 15/10/2004) FL 77+34/21 FLC 2 FAC 7+3/5 Others 2+1/1

ROBERTS Gareth (Gary)
Michael
Born: Chester, 18 March 1984
Height: 5'10" **Weight:** 11.9
Club Honours: FC '06
International Honours: E: SP-4
Gary made a bright start to the season by scoring for Ipswich in the opening game, when volleying in Alan Lee's cross. However, he seemed to lose confidence in his ability to beat defenders to get in telling crosses from the flanks and gradually drifted out of the team, making only occasional appearances as a substitute. Unable to gain a regular place at Ipswich, Gary joined Crewe in February, making an immediate debut at Leyton Orient. After playing in the front line for a further three games he returned to Portman Road and, in 2008-09, will be looking to recapture the form that prompted Jim Magilton to buy him.
Accrington Stanley (Free from Welshpool, ex Denbigh T, Bala T, Rhyl, Bangor C, on 1/2/2005) FL 14/8 FLC 2
Ipswich T (Signed on 17/10/2006) FL 40+14/3 FLC 1 FAC 4
Crewe Alex (Loaned on 12/2/2008) FL 4

ROBERTS Gareth Wyn
Born: Wrexham, 6 February 1978
Height: 5'7" **Weight:** 12.6
Club Honours: FAYC '96; AMC '07
International Honours: W: 9; B-1; U21-10
Gareth enjoyed a good season at Doncaster, with just one injury spell that kept him out of the team from early November to Christmas. Quietly and efficiently, he is a consistent performer at left-back and stories began circulating in the media towards the end of the season about other clubs casting their eyes on him. Gareth helped Rovers to beat Leeds in the play-off final at Wembley to reach the Championship.
Liverpool (From trainee on 22/5/1996. £50,000 to Panionios, Greece on 15/1/1999)
Tranmere Rov (Free from Panionios, Greece on 5/8/1999) FL 276+5/13 FLC 22 FAC 21+1 Others 12/2
Doncaster Rov (Free on 3/7/2006) FL 63+4/4 FLC 3 FAC 4 Others 9+1

ROBERTS Gary Steven
Born: Chester, 4 February 1987
Height: 5'8" **Weight:** 10.5
International Honours: E: Yth
Another product of Crewe's youth system, the former England youth international played regularly in midfield and was again among the goals last season. Gary is rated highly at Crewe and, according to requirements, can operate in a central area or on the right. He is a keen competitor and competent penalty taker, who also excels with the accuracy of his free kicks and corners.
Crewe Alex (From trainee on 7/7/2004) FL 110+12/11 FLC 2 FAC 4 Others 5

ROBERTS Jason Andre Davis
Born: Acton, 25 January 1978
Height: 5'11" **Weight:** 12.7
International Honours: Grenada: 22
Jason started the season paired with Benni McCarthy up front for Blackburn but it took Roque Santa Cruz only a matter of minutes to demonstrate that the two were fighting for one place. McCarthy was the initial choice as Santa Cruz's partner and a Carling Cup game against Birmingham did nothing to

Tony Roberts

enhance Jason's claims, particularly as he left the game with an injury. When fully fit, he asked for a transfer and seemed likely to go but nothing materialised in the transfer window. Occasionally Jason had games when opponents could not cope with him. At Fulham where he went on as an early substitute, at Bolton where he scored a last-minute winner and against the same team in the return fixture, he proved impossible to handle. This led to his re-introduction into the starting line-up in the middle of March but two goals in that period were scant reward for his efforts.

Wolverhampton W (£250,000 from Hayes on 12/9/1997)
Torquay U (Loaned on 19/12/1997) FL 13+1/6 Others 1
Bristol C (Loaned on 26/3/1998) FL 1+2/1
Bristol Rov (£250,000 on 7/8/1998) FL 73+5/38 FLC 6/3 FAC 6/7 Others 3
West Bromwich A (£2,000,000 on 27/7/2000) P/FL 75+14/24 FLC 3+1/2 FAC 6 Others 2/1
Portsmouth (Loaned on 1/9/2003) PL 4+6/1 FLC 2/3
Wigan Ath (£2,000,000 on 13/1/2004) P/FL 93/37 FLC 4+2/4 FAC 2+2/2
Blackburn Rov (£3,000,000 on 3/7/2006) PL 20+24/7 FLC 1+1 FAC 1+2/1 Others 5+2/2

ROBERTS Kevin

Born: Liverpool, 17 August 1989
Height: 6'2" **Weight:** 14.2
After making his debut in the away victory at Rochdale in August, the versatile youngster had an outstanding season for Chester and looks to have a bright future. Despite his age, Kevin put in mature performances in a variety of positions and was one of City's key performers in a disappointing season. Kevin started in central midfield, scoring his first goal at Rotherham in September, and showed his shooting prowess with a wonderful long-range effort at Wrexham. A tireless performer, Kevin also filled in at the centre of defence and on the right of Chester's back four with equal assurance. His performances were rewarded with a two-year extension to his contract.

Chester C (From juniors on 24/1/2007) FL 30+7/3 FLC 0+1 Others 0+1

ROBERTS Mark Alan

Born: Northwich, 16 October 1983
Height: 6'1" **Weight:** 12.0
Signed from Northwich in the summer, Mark started well at Accrington and quickly established himself as one of the two first-choice centre-backs, playing in Stanley's first 30 League and Cup games. Loss of form cost him a regular place and from early February he was in and out of

the side. On transfer deadline day he was allowed to return to Northwich on loan, more than playing his part in helping them to avoid relegation from the Blue Square Premier. Was out of contract in the summer and looking for a new club.

Crewe Alex (From trainee on 6/7/2003) FL 3+3 FLC 1 (Freed on 30/1/2007)
Chester C (Loaned on 31/1/2006) FL 1
Accrington Stanley (Free from Northwich Vic on 18/7/2007) FL 33+1 FLC 1 FAC 1 Others 1

ROBERTS Neil Wyn

Born: Wrexham, 7 April 1978
Height: 5'10" **Weight:** 11.0
Club Honours: Div 2 '03
International Honours: W: 4; B-1; U21-1; Yth
As the Wrexham captain, there was always total commitment from Neil who started last season in his normal position up front. When Brian Little arrived as manager, he put Neil's competitiveness to better use in midfield, where the team were suffering. It worked to a point but he returned to the forward line later. Injuries still curtail him because he puts himself on the line for his home-town club. He scored both goals in a 2-0 victory at Accrington in October and, again up front, notched the only goal of the game against Notts County. The manager surprised many by releasing Neil in May but he could still stay, depending on other contract situations.

Wrexham (From trainee on 3/7/1996) FL 58+17/17 FLC 1/1 FAC 11+1/4 Others 2+2/2
Wigan Ath (£450,000 on 18/2/2000) FL 64+61/19 FLC 7+3/2 FAC 6/1 Others 3+1
Hull C (Loaned on 25/11/2002) FL 3+3
Bradford C (Loaned on 17/9/2004) FL 3/1 Others 1
Doncaster Rov (£45,000 on 7/10/2004) FL 47+14/8 FLC 1+1 FAC 2+2 Others 1
Wrexham (Free on 3/8/2006) FL 52+3/11 FLC 2/1 FAC 0+1/1

ROBERTS Stephen (Steve) Wyn

Born: Wrexham, 24 February 1980
Height: 6'0" **Weight:** 12.7
Club Honours: AMC '05, '07
International Honours: W: 1; U21-4; Yth
Steve made only one start in Doncaster's League team in the first half of last season because of the form of the three other centre-backs at the club. He was given his chance when Matthew Mills and Gordon Greer were injured and grabbed it eagerly, winning several 'Man of the Match' awards. In March he was named in the Welsh squad, the first time for several years, for the friendly against

Luxembourg but in April, at Leyton Orient, he sustained a leg injury that kept him out for the remainder of the campaign.

Wrexham (From trainee on 16/1/1998) FL 143+7/6 FLC 3 FAC 7+1/1 Others 11+1/1
Doncaster Rov (Free on 4/7/2005) FL 58+15/1 FLC 6 FAC 2+2 Others 7+2

ROBERTSON Gregor Aedan

Born: Edinburgh, 19 January 1984
Height: 6'0" **Weight:** 12.4
International Honours: S: U21-15
Freed by Rotherham in the summer, Gregor is a tidy and effective left-back who plays a straightforward, risk-free game, and was ever-present for Chesterfield until a thigh strain forced him out in February. Concentration helps effective tackling and marking, and very few opponents caused him real headaches. His most effective position may yet be on the left of midfield, where he can spot a pass and cross well enough while offering defensive protection.

Nottingham F (From juniors at Heart of Midlothian on 8/2/2001) FL 25+11 FLC 2+2 FAC 4
Rotherham U (Free on 5/8/2005) FL 46+7/1 FLC 4
Chesterfield (Free on 11/7/2007) FL 34+1/1 FLC 1 FAC 1 Others 1

ROBERTSON Jordan

Born: Sheffield, 12 February 1988
Height: 6'0" **Weight:** 12.6
Jordan joined Oldham on a one-month loan in February. Earlier in the campaign the young striker, who is still waiting for a senior debut at Sheffield United, had similar temporary spells with Dundee United, Torquay and Northampton. In his first start for the Latics, he scored in 3-0 away win at Port Vale. A player who excels at holding up the ball up, he appeared to be settling in well before ankle ligament damage forced him into an early return to Bramall Lane for treatment.

Sheffield U (From trainee on 6/7/2006)
Torquay U (Loaned on 4/11/2006) FL 5+4/2 FAC 1+1/2
Northampton T (Loaned on 26/1/2007) FL 9+8/3
Oldham Ath (Loaned on 26/2/2008) FL 2+1/1

ROBINSON Andrew (Andy) Mark

Born: Birkenhead, 3 November 1979
Height: 5'8" **Weight:** 11.4
Club Honours: AMC '06; Div 1 '08
An exciting talent on the wide left of midfield, Andy has the ability to score from long range as well as from free

kicks around the penalty area. Having overcome an early-season hamstring injury at Cheltenham, he again contributed vital goals to Swansea through the season. Andy also displayed improved discipline when confronted with over-rigorous tackling from opponents and was deservedly among the five Swans in the PFA League One select team.
Tranmere Rov *(Free from Cammell Laird on 11/11/2002) Others 0+1*
Swansea C *(Free on 14/8/2003) FL 159+33/ 43 FLC 2+1 FAC 14+3/5 Others 14/6*

ROBINSON Ashley Paul Emmanuel
Born: Croydon, 5 December 1989
Height: 5'9" **Weight:** 14.1
Ashley is yet another graduate from the Crystal Palace Academy who found his way into the first-team squad in 2007-08. A local lad, he is a fast and tricky right-winger, who made his debut at Preston in March as an 87th-minute substitute for Victor Moses. Highly rated by the club, he hopes for more opportunities in the coming season.
Crystal Palace *(Trainee) FL 0+6*

ROBINSON Jake David
Born: Brighton, 23 October 1986
Height: 5'9" **Weight:** 10.4
Although potentially brilliant on his day, Jake has yet to reach the consistency that would turn him into a quality performer for Brighton at League One level. In and out of the side, often alternating with the equally inconsistent David Martot, the Sussex-born forward was usually employed as a winger but a return of five goals from 21 starts and another 18 appearances as a substitute was disappointing. An intelligent player, always looking to create opportunities, Jake needs to rediscover the pace, control and confidence that made him such an exciting prospect as a teenager.
Brighton & Hove A *(From trainee on 22/ 12/2003) FL 61+57/12 FLC 1+4/1 FAC 7+1/4 Others 5+1/4*

ROBINSON Paul Mark James
Born: Barnet, 7 January 1982
Height: 6'1" **Weight:** 12.1
An ever-present for Millwall last season, the central defender and club captain was outstanding. Throughout his time at the New Den, he has led by example, which endears him to the Millwall faithful. The tough-tackling central defender has quality, especially in the air where he is never overawed by any forward, and can always be relied on for much needed goals. He reached a milestone in 2007-08 when making his 150th appearance for

Paul Robinson (Millwall)

the Lions and to cap an excellent season Paul was voted Millwall's 'Player of the Season', thoroughly deserved for an exceptional Lion.
Millwall *(From trainee on 25/10/2000) FL 137+8/7 FLC 7/1 FAC 14+1/1 Others 2+1/1*
Torquay U *(Loaned on 23/12/2004) FL 12*

ROBINSON Paul Peter
Born: Watford, 14 December 1978
Height: 5'9" **Weight:** 11.12
Club Honours: Div 2 '98: Ch '08
International Honours: E: U21-3
Paul was sent off twice in five weeks, in the home League defeat by Coventry in December when the scores were level and in the 3-1 televised victory at Hull in January. Apart from this, the former Watford player was outstanding at left-back for West Bromwich, producing impressive performances at home and away. Driving his players on when captain, he worked tirelessly and often found time and space to venture forward down the left before sending over teasingly effective crosses. Like many of his colleagues, Paul was again an unlucky loser at Wembley as Albion went out of the FA Cup to Portsmouth in the semi-final. He made his 200th appearances for Albion in the penultimate game of the season, a 1-1 draw with Southampton that effectively clinched promotion. His excellent displays were recognised by a place in the PFA Championship select side.

Watford *(From trainee on 13/2/1997) P/FL 201+18/8 FLC 15+1/1 FAC 10+2 Others 5*
West Bromwich A *(£250,000 on 14/10/2003) P/FL 176+3/4 FLC 6 FAC 13 Others 3*

ROBINSON Paul William
Born: Beverley, 15 October 1979
Height: 6'2" **Weight:** 13.4
Club Honours: FAYC '97; FLC '08
International Honours: E: 41; U21-11
Having had another difficult year for club and country, the goalkeeper suffered various bouts of injury, along with dips in form and confidence, that led to him losing his first-team place for Tottenham and England. Paul was not selected for the crucial Euro 2008 qualifier against Croatia, and has since been omitted by new England coach Fabio Capello. At club level, Juande Ramos dropped him after he carried a long kick by Reading's Stephen Hunt over his own goal-line. Paul was selected for Spurs' Carling Cup victory but had to sit out the closing games while Radek Cerny kept goal. He is still capable of great reflex saves but as times been let down by a lack of confidence in his area. The former England number one is, of course, not helped by the fact that the eyes of the media often fall upon the goalkeeper as much as they do on the head coach.
Leeds U *(From trainee on 13/5/1997) PL 93+2 FLC 5/1 FAC 7 Others 12*
Tottenham H *(£1,500,000 on 16/5/2004) PL 137/1 FLC 10 FAC 12 Others 16*

ROBINSON Stephen (Steve)
Born: Lisburn, 10 December 1974
Height: 5'9" **Weight:** 11.3
Club Honours: Div 1 '05
International Honours: NI: 7; B-4; U21-1; Yth; Sch
At the start of last season, Steve and Chris Coyne were the last survivors of the Luton League One winning team still in the first-team reckoning. In central midfield, Steve had to do plenty of running, tackling and closing down as well as being responsible for creating goals. Inevitably he picked up injuries and bookings, eight in the League and FA Cup, and a sending off at Bristol Rovers. He was a regular in Mick Harford's first 11 games in charge but after being taken off at Southend, made only a single substitute appearance, at home to Brighton. After more than 200 games, his six-year stay ended when he was not retained at the end of the season.
Tottenham H *(From trainee on 27/1/1993) PL 1+1*
Bournemouth *(Free on 20/10/1994) FL 227+13/51 FLC 14/1 FAC 15+1/5 Others 16/3*

Preston NE (£375,000 on 26/5/2000) FL 6+18/1 FLC 3+1 FAC 0+1
Bristol C (Loaned on 18/3/2002) FL 6/1
Luton T (£50,000 on 20/6/2002) FL 170+15/9 FLC 6+1/1 FAC 15/2 Others 4

ROBINSON Theo

Born: Birmingham, 22 January 1989
Height: 5'11" **Weight:** 11.8
The speedy Watford forward spent a profitable season-long loan at Hereford where he was top scorer in the Bulls' promotion campaign. Tremendous pace and speed off the mark kept defenders on their toes and, allied to ability to find the net with either foot or with his head, quickly marked him as one to watch in Hereford's side. He was a first-choice for most of the campaign and after a short spell on the sidelines in February and March, he returned with a clutch of goals to assist the final stages of the promotion push.
Watford (From trainee on 5/2/2007) P/FL 0+2
Hereford U (Loaned on 9/8/2007) FL 32+11/ 13 FLC 2/1 FAC 6/2 Others 0+1

ROBSON Matthew (Matty) James

Born: Spennymoor, 23 January 1985
Height: 5'10" **Weight:** 11.2
Matty is a hard-working left-sided utility player who shows a great attitude. He was in and out of the Hartlepool first team, playing most of his games as an attacking midfielder. A product of the United youth team, Matty has been a first-team squad member for five seasons and has made well over 100 League appearances.
Hartlepool U (From trainee on 16/3/2004) FL 76+30/7 FLC 8 FAC 5+2/1 Others 10+1

ROBSON-KANU Hal

Born: Acton, 21 May 1989
Height: 5'7" **Weight:** 11.8
International Honours: E: Yth
Another transfer deadline signing for Southend, Hal's loan spell at Roots Hall from Reading was punctuated by injury, meaning that he never managed to get a decent run in the team. In a spell of five matches in March, he had to play up front rather than in his favoured wide position but responded with three goals, using his excellent first touch to good effect. He returned to Reading at the end of the season.
Reading (From trainee on 4/7/2007)
Southend U (Loaned on 31/1/2008) FL 6+2/3

ROCASTLE Craig Aaron

Born: Lewisham, 17 August 1981
Height: 6'1" **Weight:** 12.13

Having joined Port Vale after being freed by Oldham in the summer, the experienced midfield player made his debut on the opening day against Bristol Rovers before struggling for form. A strong box-to-box player, his best performance came in a 1-0 victory at Bournemouth but as the team battled against relegation changes were made and Craig was in and out of the team. In January, the new manager Lee Sinnott loaned him out to Gillingham and having appeared twice for them he returned to Vale Park after a month. Although given two more games for Vale in February he failed to make another appearance and was released on a free transfer at the end of the season.
Chelsea (Free from Slough T, ex Croydon, Gravesend & Northfleet, Ashford T, Kingstonian, on 1/9/2003)
Barnsley (Loaned on 13/2/2004) FL 4+1
Lincoln C (Loaned on 25/3/2004) FL 0+2
Hibernian (Loaned on 31/8/2004) SL 11+2 SLC 1
Sheffield Wed (Free on 3/2/2005) FLC 1+1 Others 3
Yeovil T (Loaned on 23/3/2006) FL 5+3
Oldham Ath (Free on 5/7/2006) FL 17+18/2 FLC 1/1 FAC 0+2 Others 1
Port Vale (Signed on 19/7/2007) FL 17+6/1 FLC 1 FAC 2 Others 1
Gillingham (Loaned on 10/1/2008) FL 2

ROCHA Ricardo Sergio

Born: Braga, Portugal, 3 October 1978
Height: 6'0" **Weight:** 12.8
International Honours: Portugal: 6
Although playing a part for Tottenham at the close of the previous campaign, Ricardo had to be satisfied with a place on the bench in the opening game, despite the absence of Ledley King and Michael Dawson. He played in only five of the club's early-season games and was an unused substitute eight times. Ricardo, who has the necessary defensive expertise and experience to succeed, spent various periods either injured or playing for the reserves.
Tottenham H (£3,300,000 from Benfica, Portugal, ex Famalicao, Sporting Braga, on 25/1/2007) PL 13+1 FLC 0+1 FAC 3

ROCHE Barry Christopher

Born: Dublin, 6 April 1982
Height: 6'4" **Weight:** 12.6
International Honours: RoI: Yth
Barry will have mixed feelings about his season. It began promisingly but individual errors in Chesterfield's back line increased the pressure on the goalkeeper as the season developed. Uncharacteristic mistakes came largely through a lack of experience and communication in

defence but Barry answered his critics in the best possible way by beginning to recapture better form in the closing weeks. A 'keeper of his size can be an imposing presence, and Chesterfield fans hope to see him dominate his area for many years.
Nottingham F (From trainee on 29/6/1999) FL 10+3
Chesterfield (Free on 5/8/2005) FL 126 FLC 5 FAC 4 Others 5

ROCHEMBACK Fabio

Born: Soledade, Brazil, 10 December 1981
Height: 6'0" **Weight:** 13.1
International Honours: Brazil: 7
Fabio is a versatile midfielder who can play in front of the defence, as an attacking midfielder or even as a winger. Initially he struggled to hold down a regular place for Middlesbrough, prompting Press speculation that he was unsettled on Teesside and a possible return to Portugal with Benfica was on the cards. At the start of his third full season, he was suspended for the first three games following his dismissal in a friendly game away to Hertha Berlin. When he was eligible for selection, manager Gareth Southgate had no qualms about pitching him straight back in to face Newcastle at the Riverside. Fabio scored arguably the best goal of his career when he guided an unstoppable 30-yard free kick past a disheartened Andreas Isaksson as Boro crushed ten-man Manchester City 8-1 on the last day of the campaign. His season ended as it began, with transfer speculation rife about a return to Portugal. Middlesbrough declined to take up the two-year option on Fabio, leaving him free to talk to interested clubs, and Sporting Lisbon secured his signature.
Middlesbrough (£2,500,000 from Sporting Lisbon, Portugal, ex Barcelona, on 31/8/2005) PL 60+8/5 FLC 5/1 FAC 11+1/1 Others 5+1

RODGERS Luke John

Born: Birmingham, 1 January 1982
Height: 5'7" **Weight:** 11.2
International Honours: E: SP-2
Luke made a blistering start to the season with five goals in his first nine games, the only ones Port Vale scored. A small nippy striker, Luke knows his way to goal but missed two penalties in an FA Cup replay against Chasetown as Vale suffered a giant-killing. It seemed to affect him for a period as he went 15 games without scoring. He battled on and his next goal, in the local derby victory at Crewe, appeared to re-ignite his season. A last-minute equaliser in the next game,

Luke Rodgers

a 3-3 draw with Leeds, was his last of the campaign as a knee injury sidelined him for the last few games. His 12 goals made him Vale's leading scorer.
Shrewsbury T *(From trainee on 10/7/2000)* FL 122+20/52 FLC 3/1 FAC 6+1 Others 9+2/5
Crewe Alex *(Free on 26/7/2005)* FL 18+20/9 FAC 1
Port Vale *(£30,000 on 17/1/2007)* FL 35+9/12 FLC 1/1 FAC 3/1 Others 1/1

RODRIGUEZ Jay Enrique
Born: Burnley, 29 July 1989
Height: 6'1" **Weight:** 11.0
As the son of a striker legendary in Burnley local football circles, Jay's progress ensured that he has already exceeded his dad's achievements. Given a squad place at the start of the season, he made his first-team bow just after Christmas in the home game against Bristol City. A tall and aggressive striker, he was loaned out to Stirling Albion for the final stages of the season and was offered a contract extension at Turf Moor, suggesting more of him will be seen next time around.
Burnley *(From trainee on 4/7/2007)* FL 0+1
Stirling A *(Loaned on 11/1/2008))* SL 10+1/3 SC 0+1

RODWELL Jack Christian
Born: Southport, 11 March 1991
Height: 6'1" **Weight:** 12.8
International Honours: E: Yth
The England youth international became the third youngest Everton player in history when coming on as a substitute against AZ67 in December, aged 16 years 284 days, before adding two Premier

League appearances in the course of a campaign during which he signed his first professional contract. The highly-rated defender can also play in midfield.
Everton *(From trainee on 15/3/2008)* PL 0+2 Others 0+1

[RONALDO] DOS SANTOS AVEIRO Cristiano Ronaldo
Born: Madeira, Portugal, 5 February 1985
Height: 6'0" **Weight:** 12.4
Club Honours: FAC '04; FLC '06; PL '07, '08; CS '07; UEFACL '08
International Honours: Portugal: 58; U21-15; Yth
A prodigiously gifted Manchester United and Portugal winger, who is comfortable on either flank, Ronaldo's season started with a blip when he was sent off at Portsmouth in the second Premiership game. He returned as a conquering hero to score the only goal of the Champions' League group match against his former club Sporting Lisbon. On the night he was given a standing ovation by the Sporting supporters for his muted celebration of the goal but there were plenty of occasions when the celebrations were less low key through an astonishing campaign. His scoring boots certainly did the talking as Birmingham, Wigan, Arsenal and Blackburn would readily testify. In Europe, Dynamo Kiev, Lyon and AS Roma found him too hot to handle. Off the field the plaudits continued. In December, he was runner-up to Kaka as 'European Footballer of the Year' with 277 points. In the same month, he was third in the 'FIFA World Player of the Year' awards, behind Kaká and

Lionel Messi. Undaunted, he returned to Premiership action with a match-winning double against Fulham, including a memorable volley. Two late penalties in home games against Derby and Everton were followed by a free-kick against Sunderland. In January he celebrated his first hat-trick for the Reds in the 6-0 thumping of Newcastle at Old Trafford, a result that took them to the top of the Premier League. The second in the 2-0 win against Reading took him to 23, equalling his tally for the whole of 2006-07, and in March he eclipsed George Best's 40-year-old United record of the most goals scored from the wing in one season with 42 to his name. Best scored 32 in 1967-68. Ronaldo captained United for the first time in a Premier League match against Bolton at Old Trafford and scored both goals in a 2-0 victory. In April it was reported that Real Madrid offered United a world-record £100-million for him but, if true, it was turned down. Having missed a penalty in the Nou Camp in the first leg of the Champions' League semi-final, Ronaldo had the last laugh when United beat the Spaniards 1-0 in the return leg. With the PFA 'Player of the Season' and the writers' 'Footballer of the Year' awards in the bag, the Champions' League final was a fitting climax to Ronaldo's season. He scored one and, to his distress, missed a penalty in the shoot-out with Chelsea but it fell right in the end. He is undoubtedly the Premiership's most valuable and valued player.
Manchester U *(£7,700,000 + from Sporting Lisbon, Portugal on 14/8/2003)* PL 126+37/66 FLC 8/2 FAC 21+3/12 Others 41+3/12

ROONEY Adam
Born: Dublin, 21 April 1988
Height: 5'10" **Weight:** 12.3
International Honours: RoI: U21-7; Yth
The Stoke front man brought pace and a poacher's knack to Chesterfield after joining them on loan in August but after Jamie Ward returned from injury he was played wide in midfield, a role that suited him less well, and he returned to Stoke in January. On becoming the Bury manager in February, Alan Knill was keen to bolster the striking options, signing Adam on loan, and while the striker's three goals may not have been the injection Knill was seeking his constant hard work and willingness to run endeared him to Shakers' fans. A regular in the Republic of Ireland under-21 side, Adam did have a knack of scoring important goals, none more so than his priceless equalizer in Bury's draw at Mansfield in February.

Wayne Rooney

Stoke C (From trainee on 6/9/2006) FL 2+13/4 FAC 0+4
Yeovil T (Loaned on 16/3/2007) FL 1+2
Chesterfield (Loaned on 31/8/2007) FL 11+11/7 FAC 1 Others 1
Bury (Loaned on 8/2/2008) FL 10+6/3

ROONEY John Richard
Born: Liverpool, 17 December 1990
Height: 5'10" **Weight:** 12.0
After shining as a striker in Macclesfield's youth team, for whom he scored two hat-tricks last season, John made his League debut as a 90th-minute substitute in the home win over Barnet in March. His only other appearance came when he started the final match of the season at Chester and he gave an excellent performance. John is the younger brother of Manchester United and England striker Wayne.
Macclesfield T (Trainee) FL 1+1

ROONEY Wayne Mark
Born: Liverpool, 24 October 1985
Height: 5'10" **Weight:** 12.4
Club Honours: FLC '06; PL '07, '08; CS '07; UEFACL '08
International Honours: E: 43; Yth
A hugely talented Manchester United and England striker-cum-playmaker who is widely hailed as the most complete player in world football, Wayne's injury woes returned to haunt him when he suffered a hairline fracture to a foot bone in United's opening Premiership game against Reading at Old Trafford. It was expected that the injury would keep him out for a sustained spell, but Wayne returned in September and scored twice his first comeback goal in the Champions' League group match against AS Roma at Old Trafford. Combining well with his new partner Carlos Tevez, his scoring form continued. After netting against Dynamo Kiev, he scored in successive Premiership games against Wigan, Aston Villa and Middlesbrough. In November, he damaged an ankle during training and this injury ruled him out of England's crucial Euro 2008 qualifier against Croatia. His recovery was faster than expected and he returned to training after two weeks before making his comeback against Fulham in December, Scoring against Sunderland in the final Premiership fixture of 2007, he notched further Premiership strikes against Reading, Aston Villa (2), Middlesbrough and Chelsea. An injured hip put him out of United's triumphant Champions' League semi-final against Barcelona at Old Trafford but he was back for the trip to Moscow to face Chelsea in the final.
Everton (From trainee on 20/2/2003) PL 40+27/15 FLC 4+2/2 FAC 4

Manchester U (£20,000,000 + on 31/8/2004) PL 116+11/53 FLC 5+2/2 FAC 16+4/10 Others 34+1/12

ROPER Ian Robert
Born: Nuneaton, 20 June 1977
Height: 6'3" **Weight:** 13.4
Club Honours: Div 2 '07
The battling, long-serving defender struggled for a first-team place at Walsall in the first half of last season, because of the outstanding form of Scott Dann and Anthony Gerrard, before coming back into contention after Dann's move to Coventry in February. Though lacking a little pace compared with his heyday, Ian played bravely until suffering an injury at Cheltenham in April in what turned out to be his last game for Walsall. He was released in May after 13 years of good service to his one and only League club.
Walsall (From trainee on 15/5/1995) FL 298+27/7 FLC 10+6 FAC 17+3/1 Others 16+3

ROSA Denes
Born: Budapest, Hungary, 7 April 1977
Height: 5'9" **Weight:** 11.0
International Honours: Hungary: 10
Denes did not fit into the manager's style at Wolverhampton, although he made a lively substitute appearance in the Carling Cup. He was a prolific scorer for the reserves, nine goals by the end of October, but then suffered a hernia problem and had six weeks of treatment before surgery was undertaken. Denes continued where he left off, scoring 13 for the reserves at an average of a goal a game, astonishing for a midfielder.
Wolverhampton W (Signed from Ferencvaros, Hungary on 2/1/2006) FL 6+3/2 FLC 1+1 FAC 0+1
Cheltenham T (Loaned on 9/3/2007) FL 3+1

ROSE Matthew David
Born: Dartford, 24 September 1975
Height: 5'11" **Weight:** 11.1
Club Honours: FAYC '94
International Honours: E: U21-2
The versatile Matthew was very important for injury-hit Yeovil last season as his ability to play in defence or midfield proved invaluable for manager Russell Slade. At the same time, the veteran suffered numerous injuries and had he been fully fit his performances suggest that he would have been even more influential. Matthew is still a good tackler and sound user of the ball.
Arsenal (From trainee on 19/7/1994) PL 2+3
Queens Park Rgrs (£500,000 on 20/5/1997) FL 220+22/8 FLC 7+1 FAC 5 Others 4+1
Yeovil T (Free on 23/2/2007) FL 34+5/1 FLC 0+1 Others 1+1

ROSE Michael Charles
Born: Salford, 28 July 1982
Height: 5'10" **Weight:** 11.2
Club Honours: Div 2 '05
Having missed the first few months of last season recovering from ligament reconstruction surgery, Michael returned in November and did not look back, making the Stockport left-back position his own. A number of spectacular free-kicks followed, thanks to his magical left foot, in home games against Grimsby, Accrington and Bradford. They were all of a similar type, curling in and perfectly placed, almost impossible to stop.
Manchester U (From trainee on 9/9/1999. Freed during 2001 close season)
Yeovil T (Free from Hereford U, ex Chester C, on 14/5/2004) FL 37+4/1 FLC 2 FAC 3+1 Others 0+1
Cheltenham T (Loaned on 25/8/2005) FL 3
Scunthorpe U (Loaned on 1/1/2006) FL 15 FAC 1
Stockport Co (Free on 8/7/2006) FL 47+6/6 FLC 1 FAC 3+1 Others 5+2

ROSE Richard Alan
Born: Tonbridge, 8 September 1982
Height: 6'0" **Weight:** 11.9
In his second season at Hereford, Richard proved a useful and highly competent utility defender. He began at left-back before moving to the right and had a spell in central defence, to fall in line with the team's needs, while also finding time to head the opening goal in a crucial November promotion clash with Darlington. Richard missed a spell around Christmas and the New Year with an ankle injury but returned at left-back to play a major part in Hereford's run-in. Although predominantly right-footed, this was never a handicap on the left, where his reading of the game, covering and willingness to get forward were major assets.
Gillingham (From trainee on 10/4/2001) FL 44+14 FLC 3+1 FAC 1 Others 1
Bristol Rov (Loaned on 13/12/2002) FL 9
Hereford U (Free on 27/7/2006) FL 60+4/2 FLC 4 FAC 6+2 Others 1+1

ROSE Romone Alexander Aldolphus
Born: Reading, 19 January 1990
Height: 5'9" **Weight:** 11.5
One of Queens Park Rangers' bright young prospects, Romone managed to feature for the Championship winning youth team, the reserves and AFC Wimbledon on loan as well as making his first-team debut during the final home match of last season, against West Bromwich. Talented and capable of playing wide right or up front, Romone

will hope to follow youth team-mate Angelo Balanta into the first-team picture.
Queens Park Rgrs (Trainee) FL 0+1

ROSENIOR Liam James
Born: Wandsworth, 9 July 1984
Height: 5'9" **Weight:** 11.8
Club Honours: AMC '03
International Honours: E: U21-7; Yth
Liam arrived shortly after the start of the season in a swap deal that saw Reading's Ki-Hyeon Seol going in the opposite direction to join Fulham. Reading appear to have the better of the exchange as Liam, who can operate at right-back or on the right of midfield, soon established himself. He operated wide on the right in the early stages of the season as Reading tried to fill the void left by the long-term injury to Glen Little. In the latter part of the campaign, he deputised at right-back for the injured skipper Graeme Murty and enhanced his reputation with some spirited displays. Liam scored once, in the 7-4 defeat at Portsmouth, and almost earned his team a vital point in the home game against Tottenham with a well-struck volley that forced the visiting 'keeper to a brilliant save.
Bristol C (From trainee on 15/8/2001) FL 2+20/2 FAC 0+1 Others 2+3/1
Fulham (Free on 7/11/2003) PL 76+3 FLC 3+2/1 FAC 8
Torquay U (Loaned on 19/3/2004) FL 9+1
Reading (Signed on 31/8/2007) PL 15+2 FAC 2

ROSICKY Tomas
Born: Prague, Czech Republic, 4 October 1980
Height: 5'10" **Weight:** 10.3
International Honours: Czech Republic: 67; U21
Arsenal's Czech Republic midfielder suffered another season that was hugely disrupted by injury. He is extremely gifted with a fine range of passing, is quick on and off the ball and has a tremendous capacity for long-range shooting. However, Arsenal fans were again left wondering how many times they would see Tomas in action as he endured long spells on the treatment table. His season was cut short after suffering a hamstring problem in the FA Cup tie against Newcastle in January and he did not feature again. He was also ruled out of Euro 2008. Tomas scored six times in 18 Premier League appearances and once in his five Champions' League games.
Arsenal (£6,800,000 from Borussia Dortmund, Germany, ex Sparta Prague, on 25/5/2006) PL 37+7/9 FLC 0+1 FAC 4+1/2 Others 9+2/2

ROSS Ian
Born: Sheffield, 13 January 1986
Height: 5'11" **Weight:** 11.0
International Honours: E: Yth
Accurate passing in midfield when Ian joined Rotherham on loan from Sheffield United led to his being given a contract to the end of the season. Although he did not manage to carve out an automatic place, many supporters felt he should have done. He is accurate with free kicks and always willing to have a shot at goal from any distance. Was released in the summer.
Sheffield U (From trainee on 7/7/2004) FLC 2/1
Boston U (Loaned on 26/8/2005) FL 10+1/3 Others 1
Boston U (Loaned on 27/10/2005) FL 3/1 Others 1
Bury (Loaned on 23/3/2006) FL 6+1
Notts Co (Loaned on 2/8/2006) FL 26+10/1 FLC 4 FAC 1 Others 1
Rotherham U (Free on 7/11/2007) FL 9+8

ROUSE Domaine
Born: Stretford, 4 July 1989
Height: 5'6" **Weight:** 10.10
Young Domaine is widely tipped as a rising star and good performances for Bury last season enhanced his reputation. Yet to feature in the starting line-up, seven substitute appearances showed that both managers, Chris Casper and Alan Knill, have faith in his ability as a striker. After going on as a substitute against Rochdale in the Johnstone's Paint Trophy, he scored his first senior goal with a well-taken finish and fans are keen to see Domaine fulfil his obvious potential.
Bury (From trainee on 6/11/2007) FL 0+8 Others 0+1/1

ROUTLEDGE Wayne Neville Anthony
Born: Sidcup, 7 January 1985
Height: 5'6" **Weight:** 10.7
International Honours: E: U21-12; Yth
Having signed for Tottenham in 2005, the midfielder has spent most of his time as a loan player elsewhere and was only involved in two of Spurs' early games last season before suffering a knee injury and trying to play his way back in the reserves. Martin O'Neill decided to take a gamble on Wayne when signing him for Aston Villa in the January transfer window but he has so far only played four minutes of first-team football for his new club. It will be interesting to see if the tricky, skilful wide player, who is at home on either flank, can get back to where he once was in 2008-09 under O'Neill.
Crystal Palace (From trainee on 9/7/2002) P/FL 83+27/10 FLC 5+2 FAC 2+1 Others 3

Tottenham H (£2,000,000 on 7/7/2005) PL 3+2
Portsmouth (Loaned on 30/1/2006) PL 3+10
Fulham (Loaned on 31/8/2006) PL 13+11 FLC 1 FAC 3/1
Aston Villa (£1,250,000 on 30/1/2008) PL 0+1

ROWE Thomas (Tommy)
Born: Manchester, 1 May 1989
Height: 5'11" **Weight:** 12.11
Tommy began to feature regularly for Stockport six weeks into the new season, scoring his first goal, against Notts County, and then underlining his huge potential with a stunning hat-trick at Rotherham. The Premiership scouts have been regular visitors to Edgeley Park, keeping tabs on the mercurial left-winger who played a key role at Wembley to help County win the League Two play-off final.
Stockport Co (From trainee on 23/3/2007) FL 18+10/6 FAC 0+2 Others 3+2

ROWLANDS Martin Charles
Born: Hammersmith, 8 February 1979
Height: 5'9" **Weight:** 10.10
Club Honours: Div 3 '99
International Honours: RoI: 3; U21-8
Martin hit some of the finest form of his career last season. After spending much of his time at Loftus Road deployed in wide positions, he finally made a central midfield spot his own with a succession of classy performances that saw him named both the supporters' and players' 'Player of the Year'. Almost an ever-present, missing only two games, he also contributed seven goals, including two in the fine 4-2 away win at Watford and what proved to be the winner in a 3-2 home victory over Blackpool.
Brentford (£45,000 from Farnborough T on 6/8/1998) FL 128+21/20 FLC 8+3/1 FAC 7+2 Others 17/2
Queens Park Rgrs (Free on 6/8/2003) FL 154+10/31 FLC 5/4 FAC 4 Others 3

ROYCE Simon Ernest
Born: Forest Gate, 9 September 1971
Height: 6'2" **Weight:** 12.8
Simon signed for Gillingham on a permanent basis in the summer, having been on loan from Queens Park Rangers at the end of 2006-07. He is a highly experienced goalkeeper who saved the Gills on so many occasions during the season that it is almost impossible to number them. He was voted 'Player of the Year' by fans and also won the sponsors' award. A good shot-stopper and comfortable on crosses, Gillingham supporters were keeping their fingers crossed as he entered discussions about a new contract.

Southend U (£35,000 from Heybridge Swifts on 15/10/1991) FL 147+2 FLC 9 FAC 5 Others 6
Charlton Ath (Free on 2/7/1998) PL 8
Leicester C (Free on 17/7/2000) PL 16+3 FLC 1 FAC 4
Brighton & Hove A (Loaned on 24/12/2001) FL 6
Queens Park Rgrs (Loaned on 24/8/2002) FL 16 Others 1
Charlton Ath (Free on 4/7/2003) PL 1
Luton T (Loaned on 29/10/2004) FL 2
Queens Park Rgrs (Free on 13/1/2005) FL 63 FLC 1 FAC 3
Gillingham (Free on 19/4/2007) FL 36 FLC 1 FAC 1 Others 1

ROZEHNAL David Sebastian

Born: Sternberk, Czech Republic, 5 July 1980
Height: 6'3" **Weight:** 12.8
International Honours: Czech Republic: 42; U21-8
David is a tall, angular Czech international who was signed by Newcastle during the summer to strengthen the perennially leaky defence. He arrived with a reputation as an accomplished centre-back, having been Paris St Germain's 'Player of the Year' the previous season, in which he was also chosen for the French League's 'Team of the Year'. Although he continued to represent his country, he was not the commanding presence the Tynesiders needed, at least in part because he was rarely allowed to settle in one position. Although primarily fielded at the centre of the defence, he also had outings at right-back and in midfield. The lack of continuity unsettled him, and after losing his starting place at the end of the year, he moved to Lazio in January on loan to the end of the season, an arrangement he was keen to make permanent.
Newcastle U (£2,500,000 from Paris St Germain, France, ex Sigma Olomouc, Club Brugge, on 13/7/2007) PL 16+5 FLC 1 FAC 1+2

RUDDY John Thomas Gordon

Born: St Ives, 24 October 1986
Height: 6'4" **Weight:** 15.4
International Honours: E: Yth
Everton's reserve goalkeeper went on loan to Stockport in February where he impressed in keeping a string of clean sheets and winning a 'Player of the Month' award. Unable to get a game at Goodison, County manager Jim Gannon swooped to bring John back for a second spell at the club after his number one 'keeper Conrad Logan was dismissed against Bury. The Everton shot-stopper then took over the position and his calm,

assured performances helped County to win nine and draw one of his 12 League games. Rested for the final two matches, he returned for the play-off semi-final first leg at Wycombe but it was Logan who was selected for the return and the Wembley final. John is contracted with Everton until 2009.
Cambridge U (From trainee on 3/9/2004) FL 39 FLC 1 FAC 1 Others 2
Everton (£250,000 + on 20/5/2005) PL 0+1
Walsall (Loaned on 23/9/2005) FL 5
Rushden & Diamonds (Loaned on 10/11/2005) FL 3 Others 1
Chester C (Loaned on 16/12/2005) FL 4
Stockport Co (Loaned on 14/9/2006) FL 11
Wrexham (Loaned on 9/2/2007) FL 5
Bristol C (Loaned on 21/4/2007) FL 1
Stockport Co (Loaned on 22/2/2008) FL 12 Others 1

[RUI MARQUES] MARQUES Rui Manuel

Born: Luanda, Angola, 3 September 1977
Height: 5'11" **Weight:** 12.0
International Honours: Angola: 7
Rui Marques was the pick of the Leeds' defence for much of the season with his calmness and superb reading of the game worthy of a bigger stage than League One. Many fans likened him to former favourite Lucas Radebe as the African slipped effortlessly through the gears to snuff out opposition attacks. He played in all United's League games before he went to the African Cup of Nations with Angola in January, having an excellent tournament as his country reached the quarter-finals. United won only one game during his five-game absence but he quickly slotted in at centre-back on his return, scoring in a 3-3 draw at Port Vale, his third of the season. Injury ruled him out for a four-game spell as the season came to a close and he had to be content with a place on the bench when fit. He also skippered the Leeds' side most of March while Jonathan Douglas, Alan Thompson and Andy Hughes were out. Despite interest from Championship clubs, he signed a new two-year deal with Leeds in April.
Leeds U (Signed from CS Maritimo, Portugal, ex SSV Ulm 1846, VfB Stuttgart, on 5/8/2005) FL 48+5/3 FLC 2 FAC 2 Others 1
Hull C (Loaned on 23/3/2006) FL 1

RULE Glenn Paul

Born: Birkenhead, 30 November 1989
Height: 5'11" **Weight:** 11.0
Glenn was one of a number of graduates from the Chester Academy who was given an opportunity at the Deva Stadium by Bobby Williamson. Making his debut at Carlisle as a substitute in a Johnstone's

Paint Trophy tie, the right-sided attacking midfielder made his first start at Morecambe on Boxing Day. A confident ball player, the youngster aims to make further advances after being awarded a professional contract in the summer.
Chester C (Trainee) FL 2+2 Others 0+1

RUNDLE Adam

Born: Durham, 8 July 1984
Height: 5'10" **Weight:** 11.2
A key figure in Rochdale's attacking play, Adam was the first choice on the left-wing for most of the season, missing only a handful of games. His numerous assists were vital as Dale became the third most prolific scorers in League Two, behind MK Dons and Peterborough. He weighed in with several goals, including strikes when Dale scored four against each of Shrewsbury, Chester and Notts County, and ended the season by hitting a stunning volley with his wrong foot to give Rochdale a late lifeline when they went down 3-2 to Stockport in the play-off final at Wembley.
Darlington (Trainee) FL 8+9
Carlisle U (Free on 31/12/2002) FL 25+19/1 FLC 1 Others 4+1/2 (Freed on 19/8/2004)
Mansfield T (Free from Dublin C on 14/1/2005) FL 45+8/9 FLC 1 FAC 3
Rochdale (Free on 5/7/2006) FL 57+14/9 FLC 3/1 FAC 2+1 Others 4/1

RUSSELL Alexander (Alex) John

Born: Crosby, 17 March 1973
Height: 5'9" **Weight:** 11.7
The skilful midfielder hardly had a look-in for Bristol City last season after playing in two early games and had lengthy loan spells at Northampton and Cheltenham. Loaned to Northampton at the end of August, Alex controlled midfield in his short stay at Sixfields, prompting attacks and using his experience to help the younger players. Back at Ashton Gate, but still unable to get a game, Alex joined Cheltenham on loan in January and remained at Whaddon Road for the rest of the season. The standout feature of his game is his passing ability and he added a new dimension with his creativity from the centre of midfield. Cheltenham's downturn in results in April coincided with his absence due to a hamstring injury but Alex returned for the final two matches as the Robins staved off relegation from League One. He scored a late goal in a 2-1 home win over Brighton and his spectacular goal in the 2-1 victory at Leeds was one of the highlights of the season, the crowning moment of one of Cheltenham's most memorable League victories. Alex was released by City at the

363

Darel Russell

end of the season and it was thought likely that would rejoin Torquay, one of his former clubs. Earlier, Northampton wanted to sign him on full terms after his loan expired but he felt he still had something to give in the Championship.
Rochdale *(£4,000 from Burscough on 11/7/1994) FL 83+19/14 FLC 5/1 FAC 1+1 Others 2+3*
Cambridge U *(Free on 4/8/1998) FL 72+9/8 FLC 7+1 FAC 6 Others 3*
Torquay U *(Free on 9/8/2001) FL 152+1/21 FLC 4 FAC 4/1 Others 2*
Bristol C *(Free on 1/7/2005) FL 42+14/6 FLC 1 FAC 4+3 Others 1+2*
Northampton T *(Loaned on 31/8/2007) FL 11+2/1 Others 1*
Cheltenham T *(Loaned on 11/1/2008) FL 12+1/2*

RUSSELL Darel Francis Roy
Born: Stepney, 22 October 1980
Height: 5'11" **Weight:** 11.9
International Honours: E: Yth
After four years away from Carrow Road, the popular midfielder returned to Norwich from Stoke in July. His energetic, bustling style ensures he is never far from the action and he was rewarded as runner-up in the Canaries' 'Player of the

Season' voting. A graduate of Norwich's youth policy, he ended the season on 191 appearances for City over two spells. He loves to get forward and scored five goals. He could have had more, but he has other duties as a combative figure, always working hard to deny opponents the space to play.
Norwich C *(From trainee on 29/11/1997) FL 99+33/7 FLC 8/2 FAC 6+1*
Stoke C *(£125,000 on 8/8/2003) FL 166+5/16 FLC 4+1 FAC 6*
Norwich C *(Signed on 31/7/2007) FL 37+2/4 FLC 3/1 FAC 2*

RUSSELL Samuel (Sam) Ian
Born: Middlesbrough, 4 October 1982
Height: 6'0" **Weight:** 10.13
Sam joined Rochdale on trial at the start of last season, having been released by Torquay, and was rewarded with a short-term contract, which was later extended. A regular on the bench, he took over in goal when James Spencer was injured in the week leading up to the FA Cup tie at Southend. His League debut for Dale coincided with the start of a run which saw them beaten only once in 12 games and he appeared in every match until February when he was found to have played the previous game with a broken finger. The injury subsequently required surgery, ruling out the goalkeeper for the rest of the campaign.
Middlesbrough *(From trainee on 7/7/2000)*
Darlington *(Loaned on 28/12/2002) FL 1*
Scunthorpe U *(Loaned on 22/8/2003) FL 10 FLC 1 Others 1*
Darlington *(Free on 5/8/2004) FL 107 FLC 1 FAC 5 Others 4*
Rochdale *(Free on 10/8/2007) FL 15 FAC 1 Others 1*

RUTHERFORD Paul Leslie
Born: Moreton, Cheshire, 10 July 1987
Height: 5'9" **Weight:** 11.7
An attacking right-sided midfielder with an explosive turn of pace, Paul was initially kept out of the Chester side by Richie Partridge and had to be content with occasional appearances from the substitutes' bench. The youngster was given a longer run in the side towards the end of the season when Simon Davies, the former youth-team coach at the Deva Stadium, was promoted to manager. Although Paul can fade in and out of games, his skill and unpredictability make him exciting to watch and he made some telling contributions when he played, including his first senior goal in the 2-1 victory over Lincoln.
Chester C *(Free from Greenleas on 17/10/2005) FL 17+21/1 FLC 0+2 FAC 0+1 Others 1+2*

RYAN James (Jimmy)
Born: Maghull, 6 September 1988
Height: 5'11" **Weight:** 10.10
Club Honours: FAYC '07
International Honours: RoI: Yth
Initially signed on loan from Liverpool, the young midfield player made an impressive debut for Shrewsbury in the Carling Cup victory over Colchester and turned in a 'Man of the Match performance against Fulham in the second round. Despite his busy, involved style, chances were limited and he was released at the end of the season.
Liverpool *(From trainee on 5/7/2006)*
Shrewsbury T *(Free on 14/8/2007) FL 1+3 FLC 2 Others 1*

RYAN Oliver (Ollie) Paul
Born: Boston, 26 September 1985
Height: 5'9" **Weight:** 11.0
Although he remained a regular goalscorer in the reserve team for Lincoln, Ollie found success in front of goal in the League somewhat elusive and by the time he left the Imps by mutual consent at the end of the campaign he had failed to hit the back of the net at first-team level. Is a willing runner, who may well come back to the lower reaches via a spell in non-League soccer.
Lincoln C *(From trainee on 3/8/2005) FL 8+30 FAC 0+1 Others 2*

RYAN Timothy (Tim) James
Born: Stockport, 10 December 1974
Height: 5'10" **Weight:** 11.6
Club Honours: Div 3 '04
International Honours: E: SP-14
Tim started the season as Darlington's first choice at left-back and was part of a formidable defence that conceded only five goals in the first 11 league games. He showed composure and good aerial strength but a serious injury against Stockport in mid-October ruled him out for the rest of the season. Was never adequately replaced and was sorely missed.
Scunthorpe U *(From trainee on 8/4/1993) FL 1+1 (Free to Buxton on 28/11/1994)*
Doncaster Rov *(Free from Buxton on 8/8/1996) FL 22+6 FLC 0+1 FAC 1 Others 1 (Free to Southport on 5/8/1997)*
Doncaster Rov *(Free from Southport on 24/5/2000) FL 86+2/6 FLC 5 FAC 3 Others 1+1*
Peterborough U *(Free on 20/3/2006) FL 6+1*
Boston U *(Free on 22/5/2006) FL 23/4 FLC 1 FAC 1 Others 1*
Darlington *(Signed on 4/1/2007) FL 17+1/1 Others 1*

S

SAAH Brian Ebo
Born: Hornchurch, 16 December 1986
Height: 6'1" **Weight:** 11.0
Brian missed the early part of the season through injury but regained his Leyton Orient place at centre-half following injuries to other players before he was absent at the end of the season with a hamstring problem. A dominant centre-half, who is both good in the air and on the ground, he scored against Bournemouth on Boxing Day with a shot from the edge of the penalty area.
Leyton Orient (From trainee on 1/8/2006) FL 68+10/1 FLC 1+1 FAC 3+2 Others 4+1/1

SADLER Matthew (Mat)
Born: Birmingham, 26 February 1985
Height: 5'11" **Weight:** 11.6
International Honours: E: Yth
Mat made three Premier League starts for Birmingham during the early part of Alex McLeish's tenure last season. He has a great attitude and is disciplined in defence but with Franck Queudrue and David Murphy ahead of him at left-back, he decided to move to Watford in January, going straight into the team at left-back and establishing himself with a series of assured performances. A reliable defender who was always looking to join the attack, he missed a handful of matches towards the end of the campaign because of hamstring problems.
Birmingham C (From trainee on 12/4/2002) P/FL 49+2 FLC 6 FAC 3+1
Northampton T (Loaned on 21/11/2003) FL 7 Others 1
Watford (£750,000 + on 25/1/2008) FL 14+1 FAC 1 Others 2

SAFRI Youssef
Born: Casablanca, Morocco, 1 March 1977
Height: 5'10" **Weight:** 11.8
International Honours: Morocco
Although Southampton's midfield was disappointing last season, Youssef, in the heart of it, was exempt from blame. Having arrived from Norwich in the summer, his game was to position himself in front of the back four, help to break up attacks, and launch counter offensives. He has a silky tackling technique, is rarely caught in possession and his scheming and delivery are exemplary. However, those around him often seemed incapable of reading his game and a shaky rearguard blunted his effectiveness. But he is a class act.
Coventry C (Free from Raja Casablanca,

Morocco on 25/8/2001) FL 87+4/1 FLC 6 FAC 1
Norwich C (£500,000 on 9/7/2004) P/FL 68+15/3 FLC 3+2/1 FAC 4
Southampton (£200,000 on 7/8/2007) FL 37 FLC 1 FAC 1

SAGANOWSKI Marek Miroslaw
Born: Lodz, Poland, 31 October 1978
Height: 5'10" **Weight:** 12.0
International Honours: Poland: 26
In an extremely disappointing season for Southampton, Marek never fulfilled the promise of his loan in January 2007 – until the final act. Hard-working, deceptively strong, easy on the ball and a natural poacher he struck ten Championship goals in 13 appearances during his loan. Great things were expected when he signed a two-year contract last summer but he never found the form to become a regular, although remaining in the Polish international squad. However, on the last day of the season, with Saints needing to defeat Sheffield United at St Mary's to have any hope of survival, Marek had a stupendously influential game, the high point of which was a dynamic far-post header just before half-time, bringing the score to 1-1. The 3–2 win kept the club up and guaranteed Marek a place in the pantheon of Saints' heroes.
Southampton (£680,000 from Vitoria Guimaraes, Portugal, ex LKS Lodz, Feyenoord - loan, SV Hamburg - loan, Wisla Plock, Odra Wodzislaw, Legia Warsaw, on 31/1/2007) FL 25+18/13 FLC 0+1 FAC 1 Others 2

SAGNA Bacary
Born: Sens, France, 14 February 1983
Height: 5'11" **Weight:** 11.5
International Honours: France: 2; U21

Bacary Sagna

The powerful right-back arrived at Arsenal from Auxerre in the close season and immediately impressed. He struck up an instant understanding with his fellow Frenchman on the opposite flank, Gael Clichy, and soon looked as if he had been a regular member of the Arsenal back four for several seasons. Fierce in the tackle, strong going forward and a fine all-round reader of the game, Bacary quickly won over the Gunners' crowd. He scored his first goal at Chelsea but an injury suffered later in that game brought a premature end to a highly impressive first season in English football. A fitting reward duly arrived at the end of the season as he was voted into the PFA 'Premier League Team of the Season'. His first full French honours came early in the season but, because of injury, he was left out of the French squad to contest the European Championship finals.

Arsenal (£6,000,000 from Auxerre, France on 18/7/2007) PL 29/1 FLC 1+1 FAC 1 Others 7+1

SAHA Louis

Born: Paris, France, 8 August 1978
Height: 5'11" **Weight:** 11.10
Club Honours: Div 1 '01; FLC '06; PL '07, '08
International Honours: France: 18; U21; Yth (UEFA U-18 '97)
A skilful, pacy Manchester United striker who is dangerous in the air, Louis celebrated his long-awaited return from injury in August with a Premiership goal against Sunderland, a late winner from a corner. Having both won and converted a penalty against Chelsea in Avram Grant's first match in charge of the London club, his performances earned him a recall by France after a year out. Louis came on to replace Carlos Tevez against Arsenal at the Emirates and supplied a sublime back-heeled pass to Patrice Evra. It was his first match since an injury against Roma at Old Trafford in October and he continued to be used as a substitute, his Boxing Day double against Sunderland lifting United to first place in the Premiership. There were more woes from a recurring knee injury and his last goal of the season was against Newcastle in February. Louis did not appear again after a Premiership outing against Bolton in March.

Newcastle U (Loaned from Metz, France on 8/1/1999) PL 5+6/1 FAC 1/1
Fulham (£2,100,000 from Metz, France on 29/6/2000) PIFL 100+17/53 FLC 3+3/6 FAC 10+1/3 Others 5+4/1
Manchester U (£12,825,000 on 23/1/2004) PL 52+34/28 FLC 9/7 FAC 6+4/3 Others 9+10/4

SAHAR Ben

Born: Holon, Israel, 10 August 1989
Height: 5'10" **Weight:** 12.5
International Honours: Israel: 7; U21-2; Yth
An exciting young prospect, Ben joined Queens Park Rangers on loan from Chelsea last August but suffered a ruptured appendix before his season really got going. After recovering from the operation he made nine appearances for the Rs but didn't find the back of the net before returning to Stamford Bridge. Sent out on loan for the second time in 2007-08, joining Sheffield Wednesday in February, Ben contributed some good work for the Owls while playing as a striker in a 4-4-2 formation and also as a wide midfielder in a 4-5-1. At 18, he is already a full Israeli international, is very assured on the ball and needs only to add a greater goal threat to become a top player.

Chelsea (Trainee, having been signed from Hapoel Tel Aviv, Israel for £320,000 on 15/8/2006) PL 0+3 FLC 0+1 FAC 0+1
Queens Park Rgrs (Loaned on 9/8/2007) FL 6+3
Sheffield Wed (Loaned on 21/2/2008) FL 8+4/3

ST LEDGER-HALL Sean Patrick

Born: Birmingham, 28 December 1984
Height: 6'0" **Weight:** 12.0
Sean continued to develop into a solid and reliable central defender for Preston, forming excellent partnerships with Youl Mawene and Liam Chilvers. Comfortable on the ball, he loves to burst through midfield to set up attacks and he put this flair to good use when he was asked to cover at right-back. His distribution still needs some work but his value was recognised by the fans and team-mates when he swept the board in all five 'Player of the Year' awards. Although not a big man, he combines strength with excellent tackling and his solitary goal in the home win over Coventry does not reflect his threat at set pieces.

Peterborough U (From trainee on 18/7/2003) FL 77+2/1 FLC 1 FAC 6 Others 5
Preston NE (£225,000 on 12/7/2006) FL 74+4/2 FLC 2 FAC 1

SALIFOU Moustapha

Born: Lome, Togo, 1 June 1983
Height: 5'11" **Weight:** 12.0
International Honours: Togo: 37
Signed by Aston Villa from Swiss club Wil last August, the midfield player's arrival was delayed by work permit problems. Moustapha has been compared to Zinedine Zidane in that he can keep

the ball, dribble and do anything he wants in possession. That is a premature reputation as Moustapha's involvement in Villa's team amounted to a handful of appearances from the substitutes' bench, but he is clearly viewed as a player with potential.

Aston Villa (Signed from FC Wil, Switzerland, ex Modele de Lome, RW Oberhausen, Brest, on 31/8/2007) PL 0+4

SALMON Mark Maurice

Born: Dublin, 31 October 1988
Height: 5'10" **Weight:** 11.0
Mark, a central midfield player, joined Port Vale on loan from Wolverhampton in November and made his debut as a substitute in a 3-1 defeat by Doncaster. His first start in League football was in front of more than 20,000 at Leeds. He is a good passer and not short of pace, improving as he played more games. Mark was instrumental in the 2-1 win at Gillingham in a monsoon and then maintained a regular place. His best performance for Vale was in a 3-2 defeat at Carlisle but that it was also his last as his loan spell ended after two months and he returned to Molineux.

Wolverhampton W (From trainee on 4/11/2006)
Port Vale (Loaned on 22/11/2007) FL 8+1 FAC 1

SAM Hector McLeod

Born: Mount Hope, Trinidad, 25 February 1978
Height: 5'9" **Weight:** 11.5
Club Honours: AMC '05; Div 2 '07
International Honours: Trinidad & Tobago: 20
Much was expected of this experienced striker who helped Walsall to promotion the previous season. However, he was given few starts by Notts County and was a regular substitute. Various combinations were tried but failed to yield a scoring run. Left on the sidelines after the change of management, Hector chose to move on in mid-season and his contract was terminated by mutual consent.

Wrexham (£125,000 from CL Financial San Juan Jabloteh, Trinidad on 8/8/2000) FL 77+73/45 FLC 6+1/1 FAC 4+2/1 Others 6+7/3
Port Vale (Free on 4/7/2005) FL 0+4 FLC 0+1
Walsall (Free on 20/7/2006) FL 28+14/7 FLC 2 FAC 2 Others 1
Notts Co (Free on 3/7/2007) FL 7+13/1 FLC 1 FAC 1+1/1 Others 0+1

SAM Lloyd Ekow

Born: Leeds, 27 September 1984
Height: 5'8" **Weight:** 10.7
International Honours: E: Yth

Lloyd Sam

Lloyd finally made the breakthrough in 2007-08 and became a regular on Charlton's right-wing until a hamstring injury in the home game against Preston in March. He missed three games after being sent off at Hull in October but was first choice for most of the season. Lloyd is a skilful and pacy winger who can play on either the right or left. He likes to take on defenders and is exciting to watch, not afraid to try a few tricks and dangerous in front of goal. Lloyd scored his first goal for the Addicks with a curling free kick in the Carling Cup win over Stockport and added two more, including a match-winning header at home to Stoke.

Charlton Ath *(From trainee on 5/7/2002) PL/FL 27+11/2 FLC 3+1/1 FAC 2+1*
Leyton Orient *(Loaned on 15/1/2004) FL 5+5*
Sheffield Wed *(Loaned on 24/8/2006) FL 4*
Southend U *(Loaned on 12/3/2007) FL 0+2*

SAMARAS Georgios

Born: Heraklion, Greece, 21 February 1985
Height: 6'4" **Weight:** 12.13
Club Honours: SPD '08
International Honours: Greece: 18; U21

Following the change of manager, the tall, skilful Greek striker's first-team chances at Manchester City became limited and after seven appearances, that included a last-minute winner against Norwich in the Carling Cup third round, he was loaned to Glasgow Celtic for the remainder of the campaign. As dangerous from set pieces as he is from open play, Georgios showed that he had not lost his touch when scoring six times for Celtic during his stay at Parkhead.

Manchester C *(£6,000,000 from SC Heerenveen, Holland on 31/1/2006) PL 28+27/8 FLC 3/2 FAC 5+2/2*
Glasgow Celtic *(Loaned on 12/1/2008) SL 5+11/5 SC 0+3/1 Others 0+2*

SAMBA Christopher (Chris)
Veijeany
Born: Paris, France, 28 March 1984
Height: 6'5" **Weight:** 13.3
International Honours: Congo: 20

The huge Blackburn defender had a curious season. At the start he was a colossus, master of the centre of defence and an inspiration, but he lost form in the middle of the season. Mark Hughes never lost faith in him and he recovered to end the campaign strongly. Even so the Frenchman has yet to achieve his potential, because he is a massive talent. His Optima rating for duels won indicates his competitive nature; he can be totally dominant in the air and his ability to bring down a high ball with a long outstretched

leg and have it under total control is remarkable. Late in the season, his speed was demonstrated when he ran stride for stride with Ronaldo and emerged the winner.
Blackburn Rov *(£396,000 from Hertha Berlin, Germany, ex Rouen, Sedan, on 26/1/2007) PL 46+1/4 FLC 3 FAC 5+1 Others 4/1*

SAMUEL Jlloyd
Born: Trinidad, 29 March 1981
Height: 5'11" **Weight:** 11.4
International Honours: E: U21-7; Yth
Signed from Aston Villa in the summer, the former England under-21 international made his Bolton debut in the opening day defeat by Newcastle last season and, despite filling in at times as a makeshift right-back, soon lost his place when Ricardo Gardner returned. Gardner's rib injury in March allowed Jlloyd back in and he stayed for the remainder of the campaign, contributing significantly to some fine defensive displays that played a big part in Bolton's Premiership survival. Visibly growing in confidence with each passing game, Jlloyd regained the form of his early Villa days and appeared to be enjoying his football again, so much so that he has emerged as a genuine contender to keep the left-back berth in the months ahead.
Aston Villa *(From trainee on 2/2/1999) PL 144+25/2 FLC 15+1/1 FAC 7+1 Others 5+2*
Gillingham *(Loaned on 26/10/2001) FL 7+1*
Bolton W *(Free on 30/6/2007) PL 14+6 FLC 1 Others 4*

SANDERCOMBE Timothy (Tim) Eric
Born: Enfield, 15 June 1989
Height: 6'0" **Weight:** 13.12
Tim joined Notts County from Plymouth during the summer as the second goalkeeper with a view to developing him for the future. A tall and capable youngster who handles well, he suffered an unfortunate injury just as Kevin Pilkington was also injured and was denied the chance of first-team experience.
Notts Co *(From trainee at Plymouth Arg on 3/7/2007) Others 1*

SANDWITH Kevin
Born: Workington, 30 April 1978
Height: 5'11" **Weight:** 13.6
The left-sided defender found opportunities limited at Chester in the first half of last season as Bobby Williamson favoured Laurie Wilson on the left of Chester's back four. Kevin was made available for transfer in December but, after the replacement of Williamson as manager by Simon Davies, was reinstated to the side, initially in a more

attacking left-sided role but later in the centre of midfield. His experience was invaluable at Hereford, where a stunning long-range effort helped spur City to recover from a two-goal deficit and claim a point. Kevin finished the campaign as a regular in the City side that narrowly avoided relegation before being released in the summer.
Carlisle U *(From trainee on 16/7/1996) FL 2+1 (Free to Barrow on 27/9/1998)*
Lincoln C *(Free from Halifax T, ex Telford U, Doncaster Rov, on 12/3/2004) FL 35+5/2 FAC 1 Others 4*
Macclesfield T *(Free on 4/7/2005) FL 34+1/3 FLC 2 Others 5/2*
Chester C *(Free on 24/6/2006) FL 39+15/3 FAC 3 Others 2*

SANKOFA Osei Omari Kwende
Born: Streatham, 19 March 1985
Height: 6'0" **Weight:** 12.4
International Honours: E: Yth
Osei hoped to secure Charlton's right-back spot following Luke Young's departure to Middlesbrough but suffered a thigh injury in pre-season, allowing new signing Yazz Moutaouakil to start the season. When Moutaouakil was injured in turn, Danny Mills arrived on loan and then Greg Halford signed. Osei started in the Carling Cup defeat at Luton in September but apart from a single substitute appearance at West Bromwich in December, did not even make the bench. In January he went to Brentford on loan, initially for a month, but that was soon extended to the end of the season. The centre-back or right-back started well at centre-back alongside Matt Heywood but when Heywood was injured, he lost form and was replaced by another loanee, Alan Bennett. Was released by Charlton at the end of the season.
Charlton Ath *(From trainee on 8/11/2002) P/FL 12+3 FLC 2+2*
Bristol C *(Loaned on 27/9/2005) FL 8 Others 1*
Brentford *(Loaned on 21/1/2008) FL 10+1*

SANTA CRUZ Roque Luis
Born: Ascuncion, Paraguay, 16 August 1981
Height: 6'3" **Weight:** 12.12
International Honours: Paraguay: 59
A man described by Mark Hughes as the best pound-for-pound signing of the close season after his arrival from Bayern Munich, he was a revelation, scoring within three minutes on his debut for Blackburn. Roque scored 23 goals, of all varieties, with head and foot. He is outstanding at working out where the ball will fall loose in dangerous areas and showed at Wigan that he can strike a

long-range shot with the best of them. An outstanding header, his workrate is amazing. He brings the ball under control instantly, holds it due to quick feet and lays it off well. A non-stop runner, he roams both channels and drops back to tackle in defence. Whenever the team was a man short, he was given the challenging role of dropping deep behind the front man, both doing a stint in midfield and getting up to help the front man. To add to his talents he played right-wing in the late season game against Manchester United and was outstanding.
Blackburn Rov *(£3,500,000 from Bayern Munich, Germany, ex Olimpia Ascuncion, on 31/7/2007) PL 36+1/19 FLC 2+1/3 Others 3/1*

SAPPLETON Reneil (Ricky) St Aubin
Born: Jamaica, 8 December 1989
Height: 5'10" **Weight:** 11.13
The highly-rated young Leicester striker was handed an unexpected elevation to the bench during December, making his debut in the home defeat by Southampton. Otherwise, he warmed the bench on odd occasions as his progress was generally monitored at reserve level, where he regularly hit the back of the net.
Leicester C *(From trainee at Queens Park Rgrs on 10/8/2007) FL 0+1*

SAUNDERS Sam Daniel
Born: Greenwich, 29 August 1983
Height: 5'6" **Weight:** 11.4
Club Honours: FC '07
After being part of Dagenham's promotion team the previous season, Sam started the first League game at Stockport. The right-winger scored at Southend in the Johnstone's Paint Trophy with an overhead kick that earned him the club's 'Goal of the Season' award. An ankle injury in November kept him out of the side for a month and a recurrence of the ankle problem in February meant he missed more matches, but he returned for the latter stages of the season.
Dagenham & Redbridge *(Free from Carshalton Ath, ex Welling U, Hastings T, Ashford, on 10/5/2005) FL 21+1 FLC 1 FAC 1 Others 1/1*

SAVAGE Basir (Bas) Mohammed
Born: Wandsworth, 7 January 1982
Height: 6'3" **Weight:** 13.8
Having performed so well in the second half of 2006-07, it was sad that Bas left Brighton under something of a cloud when his contract expired. Although offered new terms, the lanky, eccentric forward preférred to look for other options. Although circumstances at the

Withdean Stadium often necessitated his deployment as a target-man, Bas is at his best as an impact substitute or a wide player but the Brighton fans were still treated to his trademark moonwalk goal celebration on four occasions. Signing for Millwall on a short-term contract in February, Bas made an excellent start to his time at the New Den when coming off the bench and scoring the winner against Yeovil in his second appearance. The tall striker is good in the air, holds up the ball well to bring players into the game and creates chances with his movement.

Reading (£20,000 from Walton & Hersham on 7/2/2002) FL 6+10 FLC 1 FAC 1 (Freed during 2005 close season)

Wycombe W (Loaned on 2/9/2004) FL 2+2 Others 1

Bury (Loaned on 11/2/2005) FL 5

Bristol C (Free from Walton & Hersham, via trial at Coventry C, on 25/11/2005) FL 15+8/1

Gillingham (Free on 28/9/2006) FL 8+6/1 Others 0+1

Brighton & Hove A (Free on 2/2/2007) FL 31+5/9 FLC 0+1 FAC 3 Others 1+1/1

Millwall (Free on 25/2/2008) FL 9+2/2

SAVAGE Robert (Robbie)
William

Born: Wrexham, 18 October 1974
Height: 6'1" **Weight:** 11.11
Club Honours: FAYC '92; FLC '00
International Honours: W: 39; U21-5; Yth; Sch

Returning from a broken leg, Robbie found it difficult to recover form for Blackburn last season. His doubts about the leg were emphasised in the first week of September when he took a whack from Richard Dunne and left the field as early as the 17th minute. Although he was back the following week he never mentally adjusted and by the end of October had lost his place to Aaron Mokoena. Returning to the side in December, his ability to raise the tempo of the game and pressurise the opposition appeared to be waning and, faced with not playing, he accepted a transfer to Derby. Feeling the need for more extrovert players, Paul Jewell signed Robbie in January and made him captain. The snag was that Robbie was short of football and could do little to stop Derby's drift towards relegation. He was so concerned about his early form that he donated part of his wages to one of the club's nominated charities, feeling that he was not giving value for money. Gradually coming to terms with himself, although Derby's inevitable fate was sealed before March was out, Robbie's game in midfield depends on bustling and closing opponents and he is well aware that he faces a tough challenge in the

Championship. In the last home game of the season he returned to Ewood Park with Derby and received a warm welcome as he ran a lap of honour to thank the Rovers' fans.

Manchester U (From trainee on 5/7/1993)

Crewe Alex (Free on 22/7/1994) FL 74+3/10 FLC 5 FAC 5 Others 8/1

Leicester C (£400,000 on 23/7/1997) PL 160+12/8 FLC 15+2 FAC 12/1 Others 2+1

Birmingham C (£2,500,000 on 30/5/2002) PL 82/11 FLC 1/1 FAC 5

Blackburn Rov (£3,100,000 on 9/1/2005) PL 74+2/1 FLC 7 FAC 5+1 Others 10+1/2

Derby Co (£1,500,000 on 9/1/2008) PL 16 FAC 1

SAWYER Gary Dean

Born: Bideford, 5 July 1985
Height: 6'0" **Weight:** 10.8

Gary began last season as first-choice left-back for Plymouth. He is a cultured young defender who is strong in the tackle, good in the air, but also extremely composed on the ball. His left-wing attacking raids were often seen at Home Park and his improved crossing ability created several scoring opportunities. He scored his first senior Plymouth goal in the 4-1 home victory over Colchester in March and will be working to retain his place in Argyle's defence.

Plymouth Arg (From trainee on 8/7/2004) FL 47+6/1 FLC 2 FAC 5+1

SAYNOR Ben Kristian Grant

Born: Leeds, 6 March 1989
Height: 6'0" **Weight:** 12.5

Goalkeeper Ben was given his senior debut by Bradford in a Johnstone's Paint Trophy tie at Doncaster. Although the League Two side was well beaten 5-1, the teenager made several good saves. Was among 13 players released at the end of the season.

Bradford C (From trainee on 4/7/2007) Others 1

SCANNELL Damian

Born: Croydon, 28 April 1985
Height: 5'10" **Weight:** 11.7

Brother of Crystal Palace's Sean, Damian played exceptionally well for Blue Square South side Eastleigh, scoring seven times, before joining Southend in January. A well-built winger with a fair turn of pace, he went straight in as a substitute, replacing Mark Gower in the home game against Yeovil. The step up in conditioning needed for League One occasionally showed and Damian was restricted to short bursts from the bench. He was banned for three games after being sent off for an ill-timed tackle at Millwall in February but with a full

pre-season under his belt, there may be further opportunities.

Southend U (£5,000 from Eastleigh, ex Fisher Ath, on 31/12/2007) FL 0+9

SCANNELL Sean

Born: Croydon, 19 September 1990
Height: 5'9" **Weight:** 11.4
International Honours: RoI: U21-1; Yth

Another Croydon product of the Crystal Palace Academy to be blooded in the first team by Neil Warnock, this highly-rated 17-year-old Republic of Ireland under-21 international was awarded The Irish Examiner 'Junior Sports Award' by Sir Alex Ferguson in February. Having made his debut at Queens Park Rangers as a 60th-minute substitute in December, Sean scored his first League goal against Sheffield Wednesday, a fierce drive in the closing stages, and went on to appear frequently as Palace's wide striker. Extremely fast and able to hold off vigorous challenges, it is no surprise that he is being watched by many leading scouts.

Crystal Palace (From trainee on 6/2/2008) FL 10+13/2 FAC 1 Others 1

SCHARNER Paul

Born: Scheibbs, Austria, 11 March 1980
Height: 6'3" **Weight:** 12.13
International Honours: Austria: 15

Paul had another magnificent season at Wigan, playing a major part in their third campaign in top-flight football. Quick, tough-tackling and strong in the air he produced some solid and determined performances in the first half of the season in midfield, while his drive, enthusiasm, all-out commitment and urgency went a long way in helping the club avoid relegation. On target with five League goals, his best was an acrobatic overhead strike at West Ham. Following the arrival of Steve Bruce, Paul showed his versatility when converting from midfield to centre-half, proving to be an extremely cultured defender. He created a club record by passing Leighton Baines' number of Premier League appearances and deservedly collected Athletic's 'Player of the Year 'award. Having overturned his retirement from international football, it was surprising he was not selected to represent Austria at this summer's European Championship finals.

Wigan Ath (£2,000,000 from SK Brann Bergen, Norway on 6/1/2006) PL 73+5/10 FLC 3+1/1 FAC 3/1

SCHMEICHEL Kasper Peter

Born: Copenhagen, Denmark, 5 November 1986
Height: 6'0" **Weight:** 12.0
International Honours: Denmark: U21; Yth

An injury to Andreas Isaksson at the start of last season gave Kasper the chance to show what he could do on the Premier League stage for Manchester City. The goalkeeper certainly took it, with four clean sheets in his first seven appearances and a penalty save at Arsenal. His fine start at City continued when he signed a new four-year contract in September. At the end of October, in order to get more experience and with Joe Hart in the City goal, Kasper headed to Cardiff on an initial one-month loan deal that was extended until the end of December. The young goalie shone during his time at Ninian Park and quickly became a fans' favourite as he made some outstanding saves. Having arrived back at the City of Manchester Stadium in January and still unable to get a game, the son of the legendary Peter joined Coventry on loan in March, immediately going into the first team and playing all remaining nine games for the Sky Blues. He gave the defence a more solid look and pulled off some excellent saves, especially in the vital home game with Wolves where his handling was excellent as was his shot-stopping. He established himself in the Denmark under-21 side and was named as the 2007 Danish 'Young Sports Personality of the Year'.

Manchester C (From trainee on 9/11/2004) PL 7
Darlington (Loaned on 13/1/2006) FL 4
Bury (Loaned on 23/2/2006) FL 15
Bury (Loaned on 24/8/2006) FL 8
Bury (Loaned on 21/10/2006) FL 6
Falkirk (Loaned on 11/1/2007) SL 15 SLC 1 SC 1
Cardiff C (Loaned on 26/10/2007) FL 14
Coventry C (Loaned on 14/3/2008) FL 9

SCHMITZ Rafael

Born: Blumenau, Brazil, 17 December 1980
Height: 5'11" **Weight:** 11.9
The Brazilian signed for Birmingham on a season-long loan from Lille and proved to be a hardy customer, who was solid and carried a biting tackle. Despite seeming to be on the small side for a central defender, Rafael has a great spring to attack the ball in the air and although unable to hold down the centre-half position, he spent some time filling-in at left-back. After the new manager Alex McLeish left him out from January onwards, Rafael returned to his club in France.
Birmingham C (Loaned from Lille, France, Malutrom, Krylia - loan, on 17/7/2007) PL 12+3 FLC 0+1

SCHOFIELD Daniel (Danny) James

Born: Doncaster, 10 April 1980
Height: 5'10" **Weight:** 11.3
Danny was due to leave Huddersfield at the end of last season after ten years of great service, a combination of personal issues and the need for a fresh challenge leading to the skilful winger requesting a move. A creative midfielder with quick feet and a touch of trickery when running at opposing defences, he was always suited to the out-and-out winger's role rather than the centre of midfield, scoring twice, in the defeat at Southend, and in the final home game, a victory over Walsall. It was a fitting way to say farewell to the home fans.
Huddersfield T (£2,000 from Brodsworth MW on 8/2/1999) FL 205+43/39 FLC 9+1 FAC 13+2/1 Others 16+1/6

SCHOLES Paul

Born: Salford, 16 November 1974
Height: 5'7" **Weight:** 11.10
Club Honours: PL '96, '97, '99, '00, '01, '03, '07, '08; FAC '96, '99, '04; CS '96, '97, '03; UEFACL '08
International Honours: E: 66; Yth (UEFA-U18 '93)
A Manchester United central midfield dynamo whose imaginative distribution makes him the fulcrum of the team, Paul started with a run of ten Premiership outings before sustaining knee ligament damage after turning awkwardly in training the night before the Champions' League clash with Dynamo Kiev in October. Having previously been shortlisted for a place in the National Football Museum 'Hall of Fame' in August, being edged out by former Arsenal striker Dennis Bergkamp, he was determined to prove that his football talents were not yet a museum piece. Described by Sir Bobby Charlton in his recent autobiography as 'the one player still playing who truly epitomises the spirit of Manchester United and what is great about football,' Paul was keen to have more than an early-season strike against Portsmouth as his legacy of the season. Making his long-awaited return as a substitute in United's 3-1 win against Tottenham in the fourth round of the FA Cup, he resumed slowly following his injury before putting in the kind of performances that United fans have become accustomed to. He was 'Man of the Match' in the Premiership battle against Liverpool at Old Trafford in March and produced a similar display in the next game against Aston Villa. While goals are a bit of a rarity, he appeared in his 100th Champions' League match, in the semi-final first leg in Barcelona. His stunning goal in the return at Old Trafford earned the Reds a prized Champions' League final against Chelsea. Already guaranteed a place by Sir Alex Ferguson on that heady night in Moscow, it came full circle for Paul after he missed the 1999 final through suspension.
Manchester U (From trainee on 29/1/1993) PL 328+67/96 FLC 11+5/8 FAC 27+12/12 Others 108+12/23

SCHUMACHER Steven (Steve) Thomas

Born: Liverpool, 30 April 1984
Height: 5'10" **Weight:** 11.0
International Honours: E: Yth
Signed from Bradford in May, the central midfielder started last season as first choice for Crewe before injury compelled him to drop out for a time. Steve returned on a regular basis for Alexandra, never afraid to put his foot in when required. His only goal was a spectacular effort at Swindon.
Everton (From trainee on 12/5/2001)
Carlisle U (Loaned on 31/10/2003) FL 4 FAC 1 Others 1/1
Bradford C (Free on 6/8/2004) FL 110+7/13 FLC 3/1 FAC 7/1 Others 2+1
Crewe Alex (Signed on 29/5/2007) FL 24+2/1 FLC 1 FAC 0+1 Others 1

SCHWARZER Mark

Born: Sydney, Australia, 6 October 1972
Height: 6'5" **Weight:** 13.6
Club Honours: FLC '04
International Honours: Australia: 57; Yth
Mark completed his 12th season at Middlesbrough and, as his contract ended, became a free agent in June. The Australian number-one goalkeeper was offered a one-year extension by Middlesbrough but Mark declined, saying that he wants to play in the 2010 World Cup and needs the security of a two-year club deal. The impasse suggested an exit was on the cards after more than a decade of magnificent service to Middlesbrough. He is established as one of the best 'keepers in the Premiership and can continue to show it. After rumours that the German-speaker was contemplating a move to the Bundesliga, with Bayern Munich the favourites, he agreed to join Fulham.
Bradford C (£350,000 from Kaiserslautern, Germany, ex Blacktown, Marconi, Dynamo Dresden, on 22/11/1996) FL 13 FAC 3
Middlesbrough (£1,500,000 on 26/2/1997) P/FL 367 FLC 26 FAC 32 Others 21

SCIMECA Riccardo (Riccy)

Born: Leamington Spa, 13 June 1975
Height: 6'1" **Weight:** 12.9
Club Honours: FLC '96
International Honours: E: B-1; U21-9

Riccy suffered from injury problems and had four operations during 2006-07. Having started pre-season for Cardiff, he broke down with a groin problem and was unable to play for six months before he finally made his comeback last March. Proved his fitness over the remainder of the season, enough to earn a new one-year contract, but just failed to gain a place in the 16 for Cardiff's FA Cup final appearance against Portsmouth. At his best, Riccy, who can also play at full-back and in the centre of defence, is a commanding midfielder with excellent skills on the ball.

Aston Villa *(From trainee on 7/7/1993) PL 50+23/2 FLC 4+3 FAC 9+1 Others 5+2*
Nottingham F *(£3,000,000 on 23/7/1999) FL 147+4/7 FLC 8/1 FAC 5 Others 2*
Leicester C *(Free on 5/7/2003) PL 28+1/1 FLC 1 FAC 1*
West Bromwich A *(£100,000 on 24/5/2004) PL 29+6 FLC 2+1 FAC 2*
Cardiff C *(Free on 13/1/2006) FL 56+6/6 FAC 2+1*

SCOTLAND Jason Kelvin
Born: Morvant, Trinidad, 18 February 1979
Height: 5'9" **Weight:** 11.9
Club Honours: Div 1 '08
International Honours: Trinidad & Tobago: 28
Signed in the summer from Scottish First Division side St Johnstone, Jason finished Swansea's successful season as their leading League scorer and gained further international honours for Trinidad and Tobago. A difficult front runner to shake off the ball, his close skills and shooting power were highlighted by vital goals in a televised game at the Liberty Stadium against Bristol Rovers. Jason was one of five Swans' players nominated in the PFA League One team of the season.

Dundee U *(Signed from Defence Force, Trinidad & Tobago, ex San Juan Jabloteh, on 16/7/2003) SL 21+29/8 SLC 3+2/1 SC 2+3*
St Johnstone *(Signed on 27/8/2005) SL 65+1/33 SLC 4/4 SC 6/2 Others 5/3*
Swansea C *(Signed on 2/8/2007) FL 43+2/24 FLC 0+2/1 FAC 3+1/2 Others 1+2/2*

SCOTT Paul
Born: Wakefield, 5 November 1979
Height: 5'11" **Weight:** 12.8
As the fans' favourite, Paul showed that he is competent in any role. Although a defender by trade, he was happy to feature in the centre of Bury's midfield for most of the season, leaving the role only briefly to fill in as right-back against Morecambe. Having gained a reputation as a hard-tackling ball winner in midfield, he was thought highly enough of by boss

Chris Casper to be made captain when Dave Challinor was sidelined. News that he signed a two-and-a-half-year contract extension in December came as a relief to supporters and was followed by him receiving the 'Player of the Season' award.
Huddersfield T *(From trainee on 3/7/1998) FL 18+14/2 FLC 1+1 FAC 1 Others 1+1*
Bury *(Free on 20/8/2004) FL 145+5/10 FLC 5 FAC 10+1/2 Others 3+1/1*

SCOWCROFT James Benjamin
Born: Bury St Edmunds, 15 November 1975
Height: 6'1" **Weight:** 12.2
International Honours: E: U21-5

An experienced Crystal Palace striker, at his best when holding up play, James scored a hat-trick on the opening day of last season at Southampton and had a spell of three goals in five games over the Christmas period. A player who can adapt to differing roles to meet the team's immediate requirements, James went on to score the 100th goal of his career, against Barnsley in March.
Ipswich T *(From trainee on 1/7/1994) P/FL 163+39/47 FLC 21+4/7 FAC 9+1 Others 7+3/1*
Leicester C *(£3,000,000 on 31/7/2001) P/FL 127+6/24 FLC 6+1/1 FAC 7/3*
Ipswich T *(Loaned on 15/2/2005) FL 3+6*

James Scowcroft

Coventry C (Free on 11/7/2005) FL 37+4/3 FLC 0+1 FAC 3
Crystal Palace (£500,000 on 27/7/2006) FL 61+12/14 FAC 2 Others 0+1

SEANLA Stephane **Claude**

Born: Abidjan, Ivory Coast, 2 June 1988
Height: 5'9" **Weight:** 11.11
The young midfielder arrived at Barnet after leaving Kettering at the end of 2006-07 and did enough in pre-season to gain a contract but his first-team opportunities were limited. Claude started one League game and made two further substitute appearances before having loan spells with St Albans and Wivenhoe. Was released by Barnet at the beginning of April.
Watford (From trainee on 26/6/2006) FLC 0+1(Freed on 2/2/2007)
Barnet (Free from Kettering T on 8/8/2007) FL 1+2 FLC 0+1 Others 0+1

SEARS Frederick (Freddie)
David

Born: Hornchurch, 27 November 1989
Height: 5'8" **Weight:** 10.1
International Honours: E: Yth
Freddie, an 18-year-old youth-team player, burst on the scene for West Ham last season when he made his debut as a substitute in the home game against Blackburn. Five minutes later, he took a pass from Dean Ashton, saw his shot saved but was on hand to head in the rebound. Freddie was a breath of fresh air in West Ham's attack as his pace and awareness in front of the goal caused problems for the Rovers' defence. The following week at Everton, again as a substitute, he gave the side a lift and was unlucky to hit a post in the last minute. A bright future is predicted as he joins the many stars produced by the West Ham Academy.
West Ham U (From trainee on 11/7/2007) PL 1+6/1

SECK Mamadou

Born: Rufisque, Senegal, 23 August 1979
Height: 6'4" **Weight:** 12.13
International Honours: Senegal: 6
Sheffield United centre-half Mamadou made the switch on loan to Championship rivals Scunthorpe at the start of January to provide some defensive cover. He made only a fleeting five-minute appearance as a substitute for the Iron, when he was thrown on up front as they chased an equaliser at Southampton, before a back injury kept him sidelined.
Sheffield U (Free from Le Havre, France, ex Toulouse, Nimes, AC Ajaccio, Erciyesspor, on 18/1/2007)
Scunthorpe U (Loaned on 1/1/2008) FL 0+1

SEDGWICK Christopher (Chris) Edward

Born: Sheffield, 28 April 1980
Height: 5'11" **Weight:** 10.10
A fine example for any young professional, Chris acts as the workhorse in the Preston team and missed a place in the first-team squad just once all season. No longer possessing the pace of his earlier career, Chris continues to work tirelessly on the right wing and in his occasional central-midfield role. Although not the strongest of tacklers, he makes a real nuisance of himself and provides excellent cover for his full-back. An infrequent scorer, both his goals came before the turn of the year and included an even rarer header in the home rout of Southampton.
Rotherham U (From trainee on 16/8/1997) FL 195+48/17 FLC 10+2/3 FAC 8+5 Others 2+2/1
Preston NE (£300,000 on 23/11/2004) FL 144+11/10 FLC 2+1 FAC 10/1 Others 3+1

SEIP Marcel

Born: Winschoten, Holland, 5 April 1982
Height: 6'0" **Weight:** 13.3
Marcel is a tough-tackling Plymouth centre-back who is a superb reader of the game. He forged an excellent central defensive partnership with Krisztian Timar and was one of the main reasons why Argyle had a good defensive record. Marcel scored his only goal against Stoke at the Britannia Stadium in September. An aggravating groin injury towards the end of the campaign interrupted his progress in the team and it was agreed that a hernia operation be completed at the end of the season. Marcel's future at the club remains uncertain as the Dutch defender was put on the transfer list after a disagreement with manager Paul Sturrock.
Plymouth Arg (Free from SC Heerenveen, Holland, ex BV Veendam, on 31/8/2006) FL 68+3/3 FLC 3 FAC 6

SEMEDO Jose Victor Moreira

Born: Setubal, Portugal, 11 January 1985
Height: 6'0" **Weight:** 12.8
International Honours: Portugal: U21-5
Signed from Sporting Lisbon in the summer, Jose was extremely versatile, able to play at right-back, central defence or in midfield. He made his Charlton debut in midfield in the opening game and kept his place until early December when Matt Holland returned after injury. Even then, Jose was a regular on the substitutes' bench and missed only four League games all season, one through suspension after two yellow cards at Southampton. Jose was generally used

in central midfield, although he did deputise at right-back and started two games there. Comfortable on the ball and strong in the tackle, he looks well suited to a defensive midfield role and shows creativity with his passing.
Charlton Ath (Free from Sporting Lisbon, Portugal, ex Casa Pia, Fereinse, Cagliari - all loan spells from Sporting Lisbon, on 9/8/2007) FL 28+9 FLC 2

SENDA Daniel (Danny) Luke

Born: Harrow, 17 April 1981
Height: 5'10" **Weight:** 10.0
International Honours: E: Yth
Danny settled comfortably into Millwall's right-back position, his attacking prowess putting many a defence under pressure with penetrating runs and quality crosses. The versatile player has yet to score for the Lions but his time will come, especially with his positive attitude towards shooting. He reads the game well and it is hoped that he will sign an extension to his contract.
Wycombe W (From juniors at Southampton on 26/1/1999) FL 217+59/9 FLC 6+3 FAC 10+3 Others 14+4
Millwall (Free on 31/8/2006) FL 73+3/1 FLC 1 FAC 7 Others 2+1

SENDEROS Philippe

Born: Geneva, Switzerland, 14 February 1985
Height: 6'1" **Weight:** 13.10
Club Honours: FAC '05
International Honours: Switzerland: 31; U21; Yth
The Swiss defender once more played out a season in which there were more questions than answers about his ability to become a first-choice central defensive option for Arsenal. He still appears to be more suited to the slower and more deliberate pace of the Champions' League and is more convincing in that competition than in domestic games. Philippe was a key man in co-hosts Switzerland's squad for Euro 2008.
Arsenal (£2,500,000 from Servette, Switzerland on 18/7/2003) PL 54+10/4 FLC 16 FAC 14+1 Others 19+1

SEOL Ki-Hyeon

Born: Seoul, South Korea, 8 January 1979
Height: 6'0" **Weight:** 11.7
International Honours: South Korea: 77
Ki-Hyeon travelled with the Reading squad to his home country, Korea, for the pre-season Peace Cup tournament and played in the first three Premiership games of the campaign. It soon became apparent that he was unable to recapture his form of the previous campaign and with Reading in need of cover at

right-back the Korean international was involved in a straight swap for Fulham's Liam Rosenior. A rare starter at Fulham, he was more often used as a late substitute in the first part of the campaign, usually as a wide player, but occasionally in a more direct forward role. His pace can unsettle opposing defences but he did not feature after the FA Cup replay against Bristol Rovers in January and returned to the reserves. Ki-Hyeon continued to represent South Korea, including an appearance against North Korea in March.

Wolverhampton W (Signed from Anderlecht, Belgium on 1/9/2004) FL 50+19/ 8 FLC 3/1 FAC 4/1
Reading (£1,000,000 + on 12/7/2006) PL 24+6/4 FAC 4
Fulham (Signed on 31/8/2007) PL 4+8 FLC 1 FAC 0+2

SHACKELL Jason Philip
Born: Stevenage, 27 August 1983
Height: 5'11" **Weight:** 11.9
This product of Norwich's Academy system produced some excellent defensive displays as the Canaries fought successfully to avoid the drop to League One. An imposing figure, he is particularly strong in the air and forceful in the tackle, never shirking a challenge or afraid to put his body on the line to prevent a scoring opportunity. With greater experience has come the confidence to be more constructive with the ball at his feet and he is now prepared to pick a pass rather than just clear his lines. He poses a real threat at set-piece situations but is not yet a regular contributor of goals, something he intends to improve.
Norwich C (From trainee on 28/1/2003) P/FL 111+7/3 FLC 7 FAC 4

SHAKES Ricky Ulric
Born: Brixton, 26 January 1985
Height: 5'10" **Weight:** 12.0
International Honours: Trinidad & Tobago: 1
An outside-right with speed and a great work ethic, Ricky joined Brentford on the final day of the August transfer window, having been unattached since leaving Swindon in the summer. He scored as a substitute the following day at Bury, where he was once on loan, and hit the net at Swindon in the Johnstone's Paint Trophy a few days later. Ricky was a regular for the rest of the season, having his contract extended twice. He scored two against Wrexham in March and endeared himself to the Brentford crowd with his effort and non-stop running.
Bolton W (From trainee on 1/7/2004) FLC 1

FAC 0+1/1
Bristol Rov (Loaned on 15/2/2005) FL 0+1 Others 0+1
Bury (Loaned on 24/3/2005) FL 4+3/2
Swindon T (Free on 5/8/2005) FL 52+17/5 FLC 2 FAC 4+1 Others 1
Brentford (Free on 31/8/2007) FL 25+14/3 FAC 1+1 Others 1/1

SHARP William (Billy) Louis
Born: Sheffield, 5 February 1986
Height: 5'8" **Weight:** 12.2
Club Honours: Div 1 '07
Billy, a Sheffield United supporter, returned to Bramall Lane from Scunthorpe in the summer on a four-year deal, to the universal delight of fans. For much of the season, he vied with Jon Stead to play alongside James Beattie and although he scored in the Carling Cup, his first League goal did not arrive until March. He retained the support of the fans and after Kevin Blackwell's arrival Billy was ever-present, playing in a more forward role. Working hard, he was a threat in the penalty area and, being difficult to knock off the ball, earned two penalties. Billy was the supporters' 'Young Player of the Year'.
Sheffield U (From trainee on 7/7/2004) FL 0+2
Rushden & Diamonds (Loaned on 21/1/2005) FL 16/9
Scunthorpe U (£100,000 on 18/8/2005) FL 80+2/53 FLC 4/1 FAC 7/1 Others 1+1/1
Sheffield U (£2,000,000 on 7/8/2007) FL 21+8/4 FLC 3/2 FAC 2+2

SHARPS Ian William
Born: Warrington, 23 October 1980
Height: 6'4" **Weight:** 13.8
A strong and powerful Rotherham central defender, Ian's sound partnership with Graham Coughlan played a prominent part in the team's success in the first half of the season. Always willing to join the attack in dead-ball situations, he might well have scored more goals but his presence helped to create several for those around him. Ian missed the end of the season with a hernia problem.
Tranmere Rov (From trainee on 5/7/1999) FL 163+7/6 FLC 7/1 FAC 7 Others 9
Rotherham U (Free on 3/8/2006) FL 71/4 FLC 3/1 FAC 2+1 Others 3/1

SHAW Richard Edward
Born: Brentford, 11 September 1968
Height: 5'9" **Weight:** 12.8
Club Honours: FMC '91; Div 1 '94
The experienced defender started the season in fine form for Millwall before an injury sidelined him. During the autumn he took over as caretaker manager until

the club could find the right man and acquitted himself well. His experience and knowledge really helped the team. When Kenny Jackett came in, Richard found it hard to win a first-team place on a regular basis, but was still knocking at the door prior to being released in the summer.
Crystal Palace (From apprentice on 4/9/1986) P/FL 193+14/3 FLC 28+2 FAC 18 Others 12+1
Hull C (Loaned on 14/12/1989) FL 4
Coventry C (£1,000,000 on 17/11/1995) P/FL 296+21/1 FLC 21+2 FAC 21+1
Millwall (Free on 30/6/2006) FL 57+2 FLC 1 FAC 4 Others 1

SHAWCROSS Ryan James
Born: Buckley, 4 October 1987
Height: 6'0" **Weight:** 12.0
International Honours: E: U21-2
Ryan, a young Manchester United central defender, moved to the Potteries on loan just before the start of the season and scored Stoke's winner at Cardiff in the first match. Strong in the air and a good tackler, Ryan made his mark, continued to impress and signed full-time in the January transfer window. His partnership with Leon Cort was one of the most important for Stoke in their promotion season, especially as they scored 16 goals between them. Ryan was selected as 'Young Player of the Year' by the supporters.
Manchester U (From trainee on 6/7/2006) FLC 0+2
Stoke C (£1,000,000 + on 9/8/2007) FL 39+2/7 FLC 1/1 FAC 2

SHAWKY Mohamed Ali Abu El Yazid
Born: Port Said, Egypt, 5 October 1981
Height: 6'0" **Weight:** 11.11
International Honours: Egypt: 48
Signed from Al-Ahly last August, the Egyptian international midfielder made his first appearance for Middlesbrough in a 2-0 Carling Cup defeat at Tottenham. Mohamed started but was replaced at half-time, when the score was 0-0, by Tom Craddock. His Premiership debut at Portsmouth in late December was a winning one and Mohamed was a key member of the Egyptian squad that successfully defended their African Cup of Nations title in Ghana in February. He returned with a back injury that caused him to miss the final games of Middlesbrough's season and could even threaten his involvement in Egypt's opening 2010 World Cup qualifying matches.
Middlesbrough (£650,000 from Al-Ahly, Egypt, ex Al-Masry, on 31/8/2007) PL 3+2 FLC 1

SHEARER Scott
Born: Glasgow, 15 February 1981
Height: 6'3" **Weight:** 14.8
International Honours: S: B-1
Released last summer by Bristol Rovers, Wycombe signed the tall goalkeeper on a three-year contract. After playing in the first five games of the season, Scott was dropped in favour of Jamie Young and, shortly afterwards, had the misfortune to suffer a broken ankle in training at the end of September, thus missing the rest of the season. He returned to training in spring and should be fit for the start of the coming campaign.
Albion Rov (Signed from Tower Hearts on 6/7/2000) SL 47+2/1 SLC 1 SC 2 Others 1
Coventry C (Signed on 7/7/2003) FL 37+1 FLC 3
Rushden & Diamonds (Loaned on 18/2/2005) FL 3
Rushden & Diamonds (Loaned on 10/3/2005) FL 10
Bristol Rov (Free on 29/7/2005) FL 47 FLC 1 FAC 3 Others 2
Shrewsbury T (Loaned on 25/10/2006) FL 20 FAC 2 Others 2
Wycombe W (Free on 3/7/2007) FL 4+1 FLC 1

SHEEHAN Alan Michael Anthony
Born: Athlone, 14 September 1986
Height: 5'10" **Weight:** 11.2
International Honours: RoI: U21-5; Yth
An up-and-coming left-back or midfield player, Alan was in competition with Joe Mattock during the first half of Leicester's campaign. Scored his first Foxes' goal with a well-struck free kick against then leaders Watford and regularly supplied a stream of whipped in corners. He appeared to fall out of favour with Ian Holloway and was allowed to join Leeds on loan in January to further enhance his experience. Alan had an eventful time at Leeds, who signed him to fill the problem position. He was the sixth player to be tried at left-back and struggled at first, being dropped after four games from which the club took only three points. United then signed another left-back on loan, Stephen O'Halloran from Aston Villa, but he was seriously injured during the warm-up before his debut at Swindon and forced to return to Villa Park. Alan had to wait four games before his recall, putting in a strong display in the 2-0 win over Walsall and scoring the winner at Doncaster with a superbly struck free kick. Just as he looked settled at Elland Road, he was sent off for a two-footed tackle at Yeovil when Leeds won to seal their League One play-off place. That ruled Alan out of the final League game and

both play-off semi-finals against Carlisle, but he was on the bench at Wembley.
Leicester C (From trainee on 24/9/2004) FL 20+3/1 FLC 4+1/1 FAC 1
Mansfield T (Loaned on 8/9/2006) FL 9+1 Others 1
Leeds U (Loaned on 31/1/2008) FL 10/1

SHELTON Luton
Born: Kingston, Jamaica, 11 November 1985
Height: 5'11" **Weight:** 11.11
International Honours: Jamaica: 27
Fast and tricky, although not always at his best, many of Luton's appearances for Sheffield United were from the bench. He scored with a well-taken goal at Colchester and claimed the first against Manchester City in the FA Cup, when the ball was deflected off a balloon. His brace against Morecambe meant he scored in all three competitions. Partly through injury he played little after the arrival of Kevin Blackwell. Luton continued to represent Jamaica and played for a FIFA XI against a China/Hong Kong side in July 2007.
Sheffield U (£1,850,000 from Helsingborgs, Sweden, ex Harbour View, on 24/11/2007) P/FL 7+12/1 FLC 1+2/2 FAC 2+1/1

SHELVEY Jonjo
Born: Romford, 27 February 1992
Height: 6'1" **Weight:** 11.2
International Honours: E: Yth
Jonjo became Charlton's youngest-ever player, beating Paul Konchesky's record, when he made his debut at the age of 16 years 59 days against Barnsley at Oakwell last April. It was an incredible achievement for a player who was in the under-16 side at the start of the season. He kept his place for the final game against Coventry at the Valley and looks to have a good future. An influential midfielder, he loves to get forward and always wants the ball. He has a powerful shot and is not afraid to have a go from long range. Jonjo is tall, looks older than he is and has bags of confidence for one so young, with ability to match. He has already captained England at under-16 level.
Charlton Ath (Associated Schoolboy) FL 2

SHERINGHAM Edward (Teddy) Paul
Born: Highams Park, 2 April 1966
Height: 5'11" **Weight:** 12.5
Club Honours: Div 2 '88; FMC '92; CS '97; PL '99, '00, '01; FAC '99; EC '99
International Honours: E: 51; U21-1; Yth
Former England star Teddy became the most high-profile signing in Colchester's

history when he arrived at Layer Road from West Ham in a blaze of publicity last summer. It all began so well for the veteran striker. He scored two goals in his first three appearances, in the 2-2 draw against Barnsley and the 3-0 win at Preston, but managed only one more League goal, albeit a dramatic first-minute effort in the 2-1 success at Sheffield Wednesday in December. He was hampered by a foot problem that restricted him to only a handful of appearances in the last four months before being released in the summer.
Millwall (From apprentice on 19/1/1984) FL 205+15/93 FLC 16+1/8 FAC 12/5 Others 12+1/5
Aldershot (Loaned on 1/2/1985) FL 4+1 Others 1
Nottingham F (£2,000,000 on 23/7/1991) P/FL 42/14 FLC 10/5 FAC 4/2 Others 6/2
Tottenham H (£2,100,000 on 28/8/1992) PL 163+3/75 FLC 14/10 FAC 17/13
Manchester U (£3,500,000 on 1/7/1997) PL 73+31/31 FLC 1/1 FAC 4+5/5 Others 23+16/9
Tottenham H (Free on 16/7/2001) PL 67+3/22 FLC 6+1/3 FAC 3/1
Portsmouth (Free on 2/7/2003) PL 25+7/9 FLC 3 FAC 2+1/1
West Ham U (Free on 30/7/2004) P/FL 45+31/28 FLC 1+2 FAC 3+4/2 Others 0+1
Colchester U (Free on 17/7/2007) FL 11+8/3 FAC 1/1

SHEVCHENKO Andrei Mykolayovich
Born: Dvirkivshchyna, Ukraine, 29 August 1976
Height: 6'0" **Weight:** 11.5
Club Honours: FLC '07
International Honours: Ukraine: 80
Revered as one of the world's best-ever strikers, it cannot be said that Andrei does not put 100 per cent into his Chelsea career and he even went so far as having private lessons with Olympic gold medallist Darren Campbell to help with his pace. There were moments when his obvious class shone through, a left-footed screamer against Leicester in the Carling Cup when the Blues looked to be heading for a shock exit and two great goals against Aston Villa on Boxing Day to maintain the long unbeaten home record. Sadly, this was Sheva's last start of the season as Chelsea invested heavily in Nicolas Anelka during the January window, further reducing the Ukrainian's chances. From then on, he was reduced to sporadic substitute appearances and in the last of these, scored the Blues' final Premier League goal of the season as they strove valiantly to overhaul Manchester United. A last-minute goal-line clearance against the same opposition two weeks

earlier secured a famous victory for Chelsea and kept alive the most exciting title race since the inception of the Premier League. Andrei's omission from the Champions' League final, a stage he had graced so nobly in the past, must have been a bitter blow. Throughout the season, his former club AC Milan made statements that they would welcome back their prodigal son with open arms but Andrei remained a Chelsea player.
Chelsea *(£30,800,000 from AC Milan, Italy, ex Dynamo Kiev, on 4/7/2006) PL 30+17/9 FLC 6/5 FAC 5+2/3 Others 12+4/5*

SHIMMIN Dominic Edward
Born: Bermondsey, 13 October 1987
Height: 6'0" **Weight:** 12.6
The central defender joined Bournemouth on loan from Queens Park Rangers in December when he appeared to be on the verge of a release from Loftus Road. After two appearances for the Cherries, it was announced that he had left the club. Dominic later emerged at Crawley. A forceful left-sided defender, who is strong in the tackle, much of his time in football has been spent recovering from injury.
Queens Park Rgrs *(From trainee at Arsenal on 24/3/2005) FL 2+1 FLC 1*
Bournemouth *(Loaned on 22/11/2007) FL 1+1*

SHITTU Daniel (Danny)
Olusola
Born: Lagos, Nigeria, 2 September 1980
Height: 6'3" **Weight:** 16.0
International Honours: Nigeria: 12
Watford's giant centre-half and occasional centre-forward had an excellent season at both ends of the pitch in 2007-08. Commanding in defence, he also posed a considerable threat in opposing penalty areas and finished with nine goals, making him the Hornets' third-highest scorer. In January, Danny scored two headed goals to win the FA Cup third round tie against Crystal Palace before leaving to represent Nigeria in the African Cup of Nations, in which his team reached the semi-finals. On his return, he picked up where he left off and his powerful and athletic performances led to him being named in the PFA 'Championship Select' 'Team of the Year' and among the top-ten best players outside the Premiership. He was also inducted into the 'Show Racism the Red Card' Hall of Fame. An engaging character off the pitch, Danny runs his own football youth academy and is something of a computer expert.
Charlton Ath *(Free from Carshalton Ath on 15/9/1999)*
Blackpool *(Loaned on 16/2/2001) FL 15+2/2*

Nicky Shorey

Others 2
Queens Park Rgrs *(£250,000 on 23/10/ 2001) FL 166+3/17 FLC 5 FAC 3 Others 5*
Watford *(£1,600,000 on 7/8/2006) P/FL 64+5/8 FLC 2/1 FAC 3/2 Others 1*

SHOREY Nicholas (Nicky)
Born: Romford, 19 February 1981
Height: 5'9" **Weight:** 10.10
Club Honours: Ch '06
International Honours: E: 2; B-1
Nicky became the first Reading player to represent England at full international level for over 100 years when he won caps against Brazil and Germany in the summer of 2007. He was called up for further national training camps, even postponing his honeymoon to do so on one occasion, without increasing his total of England appearances, so concentrated on the task of helping his club retain its place in the Premiership. He was a model of consistency at left-back, missing only two matches and scoring twice, at home to Arsenal and at Aston Villa. An outstanding crosser of the ball and extremely effective from dead-ball situations, Nicky is just four games short of reaching 300 for the Royals. Reading would love to retain his services but there

was intense speculation in the media at the end of the season that he might move on to a Premiership club following relegation.

Leyton Orient *(From trainee on 5/7/1999)* FL 12+3 FAC 1

Reading *(£25,000 on 9/2/2001)* P/FL 267/12 FLC 12 FAC 13 Others 4

SHOWUNMI Enoch Olusesan

Born: Kilburn, 21 April 1982
Height: 6'3" **Weight:** 14.10
Club Honours: Div 1 '05
International Honours: Nigeria: 2

Many at Bristol City expect more from this tall, well-built forward, given his physical attributes, but Enoch rarely seemed to use his size and weight to advantage and perhaps needs a bit more devil. After appearing in City's early games, he was loaned to Sheffield Wednesday in the New Year. Wednesday wanted Enoch to help out in a striker shortage at Hillsborough but despite his best endeavours he could not notch a goal for the team. Although he played with a lot of enthusiasm he was unfortunate in front of goal. Back at Ashton Gate, he made a couple of substitute appearances as the season neared its end before being released.

Luton T *(Signed from Willesden Constantine on 5/9/2003)* FL 40+62/14 FLC 1+1/1 FAC 2+4 Others 3+1/1

Bristol C *(Free on 4/7/2006)* FL 38+12/13 FLC 2 FAC 5+1/3 Others 3/2

Sheffield Wed *(Loaned on 31/1/2008)* FL 6+4

SHUKER Christopher (Chris) Alan

Born: Liverpool, 9 May 1982
Height: 5'5" **Weight:** 10.1

A cheeky, talented right-winger with boyish enthusiasm, Chris continued to create chances for the Tranmere forwards and helped Rovers to an unbeaten ten-game League run early in the campaign. As the season wore on it became clear that a niggling thigh injury was starting to hamper Chris's ability to run past defenders and deliver his trademark crosses but he soldiered on until Boxing Day, when a challenge in the home game against Carlisle sidelined him for three months, the longest lay-off in his career. He recovered more quickly than expected as surgery revealed cartilage rather than the suspected cruciate ligament damage and made a comeback in the last six weeks of the season. Off the field, Chris is a keen horseman, and regaining his usual speed and sharpness will be his priority before next term.

Manchester C *(From trainee on 21/9/1999)*

P/FL 1+4 FLC 0+1/1

Macclesfield T *(Loaned on 27/3/2001)* FL 6+3/1

Walsall *(Loaned on 26/2/2003)* FL 3+2

Rochdale *(Loaned on 7/8/2003)* FL 14/1 FLC 1

Hartlepool U *(Loaned on 13/12/2003)* FL 14/1 FAC 1

Barnsley *(Signed on 17/3/2004)* FL 93+7/17 FLC 4/1 FAC 6 Others 2+2

Tranmere Rov *(Free on 17/7/2006)* FL 67+2/9 FLC 2 FAC 3 Others 3/1

SIBIERSKI Antoine

Born: Lille, France, 5 August 1974
Height: 6'2" **Weight:** 12.8
International Honours: France: B-1; U21

Signed by Wigan from Newcastle at the start of last season, Antoine made an immediate impact when scoring after coming off the bench on his debut at Everton. Tall and good in the air, he kept the game simple to eliminate errors and became popular with the crowd because of his commitment and wholehearted approach. One of only a handful of players to score on his Latics' Premier League debut, he created a club record by scoring in three consecutive games at the start of the campaign. His best goal, a volley on the turn in the FA Cup match against Chelsea, was voted the 'Goal of the Season' by supporters. Playing mainly up front, but occasionally as an attacking midfielder, Antoine struggled with injuries in the second half of the season and was restricted to a handful of substitute appearances.

Manchester C *(£700,000 from Lens, France, ex Lille OSC, Auxerre, Nantes, on 7/8/2003)* PL 64+28/11 FLC 3+1/2 FAC 6+4/1 Others 1/1

Newcastle U *(£2,000,000 on 31/8/2006)* PL 14+12/3 FLC 1+1/1 FAC 2 Others 8+1/4

Wigan Ath *(Free on 5/6/2007)* PL 10+20/4 FAC 1+1/1

SIDIBE Mamady (Mama)

Born: Bamoko, Mali, 18 December 1979
Height: 6'4" **Weight:** 12.4
International Honours: Mali: 8

Although his scoring record is not the best, only four goals all season, Mama's contribution to Stoke cannot be underestimated. A powerful, strong runner up front his link-up play with Ricardo Fuller was one of the reasons for their success. He was severely set back when caught up in an after-match riot in Togo, having played for Mali in the Africa Cup of Nations qualifiers. Mama was thrown through a window and needed a frightening number of stitches in a gashed arm. At one point, he was in danger of dying but came back to help

Stoke to promotion.

Swansea C *(Free from CA Paris, France, ex Racing Club Paris, on 27/7/2001)* FL 26+5/7 FLC 0+1 FAC 2/1 Others 1

Gillingham *(Free on 9/8/2002)* FL 80+26/10 FLC 4+1/1 FAC 3+1/2

Stoke C *(Free on 5/7/2005)* FL 112+8/19 FLC 3 FAC 7/1

SIDWELL Steven (Steve) James

Born: Wandsworth, 14 December 1982
Height: 5'10" **Weight:** 11.2
Club Honours: FAYC '00, '01; Ch '06
International Honours: E: U21-5; Yth

One of the most thankless tasks for a midfielder is to join a club with a host of world-class players ahead in the battle for a regular place; a fate that befell Steve when he joined Chelsea on a Bosman free in July. Steve took a calculated gamble to run down his Reading contract and secure a move to a club involved in European competition. A hard-running, tough-tackling midfielder who, despite his limited opportunities in Chelsea's star-studded midfield, proved a valuable member of the squad, particularly when African Cup of Nations demands and an injury crisis stretched personnel either side of the New Year. During this period he scored his first Chelsea goal with a rasping drive in the Carling Cup tie at Hull. But when Michael Essien and John Obi Mikel returned from Ghana and Claude Makelele, Michael Ballack and Frank Lampard recovered from injuries, his run came to an end. Steve's last appearance was at the end of January against his old club Reading. Obviously, with Steve sitting in the stands for Chelsea matches, the rumour mill swung into action with Premier League rivals keen to give him a regular berth. He is too good not to be playing week-in, week-out.

Arsenal *(From trainee on 2/7/2001)*

Brentford *(Loaned on 23/10/2001)* FL 29+1/4 FAC 2 Others 3

Brighton & Hove A *(Loaned on 9/11/2002)* FL 11+1/5

Reading *(£250,000 on 21/1/2003)* P/FL 164+4/29 FLC 7/1 FAC 9+1 Others 2

Chelsea *(Free on 3/7/2007)* PL 7+8 FLC 3+2/1 FAC 3 Others 0+2

SILK Gary Lee

Born: Newport, Isle of Wight, 13 September 1984
Height: 5'9" **Weight:** 13.7

Involved in half Notts County's League games, Gary became a versatile member of the squad in 2007-08. He began life at County as an orthodox right-back with a desire to drive forward down the flank

as often as possible, but is one of those prepared to turn his hand to anything the manager required. Was released in the summer.

Portsmouth (From trainee on 6/1/2004)
Wycombe W (Loaned on 6/7/2004) FL 19+3 FLC 1 FAC 2 Others 3
Boston U (Loaned on 13/1/2006) FL 11+3
Notts Co (Free on 12/7/2006) FL 46+17/2 FLC 4+1 FAC 3 Others 2

SILVESTRE Mikael Samy
Born: Chambray-les-Tours, France, 9 August 1977
Height: 6'0" **Weight:** 13.1
Club Honours: PL '00, '01, '03, '07; CS '03, '07; FAC '04; FLC '06; UEFACL '08
International Honours: France: 40; U21; Yth (UEFA-U18 '96)
As a stylish Manchester United defender, who keeps a cool head under pressure, Mikael was all set to battle Patrice Evra for the left-back position after the sudden and unexpected departure of Gabriel Heinze to Real Madrid in the close season. In September, however, he was stretchered off with knee-ligament damage during the Premiership match against Everton and the verdict was that he was out for the rest of the season. Sir Alex Ferguson remained hopeful that he would be back by March and that prediction came true when Mikael made his comeback in the 4-1 reserves win over Manchester City. With no undue effects from the injury, he played in the Champions' League quarter-final against AS Roma in April and in the battle between the Premiership's top two at Chelsea.
Manchester U (£4,000,000 from Inter Milan, Italy on 10/9/1999) PL 225+24/6 FLC 13+1 FAC 19+2/1 Others 69+8/3

SIMEK Franklin (Frank)
Michael
Born: St Louis, Missouri, USA, 13 October 1984
Height: 6'0" **Weight:** 11.6
International Honours: USA: 5; Yth
Showing real consistency and accomplished play as an attacking right-back, Frank was one of the brightest spots in Sheffield Wednesday's struggles. He retained his place in the United States team and was rumoured to be interesting several Premiership sides. However, he injured an ankle when he landed awkwardly at Crystal Palace in December and was eventually forced to have an operation. Frank was ruled out for the remainder of the season after a few minutes in a reserve match, when his ankle gave way again.
Arsenal (From trainee on 1/7/2002) FLC 1

Queens Park Rgrs (Loaned on 19/10/2004) FL 5
Bournemouth (Loaned on 24/3/2005) FL 8
Sheffield Wed (Free on 3/8/2005) FL 100+1/2 FLC 5 FAC 3

SIMMONDS Donovan
Ashton
Born: Walthamstow, 12 October 1988
Height: 6'0" **Weight:** 11.7
A young and speedy attacking midfield player, Donovan joined Coventry during last summer. Before that, he was at Charlton as a scholar and impressed the City manager by scoring twice in a trial against Nuneaton. In order to further his experience, Coventry loaned him out in March to Gillingham, where he was used mainly as substitute. A regular scorer in Coventry's reserve side, he is a youngster who has overcome early injuries as he seeks a career in football.
Coventry C (From trainee at West Ham U on 1/7/2007)
Gillingham (Loaned on 27/3/2008) FL 0+3

SIMMONS Paris Michael
Born: Lewisham, 2 January 1990
Height: 5'10" **Weight:** 11.12
After a torrid season in the Derby reserves, who, like the first team, won only one match, Paris earned a first taste of Premiership action as a substitute in the final game. The young striker is an Academy product and rated as one of their brighter prospects for the future.
Derby Co (Trainee) PL 0+1

SIMONSEN Steven (Steve)
Preben Arthur
Born: South Shields, 3 April 1979
Height: 6'3" **Weight:** 13.2
International Honours: E: U21-4; Yth
The experienced goalkeeper was on his way to a record number of consecutive appearances for Stoke when manager Tony Pulis decided he needed a challenge to his place in the side. Carlo Nash was signed on an emergency loan and went straight into the team for the last ten games of the season. A competent

Steve Simonsen

'keeper and a good shot-stopper, Steve never complained about being dropped to the bench and his time will surely come again.

Tranmere Rov (From trainee on 9/10/1996) FL 35 FLC 4 FAC 3
Everton (£3,300,000 on 23/9/1998) PL 28+2 FLC 2 FAC 5
Stoke C (Free on 6/8/2004) FL 155+3 FLC 3 FAC 9

SIMPSON Daniel (Danny)
Peter
Born: Eccles, 4 January 1987
Height: 5'8" **Weight:** 11.10
Club Honours: Ch '07
A young, locally born Manchester United defender, Danny made his first appearance of the season in the 2-0 Carling Cup defeat by Coventry in September. Soon after this, he made his Premiership bow against Wigan at Old Trafford as a 30th-minute substitute for the injured John O'Shea, setting up the fourth goal with a well-flighted cross for Wayne Rooney. His Champions' League debut also came in October, as a substitute against Dynamo Kiev, and his first European start was in the reverse fixture against Dynamo the following month. Danny, who signed a new three-year contract with United in August 2007, went on loan to Ipswich in March, making his debut for Town as a substitute at Scunthorpe, playing in midfield. His first start the following week against Queens Park Rangers was at right-back, a position he kept for the rest of the season. An attacking full-back, he loves getting forward and links well with the front players.
Manchester U (From trainee on 10/1/2006) PL 1+2 FLC 1 FAC 0+1 Others 2+1
Sunderland (Loaned on 29/1/2007) FL 13+1
Ipswich T (Loaned on 21/3/2008) FL 7+1

SIMPSON Jay Alistaire Frederick
Born: Enfield, 27 December 1988
Height: 5'11" **Weight:** 13.4
International Honours: E: Yth
Jay was initially signed from Arsenal on a three-month loan but this was extended for the full season, which was a great coup for Millwall. Establishing himself as a regular in the side, he became a favourite with supporters, showing great pace and trickery and the ability to work on either flank. While creating many chances for others he was also able to hit the net on his own account, finishing the season with eight goals.
Arsenal (From trainee on 2/7/2007)
Millwall (Loaned on 31/8/2007) FL 34+7/6 FAC 4/1 Others 1/1

SIMPSON Robbie
Born: Cambridge, 15 March 1985
Height: 5'10" **Weight:** 11.6
Iain Dowie signed the young striker from Cambridge United in the summer. He was not expected to be in contention for the first team but made everyone sit up when he scored on his Coventry debut as a substitute against Notts County in the Carling Cup. Several energetic substitute appearances enhanced his reputation and he earned his first start at Old Trafford. Robbie had a dream game as a wide midfielder, causing endless problems to Manchester United's defence in the Carling Cup shock. He scored a League goal in the win over Blackpool but tore a hamstring at Stoke and was out until New Year's Day. The injury seemed to drain his confidence and he lost his early season zip. After several unmemorable substitute appearances, he was recalled to the starting line-up when Leon Best was suspended and gave two hard-working performances as City picked up four points. Robbie advanced a long way in 12 months and has the temperament to succeed.
Coventry C (£40,000 + from Cambridge U, ex Cambridge C, on 1/7/2007) FL 10+18/1 FLC 1+3/1 FAC 1+1

SINCLAIR Dean Michael
Born: Luton, 17 December 1984
Height: 5'9" **Weight:** 11.3
Club Honours: FC '05
Signed from Barnet after a successful pre-season trial, Dean made his Charlton debut as a substitute in the Carling Cup tie at Swindon and started in the same competition at Luton, scoring after three minutes in a 4-1 defeat, when he slotted in Izzy McLeod's cross. Dean is a hard-working central midfielder who likes to get forward, passes well and is not afraid to get stuck in. He was loaned to Cheltenham in October, initially for a month to gain experience, becoming new manager Keith Downing's first signing. This was subsequently extended until January, but after suffering a posterior cruciate ligament injury at Swansea on Boxing Day Dean was forced to return to the Valley, spending the remainder of the season building up his fitness. Dean's 14 appearances in central midfield at Cheltenham were characterised by strong running, inventive passing and a tendency to get forward.
Norwich C (From trainee on 7/5/2003) FL 1+1
Barnet (Free on 11/8/2004) FL 81+5/8 FLC 4/1 FAC 4/2 Others 3/1

Charlton Ath (£125,000 on 31/7/2007) FLC 1+1/1
Cheltenham T (Loaned on 6/10/2007) FL 12/1 Others 2

SINCLAIR Emile Anthony
Born: Leeds, 29 December 1987
Height: 6'0" **Weight:** 11.4
Emile is an emerging young forward who progressed through Nottingham Forest's junior ranks to break through into the first-team squad last season. He became an instant hero when he scored the deciding penalty in the shoot-out against Chester in the Carling Cup on his debut and collected his first League goal against Gillingham in only his third appearance. To further his experience he was allowed to move on loan to Brentford in November but unfortunately made his first League start against Peterborough in a 7-0 defeat and then struggled to get into a poor side. Most remembered for his red boots.
Nottingham F (From juniors at Bradford C, ex Harrogate College, on 10/7/2007) FL 0+12/1 FLC 0+1 Others 0+1
Brentford (Loaned on 22/11/2007) FL 1+3

SINCLAIR Frank Mohammed
Born: Lambeth, 3 December 1971
Height: 5'9" **Weight:** 12.9
Club Honours: FAC '97; FLC '98, '00
International Honours: Jamaica: 28
After being on loan from Burnley for the last three months of 2006-07, the solid and adventurous defender signed for Huddersfield on a permanent basis in the summer, adding valuable stability at the back. Mainly operating at right-back, Frank showed his experience and organisation skill. With a good positional sense and willingness to push forward, the seasoned player enjoyed a continuous run out in the starting line-up. Frank was rewarded with the captain's armband on his return to Chelsea in the FA Cup fifth round. Niggling injuries hampered him, along with two red cards that kept him on the sidelines, otherwise the dependable defender enjoyed a fruitful personal season before he was released by the new manager.
Chelsea (From trainee on 17/5/1990) P/FL 163+6/7 FLC 17+1/2 FAC 18/1 Others 13/3
West Bromwich A (Loaned on 12/12/1991) FL 6/1
Leicester C (£2,000,000 on 14/8/1998) P/FL 153+11/3 FLC 20 FAC 10/1
Burnley (Free on 29/7/2004) FL 88+4/1 FLC 2+3 FAC 5
Huddersfield T (Free on 9/2/2007) FL 41+1 FLC 1 FAC 5

SINCLAIR James Alexander
Born: Newcastle, 22 October 1987
Height: 5'6" **Weight:** 10.5
Having made his first-team debut for Bolton the previous season, James hoped to make more of a mark in 2007-08. However, despite being used by Sammy Lee in the pre-season Peace Cup tournament, James' only first-team appearance came as a substitute in the 1-0 UEFA Cup victory at Red Star Belgrade. A phenomenally quick player, capable of playing as an out-and-out striker or at full-back, James approaches the new season optimistically.
Bolton W (From trainee on 29/6/2007) PL 0+2 Others 0+1

SINCLAIR Scott Andrew
Born: Bath, 26 March 1989
Height: 5'10" **Weight:** 10.10
International Honours: E: Yth; Sch
Chelsea recognised the potential of this highly-promising young winger by awarding him a four-year contract at the beginning of last season. After a Wembley substitute appearance in the Community Shield, he started at Hull in the Carling Cup and scored his first Chelsea goal. Scott was a regular in the 'shadow side' for domestic Cups and, given the abundance of talent in wide positions at Stamford Bridge, was a prime candidate for loan experience. His first stop was Queens Park Rangers, signing on a six-week deal in November. Scott made his debut at home to Coventry and scored his first Rangers' goal in the next game at Crystal Palace. It was a surprise when Charlton manager Alan Pardew announced Scott's loan signing in February as there were four other wingers at the club, including Lee Cook who had recently signed on loan from Fulham. Scott did not start for Charlton but came on as a substitute on three occasions, playing most of the game against Preston at the Valley after an early injury to Lloyd Sam. Although obviously gifted, his loan was terminated early by Pardew as he felt him too inexperienced for the promotion push. Scott's third loan spell was at Crystal Palace in March, having scored against them for Plymouth in 2006-07 and Rangers earlier in the season. A quick and dangerous player, the Chelsea youngster scored at Hull and signed off with a fine individual goal against Burnley.
Bristol Rov (Schoolboy) FL 0+2
Chelsea (From trainee on 28/3/2006) PL 1+2
FLC 3+1/1 FAC 2 Others 0+1
Plymouth Arg (Loaned on 17/1/2007) FL 8+7/2 FAC 2+1/2
Queens Park Rgrs (Loaned on 6/11/2007) FL 8+1/1
Charlton Ath (Loaned on 28/2/2008) FL 0+3
Crystal Palace (Loaned on 27/3/2008) FL 6/2 Others 2

SINCLAIR Trevor Lloyd
Born: Dulwich, 2 March 1973
Height: 5'10" **Weight:** 12.10
International Honours: E: 12; B-1; U21-14; Yth
The former England midfield player arrived at Cardiff from Manchester City in the summer alongside two other big names in Robbie Fowler and Jimmy Floyd Hasselbaink. Trevor was first to sign, joining the club during their pre-season tour to Portugal. Suffered a severe knee injury and thought of retiring but finished the season among Cardiff's substitutes for the FA Cup final and came off the bench for the last four minutes. Able to play either on the right or left of midfield, Trevor may have lost some of his former pace but can still open defences while looking to get his shots off. Was released at the end of the campaign.

Frank Sinclair

Blackpool (From trainee on 21/8/1990) FL 84+28/15 FLC 8 FAC 6+1 Others 8+5/1
Queens Park Rgrs (£750,000 on 12/8/1993) P/FL 162+5/16 FLC 13/3 FAC 10/2
West Ham U (£2,300,000 + on 30/1/1998) PL 175+2/37 FLC 9+1 FAC 8 Others 10/1
Manchester C (£2,500,000 on 22/7/2003) PL 65+17/5 FLC 4 FAC 7+2 Others 3/1
Cardiff C (Free on 27/7/2007) FL 14+7/1 FLC 1/1 FAC 1+3

SISSOKO Mohamed (Momo)
Lamine
Born: Rouen, France, 22 January 1985
Height: 6'2" **Weight:** 12.6
Club Honours: ESC '05; FAC '06; CS '06
International Honours: Mali: 14
For two seasons the Liverpool and Malian international holding midfielder showed such excellent form that it appeared that he would be a fixture for years to come. However, two serious injuries interrupted his progress and when he returned to fitness on the second occasion in February 2007 he found that his role in the team had been usurped by the peerless Argentine player, Javier Mascherano, who played in the 2007 Champions' League final in Athens and who was clearly manager Rafa Benitez's first choice at the start of 2007-08. Even so, Momo made a good start to the season by scoring his first and only goal for the Reds in his first start of the season at Sunderland in August, a 20-yard drive from a lay-off by Andriy Voronin. Sadly thereafter, his form vanished and although given a number of chances to stake a claim in Benitez's rotation system, his performances became steadily less assured, both losing tackles and misplacing passes. Clearly losing his first-choice status, due to circumstances beyond his control, undermined his confidence and it was probably a relief to both player and club when he accepted an offer to join Juventus in the January transfer window for £8-million. It was an anti-climactic end to what had once seemed destined to be a glittering career at Anfield.
Liverpool (£5,600,000 from Valencia, Spain, ex Auxerre, Brest - loan, on 19/7/2005) PL 42+9/1 FLC 4 FAC 6 Others 20+6

[SITO] CASTRO Luisito
Born: La Coruna, Spain, 21 May 1980
Height: 5'7" **Weight:** 11.7
Sito seemed to be the forgotten man of Portman Road until he appeared as a second-half substitute after a particularly poor first-half defensive display at Charlton. Injury and suspension meant that he was unable to put a run of appearances together but he never let the side down when he did play, mostly in

the unfamiliar left-back berth. Scored his first goal for Ipswich at Scunthorpe, when he cut in from the left, jinked past two defenders and drove in a low shot – just as he had predicted in an interview with the local newspaper before the game.
Ipswich T (Signed from Racing Ferrol, Spain on 9/8/2005) FL 48+11/1 FLC 1 FAC 2+1

SKACEL Rudolf (Rudi)
Born: Trutnov, Czech Republic, 17 July 1979
Height: 5'10" **Weight:** 12.1
Club Honours: SC '06
International Honours: Czech Republic: 4; U21-9
Although he has provided moments of genius since being heralded on his arrival as a player capable of leading the Southampton back to the Premiership, Rudi has never been able to hold down a regular first-team place in his preferred position as a wide midfielder. Throughout 2007, most of his games were at left wing-back but by December George Burley preferred Jermaine Wright, a right-footed midfielder, in that role. Burley's departure to manage Scotland was incentive for Rudi to go on loan to Hertha Berlin, where he has prospered.
Heart of Midlothian (Signed from Olympique Marseille, France, ex Hradec Kralove, Slavia Prague, Panathinaikos - loan, on 1/7/2005) SL 33+2/16 SLC 0+1 SC 4/1
Southampton (£1,600,000 on 3/8/2006) FL 45+8/4 FLC 3/1 FAC 0+1 Others 1+1

SKARZ Joseph (Joe) Peter
Born: Huddersfield, 13 July 1989
Height: 5'11" **Weight:** 13.0
Joe, another young home-grown player, opened his account by establishing himself as Huddersfield's left-back. Predominantly left sided, the accomplished defender heads and tackles solidly, also delivering good crosses into the danger area. Always dependable, he works hard when used in midfield and some displays showed a maturity beyond his years. After a run of 22 games in the squad, rotation allowed him to recharge on the sidelines but Joe continued to be involved with the first team, a good achievement for a first-year professional.
Huddersfield T (From trainee on 28/2/2007) FL 37+7 FLC 1 FAC 3+1 Others 1

SKIVERTON Terence (Terry) John
Born: Mile End, 26 June 1975
Height: 6'1" **Weight:** 13.6
Club Honours: FAT '02; FC '03; Div 2 '05
International Honours: E: SP-4
Terry's performances seem to improve every time he is on the pitch for Yeovil.

The Glovers' captain scored some crucial goals in Town's relegation battle, particularly in the 90th minute of a key game against Northampton. The battling centre-back has been the cornerstone of the Yeovil side since signing from Welling nine years ago and has seen the club grow from Conference level to playing at Wembley Stadium. A born leader, the tough-tackling defender relishes aerial challenges and is difficult to pin down at set pieces.
Chelsea (From trainee on 19/5/1993)
Wycombe W (Loaned on 17/2/1995) FL 8+2
Wycombe W (Free on 26/3/1996) FL 5+5/1 FAC 0+1 (Free to Welling U on 13/8/1997)
Yeovil T (Signed from Welling U on 3/6/1999) FL 163+7/19 FLC 5 FAC 10 Others 4

SKOKO Josip
Born: Mount Gambier, Australia, 10 December 1975
Height: 5'10" **Weight:** 12.4
International Honours: Australia: 51
As a holding player for Wigan, Josip featured mainly in the back four, using his neat distribution to turn defence into attack. A reliable player, he did his bit towards the Latics maintaining their Premiership status, sitting deep while others pressed forward. Hard-working and with good anticipation, he was always at the centre of the team's endeavours and turned in a good performance in the home match against Birmingham. Still to score in top-flight football, he retired from international football with Australia to concentrate on club matters. Out of contract at the end of the season, he has the option of a further year but may move on for regular first-team football.
Wigan Ath (Signed from Genclerbirligi, Turkey on 23/8/2005) PL 34+11 FLC 4 FAC 4
Stoke C (Loaned on 8/2/2006) FL 9/2

SKRTEL Martin
Born: Handlova, Slovakia, 15 December 1984
Height: 6'4" **Weight:** 12.12
International Honours: Solvakia: 25
An early season injury to Daniel Agger left Liverpool manager Rafa Benitez bereft of cover in the centre-back department, a situation he rectified with the signing of Slovakian international Martin from Russian champions Zenit St Petersburg during the January transfer window. After making his Premiership debut as a substitute at home to Aston Villa, he was handed his first start in the FA Cup fourth round at home to non-leaguers Havant & Waterlooville, the lowest ranked English team Liverpool have ever faced, playing in the Blue Square South five

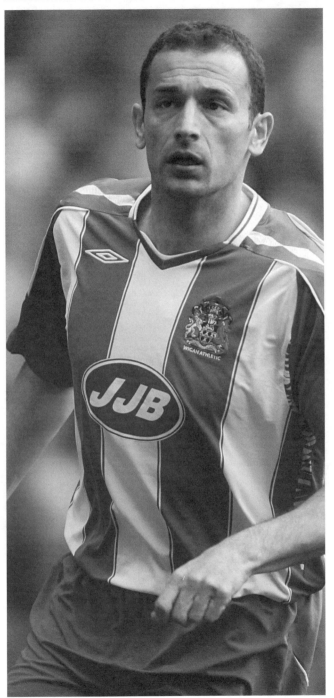

Josip Skoko

levels below them. If Benitez thought that this would be a comfortable baptism, he had a rude shock as the gallant non-Leaguers carried the game to their illustrious opponents, causing panic in the Liverpool rearguard and taking the lead twice in the first half, their second deflected off Martin. Even though the Reds recovered to win 5-2, the visitors continued to harass the Liverpool defence and rightly received a tremendous ovation from the Liverpool supporters. It is greatly to Martin's credit that he not only recovered from this nightmare debut so quickly but in his second Premiership start, away to Chelsea, he was voted 'Man of the Match'. By the end of the season he was an automatic choice, playing alongside Jamie Carragher or Sami Hyypia. In the climax to Liverpool's season, the second leg of the Champions' League semi-final away to Chelsea, he was unfortunate to be injured early in the match, perhaps a critical factor given his earlier performance at Stamford Bridge as his replacement Hyypia was unable to subdue the always dangerous Didier Drogba, who scored twice to end Liverpool's dream of a third Champions' League final in four years.
Liverpool *(£6,500,000 from Zenit St Petersburg, Russia, ex Trencin, on 14/1/2008) PL 13+1 FAC 1 Others 5*

SKUSE Cole
Born: Bristol, 29 March 1986
Height: 6'1" **Weight:** 11.5
A product of Bristol City's Academy system, Cole did not have many starts for the Robins last season. The skilful midfielder's services were frequently called upon as substitute and his energy was often seen to good effect during the closing stages of matches. Also able to play in the centre of the defence, he is a player who the club have a lot of faith in.
Bristol C *(From trainee on 29/4/2005) FL 69+43/2 FLC 1+2 FAC 5+1 Others 3+2*

SLATER Christopher (Chris) James
Born: Lichfield, 14 January 1984
Height: 6'0" **Weight:** 13.3
This utility defender was signed by Port Vale in January after his exploits with Chasetown helped them to knock Vale out of the FA Cup. He acquitted himself well during the fairy-tale run to the third round, where they were eventually beaten by Cardiff. A cool defender who never panics, he was tipped for a move when the Cup run ended and Vale secured his signature. He made his debut as a substitute at Swansea but illness limited his progress. Another three substitute

appearances followed, along with one start in a 3-0 defeat at Millwall. He was mainly used at right-back but can play in the centre.

Port Vale (Signed from Chasetown, ex trainee at Wolverhampton W, on 11/1/2008) FL 1+4

SLEATH Daniel (Danny) James

Born: Matlock, 14 December 1986
Height: 5'8" **Weight:** 11.5
This lively Mansfield midfielder and former youth team 'Player of the Year' continued his progression through the ranks at Field Mill. A regular first-team squad member early on, his opportunities were limited and before Christmas he spent a period on loan at Boston to gain some match practice. With first-team chances still limited and no reserve side where he could play on a regular basis, he left on loan for Gainsborough in March for the remainder of the season.
Mansfield T (From juniors on 27/8/2005) FL 5+9 FLC 0+1 FAC 0+1 Others 1

SLOMA Samuel (Sam) Mark

Born: Enfield, 29 October 1982
Height: 5'7" **Weight:** 11.6
Club Honours: FC '07
Sam scored Dagenham's first League goal, against Wycombe in August, and was a regular in the side at the start before a change in formation relegated him to the bench for the last two months. The left-winger still made a major contribution, going on at Darlington in the penultimate fixture to score and change the game completely as the Daggers headed for the victory they needed to retain League status. Was out of contract in the summer and looking for a new club.
Dagenham & Redbridge (Free from Thurrock, ex trainee at Wimbledon, Hampton & Richmond Borough, Aylesbury U, Wingate & Finchley, Milwaukee Wave U, on 21/7/2006) FL 22+7/2 FLC 1 FAC 3 Others 2+1

SLUSARSKI Bartosz

Born: Szamocin, Poland, 11 December 1981
Height: 6'1" **Weight:** 12.6
International Honours: Poland: 2
The Polish striker penned a two-year deal with West Bromwich, plus a further year's option in Albion's favour, to become Tony Mowbray's 12th summer signing of 2007. During the first three months of his Hawthorns career, Bartosz was limited to one late substitute appearance at Colchester in October before widening his Championship experience with two loan spells. Signing for Blackpool in

November he scored against Norwich in a 3-1 defeat and made four League starts without leaving a lasting impression at Bloomfield Road. In March, with Sheffield Wednesday in the middle of a striker crisis, he moved to Hillsborough and played a big part in helping Wednesday to avoid relegation, particularly with his vital goal at Leicester in the penultimate match. Bartosz impressed with his speed and control as an out-and-out striker, being equally comfortable coming in from the left.
West Bromwich A (£680,000 from Groclin Dyskobolia, Poland, ex Lech Poznan, Widzew Lodz - loan, Groclin Dyskobolia, Uniao Leira, on 29/8/2007) FL 0+1
Blackpool (Loaned on 21/11/2007) FL 4+2/1
Sheffield Wed (Loaned on 27/3/2008) FL 3+4/1

SMALL Wade Kristopher

Born: Croydon, 23 February 1984
Height: 5'7" **Weight:** 11.6
It was an unfulfilling season for the small, pacy winger or striker. Wade was hampered by bouts of injury throughout the campaign, so was never able to put together a consistent run for Sheffield Wednesday. Adept on either wing, he also enjoys playing as a striker, although his goals-per-game ratio does not indicate a natural scoring touch. He always gives everything, accepts being out of the side and does his best to make an impact when called from the substitutes' bench.
Wimbledon/MK Dons (From trainee on 17/7/2003) FL 88+11/12 FLC 3 FAC 10/1 Others 3/2
Sheffield Wed (Signed on 2/6/2006) FL 31+18/6 FLC 2/1 FAC 1+2

SMALLEY Deane Alfie Michael

Born: Oldham, 5 September 1988
Height: 6'0" **Weight:** 11.10
A pacy young Oldham forward, whose school was just yards from Boundary Park, Deane signed his first professional deal last summer and looks set for a bright future. A prolific youth-team marksman, he made the step up to first-team football to such good effect that he finished the campaign with a total of 45 appearances. Capable of operating wide on the right or through the middle, he was outstanding in the 1-0 FA Cup success at Everton in the FA Cup third round, giving England under 21 cap Leighton Baines problems. His scoring return of three failed to reflect his effectiveness but Deane ended his high with a goal in each of the last two League games and signed a new three-year contract.
Oldham Ath (From trainee on 3/7/2007) FL 19+20/2 FLC 1+1/1 FAC 5 Others 0+1

SMART Mapidima (Bally) Lesetja

Born: Polokwane, South Africa, 27 April 1989
Height: 5'10" **Weight:** 10.0
Club Honours: AMC '08
Bally showed up well as a speedy left-winger for Norwich in an early reserve game against MK Dons and was signed soon afterwards on a three-month loan. He made a couple of starts in Cup games but was only used off the bench in the League, showing plenty of skill and promise. Was released in the summer.
Norwich C (From trainee on 3/7/2007) FL 0+1
MK Dons (Loaned on 14/9/2007) FL 0+8 FAC 1 Others 1+1

SMERTIN Alexei

Born: Barnaul, Russia, 1 May 1975
Height: 5'9" **Weight:** 10.8
Club Honours: PL '05
International Honours: Russia: 55
The creative Russian enjoyed some good form at the beginning of the season, when he had his best run of starts. A plethora of midfielders at Fulham and in particular the arrival of Danny Murphy restricted his chances. As a central midfielder who likes to get forward, he appeared to have found the target against Bolton and Tottenham only to have both efforts credited to opponents by the dubious goals panel, rather unfairly in the case of the latter strike. A regular in the reserves, he played his part in their successful season.
Chelsea (£3,450,000 from Bordeaux, France, ex Uralan, Lokomotiv Moscow, on 26/8/2003) PL 11+5 FLC 1 FAC 3 Others 4+1/1 (Free to Moscow Dynamo, Russia on 13/3/2006)
Portsmouth (Loaned on 27/8/2003) PL 23+3 FLC 2 FAC 5
Charlton Ath (Loaned on 15/7/2005) PL 18 FLC 2 FAC 1+1
Fulham (Signed from Moscow Dynamo, Russia on 29/1/2007) PL 17+5 FLC 1 FAC 2

SMITH Nathan Adam

Born: Huddersfield, 20 February 1985
Height: 6'0" **Weight:** 12.5
Adam's involvement in Chesterfield's chase for the play-offs proved to be disappointingly peripheral. A knee injury prevented his seeing much action until November and following that he spent a month on loan at Lincoln in January, making just four substitute appearances during his brief spell at Sincil Bank. An attacking midfielder, Adam made only one start after that, with too little being seen of his pace and trickery and the former trainee's four-year spell as a Saltergate professional ended with his

release in May.

Chesterfield *(From trainee on 3/8/2004) FL 23+43/3 FLC 0+4 FAC 2+2 Others 4+1/1*
Lincoln C *(Loaned on 4/1/2008) FL 0+4*

SMITH Alan
Born: Rothwell, W. Yorkshire, 28 October 1980
Height: 5'9" **Weight:** 11.10
Club Honours: FLC '06
International Honours: E: 19; B-1; U21-10; Yth
Alan's summer arrival in Newcastle from Manchester United was lauded as a major signing and he made a good start

Alan Smith

with a scoring debut in the pre-season friendly against Sampdoria. Strong and highly competitive, he added a further England cap and started regularly for Newcastle until March when he found himself on the bench. He failed to add to his goals, largely because he oscillated between a target-man striker, a midfielder and a shield in front of the back four. His committed approach was recognised when he replaced Geremi as team captain, although he later lost the armband to Michael Owen on the arrival of new manager Kevin Keegan. While his fierce tackling brought a number of

yellow cards, the fans recognise his total commitment to the cause.
Leeds U *(From trainee on 26/3/1998) PL 148+24/38 FLC 4+2 FAC 11+4/4 Others 28+7/14*
Manchester U *(£7,000,000 on 26/5/2004) PL 43+18/7 FLC 4+2/1 FAC 2+6 Others 12+6/4*
Newcastle U *(£6,000,000 on 3/8/2007) PL 26+7 FLC 2 FAC 2*

SMITH Andrew Greg
Born: Burnley, 22 December 1989
Height: 5'10" **Weight:** 11.2
Andrew is a young Accrington striker who made his debut as a substitute against Barnet in April, although he had already been an unused sub several times as well as playing and scoring in the Lancashire Senior Cup. He has been leading scorer in the youth team in both his years as a scholar and gained valuable exposure playing for Radcliffe in the Unibond League on work experience. Andrew is one of four scholars to be offered professional terms for next season.
Accrington Stanley *(Trainee) FL 0+1*

SMITH Benjamin (Ben) James
Born: Newcastle, 5 September 1986
Height: 6'1" **Weight:** 12.11
Club Honours: AMC '07
The goalkeeper found himself on the Doncaster bench at the beginning of last season as understudy to Neil Sullivan, who had been signed in the summer. Ben's only appearances in the first team were one start and one as a substitute in the Johnstone's Paint Trophy. At the turn of the year he was loaned out to Lincoln for two months and received some good reports while making a total of nine appearances during his time at Sincil Bank before returning to Rovers.
Doncaster Rov *(Free from N/C at Stockport Co, ex trainee at Newcastle U, on 4/8/2006) FL 13 FLC 1 FAC 4 Others 6+1*
Lincoln C *(Loaned on 17/11/2007) FL 9*

SMITH Benjamin (Ben) Peter
Born: Chelmsford, 23 November 1978
Height: 5'8" **Weight:** 11.6
Ben was Hereford's key attacking midfielder in their promotion campaign and led the side for much of the season. A quality performer on the ball, he set an excellent example with his enthusiastic running and tackling and willingness to drive play forward. An incisive passer with either foot, he added some crucial goals to underline his importance, his first equaliser at Tranmere, which the fans voted their 'Away Goal of the Season' being a case in point. It was more than appropriate that Ben scored the opening

goal on the final day to ensure that Hereford's promotion party would go with a swing.

Reading *(From trainee at Arsenal on 16/4/1997) FL 0+1 (Free to Yeovil T on 6/3/1998)*
Southend U *(Free from Yeovil T on 8/6/2001) FL 0+1 (Freed during 2002 close season)*
Shrewsbury T *(Free from Hereford U on 5/6/2004) FL 19+5/4 FLC 3 FAC 2 Others 1 (Free to Weymouth on 13/1/2006)*
Hereford U *(Signed from Weymouth on 25/1/2007) FL 60+2/6 FLC 2 FAC 6/1 Others 0+1*

SMITH Daniel (Dan) Philip
Born: Plymouth, 7 June 1989
Height: 5'10" **Weight:** 10.7
Dan is an exciting young winger blessed with searing pace and more than a few tricks. A first-year professional at Plymouth after coming through the ranks at Home Park, he made his senior debut as an 85th-minute substitute against Burnley in January but had to wait until the final home game for another chance, again as a substitute against Blackpool. At the end of the season, Dan was offered a new contract by Plymouth and was considering his future.
Plymouth Arg *(From trainee on 6/7/2007) FL 0+2*

SMITH Emmanuele (Manny)
Born: Birmingham, 8 November 1987
Height: 6'2" **Weight:** 12.3
After being voted 'Man of The Match' in his one and only first-team game in the previous season, Manny waited patiently for a further opportunity. It duly came and, following a substitute appearance in November, he showed up well at the heart of the Walsall defence in the last three games of the season. At 19, Manny promises to be one of the Saddlers' players of the future.
Walsall *(From Solihull College on 19/9/2005) FL 5+2*

SMITH Gary Stephen
Born: Middlesbrough, 30 January 1984
Height: 5'8" **Weight:** 10.8
Freed by MK Dons, the industrious midfield ball-winner joined Brentford in the close season. Initially he struggled to win a place but a change of manager in December saw him selected alongside Kevin O'Connor in central midfield and he was then a virtual ever-present until the end of the season. Gary can drive the team forward after winning possession and has good passing ability.
Middlesbrough *(From trainee on 6/7/2002)*
Wimbledon *(Loaned on 22/3/2004) FL 10+1/3*

MK Dons *(Free on 6/8/2004) FL 47+24/5 FLC 0+1 FAC 3+2/1 Others 3/3*
Brentford *(Free on 1/8/2007) FL 26+3/1 FLC 0+1 FAC 0+1 Others 1*

SMITH Grant Gordon
Born: Irvine, 5 May 1980
Height: 6'1" **Weight:** 12.7
Arriving at Carlisle in mid-season from HJK Helsinki, Grant quickly established himself as an integral part of the United midfield. An energetic and bustling player, his positive performances helped inspire the club's fine run of results in February and March. Always willing to test opposing goalkeepers, he capped an excellent display at Leyton Orient with his first goal for the club and looks likely to be a key performer again this coming season.
Reading *(From trainee at Wycombe W on 7/8/1998)*
Heart of Midlothian *(Free on 19/3/1999)*
Livingston *(Free on 4/7/2000) SL 0+2 SLC 1 Others 1*
Clydebank *(Free on 2/12/2000) SL 16+1/2*
Sheffield U *(Free on 13/7/2001) FL 2+8 FAC 0+1*
Halifax T *(Loaned on 7/9/2001) FL 11 Others 1*
Plymouth Arg *(Loaned on 10/3/2003) FL 4+1/1*
Swindon T *(Free on 25/7/2003) FL 23+14/10 FLC 4 FAC 0+3 Others 4+2*
Bristol C *(Free on 1/7/2005) FL 4+7 FLC 1*
Walsall *(Loaned on 11/1/2006) FL 13/3 FAC 1 Others 1*
Dundee U *(Signed on 30/9/2006) SL 4+2 (Freed on 31/1/2007)*
Carlisle U *(Free from HJK Helsinki, Finland on 22/1/2008) FL 15+1/1 Others 2*

SMITH Jack David
Born: Hemel Hempstead, 14 October 1983
Height: 5'11" **Weight:** 11.5
For the first time since he arrived at Swindon, Jack found himself on the fringes of first-team action and will surely have been disappointed by his appearance total. But he ended strongly and did enough to be offered a further contract. Jack is a capable and dependable defender, usually at right-back although he has performed competently on the left when required.
Watford *(From trainee on 5/4/2002) FL 23+2/2 FLC 0+1 FAC 2*
Swindon T *(Free on 5/8/2005) FL 100/4 FLC 3 FAC 6 Others 1*

SMITH James
Born: Liverpool, 17 October 1985
Height: 5'10" **Weight:** 11.8
James arrived at Stockport from Liverpool

on the eve of last season, initially on loan, before making the move permanent in the January transfer window. A no-nonsense full-back who also filled in at centre-half, he proved to be a consistent performer and comfortable on the ball, qualities that made him a firm favourite with the County fans. He rounded off a fine season by helping the Hatters win the League Two play-off final at Wembley.
Liverpool *(From trainee on 15/5/2006) FLC 0+1*
Ross Co *(Loaned on 1/1/2007) SL 8 SC 1*
Stockport Co *(Free on 11/8/2007) FL 24+2 FLC 1 Others 4*

SMITH James (Jimmy) Dean
Born: Woodford, 7 January 1987
Height: 6'1" **Weight:** 10.8
International Honours: E: Yth
A pre-season ankle injury, sustained while Norwich were on tour in Holland, prevented the stylish Chelsea midfielder making a real impact at Carrow Road during his half-season loan. The injury delayed his debut until late October, by which time Norwich were struggling at the foot of the Championship. An attacking player with creative passing skills and an eye for goal, as he proved at Queens Park Rangers in 2006-2007, Norwich never saw the best of this exciting young talent but he is sure to mature into an excellent player.
Chelsea *(From trainee on 26/3/2005) PL 0+1*
Queens Park Rgrs *(Loaned on 27/9/2006) FL 22+7/6 FAC 2*
Norwich C *(Loaned on 10/8/2007) FL 6+3*

SMITH Jay Alexander
Born: Lambeth, 24 September 1981
Height: 5'7" **Weight:** 11.0
Club Honours: Div 1 '06
Having become a permanent member of Notts County's playing staff after a loan spell in the previous season, Jay suffered a series of niggling injuries and his comeback was hampered by problems with the diagnosis. More than half the season passed before he was able to return to duty in the centre of midfield. Jay is a clever player who can win the ball in a tackle as well as making himself available to receive passes. Sadly, he ended the season with a further injury.
Aston Villa *(From trainee on 7/7/2000)*
Southend U *(Free on 19/8/2002) FL 49+13/7 FLC 2 FAC 9+1/3 Others 5*
Oxford U *(Loaned on 23/3/2006) FL 5+1*
Notts Co *(Signed on 17/11/2006) FL 41+6/4 FLC 1 Others 1*

SMITH Jeffrey (Jeff)
Born: Middlesbrough, 28 June 1980
Height: 5'10" **Weight:** 11.8

Paul Smith

As a skilful left-sided midfielder, Jeff featured in most of Carlisle's games in the early weeks of the campaign before injury and a drop in form caused him to lose his place. He continued to make occasional substitute appearances and his only goal of the season, against Hartlepool on New Year's Day, was scored within two minutes of his arrival off the bench. Jeff remains a valuable member of the squad and will be looking to make more of an impact next season.

Hartlepool U (From trainee on 3/7/1998) FL 2+1 Others 1 (Free to Barrow in October 1999)
Bolton W (Free from Bishop Auckland on 21/3/2001) P/FL 1+1 FLC 2 FAC 4
Macclesfield T (Loaned on 23/11/2001) FL 7+1/2
Scunthorpe U (Loaned on 16/1/2004) FL 1
Rochdale (Loaned on 20/2/2004) FL 1
Preston NE (Signed on 4/3/2004) FL 0+5
Port Vale (Free on 5/7/2004) FL 65+23/5 FLC 4+1/1 FAC 5+1 Others 1+3/1
Carlisle U (£60,000 on 26/11/2007) FL 30+9/2 FLC 1+1 FAC 1+1 Others 2

SMITH Johann Anwar Ryan
Born: Hartford, Connecticut, USA, 25 April 1987
Height: 5'10"   **Weight:** 12.2
International Honours: USA: Yth
An extremely quick and direct left-

winger who arrived at Darlington on loan from Bolton in October and made three appearances before returning to the Reebok without having been on the losing side. He showed tremendous pace down the left and delivered a near perfect cross for Tommy Wright to head in against Stockport on his debut. With nothing better than the odd reserve match at Bolton, the striker signed on loan for Stockport in March as cover for a number of injuries. The young American made two substitute appearances for the Hatters, leaving the bench in successive games against Macclesfield and Wycombe. Was released by his parent club during the summer.

Bolton W (From trainee on 5/10/2006) PL 0+1 FLC 0+1 FAC 0+1
Carlisle U (Loaned on 31/1/2007) FL 9+5/1
Darlington (Loaned on 12/10/2007) FL 3
Stockport Co (Loaned on 20/3/2008) FL 0+2

SMITH Martin Geoffrey
Born: Sunderland, 13 November 1974
Height: 5'11"   **Weight:** 12.6
Club Honours: Div 1 '96
International Honours: E: U21-1; Yth; Sch
The cultured and vastly experienced Darlington player spent the first half of the season recovering from a knee operation and did not feature until the

last game of 2007 against MK Dons, when he appeared as a substitute to rousing applause. Alas, he managed only three more outings from the bench before his injury problem flared again and he reluctantly agreed to retire in March.

Sunderland (From trainee on 9/9/1992) P/FL 90+29/25 FLC 10+6/2 FAC 7+3/1
Sheffield U (Free on 6/8/1999) FL 24+2/10 FLC 3+1/4 FAC 3/1
Huddersfield T (£300,000 on 3/2/2000) FL 72+8/29 FLC 2+1 FAC 1 Others 1
Northampton T (Free on 7/8/2003) FL 96+8/24 FLC 1 FAC 11/4 Others 7+2/1
Darlington (Free on 1/8/2006) FL 30+8/5 FAC 2/3 Others 0+1/1

SMITH Nathan Colin
Born: Enfield, 11 January 1987
Height: 5'11"   **Weight:** 12.0
Nathan signed for Yeovil as an unknown from non-League Potters Bar, having been recommended by a former player, Steve Browne, and impressing Russell Slade with his ability. After training to be an IT technician, the last thing Nathan thought he would be doing in 2008 was playing in front of 20,000 fans at Nottingham Forest's City Ground. Remarkably, the young attack-minded full-back with the ability to play anywhere across the back four, has adapted to League One football with consummate ease since joining in March.

Yeovil T (Free from Potters Bar T on 23/3/2008) FL 6+1

SMITH Paul Daniel
Born: Epsom, 17 December 1979
Height: 6'4"   **Weight:** 14.0
Paul has excellent reflexes and was ever-present in goal for Nottingham Forest during their successful campaign. He kept 24 clean sheets, which explains why Forest achieved the best defensive record in the entire Football League. Leicester let him score against them in the rearranged Carling Cup tie, originally abandoned because of Clive Clarke's collapse at half-time with Forest leading 1-0.

Charlton Ath (Free from Walton & Hersham on 2/7/1998. Free to Walton & Hersham during 1999 close season)
Brentford (Free from Carshalton Ath on 27/7/2000) FL 86+1 FLC 3 FAC 6 Others 8+1
Southampton (£250,000 + on 28/1/2004) P/FL 14+1 FLC 2 FAC 4
Nottingham F (£500,000 on 13/7/2006) FL 91 FLC 3/1 FAC 7 Others 3

SMITH Philip (Phil) Anthony
Born: Harrow, 14 December 1979
Height: 6'1"   **Weight:** 13.12
Injury curtailed a season that Phil began as Swindon's first-choice goalkeeper. He

again impressed with some competent displays. After recovering, Phil was confined to the bench and the reserves apart from a brief recall at the end of February. His past performances prove him to be an able and reliable goalkeeper.
Millwall *(From trainee on 17/1/1998) FL 5 (Freed during 2001 close season)*
Swindon T *(Free from Crawley T, ex Folkestone Invicta, Dover Ath, Margate, on 28/7/2006) FL 46 FLC 1 FAC 3 Others 1*

SMITH Ross Graham
Born: Ontario, Canada, 4 November 1980
Height: 6'0" **Weight:** 12.7
Having signed a one-year deal for Dagenham from Ebbsfleet during the close season, Ross was in the wars throughout the campaign when operating either in a two-man centre-back unit or on the right of a defensive trio. He missed the opening month of the season because of a thigh strain and a kick on the leg in the FA Cup first round match at Hampton ruled him out for two months around Christmas. Ross then missed the last two matches after a mouth injury at Rotherham before being released in the summer.
Dagenham & Redbridge *(Free from Gravesend & Northfleet, ex Margate, on 9/7/2007) FL 23/1 FAC 1+1 Others 1+1*

SMITH Ryan Craig Matthew
Born: Islington, 10 November 1986
Height: 5'10" **Weight:** 10.10
International Honours: E: Yth
Ryan was yet another player who started last season well for Millwall, after making his move from Derby permanent, before the injury hoodoo struck and forced him to miss most of the campaign. His pace and trickery were sorely missed as his penetrating runs constantly put defenders under pressure. He can play on either flank, which makes him a player of considerable importance to the manager.
Arsenal *(From trainee on 26/11/2004) FLC 2+4*
Leicester C *(Loaned on 30/9/2005) FL 10+7/1 FAC 2*
Derby Co *(Signed on 4/8/2006) FL 5+10 FLC 1+1 FAC 1+2*
Millwall *(£150,000 on 21/3/2007) FL 14+8 FLC 1*

SMITH Thomas (Tommy) William
Born: Hemel Hempstead, 22 May 1980
Height: 5'8" **Weight:** 11.4
International Honours: E: U21-1; Yth
Tommy was a popular choice as Watford's 'Player of the Season', a fitting tribute to his consistent all-round contribution. A right-winger

or wide player, he missed only two League matches and his energy, desire and commitment were key factors in Watford's success. Personal highlights included an outstanding goal-line clearance against Sheffield United, which led to him being named in the Championship team of the week, a brace of goals at Wolverhampton, three assists at Colchester and the goal at Blackpool that clinched Watford's place in the play-offs. Tommy, who is in his second spell with the Hornets, has now made over 200 appearances for the club.
Watford *(From trainee on 21/10/1997) P/FL 114+35/33 FLC 7+3/1 FAC 5+3/2*
Sunderland *(Signed on 25/9/2003) FL 22+14/4 FAC 3+1/4 Others 0+2*
Derby Co *(Free on 29/7/2004) FL 88+2/20 FLC 2 FAC 5/1 Others 2*
Watford *(£500,000 on 30/8/2006) P/FL 76/8 FAC 6+1/1 Others 2*

SMITHIES Alexander (Alex)
Born: Huddersfield, 25 March 1990
Height: 6'1" **Weight:** 13.4
International Honours: E: Yth
The 17-year-old goalkeeper, in the final year of his scholarship with Huddersfield, was drafted into the first team in the December Yorkshire derby with Leeds because of suspension and injury to the two senior 'keepers. The England under-18 international commands his area well but conceded four goals in a difficult debut. His displays away from the limelight suggest Alex has a part to play in the club's future.
Huddersfield T *(From trainee on 3/3/2007) FL 1+1*

SOARES Thomas (Tom) James
Born: Reading, 10 July 1986
Height: 6'0" **Weight:** 11.4
International Honours: E: U21-4; Yth
A talented Crystal Palace and England under-21 international, Tom had a fine season, flourishing under the new manager Neil Warnock in the centre of a three-man midfield. Able to play wide when required, Tom is more at home in the middle where his workrate and driving runs spell danger for the opposition. He scored five times, including consecutive strikes at Stoke and Scunthorpe. His brother Louis was in the Aldershot team that won the Blue Square Premier to regain League status.
Crystal Palace *(From trainee on 9/9/2004) P/FL 124+21/10 FLC 4+1/1 FAC 1+2 Others 4*

SODJE Idoro Akpoeyere (Akpo) Ujoma
Born: Greenwich, 31 January 1981
Height: 6'2" **Weight:** 12.8

As a striker who gives everything, Akpo began the season with Port Vale but a stirring performance in a pre-season friendly against Sheffield Wednesday led to a move to Hillsborough. Before the move was finalised he made three appearances for the Vale without scoring but left with everyone's best wishes. Akpo took a few games to settle himself before a run of appearances and goals helped to establish him in the Owls' side. An ankle injury at Southampton kept him out for several matches but he came back and scored against local rivals Sheffield United. Unfortunately, he injured ankle ligaments shortly afterwards and needed an operation that will keep him out until pre-season. Strong, pacy and a real threat, he was sadly missed by Wednesday.
Huddersfield T *(Free from Erith & Belvedere on 1/9/2004) FL 1+6 Others 1+1*
Darlington *(Free on 24/3/2005) FL 18+25/9 FLC 0+1 FAC 1 Others 0+1*
Port Vale *(Free on 1/7/2006) FL 41+5/14 FLC 4/1 FAC 1/1 Others 1+1*
Sheffield Wed *(£500,000 on 30/8/2007) FL 16+3/7 FLC 0+1 FAC 1*

SODJE Efetobore (Efe)
Born: Greenwich, 5 October 1972
Height: 6'1" **Weight:** 12.0
Club Honours: GMVC '96; Div 1 '06
International Honours: Nigeria: 9
An experienced central defender, Efe was a regular member of Gillingham's defence after arriving from Southend in the summer until sustaining a nasty injury at Yeovil on live television. After being out for the best part of a month, he was unable to regain his place at the Priestfield Stadium and Bury manager Alan Knill acted quickly to sign him on loan in February. The experienced Nigerian made an instant impact, not least by hiding behind Stockport goalkeeper Conrad Logan and running round him to collect the ball after he put it down. Although prone to the occasional eccentric moment, Efe showed himself to be a solid centre-half who has the awareness to create attacking opportunities from defence.
Macclesfield T *(£30,000 from Stevenage Borough on 11/7/1997) FL 83/6 FLC 6 FAC 6/1 Others 1*
Luton T *(Free on 12/8/1999) FL 5+4 FLC 1 FAC 2+1 Others 1*
Colchester U *(Free on 23/3/2000) FL 3*
Crewe Alex *(Free on 21/7/2000) FL 86+12/3 FLC 6+2 FAC 6+3/1 Others 2*
Huddersfield T *(Free on 7/8/2003) FL 61+6/ 5 FLC 3 FAC 1 Others 4+1*
Yeovil T *(Free on 23/3/2005) FL 23+2/3 FLC 1+1 FAC 1+1 Others 1*
Southend U *(Signed on 6/1/2006) FL 35+2/2*

FLC 4
Gillingham *(Free on 7/8/2007) FL 12+1 FLC 1 FAC 1 Others 1*
Bury *(Loaned on 15/2/2008) FL 16/1*

SODJE Samuel (Sam)
Okeremute
Born: Greenwich, 29 May 1979
Height: 6'0" **Weight:** 12.0
International Honours: Nigeria: 2
Nigerian international Sam made just one
appearance for Reading, at centre-back in
the Carling Cup tie at Swansea that the
Royals won 1-0 after extra time. However,
Sam's contribution was to be booked
after 18 minutes and sent off after 58
for a second yellow card. Following
suspension, he made a handful of reserve
appearances before Charlton signed him
on loan deal for the remainder of the
season. Sam made his Charlton debut as
a last-minute substitute in the home win
over Norwich and was a sub in the next
six games, coming on in five of them. He
made his first start in the home defeat
by Queens Park Rangers in late October
and kept his place for the next 12 games
before a red card at Norwich on Boxing
Day led to a four-match suspension.
While out with an arm injury, Paddy
McCarthy and Madjid Bougherra were
the preferred central defenders but he
earned a recall against Sheffield United
in March and kept his place until he
dislocated a toe in the win at Plymouth.
Is a strong-tackling central defender who
is good in the air and also has an eye for
goal, scoring twice for Charlton.
Brentford *(Free from Margate, ex Stevenage Borough, on 2/7/2004) FL 83/12 FAC 14/2 Others 3*
Reading *(£350,000 + on 14/7/2006) PL 2+1 FLC 1+1 FAC 2+1/1*
West Bromwich A *(Loaned on 16/3/2007) FL 7/1 Others 3*
Charlton Ath *(Loaned on 31/8/2007) FL 20+7/2*

SOLANO Nolberto (Nobby)
Albino
Born: Lima, Peru, 12 December 1974
Height: 5'8" **Weight:** 10.8
International Honours: Peru: 82; Yth
One of the most popular players at
Newcastle in recent years, midfielder
Nobby began the season with a substitute
appearance in the opener against Bolton,
followed three games later by a start
in the Carling Cup against Barnsley.
However, he was then transferred to
West Ham after he requested a move
to be closer to his family who had
relocated to London. Having joined the
Hammers on the August deadline day,
the Peruvian international made his debut

Nobby Solano

as a substitute against Sunderland and changed the game when he scored within five minutes. A right-sided midfield player, his all-round experience and passing skills were invaluable to a team that was badly hit by injuries. Nobby is also brilliant at free kicks, scoring stunning goals at Derby and at home against Aston Villa. Before being released at the end of the season, he added to his international caps for Peru through the campaign.

Newcastle U (£2,763,958 from Boca Juniors, Argentina, ex Cristal Alianza Lima, Sporting, Deportivo Municipal, on 17/8/1998) PL 158+14/29 FLC 10+2 FAC 19/2 Others 27+4/7

Aston Villa (£1,500,000 on 29/1/2004) PL 44+5/8 FLC 2/1 FAC 1

Newcastle U (£1,500,000 on 31/8/2005) PL 52+6/8 FLC 5+1/2 FAC 6 Others 10+1

West Ham U (Signed on 31/8/2007) PL 14+9/4

SOMNER Matthew (Matt) James
Born: Isleworth, 8 December 1982
Height: 6'0" **Weight:** 13.2
International Honours: W: U21-2
At the start of his Notts County career, Matt demonstrated great ability as a traditional centre-half; tough and uncompromising. It was a surprise to many that he was later deployed as a midfield ball-winner. In this role, he was always competitive and eager to succeed. He began last season as the midfield anchor-man but was soon removed by new manager Ian McParland and was not seen subsequently. A hard-working professional, he deserves a chance to prove himself in his best position at centre-half. Was released at the end of the campaign.

Brentford (From trainee on 4/7/2001) FL 72+12/1 FLC 1+1 FAC 3+2/1 Others 2

Cambridge U (Free on 3/12/2004) FL 24

Bristol Rov (Free on 5/8/2005) FL 1 (Free to Aldershot T on 30/8/2005)

Notts Co (Free from Aldershot T on 30/6/2006) FL 47+7/1 FLC 3 FAC 2+1 Others 2

SONG BILONG Alexandre (Alex) Dimi
Born: Douala, Cameroon, 9 April 1987
Height: 6'0" **Weight:** 12.0
International Honours: Cameroon: 8; Yth. France: Yth;
It is fair to say that Alex had certainly not won over a majority of Arsenal fans by the time last season kicked off. Yet it was actually time spent many miles away, playing for Cameroon in the African Cup of Nations Cup in January, that could be the making of him. He was impressive throughout as Cameroon narrowly lost the final and displayed an ability to

play either in central midfield or central defence. His performances were rewarded by his appearance in the 'Team of the Tournament'. He finished the season alongside William Gallas and played in nine Premier League games, adding three in the Champions' League and three in the Carling Cup.

Arsenal (£2,500,000 from Bastia, France on 16/8/2005) PL 9+7 FLC 8/1 Others 3+3

Charlton Ath (Loaned on 30/1/2007) PL 12

SONGO'O Franck Steven
Born: Yaounde, Cameroon, 14 May 1987
Height: 6'2" **Weight:** 12.6
International Honours: France: Yth
The pacy, tricky right-winger who has yet to start a game for Portsmouth, Franck became Neil Warnock's first signing on loan for Crystal Palace in October and gave a brilliant first-half performance on his debut in a 2-0 home defeat by Watford. He never reached similar heights again at Palace. Back at Fratton Park, when Pompey were shorn of their African Cup of Nations players in January he was a 65th-minute substitute in the League defeat at Sunderland, his first appearance for the club in more than two-and-a-quarter years. Franck made an instant impact after joining Sheffield Wednesday on loan in March, his supreme skill and confidence on the ball enlivening the crowd. Given more or less a free role to roam across midfield at Wednesday, he occasionally showed signs of packing a terrific shot and possibly should have scored more than the one goal. All in all he was a really good addition for the Owls in an injury-hit season.

Portsmouth (Signed from Barcelona, Spain on 31/8/2005) PL 0+3 FLC 0+1

Bournemouth (Loaned on 20/10/2006) FL 3+1 Others 0+1

Preston NE (Loaned on 8/3/2007) FL 4+2

Crystal Palace (Loaned on 29/10/2007) FL 9

Sheffield Wed (Loaned on 7/3/2008) FL 12/1

SONKO Edrissa (Eddy)
Born: Essau, Gambia, 23 March 1980
Height: 5'9" **Weight:** 11.0
International Honours: Gambia: 14
Eddy, a Gambian international, joined Walsall from Greek club Xanthi Skoda in the summer. If at times he looked a little frail for League football, he showed considerable skill and no little opportunism in the course of his season at the Banks's Stadium. He played more than 40 games in midfield but homesickness at times affected him and he was released at the end of the season.

Walsall (Signed from Xanthi Skoda, Greece, ex Anderlecht, Roda JC Kerkrade, on 1/8/2007) FL 30+7/5 FAC 4+1

SONKO Ibrahima (Ibu)
Born: Bignona, Senegal, 22 January 1981
Height: 6'3" **Weight:** 13.7
Club Honours: Ch '06
International Honours: Senegal: 1; U21
Ibu's first game of the season for Reading came in the 4-2 defeat at Blackburn in October. It was the tall centre-back's return to action after rupturing cruciate ligaments in a knee nine months earlier. He performed well and stayed in the starting line-up for a run of 12 matches before a harsh sending-off in the home fixture against Portsmouth cost him his place. 'Superman', as he is nicknamed by the fans, made intermittent appearances towards the end of the season but the campaign ended in controversy when he, along with Emerse Fae, declined to play in the reserves, stating that he did not wish to risk injury before Senegal's international programme. He was suspended by Reading, fined two weeks wages and lost his appeal. Happily, the situation was resolved and he will be able to play an important part in Reading's bid to regain Premiership status.

Brentford (Free from Grenoble, France, ex St Etienne, on 9/8/2002) FL 79+1/8 FLC 3/1 FAC 6 Others 2

Reading (Free on 5/7/2004) P/FL 119+5/5 FLC 4 FAC 5

SONNER Daniel (Danny) James
Born: Wigan, 9 January 1972
Height: 5'11" **Weight:** 12.8
International Honours: NI: 13; B-4
The battling midfielder arrived from Port Vale last summer for his second spell with Walsall but it was soon obvious that, at 35, he was not quite the same player as in his Northern Ireland days and he was released at the end of September. Following a spell on trial at Vale, Danny joined Wrexham, along with former Walsall team-mate Paul Hall, to help in the proposed 'Great Escape'. The central midfielder added much needed fluidity to the side, not to mention character that had been absent for some time. Danny scored in a 2-2 draw at Morecambe at the end of January but sadly and perhaps crucially, an old Achilles tendon injury flared again, restricting and eventually curtailing his contribution. It is worth noting that he was on the losing side only twice in his nine appearances – and that in a relegation-bound team. Was out of contract in the summer and looking for a new club.

Burnley (From trainee at Wigan Ath on 6/8/1990) FL 1+5 FLC 0+1/1 Others 0+2 (Free to Preussen Koln, Germany during 1993 close season)

Bury (Loaned on 21/11/1992) FL 5/3 FAC 3 Others 1/1
Ipswich T *(Free from FC Erzgebirge Aue, Germany on 12/6/1996) FL 28+28/3 FLC 6+4/1 FAC 1+1 Others 0+1*
Sheffield Wed *(£75,000 on 15/10/1998) PL 42+11/3 FLC 3+1/1 FAC 4+2*
Birmingham C *(Free on 4/8/2000) FL 32+9/2 FLC 12/1 FAC 1 Others 2*
Walsall *(Free on 5/8/2002) FL 20+4/4 FLC 2 FAC 2*
Nottingham F *(Free on 6/8/2003) FL 19+9 FLC 3 FAC 1*
Peterborough U *(Free on 13/8/2004) FL 11+4 FLC 0+1 Others 1*
Port Vale *(Signed on 22/2/2005) FL 71+4/2 FLC 5 FAC 4 Others 3 (Freed on 29/9/2007)*
Walsall *(Free on 27/7/2007) FL 6 FLC 1*
Wrexham *(Free, following trial at Port Vale, on 11/1/2008) FL 9/1*

SORVEL Neil Simon
Born: Widnes, 2 March 1973
Height: 6'0" **Weight:** 12.9
Club Honours: GMVC '95, '97; FAT '96
Experienced midfielder who was a vital member of the promotion team, Neil started at the hub of Morecambe's midfield in ten of the first 11 games but lost his place to Damien Allen and failed to win it back as Sammy McIlroy used various combinations in that department. He had a spell on loan at Southport and chipped in with a couple of starts at the end of the campaign but the intelligent and popular player was among those released.
Crewe Alex *(From trainee on 31/7/1991) FL 5+4 FAC 1+1 Others 4*
Macclesfield T *(Free on 21/8/1992) FL 79+7/7 FLC 4+1 FAC 5 Others 0+1*
Crewe Alex *(Free on 9/6/1999) FL 229+21/13 FLC 17 FAC 11+1 Others 4*
Shrewsbury T *(Free on 4/7/2005) FL 59+4/5 FLC 3 FAC 2 Others 2*
Morecambe *(Free on 24/1/2007) FL 14+8 FLC 3 FAC 1 Others 2*

SOUTHALL Leslie Nicholas (Nicky)
Born: Stockton, 28 January 1972
Height: 5'10" **Weight:** 12.12
There is no substitute for experience and when Nicky was missing from the Gillingham team, there was no one capable of delivering crosses to match the quality he produced on a regular basis. Equally at home in a midfield role, he remains more suited to an attacking right-back position. Nicky has now made over 300 senior appearances for the Gills in three spells.
Hartlepool U *(From juniors at Darlington on 21/2/1991) FL 118+20/24 FLC 6+1/3 FAC 4+4 Others 6+2*
Grimsby T *(£40,000 on 12/7/1995) FL*
55+17/6 FLC 3+3/1 FAC 4+3/2
Gillingham *(Free on 9/12/1997) FL 141+13/17 FLC 6+1/1 FAC 10/3 Others 12*
Bolton W *(Free on 2/7/2001) PL 10+8/1 FLC 4 FAC 2*
Norwich C *(Loaned on 27/9/2002) FL 4+5*
Gillingham *(Free on 6/12/2002) FL 86+6/2 FLC 2 FAC 5*
Nottingham F *(Free on 4/8/2005) FL 63+4/13 FLC 1+1 FAC 7+1/1 Others 2/1*
Gillingham *(Free on 31/1/2007) FL 46+2/1 FLC 1 FAC 1 Others 2*

SOUTHAM Glen Andrew James
Born: Enfield, 10 June 1980
Height: 5'7" **Weight:** 11.10
Club Honours: FC '07
International Honours: E: SP-12
Glen signed a contract extension at the start of last season with Dagenham after playing an important midfield role in the promotion campaign and made his League debut when the Daggers opened at Stockport. An ever present until the last game of the season, his physical fitness was evident from the way he covered ground so tirelessly. Although a playmaker, he can tackle if required.
Dagenham & Redbridge *(Free from Bishops Stortford on 8/5/2004) FL 44+1/2 FLC 1 FAC 3 Others 3*

SOUTHERN Keith William
Born: Gateshead, 24 April 1981
Height: 5'10" **Weight:** 12.6
Club Honours: AMC '04
One of Blackpool's longest-serving players, Keith excelled last season, effortlessly making the step up to the Championship. An ankle injury in the middle of the campaign limited his number of starts but he again showed himself to be a tenacious box-to-box midfielder with an abundance of energy. Starting the season off with a goal against Leicester in a 1-0 win, Keith predominately played in the centre of midfield with Claus Jorgensen and should soon hit the milestone of 200 appearances for Blackpool.
Everton *(From trainee on 21/5/1999)*
Blackpool *(Free on 8/8/2002) FL 180+24/19 FLC 4+3/1 FAC 12+1/2 Others 11+1/3*

SOUZA Denis
Born: Sao Paulo, Brazil, 9 January 1980
Height: 6'3" **Weight:** 13.5
Barnsley cast their net wide in the summer and Denis joined them on a two-year contract from Belgian club Charleroi, making his debut in the first match of the season. He settled quickly at the heart of Barnsley defence, a good man-marker and powerful in the air. Denis played more times for the Reds than anyone else,
forming effective partnerships with Lewin Nyatanga and Steve Foster. He was also a threat from set plays, scoring twice.
Barnsley *(£700,000 from Charleroi, Belgium, ex Matsubara, Harelbeke - Ioan, RAEC Mons - Ioan, K Beringen-Heusden Zolder - Ioan, Standard Liege, RAEC Mons, on 8/8/2007) FL 45/2 FLC 2 FAC 5*

SPANN Silvio Reinaldo
Born: Couva, Trinidad, 21 August 1981
Height: 5'11" **Weight:** 10.13
International Honours: Trinidad & Tobago: 28
Silvio joined Wrexham from Trinidadian club W Connection in the summer after obtaining a work permit. An established Trinidad & Tobago international who has played in Italy and Japan, he missed the 2006 World Cup because he was injured only days before the team left for Germany. The loose-limbed midfielder has a fluid style with a decent shot but never realised his potential and had the unwanted record of never being on the winning side in his 11 League and Cup appearances. He scored in a 2-1 defeat at Notts County and his best moment was in the reserves, a 45-yard goal against Accrington. Although under contract he was released by Brian Little in the close season.
Wrexham *(Signed from W Connection, Trinidad & Tobago, ex Doc's Kelwalaas, W Connection, Perugia, Sambenedettese, W Connection, Dinamo Zagreb, Yokohama, on 31/8/2007) FL 7+2/1 FAC 1 Others 1*

SPARROW Matthew (Matt) Ronald
Born: Wembley, 3 October 1981
Height: 5'11" **Weight:** 10.6
Club Honours: Div 1 '07
Scunthorpe midfielder Matt stepped up to the Championship for the first time and was a regular performer during the season, either in the centre of midfield or on the right side. A hard-working player, he netted the last-minute winner against Sheffield United at the start of September but failed to score again in a struggling side. A red card in the February home match against Southampton saw him miss three matches and he started only once in the closing six games.
Scunthorpe U *(From trainee on 30/7/2001) FL 226+44/32 FLC 8+4 FAC 19+1/1 Others 9+1/1*

SPECTOR Jonathan Michael Paul
Born: Chicago, Illinois, USA, 1 March 1986
Height: 6'0" **Weight:** 12.8
International Honours: USA: 12; Yth

Jonathan Spector

Because of the many injuries that West Ham suffered, Jonathan was able to show his adaptability by playing in all the defensive positions. The versatile American was always prepared to play out of position and is a handy man to have in the squad. At Derby in November he fired home what he thought was his first goal for the club, only to have it classed as an own goal because it hit a defender on the way in. He was outstanding as a makeshift centre-half at Middlesbrough in December and continued to represent the Unites States.
Manchester U (Signed from Chicago Sockers, USA on 13/11/2003) PL 2+1 FLC 0+1 FAC 1 Others 1+2
Charlton Ath (Loaned on 11/7/2005) PL 13+7 FLC 1+1 FAC 2
West Ham U (£500,000 on 16/6/2006) PL 30+21 FLC 0+1 FAC 1+2 Others 1

SPEED Gary Andrew

Born: Deeside, 8 September 1969
Height: 5'10" **Weight:** 12.10
Club Honours: Div 2 '90, Div 1 '92; CS '92
International Honours: W: 85; U21-3; Yth
The evergreen midfield player started Bolton's first eight League games under Sammy Lee last season, but after spending some time out of the starting line-up he moved to Sheffield United

on loan, with the deal later becoming permanent. Having passed his 38th birthday early in the season, Gary has been an absolute credit to himself and the game, making well over 100 appearances for Bolton and racking up a total of 521 Premiership games, scoring 81 goals in the process. In August, he became one of only two players to score in every Premiership season when he headed home in the 3-0 victory against Reading. Moving on loan to Sheffield United in January, he went immediately into the Blades' side and adapted quickly to Championship football, so much so that he soon signed an 18-month permanent deal. Gary also stepped up to the faster tempo required when Kevin Blackwell took over as manager. He uses his experience, not only for his own performance but to influence the team on the field, particularly the other midfielders. Knowing when to stay back and when to go forward Gary was often a threat in the opposition's area at set pieces and against Bristol City scored his 100th League goal. He just likes playing.
Leeds U (From trainee on 13/6/1988) P/FL 231+17/39 FLC 25+1/11 FAC 21/5 Others 14+3/2
Everton (£3,500,000 on 1/7/1996) PL 58/16 FLC 5/1 FAC 2/1
Newcastle U (£5,500,000 on 6/2/1998) PL 206+7/29 FLC 9+2/1 FAC 22/5 Others 39/5

Bolton W (£750,000 on 21/7/2004) PL 115+6/14 FLC 4 FAC 6 Others 5+3
Sheffield U (£250,000 on 1/1/2008) FL 20/3 FAC 2

SPENCER Damian Michael

Born: Ascot, 19 September 1981
Height: 6'1" **Weight:** 14.5
Damian had an eventful season for Cheltenham, scoring twice in his first appearance to secure a rare away win at Huddersfield. He started that match on the left of midfield, then had a six-game run alongside Paul Connor in the forward line. Having returned to midfield following Steven Gillespie's recovery from injury, Damian won the admiration of the Whaddon Road crowd with enthusiastic displays and his willingness to chase anything. Crewe were also impressed and a fee was agreed in January, only for Damian to fail a medical at Gresty Road. Back at Cheltenham, he made a handful of appearances in the second half of the season but remained troubled by a knee injury and underwent an operation in April with the aim of establishing his fitness for the new season.
Bristol C (From trainee on 14/6/2000) FL 8+5/1 FLC 0+1 Others 1+3/1
Exeter C (Loaned on 22/3/2001) FL 2+4
Cheltenham T (Free on 7/8/2002) FL 115+95/32 FLC 1+4 FAC 7+9/2 Others 6+9/2

SPENCER James Matthew
Born: Stockport, 11 April 1985
Height: 6'5" **Weight:** 15.2
James was signed by Rochdale in the
summer, arriving from Stockport to
replace goalkeeper Matt Gilks, who
moved to Norwich. He initially found Gilks
a hard act to follow but came into his
own as the Dale moved up from the foot
of the table. He was injured in November
and replaced by understudy Sam Russell.
When Russell, in turn, was injured James
returned to the side but lasted only
another half-dozen games before being
ruled out for the rest of the season with a
groin problem.
Stockport Co (From trainee on 19/4/2002)
FL 90+1 FLC 2 FAC 9 Others 6
Rochdale (Signed on 5/6/2007) FL 20 FLC 2

SPENCER Scott Kernaghan
Born: Manchester, 1 January 1989
Height: 5'11" **Weight:** 12.8
Everton's Scott spent a month on loan
at Macclesfield to give Keith Alexander
an additional striking option. He made
his League debut when coming off the
bench late on at Brentford in early March,
followed by two further second half
substitute appearances before returning
to Everton at the end of his loan.
*Everton (From trainee at Oldham Ath on
8/6/2006)*
Macclesfield T (Loaned on 7/3/2008) FL 0+3

SPENDER Simon
Born: Mold, 15 November 1985
Height: 5'8" **Weight:** 11.0
Club Honours: AMC '05
International Honours: W: U21-6; Yth
Despite Wrexham's demise, Simon had
his best season in a red shirt, at least in
terms of involvement, and continued to
improve. The right-back always gave full
commitment and was never reluctant to
add support down the flank. He scored
in a 3-2 defeat at Barnet in March and
may play a big part to play in Blue Square
Premier.
*Wrexham (From trainee on 3/8/2005) FL
82+15/5 FLC 3+2 FAC 4 Others 3*

SPERONI Julian
Born: Buenos Aires, Argentina, 18 May
1979
Height: 6'0" **Weight:** 11.5
International Honours: Argentina:
U23; Yth
The Crystal Palace goalkeeper had a
brilliant season, his best since signing
from Dundee in 2004. Replacing the
experienced Gabor Kiraly, the agile former
Argentine youth international had the
best defensive record in the division with
just 42 goals against. There were several

Simon Spender

391

games in which he produced 'Man of the Match' performances, none more so than the 1-1 draw against Queens Park Rangers at Selhurst Park, when he made many superb stops to deny the visitors what should have been a comfortable victory. It was no surprise when Julian signed a new three-year contract in April.
Dundee (Signed from Platense, Argentina on 1/6/2001) SL 92 SLC 5 SC 12 Others 4
Crystal Palace (£750,000 on 14/7/2004) P/FL 60+1 FLC 6 Others 2

SPICER John William
Born: Romford, 13 September 1983
Height: 5'11" **Weight:** 11.7
International Honours: E: Yth
After his promising finish to the previous campaign, John enjoyed a good spell of first-team action for Burnley in October and November, displaying all his tenacity and attacking intentions. He was dismissed in the game at Ipswich in December and little was seen of him thereafter, the competition for places too strong after the return to favour of James O'Connor. With this likely to remain the case, he was released on the expiry of his contract.
Arsenal (From trainee on 2/7/2001) FLC 0+1
Bournemouth (£10,000 on 10/9/2004) FL 43/6 FLC 2/1 FAC 5/1
Burnley (£35,000 on 26/8/2005) FL 31+38/4 FLC 5/1

SPILLANE Michael Edward
Born: Cambridge, 23 March 1989
Height: 5'9" **Weight:** 11.10
International Honours: RoI: U21-2; Yth
Michael demonstrated his versatility in six starts for Norwich, appearing at right-back, in central defence and also at the heart of midfield. The youth team product continued to make real progress at international level, playing regularly for the Republic of Ireland under-19 and winning late season call-ups to the under-21 team. He is likely to settle eventually as a central defender, where his natural competitiveness and ball-winning skills will be to the fore. Add to that his ability on the ball, both in terms of passing and being able to create space, and he has the making of a top-quality player.
Norwich C (From trainee on 2/8/2006) FL 10+3 FLC 1+2 FAC 1+1

SPILLER Daniel (Danny)
Born: Maidstone, 10 October 1981
Height: 5'9" **Weight:** 12.3
A summer signing from Gillingham, the hard-working midfielder played the first seven games of the season for Millwall, giving some excellent performances. However, after a bad injury that was

followed by an operation, he sat out the rest of the campaign. Tenacious in the tackle and a player who hounds the opposition, he will be an asset for the Lions when fully fit.
Gillingham (From trainee on 10/7/2000) FL 89+41/6 FLC 3+2 FAC 2+1 Others 2
Millwall (Free on 5/7/2007) FL 6/1 FLC 1

SPRING Matthew (Matty) John
Born: Harlow, 17 November 1979
Height: 5'11" **Weight:** 11.5
Matty always played when available in one of the worst seasons in Luton's history, his consistency as the midfield creator with box-to-box runs and accurate passing, long or short, standing out. He has developed into a firm tackler and, as the playmaker, was always in the thick of the action. Only the fact that he was booked ten times, more than any other Luton player, prevented him being an ever-present. His ability to hit free kicks and penalties enabled him to notch double strikes over Northampton and Crewe and his 12 goals in all competitions made him Luton's joint leading scorer. With the entire squad available for transfer, rumours circulated that he will join a Championship club.
Luton T (From trainee on 2/7/1997) FL 243+7/25 FLC 16/1 FAC 18+1/3 Others 4
Leeds U (Free on 2/7/2004) FL 4+9/1 FLC 2
Watford (£150,000 on 19/8/2005) P/FL 38+7/8 FLC 4+1 Others 3/1
Luton T (£200,000 + on 18/1/2007) FL 58/10 FLC 4/2 FAC 5 Others 1/1

SPROULE Ivan
Born: Castlederg, 18 February 1981
Height: 5'9" **Weight:** 10.5
International Honours: NI: 11
Signed from Hibernian in June, the right-winger was heralded by Bristol City manager Gary Johnson as being the quickest player outside of the Premiership. He impressed in pre-season friendlies but City were not helped by the fact suspension ruled out Ivan from the opening four games. After a substitute appearance in the home Carling Cup defeat by Manchester City, he made his League debut in City's 1-0 win at Sheffield Wednesday in September and was a regular until late on in the season, when he was more often used as substitute. Like most wingers, lack of consistency is a problem but on his day he is capable of being a match winner. Ivan added to his Northern Ireland caps as a substitute in a 2-1 win over Denmark, then starting against Spain. Ivan's pace worried Hull when he went on as substitute in the Championship play-off final at Wembley

and he twice managed to get behind their blanket defence without being able to conjure up the killer cross.
Hibernian (Signed from Institute, ex Omagh T, on 1/3/2005) SL 35+36/12 SLC 5+1 SC 10+1/4 Others 4+2/2
Bristol C (£500,000 on 7/7/2007) FL 31+9/2 FLC 0+1 FAC 1 Others 0+2

SPURR Thomas (Tommy)
Born: Leeds, 13 September 1987
Height: 6'1" **Weight:** 11.5
Sheffield Wednesday had another really good season from the young defender. Originally a central defender, Tommy has settled comfortably at left-back in a back four over the last two seasons. He is good defensively and always looks to break forward but needs to improve his crossing to become a real danger to opponents. This exciting prospect developed through the club's own ranks.
Sheffield Wed (From trainee on 18/7/2006) FL 73+6/2 FLC 3 FAC 4

STACK Graham Christopher
Born: Hampstead, 26 September 1981
Height: 6'2" **Weight:** 12.6
Club Honours: FAYC '00
International Honours: RoI: U21-7; Yth
On loan from Reading, Graham was Wolverhampton's goalkeeper in two Carling Cup ties but had a torrid night against Morecambe in the second. He looked more assured as a substitute in a League match with Coventry, making some fine saves, and was a sub again later in the campaign, making another useful contribution at Palace. He did not appear for Reading at the end of the season.
Arsenal (From trainee on 18/7/2000) FLC 5
Millwall (Loaned on 13/7/2004) FL 25+1 FLC 1 FAC 1 Others 2
Reading (Signed on 18/7/2005) P/FL 1 FLC 5 FAC 4
Leeds U (Loaned on 27/10/2006) FL 12
Wolverhampton W (Loaned on 10/8/2007) FL 0+2 FLC 2

STALLARD Mark
Born: Derby, 24 October 1974
Height: 6'0" **Weight:** 13.6
An experienced striker, Mark suffered an injury-hit second season with Lincoln and managed to record just two League goals from his 25 appearances in 2007-08. Despite spending long spells on the sidelines, he remained the model professional, providing the younger members of the City squad with a work ethic and working closely with the reserve team. He was one of four players released by manager Peter Jackson at the end of the season.

Tommy Spurr

Derby Co *(From trainee on 6/11/1991) FL 19+8/2 FLC 2+1/2 FAC 2+2 Others 3/2*
Fulham *(Loaned on 23/9/1994) FL 4/3*
Bradford C *(£110,000 on 12/11/1996) FL 33+10/10 FLC 2/1 FAC 0+1 Others 3/2*
Preston NE *(Loaned on 14/2/1997) FL 4/1*
Wycombe W *(£100,000 on 7/3/1997) FL 67+3/23 FLC 5+1/1 Others 2/1*
Notts Co *(£10,000 on 3/3/1999) FL 168+17/67 FLC 13+1/8 FAC 10/3 Others 2*
Barnsley *(Free on 21/1/2004) FL 10+5/1 FLC 0+1*
Chesterfield *(Loaned on 1/10/2004) FL 7+2/2 FAC 1*
Notts Co *(Loaned on 4/2/2005) FL 16/3*
Shrewsbury T *(Free on 28/7/2005) FL 25+12/6 FLC 1+1/1 FAC 1 Others 1*
Lincoln C *(Free on 21/7/2006) FL 55+11/17 FLC 1+1/1 FAC 1 Others 3+1/3*

STALTERI Paul
Born: Toronto, Canada, 18 October 1977
Height: 5'11" **Weight:** 12.1
International Honours: Canada: 67
Tottenham's Canadian full-back spent the second half of the season on loan at Fulham and played a full part in their dramatic escape from relegation. Paul was involved in only seven Spurs' games and was never first choice, with Pascal Chimbonda ahead of him on the right and Gareth Bale and Young-Pyo Lee at left-back. When he left for Fulham on loan in January, he passed up a possible Carling Cup final appearance to join a relegation fight. He went straight into the side and kept his place for the final 13 games of the season. A defender whose positional sense allows him to time his tackles and pop up with a number of last-ditch clearances, Paul's pace enables him to link with the attack and provide support to the right-sided midfielder. He enjoyed excellent form in the final matches and was outstanding in the last game at Portsmouth. Paul continues to represent and captain Canada.
Tottenham H *(Free from Werder Bremen, Germany on 11/7/2005) PL 37+5/2 FLC 3 FAC 3+2/1 Others 4+2*
Fulham *(Loaned on 31/1/2008) PL 13*

STAM Stefan
Born: Amersfoort, Holland, 14 September 1979
Height: 6'2" **Weight:** 12.9
International Honours: Holland: U21
Stefan, an elegant Dutch central defender, is now Oldham's longest-serving player and agreed a new 12-month contract last summer. After shaking off a long-standing hamstring problem in October, he stayed injury free and enjoyed 40 consecutive appearances, his most productive run since joining the

club. Stefan maintained his reputation as a strong tackler with a cool temperament and his return improved Oldham's defensive record. Under the terms of his previous contract, he triggered a new deal after 25 starts and looks set for at least another season at Boundary Park.
Oldham Ath *(Free from Huizen, Holland, ex Grasshoppers, AFC 34, AZ Alkmaar, PSV Eindhoven, ADO Den Haag, on 16/2/2005) FL 73+11/1 FLC 1 FAC 7 Others 1+1*

STANLEY Craig
Born: Bedworth, 3 March 1983
Height: 5'8"   **Weight:** 10.5
International Honours: E: SP-4
A hard-working Morecambe midfielder, Craig was an almost ever-present despite ending the season on the transfer list. The former Hereford man was among the first names on the team sheet and signed an extended contract midway through the season. His campaign took a turn for the worse on a personal level because he fell foul of manager Sammy McIlroy when rested for a game in March and was listed as a result. He played his way back into the side at the end of the season and will hope to put the problems with his boss behind him. A real box-to-box player, he scored only twice, despite getting forward more than the previous year.
Walsall *(From trainee on 23/7/2002. Freed on 28/7/2003)*
Raith Rov *(Loaned on 21/7/2003) SL 18+1/1 SC 1 Others 3/1*
Morecambe *(Free from Hereford U, ex Telford U, on 15/7/2006) FL 41/2 FLC 3 FAC 1 Others 3*

STANTON Nathan
Born: Nottingham, 6 May 1981
Height: 5'9"   **Weight:** 11.3
International Honours: E: Yth
Nathan was still recovering from the injury sustained in 2006-07 when last season began and eventually returned, with virtually no prior match practice, after Rochdale found themselves with only two fit, eligible defenders for the FA Cup tie at Southend. Initially getting through on experience, Nathan quickly worked his way back to fitness and his presence in the centre of defence helped inspire a run of just one defeat in 12 games that propelled Dale into the play-off places. A slightly chequered disciplinary record saw him miss several games through suspension, including the first leg of the play-off semi-final, but he was back in time to play in Dale's first Wembley appearance.
Scunthorpe U *(From trainee on 19/3/1999) FL 215+22 FLC 9 FAC 16+2 Others 11+1/1*
Rochdale *(Free on 25/7/2006) FL 62 FLC 1 FAC 3 Others 3*

Richard Stearman

STAROSTA Ben Mark
Born: Sheffield, 7 January 1987
Height: 6'0" **Weight:** 12.4
International Honours: Poland: U21-5;
Yth. E: Yth
Ben joined Brentford on a five-month loan
from Sheffield United before the start of
last season and was the regular Bees' right-
back throughout that period. He defended
well but was not so effective, often due
to the lack of support, when he ventured
forward. Ben was more successful at
Bradford, where he was on loan for the
second half of the season. Capped at
under-20 level by Poland, he caught the
eye at Valley Parade with his adventurous
approach and overlapping runs but has yet
to play for his parent club.
Sheffield U (From trainee on 6/7/2006)
Brentford (Loaned on 1/8/2007) FL 20+1
FLC 1 FAC 1
Bradford C (Loaned on 21/1/2008) FL 12+3

STEAD Jonathan (Jon)
Graeme
Born: Huddersfield, 7 April 1983
Height: 6'3" **Weight:** 11.7
International Honours: E: U21-11
For much of last season Jon and Billy
Sharp were vying for the striker role at
Sheffield United, playing alongside James
Beattie. Jon used his pace to create
danger when running at opponents
either down the middle or on the flanks
and, given opportunities, finished well.
When Kevin Blackwell arrived Jon found
himself regularly on the bench but with
few opportunities even as a substitute.
Although he was involved in 43 League
games, he was not used in 19 of them.
Huddersfield T (From trainee on 30/11/
2001) FL 54+14/22 FLC 5/2 FAC 2 Others 2
Blackburn Rov (£1,200,000 on 2/2/2004) PL
32+10/8 FLC 0+1 FAC 1+3
Sunderland (£1,800,000 on 16/6/2005) P/FL
22+13/2 FLC 2+1 FAC 2
Derby Co (Loaned on 13/10/2006) FL
15+2/3
Sheffield U (£750,000 + on 11/1/2007) P/FL
24+14/8 FLC 3/2 FAC 4/1

STEARMAN Richard James
Michael
Born: Wolverhampton, 19 August 1987
Height: 6'2" **Weight:** 10.8
International Honours: E: Yth
Developing Leicester right-back who
earned his team-mates' votes as the
'Players' Player of the Season'. His three
strikes during the campaign all set up rare
victories and he also earned elevation
to the England under-21 squad but did
not advance from the substitutes' bench.
Having come through the ranks, he was
clearly affected more than most by the

club's plight and may well be a target for
Premiership outfits following the Foxes'
relegation.
Leicester C (From trainee on 30/11/2004) FL
94+22/7 FLC 8+2/4 FAC 3+1

STEELE Luke David
Born: Peterborough, 24 September 1984
Height: 6'2" **Weight:** 11.12
Club Honours: FAYC '03
International Honours: E: Yth
Luke made two League appearances
for West Bromwich in 2007-08 but was
unable to make much headway at the
Hawthorns because of Dean Kiely's form
as the number-one goalkeeper. Barnsley
signed him in January on a month's
emergency loan when Heinz Muller injured
and Tony Warner Cup-tied and Luke
made his debut two days later, giving a
heroic display against Liverpool at Anfield
in Barnsley's historic FA Cup fifth-round
victory. He returned to the Hawthorns
at the end of his loan but was back at
Oakwell near the transfer deadline. Luke
was again tremendous when Barnsley
dumped Chelsea out of the Cup and an
agreement with Albion meant he could
play in the semi-final against Cardiff.
When he signed permanently at the end
of the season, he was already a fans'
favourite and a real asset.
Peterborough U (From trainee on 26/9/
2001) FL 2
Manchester U (£500,000 on 4/3/2002)
Coventry C (Loaned on 11/9/2004) FL 32
FLC 2 FAC 2
West Bromwich A (Signed on 10/8/2006)
FL 2
Coventry C (Loaned on 23/12/2006) FL 5
FAC 2
Barnsley (Signed on 14/2/2008) FL 14 FAC 3

STEFANOVIC Dejan
Born: Belgrade, Serbia, 28 October 1974
Height: 6'2" **Weight:** 12.10
International Honours: Serbia: 23
A signing from Portsmouth late in the
summer moves period, Dejan made his
Fulham debut against Tottenham but
had to wait until mid-October to gain a
regular place. Then, he formed a solid
defensive partnership with Aaron Hughes.
An excellent reader of the game, his
ability to make last-ditch interceptions
proved crucial on more than one
occasion. He lost his place following a
red card in the FA Cup replay at Bristol
Rovers, a game in which he gave a
commanding performance on a tricky
surface. Stefan was unable to force his
way back into contention following the
arrival of Brede Hangeland.
Sheffield Wed (£2,000,000 from Red Star
Belgrade, Serbia on 22/12/1995) PL 59+7/4

FLC 2 FAC 4/1 (Free to Vitesse Arnhem,
Holland on 1/7/1999)
Portsmouth (£1,850,000 from Vitesse
Arnhem, Holland on 30/7/2003) PL 111+1/3
FLC 4+1 FAC 8
Fulham (£1,000,000 on 31/8/2007) PL 13
FAC 2

STEINSSON Gretar Rafn
Born: Siglufjordur, Iceland, 9 January 1982
Height: 6'2" **Weight:** 12.4
International Honours: Iceland: 24
Bolton's most expensive defensive
signing, this tough-tackling Icelandic
international right-back joined from
Dutch club AZ Alkmaar in the January
transfer window. Gretar was selected
as the right-back in last season's 'Dutch
League Team of the Year' and quickly
showed why with a series of energetic
and powerful displays. Soon making the
position his own, he was equally effective
when advancing down the wing as when
defending, proving to be a fine crosser
of the ball. Gretar's first three games
with the club resulted in three clean
sheets and he appeared in every League
game following his signing, being a
considerable factor in helping the Trotters
to cement their Premiership status.
Bolton W (£3,500,000 from AZ Alkmaar,
Holland, ex IA Akranes, Young Boys Berne,
on 17/1/2008) PL 16

STEPHENS Dale Christopher
Born: Bolton, 12 June 1989
Height: 5'7" **Weight:** 11.3
After starting the season on loan to
Droylsden, an injury crisis saw Dale
drafted into the centre of Bury's three-
man midfield for the FA Cup tie against
Workington. Unfortunately he did not
make the impact he wanted and was
substituted after an hour. After the
departure of Chris Casper, caretaker-
manager Chris Brass showed faith in Dale
with a place in his five-man midfield,
initially against Norwich in the FA Cup.
Dale took this with both hands and in the
next game, at home to Bradford, scored
Bury's equaliser with a strike that was
voted 'Goal of the Season'.
Bury (From trainee on 5/7/2007) FL 6+3/1
FAC 3

STERJOVSKI Mile
Born: Wollongong, Australia, 27 May
1979
Height: 5'11" **Weight:** 12.8
International Honours: Australia: 34;
U23-7; U20-6
Lengthy processing of the work
permit following his spell in Turkey
with Genclerbirligi delayed Mile's first
appearance as a Derby substitute in 2007-

08. He showed himself to be a strong runner on the right of midfield and Paul Jewell also experimented with him in attack. The Australian international, who has a variety of experience in European football, is seen as one of Derby's regulars when they return to the Championship, but is still bedding into the English game.
Derby Co *(£300,000 from Genclerbirligi, Turkey, ex Wollongong Wolves, Illawarra Lions, Sydney U, Parramatta Power, OSC Lille, FC Basle, on 31/1/2008) PL 9+3*

STEWART Damion Delano
Born: Jamaica, 8 August 1980
Height: 6'3" **Weight:** 13.8
International Honours: Jamaica: 37
Damion has been a regular in the Queens Park Rangers' defence for two seasons. The Jamaican centre-back started as first choice under John Gregory and is one of only a handful of players to survive after the new manager restructured the playing staff from top to bottom. As well as providing an imposing presence at the back, he is also an attacking menace from set pieces. He scored on the opening day, netting a last-minute equaliser against Bristol City in a thrilling 2-2 draw, and went on to bag a further four goals, equalling his total of five from the previous season.
Bradford C *(Signed from Harbour View, Jamaica on 5/8/2005) FL 20+3/1 FLC 0+1 FAC 0+1 Others 1*
Queens Park Rgrs *(Free on 31/7/2006) FL 80+4/6 FLC 2+1/1 FAC 3*

STEWART Gareth John
Born: Preston, 3 February 1980
Height: 6'0" **Weight:** 12.8
International Honours: E: Yth; Sch
The long-serving Bournemouth goalkeeper suffered plenty of bad luck during last season. He started as third in the pecking order but regained the starting position when he came on against MK Dons following an injury to Neil Moss. Gareth then enjoyed a profitable run in the side before being forced off by injury against Southend. Once back in the side yet again, he landed awkwardly against Hartlepool and broke an ankle. That proved to be his last appearance for the Cherries as it was announced in May that he was being released.
Blackburn Rov *(From trainee on 11/2/1997)*
Bournemouth *(Free on 2/7/1999) FL 163+1 FLC 3 FAC 9+1 Others 2+1*

STEWART Jordan Barrington
Born: Birmingham, 3 March 1982
Height: 5'11" **Weight:** 11.12
International Honours: E: U21-1; Yth

Jordan started last season brightly by scoring his first goal for Watford on the opening day against Wolverhampton. An attacking full-back and specialist dead-ball kicker, Jordan was one of Watford's most consistent performers in the early part of last season. However, he seemed to lose form coming up to Christmas, possibly because of the distraction of protracted contract renewal talks. In January he lost his first-team place to transfer-window signing Mat Sadler. Scored a second goal after coming on as a substitute against Burnley in March, but was released from his contract before the end of the season and agreed to join Derby.
Leicester C *(From trainee on 22/3/2000) P/FL 86+24/6 FLC 4+2 FAC 8+3*
Bristol Rov *(Loaned on 23/3/2000) FL 1+3*
Watford *(£125,000 on 5/8/2005) P/FL 92+13/2 FLC 4 FAC 5 Others 3*

STEWART William Marcus Paul
Born: Bristol, 7 November 1972
Height: 5'10" **Weight:** 11.0
Club Honours: Ch '05
International Honours: E: Sch

The veteran forward found himself dropping into central midfield for Yeovil and his excellent performances throughout the campaign saw him pick up most of the Glovers' end of season awards. Now 35, Marcus continued to show his ability to pick out passes and finish clinically, playing a key role in Yeovil's battle for League One safety. The scorer of five goals, Marcus still has that ability to lose his marker.
Bristol Rov *(From trainee on 18/7/1991) FL 137+34/57 FLC 11/5 FAC 7+1/4 Others 16+1/14*
Huddersfield T *(£1,200,000 + on 2/7/1996) FL 129+4/58 FLC 18/7 FAC 9/3*
Ipswich T *(£2,500,000 on 1/2/2000) P/FL 65+10/27 FLC 4+2/1 FAC 4/2 Others 8/7*
Sunderland *(£3,250,000 on 30/8/2002) P/FL 77+25/31 FLC 5+1/4 FAC 7+2/2 Others 2/2*
Bristol C *(Free on 29/7/2005) FL 16+11/5 FLC 1 Others 1*
Preston NE *(Loaned on 21/3/2006) FL 4 Others 1*
Yeovil T *(Signed on 30/8/2006) FL 66+1/12 FAC 1/1 Others 6/1*

Marcus Stewart

STIEBER Zoltan

Born: Budapest, Hungary, 16 October 1988
Height: 6'0" **Weight:** 12.4
International Honours: Hungary: Yth
Signed on loan for Yeovil from Aston Villa last November, the Hungarian-born midfielder immediately showed great ability at set pieces. Having come through the junior ranks at Villa to sign a professional contract at the beginning of 2007, Zoltan went out on loan with the sole purpose of picking up valuable experience. He certainly excited Town's fans with his quick feet on the left flank, where his pace helps him to reach the line before whipping crosses into the box. The scorer of one goal during his stay, he continually showed glimpses of the kind of player he might be on a regular basis in the years ahead. Was released at the end of the campaign.
Aston Villa (From trainee on 11/1/2007)
Yeovil T (Loaned on 22/11/2007) FL 14+1/1

STILLIE Derek Daniel

Born: Irvine, 3 December 1973
Height: 6'0" **Weight:** 12.0
International Honours: S: U21-14
Derek was tempted south during the summer to join Gillingham from Dundee United and was allowed to continue studying for a law degree at Medway University. The goalkeeper gained a regular place towards the end of the season when Simon Royce was injured and saved a crucial penalty in the 2-1 home win over Bournemouth. Was released at the end of the season.
Aberdeen (From Notts Co juniors on 3/5/1991) SL 22+1 SLC 2 SC 3
Wigan Ath (Free on 5/8/1999) FL 42+2 FLC 3+1 FAC 5 Others 4
Dunfermline Ath (Free on 26/5/2002) SL 96 SLC 5 SC 15 Others 1
Dundee U (Signed on 7/7/2005) SL 67 SLC 3 SC 3 Others 1
Gillingham (Signed on 1/8/2007) FL 13+1 Others 2

STIRLING Jude Barrington

Born: Enfield, 29 June 1982
Height: 6'2" **Weight:** 11.12
Club Honours: AMC '08; Div 2 '08
An immensely popular player with MK Dons fans, Jude showed there is more to his game than a prodigious long throw by putting in a string of wholehearted performances throughout the campaign. He played in almost every position apart from goal, where he would no doubt have gone given half a chance, and never let the side down wherever he featured. For such a tall player, he has a good range of skills on the

ball, was always an aerial threat when not delivering his own set pieces and thoroughly deserved his two winners' medals.
Luton T (From trainee on 9/7/1999) FL 6+4 FAC 0+2 Others 0+1 (Free to Stevenage Borough on 22/2/2002)
Oxford U (Free from Grays Ath, ex St Albans C, Hornchurch, Dover Ath, Tamworth, on 5/8/2005) FL 6+4 FLC 1 FAC 0+1 Others 2
Lincoln C (Free on 19/1/2006) FL 0+6
Peterborough U (Free on 12/7/2006) FL 14+8 FLC 1+1 FAC 2 Others 0+2
MK Dons (Signed on 8/1/2007) FL 26+24/3 FLC 2 Others 5+2

STOCK Brian Benjamin

Born: Winchester, 24 December 1981
Height: 5'11" **Weight:** 11.2
Club Honours: AMC '07
International Honours: W: U21-4
Brian had a good season in the centre of Doncaster's midfield, where he pulled the strings as the general besides rattling in a few goals with some tremendous shots from well outside the penalty area. He missed a few games in the middle of the campaign because of injury but returned to gain selection for the full Welsh squad in March for the match against Luxembourg. During the latter part of the season, when Adam Lockwood was out, Brian captained Rovers to the play-off final against Leeds at Wembley, where his drive and enthusiasm helped the team to win promotion to the Championship.
Bournemouth (From trainee on 25/1/2000) FL 113+32/16 FLC 5/1 FAC 11/1 Others 7+4/1
Preston NE (£125,000 on 14/1/2006) FL 5+3/1
Doncaster Rov (£125,000 on 12/9/2006) FL 75+1/8 FLC 2/1 FAC 6/1 Others 8+1/2

STOCKDALE David Adam

Born: Leeds, 20 September 1985
Height: 6'3" **Weight:** 13.4
David started last season at Darlington as goalkeeping understudy to the experienced Andy Oakes but was forced into action on the opening day when Oakes was sent off after 63 minutes of his debut against Wrexham. He seized this opportunity to display his capabilities and established himself in the side, limiting Oakes to only six more outings all season. He kept 20 clean sheets as he grew in confidence, showing himself to be an agile shot-stopper with a good command of his area as well as a strong kicker of a dead ball. He was linked with a move to Fulham after the play-offs.
York C (From trainee on 9/8/2005) FL 0+1
Darlington (Free on 8/8/2006) FL 46+1 FLC 3 FAC 2 Others 2

STOCKDALE Robert (Robbie) Keith

Born: Middlesbrough, 30 November 1979
Height: 5'11" **Weight:** 11.3
International Honours: S: 5; B-2; E: U21-1
Apart from a short spell out with injury in mid-season, Robbie was an ever-present for Tranmere. He is an experienced full-back who reads the game well and although he is never less than competitive, displays a mature attitude towards officials. With a liking to go forward whenever the opportunity allows, he is the provider of some useful crosses to his team-mates. Out of contract at the end of the campaign, Robbie was openly keen to stay at Prenton Park but, somewhat surprisingly, was released by the Birkenhead club shortly after the end of the season.
Middlesbrough (From trainee on 2/7/1998) P/FL 62+13/2 FLC 8+1 FAC 7
Sheffield Wed (Loaned on 13/9/2000) FL 6
West Ham U (Loaned on 23/10/2003) FL 5+2 FLC 1 FAC 1
Rotherham U (Free on 20/2/2004) FL 43/1 FLC 2
Hull C (Free on 31/1/2005) FL 12+2
Darlington (Loaned on 25/2/2006) FL 3
Tranmere Rov (Free on 3/7/2006) FL 78+2 FLC 2 FAC 4 Others 2

STOCKLEY Samuel (Sam) Joshua

Born: Tiverton, 5 September 1977
Height: 6'0" **Weight:** 12.0
Ever popular with the Wycombe supporters for his enthusiasm and commitment, Sam had a rather frustrating season, in and out of the side. He made most of his 18 starts at left-back, out of position it has to be said, preferring a central or right-sided defensive role. Sam always gives his all but, dropped in favour of Craig Woodman at the turn of the year, he had a trial with Major League Soccer club Dallas in February before signing for Port Vale at the end of the campaign.
Southampton (From trainee on 1/7/1996)
Barnet (Free on 31/12/1996) FL 177+5/2 FLC 10 FAC 4 Others 11
Oxford U (£150,000 on 13/7/2001) FL 39+2 FLC 1 FAC 1 Others 1
Colchester U (Free on 30/8/2002) FL 129+12/3 FLC 5 FAC 14+1 Others 10+1
Blackpool (Loaned on 17/3/2006) FL 3+4
Wycombe W (Free on 26/7/2006) FL 51+5/1 FLC 3+1 FAC 2+1 Others 2

STOKES Anthony

Born: Dublin, 25 July 1988
Height: 5'11" **Weight:** 11.6
Club Honours: Ch '07
International Honours: RoI: 3; B; U21-9; Yth

Manager Roy Keane has called Anthony possibly the most talented player at Sunderland and the young striker has already picked up Republic of Ireland international honours. Anthony scored one of last season's most vital goals for the Black Cats when he reacted brilliantly to force home a 93rd-minute winner at home to Derby in December. Quick and direct, he is a confident player, still young and talented enough to establish himself as one of Sunderland's main forwards.

Arsenal (From trainee on 28/7/2006) FLC 0+1
Falkirk (Loaned on 8/9/2006) SL 16/14 SLC 2/2
Sunderland (£2,000,000 on 11/1/2007) P/FL 15+19/3 FLC 1

STONE Craig Brian Raymond
Born: Strood, 29 December 1988
Height: 6'0" **Weight:** 10.5
A strong and steady midfielder, Craig looked good in the few games he played for Gillingham last season but was unable to hold down a regular place. He then spent two months on loan at Brentford, arriving in January, and deputised for the injured Kevin O'Connor. At one stage, he was on the sidelines because Brentford had more than five players on loan but played a couple more times before returning to the Gills. Released in the summer, if given a run of games the neat midfielder could be impressive.

Gillingham (From trainee on 5/7/2007) FL 5+9 FLC 1 Others 3+1/1
Brentford (Loaned on 18/1/2008) FL 5+1

STRACHAN Gavin David
Born: Aberdeen, 23 December 1978
Height: 5'11" **Weight:** 11.7
International Honours: S: U21-8; Yth
Gavin had limited chances in Peterborough's midfield in 2007-08, before being released in early January and becoming new manager Ian McParland's first permanent signing for Notts County a day later. Drafted in to provide a competitive edge and greater competence to County's central midfield area, Gavin was settling nicely to the task when injury struck after only seven games and recovery before the end of the season proved impossible.

Coventry C (From trainee on 28/11/1996) P/FL 5+11 FLC 1+3/1 FAC 2+2
Dundee (Loaned on 27/11/1999) SL 4+2
Peterborough U (Free on 14/3/2003) FL 1+1
Southend U (Free on 27/3/2003) FL 6+1
Hartlepool U (Free on 8/8/2003) FL 63+15/7 FLC 5 FAC 4+1 Others 7/1
Stockport Co (Loaned on 6/10/2005) FL 4
Peterborough U (Free on 1/1/2007) FL 13+6/3 FLC 1 FAC 2 Others 1+1
Notts Co (Free on 9/1/2008) FL 7

STREVENS Benjamin (Ben) John
Born: Edgware, 24 May 1980
Height: 6'1" **Weight:** 11.0
Club Honours: FC '05, '07
The former Barnet player established himself as Dagenham's number-one striker and did not disappoint as he ended top scorer. In 2006-07, Dagenham did not get the best out of Ben during the last four months because he had to overcome a fractured cheekbone. But in the League, his non-stop energy led to a number of goals through determined closing down of goalkeepers. Ben finished third in both the club's and Supporters Club 'Player of the Year' awards.

Barnet (Free from Wingate & Finchley on 13/1/1999) FL 44+25/9 FLC 4+2 FAC 1+1 Others 2+2 (Freed during 2006 close season)
Dagenham & Redbridge (Free from Crawley T on 1/12/2006) FL 39+7/15 FLC 0+1/1 FAC 2+1/3 Others 2/1

STRIHAVKA David
Born: Prague, Czech Republic, 4 March 1983
Height: 6'3" **Weight:** 12.12
International Honours: Czech Republic: Yth
Norwich signed the Czech Republic striker from FC Viktoria Plzen in July on a one-year loan with an option to buy him in the summer of 2008. This option was not exercised and in January, the tall, rangy front man was allowed to return to the Czech Republic to sign for Slavia Prague, for whom he scored against Tottenham in the UEFA Cup later in the season. Having finished top scorer in the Czech League in 2006-2007, great things were expected of David but his inability to adapt to the English game, combined with Norwich's poor start to the season, prevented him from making a real impact. A winning goal against Crystal Palace at Carrow Road looked as if it might kick-start his Canaries' career but it was not to be.

Norwich C (Signed from FC Viktoria Plzen, Czech Republic, ex Bohemians Prague, Sparta Prague, FK Jablonek, Bohemians Prague, Sparta Prague, Chmal Ostra, on 17/7/2007) FL 3+7/1 FLC 0+1

STUBBS Alan
Born: Liverpool, 6 October 1971
Height: 6'2" **Weight:** 13.10
Club Honours: SPD '98, '00; SLC '97, '99
International Honours: E: B-1
Alan left Everton last January after sterling service across two spells. The Kirkby-born centre-half played 13 games in the first half of the campaign, displaying his customary commitment and leadership, with a fine free kick in the 3-1 win at

Tottenham being a personal highlight. Alan left with the good wishes of all associated with the club. It would have been easy for him to stay and see out his contract with Everton but a desire to be playing regularly persuaded him to accept Derby's offer in the January transfer window. He brought with him the experience of well over 500 starts at club level, along with a good knowledge of the game, and gave some composure to an ailing defence, although a calf strain in the defeat by Chelsea at Stamford Bridge kept him out for a month. At least he could say it was 0-0 when he left, so he could hardly be blamed for a 6-1 hammering. Alan arrived knowing that Derby's real challenge is in the coming Championship campaign and, after a knee operation at the end of April, hopes to be ready for the battle.

Bolton W (From trainee on 24/7/1990) P/FL 181+21/9 FLC 23/4 FAC 16+2/2 Others 12+1
Glasgow Celtic (£3,500,000 on 10/7/1996) SL 101+5/3 SLC 8+1 SC 11 Others 16+1/2
Everton (Free on 13/7/2001) PL 117+7/3 FLC 5+2 FAC 11/1
Sunderland (Free on 3/8/2005) PL 8+2/1 FAC 1
Everton (Free on 20/1/2006) PL 43+2/3 FLC 3 FAC 1 Others 1+1
Derby Co (Free on 31/1/2008) PL 8

STURRIDGE Daniel Andre
Born: Birmingham, 1 September 1989
Height: 6'2" **Weight:** 12.0
International Honours: E: Yth
Daniel is a promising young Manchester City forward who was moved up to the senior squad in 2006-07 before forcing himself into Sven-Goran Eriksson's plans last season. After making his debut in City's shock FA Cup defeat at Sheffield United, Daniel bagged his first goal against Derby at Pride Park three days later. His uncle Dean, who played for the Rams in the 1990s, was able to comment on the goal as Radio Derby's analyst.

Manchester C (From trainee on 2/9/2007) PL 2+3/1 FAC 0+1/1

STURROCK Blair David
Born: Dundee, 25 August 1981
Height: 6'0" **Weight:** 11.1
Club Honours: Div 3 '02; Div 2 '04
Although setting off as a regular at Swindon, the arrival of further strikers meant that Blair dropped down the order and the departure of father Paul as manager added to his difficulties at the County Ground. He continued to work hard whenever selected and his six goals from all competitions was a reasonable return from the number of games played, including a well-struck effort in the home

draw with Carlisle in March. A strong-running and brave forward who can make goals as well as score them, an arm injury ended his season.

Dundee U *(From juniors on 5/9/1999)*
Brechin C *(Loaned on 8/8/2000) SL 20+7/6 SC 1+2 Others 3+1/3*
Plymouth Arg *(Free on 26/10/2001) FL 9+54/2 FLC 1/1 FAC 0+5 Others 1+1*
Kidderminster Hrs *(Free on 24/12/2004) FL 17+5/5*
Rochdale *(Free on 5/8/2005) FL 15+16/6 FLC 0+1 FAC 0+1 Others 1+1 (Freed during 2006 close season)*
Swindon T *(Free, following trial at Wrexham, on 8/12/2006) FL 20+20/6 FLC 1 FAC 3+2/2 Others 1/1*

SULLIVAN Neil

Born: Sutton, 24 February 1970
Height: 6'0" **Weight:** 12.1
International Honours: S: 28
Neil signed for Doncaster in the summer of 2007, having been released by Leeds, and the experienced goalkeeper proved to be a good acquisition with consistent performances throughout the season. He played in every League One game but reserved his best performance for the play-off final at Wembley against his old club, with an impeccable display of handling.

Wimbledon *(From trainee on 26/7/1988) P/FL 180+1 FLC 18 FAC 25*
Crystal Palace *(Loaned on 1/5/1992) FL 1*
Tottenham H *(Free on 5/6/2000) PL 64 FLC 8 FAC 9*
Chelsea *(Free on 29/8/2003) PL 4 FLC 2 FAC 1+1*
Leeds U *(Free on 5/8/2004) FL 95 FLC 8 FAC 4 Others 3*
Doncaster Rov *(Loaned on 23/11/2006) FL 3*
Doncaster Rov *(Free on 19/2/2007) FL 59 FLC 2 FAC 2 Others 6*

SUMMERFIELD Luke John

Born: Ivybridge, 6 December 1987
Height: 6'0" **Weight:** 11.0
Still only 20, Luke appeared in the Carling Cup games in August but had to wait until December for a further opportunity with Plymouth. He could not hold his place until reappearing in the final games of the season. Luke has an accurate and broad range of passing from the centre of midfield and when in the team, often took over the free kicks. His crosses into the opposition box improved and despite not appearing regularly, Luke agreed a new one-year contract at the end of the season.

Plymouth Arg *(From trainee on 1/8/2005) FL 16+15/1 FLC 1+2/1 FAC 1+3*
Bournemouth *(Loaned on 20/3/2007) FL 5+3/1*

SUMULIKOSKI Velice

Born: Struga, Macedonia, 24 April 1981
Height: 6'0" **Weight:** 12.2
International Honours: Macedonia: 50
Signed from Turkish club Bursaspor in January, Velice made a couple of cameo appearances for Ipswich from the substitutes' bench before his first start at Crystal Palace. He is composed on the ball in midfield and can pass accurately over distance, playing in team-mates to provide scoring opportunities when nothing seemed to be on. He scored against Blackpool with a tremendous shot from the edge of the area and celebrated his 50th appearance for Macedonia. A shin problem seemed to have curtailed his season but a specialist gave him the all clear to continue playing.

Ipswich T *(£600,000 from Bursaspor, Turkey, ex NK Publikum, Slovacko, Zenit St Petersburg, on 28/1/2008) FL 10+6/1*

SUN JIHAI

Born: Dalian, China, 30 September 1977
Height: 5'10" **Weight:** 10.12
International Honours: China: 71
Sun Jihai is a pacy Chinese international defender who is most comfortable playing as a full-back or wing-back. The popular Manchester City utility man also enjoys getting forward in attack with overlapping runs to deliver decent crosses. Last season, his seventh with City, was not as fruitful in terms of first-team opportunities and he made only six starts. Was out of contract in the summer and looking for a new club.

Crystal Palace *(£500,000 from Dalian Wanda, China on 10/9/1998) FL 22+1 FLC 1*
FAC 1 *(£500,000 to Dalian Wanda, China on 27/7/1999)*
Manchester C *(£2,000,000 from Dalian Wanda, China on 26/2/2002) P/FL 93+37/3 FLC 7 FAC 9 Others 5/1*

SURMAN Andrew (Drew) Ronald Edward

Born: Johannesburg, South Africa, 20 August 1986
Height: 5'10" **Weight:** 11.5
International Honours: E: U21-4
It was an up-and-down season for this talented young England international midfielder. A clever and inventive passer of the ball, it was less lack of form that saw him out of the team, more the inability of all three management teams in charge of Southampton to contrive an effective combination between midfield and defence. Ironically, given that he is an attacking midfielder, he played the season out at left wing-back, from which position he gave a bravura performance as Saints defeated Sheffield United at St Mary's on the final day to bound out of

the relegation zone.

Southampton *(From trainee on 23/8/2003) P/FL 72+17/8 FLC 3+1 FAC 3/2 Others 2/1*
Walsall *(Loaned on 28/1/2005) FL 10+4/2*
Bournemouth *(Loaned on 3/8/2005) FL 24/6 FLC 2 FAC 1 Others 1*

SUTTON John William Michael

Born: Norwich, 26 December 1983
Height: 6'0" **Weight:** 14.2
International Honours: England: Yth
After scoring 30 goals in 75 appearances for St Mirren in the Scottish Premier League, John joined Wycombe last summer on a free transfer. He replaced Jermaine Easter at the end of September and forged a useful partnership with Scott McGleish, scoring six goals by the turn of the year. A tall and elegant player, John is a natural target-man, and a cool finisher. He really needs to feed off crosses but has the misfortune to play in a team without wingers. From February, he was mostly used from the bench, dropping down the pecking order with the arrival of first Leon Knight and then Delroy Facey.

Tottenham H *(From trainee on 12/7/2001)*
Carlisle U *(Loaned on 4/10/2002) FL 7/1 FAC 1 Others 2*
Swindon T *(Free on 20/12/2002) FL 0+1 (Freed on 20/1/2003)*
Raith Rov *(Free on 19/7/2003) SL 20/13 SC 1 Others 3/3*
Millwall *(£60,000 on 30/1/2004) FL 2+2 FAC 0+1*
Dundee *(Loaned on 7/7/2004) SL 20+12/8 SLC 2 SC 0+1*
St Mirren *(Signed on 31/8/2005) SL 57+7/25 SLC 2+1/1 SC 4+1/2 Others 3/2*
Wycombe W *(Free on 3/7/2007) FL 23+20/6 FLC 1 FAC 0+1 Others 1+2*

SWAILES Daniel (Danny)

Born: Bolton, 1 April 1979
Height: 6'3" **Weight:** 13.7
Club Honours: AMC '08; Div 2 '08
MK Dons let in five goals in the first two League games but conceded only 32 more from the remaining 44 after Danny's early-season arrival from manager Paul Ince's former club Macclesfield. A tall and commanding central defender, Danny quickly linked up with Sean O'Hanlon to form a rock-like barrier at the heart of the back four and always seemed to be in the right place to clear his lines when necessary. Particularly strong in the air, rarely losing a defensive header all season, he was always a threat when going forward for set pieces and thoroughly merited his place in the PFA 'League Two Team of the Season'.

Bury *(From trainee on 9/7/1997) FL 154+10/13 FLC 4+3 FAC 9+1 Others 10+3/1*
Macclesfield T *(£40,000 on 14/1/2005) FL*

Sun Jihai

94/5 FLC 3 FAC 6 Others 8+1
MK Dons *(Signed on 20/8/2007) FL 40/4 FLC 1 FAC 1 Others 5/1*

SWEENEY Antony Thomas
Born: Stockton, 5 September 1983
Height: 6'0" **Weight:** 11.9
Antony, a popular Hartlepool midfielder, has been a tireless performer for almost six seasons. Although he struggled to find his best form in the early months, it was a surprise when he was transfer listed in January. This seemed to act as a spur and his game improved steadily. He was probably Pool's most consistent player in the second half of the season and has now signed a new contract.
Hartlepool U *(From trainee on 10/1/2002) FL 146+21/27 FLC 7/1 FAC 11 Others 11/2*

SWEENEY Peter Henry
Born: Glasgow, 25 September 1984
Height: 6'0" **Weight:** 12.0
International Honours: S: B-1; U21-8; Yth
Peter failed to make an impact as a wide midfield player for Stoke, partly because of Liam Lawrence's excellent form, and spent most of the first part of the season on loan at Walsall. The former Scotland 'B' and under-21 international showed up well in his seven games in Walsall's midfield and Saddlers' fans were disappointed when he was snapped up by Leeds in January. Dennis Wise added Peter to the Elland Road roster, knowing him from the time they worked together at Millwall. The left-winger made an instant impact on his arrival with a fine debut in a 1-0 victory at Crewe that was televised live. But within days Wise left Leeds and Peter, who is blessed with ample skill, did not have much of a look-in under new manager Gary McAllister, who generally preferred Brad Johnson on the left.
Millwall *(From juniors on 13/12/2000) FL 45+14/5 FAC 3+4 Others 0+1*
Stoke C *(Signed on 5/7/2005) FL 18+17/2 FLC 1+1 FAC 3+1*
Yeovil T *(Loaned on 31/1/2007) FL 5+3*
Walsall *(Loaned on 22/11/2007) FL 7*
Leeds U *(£250,000 on 10/1/2008) FL 6+3*

SYMES Michael
Born: Great Yarmouth, 31 October 1983
Height: 6'3" **Weight:** 12.4
The Shrewsbury striker was hampered in pre-season by a hamstring injury but, although struggling for match-fitness, managed a substitute appearance in the opening game. Michael scored three vital goals, notably in the 2-1 defeat of Grimsby in September and the only goals in victories at Wrexham and at home to Barnet. That apart, he never quite hit top form and spent the second half of the season on loan at Macclesfield. Michael featured regularly during his first two months at Moss Rose, scoring one goal with a brilliant 35-yard volley in the draw at MK Dons at the end of January. In the final matches, he was used as a substitute and remains under contract at Shrewsbury.
Everton *(From trainee on 13/2/2002)*
Crewe Alex *(Loaned on 24/3/2004) FL 1+3/1*
Bradford C *(Free on 6/8/2004) FL 6+9/3 FLC 1 FAC 1 Others 0+1*
Stockport Co *(Loaned on 31/1/2006) FL 0+1*
Shrewsbury T *(Free on 4/8/2006) FL 32+22/12 FLC 3 FAC 3 Others 7+1/4*
Macclesfield T *(Loaned on 11/1/2008) FL 10+4/1*

T

TAARABT Adel
Born: Marseille, France, 24 May 1989
Height: 5'11" **Weight:** 12.0
International Honours: France: Yth
With Adel having been at Tottenham on loan from Lens since January 2007, the deal was made permanent in the summer. Despite that, he has yet to make his full debut and was restricted last season to ten appearances off the bench. Preferring to play on the left of midfield, his skill is there for all to see, especially when he runs at defenders, and he will be looking to break through in 2008-09.
Tottenham H (Signed from RC Lens, France on 5/1/2007) PL 0+8 FAC 0+1 Others 0+3

TABB Jay Anthony
Born: Tooting, 21 February 1984
Height: 5'5" **Weight:** 9.7
International Honours: RoI: U21-10
The wide midfield player was far and away Coventry's best player, overcoming an inability to complete a consistent 90 minutes. His ability to play on either flank and cross with either foot was a major plus and some of his best performances were in a more attacking central-midfield role, such as victories at Stoke and Queens Park Rangers. His non-stop activity was impressive and he always gave good cover to his full-back. A popular and sporting player, Jay scored six goals, several of them vital, including winners at Cardiff and at home to Norwich. Jay was one of the most fouled players in the Championship but was never theatrical, always jumping straight to his feet. Jay was outstanding against Norwich, forcing the substitution of his opponent, suffering two bad tackles that earned red cards and scoring the only goal.
Brentford (From trainee on 23/7/2001) FL 95+33/20 FLC 1+2 FAC 12+5/1 Others 6+2/3
Coventry C (Free on 17/7/2006) FL 62+11/8 FLC 3+1/1 FAC 4

TAINIO Teemu
Born: Tornio, Finland, 27 November 1979
Height: 5'8" **Weight:** 10.12
Club Honours: FLC '08
International Honours: Finland: 43; U21-20; Yth
Once again, frequent injury restricted Teemu's ability to play for Tottenham on a regular basis. The Finn played a part in 26 of Tottenham's games last season, and earned a Carling Cup winners' medal from the bench against Chelsea. He was required to play across midfield,

Teemu Tainio

either in an offensive or defensive role, and also at right and left-back. With Tainio behind him in the midfield, Jermaine Jenas produced some of his best performances. Often involved in Juande Ramos' successful substitution strategies, his ability to play in so many positions to good effect helped that process. Teemu continued to represent Finland, and scored once for his country last season.
Tottenham H (Free from Auxerre, France on 12/7/2005) PL 48+13/3 FLC 3+3 FAC 5+2 Others 7+2

TAIWO Soloman
Born: Lagos, Nigeria, 29 April 1985
Height: 6'0" **Weight:** 12.10
Soloman joined Dagenham from Sutton United in October and was quickly signed on a two-year contract after impressing in the reserves. He had the unfortunate distinction of being sent off in his first two starts for the club, both for aerial challenges where it was deemed he had raised his elbow. The midfielder's main asset is his ability to pick out forwards and set them up for chances on goal.
Dagenham & Redbridge (Free from Sutton U, ex Bromley, Lindsey Wilson College, Maidenhead U, Weymouth, Bromley, on 5/10/2007) FL 4+6 Others 2

TALBOT Andrew (Drew)
Born: Barnsley, 19 July 1986
Height: 5'10" **Weight:** 11.0
Having begun to make an impact for Luton after signing in January 2007, Drew picked up a minor injury and although fully recovered by the start of last season he had to settle for the bench, making an early impact when scoring in the Carling Cup at Dagenham. Long-term injuries to Sam Parkin and Paul Peschisolido gave him an opportunity for a prolonged run. Quick and full of running, with or without the ball, he can turn a defender with his body swerve but apart from a second Carling Cup goal, was unable to find the net. When he was injured in the home game against Northampton, manager Kevin Blackwell experimented with various combinations in attack but Drew was recalled when Dean Morgan joined Southend on loan. Mick Harford played Drew up front for two games, then tried him in midfield before relegating him to the bench to give Ryan Charles an extended run. He replaced Charles against Cheltenham but was on the field only a matter of minutes before an awkward fall damaged an anterior cruciate knee ligament, an injury that will keep him out until the New Year.
Sheffield Wed (Signed from Dodworth MW on 19/2/2004) FL 5+24/4 FAC 1 Others 0+3/1

Scunthorpe U (Loaned on 12/1/2007) FL 2+1/1
Luton T (£250,000 on 26/1/2007) FL 29+13/3 FLC 2+1/2 FAC 4+1 Others 1+1

TALBOT Jason Christopher
Born: Irlam, 30 September 1985
Height: 5'8" **Weight:** 10.1
Strong tackling with a bit of pace, Jason began the season as Port Vale's left-back but was hampered by a sending off against Cheltenham. He fought his way back and managed to curb the excesses that caused a number of brushes with officials. The arrival of Adam Eckersley added to competition for his place but he continued to compete. One of his best games was in Vale's 2-0 local derby at Crewe. Although told by manager Lee Sinnott in February that he would be released at the end of the season, Jason gave 100 per cent.
Bolton W (From trainee on 23/9/2004)
Derby Co (Loaned on 25/9/2004) FL 2
Mansfield T (Loaned on 19/11/2004) FL 2
Mansfield T (Free on 5/8/2005) FL 6 FLC 2 FAC 1 Others 1
Port Vale (Free on 9/2/2006) FL 43+9 FLC 3+1 FAC 3 Others 1

TANN Adam John
Born: Fakenham, 12 May 1982
Height: 6'0" **Weight:** 11.5
International Honours: E: Yth
After a previous loan spell at Notts County, Adam was recruited on a full-time basis from Leyton Orient in the summer. He was appointed team captain by Ian McParland and relished the added responsibility, leading by example. He guarantees maximum effort, either in the centre of defence or at right-back. His commitment was recognised by the management, who chose him as their 'Player of the Year'.
Cambridge U (From trainee on 7/9/1999) FL 111+10/4 FLC 2 FAC 9+1/3 Others 15/1 (Freed on 12/10/2005)
Notts Co (Free from Gravesend & Northfleet on 3/11/2005) FL 4+1 FAC 1/1
Leyton Orient (Free on 24/1/2006) FL 21+10/2
Notts Co (Free on 3/7/2007) FL 40+1/1 FLC 1 FAC 2 Others 1

TANSEY Gregory (Greg) James
Born: Huyton, 21 November 1988
Height: 6'1" **Weight:** 12.3
The central midfielder slipped down the Stockport pecking order last season following the signing of Gary Dicker, Dominic Blizzard and the emergence of his former youth-team colleague, Paul Turnbull. But the ball-playing midfielder

remains a key member of Jim Gannon's young squad and impressed on a month-long loan at Cheshire neighbours Altrincham.
Stockport Co (From trainee on 28/7/2006) FL 7+9 FAC 1+1 Others 3

TATE Alan
Born: Easington, 2 September 1982
Height: 6'1" **Weight:** 13.9
Club Honours: AMC '06; Div 1 '08
Starting the season in Swansea's first team, the former Manchester United defender suffered a fractured and chipped knee-cap in the Carling Cup defeat of Walsall. When he returned to fitness, Alan had to be satisfied with a place on the bench until the last third of the season, when he deputised firstly for Dennis Lawrence and Garry Monk at centre-back before reverting to right-back as a replacement for Angel Rangel.
Manchester U (From trainee on 18/7/2000)
Swansea C (Loaned on 22/11/2002) FL 27
Swansea C (Loaned on 24/10/2003) FL 9 Others 1
Swansea C (Free on 6/2/2004) FL 129+13/3 FLC 3 FAC 12+1 Others 14

TAUNDRY Richard Daniel
Born: Walsall, 15 February 1989
Height: 5'9" **Weight:** 12.10
The former Walsall trainee broke through with a substitute appearance against Luton in November and immediately looked the part. Both in defence and midfield, he showed up well in the second half of the season and despite an unlucky sending off against Brighton in March, Richard was deservedly voted by fans as runner-up to Mark Bradley in the 'Young Player of the Season' stakes.
Walsall (from trainee on 6/7/2007) FL 12+9 FAC 1

TAYLFORTH Sean James
Born: Middlewich, 10 March 1989
Height: 6'3" **Weight:** 10.7
An exciting left-winger, Sean is tipped for a bright future at Bradford. His debut came in a Johnstone's Paint Trophy tie at Doncaster and he almost scored with his first touch when he drove the ball across goal from close range.
Bradford C (From trainee on 4/7/2007) FL 1 FAC 0+1 Others 1

TAYLOR Andrew (Andy)
Born: Blackburn, 14 March 1986
Height: 5'11" **Weight:** 11.7
International Honours: E: Yth
Signed on loan from Blackburn last November, Andy went straight into the Tranmere side and, after a further month's extension, his loan deal was made

permanent in January. He impressed immediately with his workrate and reading of the game; and remaining injury-free, was ever-present from his arrival until the end of the season. A skilful left-back, Andy demonstrated a natural defensive talent and a maturity beyond his years, while his accurate passes out of defence provided many assists to the forwards. His consistency won him the Rovers' Supporters' 'Young Player of the Year' award and he is rumoured to be a target for several bigger clubs.
Blackburn Rov (From trainee on 2/7/2004)
Queens Park Rgrs (Loaned on 13/1/2006) FL 1+2
Blackpool (Loaned on 15/2/2006) FL 3
Crewe Alex (Loaned on 20/10/2006) FL 4 FLC 1 Others 1
Huddersfield T (Loaned on 31/1/2007) FL 7+1
Tranmere Rov (Signed on 16/11/2007) FL 29+1/2 FAC 3

TAYLOR Andrew Derek
Born: Hartlepool, 1 August 1986
Height: 5'10" **Weight:** 10.12
Club Honours: FAYC '04
International Honours: E: U21-7; Yth
Andrew started last season as Middlesbrough's regular left-back but in November the England under-21 international required surgery for plantar fascitis, more commonly known as 'Policeman's heel'. It had been hoped that complete rest would resolve the problem but surgery proved inevitable. During his absence from the side, Austrian international Manny Pogatetz, who had made a full recovery from his double knee operation, returned from injury and made the left-back slot his own. In late January, although he was some way from full match fitness, Andrew received a personal boost when he signed a one-year contract extension that will keep him at the Riverside until June 2011. Facing stiff competition for the left-back position, Andrew made a successful return to the side and featured in the final six games.
Middlesbrough (From trainee on 2/8/2003) PL 59+7 FLC 3 FAC 11 Others 1+2
Bradford C (Loaned on 2/8/2005) FL 24 Others 2

TAYLOR Andrew (Andy) John
Born: Caistor, 30 October 1988
Height: 6'2" **Weight:** 13.0
This young forward was mostly seen as a late Grimsby substitute last term, his pace and shooting skills bringing him a good goal return against tiring defences. Unlucky not to make Town's Johnstone's

Paint Trophy final squad at Wembley, he was on target in a second round penalty shoot-out at Rotherham, having once more started from the bench.
Grimsby T (From trainee on 5/12/2006) FL 3+34/7 FAC 0+3 Others 1+1

TAYLOR Christopher (Chris) David
Born: Oldham, 20 December 1986
Height: 5'11" **Weight:** 11.0
A local lad, Chris again made fine progress at Oldham, the club he supported as a boy. Although naturally right-footed, Chris plays on the left of midfield using his trickery and pace to bamboozle opposition defenders. Rated by manager John Sheridan as potentially the club's brightest talent, he occasionally stood in as captain and also bettered his debut season's strike tally with five goals. Chris was responsible for countless assists and linked well with a variety of different full-backs. Newspaper talk continues to link the rangy prospect with other clubs but the Latics seem determined to retain the services of a player who is under contract until summer 2010.
Oldham Ath (From trainee on 15/7/2004) FL 91+9/9 FLC 1+1 FAC 8 Others 5

TAYLOR Cleveland Kenneth Wayne
Born: Leicester, 9 September 1983
Height: 5'8" **Weight:** 11.5
Club Honours: Div 1 '07
International Honours: Jamaica: Yth

Cleveland started 2007-08 in the Scunthorpe team but took time in adjusting to the step up to the Championship. A fast, direct and popular right-winger, he spent the first half of the season alternating between the starting line-up and the bench before he was sold to Carlisle, ending four good years at Scunthorpe. After prolonged negotiations, Cleveland arrived at Brunton Park at the end of the January transfer window. A skilful ball player, his United career began well with some promising displays on the right, but sadly his form dipped and he seemed to lose confidence as he struggled to regain a regular place. He will be hoping that the summer break will enable him to rediscover his undoubted potential.
Bolton W (From trainee on 5/8/2002) FAC 0+2
Exeter C (Loaned on 9/8/2002) FL 1+2
Scunthorpe U (Free on 16/11/2004) FL 121+53/15 FLC 4+2 FAC 4+6 Others 4+1
Carlisle U (£50,000 on 31/1/2008) FL 14+4 Others 0+1

TAYLOR Gareth Keith
Born: Weston-super-Mare, 25 February 1973
Height: 6'2" **Weight:** 13.8
International Honours: W: 15; U21-7
Having arrived at Tranmere from Nottingham Forest in the summer of 2006, the experienced centre-forward proved yet again that he is always a tough opponent, scoring four goals, three

Chris Taylor

403

of them vital. At home to Northampton and Hereford he scored equalisers and at Southend the winner in a 2-1 victory. However, with the return of Ian Moore to Rovers, Gareth went on loan to Doncaster on January transfer deadline day and the move was made permanent a month later. Doncaster wanted Gareth to augment a strike force, depleted by injuries, in the push for promotion from League One and his experience proved vital in pursuit of that aim as the club reached the first tier of League football for the first time in 50 years. Still a thoughtful presence in attack, he is strong and unruffled, uses his height to good advantage and can orchestrate play to his own liking and tempo.

Bristol Rov *(From trainee at Southampton on 29/7/1991) FL 31+16/16 FLC 3 FAC 1+1 Others 5*
Crystal Palace *(£750,000 on 27/9/1995) FL 18+2/1 FAC 2/1*
Sheffield U *(Signed on 8/3/1996) FL 56+28/25 FLC 8+3/2 FAC 5+2 Others 1+2*
Manchester C *(£400,000 on 26/11/1998) FL 28+15/9 FLC 2+1/1 FAC 3 Others 1+3*
Port Vale *(Loaned on 21/1/2000) FL 4*
Queens Park Rgrs *(Loaned on 14/3/2000) FL 2+4/1*
Burnley *(Free on 20/2/2001) FL 88+7/36 FLC 4+1 FAC 6/1*
Nottingham F *(£500,000 on 27/8/2003) FL 78+12/19 FLC 5+1/3 FAC 8/3*
Crewe Alex *(Loaned on 17/1/2006) FL 15/4*
Tranmere Rov *(Free on 3/7/2006) FL 55+5/10 FLC 1+1 FAC 5+1/3 Others 1*
Doncaster Rov *(Signed on 31/1/2008) FL 4+8/1 Others 0+2*

TAYLOR Jamie
Born: Crawley, 16 December 1982
Height: 5'8" **Weight:** 12.2
The former Woking striker struggled to get into the Dagenham side, as he was behind four more regular forwards, but went on as a second-half substitute at home to Wrexham and scored his first League goal. In order to improve his fitness, he was loaned to Blue Square Premier side Grays for the final two months, scoring nine goals in 13 matches.
Dagenham & Redbridge *(Free from Woking, ex Broadbridge Heath, Horsham, Aldershot T, Carshalton Ath, AFC Wimbledon, Horsham, on 1/3/2007) FL 2+10/1 FAC 0+1 Others 2+1*

TAYLOR Jason James Francis
Born: Droylsden, 28 January 1987
Height: 6'1" **Weight:** 11.3
Another strong season saw Jason make more League appearances than any other Stockport player. Usually a terrier-like central midfielder, as the season

Jason Taylor

progressed he was given more license to leave the holding role to other players and make runs from the middle of the park. However, an apparently innocuous injury against Chester, a match with little at stake, saw him miss the Hatters' successful play-off campaign.

Oldham Ath (From trainee on 18/2/2006)
Stockport Co (Free on 17/3/2006) FL 93+3/5 FLC 3 FAC 5 Others 2+3

TAYLOR Kris

Born: Stafford, 12 January 1984
Height: 5'9" **Weight:** 13.5
Club Honours: Div 2 '07
International Honours: E: Yth; Sch
Arriving from Walsall in the summer, Kris had an important part in Hereford's promotion season with his ability to play in a number of different positions making him invaluable to the squad. Kris began the campaign as a central midfielder before a spell at left back. He then moved to the left of midfield before returning for the occasional outing to central midfield. Naturally left-footed, he can hit an incisive pass which, allied to a strong work ethic, made it no surprise that he should be a member of a promotion-winning side for the second successive season.

Manchester U (From trainee on 2/2/2001)
Walsall (Free on 19/2/2003) FL 58+22/6 FLC 3 FAC 3+1 Others 4
Hereford U (Free on 24/7/2007) FL 22+9/1 FLC 0+2 FAC 4+2 Others 1

TAYLOR Maik Stefan

Born: Hildesheim, Germany, 4 September 1971
Height: 6'4" **Weight:** 14.2
Club Honours: Div 2 '99; Div 1 '01
International Honours: NI: 68; B-1; U21-1
Having taken over the goalkeeping duties from Colin Doyle four games into the season, Maik brought presence and experience to the Birmingham defence. Worked diligently and with purpose at set pieces and was always alive to danger when attackers broke through. He pulled off some superb saves when the relegation battle intensified at the end of the season to keep Blues in with a shout.

Barnet (Free from Farnborough on 7/6/1995) FL 70 FLC 6 FAC 6 Others 2
Southampton (£500,000 on 1/1/1997) PL 18
Fulham (£800,000 + on 17/11/1997) P/FL 183+1 FLC 22 FAC 20 Others 6
Birmingham C (£1,500,000 on 8/8/2003) P/FL 167 FLC 5 FAC 16

TAYLOR Martin

Born: Ashington, 9 November 1979
Height: 6'4" **Weight:** 15.0

Club Honours: FLC '02
International Honours: E: U21-1; Yth
After making just one appearance for Birmingham, a 3-0 Carling Cup defeat at Blackburn, Martin went out on loan to Norwich and enjoyed an excellent spell at Carrow Road in November and December. He was influential when playing eight times as Norwich began to turn their season around under Glenn Roeder, winning four and drawing one of those games. Predictably strong in the air and a real threat at set-plays, he proved surprisingly comfortable on the ball, always being prepared to take an extra touch to ensure possession was retained. Norwich made several bids for the defender to secure his permanent transfer but failed to meet Birmingham's valuation. After returning to St Andrew's, Martin went straight into the Birmingham team but, after two impressive performances, was red carded in the third minute for a tackle on Arsenal's Eduardo, who absolved him of blame for his broken leg and fractured ankle. Martin coped with the subsequent vilification and unjustified personal attacks with dignity and resolve but it affected him and he will be hoping to move on in 2008-09.

Blackburn Rov (From trainee on 13/8/1997) P/FL 68+20/5 FLC 17 FAC 13+2/1 Others 3+2
Darlington (Loaned on 18/1/2000) FL 4
Stockport Co (Loaned on 23/3/2000) FL 7
Birmingham C (£1,250,000 on 2/2/2004) P/FL 68+7/1 FLC 10 FAC 6+1/1
Norwich C (Loaned on 4/11/2007) FL 8/1

TAYLOR Matthew Simon

Born: Oxford, 27 November 1981
Height: 5'10" **Weight:** 11.10
Club Honours: Div 1 '03
International Honours: E: U21-3
Following Portsmouth's summer signings Matthew, a livewire left wing-back or midfielder, found the competition for places intense, particularly as the manager went for height and power. By the end of September, he had started only four games, one of them in the Carling Cup. Then, between October and mid-January, he played only 168 minutes of first-team football for Pompey, all as a substitute. Frustration and a desire for regular football led to a move to Bolton in the January transfer window and Matthew arrived at the Reebok with a reputation as a proven Premiership player and scorer of some sensational goals. The former England under-21 international made his debut in the 0-0 draw at Newcastle and despite missing a penalty at Reading

and being slightly short of match-fitness, slotted effortlessly into the Bolton side. Exceptional in his UEFA Cup debut in the home victory over Atletico Madrid, it took Matthew some time to net his first goal for Wanderers but he resolved that with a fine double against Arsenal and a late equaliser in the final game at Chelsea. Matthew aims to enhance his reputation when he embarks on his first full season with Bolton.

Luton T (From trainee on 9/2/1999) FL 127+2/16 FLC 6 FAC 10/1 Others 1
Portsmouth (£400,000 + on 3/7/2002) P/FL 139+40/23 FLC 13+1/3 FAC 10+1/3
Bolton W (£4,500,000 on 17/1/2008) PL 16/3 Others 3

TAYLOR Neil John

Born: Ruthin, 7 February 1989
Height: 5'9" **Weight:** 10.2
International Honours: W: U21-3; Yth
A product of the successful Wrexham youth structure, Neil progressed via the under-18s and reserves to make his debut as a substitute in a Carling Cup tie against Aston Villa. The young defender started in the League for the first time at Stockport in September and went on to produce some eye-catching displays, always being comfortable on the ball. Neil has a good turn of pace and is dangerous from set pieces, although he was not helped by the team's indifferent performances. He played for Wales under-17s, was under-19 captain and graduated to the under-21 side. Neil won the supporters' 'Young Player of the Year' award and, if he maintains his rate of development, is one for the future.

Wrexham (From trainee on 30/7/2007) FL 21+5 FLC 0+1

TAYLOR Ryan Anthony

Born: Liverpool, 19 August 1984
Height: 5'8" **Weight:** 10.4
International Honours: E: U21-4; Yth
Having missed the first two months of the season while completing recovery from an injury sustained in the last game of 2006-07, Ryan made his first start for Wigan at Tottenham. An outstanding prospect at right-back, he demonstrated his versatility when slotting into the left side of midfield. Hard tacking, comfortable on the ball, he has boundless energy and loves to go forward to support the attack. A long-throw expert and a dead-ball specialist, he scored his first goal of the season with a curling free-kick against Newcastle at the JJB Stadium in December. His best game was against Birmingham in April, when he scored two goals, the first a stunning left-footed half-volley.

Tranmere Rov (From trainee on 3/4/2002) FL 82+16/14 FLC 5+1/1 FAC 9+1/2 Others 8/2
Wigan Ath (£750,000 + on 21/7/2005) PL 27+17/4 FLC 4/1 FAC 3

TAYLOR Ryan David
Born: Rotherham, 4 May 1988
Height: 6'2" **Weight:** 10.10
Good work is being done with Rotherham's young players and Ryan was another to emerge through the junior ranks. He is a striker with a good left foot and an eye for goal. The more games he played, the stronger he became as he adapted to the physical side of League Two football. Ryan is good in the air, never shirks a challenge and is part of a production line on which the future of the club may depend.
Rotherham U (From trainee on 3/8/2006) FL 23+23/6 FLC 1 FAC 2+1 Others 2

TAYLOR Scott James
Born: Chertsey, 5 May 1976
Height: 5'10" **Weight:** 11.4
Club Honours: AMC '02, '04, '08
Scott missed the start of the MK Dons' 2007-08 campaign through injury and the experienced striker went on loan to Rochdale in mid-October to get some games under his belt. Briefly paired with Glenn Murray in Rochdale's attack, Scott returned to Milton Keynes after only two starts and played a late cameo role in the January Johnstone's Paint Trophy win at Gillingham before being released later that month.
Millwall (£15,000 from Staines on 8/2/1995) FL 13+15 FLC 0+2/2 FAC 1+1
Bolton W (£150,000 on 29/3/1996) P/FL 2+10/1 FLC 0+4/1 FAC 1/1
Rotherham U (Loaned on 12/12/1997) FL 10/3 Others 1
Blackpool (Loaned on 26/3/1998) FL 3+2/1
Tranmere Rov (£50,000 on 9/10/1998) FL 78+30/17 FLC 16/5 FAC 2+5
Stockport Co (Free on 10/8/2001) FL 19+9/4 FLC 2/3 FAC 0+1
Blackpool (Free on 25/1/2002) FL 97+19/43 FLC 5/4 FAC 6+1/9 Others 7+3/5
Plymouth Arg (£100,000 on 30/12/2004) FL 17+17/4 FLC 2/1 FAC 0+1
MK Dons (£100,000 on 16/1/2006) FL 16+29/5 FLC 2+1 FAC 1+2 Others 1+3
Brentford (Loaned on 8/3/2007) FL 3+3
Rochdale (Loaned on 19/10/2007) FL 2+2

TAYLOR Steven Vincent
Born: Greenwich, 23 January 1986
Height: 6'1" **Weight:** 13.0
International Honours: E: B-1; U21-25; Yth
Considering all the problems that are frequently highlighted about Newcastle's defence, the one redeeming feature

continues to be Steven who is developing into a fine centre-back. A regular starter throughout the season, interrupted only briefly by back and hamstring injuries, his early form seemed a bit erratic but as the season wore on, his reading of the game developed, he became calmer and more assured and the level of his performances continually improved. Strong and committed, he continued to appear for England under-21 side, now as captain, and was named in the full squad for the friendly against Germany in August. In November, he was voted 'North-East Young Player of the Year' by sports writers and his only goal, against Arsenal the following month, was enough to earn a point.
Newcastle U (From trainee on 30/1/2003) PL 79+5/3 FLC 6 FAC 7/1 Others 20+4/1
Wycombe W (Loaned on 12/12/2003) FL 6

TAYLOR Stuart James
Born: Romford, 28 November 1980
Height: 6'4" **Weight:** 13.4
Club Honours: PL '02; FAC '03
International Honours: E: U21-3; Yth
Stuart was the goalkeeping understudy to Scott Carson throughout the season, making just six appearances, one of them as a substitute. When Scott played, Stuart was on the bench every time but with his physique and determination he is a comforting presence in reserve.
Arsenal (From trainee on 8/7/1998) PL 16+2 FLC 4 FAC 3 Others 3+2
Bristol Rov (Loaned on 24/9/1999) FL 4
Crystal Palace (Loaned on 9/8/2000) FL 10
Peterborough U (Loaned on 15/2/2001) FL 6
Leicester C (Loaned on 18/11/2004) FL 10
Aston Villa (£1,000,000 on 1/7/2005) PL 9+3 FLC 3

TAYLOR-FLETCHER (formerly FLETCHER) Gary
Born: Widnes, 4 June 1981
Height: 5'10" **Weight:** 11.7
International Honours: E: Sch
Signed in the summer from Huddersfield, Gary made the Blackpool right-wing position his own last season as he impressed all. Formerly a striker, Gary was deployed by manager Simon Grayson to attack on the right and even from there he still managed six goals, the pick being a volley against Leicester in a 2-1 home win. Unfortunate to have suffered from a slight groin injury that resulted in him missing a few games, he was the most substituted player in the Championship in 2007-08. Gary also had the honour to score the 500,000th goal in the Football League while playing for Huddersfield.
Hull C (Loaned from Northwich Vic on 16/3/

2001) FL 1+4
Leyton Orient (£150,000 from Northwich Vic on 9/7/2001) FL 10+11/1 FLC 1/1 FAC 2
Lincoln C (Free on 14/8/2003) FL 77+3/27 FLC 1+1/1 FAC 3 Others 8/3
Huddersfield T (Free on 14/7/2005) FL 69+13/21 FLC 2+1/3 FAC 4/1 Others 3/1
Blackpool (Signed on 20/7/2007) FL 40+2/6 FLC 3 FAC 1

TEAGUE Andrew Harry
Born: Preston, 5 February 1986
Height: 6'2" **Weight:** 12.0
The Macclesfield central defender missed the start of the season as he was still recovering from a broken leg but returned to training in October after a lay-off of 11 months. As part of his recuperation programme, he went on loan to non-League sides Tamworth and Hyde before making his one senior appearance in the last match of the season at Chester. Was released in the summer.
Macclesfield T (From trainee on 4/7/2005) FL 39+5/2 FLC 1 FAC 1 Others 4+1/1

TEALE Gary Stewart
Born: Glasgow, 21 July 1978
Height: 6'0" **Weight:** 11.6
Club Honours: Div 2 '03
International Honours: S: 11; B-1; U21-6
Although retaining a place in Scotland's squad, Gary was unable to pin down a regular position with Derby and half his Premiership appearances were made as substitute. His confidence inevitably suffered and he was in direct opposition to Craig Fagan for the place on the right of midfield. Derby did not see the

Gary Taylor-Fletcher

best of Gary and he joined Plymouth on loan in February, spending the last three months of the season at Home Park. He slotted into the right of midfield following David Norris' departure and made 12 appearances for the Pilgrims, including four from the bench. A tricky player with excellent crossing ability, he returned to Derby at the end of the season but it was rumoured that Argyle manager Paul Sturrock was preparing to make an offer. Gary was named in George Burley's first Scotland squad after intermittingly playing in the Euro 2008 qualifiers under Alex McCleish.

Clydebank *(From juniors on 19/6/1996) SL 52+16/14 SLC 3+1 SC 1 Others 4*
Ayr U *(£70,000 on 2/10/1998) SL 94+7/13 SLC 5+1/1 SC 10/3 Others 4/1*
Wigan Ath *(£200,000 on 14/12/2001) P/FL 121+41/8 FLC 9+5 FAC 4+3 Others 2/2*
Derby Co *(£600,000 on 11/11/2007) P/FL 20+14/1 FLC 1 FAC 2+1 Others 0+1*
Plymouth Arg *(Loaned on 19/2/2008) FL 8+4*

TEIXEIRA Filipe de Andrade

Born: Paris, France, 2 October 1980
Height: 5'8" **Weight:** 10.4
Club Honours: Ch '08
International Honours: Portugal: U21
Signed from Paris St Germain in the summer, Filipe became only the second Frenchman to play in the League for West Bromwich. Unfortunately his season was cut short by injury in early March, after he had to leave the field during the home League game against Plymouth. Before that, Filipe proved to be an effective attacking midfielder who scored three goals in four games in September, adding two more later on in a comprehensive 4-0 League victory at Coventry.

West Bromwich A *(£600,000 from Academica de Coimbra, Portugal, ex Felgueiras, Istres, Paris St Germain, Uniao Leiria - loan, on 25/7/2007) FL 24+6/5 FLC 2+1 FAC 4*

TELFER Paul Norman

Born: Edinburgh, 21 October 1971
Height: 5'9" **Weight:** 11.6
Club Honours: SPD '06, '07
International Honours: S: 1; B-2; U21-3
Having been freed by Glasgow Celtic in the summer, the highly experienced midfield player linked up with Bournemouth and was a regular in the side in the first part of last season. However, he began to struggle with the rigours of League One football and in December Paul announced his retirement from football.

Luton T *(From trainee on 7/11/1988) FL 136+8/19 FLC 5 FAC 14/2 Others 2/1*

Filipe Teixeira

407

Coventry C (£1,500,000 on 11/7/1995) PL 178+13/6 FLC 15/2 FAC 15+4/4
Southampton (Free on 2/11/2001) PL 112+16/1 FLC 5+2 FAC 12 Others 1+1
Glasgow Celtic (£200,000 on 22/7/2005) SL 56+1/1 SLC 5 SC 3 Others 7+1
Bournemouth (Signed on 17/7/2007) FL 17+1 FAC 3 Others 3

TERRY John George
Born: Barking, 7 December 1980
Height: 6'0" **Weight:** 12.4
Club Honours: FAC '00; FLC '05, '07; PL '05, '06; CS '05
International Honours: E: 44; U21-9
The England captain had a mixed pre-season in 2007, to say the least. He signed the much-publicised lucrative contract offered by Chelsea but unfortunately his injury jinx returned with a vengeance when he broke a toe in the United States, forcing him to miss the Community Shield match against Manchester United. This was the first of a whole raft of injuries that kept the inspirational skipper of club and country sidelined for a clutch of important fixtures as Chelsea and England's iron man seemed to spend more time in hospital than an extra in Casualty. Later a fractured cheekbone was added to his list but he continued playing in a protective mask. John injured a knee in England's preparation for European Championship qualifiers and was sorely missed in the crucial defeats in Moscow and by Croatia at Wembley. His comeback lasted just six matches before a broken metatarsal against Arsenal kept him on the sidelines for 14 matches. At least he was able to end his curiously long run without a Premier League goal by heading the winner at Sunderland. John played imperiously in Chelsea's run to the Champions' League final and was outstanding in Moscow, being one kick away from lifting the trophy until fate took a hand in the cruellest fashion. With the scores tied in the shoot-out, he stepped up to take the decisive penalty but slipped at the moment of contact in the atrocious conditions and struck the post with the 'keeper sent the wrong way. John was voted into the 'FIFPro World XI' for the third consecutive time, the only player apart from Ronaldinho to be nominated for all three teams.
Chelsea (From trainee on 18/3/1998) PL 224+13/16 FLC 22+1/1 FAC 29+5/9 Others 60/6
Nottingham F (Loaned on 23/3/2000) FL 5+1

TERRY Paul Edward
Born: Dagenham, 3 April 1979
Height: 5'10" **Weight:** 12.6
Club Honours: Div 2 '05
International Honours: E: SP-3

Paul joined Leyton Orient on a free transfer from Yeovil last summer and started the season as right-back because of injuries before moving to his more favoured central-midfield position when Steve Purches recovered from injury. Paul is a tough-tackling midfielder who is equally good at defending or attacking. He was out of contract in summer.
Yeovil T (Signed from Dagenham & Redbridge, ex trainee at Charlton Ath, on 20/8/2003) FL 111+24/10 FLC 2+2 FAC 11/2 Others 4+1
Leyton Orient (Free on 27/7/2007) FL 41+2 FLC 2 FAC 2 Others 1+1

TESSEM Jo
Born: Orlandet, Norway, 28 February 1972
Height: 6'3" **Weight:** 12.13
International Honours: Norway: 9; B-1
An experienced hard-working midfielder, Jo joined Bournemouth in January on a short-term deal from Lyn Oslo in Norway. He made his debut at Cheltenham but failed to re-establish himself in the starting line-up after sustaining an injury and was not offered a new contract in the summer. A player whose main strength lay in attack, he could also back up the defence when required.
Southampton (£600,000 from Molde, Norway, ex Lyn, on 19/11/1999) PL 67+43/12 FLC 4+2/1 FAC 7+6/3 Others 0+1 (Transferred to Lyn Oslo, Norway on 10/3/2005)
Millwall (Loaned on 1/10/2004) FL 11+1/1 FLC 1
Bournemouth (Free from Lyn Oslo, Norway on 9/11/2008) FL 5+6

TEVEZ Carlos Alberto
Born: Buenos Aires, Argentina, 5 February 1984
Height: 5'10" **Weight:** 10.10
Club Honours: PL '08; UEFACL '08
International Honours: Argentina: 38; U21; Yth
A stocky and highly skilled Manchester United and Argentina forward, Carlos finally joined United in the summer following a payment of £2-million to West Ham United by his owners MSI. Making his debut in a 1-1 draw against Portsmouth in August, he set up the equaliser for Paul Scholes. He opened his Premiership account in September with a diving header in a 2-0 victory over Chelsea at Old Trafford and there were many more contributions as the season progressed. With double strikes against Middlesbrough and Derby, the potential of a Wayne Rooney – Carlos Tevez partnership was lauded by the Press. The pair continued to flourish, not only in the

Premiership but also on the European stage. Champions' League goals were celebrated by Carlos against Dynamo Kiev, Sporting Lisbon, Lyon and AS Roma. His first away goal in the Premiership was notable in the creation of United legends, at Liverpool in front of the famed Kop. A goal against Birmingham on New Year's Day and two against Newcastle in January took his Premiership tally to ten. Perhaps his most important contribution came in April when he scored a brilliant 70th-minute diving header in the Champions' League quarter-final second leg against Roma at Old Trafford, from Owen Hargreaves' superb cross to give the Reds a 1-0 victory on the night and a 3-0 aggregate. Ten days later, he scored an 88th-minute equalizer against Blackburn to keep alive United's hopes of retaining the title. With an inspiring performance against Barcelona in the Champions' League semi-final at Old Trafford, Carlos had a season covered in glory. He never stops running.
West Ham U (Loaned from Corinthians, Brazil, ex Boca Juniors, on 31/8/2006) PL 19+7/7 FAC 1 Others 2
Manchester U (Loaned from Corinthians, Brazil on 10/8/2007) PL 31+3/14 FAC 2/1 Others 6+6/4

[TEYMOURIAN] TIMOTIAN-SAMARANI Adranik
Born: Tehran, Iran, 6 March 1983
Height: 5'11" **Weight:** 11.7
International Honours: Iran: 28
Despite impressing during his debut season, with an abundance of energy and a keen eye for goal, Teymourian found first-team opportunities at Bolton harder to come by second time around. His only League start was in the defeat at Portsmouth in August and he made only a handful of appearances from the bench. He figured slightly more often in the early stages of the UEFA Cup campaign, but this lively central midfielder's opportunities continued to be limited.
Bolton W (£500,000 from Aboomoslem, Iran, ex Oghab, on 31/8/2006) PL 7+13/2 FLC 2+1 FAC 2/2 Others 2+3

THATCHER Benjamin (Ben) David
Born: Swindon, 30 November 1975
Height: 5'10" **Weight:** 12.7
International Honours: W: 7; E: U21-4; Yth
It was a frustrating season for Ben, who started Charlton's first three League games at left-back but suffered a recurring knee injury in the home game against Sheffield Wednesday and required an operation. It was mid-March before

John Terry

Ben returned at Burnley and his consistent displays helped him keep his place until he was rested for the final game. A tough tackler, whose steel was missed by Charlton when absent, he was out of contract at the end of the campaign.
Millwall (From trainee on 8/6/1992) FL 87+3/1 FLC 6 FAC 7 Others 1
Wimbledon (£1,840,000 on 5/7/1996) PL 82+4 FLC 12 FAC 5
Tottenham H (£5,000,000 on 12/7/2000) PL 29+7 FLC 6+1 FAC 3
Leicester C (£300,000 + on 17/7/2003) PL 28+1/1
Manchester C (£100,000 on 30/6/2004) PL 46+1 FLC 3 FAC 1
Charlton Ath (£500,000 + on 11/1/2007) P/FL 21+1

THELWELL Alton Anthony
Born: Islington, 5 September 1980
Height: 6'0"   **Weight:** 12.7
International Honours: E: U21-1
Alton started the season as first-choice centre-half at Leyton Orient but suffered a knee injury that interrupted his campaign. A quality centre-half who is good in the air for his size, he was out of contract during the summer.
Tottenham H (From trainee on 27/1/1999) PL 13+5 FAC 0+3
Hull C (Free on 1/7/2003) FL 33+7/1 FLC 1 Others 1
Leyton Orient (Signed on 21/10/2006) FL 47+3/1 FLC 2 FAC 4 Others 2

THIRLWELL Paul
Born: Washington, 13 February 1979
Height: 5'11"   **Weight:** 11.4
International Honours: E: U21-1
The campaign proved to be a frustrating one for Paul. Appointed team captain at Carlisle in succession to the departed Kevin Gray, he made only a handful of appearances before being sidelined with injury. An attempted mid-term comeback proved to be short-lived for this doughty midfielder but he did make a couple of substitute appearances in the last weeks of the season. For Paul, next season offers the hope of a fresh start.
Sunderland (From trainee on 14/4/1997) P/FL 55+22 FLC 6+2/1 FAC 5+2
Swindon T (Loaned on 8/9/1999) FL 12
Sheffield U (Free on 30/7/2004) FL 24+6/1 FLC 2+1 FAC 2+1
Derby Co (Signed on 5/8/2005) FL 15+6 FAC 2
Carlisle U (Free on 8/9/2006) FL 38+5 FLC 2+1 FAC 1 Others 1+1

THOMAS Anthony Christopher
Born: Hammersmith, 30 August 1982
Height: 5'11"   **Weight:** 12.8
Signed from Hemel Hempstead, Anthony

netted four goals for Barnet in his first season in League football, including one live on Sky at Dagenham. He spent time on loan at Cambridge City early in the season, returning just before Christmas. After being largely restricted to substitute appearances, the striker was more evident in the Bees' starting line-up in the closing months. Was out of contract in the summer and looking for a new club.
Barnet (Free from Hemel Hempstead T on 6/7/2007) FL 14+12/4 FLC 1 FAC 0+5 Others 0+1

THOMAS Aswad Kwame
Born: Westminster, 9 August 1989
Height: 5'10"   **Weight:** 11.6
Aswad joined Stanley on loan from Charlton in January, initially as a left-back, although he played most of his 13 games in midfield and successfully. His high spot was at Chester, when he scored twice, his first goals in League football. He also did well against Morecambe, when his cross to Paul Mullin led to the winning goal. His loan spell ended earlier than expected as he was sent off at Macclesfield and suspended. Despite that he is

remembered fondly at Stanley because his attitude was superb throughout his stay.
Charlton Ath (From trainee on 18/7/2007)
Accrington Stanley (Loaned on 31/1/2008) FL 13/2

THOMAS Daniel (Danny) Justin
Born: Leamington Spa, 1 May 1981
Height: 5'7"   **Weight:** 11.5
Almost ever-present for Macclesfield last season, having been freed by Hereford the previous summer, Danny made more appearances than any of his colleagues. Very much an attacking out-and-out left-winger who uses his extraordinary pace to good effect, he is not afraid to cut into the centre of the pitch when surging forward. He scored four goals, two of which were winning strikes, including a floated, acute-angled shot that was almost the last kick of the home match against Wrexham.
Leicester C (From trainee at Nottingham F on 13/5/1998) PL 0+3
Bournemouth (Signed on 8/2/2002) FL 35+24/2 FLC 2/1 FAC 6/1 Others 5+2
Boston U (Free on 19/3/2004) FL 55+27/8

Danny Thomas

FLC 1+1 FAC 4+3 Others 2+1
Shrewsbury T *(Free, following trials at Grimsby T and Cheltenham T, on 24/11/2006) FL 3+3 Others 1*
Hereford U *(Free on 23/11/2007) FL 15/2*
Macclesfield T *(Free on 11/7/2007) FL 43/4 FLC 1 FAC 1 Others 1*

THOMAS Jerome William
Born: Wembley, 23 March 1983
Height: 5'10" **Weight:** 11.10
Club Honours: FAYC '00, '01
International Honours: E: U21-2; Yth
Jerome is one of Charlton's most accomplished players. A gifted winger who can play on either side, he is confident, and loves to run at defenders to strike on goal as well as creating chances for others. Unlike some wingers, he is not afraid to take a knock and rarely complains if he does. With Darren Ambrose and Lloyd Sam vying for the wing positions, Jerome was not an automatic choice but he featured in the majority of the games despite spells out with illness and a hamstring injury. Jerome has a powerful shot but surprisingly failed score, although able to claim numerous assists.
Arsenal *(From trainee on 3/7/2001) FLC 1+2*
Queens Park Rgrs *(Loaned on 27/3/2002) FL 4/1*
Queens Park Rgrs *(Loaned on 29/8/2002) FL 5+1/2*
Charlton Ath *(£100,000 on 2/2/2004) P/FL 73+29/7 FLC 5+1 FAC 4+5*

THOMAS Wayne Junior Robert
Born: Gloucester, 17 May 1979
Height: 5'11" **Weight:** 11.12
The season's opener against West Bromwich proved to be Wayne's final appearance in a Burnley shirt, the big defender departing in a big-money move to Southampton with only a fraction of the fee being spent on his Turf Moor replacement, Clarke Carlisle. When Wayne arrived at Southampton, he appeared to be exactly what they needed, a match-fit centre-back. In addition, he proved to be fast for a big man and just the sort of defender who is popular with fans, never shy about getting stuck in and giving 100 per cent. Unfortunately, like most centre-backs at St Mary's, he suffered from injuries and missed about a third of the season.
Torquay U *(From trainee on 4/7/1997) FL 89+34/5 FLC 2+1/1 FAC 7/1 Others 6+4*
Stoke C *(£200,000 + on 5/6/2000) FL 188+1/7 FLC 7+1 FAC 10/1 Others 10*
Burnley *(Free on 4/7/2005) FL 46+4/1 FLC 2 FAC 1+1*
Southampton *(£1,000,000 on 16/8/2007) FL 29+1 FAC 2*

THOMPSON Alan
Born: Newcastle, 22 December 1973
Height: 6'0" **Weight:** 12.8
Club Honours: Div 1 '97; SPD '01, '02, '04, '06; SC '01, '04, '05; SLC '01, '06
International Honours: E: 1; B-1; U21-2; Yth
Former England man Alan started last season as captain of Leeds and stood by the Elland Road club in the summer while its future was being sorted out. Following that, the veteran left-sided midfielder had a sensational start to the campaign with a trademark free kick in the third minute of the opening home game, a 4-1 win over Southend, and led the club to four straight wins before the first of many frustrating injuries kicked in. When fully fit his vision and passing were a joy but he was able to start very few League One games for the Whites and welcomed a loan move to Hartlepool in January to get his fitness back. Alan soon proved a useful goal-maker in a run of seven games at Pool and manager Danny Wilson would have liked to keep him longer. Recalled by new Leeds' manager Gary McAllister, after returning from Victoria Park Alan suffered another injury and managed just one appearance, as substitute at Swindon, from the turn of the year before announcing his retirement at the end of May.
Newcastle U *(From trainee on 11/3/1991) FL 13+3 FAC 1 Others 3*
Bolton W *(£250,000 on 22/7/1993) P/FL 143+14/33 FLC 24+1/5 FAC 6+2/2 Others 7+1/1*
Aston Villa *(£4,500,000 on 12/6/1998) PL 36+10/4 FLC 3+3/1 FAC 1 Others 4+1*
Glasgow Celtic *(£2,750,000 on 1/9/2000) SL 146+12/37 SLC 8+3/2 SC 19+1/4 Others 34+4/8*
Leeds U *(Free on 12/1/2007) FL 18+6/5 Others 1*
Hartlepool U *(Loaned on 22/1/2008) FL 7/1*

THOMPSON Edward (Ed) Peter
Born: Enfield, 8 January 1983
Height: 6'0" **Weight:** 11.7
Having joined Dagenham in the summer, the goalkeeper was understudy to Tony Roberts but finally had his chance in January when the Welshman was suspended for three games. Ed made his League debut at Morecambe in January and despite his confidence and good handling, ended on the losing side. He kept a clean sheet in his second game the following week. Was released in the summer.
Dagenham & Redbridge *(Free from Wingate & Finchley on 7/8/2007) FL 3 FAC 0+1*

THOMPSON Garry
Born: Kendal, 24 November 1980
Height: 6'1" **Weight:** 12.2
The flying Morecambe right-winger, who passed 300 games for the Shrimps during the season, produced some excellent performances and quickly attracted the attention of scouts as the club enjoyed success in the Carling Cup. His pace was always a threat and he terrorised a number of left-backs. He scored some important goals and added vital assists while at the centre of transfer speculation for much of the second half of the season. Morecambe turned down a £10,000 bid from Bradford and Garry ended the season surrounded by rumours after stalling on a new contract, with several clubs said to be interested in signing him.
Morecambe *(From Lancaster & Morecambe College on 1/8/1999) FL 36+4/7 FLC 2+1/1 FAC 1 Others 3*

THOMPSON John
Born: Dublin, 12 October 1981
Height: 6'1" **Weight:** 11.11
International Honours: RoI: 1; U21-11; Yth
An unlucky centre-half, John endured a nightmare season after joining Oldham from Nottingham Forest in the summer. After breaking his nose three times in his first month at Boundary Park, the former Republic of Ireland international then missed a huge chunk of the campaign with knee problems before returning to action in mid-March. The Dubliner was just nine minutes into his first start in two months when he limped off again and subsequently underwent corrective knee surgery in April.
Nottingham F *(Signed from Home Farm, ex River Valley Rgrs, on 6/7/1999) FL 100+29/7 FLC 6+2 FAC 5+3 Others 3+1*
Tranmere Rov *(Loaned on 25/10/2006) FL 5 FAC 2*
Tranmere Rov *(Loaned on 31/1/2007) FL 7*
Oldham Ath *(Free on 13/7/2007) FL 6+1 FLC 2 FAC 0+1 Others 1+1*

THOMPSON Joseph (Joe)
Born: Rochdale, 5 March 1989
Height: 6'0" **Weight:** 9.7
Joe came on as a substitute in Rochdale's second League game of last season, but found himself pushed down the pecking order by the switch of newcomer Kallum Higginbotham into his favoured right-wing position. He did not manage a significant run in the side until the New Year but then netted his first senior goal in a crucial victory over fellow promotion contenders Darlington.
Rochdale *(From trainee on 5/7/2007) FL 9+16/1 Others 0+1*

THOMPSON Leslie Allotey
Born: Newham, 3 October 1988
Height: 5'10" **Weight:** 11.7
Having come through the Bolton Academy to be given a professional contract at the beginning of October, Leslie was loaned out to League Two Stockport three days later to further his experience. On arriving at Edgeley Park, manager Jim Gannon said that Leslie was an exciting player who would give County a different dimension up front in the absence of Anthony Pilkington and David Poole, both recovering from injury. With pace to burn, and plenty of trickery, he was used as a right-sided midfielder, who could also push up through the middle, and it was a rash tackle on him that produced a penalty at Barnet on his debut. After four games for County, he was back at Bolton before going on loan again, to Blue Square Premier side Torquay in January. Leslie was out of contract at the season's end and not offered a new deal by Bolton.
Bolton W (From trainee on 1/10/2007)
Stockport Co (Loaned on 4/10/2007) FL 3 Others 1

THOMPSON Steven (Steve)
Howard
Born: Paisley, 14 October 1978
Height: 6'2" **Weight:** 12.10
Club Honours: SC '03; SPD '05; SLC '05
International Honours: S: 16; U21-12
Steve had a tough season at Cardiff in 2006-07 and was put on the transfer list in the summer but then suffered an injury while on holiday. He had a long spell of rehabilitation, recovering from the groin injury and then regaining his place at Ninian Park. Hit his best spell of form in December but was then sent off at Bristol City and served a three-match suspension. Came off the bench for the last 20 minutes of the FA Cup final but was unable to do any damage as the Portsmouth defence held out, although his knock-downs caused consternation at times. A tall, aggressive target-man who needs to boost his tally of goals, Steve's contract takes him through to the end of the coming season.
Dundee U (From juniors on 1/8/1996) SL 81+52/18 SLC 10+4/9 SC 6+8/4
Glasgow Rgrs (Signed on 1/1/2003) SL 21+41/17 SLC 3+2/3 SC 0+5 Others 2+11/3
Cardiff C (Signed on 10/11/2006) FL 70+23/15 FLC 0+1 FAC 3+4/1

THOMSON Steven (Steve)
John
Born: Glasgow, 23 January 1978
Height: 5'8" **Weight:** 10.4
International Honours: S: Yth
The signing of this experienced midfielder

from the Scottish Premier League in January was something of a coup for Brighton, but the former Falkirk captain made it clear that he wanted to move south for domestic reasons. Installed straightaway in the Albion midfield, ostensibly as a replacement for the departed Dean Hammond, Steve went about his business in a quiet, unassuming way, making himself available and playing simple passes. Lacking the dynamism and scoring ability of Hammond, the experienced Scotsman will look to raise his game in the new season in order to make a truly significant impact.
Crystal Palace (From trainee on 9/12/1995) FL 68+37/1 FLC 8+4/2 FAC 3+1/1 Others 1+1
Peterborough U (Free on 5/9/2003) FL 58+8/3 FLC 1 FAC 5/1 Others 3
Falkirk (Signed on 1/7/2005) SL 64+8/4 SLC 7/1 SC 4+1
Brighton & Hove A (Signed on 16/1/2008) FL 20

THORNE Peter Lee
Born: Manchester, 21 June 1973
Height: 6'0" **Weight:** 13.6
Club Honours: Div 2 '96; AMC '00
Peter suffered a frustrating start to his Bradford career with injuries, after being released by Norwich in the summer, and it took the veteran striker until November to get off the mark. But goals then flowed freely as he easily finished as City's top scorer, leading the line with his clever play and knack of being in the right place at the right time.
Blackburn Rov (From trainee on 20/6/1991) Others 0+1
Wigan Ath (Loaned on 11/3/1994) FL 10+1
Swindon T (£225,000 on 18/1/1995) FL 66+11/27 FLC 5+1/4 FAC 4+2 Others 1+1/1
Stoke C (£350,000 + on 25/7/1997) FL 147+11/65 FLC 12+1/6 FAC 5+1 Others 9+3/9
Cardiff C (£1,700,000 on 13/9/2001) FL 116+10/46 FLC 4/3 FAC 6+1/1 Others 6/1
Norwich C (Free on 4/7/2005) FL 15+21/1 FLC 2+1/1 FAC 1+2
Bradford C (Free on 27/7/2007) FL 31+2/14 FAC 2/1 Others 0+1

THORNHILL Matthew (Matt)
Mark
Born: Nottingham, 11 October 1988
Height: 6'1" **Weight:** 13.10
After a Carling Cup debut as a substitute against Chester, Matt was regularly in Nottingham Forest's squad for the remainder of the season. The young midfield player had his best spell in March with three consecutive appearances. Matt makes effective late runs into the penalty area and already has two League goals.
Nottingham F (From trainee on 13/12/2007) FL 5+9/2 FLC 0+1 FAC 0+1

THORNTON Kevin Anthony
Born: Drogheda, 9 July 1986
Height: 5'7" **Weight:** 11.0
International Honours: RoI: Yth
The home-grown Coventry midfielder has outstanding skill but was given few chances by Iain Dowie and made only one start, out of position at Leicester. When Chris Coleman arrived, he wiped the slate clean and gave the promising youngster a run of games. Kevin's jinking runs and ability to attack from midfield came to the fore. He holds up the ball well, always seems to want to keep it moving and can control the tempo of the game. A beautiful threaded through pass set up Leon Best's goal against Leicester and if he can do that more often, Kevin promises to be an outstanding player over the next few seasons.
Coventry C (From trainee on 9/7/2003) FL 18+28/2 FLC 0+2 FAC 0+2

THORNTON Sean
Born: Drogheda, 18 May 1983
Height: 5'10" **Weight:** 11.0
Club Honours: Ch '05; AMC '07
International Honours: RoI: U21-12; Yth
Sean joined Leyton Orient on a free transfer during the summer from Doncaster. An attacking midfielder who is skilful on the ball and can open up opposing defences with his range of passing. Sean scored with two fantastic free kicks in the away games at Southend and Leeds.
Tranmere Rov (Trainee) FL 9+2/1 FAC 0+1 Others 0+1
Sunderland (Signed on 4/7/2002) P/FL 28+21/9 FLC 4 FAC 5+4 Others 1+1
Blackpool (Loaned on 7/11/2002) FL 1+2 Others 1
Doncaster Rov (£175,000 on 14/7/2005) FL 38+21/2 FLC 3+2/1 FAC 4+2 Others 4+3/1
Leyton Orient (Free on 9/8/2007) FL 22+9/3 FLC 1 FAC 0+1 Others 1

THORPE Lee Anthony
Born: Wolverhampton, 14 December 1975
Height: 6'1" **Weight:** 12.4
Lee was a surprise summer signing for Brentford. The experienced 'battering ram' of a centre-forward arrived from Torquay with a suspension and was then sent off on his debut against Barnet. On his return, he showed good form with four goals in eight games but failed to score again before suffering a back injury at the end of December. Lee cancelled his contract at Brentford to join Rochdale at the end of January but suffered a terrible run of bad luck. Injuries and suspension disrupted his entry to the

Lee Thorpe

Born: Enfield, 4 November 1981
Height: 5'8" **Weight:** 11.10
Club Honours: FAT '05,'06
Stuart was given a second chance to play in League football by Gillingham when he was signed on loan from Grays in November. The strong, battling midfielder initially gained a regular spot before making the move permanent in January. However, unable to sustain his early promise he rejoined Grays in March, on loan for the rest of the season.
Southend U (Free from Shimizu-S-Pulse, Japan on 30/1/2001) FL 49+30/1 FLC 1 FAC 5+1 Others 1+2 (Freed during 2003 close season)
Gillingham (Signed from Grays Ath on 22/11/2007) FL 11+1

TIERNEY Marc Peter
Born: Prestwich, 23 August 1985
Height: 5'11" **Weight:** 11.2
Marc had an excellent season for Shrewsbury, sweeping the board in all the 'Player of the Year' awards. A left-back who can also play in central defence or on the left of midfield, he started 42 League and all Cup games. He developed as the season went on and was commanding when Shrewsbury's need for points became more desperate to avoid the drop, notably against Darlington and in the 3-0 defeat of Wrexham. Marc is highly committed and strong in the tackle, his one goal coming in the 4-0 defeat of Dagenham in December.
Oldham Ath (From juniors on 8/8/2003) FL 21+16 FLC 2+1 FAC 2+2 Others 2+1
Shrewsbury T (Free on 15/1/2007) FL 60+1/ 1 FLC 2 FAC 1 Others 4

TIERNEY Paul Thomas
Born: Salford, 15 September 1982
Height: 5'10" **Weight:** 12.10
International Honours: RoI: U21-7
Paul arrived at Stockport from Blackpool last August on a half-season loan to cover for Michael Rose while he recovered from knee surgery. A solid defender who also enjoyed moving forward, he scored an excellent goal in County's Johnstone's Paint Trophy win at Macclesfield. Went back to Bloomfield Road, but failed to make an appearance there before being released in May.
Manchester U (From trainee on 18/7/2000) FLC 1
Crewe Alex (Loaned on 8/11/2002) FL 14+3/ 1 FAC 2 Others 3
Colchester U (Loaned on 30/1/2004) FL 2 FAC 1 Others 1
Bradford C (Loaned on 21/12/2004) FL 14+2
Livingston (Signed on 29/6/2005) SL 25+6 SLC 3 SC 2

side but he subsequently came off the bench to excellent effect in successive victories, netting the only goal with a looping header against his former club. Unfortunately, a serious dead-leg ruled him out for the rest of the campaign and he broke an arm in a most unlikely accident on the way to the play-off game at Darlington. Was released at the end of the campaign.
Blackpool (From trainee on 18/7/1994) FL 2+10 FLC 0+1 FAC 1 Others 1
Lincoln C (Free on 4/8/1997) FL 183+9/58 FLC 5+1/1 FAC 14/1 Others 9+1/7
Leyton Orient (Free on 3/5/2002) FL 42+13/ 12 FLC 2/1 FAC 1 Others 1+1
Grimsby T (Loaned on 6/2/2004) FL 5+1
Bristol Rov (Free on 12/3/2004) FL 25+10/4 FLC 1/1 FAC 0+1 Others 4/1
Swansea C (Signed on 8/2/2005) FL 9+9/3
Peterborough U (Loaned on 30/9/2005) FL 6 FAC 1 Others 1
Torquay U (Free on 13/2/2006) FL 49+2/11 FLC 1 FAC 3+1 Others 1

Brentford (Free on 4/7/2007) FL 17+2/4 FAC 2
Rochdale (Free on 31/1/2008) FL 5+3/1

THRELFALL Robert (Robbie) Richard
Born: Liverpool, 28 November 1988
Height: 5'11" **Weight:** 11.2
Club Honours: FAYC '06,'07
International Honours: E: Yth
On loan from Liverpool, Robbie made an excellent early impression at Hereford and looked a very useful prospect with his attacking and defensive work as he played left-back for the Bulls. An ankle injury in the second round of the FA Cup ruled him out for more than two months and seriously disrupted his season. When he was fit again, Robbie struggled to regain his earlier form and the excellent displays of others meant that his chances were limited to a couple of appearances.
Liverpool (From trainee on 26/7/2006)
Hereford U (Loaned on 2/11/2007) FL 6+3 FAC 3

Blackpool (Free on 7/6/2006) FL 8+2 FLC 1 FAC 2
Stockport Co (Loaned on 10/8/2007) FL 15+1 FLC 2 FAC 1 Others 1/1

TILL Peter

Born: Walsall, 7 September 1985
Height: 5'11" **Weight:** 11.4
Peter showed his best form for Grimsby during their march to the Johnstone's Paint Trophy Final at Wembley. On target in early round victories over Huddersfield and Rotherham, the winger also hit the penalty shoot-out decider against the Millers. He then had a spell out of the team before a February return at Notts County, Peter using his pace to good effect in a new central role behind a lone forward. His runs with the ball and constant movement caused plenty of problems for the home defence and he was Town's 'Man of the Match'.
Birmingham C (From trainee on 4/7/2005) FLC 0+1
Scunthorpe U (Loaned on 6/10/2005) FL 6+2 FAC 1 Others 1
Boston U (Loaned on 13/1/2006) FL 10+6/1
Leyton Orient (Loaned on 6/10/2006) FL 4 Others 1
Grimsby T (Free on 23/11/2006) FL 48+8/2 FLC 1 FAC 2+1 Others 6/2

TILLEN Samuel (Sam) Lee

Born: Newbury, 16 April 1985
Height: 5'9" **Weight:** 10.5
International Honours: E: Yth
A talented, pacy left-back or left-sided midfielder, Sam joined Brentford during the summer, having been a trainee at Chelsea. He was used as a substitute for the Bees in two games in August but was not selected again and moved to Iceland to play for Fram Reykjavik in January. His brother Joe is also a professional player.
Chelsea (From trainee on 1/7/2002)
Brentford (Free on 4/7/2005) FL 48+20/1 FLC 3+1 FAC 5+2 Others 3+1

TIMAR Krisztian

Born: Budapest, Hungary, 4 October 1979
Height: 6'2" **Weight:** 13.10
International Honours: Hungary: 1; U21
Krisztian completed a permanent move to Plymouth in the summer after initially joining them on loan from Ferencvaros in January 2007. It proved an excellent investment by the Home Park board as this towering, powerful centre-back built up formidable partnerships with Marcel Seip and, towards the end of the campaign, with Russell Anderson. Dangerous from set pieces, Krisztian loves to get forward and was rewarded with three goals during the season. Not only did the Hungarian manage to force

his way into the international squad, he made his full debut against Slovenia in March. Towards the end of the season, he was rewarded with the captain's armband and was thrilled to receive the supporters' 'Player of the Year' award. Unfortunately, in the final match of the season at Wolverhampton, Krisztian was involved in a nasty aerial collision that resulted in a fractured skull. He had an operation following the match and hopes to regain full fitness for the start of the coming season.
Plymouth Arg (£75,000 from Ferencvaros, Hungary, having started his career there, ex MTK Hungaria, BKV Elore, Videoton, Tatabanya, Nyiregyhaza, on 18/1/2007) FL 44+3/4 FLC 3 FAC 3

TIMLIN Michael Anthony

Born: New Cross, 19 March 1985
Height: 5'9" **Weight:** 11.8
International Honours: RoI: U21-8; Yth
Michael returned to Swindon on loan from Fulham in March until the end of the season. He had enjoyed a successful loan at the County Ground in 2006-07 and featured in every game during his latest spell. An energetic central midfielder who likes to pass the ball around, Michael signed a two-year deal at the end of the season following his release by Fulham.
Fulham (From trainee on 27/7/2002) FLC 2+1 FAC 0+1
Scunthorpe U (Loaned on 24/2/2006) FL 0+1
Doncaster Rov (Loaned on 23/3/2006) FL 3
Swindon T (Loaned on 23/11/2006) FL 18+6/1 FAC 1
Swindon T (Loaned on 13/3/2008) FL 9+1/1

TIMOSKA Sampsa

Born: Kokemaki, Finland, 12 December 1979
Height: 6'0" **Weight:** 12.0
International Honours: Finland: 2
The Finnish defender's chances at Queens Park Rangers decreased following the departure of John Gregory, the man who signed him the previous season. A combination of injuries, bad luck and a change of regime meant Sampsa was limited to a handful of starts and a few late substitute appearances. Despite his versatility across the back line he was allowed to leave the club in January, exactly a year after first joining.
Queens Park Rgrs (Free from MyPa, Finland, ex TPV Tampere, Kokkolan PV, on 9/1/2007) FL 14+7

[TININHO] FAZENDA Miguel Angelo Karim

Born: Beira, Mozambique, 13 October 1980
Height: 5'9" **Weight:** 12.0

Signed by West Bromwich from Portuguese side Beira Mar in the summer, Tininho made only three senior appearances, on the opening day of the League season at Burnley and in two Carling Cup ties. A competitive defender, he produced some fine displays for the reserves before joining Barnsley on a month's loan in January, making his debut at Queens Park Rangers in the same week. During his month at Oakwell he gave the defence balance and showed a willingness to attack. Strong in the tackle, he can deliver good crosses and a taste of Championship football benefited him.
West Bromwich A (£230,000 from Beira Mar, Portugal on 31/7/2007) FL 1 FLC 1+1
Barnsley (Loaned on 14/1/2008) FL 3 FAC 1

TODD Andrew (Andy) John James

Born: Derby, 21 September 1974
Height: 5'10" **Weight:** 11.10
Club Honours: Div 1 '97, '00
Arriving at Derby from Barnsley in the close season, Andy joining the club at which his father Colin was a major star in County's best days. Making a great start, Andy played as a defensive midfielder in the opening game against Portsmouth

Andy Todd

and marked the occasion with a fine headed goal. Curiously, he was not allowed to settle in that position, moving into the back four, and his season was disrupted by related back and hamstring injuries. He was out for four months before returning in the FA Cup tie against Sheffield Wednesday. From then on, Paul Jewell was happy to have Andy's experience and professionalism in the squad, although he struggled to reach peak fitness. He also played at right-back and, in a difficult season, went about his job conscientiously before being told he could leave on a free transfer.
Middlesbrough (From trainee on 6/3/1992) FL 7+1 FLC 1+1 Others 5
Swindon T (Loaned on 27/2/1995) FL 13
Bolton W (£250,000 on 1/8/1995) P/FL 66+18/2 FLC 14+5/1 FAC 1 Others 3
Charlton Ath (£750,000 on 18/11/1999) P/FL 27+13/1 FLC 4 FAC 6+1
Grimsby T (Loaned on 21/2/2002) FL 12/3
Blackburn Rov (£750,000 on 31/5/2002) PL 78+10/4 FLC 8 FAC 12+1/1 Others 3+1
Burnley (Loaned on 4/9/2003) FL 7 FLC 1
Derby Co (Signed on 9/7/2007) PL 14+5/1 FLC 0+1 FAC 3

TODD Andrew (Andy)
Jonathan
Born: Nottingham, 22 February 1979
Height: 6'0" **Weight:** 11.3
Club Honours: FC '06
Having left Accrington in the summer, Andy started 2007-08 as an automatic choice on the right of Rotherham's midfield and played a vital role in the club's promising start to the season. He lost his place after the first few months and, failing to regain it, went on loan to his former club, Accrington, spending the last four months of the season there. Although playing in almost every game, usually in his regular wide-right position and occasionally as a wing-back, he was not the dominant force he had been in the previous season, when he was Stanley's 'Player of the Year' and had chipped in with more than his share of goals. Despite failing to get his name on the scoresheet, he still caused defenders problems.
Nottingham F (Signed from Eastwood T on 29/2/1996)
Scarborough (Free on 5/2/1999) FL 0+1 (Freed on 5/3/1999)
Accrington Stanley (Signed from Burton A, ex Eastwood T, Ilkeston T, Worksop T, Eastwood T, Hucknall T, on 31/1/2006) FL 44+2/10 FLC 2 FAC 1 Others 3/1
Rotherham U (Free on 10/7/2007) FL 11+2 FLC 1 FAC 0+1 Others 0+1
Accrington Stanley (Loaned on 1/1/2008) FL 14+7

TODOROV Svetoslav
Born: Dobrich, Bulgaria, 30 August 1978
Height: 6'0" **Weight:** 11.11
Club Honours: Div 1 '03
International Honours: Bulgaria: 42; Yth
Joining the club on a free transfer from Portsmouth in the summer, Svetoslav was expected to be Charlton's main striker and the gifted marksman made his debut in the opening game against Scunthorpe at the Valley but suffered a slight hamstring injury and missed the next game. He was on the bench for two League games but between them started against Stockport in the Carling Cup, scoring Charlton's opener with a superb volley. He scored the winner in the local derby at Crystal Palace minutes after appearing as a substitute and, unsurprisingly, was restored to the starting line-up at Colchester, scoring Charlton's first goal but later hobbling off with severe cramp. Disaster struck in the home game against Plymouth in October when, on the half hour, he sustained a ruptured anterior cruciate ligament and a small fracture within his knee. Was released in the summer.
West Ham U (£500,000 + from Liteks Lovech, Bulgaria on 30/1/2001) PL 4+10/1 FLC 1 FAC 0+2/1
Portsmouth (£750,000 on 20/3/2002) P/FL 54+23/33 FLC 2+1 FAC 1+2
Wigan Ath (Loaned on 31/8/2006) PL 2+3
Charlton Ath (Free on 14/7/2007) FL 3+4/2 FLC 2/1

TOGWELL Samuel (Sam)
James
Born: Beaconsfield, 14 October 1984
Height: 5'11" **Weight:** 12.4
After signing a one-year extension to his Barnsley contract before the season, Sam found himself on the fringe of the starting team. Whenever offered a chance, he always gave mobility and maximum effort. Sam's tackling and harassing make him an effective ball winner and his highlight of the season was his 20-yard half-volley after just 20 seconds against Southampton. He hopes to spend less time on the bench in the months ahead.
Crystal Palace (From trainee on 31/8/2004) FL 0+1 FLC 1+2
Oxford U (Loaned on 22/10/2004) FL 3+1 FAC 1
Northampton T (Loaned on 24/3/2005) FL 7+1 Others 2
Port Vale (Loaned on 10/11/2005) FL 26+1/2 FAC 2/2 Others 1
Barnsley (Signed on 18/7/2006) FL 54+12/2 FLC 1+1 FAC 3+2

TOLLEY Jamie Christopher
Born: Ludlow, 12 May 1983
Height: 6'1" **Weight:** 11.3
International Honours: W: U21-12
Jamie missed the start of last season following a serious wrist injury that required surgery but regained full fitness towards the end of October, although it was necessary for him to wear a protective cast. On his return he found himself a bit-part player for Macclesfield as others had established themselves during his absence, but on the departure of Adam Murray in January he regained his place in the side. Jamie is a strong hard-working central midfielder who scored two powerful and important goals late in the season. Was out of contract in the summer and looking for a new club.
Shrewsbury T (From trainee on 9/1/2001) FL 142+18/14 FLC 3+2 FAC 5+3/2 Others 8+1/1
Macclesfield T (Signed on 11/8/2006) FL 42+5/3 FLC 1 FAC 2+3 Others 1

TOMKINS James Oliver Charles
Born: Basildon, 29 March 1989
Height: 6'3" **Weight:** 11.10
International Honours: E: Yth
Another youngster to come out of the West Ham Academy, James is a ball-playing central defender who is comfortable in possession. After some excellent performances in the reserves, he was given his first-team debut at Everton in March. Unlucky not to make it a scoring one when his fine header hit the bar, he kept his place for the remainder of the season and continued to improve with each game. A regular in the England under-19 side, a fine future is predicted for this young star.
West Ham U (From trainee on 3/4/2006) PL 5+1

TOMLINSON Stuart Charles
Born: Ellesmere Port, 10 May 1985
Height: 6'0" **Weight:** 11.0
A goalkeeper who came through Crewe's youth system, Stuart has had a few opportunities in the senior side but played only once last season, in the Johnstone's Paint Trophy tie at Chester. He went on loan to Burton in the Blue Square Premier in an effort to stay match-fit, only to sustain a serious knee injury that will keep him out of football for about nine months.
Crewe Alex (From trainee on 16/7/2003) FL 8+3 FLC 1+1 FAC 2 Others 2

TONER Ciaran
Born: Craigavon, 30 June 1981
Height: 6'1" **Weight:** 12.4
International Honours: NI: 2; U21-17; Yth; Sch

Ciaran's season began before the League campaign kicked-off with selection for a Northern Ireland XI against Everton. A midfield regular for Grimsby in the first half of the term, he proved lethal from the penalty spot, netting at old club Lincoln to secure a 2-1 win. A hamstring injury and competition for places then saw Ciaran out of contention over the winter months, though he returned to fitness in time to make a substitute appearance in the Johnstone's Paint Trophy final.

Tottenham H *(From trainee on 14/7/1999)*
Peterborough U *(Loaned on 21/12/2001)* FL 6 FAC 1
Bristol Rov *(Free on 28/3/2002)* FL 6
Leyton Orient *(Free on 7/5/2002)* FL 41+11/2 FLC 2 FAC 1 Others 2
Lincoln C *(Free on 4/8/2004)* FL 10+5/2 FLC 0+1 Others 1
Cambridge U *(Loaned on 19/3/2005)* FL 6+2
Grimsby T *(Free on 18/7/2005)* FL 80+14/14 FLC 2 FAC 3+1 Others 5+3/1

TONGE Dale

Born: Doncaster, 7 May 1985
Height: 5'10" **Weight:** 10.6
Freed by Barnsley, Dale was one of many newcomers at Rotherham when the season began. He soon established himself as an automatic choice at right-back, from where he was always ever willing to join in with the attack. He lost his place for a brief spell but returned again to give his best, also moving forward to play on the right side of midfield on a number of occasions.

Barnsley *(From trainee on 2/7/2004)* FL 30+15 FLC 4 FAC 3+2 Others 0+1
Gillingham *(Loaned on 20/3/2007)* FL 3
Rotherham U *(Free on 23/7/2007)* FL 31+6 FLC 1 FAC 2 Others 2

TONGE Michael William

Born: Manchester, 7 April 1983
Height: 6'0" **Weight:** 11.10
International Honours: E: U21-2; Yth
Having signed a three-year contract extension, Michael began slowly for Sheffield United and, although he was more combative, he had a disappointing first half to the season. The arrival of Kevin Blackwell revived his performances in midfield. He was more prepared to take on opponents and his passing became more influential. Able to steer clear of injury, he was involved in all but one of the League and Cup games and even if some were from the bench, his return of one goal, in the opening game, was disappointing.

Sheffield U *(From trainee on 16/3/2001)* P/FL 230+28/21 FLC 14+3/3 FAC 17+2 Others 3

TOPP Willy Adolfo

Born: Temuco, Chile, 4 March 1986
Height: 5'10" **Weight:** 11.5
International Honours: Chile: Yth
Chilean striker Willy eventually signed for Bradford from Universidad Catolica in December, three months after arriving on trial. A neat, skilful forward who likes to play just behind the front two, Willy enjoyed an outstanding debut at home to Shrewsbury the following month. Underwent groin surgery in April to correct a problem that caused him to cramp up during the later stages of games.

Bradford C *(£35,000 from Universidad Catolica, Chile, ex Deportivo Temuco - loan, Puerto Montt - loan, on 11/12/2007)* FL 6+5

TORPEY Stephen (Steve) David James

Born: Islington, 8 December 1970
Height: 6'3" **Weight:** 14.6
Club Honours: AMC '94; Div 1 '07
Released by Scunthorpe, the veteran front-man became Lincoln's first signing during the summer but his Imps' career never really took off and after 14 goalless appearances he found himself loaned out to Farsley Celtic. When that loan deal expired in January 2008, Steve had his Lincoln contract cancelled by mutual consent and joined up with Halifax.

Millwall *(From trainee on 14/2/1989)* FL 3+4 FLC 0+1
Bradford C *(£70,000 on 21/11/1990)* FL 86+10/22 FLC 6 FAC 2+1 Others 8/6
Swansea C *(£80,000 on 3/8/1993)* FL 151+11/44 FLC 9+2/2 FAC 10/5 Others 15+3/5
Bristol C *(£400,000 on 8/8/1997)* FL 53+17/13 FLC 4+1/1 FAC 3 Others 3+1
Notts Co *(Loaned on 7/8/1998)* FL 4+2/1 FLC 1+1/1
Scunthorpe U *(£175,000 on 3/2/2000)* FL 214+25/59 FLC 7/3 FAC 18+2/7 Others 11+3/5
Lincoln C *(Free on 2/7/2007)* FL 7+6 FLC 1

TORRES Fernando Jose

Born: Madrid, Spain, 20 March 1984
Height: 5'11" **Weight:** 12.4
International Honours: Spain: 54
In the history of Liverpool, only one other player has made such an immediate impact at Anfield as the Spanish international striker, who broke records galore for the Reds in his first season after being signed by manager Rafa Benitez from Atletico Madrid for a record Liverpool fee in summer. In 1977-78, Kenny Dalglish scored 30 goals, including the winner in the European Cup final against FC Brugge. By comparison Fernando scored 33 goals, including

24 in the Premiership and six in the Champions' League and if he did not reach the final, he at least scored the vital away goal in the second leg of the semi-final at Chelsea that could have been the springboard to victory. His 24 Premiership goals bettered a record set by Ruud Van Nistelrooy, 23 for Manchester United in 2001-02, for an overseas player in his Premier League debut season. He scored three hat-tricks, one in the Carling Cup at Reading and two in consecutive home games late in the season, against Middlesbrough and West Ham. He also scored in eight consecutive home games, equalling Roger Hunt's record from the 1960s. There were no tap-ins or penalties. All his goals required effort with the skill, whether it be outpacing his marker and angling a shot across the 'keeper (his first ever Liverpool goal, against Chelsea in early season), skipping daintily round defenders in the penalty area to pick his spot or shooting from long range, as in the equaliser at Middlesbrough. With so many quality strikes, it is difficult to choose the best but his goal in the 70th minute of the Champions, League quarter-final second leg against Arsenal was as good as any. Taking a knock down from Peter Crouch on the edge of the box, he turned his marker to create space for a curling shot into the far top corner. It should have been the knock-out punch but there was more drama to come before Liverpool's eventual triumph. Fernando's prolific scoring should have been the missing link in Liverpool's long overdue challenge for the title. Unfortunately, even he was subject to Benitez's rotation system and points dropped in goalless draws with Portsmouth, Birmingham, Blackburn and Manchester City, plus a dismal 1-1 draw at home to Wigan, in three of which games he did not start, left the Reds trailing far behind the top three by the turn of the year and despite a strong finish they could only manage fourth, 11 points behind the champions. At the end of the season, he came second in the PFA 'Player of the Year' poll behind the incomparable Ronaldo. His success is all the more remarkable given his slender frame, his boyish looks and his self-effacing goal celebrations, as if he cannot quite believe his own brilliance. Maybe he will never quite repeat his scoring exploits of 2007-08, but it is hard not to believe that he will be Liverpool's top scorer for years to come, a worthy successor to the likes of Hunt, Dalglish, Ian Rush, Robbie Fowler and Michael Owen. After helping Spain to the final of the European Championships, he scored the only goal

of the match against Germany and was named in the 'Team of the Tournament'.
Liverpool (£26,500,000 from Atletico Madrid, Spain on 27/7/2007) PL 29+4/24 FLC 1/3 FAC 1 Others 10+1/6

TORRES Sergio Raul
Born: Mar del Plata, Argentina, 8 November 1983
Height: 6'2" **Weight:** 12.4
Wycombe's multi-talented midfield playmaker thankfully enjoyed an almost injury-free season. Apart from missing four weeks in March with a foot injury, Sergio was pretty much ever-present, playing wide on either wing or just behind the front two. He successfully balances his exciting, surging runs from deep, with some determined tackling, tracking back when needed. He contributed five goals, the pick of which was at Grimsby in April when, showing superb ball control after receiving the ball on the edge of the area, he deftly flicking the ball out of range of the advancing 'keeper before coolly slotting home. With other clubs showing interest in him, he signed a new contract in March that will take him to June 2010.
Wycombe W (Signed from Basingstoke T on 26/8/2005) FL 57+29/6 FLC 2+3 FAC 2 Others 4+1

TOURE Kolo Abib
Born: Sokoura Bouake, Ivory Coast, 19 March 1981
Height: 5'10" **Weight:** 11.13
Club Honours: CS '02, '04; FAC '03, '05; PL '04
International Honours: Ivory Coast: 45
Arsenal's Ivory Coast defender endured, by his own high standards, an indifferent campaign, especially after returning from the African Cup of Nations. He remains, however, a hard-working and energetic centre-back who can also fill in at right-back and was even found in midfield as injuries took a firm grip of Arsene Wenger's squad. He scored the opening goal in the home win over Bolton and added one further goal during the season. Injury also played a part in Kolo's less than authoritative performances as he finished the season at right-back.
Arsenal (Signed from ASEC Mimosa, Ivory Coast on 18/2/2002) PL 177+19/8 FLC 7 FAC 18+4/3 Others 55+5/2

TOWNSEND Michael John
Born: Walsall, 17 May 1986
Height: 6'2" **Weight:** 13.12
It was a frustrating time for the young Cheltenham central defender, who missed the opportunity to build on the previous season's progress because of

injury and illness. Forced to miss the opening two matches with a pre-season ankle injury, Michael returned for a run of 14 games in autumn, when his height and power again became key features of the Town back four. He scored his second goal for the club in the 1-1 draw against Oldham but things took a turn for the worse after a 2-0 defeat at Walsall in early November. Michael succumbed to a virus and was diagnosed with labyrinthitis, a condition affecting the inner ear. After two attempted comebacks in the reserves, his season was written off early in 2008 and Michael hopes for a full recovery.
Cheltenham T (From trainee at Wolverhampton W on 10/1/2005) FL 70+4/2 FLC 1 FAC 3 Others 2+1

TOZER Ben Peter Anthony
Born: Plymouth, 15 March 1990
Height: 6'1" **Weight:** 12.11
Ben was a surprise inclusion for Swindon in an unfamiliar left-back position in the Carling Cup against Charlton in August and made a further appearance at right-back against Brentford. Eventually, he enjoyed further outings in his more accustomed central-defensive position in the Johnstone's Paint Trophy and FA Cup before his League debut as a late substitute against Bristol Rovers shortly before a four-day trial at Everton. Newcastle eventually jumped in to sign him on a four-and-a-half-year contract and he was an unused substitute in their last game at Everton.
Swindon T (Trainee) FL 1+1 FLC 1 FAC 2 Others 2
Newcastle U (£250,000 + on 8/1/2008)

TRAORE Armand
Born: Paris, France, 8 October 1989
Height: 6'1" **Weight:** 12.12
International Honours: France: Yth
Armand has great ability to attack with pace and his crossing technique is among the best at Arsenal. But his defending is not yet tight enough to command a regular place and in any case he has a formidable presence ahead of him at left-back in the shape of the ever-reliable Gael Clichy. Armand featured three times in the Premier League, twice in the Champions' League, twice in the FA Cup and in four of the Carling Cup ties. His best moments were the fine crosses he delivered for Nicklas Bendtner to score against Newcastle, in the Carling Cup, and Everton in the final home game.
Arsenal (Signed from AS Monaco, France on 16/10/2006) PL 1+2 FLC 9+1 FAC 3 Others 2

TRAORE Djimi
Born: Paris, France, 1 March 1980
Height: 6'3" **Weight:** 13.10
Club Honours: FLC '03; UEFACL '05; FAC '06
International Honours: Mali: 5; France: U21; Yth
Djimi featured in just one Premier League game on the left of defence for Portsmouth in August, but then made only two more appearances from the bench throughout the campaign in that competition. He also played in the centre of defence in two Carling Cup ties in August and September but drifted totally out of contention as the fight for places intensified. Following a cameo substitute appearance against Sunderland in the League in mid-January, he was allowed to join Rennes on loan for the rest of the season a few days later and it seems likely that this arrangement will be made permanent in the summer.
Liverpool (£550,000 from Laval, France on 18/2/1999) PL 72+16 FLC 12+2 FAC 4+1 Others 32+2/1
Charlton Ath (£2,000,000 on 10/8/2006) PL 11 FLC 1 FAC 1
Portsmouth (£1,000,000 on 11/1/2007) PL 11+2 FLC 2

TRAVIS Nicolas (Nicky) Vaughan
Born: Sheffield, 12 March 1987
Height: 6'0" **Weight:** 12.1
Nicky's spell on loan at Chesterfield from Sheffield United was over before it began. It was hoped that he would bring energy and crossing ability wide in midfield but a knee injury in his second game saw him return to Bramall Lane early for treatment. He has yet to play for United.
Sheffield U (From juniors on 7/7/2004)
Chesterfield (Loaned on 16/8/2007) FL 0+2

TREACY Keith Patrick
Born: Dublin, 13 September 1988
Height: 6'0" **Weight:** 13.2
International Honours: RoI: U21-1; Yth
Keith made his full debut for Blackburn in the disappointing FA Cup defeat by Coventry and, on a day when the shuffled team was way below par, looked in vain for somebody to help him. Having established himself in the first-team squad, a back injury kept him out for four months and the midfield player was only just returning when the season ended. He remains one of the club's hopes for the future, a skilful player with a good left foot.
Blackburn Rov (From trainee on 20/10/2005) FLC 0+1 FAC 1
Stockport Co (Loaned on 23/11/2006) FL 2+2

TREMARCO Carl Philip
Born: Liverpool, 11 October 1985
Height: 5'11" **Weight:** 12.3
With the arrival of Andy Taylor from Blackburn and the continuing good form of Shane Cansdell-Sheriff, Carl found himself as Tranmere's third-choice left-back in 2007-08. A naturally defensive player who can also perform on the left of midfield, Carl understandably felt he needed regular football and was transferred to Wrexham in January after manager Brian Little went back to one of his former clubs to sign him. Bringing much needed stability to the defence, Carl maintained his place until mid-March but ankle and hamstring injuries kept him sidelined until the final game. One of only two non-contract players to be offered new terms by Wrexham, he signed a two-year deal.
Tranmere Rov (From trainee on 2/4/2004) FL 34+18/1 FAC 2 Others 3+1
Wrexham (Free on 18/1/2008) FL 10

TRIMMER Lewis
Born: Norwich, 30 October 1989
Height: 5'7" **Weight:** 10.0
The 18-year-old youth team 'Player of the Year' for 2006-07, Lewis' contributions were made from the Mansfield bench last season with the squad short on resources through injury to senior players. Highly thought of when he arrived at Field Mill as a centre-forward in the summer of 2006, he looks to come good.
Mansfield T (From juniors on 15/12/2006) FL 0+3

TROTMAN Neal Anthony
Born: Manchester, 26 April 1987
Height: 6'2" **Weight:** 13.7
This all-action young central defender was a revelation after injuries had unexpectedly catapulted him into early first-team action at Oldham last season. Despite having only previously made just one League appearance, the burly and committed presence quickly formed an impressive partnership with Stefan Stam and in late-January, after making 23 appearances for the Latics, it was no surprise when a substantial bid from Preston was accepted by the club. Having made good progress at Oldham, the chance to move to the Championship was too good to turn down. Following recovery from injury and several selections on the bench, Neal made his debut as an early substitute at Plymouth in April and, proving to be strong in the air and quick across the ground, he was given his first start at Deepdale on his 21st birthday. Neal looks a good prospect and Preston fans will watch his development with interest.

Oldham Ath (From trainee at Burnley on 15/9/2006) FL 16+2/1 FLC 0+1 FAC 3+1/2 Others 1
Preston NE (£500,000 on 31/1/2008) FL 2+1

TROTTER Liam Antony
Born: Ipswich, 24 August 1988
Height: 6'2" **Weight:** 12.2
Club Honours: FAYC '05
Liam was again used sparingly in the Ipswich team, although incidents seem to follow him when he is involved. He came off the bench against Colchester and headed in a second-half corner to set his side on the way to victory. Liam made his full debut at Sheffield United in November and then played his part in the home win over West Bromwich on New Year's Day, when his physical commitment was outstanding. Four days later, the midfield player suffered the bitter disappointment of being sent off for a challenge on Portsmouth's Pedro Mendes in the FA Cup.
Ipswich T (From trainee on 30/8/2006) FL 2+5/1 FAC 1+1
Millwall (Loaned on 31/8/2006) FL 1+1 Others 0+1

TRUNDLE Lee Christopher
Born: Liverpool, 10 October 1976
Height: 6'0" **Weight:** 13.3
Club Honours: AMC '06
Bristol City's capture of the renowned goalscorer from Swansea just before the start of last season was thought to be exactly what the club needed to ensure they did not suffer the fate that befell them in 1999, the last time they played at Championship level. In the event, City were occupied at the top end of the table, although the enigmatic striker found it difficult to settle at Ashton Gate. There was no denying his wide range of ball skills but after scoring two against Scunthorpe in August, goals were elusive. Lee was in and out of the side until coming good at the end of the campaign, finding his best form as City stormed through to the Championship play-off final. Despite being tightly marked at Wembley, Lee had a couple a good chances and in the 85th minute connected sweetly with his favoured left-foot in the penalty area. The ball was destined for the net until Hull's Michael Turner's thrust out a foot to effect a

Lee Trundle

crucial block and divert it for a corner.
Wrexham *(£60,000 from Rhyl, ex Burscough, Chorley, Stalybridge Celtic, Southport, on 16/2/2001) FL 73+21/27 FLC 0+2 FAC 1 Others 4+1/3*
Swansea C *(Free on 14/7/2003) FL 135+8/77 FLC 3 FAC 13+1/7 Others 5+8/1*
Bristol C *(£1,000,000 on 31/7/2007) FL 21+14/5 FLC 1+1 FAC 0+1 Others 3/1*

TUDGAY Marcus
Born: Shoreham, 3 February 1983
Height: 6'3" **Weight:** 13.2
Marcus took time to really find a rhythm for Sheffield Wednesday and did not score his first goal until his 12th game, at Stoke. Always a lively forward, he links play well and has a steady, if not spectacular, scoring ratio. He became the Owls' leading scorer with eight, including one at his old club Derby in the FA Cup, but was then injured at Coventry in mid-March. An operation was necessary to clean out a knee cartilage, so he missed the tense final games of the season.
Derby Co *(From trainee on 16/7/2002) FL 53+39/17 FLC 2 FAC 4+1/1*
Sheffield Wed *(Signed on 1/1/2006) FL 80+13/23 FLC 3 FAC 5/1*

TUDOR Shane Anthony
Born: Wolverhampton, 10 February 1982
Height: 5'8" **Weight:** 11.2
The right-winger signed by Port Vale in summer from Leyton Orient began the 2007-08 campaign with high hopes and was a regular choice, hoping to replicate the form he showed against the Vale the previous season. His best game was in a 1-0 victory at Bournemouth, Vale's first win of the season, but it proved to be isolated and as results suffered, so did Shane's form. He was used on the bench, but niggling knee injuries cropped up and he never found his free flowing form. Shane missed a penalty in a shoot-out defeat at Morecambe in the Johnstone's Paint Trophy and was then left out by new manager Lee Sinnott before joining Shrewsbury on loan in November. Unfortunately, he injured a knee on his first day with the Shrews, making no appearances for them, and after failing to recover sufficiently his season ended in March when he had a knee operation.
Wolverhampton W *(From trainee on 9/8/1999) FL 0+1*
Cambridge U *(Free on 22/11/2001) FL 109+12/21 FLC 4/1 FAC 11/2 Others 12/2*
Leyton Orient *(Free on 12/7/2005) FL 57+9/6 FLC 2 FAC 7/1*
Port Vale *(Free on 25/7/2007) FL 8+6 FLC 1 FAC 0+1 Others 1*

TUDUR JONES Owain
Born: Bangor, 15 October 1984
Height: 6'2" **Weight:** 12.0
Club Honours: AMC '06
International Honours: W: 2; U21-3
Owain's frustrating start to the season saw the Swansea midfielder's knee injury restrict him to the reserve team in September, only to suffer an ankle injury that kept him sidelined once more. He was called into the Wales squad for training in November, after just three substitute appearances for the Swans, and made his international debut as a second-half substitute in Luxembourg in March. In the final home game of the season, against Leyton Orient, Owain made his first start since November 2006 and hopes for a campaign free of such setbacks.
Swansea C *(£5,000 from Bangor C on 4/8/2005) FL 22+11/3 FLC 1 FAC 1 Others 5+3/1*

[TUGAY] KERIMOGLU Tugay
Born: Istanbul, Turkey, 24 August 1970
Height: 5'9" **Weight:** 11.6
Club Honours: SPD '00; SC '00; FLC '02
International Honours: Turkey: 94
Tugay was reduced to cameo roles as Blackburn prepared for life without him. Even so, his stunning strike against Reading won the club's 'Goal of the Season'. Although there were signs that he is unable to cover as much ground as of old, he remained supreme in possession, using his massive array of tricks and feints to keep the ball from the opposition. He was also the player most likely to slip a pass through a defence. His contract has ended and there is no sign yet that the club will offer him a new one, which resulted in an emotional (possible) goodbye after the last home game of the season.
Glasgow Rgrs *(Signed from Galatasaray, Turkey on 15/11/2000) SL 26+16/4 SLC 2+1 SC 3+4 Others 6*
Blackburn Rov *(£1,300,000 on 20/7/2001) PL 168+36/9 FLC 17+1 FAC 15+3/1 Others 16+2/1*

[TUNCAY] SANLI Tuncay
Born: Sakarya, Turkey, 16 January 1982
Height: 5'11" **Weight:** 11.4
International Honours: Turkey: 58
Tuncay, a world-class footballer of significant standing, arrived at Middlesbrough on a free transfer from Turkish giants Fenerbahce in the summer, a move that was regarded as so important that manager Gareth Southgate personally collected the Turkish international from the airport. Revered as a superstar in his native Turkey, it took time for Tuncay to receive a work

permit and he needed further time to adjust to the rigours of the Premiership but it proved well worth the wait for Boro fans. He played 12 league games without a goal before he scored his first in December in a 1-1 draw at Reading. His second came a week later at the Riverside in a 2-1 victory over Arsenal and a third in as many games in a 1-0 victory over Derby, a superb volley. He ended the season as second-top scorer on eight and with a busy Euro 2008 tournament ahead of him. Boro fans anticipate more goals this coming season.
Middlesbrough *(Free from Fenerbahce, Turkey, ex Sakaryaspor, on 10/7/2007) PL 27+7/8 FLC 1 FAC 1+2*

TUNNICLIFFE James
Born: Denton, 7 January 1989
Height: 6'4" **Weight:** 12.3
The highly-promising young Stockport central defender's opportunities were limited at Edgeley Park by the form of Ashley Williams, Gareth Owen, Michael Raynes and then the signing of Jim McNulty. Having returned from a loan to Blue Square Premier Northwich, James was given a starting place in the final League game when he underlined his potential with a faultless performance against Brentford.
Stockport Co *(From trainee on 7/7/2006) FL 5+6 FAC 1 Others 1+1*

TURNBULL Paul Daniel
Born: Handforth, 23 January 1989
Height: 6'0" **Weight:** 12.7
Paul could be regarded as Stockport's success story of last season. His first start came when Jim Gannon made changes for a Johnstone's Paint Trophy game at Macclesfield and the powerful midfielder did enough to keep his place until a knee injury against Chesterfield at the end of January sidelined him. Allowed to go out on loan to Altrincham to regain full match-fitness, Paul returned in time to help County win promotion via the play-offs.
Stockport Co *(From trainee on 15/5/2006) FL 12+8 FAC 2 Others 6*

TURNBULL Ross
Born: Bishop Auckland, 4 January 1985
Height: 6'4" **Weight:** 13.5
International Honours: E: Yth
In late July, the highly-rated Middlesbrough number-three goalkeeper behind Australians Mark Schwarzer and Brad Jones, agreed to a season-long loan with Cardiff, the fifth club that he has been loaned out to in his relatively short career. Never quite settling at Cardiff, despite keeping three clean sheets in eight

games, the loan was cut to two months when Ross was recalled to the Riverside because of injuries, first to Schwarzer and then Jones. At that point, the consistency of Schwarzer and Jones had limited him to three games in five seasons for Middlesbrough. In early December he played in a famous 2-1 victory over Arsenal, then unbeaten in the Premiership, at the Riverside. Unsurprisingly, Ross rated it as the highlight of his career so far. He was a substitute for Boro when Cardiff won 2-0 at the Riverside in the FA Cup.
Middlesbrough (From trainee on 6/7/2002) PL 5 FLC 1
Darlington (Loaned on 14/11/2003) FL 1
Barnsley (Loaned on 22/4/2004) FL 3
Bradford C (Loaned on 6/8/2004) FL 2
Barnsley (Loaned on 6/10/2004) FL 23 FAC 1
Crewe Alex (Loaned on 4/8/2005) FL 29
Cardiff C (Loaned on 31/7/2007) FL 6 FLC 2

TURNBULL Stephen

Born: South Shields, 7 January 1987
Height: 5'10" **Weight:** 11.0
A cultured young midfield player who failed to break into the Hartlepool squad, Stephen was limited to one appearance as a substitute for five minutes in a disappointing defeat at Doncaster. He enjoyed success as captain of the reserves, leading them to the Pontins Holidays League Division One East Championship, but a player who once looked destined for greater things was released at the end of the season.
Hartlepool U (From trainee on 4/7/2006) FL 16+8 FLC 0+1
Bury (Loaned on 22/11/2006) FL 4+1 FAC 1
Rochdale (Loaned on 1/3/2007) FL 2+2

TURNER Benjamin (Ben)
Howard
Born: Birmingham, 21 January 1988
Height: 6'4" **Weight:** 14.4
International Honours: E: Yth
After progressing through Coventry's Academy, the strapping central defender was given a shock call for the Carling Cup victory at Old Trafford – his first game of the season – and came through with flying colours. He showed composure and kept his place until January. While seemingly at fault for the late West Ham winner in the next round of the Carling Cup, he gave some outstanding displays alongside Elliott Ward and Arjan De Zeeuw. The timing of his tackles improved and he marked more tightly, while his heading was excellent. Ben was rested after the Leicester game and had the misfortune to suffer a training injury that ruled him out for the remainder of the season.
Coventry C (From trainee on 1/7/2006) FL 20+1 FLC 2+1 FAC 3

Peterborough U (Loaned on 15/9/2006) FL 7+1 FLC 1 Others 1
Oldham Ath (Loaned on 23/2/2007) FL 1

TURNER Christopher (Chris)
Jack Michael
Born: Burnley, 26 August 1990
Height: 5'10" **Weight:** 11.7
A second-year scholar at Accrington, Chris usually plays on the right of midfield. Graduating to the reserve team last season, he earned selection for the squad in the home game against Wycombe and went on briefly late in the game. Although this was his only appearance, his progress had been noted and he was rewarded with his first professional contract in the summer.
Accrington Stanley (Trainee) FL 0+1

TURNER Michael Thomas
Born: Lewisham, 9 November 1983
Height: 6'4" **Weight:** 12.6
Dropped to the bench for the first game of last season, Michael bounced back in fine style and struck up an outstanding partnership at the heart of Hull's defence with experienced new signing Wayne Brown. Missing only one further game through suspension, the tall right-sided centre-back prospered as the Tigers enjoyed the best-ever season by winning the Championship play-offs. His superb performance was one of the highlights of the memorable final win against Bristol City at Wembley as promotion to the Premier League was secured. Michael also played an important role at the other end of the pitch, scoring in four consecutive home games during the crucial end of season run-in. His magnificent contribution was recognised when he was named the club's and the supporters' 'Player of the Year', the players' 'Player of the Year' and the away match 'Player of the Year'. In April, one of the Tigers' most valuable assets extended his contract at the KC Stadium to June 2011 in April.
Charlton Ath (From trainee on 6/3/2001)
Leyton Orient (Loaned on 26/3/2003) FL 7/1
Brentford (Signed on 6/8/2003) FL 91/3 FLC 1 FAC 14 Others 4
Hull C (£350,000 on 12/7/2006) FL 86+1/8 FLC 6 FAC 3 Others 3

TWISS Michael John
Born: Salford, 26 December 1977
Height: 5'11" **Weight:** 13.3
Club Honours: AMC '01
An up-and-down time for the talented former Manchester United player who many thought would star for Morecambe on the League stage. His season never really got going and the harshest of red cards against Rochdale in October did not help. Michael suffered some niggling

injuries that ruled him out for periods but still chipped in with six goals. He is capable of doing the unexpected and again won the club's 'Goal of the Season' award. His left foot delivers of the most powerful shots in League Two and Morecambe fans hope to see him back at his best.
Manchester U (From trainee on 5/7/1996) FLC 1 FAC 0+1
Sheffield U (Loaned on 7/8/1998) FL 2+10/1 FAC 2+2
Port Vale (Free on 27/7/2000) FL 15+3/3 FLC 2 FAC 0+2 Others 1+1 (Freed during 2001 close season)
Morecambe (Free from Chester C, ex Leigh RMI, on 8/5/2004) FL 27+9/6 FLC 3 Others 5+1

TYLER Mark Richard
Born: Norwich, 2 April 1977
Height: 6'0" **Weight:** 12.9
International Honours: E: Yth
It was a surprise when the long-serving goalkeeper did not start the season as Peterborough's first choice, but he fought his way back into the side before the Posh splashed out a club record fee on Joe Lewis. Still a competent and agile 'keeper, Mark went on loan to Hull at the end of January as cover for Bo Myhill after the club's second string Matt Duke had been hospitalised but failed to get a game. Despite Peterborough being prepared to listen to sensible offers, Mark, who still has plenty to offer, says he is happy to stay and fight for his place. He is already a legend at London Road for his excellent service over almost 14 years.
Peterborough U (From trainee on 7/12/1994) FL 412+1 FLC 16 FAC 33 Others 24

TYSON Nathan
Born: Reading, 4 May 1982
Height: 5'10" **Weight:** 11.12
International Honours: E: Yth
Nathan had a late start to the season for Nottingham Forest after a summer knee operation. In a Forest formation catering for only one main striker, Nathan was often played as a left-sided forward, allowed him to use his considerable pace with great effect in creating goals for himself or other players. He suffered a number of niggling hamstring injuries during the promotion campaign but Forest were always more dangerous when he was fit.
Reading (From trainee on 18/3/2000) FL 9+24/1 FLC 0+2 FAC 2+1 Others 0+2
Swansea C (Loaned on 30/8/2001) FL 7+4/1
Cheltenham T (Loaned on 22/3/2002) FL 1+7/1
Wycombe W (Free on 2/1/2004) FL 76+2/42 FLC 3/2 FAC 3 Others 1+2
Nottingham F (£675,000 on 11/11/2005) FL 66+20/26 FLC 1/1 FAC 7+1/4 Others 2

UV

UDDIN Anwar
Born: Stepney, 1 November 1981
Height: 6'2" **Weight:** 13.0
Club Honours: FC '07
Anwar became the first Asian player to captain a League team when he led out Dagenham at Stockport on the opening day. The central defender led by example and his powerful presence in the side was inspirational. He operated either in a two-man centre-back unit or as the middle man of a defensive trio before missing the last three matches of the season with a thigh strain.
West Ham U (From trainee on 9/7/2001)
Sheffield Wed (Free on 28/2/2002)
Bristol Rov (Free on 2/7/2002) FL 18+1/1 FLC 1 Others 1+1
Dagenham & Redbridge (Free on 4/8/2004) FL 40+1/1 FLC 1 FAC 2+1 Others 2

UGARTE Juan
Born: San Sebastian, Spain, 7 November 1980
Height: 5'10" **Weight:** 11.11
Club Honours: AMC '05
Unfortunately, the sum total of Juan's Wrexham season in 2007-08 was a 68th-minute substitute appearance at Stockport in September. The knee and hamstring injuries that hampered him from the start of the previous campaign finally caught up with him in January, when his contract was cancelled by mutual consent. So the Spaniard, who wrote himself into the North Wales club's history books in sensational fashion in 2004-05, finally bowed out in a sad way. Ironic too that such a prolific scorer was needed more than anything else in Wrexham's season as they too bowed out of the League after 87 years. One of the most popular players ever at Wrexham, he said goodbye to the crowd before the MK Dons game and announced his retirement at 27.
Wrexham (Free from Dorchester T, ex Real Sociedad, Barakaldo, on 1/11/2004) FL 23+7/17 FAC 1+1 Others 5+1/6
Crewe Alex (Free on 4/7/2005) FL 0+2 FLC 1 (Freed during 2006 close season)
Wrexham (Loaned on 21/10/2005) FL 1
Wrexham (Loaned on 31/1/2006) FL 1
Wrexham (Free, following long-term injury, on 23/11/2006) FL 0+3 FAC 0+1

UNSWORTH David Gerald
Born: Chorley, 16 October 1973
Height: 6'1" **Weight:** 14.2
Club Honours: FAC '95; CS '95
International Honours: E: 1; U21-6; Yth
David proved an excellent acquisition for Burnley in the August transfer window. Rarely an automatic choice, he nevertheless figured in more than half of the Clarets' Championship games as the back four was switched around through injury or suspension. Defensive howlers were too frequent at Turf Moor but David was rarely if ever the perpetrator, his coolness, determination and sheer experience often getting the side out of trouble. His only goal came in the home draw against Leicester. He was offered a new contract at the end of the season to include coaching duties so it may be that, if he does stay, his main contribution in the future will be behind the scenes.
Everton (From trainee on 25/6/1992) P/FL 108+8/11 FLC 5+2 FAC 7 Others 4/1
West Ham U (£1,000,000 + on 18/8/1997) PL 32/2 FLC 5 FAC 4
Aston Villa (£3,000,000 on 28/7/1998)
Everton (£3,000,000 on 22/8/1998) PL 164+24/23 FLC 10+1/1 FAC 16+1/4
Portsmouth (Free on 16/7/2004) PL 15/2 FLC 3 FAC 1
Ipswich T (Loaned on 23/1/2005) FL 16/1
Sheffield U (Signed on 22/8/2005) P/FL 38+1/4 FLC 1
Wigan Ath (Free on 5/1/2007) PL 6+4/1
Burnley (Free on 13/8/2007) FL 26+3/1 FLC 2

UPSON Matthew (Matty) James
Born: Diss, 18 April 1979
Height: 6'1" **Weight:** 11.4
Club Honours: PL '02
International Honours: E: 8; U21-11; Yth
The West Ham central defender was a rock at the back last season. Against Manchester United in December he was superb as he nullified the threat of Ronaldo and Carlos Tevez and, late in the game, headed the winning goal. His excellent form prompted new England manager Fabio Capello to play Matty in his first England team against Switzerland. He was ever-present in the League until the game at Liverpool in March, when he sustained a calf injury that forced him to miss the remainder of the season.
Luton T (From trainee on 24/4/1996) FL 0+1 Others 1
Arsenal (£1,000,000 on 14/5/1997) PL 20+14 FLC 8 FAC 3+1 Others 8+2
Nottingham F (Loaned on 8/12/2000) FL 1
Crystal Palace (Loaned on 2/3/2001) FL 7
Reading (Loaned on 6/9/2002) FL 13+1 FLC 1/1
Birmingham C (£2,000,000 + on 23/1/2003) P/FL 112+1/5 FLC 7 FAC 8
West Ham U (£6,000,000 + on 31/1/2007) PL 31/1 FLC 2 FAC 2

John Utaka

UTAKA John Chukwudi
Born: Legugnu, Nigeria, 8 January 1982
Height: 5'10" **Weight:** 12.12
Club Honours: FAC '08
International Honours: Nigeria: 12
John joined Portsmouth from Rennes in the middle of July and the Nigerian international soon showed that he had explosive qualities of pace, strength and power. In particular, he possesses the considerable ability of being able to run at defenders. He prefers to play up front but has been used wide on the right more often. John scored on his debut at Derby on the opening day and then netted a fantastic goal two games later after sprinting from the halfway line and side-stepping the Bolton goalkeeper. After the African Cup of Nations, during which he appeared in all three of Nigeria's qualifying games, injuries restricted his League appearances and he missed Pompey's FA Cup semi-final win. He laid on the goal for Nwankwo Kanu as Pompey won the FA Cup final against Cardiff.
Portsmouth (£7,000,000 from Rennes, France, ex Enuga Rgrs, Ismaily FC, Al-Sadd, RC Lens, on 18/7/2007) PL 25+4/5 FLC 2+1 FAC 4

VALENCIA Luis Antonio
Born: Lago Agrio, Ecuador, 4 August 1985
Height: 5'10" **Weight:** 12.4
International Honours: Ecuador: 29

An Ecuador midfielder, Antonio started last season for Wigan on another loan deal from Spanish side Villareal before completing his permanent move in the January transfer window. A skilful right-winger who likes to take on defenders and is exciting to watch, he is confident enough to try a few tricks and is dangerous in front of goal. Most of Wigan's attacking moves went through him and he delivered a string of crosses into the penalty box. After missing a month out following surgery on a knee injury in September, Antonio was a near ever-present for the rest of the campaign, scoring three league goals. His first goal was in the home game against Derby and his best game was at Aston Villa. The Latics made absolutely certain of their Premier League status in this game and Antonio scored twice, the second a lovely finish from a tight angle following a run though the defence.
Wigan Ath (Signed from Villareal, Spain, ex CD El Nacional, Recreativo - loan, on 10/8/ 2006) PL 47+6/4 FAC 1

VALENTE Nuno Jorge

Born: Lisbon, Portugal, 12 September 1974
Height: 6'0" **Weight:** 12.4
International Honours: Portugal: 33; U21
The presence of Joleon Lescott and Leighton Baines on Everton's left flank, combined with a couple of niggling injuries, restricted the opportunities for this experienced and classy Portuguese international. But whenever his presence was required in the first team, the full-back played with composure and was duly rewarded with another one-year deal at the conclusion of the season.
Everton (£1,500,000 from Porto, Portugal on 31/8/2005) PL 38+5 FLC 5 FAC 5 Others 5

VALENTINE Ryan David

Born: Wrexham, 19 August 1982
Height: 5'10" **Weight:** 11.11
International Honours: W: U21-8; Yth
Ryan continued as Wrexham's full-back last season, always presenting a tough challenge to opponents with strong, determined play. His game suffered as Wrexham struggled and when new manager Brian Little arrived, and with Ryan's contract due to run out at the end of the season, he rejoined Darlington in January. It was a surprise return by Ryan from his home-town club but, always reliable on either side of defence with his firm tackling and strong runs forward, he was also used in midfield in an effort to find an effective combination. His cumulative total of appearances for

Darlington is now just under 200, the second highest among the current squad.
Everton (From trainee on 1/9/1999)
Darlington (Free on 8/8/2002) FL 151+11/4 FLC 4 FAC 6 Others 4
Wrexham (Free on 3/8/2006) FL 46+2/2 FLC 3 FAC 2 Others 2
Darlington (Free on 18/1/2008) FL 13+4

VAN DER SAR Edwin

Born: Leiden, Holland, 29 October 1970
Height: 6'5" **Weight:** 13.6
Club Honours: FLC '06; PL '07; '08; CS '07; UEFACL '08
International Honours: Holland: 128
An outstanding Manchester United and Dutch international goalkeeper with a wealth of experience both at home and abroad, Edwin began the season in inspiring fashion, saving all three of Chelsea's penalties in the shoot-out finale as United recorded their 16th FA Community Shield victory at Wembley in August. He was to end, more famously, in the same way nine months later. Edwin conceded only two goals in United's first eight Premiership matches as they showed every intention of clinging to their crown. Although the season became a bit of a mixed bag for him because of a niggling groin injury, he put in some excellent performances at home and abroad. He signed a one-year extension to his contract in December and his inspiring, totally unflappable form in the Champions' League helped United to a Moscow final. Edwin became the hero of the hour for United that night, saving Nicolas Anelka's spot kick in the sudden-death shoot-out to give United their third European Cup success. Though it is still difficult to see any world-class 'keeper replacing him at Old Trafford, Edwin has already hinted at retirement, but the prospect of one-year rolling deals and more trophies might persude him to put such ideas off for the immediate future.
Fulham (£7,000,000 from Juventus, Italy, ex Noordwijk, Ajax, on 10/8/2001) PL 126+1 FLC 1 FAC 15 Others 11
Manchester U (£2,000,000 on 10/6/2005) PL 99 FLC 3 FAC 9 Others 31

VAN HOMOET Marciano

Born: Rotterdam, Holland, 7 March 1984
Height: 5'9" **Weight:** 11.11
A summer free transfer from Sparta Rotterdam, Barnsley signed Marciano Bruma but under EEC regulations, he had to re-register as Marciano Van Homoet, the name on his birth certificate. He missed the start of the season because of a broken bone in his hand and had to wait until December for his debut. The Dutchman soon became the regular right-back,

characterised by marauding runs down the flank. Very quick, he was a major asset in Barnsley's exciting FA Cup run.
Barnsley (Signed from Sparta Rotterdam, Holland on 19/7/2007) FL 17+2 FAC 4+1

VAN PERSIE Robin

Born: Rotterdam, Holland, 6 August 1983
Height: 6'1" **Weight:** 11.2
Club Honours: CS '04; FAC '05
International Honours: Holland: 28; U21
Arsenal's extravagantly gifted Dutchman remains one of the most talented players in Europe. Sadly, he also continues to be one of the most prone to injuries. He started last season with the equaliser in the opening game against Fulham and scored five times in his first seven Premier League games but the rest of his campaign was wrecked by a combination of injuries. Robin managed only 15 League appearances, still scoring seven times. He played in seven Champions' League matches, adding two goals, and started one Carling Cup tie. After three injury-affected seasons, Arsenal fans hope that Robin will finally enjoy a campaign free of problems. A late thigh injury cast doubts on his Holland place for Euro 2008 before he recovered to play a part in the competition, playing all four games and scoring twice.
Arsenal (£2,750,000 from Feyenoord, Holland on 17/5/2004) PL 55+32/28 FLC 7+1/ 5 FAC 6+2/3 Others 16+14/7

VARGA Stanislav (Stan)

Born: Lipany, Slovakia, 8 October 1972
Height: 6'2" **Weight:** 14.8
Club Honours: SPD '04, '06; SC '04, '05; Ch '07
International Honours: Slovakia: 54
The first new arrival under Owen Coyle's management at Burnley was the big Slovakian international defender, signed on loan from Sunderland in January, having failed to make their team in 2007-08. A baptism of fire in the FA Cup game against Arsenal proved well within his capabilities and for two months he was a commanding and imposing presence at the heart of the back four before injury kept him out for most of the final run-in. Was released in the summer.
Sunderland (£650,000 + from SK Slovan Bratislava, Slovakia, ex Tatran Presov, on 14/ 8/2000) PL 18+3/1 FLC 5+1 FAC 5+1
West Bromwich A (Loaned on 25/3/2002) FL 3+1
Glasgow Celtic (Free on 11/2/2003) SL 79+1/10 SLC 3+1/1 SC 10/2 Others 22/1
Sunderland (Signed on 31/8/2006) FL 20/1 FAC 1
Burnley (Loaned on 4/1/2008) FL 10 FAC 1

VARNEY Luke Ivan
Born: Leicester, 28 September 1982
Height: 5'11" **Weight:** 11.7
Signed from Crewe in the summer, Luke missed the early games with an ankle injury but eventually made his Charlton debut at Colchester in mid-September. He started the next nine games alongside Chris Iwelumo before being relegated to the bench as Charlton adopted a system with Iwelumo on his own up front. When they reverted to two in attack, Luke was normally one of the chosen strikers, although he also featured wide on the right in a handful of games. He is more effective in the middle and although he took time to get going, ended with a respectable eight goals, two of them in the 2-0 win over Crystal Palace at the Valley. The first of those was chosen by Charlton supporters as their 'Goal of the Season'. Luke has pace, good ball control and an eye for goal and will aim to strike more often.
Crewe Alex (Signed from Quorn on 25/3/2003) FL 68+27/27 FLC 4+1/1 FAC 2+1 Others 5/7
Charlton Ath (£2,000,000 on 21/5/2007) FL 23+16/8 FLC 0+1 FAC 2

VASKO Tamas
Born: Budapest, Hungary, 20 February 1984
Height: 6'4" **Weight:** 14.12
International Honours: Hungary: 10
This Hungarian international central defender, who joined Bristol City on a season-long loan from Ujpest, took time to adjust to English football. While he started ten times, he was usually more effective when coming off the substitutes' bench. The highlight of his season was when he slid in to score City's 67th-minute winner at Burnley. At the end of the season, City decided against taking up the option of a permanent three-year deal and Tamas returned to his Budapest club.
Bristol C (Loaned from Ujpest, Hungary, ex FC Tatanbaya - loan, on 10/8/2007) FL 8+11/1 FLC 1 FAC 1

VASSELL Darius
Born: Birmingham, 13 June 1980
Height: 5'7" **Weight:** 12.0
International Honours: E: 22; U21-11; Yth
As a former England regular, Darius is a versatile Manchester City attacker, equally effective playing wide in midfield or as an out-and-out striker. Renowned for his lightning pace and commitment, he has built a good rapport with Blues' fans since his arrival. After forming a good partnership with Andrew Cole in his first

Darius Vassell

year, Darius showed his versatility to great effect last season. Either as the lone striker or from out wide, he gave some excellent performances, even when City's results began to slip towards the end of the season.
Aston Villa (From trainee on 14/4/1998) PL 107+55/35 FLC 10+7/5 FAC 4+4/1 Others 3+11/4
Manchester C (£2,000,000 on 27/7/2005) PL 85+10/17 FLC 2+1/1 FAC 11/3

VAUGHAN David Owen
Born: Abergele, 18 February 1983
Height: 5'7" **Weight:** 10.10
International Honours: W: 13; U21-8; Yth
A very experienced player and a graduate of the Crewe youth system, David went on as a substitute in the opening game of last season against Brighton before being transferred to Real Sociedad. An experienced Welsh international who can operate wide on the left of the attack or at the back when required, he gave Alexandra great service in more than six years since he signed as a professional at Gresty Road.
Crewe Alex (From trainee on 6/2/2001) FL 166+19/18 FLC 10 FAC 9/1 Others 5/1

VAUGHAN James
Born: Liverpool, 6 December 1986
Height: 5'8" **Weight:** 11.7

This was yet another season that brought more frustration for the gifted young Everton striker. After impressing initially in pre-season, James dislocated a shoulder at Preston in a friendly and was out of action until late autumn. After scoring on his return as a substitute against Birmingham, James was used from the bench to good effect before a knee injury, sustained in training, ended his season in March. At his best, James is a real handful for defenders, with both strength and pace, and after successful surgery in the United States, everyone at Goodison hopes that the Premier League's youngest-ever scorer will be fit for the new campaign.
Tranmere Rov (From trainee on 2/7/2004)
Chester C (Free on 28/1/2006) FL 34+2 FLC 1 Others 1+1

VAUGHAN James Oliver
Born: Birmingham, 14 July 1988
Height: 5'11" **Weight:** 12.8
International Honours: E: U21-1; Yth
The young Chester defender was a regular on the right at the start of last season but, after an injury in September, missed three months of the campaign and was replaced by Simon Marples. James returned at the end of December and continued to line up on the right of City's four-man defence. Hard-working and enthusiastic, James is strong in the tackle and, when given the opportunity, has the ability to get forward and supplement the attack with some telling crosses. He was given a two-year extension to his contract.
Everton (From trainee on 14/9/2005) PL 7+18/6 FLC 0+2 FAC 1+1 Others 0+2/1

VAZ TE Ricardo Jorge
Born: Lisbon, Portugal, 1 October 1986
Height: 6'2" **Weight:** 12.7
International Honours: Portugal: U21-3; Yth
Last season was extremely frustrating for Ricardo, at a time when he was looking to establish himself as a regular at Bolton. In what turned out to be his only League appearance, Ricardo started the opening-day defeat by Newcastle but was forced to withdraw at half-time with a ligament injury that kept him out of action for the first half of the campaign. Ricardo's only other appearance came in the UEFA Cup defeat by Sporting Lisbon in March. A naturally gifted and pacy forward, he will hope to figure more regularly.
Bolton W (From trainee on 20/10/2004) PL 10+46/3 FLC 3+1/1 FAC 5+6/2 Others 1+4/1
Hull C (Loaned on 9/3/2007) FL 1+5

VELASCO Juan
Born: Sevilla, Spain, 15 May 1977
Height: 5'10" **Weight:** 11.13
International Honours: Spain: 4
Released by Espanyol at the end of 2006-2007, the former Spanish international joined Norwich as a free agent in February and made three appearances before an injury curtailed his progress. Having also played for Seville, Celta Vigo and Atletico Madrid in Spain, it came as no surprise to see his calm assurance on the ball and his excellent distribution. However, after not playing for eight months he found it hard to come to terms with the pace of games, possibly a factor in bringing about his injury. He was released by Norwich in May.
Norwich C (Free from Espanyol, Spain, ex Seville, Celta Vigo, Atletico Madrid, on 21/2/2008) FL 2+1

VERNON Scott Malcolm
Born: Manchester, 13 December 1983
Height: 6'1" **Weight:** 11.6
Scott was not Blackpool's first-choice striker at the start of last season and by January had decided to make a move in search of regular action, eventually joining Colchester. Before that, he scored four goals for the Tangerines, the pick, ironically, being the brace against Colchester in a 2-0 win in December. Scott was an 11th-hour signing for Colchester at the end of the January window and the talented striker soon turned from villain to hero with another brace, this time in Colchester's 2-0 win over East Anglian rivals Ipswich. A classy finisher, Scott also hit the back of the net in the earlier 2-1 home win over Preston, after coming on as a substitute, and executed a stunning overhead kick in the 3-3 draw at Scunthorpe on the final day.
Oldham Ath (From trainee on 3/7/2002) FL 43+32/20 FLC 1 FAC 3+2/1 Others 5+2/6
Blackpool (Loaned on 10/9/2004) FL 4/3
Blackpool (Signed on 17/6/2005) FL 37+33/16 FLC 5/2 FAC 4+2/1 Others 0+2/1
Colchester U (Loaned on 17/3/2006) FL 4+3/1
Colchester U (Signed on 31/1/2008) FL 8+9/5

VIAFARA Jhon Eduis
Born: Robles, Colombia, 27 October 1978
Height: 6'1" **Weight:** 13.5
International Honours: Colombia
Distribution skills apart, Jhon is a top-class Southampton midfielder, fleet-footed; with an excellent touch on the ball. A subtle dispossessor of opponents and with a useful cross, he was inspirational during 2006–07. Last season Jhon lacked

his customary spark and was not the influence of old. Being left out in favour of less talented footballers as a succession of managers attempted to find a winning midfield combination was unlikely to help his mood. He played himself back into the team for the relegation climax against Sheffield United at St Mary's and played a crucial part in the victory that kept Saints up.
Portsmouth (£1,500,000 from Once Caldas, Colombia on 21/7/2005) PL 10+4/1 FLC 0+1
Southampton (Signed on 4/8/2006) FL 59+17/5 FLC 2 FAC 3 Others 2/2

VIDARSSON Bjarni Thor
Born: Reykjavik, Iceland, 5 March 1988
Height: 6'1" **Weight:** 11.8
International Honours: Iceland: U21; Yth
As a product of Everton's Academy, the midfielder made his first-team bow in the away win over AZ67 in the UEFA Cup in December before joining Dutch side FC Twente on loan until the end of the season. An elegant performer, Bjarni has represented Iceland at all levels up to under-21. Was released at the end of the campaign.
Everton (From trainee on 21/3/2006) Others 0+1
Bournemouth (Loaned on 8/2/2007) FL 4+2/1

VIDIC Nemanja
Born: Subotica, Serbia, 21 October 1981
Height: 6'2" **Weight:** 13.3
Club Honours: PL '07, '08; CS '07; UEFACL '08
International Honours: Serbia: 31
A solid and outstanding Manchester United and Serbia central defender, Nemanja is now recognised as one of the best in the Premiership. His strength and commitment were key features as United mounted their perennial quest for honours. Already comparisons have been made with another former Reds defensive hero, Steve Bruce, and Nemanja's immense performances at the back showed similar courage and determination. Having signed a two-year contract in November to keep him at Old Trafford until 2012, it was no coincidence that the Reds suffered a slight dip in form when he was ruled out by injury following the 2-0 win over AS Roma in the Champions' League quarter-final in Rome. Missing key games against Middlesbrough and Arsenal in April, he returned to face Chelsea in the top of the table clash at Stamford Bridge. The Reds conceded just 21 Premiership goals, beating their previous best of 25 in the1997-98 campaign. Much of that was

due to Nemanja's influence in the heart of defence.
Manchester U (£7,200,000 from Spartak Moscow, Russia on 4/1/2006) PL 66+2/4 FLC 0+2 FAC 10 Others 18/1

VIDUKA Mark Anthony
Born: Melbourne, Australia, 9 October 1975
Height: 6'2" **Weight:** 13.9
Club Honours: SLC '00
International Honours: Australia: 43; U23; Yth
Mark was signed in the summer to become the focus of Newcastle's attack but a series of niggling injuries limited his contribution. His first Newcastle goal came on his return to former club Middlesbrough in August but hamstring and calf injuries reduced his availability and he was never able to secure an unbroken run of starts until the closing stages of the season. Then a new three-man attacking formation was used, with Mark as the spearhead, and Newcastle's fortunes were turned around with an unbeaten run that banished all relegation fears. It was clear that his subtle touch, so delicate for a big man, his strength in possession and his awareness of colleagues' positioning had been sorely missed, as it was key to drawing the best out of fellow attackers Oba Martins and Michael Owen.
Glasgow Celtic (Signed from NK Croatia Zagreb, Croatia, ex Melbourne Knights, on 2/12/1998) SL 36+1/30 SLC 4/1 SC 3/3 Others 4/1
Leeds U (£6,000,000 on 25/7/2000) PL 126+4/59 FLC 3/1 FAC 8/5 Others 25/7
Middlesbrough (£4,500,000 on 8/7/2004) PL 56+16/26 FLC 4/1 FAC 9+3/7 Others 11+2/8
Newcastle U (Free on 9/7/2007) PL 19+7/7 FAC 2

VIGNAL Gregory
Born: Montpellier, France, 19 July 1981
Height: 5'11" **Weight:** 12.3
Club Honours: FAC '01; UEFAC '01; ESC '01; FLC '03
International Honours: France: U21; Yth (UEFA-U18 '00)
Signed on loan from Lens in the summer, the vastly experienced left wing-back, despite his stature, looked a little lightweight at the beginning of the season and did not establish a regular place at Southampton until the New Year. A more effective counter-attacker than defender, with a very sweet left-foot especially in dead-ball situations, he became increasingly influential. So much so that he was fielded with an arm in a splint through February and March, after

breaking it against Norwich. A hamstring injury prematurely ended his season in mid-April.

Liverpool *(£500,000 from Montpellier, France on 29/9/2000) PL 7+4 FLC 3 FAC 0+1 Others 4+1*
Glasgow Rgrs *(Loaned on 5/8/2004) SL 29+1/3 SLC 4 SC 1 Others 6+1*
Portsmouth *(Free on 12/7/2005) PL 13+1 FLC 1 FAC 2 (Freed during 2006 close season)*
Southampton *(Loaned from RC Lens, France on 1/8/2007) FL 20/3 FLC 0+1 FAC 2/1*

VILLA Emanuel Alejandro
Born: Casilda, Argentina, 24 February 1982
Height: 5'11" **Weight:** 12.2
World Cup winning manager Cesar Luis Menotti resigned after Mexican club UAG Tecos sold Emanuel to Derby last January, but later maintained that was not the reason for his departure. Although the Argentine striker found it hard to adjust in a struggling team and did not seal a regular starting place there was promise in his displays. He is strong in possession and holds up play well. Despite not being especially tall, he is effective in the air and two goals against Fulham helped to settle him. The hope is that he will be fully integrated for Derby's return to Championship action and a settled team would undoubtedly help him.
Derby Co *(£2,000,000 from UAG Tecos, Mexico, ex Huracan, Atletico Rafaela, Rosario Central, Atlas, on 8/1/2008) PL 9+7/3 FAC 1*

VINCENT Ashley Derek
Born: Oldbury, 26 May 1985
Height: 5'10" **Weight:** 11.8
Ashley returned to action with Cheltenham in August after missing most of 2006-07 with a knee injury. He appeared to have lost none of his pace and made a number of appearances as a wide midfielder on either the right or left. He also made a couple of appearances in his preferred position of striker. Ashley scored one of the goals of the season to earn a draw from the local derby against Swindon in August and followed it with another strike against Swansea a month later. A speedy player who likes to run with the ball and take on defenders, Ashley's form in the second half of the season earned him the offer of a new contract from manager Keith Downing.
Cheltenham T *(From trainee at Wolverhampton W on 2/7/2004) FL 34+47/5 FLC 2+3 FAC 1+3 Others 4+2/2*

VINCENT James Michael
Born: Manchester, 27 September 1989
Height: 5'11" **Weight:** 11.5
The final week of last season proved

memorable for James, another graduate from Stockport's hugely successful Centre of Excellence. On the Monday the talented central midfielder was given his first professional contract and on the Saturday he came off the bench against Brentford to make his debut. James will aim for a regular place in 2008-09.
Stockport Co *(Trainee) FL 0+1*

VINCENT Jamie Roy
Born: Wimbledon, 18 June 1975
Height: 5'10" **Weight:** 11.8
Jamie, an experienced and dependable defender, was another whose season at Swindon was disrupted by injury. Left-back is his natural position but he often displays his versatility by covering at centre-back. Arguably, he gave some of his most assured performances there, as demonstrated by his commanding display in the late-season victory at Bristol Rovers, when he kept Paul Lambert quiet despite a considerable height disadvantage. Jamie agreed terms for another season.

Crystal Palace *(From trainee on 13/7/1993) FL 19+6 FLC 2+1/1 FAC 1*
Bournemouth *(Loaned on 18/11/1994) FL 8*
Bournemouth *(£25,000 + on 30/8/1996) FL 102+3/5 FLC 7+1 FAC 8 Others 9/1*
Huddersfield T *(£440,000 + on 25/3/1999) FL 54+5/2 FLC 3+2 FAC 2*
Portsmouth *(£800,000 on 23/2/2001) FL 43+5/1 FLC 1*
Walsall *(Loaned on 17/10/2003) FL 12 FAC 0+1*
Derby Co *(Free on 16/1/2004) FL 22/2 FLC 1*
Millwall *(Loaned on 5/8/2005) FL 15 FLC 2*
Yeovil T *(Free on 31/1/2006)*
Millwall *(Loaned on 15/3/2006) FL 3+1*
Swindon T *(Free on 28/7/2006) FL 66 FLC 1 FAC 3 Others 1*

VINE Rowan Lewis
Born: Basingstoke, 21 September 1982
Height: 6'1" **Weight:** 12.2
Club Honours: Div 1 '05
Rowan made two Carling Cup appearances for Birmingham before joining Queens Park Rangers on loan in October, making the move permanent

Ashley Vincent

Rowan Vine

in January. Generally seen as a striker, Rowan found some of his best form for Rangers, drifting in from wide positions and excelling either on the right or left. Although he scored seven times, it was more his overall play and silky ball skills that proved vital in the club's renaissance. After really hitting his stride, his season was cruelly ended when he became the third Rangers' player to suffer a badly broken leg, at the end of March. Rowan is concentrating on a return to the side in the new campaign.

Portsmouth *(From trainee on 27/4/2001)* FL 3+10

Brentford *(Loaned on 7/8/2002)* FL 37+5/10 FLC 1+1/1 FAC 3/2 Others 3

Colchester U *(Loaned on 7/8/2003)* FL 30+5/6 FLC 1 FAC 5+2/4 Others 4+2/2

Luton T *(Signed on 6/8/2004)* FL 90+12/31 FLC 2+2/1 FAC 5/1

Birmingham C *(£2,500,000 on 12/1/2007)* P/FL 10+7/1 FLC 2

Queens Park Rgrs *(£1,000,000 on 2/10/2007)* FL 31+2/6

VIRGO Adam John
Born: Brighton, 25 January 1983
Height: 6'2" **Weight:** 13.7
Club Honours: SPD '06
International Honours: S: B-1
Versatile Adam signed for Colchester on a season's loan from Glasgow Celtic and although his preferred position is centre-half, actually began the campaign as an emergency striker coming off the bench. However, he soon became a regular at the heart of defence, where he looked composed and made some terrific last-ditch challenges. In what was a tricky season, there was no settled back four so Adam was under pressure for most

games and was allowed to return to Celtic after the season.

Brighton & Hove A *(From juniors on 4/7/2000)* FL 65+8/10 FLC 2 FAC 1 Others 4+2/1

Exeter C *(Loaned on 29/11/2002)* FL 8+1

Glasgow Celtic *(£1,500,000 on 20/7/2005)* SL 3+7 SLC 1 SC 0+1

Coventry C *(Loaned on 7/8/2006)* FL 10+5/1 FAC 1

Colchester U *(Loaned on 18/8/2007)* FL 30+6/1 FAC 1

VOGEL Johann
Born: Geneva, Switzerland, 8 March 1977
Height: 5'9" **Weight:** 11.4
International Honours: Switzerland: 94; U21-7
Johann had not played in ten months for Real Betis when he was signed by Blackburn after a two-week trial. By April he was in the first team and, although still coming to terms with the Premiership, proved a welcome addition. A player who stays on his feet and is mobile, he patrols the centre of the midfield and finds it easy to slide from marking one player to another. Shrewd at spotting where he can win the ball, he likes to pass it around and always appears to have an option. In the few games he played, he has yet to thread the crucial ball past the defence but he has the vision to achieve this once he is accustomed to the other players.

Blackburn Rov *(Signed from Real Betis, Spain, ex Grasshoppers, PSV Eindhoven, AC Milan, on 25/3/2008)* PL 6

VOKES Samuel (Sam) Michael
Born: Lymington, 21 October 1989
Height: 5'10" **Weight:** 11.13
International Honours: W: 2; U21-9
Another big season for the young striker who, as well as being a regular for Bournemouth, firmly established himself in the Wales under-21 side. Still eligible for the youth team, Sam was the club's equal top scorer and his hold-up play won him many admirers. Several higher division clubs monitored his progress and, at the end of the season, he joined Wolverhampton in a transfer that the administrator said was vital for the survival of the club.

Bournemouth *(From Brockenhurst College on 29/11/2007)* FL 38+16/16 FLC 1 FAC 1+1 Others 2

VOLZ Moritz
Born: Siegen, Germany, 21 January 1983
Height: 5'11" **Weight:** 12.10
Club Honours: FAYC '00, '01
International Honours: Germany: U21-10; Yth

Despite making fewer than a dozen Premiership appearances for Fulham, Moritz remained a popular figure at Craven Cottage. Although nominally a right-back, he made only one start in that position, against his former club Arsenal in January, and was used in varied midfield roles, a throwback to the previous season when he enjoyed some success there. He was outstanding in the New Year's Day clash with Chelsea, his forceful run earning a penalty. A committed tackler who enjoys going forward with the ball, he was a regular in the reserves, usually in central midfield.

Arsenal *(Free from Schalke 04, Germany on 25/11/2000)* FLC 1+1

Wimbledon *(Loaned on 3/2/2003)* FL 10/1

Fulham *(£2,200,000 on 8/8/2003)* PL 115+10/2 FLC 5+1 FAC 13/2

VORONIN Andriy Viktorovych
Born: Odessa, Ukraine, 21 July 1979
Height: 5'10" **Weight:** 11.11
International Honours: Ukraine: 51
The pony-tailed Ukranian international striker was a surprise signing by Liverpool in the summer, even though he arrived on a Bosman transfer from German club, Bayer Leverkusen. Andriy had spent most of his career in Germany after being signed as a teenager by Borussia Monchengladbach but did not make the grade there and drifted down a grade with Mainz for three seasons before returning to the top level with FC Cologne. Even so, it was only at the age of 25 that he started to show some consistency with Bayer Leverkusen, where he was top scorer in two seasons. It is probable that Rafa Benitez regarded him as a squad player but he made an excellent start to his Anfield career with a stunning 25-yard volley in the early Champions' League match in Toulouse, plus goals at Sunderland and at home to Derby and Tottenham in the Premier League. He was also praised for his contribution to Liverpool's 8-0 rout of Besiktas in the Champions League, even though he did not score. Thereafter his performances lacked zip, with Liverpool supporters unable to comprehend why he was often preferred to the unlucky Peter Crouch. In January he was sidelined by an ankle injury incurred in training and did not return to action until April, scoring in two end-of-season games at Fulham and Tottenham.

Liverpool *(Free from Bayer Leverkusen, Germany, ex Chornomorets Odessa, Borussia Moenchengladbach, FSV Mainz 05, FC Cologne, on 12/7/2007)* PL 13+6/5 FLC 1 FAC 0+1 Others 4+3/1

W

WAGHORN Martyn Thomas

Born: South Shields, 23 January 1990
Height: 5'10" **Weight:** 13.0
Teenage striker Martyn was handed his full debut against Manchester United last December and although Sunderland lost 4-0, he gave a good account of himself. A pacy forward, Martyn was awarded a new two-and-a-half-year contract in February and his form in the youth and reserve teams has many at The Stadium of Light believing he has a bright future.
Sunderland (From trainee on 1/2/2008) PL 1+2 FAC 1

WAGSTAFF Scott Andrew

Born: Maidstone, 31 March 1990
Height: 5'10" **Weight:** 10.3
Charlton's under-18 side captain, Scott missed only one reserve game and made his senior debut as a second-half substitute at Barnsley in the penultimate game, having been an unused sub the previous week. He made a second substitute appearance in the final fixture against Coventry at the Valley. A skilful winger who can play on either flank or up front, Scott is comfortable on the ball, hard-working and likes to run at defenders.
Charlton Ath (Trainee) FL 0+2

WAINWRIGHT Neil

Born: Warrington, 4 November 1977
Height: 6'0" **Weight:** 11.5
In Neil's sixth full season with Darlington, he started only six times in 2007-08 with a further 11 outings from the bench. After loans to Shrewsbury and Mansfield, he was recalled towards the end of the season and made his 200th start in Darlington's final home game, against Dagenham. Neil is at his best when running at defenders on the right and can cut in effectively towards goal. He is the leader of the current squad in total appearances, with 280 outings for Darlington. The experienced right-winger signed for Shrewsbury on loan in October and made his debut as a substitute in a 0-0 draw with Mansfield. However, Neil's time at the New Meadow did not work out well and he left after being involved in three games. At Mansfield he replaced Will Atkinson in March in the hope that his experience would help the Stags out of the relegation mire. When he did not achieve a regular place, Darlington refused to extend his stay beyond the original month. Was released at the end of the campaign.

Wrexham (From trainee on 3/7/1996) FL 7+4/3 FAC 1 Others 1
Sunderland (£100,000 + on 9/7/1998) P/FL 0+2 FLC 5+1
Darlington (Loaned on 4/2/2000) FL 16+1/4
Halifax T (Loaned on 13/10/2000) FL 13 FAC 1 Others 2
Darlington (£50,000 on 17/8/2001) FL 167+68/24 FLC 2+3 FAC 10+3/2 Others 7+3
Shrewsbury T (Loaned on 25/10/2007) FL 2+1
Mansfield T (Loaned on 21/3/2008) FL 1+4

WALCOTT Theo James

Born: Stanmore, Middlesex, 16 March 1989
Height: 5'7" **Weight:** 10.10
International Honours: E: 2; B-1; U21-15; Yth
Theo started the season on the fringes of the Arsenal side and ended it by scoring the final goal, a winner at Sunderland. He has shown enough to suggest he will play a major part in Arsenal's future. Quick, skilful and with an eye for goal, Theo has only really been lacking confidence in his attempt to move his Gunners' career forward. This was a season when he scored goals, made goals and became a paid-up member of the side. He scored four times in his 25 Premier League outings, twice in nine Champions' League ties and made one FA Cup appearance. He also scored once in his four Carling Cup games. Theo's breakthrough moment was his dazzling run at Anfield, when he sprinted virtually the length of the pitch to set up Arsenal's equaliser. That was an exciting glimpse of what lies ahead for the talented youngster.
Southampton (Trainee) FL 13+8/4 FLC 0+1 FAC 0+1/1
Arsenal (£9,100,000 on 20/3/2006) PL 16+25/4 FLC 10/2 FAC 3+2 Others 4+11/2

WALKER James Luke Newton

Born: Hackney, 25 November 1987
Height: 5'11" **Weight:** 11.13
International Honours: E: Yth
The Charlton striker enjoyed a successful loan spell at Yeovil, after signing in October, scoring three goals in 15 games. His powerful performances lightened the Glovers' early season and his goals were missed when he returned to the Valley. Unable to get a game with his parent club, James had impressed Southend manager Steve Tilson during his spell at Yeovil and when the transfer window reopened in January, Southend tabled a £200,000 bid for him. Having looked set to move to Roots Hall, a heart problem was detected in his medical and James was advised by specialists to take an immediate break from the game. After some five weeks of extensive tests and treatment, he was cleared to resume his career and Southend opted to take him on loan for the rest of the campaign. James made an immediate impact, scoring the winner as a substitute against Bournemouth on his debut, and started every match after that, forming a great understanding with Lee Barnard. Possesses excellent body strength, James created a happy ending for himself and Southend.
Charlton Ath (From trainee on 9/12/2004)
Hartlepool U (Loaned on 1/1/2006) FL 1+3
Bristol Rov (Loaned on 27/9/2006) FL 3+1/1 Others 1
Leyton Orient (Loaned on 23/11/2006) FL 9+5/2 FAC 1+1/1
Notts Co (Loaned on 15/3/2007) FL 2+6
Yeovil T (Loaned on 19/10/2007) FL 11+2/3 FAC 1 Others 1
Southend U (Loaned on 15/2/2008) FL 14+1/4 Others 2

WALKER Richard Martin

Born: Birmingham, 8 November 1977
Height: 6'0" **Weight:** 12.0
Club Honours: AMC '02
Bristol Rovers' leading scorer for the previous two seasons, Richard, who had signed a new contract in the summer, struggled to hold down a regular place in the starting line-up. His only goals were the four penalties he converted in the first half of the season and he failed to feature much after Christmas.
Aston Villa (From trainee on 13/12/1995) PL 2+4/2 FLC 1+1 FAC 0+1 Others 1
Cambridge U (Loaned on 31/12/1998) FL 7+14/3 Others 1+2/1
Blackpool (Loaned on 9/2/2001) FL 6+12/3
Wycombe W (Loaned on 13/9/2001) FL 10+2/3 FAC 1/1
Blackpool (£50,000 + on 21/12/2001) FL 38+24/12 FLC 0+1 FAC 1+2 Others 3+1/3
Northampton T (Loaned on 21/10/2003) FL 11+1/4 FAC 4/2 Others 3/2
Oxford U (Free on 17/3/2004) FL 3+1
Bristol Rov (Free on 2/8/2004) FL 115+28/46 FLC 4+2/2 FAC 9+4/5 Others 12+2/9

WALKER Richard Stuart

Born: Stafford, 17 September 1980
Height: 6'2" **Weight:** 13.0
Having been released by Port Vale, Richard spent the final two months of last season at Macclesfield, using his height and experience to good effect in the centre of a five-man defence. His arrival at the Moss Rose helped to strengthen that part of the team.
Crewe Alex (From trainee on 6/7/1999) FL 82+18/6 FLC 5+1/1 FAC 3+1 Others 4
Port Vale (Free on 1/7/2006) FL 12+4 FLC 3+1/1 FAC 1 Others 1
Wrexham (Loaned on 22/3/2007) FL 3
Macclesfield T (Free on 6/3/2008) FL 10

WALLACE Ross

Born: Dundee, 23 May 1985
Height: 5'8" **Weight:** 10.0
Club Honours: SC '04; SPD '06; SLC '06; Ch '07
International Honours: S: B-1; U21-4; Yth

Ross is a talented outside-left at Sunderland who showed his versatility when starting at left-back and laying on the winning goal for Michael Chopra in the first match of 2007-08, against Tottenham. He followed that by creating Stern John's last-minute equaliser at Birmingham four days later. However, Danny Collins' excellent form at left-back pushed Ross further up the field and he scored the winner against Reading, before striking at the Emirates Stadium when Sunderland lost narrowly to Arsenal. Ross was surprisingly transfer-listed by Roy Keane in January, after which he sustained knee-ligament damage in a training-ground accident.

Glasgow Celtic (From juniors on 12/5/2002) SL 18+19/1 SLC 3+1/3 SC 2+2 Others 1+6
Sunderland (Signed on 31/8/2006) P/FL 38+15/8 FLC 1 FAC 1

WALLWORK Ronald (Ronnie)

Born: Manchester, 10 September 1977
Height: 5'10" **Weight:** 12.9
Club Honours: FAYC '95; PL '01
International Honours: E: Yth

Ronnie, an experienced midfielder, joined Huddersfield on loan from West Bromwich last September to influence the engine room. Unselfish throughout, he caught the eye with some battling displays and was instrumental in an upturn of results. As well as giving additional bite, he scored three times with some great strikes from distance. Always at the heart of the action, Ronnie clears the ball thoughtfully and distributes it with great accuracy, but found it hard to establish himself after signing for Sheffield Wednesday in January. A player who holds up play well and can create, he offers stability and experience to a very young squad.

Manchester U (From trainee on 17/3/1995) PL 4+15 FLC 4+1 FAC 1+1 Others 1+1
Carlisle U (Loaned on 22/12/1997) FL 10/1 Others 2
Stockport Co (Loaned on 18/3/1998) FL 7
West Bromwich A (Free on 2/7/2002) P/FL 86+7/2 FLC 6+1/1 FAC 7
Bradford C (Loaned on 22/1/2004) FL 7/4
Barnsley (Loaned on 23/11/2006) FL 2
Huddersfield T (Loaned on 28/9/2007) FL 16/3 FAC 2
Sheffield Wed (Free on 11/1/2008) FL 4+3

Ross Wallace

WALTERS Jonathan (Jon) Ronald

Born: Birkenhead, 20 September 1983
Height: 6'1" **Weight:** 12.0
International Honours: Rol: U21-1; Yth

The return of Pablo Counago in the summer led to a change of role for Jon. To enable him to play alongside Counago and Alan Lee, Ipswich decided to move Jon to an attacking role on the right of midfield. He proved that he had adequate defensive capabilities in the first few games of the season and being out on the right meant that he was not picked up by opposing central defenders, enabling him to ghost in unnoticed for scoring opportunities. This new position also gave another focal point for his goalkeeper and defenders to direct their clearances. Jon's best performance was probably against Bristol City, when he scored a hat-trick in a 6-0 win. He was voted 'Player of the Year' both by fellow players and supporters.

Blackburn Rov (From trainee on 3/8/2001)
Bolton W (Signed on 30/4/2002) PL 0+4 FLC 1 FAC 0+1
Hull C (Loaned on 24/2/2003) FL 11/5
Barnsley (Loaned on 12/11/2003) FL 7+1 FAC 3 Others 0+1
Hull C (£50,000 on 5/2/2004) FL 9+28/2 FLC 1 FAC 0+2/1 Others 1
Scunthorpe U (Loaned on 4/2/2005) FL 3
Wrexham (Free on 3/8/2005) FL 33+5/5 FLC 1 FAC 1 Others 1
Chester C (Free on 1/8/2006) FL 24+2/9 FLC 1 FAC 5/1 Others 0+1
Ipswich T (Signed on 27/1/2007) FL 50+6/17 FLC 1

WALTON Simon William

Born: Sherburn-in-Elmet, 13 September 1987
Height: 6'1" **Weight:** 13.5

Simon was one of Queens Park Rangers' unluckiest players. He joined from Charlton in the summer and, within a restricted budget, was a big signing for John Gregory. Unfortunately, he broke a leg in a pre-season friendly against Fulham and by the time he was fully fit, Rangers had become a very different club. Despite making his debut and four substitute appearances under new manager Luigi De Canio, Simon was allowed to move to Hull on loan in January and made his debut less than a day after becoming aware of the Tigers' interest. Skipper Ian Ashbee was ruled out with a late illness and Simon was drafted in against Coventry, having barely met his new team-mates. It was a winning start and he remained at the KC Stadium until the end of the season when Hull reached Wembley for the first time in the Championship play-off final and won promotion to the Premier League. Simon was mainly used as defensive midfield cover as well as being on standby at centre-back.

Leeds U (From trainee on 14/9/2004) FL 26+8/3 FLC 1+1 FAC 2
Charlton Ath (£500,000 + on 10/7/2006)
Ipswich T (Loaned on 18/8/2006) FL 13+6/3
Cardiff C (Loaned on 31/1/2007) FL 5+1
Queens Park Rgrs (£200,000 on 9/8/2007) FL 1+4
Hull C (Loaned on 29/1/2008) FL 5+5

WARD Darren

Born: Worksop, 11 May 1974
Height: 6'2" **Weight:** 14.2
Club Honours: Div 3 '98; Ch '07
International Honours: W: 5; B-1; U21-2

As Sunderland's back-up goalkeeper, Darren deputised for Craig Gordon four times last season, beginning with a 3-0 Carling Cup reverse at League One Luton. However, his three Premier League games were more successful with a win over Derby and a draw with Aston Villa on either side of a 2-0 defeat at Chelsea, a game in which Darren acquitted himself extremely well.

Mansfield T (From trainee on 27/7/1992) FL 81 FLC 5 FAC 5 Others 6
Notts Co (£160,000 on 11/7/1995) FL 251 FLC 18 FAC 23 Others 10
Nottingham F (Free on 21/5/2001) FL 123 FLC 8 FAC 4 Others 2
Norwich C (Signed on 6/8/2004) P/FL 0+1 FLC 1 FAC 0+1
Sunderland (Free on 4/8/2006) P/FL 33 FLC 1 FAC 1

WARD Darren Philip

Born: Harrow, 13 September 1978
Height: 6'0" **Weight:** 12.6

Following his arrival at Wolverhampton from Crystal Palace during the summer, Darren's partnership with Gary Breen was not working smoothly and he was dropped for four games before returning to team up with Jody Craddock. Darren is good in the air and the team had a good defensive record during his 24-game spell, conceding only two in one seven-match sequence. He did not quite maintain the standard, being dropped, recalled for a couple of games and then slipping out of the first-team squad.

Watford (From trainee on 13/2/1997) P/FL 56+3/2 FLC 6/1 FAC 2 Others 0+1
Queens Park Rgrs (Loaned on 17/12/1999) FL 14 FAC 1
Millwall (£500,000 on 3/10/2001) FL 135+7/4 FLC 3 FAC 12 Others 4
Crystal Palace (£1,100,000 on 1/6/2005) FL 62+1/5 FLC 1 FAC 4/1 Others 1
Wolverhampton W (£500,000 on 4/7/2007) FL 30 FAC 2

WARD Elliott Leslie

Born: Harrow, 19 January 1985
Height: 6'2" **Weight:** 12.0

After being Coventry's regular centre-half in the previous campaign, Elliott had stiff competition in the first half of last season. He missed the Colchester home game with injury and could not regain his place because of the form of Ben Turner and Arjan De Zeeuw. Elliott loves the big game and was a rock in Coventry's victories at Manchester United, Blackburn and West Bromwich. Although dropped following a debacle at Blackpool, he was a virtual ever-present after regaining his place in January. Elliott is big-hearted and can win the ball in the air against most Championship strikers. At Blackburn he took over penalty duties from Michael Doyle and converted six, including two in one game at Colchester, and scored the vital home goal against Wolverhampton with a delicate header.

West Ham U (From trainee on 23/1/2002) P/FL 13+2 FLC 3 Others 3
Bristol Rov (Loaned on 29/12/2004) FL 0+3
Plymouth Arg (Loaned on 22/11/2005) FL 15+1/1
Coventry C (£1,000,000 on 7/7/2006) FL 74+2/9 FLC 3 FAC 3/1

WARD Gavin John

Born: Sutton Coldfield, 30 June 1970
Height: 6'3" **Weight:** 14.12
Club Honours: Div 3 '93; WC '93; AMC '00

On leaving Tranmere in the summer, the veteran goalkeeper was signed by Chester not only to help on the coaching side but to compete for the number-one jersey with John Danby. However, he was unable to break into the side and his only appearance was as a second-half substitute for Danby in the Johnstone's Paint Trophy tie against Crewe. In January, Gavin moved across the border to sign for Wrexham on an 18-month deal. A regular starter at the Racecourse in the attempt to beat the dreaded drop, Gavin blew hot and cold on occasions although, as so often happens, he produced his best display at former club Chester in March, one outstanding save helping Wrexham to an important three points.

Shrewsbury T (From trainee at Aston Villa on 26/9/1988)
West Bromwich A (Free on 18/9/1989) FLC 1
Cardiff C (Free on 5/10/1989) FL 58+1 FAC 1 Others 7
Leicester C (£175,000 on 16/7/1993) P/FL 38 FLC 3 FAC 0+1 Others 4
Bradford C (£175,000 on 13/7/1995) FL 36 FLC 6 FAC 3 Others 2
Bolton W (£300,000 on 29/3/1996) P/FL 19+3 FLC 2 FAC 4
Burnley (Loaned on 14/8/1998) FL 17
Stoke C (Free on 25/2/1999) FL 79 FLC 7 FAC 2 Others 12
Walsall (Free on 9/8/2002) FL 5+2
Coventry C (Free on 4/8/2003) FL 12 FAC 3
Barnsley (Loaned on 29/4/2004) FL 1
Preston NE (Free on 6/8/2004) FL 6+1 FLC 1
Tranmere Rov (Free on 3/7/2006) FL 36+2/1 FLC 1 FAC 2
Chester C (Free on 2/7/2007) Others 0+1
Wrexham (Free on 8/1/2008) FL 22

WARD Jamie John

Born: Birmingham, 12 May 1986
Height: 5'5" **Weight:** 9.4
International Honours: NI: U21-7; Yth

Troublesome hamstrings threatened to ruin Jamie's season before it started but Chesterfield's physios found a way to manage the problem. They were rewarded with many lively performances on the wing, where his speed off the mark tormented defences and brought 12 League goals. Fans voted Jamie's stunning volley in the 4-1 defeat of Shrewsbury in April as the 'Goal of the Season'.

Aston Villa (From trainee on 16/5/2004)
Stockport Co (Loaned on 7/3/2006) FL 7+2/1
Torquay U (Free on 18/7/2006) FL 21+4/9 FLC 1 FAC 2/2 Others 0+1
Chesterfield (Signed on 31/1/2007) FL 35+9/15 FLC 1

WARD Nicholas (Nick)

Born: Perth, Australia, 24 March 1985
Height: 6'0" **Weight:** 12.6
International Honours: Australia: U23-2; Yth

A young Australian attacking midfielder who can also perform well in a more central position, Nick returned home in December, having made only two appearances for Queens Park Rangers in the early stages of the season.
Queens Park Rgrs *(Signed from Perth Glory, Australia on 20/7/2006) FL 11+9/1 FLC 2 FAC 1*
Brighton & Hove A *(Loaned on 31/1/2007) FL 6+2/1*

WARD Stephen Robert
Born: Dublin, 20 August 1985
Height: 5'11" **Weight:** 12.1
International Honours: RoI: B; U21-3; Yth
With four established strikers at Wolverhampton, it seemed Stephen might have to go out on loan. However, injury to new signing Matt Jarvis meant he played on the left-wing. He worked hard, started most games, and as a substitute at Cardiff helped to turn the match. Stephen had a couple of chances to score against Bristol City but was not often seen as a striker. In fact, he sometimes played deep and did not shirk his defensive duties. Stephen, who played for Republic of Ireland 'B', was involved in all but two of Wolverhampton's matches until January but then suffered patella tendinitis and was seen only briefly towards the end of the season.
Wolverhampton W *(Signed from Bohemians, ex Portmarnock, on 19/1/2007) FL 34+13/3 FLC 0+1 FAC 1+1 Others 0+2*

WARLOW Owain James
Born: Pontypridd, 3 July 1988
Height: 6'0" **Weight:** 12.0
International Honours: W: U21-2
Having received Lincoln's 2006-07 'Young Player of the Season' award, the midfielder's appearances last season came mainly in the first half of the campaign, and mostly as a substitute, as he struggled to hold down a regular first-team berth. Struggling for consistency, although he did start six consecutive games in the latter part of 2007, Owain is highly thought of at the club as a speedy left-sided player with good skills and an ability to take on defenders. The coming season will be an important one for him.
Lincoln C *(From trainee on 6/7/2006) FL 6+16 FLC 0+1 FAC 1+1 Others 1*

WARNE Paul
Born: Norwich, 8 May 1973
Height: 5'9" **Weight:** 11.2
After Paul's hugely successful 2006-07 season for Oldham, Yeovil moved quickly to snap up the forward after his surprising release in the summer. Unfortunately, the

veteran suffered an injury-hit season and struggled to gain full fitness in order to string games together after Christmas. Only one goal in the campaign was a poor reward for all the hard work Paul put in but he remained a team player who created chances for others by his dogged persistence.
Wigan Ath *(£25,000 from Wroxham on 30/7/1997) FL 11+25/3 FLC 0+1 FAC 1 Others 1+2/1*
Rotherham U *(Free on 15/1/1999) FL 173+57/28 FLC 6+6/1 FAC 10/1 Others 5*
Mansfield T *(Loaned on 26/11/2004) FL 7/1*
Oldham Ath *(Free on 4/7/2005) FL 80+6/18 FLC 2 FAC 8/3 Others 4*
Yeovil T *(Free on 18/7/2007) FL 26+7/1 FLC 1 FAC 0+1 Others 2*

WARNER Anthony (Tony) Randolph
Born: Liverpool, 11 May 1974
Height: 6'4" **Weight:** 13.9
Club Honours: Div 2 '01
International Honours: Trinidad & Tobago: 1
An injury to Antti Niemi gave Tony the opportunity to start last season as Fulham's first-choice goalkeeper in the opening three games and he gave a particularly sound performance on the first day at Arsenal. These were his only Premiership appearances, although he enjoyed an outstanding game in the FA Cup replay at Bristol Rovers in January. After a brief loan spell at Barnsley, he was Fulham's regular substitute goalkeeper for the final months of the season. Barnsley signed Tony on an initial month's loan at the end of January after Heinz Muller was injured and he made his debut two days later at Coventry, unfortunately in a 4-0 defeat. He performed excellently in his next match against West Bromwich, showing good shot-stopping and command of the area, but he was Cup-tied and unable to play against Liverpool. With Luke Steele performing heroics and keeping his place, Tony returned to Fulham at the end of his month before being released in the summer.
Liverpool *(From juniors on 1/1/1994)*
Swindon T *(Loaned on 5/11/1997) FL 2*
Glasgow Celtic *(Loaned on 13/11/1998) SL 3*
Aberdeen *(Loaned on 31/3/1999) SL 6*
Millwall *(Free on 16/7/1999) FL 200 FLC 10 FAC 10 Others 5*
Cardiff C *(Free on 3/7/2004) FL 26 FLC 2 FAC 2*
Fulham *(£100,000 on 12/8/2005) PL 19+2 FLC 2 FAC 3*
Leeds U *(Loaned on 4/8/2006) FL 13 FLC 1*
Norwich C *(Loaned on 2/3/2007) FL 13*
Barnsley *(Loaned on 31/1/2008) FL 3*

WARNOCK Stephen
Born: Ormskirk, 12 December 1981
Height: 5'7" **Weight:** 12.1
Club Honours: ESC '05
International Honours: E: 1; Yth; Sch
A call-up to the England squad for the post-season friendlies was no more than the Blackburn left-back deserved, given his performances. A razor-sharp tackler with great judgement, he could also overlap with gusto, his cross for Roque Santa Cruz's goal at Wigan being a perfect example. Midway through the season, he began to lose consistency and attacked less frequently so that he could concentrate on basics but by the end he was back to his old, swashbuckling self.
Liverpool *(From trainee on 27/4/1999) PL 27+13/1 FLC 7+1 FAC 2+1 Others 10+6*
Bradford C *(Loaned on 13/9/2002) FL 12/1*
Coventry C *(Loaned on 31/7/2003) FL 42+2/3 FLC 2 FAC 2+1*
Blackburn Rov *(£1,500,000 on 23/11/2007) PL 50/2 FLC 1+1 FAC 5 Others 8/1*

WARRINGTON Andrew (Andy) Clifford
Born: Sheffield, 10 June 1976
Height: 6'3" **Weight:** 12.13
Club Honours: Div 3 '04
Andy arrived at Rotherham from Bury during the summer as a vastly experienced goalkeeper and soon showed he had fully recovered from previous injury problems with a number of outstanding performances to win him several 'Man of the Match' awards. Had it not been for the bravery that saw him pull off many one-on-one saves, the number of goals conceded would have been much higher. He saved points

Andy Warrington

for the club through his alertness to situations.

York C *(From trainee on 11/6/1994) FL 61 FLC 7 FAC 4 Others 4*
Doncaster Rov *(Free on 8/6/1999) FL 89 FLC 7 FAC 3*
Bury *(Free on 23/11/2006) FL 20 FAC 1*
Rotherham U *(Free on 11/7/2007) FL 46 FLC 1 FAC 2 Others 1*

WATSON Benjamin (Ben)
Born: Camberwell, 9 July 1985
Height: 5'10" **Weight:** 10.11
International Honours: E: U21-2
The young ginger-headed England under-21 international midfielder had another fine season for Crystal Palace in 2007-08. A dead-ball specialist, who is a constant danger from free kicks, corners and penalties, Ben scored four times from the spot, including one as Palace qualified for the play-offs, and added to his reputation as a tough-tackling player who can distribute the ball effectively. At Bristol City, he scored with a long-range header before ending the season by missing a penalty. Ben is now approaching 160 appearances in his four years as a professional with Palace.
Crystal Palace *(From trainee on 12/8/2004) P/FL 127+24/13 FLC 7+3 FAC 5 Others 3+1/2*

WATSON Kevin Edward
Born: Hackney, 3 January 1974
Height: 6'0" **Weight:** 12.6
After three superb seasons at Colchester, during which he hardly missed a game, Kevin endured one to forget. His campaign was completely ruined by injuries, starting off in pre-season before being dogged by Achilles tendon and calf problems that restricted him to seven appearances. The central midfielder played the whole of November but was always struggling for sharpness, and a return to action against Wolverhampton at the beginning of March backfired. He rushed back too soon and was duly released by Colchester at the end of the season.
Tottenham H *(From trainee on 15/5/1992) PL 4+1 FLC 1+1/1 FAC 0+1 Others 4*
Brentford *(Loaned on 24/3/1994) FL 2+1*
Bristol C *(Loaned on 2/12/1994) FL 1+1*
Barnet *(Loaned on 16/2/1995) FL 13*
Swindon T *(Free on 15/7/1996) FL 39+24/1 FLC 2+2 FAC 1+2*
Rotherham U *(Free on 31/7/1999) FL 109/7 FLC 6/1 FAC 7 Others 3*
Reading *(Loaned on 2/11/2001) FL 6*
Reading *(£150,000 + on 14/3/2002) FL 40+20/2 FLC 2 FAC 0+1 Others 0+1*
Colchester U *(Free on 12/7/2004) FL 132+3/3 FLC 5 FAC 10/1 Others 3+1*

WATSON Stephen (Steve) Craig
Born: North Shields, 1 April 1974
Height: 6'0" **Weight:** 12.7
International Honours: E: B-1; U21-12; Yth
Sheffield Wednesday's versatile veteran endured a frustrating season. Steve spent time out because of hamstring problems, so was never able to stamp his authority on the side. He can play in midfield, central defence or full-back and also captains the Owls when in the side. The highlight of his season was his last-minute equaliser at his old club, West Bromwich, but injuries made it a disappointing time for him.
Newcastle U *(From trainee on 6/4/1991) P/FL 179+29/12 FLC 10+6/1 FAC 13+4 Others 18+4/1*
Aston Villa *(£4,000,000 on 15/10/1998) PL 39+2 FLC 7+1/1 FAC 4*
Everton *(£2,500,000 on 12/7/2000) PL 106+20/14 FLC 7+1/1 FAC 2+1/1*
West Bromwich A *(Free on 5/7/2005) P/FL 38+4/1 FLC 2*
Sheffield Wed *(Free on 9/2/2007) FL 31+3/2 FLC 1 FAC 1/1*

WATT Philip (Phil) Alexander
Born: Rotherham, 10 January 1988
Height: 5'11" **Weight:** 11.5
A pre-season injury to Lee Beevers meant that the right-sided defender marked the start of the 2007-08 campaign by making his League debut for Lincoln against Shrewsbury. Beevers' subsequent return to fitness saw Phil make just one further appearance, as a substitute against Nottingham Forest in the first round of the FA Cup, before he left the Imps by mutual consent shortly after he returned from a loan spell at non-League Corby.
Lincoln C *(From trainee on 6/7/2006) FL 1 FAC 0+1*

WAY Darren
Born: Plymouth, 21 November 1979
Height: 5'7" **Weight:** 11.0
Club Honours: FAT '02; FC '03; Div 2 '05; AMC '06
International Honours: E: SP-3
Darren's long-standing shin injury kept him out at the start of Swansea's 2007-08 season and after a couple of reserve appearances in late September he injured a hamstring the following month. To get match fit, Darren returned to his former club Yeovil on loan in November and played eight games, scoring once, while performing at a level reminiscent of his first spell at Huish Park. Injury problems forced Swansea to recall Darren and he made his first start for the Swans, against MK Dons, in the Johnstone's Paint Trophy

Southern final first leg and appeared three more times before the end of the campaign. Ever since leaving Yeovil, the central midfielder struggled to achieve fitness and can only hope his fortunes change in the coming season.
Norwich C *(From trainee on 11/9/1998)*
Yeovil T *(Free on 19/8/2000) FL 98+1/13 FLC 5/1 FAC 8/3 Others 2*
Swansea C *(£150,000 on 23/1/2006) FL 6+10 Others 3+2*
Yeovil T *(Loaned on 15/11/2007) FL 7/1*

WEALE Christopher (Chris)
Born: Chard, 9 February 1982
Height: 6'2" **Weight:** 13.3
Club Honours: FAT '02; FC '03; Div 2 '05
International Honours: E: SP-4
The Bristol City goalkeeper was recalled from an early-season loan at Hereford when Adriano Basso was injured in the opener against Queens Park Rangers. Chris played in the next four games, only one of which was lost, 2-1 to Manchester City in the Carling Cup, before taking an almost regular place on the substitutes' bench. He played a small part in Hereford's successful season after being drafted in as an emergency loan for the opening game following an injury to first-choice 'keeper Wayne Brown. Chris impressed with his safe handling as he kept a clean sheet but injury problems at his home club forced an immediate recall to Ashton Gate.
Yeovil T *(From juniors on 5/6/2000) FL 97+1 FLC 5 FAC 11 Others 2*
Bristol C *(Free on 4/7/2006) FL 2+2 FLC 2 FAC 1*
Hereford U *(Loaned on 9/8/2007) FL 1*

WEAVER Nicholas (Nicky) James
Born: Sheffield, 2 March 1979
Height: 6'3" **Weight:** 13.6
Club Honours: Div 1 '02
International Honours: E: U21-10
An experienced goalkeeper, Nicky was signed by Charlton on a free transfer from Manchester City in the summer and immediately given the number-one jersey. He missed only one League game, through suspension after he was dismissed for handling outside the penalty area in the second minute at Plymouth. Nicky is an assured 'keeper who handles well and is a competent shot-stopper. He is comfortable with crosses and commands his area, keeping 13 clean sheets in League and Cup games, including four in a row in November. Nicky had a consistent season and his best performance was in a 2-0 victory at Preston.
Mansfield T *(Trainee) FL 1*

Nicky Weaver

Manchester C *(£200,000 on 2/5/1997) P/FL 170+2 FLC 15 FAC 16 Others 4*
Sheffield Wed *(Loaned on 4/11/2005) FL 14*
Charlton Ath *(Free on 9/8/2007) FL 45 FLC 1 FAC 2*

WEBB Luke Alexander
Born: Nottingham, 12 September 1986
Height: 6'0" **Weight:** 12.1
Injuries played a major part in destroying what should have been a big season for Luke. A regular substitute in Hereford's early matches, he came off the bench to score at Morecambe and, in a rare start, grabbed both goals against Brentford. Lionel Ainsworth's departure for Watford should have opened the door for Luke but a training injury meant that he was unfit when the chance came. After a couple more substitute appearances, further injury necessitated a back operation that ended his season. Was out of contract in the summer and looking for a new club.
Coventry C *(From trainee at Arsenal, via trial at Wycombe W, on 1/8/2005)*
Hereford U *(Free on 31/8/2006) FL 16+19/3 FAC 3/2 Others 2*

WEBB Sean Michael
Born: Dungannon, 4 January 1983
Height: 6'2" **Weight:** 12.5
International Honours: NI: 4; U21-6; Yth
Having arrived from Ross County on the last day of the August transfer window, international call-ups and injuries prevented the centre-back from making his Accrington debut until mid-

September. He was in for four games but that was his longest run of the season. From then on, he was in and out the side or on the bench and will look back on his first season in English football as a disappointment, particularly as he did not add to his four Northern Ireland caps.
Ross Co *(Signed from Dungannon Swifts on 4/8/2001) SL 43+6/1 SLC 4 SC 1+1 Others 3+2/2*
St Johnstone *(Signed on 3/6/2004) SL 15+4 SC 1 Others 1*
Ross Co *(Signed on 31/5/2005) SL 32+3/1 SLC 2/1 SC 3 Others 2*
Accrington Stanley *(Free on 31/8/2007) FL 18 FAC 1*

WEBB Thomas (Tom) James Jonathan
Born: Chelmsford, 17 April 1989
Height: 5'9" **Weight:** 11.2
Striker Tom scored regularly for the reserves but made only one brief appearance for Colchester's first team as a late substitute in the Carling Cup defeat at Shrewsbury during the first week of the season. He enjoyed some action on loan at Folkestone Invicta before being released by the U's at the end of the campaign.
Colchester U *(From trainee on 4/7/2007) FLC 0+1*

WEBBER Daniel (Danny) Vaughn
Born: Manchester, 28 December 1981
Height: 5'9" **Weight:** 10.8
International Honours: E: Yth

Danny was in and out of the Sheffield United side at the start of last season, despite scoring twice at Scunthorpe. He finally had a run of games in October and November, when he caused problems with his speed and tricky footwork on the flanks, but his season came to an early end in November due to a persistent knee injury.
Manchester U *(From trainee on 7/1/1999) FLC 1+1 Others 0+1*
Port Vale *(Loaned on 23/11/2001) FL 2+2 Others 0+1*
Watford *(Loaned on 28/3/2002) FL 4+1/2*
Watford *(Loaned on 13/8/2002) FL 11+1/2*
Watford *(Signed on 7/7/2003) FL 48+7/17 FLC 3+1 FAC 1+3*
Sheffield U *(£500,000 on 24/3/2005) P/FL 51+27/19 FLC 4+1/1 FAC 1*

WEIR-DALEY Spencer
Born: Leicester, 5 September 1985
Height: 5'9" **Weight:** 10.11
Spencer turned down the opportunity of a renewed contract at Nottingham Forest to cross Trent Bridge in search of more regular first-team football at Notts County. He is a clever striker who comes alive in the penalty area and has a good touch. He looks on every pass in his direction as a chance to make or score a goal but his opportunities were restricted as physically stronger players were chosen ahead of him. He remains a real hope for the future.
Nottingham F *(From trainee on 9/1/2004) FL 0+7/1 FLC 1+1 Others 1+1/1*
Macclesfield T *(Loaned on 31/8/2006) FL 5+2/2 Others 1*
Lincoln C *(Loaned on 1/1/2007) FL 4+7/5*
Bradford C *(Loaned on 22/3/2007) FL 2+3/1*
Notts Co *(Signed on 6/7/2007) FL 12+18/3 FLC 0+1 FAC 0+2 Others 1*

WELLENS Richard (Richie) Paul
Born: Manchester, 26 March 1980
Height: 5'9" **Weight:** 11.6
Club Honours: AMC '02, '04
International Honours: E: Yth
Richie was signed by Doncaster from Oldham in the summer and proved to be a mainstay of the team in the midfield. Hard-working, comfortable and skilful on the ball, he loves to get forward and was just behind the strikers with his goal tally. Richie was named in the PFA 'League One Select' team and battled through the play-off final against Leeds at Wembley with a double hernia.
Manchester U *(From trainee on 19/5/1997) FLC 0+1*
Blackpool *(Signed on 23/3/2000) FL 173+15/16 FLC 8+1 FAC 10+2/2 Others 12+5/1*

Oldham Ath (Signed on 4/7/2005) FL 87/8
FLC 2 FAC 8 Others 3+1
Doncaster Rov (Free on 23/7/2007) FL 45/6
FLC 2/1 FAC 2 Others 3+1

WELSH Andrew (Andy) Peter
David
Born: Manchester, 24 January 1983
Height: 5'8" **Weight:** 9.8
International Honours: S: Yth
Released by Sunderland in March 2007,
Andy moved to Toronto before being
signed by Blackpool in September and
was expected to have a major impact,
considering his previous experience in the
Championship. Although a nippy left-
winger with good crossing ability, it was
apparent from his substitute appearances
that he was finding life difficult at
Bloomfield Road. He made only three
League starts before being released at the
end of the campaign.
Stockport Co (From trainee on 11/7/2001) FL
44+31/3 FLC 1+2 FAC 2 Others 3+2
Macclesfield T (Loaned on 30/8/2002) FL
4+2/2
Sunderland (£15,000 on 24/11/2004)
P/FL 15+6/1 FLC 1+1 FAC 1+1/1 (Freed on
23/3/2007)
Leicester C (Loaned on 1/3/2006) FL 4+6/1
Leicester C (Loaned on 16/10/2006) FL 4+3
—FLC 1
Blackpool (Free from Toronto FC, Canada on
31/8/2007) FL 3+18 FLC 1+1 FAC 1

WELSH John Joseph
Born: Liverpool, 10 January 1984
Height: 5'7" **Weight:** 11.6
International Honours: E: U21-8; Yth
John joined Chester on a one-month loan
at the start of January in order to gain
match fitness following a serious leg injury
in March 2007. After a tentative start the
powerful midfielder began to make his
presence felt at the Deva Stadium before
returning to Hull after six appearances
for the Blues. He did not play for Hull in
2007-08.
Liverpool (From trainee on 29/1/2001) PL
2+2 FLC 0+3 FAC 1 Others 0+2
Hull C (Signed on 23/8/2005) FL 38+12/3
FLC 3+1
Chester C (Loaned on 1/1/2008) FL 6

WELSH-ELLIOTT Ishmael
Born: Deptford, 4 September 1987
Height: 5'7" **Weight:** 10.10
Unable to secure a place at Yeovil early
last season, Ishmael went on loan to
Torquay in order to stay match fit and
was a regular until arriving back at Huish
Park. A player whose main attribute is his
ability to get down the wing and whip in
crosses, Ishmael managed three substitute
appearances for Yeovil in January before

another loan, this time to Forest Green.
Released at the end of the campaign, he
was snapped up by Blue Square Premier
side Grays.
Yeovil T (From trainee at West Ham U on
1/8/2006) FL 4+17/1 FLC 1 FAC 0+1 Others 1

WERLING Dominik Patrick
Born: Ludwigshafen, Germany, 13
December 1982
Height: 5'8" **Weight:** 10.7
Taken on six months loan from
Sakaryaspor in July, Dominik made his
Barnsley debut as a substitute on the
opening day and left the club when his
loan expired. Dominik soon became a fans'
favourite. He was strong in the tackle at
left- back and needed no urging to get
forward. Dominik's hammer of a left foot
made him a danger at free kicks and he
went close several times before hitting in a
35-yard spectacular against Plymouth.
Barnsley (Loaned from Sakaryaspor, Turkey,
ex Armenia Bielfeld, Union Berlin, Crailsheim,
on 17/7/2007) FL 16+1/1 FLC 2

WESOLOWSKI James Peter
Born: Sydney, Australia, 25 August 1987
Height: 5'7" **Weight:** 10.10
International Honours: Australia: Yth
The highly-talented Leicester midfielder
picked up the odd injury and found himself
in and out of the first team, particularly
under Ian Holloway. James' only goal of
the season was enough to secure a Carling
Cup victory in the Foxes' first-ever trip to
Accrington and he may yet develop into
a regular for both City and Australia in
coming seasons.
Leicester C (From trainee on 24/9/2004) FL
29+17 FLC 5/1 FAC 1+2/1

WESSELS Stefan
Born: Rahden, Germany, 28 February
1979
Height: 6'2" **Weight:** 13.3
International Honours: Germany: U21-1
Having arrived from FC Cologne, the
German 'B' international was the first
player from his country to appear for
Everton when making his debut against
Manchester United in September 2007.
The goalkeeper had an impressive first
game in place of Tim Howard and made
six other appearances in the campaign,
performing soundly, but was released at
the end of his year's contract.
Everton (Free from FC Cologne, Germany, ex
Bayern Munich, on 24/8/2007) PL 2 FLC 2 FAC
1 Others 2

WESTLAKE Ian John
Born: Clacton, 10 July 1983
Height: 5'9" **Weight:** 12.0
Ian suffered another frustrating season

at Leeds in 2007-08. Niggling injuries did
not help but he made an impact as Leeds
maintained their stunning start to the
season to eat away the points' penalty
caused by entering administration. Ian was
credited with United's last-gasp equaliser
at Walsall and scored the only goal of the
game as Leeds won at Macclesfield in the
first round of the Carling Cup. Having
been out of action since the 1-1 draw at
Luton towards the end of January, Ian
went on loan to Brighton at the beginning
of March and, as a left-sided midfielder, he
added balance to a side sitting just behind
Leeds in League One. Although he could
not quite maintain the high quality of his
initial impact, he scored two goals before
returning to United for the play-offs.
Ipswich T (From trainee on 9/8/2002) FL
90+24/15 FLC 3+2/1 FAC 3 Others 4
Leeds U (Signed on 4/8/2006) FL 29+18/1 FLC
2+1/1 FAC 1 Others 1
Brighton & Hove A (Loaned on 4/3/2008)
FL 11/2

WESTON Curtis James
Born: Greenwich, 24 January 1987
Height: 5'11" **Weight:** 11.9
Curtis hooked up with manager Dennis
Wise for the third time in his career when
he joined Leeds just before the start of the
season, having been released by Swindon.
He had played for the ex-England
midfielder at Millwall and Swindon and
was in the United side that kicked off life
in the third tier of English football for the
first time with a 2-1 victory at Tranmere.
That was his only League One start for
the Whites and he was generally confined
to the reserves, the bench or Cup duties,
scoring his only goal in the last minute
of United's 3-0 romp over Northampton
at Elland Road. To get some more action,
Curtis joined Championship strugglers
Scunthorpe in March, on loan until the
end of the season, but found opportunities
restricted at Glanford Park. He started
only two matches on the right of midfield
but showed great pace in his fleeting
appearances, helping to create a goal
against Ipswich with a blistering run.
Millwall (From trainee on 17/3/2004) FL 2+2
FAC 0+2
Swindon T (Free on 12/7/2006) FL 21+6/1
FLC 0+1 FAC 2 Others 1
Leeds U (Free on 10/8/2007) FL 1+6/1 FLC
0+1 FAC 1+1 Others 1
Scunthorpe U (Loaned on 4/3/2008) FL 2+5

WESTON Myles Arthur Eugene
Wesley
Born: Lewisham, 12 March 1988
Height: 5'11" **Weight:** 12.0
The hugely talented young left-winger
became a permanent recruit from

Charlton, having previously spent time on loan at Notts County. Myles experienced real difficulty with fitness, usually because of strains that were reckoned to be related to his physical development. He can terrorise defenders and opponents often use two players to block his exhilarating dashes down the wing. His incredible run, leaving four Wycombe players in his wake, created the goal that kept County in the League.

Charlton Ath *(From trainee on 16/6/2006)*
Notts Co *(Free on 15/3/2007) FL 15+14 FLC 0+1 FAC 1*

WESTON Rhys David

Born: Kingston, 27 October 1980
Height: 6'1" **Weight:** 12.3
International Honours: W: 7; U21-4; E: Yth, Sch

Signed from Port Vale in summer, the Welsh international right-sided defender quickly found his feet at the back for Walsall, being equally impressive when defending or going forward. Rhys was absent only three times and was voted runner up to Anthony Gerrard as Walsall 'Player of the Season'. He is likely to be a key figure as the Saddlers prepare for a new campaign.

Arsenal *(From trainee on 8/7/1999) PL 1 FLC 1+1*
Cardiff C *(£300,000 on 21/11/2000) FL 170+12/2 FLC 10 FAC 14+1 Others 7 (Free to Viking FK, Norway on 31/8/2006)*
Port Vale *(Free from Viking FK, Norway on 9/2/2007) FL 15*
Walsall *(Free on 23/7/2007) FL 43+1 FAC 5 Others 1*

WESTWOOD Ashley Michael

Born: Bridgnorth, 31 August 1976
Height: 6'0" **Weight:** 12.8
Club Honours: FAYC '95
International Honours: E: Yth

On loan to Port Vale from Chester, the experienced central defender had an excellent debut in a 1-0 victory at Bournemouth, using his experience to help a very young team. Unfortunately, a sending off at Luton disrupted his season and Ashley began to struggle as results faltered. Injury cut short his loan in December and he returned to the Deva Stadium before joining Stevenage on a free transfer to be nearer his Northampton home.

Manchester U *(From trainee on 1/7/1994)*
Crewe Alex *(£40,000 on 26/7/1995) FL 93+5/9 FLC 8 FAC 9/2 Others 10*
Bradford C *(£150,000 on 20/7/1998) P/FL 18+6/2 FLC 1 FAC 2+1 Others 1+1*
Sheffield Wed *(£150,000 + on 10/8/2000) FL 79+3/5 FLC 10+2/4 FAC 2*
Northampton T *(Free on 15/7/2003) FL*

Chris Westwood

27+4/2 FAC 2+1 Others 1
Chester C (Free on 2/8/2006) FL 21/3 FLC 1
FAC 2 Others 1
Swindon T (Loaned on 2/3/2007) FL 8+1
Port Vale (Loaned on 30/8/2007) FL 11+1
FAC 1 Others 1

WESTWOOD Christopher (Chris) John

Born: Dudley, 13 February 1977
Height: 6'0" **Weight:** 12.2
Club Honours: Div 2 '07
Having been signed from Walsall in
the summer, Chris persuaded many
Peterborough fans that his presence
in the centre of defence was the
main reason Posh earned promotion.
Marshalling the defence and leading from
the front, he proved to be a fine reader
of the game, thus helping the younger
players around him.
Wolverhampton W (From trainee on 3/7/
1995) FL 3+1/1 FLC 1+1 (Freed during 1998
close season)
Hartlepool U (Signed from Telford U on
24/3/1999) FL 244+6/7 FLC 8 FAC 15/2
Others 20
Walsall (Free on 1/7/2005) FL 64+5/5 FLC 3
FAC 1+1 Others 2
Peterborough U (Free on 12/7/2007) FL
35+2 FLC 1+1 FAC 2 Others 2

WESTWOOD Keiren

Born: Manchester, 23 October 1984
Height: 6'1" **Weight:** 13.10
Club Honours: Div 2 '06
Keiren had an exceptional season as
Carlisle's goalkeeper, being the club's
only ever-present and the clear winner
in the 'Player of the Season' awards. A
superb shot-stopper as was demonstrated
not least in the play-off game at Leeds,
where he made several exceptional saves.
Recognition of his talents also came
from his fellow professionals who chose
him for the PFA 'League One Select'.
Statistically the best 'keeper in the club's
history, he has now received a call up to
the full Northern Ireland squad and looks
certain to be playing regularly at a higher
level before much longer.
Manchester C (From juniors on 25/10/2001)
Carlisle U (Free on 13/9/2004) FL 127 FLC
3+1 FAC 4 Others 11

WETHERALL David

Born: Sheffield, 14 March 1971
Height: 6'3" **Weight:** 13.12
International Honours: E: Sch
The Bradford captain brought down the
curtain on his playing career with another
consistent season, not missing a single
League match. David, who clocked up
300 League games as a centre-half for
the club, will take over as first-team coach

but will retain his playing registration in
case of emergencies.
Sheffield Wed (From trainee on 1/7/1989)
Leeds U (£125,000 on 15/7/1991) P/FL
188+14/12 FLC 19+1/2 FAC 21+3/4 Others 4
Bradford C (£1,400,000 on 7/7/1999) P/FL
301+3/18 FLC 11/2 FAC 11/1 Others 4

WHALEY Simon

Born: Bolton, 7 June 1985
Height: 5'11" **Weight:** 11.7
Simon remains something of an enigma,
being potentially one of Preston's most
exciting players but too often frustrating
fans and team-mates alike. Included in
virtually every squad, his return of 33
games and 14 substitute appearances
should have included more starts but he
is very much a confidence player. At his
best a penetrating winger on either flank,
with a dangerous whipped cross and a
powerful long-range shot. He missed a
vital penalty against Portsmouth in the
FA Cup and that seemed to knock him
back for the rest of the season. Simon will
be hoping for greater consistency and a
return to the form that can light up the
dullest winter day.
Bury (From trainee on 30/10/2002) FL
48+25/11 FLC 2 FAC 2+2 Others 1+5
Preston NE (£250,000 on 9/1/2006) FL
67+32/13 FLC 2/1 FAC 4+2/2 Others 0+2

WHALLEY Shaun James

Born: Prescot, 7 August 1987
Height: 5'9" **Weight:** 10.7
As the son of the former Preston player
Neil Whalley, Shaun was a regular
member of Accrington's squad, though
more than half his appearances were
as a substitute. On his day he can be a
devastating wide man with a terrific turn
of speed but at other times can frustrate.
However, Shaun ended the season on a
high note when he gave a tremendous
display at Wrexham, easily his best
Stanley performance, and capped it with
a brilliant solo goal. Was released in the
summer.
Chester C (Free from Southport on 17/9/
2004) FL 0+3 Others 0+2 (Free to Runcorn
Halton in August 2005)
Accrington Stanley (Signed from Witton A
on 8/11/2006) FL 27+24/5 FLC 0+1 FAC 0+1
Others 1+1

WHARTON Benjamin (Ben) Francis

Born: Stockport, 17 June 1990
Height: 6'1" **Weight:** 13.0
A junior with Stockport, Ben was a
second-year scholar who first appeared
in Rochdale's first team in the pre-season
game against Oldham. The top scorer
in the youth and reserve teams, with

24 goals all told, he made his League
debut as a substitute in Dale's victory at
Accrington in December. Despite his goals
record, he was not offered a professional
contract at the end of the season, largely
due to limitations on the overall wage bill.
Rochdale (Trainee) FL 0+1

WHEATER David James

Born: Redcar, 14 February 1987
Height: 6'4" **Weight:** 12.12
Club Honours: FAYC '04
International Honours: E: U21-6; Yth
David started last season as a
Middlesbrough reserve, one of five
centre-backs at the Riverside, and ended
it as England under-21 captain, against
Wales in May, and a potential England
player. Showing a maturity far beyond
his years, he established himself, in
his tremendous first full season, as a
Premiership regular at the Riverside
but remains determined to keep both
feet on the ground with the words: "I
didn't expect to be at Middlesbrough
this season. I thought I may have been
going out on loan, but the manager
put me in and it's just gone on from
there". Middlesbrough rewarded the
'Redcar Rock' with a three-and-a-half-
year contract in March and there was
more good news to come when Fabio
Capello picked him in a 31-man squad
for England's friendlies against the United
States and Trinad & Tobago. Watch out
for this young man.
Middlesbrough (From trainee on 16/2/
2005) PL 39+3/4 FLC 2 FAC 4/1 Others 0+1
Doncaster Rov (Loaned on 10/2/2006)
FL 7/1
Wolverhampton W (Loaned on 29/9/2006)
FL 1
Darlington (Loaned on 1/1/2007) FL 15/2
Others 1

WHELAN Glenn David

Born: Dublin, 13 January 1984
Height: 6'0" **Weight:** 12.5
International Honours: RoI: 2; B; U21-
18; Yth
Glenn was another quality player to
leave Sheffield Wednesday last season,
being transferred to Stoke in January. An
extremely hard-working, skilful link-up
midfield player, who has a reasonable
goals ratio, his sale was unpopular with
Owls' fans but the club's finances dictated
it. Having been a key member of the side
since arriving from Manchester City, the
Republic of Ireland under-21 international
moved to the Britannia Stadium in the
last few minutes of the transfer window.
As a midfield general and ball winner,
Glenn was a regular in the side for the
remainder of the campaign, scoring

against Crystal Palace with a thunderous 25-yard effort. An important piece in the jigsaw assembled by manager Tony Pulis, he will be looking forward to Premier League football in 2008-09.

Manchester C (From trainee on 25/1/2001) Others 0+1
Bury (Loaned on 29/9/2003) FL 13 FAC 1 Others 1
Sheffield Wed (Free on 7/7/2004) FL 136+6/12 FLC 8/2 FAC 6/1 Others 3/1
Stoke C (£500,000 on 31/11/2008) FL 13+1/1

WHELPDALE Christopher (Chris) Mark

Born: Harold Wood, 27 January 1987
Height: 6'0" **Weight:** 12.8
A wide attacking Peterborough midfielder who improved as the season progressed, Chris was signed from Billericay and initially found the pace in League Two very tiring. Now accustomed to the requirements of League football, he is still learning and shows much promise.
Peterborough U (Free from Billericay T, ex Maldon T, on 17/5/2007) FL 29+6/3 FLC 2 FAC 4 Others 1

WHING Andrew (Andy) John

Born: Birmingham, 20 September 1984
Height: 6'0" **Weight:** 12.0
Although experiencing a rocky patch in the middle of the campaign as, indeed, did the whole team, Andy can be pleased with his first full season at Brighton, having firmed up his initial loan move from Coventry. Despite appearing somewhat laid-back on the pitch, he is an accomplished and reliable right-back who always looks to get forward to deliver an incisive cross. Missing only a handful of games through illness or suspension, Andy was unlucky not to have scored. Now a defender of some experience at Championship and League One level, he looks set for a solid future.
Coventry C (From trainee on 7/4/2003) FL 87+19/2 FLC 4+3 FAC 5+1
Brighton & Hove A (Loaned on 7/10/2006) FL 12 Others 3
Brighton & Hove A (Free on 3/7/2007) FL 42 FLC 1 FAC 3 Others 1+1

WHITAKER Daniel (Danny) Philip

Born: Wilmslow, 14 November 1980
Height: 5'10" **Weight:** 11.2
The Port Vale playmaker has an eye for goal and was a regular in the side despite the struggle against relegation. Very skilful, he can play in the centre or on either flank and was one of the club's plus points. Danny scored seven goals, including one against Gillingham that was chosen as the 'Goal of the

Season'. After voting had closed, he scored an even better one, at Brighton with a dipping 30-yard shot in a 3-2 victory to cap his best performance of the campaign. He plays better alongside a good ball-winner but will always score goals. Danny rejected the offer of a new contract.
Macclesfield T (Signed from Wilmslow Albion on 5/7/2000) FL 156+15/23 FLC 6/5 FAC 12/2 Others 12+1/2
Port Vale (Free on 8/7/2006) FL 80+6/14 FLC 5/1 FAC 5/1 Others 2

WHITBREAD Zak Benjamin

Born: Houston, Texas, USA, 4 March 1984
Height: 6'2" **Weight:** 11.6
International Honours: USA: U23
Following a long lay off from the previous season, continuing into 2007-08, Zak finally broke back into the Millwall team when Richard Shaw was absent. After a few games he sustained another injury that sidelined him for several weeks. Having recovered both fitness and a first-team place, he gave some excellent performances, forging a strong partnership in the centre of defence with Paul Robinson. His strength in the air and an eye for picking out players with quality long passes make him one of the best central defenders in the League One.
Liverpool (From trainee on 8/5/2003) FLC 4 FAC 1 Others 1+1
Millwall (Free on 24/11/2005) FL 59+3/3 FLC 3 FAC 8 Others 2

WHITE Alan

Born: Darlington, 22 March 1976
Height: 6'1" **Weight:** 13.2
An experienced defender who arrived at Darlington from Notts County in the summer to achieve the ambition of playing for the team of his birthplace after spells with seven other clubs over a period of 13 years. He formed a formidable partnership in the centre of defence with the equally experienced Stephen Foster. Alan is powerful in the air and clears his lines effectively with his strong no-nonsense approach to defending. He scored only one goal, in the 4-0 rout of Grimsby at Blundell Park in December, but went close on a number of occasions from set pieces.
Middlesbrough (From trainee on 8/7/1994) Others 1
Luton T (£40,000 on 22/9/1997) FL 60+20/3 FLC 3+3 FAC 2 Others 4
Colchester U (Loaned on 12/11/1999) FL 4 Others 1
Colchester U (Free on 19/7/2000) FL 128+11/4 FLC 7+1 FAC 6+2 Others 6
Leyton Orient (Free on 6/7/2004) FL 26 FLC

1 FAC 2 Others 2
Boston U (Free on 4/3/2005) FL 48/4 FLC 1 FAC 3 Others 1/1
Notts Co (Free on 3/7/2006) FL 32+3/5 FLC 3 FAC 1 Others 1
Peterborough U (Loaned on 20/3/2007) FL 7/3
Darlington (Free on 4/7/2007) FL 35/1 FLC 1 FAC 2 Others 3

WHITE Jason Lee

Born: Sutton-in-Ashfield, 28 January 1984
Height: 6'3" **Weight:** 12.7
At the start of last season, Jason was at last established as the number-one goalkeeper at Mansfield before suffering a loss of confidence and surrendering his place to Carl Muggleton. The veteran was first choice for the remainder of the campaign but Jason filled in on the rare occasions when Muggleton was unfit.
Mansfield T (From trainee on 9/8/2002) FL 49+4 FLC 3 Others 3

WHITE John Alan

Born: Maldon, 26 July 1986
Height: 5'10" **Weight:** 12.1
John is a local boy who came of age in a big way during the second half of the season. A product of Colchester's youth system, he started only two League games before the turn of the year, both at right-back in the first month. But he benefited from a loan to Blue Square Premier side Stevenage and returned to Layer Road to be transformed into the U's regular left-back. He played the last 20 games of the season, with the previous occupant of the position, George Elokobi, having moved to Wolverhampton in January. John improved steadily and one of his best performances was in the 1-1 draw at Burnley.
Colchester U (From trainee on 23/2/2005) FL 77+15 FLC 2+1 FAC 8 Others 1+1

WHITEHEAD Dean

Born: Abingdon, 12 January 1982
Height: 5'11" **Weight:** 12.1
Club Honours: Ch '05, '07
Sunderland's club captain, Dean suffered a serious knee injury in training last August, damaging a cruciate ligament, and it was initially feared that he would miss the whole season. He made a remarkable recovery and was back to lead the team in November. Dean not only operated in his usual central midfield role but also at right-back and in either position was a positive influence. Is a player who leads by example, covering most of the field and always available to take charge in the midfield. His only goal of the season was worth waiting for, a

spectacular side-footed volley at home to Manchester City in April.

Oxford U *(From trainee on 20/4/2000) FL 92+30/9 FLC 5+1 FAC 3+2 Others 1+2*
Sunderland *(Signed on 2/8/2004) P/FL 146+5/13 FLC 2+3 FAC 6/1*

WHITLEY Jeffrey (Jeff)
Born: Ndola, Zambia, 28 January 1979
Height: 5'8" **Weight:** 11.2
Club Honours: Ch '05
International Honours: NI: 20; B-2; U21-17

Although Jeff missed Wrexham's all-important game against Boston in 2006-07 and struggled with well-documented personal problems, Brian Little took a chance on him just before Christmas. Signed on non-contract terms in the hope he would add much-needed experience to central midfield, Jeff stated he wanted to make amends to the fans but was unable to make a real impression in a struggling side.

Manchester C *(From trainee on 19/2/1996) P/FL 96+27/8 FLC 9+1 FAC 2+2 Others 4*
Wrexham *(Loaned on 14/1/1999) FL 9/2*
Notts Co *(Loaned on 21/3/2002) FL 6*
Notts Co *(Loaned on 18/10/2002) FL 12 FAC 1 Others 1*
Sunderland *(Free on 7/8/2003) FL 65+3/2 FLC 2 FAC 5 Others 2*
Cardiff C *(Free on 2/8/2005) FL 32+2/1 FLC 3 FAC 1 (Freed during 2007 close season)*
Stoke C *(Loaned on 18/8/2006) FL 0+3 FLC 1*
Wrexham *(Loaned on 16/2/2007) FL 11/1*
Wrexham *(Free, following a spell on the sidelines, on 18/1/2008) FL 5+6*

WHITTINGHAM Peter Michael
Born: Nuneaton, 8 September 1984
Height: 5'10" **Weight:** 10.5
Club Honours: FAYC '02
International Honours: E: U21-17; Yth

Among the most technically gifted players in the Championship, Peter scored an outstanding goal in Cardiff's FA Cup win at Middlesbrough and made a significant contribution to their progress over the season. Although he can often drift in and out of games, defenders never dare leave him alone as he can become a match winner in a flash. Is a lively midfielder with a powerful shot and despite being naturally left-footed, can cross from either side and needs little space in which to work.

Aston Villa *(From trainee on 2/11/2002) PL 32+24/1 FLC 6+3/1 FAC 1*
Burnley *(Loaned on 14/2/2005) FL 7 FAC 2*
Derby Co *(Loaned on 16/9/2005) FL 11*
Cardiff C *(£350,000 on 11/1/2007) FL 43+17/9 FLC 2+2/1 FAC 6/3*

Peter Whittingham

WHITTLE Justin Philip
Born: Derby, 18 March 1971
Height: 6'1" **Weight:** 12.12
Justin began the season in his usual central defensive role for Grimsby, contributing a rare goal in a 2-1 victory over Lincoln, enabling the Mariners to claim their first League win at Sincil Bank for almost 50 years. He maintained his place in the side until November when sustaining a freak ankle injury celebrating the Johnstone's Paint Trophy success over Doncaster, thereafter being restricted mostly to the substitutes' bench. The veteran defender returned to captain Grimsby to a 4-0 success at Morecambe before he was released at the end of the season.
Glasgow Celtic (Signed from Army during 1994 close season)
Stoke C (Free on 20/10/1994) FL 66+13/1 FLC 3+4 FAC 2 Others 7/1
Hull C (£65,000 on 27/11/1998) FL 184+9/2 FLC 9 FAC 8+2 Others 7/1
Grimsby T (Free on 2/8/2004) FL 118+9/3 FLC 7 FAC 4+1 Others 7+1

WIDDOWSON Joseph (Joe)
Born: Forest Gate, 29 March 1989
Height: 6'0" **Weight:** 12.0
A young defender who came to Rotherham on loan from West Ham, Joe only made a handful of appearances at left-back, where he displayed promise. He has yet to appear for the Hammers.
West Ham U (From trainee on 6/7/2007)
Rotherham U (Loaned on 12/2/2008) FL 3

WILBRAHAM Aaron Thomas
Born: Knutsford, 21 October 1979
Height: 6'3" **Weight:** 12.4
Club Honours: AMC '08; Div 2 '08
Aaron is a tall and well-balanced striker who began his third season for MK Dons on the bench for the first half of the season was more often than not a starter as he competed with half-a-dozen other forwards for the attacking berths. An injury then kept him out for a month over Christmas but once he returned to full fitness he showed some of his best form, the seven goals he scored from the last ten games helping the Dons complete the Johnstone's Paint Trophy and League Two double and making him the fourth of the club's players to hit double figures for the season.
Stockport Co (From trainee on 29/8/1997) FL 118+54/35 FLC 5+2/1 FAC 3+1 Others 2
Hull C (£100,000 on 9/7/2004) FL 10+9/2 FAC 1
Oldham Ath (Loaned on 29/10/2004) FL 4/2 Others 1
MK Dons (Free on 8/7/2005) FL 75+23/21 FLC 4+1/2 FAC 2+3 Others 4+1/2
Bradford C (Loaned on 3/3/2006) FL 5/1

WILES Simon Peter
Born: Preston, 22 April 1985
Height: 5'11" **Weight:** 11.4
Simon spent the first half of the season on loan at Macclesfield, although much of his time was on the substitutes' bench. Usually he was introduced for the final 20 minutes of matches, but it was often ample time to show his pace and ability to make pin-point passes into the box. Although Macclesfield offered him a permanent contract, Simon opted to remain at Blackpool.
Blackpool (From trainee on 10/5/2004) FL 14+17/3 FLC 1 FAC 1 Others 3+3
Macclesfield T (Loaned on 31/10/2006) FL 2 FAC 2
Macclesfield T (Loaned on 31/1/2007) FL 0+5
Macclesfield T (Loaned on 18/7/2007) FL 1+16 FLC 0+1 FAC 0+1 Others 2

WILHELMSSON Christian
Born: Malmo, Sweden, 8 December 1979
Height: 5'10" **Weight:** 10.11
International Honours: Sweden: 51
Arriving at Bolton on loan from Nantes with an impressive reputation, having spent some of the previous season on loan with Italian giants Roma, Christian failed to make a significant impact. A Swedish international winger, with appearances at Euro 2004 and the 2006 World Cup under his belt, he made his first start in the Carling Cup victory at Fulham but was then on the substitutes' bench more often than not. Having seemingly found it difficult to come to terms with life in the Premier League, it was no real surprise when Christian left in January to join Deportivo la Coruna.
Bolton W (Loaned from Nantes, France, ex Mjalby, Stabaek, Anderlecht, AS Roma - loan, on 10/8/2007) PL 0+8 FLC 1 FAC 0+1 Others 3

WILKINSON Andrew (Andy) Gordon
Born: Stone, 6 August 1984
Height: 5'11" **Weight:** 11.0
Andy is established as one of the unluckiest players at Stoke as he continues to spend more than his fair share of time on the treatment table. A central defender or full-back of considerable promise, he has a good future at the Britannia Stadium if he can overcome his injury problems. Even in the last match of the season he needed stitches in an ankle when a player's studs went into a vein. Andy is a local boy and popular at the club but needs a turn of fortune.
Stoke C (From trainee on 8/7/2002) FL 23+14 FLC 1+1 FAC 1+1 Others 0+1

Partick T (Loaned on 13/7/2004) SL 9+3/1 SLC 2 Others 1+2
Shrewsbury T (Loaned on 8/3/2005) FL 9
Blackpool (Loaned on 23/11/2006) FL 5+2

WILLIAMS Adrian (Adie)
Born: Reading, 16 August 1971
Height: 6'2" **Weight:** 13.2
Club Honours: Div 2 '94
International Honours: W: 13
A brief substitute appearance for Swindon in the home victory over Hartlepool in December seems to have brought down the curtain on Adie's playing career. Entering the fray as a late replacement, he managed only four minutes before himself being substituted. After that, he had a few outings in the reserves as he plans to concentrate on the coaching role he has been offered.
Reading (From trainee on 4/3/1989) FL 191+5/14 FLC 17/1 FAC 16/2 Others 14/2
Wolverhampton W (£750,000 on 3/7/1996) FL 26+1 FLC 3 FAC 2+2 Others 2/1
Reading (Loaned on 15/2/2000) FL 5/1 Others 1
Reading (Free on 26/3/2000) FL 130+2/3 FLC 8+1 FAC 3 Others 5
Coventry C (Free on 2/11/2004) FL 33+2/2 FLC 1 FAC 5
Millwall (Loaned on 12/9/2005) FL 12/1
Swindon T (Free on 5/7/2006) FL 27+1 FAC 3

WILLIAMS Andrew (Andy)
Born: Hereford, 14 August 1986
Height: 5'11" **Weight:** 11.2
Recruited from Hereford in the summer, the 21-year-old striker scored on his League debut for Bristol Rovers at Port Vale after coming off the bench but generally found it hard to add to his total. However, he scored a superb goal in December against Carlisle and followed it up with the winner at Southend on New Year's Day.
Hereford U (From Pershore College on 14/3/2006) FL 30+11/8 FLC 1+1 FAC 2+2 Others 0+1
Bristol Rov (Signed on 19/7/2007) FL 19+22/4 FLC 1+1/1 FAC 7+1/1 Others 1

WILLIAMS Anthony Simon
Born: Maesteg, 20 September 1977
Height: 6'1" **Weight:** 13.5
International Honours: W: U21-16; Yth
Following a period on loan at Wrexham towards the end of 2006-07, Anthony was signed on a permanent basis from Carlisle in the summer. The goalkeeper picked up where he had left off and became an important factor in the fight to keep the Dragons in the League. He was not helped by constant changes to the defence in front of him and his

Ben Williams

confidence faltered. Replaced in January when Gavin Ward arrived, he was in the reserves from then on and despite the fact that he had 12 months of his contract to run, was told he could leave in the close-season.

Blackburn Rov *(From trainee on 4/7/1996)*
Macclesfield T *(Loaned on 7/1/1999) FL 4*
Bristol Rov *(Loaned on 24/3/1999) FL 9*
Gillingham *(Loaned on 5/8/1999) FL 2 FLC 2*
Macclesfield T *(Loaned on 28/1/2000) FL 11*
Hartlepool U *(Free on 7/7/2000) FL 131 FLC 2 FAC 4 Others 9*
Stockport Co *(Loaned on 23/1/2004) FL 15*
Grimsby T *(Free on 21/7/2004) FL 46 FLC 2 FAC 1 Others 1*
Carlisle U *(Free on 1/8/2005) FL 11 FLC 2 Others 1*
Bury *(Loaned on 10/1/2006) FL 3*
Wrexham *(Free on 21/3/2007) FL 31 FAC 1 Others 1*

WILLIAMS Ashley Errol

Born: Wolverhampton, 23 March 1984
Height: 6'0" **Weight:** 11.2
International Honours: W: 3

Not even Ashley could have foreseen how successfully his season would turn out. A rock at the back for Stockport, alongside Gareth Owen, he suffered a ruptured ligament against Peterborough in November and was out of the side for two months. On his return, it was as if he'd never been away, his calm, composed defending helping Stockport's push for promotion. By the end of March his fantastic form as a central defender earned him selection for Wales against Luxembourg when still a League Two player and was quickly followed by a move to would-be League One champions Swansea. Initially signing for the Swans on loan in March, with a permanent transfer on the cards at the end of the season, the composed defender made his Swansea debut in a top-of-the-table clash at Carlisle and looked a class act.

Stockport Co *(Free from Hednesford T on 31/12/2003) FL 159+3/3 FLC 5 FAC 6/1 Others 3*
Swansea C *(Loaned on 27/3/2008) FL 3*

WILLIAMS Benjamin (Ben) Philip

Born: Manchester, 27 August 1982
Height: 6'0" **Weight:** 13.4
International Honours: E: Sch

Having been on the Crewe staff since 2004, Ben is now firmly established as the number-one goalkeeper. Unfortunate to have been forced to spend a long spell out of action through a serious illness earlier in his career, Ben has now made a full recovery and was an ever-present in Alexandra's League One games last season. Out of contract in the summer, he is a firm favourite with the fans as a solid and reliable 'keeper who stays cool under pressure.

Manchester U *(From juniors on 3/7/2001)*
Chesterfield *(Loaned on 30/12/2002) FL 14*
Crewe Alex *(Free on 19/3/2004) FL 134+1 FLC 7 FAC 2 Others 4*

WILLIAMS Daniel (Danny) Ivor Llewellyn

Born: Wrexham, 12 July 1979

Height: 6'1" **Weight:** 13.0
Club Honours: AMC '05
International Honours: W: U21-9
After his influential displays from
midfield helped to keep Wrexham up in
the previous campaign, Danny started
as a regular in defence or midfield.
Unfortunately, a back problem that had
bothered him for a considerable time
reached the stage of needing urgent
attention and an operation put him
out of action from mid-October until
early April. To say he was sorely missed
would be an understatement and he was
expected to be invaluable as Wrexham
attempt to bounce back from the Blue
Square Premier, especially as a loan to
Kidderminster went so well. However, he
was released with many others in Brian
Little's May clear-out.
Liverpool (From trainee on 14/5/1997)
Wrexham (Free on 22/3/1999) FL 38+1/3
FLC 4 FAC 4/1 Others 1
Kidderminster Hrs (Free on 11/7/2001) FL
108+3/8 FLC 2 FAC 7 Others 5+1
Bristol Rov (Free on 25/3/2004) FL 6/1
Wrexham (Free on 3/8/2004) FL 117+4/7
FLC 6 FAC 4/1 Others 5+1/1

WILLIAMS Darren
Born: Middlesbrough, 28 April 1977
Height: 5'10" **Weight:** 11.12
Club Honours: Div 1 '99
International Honours: E: B-1; U21-2
The experienced right-back left
Hartlepool for regular football and found
that with Bradford. Darren is a strong
defender who is good in the air and can
fill in at centre-half if required. He faced
a fight for his place when Ben Starosta
arrived on loan from Sheffield United
and was released in the summer.
York C (From trainee on 21/6/1995) FL
16+4 FLC 4+1 FAC 1 Others 3/1
Sunderland (£50,000 on 18/10/1996) P/FL
155+44/4 FLC 20+2/2 FAC 11+2 Others
4+1
Cardiff C (Free on 23/9/2004) FL 17+3
Hartlepool U (Free on 5/8/2005) FL 52+13
FLC 4 FAC 4 Others 1
Bradford C (Free on 2/8/2007) FL 28 FLC
1 FAC 2

WILLIAMS Eifion Wyn
Born: Anglesey, 15 November 1975
Height: 5'11" **Weight:** 11.12
International Honours: W: B-1; U21-2
Anglesey boy Eifion joined Wrexham
in the summer from Hartlepool as a
striker but was surprisingly used more
in midfield just behind the front men,
no doubt to exploit his strong running
and industry. He was often on the bench
in his 16 League and Cup appearances
and scored once, at Bury in early

December. It proved to be his final game
for the Dragons as, in the process of
bravely knocking the ball into net under
pressure, he suffered a bad hamstring
injury that kept him out for months.
Eifion announced his retirement from
playing in March because of his ongoing
fitness problems.
Torquay U (£70,000 from Barry T on
25/3/1999) FL 84+27/24 FLC 4+1 FAC 3
Others 3
Hartlepool U (£30,000 on 6/3/2002) FL
175+33/50 FLC 4+2/2 FAC 10+3/1 Others
10+2/3
Wrexham (Free on 25/7/2007) FL 7+6/1 FLC
1 FAC 1 Others 1

WILLIAMS Gavin John
Born: Pontypridd, 20 June 1980
Height: 5'10" **Weight:** 11.5
Club Honours: FC '03; Div 2 '05
International Honours: W: 2
Gavin continued to be dogged by injury
during the early part of the season and
when he did eventually return to the
Ipswich side was unable to produce
anything like his best form. He was able
to put a run of appearances together
during December but lost his place
following the arrival of more midfield
players in January and struggled to
regain it.
Yeovil T (£20,000 from Hereford U on
16/5/2002) FL 54+1/11 FLC 1+1 FAC 5/3
Others 2/1
West Ham U (£250,000 on 9/12/2004) P/FL
7+3/1 FLC 1
Ipswich T (£300,000 on 9/11/2005) FL
47+7/3 FAC 4+1

WILLIAMS Marc Richard
Born: Colwyn Bay, 27 July 1988
Height: 5'9" **Weight:** 11.2
International Honours: W: U21-2; Yth
Marc turned full-time professional
for Wrexham in the summer. A fiery
competitor who does not allow
opponents time on the ball, he
continued to progress although,
disappointingly, was not given an
extended run. Has time on his side to
become a regular with his infectious
enthusiasm and eye for a chance. Marc
shows good movement and commitment
and wins plenty in the air despite being
on the small side for a striker. He scored
in his first two starts, at Stockport in a
2-1 defeat and the only goal against
Lincoln at the Racecourse, both at the
end of September. He was a substitute
for the Welsh under-21s against Israel
in a European qualifier and scored twice
before being sent off near the end.
Wrexham (From trainee on 3/8/2006) FL
24+15/4 FLC 0+2 FAC 0+2 Others 0+1

WILLIAMS Marcus Vincent
Born: Doncaster, 8 April 1986
Height: 5'8" **Weight:** 10.9
Club Honours: Div 1 '07
Young Scunthorpe left-back Marcus
took a while to adjust to the step up
to the Championship. He lost his place
in September, returning in November
and staying in the team for all but a
five-game spell during the remainder of
the campaign. A talented player, who is
quick and comfortable on the ball, he
was watched by a number of bigger clubs
during the season.
Scunthorpe U (From trainee on 3/8/2005) FL
89+14 FLC 5 FAC 6+2 Others 2+1

WILLIAMS Marvin Travis
Born: Sydenham, 12 August 1987
Height: 5'11" **Weight:** 11.6
Released by Millwall during the summer,
the speedy young striker was snapped
up by Yeovil in time for 2007-08 and his
pace was crucial in the battle to avoid
relegation. This was epitomised by his
terrific cross for Terry Skiverton's goal at
Swansea to secure the Glovers' League
One safety. Although Marvin suffered
with a series of injuries, he showed
glimpses of what Yeovil fans can expect
once he gets a string of games under
his belt.
Millwall (From trainee on 11/1/2006) FL
27+24/7 FAC 3/1 Others 1
Torquay U (Loaned on 6/3/2007) FL 2/1
Yeovil T (Signed on 9/8/2007) FL 8+15 FLC 1

WILLIAMS Michael (Mike) Paul John
Born: Colwyn Bay, 27 October 1986
Height: 5'11" **Weight:** 13.0
International Honours: W: U21-13
The brother of Marc and a fellow
Welsh under-21 international, Mike
is an important member of that
emerging squad but was used sparingly
at Wrexham. He had a regular place
during February and March as Wrexham
struggled to escape from the relegation
positions. Like his younger brother, he
needs an extended run in the side to
prove his capabilities, both as a central
and a left-sided defender. Has the
potential and versatility to succeed in
helping Wrexham back into the League
while furthering his own career.
Wrexham (From trainee on 5/8/2006) FL
42+19 FLC 2 FAC 3 Others 2

WILLIAMS Robert (Robbie)
Born: Liverpool, 12 April 1979
Height: 6'1" **Weight:** 12.8
Club Honours: FC '06
Robbie is Accrington's longest-serving
player and last season was a great

disappointment to him, particularly as the previous campaign had been his best ever. He missed the last three-and-a-half months with a knee injury that had affected his play at the centre of Stanley's defence and eventually needed an operation. He will hope to come back stronger than ever in 2008-09.

Accrington Stanley (Free from St Dominic's on 3/8/1999) FL 66+3/3 FLC 3 FAC 1 Others 4/1

WILLIAMS Robert (Robbie)
Ian
Born: Pontefract, 2 October 1984
Height: 5'10" **Weight:** 11.13
Originally a summer target, Robbie's move to Huddersfield was compromised when the left-sided Barnsley defender was injured as the transfer was about to take place. Robbie was signed later but had to wait until the December derby against Leeds for his debut. He showed quality both defensively and in attack as he supplied some accurate passes and crosses. The man from Pontefract made the left-back berth his own, always one to put in the important blocking tackles. Robbie strikes the ball well in dead-ball situations, never more so than with his first goal in the draw at Brighton. A move to wing-back allowed him to add to that with a great strike in the home derby with Doncaster.

Barnsley (From trainee on 2/7/2004) FL 44+22/4 FLC 5/1 FAC 3+1 Others 1+2
Blackpool (Loaned on 21/3/2007) FL 9/4 Others 3/1
Huddersfield T (Signed on 24/8/2007) FL 24+1/2 FAC 3

WILLIAMS Thomas (Tom)
Andrew
Born: Carshalton, 8 July 1980
Height: 6'0" **Weight:** 11.8
International Honours: Cyprus: 1
Out of contract at Swansea, Tom was Wycombe manager Paul Lambert's last signing of the summer, agreeing a two-year contract. In and out of the side for the first part of the season, he started a run of five consecutive games at left-back in October, winning the PFA Fans' 'Player of the Month' on the back of his attacking raids down the left. Tom has a special ability to push the ball past a defender from a standing start and beat him to it. The run came to an end after an error led to defeat by Swindon in the FA Cup. Dropped for the next game, Tom did not react well and he made no further appearances, moving in January for his third spell at Peterborough. He started only the last three games but showed what a good player he is with two 'Man

of the Match' awards. Sometimes seen as a showman, with pace and no lack of confidence, Tom has plenty to offer.

West Ham U (£60,000 from Walton & Hersham on 3/4/2000)
Peterborough U (Free on 22/3/2001) FL 32+4/2 FLC 1+1 FAC 4+1 Others 1
Birmingham C (£1,000,000 on 12/3/2002) FL 4
Queens Park Rgrs (Loaned on 8/8/2002) FL 22+4/1 FLC 1 FAC 2 Others 2+2
Queens Park Rgrs (Loaned on 4/8/2003) FL 4/1
Peterborough U (Free on 1/2/2004) FL 20+1/1 FAC 1
Barnsley (Free on 4/6/2004) FL 38+1 FLC 2 FAC 1 Others 1
Gillingham (Free on 1/9/2005) FL 13 FLC 1+1 FAC 1 Others 2
Swansea C (£50,000 on 1/1/2006) FL 30+16 FLC 0+1 FAC 2 Others 0+3
Wycombe W (Free on 7/8/2007) FL 6+4 FLC 1 FAC 1 Others 1
Peterborough U (Signed on 1/1/2008) FL 3+4

WILLIAMSON Lee Trevor
Born: Derby, 7 June 1982
Height: 5'10" **Weight:** 10.4
A tidy, hard-working central midfield player who tackles cleanly and passes well, Lee was one of Watford's most consistent players. He scored his first goal for the Hornets against Sheffield United and an outstanding second from a free kick at Plymouth. There is never any doubting his commitment.

Mansfield T (From trainee on 3/7/2000) FL 114+30/3 FLC 3+3 FAC 8+1 Others 7
Northampton T (Signed on 9/9/2004) FL 31+6 FLC 1 FAC 2/1 Others 3/1
Rotherham U (Signed on 28/7/2005) FL 54+2/9 FLC 3/1 FAC 1+1 Others 1
Watford (Signed on 5/1/2007) P/FL 31+6/2 FAC 1 Others 2

WILLIAMSON Michael (Mike) James
Born: Stoke, 8 November 1983
Height: 6'4" **Weight:** 13.3
Sidelined for 12 months with a cruciate knee-ligament injury, Mike finally returned to Wycombe's first team in February in his usual central defensive role. Frequently used as substitute to begin with, Mike replaced the injured David McCracken and held his place until the end of the season, putting in a run of excellent performances. As one of Wycombe's most talented players, he is a superbly assured defender who dominates his opponents without fouling, is near unbeatable in the air and always a threat when coming up for set pieces.

Torquay U (Trainee) FL 3 Others 1

Southampton (£100,000 on 21/11/2001)
Torquay U (Loaned on 15/9/2003) FL 9+2 Others 1
Wycombe W (Free on 20/7/2004) FL 110+11/8 FLC 9/1 FAC 4 Others 8+1

WILLIAMSON Sam James
Born: Macclesfield, 15 October 1987
Height: 5'8" **Weight:** 11.9
Another product of Manchester City's flourishing Academy, Sam made his first-team debut as a substitute for the injured Richard Dunne in City's 3-1 victory over Portsmouth in April. The versatile young defender made a solid start to what is hoped will be a successful career with the Blues.

Manchester C (From trainee on 3/7/2006) PL 0+1

WILLOCK Calum Daniel
Born: Lambeth, 29 October 1981
Height: 5'11" **Weight:** 12.7
International Honours: St Kitts: 3; E: Sch
Having been freed by Brentford, the burly striker joined Port Vale on a six-month contract. Calum made his debut on the opening day against Bristol Rovers as a substitute and within four minutes won a penalty that produced an equaliser. He did the same thing in the next game, a Carling Cup tie against Wrexham, and became a regular member of the squad. A strong player who holds up the ball well, he scored his first goal at Morecambe in the FA Cup and followed with a quite brilliant strike in the next game at Oldham. Further goals followed at Gillingham and against Luton, sparking the offer of a new contract. Calum declined, preferring to join Stevenage in the Blue Square Premier to be nearer his London-based family.

Fulham (From ADT College, Putney on 18/7/2000) P/FL 0+5
Queens Park Rgrs (Loaned on 7/11/2002) FL 3
Bristol Rov (Loaned on 8/8/2003) FL 0+5
Peterborough U (£25,000 on 13/10/2003) FL 60+19/23 FAC 4+3/3 Others 4
Brentford (Signed on 31/1/2006) FL 23+18/4 FLC 0+1 Others 0+1
Port Vale (Free on 10/8/2007) FL 8+7/3 FLC 1 FAC 3/1 Others 0+1

WILNIS Fabian
Born: Surinam, 23 August 1970
Height: 5'8" **Weight:** 12.6
Fabian continued to be an ideal player to have in a squad. He did not play regularly for Ipswich but, when called on, always gave of his best and never let the side down, whether at full-back or in central defence. His appearance as a substitute at

Plymouth was notable for all the wrong reasons as he was red-carded after being on the pitch for only four minutes. It was the fourth time he had been sent off in his Town career and three of the four have been against Plymouth, two of them decisions by the same referee. Fabian spent a considerable amount of time coaching Ipswich youngsters during the season and, as his playing contract was not renewed, is likely to concentrate on that side of the game in the future, possibly at Portman Road.

Ipswich T (£200,000 from De Graafschap, Holland, ex NAC Breda, on 6/11/1999) P/FL 255+27/6 FLC 11+4 FAC 14 Others 13+1

WILSON Brian Jason
Born: Manchester, 9 May 1983
Height: 5'10" **Weight:** 11.0
Brian started the season in Bristol City's side but was unable to hold a regular place following a goalless draw at Preston in late September. The winger played well in City's home defeat by Plymouth before being surprisingly substituted at half-time. Given an opportunity in City's vital game at Stoke, where victory may well have brought automatic promotion, he was again replaced during the interval.

Stoke C (From trainee on 5/7/2001) FL 1+5 FLC 0+1 Others 1
Cheltenham T (Loaned on 12/12/2003) FL 7 FAC 1
Cheltenham T (Signed on 25/3/2004) FL 105+13/15 FLC 5/1 FAC 9/1 Others 10+1/2
Bristol C (£100,000 on 12/1/2007) FL 33+4/1 FLC 1 FAC 1

WILSON Che Christian Aaron Clay
Born: Ely, 17 January 1979
Height: 5'9" **Weight:** 11.3
Club Honours: Div 1 '06
Che signed a new one-year deal with Southend during the close season despite his opportunities being restricted in 2006-07. With Steve Hammell injured during pre-season, Che was thrust into the team for the opening matches. Always a competent defender, he lost his place when Hammell was fit, with manager Steve Tilson preferring the Scot's more attacking tendencies. Che played regularly in the reserves until Christmas when an Achilles injury that eventually required surgery ended his season. Was released at the end of the campaign.

Norwich C (From trainee on 3/7/1997) FL 16+6 FLC 3
Bristol Rov (Free on 13/7/2000) FL 74+1 FLC 7 FAC 6 Others 3+1 (Free to Cambridge C during 2002 close season)
Southend U (Free from Cambridge C on

30/7/2003) FL 98+8/2 FLC 2+1 FAC 5 Others 12+2
Brentford (Loaned on 16/1/2007) FL 3
Rotherham U (Loaned on 22/3/2007) FL 5+1

WILSON Kelvin James
Born: Nottingham, 3 September 1985
Height: 6'2" **Weight:** 12.3
Kelvin returned to his home city when Nottingham Forest signed him from Preston shortly before the start of the season. The former Notts County player immediately became a regular on the other side of the Trent with some outstanding performances at the heart of the defence. He was equally impressive when Forest changed formation to a back three during a run of poor away results. His maturity and ready acceptance of responsibility made him a natural choice as captain when Ian Breckin was not in the side.

Notts Co (From trainee on 20/7/2004) FL 71+7/3 FLC 2+1/1 FAC 5 Others 2
Preston NE (Signed on 10/3/2006) FL 16+1/1 FLC 1 FAC 2/1
Nottingham F (£300,000 on 20/7/2007) FL 40+2 FLC 2 FAC 3

WILSON Laurence (Laurie) Thomas
Born: Huyton, 10 October 1986
Height: 5'10" **Weight:** 11.0
International Honours: E: Yth
As a speedy left-sided player, Laurie was a virtual ever-present in the Chester defence. The arrival of Kevin Ellison during the summer saw him continue to play in a more defensive role than he would probably have liked but his pace was an asset and his improved tackling marked him as a reliable performer for the Blues. Laurie likes to press forward when given the opportunity and has the ability to go past defenders and deliver telling crosses. He also has a lethal shot and both goals he scored during the season were long-range blockbusters, against Macclesfield and Accrington.

Everton (From trainee on 12/11/2004)
Mansfield T (Loaned on 10/2/2006) FL 14+1/1
Chester C (Free on 1/8/2006) FL 74+7/3 FLC 2 FAC 6/2 Others 4/2

WILSON Marc David
Born: Belfast, 17 August 1987
Height: 6'2" **Weight:** 12.7
International Honours: RoI: U21-1; Yth. NI: Yth
A tall Portsmouth player who can operate in midfield or the centre of defence, Marc spent much of the previous season on loan at Bournemouth and returned for a short spell early in 2007-08. Following

that, he moved to Luton on loan in November to add craft and extra fire-power to a struggling side and after making his debut on the right of midfield at Walsall he was switched to the centre and then had two games on the left. Each time, Marc added a different dimension but as his loan coincided with Luton going into administration, he had to return to his parent club. Back at Fratton Park, he finally broke into Portsmouth's squad when he was an unused substitute in three Premier League games in the second half of the season. Still awaiting his debut, Marc was in the Republic's under-21 squad for the Intercontinental Cup in Malaysia in May.

Portsmouth (From trainee on 7/7/2005)
Yeovil T (Loaned on 10/3/2006) FL 1+1
Bournemouth (Loaned on 5/1/2007) FL 19/3
Bournemouth (Loaned on 21/9/2007) FL 7 Others 1
Luton T (Loaned on 16/11/2007) FL 4

WILSON Mark Antony
Born: Scunthorpe, 9 February 1979
Height: 5'11" **Weight:** 13.0
Club Honours: AMC '07
International Honours: E: U21-2; Yth; Sch
Mark held a regular place in the Doncaster midfield for the first half of the season before losing out to Paul Green, who turned in some terrific performances to keep him on the substitutes' bench. Mark's last starting appearance was at home to Gillingham in mid-March but he was on the field for only 20 minutes before being forced off by a severe groin injury that effectively finished his season.

Manchester U (From trainee on 16/2/1996) PL 1+2 FLC 2 Others 3+2
Wrexham (Loaned on 23/2/1998) FL 12+1/4
Middlesbrough (£1,500,000 on 9/8/2001) PL 6+10 FLC 5/2 FAC 2+1 (Freed during 2005 close season)
Stoke C (Loaned on 14/3/2003) FL 4
Swansea C (Loaned on 12/9/2003) FL 12/2 Others 1
Sheffield Wed (Loaned on 22/1/2004) FL 3
Doncaster Rov (Loaned on 2/9/2004) FL 1+2 Others 1
Livingston (Loaned on 24/1/2005) SL 4+1 SC 1
Doncaster Rov (Free from Dallas Burn, USA, via trial at Bradford C, on 15/11/2006) FL 40+13/2 FLC 1+1 FAC 1 Others 3+3

WINDASS Dean
Born: Hull, 1 April 1969
Height: 5'10" **Weight:** 12.6
In the words of the song, fairy tales do come true... if you're young at heart. In his 40th year, when he became Hull's fourth oldest player ever, the striker

continued to defy time as he played a truly inspirational role in the season that his home-town club ended in their highest-ever League position. The scarcely credible ending came in the play-off final, his and the club's first visit to Wembley. Having made his loan from Bradford permanent in the summer, Dean struck the only goal of the game against Bristol City with a sensational 18-yard volley. It meant his beloved Tigers were promoted to the top flight for the first time in their history. His usual prolific supply of goals took him to a career total of 200 in English football (not to mention 31 for Aberdeen) with another crucial strike in the play-off semi-final at Watford. The romance appeared to come to a shuddering halt in February, when an exploratory operation became complicated by a cyst at the back of a knee. Typically, Hull's 'Roy of the Rovers' missed only seven games before returning to pen another glorious and emotional chapter in his remarkable story. It's been asked before but who does write his scripts?

Hull C *(Free from North Ferriby U on 24/10/1991)* FL 173+3/57 FLC 11/4 FAC 6 Others 12/3
Aberdeen *(£700,000 on 1/12/1995)* SL 60+13/21 SLC 5+2/6 SC 7/3 Others 6/1
Oxford U *(£475,000 on 6/8/1998)* FL 33/15 FLC 2 FAC 3/3
Bradford C *(£950,000 + on 5/3/1999)* P/FL

Dean Windass

64+10/16 FLC 6/2 FAC 2 Others 6/3
Middlesbrough *(£600,000 + on 15/3/2001)* PL 16+21/3 FLC 2 FAC 4+3
Sheffield Wed *(Loaned on 6/12/2001)* FL 2
Sheffield U *(Loaned on 11/11/2002)* FL 4/3
Sheffield U *(Signed on 16/1/2003)* FL 16/3 Others 2
Bradford C *(Free on 14/7/2003)* FL 138+4/60 FLC 5/4 FAC 7/2 Others 1
Hull C *£150,000 on 18/1/2007)* FL 44+11/19 FLC 0+1 FAC 0+1/2 Others 3/2

WINN Peter Henry
Born: Cleethorpes, 19 December 1988
Height: 6'0" **Weight:** 11.9
Young Scunthorpe striker Peter got his first brief chance of the season in the first team when he made his League debut in the 5-0 defeat at West Bromwich in December. A quick player who can perform on the left-wing or down the middle, he made further appearances as a substitute in the closing three League games.
Scunthorpe U *(From trainee on 23/7/2007)* FL 0+4 Others 1+1

WINTER Jamie
Born: Dundee, 4 August 1985
Height: 5'10" **Weight:** 13.4
Released by Aberdeen in the summer and despite lacking a proper pre-season, Jamie started as a first choice in midfield for Chesterfield but tenacious tackling brought bookings and an early suspension. He was forced to wait until December to reclaim a place but he then displayed his best form. Jamie is well-suited to a slightly deeper midfield role, where neat passes can link with advancing full-backs, and he can bring the ball forward himself. He is the son of Gordon Winter, the former St Johnstone and Forfar player.
Leeds U *(From trainee on 17/10/2002)*
Aberdeen *(Free on 11/1/2005)* SL 13+6/1 SLC 2/1 SC 1
St Johnstone *(Loaned on 26/1/2006)* SL 5+3
Chesterfield *(Free on 2/8/2007)* FL 20+5 FLC 1 Others 1

WISEMAN Scott Nigel Kenneth
Born: Hull, 9 October 1985
Height: 6'0" **Weight:** 11.6
International Honours: E: Yth
The energetic, young right-sided defender signed for Darlington in the summer after impressing on loan from Hull in the last ten League games of the previous season. He is quick to the ball with good distribution and enjoys getting forward down the flank, but was limited to two League starts and five substitute appearances. Was out of contract in the summer.

Hull C *(From trainee on 8/4/2004)* FL 10+6 FLC 1 FAC 0+1 Others 0+1
Boston U *(Loaned on 18/2/2005)* FL 1+1
Rotherham U *(Loaned on 4/8/2006)* FL 9+9/1 FLC 1+1 Others 1
Darlington *(Free on 8/3/2007)* FL 12+5 FAC 1 Others 2

WOLFENDEN Matthew (Matty)
Born: Oldham, 23 July 1987
Height: 5'9" **Weight:** 11.1
Matty was handed a new two-year deal last summer and the young locally-born striker enjoyed his most fruitful season to date with Oldham. A product of the youth system and a regular scorer at reserve level, Matty made 22 appearances in all competitions, mostly as a substitute, and netted three times, including his first League goals, against Crewe and Port Vale. Although not the tallest of front men, he is a hard-working and tenacious prospect.
Oldham Ath *(From trainee on 19/7/2006)* FL 7+27/2 FLC 0+1 FAC 2+2 Others 0+3/2

WOOD Christopher (Chris) Hayden
Born: Worksop, 24 January 1987
Height: 6'0" **Weight:** 11.4
Chris is a former Mansfield youth team player who continued to progress and had a splendid game at right-back against Rotherham in the Johnstone's Paint Trophy game in September. He was given his first League outing of the season at Accrington and was named 'Man of the Match'. The following week at Field Mill he was stretchered off with an ankle injury before returning to the squad at Christmas and being a regular on the bench.
Mansfield T *(From trainee on 4/8/2006)* FL 9+6 FAC 0+1 Others 1+2

WOOD Richard Mark
Born: Ossett, 5 July 1985
Height: 6'3" **Weight:** 11.11
A long absence because of a dislocated shoulder, suffered in October at home to Scunthorpe, disrupted Richard's season. A classy, pacy central defender, he was out for almost four months but came back as good as new to blend well with young Mark Beevers. He reads the game intelligently and captained Sheffield Wednesday in a solid back four. Richard's progress has been hampered by injuries in the last few seasons, so with luck he is now due for a clear spell. He certainly has the potential to play at a higher level than the Championship.
Sheffield Wed *(From trainee on 7/4/2003)* FL 110+8/5 FLC 5+1/1 FAC 2+2 Others 5+1

WOODARDS Daniel (Danny) Mark
Born: Forest Gate, 7 October 1983
Height: 5'11" **Weight:** 11.1
Into his second season with Crewe after arriving from Exeter in January 2007, Danny is now firmly entrenched at right-back and has become a competent and much valued member of the defence. Confident in the tackle and a good passer of the ball, his only absences from the side in 2007-08 were through injury.
Chelsea (From trainee on 11/7/2003. Freed during 2005 close season)
Crewe Alex (£30,000 + from Exeter C on 31/1/2007) FL 45+2 FLC 1 FAC 2 Others 1

WOODGATE Jonathan Simon
Born: Middlesbrough, 22 January 1980
Height: 6'2" **Weight:** 13.0
Club Honours: FAYC '97
International Honours: E: 7; U21-1; Yth
Jonathan spent the previous season on loan to Middlesbrough from Real Madrid, where he made only 12 appearances in 32 months. In April 2007 there was considerable speculation that he would join Newcastle but Middlesbrough announced him as their first summer signing on a four-year contract. He missed the opening games with a knee injury but returned to the side in late August for the 2-2 home draw against Newcastle. Named the North-East 'Player of the Year' at the Prince's Trust in October, hamstring problems interrupted him in November and when the January transfer window opened, news broke that Jonathan had become increasingly unsettled. Manager Gareth Southgate weighed up the situation and decided that Boro were well stocked in central defence with David Wheater, Robert Huth, Chris Riggott and Manny Pogatetz, and was prepared to let him leave. Newcastle and Tottenham led the pack of interested clubs, with Kevin Keegan's United as favourites, but he ended at White Hart Lane. When the centre-back was signed by Spurs, their fans were naturally concerned because of his poor fitness record in recent years, but he proved to be a fantastic signing and in his debut at Everton, demonstrated what a cultured and classy player he is. Jonathan played in 17 games, including the Carling Cup final, when he scored the winning goal with his header past Petr Cech in extra-time. His courage in the challenge was decisive as he had the rub of the green and scored with a rebound when the Chelsea goalkeeper tried to clear. Jonathan's only other goal during the campaign also came against Chelsea, a header in the 4-4 draw. A player who

reads the game very well and has good positional sense, winning the ball with head or feet, he is cool under pressure and his England career was revived in the end-of-season friendlies.
Leeds U (From trainee on 13/5/1997) PL 100+4/4 FLC 7 FAC 11 Others 20
Newcastle U (£9,000,000 on 31/1/2003) PL 28 FAC 2 Others 7 (£13,400,000 to Real Madrid, Spain on 20/10/2005)
Middlesbrough (£7,000,000 from Real Madrid, Spain on 31/8/2006) PL 46 FAC 6
Tottenham H (£8,000,000 on 29/1/2008) PL 12/1 FLC 1/1 Others 4

WOODMAN Craig Alan
Born: Tiverton, 22 December 1982
Height: 5'9" **Weight:** 9.11
Released by Bristol City last summer, Craig signed for Wycombe on a two-year contract. He started the first two matches at left-back but then became a fringe player, not starting another game until late December. Immediately stamping his authority on the left-back position, holding it until the end of the season, Craig proved to be a very accomplished player. A safe and dependable defender and very effective pushing down the left wing, he likes to finish with a dangerous out-swinging cross.
Bristol C (From trainee on 17/2/2000) FL 71+19/1 FLC 3 FAC 4+2 Others 13
Mansfield T (Loaned on 25/9/2004) FL 8/1 Others 1
Torquay U (Loaned on 6/12/2004) FL 20+2/1
Torquay U (Loaned on 3/11/2005) FL 2 FAC 2
Wycombe W (Free on 1/8/2007) FL 27+2 FLC 1 Others 3

WOODS Martin Paul
Born: Airdrie, 1 January 1986
Height: 5'11" **Weight:** 11.11
International Honours: S: U21-2; Yth
Having joined Doncaster on a free transfer during the close season from neighbours Rotherham, who had been relegated to League Two, Martin started 2007-08 in Rovers' first team before suffering a foot injury and being unable to regain his place. In February, to play his way back into contention, the midfielder went on loan to Yeovil who needed cover for their injury-depleted squad. Although his cultured left foot briefly helped Yeovil in their battle to keep out of relegation trouble, Martin also suffered injury problems there before returning to the Keepmoat Stadium after just three games and failed to make any further appearances during the campaign. An attacking left-sided midfielder, noted for long-range shooting and free kicks, he

will be hoping for better in 2008-09.
Leeds U (From trainee on 3/11/2003) FL 0+1
Hartlepool U (Loaned on 10/9/2004) FL 3+3 FLC 1 Others 1
Sunderland (Free on 7/7/2005) PL 1+6 FLC 1
Rotherham U (Free on 4/8/2006) FL 31+5/4 FLC 2 Others 1
Doncaster Rov (Free on 28/7/2007) FL 7+8 FLC 2 FAC 2 Others 2+1/2
Yeovil T (Loaned on 15/2/2008) FL 3

WOODTHORPE Colin John
Born: Ellesmere Port, 13 January 1969
Height: 5'11" **Weight:** 11.8
Colin earned a six-month contract extension with Bury in August that was then extended to the end of the season after Christmas. Although personal issues threatened to disrupt his season, his professionalism shone through. Dependable and solid, he was a rock at left-back in the five-man defence used by Chris Casper and Keith Alexander, but Alan Knill's preference for a back four and Colin's ageing legs meant he lost his place to David Buchanan.
Chester C (From trainee on 23/8/1986) FL 154+1/6 FLC 10 FAC 8+1 Others 18/1
Norwich C (£175,000 on 17/7/1990) P/FL 36+7/1 FLC 0+2 FAC 6 Others 1+1
Aberdeen (£400,000 on 20/7/1994) SL 43+5/1 SLC 5+1/1 SC 4 Others 5+2
Stockport Co (£200,000 on 29/7/1997) FL 114+39/4 FLC 12+1/2 FAC 4+1/1
Bury (Free on 23/8/2002) FL 171+10/1 FLC 4+1 FAC 12+1 Others 12/1

WOOLFE Nathan Brett
Born: Manchester, 6 October 1988
Height: 5'11" **Weight:** 12.5
Nathan is a Bolton Academy prospect who has progressed to the first team, making his debut as a substitute in the UEFA Cup defeat at Sporting Lisbon last season. A promising left-back who impressed for the reserves on a consistent basis with a string of assured and measured performances, he will look for further first-team opportunities.
Bolton W (From trainee on 8/7/2007) Others 0+1

WORDSWORTH Anthony Daniel
Born: Camden, 3 January 1989
Height: 6'1" **Weight:** 12.0
A product of the Colchester youth team, this cultured midfielder made his senior debut as a substitute in the 1-0 defeat at Shrewsbury in the Carling Cup in the first week of last season. That was on the back of an impressive pre-season, during which he scored several goals. Seven months later, he made his League debut as a late substitute in the 1-1 home draw

Jonathan Woodgate

against Cardiff and enjoyed his first start three days later in the home defeat by Hull. Despite restricted opportunities, he showed up as a good passer of the ball.
Colchester U (From trainee on 4/7/2007) FL 1+2 FLC 0+1

WORLEY Harry
Born: Warrington, 25 November 1988
Height: 6'4" **Weight:** 13.3
After signing on loan from Chelsea last August, Harry played as a central defender for the first 45 minutes of his only game for Carlisle before returning to Stamford Bridge. In March, signed on loan by the Leicester manager Ian Holloway with a view to a permanent deal in the summer, Harry was handed a surprise City debut from the bench at Sheffield United. It was an even bigger shock when he was picked as a midfield anchor in the crucial final-day clash at Stoke. Harry did not let anyone down on either occasion and, between times, impressed several onlookers in the reserves.
Chelsea (From trainee, having been signed from Stockport Co juniors for £150,000, on 5/12/2005)
Doncaster Rov (Loaned on 6/3/2007) FL 10
Carlisle U (Loaned on 31/8/2007) FL 1
Leicester C (Signed on 6/3/2008) FL 1+1

WORRALL David Richard
Born: Manchester, 12 June 1990
Height: 6'0" **Weight:** 11.3
Midfielder David made his senior debut for West Bromwich while still an Academy player, as a second-half substitute in the Carling Cup win over Bournemouth in August. He is a youngster with a fine future.
Bury (Trainee) FL 0+1
West Bromwich A (From trainee on 8/8/2007) FLC 0+1

WORTHINGTON Jonathan (Jon) Alan
Born: Dewsbury, 16 April 1983
Height: 5'9" **Weight:** 11.0
Huddersfield's club captain suffered another season of heartache in the treatment room as a string of injuries blighted him, hamstring, hernia and ankle problems taking their toll. Jon is a home-grown talent who tackles strongly and drives the side forward with real purpose when he competes in the midfield engine room. He can play a holding role or contribute by seeking probing passes for the strikers. Always one for the crunching tackle, he plays with his heart on his sleeve and was sent off in the Yorkshire derby against Leeds. When fully fit, Jon is an early name on the team-sheet

and should continue to be as the team remoulds.
Huddersfield T (From trainee on 10/9/2001) FL 172+22/12 FLC 5 FAC 7 Others 9/1

WOTTON Paul Anthony
Born: Plymouth, 17 August 1977
Height: 5'11" **Weight:** 12.0
Club Honours: Div 3 '02; Div 2 '04
This Plymouth legend struggled to regain his fitness following a nasty knee injury in December 2006, but after all his sheer hard work and determination it was a pleasure to see him in an Argyle shirt again some 14 months later. He returned to his beloved Home Park as a substitute against Barnsley in February and went on to make five starting appearances, scoring a customary penalty in the 2-2 home draw against Preston in April. That was the final appearance for his home-town club as it was then announced that manager Paul Sturrock would not be offering the club captain a further contract. After 13 years as a professional at Home Park, Paul will forever be remembered as the skipper when Plymouth lifted titles in 2002 and 2004.
Plymouth Arg (From trainee on 10/7/1995) FL 359+35/54 FLC 10+1/2 FAC 23/5 Others 9+1/2

WRACK Darren
Born: Cleethorpes, 5 May 1976
Height: 5'9" **Weight:** 12.10
Club Honours: Div 2 '07
Having come back bravely from a broken leg in 2005-06, Darren played regularly in the Walsall midfield in his Testimonial year and after he missed only eight games all season, Saddlers' fans were disappointed that this consistent midfielder was released at the end of the campaign. A big favourite at the Banks' Stadium in his ten years with Walsall, Darren could always be relied upon to perform at his utmost wherever he was played.
Derby Co (From trainee on 12/7/1994) FL 4+22/1 FLC 0+3 FAC 0+2
Grimsby T (£100,000 + on 19/7/1996) FL 5+8/1 Others 0+1
Shrewsbury T (Loaned on 17/2/1997) FL 3+1 Others 1
Walsall (Free on 6/8/1998) FL 289+47/46 FLC 13+1/1 FAC 19+2/3 Others 11+2/2

WRIGHT Alan Geoffrey
Born: Ashton-under-Lyne, 28 September 1971
Height: 5'4" **Weight:** 9.9
Club Honours: FLC '96
International Honours: E: U21-2; Yth; Sch
Veteran defender Alan was without a club at the start of the season and spent the

first two months training with the youth squad at his former club Sheffield United. Shortly after taking over as Cheltenham manager, Keith Downing offered him the chance to join on a non-contract basis and Alan made his debut against Swindon in the Johnstone's Paint Trophy. He proved his fitness immediately and won over the fans with a series of assured displays at left-back, his vast experience helping to steady the back four and earning him a full-time contract in the process. Alan missed only three games in the remainder of the season with a slight ankle injury and his performances, which included a spectacular goal from a free-kick against Crewe, earned him a further contract offer.
Blackpool (From trainee on 13/4/1989) FL 91+7 FLC 10+2 FAC 8 Others 11+2
Blackburn Rov (£400,000 on 25/10/1991) P/FL 67+7/1 FLC 8 FAC 5+1 Others 3
Aston Villa (£1,000,000 on 10/3/1995) PL 255+5/5 FLC 18 FAC 25 Others 26
Middlesbrough (Free on 12/8/2003) PL 2
Sheffield U (Free on 31/10/2003) P/FL 36+6/1 FLC 3+1 FAC 3+1 (Freed during 2007 close season)
Derby Co (Loaned on 23/2/2006) FL 7
Leeds U (Loaned on 12/10/2006) FL 1
Cardiff C (Loaned on 23/11/2006) FL 6+1
Doncaster Rov (Loaned on 16/2/2007) FL 3
Nottingham F (Loaned on 16/3/2007) FL 9 Others 2
Cheltenham T (Free, following trial at Oldham Ath, on 8/10/2007) FL 33/1 FAC 2 Others 1

WRIGHT Andrew David
Born: Liverpool, 15 January 1985
Height: 6'1" **Weight:** 13.7
Former Liverpool trainee Andrew returned from a spell at university in the United States to join Championship side Scunthorpe on trial before Christmas. He won a contract for the rest of the season and did well in the reserves, playing either at full-back or in the midfield holding role. His first-team experience was brief, two minutes as a stoppage-time substitute in the home defeat against Ipswich in March.
Scunthorpe U (Free from University of West Virginia, USA, ex trainee at Liverpool, on 14/1/2008) FL 0+2

WRIGHT Benjamin (Ben)
Born: Munster, Germany, 1 July 1980
Height: 6'2" **Weight:** 14.0
Having joined Lincoln from Viking Stavanger in the summer of 2007 following six years in Norway, Ben's Imps' career only seemed to come to life following the appointment of manager Peter Jackson, who gave him a regular

place up front in the starting line-up. The striker repaid Jackson by ending the season as City's leading scorer with 15 goals, a fine return for a player who was experiencing his first full season of League action. A thinking player who has the ability to be in the right place at the right time, he has good ball control for a tall man and brings others into the game.
Bristol C (£30,000 + from Kettering T on 10/3/1999) FL 0+2 (Freed on 18/12/2000)
Lincoln C (Free from IK Start, Norway, ex Viking Stavanger, Moss FK - loan, on 1/8/2007) FL 26+8/15 FLC 1 FAC 2 Others 0+1

WRIGHT David
Born: Warrington, 1 May 1980
Height: 5'11" **Weight:** 10.8
International Honours: E: Yth
A versatile full-back who can play on either side, David was an integral part of Ipswich's defence for much of the season. A good tackler who is happy to join in with his attack, he scored two vital goals during the campaign. The first was against Bristol City, when he met Alan Lee's cross with a diving header that any striker would have been proud of, and against West Bromwich he started the move that he finished by deftly heading Jon Walters' cross into the corner of the net.
Crewe Alex (From trainee on 18/6/1997) FL 206+5/3 FLC 10+1 FAC 12 Others 3+1
Wigan Ath (£500,000 on 28/6/2004) P/FL 26+19 FLC 3 FAC 1
Norwich C (Loaned on 17/11/2005) FL 5
Ipswich T (Signed on 12/1/2007) FL 58+2/3 FLC 1 FAC 2

WRIGHT Jermaine Malaki
Born: Greenwich, 21 October 1975
Height: 5'9" **Weight:** 11.9
International Honours: E: Yth
Victimisation by the Southampton boo-boys early in the season after some less than impressive defensive displays was manifestly unjust, given that Jermaine makes no claim to being a right-back or indeed a left-back. However, he is a conscientious, diligent team-player, always available for a pass no matter how badly things are going, which is probably why he was invariably selected ahead of designated defenders. By December he had silenced the criticism and was a crucial component in the side that fended off relegation. Was released at the end of the campaign.
Millwall (From trainee on 27/11/1992)
Wolverhampton W (£60,000 on 29/12/1994) FL 4+16 FLC 1+3/1 Others 0+1
Doncaster Rov (Loaned on 1/3/1996) FL 13
Crewe Alex (£25,000 on 19/2/1998) FL 47+2/5 FLC 5 FAC 1

Ipswich T (£500,000 on 23/7/1999) P/FL 147+37/10 FLC 15+2 FAC 8+1/1 Others 10+1
Leeds U (Free on 2/7/2004) FL 36+2/3 FLC 1 FAC 1
Millwall (Loaned on 13/9/2005) FL 15/2 FLC 1
Southampton (Free on 8/2/2006) FL 87+4/1 FLC 2+1 FAC 6

WRIGHT Joshua (Josh) William
Born: Bethnal Green, 6 November 1989
Height: 5'9" **Weight:** 11.10
International Honours: E: Yth
After joining Barnet on loan from Charlton in September for three months, Josh quickly became a first-team regular

with some excellent performances alongside Neal Bishop in the centre of midfield. He returned to Charlton in early December but Paul Fairclough negotiated another loan in January, keeping the 18-year-old Josh at Underhill until the end of the season. Despite being a Charlton player, Josh became very popular with the Barnet crowd, who voted him their 'Young Player of the Year'.
Charlton Ath (From trainee on 4/7/2007)
Barnet (Loaned on 31/8/2007) FL 31+1/1 FAC 3

WRIGHT Mark Anthony
Born: Wolverhampton, 24 February 1982
Height: 5'11" **Weight:** 11.4
Club Honours: Div 2 '07, '08; AMC '08

Mark Wright

Signed in the summer after his surprising release by Walsall, the fact that Mark ended the season as MK Dons' leading scorer with 13 League goals shows what a big contribution he made to the title-winning success. But there is more to his game as he provided several assists from his dashing flank play. Most often used on the right, he sometimes switched over to cut inside from the left and scored a hat-trick from that position in the February draw at Shrewsbury. He was not reluctant to track back into defence whenever necessary and all told proved to be an inspired signing by manager Paul Ince.

Walsall *(From trainee on 26/1/2001) FL 94+30/9 FLC 3+2 FAC 6 Others 6*
MK Dons *(Free on 19/7/2007) FL 29+5/13 FLC 1+1 FAC 1 Others 3+1/2*

WRIGHT Richard Ian
Born: Ipswich, 5 November 1977
Height: 6'2" **Weight:** 13.0
Club Honours: FAC '02; PL '02
International Honours: E: 2; U21-15; Yth; Sch

West Ham signed the experienced goalkeeper from Everton at the start of last season and while being an excellent shot-stopper and a 'keeper who commands his area well, Robert Green's consistent form meant that he was used only in three Carling Cup games. With three goalkeepers crocked, Southampton manager Nigel Pearson was obliged to cast around and was fortunate indeed that he managed to loan Richard from West Ham in March. Quite why Richard has been so deeply in the shadows for the last four seasons is hard to fathom as, for the last seven games of the campaign, he exhibited the sort of form that made him an England international, steadying what was, at best, a poor defence. If any one player at Southampton deserved a special accolade for keeping Saints in the Championship, Richard would be a hot favourite.

Ipswich T *(From trainee on 2/1/1995) P/FL 240 FLC 27 FAC 13 Others 11*
Arsenal *(£6,000,000 on 13/7/2001) PL 12 FLC 1 FAC 5 Others 4*
Everton *(£3,500,000 + on 26/7/2002) PL 58+2 FLC 7 FAC 4*
West Ham U *(Free on 6/7/2007) FLC 3*
Southampton *(Loaned on 20/3/2008) FL 7*

WRIGHT Stephen John
Born: Liverpool, 8 February 1980
Height: 6'2" **Weight:** 12.0
Club Honours: UEFAC '01; Ch '05
International Honours: E: U21-6; Yth
A strong right-back, Stephen signed for Stoke on loan from Sunderland just before the season got under way and shared the duties with another loan player, Gabby Zakuani. A leg injury ruled out Stephen and not long after reclaiming his position, he was recalled to the Stadium of Light. Was out of contract in the summer and looking for a new club.

Liverpool *(From trainee on 13/10/1997) PL 10+4 FLC 1+1 FAC 2 Others 2+1/1*
Crewe Alex *(Loaned on 6/8/1999) FL 17+6 FLC 1*
Sunderland *(£3,000,000 on 15/8/2002) P/FL 88+4/2 FLC 1+2 FAC 10*
Stoke C *(Loaned on 7/8/2007) FL 14+2 FLC 1*

WRIGHT Thomas (Tommy) Andrew
Born: Kirby Muxloe, 28 September 1984
Height: 6'0" **Weight:** 11.12
International Honours: E: Yth
Tommy led the Darlington line very effectively throughout the season despite having to link with various other strike-partners due to injuries. He managed to stay relatively injury-free, appearing in all but seven of the 50 League and Cup games played. Tommy is a hard-running and energetic striker, very strong in helping the ball on in the air, upsets defences with his direct approach and scores opportunist goals. He ended as top scorer with 13 goals in the League and two in the Cups.

Leicester C *(From trainee on 10/6/2003) P/FL 3+18/2 FLC 1 FAC 0+2*
Brentford *(Loaned on 12/9/2003) FL 18+7/3*
Blackpool *(Loaned on 31/8/2005) FL 10+3/6 Others 2*
Barnsley *(£50,000 on 1/1/2006) FL 11+23/2 FLC 2 FAC 1+1 Others 0+3*
Walsall *(Loaned on 23/11/2006) FL 5+1/2*
Darlington *(Signed on 16/1/2007) FL 46+7/17 FLC 1/1 FAC 2/1 Others 2*

WRIGHT-PHILLIPS Bradley Edward
Born: Lewisham, 12 March 1985
Height: 5'8" **Weight:** 11.0
International Honours: E: Yth
Fast and capable of breathtaking sleight-of-foot, Bradley is a talented young Southampton forward who can devastate defences and delight spectators at one moment, only to reverse the process at the next. Is a player with great potential, but questions were raised about his future at the club following a well-documented expose.

Manchester C *(From trainee on 2/7/2002) PL 1+31/2 FLC 0+2 FAC 2+4*
Southampton *(£1,000,000 on 20/7/2006) FL 42+36/16 FLC 4/3 FAC 3+2*

WRIGHT-PHILLIPS Shaun Cameron
Born: Greenwich, 25 October 1981
Height: 5'6" **Weight:** 10.1
Club Honours: Div 1 '02; PL '06; CS '05; FLC '07
International Honours: E: 19; U21-6
Shaun started last season in top form and was less of a peripheral figure, playing the best football of his Chelsea career and scoring vital goals for club and country. He switched to a central midfield role alongside Michael Ballack during the Blues' manpower shortage of January and February and was instrumental in the club's record-equalling run of nine consecutive victories. He was absolutely outstanding in the Carling Cup semi-final first-leg victory with a decisive hand in both goals, scoring with a delightful curling shot and, with his spring-heeled leap, forcing an unfortunate defender into an own-goal. Although Shaun started the Carling Cup final he suffered from the fallout of the disappointing defeat and barely had a look-in for the rest of the season as Florent Malouda returned from injury and claimed the wide-left midfield spot. A further blow followed when he was omitted from England's squad for the end-of-season friendlies, a personal anti-climax to a season that had promised so much.

Manchester C *(From trainee on 28/10/1998) P/FL 130+23/26 FLC 9+4/3 FAC 8+1/1 Others 4+2/1*
Chelsea *(£21,000,000 on 19/7/2005) PL 43+38/4 FLC 7+2/1 FAC 11+3/4 Others 4+16/1*

WYLDE Michael Joseph
Born: Birmingham, 6 January 1987
Height: 6'2" **Weight:** 13.2
Michael made one appearance for Cheltenham after missing the start of the season with a broken jaw, sustained in a clash of heads with a team-mate during a pre-season friendly. Upon making a full recovery, he played against Brighton in the Johnstone's Paint Trophy and made 14 appearances for the reserves. After starting as a left-back, Michael is now regarded as a central defender and spent the final part of the campaign on loan with Kidderminster in the Blue Square Premier. Was released in the summer.

Cheltenham T *(From trainee on 7/7/2006) FL 4+4 FLC 0+1 FAC 0+1 Others 1+2*

XYZ

YAKUBU Ayegbeni
Born: Benin City, Nigeria, 22 November 1982
Height: 6'0" **Weight:** 13.1
Club Honours: Div 1 '03
International Honours: Nigeria: 41
Ayegbeni scored 35 League and Cup goals in just two years for Middlesbrough but, at the start of last season, made it abundantly clear that he wanted to leave the Riverside. In what proved to be his final game, a defeat at Wigan, as a forlorn figure he was booed by the supporters. Soon after the Wigan game, Ayegbeni met Everton for talks and speculation was ended by a transfer. The Nigerian fully justified his status as Everton's record signing by scoring 21 goals. Although scoring on his Toffees' debut at Bolton, the centre-forward struggled early in his Goodison career, finding it difficult to adapt to new surroundings, before a goal at Derby in October began a run of eight in seven League matches, including a hat-trick against Fulham. After appearing in the African Cup of Nations, he continued his good form with another hat-trick against SK Brann in the UEFA Cup and although his form dipped near the end of the campaign he ended it with two goals against Newcastle on the final day. A cool finisher with greater skill and awareness than he is given credit for, it is hoped that cries of 'Feed the Yak' will be heard at Goodison Park for several more seasons.
Portsmouth (£1,800,000 from Maccabi Haifa, Israel, ex Okomo Oil, Julius Berger, Hapoel Kfar-Saba, on 13/1/2003) P/FL 76+5/ 35 FLC 2+3/4 FAC 6/3
Middlesbrough (£7,500,000 on 13/7/2005) PL 67+6/25 FLC 1+1 FAC 15/8 Others 5+9/2
Everton (£11,250,000 on 30/8/2007) PL 26+3/15 FLC 3/3 FAC 0+1 Others 7/3

YAKUBU Ismail Salami
Born: Kano, Nigeria, 8 April 1985
Height: 6'1" **Weight:** 12.9
Club Honours: FC '05
International Honours: E: SP
Appointed club captain just before the season started and despite being only 22, Ismail is currently Barnet's longest-serving player. He was once again a rock at the heart of the Bees' defence. Ismail scored the winning goal in Barnet's surprise 1-0 away win over eventual champions MK Dons in January and another at home to Wrexham in a 3-2 win. Unfortunately, that was his final appearance of the season, as injury ruled him out for the

final eight games.
Barnet (From juniors on 30/4/2005) FL 82+1/ 4 FLC 2 FAC 11/2 Others 4

YAO Sosthene Aubin
Born: Ivory Coast, 7 August 1987
Height: 5'4" **Weight:** 11.9
A diminutive, pacy wide player, Sosthene made a series of substitute appearances for Cheltenham and started one match, against Southend in the Carling Cup. Normally a right-sided player but also capable of playing on the left or up front, Sosthene made 14 reserve appearances before departing in February and finishing the season with Bishop's Stortford in the Blue Square South.
Cheltenham T (From trainee on 28/4/2006) FL 2+21 FLC 1+1 FAC 0+2 Others 0+2

YATES Adam
Born: Stoke-on-Trent, 28 May 1983
Height: 5'10" **Weight:** 10.9
International Honours: E: SP-3
The regular Morecambe right-back had a consistent first season in the League, making more than 40 starts. A former Crewe trainee who was signed from Leek, Adam was an integral part of the promotion-winning side and carried that form into the next grade. Always keen to get forward and put in dangerous crosses, he provided some useful assists but did not repeat his goals of the promotion season.
Crewe Alex (From trainee on 6/2/2001. Freed during 2004 close season)
Morecambe (Signed from Leek T on 11/8/ 2006) FL 42+2 FLC 3 FAC 1 Others 6

Adam Yates

YATES Jamie
Born: Sheffield, 24 December 1988
Height: 5'7" **Weight:** 10.11
Jamie, another of the Rotherham home-produced youngsters, is a speedy winger who is not afraid to take on more experienced defenders. He scored a couple of goals in a home win against Morecambe and was invariably used as a substitute before he forced his way into the starting line-up towards the end of the season.
Rotherham U (From trainee on 1/7/2007) FL 5+18/3 FAC 1+1 Others 1

YEATES Mark Stephen Anthony
Born: Dublin, 11 January 1985
Height: 5'9" **Weight:** 10.7
International Honours: RoI: U21-4; Yth
Signed from Tottenham during the summer, it was a season of two halves for the talented winger. Mark took the Championship by storm during the opening three months, scoring seven goals in Colchester's first 11 League games, several of them from long-range free-kicks. He scored two such crackers to earn the U's a 2-2 draw at Blackpool and also netted a brace in the shock home win over high-flying West Bromwich. But he was less happy when missing a penalty at East Anglian rivals Ipswich when the U's were leading 1-0. They ended by losing 3-1, after which they slid down the table. Worse still, he dislocated a shoulder at home to Sheffield United at the beginning of January, needed an operation and was out for the rest of the season.
Tottenham H (From trainee on 25/7/2002) PL 1+2 FAC 0+1
Brighton & Hove A (Loaned on 14/11/2003) FL 9 Others 1
Swindon T (Loaned on 27/8/2004) FL 3+1
Colchester U (Loaned on 5/8/2005) FL 42+2/ 5 FLC 1 FAC 5/1 Others 1+1
Hull C (Loaned on 10/8/2006) FL 2+3 FLC 1+1
Leicester C (Loaned on 31/1/2007) FL 5+4/1
Colchester U (£100,000 on 27/7/2007) FL 29/8 FLC 1 FAC 1

YEO Simon John
Born: Stockport, 20 October 1973
Height: 5'10" **Weight:** 11.8
This experienced goal-poacher started last season competing for the second striker's position at Chester alongside John Murphy. Two goals against Dagenham at the end of August seemed to secure his position but he returned to the bench in October. Although scoring as a substitute against Shrewsbury and Hereford, Simon was overlooked in favour of Chris Holroyd and Nathan Lowndes and in January went

on loan to Bury for the remainder of the campaign. Following that, City struggled to find the back of the net and lacked a player with Simon's natural scoring ability. Earlier, he had been a pre-season target for Bury director of football Keith Alexander but a deal could not be struck at the time. Featuring at Bury from the bench in four consecutive games as Chris Casper showed faith in the new recruit, the sackings of Casper and Alexander did not damage Simon's chances as caretaker boss Chris Brass used him in his three League games in charge. However, the new manager Alan Knill did not share their view and Simon's opportunities were severely restricted by the arrival of Adam Rooney on loan. Unable to get a game after mid-March, he was released by Chester at the end of the season and was reported to be joining Macclesfield.
Lincoln C (Free from Hyde U on 7/8/2002) FL 73+49/37 FLC 2+1/2 FAC 4/1 Others 8+6/6 (Freed during 2005 close season)
Lincoln C (Free from New Zealand Knights on 1/1/2006) FL 11+1/5 Others 1+1
Peterborough U (Free on 3/8/2006) FL 8+5/2 FLC 1 FAC 0+2
Chester C (Signed on 31/1/2007) FL 21+15/8 FLC 1 FAC 1 Others 2
Bury (Loaned on 3/1/2008) FL 0+8

YOBO Joseph
Born: Kano, Nigeria, 6 September 1980
Height: 6'2" **Weight:** 11.6
International Honours: Nigeria: 59
The Nigerian international continued to cement his reputation as one of the most effective centre-halves in the top flight in an excellent campaign, during which he captained Everton for the first time. Having eradicated the occasional errors that blighted his early Goodison career, the powerful defender formed strong partnerships with either Phil Jagielka or Joleon Lescott and continued to demonstrate his usual pace and power. He was often at his best against the stronger teams. Despite being absent when on duty for Nigeria in the African Cup of Nations, Joseph enjoyed a consistent campaign and passed 200 matches for Everton.
Everton (£4,500,000 from Olympique Marseille, France, ex Mechelen, Standard Liege, on 6/8/2002) PL 164+12/6 FLC 11 FAC 4+1 Others 11/1

YORKE Dwight Eversley
Born: Canaan, Tobago, 3 November 1971
Height: 5'10" **Weight:** 12.4
Club Honours: FLC '96; FAC '99; PL '99, '00, '01; EC '99; Ch '07
International Honours: Trinidad &

Tobago: 59
A vastly experienced and much decorated player, Dwight, although recognised throughout his career as a striker, operated for Sunderland in midfield during 2007-08, where his excellent short passing, sensible use of the ball and intelligent reading of the game were evident. Dwight picked up a red card at one of his former clubs, Blackburn, in December and his only goal was a consolation effort in the 7-1 mauling at Everton in November. Was released at the end of the campaign.
Aston Villa (£120,000 from Signal Hill, Tobago on 19/12/1989) P/FL 195+36/73 FLC 20+2/8 FAC 22+2/14 Others 10/3
Manchester U (£12,600,000 on 22/8/1998) PL 80+16/48 FLC 3/2 FAC 6+5/3 Others 31+11/12
Blackburn Rov (£2,000,000 on 26/7/2002) PL 42+18/12 FLC 5/4 FAC 3+1/3 Others 4+1
Birmingham C (Signed on 31/8/2004) PL 4+9/2 FLC 2 FAC 0+1 (Freed on 26/4/2005)
Sunderland (Free from Sydney FC, Australia on 31/8/2006) P/FL 45+7/6 FLC 0+1 FAC 0+1

YOUGA Kelly Alexandra
Born: Bangui, Central African Republic, 22 September 1985
Height: 6'1" **Weight:** 12.0
Kelly is a talented left-sided Charlton defender who is extremely comfortable on the ball, loves to get forward and is surprisingly skilful. He started 2007-08 at Scunthorpe, joining the Iron in July on a six-month loan, and played a key role for them in the first half of the season. Excellent on the ball, he did well in either full-back role but looked more comfortable on the left.

Kelly Youga

Although two red cards in successive matches hampered his progress he returned to net his first League goal in his final appearance against Barnsley on New Year's Day. Scunthorpe wanted to sign him permanently but Charlton preferred to keep him and, after being recalled, he was drafted in for his long awaited Athletic debut in the FA Cup tie against West Bromwich at the Valley. He performed brilliantly and kept his place, missing only one of the next 11 games, due to suspension, but when Charlton manager Alan Pardew made wholesale changes after the home defeat by Preston in early March Kelly lost out to fit again Ben Thatcher. After spending time on the sidelines, Kelly returned for the final game and was rewarded with a new three-year contract.
Charlton Ath (Free from Lyon, France on 30/6/2005) FL 11 FAC 2
Bristol C (Loaned on 14/10/2005) FL 4 FAC 1
Bradford C (Loaned on 31/1/2007) FL 11
Scunthorpe U (Loaned on 11/7/2007) FL 18+1/1 FLC 1

YOUNG Ashley Simon
Born: Stevenage, 9 July 1985
Height: 5'9" **Weight:** 9.13
International Honours: E: 3; U21-10
As a player with pace and an eye for goal, Ashley is just as capable of scoring from free kicks as from open play and his crossing ability and delivery from set pieces helped him weigh in with a healthy number of assists for Aston Villa's front men last season. A right-footed player who operates mainly on the left, Ashley was given more of a licence to roam, playing at the front of a midfield

diamond. He also contributes defensively, being willing to track back when needed, and missed only two games all season. His exciting potential is being translated into consistent achievement and he was rewarded with a place in the PFA Premier League select team. He scored eight goals, an invaluable contribution from one whose primary role is as a creator rather than a finisher and his energy, workrate, pace and accurate crossing impress everyone and make him popular with the fans. He was 'Man of the Match' in the England under-21 side's friendly against Slovakia and scored twice in their European Championship semi-finals against Holland. Was promoted to the full England side as a substitute for his debut in a friendly in Austria and played for England against Switzerland.

Watford (From juniors on 12/7/2002) P/FL 73+25/19 FLC 7+1/2 FAC 0+1 Others 3/1
Aston Villa (£8,000,000 + on 23/1/2007) PL 48+2/10 FLC 0+1 FAC 1

YOUNG Jamie lain

Born: Brisbane, Australia, 25 August 1985
Height: 5'11"　**Weight:** 12.9
International Honours: E: Yth
Jamie was hoping to pin down the number-one goalkeeping spot at Wycombe last season, but the arrival of Scott Shearer in the summer saw him relegated to the substitutes' bench. He was elevated to first choice in September, at Scott's expense, but in his third game back he suffered a hamstring injury that sidelined him until January. Jamie then spent the rest of the campaign as understudy to on-loan 'keeper Frank Fielding, making a half-time substitute appearance in the final League game of the season. In the majority of supporters' eyes, Jamie is good enough to be first choice so it will be interesting to see if he can grab the number-one spot.

Reading (From trainee on 20/10/2003) FL 0+1
Rushden & Diamonds (Loaned on 21/7/2005) FL 19+1 FLC 1 FAC 3
Wycombe W (Free on 3/8/2006) FL 20+3 FLC 3 FAC 2

YOUNG Luke Paul

Born: Harlow, 19 July 1979
Height: 5'11"　**Weight:** 12.4
Club Honours: FLC '99
International Honours: E: 7; U21-12; Yth
Luke, a classy, sure-footed, attacking full-back, was in the second year of a four-year contract at the Valley when Charlton, who used three managers during that time, were relegated from

the Premiership at the end of 2006-07. It came as no surprise when the England international asked for a transfer and immediately attracted the attention of Aston Villa, Bolton, Newcastle and Middlesbrough. Having opted for Middlesbrough on a four-year contract, Luke made his debut against Newcastle at the Riverside Stadium in late August. He settled immediately and from then on was a permanent fixture for the remaining 42 League and Cup games, his one goal being an absolute classic.

Tottenham H (From trainee on 3/7/1997) PL 44+14 FLC 1+3 FAC 9+2 Others 2+1
Charlton Ath (£3,000,000 + on 27/7/2001) PL 181+6/4 FLC 12 FAC 9
Middlesbrough (£2,500,000 on 10/8/2007) PL 35/1 FLC 2 FAC 5

YOUNG Matthew Geoffrey

Born: Woodlesford, 25 October 1985
Height: 5'8"　**Weight:** 11.3
An Academy product, Matthew adapted well in his early-season forays in Huddersfield's midfield. He works hard and is versatile, able to play in midfield or at full-back. Added nine senior appearances before being released at the end of 2007-08.

Huddersfield T (From trainee on 8/7/2005) FL 20+19/2 FAC 0+1 Others 1+1

YOUNG Neil Anthony

Born: Harlow, 31 August 1973
Height: 5'9"　**Weight:** 12.0
Last season was frustrating for the Bournemouth right-back and at the end of the campaign he announced his retirement, stating that he was emigrating to Australia. Although Neil passed 500 appearances for the club he joined in 1994, he spent a short time on loan at Weymouth and rather more time on the treatment table before returning to the squad to play his part in the final battle to avoid relegation.

Tottenham H (From trainee on 17/8/1991)
Bournemouth (Free on 11/10/1994) FL 408+21/4 FLC 24+1 FAC 28 Others 23

ZAABOUB Sofiane

Born: Melun, France, 23 January 1983
Height: 5'10"　**Weight:** 11.0
After started as a regular on Swindon's left flank, Sofiane began to be seen less frequently. He was often used from the bench but increasingly overlooked as the season drew to a close. He would like to have made a greater contribution and it was no real surprise when he was released at the end of the season. Is a skilful performer who can sometimes prove a real handful with the ability to supply dangerous crosses.

Swindon T (Free from FC Brussels, Belgium, ex St Etienne, Modena, Real Jaen, on 9/11/2006) FL 41+15/1 FLC 0+1 FAC 4+2 Others 1

ZAKUANI Gabriel (Gabby)

Born: Kinshasa, DR Congo, 31 May 1986
Height: 6'0"　**Weight:** 10.10
International Honours: DR Congo: 1
Gabby had a spell on loan at Stoke in 2006-07 and the Potters again took him from Fulham in August, this time for a full season. His main strength is as a central defender but City used him successfully at right-back. A leg injury sustained in February brought a premature end to Gabby's season except for one final substitute appearance.

Leyton Orient (From trainee on 1/6/2005) FL 84+3/3 FLC 2 FAC 7 Others 2
Fulham (£1,000,000 on 12/7/2006) FLC 1 FAC 0+1
Stoke C (Loaned on 30/1/2007) FL 9
Stoke C (Loaned on 31/8/2007) FL 11+8 FAC 1

ZAMORA Robert (Bobby) Lester

Born: Barking, 16 January 1981
Height: 6'0"　**Weight:** 11.0
Club Honours: Div 3 '01; Div 2 '02
International Honours: E: U21-6
It was a disappointing season for the West Ham striker as, after playing in the opening games, he picked up a knee injury and did not figure again until the match against Blackburn in March. He is always a threat and his link up-play is superb. Scored his only goal of the campaign when heading the opener in the victory over Derby in April and was involved in both goals against Newcastle.

Bristol Rov (From trainee on 1/7/1999) FL 0+4 FLC 0+1 FAC 0+1
Brighton & Hove A (Loaned on 11/2/2000) FL 6/6
Brighton & Hove A (£100,000 on 10/8/2000) FL 117+2/70 FLC 4/2 FAC 6/4 Others 1/1
Tottenham H (£1,500,000 on 22/7/2003) PL 6+10 FLC 1/1 FAC 0+1
West Ham U (Signed on 3/2/2004) P/FL 85+45/30 FLC 5/4 FAC 3+6/2 Others 7+1/4

ZARATE Mauro Matias

Born: Buenos Aires, Argentina, 18 March 1987
Height: 5'10"　**Weight:** 10.10
International Honours: Argentina: U20
Brought in on loan from Qatar's Al-Sadd in January and after getting used to England and the Premier League, Mauro burst into the spotlight for Birmingham with his first goal at Reading. He followed that up with two brilliant finishes on

his first start at St Andrew's against Manchester City. An elusive dribbler who could beat players with ease, he often went on mazy runs that electrified the Blues' forward play and excited the fans. Although unpredictable, possessing a low centre of gravity to go with his pace, he could play up front or on either wing and quickly became a favourite, who was eyed up by other clubs. Unfortunately, relegation meant his loan was not made permanent.

Birmingham C (Loaned from Al-Sadd, Qatar, ex Velez Sarsfield, on 21/1/2008) PL 6+8/4

ZHENG ZHI
Born: Shenyang, China, 20 August 1980
Height: 5'11" **Weight:** 11.5
International Honours: China: 41
Having been on loan at Charlton the previous season, China's international captain was signed permanently from Chinese club Shandong Luneng for a fee that could rise to £2m. Zheng Zhi is a dynamic central midfielder, who can also play wide or up front. He likes to get forward into scoring positions but is also a fierce tackler and good in the air. Reading the game well and improving his first touch as he adapted to the Championship, 'ZiZi' was a regular for most of the season and joint second top scorer with nine goals. His goal at Norwich on Boxing Day was probably the best of the bunch, when he collected a pass from Jose Semedo, dummied a defender and hit a low shot under the goalkeeper. A groin injury ruled him out of the last two games and the best is yet to come for 'ZiZi' as he acclimatises himself to the English game.

Charlton Ath (£2,000,000 from Shandong Luneng, China, ex Liaoning Chuangye, Shenzhen Kingsway, on 8/1/2007) P/FL 46+8/8 FLC 1/1 FAC 2/1

ZOKORA Didier Alain
Born: Abidjan, Ivory Coast, 14 December 1980
Height: 5'10" **Weight:** 11.0
Club Honours: FLC '08
International Honours: Ivory Coast: 77
Didier played a full part in Tottenham's season, participating in 43 games. He remains a first choice for the Ivory Coast and played in all six of their games in the African Cup of Nations as they reached the third-place play-off. Didier played not only in his primary defensive midfield slot but in every position across the back four for Spurs, all to good effect. He is a swift and tenacious defender, with good heading ability. Didier's form for his club improved as the season progressed and he never lost his enthusiasm after

Calvin Zola-Makongo

the Carling Cup final, a period in which the team's commitment seemed to flag. A good passer of the ball who makes plenty of forward runs, his only strike in Tottenham's colours was a successful penalty in the shoot-out against PSV Eindhoven in the UEFA Cup.

Tottenham H (£8,200,000 from St Etienne, France, ex ASEC Mimosas Abidjan, KRC Genk, on 7/7/2006) PL 51+8 FLC 5+1 FAC 6 Others 19

ZOLA-MAKONGO Calvin
Born: Kinshasa, DR Congo, 31 December 1984
Height: 6'1" **Weight:** 12.0
Calvin was affected by a series of niggling injuries in the early part of last season and

only really got into his stride for Tranmere from December. In the Peter Crouch mould of strikers, his height and slight build can make him seem gangly and awkward in front of goal but he cleverly uses this to his advantage, scoring the majority of his five League goals from close range. Although under contract at Prenton Park until 2009, Calvin is rumoured to be interesting other League One sides, despite having yet to fulfil his undoubted potential to the maximum.

Newcastle U (From trainee on 17/1/2002)
Oldham Ath (Loaned on 30/8/2003) FL 21+4/5 FAC 1/1 Others 2/1
Tranmere Rov (Free on 9/7/2004) FL 55+41/16 FLC 2+2/1 FAC 4+2 Others 1+1/1

FA Barclays Premiership and Coca-Cola Football League Clubs
Summary of Appearances and Goals for 2007-08

KEY TO TABLES: P/FL = Premier/Football League. FLC = Football League Cup. FAC = FA Cup. Others = Other first team appearances.
Left hand figures in each column list number of full appearances + appearances as substitute. Right hand figures list

ACCRINGTON STANLEY (DIV 2: 17th)

Player	P/FL App	P/FL Goals	FLC App	FLC Goals	FAC App	FAC Goals	Others App
ARTHUR Kenny	24		1				
BELL Jay	2						
BOCO Romauld	6 + 5		1				1
BRANCH Graham	19 + 3						
BROWN David	8 + 7				1		1
CARDEN Paul	4						
CAVANAGH Peter	19	1	1		1	1	
CRANEY Ian	34	7					
DENNEHY Billy	2 + 5						
DOUGHTY Philip	3						
D'SANE Roscoe	18 + 4	7			1		1	1
DUNBAVIN Ian	22 + 1				1		1
EDWARDS Philip	28 + 3	1			1		
GRANT Robert	5 + 2						
HARRIS Jay	38 + 3	1					
KEMPSON Darran	8	1					
KING Mark	4 + 2						
McEVILLY Lee	3 + 8		1		0 + 1		
McGIVERN Leighton	2 + 10	1					0 + 1
McGRAIL Chris	0 + 1						0 + 1
MANGAN Andy	3 + 4	1					
MANNIX David	9 + 3						
MILES John	12 + 4		1		0 + 1		1
MULLIN Paul	43	12	1		1	1	1
MURPHY Peter	2						
PROCTOR Andy	40 + 3	10	1		1		1	1
RICHARDSON Leam	33 + 4	1	1		1		
ROBERTS Mark	33 + 1		1		1		
SMITH Andrew	0 + 1						
THOMAS Aswad	13	2					
TODD Andy	14 + 7						
TURNER Chris	0 + 1						
WEBB Sean	18				1		
WHALLEY Shaun	14 + 17	3	0 + 1		0 + 1		0 + 1
WILLIAMS Robbie	23 + 3		1		1		

ARSENAL (PREM: 3rd)

Player	P/FL App	P/FL Goals	FLC App	FLC Goals	FAC App	FAC Goals	Others App
ADEBAYOR Emmanuel	32 + 4	24	0 + 1	1	1 + 1	2	7 + 2	3
ALMUNIA Manuel	29						9
BARAZITE Nacer			0 + 2				
BENDTNER Nicklas	7 + 20	5	5	1	2	1	3 + 3	2
CLICHY Gael	37 + 1				1		10
DENILSON	4 + 9		5	2	1		3 + 1
DIABY Abou	9 + 6	1	4 + 1	1	2		5 + 1	2
DIARRA Lassana	4 + 3		3				1 + 2
DJOUROU Johan	1 + 1		1				
EBOUE Manu	20 + 3		1		2		8 + 2
EDUARDO	13 + 4	4	3 + 2	4	2 + 1	1	4 + 2	3
FABIANSKI Lukasz	3		5				
FABREGAS Cesc	32	7	0 + 1		1		9 + 1	6
FLAMINI Mathieu	30	3			1 + 1		8
GALLAS William	31	4	1		2		8
GIBBS Kieran			1 + 1				
GILBERTO	12 + 11	1	3		2 + 1		3 + 4
HLEB Alexander	29 + 2	2	1		1 + 1		8	2
HOYTE Justin	2 + 3		5		2 + 1		2
LANSBURY Henri			0 + 1				
LEHMANN Jens	6 + 1				3		3
MERIDA Fran			0 + 3				
RANDALL Mark	0 + 1		1 + 1				
ROSICKY Tomas	15 + 3	6			1		3 + 2	1
SAGNA Bacary	29		1		1		7 + 1
SENDEROS Philippe	14 + 3	2	3		2 + 1		8 + 1
SONG Alex	5 + 4		3				2 + 1
TOURE Kolo	29 + 1	2			2		9
TRAORE Armand	1 + 2		4		2		2
VAN PERSIE Robin	13 + 2	7	1				6 + 1	2
WALCOTT Theo	11 + 14	4	4		1	1	4 + 5	2

ASTON VILLA (PREM: 6th)

Player	P/FL App	P/FL Goals	FLC App	FLC Goals	FAC App	FAC Goals	Others App
AGBONLAHOR Gabby	37	11	2		1		
BARRY Gareth	37	9	2		1		
BERGER Patrik	0 + 8		0 + 1				
BOUMA Wilfred	38	1			1		
CAHILL Gary	0 + 1		1				
CAREW John	32	13			1		
CARSON Scott	35				1		
DAVIES Curtis	9 + 3	1	1		1		
GARDNER Craig	15 + 8	3	1		0 + 1		
HAREWOOD Marlon	1 + 22	5	2	1	1		
KNIGHT Zat	25 + 2	1	1				
LAURSEN Martin	38	6			1		
MALONEY Shaun	11 + 11	4	2	2	0 + 1	1	
MELLBERG Olof	33 + 1	2	2		1		
MOORE Luke	8 + 7	1	1 + 1	1	0 + 1		
OSBOURNE Isaiah	1 + 7		2				
PETROV Stilian	22 + 6	1	1 + 1		1		
REO-COKER Nigel	36		2	1	1		
ROUTLEDGE Wayne	0 + 1		1				
SALIFOU Moustapha	0 + 4						
TAYLOR Stuart	3 + 1		2				
YOUNG Ashley	37	8	0 + 1		1		

BARNET (DIV 2: 12th)

Player	P/FL App	P/FL Goals	FLC App	FLC Goals	FAC App	FAC Goals	Others App
ADOMAH Albert	22	5					
AKURANG Cliff	17 + 4	7			3		
ANGUS Stev	1						
BECKWITH Rob	9				2		
BIRCHALL Adam	36 + 6	11	1		1		4 + 2	2	1	1
BISHOP Neal	39		2		1		6		1
BURTON-GODWIN Sagi	29 + 1	1	1		2		1
CAREW Ashley	18 + 15	1	1		5		1
DEVERA Joe	41			1			6		1
GILLET Kenny	30 + 1				6		
GRAZIOLI Giuliano	2 + 9				1 + 2		
HARRISON Lee	37 + 1	1			4		1
HART Danny	0 + 2						
HATCH Liam	10 + 11	6			2	2	0 + 1
HENDON Ian	2 + 2		1				
LEARY Michael	19 + 3	1	1		3 + 1		1
MINTO-ST AIMIE Kieron	5 + 5						
NICOLAU Nicky	31 + 7	2	1		4 + 2		1
NORVILLE Jason	5 + 3	1			1		
O'CEARUILL Joe	9 + 5				1 + 2		1
PARKES Jordan	7 + 3						
PORTER Max	26 + 4	1	0 + 1		3 + 1		1
PUNCHEON Jason	37 + 4	10	1	1	5		1
SEANLA Claude	1 + 2		0 + 1				0 + 1
THOMAS Anthony	14 + 12	4	1		0 + 5		0 + 1
WRIGHT Josh	31 + 1	1			3		
YAKUBU Ismail	28	2			6	1	

BARNSLEY (CHAMP: 18th)

Player	P/FL App	P/FL Goals	FLC App	FLC Goals	FAC App	FAC Goals	Others App
ADAM Jamil	0 + 1						
ANDERSON	20				1		
BUTTERFIELD Jacob	1 + 2		0 + 1		0 + 1		
CAMPBELL-RYCE Jamal	34 + 3	3			4 + 1	1	
CHRISTENSEN Kim	0 + 12	1	0 + 1				
COLGAN Nick	1						
COULSON Michael	1 + 11		0 + 1		0 + 3	1	
DEVANEY Martin	24 + 10	4	1		3 + 1		
FERENCZI Istvan	25 + 12	5	0 + 1	1	4		
FOSTER Steve	41	1			5		2
HASSELL Bobby	17 + 3				5		
HOWARD Brian	41	13	1		5		1
JOHNSON Andy	4				5		
KOZLUK Rob	24		2		3 + 1		
LEON Diego	16 + 2	1			1 + 1		
LETHEREN Kyle					0 + 1		
McCANN Grant	11 + 8	3	1 + 1		1		
MACKEN Jon	28 + 1	8					
MATTIS Dwayne	0 + 1		1				
MOSTTO Miguel	7 + 7	1	2		1		
MULLER Heinz	28		2		2		
NARDIELLO Danny	8 + 3	1			2		
NYATANGA Lewin	40 + 1	1	2				
ODEJAYI Kayode	23 + 16	3	1		3 + 2	1	
REID Paul	2 + 1		1	1			
RICKETTS Rohan	2 + 8		2		1		
SOUZA Denis	45	2	2		5		

	P/FL App	Goals	FLC App	Goals	FAC App	Goals	Others App
STEELE Luke	14				3		
TININHO	3						
TOGWELL Sam	10 + 12	1	1 + 1		1 + 2		
VAN HOMOET Marciano	17 + 2				4 + 1		
WARNER Tony	3						
WERLING Dominik	16 + 1	1	2				
BIRMINGHAM CITY (PREM: 19th)							
ALUKO Sone			0 + 1				
DANNS Neil	0 + 2		2				
DE RIDDER Daniel	6 + 4		1		1		
DJOUROU-GBADJERE Johan	13						
DOYLE Colin	3		0 + 1				
FORSSELL Mikael	21 + 9	9	1		1		
JAIDI Radhi	18		1		1		
JEROME Cameron	21 + 12	7			0 + 1		
JOHNSON Damien	17		1				
KAPO Olivier	22 + 4	5					
KELLY Stephen	38		1		1		
KINGSON Richard	1		2				
LARSSON Sebastian	32 + 3	6	1		1		
McFADDEN James	10 + 2	4					
McSHEFFREY Gary	24 + 8	3	1		1	1	
MUAMBA Fabrice	37		2		1		
MURPHY David	14		1				
NAFTI Mehdi	19 + 7		1				
O'CONNOR Garry	5 + 18	2	2	1	1	1	
OUBINA Borja	1 + 1						
PALACIOS Wilson	4 + 3		0 + 1				
PARNABY Stuart	4 + 9		2				
QUEUDRUE Franck	14 + 2				1		
RIDGEWELL Liam	35	1	1		1		
SADLER Mat	3 + 2		2				
SCHMITZ Rafael	12 + 3		0 + 1				
TAYLOR Maik	34						
TAYLOR Martin	4		1				
VINE Rowan							
ZARATE Mauro	6 + 8	4					
BLACKBURN ROVERS (PREM: 7th)							
BENTLEY David	37	6	3	1	1	1	6 1
BERNER Bruno	2		1				
DERBYSHIRE Matt	4 + 19	3	2 + 1	1	0 + 1		1 + 5 2
DUNN David	25 + 6	1	3				3 + 1
EMERTON Brett	31 + 2	1	1 + 1		1		3 + 1
FRIEDEL Brad	38		3		1		6
KHIZANISHVILI Zurab	10 + 3		1 + 1		1		0 + 1
McCARTHY Benni	21 + 10	8	1 + 1	1	1		3 + 1 2
MOKOENA Aaron	8 + 10		2 + 1		1		3 + 1
NELSEN Ryan	22				0 + 1		5
OLSSON Martin	0 + 2		1				0 + 1
OOIJER Andre	23 + 4		1				6
PEDERSEN Morten Gamst	32 + 5	4	2		0 + 1		5 + 1 1
REID Steven	20 + 4		1				
RIGTERS Maceo	0 + 2		0 + 1		1		1 + 2
ROBERTS Jason	11 + 15	3	1				4 2
SAMBA Chris	33		3		1		4 1
SANTA CRUZ Roque	36 + 1	19	2 + 1	3			3 1
SAVAGE Robbie	10 + 2		1				4 + 1
TREACY Keith			0 + 1		1		
TUGAY	12 + 8	2	1		1		3 + 2
VOGEL Johann	6						
WARNOCK Stephen	37	1	1 + 1				6 1
BLACKPOOL (CHAMP: 19th)							
BARKER Shaun	46	2	4				
BURGESS Ben	25 + 10	9	0 + 1	1	1		
COID Danny	9 + 4		1 + 1				
CRAINEY Stephen	37 + 3	1	2		1		
DICKOV Paul	7 + 4	6					
EVANS Rhys							
EVATT Ian	27 + 2		2		1		
FLYNN Mike	20 + 8	3	3		1		
FORBES Adrian	0 + 2		1				
FOX David	16 + 12	1	4		1	1	
GORKSS Kaspars	39 + 1	5	3 + 1	2			
GREEN Stuart	1 + 5						
HILLS John	1 + 3	3	3		1		
HOLT Grant	0 + 4						
HOOLAHAN Wes	43 + 4	5	1 + 3	1	0 + 1		
JACKSON Matt	2 + 1						
JACKSON Mike	23 + 2		3 + 1	1	1		
JORGENSEN Claus	30 + 7	4			0 + 1		

	P/FL App	Goals	FLC App	Goals	FAC App	Goals	Others App
McMAHON Tony	2						
McPHEE Stephen	16 + 3	4					
MARTIN Joe	1						
MORRELL Andy	23 + 15	5	1 + 3		0 + 1		
PARKER Keigan	10 + 11		4				
RACHUBKA Paul	46		2		1		
SLUSARSKI Bartosz	4 + 2	1					
SOUTHERN Keith	29 + 1	3	1 + 1				
TAYLOR-FLETCHER Gary	40 + 2	6	3		1		
VERNON Scott	6 + 9	4	3		1		
WELSH Andy	3 + 18		1 + 1		1		
BOLTON WANDERERS (PREM: 16th)							
AL-HABSI Ali	10		1				4
ALONSO Mikel	4 + 3		2				2 + 1
ANELKA Nicolas	18	10					2 + 2 1
BRAATEN Daniel	0 + 6	1	1 + 1		1		3 + 2
CAHILL Gary	13						4
CAMPO Ivan	25 + 2	1	0 + 1				2 + 1
CID Gerald	6 + 1		1		1		5
COHEN Tamir	3 + 7	1			1		
DAVIES Kevin	31 + 1	3	1		1		8 1
DIOUF El Hadji	30 + 4	4	1		1		2 + 4 2
DZEMAILI Blerim					0 + 1		
FAYE Abdoulaye	1						
GARDNER Ricardo	25 + 1						4 1
GIANNAKOPOULOS Stelios	1 + 14	2	1 + 1	1	1		4 + 4 1
GUTHRIE Danny	21 + 4		2	1			6 + 1
HELGUSON Heidar	3 + 3	2					2
HUNT Nicky	12 + 2		1		1		8
JAASKELAINEN Jussi	28		1				6
McCANN Gavin	21 + 10	1	2				8 2
MEITE Abdoulaye	21		2		0 + 1		5 + 1 1
MICHALIK Lubo	5 + 2		1 + 1		1		3
NOLAN Kevin	33	5	1				5
O'BRIEN Andy	31 + 1		1		1		7 + 1
O'BRIEN Joey	15 + 4		1		1		4 + 1
RASIAK Grzegorz	2 + 5						
SAMUEL JLloyd	14 + 6		1				4
SINCLAIR James							0 + 1
SPEED Gary	11 + 3	1					3
STEINSSON Gretar	16						
TAYLOR Matthew	16	3					3
TEYMOURIAN	1 + 2		0 + 1				2 + 3
VAZ TE Ricardo	1						1
WILHELMSSON Christian	0 + 8		1		0 + 1		3
WOOLFE Nathan							0 + 1
BOURNEMOUTH (DIV 1: 21st)							
ANDERTON Darren	20	3	1				
BARTLEY Marvin	14 + 6	1			0 + 1		
BEGOVIC Asmir	8						1
BRADBURY Lee	33 + 2	3			2		2 2
CHRISTOPHE Jean-Francois	5 + 5	1	1				
COOPER Shaun	33 + 5	1	0 + 1		3	1	2
CUMMINGS Warren	31 + 1	2	1		2		1
FINLAY Matt	0 + 1						
FORDE David	11						
FRANKS Billy	1						
GARRY Ryan	6 + 2		0 + 1				
GOLBOURNE Scott	5				2	1	1
GOWLING Josh	36 + 1		1		3		2
GRADEL Max-Alain	31 + 3	9	1		2	1	1
HENRY James	8 + 3	4					1
HOLLANDS Danny	37	4			3	1	2 + 1
HUTCHINGS Steve	0 + 1						
KARACAN Jem	11 + 2	1			3	1	1
LALLANA Adam	2 + 1						1
McQUOID Josh	2 + 3				0 + 2		0 + 1
MOSS Neil	7		1		1		2
NEWMAN Rob							0 + 1
O'CONNOR Garreth	5 + 1		1				1 + 1
OSEI-KUFFOUR Jo	37 + 5	12	1		3		1
PARTINGTON Joe	0 + 6	1					1
PEARCE Alex	11						1
PEARCE Jason	30 + 3	1	1		2 + 1		1
PERRETT Russ	10						1
PITMAN Brett	14 + 25	6	0 + 1		2 + 1		1 + 2
PRYCE Ryan	2 + 2						
SHIMMIN Dominic	1 + 1						
STEWART Gareth	18		2		0 + 1		1
TELFER Paul	17 + 1		3				3
TESSEM Jo	5 + 6						

	P/FL App	P/FL Goals	FLC App	FLC Goals	FAC App	FAC Goals	Others App
VOKES Sam	30 + 11	12	1		1		2
WILSON Marc	7						1
YOUNG Neil	18 + 3		1				1
BRADFORD CITY (DIV 2: 10th)							
AINGE Simon	0 + 4						1
BENTHAM Craig	0 + 3						1
BOWER Mark	25 + 2	3	1				
BROWN David	0 + 5	1					1
BULLOCK Lee	12	1					
CLARKE Matt	15 + 2	1			2		1
COLBECK Joe	27 + 6	6	1				1
CONLON Barry	21 + 21	7	1		0 + 2		1
DALEY Omar	37 + 4	4	1		2		
EVANS Paul	19 + 6		1		2		
EVANS Rhys	4						
HARBAN Tom	6						1
HECKINGBOTTOM Paul	44		1		1		1
JOHNSON Eddie	30 + 2	4	1		1		
JOYNES Nathan	1 + 1						0 + 1
LAW Nicky	10	2					
LOACH Scott	20						
MEDLEY Luke	1 + 8	2					
MONCUR Thomas	6 + 1						
N'DUMBU-NSUNGU Guy	17 + 1	6	0 + 1		2		
NIX Kyle	31 + 9	6	1	1	2		1	1
O'BRIEN Luke	2				1		0 + 1
PENFORD Tom	13 + 2	1			0 + 1		
PHELAN Scott	8 + 5				1 + 1		1
RHODES Alex	11 + 17	3	0 + 1		0 + 1		
RICKETTS Donovan	22		1		2		
SAYNOR Ben					1		
STAROSTA Ben	12 + 3						
TAYLFORTH Sean	1				0 + 1		1
THORNE Peter	31 + 2	14			2	1	0 + 1
TOPP Willy	6 + 5						
WETHERALL David	46	2	1		2		
WILLIAMS Darren	28		1		2		
BRENTFORD (DIV 2: 14th)							
BASEY Grant	8		1				1
BENNETT Alan	11		1				
BROOKER Paul	0 + 1		1				
BROWN Simon	26				1		
BROWN Wayne	7 + 4	1			1		
CHARLES Darius	8 + 9				1 + 1		
CONNELL Alan	35 + 7	12	1		1		1
DICKSON Ryan	30 + 1						
ELDER Nathan	16 + 1	4					
EMANUEL Lewis	3						
HAMER Ben	20		1				
HEYWOOD Matt	30 + 2	1	1		2		1
IDE Charlie	16 + 3		1		2	1	0 + 1
MACKIE John	14		1		1		
MASTERS Clark	0 + 1				1		
MILSOM Rob	5 + 1				1		
MONTAGUE Ross	7 + 3	1					
MOORE Sammy	13 + 7	2	1		2		1
MOUSINHO John	13 + 10	2	1				
O'CONNOR Kevin	36 + 1	3	1		2		1
OSBORNE Karleigh	25 + 4	1			0 + 1		1
PARKES Jordan	0 + 1						
PEAD Craig	27 + 5				2		0 + 1
PETERS Ryan	0 + 4		0 + 1				0 + 1
PETTIGREW Adrian	9 + 2		1		1		1
POOLE Glenn	42 + 3	14	1		2		1
REID Reuben	1 + 9	1					
SANKOFA Osei	10 + 1						
SHAKES Ricky	25 + 14	3			1 + 1		1	1
SINCLAIR Emile	1 + 3						
SMITH Gary	26 + 3	1	0 + 1		0 + 1		1
STAROSTA Ben	20 + 1	1			1		
STONE Craig	5 + 1						
THORPE Lee	17 + 2	4			2		
TILLEN Sam	0 + 1		0 + 1				
BRIGHTON & HOVE ALBION (DIV 1: 7th)							
BOWDITCH Dean	5						
BUTTERS Guy	19 + 2	1	1		2 + 1		1
COX Dean	40 + 2	6	1		4		3	1
DIXON Jonny	2 + 2						
EL-ABD Adam	31 + 4	1	1		4	1	3
ELDER Nathan	1 + 8	1			0 + 2		1 + 2
ELPHICK Tommy	39	2	1		2		2
FOGDEN Wes	1 + 2						1
FORSTER Nicky	39 + 2	15	1		4	2	2	2
FRASER Tommy	15 + 9		1		3 + 1		2 + 1
GARGAN Sam	0 + 1						
GATTING Joe	0 + 9						
HAMMOND Dean	24	5	1		3	1	1 + 1
HART Gary	2 + 5						0 + 1
HINSHELWOOD Adam	0 + 1						
KUIPERS Michel	46		1		4		3
LOFT Doug	1 + 12				0 + 3	1	1
LYNCH Joel	18 + 4	1	1		2 + 1		2
McFAUL Shane	0 + 1						
MARTOT David	17 + 9	1			0 + 2		2 + 1	1
MAYO Kerry	10 + 5						
MURRAY Glenn	20 + 1	9					
O'CALLAGHAN George	13 + 1				1		2
RACON Therry	8						
REID Paul	3 + 4		0 + 1		1		
RENTS Sam	4 + 1		0 + 1		0 + 1		0 + 1
REVELL Alex	14 + 7	6	1		1	1	1
RICHARDS Matt	28				3		2
ROBINSON Jake	16 + 18	4			4		1	1
SAVAGE Bas	17 + 4	3	0 + 1		3		1 + 1	1
THOMSON Steve	20						
WESTLAKE Ian	11	2					
WHING Andy	42		1		3		1 + 1
BRISTOL CITY (CHAMP: 4th)							
ADEBOLA Dele	16 + 1	6					3
BASSO Adriano	44				1		3
BETSY Kevin	0 + 1		1				1
BROOKER Steve	1 + 3	1					
BYFIELD Darren	17 + 16	8					0 + 1
CAREY Louis	33		1				3	1
CARLE Nick	14 + 3						3
ELLIOTT Marvin	44 + 1	5	2		1		3
FONTAINE Liam	32 + 6	1	2		1	1	1 + 2
HENDERSON Stephen	0 + 1						
JEVONS Phil	0 + 2		1 + 1	2			
JOHNSON Lee	39 + 1	1	1		1		0 + 3
KEOGH Richard	1						
McALLISTER Jamie	40 + 1		2		1		3
McCOMBE Jamie	25 + 9	3					2
McINDOE Michael	45	6	1				3	1
MURRAY Scott	4 + 10	3	2		0 + 1		3	1
NOBLE David	16 + 10	2			1		3
ORR Bradley	42	4	1 + 1	1	1		3
RUSSELL Alex	1		1				
SHOWUNMI Enoch	10 + 7	3	1		0 + 1		
SKUSE Cole	5 + 20		0 + 1				
SPROULE Ivan	31 + 9	2	0 + 1		1		0 + 2
TRUNDLE Lee	21 + 14	5	1 + 1		0 + 1		3	1
VASKO Tamas	8 + 11	1	1		1		
WEALE Chris	2 + 1				2		
WILSON Brian	16 + 2	1	1		1		
BRISTOL ROVERS (DIV 1: 16th)							
ANDREWS Wayne							1
ANTHONY Byron	19 + 1	1	2				1
CAMPBELL Stuart	46		2		7		1
CARRUTHERS Chris	13 + 4		2		3 + 1		1
CLOUGH Charlie	0 + 1						
COLES Danny	24	1			6	2	
DISLEY Craig	41 + 3	6	2	1	5 + 1	2	1
ELLIOTT Steve	33	3	2		3		0 + 1
GREEN Ryan	12				1		1
GROVES Matt	0 + 1				0 + 1		1
HALDANE Lewis	22 + 10	1	1 + 1		2 + 1		0 + 1
HINTON Craig	21 + 3	2			7 + 1	3	1
IGOE Sammy	9 + 12		0 + 1		3 + 3		
JACOBSON Joe	34 + 6	1	1 + 1		7		
KLEIN-DAVIES Josh	2 + 8	1					
LAMBERT Rickie	42 + 4	14	1 + 1		8	6	1
LESCOTT Aaron	34		2		7		
LINES Chris	25 + 3				6 + 2		1
PARRINELLO Tom					0 + 1		
PHILLIPS Steve	46		2		8		1
PIPE David	37 + 3	2	2		7		1
PULIS Tony	0 + 1						
REECE Charlie	0 + 1						

	P/FL		FLC		FAC		Others	
	App	Goals	App	Goals	App	Goals	App	
RIGG Sean	14 + 17	1	0 + 1		1 + 4		1	
WALKER Richard	12 + 12	4	2		0 + 4		0 + 1	
WILLIAMS Andy	19 + 22	4	1 + 1	1	7 + 1	1	1	
BURNLEY (CHAMP: 13th)								
AKINBIYI Ade	14 + 25	8	2 + 1	1	0 + 1			
ALEXANDER Graham	43	1	0 + 1		1			
BLAKE Robbie	41 + 4	9	1 + 2	1	1			
CALDWELL Steve	26 + 3	2	2		1			
CARLISLE Clarke	32 + 1	2	2					
COLE Andrew	8 + 5	6						
DUFF Michael	8	1	2					
ELLIOTT Wade	45 + 1	2	1		1			
FOSTER Steve			1					
GRAY Andy	25	11	1 + 1	2	1			
GUDJONSSON Joey	13 + 15	1	1		0 + 1			
HARLEY Jon	31 + 2		0 + 1		1			
JENSEN Brian	19		2					
JONES Steve	1 + 16	1	2 + 1		0 + 1			
JORDAN Stephen	20 + 1		3					
KIRALY Gabor	27		1		1			
LAFFERTY Kyle	34 + 3	5	2		1			
McCANN Chris	34 + 1	5	1		1			
MacDONALD Alex	0 + 2							
MAHON Alan	13 + 13	1	2 + 1					
O'CONNOR Garreth	0 + 1							
O'CONNOR James	24 + 5	3	2 + 1		1			
RANDALL Mark	2 + 8							
RODRIGUEZ Jay	0 + 1							
SPICER John	9 + 15		3					
THOMAS Wayne	1							
UNSWORTH David	26 + 3	1	2					
VARGA Stan	10				1			
BURY (DIV 2: 13th)								
ADAMS Nicky	41 + 2	12	1		5	1	3	
ANANE Ricky					0 + 1		1	
BAKER Richie	21 + 11	1	0 + 1		4 + 1		1 + 1	
BARRY-MURPHY Brian	27 + 4	1	1		3 + 1		3	
BELFORD Cameron	0 + 1							
BENNETT Elliott	18 + 1	1						
BISHOP Andy	37 + 7	19	0 + 1		5	5	2	1
BUCHANAN David	24 + 11		1		4 + 1		3	
BULLOCK Lee	8							
CHALLINOR Dave	26		1		2		3	
DEAN James	3 + 1		1				1	
DORNEY Jack	3 + 4				0 + 2		0 + 2	
FUTCHER Ben	40		1		4	1	2	1
HASLAM Steve	37	1			5		3	
HUGHES Liam	1 + 3				0 + 1			
HURST Glynn	29 + 13	6	1		1 + 1		2 + 1	2
MANGAN Andy	7 + 13	4	0 + 1		1 + 2		0 + 2	
MORGAN Paul	20		1		1			
PARRISH Andy	17 + 9	1	1		3		3	
PROVETT Jim	32		1		5		3	
RANDOLPH Darren	14							
RICHARDSON Marcus	1							
ROONEY Adam	10 + 6	3						
ROUSE Domaine	0 + 6						0 + 1	1
SCOTT Paul	40	6	1		4	1	1 + 1	
SODJE Efe	16	1						
STEPHENS Dale	4 + 2	1			3			
WOODTHORPE Colin	30 + 1	1			5		2	
YEO Simon	0 + 8							
CARDIFF CITY (CHAMP: 12th)								
BLAKE Darcy	4 + 4		0 + 1		0 + 3			
BROWN Jon	0 + 2							
CAPALDI Tony	43 + 1		4		6			
ENCKELMAN Peter	15 + 1				4			
FEENEY Warren	1 + 4		1					
FOWLER Robbie	10 + 3	4	3	2				
GREEN Matty			0 + 1					
GUNTER Chris	11 + 2		2 + 2					
HASSELBAINK Jimmy Floyd	33 + 3	7	3	1	4 + 1	1		
JOHNSON Roger	41 + 1	5	4	1	6	1		
LEDLEY Joe	38 + 3	10	2 + 1		4	1		
LOOVENS Glenn	36		1		6			
MacLEAN Steve	6 + 9	1	1 + 1		1			
McNAUGHTON Kevin	35	1	2		6	1		
McPHAIL Stephen	42 + 1	3	4		5			
OAKES Mike	11		2		2			
PARRY Paul	37 + 4	10	3 + 1		5	1		
PURSE Darren	12 + 6	1	3	1				
RAE Gavin	40 + 5	4	4		6			
RAMSEY Aaron	11 + 4	1	0 + 1		3 + 2	1		
SCHMEICHEL Kasper	14							
SCIMECA Riccy	4 + 5				0 + 1			
SINCLAIR Trevor	14 + 7	1	1	1	1 + 3			
THOMPSON Steve	17 + 19	5	0 + 1		1 + 4	1		
TURNBULL Ross	6		2					
WHITTINGHAM Peter	25 + 16	5	2 + 2	1	6	3		
CARLISLE UNITED (DIV 1: 4th)								
ANYINSAH Joe	10 + 2	3					2	
ARANALDE Zigor	27		2		2	1	2	
ARNISON Paul	7 + 10		2				2	
BRIDGE-WILKINSON Marc	44 + 1	6	1		2		4	2
BRITTAIN Martin	0 + 1		1					
CAMPION Darren	1 + 1							
CARLTON Danny	5 + 26		1 + 1		0 + 2		1 + 1	
DOBIE Scott	8 + 7	4					2	
GALL Kevin	10 + 11	1	1 + 1		2		1 + 1	2
GARNER Joe	30 + 1	14	1		2		0 + 1	
GRAHAM Danny	39 + 6	14	2	1	2		4	2
HACKNEY Simon	39 + 4	8	1 + 1		1 + 1		2 + 2	
HORWOOD Evan	19						2	
JOYCE Luke	1 + 2	1						
KEOGH Richard	7							
LIVESEY Danny	45	6	2		2		4	
LUMSDON Chris	38 + 2		1		2		4	
McDERMOTT Neale			0 + 1					
MADINE Gary	1 + 10						0 + 1	
MURPHY Peter	33 + 3	3			2		3	
RAVEN David	43	1	2		2		3	
REID Paul	1							
SMITH Grant	15 + 1	1					2	
SMITH Jeff	13 + 9	1	1 + 1		1 + 1		2	
TAYLOR Cleveland	14 + 4						0 + 1	
THIRLWELL Paul	9 + 4		2				0 + 1	
WESTWOOD Keiren	46		2		2		4	
WORLEY Harry	1							
CHARLTON ATHLETIC (CHAMP: 11th)								
AMBROSE Darren	29 + 8	7	2 + 1	1	2	1		
ARTER Harry			0 + 1					
BASEY Grant	8	1			0 + 1			
BENT Marcus	3	1	1					
BOUGHERRA Madjid	24 + 5	2	2		2			
COOK Lee	4 + 5							
DICKSON Chris	0 + 2		0 + 1		0 + 2	1		
ELLIOT Rob	0 + 1							
FAYE Amdy	0 + 1		1					
FORTUNE Jon	25 + 1	2	2 + 1					
GRAY Andy	10 + 6	2						
HALFORD Greg	16	2						
HOLLAND Matt	28 + 3	1	1		2			
IWELUMO Chris	32 + 14	10	0 + 2		0 + 2			
LITA Leroy	8	3						
McCARTHY Paddy	27 + 2	2	2	1	2			
McLEOD Izale	2 + 16	1	3		2			
MILLS Danny	19							
MOUTAOUAKIL Yazz	7 + 3		2		2			
POWELL Chris	16 + 1	1	2					
RACON Therry	1 + 3		2					
RANDOLPH Darren	1		2					
REID Andy	21 + 1	5	1	1				
SAM Lloyd	24 + 4	2	2	1	2			
SANKOFA Osei	0 + 1		1					
SEMEDO Jose	28 + 9		2					
SHELVEY Jonjo	2							
SINCLAIR Dean			1 + 1	1				
SINCLAIR Scott	0 + 3							
SODJE Sam	20 + 7	2						
THATCHER Ben	11							
THOMAS Jerome	20 + 12				0 + 1			
TODOROV Svetoslav	3 + 4	2	2	1				
VARNEY Luke	23 + 16	8	0 + 1		2			
WAGSTAFF Scott	0 + 2							
WEAVER Nicky	45		1		2			
YOUGA Kelly	11				2			
ZHENG ZHI	38 + 4	7	1	1	2	1		
CHELSEA (PREM: 2nd)								
ALEX	22 + 6	2	3		2		5 + 1	1
ANELKA Nicolas	10 + 4	1	2		2 + 1	1	0 + 5	

	P/FL		FLC		FAC		Others	
	App	Goals	App	Goals	App	Goals	App	Goals
BALLACK Michael	16 + 2	7	1 + 2		1 + 1		7	2
BELLETTI Juliano	20 + 3	2	6		2		4 + 3	
BEN HAIM Tal	10 + 3		3 + 2		2		2 + 1	
BRIDGE Wayne	9 + 2		4 + 1		3		3	
CARVALHO Ricardo	21	1	4		2		11	
CECH Petr	26		3		1		10	
COLE Ashley	27	1	1 + 1		1		11	
COLE Joe	28 + 5	7	2 + 3	1	2 + 1		13 + 1	2
CUDICINI Carlo	10		2		2		4 + 1	
DIARRA Lassana							0 + 1	
DROGBA Didier	17 + 2	8	1		1	1	11	6
ESSIEN Michael	23 + 4	6	3 + 1		1 + 1		12 + 1	
FERREIRA Paulo	15 + 3		1 + 1		2 + 1		5	
HILARIO	2 + 1		1		1		0 + 1	
JOHNSON Glen	1 + 1						1	
KALOU Salomon	24 + 6	7	2 + 2	2	2 + 1	1	5 + 6	1
LAMPARD Frank	23 + 1	10	3	4	1	2	11 + 1	4
MAKELELE Claude	15 + 3		1 + 1		1		12 + 1	
MALOUDA Florent	16 + 5	2	2 + 1		2		9 + 3	2
MIKEL Jon Obi	21 + 8		3		2		2 + 3	
PIZARRO Claudio	4 + 17		3 + 1		1		1 + 2	
SHEVCHENKO Andrei	8 + 9	5	2		2	2	2 + 3	1
SIDWELL Steve	7 + 8		3 + 2	1	3		0 + 2	
SINCLAIR Scott	0 + 1		3		1		2	
TERRY John	23	1	2		2		10	
WRIGHT-PHILLIPS Shaun	20 + 7	2	5	1	3	1	3 + 3	

CHELTENHAM TOWN (DIV 1: 19th)

	P/FL		FLC		FAC		Others	
	App	Goals	App	Goals	App	Goals	App	Goals
ARMSTRONG Craig	13 + 1							
BIRD David	46	4	1		2		2	
BROOKER Steve	14	5						
BROWN Scott	9 + 11							
CAINES Gavin	22 + 6	2			2		1 + 1	
CONNOLLY Adam	3 + 12				2		2	
CONNOR Paul	26 + 13	4	1		2		2	1
D'AGOSTINO Michael	14 + 11							
DUFF Shane	30		1		2			
FINNIGAN John	10	1	1	1				
GALLINAGH Andy	24 + 2		1				1 + 1	
GILL Ben	0 + 2		0 + 1		1		0 + 2	
GILL Jerry	43		1		2		1	
GILLESPIE Steven	35 + 2	14	1		2	2	1	
HIGGS Shane	46		1		2		2	
KEOGH Richard	10							
LEDGISTER Aaron			0 + 1					
LINDEGAARD Andy	31 + 11	2	1					
MADJO Guy	2 + 3							
MYRIE-WILLIAMS Jennison	7 + 5				1		1	1
REID Craig	2 + 6		1		0 + 2		1	1
RIDLEY Lee	8				1			
RUSSELL Alex	12 + 1	2						
SINCLAIR Dean	12	1					2	
SPENCER Damian	22 + 8	3			2		1	
TOWNSEND Michael	13	1					1	
VINCENT Ashley	19 + 18	2	0 + 1		1		0 + 1	
WRIGHT Alan	33	1			2		1	
WYLDE Michael							1	
YAO Sosthene	0 + 5		1		0 + 2		0 + 1	

CHESTER CITY (DIV 2: 22nd)

	P/FL		FLC		FAC		Others	
	App	Goals	App	Goals	App	Goals	App	Goals
BOLLAND Phil	2						1	
BUTLER Paul	35	2	1		1		1	
CARROLL Neil	1							
DANBY John	46		1		1		2	
DINNING Tony	20	2			1		1	
ELLISON Kevin	36	11	1		1		1	
GRANT Tony	15 + 4	1	1		1		1	
HAND Jamie	0 + 1		1					
HOLROYD Chris	14 + 11	4	0 + 1				0 + 1	1
HUGHES Mark	39 + 4	4	1		1		2	
KELLY Shaun	7 + 3							
LINDFIELD Craig	5 + 2							
LINWOOD Paul	42	1	1		1		2	
LOWNDES Nathan	8 + 4		1		1		0 + 1	
McMANUS Paul	9 + 10	1			0 + 1		1	
MARPLES Simon	16						1	
MITCHELL Andy	0 + 4							
MURPHY John	39	9			1			
NEWTON Sean	2							
PALETHORPE Phil	0 + 1							
PARTRIDGE Richie	34 + 2	5			2		2	2
ROBERTS Kevin	30 + 7	3	0 + 1				0 + 1	
RULE Glenn	2 + 2						0 + 1	
RUTHERFORD Paul	10 + 13	1	0 + 1		0 + 1		0 + 1	
SANDWITH Kevin	12 + 10	1					1	
VAUGHAN James	29 + 1	1	1				1	
WARD Gavin							0 + 1	
WELSH John	6							
WILSON Laurie	40	2	1		1		2	
YEO Simon	7 + 14	4	1		1		2	

CHESTERFIELD (DIV 2: 8th)

	P/FL		FLC		FAC		Others	
	App	Goals	App	Goals	App	Goals	App	Goals
ALGAR Ben	1 + 1						0 + 1	
ALLISON Wayne	0 + 9		1				1	1
BARNES Michael	1 + 2							
BASTIANS Felix	12		1		1			
COOPER Kevin	2 + 5	1			1			
DAVIES Gareth	0 + 1							
DOWNES Aaron	38 + 2	2	1		1			
DOWSON David	9 + 3	3						
DYER Bruce	0 + 3							
FLETCHER Steve	23 + 15	5			1			
GRAY Kevin	10 + 5						1	
HARTLEY Peter	12							
HAWKINS Colin	5							
JACKSON Jamie	0 + 4						1	
JORDAN Michael	1							
KERRY Lloyd	8 + 5	2						
KOVACS Janos	41	2	1				1	
LAW Josh							0 + 1	
LESTER Jack	35 + 1	23	1		1	1	1	1
LEVEN Peter	42	6	1		1			
LOWRY Jamie	41 + 1	6	0 + 1				1	
MOLONEY Brendon	8 + 1	1						
NIVEN Derek	38	3	1				1	
O'HARE Alan	4 + 9						0 + 1	
OWENS Graeme	2 + 2							
PICKEN Phil	34 + 3		1				1	
ROBERTSON Gregor	34 + 1	1	1				1	
ROCHE Barry	45		1		1		1	
ROONEY Adam	11 + 11	7			1			
SMITH Adam	2 + 6		0 + 1		0 + 1			
TRAVIS Nicky	0 + 2							
WARD Jamie	27 + 8	12	1				1	
WINTER Jamie	20 + 5							

COLCHESTER UNITED (CHAMP: 24th)

	P/FL		FLC		FAC		Others	
	App	Goals	App	Goals	App	Goals	App	Goals
BALDWIN Pat	23 + 3		1		1			
BALOGH Bela	10 + 7							
CONNOLLY Matt	13 + 3	2						
COUSINS Mark	0 + 2							
COYNE Chris	16		1					
DAVISON Aidan	6							
DUGUID Karl	37		1		0 + 1			
ELITO Medy	7 + 4	1						
ELOKOBI George	17	1	1		1			
GERKEN Dean	40		1		1			
GRANVILLE Danny	14 + 5		1					
GUTTRIDGE Luke	5 + 9		1		1			
GUY Jamie	0 + 11				0 + 1			
HAMMOND Dean	11 + 2							
HEATH Matt	5							
IFIL Phil	20							
IZZET Kem	35 + 4	1	0 + 1		1			
JACKSON Johnnie	46	7	1		1			
LISBIE Kevin	39 + 3	17	1		1			
McLEOD Izzy	0 + 2							
McLEOD Kevin	21 + 7	4	1		1			
PLATT Clive	34 + 7	8	1					
SHERINGHAM Teddy	11 + 8	3			1	1		
VERNON Scott	8 + 9	5						
VIRGO Adam	30 + 6	1	1		1			
WATSON Kevin	7							
WEBB Tom			0 + 1					
WHITE John	21		1					
WORDSWORTH Anthony	1 + 2		0 + 1					
YEATES Mark	29	8	1		1			

COVENTRY CITY (CHAMP: 21st)

	P/FL		FLC		FAC		Others	
	App	Goals	App	Goals	App	Goals	App	Goals
ADEBOLA Dele	15 + 11	4	2 + 1	1	2	1		
ANDREWS Wayne	0 + 1							
BEST Leon	29 + 5	8	3	1	2 + 1			
BIRCHALL Chris	1		0 + 1		0 + 1			
BORROWDALE Gary	20 + 1		3		2			
CAIRO Ellery	4 + 3		2					
DANN Scott	14 + 2							

Player	P/FL App	Goals	FLC App	Goals	FAC App	Goals	Others App	Goals
DAVIS Liam	2 + 4				1			
DE ZEEUW Arjan	16 + 1		1		1			
DOYLE Micky	42	7	4		3			
DUFFY Richard	2							
FOX Danny	18	1						
GRAY Julian	20 + 6	3	2		1			
HALL Marcus	17 + 1		1 + 1		1			
HAWKINS Colin			1					
HINES Zavon	0 + 7	1						
HUGHES Michael	16 + 2				2			
HUGHES Stephen	32 + 5	1	3		1	1		
KONSTANTOPOULOS Dimi	21				2			
KYLE Kevin	7 + 6	2	0 + 1					
McKENZIE Leon	9 + 2	2						
McNAMEE David	12 + 1		1 + 1					
MARSHALL Andy	16		4		1			
MIFSUD Michael	34 + 7	10	3	4	3	3		
OSBOURNE Isaac	37 + 5		4		3			
PAGE Robert			2					
SCHMEICHEL Kasper	9							
SIMPSON Robbie	10 + 18	1	1 + 3	1	1 + 1			
TABB Jay	40 + 2	5	3 + 1	1	3			
THORNTON Kevin	9 + 10	1			0 + 1			
TURNER Ben	19		2 + 1		1			
WARD Elliott	35 + 2	6	2		3	1		

CREWE ALEXANDRA (DIV 1: 20th)

Player	P/FL App	Goals	FLC App	Goals	FAC App	Goals	Others App	Goals
ABBEY George	20 + 3							
ANYINSAH Joe	6 + 2							
BAILEY James	0 + 1							
BAILEY Matt	0 + 2				1			
BARNARD Lee	9 + 1	3						
BASEYA Cedric	1 + 2				0 + 1			
BAUDET Julien	35	1	1		1		1	
BENNETT Elliott	4 + 5	1			0 + 2			
BOPP Eugene	5 + 5	1	0 + 1				1	
BOYLE Pat	17							
BROWN Junior	0 + 1							
CARRINGTON Mark	3 + 6		0 + 1				0 + 1	
CHURCH Simon	11 + 1	1			2			
COX Neil	21 + 6				2	1		
DANIEL Colin	0 + 1							
DICKSON Chris	2 + 1							
FARQUHARSON Nick							1	
GRAY David	1							
JONES Steve	2 + 2	1						
JONES Billy	22		1		2		1	
LOWE Ryan	16 + 11	4			2		1	1
LUNT Kenny	14							
LYNCH Ryan	1 + 1						0 + 1	
McCREADY Chris	32 + 2	1	1		2	1		
MAYNARD Nicky	25 + 2	14			0 + 1			
MILLER Shaun	5 + 10	1	1				0 + 1	
MOORE Byron	25 + 8	3	1		2			
MORGAN Dean	7 + 2	1						
O'CONNOR Michael	17 + 6							
O'DONNELL Danny	19 + 8	1					1	
POPE Tom	15 + 11	7	1				1	
RIX Ben	21 + 4	1			2		1	
ROBERTS Gary M	4							
ROBERTS Gary S	40 + 2	6	1		2			
SCHUMACHER Steve	24 + 2	1	1		0 + 1		1	
TOMLINSON Stuart							1	
VAUGHAN David	0 + 1							
WILLIAMS Ben	46		1		2			
WOODARDS Danny	36		1		2		1	

CRYSTAL PALACE (CHAMP: 5th)

Player	P/FL App	Goals	FLC App	Goals	FAC App	Goals	Others App	Goals
ASHTON Nathan	1							
BOSTOCK John	1 + 3				1			
BUTTERFIELD Danny	25 + 5		1				2	
CORT Leon	12							
CRAIG Tony	13		1					
DANNS Neil	2 + 2							
DERRY Shaun	30						2	
DICKOV Paul	6 + 3							
FLETCHER Carl	17 + 11	1			1			
FLINDERS Scott			1		1			
FONTE Jose	17 + 5	1	1		1		1 + 1	
FREEDMAN Dougie	4 + 15	1	1	1				
GRABBAN Lewis	0 + 2		0 + 1					
GREEN Stuart	7 + 3	2	1					
HALL Ryan	0 + 1				0 + 1			
HALLS John	5							
HILL Clint	28	3			0 + 1		2	
HILLS Lee	6 + 6	1			1			
HUDSON Mark	45	2	1		1		2	
HUGHES Jeff	4 + 6							
IDRIZAJ Besian	3 + 4							
IFILL Paul	5 + 8	2					0 + 2	
KENNEDY Mark	8							
KUDJODJI Ben	0 + 1							
KUQI Shefki	2 + 6		1					
LAWRENCE Matt	36 + 1	1	0 + 1		1		1 + 1	
MARTIN Dave	2 + 7	1						
MORRISON Clinton	33 + 10	16	0 + 1		1		2	
MOSES Victor	9 + 4	3			0 + 1		1 + 1	
REID Kyel	0 + 2							
ROBINSON Ashley	0 + 6							
SCANNELL Sean	10 + 13	2			1		1	
SCOWCROFT James	35 + 3	9			1		0 + 1	
SINCLAIR Scott	6	2					2	
SOARES Tom	38 + 1	6	1				2	
SONGO'O Franck	9							
SPERONI Julian	46						2	
WATSON Ben	41 + 1	5	1		1		2	2

DAGENHAM & REDBRIDGE (DIV 2: 20th)

Player	P/FL App	Goals	FLC App	Goals	FAC App	Goals	Others App	Goals
ARBER Mark	16	1						
BAIDOO Shabazz	1 + 2							
BENSON Paul	19 + 3	6			2	3	2	
BOARDMAN Jon	22 + 5		1		3		2	
COOK Anthony	0 + 1							
FOSTER Danny	31 + 1	1	1		3			
GAIN Peter	18	1						
GOODWIN Lee	0 + 1							
GRAHAM Richie	4 + 3						0 + 1	
GREEN Dominic	2 + 10							
GRIFFITHS Scott	41		1		3		3	
HALL Ryan	2 + 6	2						
HUKE Shane	31 + 5	2	0 + 1		3	1	3	
MOORE Chris	13 + 13	2	1		2		1 + 2	1
NURSE Jon	23 + 7	1	1		1 + 1	1	0 + 2	
OKUONGHAE Magnus	9 + 1						1	
PATTERSON Marlon	5 + 1							
RAINFORD Dave	28 + 1	8	1		1		3	
ROBERTS Tony	43		1		3		3	
SAUNDERS Sam	21 + 1	1	1		1		1	
SLOMA Sam	22 + 7	2	1		3		2 + 1	
SMITH Ross	23	1			1 + 1		1 + 1	
SOUTHAM Glen	44 + 1	2	1		3		3	
STREVENS Ben	39 + 7	15	0 + 1	1	2 + 1	3	2	
TAIWO Soloman	4 + 6						2	
TAYLOR Jamie	2 + 10	1			0 + 1		2 + 1	
THOMPSON Ed	3				0 + 1			
UDDIN Anwar	40 + 1	1	1		2 + 1		2	

DARLINGTON (DIV 2: 6th)

Player	P/FL App	Goals	FLC App	Goals	FAC App	Goals	Others App	Goals
ABBOTT Pawel	16 + 8	9	1		0 + 2			
AUSTIN Neil	23 + 6	2			1			
BARRAU Xavier	0 + 1				0 + 1		1	
BLUNDELL Gregg	17 + 19	6	0 + 1		2	1	1	
BRACKSTONE John	3		1		2			
BURGESS Kevin					0 + 1			
COLBECK Joe	4 + 2	2						
CUMMINS Micky	31 + 9	6	0 + 1		1 + 1		2 + 1	
FORAN Richie	11 + 1	2						
FOSTER Stephen	42	2	1		2		3	
GALL Kevin	7 + 1							
GREEN Matty	3 + 1						0 + 1	
HARTY Ian	0 + 1		0 + 1					
HODGE Bryan	7							
JOACHIM Julian	40	6	1		2		3	
KAZIMIERCZAK Prez	0 + 1							
KELTIE Clark	21 + 6	4			2		2	1
KENNEDY Jason	13	2					2	1
McBRIDE Kevin	3 + 3	1	1					
MAIN Curtis	0 + 1							
MAYO Paul	7	1						
MILLER Ian	18 + 10	2					0 + 1	1
N'DUMBU-NSUNGU Guy	4 + 4	3					0 + 2	
NELTHORPE Craig	4 + 3						0 + 1	
OAKES Andy	6						1	
PALMER Chris	4		1					
PARKER Ben	13						1	
PURDIE Rob	30 + 9	1	1		2		3	

	P/FL App	Goals	FLC App	Goals	FAC App	Goals	Others App	Goals
RAVENHILL Ricky	25 + 10	3	1		1		3	
REAY Sean	0 + 1							
RIDLEY Lee	6							
RYAN Tim	13						1	
SMITH Johann	3							
SMITH Martin	0 + 4							
STOCKDALE David	40 + 1		1		2		2	
VALENTINE Ryan	13 + 4							
WAINWRIGHT Neil	5 + 9						1 + 2	
WHITE Alan	35	1	1		2		3	
WISEMAN Scott	2 + 5				1		2	
WRIGHT Tommy	37 + 3	13	1	1	2	1	2	

DERBY COUNTY (PREM: 20th)

	P/FL App	Goals	FLC App	Goals	FAC App	Goals	Others App	Goals
ADDISON Miles	1							
BARNES Giles	14 + 7	1			2 + 1	1		
BEARDSLEY Jason			1					
BYWATER Steve	18		1					
CAMARA Mo	1		1	1				
CARROLL Roy	14							
DAVIS Claude	19				2			
EARNSHAW Robert	7 + 15	1	1		0 + 2	1		
EDWORTHY Marc	7 + 2				2			
FAGAN Craig	17 + 5		1		2			
FEILHABER Benny	1 + 9							
GHALY Hossam	13 + 2							
GRIFFIN Andy	13 + 2							
HOWARD Steve	14 + 6	1	0 + 1					
JOHNSON Michael	1 + 2				0 + 1			
JONES David	11 + 3	1	1					
LEACOCK Dean	22 + 4		1					
LEWIS Eddie	22 + 2				2 + 1			
McEVELEY Jay	21 + 8	2	1					
MACKEN Jon	0 + 3				0 + 1			
MALCOLM Bob	1		1					
MEARS Tyrone	22 + 3	1			1			
MILLER Kenny	30	4			3	2		
MILLS Danny	2				1			
MOORE Darren	29 + 2		1		1 + 1			
NYATANGA Lewin	2		1		2			
OAKLEY Matt	19	3			1			
PEARSON Stephen	23 + 1		0 + 1		2			
PRICE Lewis	6				3			
ROBERT Laurent	3 + 1							
SAVAGE Robbie	16				1			
SIMMONS Paris	0 + 1							
STERJOVSKI Mile	9 + 3							
STUBBS Alan	8							
TEALE Gary	9 + 9		1		2 + 1			
TODD Andy	14 + 5	1	0 + 1		3			
VILLA Emanuel	9 + 7	3			1			

DONCASTER ROVERS (DIV 1: 3rd)

	P/FL App	Goals	FLC App	Goals	FAC App	Goals	Others App	Goals
COPPINGER James	31 + 8	3	1		1 + 1		4	3
DYER Bruce							0 + 1	
ELLIOTT Stuart	1 + 9							
GREEN Paul	26 + 12	5			1		6	1
GREER Gordon	10 + 1	1	1 + 1		2		2	
GUY Lewis	13 + 16	6	1 + 1		1 + 1		4 + 2	2
HAYTER James	21 + 13	7	2	1	2	2	2 + 2	1
HEFFERNAN Paul	18 + 9	7	2	1			3	1
HIRD Sam	3 + 1						4 + 1	
LEE Graeme	0 + 1							
LOCKWOOD Adam	39	3	2		2		0 + 1	
McCAMMON Mark	23 + 9	4	0 + 2	1	1	1	1 + 4	2
McDAID Sean	14 + 10	1	1 + 1		1			
MILLS Matthew	29 + 5	3	1				6	
NELTHORPE Craig	0 + 2				0 + 1		0 + 1	
O'CONNOR James	40		2		2		5	
PRICE Jason	18 + 11	7			0 + 2		4	1
ROBERTS Gareth	35 + 2	3	2		1		5	
ROBERTS Steve	20 + 5				0 + 1		2 + 1	
SMITH Ben							1 + 1	
STOCK Brian	40	5			2		4	1
SULLIVAN Neil	46		2		2		5	
TAYLOR Gareth	4 + 8	1			0 + 2			
WELLENS Richie	45	6	2	1	2		3 + 1	
WILSON Mark	23 + 8	1	1 + 1				1	
WOODS Martin	7 + 8		2		2		2 + 1	2

EVERTON (PREM: 5th)

	P/FL App	Goals	FLC App	Goals	FAC App	Goals	Others App	Goals
ANICHEBE Victor	10 + 17	1	1 + 3		0 + 1		1 + 8	4
ARTETA Mikel	27 + 1	1	2				6 + 1	3
BAINES Leighton	13 + 9		0 + 1		1		3 + 2	
CAHILL Tim	18	7	3 + 1	1			6	2
CARSLEY Lee	33 + 1	1	5		1		9	
FERNANDES	9 + 3						1 + 1	
GRAVESEN Thomas	1 + 7		0 + 1	1			1 + 2	
HIBBERT Tony	22 + 2		2		1		4 + 4	
HOWARD Tim	36						8	
JAGIELKA Phil	27 + 7	1	5		1		7 + 2	1
JOHNSON Andy	20 + 9	6	2		1		6 + 1	4
LESCOTT Joleon	37 + 1	8	5		0 + 1		10	2
McFADDEN James	5 + 7	2	3		2	2	5	1
NEVILLE Phil	37		2		4 + 1		8	
OSMAN Leon	26 + 2	4	4		1		7	2
PIENAAR Steven	25 + 3	2	3		1		8	
RODWELL Jack	0 + 2						0 + 1	
STUBBS Alan	7 + 1	1	2		1		1 + 1	
VALENTE Nuno	8 + 1		3				3	
VAUGHAN James	0 + 8	1	0 + 2		1		0 + 2	1
VIDARSSON Bjarni							0 + 1	
WESSELS Stefan	2		2		1		2	
YAKUBU Ayegbeni	26 + 3	15	3	3	0 + 1		7	3
YOBO Joseph	29 + 1	1	1		2		7	

FULHAM (PREM: 17th)

	P/FL App	Goals	FLC App	Goals	FAC App	Goals	Others App	Goals
ANDREASEN Leon	9 + 4							
ASHTON Nathan	1							
BAIRD Chris	17 + 1		1		1 + 1			
BOCANEGRA Carlos	18 + 4	1	2		2			
BOUAZZA Hameur	15 + 5	1	1		1			
BROWN Wayne					1			
BULLARD Jimmy	15 + 2	2			1			
CHRISTANVAL Philippe	0 + 1							
DAVIES Simon	36 + 1	5	2		0 + 1			
DAVIS Steven	22		2		0 + 1		1	
DEMPSEY Clint	29 + 7	6	2		2			
DIOP Pape Bouba	0 + 2							
HANGELAND Brede	15							
HEALY David	15 + 15	4	1 + 1	1	2	1		
HUGHES Aaron	29 + 1		1		1			
JOHN Collins	0 + 2		0 + 1					
JOHNSON Eddie	4 + 2							
KAMARA Diomansy	17 + 11	5	1 + 1	1				
KELLER Kasey	13		1					
KNIGHT Zat	4							
KONCHESKY Paul	33		2		2			
KUQI Shefki	3 + 7							
McBRIDE Brian	14 + 3	4						
MURPHY Danny	28 + 5	5	1		1		1	1
NEVLAND Erik	2 + 6	2						
NIEMI Antti	22							
OMOZUSI Elliott	8		0 + 1					
PEARCE Ian	0 + 1		1					
SEOL Ki-Hyeon	4 + 8		1		0 + 2			
SMERTIN Alexei	11 + 4		1		1			
STALTERI Paul	13							
STEFANOVIC Dejan	13				2			
VOLZ Moritz	5 + 4		1		2			
WARNER Tony	3		1		1			

GILLINGHAM (DIV 1: 22nd)

	P/FL App	Goals	FLC App	Goals	FAC App	Goals	Others App	Goals
ARMSTRONG Craig	12 + 1		1				2	1
BA Georges	1 + 3							
BENTLEY Mark	32 + 1	2	1		1		1 + 1	1
BROWN Aaron	10 + 1	1	1		1		2	1
BYGRAVE Adam	13 + 2						1	
CLOHESSY Sean	16 + 1						2	
COGAN Barry	9 + 7	1	0 + 1		1		3	
COX Ian	20		1		1		1	
CROFTS Andrew	41	5	1		0 + 1			
CULLIP Danny	11							
CUMBERS Luis	2 + 4						0 + 1	
DICKSON Chris	9 + 3	7					2	4
FACEY Delroy	27 + 5	3	0 + 1		1		1	
FREEMAN Luke	0 + 1				0 + 1		0 + 1	
FULLER Barry	9 + 1							
GRAHAM David	7 + 9	3	1		1	1	0 + 1	
GRIFFITHS Leroy	4 + 20	2					0 + 1	
HAMILTON-OMOLE Marvin	3 + 2						1	
HOWARD Charlie	1						1 + 1	
JACKSON Simeon	14 + 4	4					1	
JUPP Duncan	2						1	
KING Simon	39 + 3		1		1		3	
LEWIS Stuart	6 + 4							

	P/FL		FLC		FAC		Others	
	App	Goals	App	Goals	App	Goals	App	
LOMAS Steve	8				1			
MAHER Kevin	7							
MILLER Adam	26 + 2	3						
MULLIGAN Gary	15 + 15	5	1		0 + 1		2	
NOWLAND Adam	4 + 1						0 + 1	
NUTTER John	23 + 1	1					1	
OLI Dennis	17 + 5	4					0 + 1	1
PUGH Andy	0 + 2		0 + 1					
RICHARDS Garry	12 + 2	1						
ROCASTLE Craig	2							
ROYCE Simon	33		1		1		1	
SIMMONDS Donovan	0 + 3							
SODJE Efe	12 + 1		1		1		1	
SOUTHALL Nicky	31 + 2	1	1		1		2	
STILLIE Derek	13 + 1						2	
STONE Craig	4 + 5		1				3	1
THURGOOD Stuart	11 + 1							
GRIMSBY TOWN (DIV 2: 16th)								
ATKINSON Rob	24	1			1		4	
BARNES Phil	42		1		1		7	
BENNETT Ryan	28 + 12	1	1		3		4	
BIRD Matthew	0 + 2							
BOLLAND Paul	33 + 2	4	1		2 + 1	1	6	1
BORE Peter	4 + 13	2	0 + 1		0 + 1		0 + 4	
BOSHELL Danny	38 + 2	6	1		1		6	1
BUTLER Martin	15 + 6	6			1			
CLARKE Jamie	27 + 2	2			2		6 + 1	1
FENTON Nick	40 + 2	2	1		3		7	1
HEGARTY Nick	27 + 3	4			1 + 1		5	
HIRD Sam	17				1			
HUNT James	32 + 5		1		3		5	
JARMAN Nathan	5 + 2						0 + 1	
JONES Gary	15 + 21	4	0 + 1		3	1	2 + 4	
LOGAN Shaleum	5	2						
MONTGOMERY Gary	4 + 1				2			
MULLIGAN Dave	4 + 2						1	
NEWEY Tom	42	1	1		3		6	
NORTH Danny	21 + 6	9	0 + 1	1	2		6 + 1	
RANKIN Isaiah	12 + 5		1				1	1
TAYLOR Andy	1 + 25	5			0 + 2		1 + 1	
TILL Peter	31 + 3	2	1		2 + 1		6	2
TONER Ciaran	25 + 5	3	1		2 + 1		2 + 1	1
WHITTLE Justin	14 + 4	1	1		0 + 1		2 + 1	
HARTLEPOOL UNITED (DIV 1: 15th)								
ANTWI Godwin	27	1	2		1 + 1		3	
BARKER Richie	31 + 5	13	2		2	2	3	1
BOLAND Willie	32 + 2		2		1		1	
BROWN James	31 + 4	10	2		2	1	2	2
BUDTZ Jan	28		2		2		2	
BULLOCK Lee	0 + 1							
CLARK Ben	14 + 5	1			1		2	
COLES Danny	3							
COLLINS Sam	10	2						
CRADDOCK Tom	1 + 3							
ELLIOTT Robbie	14 + 1						1	
FOLEY David	11 + 23		0 + 2	2			0 + 2	1
GIBB Ali	4 + 2		0 + 1				1 + 2	
HUMPHREYS Ritchie	43 + 2	3	1		2		2	
LEE Graeme	3							
LEE-BARRETT Arran	18						1	
LIDDLE Gary	41	2	2		1 + 1	1	2	
McCUNNIE Jamie	23 + 6	1	2		2		2 + 1	
MACKAY Michael	10 + 14	5			1 + 1		1 + 2	1
MONKHOUSE Andy	21 + 4	2	0 + 1		0 + 2			
MOORE Ian	22 + 2	6	2	1	2	1	2	1
NELSON Michael	44 + 1	2	2		2		2	
NOLAN Eddie	11				1			
PORTER Joel	24 + 15	9	0 + 2		0 + 1	1	1 + 2	3
ROBSON Matty	6 + 11	1	2				3	
SWEENEY Antony	27 + 9	4	1		2		2	
THOMPSON Alan	7	1						
TURNBULL Stephen	0 + 1							
HEREFORD UNITED (DIV 2: 3rd)								
AINSWORTH Lionel	13 + 2	4	2	3	2	1		
BECKWITH Dean	38	2	2		5		1	
BENJAMIN Trevor	15 + 19	10	2		6	1	1	
BROADHURST Karl	22 + 1		2		1			
BROWN Wayne	44		2		6			
COLLINS Lee	14 + 2				4			
DIAGOURAGA Toumani	41	2	2		6		1	

	P/FL		FLC		FAC		Others	
	App	Goals	App	Goals	App	Goals	App	
EASTON Clint	36 + 3	3	2	1	2 + 1		1	
ESSON Ryan	1							
GLEESON Stephen	3 + 1							
GUINAN Steve	20 + 8	3	0 + 2		0 + 2			
GWYNNE Sam	9 + 6				2 + 1		0 + 1	
HOOPER Gary	19	11						
IGOE Sammy	4							
INGHAM Mike							1	
JOHNSON Simon	22 + 11	5	0 + 1		3 + 1	1	1	
McCLENAHAN Trent	38	1	2		3 + 1		1	
McCOMBE John	23 + 4				3 + 1	1	1	
MacDONALD Sherjill	7	6						
PALMER Marcus	0 + 1							
ROBINSON Theo	32 + 11	13	2	1	6	2	0 + 1	
ROSE Richard	31	1	2		4 + 1		1	
SMITH Ben	42 + 2	5	2		6	1	0 + 1	
TAYLOR Kris	22 + 9	1	0 + 2		4 + 2		1	
THRELFALL Robbie	6 + 3				3			
WEALE Chris	1							
WEBB Luke	3 + 11	3					1	
HUDDERSFIELD TOWN (DIV 1: 10th)								
AKINS Lucas	0 + 3						0 + 1	
BECKETT Luke	25 + 11	8	1		3 + 2	4	1	
BERRETT James	10 + 5	1			2			
BOOTH Andy	28 + 10	9	0 + 1		2 + 1			
BRANDON Chris	25 + 3	2	1		2	1	1	
BROADBENT Danny	0 + 5							
CADAMARTERI Danny	10 + 2	3			1 + 1			
CLARKE Nathan	44	2	1		4		1	
CLARKE Tom	2 + 1						0 + 1	
COLLINS Michael	35 + 6	2	1		3 + 2	1	1	1
GLENNON Matty	45		1		5		1	
HARDY Aaron	5 + 1		0 + 1				1	
HOLDSWORTH Andy	43 + 1	3			5		1	
JEVONS Phil	17 + 4	7			3 + 1	2		
KAMARA Malvin	33 + 10	3	1		3 + 2	2	1	
KEOGH Richard	9	1					1	
KILLOCK Shane	1							
MIRFIN David	23 + 6	1	1		3 + 1			
PAGE Robert	18	1			2			
RACCHI Danny	0 + 3							
SCHOFIELD Danny	19 + 6	2	1		4 + 1		1	
SINCLAIR Frank	28 + 1		1		5			
SKARZ Joe	22 + 5		1		2 + 1		1	
SMITHIES Alex	1 + 1							
WALLWORK Ronnie	16	3			2			
WILLIAMS Robbie	24 + 1	2			3			
WORTHINGTON Jon	19 + 6		1		1			
YOUNG Matthew	4 + 4						0 + 1	
HULL CITY (CHAMP: 3rd)								
ASHBEE Ian	42	3	1 + 2				3	
ATKINSON Will					0 + 1			
BARMBY Nick	5 + 10	1			1		3	2
BRIDGES Michael	1 + 6		2	1				
BROWN Wayne	41	1	3				3	
CAMPBELL Fraizer	32 + 2	15					3	
CLEMENT Neil	4 + 1							
COLES Danny	1							
COLLINS Sam					1			
DAWSON Andy	24 + 5	1	1 + 1				3	
DELANEY Damien	20 + 2		3		1			
DOYLE Nathan	0 + 1		1		1		0 + 2	1
DUKE Matt	3		1					
ELLIOTT Stuart	3 + 4		3	1	1			
FAGAN Craig	4 + 4						0 + 3	
FEATHERSTONE Nicky	0 + 6		2 + 1					
FOLAN Caleb	18 + 11	8			1		0 + 3	1
FRANCE Ryan	3 + 10				1			
GARCIA Richard	35 + 3	5	1 + 1	1	0 + 1		3	1
HUGHES Bryan	26 + 9	1	1				3	
LIVERMORE David	9 + 11	1	3		1			
McPHEE Stephen	7 + 12	2	3	1				
MARNEY Dean	35 + 6	6	0 + 2		1		0 + 1	
MYHILL Bo	43		2		1		3	
OKOCHA Jay Jay	10 + 8		1					
PEDERSEN Henrik	18 + 3	4	1					
RICKETTS Sam	44		1 + 1				3	
TURNER Michael	44	5	3		1		3	
WALTON Simon	5 + 5							
WINDASS Dean	29 + 8	11	0 + 1		0 + 1	2	3	2

IPSWICH TOWN (CHAMP: 8th)

Player	P/FL App	P/FL Goals	FLC App	FLC Goals	FAC App	FAC Goals	Others App
ALEXANDER Neil	29		1		1		
BRUCE Alex	35+1		1		1		
BYWATER Steve	17						
CASEMENT Chris	2+1						
CLARKE Billy	9+11		0+1		1		
COUNAGO Pablo	35+8	12	1		1		
DE VOS Jason	46	2	1				
GARVAN Owen	39+4	2	1	1	1		
HARDING Dan	29+1	1	1				
HAYNES Danny	18+23	7	0+1		1		
KUQI Shefki	2+2						
LEE Alan	37+8	11	1	1	0+1		
LEGWINSKI Sylvain	9+6	2	0+1				
MILLER Tommy	32+5	5	1				
NAYLOR Richard	6+1				0+1		
NORRIS David	9	1					
O'CALLAGHAN George	1						
PETERS Jaime	0+5				0+1		
QUINN Alan	14+2	1	1				
RHODES Jordan	0+8	1	1				
ROBERTS Gary	10+11	1	1		1		
SIMPSON Danny	7+1						
SITO	11+2	1	1		1		
SUMULIKOSKI Velice	10+6	1	1				
TROTTER Liam	2+4	1	1		1		
WALTERS Jon	39+1	13	1		1		
WILLIAMS Gavin	10+3				1		
WILNIS Fabian	9+4				1		
WRIGHT David	39+2	2	1		1		

LEEDS UNITED (DIV 1: 5th)

Player	P/FL App	P/FL Goals	FLC App	FLC Goals	FAC App	FAC Goals	Others App	Others Goals
AMEOBI Tomi			1				0+1	
ANDREWS Wayne	1						1	
ANKERGREN Casper	43		2		2		3	
BAYLY Rob			0+1					
BECKFORD Jermaine	40	20	0+2		2		3	
CAROLE Seb	17+11	3	2		2		1+1	
CLAPHAM Jamie	12+1				0+1		0+1	
CONSTANTINE Leon	1+3	1			0+2		1	1
DA COSTA Filipe	0+4				0+1		1+1	
DELPH Fabian	0+1		0+1					
DE VRIES Mark	1+5	1					2	
DOUGLAS Jonathan	22+2	3	2		1		3+1	
ELDING Anthony	4+5	1						
ELLIOTT Tom			1					
FLO Tore Andre	4+18	3						
FREEDMAN Dougie	9+2	5					3	1
GARDNER Scott	1		1					
HEATH Matt	25+1	1	2		2		1+1	
HOWSON Jonny	21+5	3	2		2		5	2
HUGHES Andy	32+8	1	1		1		0+2	
HUNTINGTON Paul	12+5	1			2		5	1
JOHNSON Brad	18+3	3					3	
KANDOL Tresor	32+9	11	2		2		0+3	
KENTON Darren	16							
KILKENNY Neil	16	1					3	
KISHISHEV Radostin	5+2							
LEWIS Eddie	1		1					
LUCAS David	3				0+1		2	
MADDEN Simon							1	
MICHALIK Lubo	17						3	
PARKER Ben	6+3		2		2		2	
PRUTTON David	38+5	4	2				4	
RICHARDSON Frazer	39	1	1		1		4	
RUI MARQUES	34+2	3	1		1		1	
SHEEHAN Alan	10	1						
SWEENEY Peter	6+3							
THOMPSON Alan	9+4	3					1	
WESTLAKE Ian	10+10	1	0+1	1	1		1	
WESTON Curtis	1+6	1	0+1		1+1		1	

LEICESTER CITY (CHAMP: 22nd)

Player	P/FL App	P/FL Goals	FLC App	FLC Goals	FAC App	FAC Goals	Others App
ALNWICK Ben	8						
BELL David	6						
BORI Gabor	4+2						
CAMPBELL DJ	17+11	4	2+2	1			
CHAMBERS Ashley	1+4						
CHAMBERS James	15+9		2+1				
CLAPHAM Jamie	11						
CLARKE Clive	2						
CLEMENCE Stephen	30+1	2	3		1		
CORT Carl	7+7		1	1			
DE VRIES Mark	5+1	1	1+1				
ETUHU Kelvin	2+2						
FRYATT Matty	21+9	2	3+1	1	1		
FULOP Marton	24		3				
HAYES Jonny	1+6						
HAYLES Barry	9+9	2			1		
HENDERSON Paul	14		1		1		
HENDRIE Lee	9	1					
HOWARD Steve	20+1	6			1		
HUME Iain	34+6	11	3		1		
JOHN Collins	7+4	2					
KAEBI Hossein	2+1						
KENTON Darren	6+4		2+1		1		
KING Andy	5+6	1			0+1		
KISHISHEV Radostin	2+5		2				
KISNORBO Patrick	41	3	3		1		
LACZKO Zsolt	5+4						
McAULEY Gareth	43+1	2	4	1	1		
MATTOCK Joe	26+5		2				
MAYBURY Alan	1		0+2				
NEWTON Shaun	7+3		1				
N'GOTTY Bruno	30+8		4		0+1		
OAKLEY Matt	20						
ODHIAMBO Eric			0+1				
PORTER Levi			0+1				
SAPPLETON Ricky	0+1						
SHEEHAN Alan	17+3	1	3	1	1		
STEARMAN Richard	37+2	2	2+2	1	1		
WESOLOWSKI James	15+7		2	1	1		
WORLEY Harry	1+1						

LEYTON ORIENT (DIV 1: 13th)

Player	P/FL App	P/FL Goals	FLC App	FLC Goals	FAC App	FAC Goals	Others App
BARCHAM Andy	15+10	1					
BOYD Adam	40+4	14	1+1	1	2	2	1
CHAMBERS Adam	45	3	1+1		2		2
CORDEN Wayne	17+9		1		1+1		1
DANIELS Charlie	24+7	2	1+1		2		1+1
DEMETRIOU Jason	31+12	3	2		2		2
ECHANOMI Efe	0+14		1+1		0+1		1+1
FORTUNE Clayton	0+1						
GRAY Wayne	30+8	8	2		2	2	1
IBEHRE Jabo	18+13	7			0+1		1
MELLIGAN John	25+7	3	2		1+1		2
MKANDAWIRE Tamika	35	3	2		2		1
MORRIS Glenn	16				1		2
NELSON Stuart	30		2		1		1
OJI Sam	9+4						2
PALMER Aiden	23		2				1
PIRES Loick	0+1						
PURCHES Steve	35+2	1			2		0+1
SAAH Brian	23+2	1			1		1
TERRY Paul	41+2		2		2		1+1
THELWELL Alton	27+1		2		1		1
THORNTON Sean	22+9	3	1		0+1		1

LINCOLN CITY (DIV 2: 15th)

Player	P/FL App	P/FL Goals	FLC App	FLC Goals	FAC App	FAC Goals	Others App	Others Goals
AMOO Ryan	10+3	1	1		0+1		1	
BEEVERS Lee	37		1				1	
BENCHERIF Hamza	11+1	1	1				1	
BROWN Nat	23+4		1					
CLARKE Shane	11+5							
CROFT Gary	20						2	
DODDS Louis	38+3	9	0+1				2	
DUFFY Ayden	3+1							
FORRESTER Jamie	37+3	12	1	1	2	1	0+1	
FRECKLINGTON Lee	31+3	4	1		2		1	
GREEN Paul	36		1	1	2		1	
HAND Jamie	19+6						1	
HONE Daniel	20+3	1			2			
JOHN-LEWIS Lenny	15+6	3			0+1		1	
KERR Scott	33+3	1	1		2		1	
KING Gary	3+3	1						
MARRIOTT Alan	34		1		2		1	
MOSES Adie	16+2	1	1		2			
N'GUESSAN Dany	23+14	7	1		1+1		0+1	
PEMBLETON Martin	4+2							
RIDLEY Lee	15							
RYAN Ollie	4+11				1			
SMITH Adam	0+4							
SMITH Ben	9							
STALLARD Mark	14+11	2	0+1		1		2	
TORPEY Steve	7+6							

Player	P/FL App	P/FL Goals	FLC App	FLC Goals	FAC App	FAC Goals	Others App
WARLOW Owain	6 + 11		0 + 1		1 + 1		1
WATT Phil	1				0 + 1		
WRIGHT Ben	26 + 8	15	1		2		0 + 1
LIVERPOOL (PREM: 4th)							
AGGER Daniel	4 + 1						1
ALONSO Xabi	16 + 3	2			3		4
ARBELOA Alvaro	26 + 2		3		1		8 + 1
AURELIO Fabio	13 + 3	1	3		0 + 1		7 + 2
BABEL Ryan	15 + 15	4	2		4	1	8 + 5	5
BENAYOUN Yossi	15 + 15	4	1 + 2	1	3	3	7 + 4	3
CARRAGHER Jamie	34 + 1		3		3 + 1		13
CROUCH Peter	9 + 12	5	3		4	2	5 + 3	4
EL ZHAR Nabil			1 + 1	1	0 + 1		
FINNAN Steve	21 + 3		1		3		6 + 1
GERRARD Steven	32 + 2	11	1 + 1	1	1 + 2	3	13	6
HOBBS Jack	1 + 1		2 + 1				
HYYPIA Sami	24 + 3	1			4	1	12 + 1	2
INSUA Emiliano	2 + 1						
ITANDJE Charles			3		4		
KEWELL Harry	8 + 2		0 + 1		0 + 1		1 + 2
KUYT Dirk	24 + 8	3			2 + 2	1	10 + 2	7
LETO Sebastian			2				2 + 1
LUCAS	12 + 6		3		3 + 1	1	2 + 5
MASCHERANO Javier	25	1	0 + 1		1 + 1		13
PENNANT Jermaine	14 + 4	2			2		2 + 3
PLESSIS Damien	2						
REINA Pepe	38						14
RIISE John Arne	22 + 7		0 + 1		4		5 + 5
SISSOKO Momo	6 + 3	1	2				2 + 1
SKRTEL Martin	13 + 1				1		5
TORRES Fernando	29 + 4	24	1		3	1	10 + 1	6
VORONIN Andriy	13 + 6	5	1		0 + 1		4 + 3	1
LUTON TOWN (DIV 1: 24th)							
ALNWICK Ben	4						
ANDREW Calvin	19 + 20	2	0 + 2		4 + 1	2	2
ASAFU-ADJAYE Ed	7						
BEAVAN George	1 + 1						
BELL David	32	4	3	1	5		1
BRILL Dean	37		3		5		2
BRKOVIC Ahmet	0 + 1		0 + 1				1 + 1
CHARLES Ryan	6 + 1	1					
COYNE Chris	18		3		4	1	
CURRIE Darren	25 + 6	2	1 + 1		4 + 1		
DAVIS Sol	15						
EDWARDS David	18 + 1	4	2		4		1
EMANUEL Lewis	15 + 2	2	1				1
FOJUT Jaroslaw	15 + 1	2	2		3	1	2
FORDE David	5		1				
FURLONG Paul	24 + 8	8	3 + 1	2	1 + 1		1	2
GOODALL Alan	25 + 4	1	1	3	2 + 1		1
GRANT Anthony	1 + 3				0 + 1		
HOWELLS Jake	0 + 1						
HUTCHISON Don	15 + 6		1		2		2	1
JACKSON Richard	27 + 2		3		4		1
KEANE Keith	27 + 1		1 + 1		2 + 1		1
LANGLEY Richard	0 + 1						
McVEIGH Paul	15 + 10		1 + 3		0 + 2		1 + 1
MORGAN Dean	8 + 8	1	3 + 1				0 + 1
O'LEARY Stephen	10 + 6				0 + 1		0 + 1
PARKIN Sam	12 + 7	5	1				
PERRY Chris	35	1	3		4		2
PESCHISOLIDO Paul	2 + 2						0 + 1	1
ROBINSON Steve	24 + 3		3	1	3		1
SPRING Matty	44	9	4	2	5		1	1
TALBOT Drew	16 + 11		2 + 1	2	3 + 1		1 + 1
WILSON Marc	4						
MACCLESFIELD TOWN (DIV 2: 19th)							
ASHMORE James	7 + 1						
ASHTON Neil	19	1					
BLACKMAN Nick	1 + 10	1					
BRAIN Jonny	29				2		
BRISLEY Shaun	9 + 1	2					
CRESSWELL Ryan	19	1					
DENNIS Kristian	0 + 1	1					
DIMECH Luke	23 + 3		1		1		1
DOUGHTY Phil	5 + 1						
DUNFIELD Terry	40 + 1	1	1		1		
EDGHILL Richard	13 + 2		1				
EVANS Gareth	20 + 22	7	0 + 1		1		0 + 2
FLYNN Matthew							0 + 1

Player	P/FL App	P/FL Goals	FLC App	FLC Goals	FAC App	FAC Goals	Others App
GREEN Franny	35 + 6	11	1		0 + 1		1
GRITTON Martin	27 + 4	8			1	1	2
HADFIELD Jordan	0 + 2						2
HESSEY Sean	26						
HUSBANDS Michael	2		1				1	1
JENNINGS James	5 + 6						1 + 1
LEE Tommy	17 + 1		1		1		
McINTYRE Kevin	22 + 1	2	1		1		1
McNULTY Jimmy	13 + 6	1			1		2
MILLAR Christian	0 + 2						
MORLEY Dave	2 + 2	1			1		2
MURRAY Adam	22 + 1	1	1				
ONIBUJE Fola	0 + 1						
REGAN Carl	18 + 2		1		1		1
REID Izak	17 + 8	2					1 + 1
REID Levi	29 + 2	2	1		1		2
ROONEY John	1 + 1						
SPENCER Scott	0 + 3						
SYMES Michael	10 + 4	1					
TEAGUE Andrew	1						
THOMAS Danny	43	4	1		1		1
TOLLEY Jamie	20 + 4	2			0 + 1		
WALKER Richard	10						
WILES Simon	1 + 16		0 + 1		0 + 1		2
MANCHESTER CITY (PREM: 9th)							
BALL Michael	19 + 9		3 + 1		3		
BENJANI	13	3					
BIANCHI Rolando	7 + 12	4	3		1		0 + 2
BOJINOV Valeri	1 + 2						
CAICEDO Felipe	0 + 10						
CASTILLO Nery	2 + 5				2		
CORLUKA Vedran	34 + 1		3		2		
DABO Ousmane	0 + 1						
DICKOV Paul	0 + 1						
DUNNE Richard	36		3		3		
ELANO	29 + 5	8	2		1	2	1
ETUHU Kelvin	2 + 4	1	0 + 1		0 + 1	1	
EVANS Ched	0 + 1						
FERNANDES Gelson	21 + 5	2	2 + 1		1 + 2		
GARRIDO Javier	21 + 6		2				
GEOVANNI	2 + 17	3	2 + 1		0 + 1		
HAMANN Didi	26 + 3		2		3		
HART Joe	26		3		3		
IRELAND Stephen	32 + 1	4	3		2 + 1	1	
ISAKSSON Andreas	5		1				
JOHNSON Michael	23	2	2				
LOGAN Shaleum			2				
MPENZA Emile	8 + 7	2	1 + 1	1	1		
ONUOHA Nedum	13 + 3	1	2 + 1		2		
PETROV Martin	34	5	3		3		
RICHARDS Micah	25		2		2		
SAMARAS Georgios	2 + 3		2	1			
SCHMEICHEL Kasper	7						
STURRIDGE Daniel	2 + 1	1			0 + 1	1	
SUN JIHAI	7 + 7		2				
VASSELL Darius	21 + 6	6	1 + 1		3		
WILLIAMSON Sam	0 + 1						
MANCHESTER UNITED (PREM: 1st)							
ANDERSON	16 + 8		1		2 + 2		6 + 3
BARDSLEY Phil			1				
BROWN Wes	34 + 2	1	0 + 1		4		10 + 1
CAMPBELL Fraizer	0 + 1		0 + 1				
CARRICK Michael	24 + 7	2	0 + 1		3 + 1		12 + 1
DONG Fangzhuo	1 + 3		1				0 + 1
EAGLES Chris			1				1
EVANS Jonny			1				1 + 1
EVRA Patrice	33				4		11
FERDINAND Rio	35	2			4		12	1
FLETCHER Darren	5 + 11		1		2	2	5 + 2
FOSTER Ben	1						
GIGGS Ryan	26 + 5	3			2		5 + 5	3
HARGREAVES Owen	16 + 7	2			2 + 1		5 + 3
KUSZCZAK Tomasz	8 + 1		1		0 + 1		3 + 2
MARTIN Lee			1				
NANI	16 + 10	3	1		2	1	7 + 5
NEVILLE Gary							0 + 1	1
O'SHEA John	10 + 18		1		1 + 1		5 + 2
PARK Ji-Sung	8 + 4	1			2		4
PIQUE Gerard	5 + 4		1				3	2
RONALDO	31 + 3	31			3	3	12	8
ROONEY Wayne	25 + 2	12			3 + 1	2	11 + 1	4

	P/FL App	P/FL Goals	FLC App	FLC Goals	FAC App	FAC Goals	Others App
SAHA Louis	6 + 11	5			1 + 1		3 + 2
SCHOLES Paul	22 + 2	1			1 + 2		7
SILVESTRE Mikael	3						2 + 1
SIMPSON Danny	1 + 2		1		0 + 1		2 + 1
TEVEZ Carlos	31 + 3	14			2	1	6 + 6 4
VAN DER SAR Edwin	29				4		11
VIDIC Nemanja	32	1			3		10
MANSFIELD TOWN (DIV 2: 23rd)							
ARNOLD Nathan	21 + 11	4	1		1 + 1		1
ATKINSON Will	10 + 2						
BELL Lee	23	1	1		3 + 1		
BOULDING Micky	43	22	1		3	3	
BOULDING Rory	4 + 7		0 + 1		2 + 1	1	0 + 1
BRIGGS Keith	10 + 3						
BROWN Simon	15 + 14	4			2 + 1		
BULLOCK Lee	5						
BURRELL Warren	0 + 1						
BUXTON Jake	40	2	1		4		1
DAWSON Stephen	43	2	1		4		1
D'LARYEA Jon	23 + 6				3 + 1		
GOWARD Ryan	0 + 2						
HAMSHAW Matt	45		2		4	1	1
HOLMES Ian	4 + 12	1			1 + 1	2	1
HORLOCK Kevin	0 + 5						
JELLEYMAN Gareth	37 + 2		1		4	1	1
JOHN-BAPTISTE Alex	25				1		
KITCHEN Ashley	1				0 + 1		
LOUIS Jefferson	14 + 4	4					
McALISKEY John	9 + 7	2	1		0 + 2		1
McALLISTER Sean	5 + 2						
McINTOSH Martin	9 + 2	1	1				
MARTIN Dan	21 + 5		1		4		0 + 1
MUGGLETON Carl	36		1		4		1
MULLINS Johnny	42 + 1	2	1	1	4		1
REET Danny	0 + 2						0 + 1
SLEATH Danny	2 + 5		0 + 1		0 + 1		1
TRIMMER Lewis	0 + 2						
WAINWRIGHT Neil	1 + 4						
WHITE Jason	10 + 3						
WOOD Chris	8 + 5						1
MIDDLESBROUGH (PREM: 13th)							
ALIADIERE Jeremie	26 + 3	5			2		
ALVES Afonso	7 + 4	6			2 + 1		
ARCA Julio	23 + 1				5		
BOATENG George	29 + 4	1	1 + 1		1 + 2		
CATTERMOLE Lee	10 + 14	1	2		2		
CRADDOCK Tom	1 + 2		0 + 1				
DAVIES Andrew	3 + 1		1 + 1				
DOWNING Stewart	38	9	2		4 + 1	1	
GROUNDS Jonathan	5				2		
HINES Seb	0 + 1		0 + 1		1		
HUTCHINSON Ben	0 + 8	1			1		
HUTH Robert	9 + 4	1			3		
JOHNSON Adam	3 + 16	1	1		2 + 2		
JONES Brad	1				2		
LEE Dong-Gook	5 + 9		2	1	1 + 1	1	
McMAHON Tony	0 + 1				1		
MIDO	8 + 4	2	0 + 1		2 + 2		
O'NEIL Gary	25 + 1				2 + 1		
OWENS Graeme			0 + 1				
POGATETZ Manny	23 + 1				5		
RIGGOTT Chris	9 + 1	1	1				
ROCHEMBACK Fabio	21 + 5	1	2	1	5		
SCHWARZER Mark	34				5		
SHAWKY Mohamed	3 + 2		1				
TAYLOR Andrew	18 + 1		2				
TUNCAY	27 + 7	8	1		1 + 2		
TURNBULL Ross	3						
WHEATER David	34	3	2		4	1	
WOODGATE Jonathan	16						
YAKUBU Ayegbeni	2						
YOUNG Luke	35	1	2		5		
MILLWALL (DIV 1: 17th)							
AKINFENWA Adebayo	1 + 6				1 + 1		
ALEXANDER Gary	32 + 4	7	1		3	1	0 + 1
ARDLEY Neal	0 + 1						
BAKAYO Zoumana	5 + 5				2 + 1		
BARRON Scott	7 + 5		0 + 1		2 + 1		1
BIGNOT Marcus	17 + 5				3		
BOWES Gary	0 + 1						

	P/FL App	P/FL Goals	FLC App	FLC Goals	FAC App	FAC Goals	Others App
BRAMMER Dave	23				1 + 1		
BRKOVIC Ahmet	15 + 10	2			2	1	
COCHRANE Justin	0 + 1						
CRAIG Tony	5	1					
DAY Chris	5		1				1
DOUGLAS Rab	7						
DUNNE Alan	17 + 2	3	1		2	1	1
EDWARDS Preston	0 + 1						0 + 1
EVANS Rhys	21				1		
FORBES Adrian	6 + 5				2 + 1		
FRAMPTON Andy	28 + 2	1	1		3		1
FUSEINI Ali	31 + 6	2			4		
GAYNOR Ross	1 + 2				2 + 1		
GRABBAN Lewis	10 + 3	3			1		
HACKETT Chris	1 + 5						1
HARRIS Neil	19 + 8	3	1		1 + 1		1
HODGE Bryan	10				3		
HOSKINS Will	9 + 1	2			2	2	
KARACAN Jem	7						0 + 1
KILBEY Tom							0 + 1
LAIRD Marc	16 + 1	1			1		
MARTIN Dave	7 + 4	2					
MAY Ben	4 + 4		1		1 + 1	1	1 1
O'HARA Jamie	10 + 4	2			1		
PIDGELEY Lenny	13				4		
ROBINSON Paul	45	3	1		5		1
SAVAGE Bas	9 + 2	2			1		
SENDA Danny	39 + 1	1	1		3		1
SHAW Richard	16 + 2						
SIMPSON Jay	34 + 7	6			4	1	1 1
SMITH Ryan	9 + 1				1		
SPILLER Danny	6	1	1				
WHITBREAD Zak	21 + 2	3	1		3		1
MILTON KEYNES DONS (DIV 2: 1st)							
ABBEY Nathan			2		1		
ANDREWS Keith	40 + 1	12			4		2
BALDOCK Sam	0 + 5		0 + 1		1 + 2		
BROUGHTON Drewe	2 + 11		1	1	1		2 + 2
CAMERON Colin	21 + 8	3			0 + 1		4 + 1 1
CARAYOL Mustapha			1				0 + 1
CARBON Matt	0 + 3						0 + 1
DIALLO Drissa	30		2		1		4
DOBSON Craig	1						
DYER Lloyd	43 + 2	11	0 + 2				3
EDDS Gareth	2 + 5		1 + 1		1		0 + 1
GALLEN Kevin	15 + 9	8	1 + 1	1	1		4
GUERET Willy	46						6
HADFIELD Jordan	6 + 7						
HOWELL Luke	8		1				2
JOHNSON Jemal	17 + 22	5			1	1	6 2
KNIGHT Leon	15 + 2	4	1		1		
LEWINGTON Dean	45		1		1		6
LIVERMORE Jake	0 + 5						
McGOVERN Jon-Paul	2 + 1		2		1		
MILES John	7 + 5						
MURPHY Kieran	1 + 2		2				
NAVARRO Alan	38 + 1	3	2		1		5
O'HANLON Sean	41 + 2	4	1		1		6 1
REGAN Carl	8 + 1	1					
SMART Bally	0 + 8				1		1 + 1
STIRLING Jude	21 + 13	2	2				3 + 2
SWAILES Danny	40	4	1		1		5 1
TAYLOR Scott							0 + 2
WILBRAHAM Aaron	28 + 7	10	1 + 1		0 + 1		1 + 1
WRIGHT Mark	29 + 5	13	1 + 1		1		3 + 1 2
MORECAMBE (DIV 2: 11th)							
ADAMS Danny	42		3		1		4
ALLEN Damien	16 + 4	2	2				2
ARTELL Dave	34 + 2	3	3	1			5
BAKER Carl	40 + 2	10	3	1	1		2
BENTLEY Jim	43	6	3	1	1		2
BLINKHORN Matty	36 + 5	10	1 + 1		0 + 1		5 1
BURNS Jamie	4 + 3		0 + 1				2 + 1 1
CRESSWELL Ryan	2						
CURTIS Wayne	16 + 20	2	0 + 1		1		2 + 2
DAVIES Scott	10						3
DRENCH Steven	3 + 1						2
DRUMMOND Stewart	17 + 1	2					1 + 1
GRAND Simon	4 + 2	1	0 + 1		1		3 + 1
HOWARD Mike	2 + 2						3 + 1
HUNTER Garry	19 + 19	1	0 + 3		0 + 1		5 1

	P/FL		FLC		FAC		Others
	App	Goals	App	Goals	App	Goals	App
JALAL Shwan	12						
JARVIS Paul							0 + 1
LANGFORD Andy							0 + 1
LEWIS Joe	19		3				
LLOYD Paul	1 + 6						1 + 2
LOACH Scott	2						1
McLACHLAN Fraser	1		1				
McSTAY Henry	12 + 1						1
NEWBY Jon	11 + 21	6	0 + 1	1	1		3 + 2 3
SORVEL Neil	14 + 8		3		1		2
STANLEY Craig	41	2	3		1		3
THOMPSON Garry	36 + 4	7	2 + 1	1	1		3
TWISS Michael	27 + 9	6	3		1		5 + 1
YATES Adam	42 + 2		3		1		6

NEWCASTLE UNITED (PREM: 12th)

	P/FL		FLC		FAC		Others
	App	Goals	App	Goals	App	Goals	App
AMEOBI Shola	2 + 4		2				
BARTON Joey	20 + 3	1					
BEYE Habib	27 + 2	1	1				
BUTT Nicky	35		0 + 2		2		
CACAPA	16 + 3	1	1		2	1	
CARR Stephen	8 + 2				2		
CARROLL Andy	1 + 3				0 + 2		
DIATTA Lamine	0 + 2						
DUFF Damien	12 + 4				3	1	
EDGAR David	2 + 3		0 + 1				
EMRE	6 + 8	1	1 + 1		1		
ENRIQUE	18 + 5		2		3		
FAYE Abdoulaye	20 + 2	1	1		1		
GEREMI	24 + 3	1	1		1		
GIVEN Shay	19		2		3		
HARPER Steve	19 + 2						
LUA-LUA Kazenga	0 + 2				0 + 3		
MARTINS Oba	23 + 8	9	1 + 1	1			
MILNER James	25 + 4	2	1		2	1	
N'ZOGBIA Charles	27 + 5	3	2		3		
OWEN Michael	24 + 5	11	1		3	1	
RAMAGE Peter	0 + 3						
ROZEHNAL David	16 + 5		1		1 + 2		
SMITH Alan	26 + 7		2		2		
SOLANO Nobby	0 + 1		1				
TAYLOR Steven	29 + 2	1	2		3		
VIDUKA Mark	19 + 7	7			2		

NORTHAMPTON TOWN (DIV 1: 9th)

	P/FL		FLC		FAC		Others
	App	Goals	App	Goals	App	Goals	App
AISTON Sam	0 + 1		0 + 1		0 + 1		
AKINFENWA Adebayo	13 + 2	7					
BOWDITCH Dean	7 + 3	2					
BRANSTON Guy	3				0 + 1		
BUNN Mark	45		2		4		1
BURNELL Joe	26 + 7		1		3 + 1		
COKE Giles	11 + 9	5					
CROWE Jason	44	4	2		3		0 + 1
DOIG Chris	15	1	2		1		1
DOLMAN Liam	27 + 3				4		1
DUNN Chris	1						
DYER Alex	3 + 3	1	1		0 + 1		1
GILLIGAN Ryan	28 + 10	4	1		3		0 + 1
GYEPES Gabor	13						
HAYES Jonny	5 + 6						
HENDERSON Ian	9 + 14		2		1 + 1		
HOLT Andy	29 + 7	2	2		4		
HUBERTZ Poul	33 + 7	13	2		4		1
HUGHES Mark	34 + 1	1	2		4		1
JACKMAN Danny	34 + 5	1	1		4		
JOHNSON Brad	22 + 1	3	2	1	2 + 1	1	1
JOHNSON Brett	10 + 6		0 + 2				
JONES Daniel	27 + 6	3	1 + 1		1 + 2		1
KIRK Andy	25	8	1	1	2 + 1	2	0 + 1
LARKIN Colin	14 + 19	2	0 + 2		4	1	1
LITTLE Mark	17						
MAY Danny	0 + 2						1
RUSSELL Alex	11 + 2						1

NORWICH CITY (CHAMP: 17th)

	P/FL		FLC		FAC		Others
	App	Goals	App	Goals	App	Goals	App
BATES Matty	2 + 1						
BERTRAND Ryan	18				1 + 1		
BRELLIER Julien	8 + 2		1				
BROWN Chris	8 + 6	1	2 + 1				
CAMARA Mo	20 + 1				1 + 1		
CHADWICK Luke	9 + 4	1	0 + 1				
CROFT Lee	19 + 22	1	2 + 1		1 + 1		
CURETON Jamie	29 + 12	12	2	2	2		

	P/FL		FLC		FAC		Others
	App	Goals	App	Goals	App	Goals	App
DOHERTY Gary	32 + 2		3		2	1	
DRURY Adam	9		1				
DUBLIN Dion	28 + 9	7	1 + 1	1	1 + 1	1	
EVANS Ched	20 + 8	10					
FOTHERINGHAM Mark	26 + 2	2	1		1		2
GIBBS Kieran	6 + 1						
HARTSON John	2 + 2						
HENRY James	1 + 2						
HUCKERBY Darren	26 + 8	5	1		2		
JARVIS Rossi	4		1				
JARVIS Ryan	0 + 1				1 + 1		
LAPPIN Simon	15	1	3	1			
MARSHALL David	46		3		2		
MARTIN Chris	3 + 4		1 + 1		1		
MURRAY Ian	8 + 1		2				
OTSEMOBOR Jon	41 + 2	1	3		0 + 1		
PATTISON Matty	22 + 5				2		
PEARCE Alex	8 + 3						
RIGTERS Maceo	0 + 2						
RUSSELL Darel	37 + 2	4	3	1	2		
SHACKELL Jason	36 + 3		2		1		
SMITH Jimmy	6 + 3						
SPILLANE Michael	4 + 2		1		1		
STRIHAVKA David	3 + 7	1	0 + 1				
TAYLOR Martin	8	1					
VELASCO Juan	2 + 1						

NOTTINGHAM FOREST (DIV 1: 2nd)

	P/FL		FLC		FAC		Others
	App	Goals	App	Goals	App	Goals	App
AGOGO Junior	27 + 8	13	1 + 1		1 + 2		1
BASTIANS Felix	0 + 1		1				1
BENNETT Julian	33 + 1	4	2		2		1
BRECKIN Ian	22 + 6	1			2		1
BYRNE Mark	0 + 1						
CHAMBERS Luke	40 + 2	6	2		3	1	2
CLINGAN Sammy	40 + 2	1	2		2		
COHEN Chris	40 + 1	2	1		3		
COMMONS Kris	29 + 10	9	2		2 + 1	1	1
DAVIES Arron	9 + 10	1			1 + 2		
DOBIE Scott	1 + 1		1				
HOLT Grant	22 + 10	3	1 + 1		1		
HOSKINS Will	2						
LENNON Neil	15 + 3		2		1		0 + 1
LOCKWOOD Matt	11				1		
McCLEARY Garath	3 + 5	1					
McGUGAN Lewis	24 + 9	6			3	1	
MOLONEY Brendon	2						
MORGAN Wes	37 + 5	1	2		1		1
ORMEROD Brett	13	2					1
PERCH James	19 + 11		0 + 1		1 + 1		1
POWER Alan	0 + 12	1	0 + 1				0 + 1
SINCLAIR Emile	0 + 1						
SMITH Paul	46		2	1	3		1
THORNHILL Matt	5 + 9	2	0 + 1		0 + 1		1
TYSON Nathan	26 + 8	9	1	1	3	2	1
WILSON Kelvin	40 + 2		2		3		

NOTTS COUNTY (DIV 2: 21st)

	P/FL		FLC		FAC		Others
	App	Goals	App	Goals	App	Goals	App
BASTIANS Felix	5						
BRANSTON Guy	1						
BUTCHER Richard	46	12	1		1 + 1		2
CANOVILLE Lee	32 + 3		1		2		
CORDEN Wayne	7 + 2						
CROW Danny	13 + 1	2					
DUDFIELD Lawrie	26 + 7	1	1		2	2	1
EDWARDS Mike	19	1					
FROST Stef	0 + 2						0 + 1
GIBB Ali	9						
HOULT Russell	14						
HUNT Stephen	36 + 1	2	1		1		1
JARVIS Ryan	17	2					
JOHNSON Michael	11 + 1	1					
LEE Jason	22 + 9	1	1		0 + 1		1
LINDFIELD Craig	3	1	1		1		
McCANN Austin	13 + 9						1
MacKENZIE Neil	24 + 5	6	1		2		1
MAYO Paul	27 + 2				2		1
PARKINSON Andy	11 + 12				1		0 + 1
PEARCE Krystian	8	1			1		
PILKINGTON Kevin	32		1		2		
SAM Hector	7 + 13	1	1		1 + 1	1	0 + 1
SANDERCOMBE Tim							1
SILK Gary	22 + 11	2	0 + 1		2		1
SMITH Jay	16 + 4		1				1

Michael Owen (Newcastle United)

	P/FL App	P/FL Goals	FLC App	FLC Goals	FAC App	FAC Goals	Others App
SOMNER Matt	12 + 4				1 + 1		1
STRACHAN Gavin	7						
TANN Adam	40 + 1	1			2		1
WEIR-DALEY Spencer	12 + 18	3	0 + 1		0 + 2		1
WESTON Myles	14 + 11		0 + 1		1		

OLDHAM ATHLETIC (DIV 1: 8th)

	P/FL App	P/FL Goals	FLC App	FLC Goals	FAC App	FAC Goals	Others App
ALESSANDRA Lewis	12 + 3	2			0 + 1		
ALLOTT Mark	34 + 8	4	1		5		2
BERESFORD Marlon	5						1
BERTRAND Ryan	21		1				2
BLACK Paul	0 + 2						
CHALMERS Aaron	0 + 2						
CONSTANTINE Leon	7 + 1	2					
CROSSLEY Mark	38				5		
DAVIES Craig	31 + 1	10	2	1	5	1	2	1
EARDLEY Neal	40 + 2	6	2		5		1
GIDDINGS Stuart	2		1				
GREGAN Sean	15		2				2
HAZELL Reuben	32 + 2	1			3 + 1		1
HUGHES Lee	15 + 3	7			3	1	
JARRETT Jason	12 + 3	3					
KAMUDIMBA KALALA Jean-Paul	14 + 6		2	1	2		2
KELLY Ashley	0 + 1						
KILKENNY Neil	19 + 1	1	1	1	3		1
LIDDELL Andy	16 + 2	2	1 + 1				1	1
LIVERMORE David	10	1					
LOMAX Kelvin	17 + 4				1		0 + 1
McDONALD Gary	31 + 4	4	1 + 1		5	2	1
O'DONNELL Richard	3 + 1						
PEARSON Mike	0 + 1						
RICKETTS Michael	8 + 1	2	2				1
ROBERTSON Jordan	2 + 1	1					
SMALLEY Deane	19 + 18	2	1 + 1	1	5		0 + 1
STAM Stefan	34 + 2				5		
TAYLOR Chris	40 + 2	5	1 + 1		4		2
THOMPSON John	6 + 1		2		0 + 1		1 + 1
TROTMAN Neal	16 + 1	1	0 + 1		3	1	1
WOLFENDEN Matty	7 + 18	2	0 + 1		1 + 1		0 + 2	1

PETERBOROUGH UNITED (DIV 2: 2nd)

	P/FL App	P/FL Goals	FLC App	FLC Goals	FAC App	FAC Goals	Others App
BLACKETT Shane	9 + 2		2				1
BLANCHETT Danny	1						
BOYD George	41 + 5	12	1	1	4	1	2	1
BRANSTON Guy	1 + 1						
CHARNOCK Kieran	10				2		2
CROW Danny	2 + 2	2	1 + 1				
DAY Jamie	42		3	2	3		1 + 1
GNAPKA Claude	25 + 3				2 + 1		1
HATCH Liam	1 + 10						
HOWE Rene	2 + 13	1			0 + 2		1
HUGHES Jeff	2 + 5	1			1 + 1		
HYDE Micah	33 + 4		1		3		2
JALAL Shwan	7		2				1
KEATES Dean	33 + 7	5	1 + 1		2 + 1		
LEE Charlie	32 + 10	6	1 + 1		3 + 1	1	1 + 1	1
LEWIS Joe	22				1		
LOW Josh	9 + 6	2	2		0 + 2		1
MACKAIL-SMITH Craig	34 + 2	12			4	7	0 + 1
McKEOWN James	0 + 1						
McLEAN Aaron	45	29	2		4	3	2	1
MITCHELL Scott	1 + 4				0 + 1		
MORGAN Craig	41		2		1		4		1
NEWTON Adam	26 + 6		2		2		1
POTTER Alfie	0 + 2		0 + 1				
RENDELL Scott	3 + 7	3					
STRACHAN Gavin	0 + 3		1				1 + 1
TYLER Mark	17				3		1
WESTWOOD Chris	35 + 2		1 + 1		2		2
WHELPDALE Chris	29 + 6	3	2		4		1
WILLIAMS Tom	3 + 4						

PLYMOUTH ARGYLE (CHAMP: 10th)

	P/FL App	P/FL Goals	FLC App	FLC Goals	FAC App	FAC Goals	Others App
ABDOU Nadjim	22 + 9	1	1				
ANDERSON Russell	14						
BARNES Ashley			0 + 1				
BUZSAKY Akos	8 + 3		2				
CHADWICK Nick	3 + 6	2	2 + 1		0 + 1		
CLARK Chris	8 + 4				1		1
CONNOLLY Paul	42	1	3		2		
DICKSON Ryan			0 + 1				
DJORDJIC Bojan	1		0 + 1				

	P/FL App	P/FL Goals	FLC App	FLC Goals	FAC App	FAC Goals	Others App
DOUGLAS Rab	1						
DOUMBE Mathias	10 + 2				2		
EASTER Jermaine	20 + 12	6			2		
EBANKS-BLAKE Sylvan	19 + 6	11	3	1	3	1	
FALLON Rory	13 + 16	7	0 + 2		1		
FOLLY Yoann	1 + 3				0 + 1		
GOSLING Dan	5 + 5						
HALMOSI Peter	41 + 2	8	2		2		1
HAYLES Barry	21 + 2	2	1				
HODGES Lee	20 + 7		2		1	1	1
JUTKIEWICZ Lukas	1 + 2				0 + 2		
LAIRD Scott			1				
LARRIEU Romain	15						
McCORMICK Luke	30		3		2		
MACKIE Jamie	4 + 9	3					
MacLEAN Steve	14 + 3	3					
MARTIN Lee	10 + 2	2					
NALIS Lilian	35 + 5	1	1		2		
NORRIS David	27	5	2		1		
PATERSON Jim	7 + 1	1					
REID Reuben			1 + 1				
SAWYER Gary	28 + 3	1	2		1 + 1		
SEIP Marcel	32 + 2	1	3		1		
SMITH Dan	0 + 2						
SUMMERFIELD Luke	5 + 2		1 + 1	1	1		
TEALE Gary	8 + 4						
TIMAR Krisztian	36 + 2	3	3		1		
WOTTON Paul	5 + 3	1					

PORTSMOUTH (PREM: 8th)

	P/FL App	P/FL Goals	FLC App	FLC Goals	FAC App	FAC Goals	Others App
ASHDOWN Jamie	3		2				
AUBEY Lucien	1 + 2						
BAROS Milan	8 + 4				1 + 3		
BENJANI	21 + 2	12	3		1		
CAMPBELL Sol	31		1		5		
CRANIE Martin	1 + 1		1				
DAVIS Sean	18 + 4		1		0 + 2		
DEFOE Jermain	12	8					
DIARRA Lassana	11 + 1	1			5		
DIOP Pape Bouba	25				4 + 1		
DISTIN Sylvain	36		3		6		
HREIDARSSON Hermann	30 + 2	3	0 + 1		6		
HUGHES Richard	8 + 5		2		0 + 2		
JAMES David	35		1		6		
JOHNSON Glen	29	1	1		6		
KANU Nwankwo	13 + 12	4	0 + 1	1	5	2	
KRANJCAR Niko	31 + 3	4	2		6	1	
LAUREN	11 + 4				1 + 1		
MENDES Pedro	14 + 4		3		3		
MUNTARI Sulley	27 + 2	4			4	1	
MVUEMBA Arnold	3 + 5		1 + 1		1 + 1		
NUGENT David	5 + 10		2 + 1	2	1 + 3	1	
O'NEIL Gary	2		0 + 1				
PAMAROT Noe	14 + 4	1	3		2	1	
SONGO'O Franck	0 + 1						
TAYLOR Matthew	3 + 10	1	1 + 1				
TRAORE Djimi	1 + 2		2				
UTAKA John	25 + 4	5	2 + 1		4		

PORT VALE (DIV 1: 23rd)

	P/FL App	P/FL Goals	FLC App	FLC Goals	FAC App	FAC Goals	Others App
ANYON Joe	44		1		3		1
ATKINSON Will	3 + 1						
CARDLE Joe	4 + 5						
CHAPMAN Luke	0 + 1						
DAVIDSON Ross	0 + 3						
ECKERSLEY Adam	18	1					
EDWARDS Paul	17 + 8	2	0 + 1		2		1
GLOVER Danny	9 + 6	1					0 + 1
HARSLEY Paul	39 + 2	5			1		
HERD Chris	11	2					
HOWLAND David	17	1					
HULBERT Robin	15 + 7				3		
LAIRD Marc	7	1			0 + 1		
LAWRIE James	0 + 6				0 + 1		
LOWE Keith	24 + 4	3	1		2		
McGOLDRICK David	15 + 2	2					1
McGREGOR Mark	18 + 2		1		2		
MARTIN Chris	2						
MIKAELSSON Tobias	5 + 1						
MILES Colin	1 + 2		0 + 1		0 + 1		
MILLER Justin	12 + 2				1		1	1
MULLIGAN Dave	10 + 3	1					
O'LOUGHLIN Charlie	0 + 3						

Player	P/FL App	P/FL Goals	FLC App	FLC Goals	FAC App	FAC Goals	Others App
PEARCE Krystian	11 + 1						
PERRY Kyle	9 + 7						
PILKINGTON George	45	2	1		3	1	1
PROSSER Luke	3 + 2						
RICHARDS Marc	19 + 10	5	0 + 1		0 + 1		1
RICHMAN Simon	6						
ROCASTLE Craig	17 + 6	1	1		2		1
RODGERS Luke	29 + 7	9	1	1	3	1	1
SALMON Mark	8 + 1				1		
SLATER Chris	1 + 4						
SODJE Akpo	3						
TALBOT Jason	21 + 4		1		3		
TUDOR Shane	8 + 6		1		0 + 1		1
WESTWOOD Ashley	11 + 1				1		1
WHITAKER Danny	36 + 5	7	1		3		
WILLOCK Calum	8 + 7	3	1		3	1	0 + 1

PRESTON NORTH END (CHAMP: 15th)

Player	P/FL App	P/FL Goals	FLC App	FLC Goals	FAC App	FAC Goals	Others App
AGYEMANG Patrick	11 + 11	4					
ALEXANDER Graham	3						
BEATTIE Craig	1 + 1						
BROWN Chris	17	5			2		
CARROLL Andy	7 + 4	1	0 + 1				
CARTER Darren	30 + 9	4	1		3		
CHAPLOW Richard	7 + 5	3			0 + 1		
CHILVERS Liam	27 + 1				3		
DAVIDSON Callum	39 + 1	4			3		
GALLAGHER Paul	15 + 4	1					
HALLS John	4						
HART Michael	2						
HAWLEY Karl	20 + 5	3	0 + 1		3	2	
HENDERSON Wayne	3		1				
HILL Matt	21 + 5		1		1 + 1		
JONES Billy	28 + 1		1		1		
LONERGAN Andy	43				3		
McKENNA Paul	33				3		
MAWENE Youl	36 + 2	3	1		3		
MELLOR Neil	12 + 24	9	1		1 + 2	1	
NEAL Lewis	8 + 9	2			1		
NICHOLLS Kevin	17 + 1		1		0 + 1		
ORMEROD Brett	8 + 10	1	1		0 + 1		
PRISKIN Tamas	4 + 1	2					
PUGH Danny	5 + 2		1	1			
ST LEDGER-HALL Sean	34 + 3	1	1		1		
SEDGWICK Chris	40 + 2	2	0 + 1		1		
TROTMAN Neal	2 + 1						
WHALEY Simon	29 + 14	4	1		3	2	

QUEENS PARK RANGERS (CHAMP: 14th)

Player	P/FL App	P/FL Goals	FLC App	FLC Goals	FAC App	FAC Goals	Others App
AGYEMANG Patrick	17	8			0 + 1		
AINSWORTH Gareth	16 + 8	3			1		
BAILEY Stefan	1		1				
BALANTA Angelo	6 + 5	1			0 + 1		
BARKER Chris	25				1		
BIGNOT Marcus	0 + 2		1				
BLACKSTOCK Dexter	26 + 9	6			1		
BOLDER Adam	20 + 4	2	1		1		
BUZSAKY Akos	24 + 3	10			1		
CAMP Lee	46		1		1		
CONNOLLY Matt	18 + 2				1		
CRANIE Martin	6						
CULLIP Danny	5 + 1		1				
CURTIS John	3 + 1		0 + 1				
DELANEY Damien	17	1					
EPHRAIM Hogan	20 + 9	3			1		
HALL Fitz	14				1		
JARRETT Jason	1 + 1						
LEE Kieran	2 + 5				0 + 1		
LEIGERTWOOD Mikele	33 + 7	5					
MAHON Gavin	11 + 5	1			1		
MALCOLM Bob	10 + 1						
MANCIENNE Michael	26 + 4		1				
MINTO-ST AIMIE Kieron	0 + 1						
MOORE Stefan	5 + 6	1	1				
NARDIELLO Danny	4 + 4						
NYGAARD Marc	6 + 13	1	1		1		
REHMAN Zesh	17 + 4		1				
ROSE Romone	0 + 1						
ROWLANDS Martin	43 + 1	6	1	1	1		
SAHAR Ben	6 + 3						
SINCLAIR Scott	8 + 1	1					
STEWART Damion	35 + 4	5	0 + 1		1		
TIMOSKA Sampsa	3 + 4						

Player	P/FL App	P/FL Goals	FLC App	FLC Goals	FAC App	FAC Goals	Others App
VINE Rowan	31 + 2	6					
WALTON Simon	1 + 4						
WARD Nick	0 + 1		1				

READING (PREM: 18th)

Player	P/FL App	P/FL Goals	FLC App	FLC Goals	FAC App	FAC Goals	Others App
BIKEY Andre	14 + 8	3	1		1		
CISSE Kalifa	11 + 11	1	1		2		
CONVEY Bobby	12 + 8		2	1	2		
COX Simon			0 + 1		0 + 1		
DE LA CRUZ Ulises	3 + 3		2		2		
DOYLE Kevin	34 + 2	6					
DUBERRY Michael	12 + 1		2		1		
FAE Emerse	3 + 5		2		1		
FEDERICI Adam			2		2		
GOLBOURNE Scott	1		0 + 1				
GUNNARSSON Brynjar	18 + 2		2				
HAHNEMANN Marcus	38						
HALLS John	0 + 1		2		1		
HARPER James	38	6	2		1		
HENRY James			0 + 1				
HUNT Stephen	37	5	0 + 1		1 + 1	2	
INGIMARSSON Ivar	33 + 1	2			1		
KEBE Jimmy	1 + 4						
KITSON Dave	28 + 6	10	1 + 1		1		
LITA Leroy	10 + 4	1	2	1	2		
LITTLE Glen	0 + 2						
LONG Shane	7 + 22	3	1		2		
MATEJOVSKY Marek	10 + 4	1					
MURTY Graeme	28						
OSTER John	12 + 6						
PEARCE Alex			0 + 1		1 + 1		
ROSENIOR Liam	15 + 2				2		
SEOL Ki-Hyeon	2 + 1						
SHOREY Nicky	36	2	1		1		
SODJE Sam			1				
SONKO Ibu	15 + 1						

ROCHDALE (DIV 2: 5th)

Player	P/FL App	P/FL Goals	FLC App	FLC Goals	FAC App	FAC Goals	Others App	Others Goals
ATKINSON Rob	0 + 2							
BASHAM Chris	5 + 8							
BOWYER George	0 + 1							
BRANSTON Guy	4		1				1	
BUCKLEY Will	1 + 6						0 + 1	
CROOKS Lee	5 + 4				1		1	
DAGNALL Chris	7 + 7	7	2				3	2
D'ARYEA Nathan	2 + 4		1		1		2	
DOOLAN John	19 + 6		1				0 + 2	
EVANS Rapha	1							
HIGGINBOTHAM Kallum	22 + 11	3			1		3 + 1	
HOLNESS Marcus	13 + 6						1 + 1	
HOWE Rene	19 + 1	9					2 + 1	
JONES Gary	43	7	2		1		4	
KENNEDY Tom	43	2	2		1		4	
LEE Tommy	11						3	
LE FONDRE Adam	30 + 16	16	0 + 2		1	1	2 + 2	
LOMAX Kelvin	10							
McARDLE Rory	42 + 1	2	2		1		3	1
McEVILLY Lee	3 + 4	3						
MUIRHEAD Ben	18 + 13		2				0 + 3	
MURRAY Glenn	21 + 2	9	2	1	1		1	
PERKINS David	40	4	1		1		3	1
PRENDERGAST Rory	2 + 12		0 + 2	1	0 + 1		1	1
RAMSDEN Simon	35		2				4	
RUNDLE Adam	37 + 5	5	2		0 + 1		4	1
RUSSELL Sam	15				1		1	
SPENCER James	20		2				2	
STANTON Nathan	27				1		2	
TAYLOR Scott	2 + 2							
THOMPSON Joe	4 + 7	1					0 + 1	
THORPE Lee	5 + 3	1						
WHARTON Ben	0 + 1							

ROTHERHAM UNITED (DIV 2: 9th)

Player	P/FL App	P/FL Goals	FLC App	FLC Goals	FAC App	FAC Goals	Others App
ANNERSON Jamie							1
BEAN Marcus	11 + 1	1					2
BROGAN Steve	28 + 1	3	1		2	1	1 + 1
CAHILL Tom	5 + 2						0 + 1
COUGHLAN Graham	45		1		2		1
CRESSWELL Ryan	1 + 2						1
DUNCUM Sam	0 + 2		0 + 1				0 + 1
DYER Bruce	3						
GREEN Jamie	6 + 3	1					1
HAGGERTY David	0 + 1						

Name	P/FL App	P/FL Goals	FLC App	FLC Goals	FAC App	FAC Goals	Others App
HARRISON Danny	44	4	1	1	2		2
HOLMES Derek	33 + 4	11	1				1 + 1
HOLMES Peter	19 + 5	2	1		0 + 1		1
HUDSON Mark	30 + 1	9			2		
HURST Paul	8 + 3		1		1 + 1		1 + 1
JOSEPH Marc	34 + 2	4	0 + 1				1
KING Liam	0 + 1						
MILLS Pablo	32 + 1	1			1		
NEWSHAM Marc	11 + 14	4	0 + 1		1 + 1		2
O'GRADY Chris	35 + 3	9	1		2	1	1
PETTIGREW Adrian	3 + 1						
ROSS Ian	9 + 8						
SHARPS Ian	33	2	1		2		2
TAYLOR Ryan	22 + 13	6			2		1
TODD Andy	11 + 2		1		0 + 1		0 + 1
TONGE Dale	31 + 6		1		2		2
WARRINGTON Andy	46		1		2		1
WIDDOWSON Joe	3						
YATES Jamie	3 + 17	3			1 + 1		
SCUNTHORPE UNITED (CHAMP: 23rd)							
AMEOBI Tomi	0 + 9				0 + 1		
BARACLOUGH Ian	17						
BUTLER Andy	34 + 2	2	0 + 1				
BYRNE Cliff	25		1		1		
CORK Jack	32 + 2	2			1		
CROSBY Andy	38	4	1		1		
FORTE Jonathan	18 + 20	4	0 + 1		0 + 1		
GOODWIN Jim	39 + 1	3	0 + 1		1		
HAYES Paul	32 + 8	8	1		1		
HOBBS Jack	7 + 2	1					
HORSFIELD Geoff	11 + 1						
HURST Kevan	31 + 2	1	1		1		
IRIEKPEN Izzy	12 + 5	1	1				
LILLIS Josh	1 + 2		1		0 + 1		
LOGAN Shaleum	4						
McCANN Grant	12 + 2	1					
MARTIS Shelton	3				1		
MAY Ben	6 + 15	1			1		
MORRIS Ian	20 + 5	3			1		
MURPHY Joe	45				1		
PATERSON Martin	34 + 6	13	1	1	1		
SECK Mamadou	0 + 1						
SPARROW Matt	24 + 8	1	1		1		
TAYLOR Cleveland	12 + 8		1		1		
WESTON Curtis	2 + 5						
WILLIAMS Marcus	29 + 5		1		1		
WINN Peter	0 + 4						
WRIGHT Andrew	0 + 2						
YOUGA Kelly	18 + 1	1	1				
SHEFFIELD UNITED (CHAMP: 9th)							
ARMSTRONG Chris	27 + 5	3	2 + 1		1 + 1		
BARDSLEY Phil	16						
BEATTIE James	36 + 3	22			2		
BENNETT Ian	6 + 1		1		2		
BROMBY Leigh	11		2 + 1		2		
CAHILL Gary	16	2					
CARNEY Dave	18 + 3	2	3		1 + 1	1	
COTTERILL David	15 + 1						
EHIOGU Ugo	5 + 5						
GEARY Derek	19 + 2		3		4		
GILLESPIE Keith	23 + 12	2	0 + 1		1 + 1		
HALLS John	5 + 1						
HENDRIE Lee	7 + 5	1	1		1	1	1
HORSFIELD Geoff			0 + 2	1			
HULSE Rob	10 + 11				0 + 3		
KENNY Paddy	40		3		4		
KILGALLON Matt	39 + 1	2	3		3		
LAW Nicky	0 + 1		1	1			
LEIGERTWOOD Mikele	1 + 1		2				
LUCKETTI Chris	4 + 2		3	1			
MARTIN Lee	5 + 1				2 + 1		
MONTGOMERY Nick	18 + 2		2		1		
MORGAN Chris	25	2	2		3		
NAYSMITH Gary	38		2		3		
QUINN Alan	4 + 4		2 + 2				
QUINN Stephen	15 + 4	2	2		4		
SHARP Billy	21 + 8	4	3	2	2 + 2		
SHELTON Luton	5 + 10	1	1 + 2	2	2 + 1	1	
SPEED Gary	20	3					
STEAD Jon	12 + 12	3	3	2	4	1	
TONGE Michael	37 + 8	1	2 + 2		2 + 1		
WEBBER Danny	8 + 6	3	1 + 1	1			

Name	P/FL App	P/FL Goals	FLC App	FLC Goals	FAC App	FAC Goals	Others App
SHEFFIELD WEDNESDAY (CHAMP: 16th)							
BEEVERS Mark	26 + 2				2	1	
BODEN Luke	0 + 2		0 + 1				
BOLDER Adam	11 + 2	2					
BRUNT Chris	1						
BULLEN Lee	17 + 5	1	0 + 1		2		
BURCH Rob	2						
BURTON Deon	23 + 17	7	2 + 1	2	0 + 2		
CLARKE Leon	2 + 6	3	0 + 1		0 + 1		
ESAJAS Etienne	5 + 13				1		
FOLLY Yoann	7 + 3		0 + 1	1			
GILBERT Peter	9 + 1		1				
GRANT Lee	44		2		2		
HINDS Richard	30 + 8	2	2		2		
JEFFERS Francis	7 + 3	2	1		1		
JOHNSON Jermaine	30 + 5	1	3		2		
JOHNSON Michael	13						
KAVANAGH Graham	21 + 2	2	1				
LUNT Kenny	3 + 1		2 + 1		0 + 1		
McALLISTER Sean	5 + 3						
O'BRIEN Burton	26 + 7	3	1		1		
SAHAR Ben	8 + 4	3					
SHOWUNMI Enoch	6 + 4						
SIMEK Frankie	17		3				
SLUSARSKI Bartosz	3 + 4	1					
SMALL Wade	18 + 11	4	2	1	1		
SODJE Akpo	16 + 3	7	0 + 1		1		
SONGO'O Franck	12	1					
SPURR Tommy	40 + 1	2	2		2		
TUDGAY Marcus	29 + 6	7	3		2	1	
WALLWORK Ronnie	4 + 3						
WATSON Steve	20 + 3	2	1		1	1	1
WHELAN Glenn	25		2		3	1	2
WOOD Richard	26 + 1	2	3				
SHREWSBURY TOWN (DIV 2: 18th)							
ASHTON Neil	6 + 9						1
BARNES Michael	2						
BEVAN Scott	5						
BRIGGS Keith	1 + 1	1					
CONSTABLE James	7 + 7	4					
COOKE Andy	10 + 4	5	0 + 1				
DAVIES Ben	26 + 1	6					
DRUMMOND Stewart	22 + 1	3	1		1		
ESSON Ryan			2				
GARNER Glyn	41				1		
HALL Asa	13 + 2	3					
HALL Danny	7 + 8		0 + 1		1		1
HERD Ben	42 + 3	1			0 + 1		0 + 1
HIBBERT Dave	36 + 8	12	1 + 1		1		1
HUMPHREY Chris	7 + 18		2				1
HUNT David	22 + 5	2	1 + 1				
JONES Luke	6 + 1						
KEMPSON Darran	18 + 5		2	1			1
LANGMEAD Kelvin	39	1	1		1		1
LEE Graeme	4 + 1						
LESLIE Steven	10 + 7	1	2		1		0 + 1
McINTYRE Kevin	22	2					
MacKENZIE Chris	3						1
MADJO Guy	10 + 5	3					
MEREDITH James	3						
MOSS Darren	28 + 3	2	1		1		1
MURDOCK Colin	29	2	1		1		
NICHOLSON Stuart	6 + 8	1			1		1
ONIBUJE Fola			1 + 1				
PUGH Marc	27 + 10	4			1		
RYAN Jimmy	1 + 3		2				1
SYMES Michael	12 + 9	3	2		1		1
TIERNEY Marc	42 + 1	1	2		1		1
WAINWRIGHT Neil	2 + 1						
SOUTHAMPTON (CHAMP: 20th)							
BASEYA Cedric	0 + 1						
BENNETT Alan	10		1				
BIALKOWSKI Bartosz	1		1				
DAILLY Christian	11						
DAVIES Andrew	22 + 1				2		
DAVIS Kelvin	35				3		
DYER Nathan	15 + 2	1	1	1			
EUELL Jason	31 + 7	3			3		
GILLETT Simon	0 + 2						
HAMMILL Adam	12 + 13				2 + 1		

Player	P/FL App	Goals	FLC App	Goals	FAC App	Goals	Others App	Goals
IDIAKEZ Inigo	14 + 7	1			1 + 1			
IFIL Phil	11 + 1							
JOHN Stern	35 + 5	19			1 + 1			
JONES Kenwyne	1	1						
LALLANA Adam	0 + 5	1						
LICKA Mario	10 + 2		1					
LUCKETTI Chris	4							
McGOLDRICK David	2 + 6		0 + 1		0 + 2			
MAKIN Chris	5		1					
O'HALLORAN Stephen	0 + 1							
OSTLUND Alexander	8 + 4				1			
PEARCE Ian	1							
PERICARD Vincent	1 + 4							
PERRY Chris	6							
POKE Michael	3 + 1							
POWELL Darren	10	1			3			
RASIAK Grzegorz	13 + 10	6	1	1	2	1	1	
SAFRI Youssef	37		1		1			
SAGANOWSKI Marek	14 + 16	3	0 + 1		1			
SKACEL Rudi	13 + 3	1	1		0 + 1			
SURMAN Drew	35 + 5	2	1		3	2		
THOMAS Wayne	29 + 1				2			
VIAFARA Jhon	30 + 10	3			1			
VIGNAL Gregory	20	3	0 + 1		2	1		
WRIGHT Jermaine	33 + 3		1		3			
WRIGHT Richard	7							
WRIGHT-PHILLIPS Bradley	27 + 12	8	1		2 + 1			

SOUTHEND UNITED (DIV 1: 6th)

Player	P/FL App	Goals	FLC App	Goals	FAC App	Goals	Others App	Goals
BAILEY Nicky	42 + 2	9	3		5	2	3	1
BARNARD Lee	11 + 4	9			0 + 1		2	
BARRETT Adam	45	6	3	1	4		3	
BLACK Tommy	29 + 9	2	2 + 1		1 + 1		2	
BRADBURY Lee	1		1	3				
CAMPBELL-RYCE Jamal	2		1					
CLARKE Leon	16	8						
CLARKE Peter	45	4	2		5		3	
COLLIS Steve	20		2		3		1	
FLAHAVAN Darryl	26		2		2		2	
FORAN Richie	0 + 6		0 + 1				1	1
FRANCIS Simon	24 + 3	2	1 + 1		4	1	2	
GILBERT Kerrea	5				1			
GOWER Mark	40 + 2	9	1		4		2	
GRANT Anthony	0 + 10							
HAMMELL Steve	16	2			4			
HARROLD Matt	12 + 4		2	2	2	1	1	
HOOPER Gary	9 + 4	2	1 + 1		2 + 1		0 + 1	
HUNT Lewis	23 + 1		2 + 1		5		1	
LOKANDO Peggy			0 + 1					
McCORMACK Alan	42	8			4		3	1
MacDONALD Charlie	11 + 14	1	2 + 1	1	2 + 2	3	0 + 2	
MAHER Kevin	18 + 1		1		3			
MORGAN Dean	6 + 2				3	3		
MOUSSA-NYINZAPA Franck	6 + 10		2 + 1		1 + 1		1	
MULGREW Charlie	18	1					2	
ODHIAMBO Eric	2 + 3						1	
REVELL Alex	5 + 3						0 + 2	
RICHARDS Garry	8 + 2		2		1		1	
ROBSON-KANU Hal	6 + 2	3						
SCANNELL Damian	0 + 9							
WALKER James	14 + 1	4					2	
WILSON Che	4 + 2		1					

STOCKPORT COUNTY (DIV 2: 4th)

Player	P/FL App	Goals	FLC App	Goals	FAC App	Goals	Others App	Goals
ADAMSON Chris					2			
BLIZZARD Dominic	22 + 5	1	1 + 1	1	1		1	
BOWLER Michael	4 + 1		1				2	
BRIGGS Keith	5 + 8						1	
DICKER Gary	29 + 1		2				4	
DICKINSON Liam	34 + 6	19	0 + 1		1		6	2
ELDING Anthony	18 + 7	13	2	1	2		3	1
GLEESON Stephen	4 + 2						2 + 1	1
GRIFFIN Adam	19 + 9	1	1 + 1		1		1	
HAVERN Gianluca	1	1						
LOGAN Conrad	34		2				5	
LOGAN Shaleum	6 + 1							
LOWE Ryan	4							
McNEIL Matty	17	2	2	1	2	2	1 + 1	1
McNULTY Jimmy	11						2 + 1	
McSWEENEY Leon	5 + 6	1			1 + 3			
MORGAN-SMITH Amari	0 + 1							
NOWLAND Adam	4							
OWEN Gareth	35 + 1		2		2		4	
PILKINGTON Anthony	23 + 6	6	0 + 2		0 + 1		4 + 1	2
POOLE David	13 + 9	2	1		0 + 1		1	
PROUDLOCK Adam	18 + 15	8	1	1	1 + 1		1 + 1	1
RAYNES Michael	20 + 7				2		3 + 1	
ROSE Michael	25 + 3	3			1 + 1		4 + 1	
ROWE Tommy	17 + 7	6			0 + 1		3 + 2	
RUDDY John	12						1	
SMITH James	24 + 2		1				4	
SMITH Johann	0 + 2							
TANSEY Greg	5 + 8				1 + 1		1	
TAYLOR Jason	40 + 2	4	2		2		1 + 2	
THOMPSON Leslie	3							
TIERNEY Paul	15 + 1		2		1		1	1
TUNNICLIFFE James	1 + 4						1 + 1	
TURNBULL Paul	12 + 7				2		6	
VINCENT James	0 + 1						1	
WILLIAMS Ashley	26		2				1	

STOKE CITY (CHAMP: 2nd)

Player	P/FL App	Goals	FLC App	Goals	FAC App	Goals	Others App
AMEOBI Shola	3 + 3						
BOTHROYD Jay	1 + 3						
BUXTON Lewis	0 + 4						
CORT Leon	33	8			2		
CRADDOCK Jody	4						
CRESSWELL Richard	42 + 1	11	0 + 1	1	2		
DELAP Rory	44	2	1		1		
DIAO Salif	8 + 3				0 + 1		
DICKINSON Carl	19 + 8		1		1 + 1		
EUSTACE John	20 + 6		1		2		
FULLER Ricardo	39 + 3	15			2		
GALLAGHER Paul	2 + 5						
GRIFFIN Andy	15						
HIGGINBOTHAM Danny	1		1				
HILL Clint	4 + 1						
HOULT Russell	1		1				
LAWRENCE Liam	40 + 1	14	1		2	1	
MATTEO Dominic	14						
NASH Carlo	10						
PARKIN Jon	4 + 25	2	1		1 + 1		
PEARSON Stephen	3 + 1						
PERICARD Vincent	2 + 3				0 + 1		
PHILLIPS Demar	0 + 2						
PUGH Danny	27 + 3				2		
PULIS Tony	0 + 1		1		0 + 2		
RIGGOTT Chris	9						
SHAWCROSS Ryan	39 + 2	7	1	1	2		
SIDIBE Mama	33 + 2	4	1		1		
SIMONSEN Steve	35 + 1				2		
SWEENEY Peter	0 + 5		0 + 1				
WHELAN Glenn	13 + 1	1			1		
WILKINSON Andy	16 + 7		0 + 1		1		
WRIGHT Stephen	14 + 2		1				
ZAKUANI Gabby	11 + 8				1		

SUNDERLAND (PREM: 15th)

Player	P/FL App	Goals	FLC App	Goals	FAC App	Goals	Others App
ANDERSON Russell	0 + 1		1				
BARDSLEY Phil	11						
CHOPRA Michael	21 + 12	6	1		0 + 1		
COLE Andrew	3 + 4				0 + 1		
COLLINS Danny	32 + 4	1			1		
CONNOLLY David	1 + 2		0 + 1		0 + 1		
EDWARDS Carlos	11 + 2				1		
ETUHU Dickson	18 + 2	1	1				
EVANS Jonny	15				1		
FULOP Marton	1						
GORDON Craig	34				1		
HALFORD Greg	8		1				
HARTE Ian	3 + 5						
HIGGINBOTHAM Danny	21	3					
JOHN Stern	0 + 1		1		1		
JONES Kenwyne	33	7					
KAVANAGH Graham					1		
LEADBITTER Grant	17 + 14	2	1		0 + 1		1
McSHANE Paul	20 + 1				1		
MILLER Liam	16 + 8	1	1		1		
MURPHY Daryl	20 + 8	3	1		1		1
NOSWORTHY Nyron	29		1		1		
O'DONOVAN Roy	4 + 13		0 + 1		1		
PRICA Rade	0 + 6	1					
REID Andy	11 + 2	1					
RICHARDSON Kieran	15 + 2	3			1		
STOKES Anthony	8 + 12	1	1				
WAGHORN Martyn	1 + 2				1		

Michael Chopra (Sunderland)

	P/FL		FLC		FAC		Others	
	App	Goals	App	Goals	App	Goals	App	
WALLACE Ross	18 + 3	2	1					
WARD Darren	3		1					
WHITEHEAD Dean	27	1			1			
YORKE Dwight	17 + 3	1	0 + 1					
SWANSEA CITY (DIV 1: 1st)								
ALLEN Joe	2 + 5		2		2 + 1		2 + 1	
AMANKWAAH Kevin					1		2 + 1	
ANDERSON Paul	22 + 9	7	2	1	3		5	2
AUSTIN Kevin	17 + 2		2		4		3 + 1	
BAUZA Guillem	12 + 16	7	2		3 + 2	4	5	2
BODDE Ferrie	33	6			1	1	1 + 1	
BRANDY Febian	2 + 17	3					2	
BRITTON Leon	35 + 5		1 + 1		4 + 1	1	0 + 1	
BUTLER Tommy	29 + 13	6			2 + 1		2 + 3	
CRANEY Ian	0 + 1		2				1	
DE VRIES Dorus	46		2		4		6	
DUFFY Darryl	12 + 8	1	0 + 2		1 + 3		3 + 2	1
FEENEY Warren	7 + 3	5			1 + 1	1	0 + 1	
KNIGHT David					1			
LAWRENCE Dennis	40	2	1		2		2 + 1	
MacDONALD Shaun	0 + 1						0 + 2	
MONK Garry	32	1	2		3		6	
O'LEARY Kris	5 + 6		2		2		4	
ORLANDI Andrea	1 + 7				2 + 2		3	
PAINTER Marcos	29 + 1		1		2		4	
PRATLEY Darren	39 + 3	5			3	1	3 + 2	
RANGEL Angel	43	2	1		4		4	
ROBINSON Andy	34 + 6	8	1 + 1		3 + 1	2	2	

	P/FL		FLC		FAC		Others	
	App	Goals	App	Goals	App	Goals	App	
SCOTLAND Jason	43 + 2	24	0 + 2	1	3 + 1	2	1 + 2	2
TATE Alan	18 + 3	1	1		4		3	
TUDUR JONES Owain	2 + 6							
WAY Darren	0 + 2						2	
WILLIAMS Ashley	3							
SWINDON TOWN (DIV 1: 13th)								
ADAMS Steve	2		1		0 + 1		2	
ALJOFREE Hasney	38 + 1	2	1		4	1		
ALLEN Chris	7 + 1				0 + 1		1 + 1	
ALMEIDA Mauro							1	
ARRIETA Ibon	0 + 4		0 + 1				1	1
ASHIKODI Moses	4 + 6							
BLACKBURN Chris	4 + 3						2	2
BREZOVAN Petr	31		1		4		2	
COLLINS Sam	3 + 1							
COMMINGES Miguel	32 + 8		1		4		2	
CORR Barry	7 + 10	5			2 + 1			
COX Simon	35 + 1	15					1 + 1	1
EASTON Craig	40	6	1		3		1	
IFIL Jerel	39 + 1	1	1		2			
JOYCE Ben	0 + 3	1						
KANYUKA Patrick	3 + 1							
KENNEDY Callum							1	
McGOVERN Jon-Paul	34 + 7	2			3	1	2	
MACKLIN Lloyd							0 + 1	
McNAMEE Anthony	18 + 1	2						
MOHAMED Kaid	3 + 8				0 + 1		1 + 1	
MORRISON Sean	1 + 1							
NICHOLAS Andy	8 + 3	1						
PAYNTER Billy	23 + 13	8			3 + 1	2		
PEACOCK Lee	36 + 1	6	1		3			
POOK Michael	13 + 9	1	0 + 1		3		1	
ROBERTS Chris	16 + 11	5	1		1 + 3	1	0 + 1	
SMITH Jack	21	1	1		2			
SMITH Phil	15							
STURROCK Blair	13 + 8	3	1		3 + 1	2	1	1
TIMLIN Michael	9 + 1	1						
TOZER Ben	1 + 1		1		2		2	
VINCENT Jamie	32				2			
WILLIAMS Adie	0 + 1							
ZAABOUB Sofiane	18 + 11		0 + 1		3		1	
TOTTENHAM HOTSPUR (PREM: 11th)								
ASSOU-EKOTTO Benoit	1						1	
BALE Gareth	8	2	1	1			1 + 2	
BENT Darren	11 + 16	6	0 + 1				4 + 4	2
BERBATOV Dimitar	33 + 3	15	6	1	2	2	7 + 1	5
BOATENG Kevin	7 + 6		1 + 2		1 + 1		1 + 2	
CERNY Radek	13		2		2		3	
CHIMBONDA Pascal	31 + 1	2	6	1	2		9	
DAWSON Michael	26 + 1	1	4		3		5 + 1	1
DEFOE Jermain	3 + 16	4	2 + 3	1	1 + 1		2 + 3	3
GARDNER Anthony	4	1					2	
GILBERTO	3 + 3	1					1	
GUNTER Chris	1 + 1				1 + 1			
HUDDLESTONE Tom	18 + 10	3	1 + 3	1	1 + 1		7 + 2	
HUTTON Alan	14		1					
JENAS Jermaine	28 + 1	4	6	2	3		6 + 1	
KABOUL Younes	19 + 2	3	3 + 1		1		3	1
KEANE Robbie	32 + 4	15	4 + 1	2	3	2	7 + 3	4
KING Ledley	4		3		1		2	
LEE Young-Pyo	17 + 1		4		2		6	
LENNON Aaron	25 + 4	2	6	1	2 + 1		8 + 1	
MALBRANQUE Steed	35 + 2	4	5	2	3		9 + 1	1
O'HARA Jamie	9 + 8	1	1 + 1		1 + 1		1 + 3	1
ROBINSON Paul	25		4		1		7	
ROCHA Ricardo	4 + 1							
ROUTLEDGE Wayne	1 + 1							
STALTERI Paul	3				0 + 1		2 + 1	
TAARABT Adel	0 + 6				0 + 1		0 + 3	
TAINIO Teemu	6 + 10		2 + 3		2		2 + 1	
WOODGATE Jonathan	12	1	1	1			4	
ZOKORA Didier	25 + 3		3 + 1		1		10	
TRANMERE ROVERS (DIV 1: 11th)								
ACHTERBERG John	5						1	
AHMED Adnan	3 + 3						1	
CANSDELL-SHERIFF Shane	43 + 1	3	1		4			
CHORLEY Ben	30 + 1	1	1		2 + 1		1	
COOPER Kevin	3 + 1							
COYNE Danny	41		1		4			
CURRAN Craig	1 + 34	2	0 + 1		1 + 2		1	

	P/FL App	P/FL Goals	FLC App	FLC Goals	FAC App	FAC Goals	Others App
DAVIES Steve	8 + 2	2	1				1
GOODISON Ian	42		1		2		0 + 1
GREENACRE Chris	36 + 4	11	1		2	3	
HENRY Paul	1 + 1						
JENNINGS Steve	39 + 2	2	1		4	2	1
JONES Mike	4 + 5	1			0 + 1		0 + 1
KAY Antony	30 + 8	6			4	1	1
McLAREN Paul	43	4	1		4		
MOORE Ian	17	3					
MULLIN John	4 + 6				0 + 2		
MYRIE-WILLIAMS Jennison	21 + 4	3			1		
SHUKER Chris	22 + 1	3	1		2		1
STOCKDALE Robbie	43 + 1		1		4		1
TAYLOR Andy	29 + 1	2			3		
TAYLOR Gareth	19 + 4	3	0 + 1		3 + 1	1	
TREMARCO Carl	4 + 4				1		1
ZOLA-MAKONGO Calvin	18 + 12	5	1		3 + 1		

WALSALL (DIV 1: 12th)

	P/FL App	P/FL Goals	FLC App	FLC Goals	FAC App	FAC Goals	Others App
BETSY Kevin	16	2					
BOERTIEN Paul	20		1		0 + 1		1
BRADLEY Mark	29 + 6	3			5		
BRITTAIN Martin	0 + 1				0 + 2		
BUTLER Martin	5	1					1
CARNEIRO Carlos	2 + 1		1				1
CRADDOCK Josh	0 + 1						
DANN Scott	28	3	1		5		
DEENEY Troy	16 + 19	1			2 + 2		0 + 1
DE MONTAGNAC Ishmel	10 + 20	3			3 + 2	1	1
DOBSON Michael	21 + 3	1	1		0 + 1		1
FOX Danny	21 + 1	3	1		4		1
GERRARD Anthony	44	3	1		4		1
HALL Paul	7 + 12	1	1		2 + 1		1
HOLMES Lee	19	4					
INCE Clayton	46		1		5		1
McDERMOTT David	1 + 12				0 + 1		0 + 1
MATTIS Dwayne	4						
MOONEY Tommy	36	11	1		3	1	
MOORE Stefan	3 + 2	1					
N'DOUR Alassane	3 + 6	1					
NICHOLLS Alex	7 + 12	2	0 + 1		2 + 2	1	0 + 1
RICKETTS Michael	12	3			4	2	
ROPER Ian	19	1			1		1
SMITH Manny	4						
SONKO Eddy	30 + 7	5			4 + 1		
SONNER Danny	6		1				
SWEENEY Peter	7						
TAUNDRY Richard	12 + 9				1		
WESTON Rhys	43 + 1				5		1
WRACK Darren	35 + 2	1	1		5		1

WATFORD (CHAMP: 6th)

	P/FL App	P/FL Goals	FLC App	FLC Goals	FAC App	FAC Goals	Others App
AINSWORTH Lionel	3 + 5						1 + 1
AVINEL Cedric			2				
BANGURA Al	3 + 4		2		1		
BROMBY Leigh	16	1					2
CAMPANA Alex			1 + 1	1			
DAVENPORT Calum	1						
DE MERIT Jay	30 + 5	1			2		1 + 1
DOYLEY Lloyd	36				2		1
ELLINGTON Nathan	18 + 16	4			1 + 1		2
EUSTACE John	13						2
FORBES Kieron			0 + 1				
FRANCIS Damien	6 + 5	2			1		
HENDERSON Darius	34 + 6	12			1		1 1
HOSKINS Will	0 + 1		2				
JACKSON Matt	6		2				
JOHN Collins	3 + 2						
JOHNSON Adam	11 + 1	5					
KABBA Steve	7 + 7	1	1		1		
KING Marlon	25 + 2	11			1		
LEE Richard	34 + 1		2		2		2
McANUFF Jobi	31 + 8	2			2		2
MACKAY Malky					1		
McNAMEE Anthony			2				
MAHON Gavin	19						
MARIAPPA Adrian	13 + 12		2		0 + 2		1
OSBORNE Junior			0 + 1				
O'TOOLE John-Joe	23 + 12	3	0 + 1		1	1	0 + 1
PARKES Jordan			2				
POOM Mart	12						
PRISKIN Tamas	7 + 7	1	2	1	1 + 1		0 + 2
RINALDI Douglas			2				

	P/FL App	P/FL Goals	FLC App	FLC Goals	FAC App	FAC Goals	Others App
SADLER Mat	14 + 1				1		2
SHITTU Danny	37 + 2	7			1	2	1
SMITH Tommy	44	7			1 + 1		2
STEWART Jordan	33 + 6	2			1		
WILLIAMSON Lee	27 + 5	2			1		2

WEST BROMWICH ALBION (CHAMP: 1st)

	P/FL App	P/FL Goals	FLC App	FLC Goals	FAC App	FAC Goals	Others App
ALBRECHTSEN Martin	28 + 4	2	3		6		
BARNETT Leon	30 + 2	3			4		
BEATTIE Craig	6 + 15	3	3	1	1 + 1		
BEDNAR Roman	18 + 11	13			5	4	
BRUNT Chris	22 + 12	4	1		3 + 3	1	
CESAR Bostjan	19 + 1	1	2		2		
CHAPLOW Richard	2 + 3		2				
CLEMENT Neil	8 + 1		1		1		
ELLINGTON Nathan	0 + 3		2		1		
GERA Zoltan	33 + 10	8	1	1	4 + 1	1	
GREENING Jonathan	46	1	2 + 1		5		
HODGKISS Jared	3 + 1		3		1		
HOEFKENS Carl	42				5		
KIELY Dean	44		3		6		
KIM Do-Heon	1 + 3	1			0 + 3		
KOREN Robert	38 + 2	9	0 + 1		4 + 1	1	
MacDONALD Sherjill	0 + 10		0 + 2		0 + 3		
MARTIS Shelton	2		1				
MILLER Ishmael	24 + 10	9	1	2	3 + 2	5	
MOORE Luke	3 + 7						
MORRISON James	25 + 10	4	2		5 + 1	2	
NICHOLSON Stuart			0 + 1				
PELE	13 + 8	2			2 + 1		
PHILLIPS Kevin	29 + 6	22			1 + 2	2	
ROBINSON Paul	43	1	1		4		
SLUSARSKI Bartosz	0 + 1						
STEELE Luke	2						
TEIXEIRA Filipe	24 + 6	5	2 + 1		4		
TININHO	1		1 + 1				
WORRALL David			0 + 1				

WEST HAM UNITED (PREM: 10th)

	P/FL App	P/FL Goals	FLC App	FLC Goals	FAC App	FAC Goals	Others App
ASHTON Dean	20 + 11	10	2	1	2		
BELLAMY Craig	7 + 1	2	1	2			
BOA MORTE Luis	18 + 9	4	4		1		
BOWYER Lee	12 + 3	4	2 + 1		1 + 1		
CAMARA Henri	3 + 7						
COLE Carlton	21 + 10	4	3 + 1	2	1 + 1		
COLLINS James	2 + 1		1 + 1				
COLLISON Jack	1 + 1						
DYER Kieron	2		1				
ETHERINGTON Mattie	15 + 3	3	1		2		
FAUBERT Julien	4 + 3				0 + 1		
FERDINAND Anton	22 + 3	2	2		2		
GABBIDON Danny	8 + 2		3 + 1				
GREEN Robert	38		1		2		
LJUNGBERG Freddie	22 + 3	2	2		1		
McCARTNEY George	38	1	4		2		
MULLINS Hayden	32 + 2		4		1		
NEILL Lucas	34		4		2		
NOBLE Mark	25 + 6	3	1 + 2		2		
PANTSIL John	4 + 10		0 + 2		1		
PARKER Scott	17 + 1	1	2				
REID Kyel	0 + 1				0 + 2		0 + 1
SEARS Freddie	1 + 6	1					
SOLANO Nobby	14 + 9	4					
SPECTOR Jonathan	13 + 13		0 + 1		0 + 1		
TOMKINS James	5 + 1						
UPSON Matty	29	1	2		2		
WRIGHT Richard					3		
ZAMORA Bobby	11 + 2	1	1				

WIGAN ATHLETIC (PREM: 14th)

	P/FL App	P/FL Goals	FLC App	FLC Goals	FAC App	FAC Goals	Others App
AGHAHOWA Julius	2 + 12		0 + 1		0 + 2		
BENT Marcus	25 + 6	7			1		
BOYCE Emmerson	24 + 1	1	1		1		
BRAMBLE Titus	26	2			1		
BROWN Michael	27 + 4		1		1 + 1		
CAMARA Henri			1				
COTTERILL David	2		1		0 + 1	1	
EDMAN Erik	5						
FIGUEROA Maynor	1 + 1						
FOLAN Caleb	1 + 1	1					
GRANQVIST Andreas	13 + 1		1		1		
HAGEN Erik	1						
HALL Fitz	0 + 1	1					

471

	P/FL App	Goals	FLC App	Goals	FAC App	Goals	Others App
HESKEY Emile	27 + 1	4			2		
KILBANE Kevin	33 + 2	1	1		2		
KING Marlon	8 + 7	1					
KIRKLAND Chris	37				1		
KOUMAS Jason	21 + 9	1	0 + 1		1 + 1		
LANDZAAT Denny	19	3					
MELCHIOT Mario	31		1		1		
OLEMBE Saloman	2 + 6				1		
PALACIOS Wilson	16				1		
POLLITT Mike	1		1		1		
SCHARNER Paul	37	4			2	1	
SIBIERSKI Antoine	10 + 20	4			1 + 1	1	
SKOKO Josip	7 + 5				1		
TAYLOR Ryan	12 + 5	3			2		
VALENCIA Antonio	30 + 1	3			1		

WOLVERHAMPTON WANDERERS (CHAMP: 7th)

	P/FL App	Goals	FLC App	Goals	FAC App	Goals	Others App
BENNETT Elliott			2				
BOTHROYD Jay	13 + 9	3			3	1	
BREEN Gary	18 + 1				1		
CLAPHAM Jamie			0 + 1				
COLLINS Neill	34 + 5	3	1		2	1	
CRADDOCK Jody	22 + 1	1	1	1	1		
EASTWOOD Freddy	10 + 21	3	2	1	0 + 2		
EBANKS-BLAKE Sylvan	20	12					
EDWARDS David	10	1					
EDWARDS Rob	4 + 4	1	2		1 + 1		
ELLIOTT Stephen	18 + 11	4			1 + 1		
ELOKOBI George	15						
FOLEY Kevin	42 + 2	1	2		3		
GIBSON Darron	15 + 6	1			1 + 2		
GLEESON Stephen			1				
GRAY Michael	29 + 4	3	1		2 + 1		
HENNESSEY Wayne	46				3		
HENRY Karl	38 + 2	3	2		2		
JARVIS Matt	17 + 9	1			2		
JONES Daniel	0 + 1						
KEOGH Andy	33 + 10	8	2	1	3	2	
KIGHTLY Michael	20 + 1	4	1 + 1		0 + 2	1	
KYLE Kevin	3 + 9	1			1		
LITTLE Mark	0 + 1						
MULGREW Charlie			2				
OLOFINJANA Seyi	35 + 1	3			1		
POTTER Darren	11 + 7		1 + 1		3		
ROSA Denes			0 + 1				
STACK Graham	0 + 2		2				
WARD Darren	30				2		
WARD Stephen	23 + 6		0 + 1		1		

WREXHAM (DIV 2: 24th)

	P/FL App	Goals	FLC App	Goals	FAC App	Goals	Others App
AISTON Sam	13 + 6						
BAYNES Wes	10 + 2	2					
BOLLAND Phil	18						
BROUGHTON Drewe	16	2					
CARVILL Michael	5 + 3						1
COLLINS Matty	2				1		
CROWELL Matty	3 + 3						1
DONE Matty	13 + 13		1		1		1
DUFFY Rob	0 + 6						
EVANS Gareth	10 + 3				1		
EVANS Steve	30 + 1	3	1				1
FLEMING Andy	2 + 2						
GARRETT Robbie	9 + 3				1		
HALL Paul	7 + 4	1					
HOPE Richard	33		1		1		1
JOHNSON Josh	0 + 7		0 + 2				
JONES Mark	14 + 2		1				
JONES Michael	2		2				
LLEWELLYN Chris	38 + 2	3	2		1		1
MACKIN Levi	8 + 1	1	2				
MURTAGH Conall	3 + 1		1 + 1				
NICHOLSON Stuart	9 + 4						
PEJIC Shaun	17 + 2		2		0 + 1		0 + 1
PROCTOR Michael	23 + 17	11	2	1			0 + 1
ROBERTS Neil	35 + 1	8	1		0 + 1	1	
SONNER Danny	9	1					
SPANN Silvio	7 + 2	1			1		1
SPENDER Simon	32 + 2	1	2		1		
TAYLOR Neil	21 + 5		0 + 1				
TREMARCO Carl	10						
UGARTE Juan	0 + 1						
VALENTINE Ryan	14		2		1		1
WARD Gavin	22						
WHITLEY Jeff	5 + 6						

	P/FL App	Goals	FLC App	Goals	FAC App	Goals	Others App
WILLIAMS Anthony	22				1		1
WILLIAMS Danny	11 + 4		1				
WILLIAMS Eifion	7 + 6	1	1		1		1
WILLIAMS Marc	11 + 8	3	0 + 2		0 + 1		0 + 1
WILLIAMS Mike	15 + 3						1

WYCOMBE WANDERERS (DIV 2: 7th)

	P/FL App	Goals	FLC App	Goals	FAC App	Goals	Others App
ANTWI Will	6						1
BLOOMFIELD Matt	26 + 9	4	1		1	1	1
BOUCAUD Andre	2 + 8						1
BULLOCK Martin	17 + 8		1		1		
CHRISTON Lewis	2						0 + 1
DALY George	0 + 2						
DOHERTY Tommy	21 + 3						2
DOUGLAS Rab	3						
DUNCAN Derek							0 + 1
EASTER Jermaine	6	2					1
FACEY Delroy	4 + 2	1					2	1
FIELDING Frank	36				1		2
HERD Chris	3 + 1						
HOLT Gary	42 + 1	2			1		2
JOHNSON Leon	44 + 1		1		1		3
KAZIMIERCZAK Prez	2						1
KNIGHT Leon	12 + 8	5					0 + 2
LENNON Neil	8 + 1						
McCRACKEN David	35 + 2	1	1		1		1
McGLEISH Scott	45 + 1	25	0 + 1		1		2
MARTIN Russell	44		1		1		3
OAKES Stefan	23 + 11	3	1		1	1	2
PALMER Chris	1						
PHILLIPS Matt	1 + 1						0 + 1
REID Reuben	1 + 10	1					1
RICE Robbie	0 + 1						
SHEARER Scott	4 + 1		1				
STOCKLEY Sam	18 + 4				0 + 1		
SUTTON John	23 + 20	6	1		0 + 1		1 + 2
TORRES Sergio	36 + 6	5	1		1		2
WILLIAMS Tom	6 + 4		1		1		1
WILLIAMSON Mike	7 + 5						1
WOODMAN Craig	27 + 2		1				3
YOUNG Jamie	3 + 1						

YEOVIL TOWN (DIV 1: 18th)

	P/FL App	Goals	FLC App	Goals	FAC App	Goals	Others App
ALCOCK Craig	5 + 3		0 + 1		1		2 + 1
BARRY Anthony	25 + 11		1		1		3
BEGOVIC Asmir	2						
BETSY Kevin	5		1				1
BIRCHAM Marc	9 + 4						
BRIDCUTT Liam	6 + 3						
CHRISTOPHE Jean-Francois	4 + 1						
CHURCH Simon	2 + 4						
COCHRANE Justin	6 + 6	2	0 + 1				
DEMPSEY Gary	10 + 6	2			0 + 1		1
DOMORAUD Wilfried	0 + 5						0 + 1
DOWNES Aidan	3 + 2	1					
FLINDERS Scott	9						
FORBES Terrell	41		1		1		3
GILLETT Simon	3 + 1						0 + 1
GUYETT Scott	34		1		1		2
HUGHES Jerahl	0 + 1						0 + 1
JONES Nathan	29 + 2	1	1		1		3
JONES Richie	6 + 3						1 + 1
KIRK Andy	15 + 4	4					
KNIGHTS Darryl	0 + 3						0 + 1
LARRIEU Romain	6						1
LYNCH Mark	12 + 2		1		0 + 1		1
MAHER Stephen	4 + 2						0 + 1
MILDENHALL Steve	29		1		1		2
MORRIS Lee	0 + 1	1					
OWUSU Lloyd	31 + 12	9	1	1	1		3	1
PELTIER Lee	34		1		1		2
PETERS Jaime	12 + 2	1					
ROSE Matthew	27 + 3	1	0 + 1				1 + 1
SKIVERTON Terry	27 + 4	5			1		1
SMITH Nathan	6 + 1						
STEWART Marcus	35 + 1	4			1	1	3
STIEBER Zoltan	14 + 1	1					
WALKER James	11 + 2	3					1
WARNE Paul	26 + 7	1	1		0 + 1		2
WAY Darren	7	1					
WELSH Ishmael	0 + 3						
WILLIAMS Marvin	8 + 15		1				
WOODS Martin	3						

Stop Press: Transfers

These are the reported transfers between the beginning of June and 11 July 2008 that relate to players appearing within these pages who will start with new P/FL clubs in 2008-2009. Moves are only listed if not mentioned within the text. This list does not include players who were released at the end of the season and moved into non-League football.

ABDOU Nadjim (Plymouth Argyle - Millwall) Free
AGOGO Junior (Nottingham Forest - Zamalek Sporting Club) Undisclosed
ALBRECHTSEN Martin (West Bromwich Albion - Derby County) Undisclosed
ADAMS Nicky (Bury - Leicester City) Undisclosed
AMANKWAAH Kevin (Swansea City - Swindon Town) Free
ARNISON Paul (Carlisle United - Bradford City) Free
AUSTIN Kevin (Swansea City - Chesterfield) Free
BARRY Anthony (Yeovil Town - Chester City) Free
BASEYA Cedric (Southampton - Lille) Free
BREEN Gary (Manchester City - Hereford United) Undisclosed
BROWN Aaron (Gillingham - Lincoln City) Free
BROWN Nat (Lincoln City - Wrexham) Free
BROWN Wayne (Hereford United - Bury) Undisclosed
BURCH Rob (Sheffield Wednesday - Lincoln City) Free
BUTLER Andy (Scunthorpe United - Huddersfield Town) Free
CANSDELL-SHERIFF Shane (Tranmere Rovers - Shrewsbury Town) Free
CARLE Nick (Bristol City - Crystal Palace) Undisclosed
CLINGAN Sammy (Nottingham Forest - Norwich City) Free
COLE Andrew (Sunderland - Nottingham Forest) Free
COLLIS Steve (Southend United - Crewe Alexandra) Free
CONSTANTINE Leon (Leeds United - Northampton Town) Free
CROUCH Peter (Liverpool - Portsmouth) £9,000,000
DAVIES Curtis (West Bromwich Albion - Aston Villa) Undisclosed
DAVIES Steve (Tranmere Rovers - Derby County) Free
DAVIS Liam (Coventry City - Northampton Town) Free
DE RIDDER Daniel (Birmingham City - Wigan Athletic) Free
DIAGOURAGA Toumani (Watford - Hereford United) Free
DICKINSON Liam (Stockport County - Derby County) £750,000
DONE Matty (Wrexham - Hereford United) Undisclosed
DUFFY Darryl (Swansea City - Bristol Rovers) Free
DUGUID Karl (Colchester United - Plymouth Argyle) Undisclosed

DYER Lloyd (MK Dons - Leicester City) Free
FAGAN Craig (Derby County - Hull City) £750,000
FLAHAVAN Darryl Flahavan (Southend United - Crystal Palace) Free
FORDE David (Cardiff City - Millwall) Free
FORTUNE Clayton (Leyton Orient - Darlington) Free
FURLONG Paul (Luton Town - Southend United) Free
GEOVANNI (Manchester City - Hull City) Free
GERA Zoltan (West Bromwich Albion - Fulham) Free
GILLESPIE Steven (Cheltenham Town - Colchester United) Undisclosed
GOODWIN Jim (Scunthorpe United - Huddersfield Town) Free
GOWER Mark (Southend United - Swansea City) Free
GRANVILLE Danny (Colchester United - Leyton Orient) Free
GRIFFIN Adam (Stockport County - Darlington) Free
HALFORD Greg (Sunderland - Sheffield United) Season-long loan
HALL Danny (Gretna - Chesterfield) Free
HAMSHAW Matt (Mansfield Town - Notts County) Free
HARRIS Jay (Accrington Stanley - Chester City) Free
HESSEY Sean (Chester City - Macclesfield Town) Free
HEYWOOD Matt (Brentford - Grimsby Town) Free
HOLMES Derek (Rotherham United - St Johnstone) Free
HOLT Grant (Nottingham Forest - Shrewsbury Town) £170,000
HOOLAHAN Wes (Blackpool - Norwich City) Undisclosed
HOPE Richard (Wrexham - Grimsby Town) Free
HOULT Russell (Stoke City - Notts County) Free
HUGHES Jeff (Crystal Palace - Bristol Rovers) Undisclosed
HUME Iain (Leicester City - Barnsley) £1,200,000
IBEHRE Jabo (Leyton Orient - Walsall) Free
ISAKSSON Andreas (Manchester City - PSV Eindhoven) Undisclosed
JACKSON Michael (Blackpool - Shrewsbury Town) Free
JARVIS Ryan (Norwich City - Leyton Orient) Free
JOHN-BAPTISTE Alex (Mansfield Town - Blackpool) Undisclosed
JONES David (Derby County - Wolverhampton Wanderers) Undisclosed
JONES Richie (Manchester United - Hartlepool United) Free
KENNEDY Mark (Crystal Palace - Cardiff City) Free
KEWELL Harry [Liverpool - Galatasaray) Free
KOVACS Janos (Chesterfield - Lincoln City) Tribunal
LAFFERTY Kyle (Burnley - Glasgow Rangers) £3,000,000
LEE Graeme (Doncaster Rovers - Bradford City) Free
LEVEN Peter (Chesterfield - Milton Keynes Dons) Undisclosed

LITTLE Glen (Reading - Portsmouth) Undisclosed
LIVERMORE David (Hull City - Brighton & Hove Albion) Free
LOCKWOOD Matt (Nottingham Forest - Colchester United) Undisclosed
LUCKETTI Chris (Sheffield United - Huddersfield Town) Free
McAULEY Gareth (Leicester City - Ipswich Town) Undisclosed
McCAMMON Mark (Doncaster Rovers - Gillingham) Free
McCARTHY Patrick (Charlton Athletic - Crystal Palace) Undisclosed
MacDONALD Charlie (Southend United - Brentford) Undisclosed
McLAREN Paul (Tranmere Rovers - Bradford City) Free
McLEOD Kevin (Colchester United - Brighton & Hove Albion) Free
MANNIX David (Accrington Stanley - Chester City) Free
MARTIN Joe (Tottenham Hotspur - Blackpool) Undisclosed
MATTIS Dwayne (Barnsley - Walsall) Free
MEDLEY Luke (Bradford City - Barnet) Free
MILDENHALL Steve (Yeovil Town - Southend United) Free
MILLER Kenny (Derby County - Glasgow Rangers) £2,000,000
MOORE Darren (Derby County - Barnsley) Free
MOUSINHO John (Brentford - Wycombe Wanderers) Free
MUAMBA Patrice (Birmingham City - Bolton Wanderers) £5,000,000
MULLINS Johnny (Mansfield Town - Stockport County) Undisclosed
MURDOCK Colin (Shrewsbury Town - Accrington Stanley) Free
NEWTON Adam (Peterborough United - Brentford) Free
NOWLAND Adam (Lancaster City - Notts County) Free
OAKES Stefan (Wycombe Wanderers - Lincoln City) Free
O'BRIEN Burton (Sheffield Wednesday - Falkirk) Free
O'CALLAGHAN George (Cork City - Tranmere Rovers) Free
O'CONNOR James (Burnley - Sheffield Wednesday) Free
PATERSON Martin (Scunthorpe United - Burnley) £1,000,000
PERKINS David (Rochdale - Colchester United) Undisclosed
PERRY Chris (Luton Town - Southampton) Free
PHILLIPS Kevin (West Bromwich Albion - Birmingham City) Free
POOLE David (Stockport County - Darlington) Free
POWER Alan (Nottingham Forest - Hartlepool United) Free
PROUDLOCK Adam (Stockport County - Darlington)

Free
PUNCHEON Jason (Barnet - Plymouth Argyle) £250,000
RAMSEY Aaron (Cardiff City - Arsenal) Undisclosed
RANDOLPH Darren (Charlton Athletic - Hereford United) Season-long loan
REID Paul (Barnsley - Colchester United) Free
RHODES Alex (Bradford City - Rotherham United) Free
RIISE John Arne (Liverpool - Roma) £4,000,000
ROBERTS Steve (Doncaster Rovers - Walsall) Free
ROCHE Barry (Chesterfield - Morecambe) Free
ROZEHNAL David (Newcastle United - Lazio) £2,900,000
RUSSELL Alex (Bristol City - Cheltenham Town) Free
SANKOFA Osei (Charlton Athletic - Southend United) Free
SCHOFIELD Danny (Huddersfield Town - Yeovil Town) Free
SHEEHAN Alan (Leicester City - Leeds United) Undisclosed
SHOWUNMI Enoch (Bristol City - Leeds United) Free
SIDWELL Steve (Chelsea - Aston Villa) £5,000,000
SAVAGE Bas (Millwall - Tranmere Rovers) Free
SINCLAIR Frank (Huddersfield Town - Lincoln City) Free
SODJE Efe (Gillingham - Bury) Free
SONKO Edrissa (Walsall - Tranmere Rovers) Free
SPICER John (Burnley - Doncaster Rovers) Free
STEARMAN Richard (Leicester City - Wolverhampton Wanderers) Undisclosed
STEPHENS Dale (Bury - Oldham Athletic) Tribunal
STOCKDALE Robbie (Tranmere Rovers - Grimsby Town) Free
SUN JIHAI (Manchester City - Sheffield United) Free
TEYMOURIAN (Bolton Wanderers - Fulham) Free
VIRGO Adam (Glasgow Celtic - Brighton & Hove Albion) Free
WAINWRIGHT Neil (Darlington - Morecambe) Undisclosed
WALKER Richard (Bristol Rovers - Shrewsbury Town) Season-long loan
WAY Darren (Swansea City - Yeovil Town) £50,000
WESTWOOD Keiren (Carlisle United - Coventry City) £500,000
WHALLEY Shaun (Accrington Stanley - Wrexham) Free
WHITAKER Danny (Port Vale - Oldham Athletic) Free
WILLIAMS Ben (Crewe Alexandra - Carlisle United) Free
WILLIAMS Gavin (Ipswich Town - Bristol City) Undisclosed
WILLIAMS Marvin (Yeovil Town - Brentford) Undisclosed
WOTTON Paul (Plymouth Argyle - Southampton) Free
WRIGHT Jermaine (Southampton - Blackpool) Free
ZAABOUB Sofiene (Swindon Town - Walsall) Free
ZOLA-MAKONGO Calvin (Tranmere Rovers - Crewe Alexandra) £200,000